Dreamweaver CS4

THE MISSING MANUAL

The book that
should have been
in the box®

Dreamweaver CS4

THE MISSING MANUAL®

David Sawyer McFarland

POGUE PRESS™
O'REILLY®
Beijing • Cambridge • Farnham • Köln • Sebastopol • Tokyo

Dreamweaver CS4: The Missing Manual
by David Sawyer McFarland

Printed in the United States of America.

Published by O'Reilly Media, Inc., 1005 Gravenstein Highway North, Sebastopol, CA 95472.

O'Reilly books may be purchased for educational, business, or sales promotional use. Online editions are also available for most titles (*safari.oreilly.com*). For more information, contact our corporate/institutional sales department: (800) 998-9938 or *corporate@oreilly.com.*

Printing History:

November 2008: First Edition.

ISBN: 978-0-596-52292-6

[LSI] [2011-05-13]

Table of Contents

The Missing Credits

About the Author

David Sawyer McFarland is president of Sawyer McFarland Media, Inc., a Web development and training company in Portland, Oregon. He's been building Web sites since 1995, when he designed his first Web site: an online magazine for communication professionals. He's served as the Webmaster at the University of California at Berkeley and the Berkeley Multimedia Research Center, and he has helped build, design, and program numerous Web sites for clients including Macworld.com, among others.

In addition to building Web sites, David is also a writer, trainer, and instructor. He's taught Dreamweaver at the UC Berkeley Graduate School of Journalism, the Center for Electronic Art, the Academy of Art College, Ex'Pressions Center for New Media, and the Art Institute of Portland. He currently teaches in the Multimedia Program at Portland State University. He's written articles about Dreamweaver and the Web for *Practical Web Design*, *MX Developer's Journal*, *Macworld* magazine and CreativePro.com.

David is also the author of *CSS: The Missing Manual*, and *JavaScript: The Missing Manual.*

David has used Dreamweaver since version 2, and has been a member of the Dreamweaver Advisory Council. He welcomes feedback about this book by email: *missing@sawmac.com*. (If you're seeking technical help, however, please refer to the sources listed in Appendix Getting Help.)

About the Creative Team

Peter Meyers (editor) is the managing editor of O'Reilly Media's Missing Manual series. He lives with his wife, daughter, and cats in New York City. Email: *meyers@oreilly.com.*

Sohaila Abdulali (copy editor) is a freelance writer and editor. She has published a novel, several children's books, and numerous short stories and articles. She recently finished an ethnography of an aboriginal Indian woman. She lives in New York City with her husband Tom and their small but larger-than-life daughter, Samara. She can be reached through her Web site at *www.sohailaink.com*.

Nellie McKesson (production editor) lives in Jamaica Plain, Mass., and spends her spare time making t-shirts for her friends to wear (*mattsaundersbynellie.etsy.com*), and playing music with her band (*myspace.com/drmrsvandertrampp*). Email: *nellie@oreilly.com.*

Ron Strauss (indexer) is a full-time freelance indexer specializing in information technology. When not working, he moonlights as a concert violist and alternative medicine health consultant. Email: *rstrauss@mchsi.com*.

Deborah Pang Davis (Chia Vet Web site designer) created Cococello, a print and Web design boutique in beautiful Portland, Oregon. Before launching Cococello, she had the privilege of working at, among others, National Geographic Traveler, The Chicago Tribune, Toronto's Globe and Mail, and The Seattle Times. She knew early on that life for her never included pantyhose or the pantsuit. She can be reached through her Web site at *www.cococello.com*.

John C. Bland II (technical reviewer) is co-founder of Katapult Media Inc. (*www.katapultmedia.com*) which focuses on software and Web development using technologies such as ColdFusion, the Flash platform, PHP, Java, and the .NET platform. Through Katapult, he works diligently on custom software and Web products. As the manager of the Arizona Flash Platform User Group, John continues to put back into the community which helped mold him into the developer he is today. John blogs regularly on his blog: Geek Life (*www.johncblandii.com*).

Murray Summers (technical reviewer), a biochemist by training, has spent the last 20 years working in the computer industry. In 1998, Murray started his Web site production company, Great Web Sights (*www.great-web-sights.com*). He's an Adobe Community Expert, and previously a Team Macromedia member, a Macromedia Certified Web Site Developer, and Dreamweaver Developer. Murray has also contributed chapters and authored books about Web development.

Acknowledgements

Many thanks to all those who helped with this book, including Deb Pang Davis, the design mastermind behind ChiaVet.com, and my technical editor, Murray Summers, whose prolific critiques have provided a comfortable safety net to protect me from any embarrassing gaffes. Thanks also to my students who've helped me understand Dreamweaver better and always seem to come up with at least one question that I have no answer for.

Finally, thanks to David Pogue whose unflagging enthusiasm and boundless energy never fails to inspire; to my editor, Peter Meyers, who has helped make my words sharper and my writing clearer (and who also has had to endure long weekends of work to make sure this book got finished on time); to my wife, Scholle, for being such a strong supporter of my writing and a wonderful partner in my life; my mom and Doug; Mary, David, Marisa and Tessa; Phyllis and Les; my son, Graham, who has taught me that robots, spaceships, *Star Wars*, and Legos are much more important than writing books; and to my daughter, Kate, who helped the most by graciously agreeing to sleep through the night while I was writing this book.

—David Sawyer McFarland

The Missing Manual Series

Missing Manuals are witty, superbly written guides to computer products that don't come with printed manuals (which is just about all of them). Each book features a handcrafted index and cross-references to specific pages (not just chapters).

Recent and upcoming titles include:

Access 2007: The Missing Manual by Matthew MacDonald

AppleScript: The Missing Manual by Adam Goldstein

AppleWorks 6: The Missing Manual by Jim Elferdink and David Reynolds

CSS: The Missing Manual by David Sawyer McFarland

Creating a Web Site: The Missing Manual, Second Edition by Matthew MacDonald

David Pogue's Digital Photography: The Missing Manual by David Pogue

Dreamweaver CS3: The Missing Manual by David Sawyer McFarland

eBay: The Missing Manual by Nancy Conner

Excel 2003: The Missing Manual by Matthew MacDonald

Excel 2007: The Missing Manual by Matthew MacDonald

Facebook: The Missing Manual by E.A. Vander Veer

FileMaker Pro 8: The Missing Manual by Geoff Coffey and Susan Prosser

FileMaker Pro 9: The Missing Manual by Geoff Coffey and Susan Prosser

Flash CS3: The Missing Manual by E.A. Vander Veer and Chris Grover

Flash CS4: The Missing Manual by Chris Grover

FrontPage 2003: The Missing Manual by Jessica Mantaro

Google Apps: The Missing Manual by Nancy Conner

The Internet: The Missing Manual by David Pogue and J.D. Biersdorfer

iMovie 6 & iDVD: The Missing Manual by David Pogue

iMovie '08 & iDVD: The Missing Manual by David Pogue

iPhone: The Missing Manual by David Pogue

iPhoto '08: The Missing Manual by David Pogue

iPod: The Missing Manual, Seventh Edition by J.D. Biersdorfer

JavaScript: The Missing Manual by David Sawyer McFarland

Mac OS X: The Missing Manual, Tiger Edition by David Pogue

Mac OS X: The Missing Manual, Leopard Edition by David Pogue

Microsoft Project 2007: The Missing Manual by Bonnie Biafore

Office 2004 for Macintosh: The Missing Manual by Mark H. Walker and Franklin Tessler

Office 2007: The Missing Manual by Chris Grover, Matthew MacDonald, and E.A. Vander Veer

Office 2008 for Macintosh: The Missing Manual by Jim Elferdink

PCs: The Missing Manual by Andy Rathbone

Photoshop CS4: The Missing Manual by Lesa Snider King

Photoshop Elements 7: The Missing Manual by Barbara Brundage

Photoshop Elements 6 for Mac: The Missing Manual by Barbara Brundage

PowerPoint 2007: The Missing Manual by E.A. Vander Veer

QuickBase: The Missing Manual by Nancy Conner

QuickBooks 2008: The Missing Manual by Bonnie Biafore

QuickBooks 2009: The Missing Manual by Bonnie Biafore

Quicken 2008: The Missing Manual by Bonnie Biafore

Quicken 2009: The Missing Manual by Bonnie Biafore

Switching to the Mac: The Missing Manual, Tiger Edition by David Pogue and Adam Goldstein

Switching to the Mac: The Missing Manual, Leopard Edition by David Pogue

Wikipedia: The Missing Manual by John Broughton

Windows XP Home Edition: The Missing Manual, Second Edition by David Pogue

Windows XP Pro: The Missing Manual, Second Edition by David Pogue, Craig Zacker, and Linda Zacker

Windows Vista: The Missing Manual by David Pogue

Windows Vista for Starters: The Missing Manual by David Pogue

Word 2007: The Missing Manual by Chris Grover

Your Brain: The Missing Manual by Matthew MacDonald

Introduction

The World Wide Web continues to evolve, growing in scope and complexity, with new features popping up every year to make the Web look and work better. Even people building personal Web sites now use various programming languages and server technologies to dish up content. Throughout its history, Dreamweaver has managed to keep pace with this changing landscape with each new version.

Dreamweaver CS4 is no exception: It's capable of doing more than any previous version. Whether you're creating database-enabled PHP pages, adding your favorite site's XML-based news feeds directly to your home page, using Cascading Style Sheets (CSS) for cutting-edge design effects, dipping into the dynamic world of JavaScript and AJAX, or simply sticking to straightforward HTML pages, Dreamweaver has just about all the tools you need.

Any enterprising designer can create Web pages, Cascading Style Sheets, and even JavaScript programs with a simple text editor. In fact, Dreamweaver CS4 provides powerful text-editing abilities for creating basic text files or complex database-driven Web pages. But why go to all that trouble when Dreamweaver's *visual* page-building approach makes your job of creating beautiful and complex Web sites so much easier? Whether you're new to building Web pages or a hard-core, hand-coding HTML jockey, Dreamweaver is a powerful tool that lets you build Web sites quickly and efficiently, without compromising the quality of your code.

What Dreamweaver Is All About

Dreamweaver is a complete Web site production and management program. It works with Web technologies like HTML, XHTML, CSS, and JavaScript.

The enhancements in the latest version, in fact, make it easier than ever to design and lay out Web sites. Cascading Style Sheet support lets you access the latest Web techniques for creating fast-loading, easily modified Web page designs; while the "Spry" technology provides one-click access to complex, interactive layout options like drop-down menus. Dreamweaver also includes plenty of tools for managing Web sites once you've built them. You can check for broken links, use templates to streamline site-wide page changes, and reorganize your site in a flash with the program's site management tools.

Note: Get used to the acronym CSS, which you'll encounter frequently in this book. It stands for Cascading Style Sheets, a formatting language used to design HTML Web pages. Dreamweaver CS4 continues to integrate advanced CSS creation, testing, and editing tools into Dreamweaver.

It's also a serious tool for creating *dynamic* (database-driven) Web sites. You can now turn your company's database of products into an easily updated online catalog—or turn that cherished recipe collection into an online culinary resource for an adoring public. You can even create Web pages for updating and deleting database records, meanwhile keeping designated areas of your site secure from unauthorized visitors. Best of all, Dreamweaver CS4 does the programming for you.

If you've never used Dreamweaver before, but have already built one or more Web sites, you won't have to start from scratch. Dreamweaver happily opens Web pages and Web sites that were created in other programs without destroying any of your carefully handcrafted code.

Why Dreamweaver?

There are other Web design programs—dozens of them, in fact. But Dreamweaver has become one of the leading programs thanks to key benefits like these:

- **Visual page building**. If you've spent any time using a text editor to punch out the HTML code for your Web pages, you know the tedium involved in adding even a simple item like a photograph to a Web page. When your boss asks you to add her photo to the company home page, you launch your trusty text editor and type something like this: *<img src="images/staff/bigcheese.jpg" width="100" height="150" alt="The Boss">*.

  Not only is this approach prone to typos, but it also separates you from what you want the page to *look* like.

  Dreamweaver, on the other hand, takes a *visual* approach to building Web pages. If you put an image on your page, Dreamweaver shows you the picture on the screen. As in a word processor, which displays documents onscreen as they look when printed, Dreamweaver provides a very close approximation of what your Web page will look like in a Web browser.

- **Complex interactivity, simply.** You've probably seen Web pages where an image (on a navigation bar, for example) lights up or changes appearance when you move your mouse over it.

  Dynamic effects like this—mouse rollovers, alert boxes, and navigational pop-up menus—usually require programming in JavaScript, a programming language that most Web browsers understand. While JavaScript can do amazing things, it requires time and practice to learn.

  Dreamweaver CS4 includes an easy to use and innovative JavaScript-based technology called Spry. With Spry, you can easily create interactive, drop-down menus (Chapter 5), add advanced layout elements like tabbed panels (Chapter 12), and add sophisticated form validation to prevent visitors to your site from submitting forms without providing the proper information (Chapter 11).

- **Solid code.** Every now and then, even in Dreamweaver, you may sometimes want to put aside the visual view and look at the underlying HTML code of a page. You may want to tweak the HTML that Dreamweaver produces, for example, or you may be a long-time HTML hand-coder wondering what Dreamweaver offers you.

  Adobe realized that many professional Web developers still do a lot of work "in the trenches," typing HTML, CSS and JavaScript code by hand. In Dreamweaver, you can edit the raw HTML to your heart's content. Switching back and forth between the visual mode—called Design view—and Code view is seamless and, best of all, nondestructive. Unlike many visual Web page programs, where making a change in the visual design mode stomps all over the underlying HTML code, Dreamweaver respects hand-typed code and doesn't try to rewrite it (unless you ask it to).

  You can even use "Split view" to see your HTML code side-by-side with a visual representation of your page. This lets you work in either Code or Design view, without missing a beat as you switch between the two. In addition, Dreamweaver can open many other types of files commonly used in Web sites, such as external JavaScript files (.js files), so you don't have to switch to another program to work on them. Dreamweaver CS4 also introduces a new "related files" toolbar which lists all JavaScript, CSS, or server-side files used by the current document. For hand-coders this means that editing a page's CSS or JavaScript is just a click away (instead of a time-draining File → Open...hunt around for that danged file). Chapter 10 has the full scoop on how Dreamweaver handles writing and editing code.

- **Site management tools.** Rarely will you build just a single Web page. More often, you'll be creating and editing pages that work together to form part of a Web site. Or you may be building an entire Web site from scratch.

Either way, Dreamweaver's site management tools make your job of dealing with site development easier. From managing links, images, pages, and other media to working with a team of people and moving your site onto a Web server, Dreamweaver automates many of the routine tasks every Webmaster faces. Part 4 of this book looks at how Dreamweaver can help you build and maintain Web sites.

- **Database-driven Web sites.** Data makes the world go round. Whether you're a human-resource records manager or a high school teacher, you probably keep track of a lot of information. Today, companies and individuals store reams of information in database systems like Microsoft Access or Oracle 10g. Dreamweaver CS4 can help you bring that information to life on the Web without having to learn a lot of programming along the way. From accessing information—such as the latest items in your company's product catalog—to updating and editing databases online, Dreamweaver CS4 can help you build database-driven Web sites. Part 6 of this book offers a gentle introduction to building dynamic Web sites.

UP TO SPEED

Hand Coding vs. WYSIWYG Editors

Creating Web pages in a text editor was long considered the best method of building Web sites. The precise control over HTML available when code is written by hand was (and often still is) seen as the only way to assure quality Web pages.

Hand coding's reputation as the only way to go for pros is fueled by the behavior of many visual page-building programs that add unnecessary code to pages—code that affects how a page appears and how quickly it downloads over the Internet.

But hand coding is time-consuming and error-prone. One typo can render a Web page useless.

Fortunately, Dreamweaver brings solid code writing to a visual environment. Since its earliest incarnation, Dreamweaver has prided itself on its ability to produce clean HTML and its tolerance of code created by other programs—including text editors. In fact, Dreamweaver includes a powerful built-in text-editing mode that lets you freely manipulate the HTML of a page—or any other code, including JavaScript, Visual Basic, XML, PHP, or ColdFusion Markup Language.

But the real story is that the code produced when working in the visual mode is as solid and well written as hand coding. Knowing this, you should feel free to take advantage of the increased productivity that Dreamweaver's visual-editing mode brings to your day-to-day work with its one-click objects, instant JavaScript, and simplified layout tools. Doing so won't compromise your code, and will certainly let you finish your next Web site in record time.

Besides, no Web design program is really WYSIWYG (what you see is what you get). Because every browser interprets the HTML language slightly differently, Web design is more like WYSIRWYGOAGD: what you see is roughly what you'll get, on a good day.

Finally, if you have experience hand-coding HTML and CSS, you'll be pleasantly surprised by the powerful text-editing capabilities of Dreamweaver CS4. In fact, even though Dreamweaver has developed a reputation as a *visual* Web page editor, it's also one of the best text-editing programs on the market. Many of the improvements made in Dreamweaver CS4 are aimed specifically at people who spend time looking at the raw HTML, CSS, and JavaScript code on a Web page.

- **Have it your way.** As if Dreamweaver didn't have enough going for it, the engineers at Adobe have created a software product that is completely customizable, or, as they call it, *extensible*. Anyone can add to or change the menus, commands, objects, and windows in the program.

  Suppose, for example, that you hardly ever use any of the commands in the Edit menu. By editing one text file in the Dreamweaver Configuration folder, you can get rid of any unwanted menu items—or even add new commands of your own creation. This incredible flexibility lets you customize the program to fit your work methods, and even add features that Adobe's programmers never imagined. Best of all, the Adobe Exchange Web site includes hundreds of free and commercial extensions to download and add to Dreamweaver. See Chapter 21 for details.

  Dreamwever CS4 also sports a completely new interface that lets you configure the program's many panels, toolbars, and inspectors in nearly an unlimited number of ways—all of which ensures that the program fits nearly every screen size available and conforms to just about every Web design workflow.

- **Part of the Creative Suite.** Since Adobe purchased Macromedia (the original creator of Dreamweaver), Web designers now have access to a much larger family of design tools including Adobe Photoshop and Illustrator. Ultimately all these Adobe programs will work together seamlessly and share a common appearance. Dreamweaver CS4 now sports the same interface as the rest of the Creative Suite, so if you're a long time Photoshop or Illustrator user, you'll feel at home with the revamped design. In addition, Dreamweaver CS4 expands on the Photoshop integration added in the last version of Dreamweaver. Now, you can use Adobe's "Smart Object" technology to keep your site's graphics in sync with any changes you make to an original Photoshop file (see page 217).

What's New in Dreamweaver CS4

If you've never used Dreamweaver before, see Chapter 1 for a welcome and the grand tour. If you're upgrading from Dreamweaver CS3 or some other version, you'll find that Dreamweaver CS4 offers a host of new features.

- **New Look.** When Adobe bought Dreamweaver from Macromedia, they pretty much left the program's user interface alone. In CS4, Dreamweaver now shares the same look and feel as other programs in the Creative Suite like Photoshop and Illustrator. Not only do the buttons, panels, windows, and toolbars look different compared to previous versions of Dreamweaver, they can now be configured in many different ways to match the way you want to work. You'll learn more about this in Chapter 1.

  The Property inspector (see page 30) has also been revamped. In addition to a cosmetic makeover, it also works differently, making a clear distinction between its two uses as an HTML building tool and a CSS creation tool.

- **Coding Improvements.** Adobe realized that a lot of Dreamweaver users actually spend a fair amount of time in Code view—tweaking HTML, coding CSS, and writing JavaScript programs. Even if the visual Design view is where you feel most comfortable, going into Code view can sometimes make your work more accurate and go faster. With that in mind, Dreamweaver CS4 offers many new features meant to make working in Code view better. First of all, many Web pages actually rely on other external files such as Cascading Style Sheets and external JavaScript files. A new, Related Files toolbar gives one click access to every CSS, JavaScript or server-side programming file the current Web document depends on.

  In addition, you can now view Code and Design view in a side-by-side Split view (previous versions could only display the two views on top of each other—not exactly an optimum use of the space on most widescreen displays.) In this way, you can have the best of both worlds without having to repeatedly switch back and forth—this improvement alone is a great way for visual designers to get comfortable with and learn HTML, CSS, and JavaScript code, and for hand-coders to get used to Dreamweaver's visual display.

- **More Spry goodies.** Dreamweaver CS3 introduced a powerful set of JavaScript Web page enhancements based on Adobe's "Spry Framework" (a collection of JavaScript programs developed by Adobe). These new features made it easy to add pop-up navigational menus, validate HTML forms, include complex, animated visual effects, and add interactive data tables. The Spry Menu Bar, for example, lets you quickly and easily add a pop-up navigational menu to your site—without you having to learn all the messy JavaScript and CSS to make it happen.

  While Dreamweaver CS4 doesn't add as many cool new JavaScript goodies as the last version, you'll find new form validation tools for making sure a visitor registering on a Web site provides a tricky-enough password, and that at least one button is selected in a group of radio buttons (see Chapter 11). And the new Spry Tooltip, presented in Chapter 12, lets you add pop-up information bubbles that appear when a visitor mouses over an element on the page; for example, you can provide supplemental information such as details about a photo that a visitor moves his mouse over.

  In addition, the Spry Dataset tool has been improved, letting you use info from a basic HTML table to create an engaging, interactive page that lets you present lots of information in a compact page design—all updated with new information as a visitor clicks around the page. Chapter 12 has the details.

- **JavaScript Programming benefits.** While Dreamweaver's Spry tools make it easy to add sophisticated programming to a page, many Web designers want more interactivity than Dreamweaver offers. JavaScript plays a big role in many modern Web sites, and lots of Web designers are choosing to dip their toes into the JavaScript pool (if you are too, *JavaScript: The Missing Manual* is a great place to start). Dreamweaver CS4 offers many new features aimed at making

JavaScript programming easier. JavaScript code-hinting saves your weary fingers by automatically completing JavaScript programming terms and anticipating what you'll type next.

The new Live Mode actually lets you preview what your page will look like and how its JavaScript will perform without having to leave the program—Apple's WebKit browser is now built-into Dreamweaver to give you a high-fidelity representation of your Web page. In addition, a "pause JavaScript" function lets you stop a JavaScript program in mid-stream—for example, you can mouse over a Spry navigation menu, see a pop-menu of options appear, and then freeze the page with the menu open. Besides just looking cool, this neat feature lets you analyze the CSS of a dynamic element (like the pop-opened menu) and see which styles are affecting it, so you can tweak the display to be just perfect.

- **Greater Photoshop integration.** Dreamweaver CS3 added integrated support for Photoshop, so that a Web designer could copy from Photoshop and paste into Dreamweaver. It all happened thanks to an image optimization window in Dreamweaver which streamlined the process of turning a Photoshop document into a graphic format ready for the Web. CS4 adds support for Adobe "Smart Objects" so you can maintain a connection between a high-quality Photoshop file and the smaller, lower quality Web version of the image. If you edit the original graphic file in Photoshop, Dreamweaver automatically updates the Web version, skipping all those intermediate steps usually required to optimize a Photoshop image for the Web.
- **And more.** Dreamweaver CS4 also includes lots of little enhancements, such as improved FTP performance for more quickly transferring files to a Web server, a more industry-standard method of embedding Flash movies into a Web page (page 597), the ability to share your Dreamweaver screen with other users over the Web, support for Adobe's InContext Editing service to make it easier for non-Web designers to update pages that you build for them, and more.

Note: Adobe occasionally issues updates to Dreamweaver. To make sure you're using the latest version, visit the Adobe Web site at *www.adobe.com/products/dreamweaver/*.

HTML, XHTML, CSS, and JavaScript 101

Underneath the hood of any Web page—whether it's your uncle's "Check out this summer's fishin'" page or the front door of a billion-dollar online retailer—is nothing more than line after line of ordinary typed text. With its use of simple commands called *tags*, HTML (Hypertext Markup Language) is still at the heart of most of the Web.

The HTML code that creates a Web page can be as simple as this:

```
<html>
<head>
<title>Hey, I am the title of this Web page.</title>
</head>
<body>
<p>Hey, I am some body text on this Web page.</p>
</body>
</html>
```

While it may not be exciting, the HTML shown here is all you need to make an actual Web page.

Of Tags and Properties

In the example above—and, indeed, in the HTML code of any Web page you examine—you'll notice that most commands appear in *pairs* that surround a block of text or other commands.

These bracketed commands constitute the "markup" part of the Hypertext Markup Language and are called *tags*. Sandwiched between brackets, tags are simply instructions that tell a Web browser how to display the Web page.

The starting tag of each pair tells the browser where the instruction begins, and the ending tag tells it where the instruction ends. An ending tag always includes a forward slash (/) after the first bracket symbol (<), which tells the browser that it is a closing tag.

Fortunately, Dreamweaver can generate all these tags *automatically*. There's no need for you to memorize or even type these commands (although many programmers still enjoy doing so for greater control). Behind the scenes, Dreamweaver's all-consuming mission is to convert your visual designs into underlying codes like these:

- The <html> tag appears once at the beginning of a Web page and again (with an added slash) at the end. This tag tells a Web browser that the information contained in this document is written in HTML, as opposed to some other language. All the contents of a page, including other tags, appear between the opening and closing <html> tags.

  If you were to think of a Web page as a tree, the <html> tag would be its trunk. Springing from the trunk are two branches that represent the two main parts of any Web page: the head and the body.

- The *head* of a Web page, surrounded by <head> tags, contains the title of the page. It may also provide other, invisible information (such as search keywords) that browsers and Web search engines can exploit.

  In addition, the head can contain information that the Web browser uses for displaying the Web page and adding interactivity. CSS styles and JavaScript code, for example, can be stored in the head (as can links to external files containing either of these elements). In fact, Dreamweaver's Spry widgets (Chapter 12) achieve their interactive effects with the help of JavaScript code that's stored in separate files and linked to from a page's head.

- The *body* of a Web page, as set apart by its surrounding <body> tags, contains all the information that appears inside a browser window—headlines, text, pictures, and so on.

  In Dreamweaver, the blank white portion of the document window represents the body area (see Figure I-1). It resembles the blank window of a word processing program.

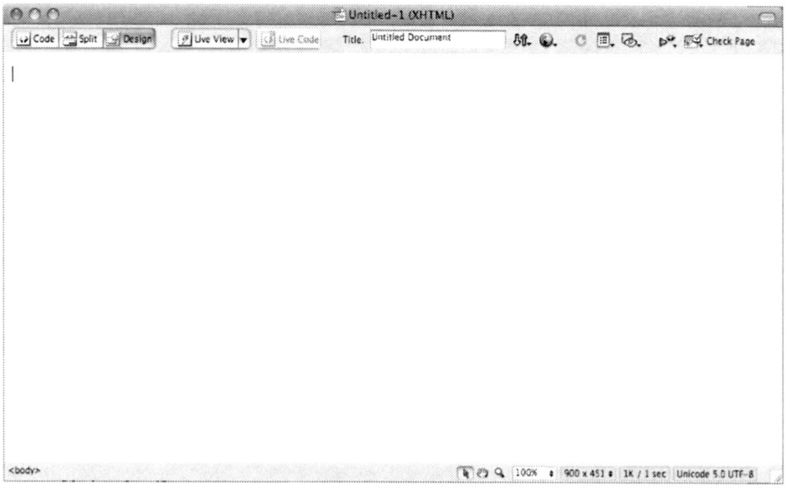

Figure I-1: *The document window displays your page as you build it. You can add text, graphics, and other elements to it, and–thanks to Dreamweaver's visual approach–see a close approximation of how the page will appear in a Web browser.*

Most of your work with Dreamweaver involves inserting and formatting text, pictures, and other objects in the body of the document. Many tags commonly used in Web pages appear within the <body> tag. Here are a few:

- You can tell a Web browser where a paragraph of text begins with a <p> (opening paragraph tag), and where it ends with a </p> (closing paragraph tag).

- The <strong> tag is used to emphasize text. If you surround some text with it and its partner tag, </strong>, you get boldface type. The HTML snippet <strong>Warning!</strong> would tell a Web browser to display the word "Warning!" in bold type on the screen.

- The <a> tag, or anchor tag, creates a link (hyperlink) in a Web page. A link, of course, can lead anywhere on the Web. How do you tell the browser where the link should point? Simply give address instructions to the browser inside the <a> tags. For instance, you might type *<a href="http://www.missingmanuals.com/">Click here!</a>*.

The browser knows that when your visitor clicks the words "Click here!" it should go to the Missing Manuals Web site. The *href* part of the tag is called, in Dreamweaver, a *property* (you may also hear the term *attribute*), and the URL (the Uniform Resource Locator, or Web address) is the *value*. In this example, *http://www.missingmanuals.com* is the value of the *href* property.

Fortunately, Dreamweaver exempts you from having to type any of these codes and provides an easy-to-use window called the *Property inspector* for adding properties to your tags and other page elements. To create links the Dreamweaver way (read: the easy way), turn to Chapter 5.

Note: For a full-fledged introduction to HTML, check out *Creating a Web Site: The Missing Manual*. For a primer that's geared to readers who want to master CSS, pick up a copy of *CSS: The Missing Manual*. And if you want to add interactivity to your Web pages (beyond the cool, ready-to-use features offered by Dreamweaver) then you might be interested in *JavaScript: The Missing Manual*.

XHTML, Too

Like any technology, HTML has evolved over time. Although standard HTML has served its purpose well, it's always been a somewhat sloppy language. Among other things, it allows uppercase, lowercase, or mixed-case letters in tags (<body> and <BODY> are both correct, for example) and permits unclosed tags (so that you can use a single <p> tag without the closing </p> to create a paragraph). While this flexibility may make page writing easier, it also makes life more difficult for Web browsers, smart phones, and other technologies that must interact with data on the Web. Additionally, HTML doesn't work with one of the hottest Internet languages: XML, or Extensible Markup Language (see page 522 for a quick intro to XML). In fact, XHTML is just an "XML-ified" version of HTML.

To keep pace with the times, an improved version of HTML called XHTML was introduced back in 2000 and you'll find it used frequently on many sites. Dreamweaver CS4 can create and work with XHTML files as well as plain HTML. If you understand only HTML, don't worry—XHTML isn't a revolutionary new language that takes years to learn. It's basically HTML, but with somewhat stricter guidelines. For example, the HTML page code shown on page 8 would look like *this* in XHTML:

```
<!DOCTYPE html PUBLIC "-//W3C//DTD XHTML 1.0 Transitional//EN"
"http://www.w3.org/TR/xhtml1/DTD/xhtml1-transitional.dtd">
<html xmlns="http://www.w3.org/1999/xhtml">
<head>
<title>Hey, I am the title of this Web page.</title>
<meta http-equiv="Content-Type" content="text/html; charset=iso
8859-1" />
</head>
<body>
<p>Hey, I am some body text on this Web page.</p>
</body>
</html>
```

Notice that everything below the <head> is *nearly* the same as the HTML page. The information that begins the page, however, is how the page identifies which standards it conforms to. In this case, it merely says that the page is using a particular brand of HTML, called XHTML, and more specifically a type of XHTML called Transitional 1.0. (Don't worry—Dreamweaver automatically writes all of this code when you create a new XHTML page.)

As you can see, the real code used to make the page is much like HTML. To make an XHTML file comply with XML, however, there are a few strict rules to keep in mind:

- **Begin the page with a document-type declaration and a namespace.** That's the first few lines in the code above. They simply state what type of document the page is and point to files on the Web that contain definitions for this type of file. This document-type declaration (or DTD) is also important as it affects how Web browsers display a Web page—stick with any of the DTDs Dreamweaver writes and you'll be OK.
- **Tags and tag attributes must be lowercase.** Unlike in HTML, typing the tag <BODY> in an XHTML file is incorrect. It must be lowercase like this: <body>.
- **Quotation marks are required for tag attributes.** For example, a link written like this: <a href=*http://www.missingmanuals.com* > is valid in HTML, but doesn't work in XHTML. You have to enclose the value of the *href* property in quotes: <a href="*http://www.missingmanuals.com*">.
- **All tags (even empty tags) must be closed.** To create a paragraph in XHTML, for example, you must begin with <p> and end with </p>. However, some tags don't come in pairs. These tags, called *empty tags*, have no closing tag. The line break tag is one example. To close an empty tag, you must include a backslash at the end of the tag, like this: <br />.

If all this seems a bit confusing, don't worry. All these strict XHTML rules are built into Dreamweaver, so creating an XHTML page using Dreamweaver's visual design tools won't feel one bit different from creating an old-style HTML page. (For more information on creating an XHTML page in Dreamweaver, see page 44.) In fact, with just a couple of exceptions discussed on page 46, it doesn't really matter which version of HTML or XHTML you use—pick one and let Dreamweaver take care of the rest.

Note: When XHTML was introduced it was heralded as the next big thing, and an intermediate step in the transition to XML as the prime language of the Web. History proves that that prediction was a bit grandiose. As it turns out, the complexity of moving to XML has kept browser manufacturers from following the XML path laid down by the W3C–the group responsible for coming up with many Internet technologies. Now, the W3C is working on a new version of HTML, called HTML 5, which is a move *away* from XML and back to plain HTML–albeit an enhanced version of HTML. Since all the browser manufacturers are behind HTML 5 (and some browsers are already adopting parts of it), it's a good bet that down the line HTML 5 will be the new big thing. So if your know-it-all co-worker says that you MUST use XHTML because it's the future, just say "What about HTML 5?" That should keep him quiet. To learn more about HTML 5 visit *www.w3.org/html/wg/html5/*.

Adding Style with Cascading Style Sheets

HTML used to be the only language you needed to know. You could build pages with colorful text and graphics and make words jump out using different sizes, fonts, and colors. But today, you can't add much visual sophistication to a site without CSS. CSS is a formatting language used to make text look good, add sophisticated layout to pages, and basically add style to your site.

From now on, think of HTML as merely the language you use to give organization to a page. It helps identify and structure the stuff you want the world to know about. Tags like <h1>, <h2>, and <title> denote headlines and assign them relative importance: a *heading 1* is more important than a *heading 2* (and can also affect how a search engine like Google adds a page to its search listings [see page 96]). The <p> tag indicates a basic paragraph of information. Other tags provide further structural clues: for example, a <ul> tag identifies a bulleted list (to make a list of recipe ingredients more intelligible).

Cascading Style Sheets, on the other hand, add design flair to the highly structured HTML content, making it more beautiful and easier to read. Essentially, a CSS style is just a rule that tells a Web browser how to display a particular element on a page—for example, to make a <h1> tag appear 36 pixels tall, in the Verdana font and the color orange.

But CSS is more powerful than that. You can use it to add borders, change margins, and even control the exact placement of an element on a page.

If you want to be a Web designer, you need to get to know Cascading Style Sheets. You'll learn more about this exciting technology throughout this book. In fact, it's so important for current Web design, that this edition of *Dreamweaver: The Missing Manual* includes expanded coverage and examples of CSS in most chapters.

Adding Interactivity with JavaScript

A normal Web page—just regular HTML and CSS—isn't very responsive: Web visitors basically interact with a Web page by clicking a link to load a new Web page. While we've grown accustomed to the "click-and-wait" slowness of the Web, we're also used to the way our computers' desktop programs react immediately to our every mouse-click. JavaScript is a programming language that lets you super charge your HTML with animation, interactivity, and dynamic visual effects. JavaScript also can make a Web page more useful, by supplying immediate feedback to Web site visitors. For example, a JavaScript-powered shopping cart page can instantly display a total cost, with tax and shipping, the moment a visitor selects a product to buy; or JavaScript can produce an error message immediately after someone attempts to submit a Web form that's missing necessary information.

JavaScript's main selling point is its immediacy. It lets Web pages respond instantly to the actions of someone interacting with a page: clicking a link, filling out a form, or merely moving the mouse around the screen. JavaScript doesn't suffer from the frustrating delay associated with "server-side" programming languages like PHP which rely on communication between the Web browser and the Web server—in other words, constantly loading and reloading Web pages. JavaScript lets you create Web pages that feel and act more like desktop programs than Web pages.

If you've visited Google Maps (*http://maps.google.com/*) you've seen JavaScript in action. Google Maps lets you view a map, zoom in to get a detailed view of streets, and zoom out to get a birds-eye view of how to get across town, the state, or the nation. While there have been lots of map Web sites before Google, those sites always required reloading multiple Web pages (a usually slow process) to get to the information you wanted. Google Maps, on the other hand, works without page refreshes: It responds immediately to your choices.

The programs you create with JavaScript can range from the really simple (such as popping-up a new browser window with a Web page in it) to full blown "Web applications" such as Google Docs (*http://docs.google.com/*), which let you create presentations, edit documents, and create spreadsheets using your Web browser—all with the feel of a program running directly on your computer.

While JavaScript programming can be difficult, Dreamweaver has plenty of tools to let you add sophisticated interactivity to your Web sites—from animations to drop-down navigation menus—in just a few mouse clicks.

The Very Basics

You'll find very little jargon or nerd terminology in this book. You will, however, encounter a few terms and concepts that you'll encounter frequently in your computing life:

- **Clicking.** This book gives you three kinds of instructions that require you to use your computer's mouse or trackpad. To *click* means to point the arrow cursor at something on the screen and then—without moving the cursor at all—press and release the clicker button on the mouse (or laptop trackpad). To *double-click*, of course, means to click twice in rapid succession, again without moving the cursor at all. And to *drag* means to move the cursor while holding down the button.

- **Keyboard shortcuts.** Every time you take your hand off the keyboard to move the mouse, you lose time and potentially disrupt your creative flow. That's why many experienced computer fans use keystroke combinations instead of menu commands wherever possible. Ctrl+B (⌘-B for Mac folks), for example, is a keyboard shortcut for boldface type in Dreamweaver (and most other programs).

  When you see a shortcut like Ctrl+S (⌘-S), it's telling you to hold down the Ctrl or ⌘ key and, while it's down, type the letter S, and then release both keys. (This command, by the way, saves changes to the current document.)

- **Choice is good.** Dreamweaver frequently gives you several ways to trigger a particular command—by selecting a menu command, *or* by clicking a toolbar button, *or* by pressing a key combination, for example. Some people prefer the speed of keyboard shortcuts; others like the satisfaction of a visual command available in menus or toolbars. This book lists all the alternatives; use whichever you find most convenient.

About This Book

Despite the many improvements in software over the years, one feature has grown consistently worse: documentation. Until version 4, Dreamweaver came with a printed manual. But since MX 2004, all you get is a *Getting Started* booklet. To get any real information, you need to delve into the program's online help screens.

But even if you have no problem reading a help screen in one window as you work in another, something's still missing. At times, the terse electronic help screens assume you already understand the discussion at hand, and hurriedly skip over important topics that require an in-depth presentation. In addition, you don't always get an objective evaluation of the program's features. Engineers often add technically sophisticated features to a program because they *can*, not because you need them. You shouldn't have to waste your time learning tools that don't help you get your work done.

The purpose of this book, then, is to serve as the manual that should have been in the box. In this book's pages, you'll find step-by-step instructions for using every Dreamweaver feature, including those you may not even have quite understood, let alone mastered, such as Libraries, Layout view, Behaviors, and Dreamweaver's Spry tools. In addition, you'll find honest evaluations of each tool to help you determine which ones are useful to you, as well as how and when to use them.

Note: This book periodically recommends *other* books, covering topics that are too specialized or tangential for a manual about using Dreamweaver. Careful readers may notice that not every one of these titles is published by Missing Manual parent O'Reilly Media. While we're happy to mention other Missing Manuals and books in the O'Reilly family, if there's a great book out there that doesn't happen to be published by O'Reilly, we'll still let you know about it.

Dreamweaver CS4: The Missing Manual is designed to accommodate readers at every technical level. The primary discussions are written for advanced-beginner or intermediate computer users. But if you're new to building Web pages, special sidebar articles called "Up To Speed" provide the introductory information you need to understand the topic at hand. If you're a Web veteran, on the other hand, keep your eye out for similar shaded boxes called "Power Users' Clinic". They offer more technical tips, tricks, and shortcuts for the experienced computer fan.

About → These → Arrows

Throughout this book, and throughout the Missing Manual series, you'll find sentences like this one: "Open the System → Library → Fonts folder." That's shorthand for a much longer instruction that directs you to open three nested folders in sequence, like this: "On your hard drive, you'll find a folder called System. Open that. Inside the System folder window is a folder called Library; double-click it to open it. Inside *that* folder is yet another one called Fonts. Double-click to open it, too."

Similarly, this kind of arrow shorthand helps to simplify the business of choosing commands in menus, as shown in Figure I-2.

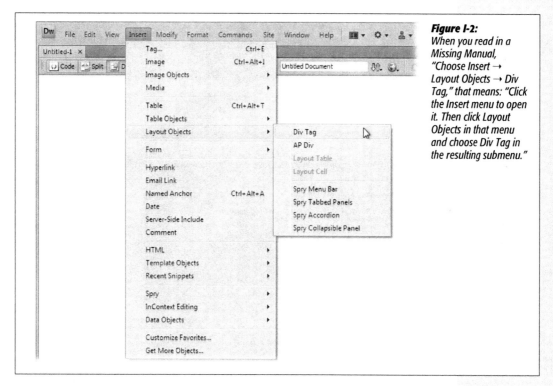

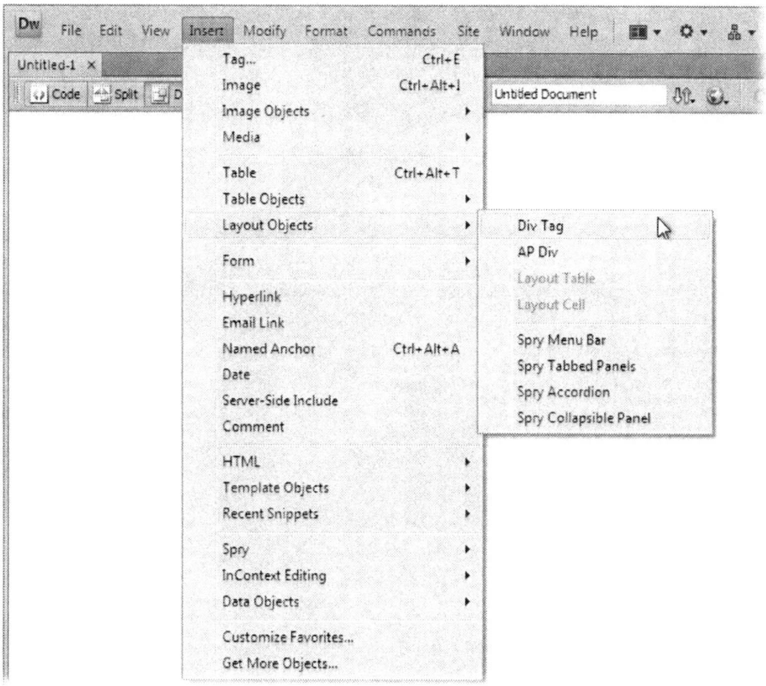

Figure I-2:
When you read in a Missing Manual, "Choose Insert → Layout Objects → Div Tag," that means: "Click the Insert menu to open it. Then click Layout Objects in that menu and choose Div Tag in the resulting submenu."

Macintosh and Windows

Dreamweaver CS4 works almost precisely the same way in its Macintosh and Windows versions. Every button in every dialog box is exactly the same; the software response to every command is identical. In this book, the illustrations have been given even-handed treatment, alternating between the various operating systems where Dreamweaver feels at home (Windows XP, Windows Vista, and Mac OS X).

One of the biggest differences between Mac and Windows software is the keystrokes, because the Ctrl key in Windows is the equivalent of the Macintosh ⌘ key.

And the key labeled Alt on a PC (and on non-U.S. Macs) is the equivalent of the Option key on American Mac keyboards.

Whenever this book refers to a key combination, therefore, you'll see the Windows keystroke listed first (with + symbols, as is customary in Windows documentation); the Macintosh keystroke follows in parentheses (with - symbols, in time honored Mac fashion). In other words, you might read, "The keyboard shortcut for saving a file is Ctrl+S (⌘-S)."

About the Outline

Dreamweaver CS4: The Missing Manual is divided into six parts, each containing several chapters:

- **Part One: Building a Web Page**, explores Dreamweaver's interface and takes you through the basic steps of building a Web page. It explains how to add text and format it, how to link from one page to another, how to spice up your designs with graphics, and introduces you to Cascading Style Sheets.
- **Part Two: Building a Better Web Page**, takes you deeper into Dreamweaver and provides in-depth CSS coverage. In addition, you'll get step-by-step instructions for creating advanced page layouts, as well as advice on how to view and work with the underlying HTML code of a page.

Note: Previous versions of this book contained a chapter on HTML frames–a method of displaying several Web pages in a single Web browser window. This technique is going the way of the dodo bird. Since Dreamweaver CS4 is full of so many useful and exciting features and this book's already bursting at its seams (if we added any more pages, we'd have to issue a medical warning to those with bad backs), the frames chapter has been moved online. You can find it, free of charge, at *www.sawmac.com/missing/dw8/appc.pdf*.

- **Part Three: Bringing Your Pages to Life**, helps you add interactivity to your site. From using forms to collect information from your site's visitors to adding interactive page widgets like tabbed interfaces with the Spry framework, this section guides you through adding animation, multimedia, and other interactive effects with ease.
- **Part Four: Building a Web Site**, covers the big picture: managing the pages and files in your Web site, testing links and pages, and moving your site onto a Web server connected to the Internet. And since you're not always working solo, this section also covers features that let you work with a team of Web developers.
- **Part Five, Dreamweaver Power**, shows you how to take full advantage of such time-saving features as Libraries, Templates, and History panel automation. It also covers Dreamweaver's Extension Manager, a program that can add hundreds of new free and commercial features to the program.

- **Part Six: Dynamic Dreamweaver**, presents a gentle introduction to the often confusing and complex world of database-driven Web sites. You'll learn what you need to know to build a dynamic Web site; how to connect Dreamweaver to a database; and how to use Dreamweaver to build pages that can display database information as well as add, edit, and delete database records. The last chapter of this section covers the powerful XSLT tools for converting XML files (including RSS feeds) into browser-ready Web designs.

At the end of the book, two appendixes provide a list of Internet resources for additional Web design help and a menu-by-menu explanation of Dreamweaver CS4.

Living Examples

This book is designed to get your work onto the Web faster and more professionally; it's only natural, then, that half the value of this book also lies on the Web.

As you read the book's chapters, you'll encounter a number of *living examples*—step-by-step tutorials that you can build yourself, using raw materials (like graphics and half-completed Web pages) that you can download from either *www.sawmac.com/dwcs4/* or from this book's "Missing CD" page at *www.missingmanuals.com*. You might not gain very much from simply reading these step-by-step lessons while relaxing in your porch hammock. But if you take the time to work through them at the computer, you'll discover that these tutorials give you unprecedented insight into the way professional designers build Web pages.

You'll also find, in this book's lessons, the URLs of the finished pages, so that you can compare your Dreamweaver work with the final result. In other words, you won't just see pictures of Dreamweaver's output in the pages of the book; you'll find the actual, working Web pages on the Internet.

About MissingManuals.com

At *www.missingmanuals.com*, you'll find articles, tips, and updates to *Dreamweaver CS4: The Missing Manual*. In fact, we invite and encourage you to submit such corrections and updates yourself. In an effort to keep the book as up to date and accurate as possible, each time we print more copies of this book, we'll make any confirmed corrections you've suggested. We'll also note such changes on the Web site, so that you can mark important corrections into your own copy of the book, if you like. (Click the book's name, and then click the Errata link, to see the changes.)

In the meantime, we'd love to hear your own suggestions for new books in the Missing Manual line. There's a place for that on the Web site, too, as well as a place to sign up for free email notification of new titles in the series. And while you're online, you can also register this book at *www.oreilly.com* (you can jump directly to the registration page by going here: *https://epoch.oreilly.com/register/default.orm*. Registering means we can send you updates about this book, and you'll be eligible for special offers like discounts on future editions.

Safari® Books Online

When you see a Safari® Books Online icon on the cover of your favorite technology book, that means the book is available online through the O'Reilly Network Safari Bookshelf.

Safari offers a solution that's better than e-books. It's a virtual library that lets you easily search thousands of top tech books, cut and paste code samples, download chapters, and find quick answers when you need the most accurate, current information. Try it for free at *http://safari.oreilly.com*.

1

Part One: Building a Web Page

CHAPTER

1

Dreamweaver CS4 Guided Tour

Dreamweaver CS4 is a powerful program for designing and building Web sites. If you're brand-new to Dreamweaver, then turn to page 1 to get an overview of what this program can do and what's new in this latest version. This chapter provides a basic overview of the different windows, toolbars, and menus that you'll use every time you build a Web page. You'll also learn to set up the program so you can begin building Web pages. And, because *doing* is often a better way to learn than just *reading*, you'll get a step-by-step tour of Web page design—the Dreamweaver way—in the tutorial at the end of this chapter.

The Dreamweaver CS4 Interface

Dreamweaver CS4's interface is a big departure from previous versions of the program. Adobe has scrapped the original Dreamweaver look and feel, and replaced it with one that's shared by other programs in the "Creative Suite" like Photoshop, Illustrator, and Flash. Even long-time Dreamweaver owners will have a little learning to do to get up to speed with the program's new layout. And not only is the program's look different, but the interface is very customizable: You can display the various windows in a variety of different ways to match your monitor size and how *you* want to work with the program.

Out-of-the-box, Dreamweaver organizes its various windows as a unified whole (see Figure 1-1). That is, the edges of all the different windows touch; resizing one window affects the others around it. This type of interface is common on Windows computers, but Mac fans who are accustomed to independent floating windows might find this type of look strange. Give it a chance. As you'll soon see, this design has some benefits. (But, if you just can't stand this locked-in-place style, you can detach the various panels, and then place them wherever you'd like on the screen.)

Many of the program's individual windows are used to assist with specific tasks, like building style sheets, and are described in the relevant chapters. But you'll frequently interact with four main groups of windows: the document window, the application bar, the Property inspector, and panel groups.

Note: The look of these windows depends on what kind of computer you're using (Windows or Macintosh) and what changes you've made to the program's preference settings.

Even so, the features and functions generally work the same way no matter what your situation. In this book, where the program's operation differs dramatically in one operating system or the other, special boxes and illustrations (labeled "For Macs Only" or "For Windows Only") will let you know.

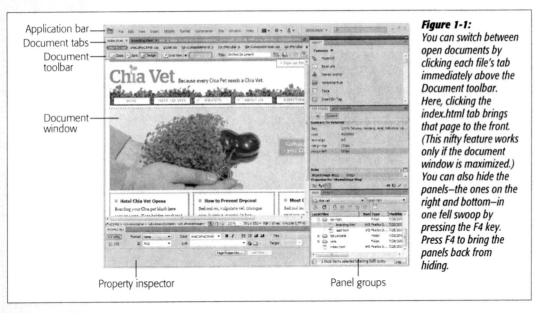

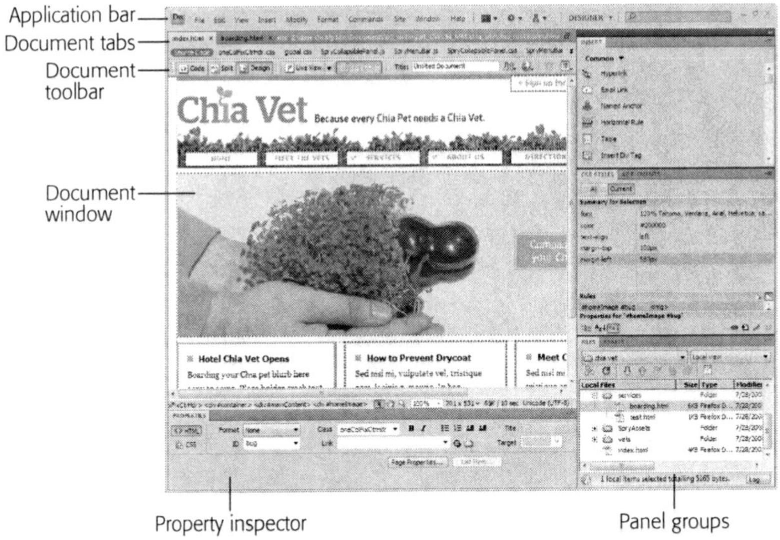

Figure 1-1: *You can switch between open documents by clicking each file's tab immediately above the Document toolbar. Here, clicking the index.html tab brings that page to the front. (This nifty feature works only if the document window is maximized.) You can also hide the panels—the ones on the right and bottom—in one fell swoop by pressing the F4 key. Press F4 to bring the panels back from hiding.*

The Document Window

You build Web pages in the *document window*. As in a word processor, simply click inside the document window, and then type to add text to the page. You'll work in this window as you build a page, and you'll open new document windows as you add or edit pages for your site.

Several other screen components provide useful information about your document. These components may appear in different locations on Windows computers and on Macs (see Figure 1-1 and Figure 1-2, respectively), but they work the same way. For example:

- **Title bar** (**Mac only**). The title bar shows the name of the file on which you're currently working. In addition, if the Web page is XHTML-compliant (see page 10), then that's indicated in parentheses. For instance, in the example shown in Figure 1-2 the Web page is written in XHTML, and saved as a file named *index.html.*
- **Document tabs.** When more than one Web document is open, small tabs appear at the top of the document window—one for each file. The name of the file appears in the tab; to switch to another open file, just click its tab. In Windows, the Document tab bar also displays the location on your computer for the file currently being viewed (see Figure 1-1).
- **Related files bar.** The related files bar is new in Dreamweaver CS4. It lists all CSS, JavaScript, or server-side programming pages (like ASP or PHP) that the current Web page uses. You'll learn more about external files such as external style sheets (page 113), external JavaScript files (page 426), and server side pages (section 6) later in this book. But as a quick summary, it's very common in current Web design to use other files to supply design and interactivity to a page of HTML. Web designers frequently work on these files, so this new related files bar lets you quickly jump to and work on an external style sheet or JavaScript file.
- **Document toolbar.** The Document toolbar (see Figure 1-2) lets you change the title of a page, switch between Design and Code views, jump to Live view (to see how the page will look and work in a Web browser), preview the page in different Web browsers, check if the HTML code for the page is valid (that is, written correctly), and change the look of the document window. You'll read about its various buttons and menus in the relevant chapters of this book, but you'll want to be aware of the Code, Split, and Design buttons (circled in Figure 1-2). Those buttons let you see, respectively, just the raw HTML of the file you're working on; a split view showing that code in one half of the window and the visual, design view in the other half; and, finally, a button for showing just the design of the page. In this book, we'll assume that you're in Design view (the visual, "this is what your page will pretty much look like in a browser" view) most of the time. (To make the toolbar visible if it's not already, choose View → Toolbars → Document.)

Note: You might find two other toolbars, the Standard toolbar and Style Rendering toolbar, useful. The Standard toolbar is common on many Windows programs and includes buttons for frequent file and editing tasks like creating a new page, opening a page, saving one or all open documents, cutting, copying, pasting, and undoing and redoing actions. (This toolbar is hidden until you summon it by choosing View → Toolbars → Standard.) The Style Rendering toolbar comes in handy when working with CSS. You'll learn how to use it on page 324.

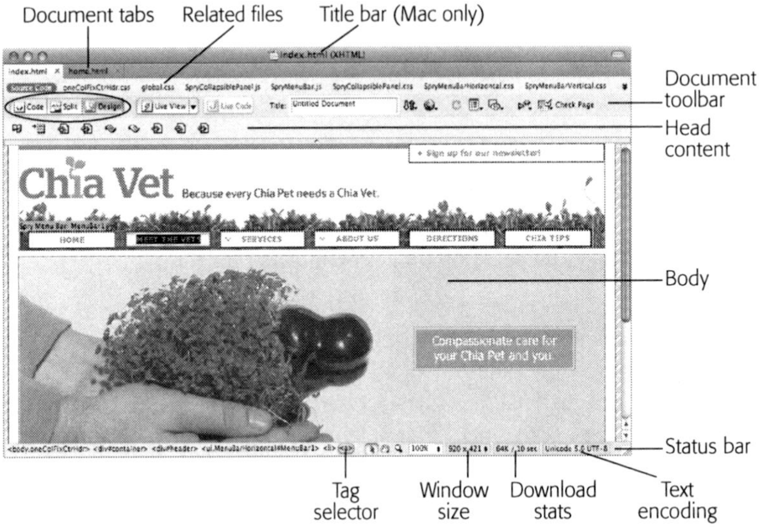

***Figure 1-2:** A document window like this represents each Web page; here's where you add text, graphics, and other objects as you build a page. The status bar at the bottom of the window provides some added useful information. It shows you how quickly the page will download over a 56k modem (who has that anymore? Page 665 tells you how to change this setting). In addition, the status bar lists the page's text encoding–encoding refers to the characters the computer uses to represent text on the page. Pages you build nowadays use UTF-8, which lets you include lots of different characters–including letters from other non-Latin based languages. On page 76, you'll see how UTF-8 lets you easily include fancy typographic characters like em-dashes and real ellipses.*

- **Head content.** Most of what you put on a Web page winds up in the body of the page, but some elements are specific to the region of the page called the *head* (see Figure 1-2). This is where you put things like the page's title, the *meta tags* (keywords) that provide information for some search engines and browsers, JavaScript scripts, and CSS information (Chapter 6).

  None of this information is actually visible on your Web page once it's "live" on the Internet. But while working in Dreamweaver, you can have a look at it by choosing View → Head Content. You'll see a row of icons representing the different bits of information in the head.

- **The Tag selector** (labeled in Figure 1-2) is also extremely useful. It provides a sneak peek at the HTML that, behind the scenes, composes your Web page. It indicates how tags are nested in the document based on what you've selected or the insertion point's location.

  You can also use the Tag selector to select an HTML tag and all the information nested inside it. For instance, say the insertion point is somewhere in the middle of a paragraph; clicking the <p> tag selects that paragraph and everything inside it. This feature is very useful when you want to set properties (see page 30),

GEM IN THE ROUGH

The Window Size Pop-Up Menu

Creating pages that look good on different monitors set to a wide range of resolutions is one of the most difficult tasks facing Web designers. After all, not everyone has a 21-inch monitor or views Web sites with the browser window maximized to fill the whole screen. Nothing's more dispiriting than spending a solid week designing the coolest-looking Web page, only to have your client call up to say that your design doesn't fit his 17-inch monitor (a painfully common story).

You could simulate browser windows of different sizes by dragging the resize handle at the lower-right corner of the document window. But Dreamweaver has a better tool for such experiments: the Window Size pop-up menu on the status bar at the bottom of your document window. Clicking the black arrow next to the window-size stats lets you choose a different setting for the document window, as shown here. Use this feature to test how your page will look inside different-size browser windows. The numbers indicate the width and height in pixels.

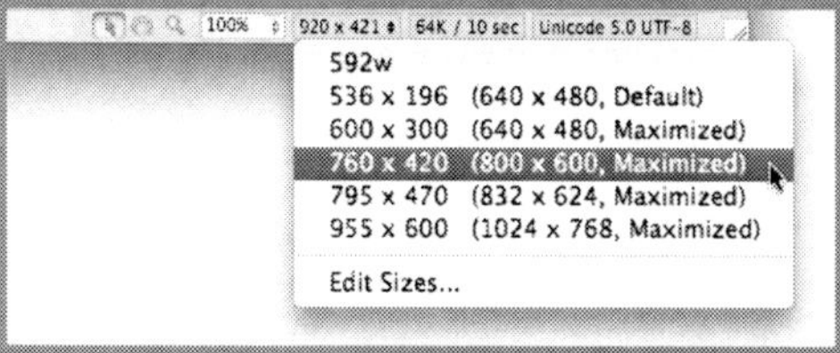

(Note to Windows folks: If your document window is maximized, this feature doesn't work. Choose Window → Cascade to "unlock" the document window from its space on the screen. Now you're free to resize the window and use the Window Size pop-up menu. However, this gets rid of the nifty document tabs that let you quickly switch between open documents—as pictured in Figure 1-1. To get them back, in the document window, just click the Maximize window button.)

The first pair of numbers indicates the amount of usable space in the document window; the numbers in parentheses indicate the resolution of the monitor. The fourth option shown here, in other words, indicates that if someone has an 800 × 600 monitor and maximizes the browser window, she has 760 × 420 pixels of space to display a Web page. (Even though a monitor's resolution is, say, 800 × 600, after you subtract the space required to display the browser's toolbar, location bar, status bar, and other "chrome," 760 × 420 pixels of space will be visible when a Web page is opened.)

In any case, note that the Window Size pop-up menu doesn't actually set the size of your Web page or add any code to your page; Web pages are usually fluid, and can grow or shrink to the size of each visitor's browser window. For techniques that let you exercise greater control over your page presentation, see Chapter 8.

add behaviors (Chapter 13), or precisely control the application of styles (Chapter 4).

You'll make good use of the Tag selector in the tutorials to come. For experienced Dreamweaver fans, it's one of the program's most popular tools.

Tip: In Design view, clicking the <body> tag in the Tag selector is usually the same as pressing Ctrl+A (⌘-A) or choosing Edit → Select All: It selects everything in the document window. However, if you've clicked inside a table (Chapter 7), or inside a <div> tag (see page 333), choosing Edit → Select All selects only the contents of the table cell or <div> tag. In this case, you need to press Ctrl+A (⌘-A) several times to select everything on a page. After selecting everything this way, you can press the Delete key to instantly get rid of everything in your document.

Careful, though: Pressing Ctrl+A (⌘-A) or choosing Edit → Select All in Code view selects all the code. Deleting *this* gives you an empty file—and an invalid Web page.

The Insert Panel

Dreamweaver CS4 provides many different windows for working with the various technologies required to build and maintain a Web site. Most of Dreamweaver's windows are called *panels* and they sit in tidy groups on the right edge of your screen. The various panels and their uses will come up in relevant sections of this book, and you'll learn about how to organize panels on page 32. But two panels are worth mentioning up front: the Insert panel and the Files panel.

The Insert panel replaces the Insert bar that appeared in previous versions of Dreamweaver. If the document window is your canvas, then the Insert panel holds your brushes and paints, as shown in Figure 1-3. While you can add text to a Web page simply by typing in the document window, adding elements like images, horizontal rules, forms, and multimedia elements is simplified by the Insert panel's click-to-add approach. Want to put a picture on your Web page? Just click the Images icon.

Note: Adding elements to your Web page this way may feel like magic, but the Insert panel is really just a quick way to add code to a page, whether it's HTML, XHTML, JavaScript, or server-side code like PHP (see Part 6 of this book). Clicking the Images icon, for instance, simply inserts the <img> tag into the underlying HTML of your page. Of course, Dreamweaver's visual approach hides that messy code and cheerfully displays a picture on the page.

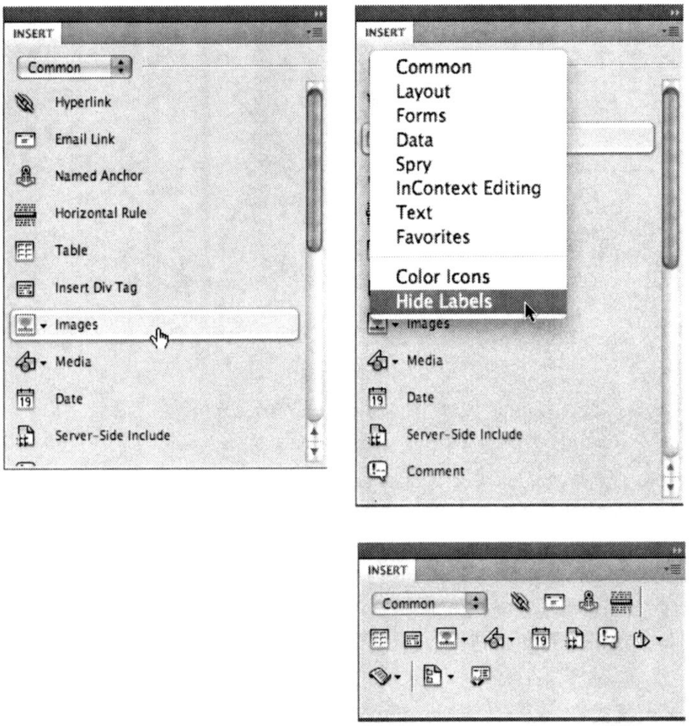

Figure 1-3: *The Insert panel normally displays the objects under each drop-down menu category in a single list with an icon and a name–for example, the picture of an envelope and the label "Email link" (top left). Unfortunately, this tall list takes up a lot of screen real estate. You can display the Insert panel's buttons in a more compact way by hiding the labels. When you choose Hide Labels from the panel's category menu (top right image), the icons are displayed side by side in rows, taking up a lot less space (bottom right image). You'll see this panel style throughout the book.*

When you first start Dreamweaver, the Insert panel is open. If you ever close it by mistake, you can open it again by choosing Window → Insert or by pressing Ctrl+F2 (⌘-F2). On the other hand, if space is at a premium on your screen, then you can close the Insert panel and use the Insert *menu* instead. Its commands duplicate all the objects available from the Insert panel.

The Insert panel offers seven sets of objects, each available by selecting an option from the menu at the top of the panel (see Figure 1-3, top right):

- **Common objects.** In addition to images, tables, and email links—which you'll use frequently in everyday Web design—this category of the Insert panel offers access to Dreamweaver's *template* features. Templates let you build basic Web page designs that you can use over and over again in your site, speeding up your production process and facilitating easy updates. See Chapter 18 for details.
- **Layout objects.** The objects in this category help you control the layout of a Web page by organizing a page's contents using CSS or HTML tables. In addition, this panel includes Dreamweaver's Spry widgets that let you add sophisticated, interactive page elements such as drop-down navigation menus and animated, collapsible panels, so you can fit more information in less space on a Web page (see Chapter 12).
- **Form objects.** Want to get some input from visitors to your Web site? You can use forms to receive their comments, collect credit card information for online sales, or gather any other kind of data. The Forms category lets you add form elements like radio buttons, pull-down menus, and text boxes (see Chapter 12). Dreamweaver CS4 includes sophisticated form validation so you can make sure that visitors input the correct information *before* they submit the form.
- **Data.** Dreamweaver makes connecting your Web pages to databases as easy as clicking a few buttons. (OK, *almost* as easy; see Part 6 for details.) The Data category provides many powerful tools for building dynamic pages: controls that add records to your database, for example, or that update information already in a database. Dreamweaver CS4 also includes several data tools that don't require a complicated database setup. The Spry dataset feature lets you display interactive data in a table, so visitors can sort the data by column and even change what's displayed on the page by interacting with the data—all without having to reload an additional Web page (Spry datasets are discussed on page 518).

Tip for Long-Time Dreamweaver Users: In previous versions the program's buttons were in color; now the buttons in the Insert panel are black and white–if you liked it better the old way, just right-click the Insert panel, and then choose Color Icons. Better yet, you can move the Insert panel back to its old location above the document window by selecting Classic from the Workspace switcher menu (see Figure 1-6). This action not only brings back the old Insert *bar*, but also adds color to all the buttons.

- **Spry.** Spry is a technology from Adobe that lets you easily add interactive features to your site: from drop-down navigation menus to animated effects to complex displays of data. Basically, Spry is a simple way for Web designers to insert complex JavaScript programming into Web sites. The Spry category gathers together all the different Spry features available in Dreamweaver CS4. You'll find the same buttons spread throughout the Insert panel; for example, the Spry tools related to form validation also appear in the Form objects category, while the Spry dataset buttons are also available from the Data category.

- **InContext Editing.** If you build Web sites that are updated by non-Web savvy folk, Adobe offers a commercial service named InContext Editing, which lets average people edit Web pages using a simple Web-based interface. If you're a freelance Web designer and you want to hand-off routine Web site maintenance chores to your clients, then this service might be for you. The box on page 741 has more on this feature.

- **Text objects.** To format type—make it bold or italic, for instance—you can turn to the Text category. Most of the buttons here aren't technically objects; they don't insert new objects onto the page. Instead, they format text already present on the page. For the most part, the Property inspector offers the same formatting options and is a more common tool for formatting text.

Note: You might find it disorienting to use the options found in the Text objects category. Some "text objects" create incomplete HTML and actually dump you into the raw HTML of the page, leaving the nice visual Design view behind. In general, the Property inspector and Text menu let you do everything in this tab–more quickly and more safely.

- **Favorites.** Perhaps the most useful category, Favorites can be anything you want it to be. That is, after you've discovered which objects you use the most (like the Image command, if you work with a lot of graphics), you can add them to this personal category. You may find that once you've customized this category, you'll never again need the other categories in the Insert panel. For instructions on adding objects to your Favorites, see the box on the opposite page.

- **ASP, PHP, ColdFusion.** If you're building database-driven Web pages, you'll discover yet another category of objects. The exact name of the category depends on the server model you're using (PHP, Microsoft's Active Server Pages, or Adobe's ColdFusion server, for example), but it always contains frequently used code snippets for the appropriate programming language. See Part 6 for more on working with these technologies.

The Files Panel

The Files panel is another panel you'll turn to frequently (see Figure 1-4). It lists all the Web files—Web pages, graphics, Flash movies, and so on—that make up your Web site. It gives you a quick way to open Web pages that you wish to work on (in the panel, just double-click the file name). It also lets you switch between different sites that you're building or maintaining, and provides some valuable tools for organizing your files. If the Files panel isn't open, summon it by choosing Window → Files or by pressing F8 (Shift-⌘-F on Macs).

FREQUENTLY ASKED QUESTION

Adding Favorite Objects to the Insert Panel

Help! I'm tired of wading through so many pull-down menus to find all my favorite Dreamweaver objects. How can I see all of my most used objects in one place?

Dreamweaver includes a marvelous productivity tool: the Favorites category of the Insert Panel. It lets you collect your most used objects into a single place, without any interference from the buttons for HTML tags and objects you never use. Maybe you use the Common category's Email Link object all the time, but never touch the Named Anchor object. This is the timesaving feature for you.

To add objects to the Favorites category, right-click (Control-click) anywhere on the Insert bar. From the shortcut menu, choose Customize Favorites to open the Customize Favorite Objects window. All the objects available in all the Insert bar categories appear in the left-hand list. Select an object, and then click the >> button to add it to your Favorites. (You can view the objects for just one category by selecting the category from the "Available objects" menu.) Repeat with other objects, if you like.

To rearrange the order of the toolbar buttons, click one, and then click the up or down arrow to move its location on the panel. Depending on how you display the panel buttons (with or without labels, as described on page 26), buttons listed higher in the list appear either toward the top of the panel or toward the beginning of the rows of buttons. You can even use the Add Separator button to insert a thin gray line between buttons on the Insert panel—to separate one group of similar objects (graphic-related objects, say) from another (such as form objects). Unfortunately, you can't group Favorite objects into submenus. Each item you add is a single button on the Insert bar.

To delete a button or separator from the list, select it, and then click the trash icon. Click OK to close the window and create your new list of Favorite objects, which are now available under the Favorites category of the Insert panel.

After you've created your Favorites tab, you can always add more objects (or delete ones you no longer need) by right-clicking (Control-clicking) the Insert bar, and then, from the shortcut menu, choosing Customize Favorites.

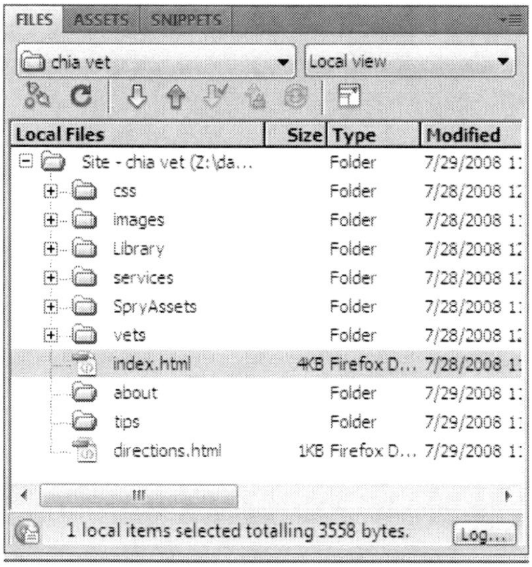

Figure 1-4:
The Files panel provides a bird's-eye view of your site's files. But it's more than just a simple list—it also lets you quickly open files, rename and rearrange them in the site, and more. You'll learn about the Files panel in detail on page 625.

To use the Files panel effectively, you need to "Define a site" for each site you work on—defining a site is specific to Dreamweaver, and one of the most important steps in using Dreamweaver correctly. You'll learn how later in this chapter, starting on page 37.

The Property Inspector

After dropping in an image, table, or anything else from the Insert panel, you can use the Property inspector to fine-tune its appearance and attributes. Suppose, for example, that your boss has decided she wants her picture to link to her personal blog. After highlighting her picture in the document window, you would then use the Property inspector to add a link to her blog.

The Property inspector (Figure 1-5) is a chameleon. It's aware of what you're working on in the document window—a table, an image, some text—and displays the appropriate set of properties (that is, options). You use the Property inspector extensively in Dreamweaver.

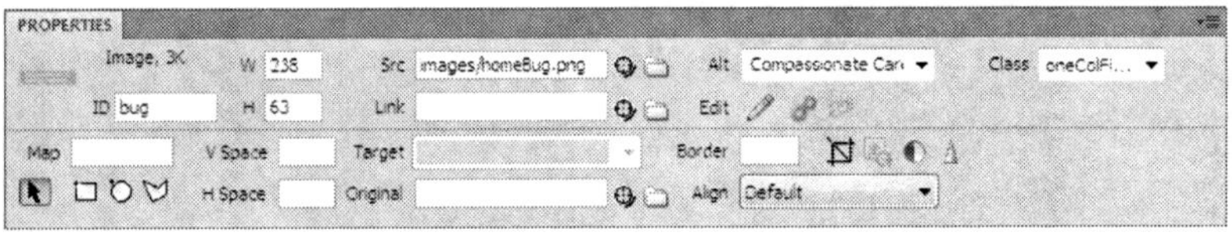

***Figure 1-5:** If you don't see the Property inspector, then you can open it by choosing Window → Properties, or pressing Ctrl+F3 (⌘-F3).*

For now, though, here are two essential tips to get you started:

- In the Property inspector, double-click any blank gray area to hide or show the bottom half of the inspector, where Dreamweaver displays an additional set of advanced options. (It's a good idea to leave the inspector fully expanded most of the time, since you may otherwise miss some useful options.)
- At its heart, the Property inspector is simply a display of the attributes of HTML tags. The *src* (source) attribute of the <img> (image) tag, for instance, tells a Web browser where to look for an image file.

  You can most easily make sure you're setting the properties of the correct object by clicking its tag in the Tag selector (see page 24).

The Application Bar

The Application bar is new in Dreamweaver CS4. Its main purpose in life is to let you switch between different document views (for example, between Code and Design view), to choose a configuration of the program's windows, and to give you a shortcut for getting help, defining sites, and downloading extensions. You can also get all the options here from the program's main menus. Figure 1-6 shows its location in Windows (top) and on a Mac (bottom). Here's what it offers:

- **Code/Design View** menu lets you switch between the visual Design view (what the page will look like in a Web browser) and the raw HTML. You can also choose to show both the design and code at the same time. Page 395 has more on that option (called Split view).
- The **Extensions** menu gives you quick access to the Extension Manager as well as to the Adobe Exchange Web site. Extensions are add-on features (some are free and some cost money) that let you do more with Dreamweaver. Extensions are discussed on page 804.
- The **Sites** menu lets you "define" a new site or "manage" the sites you already have. You'll learn a lot more about Dreamweaver sites later in this chapter on page 37, but basically a site is a way to let Dreamweaver know where you keep all the files for one particular site. If you're designing more than one Web site, then you can define multiple sites within Dreamweaver.
- The **Workspace** switcher lets you re-organize the program's layout of windows. You can choose one of the workspaces supplied by Dreamweaver, or, as discussed on page 24, you can create your own layout of windows to create the ultimate workspace for your sites.
- The **Community Help** box is a search function. But unlike the normal "Help" box you find in most programs, this search field lets you search the entire Internet for useful information related to Dreamweaver. Type a search term in the box, and then hit Enter (Return) and a Web browser launches, loading a page on Adobe's Web site which lists many resources to help answer your questions. This help function is a bit better than just using Google—you never know what that'll turn up—since the sites that are searched have all been hand-picked by Adobe. That way you know you won't be getting any "helpful" advice from the blogger down the street who just bought Dreamweaver and decided to post his thoughts on the program.

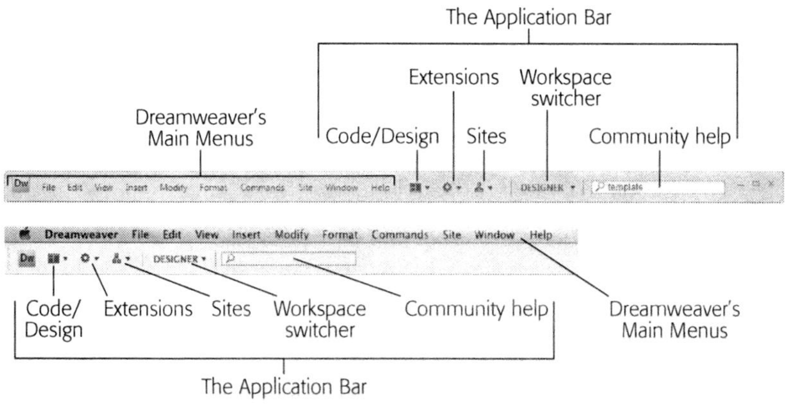

Figure 1-6: *The Application bar is new to Dreamweaver CS4 and looks slightly different on Windows (top) and Macs (bottom).*

Organizing Your Workspace

Dreamweaver's basic user interface includes the document window, Application bar, Property inspector and panel groups on the right edge of the screen (see Figure 1-7). All these windows act like a unified whole; that is, if you resize one window, the other windows also resize to fit the space. For example, you can drag the left edge of the panel groups (circled in Figure 1-7) and drag it to the left to make the panels wider, or to the right to make them thinner. The other windows that touch the panels (the document window and Property inspector) change their widths accordingly. This kind of joined-at-the-hip interface is common in Windows applications, but may feel a bit weird for Mac enthusiasts. (If you prefer the "floating palette" look and feel common to a lot of programs, you can set up Dreamweaver that way as well—see the opposite page.)

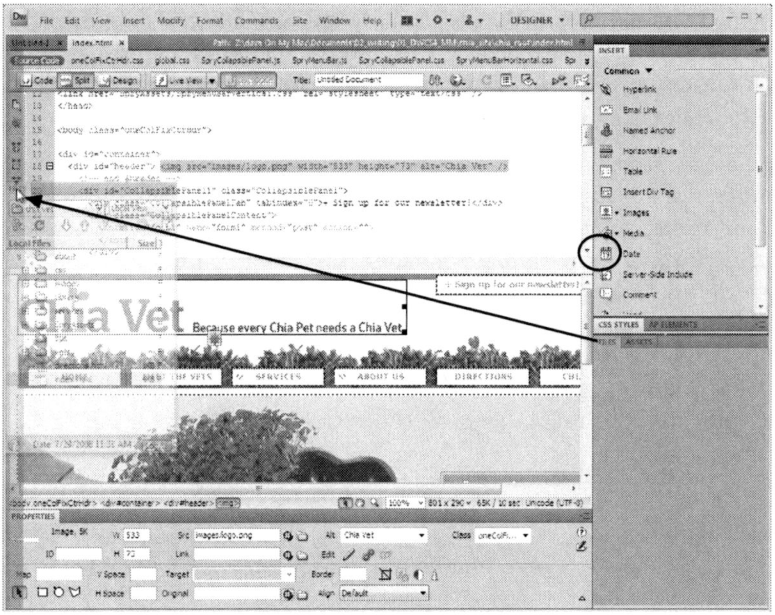

Figure 1-7: *You can move individual tabs to other parts of the screen–you're not limited to keeping all the tabs on the right side. In this figure, the Files panel is being dragged to the left edge of the screen. A ghosted version of the tab appears as you drag it around the screen. When you see a thick blue line on the screen's edge, drop the tab to create a panel that takes up the entire edge of the screen. In other words, in this figure, dropping the Files panel tab creates a full-height column on the left edge composed entirely of the Files panel–the document window and Properties inspector move to the right to make room. This technique is particularly good if you have a very wide monitor, since it lets you display the Files panel (which often contains lots of files) by itself and at full screen height. (The "Collapse to Icons" button labeled here is discussed under "Iconic Panes" on page 34.)*

You can control the panel in many different ways to help customize your workspace:

- You can open a particular panel from the Window menu. For example, to open the Files panel, choose Window → Files.
- Double-click on a panel's tab to open it. Double-click the tab again, and the tab (and any other tabs grouped with it) closes.
- Drag the line between an open panel and another panel to resize a panel. For example, if you want to make the Insert panel (pictured in Figure 1-7) taller, then grab the thick border line between that panel and the panel group containing the CSS Styles and AP Elements tabs.
- To completely close a panel, so that even its tab no longer appears, right-click (Ctrl-click) the tab, and then choose Close. (Choose Close Tab Group to hide the tab and any other tabs it's grouped with.)
- If you want to hide all windows *except* for documents, then choose Window → Hide Panels or press F4—a useful trick when you want to maximize the amount of your screen dedicated to showing the actual Web page you're working on. To bring back all of Dreamweaver's administrative windows, press F4 again or choose Window → Show Panels.

Floating panels

As mentioned in Figure 1-7, you can drag a panel by its tab to another part of the screen. Dragging it to the edge of the screen docks the panel on that edge. However, if you drag a panel and drop it when it's not near a screen's edge, then it becomes a floating panel (see Figure 1-8). Floating panels are often nuisances, since they hide whatever's beneath them, so you often end up having to move them out of the way just to see what you're doing. However, they come in very handy when you have two monitors. If that's the case, you can dedicate your main monitor to the document window and Property inspector (and maybe your most important panels), and then drag a bunch of floating panels onto your second screen.

To "unfloat" a floating panel, simply drag it to the edge of your screen (if you have more than one monitor, drag the panel to one of the edges of your *main* monitor). If you already have panels at that edge, drag the panel to either the bottom of the panels (to dock it at the bottom of the column of panels), between other panel groups (to insert that panel in its own group between other panels) or next to another panel's tab to group the panels together.

Tip: Drag a panel to either side of a docked column of panels to create a second column. In other words, you can create two, side by side, columns of panels.

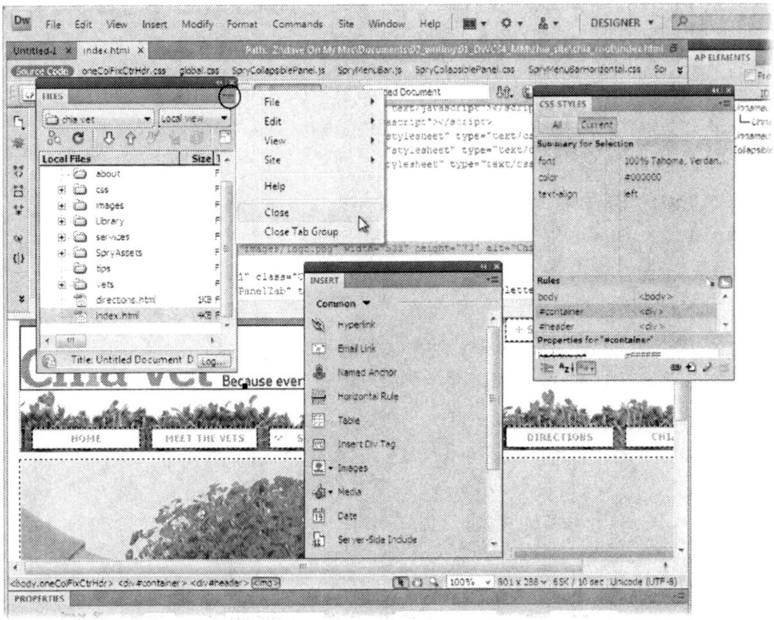

Figure 1-8: *Here, the Files, Insert and CSS Styles panels are floating. Each panel has its own Context menu icon (circled on Files panel at left side of image). Clicking the button reveals a shortcut menu that lets you work with features specific to that panel. This menu also offers generic panel actions, such as closing the panel.*

Iconic panes

As if you didn't already have enough ways to organize your panels, Dreamweaver CS4 introduces yet another way to display panels. By clicking the "Collapse to Icons" button at the top right of a column of panels (see Figure 1-7) you can shrink the panels to a group of much smaller icons (see Figure 1-9). To re-open the controls for a particular panel you've just shrunk, just click the icon. For example, in Figure 1-9, clicking the CSS Styles icon opens the CSS Styles panel to the left. Once you finish working with the panel, and click elsewhere on the screen, the pop-up panel disappears. This so-called iconic view is particularly good if you have a small monitor and need to preserve as much screen real estate as possible.

Workspace Layouts

Sometimes too much choice is a bad thing, and even though the new user interface changes in Dreamweaver CS4 mean you can pretty much organize the windows and panels any way you like, it also means you can easily accidentally click or drag the wrong spot and suddenly find panels strewn across the screen or completely gone.

Fortunately, Dreamweaver includes a wonderful, timesaving productivity enhancer that ensures you always have your windows organized the way you want, and you can quickly return to that setup if you accidentally move your panels. The Workspace Layouts feature lets you save the position and size of Dreamweaver's panels and windows as a "layout," which you can return to by simply selecting the layout's name from the Workspace Switcher menu in the Application bar (see Figure 1-6) or by choosing Window → Workspace Layout.

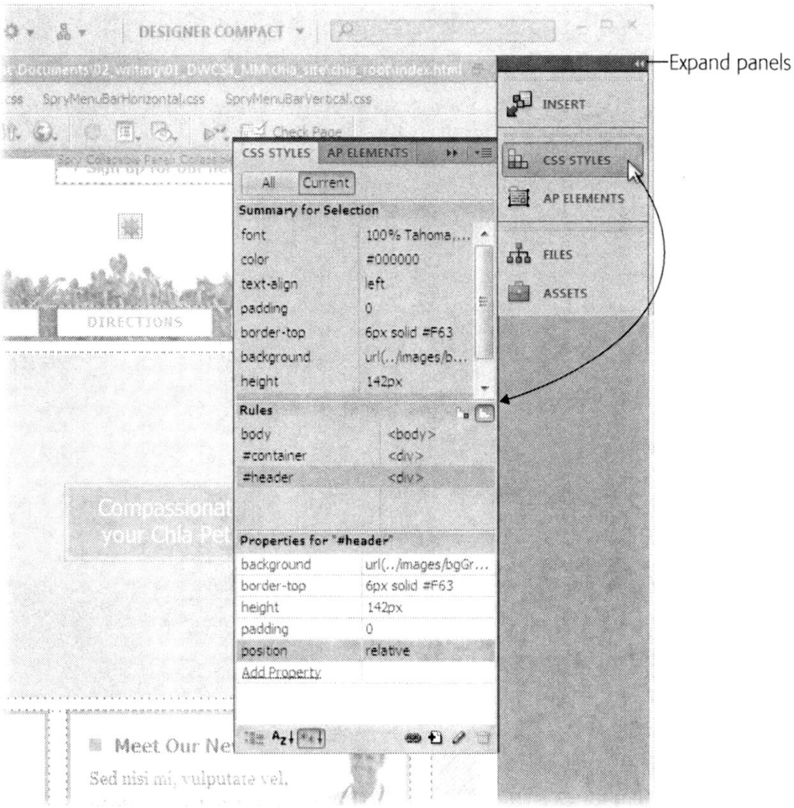

Figure 1-9: *Iconic panes let you preserve screen real estate. To return to normal width panels, click the Expand Panels button.*

For example, when you're working on a database-driven Web site, you may like to have the Application panel group and the Snippets panel open, but keep the CSS panel tucked away. When working on a design-heavy site, on the other hand, you probably want the CSS panel open, but could care less about the Tag Inspector. You can create a different layout for each situation, and then simply switch between them.

Tip: Dreamweaver CS3 veterans should check out the "Classic" layout, which puts the Insert panel back up at the top of the screen and makes Dreamweaver CS4's new, stylish black-and-white icons return to their vibrant, colorful selves.

In addition, Dreamweaver CS4 comes pre-programmed with eight layouts designed to configure interface to match the needs of designers, coders, application developers, and those who like to spread their windows and panels across two monitors. You should try each layout (use the Workspace switcher menu in the Application bar [Figure 1-6]) to see which workspace you like best. You can then tweak that layout by closing or opening other panels, rearranging panels, and so on, until you find the perfect layout for you. Then just save that layout (as described below) so you can call it up anytime you'd like. Here are a few other tips when you're ready to lay down a custom layout:

- Open the panels you work with most frequently. For example, choose Window → Files to open the Files panel.
- Increase or decrease the height of a panel by dragging up or down the empty space to the right of a panel or panel-group name (see Figure 1-10).

Figure 1-10: *Resizing a panel is as easy as dragging up or down (circled at bottom of Insert panel on right). If you're lucky enough to have a large monitor, it's often helpful to put the Files panel by itself on either the left or right side of the screen.*

- You can move a panel to another area of your screen by dragging its tabs as described on page 32 (see Figure 1-7). This trick is especially useful if you have a large monitor, since you can place one group of panels on the right edge of the monitor and another group either next to the first or on the left side of the monitor. As described on page 33, you can also create floating panels. If you've got two monitors hooked up to your computer, then you can then spread the panels across both monitors.
- Choose the Insert panel category containing the objects you use most frequently—for example, if you're always building Web forms, then select the Forms category. (Better yet, collect your favorite objects onto a single tab, as described on page 29.)

To save your layout, select New Workspace from the Workspace switcher menu in the Application bar (see Figure 1-11) or, alternatively, choose Window → Workspace Layout → New Workspace. The Save Workspace dialog box appears; type a name for the layout, and then click OK. (If you type the same name as a layout you've already saved, Dreamweaver lets you know and gives you the option to replace the old layout with this new layout. You have to do this to update a layout you've previously created.) Dreamweaver saves your new layout.

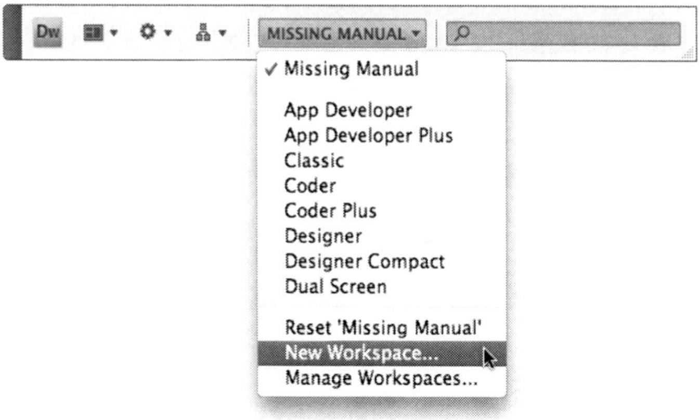

Figure 1-11: *The Application bar's Workspace switcher menu lets you choose one of the eight workspaces already set up in the program, or a workspace you've created. For example, the Missing Manual option pictured here is a custom workspace. If you accidentally move a panel out of position, you can return the current workspace to its original setup by selection the Reset option at the bottom of this menu.*

Tip: This feature is also handy if you share your computer with other people. You can create your own Workspace Layout—use your own name when naming the layout—with all the panels and windows exactly where you like them. Then, when you go to use the computer and the bozo before you has rearranged the entire workspace, just select your layout from the Application bar or the Window → Workspace Layouts menu.

To switch to a layout you've already saved, simply select your workspace from the Application bar (see Figure 1-11) or choose Window → Workspace Layout → *The Name of Your Layout*. After a brief pause, Dreamweaver switches to the selected layout.

Setting Up a Site

Whenever you build a new Web site or want to edit an existing one you've created elsewhere, you have to begin by introducing Dreamweaver to it—a process called *defining a site*. This is *the* most important first step when you start using Dreamweaver, whether you plan to whip up a five-page Web site, build a thousand-page online store, or edit the site your sister built for you. At its most basic, defining a site lets Dreamweaver know where you store your Web pages on your computer, and makes sure Dreamweaver correctly inserts images and adds links to the pages of your site. In addition, if you want to take advantage of Dreamweaver's many timesaving site management tools such as the link checker (see page 644), Library items (Chapter 17), Templates (Chapter 18), and FTP tool for moving your Web files to a Web server (Chapter 16), then you *have* to define a site.

Dreamweaver gives you two methods for defining a site: the hold-you-by-the-hand Site Definition wizard, and the advanced "Get out of my way, I know what I'm doing" approach.

The Site Definition Wizard

Dreamweaver's Site Definition Wizard steps you through a series of screens, prompting you for information about your Web site setup.

1. **Choose Site → New Site.**

   The Site Definition window appears. To use the wizard, make sure the Basic tab is selected (see Figure 1-12).

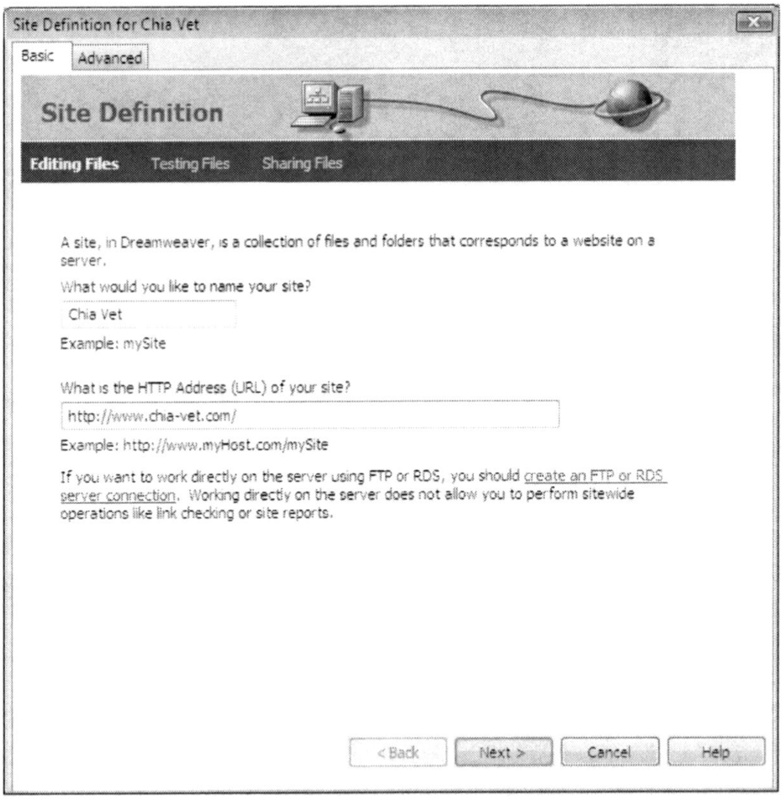

Figure 1-12: *The Site Definition window's Basic tab takes you step by step through the process of setting up a new site. Each stage of the process–Editing Files, Testing Files, and Sharing Files–is clearly labeled. Depending on the type of site you're building and which Dreamweaver features you plan on using, you're taken through a series of simple questions that help you set up your site.*

2. **Type the name of your site in the first field.**

   The name you type here is solely for your own reference, to help you identify the site in Dreamweaver's Files panel. It won't appear on the Web. Dreamweaver also asks for your site's Web address.

3. **Type the Web address for your Web site. For example, *http://www.chia-vet.com.***

   This step is optional. If you don't yet have a Web address, then you can leave this blank. In some cases, you may need to add some more information after the domain name. For example, the address for your Web site might look something like this: *http://www.somecollege.edu/~bob*. Or you might be responsible for maintaining just part of a larger site—sometimes called a "sub site." Regardless, just type the address you normally type into a Web browser to visit your site. For example, *http://www.mybigcompany.com/marketing*.

Note: If you're using site-root relative paths for linking to the pages in your site, step 3 above is critical. See page 163 for the gory details.

---

4. **Click the Next button to proceed to the next screen.**

   In the next step, you'll tell Dreamweaver whether you plan on building regular Web pages or pages that require a special server for creating the dynamic, database-driven Web sites discussed in Part 6 of this book.

5. **Unless you're creating a database-driven site, choose "No, I do not want to use a server technology", and then click Next.**

   For creating basic Web pages, you don't need any server technology. To learn about defining a site for database-driven Web sites like those described in Part 6 of this book, see page 824.

   In the next steps, you'll tell Dreamweaver how you want to work on the files in your site, and where you'll store those files.

6. **Choose either "Edit local copies on my machine" or "Edit directly on server using local network" (see Figure 1-13).**

   The first option—*Edit local copies*—is the most common. Typically, Web designers have two sets of files: the *local site* on their hard drives and the *remote site* on the Web (see the box on page 43). The local site lets you keep your works in progress on your computer, while the remote site contains the completed pages that the world can view with a Web browser.

   The second option (*Edit directly on server*) isn't a very good idea. Working directly on the live version of the site—the one anyone with a Web browser can see—exposes your half-finished pages, with their typos and missing pictures, to your audience. Much better to perfect a page on your own computer, and then, when it's finished, move it to the Web server.

7. **Click the folder icon next to the label, "Where on your computer do you want to store your files?"**

   The Choose Local Root Folder window opens, so that you can choose a folder on your hard drive to serve as your *local site's root folder*. This folder is where on your computer you'll store the HTML documents and graphics, CSS, and other Web files that make up your Web site.

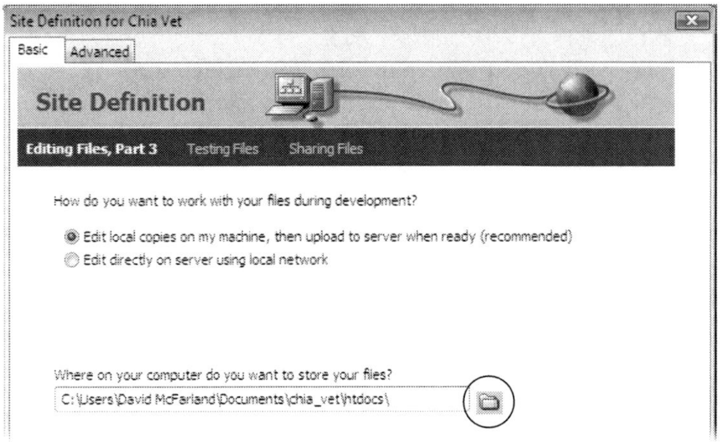

Figure 1-13:
You see the folder icon (circled) everywhere in Dreamweaver CS4. It lets you select a folder or file, which you do when you create links, add images, and, yes, select a local root folder for your site.

8. **Browse to and select the folder containing your site's files (see Figure 1-14).**

   If you're starting a Web site from scratch, then you can also create a new empty folder at this point. You then save your Web pages and graphics into this folder as you build your site.

   For more on root folders and organizing Web sites, see Chapter 15. For now, the fact to burn into your brain is that all the files that will constitute your Web site must live in the folder you select—this folder is called the *local root folder*. (You can have subfolders with Web files *inside* the local root folder; you just can't have any files *outside* this root folder.)

Tip: Another way to think of the local root folder: It's the folder on your computer in which you'll put your site's home page.

9. **Click Next.**

   Now Dreamweaver asks how you want to connect to your *remote server*—the computer that will dish up the finished Web files to your adoring public.

10. **Choose one of the options from the "How do you connect to your remote server?" menu.**

    To just get started building Web pages, choose None. You'll use this option in all of the tutorials in this book. In Chapter 17, you'll learn how to use other options, such as FTP, from this menu to move your files to your Web server using Dreamweaver. Even if you don't select a remote server now, you can always return to the Site Definition window later to tell Dreamweaver where to put your finished Web pages.

11. **Click Next.**

    A summary of your settings appears (see Figure 1-15).

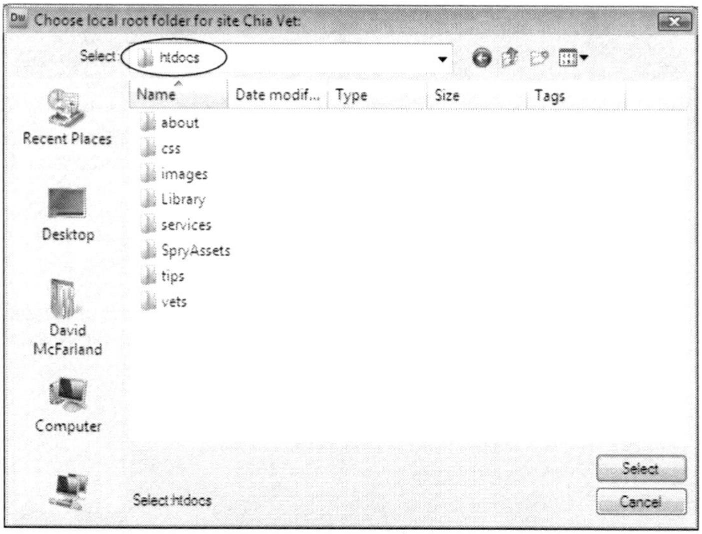

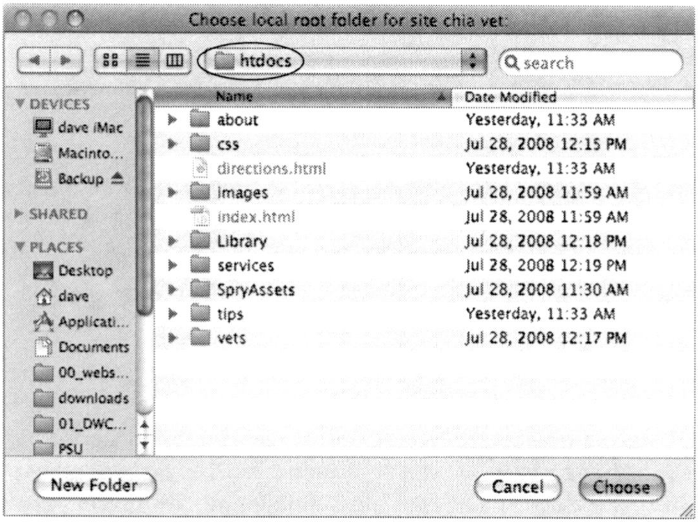

***Figure 1-14:** The dialog box for selecting a folder in Windows (top) is pretty much the same as the one for Macs (bottom). You can verify which folder you're about to select by looking in the Select field for Windows (circled in top image) or in the path menu on a Mac (circled in bottom image).*

12. **Click Done.**

After defining the site, Dreamweaver creates a *site cache* for your Web site. That's a small database that tracks pages, links, images, and other components of your site. The cache helps Dreamweaver's site management tools avoid breaking links, lets Dreamweaver warn you when you're about to delete important files, and lets you reorganize your site quickly. If you're creating a brand-new site or have a small site with just a few files, you may not even notice this site cache creation happening.

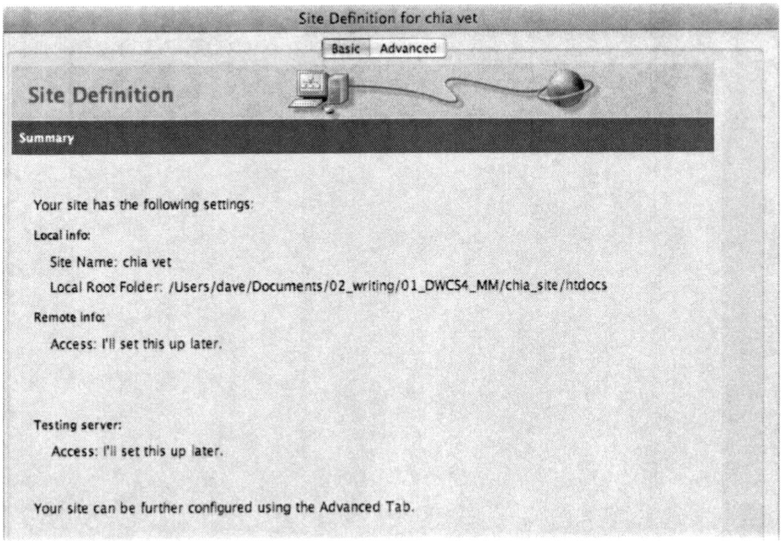

Figure 1-15: *After you've finished the Site Definition Wizard, Dreamweaver summarizes the settings you selected. Nothing's set in stone, however. If you later decide to connect to a Web server to upload your Web pages or use Dreamweaver's database tools, you can always change your site options as described on page 622.*

Defining a site doesn't actually do anything to your computer; it doesn't create a home page or add a folder, for example. It merely prepares Dreamweaver for working on a site.

Note: Dreamweaver lets you define *multiple* Web sites, a handy feature if you're a Web designer with several clients, or if your company builds and manages more than one site. To define an additional site, choose Site → New Site, and then repeat the steps starting on page 38. You can then switch from one site to another using the Sites menu in the Files panel (see Figure 15-6 on page 626).

Defining a Site the Fast Way

Although the Site Definition Wizard is a nearly foolproof way to define a site, clicking through each of its steps can get tedious. If you want to get started building Web pages (or editing a Web site you've already created) right away, then you just need to provide a few details using the Site Definition window's Advanced tab.

1. **Choose Site → New Site to open the Site Definition window, and then select the Advanced tab (see Figure 1-16).**

   The number of options in the Advanced view of the Site Definition window may seem overwhelming. But to get started building a Web site, you need to supply only a few pieces of information under the Local Info category of this window. The other categories are for more advanced site setups, which you'll learn about later in this book. For example, the Remote Info category is for setting up Dreamweaver to move files to your Web server and is discussed in Chapter 17, while the Testing Server category is used for the database-driven Web sites detailed in Part 6 of this book.

UP TO SPEED

Terms Worth Knowing About

During the tutorial in these pages—and, indeed, everywhere in Dreamweaver—you'll encounter a few terms frequently heard at Web designer luncheons:

Root folder. The first rule of managing a Web site is that every piece of the site you're working on—Web page (HTML) documents, graphic images, sound files, and so on—must sit in a single folder on your hard drive. That master folder is the *root* folder for your Web site, and because it's sitting on your computer it's called the *local* root folder. The *root* is the master, outer, main folder—think of that folder as the edge of the known universe for that site: Nothing exists outside the root. Of course, to help organize your site's files, you can include any number of subfolders inside the root folder. (When you've finished creating your Web site, you'll move files in this folder onto a Web server for the world to see. The folder you place your Web files into on a Web server is called the *remote root folder*.)

Local site. The usual routine for creating Web pages goes like this: First you create the page on your own computer—using a program like Dreamweaver—and then you upload it to a computer on the Internet called a Web server, where your handiwork becomes available to the masses. In other words, almost every Web site exists in two places at once. One copy is on the Internet, where everyone can get at it. The other, original copy is on some Web designer's hard drive.

The copy on your own computer is called the *local site*, or the development site. Think of the local site as a sort of staging ground, where you build your site, test it, and modify it. Because the local site isn't on a Web server and can't be accessed by the public, you can freely edit and add to it without affecting the pages your visitors are viewing, meanwhile, on the remote site.

Remote site. When you've added or updated a file, you move it from the local site to the remote site. The *remote*, or live, site is a mirror image of the local site. Because you create it by uploading your local site, it has the same organizational folder structure as the local site, and contains the same files. Only polished, fully functional pages go online to the remote site; save the half-finished, typo-ridden drafts for your local site. Chapter 16 explains how to use Dreamweaver's FTP features to define and work with a remote site.

(If you're using Dreamweaver's database features, by the way, you'll encounter yet another term: a *testing server*. You'll find the lowdown on this kind of site, which is used to test database features, on page 821.)

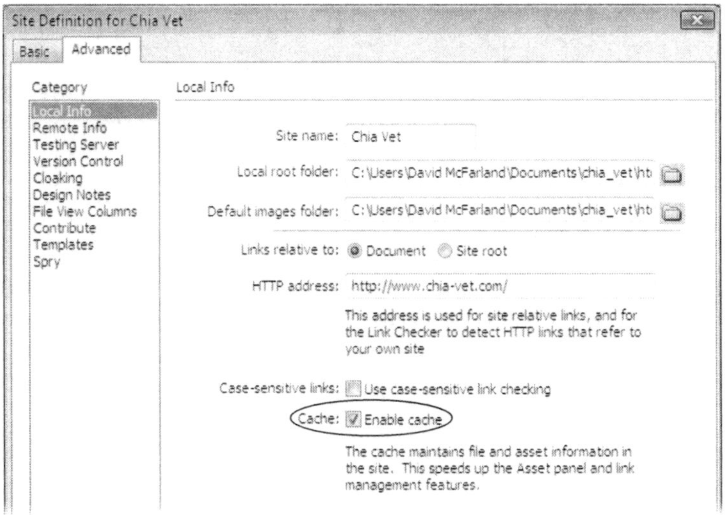

Figure 1-16:
Make sure the "Enable cache" box (circled) is turned on. This step speeds up Dreamweaver's site management features such as link checking. If you have a really large site with thousands of pages and files, then creating the cache can take several minutes, so you might be tempted to disable this feature. Don't. With the cache enabled, Dreamweaver can make sure you don't accidentally delete a page that thousands of other pages link to, or help update links when you move a page to another location in your site.

2. **In the Category list, make sure Local Info is selected, and then, in the "Site name" field, type a name for your site.**

   The name you type here is solely for your own reference, to help you identify the site in Dreamweaver's files panel; it won't appear on the Web.

3. **Click the folder icon to the right of the "Local root folder" field.**

   The Choose Local Root Folder window opens, where you can choose a folder on your hard drive that will serve as your *local site's root folder*. This folder is the folder on your computer where you'll store the HTML documents and graphics, CSS, and other Web files that make up your Web site.

4. **Browse to and select the folder containing your site's files.**

   Figure 1-14 demonstrates the process for Windows and Macs. If you're creating a new site, you can also create a new folder at this point using the New Folder button in this window.

   You can also let Dreamweaver know where you plan on storing the images for the site by selecting a folder for the "Default images folder" field. This step is optional, but comes in handy if you insert an image from the desktop or another folder outside your local root folder as described on page 216.

Note: Because defining a site is such an important step, you can find a video about the process on this book's Web site at *www.sawmac.com/dwcs4/define*.

5. **Type the Web address of your site in the HTTP address field. For example, *http://www.chia-vet.com.***

   This step is also optional. Just type the address you'd normally type into a Web browser to view your site. If you don't yet have a Web address, then you can leave this blank.

6. **Click OK to finish the process.**

   Dreamweaver creates a site cache as described in step 12 on page 41. Your site's files (if there are any yet) appear in the Files panel. Now you're ready to create Web pages and take advantage of Dreamweaver's powerful site building tools.

Creating a Web Page

After defining a site, you'll want to start building pages. Just choose File → New or press Ctrl+N (⌘-N on a Mac) to open the New Document window (see Figure 1-17). The New Document window is a little overwhelming. You have so many options it's hard to know where to start. Fortunately, when you just want to create a new HTML file, you can skip most of these options.

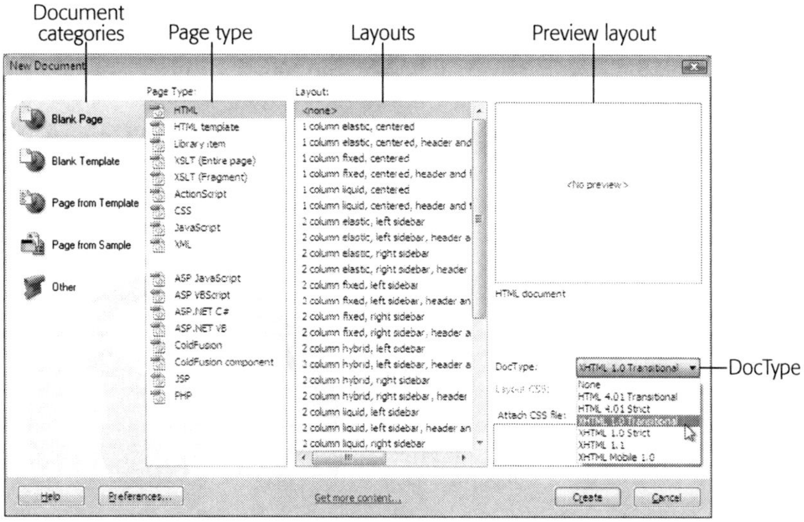

***Figure 1-17:** The New Document window lets you create nearly every Web document type under the sun. Dreamweaver CS4 also includes many prepackaged designs including lots of advanced page layouts using the latest Web design techniques. If you select one of those designs in the Layout list, then, in the upper-right corner of the window, you see a preview of the layout.*

To create a basic HTML file for a Web page:

1. **From the left-hand list of document categories, choose Blank Page.**

   The Blank Page category lets you create a new empty document—this might be a Web page or something a bit more esoteric like an XML file (see page 522 for more on XML), an external JavaScript file, or one of the several server-driven pages such as PHP or ASP (which are discussed in Part 6).

   Both the Blank Template and "Page from Template" categories relate to Dreamweaver's Template feature discussed in Chapter 19. The "Page from Sample" category lets you choose from several different files with already-created designs—it's best to avoid these. The designs in this category are old and left over from earlier versions of the program; they generally aren't very attractive and don't use the best techniques for building a Web page. Dreamweaver CS4 does ship with some very useful page layouts that you can access from the Blank Page category. (You'll learn about these designs in Chapter 9.) The last category, Other, lets you create documents for different programming languages like ActionScript or Java—unless you're a Flash or Java programmer, you probably won't ever need these.

2. **From the Page Type list, choose HTML.**

   You can also create other types of documents, most of which you'll learn more about later in this book, such as PHP or ASP for database-driven sites (see Part 6 of this book), XSLT files for processing XML (Chapter 26), templates (Chapter 19), library items (Chapter 18), or CSS files (Chapter 4).

3. **From the Layout list, choose "<none>".**

   "<none>" creates a blank document. The other choices ("1 column elastic, centered", "1 column elastic, centered, header and footer", and so on) are predesigned page layouts. These designs (not to be confused with the designs under the "Page from Sample" category) use CSS, which you'll learn much more about starting in Chapter 4. Because CSS-based layout can be tricky, Dreamweaver includes all the code you need to create many of the most common types of these page designs. You'll learn more about this great feature in Chapter 9.

4. **Select a document type from the DocType menu.**

   Selecting a document type identifies the type of HTML you'll be using on the page. It affects how Dreamweaver writes the HTML code and how a Web browser understands it. Fortunately, since Dreamweaver writes all the code for you, you don't need to worry about the subtle differences between the different types.

   XHTML 1.0 Transitional is the normal setting in Dreamweaver, but HTML 4.01 Transitional, HTML 4.01 Strict, and XHTML 1.0 Strict are also fine choices. The transitional doc types let you use a few HTML tags and properties that have been phased out of the strict types. Most notably, transitional doc types can use the "target" property for links—a simple way to force links to open in a new browser window.

   If you don't really understand or care about doc types, just select XHTML 1.0 Transitional. But make sure you avoid None (which can force browsers to display pages in what's called "quirks mode" and makes perfecting designs difficult) and XHTML 1.1 (which requires a special setting on your Web server to work properly).

Note: If you don't want to deal with the New Document window every time you create a new page, choose Edit → Preferences in Windows or Dreamweaver → Preferences on Mac. In the Preferences dialog box, click the New Document category, and then turn off the "Show New Document Dialog on Control-N" checkbox.

While you're at it, you can also specify what kind of file you want Dreamweaver to create whenever you press Ctrl+N (⌘-N). For example, if you usually create plain HTML files, then choose HTML. But if you usually create dynamic pages (like the PHP pages described in Part 6), then choose a different type of file–PHP, for example.

With these settings, pressing Ctrl+N (⌘-N) instantly creates a new blank document. (Choosing File → New, however, still opens the New Document window.)

---

5. **Click Create.**

   Dreamweaver opens a new, blank Web page ready for you to save and title (see Figure 1-18).

6. **Choose File → Save.**

   The Save As dialog box appears. You need to save the file somewhere inside the local root folder. You can save it inside any subfolders within the root folder as well.

7. **Type a name for the file, and then click Save.**

   Make sure the name doesn't contain spaces or any characters except letters, numbers, hyphens, and underscores, and that it ends in either .html or .htm.

   Although most operating systems let you save files with long names, spaces, and characters like #, $, and &, some browsers and servers have trouble interpreting anything other than letters and numbers.

   Furthermore, Web servers rely on file extensions like .htm, .html, .gif, and .jpg to know whether a file is a Web page, graphic, or some other type of file. Dreamweaver for Windows automatically adds the extension to your saved document names. But on the Mac—which lets you save files without extensions—make sure the file ends in the suffix .html or .htm when you save a Dreamweaver document.

8. **At the top of the document window, click inside the Title box, and then type a name for the page (see Figure 1-18).**

   Every new document Dreamweaver creates has the unflattering title Untitled Document. If you do a quick search on Google for "Untitled Document", you'll find (at the time of this writing) 44,400,000 results—that's half a million more pages than the last edition of *Dreamweaver: The Missing Manual* (obviously there are still some people who need to pick up a copy of this book). Dreamweaver probably created many of those pages. You should change this to a descriptive title indicating the main topic of the page: for example, "Contact Chia Vet", "About Chia Vet's Chia Pet Services", or "Technical Specifications for the Anodyne 3000 Indoor Lawn Mower". Not only is replacing "Untitled document" more professional, but providing a descriptive title can improve a Web page's ranking among search engines. In addition, the title appears on Google's, Yahoo's, and MSN's search listings.

The Dreamweaver Test Drive

Although reading a book is a good way to learn the ins and outs of a program, nothing beats sitting in front of your computer and taking a program through its paces. Many of this book's chapters, therefore, conclude with hands-on training: step by step tutorials that take you through the creation of a real, working, professionally designed Web site for the fictional company Chia Vet.

The rest of this chapter, for example, introduces Dreamweaver by taking you step by step through the process of building a Web page. It shouldn't take more than an hour. When it's over, you'll have learned the basic steps of building any Web page:

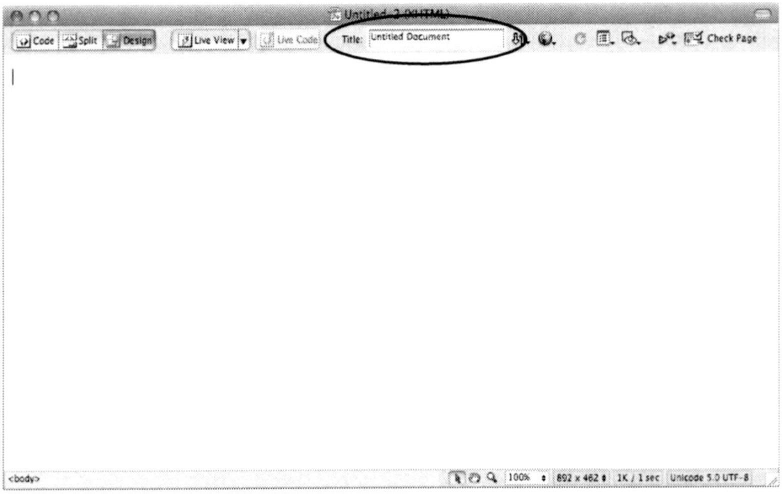

Figure 1-18:
A new blank Web page. Always remember to title the page by clicking inside the Title box at the top of the document window (circled), and then entering a descriptive title.

creating and saving a new document, adding and formatting text, inserting graphics, adding links, and making the program work for you (the finished tutorial is pictured in Figure 1-35).

If you're already using Dreamweaver and want to jump right into the details of the program, feel free to skip this tutorial. (And if you're the type who likes to read first and try second, read Chapters 2 through 5, and then return to this point to practice what you've just learned.)

Note: The tutorial in this chapter requires the example files from this book's Web site, *www.sawmac.com/dwcs4/*. Click the Download Tutorials link to download the files. The tutorial files are stored as ZIP files, a type of file that compresses a lot of different files into one, smaller file.

Windows folks should download the file, and then double-click it to open the archive. Click the Extract All Files option, and then follow the instructions of the Extraction Wizard to unzip the files and place them on your computer. Mac users, just double-click the file to decompress it.

After you've downloaded and decompressed the files, you should have a MM_DWCS4 folder on your computer, containing all the tutorial files for this book.

Phase 1: Getting Dreamweaver in Shape

Before you get started working in Dreamweaver, you need to make sure the program's all set up to work for you. In the following steps, you'll double-check some key Dreamweaver preference settings, and organize your workspace using the Workspace Layout feature.

First, make sure the preferences are all set:

1. **If it isn't already open, start Dreamweaver.**

   Hey, you've got to start with the basics, right?

2. **Choose Edit → Preferences (Windows) or Dreamweaver → Preferences (Mac).**

   The Preferences dialog box opens, listing a dizzying array of categories and options (see Figure 1-19).

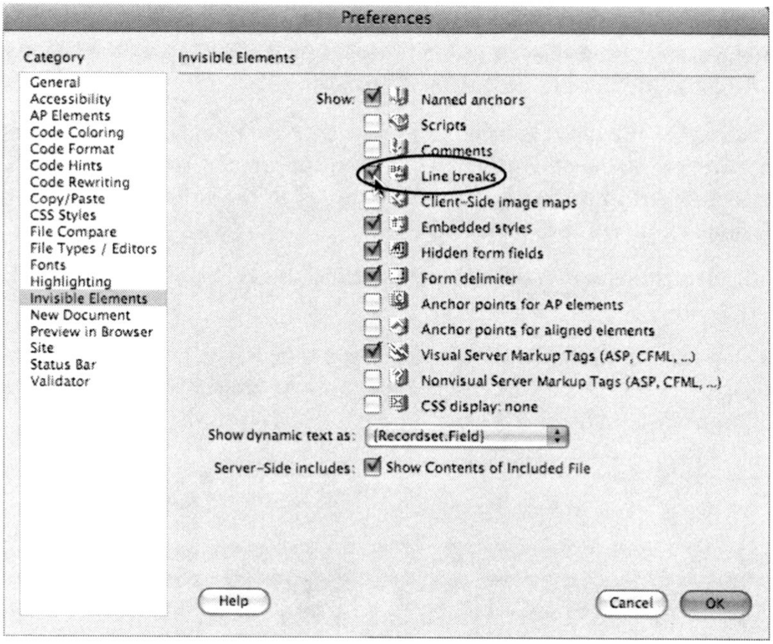

***Figure 1-19:** Dreamweaver's Preferences dialog box is a smorgasbord of choices that let you customize the program to work and look the way you want.*

3. **In the Preferences dialog box, select the Invisible Elements category, and then turn on the fourth checkbox from the top, labeled Line Breaks (see Figure 1-19, circled).**

   Sometimes, when pasting text from other programs like Microsoft Word or an email program, separate paragraphs come into Dreamweaver as a single paragraph broken up with invisible characters called *line breaks* (for you HTML-savvy readers, this is the <br> tag). Normally you can't see this character in Dreamweaver's Design view. This setting makes the line break character visible—represented in the document window by a little gold shield—so that you can easily select and remove it.

4. **Click OK.**

   The Preferences dialog box closes. You're ready to get your workspace in order. As noted at the beginning of this chapter, Dreamweaver has many different windows that help you build Web pages. For this tutorial, though, you need only three: the Insert panel, the document window, and the Property inspector. But, for good measure (and to give you a bit of practice), you'll open another panel and rearrange the workspace a little. To get started, you'll make sure Dreamweaver is displaying the default Designer workspace.

5. **From the Workspace switcher on the Application bar, select Designer** (see Figure 1-20).

   If Designer is already selected, choose "Reset 'Designer'", which moves any panels that have been resized, closed, or repositioned back to their original locations. The Designer workspace built into Dreamweaver puts the Property inspector at the bottom of the screen, opens the Insert and Files panels on the right edge, and also displays a group of closed panels containing the CSS styles and AP (absolutely positioned) elements panels.

   As you can see, the Insert Panel in its normal configuration takes up a lot of vertical space, giving the other panels a cramped appearance. Fortunately, you can change how Dreamweaver displays the buttons in the Insert Panel—but you can't do that unless a Web page is open.

6. **On the Dreamweaver Welcome screen, click the HTML button** (circled in Figure 1-20).

   This step opens a blank, new Web page—you won't actually do anything with this page, but notice that the Insert Panel buttons are active. Next you'll hide the button labels on the Insert panel.

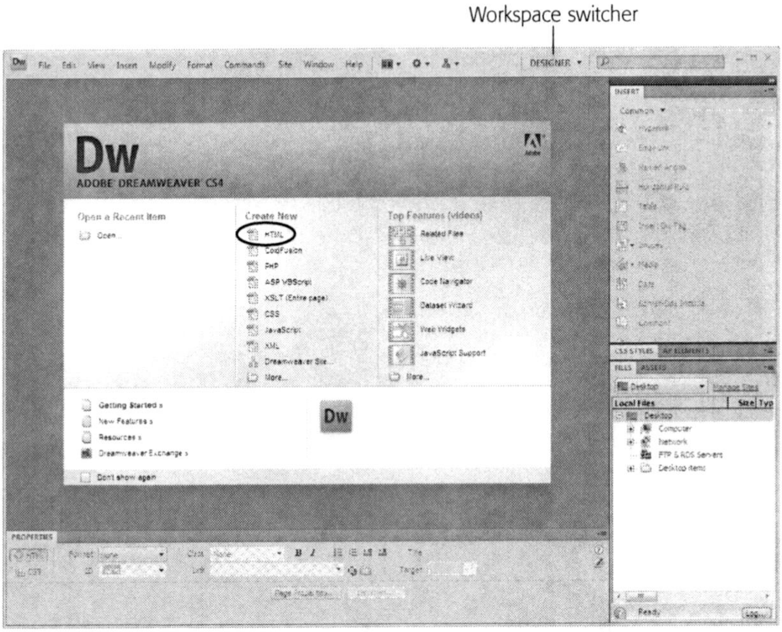

Figure 1-20: *The Dreamweaver Welcome screen pictured in the middle of this figure lists recently opened files in the left column. Clicking one of the file names opens that file for editing. The middle column provides a quick way to create a new Web page or define a new site. In addition, you can access introductory videos and other getting-started materials from this screen. You see the Welcome screen only when no other Web files are open.*

7. **From the Insert Panel's category menu, select Hide Labels (see Figure 1-3).**

   Without labels, the buttons in the Insert panel form nice compact rows, saving lots of space. As you use Dreamweaver you'll get used to what the buttons do, but in the meantime, simply hovering the mouse over a button produces a pop-up tooltip with the button's explanatory label.

   You don't need that new page you created in step 6, so you can close it.

8. **Click the document window's close button, or choose File → Close.**

   Next, you'll expand the CSS styles panel—one of the most frequently used panels in the program.

9. **Double-click the CSS styles tab to expand the panel.**

   This panel contains lots of information and tools, so it needs space. Next, you'll resize this panel to make it taller.

10. **Drag the thick line that appears between the top of the CSS styles panel and the bottom of the Insert panel (circled in Figure 1-21) until there's no empty space below the last row of icons in the Insert panel.**

    The Files panel could use a little more space as well.

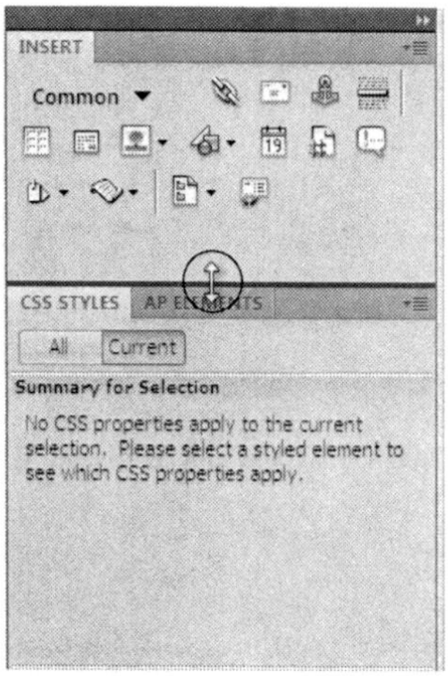

Figure 1-21:
Make a panel taller or shorter by dragging the thick line separating two groups of panels.

11. **Repeat step 9 to make the Files panel a bit taller.**

    Now the workspace looks great. It has the most common panels you'll be working with for this tutorial (and for much of your Web page building). Since this arrangement of windows is so useful, you'll want to save this as a layout (ok, maybe you don't want to save this layout…just play along).

12. **From the Application Bar's Workspace switcher menu, choose New Workspace...**

    The Save Workspace window appears, waiting for you to name your new layout.

13. **Type *Missing Manual* (or any name you like), and then click OK.**

    You've just created a new workspace layout. To see if it works, you'll switch to another one of Dreamweaver's Workspace layouts, see how the screen changes, and then switch back to your new setup.

14. **From the Workspace switcher menu, choose App Developer Plus.**

    This step moves the panels around quite a bit, and even displays some panels in Dreamweaver CS4's new iconic mode (as described on page 34). This layout's a bit too complicated for our needs, so you'll switch back.

15. **From the Workspace switcher menu, choose Missing Manual (or whatever name you gave in step 13).**

    Voilà! Dreamweaver sets up everything the way you want it. You can create multiple layouts for different Web sites or different types of sites.

Phase 2: Creating a Web Site

As discussed on page 37, whenever you want to use Dreamweaver to create or edit a Web site, your first step is always to show the program where the *root folder* is—the master folder for all your Web site files. You do this by *defining a site*, like so:

1. **Choose Site → New Site.**

   The Site Definition window appears. You have a basic and an advanced method for defining a site. You'll learn the basic method first, so make sure the Basic tab is selected (see Figure 1-12).

2. **Type *Tutorial 1* in the Site Name field.**

   The name you type here is solely for your own reference, to help you identify the site in Dreamweaver's Site menu. Dreamweaver also asks for the Web address for your site. You're working on the fictitious Chia Vet Web site.

3. **In the HTTP Address field, type *http://www.chia-vet.com*. Click Next.**

   In the next step, you'll tell Dreamweaver whether you plan on building regular Web pages or pages that require a special server for creating the dynamic, database-driven Web sites discussed in Part 6 of this book.

4. **Click "No, I do not want to use a server technology". Click Next.**

   In this tutorial, you'll build a basic Web page.

   In the next steps, you'll tell Dreamweaver how you want to work on the files in your site and where you'll store those files. In this example, you'll use one of the folders you downloaded from this book's Web site (at other times, you'll choose or create a folder of your own).

5. **Click "Edit local copies on my machine".**

   Next, you need to tell Dreamweaver where it can find the tutorial files.

6. **Click the folder icon next to the label, "Where on your computer do you want to store your files?"**

   The Choose Local Root Folder window opens, so that you can choose a folder on your hard drive that will serve as your *local root folder*. (This is the folder on your computer where you'll store the HTML documents and graphics, CSS, and other Web files that make up your Web site.)

7. **Browse to and select the Chapter01 folder located inside the MM_DWCS4 folder you downloaded earlier. Click the Select (Choose) button to set this folder as the local root folder.**

   This process is discussed on page 40 (see Figure 1-14). At this point, you've given Dreamweaver all the information it needs to successfully work with the tutorial files; you just need to skip through a few more screens and you're ready to get going.

Note: You'll find finished versions of all of the tutorials from this book in the MM_DWCS4 folder. The finished version of this tutorial is located in the Chapter01_finished folder.

8. **Click Next.**

   Dreamweaver asks how you want to connect to your *remote server*—the computer that will dish up the finished Web files to your adoring public.

9. **From the "How do you connect to your remote server?" menu, choose None, and then click Next.**

   Dreamweaver can move your files to a Web server automatically, as you'll learn in Chapter 17.

   After clicking Next, you see a summary of your settings. If you made a mistake, click Back to return to the appropriate step in the process and make changes.

10. **Click Done.**

    After defining the site, Dreamweaver creates a *site cache* for your Web site (see page 41). Since there are hardly any files in the Chapter01 folder, you may not even notice this happening—it goes by in the blink of an eye.

Phase 3: Creating and Saving a Web Page

"Enough already! I want to build a Web page," you're probably saying. You'll do just that in this phase of the tutorial:

1. **Choose File → New.**

   The New Document window opens (see Figure 1-17). Creating a blank Web page involves a few clicks.

2. **From the left-hand list of document categories, select Blank Page; in the Page Type list, highlight HTML; and from the Layout list, choose <none>. From the DocType menu in the bottom right of the window, select "XHTML 1.0 Transitional".**

   The window should look like Figure 1-17. XHTML actually has two "flavors." The "Transitional" type keeps your pages compatible with older browsers, and gives you a wider range of HTML properties to work with. If you've grown up with regular HTML, it's perfectly fine to select "HTML 4.01 Transitional".

3. **Click Create.**

   Dreamweaver opens a new, blank XHTML page. Even though the underlying code for an XHTML page is different in some ways from that of a plain HTML page, you have nothing to worry about: Dreamweaver manages all that code so you don't have to.

   If you see a bunch of strange text in the window, what you're looking at is the underlying HTML; you're in either Code or Split view. At the top left of the document window, click the Design button to tell Dreamweaver to display the page in its visual layout mode.

4. **Choose File → Save.**

   The Save As dialog box opens.

   Always save your pages right away. This habit prevents serious headaches if the power goes out as you finish that beautiful—but unsaved—creation.

5. **Save the page in the Chapter01 folder as *directions.html.***

   You could also save the page as *directions.htm*; both .html and .htm are valid.

   Make sure you save this page in the correct folder. In Phase 2 (page 52), you defined the Chapter01 folder as the root of the site—the folder that holds all the pages and files for the site. If you save the page in a different folder, Dreamweaver gets confused and its site management features don't work correctly.

Tip: When saving a file, you can quickly jump to the current site's root folder. In the Save As dialog box, click the Site Root button–this takes you right to the root folder. This little trick also works when opening or linking to a file.

6. **If the document window toolbar isn't already open, choose View → Toolbars → Document to display it.**

   The toolbar at the top of the document window provides easy access to a variety of tasks you'll perform frequently, such as titling a page, previewing it in a Web browser, and looking at the HTML source code.

7. **In the toolbar's Title field, select the text "Untitled Document", and then type *Directions to Chia Vet Headquarters.***

   The Title field lets you set a page's title—the information that appears in the title bar of a Web browser. The page title is also what shows up as the name of your Web page when someone searches the Web using a search engine like Yahoo or Google. In addition, a clear and descriptive title that identifies the main point of the page can also help increase a page's ranking among the major search engines.

8. **On the Property inspector, click the Page Properties button, or choose Modify → Page Properties.**

   The Page Properties dialog box opens (see Figure 1-22), letting you define the basic attributes of each Web page you create. Six categories of settings let you control properties like text color, background color, link colors, and page margins.

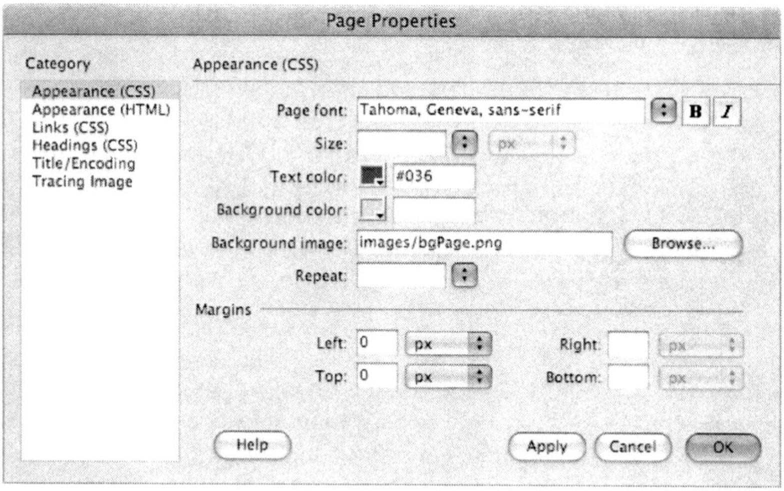

***Figure 1-22:** Dreamweaver CS4 clearly indicates which property settings use CSS and which rely on HTML. You should avoid the category labeled Appearance (HTML). The options in that category add old, out-of-date code to your Web pages.*

9. **From the "Page font" menu, select "Tahoma, Geneva, sans-serif".**

   This sets a basic font (and two backup fonts, in case your visitor's machine lacks Tahoma) that Dreamweaver will automatically use for all text on the page.

   As you'll see later in this tutorial, though, you can always specify a different font for selected text.

   Next, you'll set a basic text color for the page.

10. **Next to the "Text color" label, click the small gray box. From the pop-up color palette, choose a color (a dark color like a royal blue works well).**

    Unless you intervene, all Web page text starts out black in Dreamweaver; now, the text on this page will be the color you selected. In the next step, you'll add an image to the background of the page to liven it up.

Note: Alternatively, you could type a color, like *#333333*, into the box beside the palette square. That's *hexadecimal* notation, which is familiar to HTML coding gurus. Both the palette and the hexadecimal color-specifying field appear fairly often in Dreamweaver (see the box on page 59).

11. **To the right of the "Background image" field, click the Browse button.**

    The Select Image Source window appears (see Figure 1-23). Use this window to navigate to and select a graphic.

12. **Click the Site Root button at the top of the window (bottom of the window on Macs). Open the folder named *images*, select the file named *bgPage.png*, and then click the OK (Choose on a Mac) button.**

    In Dreamweaver, you can also just double-click a file to select it *and* close the window you used to select that file. For example, you can accomplish both steps—selecting the *bgPage.png* file *and* clicking the OK button—by just double-clicking the file.

to Windows Users: Normally Windows doesn't display a file's extension. So when you navigate images folder in step 13 above, you might see *bgPage* instead of *bgPage.png*. Since file extensions important way people (and Web servers) can identify the different types of files used on a Web site, you may want to display extensions. Here's how: In Windows Explorer, navigate to and select the MM_DWCS4 folder (the folder containing this book's tutorials). If you're using Windows XP, choose Tools → Folder Options. If you're on Vista, choose Organize → "Folder and Search Options". In the Folder Options window, select the View tab, and then turn off the "Hide extensions for known file types" checkbox. To apply this setting to all the files on your computer, click the "Apply to Folders" button, and then click OK; to apply it just to the tutorials, click OK.

13. **In the Left and Top margin boxes, type *0*.**

    This step removes the little bit of space Web browsers insert between the contents of your Web page and the top and left sides of the browser window. The size of this margin varies from browser to browser, so it's good to set this value yourself (even if you want to insert space on top and to the left of the page) to make sure the page appears consistently across the different browsers.

    If you like, you can change this setting to make the browser add more space to the top and left side of the page. In fact, you can even add a little extra empty space on the *right* side of a page. (The right margin control is especially useful for languages that read from right to left, like Hebrew or Arabic.) Note, however, that the *bottom* margin has no effect on the page display.

14. **Click the Links category, and then add the following properties: in the Link color field, type *#EC6206*; in the "Visited links" field, type *#93BD00*; in the "Rollover links" field, type *#779A00*; and in the "Active links" color field, type *#CAE0EC* (see Figure 1-24).**

    These hexadecimal codes specify specific Web page colors (see page 59 for more about this notation).

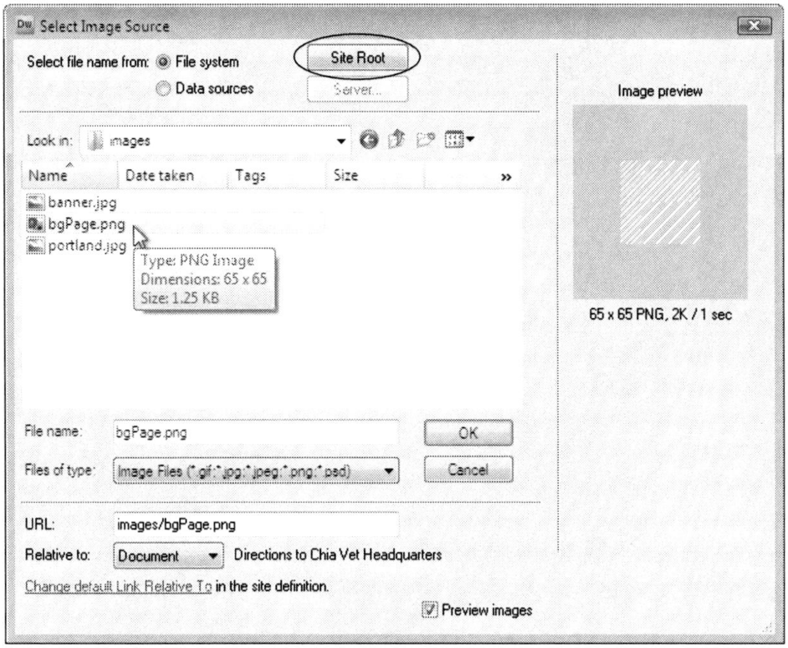

Figure 1-23: *Use the Select Image Source window when inserting graphics onto a Web page. The Site Root button (circled) gives you a quick way to immediately jump to the local site root–a nifty way to always know where you are when searching for a file. On the Mac, the Site Root button appears at the bottom right of the window.*

Links come in four varieties: regular, visited, active, and rollover. A *regular* link is a plain old link, unvisited, untouched. A *visited* link is one you've already been to, as noted in a browser's History list. An *active* link is one at the very moment you click it. And finally, a *rollover* link indicates how the link looks when someone mouses over it. You can choose different colors for each of these link states.

While it may seem like overkill to have four different colors for links, the regular and visited link colors can provide very useful feedback to Web visitors by indicating which links they've already followed and which remain to be checked out. For its part, the rollover link gives instant feedback, changing color as soon as a visitor moves the mouse cursor over it. The active link color isn't that useful for someone using his mouse to navigate a site—since clicking happens so fast, he probably won't even notice the active link color. However, with some browsers you can tab from link to link, and press the Enter key to follow the link. In this case, the active color is used to highlight a link to which a visitor just tabbed.

Note: Although Dreamweaver uses the term *rollover* link, in the world of Cascading Style Sheets, this is called a *hover* link.

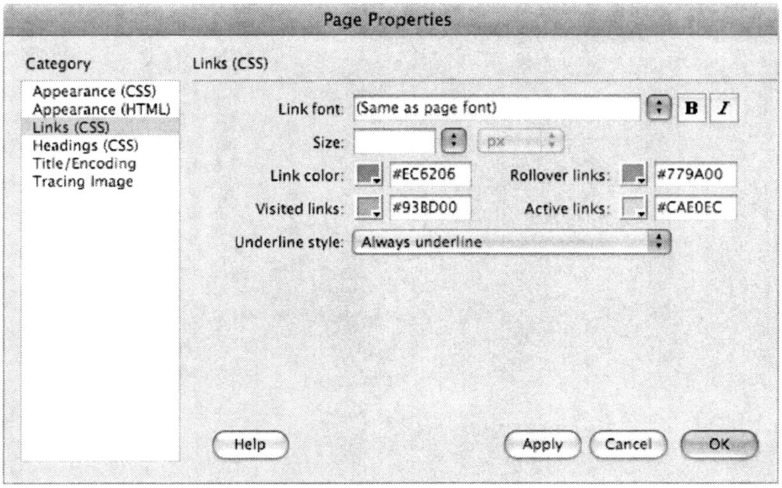

Figure 1-24: *You can set several different properties for links using the Links category of the Page Properties dialog box. You can choose a different font and size for links, as well as specify colors for four different link states. Finally, you can choose whether (or when) links are underlined. Most browsers automatically underline links, but you can override this behavior with the help of this dialog box and Cascading Style Sheets (see page 181).*

15. **Click OK to close the window and apply these changes to the page.**

    You return to your document window. You see an asterisk next to the file name at the top of the document window—Dreamweaver is trying to tell you that you've made changes to the page since you last saved it (see circled image in Figure 1-25).

Figure 1-25: *An asterisk next to the name (circled) means that you've made changes to the file, but haven't yet saved it–quick, hit Ctrl+S (⌘-S on a Mac)!*

16. **Choose File → Save (or press Ctrl+S [⌘-S]).**

    Save your work frequently. (This isn't a Web technique as much as a computer-always-crashes-when-you-least-expect-it technique.)

Phase 4: Adding Images and Text

Now you'll add the real meat of your Web page: words and pictures.

1. **On the Insert panel's Common category, from the Image menu, select Image (see Figure 1-26).**

   Alternatively, choose Insert → Image. Either way, the Select Image Source dialog box opens.

UP TO SPEED

Using Dreamweaver's Color Box

That innocent-looking gray box in the Property inspector, the Modify Page Properties window, and various boxes throughout Dreamweaver is called the *color box*. You can use it to choose a color for the selected Web page element in any of three ways.

First, you can click one of the colors on the pop-up rainbow palette that appears when you click the color box.

Second, you can use the eyedropper cursor that appears when you click the color box. This cursor is "loaded," meaning you can click any spot on your screen—even outside the dialog box—to select a color, a trick that comes in handy when you want to use a color from a graphic in your document. You can even sample a color from another application (from any visible window, Dreamweaver or not): Just move the eyedropper over the color, and then click. (This click may take you out of Dreamweaver. Just return to Dreamweaver, and you see that the color you sampled has been applied.)

Finally, you can click the Color Picker icon, shown here, to launch the Mac or Windows color-picker dialog box, which lets you choose from millions of possible colors.

If you decide you don't want to add color, or want to remove a color you've already applied, click the Default Color button. Without a specific color setting, Web browsers use default colors for the element in question. For instance, text on a Web page is usually black unless you specify otherwise.

Next to the color box in any Dreamweaver dialog box is a blank text field. If you know your Web colors, then you can type their *hex* codes into this box, which is sometimes faster and more precise than clicking the rainbow palette.

The Palette Options menu is of limited use. It lets you select a different set of (very limited) rainbow colors for your palette. The first two choices, for example, contain the outdated Web-safe color palette—a limited collection of 216 colors that display accurately on any computer screen. The Web-safe palette made sense back when graphics cards were expensive and dinosaurs ruled the earth. Today, however, most monitors can show millions of different colors. Likewise, the Grayscale palette offers 256 somber shades of gray (you'll find them useful primarily when building Ingmar Bergman tribute sites). To really exercise your color creativity, use your computer's color-picker, and select from the millions of colorful options available to computers today.

In a hex code, a Web color is represented by a six-digit code like this: #FE3400. (Hexadecimal notation is a system computers use for counting. In this system, you count like this: 0, 1, 2, 3, 4, 5, 6, 7, 8, 9, A, B, C, D, E, F. The # tells the computer that the following sequence is a series of hexadecimal numbers—in this case, three pairs of them.) The best way to learn a color's hex value is to choose the color you want by clicking on it in the palette, and then looking at the code that Dreamweaver writes in the text box next to it. Hex colors are composed of three pairs of numbers, for example #FE3400 is really, FE, 34 and 00. Each pair represents a number for red, green, or blue, which together make up a color. You sometimes see only 3 numbers like this: #F00—this is shorthand and is used when both numbers in a pair are the same. For example, #FF0011 can be shortened to just #F01.

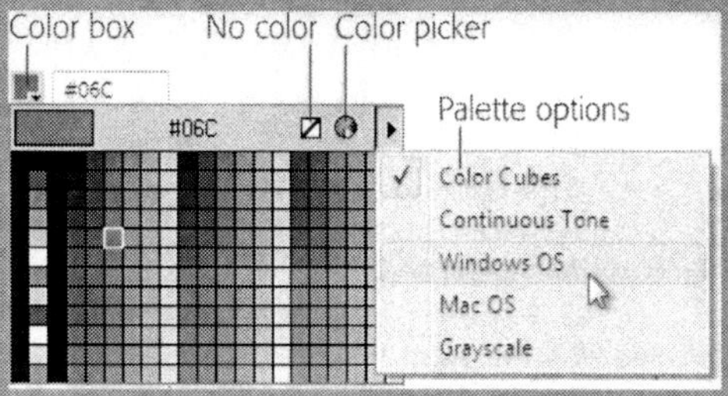

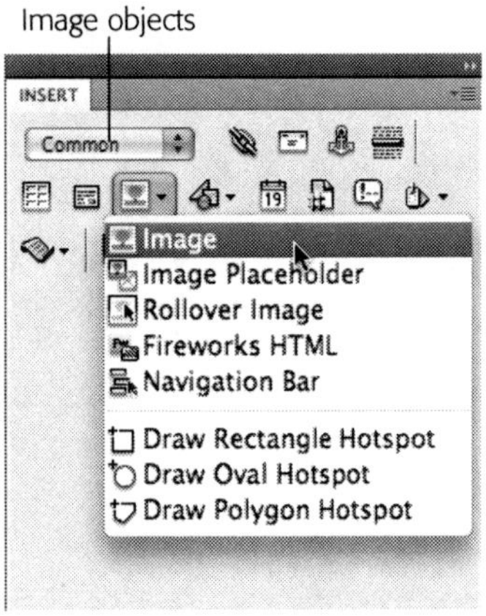

Figure 1-26:
Some of the buttons on Dreamweaver CS4's Insert panel do double duty as menus (the buttons with the small, black, down-pointing arrows). Once you select an option from the menu (in this case, the Image object), it becomes the button's current setting. If you want to insert the same object again (in this case, an image), you don't need to use the menu–just click the button.

2. **Browse to the *images* folder in the Chapter01 folder, and then double-click the graphics file called *banner.jpg*.**

   The Image Tag Accessibility window appears. Fresh out of the box and onto your computer, Dreamweaver has several accessibility preferences automatically turned on. These preferences are aimed at making your Web pages more accessible to people who use alternative devices for viewing Web sites—for example, people with viewing disabilities who require special Web browser software such as a screen reader, which literally reads the contents of a Web page out loud. Of course, images aren't words, so they can't be spoken. But you can add what's called an *alt* property. This is a text description of the graphic that's useful not only for screen-reading software, but also for people who deliberately *turn off* pictures in their Web browsers so Web pages will load faster. (Search engines also look at alt properties when indexing a page, so an accurate alt description can also help your site's search engine rankings.)

Note: If you don't see the Image Tag Accessibility window, type Ctrl+U (⌘-U) to open the Preferences panel, select the Accessibility category, turn on the Images checkbox, and then click OK.

3. **In the Alternate Text box, type *Chia Vet*. Click OK to add the image to the page.**

   The banner picture appears at the top of the page, as shown in Figure 1-27. A thin border appears around the image, indicating that it's selected. The Property inspector changes to reflect the properties of the image.

Note: You can also add or edit the *alt* text in the Property inspector (Figure 1-27).

4. **Deselect the image by clicking anywhere in the document window, or by pressing the right arrow key.**

   Keep your keyboard's arrow keys in mind—they're a great way to deselect a page element *and* move your cursor into place for adding text or more images.

Figure 1-27: *When you select an image in the document window, the Property inspector reveals its dimensions. In the top-left corner of the inspector, a small thumbnail image appears, as does the word "Image" (to let you know an image is selected) and the image's file size (in this case, 29 KB). The other image properties are described in Chapter 6.*

5. **Press Enter to create a new paragraph. Type *Directions to Chia Vet Headquarters*.**

   Notice that the text is a dark color and uses the Tahoma (or, if you don't have Tahoma installed, the Geneva) font; these are the properties you set up earlier in the Page Properties dialog box. The Property inspector now displays text formatting options.

Note: The key called Enter on a Windows keyboard is named Return on most Macintosh keyboards. On the Mac, you can press either Return or Enter.

---

6. **In the Property inspector, click the HTML button, and then, from the Format menu, choose Heading 1 (see Figure 1-28).**

   The text you just typed becomes big and bold—the default style for Heading 1. This Format menu offers a number of different paragraph types. The text doesn't stand out enough, so you'll change its color next.

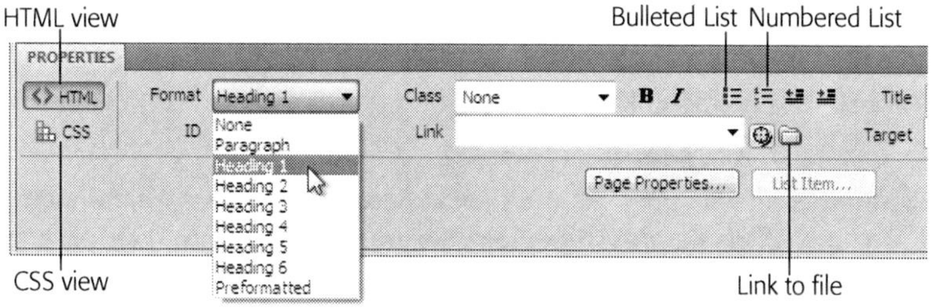

Figure 1-28: *The Property inspector includes two views: HTML and CSS. The HTML view, shown here, lets you control the HTML tags applied to text: created bulleted lists, paragraphs, create links, and so on. The CSS view provides a simple interface for creating Cascading Style Sheets so you can format text to look great.*

7. **Select the text you just typed.**

   You can do so either by dragging carefully across the entire line or by triple-clicking anywhere inside the line. (Unlike the Format menu, which affects an entire *paragraph* at a time, most options in the Property inspector—like the one you'll use next—apply only to *selected* text.)

8. **In the Property inspector, click the CSS button to switch to CSS properties. From the "Targeted rule" menu, choose "New CSS Rule". In the color field in the Property inspector, type *#EC6206* (or select a color using the color box, if you prefer), and then hit Enter.**

   The New CSS Rule window appears. This window (which you'll learn a lot more about in Chapter 4), lets you create new CSS styles. In this case, you'll be creating a type of style, called a tag style, which applies to any heading 1 (or <h1> tag) on the page.

9. **From the top menu, select "Tag (redefines an HTML element)".**

   Notice that the field below that menu changes to display h1. This is called a selector—and is simply the instruction that tells a Web browser how to apply the style you're about to create. In this case, you're redefining how <h1> tags look.

   Don't worry about any of the other settings in this window; you'll learn the details soon.

10. **Click OK.**

    Dreamweaver has just created a new CSS style. Now, wasn't that easy? Next you'll add more text.

11. **Click to the right of the heading text to deselect it. Press Enter to create a new paragraph below the headline.**

    While you may type a headline now and again, you'll probably get most of your text from word processing documents or emails from your clients, boss, or coworkers. To get that text into Dreamweaver, you simply copy it from another document, and then paste it into your Web page.

12. **In the Files panel, double-click the file *directions.txt* to open it.**

    This file is just plain text. No formatting, just words. To get it into your document, you'll copy and paste it.

13. **Click anywhere inside the text, and then choose Edit → Select All, followed by Edit → Copy. Click the *directions.html* tab to return to your Web page and, finally, choose Edit → Paste.**

    You should see a few gold shields sprinkled among the text (circled in Figure 1-29). If you don't see them, make sure you completed step 3 on page 49. These shields represent line breaks—spots where text drops to the next line without creating a new paragraph. You'll often see these appear in pasted text. In this case, you need to remove them, and then create separate paragraphs.

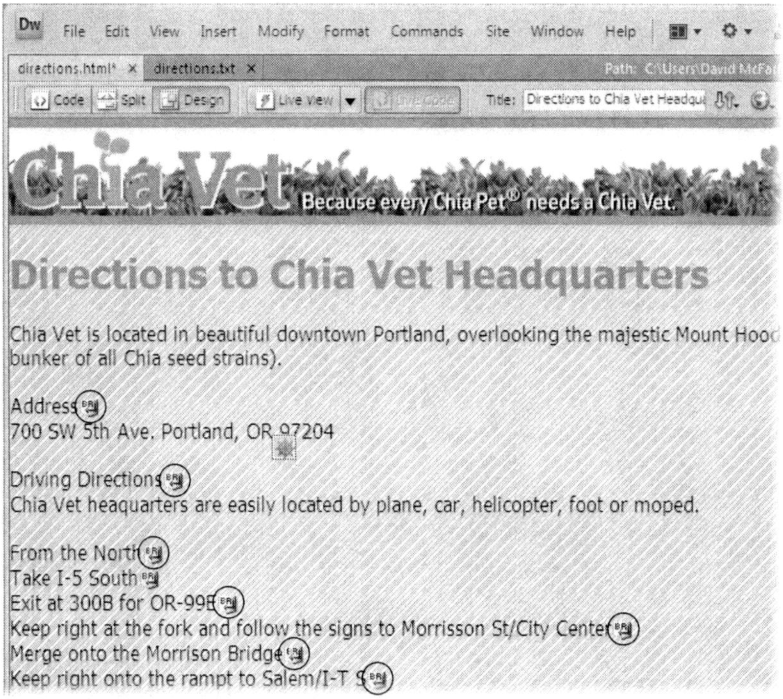

***Figure 1-29:** Line breaks (circled) often crop up when you copy and paste text from other programs into Dreamweaver. Follow the steps on page 49 to make sure the line breaks are visible in Design view.*

14. **Click one of the gold shields, and then press Enter. Repeat for any other gold shields in the document window.**

    This action deletes the line break (actually the
 HTML tag) and creates two paragraphs out of one. At this point, the pasted text is just a series of paragraphs. To give it some structure, you'll add headings and two numbered lists.

15. **Click in the paragraph with the text line "Address". In the Property inspector, click the HTML button, and then choose Heading 2 from the Format menu.**

    This step changes the paragraph to a headline—making it bigger and bolder.

16. **Repeat the last step for the lines of text "Driving Directions" and "For Geocachers" (near the end of the page).**

    You now have one heading 1 and three heading 2 headlines. To further structure the contents of this page, you'll add one last level of headlines.

17. **Click in the paragraph with the text line "From the North", and then choose Heading 3 in the Format menu. Repeat this step for the text "From the South".**

    To add a bit more style to this page, you'll format the heading 3 headlines next.

18. **Triple-click the headline "From the South" to select it. In the Property inspector, click the CSS button. In the field next to the color box, type *#779A00,* and then hit Enter.**

The New CSS Rule window appears again. Now you'll create a style for formatting <h3> tags.

19. **From the top menu, select "Tag (redefines an HTML element)".**

    You should see h3 in the middle field.

20. **Click OK.**

    Notice that the text changes to green. You'll see that the headline "From the North" is also green. The style you just created applies to all <h3> tags.

21. **Triple-click one of the green headlines. In the Property inspector, click the I (for Italics) button.**

    This action italicizes the text and updates the h3 stsyle you created earlier. Notice that the other heading 3 headline is now italicized.

22. **Select the seven paragraphs under the "From the North" headline. For example, drag from the start of the first paragraph down to the end of the seventh paragraph.**

    You can also drag up starting from the end of the last paragraph. Either way, you've selected all seven paragraphs listing driving directions to Chia Vet headquarters.

23. **On the Property inspector, click the HTML button, and then click the Numbered List button (see Figure 1-28).**

    The paragraphs turn into a single, step-by-step, numbered list. You'll now do the same for the other set of directions.

24. **Repeat steps 22 and 23 for the six paragraphs below the "From the South" headline.**

    Now you see two numbered lists (called "ordered lists" in HTML-speak). Finally, you'll highlight the company name where it appears in the text.

25. **Near the top of the page, select "Chia Vet" at the beginning of the sentence that starts with "Chia Vet is located in".**

    You'll make the name bold.

26. **Make sure the HTML button is pressed in the Property inspector, and then click the B button.**

    The text changes appearance but the New CSS Rule window doesn't appear. Even though you find the B (for bold) button on both the HTML and CSS views of the Property inspector, they do different things. When the HTML button is selected, the B button inserts the HTML <strong> tag—used to strongly emphasize text. When the CSS button is pressed, the B button adds CSS code to make the text look bold. It's a subtle but important difference that you'll read about on page 108. In this case, you want to use the HTML <strong> tag to emphasize your company's name.

27. **Repeat step 26 for both the "Chia Vet" text that appears about halfway down the page and the text "Chia-Vet.com" at the very bottom of the page. Save the page.**

    A few more design touches remain to be added to the page, but first you should see how the page looks in a real Web browser.

Phase 5: Preview Your Work

Dreamweaver is as close as a Web design program can be to a WYSIWYG application, meaning that for the most part, What You See (in the document window) Is What You'll Get (on the Web).

At least that's how it's supposed to work. But Dreamweaver may display *more* information than you'll see on the Web (including "invisible" objects and table borders) and may display *less* (it sometimes has trouble rendering complex designs).

Furthermore, much to the eternal woe of Web designers, different Web browsers display pages differently. Pages viewed in Internet Explorer don't always look the same in other browsers like Firefox or Safari. In some cases, the differences may be subtle (for example, text may be slightly larger or smaller). Or they can be dramatic: Some of the advanced page-layout techniques described in Chapter 9 can look *awful* in older Web browsers (you'll learn how to deal with many of these problems throughout this book).

Note: If you don't happen to have a Windows computer, a Mac, and every browser ever made, y take advantage of a free service that creates screenshots of your site using a wide range of brows operating systems. Check out *www.browsershots.org*.

If you're designing Web pages for use on a company intranet and have to worry about only the one Web browser your IT department has put on everyone's computer, you're lucky. Most people have to deal with the fact that their sites must withstand scrutiny from a wide range of browsers, so it's a good idea to preview your Web pages using whatever browsers you expect visitors to your Web sites to use. Fortunately, Dreamweaver lets you preview a Web page using any browser you have installed on your computer.

Before you can preview a page, you need to set up your list of browsers in the program's preference window, like this:

1. **Choose File → "Preview in Browser" → Edit Browser List.**

   The "Preview in Browser" preferences window opens (see Figure 1-30). When you install Dreamweaver, it detects which browsers are already installed on your computer; a list of those browsers appears in the browsers list in this window. If you installed a browser after you installed Dreamweaver, then it doesn't appear in this list, so you need to follow steps 2 and 3 next; otherwise, skip to step 4.

2. **Click the + button.**

   The Add Browser or Select Browser window opens.

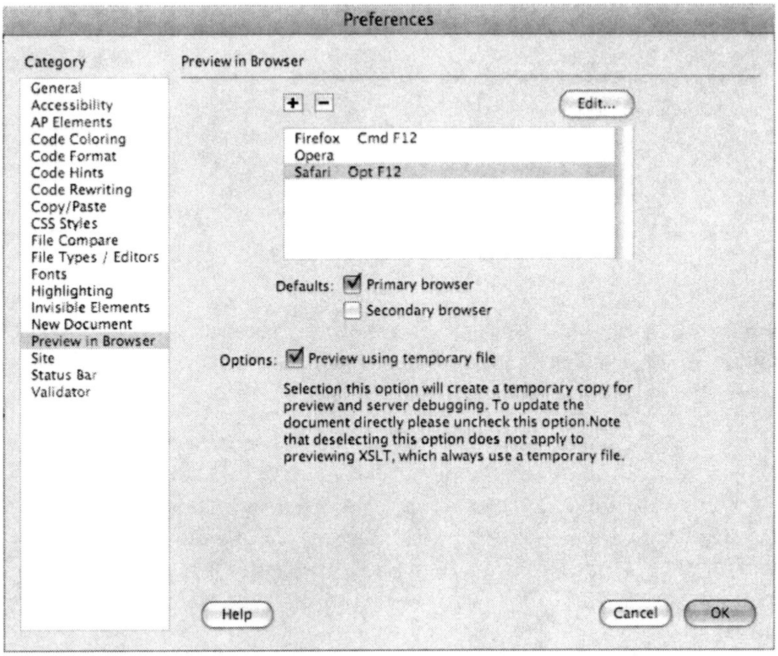

Figure 1-30: *Dreamweaver can launch a Web browser and load a page in it so you can preview your design. One option–"Preview using temporary file"–comes in handy when working with Cascading Style Sheets, as described in the Note on page 159.*

3. **Click the Browse button. Search your hard drive to find a browser you wish to add to this list.**

   Dreamweaver inserts the browser's default name in the Name field of the Add Browser window. If you wish to change its name for display purposes within Dreamweaver, select it, and then type a new name. (But don't do this *before* selecting the browser, since Dreamweaver erases anything you've typed as soon as you select a browser.)

4. **In the window's Browser list, select the browser you most commonly use. Turn on the Primary Browser box. Click OK.**

   You've just designated the browser as your *primary* browser while working in Dreamweaver. You can now preview your pages in this browser with a simple keyboard shortcut: F12 (Option-F12 on a Mac).

   If you like, you can also choose a secondary browser, which you can launch by pressing the Ctrl+F12 (⌘-F12) key combination.

   Now you're ready to preview your document in a real, bona fide Web browser. Fortunately, Dreamweaver makes it easy.

5. **Press the F12 key (Option F12 on a Mac) or choose File → "Preview in Browser" and, from the menu, select a browser.**

   The F12 key (Option-F12 on Mac) is the most important keyboard shortcut you'll learn. Macintosh fans: Unfortunately, Apple has assigned the F12 key to the Dashboard program, so it takes two keys to preview the page—Option and F12 (however, you can change this setting by creating your own keyboard shortcuts as described on page 799). This keyboard shortcut opens the Web page in your primary browser, letting you preview your work.

If you're using a Macintosh laptop, you may have to press Option-F12 and the function (fn) key in the lower-left corner of the keyboard.

You can also use the "Preview in Browser" menu in the document window to preview a page (see Figure 1-31).

Figure 1-31: *The "Preview in Browser" menu in the document window is another way to preview a page. This menu has the added benefit of letting you select any browser, not just the ones you've assigned keyboard shortcuts to.*

6. **When you're done previewing the page, go back to Dreamweaver.**

   Do so using your favorite way to switch programs on your computer—by using the Windows taskbar, or the Dock in Mac OS X.

Phase 6: Finishing the Page

You've covered most of the steps you need to finish this Web page. Now you just need to add a graphic, format the copyright notice, and provide a little more structure to the appearance of the page.

1. **In the "Address" headline, click just before the "A".**

   This step places the cursor at the beginning of the headline. You'll insert a graphic here.

2. **From the Common category on the Insert panel, click the Image button (see Figure 1-26).**

   You can also choose Insert → Image or use the keyboard shortcut Ctrl+Alt+I (⌘-Alt-I).

3. **Browse to the *images* folder in the Chapter01 folder, and double-click the graphics file called *portland.jpg*.**

   Again, the Image Tag Accessibility window appears. You need to provide a good description for this image.

Note to Windows Users: As noted above (page 56) Windows doesn't display a file's extension (unless you tell it to). So when you navigate to the *images* folder in step 3 above, you might see *portland* instead of *portland.jpg*.

4. **Type *Portland skyline,* and then press OK.**

   Look at the Property inspector. It displays properties specific to images. You'll learn more about these options in Chapter 6, but now you'll learn a quick way to make text wrap around an image.

5. **In the Property inspector's lower-right corner, from the Align pop-up menu, choose Right.**

   The image moves to the right edge of the page and text wraps around its left side. (The Left option moves the image to the left, letting text wrap around the image's right side.)

   At the bottom of the page is a copyright notice. It's not really related to the content of the page, so you'll add a line to visually separate the copyright from the rest of the page.

Note: Although the left and right options for an image's align property are quick ways to force text to wrap around an image, they aren't valid options for the "strict" versions of HTML or XHTML (see page 49). CSS provides a more flexible technique–known as a *float*–to achieve this same effect. You'll learn about it on page 231.

6. **Scroll to the bottom of the page, click before the letter C in "Copyright 2009", and then choose Insert → HTML → Horizontal Rule.**

   A gray line appears above the copyright notice. The copyright appears a little big, so you'll format it next.

Note: You can also add a line above a paragraph of text using the CSS *border* property. See page 231.

7. **Select all the text in the copyright paragraph.**

   You can either triple-click inside the paragraph or drag from the beginning of the paragraph text to the end.

8. **Click the CSS button in the Property inspector, and then, from the Size menu, choose *12*.**

   The New CSS Rule window opens again. This time you want to create a style that applies only to this one paragraph of text—not every paragraph—so you need to use what's called a class style.

9. **Type *copyright* in the selector field (circled in Figure 1-32), and then click OK.**

   You've created another style. Notice that the copyright notice text gets smaller.

   The legal department of Chia Vet headquarters has decided that every page on the site must link to an official corporate statement. You'll add a link for that next.

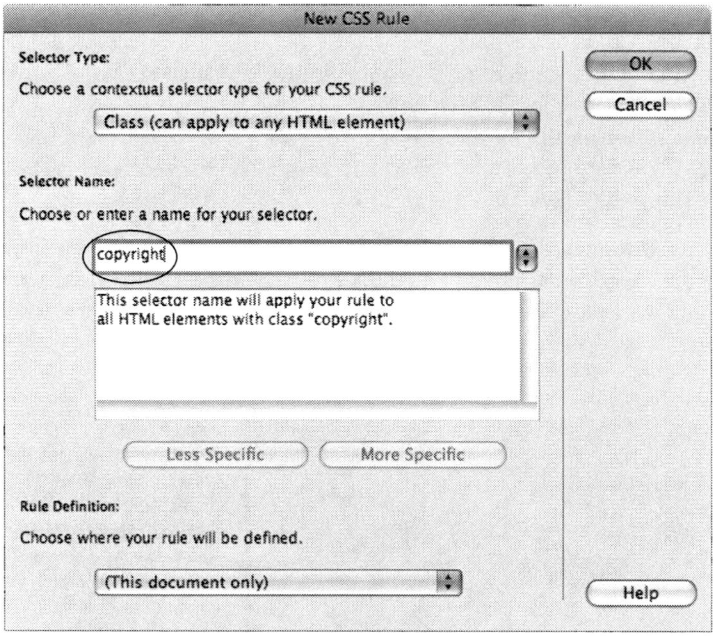

Figure 1-32: *The New CSS Rule window lets you create CSS styles. You can choose among many different types of styles. In this case, you're creating a class style named copyright. Class styles work a lot like styles in Word processing programs–to use them, you select the text you wish to format, and then apply the style.*

10. **At the bottom of the page, select the text "Read our full legal statement".**

    To create a link, you just need to tell Dreamweaver which page you want to link to. You have several ways to do this. Using the Property inspector is the easiest.

11. **In the Property inspector, click the HTML button; click the folder icon that appears to the right of the link field (see Figure 1-28).**

    The Select File dialog box appears.

12. **Click the Site Root button (top of the dialog box in Windows; bottom of dialog box on a Mac), and double click the file named *legal.html*.**

    The Site Root button jumps you right to the folder containing your site. It's a convenient way to quickly move to your root folder. Double-clicking the file inserts the HTML needed to create a link.

    If you preview the page in a Web browser, it looks all right…well, not really. The text is kind of hard to read against the blue striped background, the text is too wide if you expand your Web browser on a large monitor, and the photo is hanging way out on the right of the browser. To fix these problems, you'll create a new layout element—a box to contain all of the content on the page.

13. **Click anywhere inside the page, and then choose Edit → Select All or press Ctrl+A (⌘-A on a Mac).**

    The contents of the page are selected. You'll wrap all text and images in a <div> tag to create a kind of container for the page contents.

14. **Choose Insert → Layout Objects → Div Tag.**

    The Insert Div Tag window opens (see Figure 1-33). A <div> tag simply provides a way to organize content on a page by grouping related HTML—think of it as a box containing other HTML tags. For example, to create a sidebar of navigation links, news headlines, and Google ads, you would wrap them all in a <div> tag. It's a very important tag when creating CSS-based layouts. You'll read more about the <div> tag on page 333.

    Next, you need to create a style to provide the instructions needed to format this new <div> tag. You've already used the Property inspector to create a style, but that only works for text. To format other tags, you need to create a style in another way.

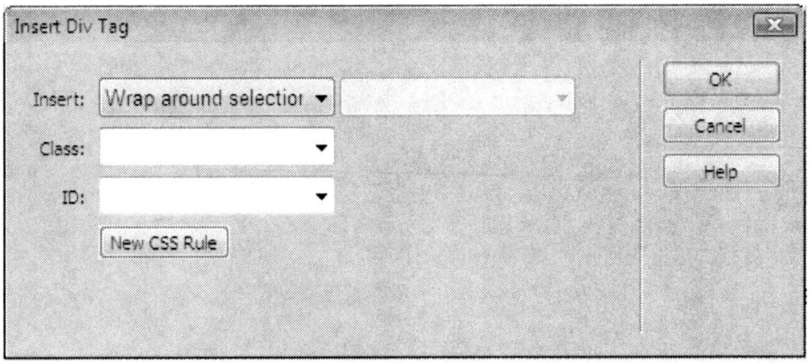

***Figure 1-33:** The Insert Div Tag window provides an easy way to divide sections of a Web page into groups of related HTML–like the elements that make up a banner, for example. You'll learn about all the different functions of this window on page 335.*

15. **Click the New CSS Rule button.**

    The New CSS Rule window appears (a CSS style is technically called a "rule"). This window lets you determine what type of style you're creating, the style's name, and where the style information should be stored. You'll learn all the ins and outs of this window in Chapter 4.

16. **From the top menu, choose ID, and then type *#wrapper* in the "Choose or enter a name" field. Make sure "This document only" is selected in the bottom menu. Click OK.**

    There's a lot going on in this box, but don't worry about the details at this point. You'll learn everything there is to know about creating styles later in this book. This part of the tutorial is intended to give you a taste of some of a Web designer's daily Web page building duties. So just relax and follow along.

    After closing the New CSS Rule window, the "CSS Rule definition" window appears (see Figure 1-34). This window is the command center for defining the formatting properties such as text color, font, and size for a style. CSS has quite a few properties, which Dreamweaver divides into eight categories. First, you'll add a background color for this <div>.

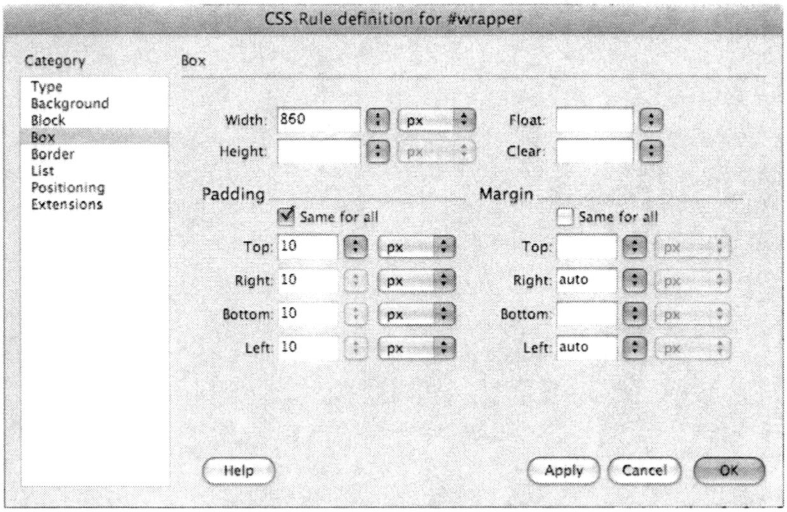

***Figure 1-34:** The "CSS Rule definition" window lets you set over 60 different CSS properties (divided into eight different categories) that control the formatting of everything from text to images to entire Web pages.*

17. **From the left-hand list of categories, select Background. Click the color box that appears to the right of Background-color, and then select a white swatch.**

    This action adds a white background to the box, making sure the text stands out. Next you'll set a specific width for the box, and center it in the middle of the browser window.

18. **Click the Box category, and then, in the width box, type *860*.**

    This step makes the box 860 pixels wide—the same width as the banner. To make sure the text doesn't butt right up against the edge of the box, you'll add a little space (called *padding*) around the inside of this style.

19. **In the Top box under Padding, type *10* (make sure the "Same for all" check-box is turned on).**

    This action adds 10 pixels of space inside the box, essentially pushing the text and the graphics away from the edges of the box.

20. **Under the Margin settings, uncheck the "Same for all" box, and then, from both the right and left margin menus, select "auto".**

    The auto property for the right and left margin is your way of telling a Web browser to automatically supply a left and right margin—in this case, as you'll see in a moment, it has the effect of centering the <div> in the middle of a browser window.

21. **The CSS Rule Definition window should now look like Figure 1-34. Click OK to complete the style.**

    The Insert Div Tag window reappears, and the name of the style you just created—wrapper—appears in a box labeled ID.

22. **In the Insert Div Tag window, click OK.**

This inserts the new <div> tag and at the same time applies the style you just created. Now it's time to view your handiwork.

23. **Choose File → Save. Press the F12 key (Option-F12 on a Mac) to preview your work in your browser (Figure 1-35).**

Test the link to make sure it works. Resize your browser and watch how the page content centers itself in the middle of the window.

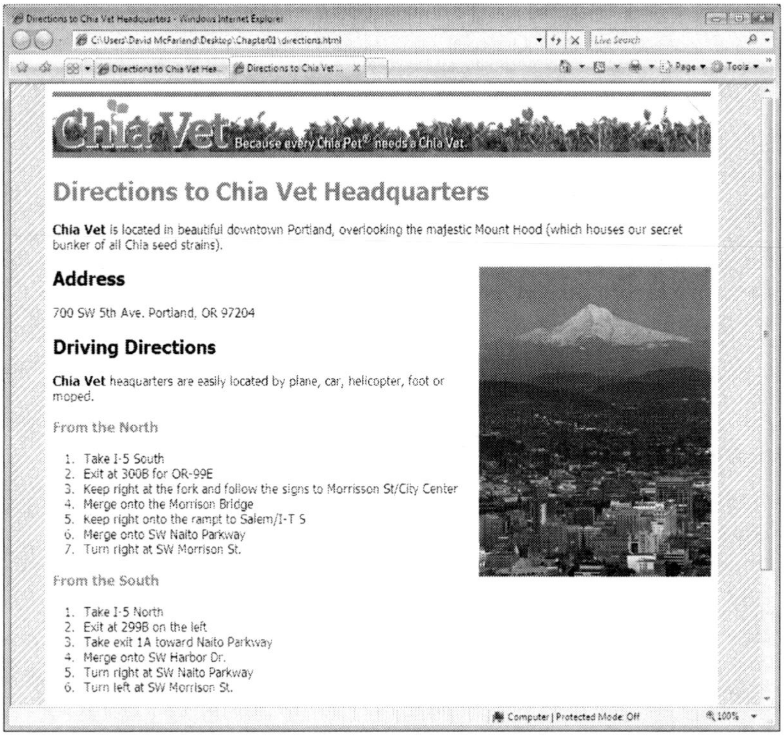

***Figure 1-35:** The finished tutorial file should look like this. You may notice that the white space above the banner logo is bigger in browsers other than Internet Explorer. (The reason for this–and how to fix it–is explained on page 356.) That's just one of those funny browser inconsistencies that drive Web designers crazy (and not in a "funny ha-ha" kind of way).*

Congratulations! You've just built your first Web page in Dreamweaver, complete with graphics, formatted text, and links. If you'd like to compare your work with the finished product, you'll find another folder, Chapter01_finished, in the Tutorials folder.

Much of the work of building Web sites involves using the procedures covered in this tutorial—defining a site, adding links, formatting text, placing graphics, creating styles, and inserting divs. The next few chapters cover these basics in greater depth and introduce other important tools, tips, and techniques for using Dreamweaver to build great Web pages.

CHAPTER

2

Adding Text to Your Web Pages

Nowadays, streaming video, audio, and high-quality graphics are what draw most people to Web sites. After all, it's exciting to hear the latest song from your favorite band, see a preview of a yet-to-be released blockbuster, and tune in to YouTube to see the kid down the street embarrass himself in front of a billion Web viewers.

But the fact is, the Web is primarily woven with *words*. iPhone 3G reviews, Brad Pitt and Angelina Jolie gossip, and countless personal blogs about cats still drive people to the Web. As you build Web pages and Web sites, you'll spend a lot of your time adding and formatting *text*. To get your message across effectively, you need to understand how Dreamweaver works with text.

This chapter covers the not-always-simple act of getting text *into* your Dreamweaver documents. In Chapter 3, you can read about formatting this text so that it looks professionally designed.

Adding Text in Dreamweaver

In many ways, Dreamweaver works like a word processing program. When you create a new document, the blinking cursor appears at the top of the page, ready for you to begin typing. When you finish a paragraph, you press Enter or Return to start a new one. Text, as well as anything else you add to a Web page, starts at the top of the page and works its way to the bottom.

Adding Special Characters

Many useful special characters—such as copyright or trademark symbols—don't appear on your keyboard, making them difficult or impossible to type. The Insert bar's Text tab lets you use a variety of symbols and international characters quickly by clicking an icon.

To open the Text tab:

1. **On the Insert panel, choose the Text category.**

   If the Insert panel isn't visible, choose Window → Insert to open it, or use the keyboard shortcut Ctrl+F2 (⌘-F2).

   The panel shown in Figure 2-1 appears. Many of the options let you add common HTML tags like the <b> (bold) and <strong> (strong) tags, most of which you can apply more easily using the Property inspector or keyboard shortcuts, as discussed in the next chapter. This panel also features less frequently used tags like <abbr> (abbreviation) or <dl> (definition list). You can satisfy your curiosity about these tags by using Dreamweaver's HTML reference (see page 422), but their names give you an idea of when you might want to use them.

   The last option on the panel is actually a menu that offers a wide range of symbols and international characters. Unlike regular Western characters, such as *a* or *z*, these special characters are represented in HTML by a code name or number. For instance, a trademark symbol (™) is written in HTML as *™*.

Tip: If you like card games or just want to add a heart to a Web page without using a graphic, go to Code view and type *♥* to get a heart character, *♦* for a diamond, *♠* for a spade, or *♣* for a club. (Don't forget the ; at the end of each–that's part of the code).

2. **From the menu at the end of the Insert panel, select the symbol you wish to insert (see Figure 2-1).**

   Dreamweaver inserts the appropriate HTML code into your Web page. (Alternatively, you can select the Other Characters option to bring up the wider-ranging Insert Other Character dialog box shown in Figure 2-1.)

Note: If you set the encoding of your Web page to anything other than Western European or Unicode (UTF-8) in the Page Properties window (by choosing Modify → Page Properties, and then clicking the Title/ Encoding category), you can reliably insert only line breaks and nonbreaking spaces. The other special characters available from the Character category of the Objects panel may not work (see the box on page 86 for more about how encoding works).

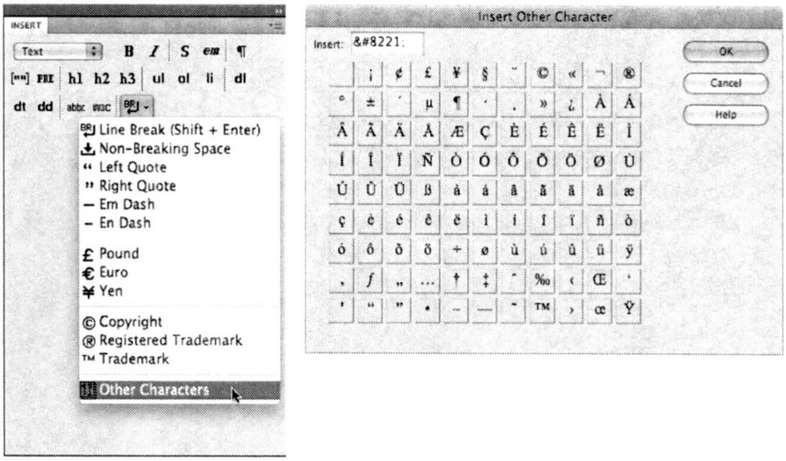

Figure 2-1: *Selecting Other Characters from the Text panel (left) brings up the Insert Other Character dialog box (right). However, there are even more characters in the Western alphabet than this dialog box lists. You can find a table listing these characters and their associated entity names and numbers at www.evolt.org/article/ala/17/21234/. (Note, normally the Insert Panel includes text labels next to each button; in this figure the labels for the Insert Panel are hidden so that more buttons fit in the panel. If you don't know how to hide the labels, you can learn on page 26.)*

Line Breaks

Pressing Enter creates a new paragraph, exactly as in a word processor. Unfortunately, Web browsers add extra space above and below paragraphs—which is a real nuisance if you're trying to create several single-spaced lines of text, like this:

702 A Street
Boring, OR
97009 USA

Here, each part of the address is on its own line, but it's still just a single paragraph (and shares the overall formatting of that paragraph, as you'll learn in the next chapter).

Tip: If you want to *entirely* dispense with the space that browsers insert between paragraphs, don't use line breaks each time. Instead, use CSS to eliminate the top and bottom margins of the <p> tag, as described in the Tip on page 144.

To create this single-spaced effect, you need to insert a *line break* at the insertion point, using one of these techniques:

- On the Insert panel's Text category, from the Characters menu, select Line Break (the first menu option at top in Figure 2-1).

POWER USERS' CLINIC

Keyboard Shortcuts for Special Characters

Dreamweaver CS4 uses UTF-8 (also called Unicode) encoding when you create a new page (unless you specify otherwise). Without getting into the messy details, basically UTF-8 lets you include almost any type of character available to the languages of the world–it lets a Chinese speaker embed actual Chinese characters into a page, for example. When you use the Other Characters window (Figure 2-1), Dreamweaver inserts what's called an HTML entity–a code that replaces the real character: for example, the © symbol is represented by *©*. But UTF-8 lets you add the actual symbol to a page–the trick is knowing how to do that with the keyboard.

On the Mac, you have a handful of keyboard shortcuts for directly typing a special character like a copyright symbol onto a page. Here are a few of the most common: Option+; to get a true ellipses (three periods in a row); Option+Shift+- for an em-dash (–); Option+] for opening single quote ('); Option+Shift+] for closing single quote ('); Option+[for opening double-quote ("); Option+Shift+[for closing double-quote ("); and Option+G for a copyright symbol(©). You can also use the Mac Character Palette to insert unusual symbols using Unicode (for information on the Mac character palette visit *http://tinyurl.com/6fg8d7*).

In Windows, you must press the Alt key, type the Unicode value using your keyboard's numeric keypad, and then release the Alt key. Note that you can't use the regular number keys for this–you must use the numeric keypad. For example, to add an em-dash, hold down the Alt key, type *0133*, and then release the Alt key. Here are a few others: open single quote is Alt+0145; closing single quote is Alt+0146; opening double-quote is Alt+0147; and closing double-quote is Alt+0148. You can also use the Windows character map to insert special symbols and characters. (Visit *http://tinyurl.com/5blqek* to learn how to use the Windows character map.)

- Choose Insert → HTML → Special Characters → Line Break.
- Press Shift+Enter.

Note: When you insert a line break in Dreamweaver, you may get no visual hint that it's even there; after all, a regular paragraph break and a line break both create a new line of text.

This scenario is especially likely if you copy text from programs other than Microsoft Word or Excel. Text from other programs–especially email programs–can be loaded with an infuriating number of line breaks. To add to the confusion, a line break may go unnoticed if it occurs at the end of a long line. Your only hope is to make line breaks visible.

To do so, choose Edit → Preferences (or Dreamweaver → Preferences on the Mac), or press Ctrl+U (⌘-U). Click the Invisible Elements category. Make sure the Line Breaks checkbox is turned on. Now you see each line break appear as a small gold shield. (If after doing this, you still don't see the line break character, choose View → Visual Aids, and make sure the Invisible Elements checkbox is turned on.)

You can select a line break by clicking the shield, and then delete it like any page element. Better yet, select the shield, and then hit Enter or Return, to eliminate the line break *and* create a new paragraph.

Another way to avoid pasting some hidden line breaks is the Paste Special command (see page 80).

Nonbreaking Spaces

Sometimes the way a sentence breaks over two lines in your text can distort what you're trying to say, as shown in Figure 2-2. In this case, a *nonbreaking space* can save the day. It looks just like a regular space, but it acts as glue that prevents the words on either side from being split apart at the end of a line. For example, adding a nonbreaking space between the words "Farmer" and "Says" in Figure 2-2 ensures that those words won't get split across a line break, and helps clarify the presentation and meaning of this headline.

To insert a nonbreaking space between two words, delete the regular space already between the words (for example, by clicking after the space and pressing the backspace key), and then do one of the following:

- On the Insert panel's Text category, from the Characters menu, select Non-Breaking Space (the second menu option in Figure 2-1, left).
- Choose Insert → HTML → Special Characters → Non-Breaking Space.
- Press Ctrl+Shift+Space bar (⌘-Shift-Space bar).

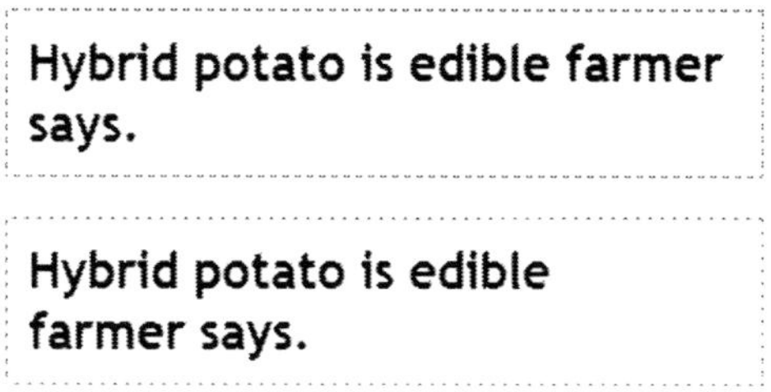

Hybrid potato is edible farmer
says.
Hybrid potato is edible
farmer says.

Figure 2-2:
Headlines sometimes split between lines leaving a single word alone on a line (top)—in typography this is known as a "widow." Adding a nonbreaking space (bottom) can prevent widows and clarify a headline's meaning.

Multiple Spaces

You may have noticed that if you type more than one space in a row, Dreamweaver ignores all but the first space. This isn't a glitch in the program; it's standard HTML. Web browsers ignore any spaces following the first one.

Therefore, a line like "Beware   of   llama," with several spaces between each word, would appear on a Web page like this: "Beware of llama." Not only do Web browsers ignore multiple spaces, but they also ignore any spaces that aren't *between* words. So if you hit the space bar a couple of times to indent the first line of a paragraph, you're wasting your time. A Web browser doesn't display any of those spaces (Dreamweaver doesn't display those spaces either).

This feature makes good sense, because it prevents Web pages from being littered with extraneous spaces that many people insert when writing HTML code. (Extra spaces in a page of HTML often make the code easier to read.)

There may be times, however, when you *want* to add more space between words. For example, consider the text navigation bar at the bottom of a Web page, a common Web page element that lists the different sections of a Web site. Visitors can click one of the section titles to jump directly to a different area of the site. For clarity, many designers like to add multiple spaces between the text links, like this:

News   Classifieds   Jobs

Or, you might want to add space at the beginning of the first line of a paragraph to create the kind of indent that's common to paragraphs in some books (but not this one). One simple way to add space is to insert multiple nonbreaking spaces as described on page 77. A Web browser *will* display every nonbreaking space it encounters, so you can add multiple nonbreaking spaces between words, letters, or even at the beginning of paragraphs. This technique has a few downsides, though: You have to type a bunch of nonbreaking spaces, which takes work, and adds code to your Web page, making it download a bit slower.

You can enlist Cascading Style Sheets (CSS) to add space as well. While you won't get in-depth detail on CSS until Chapter 4, here are a few CSS properties (formatting rules) to tuck in the back of your mind when you need to add space to your text:

- To indent the first line of a paragraph, use the *text indent* property (page 145).
- To add space between words in a paragraph, use the *word spacing* property (page 144).
- To add space between letters like this, use *letter spacing* (page 144).
- And, if you want to increase the space between text links as in the example above, you can add either left and right *margins* or *padding* to each link (page 343).

Note: If you often add multiple spaces, Dreamweaver offers a shortcut. Choose Edit → Preferences to open Dreamweaver's Preferences window (on a Mac, choose Dreamweaver → Preferences instead). Click the General category. Then, under "Editing options", turn on "Allow multiple consecutive spaces". Now, whenever you press the space bar more than once, Dreamweaver inserts *nonbreaking* spaces.

In fact, Dreamweaver is even smarter than that. It inserts a regular space if you press the space bar just once, a nonbreaking space followed by a regular space if you hit the space bar twice, and multiple nonbreaking spaces followed by a final *regular* space if you hit the space bar repeatedly. Since nonbreaking spaces act like glue that keeps words stuck together (see the previous section), the extra regular spaces let the lines break normally, if necessary.

Adding a Date to Your Page

The Insert panel's Common category offers an icon called Date (it looks like the page of a calendar). Clicking this icon or choosing Insert → Date opens the Insert Date dialog box (Figure 2-3), which lets you insert today's date, as your computer understands it, onto your Web page in progress. You can also specify whether to include the day of the week and the current time.

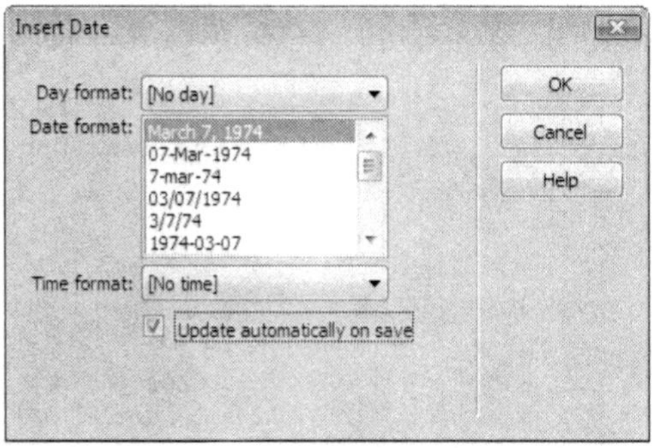

Figure 2-3:
When you insert a Date object (a placeholder for the actual date) onto a Web page, you have several additional options: If you want to add the day of the week, choose the format you want from the "Day format" pop-up menu. You may also choose to add the current time in hours and minutes–in either military time (22:18) or regular time (10:18 PM)–from the "Time format" pop-up menu.

Select the format you wish from the Date Format list. You have 13 different formats to choose from, such as March 7, 1974 or 3/7/74.

You may wonder why Dreamweaver includes an insert-date function anyway. How hard is it to type *Thursday, July 12*?

Actually, the real value of the Insert Date feature lies in the "Update automatically on save" checkbox. Choosing this option forces Dreamweaver to *update* the date each time you save the document.

You can use this feature to stamp a Web page with a date that indicates when the contents were last updated. For example, you might type *This page was last revised on*: and then choose Insert → Date and select the "Update automatically on save" option. Now, each time you make a change to the page, Dreamweaver automatically changes the date to reflect when you saved the document. You never again have to worry about it.

Copying and Pasting Text

If you're building Web sites as part of a team or for clients, your writers are likely to send you their copy in the form of word processing documents. If the text comes in a Microsoft Word document or Excel spreadsheet, you're lucky. Dreamweaver includes commands for pasting text from these two types of files. If you're using Windows, you can even import those kinds of files directly into a Web page using File → Import → Word/Excel Document (see page 85).

Simple Copy and Paste

For non–Microsoft-spawned text, you can, of course, still simply copy and paste like generations of Web designers before you.

Open the document in whatever program created it—WordPad, TextEdit, your email program, or whatever. Select the text you want (by dragging through it, for example), or choose Edit → Select All (Ctrl+A [⌘-A]) to highlight all text in the document. Then choose Edit → Copy, or press Ctrl+C (⌘-C), to copy it. Switch to Dreamweaver, click in the document window where you wish the text to go, and then choose Edit → Paste (Ctrl+V [⌘-V]).

This routine pastes the text into place. Unfortunately, you lose all text formatting (font type, size, color, bold, italic, and so on) in the process, as shown in Figure 2-4.

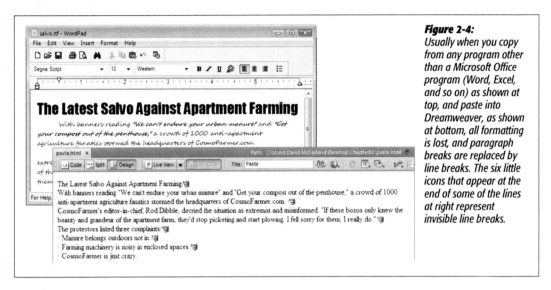

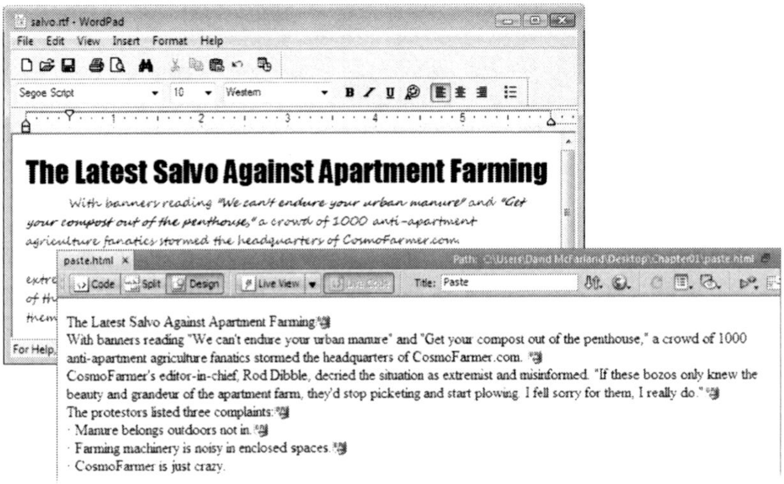

Figure 2-4: *Usually when you copy from any program other than a Microsoft Office program (Word, Excel, and so on) as shown at top, and paste into Dreamweaver, as shown at bottom, all formatting is lost, and paragraph breaks are replaced by line breaks. The six little icons that appear at the end of some of the lines at right represent invisible line breaks.*

Furthermore, you may find that pasted paragraphs are separated by line break characters, not standard carriage returns. Strangely enough, this means that when you paste in a series of paragraphs, Dreamweaver treats them as though they were one gargantuan paragraph. These line break characters can pose problems when trying to format what you *think* is a single paragraph. To identify these line breaks, see the Note on page 76.

Tip: If you *have* to copy and paste text from other programs, you do have one way to get paragraphs (and not just lines separated by the line break character) when you paste into Dreamweaver. Just make sure whoever's typing up the original documents inserts an empty paragraph between each paragraph of text. Pressing Enter (or Return) twice at the end of a paragraph inserts an empty paragraph. When you copy and paste, Dreamweaver removes the empty paragraphs *and* pastes the text as regular paragraphs.

Paste Special

Dreamweaver also includes a Paste Special command which supports four different types of paste methods, ranging from plain text to highly formatted HTML. In actual use, however, only the first two are supported for *all* pasting operations. The last two are available only when pasting from Microsoft Word or Excel.

- **Text only.** This option is the most basic of all. Text is pasted without any formatting whatsoever. Even paragraphs and line breaks are ignored, so you end up with essentially one long sentence. Though you won't want this effect often, it can come in handy when you copy a long paragraph of text from an email program that's added unnecessary line breaks at the end of each line of email text.
- **Text with structure.** Dreamweaver tries to preserve the structure of the text, including paragraphs, headers, bulleted lists, and so on. This option doesn't keep formatting applied to text, such as bold or italics. Most non–Microsoft Office copied text is pasted using this method. In most cases, however, Dreamweaver ends up preserving only paragraphs, and misses bulleted lists and headers.
- **Basic formatting.** When pasting with Basic formatting, Dreamweaver includes the same elements as the "Text with structure" option, but also includes text formatting such as bold, italics, and underlining. This is the method Dreamweaver uses when pasting Microsoft Word or Excel information, as described in the next section.
- **Full formatting.** This option includes everything offered by Basic formatting, but also attempts to paste CSS information that can control the font size and color, paragraph margins, and more. Full formatting is available only when copying and pasting from Word or Excel (see the next section).

Note to Windows Users: You can copy an entire page of HTML from Firefox or Internet Explorer, and then paste it into Dreamweaver. Click inside a Web page, press Ctrl+A to select the entire page, and then press Ctrl+C to copy the HTML. Then switch to Dreamweaver, click inside an empty page, and press Ctrl+V to paste. All the HTML is copied, and even graphics appear. This text comes in with "full formatting," but note that no style sheets come along for the ride.

You can override Dreamweaver's default behavior and choose a different method for pasting by using the Paste Special command. Choose Edit → Paste Special to open the Paste Special window (see Figure 2-5). Here, you can choose which of the four techniques you wish to use...sort of. You're limited to what Dreamweaver can paste. For non–Microsoft Office products, you can use only the first two options—the others are grayed out—whereas with text copied from Word or Excel, you can choose from any of the four.

For text copied from most programs, it's best to use "Text with structure" and keep the "Retain line breaks" checkbox checked. You'll still have to manually replace line breaks with paragraphs as described in the note on page 76, but without the "Retain line breaks" option selected, Dreamweaver removes single carriage returns, resulting in one long paragraph of text.

For Word or Excel information, there are a few options worth considering, as described next.

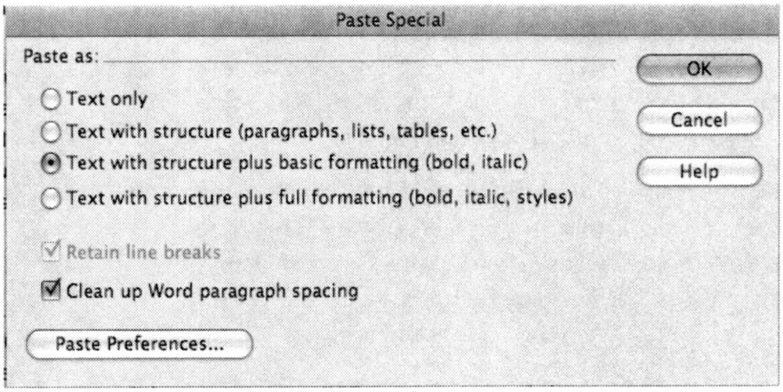

Figure 2-5: *The Paste Special command lets you paste text copied from other programs. If you want Dreamweaver to apply the same setting each time you use the Paste Special command, click the Paste Preferences button. This opens the Preferences window. Select whatever settings–Basic formatting, for example–that you want Dreamweaver to apply every time you use the Paste Special command.*

Pasting Text from Word: The Basic Method

While text from other applications doesn't retain much beyond paragraph formatting when pasted into Dreamweaver, Dreamweaver includes both basic and advanced methods of copying and pasting Word text.

Frequently, you'll just want to preserve basic formatting like bold or italic text, headlines, and bulleted lists. You won't need (and in most cases, won't want) more extravagant formatting like different fonts, colors, or margin settings. After all, you're the Web designer, and you'll use your own design sense—and Dreamweaver's CSS-based formatting tools—to add beauty to basic text.

Pasting Word text works like any copy/paste action described in the previous section. Just select the text in Word, copy it, switch to Dreamweaver, and then choose Edit → Paste to drop it into a Web page. You don't have to spend a lot of time reformatting the pasted text (see bottom-left image in Figure 2-6), since many basic formatting options are preserved:

- Any paragraphs formatted with Word's built-in Heading styles (Heading 1, Heading 2, and so on) get the HTML heading tags <h1> (or heading 1), <h2>, <title>, and so on.
- Paragraphs remain paragraphs...most of the time. Actually, how Dreamweaver pastes paragraphs depends on both how the paragraphs are formatted in Word and whether the Paste Special window's "Clean up Word paragraph spacing" setting is turned on (see Figure 2-5). If this option is selected, paragraphs you paste from Word appear as one large paragraph with line break characters at the end of each paragraph. Not the best method. To get Dreamweaver to paste each paragraph as a paragraph, choose Edit → Paste Special, turn off the "Clean up Word paragraph spacing" checkbox, and then click OK.

Note: If the Word document you're copying from has an empty line between each paragraph (in other words, an empty paragraph generated by pressing the Enter key twice after each paragraph), then make sure you *do* have the "Clean up Word paragraph spacing" checkbox turned on. This precaution eliminates those empty paragraphs.

- Bold and italic text maintain their look in Dreamweaver. (The actual HTML tags, however, can vary, as described on page 108.)
- Basic alignment options (left, right, and center) remain intact. Justified text, on the other hand, gets pasted as left-aligned text. (You can compensate for this small oversight by using the justified alignment option on the Property inspector, described on page 98.)
- Numbered lists come through as numbered lists in Dreamweaver (see page 100) *if* you used Word's automatic numbered-list feature to create them.

Tip: Suppose you've copied some HTML code, maybe out of the Source view of an actual Web page in a Web browser, or from a "How to Write HTML" Web site. You'll notice that when you paste it into Dreamweaver's Design view, all the HTML tags appear in the document window, complete with brackets (< >) and other assorted messiness. To get HTML into a page (and make it work like HTML), you have to go into Code view and paste the HTML directly into the page's code. Code view is discussed in depth on page 395.

- If you use Word's built-in list-bulleting feature, you end up with a proper HTML bulleted list (see page 100). If you create your own bulleted list style in Word, make sure to select the "list" type when creating the style; otherwise, copying and pasting a custom bulleted list might just paste plain paragraphs of text, not a bulleted list.
- Graphics from Word documents get pasted as graphics. In fact, even if the original graphics aren't in a Web-ready format (if they're BMP, TIFF, or PICT files, for example), Dreamweaver converts them to either the GIF or JPEG formats understood by Web browsers. Dreamweaver even copies the files to your local site root *and* links them correctly to the page. (Chapter 6 covers images in depth.)

Note: Keep in mind a couple of caveats when pasting from Word. First, you can't copy and paste more than a couple hundred KB worth of text, so you have to transfer really long documents in pieces (or better yet, spread them out among multiple Web pages). And second, this feature works only with versions of Word later than Office 97 (for Windows) or Office 98 (for Mac).

Pasting Text with Word Formatting

If you simply must keep that three-inch-tall, crazy-cartoon-like orange font, you can turn to the Full Formatting option of the Paste Special command. After copying text from Word and returning to Dreamweaver, choose Edit → Paste Special or press Ctrl+Shift+V (⌘-Shift-V). When the Paste Special window appears, choose the Full Formatting option, and then click OK. (If you want to make your Paste Special selection the default setting in Dreamweaver, click the Paste Preferences button to open the Preferences Window. Choose the setting you want -- for example, "Text with full structure and formatting"-- and click OK to make that choice the default setting for the Paste Special command.)

Dreamweaver pastes the text with as much formatting as possible, including margins, fonts, and text colors and sizes (see bottom-right image in Figure 2-6). Behind the scenes, Dreamweaver pastes the text *and* adds CSS code that attempts to approximate the look of the text in Word.

Unfortunately, all this extra code increases the document's file size and download time, and can interfere with future formatting changes. What's worse, most of your visitors won't even be able to *see* some of this formatting—such as uncommon fonts. For these reasons, use this feature with caution.

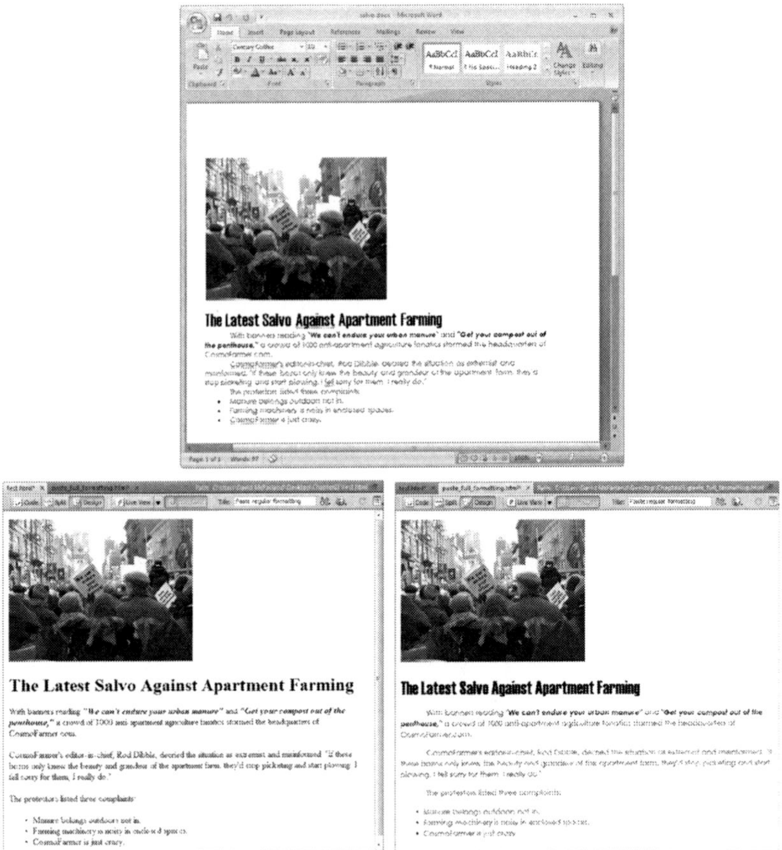

Figure 2-6: *Dreamweaver lets you paste Word text (and graphics)–like the contents of the Word file (top)–into a Web page, while preserving basic formatting options like headlines, italics, paragraphs, and bold (bottom left). The Paste Special command lets you preserve more advanced formatting such as fonts, colors, sizes, and margins (bottom right). But this special treatment comes at a price: The file size of the page on the bottom right is about 10% larger than the one on the bottom left.*

Pasting Excel Spreadsheet Information

Dreamweaver also lets you paste information from Microsoft Excel. Options include a basic method—using the standard Ctrl+V (⌘-V) or Edit → Paste—and a format-rich method, using the Full Formatting option of the Paste Special window: choose Edit → Paste Special (or press Ctrl+Shift+V [⌘-Shift-V]), choose Full Formatting from the Paste Special window, and then click OK. Both methods paste spreadsheet information as an HTML table composed of cells, rows, and columns. (See Chapter 7 for more on tables.)

But unlike pasting from Word, the basic Paste command from Excel preserves *no* formatting: It doesn't even hang on to bold and italics. The Full Formatting option, however, preserves advanced formatting like fonts, font sizes, text colors, and cell background colors.

Importing Word and Excel Documents (Windows)

Windows fans can also import material directly from a Word or Excel file into any Dreamweaver document. Just place the cursor where you wish to insert the text or spreadsheet, and then choose File → Import → Word Document (or Excel Document). An Open File dialog box appears; find and double-click the Word or Excel document you wish to import.

Dreamweaver captures the information just as if you'd used Edit → Paste. That is, for Word documents, Dreamweaver carries over basic formatting like bold, italics, headlines, and paragraphs, and imports and converts images. The importing process doesn't create style sheets or apply advanced formatting. For Excel documents, you get just an organized table of data—no formatting.

Selecting Text

After you get text into your Dreamweaver document, you'll undoubtedly need to edit it. You'll delete words and paragraphs, move sentences around, add words, and fix typos.

The first step in any of these procedures is learning how to select text, which works much as it does in word processors. You drag across text to highlight it, or just click where you wish the selection to begin, and then hold down the Shift key as you click at the end of the selection. You can also use shortcuts like these:

- To select a word, double-click it.
- To select a paragraph, triple-click anywhere in it.
- To select a line of text, move your cursor to the left of the line of text until the cursor changes from an I-beam to an arrow, signaling that you've reached the left-margin selection strip. Click once to highlight one line of text, or drag vertically in this selection strip to select multiple lines.
- While pressing Shift, use the left and right arrow keys to select one letter at a time. Use Ctrl+Shift (⌘-Shift) and the left and right arrow keys to select one *word* at a time.
- Ctrl+A (⌘-A) selects everything in the body of the page—text, graphics, and all. (Well, this isn't 100 percent true: If you're using tables or <div> tags [page 333] to organize a page, then Ctrl+A may select just the text within a table or <div> tag; clicking the <body> tag in the Tag selector [page 24] is a more sure-fire method of selecting everything on a page.)

POWER USERS' CLINIC

Decoding Encoding

In some cases, when you copy a symbol like © from Word, and then paste it into Dreamweaver, you see *©* in the HTML. Other times you see the actual symbol (©). What you get in the HTML depends on the type of *encoding* used on your Web page. If you don't work with languages other than English, encoding isn't much of an issue; you can work happily without ever worrying about how Dreamweaver encodes HTML for a Web page. But if you commonly need to type characters that don't appear on the standard English keyboard, such as Chinese, Kanji, or simply the accented letters of French or Spanish, Dreamweaver's encoding method is helpful.

Computers don't think in terms of letters or any of the other symbols we humans normally use to communicate with each other. Computers think in terms of bits and bytes. Every letter or symbol displayed on a Web page is represented by a numeric code. The process of converting a symbol to the proper code is called *encoding*. But since the world is filled with many different symbols—Latin, Chinese, Kanji, Arabic, Cyrillic, Hebrew, and so on—there are many different *encoding schemes* used to accommodate all the different alphabets of the world. Versions of Dreamweaver prior to CS3 used Western Latin encoding, which handles most of the characters used in English and Western European languages. But it doesn't handle all symbols. That's why when you copy a © symbol from Word and paste it into a Web page with Western Latin encoding, you end up with *©* in your HTML instead of the copyright symbol. *©* is called an *entity*, and Web browsers know that when they see that they should display a true copyright symbol.

Dreamweaver uses a newer type of encoding when creating a Web page—Unicode. Unicode (which Dreamweaver refers to as *Unicode 4.0 (UTF-8)*, or *UTF-8* for short) accommodates many of the alphabets of the world, so you can mix Kanji with Cyrillic with English on a single Web page, and all of those alphabets will display fine in a Web browser. A page that's encoded with Unicode also produces slightly different HTML when pasting symbols from other programs. Instead of using entities in the page like *”* for a curly right quotation mark, you see the actual character (") in the HTML of the page. This quality generally makes HTML much easier to read. However, if you've previously built a site using a different encoding like *Japanese (Shift JIS)*—yes, that's the actual format name—you may want to stick to that method.

You probably won't ever need to change Dreamweaver's encoding scheme, but if you're updating a site and wish to upgrade to the new Unicode encoding (maybe so you can type © instead of *©* in your HTML) just choose Modify → Page Properties, click the Title/Encoding category, and then select a method from the encoding menu. If you want to change the default encoding for all new documents (for example, if you absolutely must stick with the Shift JIS encoding to match the encoding method of other pages on your site) choose Edit → Preferences (Dreamweaver → Preferences on a Mac), click the New Document category, and then select an option from the Default Encoding menu. Note that if, later on, you switch back to Unicode 4.0 (UTF-8), make sure you select "C (Canonical Decomposition)" from the "Normalization" field, and leave the "Include Unicode Signature" checkbox *turned off* (otherwise the page may not display correctly in current browsers).

Finally, if you use the Insert Special Character menu (page 74), then Dreamweaver always inserts an HTML entity (*®*, for example) instead of the actual symbol (™), even when working with a UTF-8 page. You can, however, type many of these symbols on your keyboard as described in the Power Users' Clinic on page 76.

Once you've selected text, you can cut, copy, or delete it. To move text to another part of the Web page, or even to another Dreamweaver document, use the Cut, Copy, and Paste commands in the Edit menu. You can also move text around by dragging and dropping it, as shown in Figure 2-7.

Once copied, the text remains on your Clipboard and can be placed again and again (until you copy something else to the Clipboard, of course). When you cut (or copy) and paste *within* Dreamweaver, all the code affecting that text comes along for the ride. If you copy a paragraph that includes bold text, for example, then you copy the HTML tags both for creating a paragraph and for producing bold text.

Note: Not *all* formatting necessarily comes along for the ride. With Dreamweaver's support for Cascading Style Sheets, most of your text formatting includes some CSS formatting, and, unfortunately, cutting and pasting text from one document to another does *not* also copy the CSS code. So on some occasions, you may copy text from one document, paste it into another, and find that the formatting disappears. See the Note on page 127 for details on this.

To delete any selection, press Delete or choose Edit → Clear.

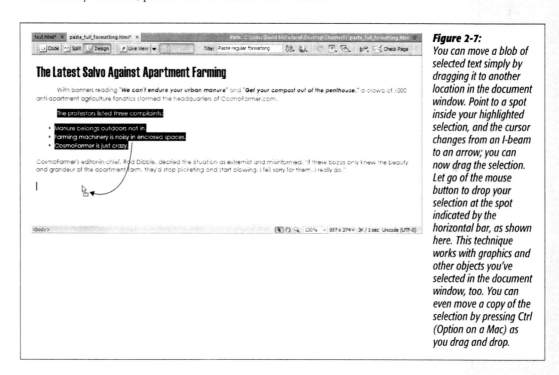

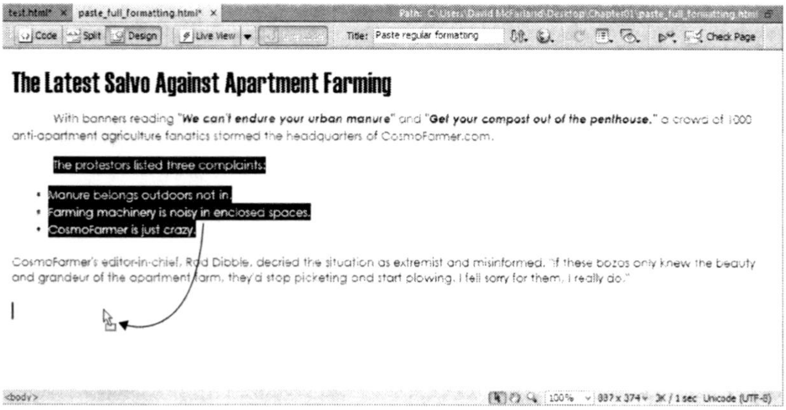

Figure 2-7: *You can move a blob of selected text simply by dragging it to another location in the document window. Point to a spot inside your highlighted selection, and the cursor changes from an I-beam to an arrow; you can now drag the selection. Let go of the mouse button to drop your selection at the spot indicated by the horizontal bar, as shown here. This technique works with graphics and other objects you've selected in the document window, too. You can even move a copy of the selection by pressing Ctrl (Option on a Mac) as you drag and drop.*

Spell Checking

You spend a lot of time perfecting your Web pages, making sure the images look great, the text is properly formatted, and everything aligns to make a beautiful visual presentation. But one step is often forgotten, especially given the hyper-speed development process of the Web—making sure your Web pages are free from typos.

GEM IN THE ROUGH

Clean Up Word

From Word, you can save any document as a Web page, essentially turning a Word document into HTML. This method's drawback is that Word produces hideous HTML code. One look at it, and you'd think that your cat fell asleep on the keyboard.

Here's what's happening: To let you reopen the document as a Word file when the time comes, Word injects reams of information that adds to the file size of the page. This is a particular problem with the latest versions of Word, which add loads of XML and Cascading Style Sheet information.

Fortunately, Dreamweaver's Clean Up Word HTML command can strip out most of that unnecessary code and produce leaner Web pages. To use it, open the Word HTML file just as you would any other Web page, by choosing File → Open. Once the file is open, choose Commands → Clean Up Word HTML.

The Clean Up Word HTML dialog box opens; Dreamweaver automatically detects whether the HTML was produced by Word 97/98 or a later version of Word, and then applies the appropriate rules for cleaning up the HTML.

Spelling mistakes give an unprofessional impression and imply a lack of attention to detail. Who wants to hire an "illustraightor" or "Web dezyner"? Dreamweaver's spell checking feature can help you.

About Dictionaries

Before you start spell checking, you should make sure that the correct *dictionary* is selected. Dreamweaver comes with 15 dictionaries for 12 different languages, including three English variations and both Iberian and Brazilian Portuguese. When it checks your spelling, the program compares the text in your document against the list of words in one of these dictionaries.

To specify a dictionary, choose Edit → Preferences (Dreamweaver → Preferences in Mac OS X)—or press Ctrl+U (⌘-U)—to open the Preferences dialog box. Select the General category, and then, from the Spelling Dictionary pop-up menu at the bottom of the window, choose a language.

Performing the Check

Once you've selected a dictionary, open the Web page whose spelling you wish to check. You can check as much or as little text as you like, as follows:

1. **Highlight the text (which can be even a single word).**

   If you want to check the *entire* document, make sure that nothing is selected in the document window. (One good way to make sure nothing is selected is to click in the middle of a paragraph of text.) Like spell checkers in other programs, you must place the cursor at the beginning of the document to begin spell checking from the top of the page.

Note: Unfortunately, Dreamweaver doesn't offer a site-wide spell checking feature. You must check each page individually.

2. **Choose Text → Check Spelling (or press Shift+F7).**

   The Check Spelling dialog box opens (see Figure 2-8). If the selected word isn't in Dreamweaver's dictionary, then it appears in the top field of the box, along with a list of suggested alternative spellings.

   The first suggestion is listed in the "Change to" field.

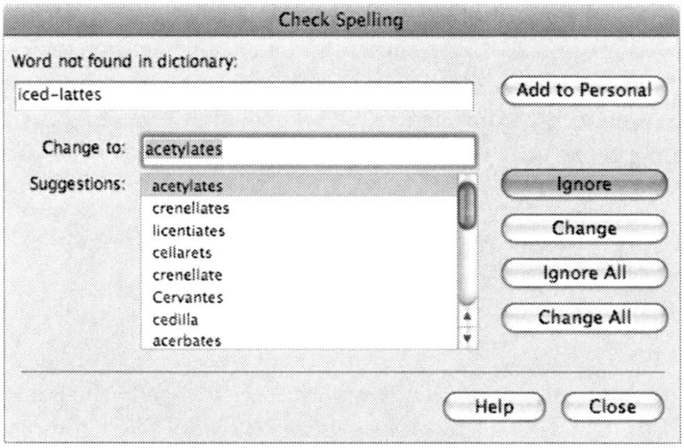

Figure 2-8:
Dreamweaver's spell checking feature checks only words in the document window. It can't check the spelling of comments, <alt> tags, or any text that appears in the head of the document with the exception of the page's title. Nor can you spell check an entire Web site's worth of pages with a single command; you need to check each Web page individually.

3. **If the "Change to" field is correct, click Change.**

   If Dreamweaver has correctly flagged the word as misspelled but the correct spelling isn't in the "Change to" field, double-click the correct spelling in the list. If the correct spelling isn't in the list, type it yourself in the "Change to" box.

   Then click the Change button to correct this one instance, or click Change All to replace the misspelled word everywhere it appears in the document.

   Dreamweaver makes the change and moves on to the next questionable spelling.

4. **If the word is actually correctly spelled (but not in Dreamweaver's dictionary), click Ignore, Ignore All, or "Add to Personal".**

   If you want Dreamweaver to ignore this word *every* time it appears in the document, rather than just this instance of it, click Ignore All.

   On the other hand, you'll probably use some words that Dreamweaver doesn't have in its dictionaries. You may, for instance, use a client's name throughout your Web pages. If that name isn't in Dreamweaver's dictionary, Dreamweaver consistently claims that it's a spelling error.

   To teach Dreamweaver the client's name so that the Check Spelling dialog box doesn't pop up each time you spell check, click "Add to Personal". Dreamweaver adds the word to your personal dictionary, which is a special dictionary file that Dreamweaver also consults when checking your spelling.

After you click Ignore or Change, Dreamweaver moves on to the next word it doesn't recognize. Begin again from step 3. If you didn't begin the spell check at the beginning of the document, once Dreamweaver reaches the end of the document, it asks if you wish to continue spell checking from the beginning.

5. **To end spell checking, click Close.**

Undo, Redo, and the History Panel

One of the great consciousness-altering moments of the 20th century was the introduction of the Undo command. After a long day in front of the computer, the ability to undo any action seems quite natural. (Unfortunately, reaching for the Ctrl+Z keys after spilling grape juice on Grandma's antique tablecloth still doesn't work in the real world.)

Fortunately, most steps you take in Dreamweaver can be reversed with either the Undo command or the History panel.

Undo

Like most computer programs these days, Dreamweaver lets you undo the last step you took by pressing Ctrl+Z (⌘-Z), or by choosing Edit → Undo. (This command changes to reflect your most recent action. If you just deleted some text, for example, it says Edit → Undo Delete.) When you're feeling indecisive, you can *redo* the action you just undid by choosing Edit → Redo or by pressing Ctrl+Y (⌘-Y).

You're not limited to a single undo, either. You can undo multiple steps—up to 50 of them, or whatever number you specify in Preferences. Choose Edit → Preferences (on the Mac, it's Dreamweaver → Preferences) to open this dialog box, click the General category from the Category list, and change the number in the "Maximum Number of History Steps" box. (Note, however, that the more steps Dreamweaver remembers, the more memory the program needs. If you set this number very high or your computer doesn't have a lot of memory, you may find your computer acting sluggish.)

Tip: You can even undo actions *after you've saved* a document (although not after you've closed it). Unlike many programs, Dreamweaver doesn't erase the list of actions you've performed when a page is saved. This means you can feel free to save as often as you want—a wise safeguard against crashes and other mishaps—without losing the ability to undo what you've done.

History Panel

You may wonder why the Preferences setting for the Undo command refers to "History Steps". It's because Dreamweaver creates a *history* for a document as you work on it. Each time you add text, insert a graphic, change the background color of the page, or do anything else to a document, Dreamweaver adds a new step to a list of previous actions.

FREQUENTLY ASKED QUESTION

Editing Your Personal Dictionary

Oops! I added a word to my personal dictionary by accident! How do I undo that?

If you click "Add to Personal" accidentally, you'll probably want to fix your mistake—but there's no obvious way to remove words from your Personal dictionary!

Your personal dictionary is stored in a file called *Personal Dictionary MX.tlx*. For Windows XP, you can find this file in your application-data folder, usually on the C: drive under Documents and Settings → [your name] → Application Data → Adobe → Dreamweaver CS4 → Common. (Note: The Application Data folder is usually hidden in Windows. If you don't see it, you need to use Folder Options—located in the Control Panel—to reveal hidden folders and files.) Vista users can find the file in C: → Users → [your name] → AppData → Roaming → Adobe → Dreamweaver CS4 → Common (as with Windows XP, the AppData folder is usually hidden, so you need to show all files by gsoing to the Appearance & Personalization section of the Control Panel to make it appear). If you use a Mac, look inside your Home → Library → Application Support → Adobe → Dreamweaver CS4 → Common folder.

Make a backup copy of this file, just in case. Then, open it in Dreamweaver by choosing File → Open, and then navigating to the .tlx file. Although the file is a text file, the .tlx extension isn't a recognized document type in Dreamweaver. You need to select "All files" (NOT "All Documents") from the "Files Of Type" menu (Windows) or Enable pop-up menu (Mac) before you can open the personal dictionary.

Don't touch the first line of the file, which indicates what language the dictionary uses. Each line thereafter lists a word followed by a tab and the letter *i*.

To delete an entry, delete its entire line. You can also add a word by manually typing the word, a tab, and the letter *i*. (Dreamweaver's spell checking engine uses that little *i* for its own purposes.)

All of these steps are listed in the History panel (see Figure 2-9). To see it, choose Window → History.

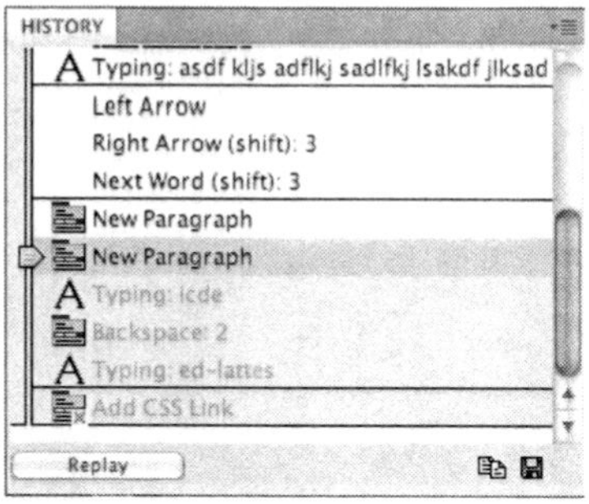

Figure 2-9:
The History panel can do a lot more than undo actions. You can also use it for automating many routine tasks that you perform while building your Web pages. To find out how, see page 777.

Each row in the panel represents one action or step, and includes a description. For instance, hitting Return or Enter while typing in the document creates a step called New Paragraph. Steps are listed in the order you perform your actions, with the most recent actions at the bottom and earliest action at the top of the list.

But the History panel isn't just a dull document to pore over—it's a living, multiple-step Undo command. Use the History slider on the left-hand side of the History panel to move to any step in the history list. To undo one action, for example, drag the slider up one step. When you do this, you'll notice that the slider's former position step is grayed out. Steps that are dimmed represent future steps, so moving the slider down one step is the equivalent of choosing Edit → Redo.

You can undo or redo multiple steps by moving the slider up or down the list. Alternatively, you can click the track to the left of a step to move the slider to that step.

If you want to eliminate all the history steps for a document—to free up some of your computer's memory, for example—from the History panel's context menu, select Clear History. But be careful: This action is the one action you can't undo.

CHAPTER

3

Text Formatting

Getting text onto a Web page (Chapter 2) is a good start, but effective communication requires effective design. Large, bold headlines help readers scan a page's important topics. Colorful text focuses attention. Bulleted sentences crystallize and summarize ideas. Just as a monotonous, low-key voice puts a crowd to sleep, a vast desert of plain HTML text is sure to turn visitors away from the important message of your site. In fact, text formatting could be the key to making your *Widgets Online 2009 Sale-a-thon* a resounding success instead of an unnoticed disaster. Figure 3-1 shows two model examples of good—and bad—text formatting.

To help get your point across, Dreamweaver provides the tools you need to format text in compelling and eye-catching ways, but it's important to understand the difference between the two methods Dreamweaver uses. You can format text using either *HTML* or *Cascading Style Sheets (CSS)*. Using HTML, you're not so much affecting the look of text (though different HTML tags do display differently in a Web browser), but changing its structure. For example the <h1> (heading 1) tag is used to indicate the most important heading on the page, while the <ol> (ordered list) tag is used to list a series of numbered steps. In contrast, you use CSS to add visual appeal to text by changing fonts, applying color, adjusting font size and a lot more.

The fundamental difference between HTML and CSS is so important, Dreamweaver CS4 introduces a new Property inspector that clearly separates these two technologies, so you'll always know when you're applying which (see Figure 3-2). In this chapter, we'll cover the use of HTML tags to structure text on a Web page; in the next chapter, we'll get started with CSS to create beautiful typography.

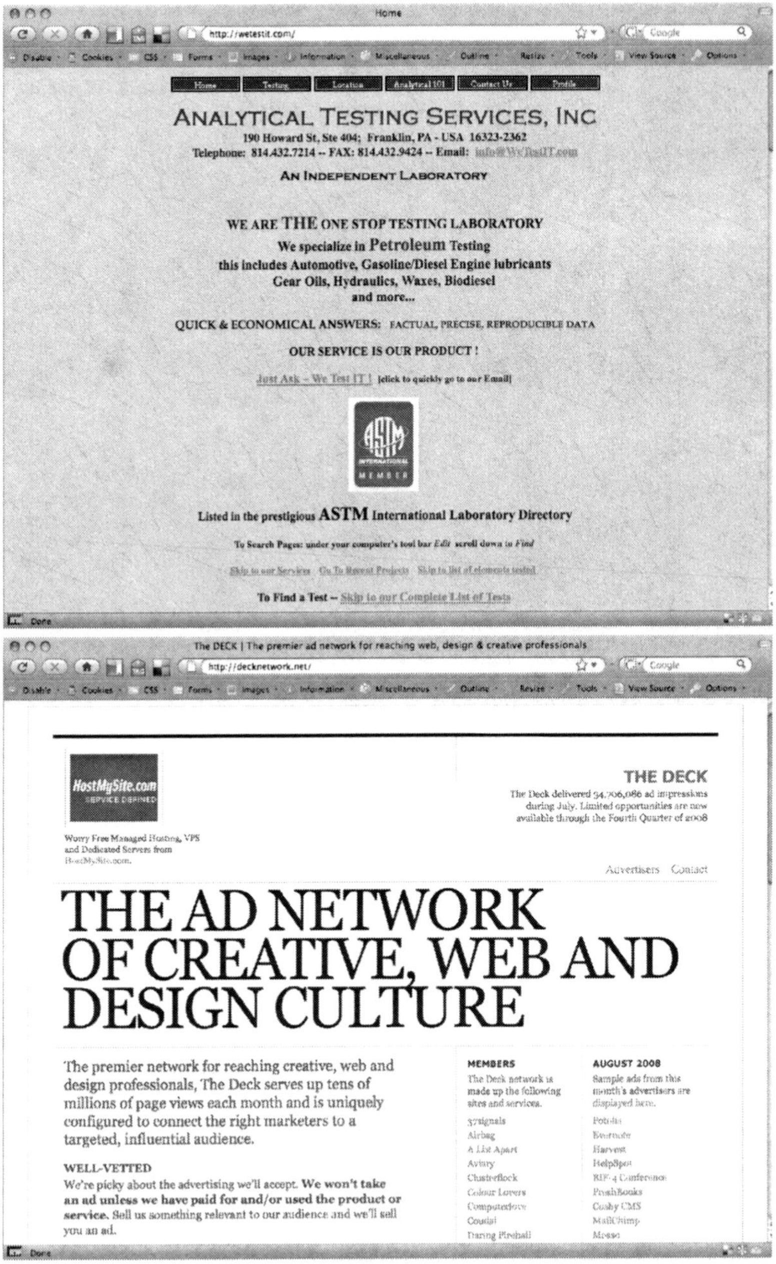

Figure 3-1:
Both these pages use different fonts, colors, and sizes to display text, but the one at bottom uses large, bold type to immediately direct your attention to the site's purpose. Other areas of the page use different type size and color to indicate their relative importance. In the page at top, by contrast, nothing really stands out. Even the site's name is so close in size to the other text on the page that it doesn't make much of a statement. Throughout the page the text shares similar font sizes and types, making it difficult to focus your attention on any one area.

Paragraph Formatting

Just as you use paragraphs to help organize your thoughts into clear, well-structured, and cohesive units when writing a paper or letter, you organize content on Web pages into blocks of information within HTML tags (see page 7 for more about tags). The most basic block of information is a simple paragraph, indicated in HTML by a paragraph tag, like this:

```
<p>Hello. This is one paragraph on this Web page.</p>
```

To a Web browser, everything between the opening <p> and closing </p> tags is considered part of the same paragraph. Many Dreamweaver formatting options—headlines, lists, indents, and alignment, for example—can apply only to an entire paragraph at a time, as opposed to individual words. In a word processor, you'd call this kind of formatting *paragraph* formatting; in Web design, it's called *block-level* formatting. Either way the idea is exactly the same: The formatting you apply affects an entire paragraph (that is, a *block* of text, whether that's just one sentence or several sentences) at a time. (*Character-level* formatting, on the other hand, can be applied to individual words or even letters. Bold and italic fall into this category, as described later in this chapter.)

Paragraphs

When you create a new document in Dreamweaver and start typing, the text you type has no paragraph formatting at all, as indicated by the word None in the Format menu at the left side of the Property inspector (see Figure 3-2). (*None* isn't an HTML tag; it just means that your text isn't surrounded by *any* of the paragraph tags used in this menu—<p>, <h1>, and so on.)

When you press Enter or Return, you create a new paragraph, complete with opening and closing <p> tags, as shown earlier, but your newly born paragraph still has no design applied to it. When your Web site visitors look at it, the font and size of your type are determined by their own Web browser preference settings. It may not look exactly like the typography you saw in Dreamweaver.

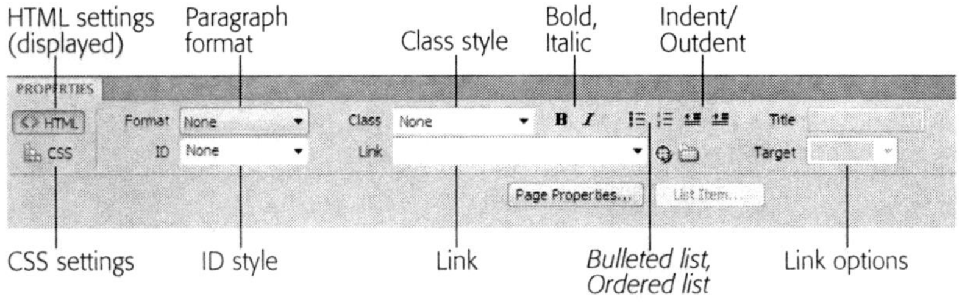

***Figure 3-2:** The HTML properties include both paragraph and character-level formatting options. The choices labeled here in bold apply to an entire paragraph. The other options represent inline, or character-level, formatting options; they apply only to the currently selected text.*

UP TO SPEED

Separating Structure from Presentation

HTML isn't about good looks or fancy design. The HTML tags you use to format text instead give structure to a Web page, providing valuable insight for the viewer into the organization of content on a page.

For example, the Heading 1 (<h1>) tag indicates a headline of the highest level and, therefore, greatest importance; the smaller Heading 2 (<h2>) tag represents a headline of slightly lower importance: a subhead. You'll see this kind of structure in this book. Each section begins with a headline ("Paragraph Formatting," on page 95, for example), and includes subheads that further divide the content into logical blocks of information.

Structure is more about organizing content than making it look pretty. Whether or not the headlines in this book used different colors and fonts, the fundamental organization—chapter title, main headlines, subheads, bulleted lists, numbered step by step instructions, and paragraphs of information—would remain the same.

HTML is actually intended to provide structure to a document, rather than making it look good. In fact, for some types of visitors (people who can't see, computer spiders that crawl Web sites for information, search engines, or text-only browsers, for example), what a Web page looks like—its presentation—is irrelevant. What matters are the cues that let the visitor know what the content means.

For a while, HTML did double duty, giving structure through tags like <h1>, <ul> (for bulleted lists), and <p> (for a paragraph of information), *and* providing visual design with tags like <font> (for setting font types, colors, and sizes).

Today, however, the World Wide Web Consortium (W3C, the main organization for determining the current and future standards for the Web), as well as most professional Web designers, consider this approach outmoded. The W3C has officially *deprecated* HTML tags that add design to a page, like the <font> tag, which means that future versions of HTML (and possibly future versions of Web browsers) won't recognize them.

Dreamweaver CS4 takes the same approach by splitting the Property inspector into two sections—HTML for structuring text and CSS for styling it.

CSS provides much more advanced and beautiful design possibilities than HTML ever did. In other words, let HTML provide the structure; let CSS create the presentation. HTML gives order, while CSS makes everything look good.

Chapter 4 introduces CSS, and Chapter 8 covers it in depth. In addition, throughout the book, you'll find notes that indicate when you can use CSS instead of HTML to better achieve your design goals.

You can add the Paragraph format to any block of text. Since this formatting option affects all the text in the block, you don't need to select any text as a first step. Simply click anywhere inside the block of text, and then do one of the following:

- In the Property inspector (Figure 3-2), from the Format menu, choose Paragraph.
- Choose Format → Paragraph Format → Paragraph.
- Press Ctrl+Shift+P (⌘-Shift-P).

Note: Much to the chagrin of Web designers, Web browsers display a line's worth of blank space before and after block-level elements like headings and paragraphs. This visual gap is distracting, but unfortunately, you can't get rid of it with regular HTML.

However, many of the formatting limitations of HTML, including this one, go away when you use CSS. See page 144 to fix this problem.

Headlines

Headlines announce information ("The Vote Is In!") and help organize content. Just as this book uses different levels of headings to introduce its topics—from chapter titles all the way down to subsections—the HTML heading tag comes in a variety of sizes used to indicate importance.

Headlines range in size from 1 (most important) to 6 (least important), as shown in Figure 3-3. They provide organization to a document, much like an outline has headings, subheads, and sub-subheads.

To turn a paragraph into a headline, click anywhere inside the line, or block, of text and then do one of the following:

- In the Property inspector, from the Format menu, select one of the heading levels (Heading 1 through Heading 6).
- Choose Format → Paragraph Format → Heading 1 (or Heading 2, Heading 3, and so on).
- Press Ctrl+1 (⌘-1), for the Heading 1 style, Ctrl+2 (⌘-2) for Heading 2, and so on.

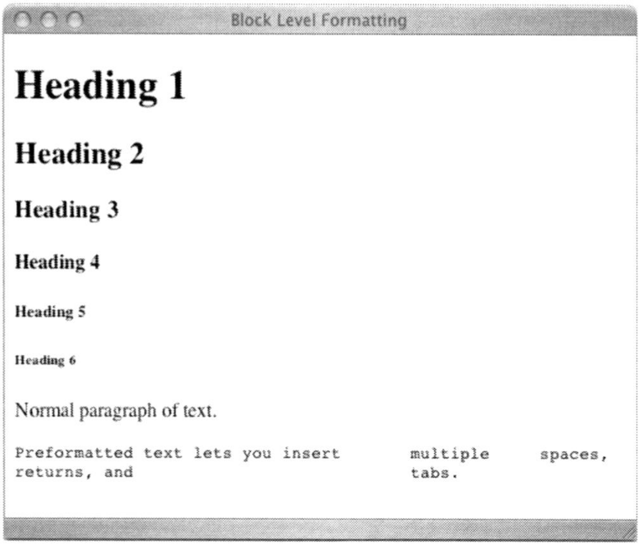

Figure 3-3:
You can apply any of eight basic paragraph formats to a block of text: Headings 1 through 6, Paragraph, and Preformatted. If you don't add any special modifications to the individual paragraph formats, then they vary in size, font, and boldness, as you can see here.

Preformatted Text

Web browsers normally ignore extra spaces, tabs, and other blank space characters in the underlying HTML when displaying a Web page. However, using the Preformatted paragraph format, you can override this behavior. Preformatted paragraphs display *every* text character in a paragraph, including tabs, multiple spaces, and line breaks, so you don't have to resort to multiple nonbreaking space characters (see page 77) to insert more than one space in a row.

The original idea behind the Preformatted format was to display tabular data—as in a spreadsheet—without the use of tables. That's why preformatted paragraphs show up in a *monospaced* font like Courier. In monospaced fonts, each letter of the alphabet, from i to w, is the same width and takes up the same horizontal space on a page, making it easy to align letters in columns. That's also why, when you use this paragraph style, you can use tabs to align text in columns. (When you use any other paragraph format, Web browsers ignore tabs.) These days, however, Dreamweaver's table feature is a much more superior method when you want to display data in columns; see Chapter 7.

Nonetheless, the Preformatted format can still be useful—when displaying sample HTML or programming code, for example. You can add the Preformatted format to any block of text. Simply click inside the block of text, and then take one of these two steps:

- In the Property inspector, choose Format → Preformatted.
- Choose Format → Paragraph Format → Preformatted Text.

Keep in mind that preformatted text appears exactly as you enter it. Unlike normal paragraph text, lines of preformatted text don't automatically wrap if they're wider than the window. That means if you present your site visitors with a really long line of preformatted text, then they have to scroll horizontally to see all of it. To end a line of preformatted text and create another, you must press the Enter or Return key to create a manual line break.

Paragraph Alignment

All text in a Web page starts out aligned with the left edge of the page (or, in the case of tables, to the left edge of a table cell). But sometimes you may want to center text in the middle of the page—perhaps an elegantly centered title—or align it to the right side. You can even create nice straight margins on both sides of a paragraph using the justification option.

Note: Although justified text looks elegant in a book, the limited resolution of computer monitors can make small type that's justified difficult to read.

The best way to align text is to create a CSS style and set the *text-align* property to left, right, center or justified. In fact, Dreamweaver CS4 has moved all alignment options for the Property inspector to the CSS view of the inspector—you'll learn how to use these settings on page 145.

However, it's *possible* to use HTML properties to align text. It's just not the way most pros do it, but it can come in handy when you want to whip out a page quickly or you have to create HTML emails (which usually don't do so well with CSS).

To change a paragraph's alignment the HTML way, click inside a paragraph, and then do one of the following:

- Choose Format → Align → Left, Center, Right, or Justify.

- Use one of the following keyboard shortcuts:

  Left: Ctrl+Alt+Shift+L (Shift-Option-⌘-L)
  Centered: Ctrl+Alt+Shift+C (Shift-Option-⌘-C)
  Right: Ctrl+Alt+Shift+R (Shift-Option-⌘-R)
  Justify: Ctrl+Alt+Shift+J (Shift-Option-⌘-J)

Note: You can remove an alignment by reapplying the *same* alignment. For instance, if you've right-aligned a paragraph, choosing Format → Align → Right removes all alignment information and returns that paragraph to its original setting.

Indented Paragraphs

Dreamweaver's Property inspector includes a button that looks like the indent buttons on the formatting toolbars of word processors. However, that button doesn't really create an indent; it actually inserts the HTML blockquote tag (it also comes in handy with lists, as described on page 104). That tag is used for setting apart text as a block of quoted material, such as an excerpt from a book, or part of a famous speech. However, since a blockquote is indented on the left and right edges, some novice Web designers use the tag to indent text.

This method isn't a good idea for a couple of reasons. First, that tag is used to indicate quoted material, so it doesn't make sense for a regular paragraph of text. In addition, you don't have any control over how *much* space is added to the margins of the paragraph. Most Web browsers insert about 40 pixels of blank space on the left and right side of a blockquote.

As you'll see on page 343, CSS gives you precise control over indented elements using the margin or padding properties. However, if you do want to quote passages of text from another source, you should use the blockquote tag. To do so, just click inside a paragraph or any block-level element (like a heading), and then do one of the following:

- On the Property inspector, click the Blockquote button (see Figure 3-2, where it's labeled Indent).
- Choose Format → Indent.
- Press Ctrl+Alt+] (⌘-Option-]).

If you ever want to remove the block quote, you can use Dreamweaver to *outdent* it, of course. (Yes, *outdent* is a real word—ever since Microsoft made it up.)

To remove a <blockquote> tag, click inside the paragraph, and then do one of the following:

- On the Property inspector, click the Outdent button (see Figure 3-2).
- Choose Format → Outdent.
- Press Ctrl+Alt+[(Option-[).

Creating and Formatting Lists

Lists organize the everyday information of our lives: to-do lists, grocery lists, least favorite celebrity lists, and so on. On Web pages, lists are indispensable for presenting groups of items such as links, company services, or a series of instructions.

HTML offers formatting options for three basic categories of lists (see Figure 3-4). The two most common types of lists are *bulleted* (called *unordered lists* in HTML-speak) and *numbered* (called *ordered* in HTML). The third and lesser-known list type, a *definition* list, comes in handy for creating glossaries or dictionary-like entries.

Bulleted and Numbered Lists

Bulleted and numbered lists share similar formatting. Dreamweaver automatically indents items in either type of list, and automatically precedes each list item by a character—a bullet, number, or letter, for example:

- Unordered or bulleted lists, like this one, are good for groups of items that don't necessarily follow any sequence. They're preceded by a bullet.
- Ordered lists are useful when presenting items that follow a sequence, such as the numbered instructions in the following section. Instead of a bullet, a number or letter precedes each item in an ordered list. Dreamweaver suggests a number (1, 2, 3, and so on), but you can substitute Roman numerals, letters, and other variations.

You can create a list from scratch within Dreamweaver, or add list formatting to text already on a Web page.

Creating a new bulleted or numbered list

When making a new list in Dreamweaver, you start by choosing a list format, and then typing the list items:

1. **In the document window, click where you wish to start a list.**

   See Chapter 2 for full details on adding text to a Web page.

2. **In the Property inspector, click the Ordered or Unordered List button to apply the list format (see Figure 3-2). (The Unordered option is also known as Bulleted.)**

   Alternatively, you can choose Format → List → Unordered List or Ordered List. Either way, the first bullet or number appears automatically in your document.

3. **Type the first list item, and then press Enter or Return. Repeat until you've added all items in the list.**

   The text you type appears (*Organic Compost*, for example, in the bulleted list in Figure 3-4) after the bullet or number. When you press Return, a new bullet or number appears, ready for your next item. (If you just want to move to the next line *without* creating a new bullet, then insert a line break by pressing Shift+Enter [Shift-Return].)

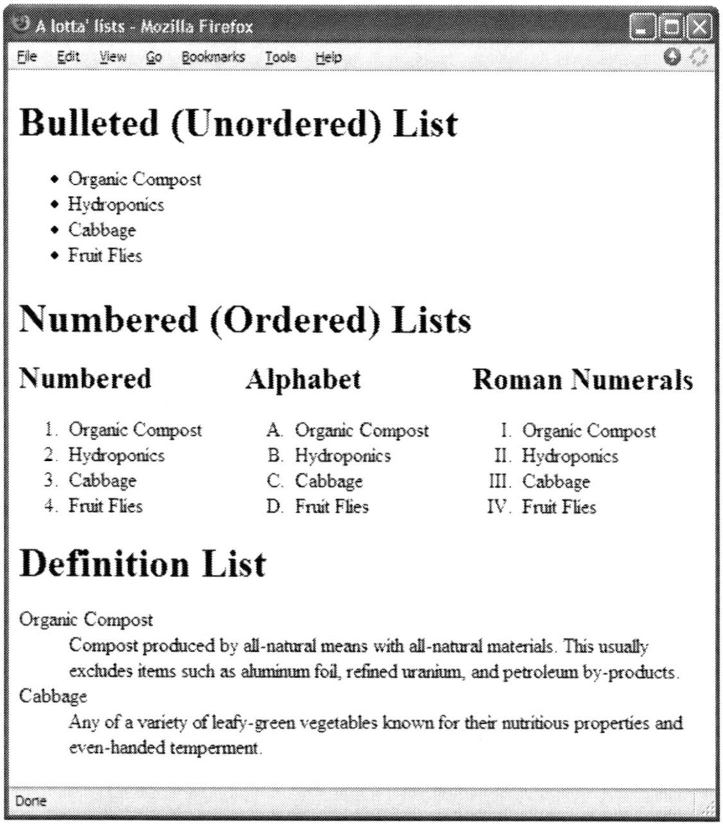

Figure 3-4: *HTML has several predefined list formats, including bulleted lists and definition lists, both of which let you organize information into orderly units. Once you've told Dreamweaver that you intend to create a bulleted or numbered list, it automatically adds the bullets or the numbering for you.*

4. **When you've finished the list, press Enter or Return twice.**

   The double carriage return ends the list and creates a new empty paragraph.

Formatting existing text as a list

You may have several paragraphs of text that you've already typed or pasted in from another program. You can easily change any such group of paragraphs into a list:

1. **Select the text you wish to turn into a list.**

   The easiest way to select text is to drag from the first list item straight down to the last list item. Lists are block-level elements; each paragraph, whether it's a headline or regular paragraph, becomes one bulleted or numbered item in the list. In other words, you don't actually need to select all the text in either the first or last paragraph.

2. **Apply the list format.**

   As when creating a list from scratch as described above, in the Property inspector, click either the Unordered or Ordered List button, or choose from the Format → List submenu. The selected paragraphs instantly take on the list formatting, complete with bullets and automatic numbering.

Note: You may sometimes run into this problem: You select what looks like a handful of paragraphs and apply the list format, but only one bullet (or number) appears. This glitch arises when you've used the line break <br> tag to move text down a line in a paragraph. While it's true that using the <br> tag visually separates lines in a paragraph into separate blocks, the text is still part of single paragraph, which appears as only *one* bulleted or numbered item. The presence of multiple <br> tags can be a real problem when pasting text from other programs. See page 75 for more on the <br> tag and how to get rid of these pesky critters.

Whichever way you started making a list—either by typing from scratch or reformatting existing text—you're not stuck with the results of your early decisions. You can add onto lists, add extra spaces, and even renumber them, as described in the following section.

Reformatting Bulleted and Numbered Lists

HTML tags define lists, just as they define other Web page features. Making changes to an existing list is a matter of changing those tags, using Dreamweaver's menu commands and Property inspector tools.

Note: Web browsers generally display list items stacked directly one on top of the other. If you want to add a little breathing room between each list item, use the CSS *margin* properties, as described on page 343, to add space between each list item (the <li> tag).

Adding new items to a list

Once you've created a list, you can easily add items. To add an item at the beginning of a list, click before the first character of the first list item, type the item you wish to add, and then press Enter or Return. Dreamweaver makes your newly typed item the first in the list, adding a bullet or number accordingly (and renumbering the other list items, if necessary).

To add an item at the middle or end of a list, click at the end of the *previous* list item, and then press Enter or Return. The insertion point appears after a new bullet or number; type your list item on this new line.

Formatting bullets and numbers

Bulleted and numbered lists aren't limited to just the standard round, black bullet or the numbers 1, 2, and 3. You can choose from two bullet types and a handful of different numbering schemes. Here's how to change these settings:

1. **Click once inside any list item.**

   Strangely enough, you can't change the properties of a list if you've first selected the entire list, an entire single list item, or several list items.

2. **Open the List Properties dialog box (Figure 3-5).**

   To do so, either click the List Item button in the bottom half of the Property inspector or choose Format → List → Properties. (If the list is inside a table cell, your only choice is to use the Format menu. In this situation, the List Item button doesn't appear in the Property inspector.)

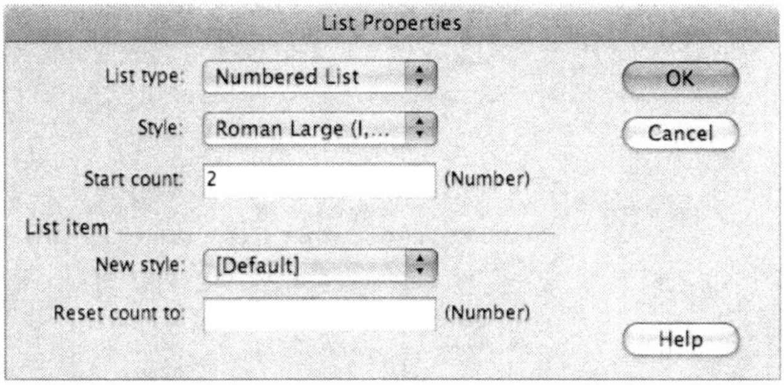

Figure 3-5: *The List Properties dialog box lets you set the type and style of a list. For example, if you select a Numbered List, you can choose from five different styles: Number (1, 2, 3); Roman Small (i, ii, iii); Roman Large (I, II, III); Alphabet Small (a, b, c); and Alphabet Large (A, B, C).*

3. **Skip the "List type" pop-up menu.**

   The List type menu lets you turn a numbered list into a bulleted list, or vice versa. But why bother? You can achieve the same thing by simply selecting a bulleted list and clicking the numbered list button in the Property inspector and vice versa. In addition, this menu has two other options—Directory List and Menu List—which insert obsolete HTML that should be avoided.

4. **Choose a bullet or numbering style.**

   Bulleted lists can have three different styles: *default, bullet*, and *square*. In most browsers, the default style is the same as the bullet style (a simple, solid, black circle). As you might guess, the square style uses a solid black square for the bullet character.

   Numbered lists, on the other hand, have a greater variety of style options. Dreamweaver starts you off with a simple numbering scheme (1, 2, 3, and so on), but you can choose from any of five styles for ordered lists, as explained in Figure 3-5.

Note: You can achieve the same effect as step 4 above using CSS. Not only does CSS give you wider options–for example, you can use a graphic you created as a bullet–but you avoid inserting obsolete HTML.

5. **Set the starting number for the list.**

   You don't have to begin a numbered list at 1, A, or the Roman numeral I. You can start it at another number, if you wish—a trick that can come in handy if, for example, you're creating a Web page to explain how to rebuild a car's engine. As part of each step, say you want to include a photograph. You create a numbered list, type in the directions for step 1, hit Return, and then insert an image (as described in Chapter 5). You hit Return again, and then type in the text for step 2. Unfortunately, the photo, because it's technically an item in an ordered list, now has the number 2 next to it, and your real step 2 is listed as 3!

   If you remove the list formatting from the photo to get rid of the 2, then you create one list above it and another below it (as described on page 100). Step 2, *below* the photo, now thinks it's the beginning of a new list—and starts over with the number 1! The solution is to make the list below the photo think it's a *new* list that begins with 2.

   To start the list at something other than 1, in the "Start count" field, type the starting number (Figure 3-5). You must enter a number, even if you want the list to use letters. So to begin a list at D instead of A, in the "Start count" field, type *4*.

   In fact, you can even change the style of a *single* list item. For instance, you could change the third item in a numeric list from a 3 to the letter C. (Of course, just because you can doesn't mean you should. Dreamweaver is very thorough in supporting the almost overwhelming combination of options available in HTML, but, unless you're building a Dadaist revival site, how often do you want a list that's numbered 1, 2, C, iv, 1?)

6. **Click OK to apply the changes.**

Note: Most of the settings in the List Properties dialog box produce invalid HTML for both strict versions of HTML and XHTML. If you use this dialog box, stick to XHTML transitional or HTML transitional documents (see page 46 for more on picking a Document type).

Nested lists

Some complex outlines require multiple *levels* of lists. Legal documents, for instance, may list major clauses with capital letters (A, B, C, and so on) and use Roman numerals (i, ii, iii, and so on) for subclauses (see Figure 3-6).

You can easily create such nested lists in Dreamweaver using the Property inspector's indent button; Figure 3-6 shows the steps.

You can change the style of a nested list—for example, change the nested list in Figure 3-6, middle, into a bulleted list—by clicking the appropriate list type in the Property inspector. Changing the nested list's type doesn't affect the list type used for the un-nested (that is, the outer) list. In other words, changing the nested list in Figure 3-6, middle, from a numbered list to a bulleted list doesn't change the outer list to a bulleted list.

Tip: You can also created a nested list by hitting the Tab key to indent a list item to another level. Shift-Tab outdents the list item.

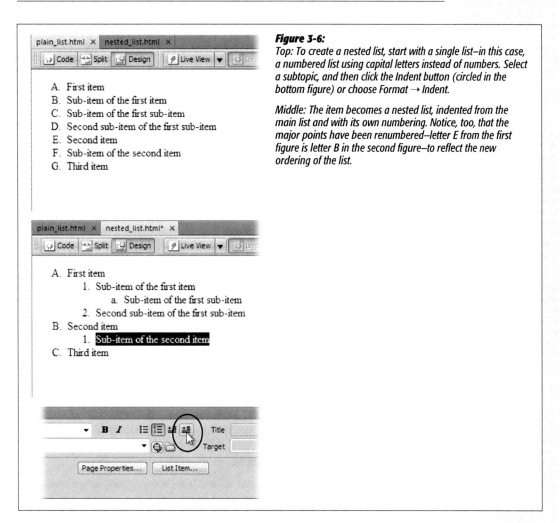

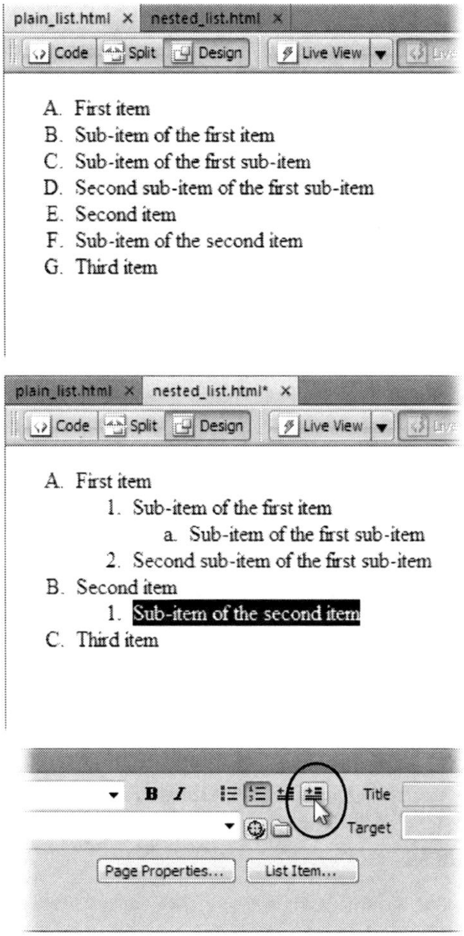

Figure 3-6:
Top: To create a nested list, start with a single list–in this case, a numbered list using capital letters instead of numbers. Select a subtopic, and then click the Indent button (circled in the bottom figure) or choose Format → Indent.

Middle: The item becomes a nested list, indented from the main list and with its own numbering. Notice, too, that the major points have been renumbered–letter E from the first figure is letter B in the second figure–to reflect the new ordering of the list.

Definition Lists

Definition lists can be used to display items in a dictionary or glossary, or whenever you need to present a term and its definition. Each item in a definition list is composed of two parts: a word or term, and a definition.

As you can see in Figure 3-4, definition lists aren't as fancy as they sound. The first item in the list—the word or term—is presented on its own line with no indent, and the second item—the definition—appears directly underneath, indented.

FREQUENTLY ASKED QUESTION

When Not to Approach the Insert Panel

I like the convenience of the Insert panel. Should I use its Text category for formatting text?

In a word, no. Unlike most of the other categories in the Insert panel, people use the Text category mainly when working in Code view (see Chapter 10) or to insert special characters like the copyright symbol, as described on page 74. It contains many of the same formatting options as the Property inspector; the *h1*, *h2*, and *h3*, for instance, are the same as Headings 1, 2, and 3 in the Property inspector's Format pop-up menu.

However, using some of the options, such as *li*, can generate invalid HTML if not used correctly. Furthermore, despite its usual tidiness, Dreamweaver doesn't clean up code produced this way.

In fact, some of these options, when used in Design view, actually split the document window in two, showing the HTML code on top and Design view on bottom. This arrangement is confusing if you're not accustomed to seeing—or just uninterested in—the raw HTML code. All major text-formatting options are available from the Property inspector and Format menu. If you stick to these two tools, you can safely avoid the Text category.

Note: Behind the scenes, Dreamweaver creates an entire definition list using the <dl> tag. Each item in the list is then composed of two tags: <dt> for the definition term or word, and <dd> for the definition itself.

You can't create a definition list using the Property inspector. Instead, start by creating a list of definitions and terms: Each term and definition should be in its own paragraph, and the definition should immediately follow the term. Next, highlight the paragraphs that contain the terms and definitions, and then choose Format → List → Definition List.

To turn a definition list *back* to regular paragraphs, select it, and then choose Format → List → None, or, in the Property inspector, click the Outdent button.

Removing and Deleting List Items

Dreamweaver lets you take items out of a list in two ways: either by removing the list *formatting* from an item or items (and changing them back into normal paragraphs) or by deleting their text outright.

Removing list items

To remove list formatting from one or more list items (or an entire list), highlight the lines in question, and then choose Format → List → None (or, on the Property inspector, just click the Outdent button). You've just removed all list formatting; the text remains on the screen, now formatted as standard paragraphs. (For nested lists, you need to click the Outdent button several times.)

If you reformat an item in the middle of a list using this technique, it becomes a regular paragraph. Dreamweaver turns the items above and below it into separate lists.

Deleting list items

You can easily delete a list or list item with the Tag selector in the document window's status bar (see Figure 3-7). To delete an entire list, click anywhere inside the list, click its tag in the Tag selector—<ul> for a bulleted list or <ol> for a numbered list—and then press Delete. You can also, of course, drag through all the text in the list, and then press Delete.

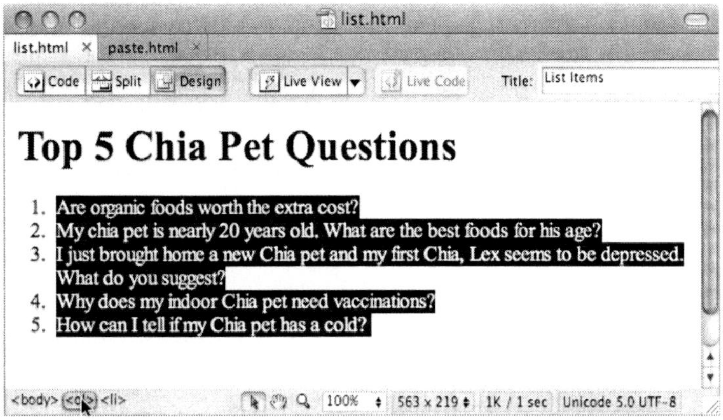

Figure 3-7:
The Tag selector (in the bottom left of the document window) is a great way to quickly and accurately select an HTML tag and its contents. Clicking the <ol> (ordered list) tag, for instance, selects the entire numbered list, as shown here. Clicking the <li> tag selects just one list item.

To delete a single list item, click that item in the document window, click the <li> tag in the Tag selector, and then press Delete.

Tip: You can rearrange a list by dragging a list item to another position within the list. If it's an ordered list (1, 2, 3, and so on), Dreamweaver automatically renumbers the list. For example, if you select an item numbered 4 and drag it to the second position in the list, then Dreamweaver changes the item to 2, and renumbers all items that follow.

However, selecting a list item can be tricky. If you simply drag to select the text, you don't actually select the list item itself, with all its formatting and numbering. To be sure you've selected a list item, in the document window's status bar, click the <li> tag in the Tag selector (see Figure 3-7). Now, when you drag the selection to a new position in the list, the number (or bullet) follows. You can also select a list item in this way, copy or cut it, and then paste it back into the list in another position.

Text Styles

The simple formatting applied by a paragraph format isn't much to write home about, much less to advertise on a résumé. Heading 1, for instance, is generally displayed in black and bold using a large Times New Roman font. As mentioned in the box on page 96, this type of paragraph formatting is intended to provide structure, not good looks.

In the next chapter you'll learn how to make your Web pages stand out using Cascading Style Sheets. With CSS you can apply different fonts, colors, and sizes to your text. However, you can also apply a handful of HTML tags to a selection of text. Dreamweaver refers to these as *styles*, but in reality they're intended to provide more information about the text—for example, if you have a "Learn HTML" Web page, then you can apply the *code* tag to some programming code you want to display on the page.

As shown in Figure 3-8, HTML offers a host of different text styles, some of which fulfill obscure purposes. For instance, the Code and Variable styles are intended for formatting the display of programming code, while the Sample style represents the output from a computer program—not exactly styles you'll need often in promoting, say, your *Cheeses of the World* mail-order company.

To use these styles, select the text (using any of the methods described on page 85), and then apply a format from the Format → Style menu. (You can also use the Property inspector to apply the <strong> or <em> tags to emphasize text by making it bold or italic.)

Note: Use italics with care. While italics are frequently used in printed material to add *emphasis* or when referencing a book title, they can be difficult to read on a computer screen, especially at small type sizes.

Unless you intend to include content whose meaning is supported by the tag (for example, you include some sample computer code on a page, so you format it with the Code style), you're better off avoiding such styles. But if you think one of them might come in handy, you can find more about these styles by consulting Dreamweaver's built-in HTML reference; see page 422. In particular, avoid the underline and strikethrough styles: Both have been deprecated (see page 96) in the HTML 4 standard, and may produce no effect in future browser versions. (You can, however, turn to the text-formatting abilities of CSS to put lines through and under any text you'd like. See page 143 for more.)

UP TO SPEED

When Bold and Italic Are Neither

You may be confused by the HTML code that Dreamweaver produces when making text bold or italic. Instead of using the <b> tag–the traditional HTML code for bold–Dreamweaver uses the <strong> tag. And instead of <i> for italics, clicking the Property inspector's I button gets you <em>, or the emphasis tag. That's because Adobe decided to follow industry practices rather than stick to an old tradition.

For most purposes, <strong> and <em> behave identically to <b> and <i>. They look the same–bolded or italicized–in most browsers. However, when encountered by screen readers (software or equipment that reads Web pages aloud for the benefit of the visually impaired), the <strong> tag triggers a loud, strong voice. The <em> tag also brings an emphasis to the voice of screen readers, though with less strength than the <strong> tag.

Since most Web browsers simply treat the <strong> tag like the <b> tag, and the <em> tag like the <i> tag, you'll probably never notice the difference. However, if you prefer the simple <b> and <i> tags, choose Edit → Preferences. Select the General category, and then turn off the checkbox labeled "Use <strong> and <em> in place of <b> and <i>".

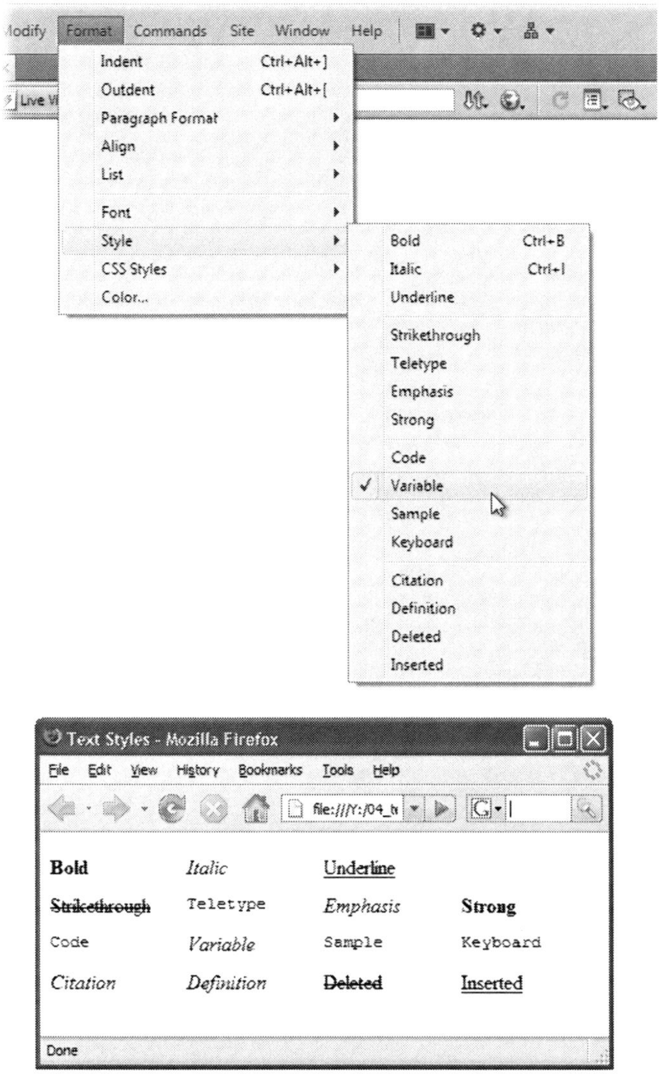

Figure 3-8:

Top: While the Property inspector lets you apply bold and italic styles to text, the Format → Style menu offers a larger selection of text styles. Don't be confused by the term "styles," which, in this case, merely refers to different HTML tags. They're unrelated to CSS styles and are intended to identify very specific types of text, like citations from a book or magazine.

Bottom: As you can see, the many style options are usually displayed in bold, italics, the browser's monospaced font (usually Courier), or some combination of the three. But don't worry about how they look "out of the box"–as you'll learn in the next chapter, by applying CSS you can make any of those tags appear anyway you wish.

CHAPTER

4

Introducing Cascading Style Sheets

What you see on a Web page when you use garden-variety HTML tags like <h1>, <p>, and <ul>, pales in comparison to the text and styling on display in, say, a print magazine. If Web designers had only HTML to make their sites look great, the Web would forever be the ugly duckling of the media world. HTML doesn't hold a candle to the typographic and layout control you get when creating a document in even the most basic word processing program.

Fortunately for us designers, we can change the ho-hum appearance of HTML using a technology called Cascading Style Sheets. CSS gives you the tools to make HTML look beautiful. If you think of HTML as the basic structure of a house (the foundation, walls, and rooms), then CSS is the house's interior decoration (the paint, carpeting, and the color, style, and placement of furniture). CSS gives you much greater control over the layout and design of your Web pages. Using them, you can add margins to paragraphs (just as in a word processor), colorful and stylish borders to images, and even dynamic rollover effects to text links. Best of all, Dreamweaver's streamlined approach lets you combine many of these design properties into powerful *style sheets* that let you control pages throughout your site.

CSS is a large topic. It's also the heart of today's cutting edge Web design. So instead of dedicating just a single chapter to the topic, this book provides instruction in the fine art of using CSS in nearly every chapter. In this chapter, you'll learn the basics of CSS, and how to use Dreamweaver CS4's powerful CSS tools. In the next few chapters you'll learn how CSS can improve the look of common Web page elements like links, images, and tables. Once you're comfortable with the basics, you'll find in-depth information on CSS in Chapter 8. And, in Chapter 9, you'll learn how to harness the power of CSS to fully control the layout of a Web page.

Cascading Style Sheet Basics

If you've used styles in programs like Microsoft Word or Adobe InDesign, CSS will feel familiar. A *style* is simply a rule describing how to format a particular piece of HTML. (A *style sheet* is a collection of these styles.)

You can create a single style, for example, that formats text with the font Arial, colored red, and with a left margin of 50 pixels. You can also create styles specifically for working with images; for instance, a style can align an image along the right edge of a Web page, surround the image with a colorful border, and place a 50-pixel margin between the image and the surrounding text.

Once you've created a style, you can apply it to text, images, or other elements on a page. For example, you could select a paragraph of text, and then apply a style to instantly change the text's size, color, and font. You can also create styles for specific tags, so that all <h1> tags in your site, for example, are displayed in the same style, no matter where they appear.

Why Use CSS?

In the past, HTML alone provided basic formatting options for text, images, tables, and other Web page elements. But today, professional Web designers use CSS to add style to their pages. In fact, the older HTML tags that were used to format text and other page elements have mostly been phased out by the World Wide Web Consortium (W3C), the organization responsible for defining standards for the Web, in favor of CSS. And following along with industry practice, Dreamweaver CS4 has made it impossible (unless you write the code yourself) to add obsolete HTML tags such as the <font> tag.

CSS has many benefits over just using HTML to design your pages. With CSS, you can format paragraphs to resemble those that appear in a book or newspaper (the first line indented and no space between each paragraph, for example), and control the leading (the space between lines of type in a paragraph). When you use CSS to add a background image to a page, you get to decide how (and whether) it tiles (repeats). HTML can't even begin to do any of these things.

Even better, CSS styles take up much less space than HTML's formatting options, such as the much-hated <font> tag. You can usually save a lot of kilobytes on text-heavy Web pages using CSS while maintaining a high level of formatting control. As a result, your pages look great *and* load faster.

Style sheets also make updating your site easier. You can collect all your styles into a separate file that's linked to every page in your site. When you edit a style in the style sheet file (called an *external style sheet*), that change immediately ripples through your site, *wherever* that style is used. You can thus completely change the appearance of a site by simply editing a single style sheet file.

POWER USERS' CLINIC

Getting to Know (and Love) CSS

Cascading Style Sheets are an exciting—and complex—addition to your Web building toolkit, worthy of entire books and Web sites. For example:

- For an excellent tutorial on CSS, visit W3 Schools' CSS tutorials at *www.w3schools.com/css/*.
- If you want to get help and learn more about CSS, the CSS-Discuss mailing list (*www.css-discuss.org*) gives you access to a great community of CSS enthusiasts. Just be prepared for an overflowing inbox, and be aware of the etiquette spelled out on the list's home page.
- You'll also find a helpful collection of wisdom generated on the CSS-Discuss Wiki at *http://css-discuss.incutio.com*. This site provides insider tips, tricks, and resources for solving many common CSS problems.
- For the ultimate source of information, turn to the World Wide Web Consortium's Web site: *www.w3.org/Style/CSS*. The W3C is the body responsible for many of the standards that drive the Web—including HTML and CSS. (Beware: This site is the ultimate authority on the matter, and reads like a college physics textbook.)
- For a great list of CSS-related sites, visit the Information and Technology Systems and Services Web site at the University of Minnesota, Duluth: *www.d.umn.edu/itss/support/Training/Online/webdesign/css.html*.
- If you just love to curl up by the fireplace with a good computer book, try *CSS: The Missing Manual* by David McFarland (hey, that name rings a bell). It's written in the same style as this book, with in-depth coverage of CSS and step-by-step tutorials that guide you through every facet of this complicated technology.
- Finally, you don't have to look any further than your own desktop for the ultimate reference to each CSS property. Dreamweaver's built-in Reference window provides instant access to concise information on Cascading Style Sheets (see page 422).

CSS may sound like a cure-all for HTML's anemic formatting powers, but, truth be told, it is a bit tricky to use. For example, CSS support varies from browser to browser, so you need to test your pages thoroughly in a wide variety of browsers. Even modern browsers—like Internet Explorer 7 for Windows, Firefox, Opera, and Safari—have their share of weird CSS behavior.

Fortunately, Dreamweaver CS4 is better than ever at displaying complex CSS-based designs, so you can develop your general design in Dreamweaver, and then use the preview feature to fine-tune your designs for different browsers. (The Check Browser Compatibility tool described on page 130 is also a big help in troubleshooting CSS problems.)

Internal vs. External Style Sheets

Each new style you create gets added to a style sheet that's stored either in the Web page itself (in which case it's an *internal style sheet*), or in another file called an *external style sheet*.

Note: You may hear the term "embedded style sheet." It's the same thing as an internal style sheet.

Internal style sheets appear in the <head> portion of a Web page, and contain styles that apply only to that page. An internal style sheet is a good choice when you have a very specific formatting task for a single page. For example, perhaps you want to create styles to format the text and table of a chart that appears only on a single page.

Note: It's often easier, when creating a new design, to add styles to an internal style sheet. Once you're satisfied with the design, you can then export the styles to an external style sheet–for use by all your site's pages–as described on page 311.

An external style sheet, on the other hand, contains only styles—no HTML—and you can link it to numerous pages. In fact, you can link it to every page on your Web site to provide a uniform, sitewide set of styles. For instance, you can put a headline style in an external style sheet, and link that sheet to every page in the site. Every headline on every page then shares the same look—instant design consistency! Even better, when the boss (or the interior decorator in you) calls up and asks you to change the color of the headlines, you need to edit only a single file—the external style sheet—to update hundreds or even thousands of Web pages.

You can create both types of style sheets easily in Dreamweaver, and you aren't limited to choosing one or the other. A single Web page can have both an external (for styles that apply to the whole site) and an internal style sheet (for page-specific formatting). You can even attach multiple external style sheets to a single page.

Types of Styles

Styles come in several different flavors. The most common are *class*, *ID*, and *tag* styles.

A *class style* is one that you create, name, and attach manually to text or an HTML tag. Class styles work much like styles in word processing and page layout programs. If you want the name of your company to be displayed in bold and red wherever it appears in the text of a Web page, you can create a class style named *Company* with boldface and red text-color formatting. You would then select your company's name on the page, and apply this style.

An *ID* is a type of style that lets you format a *unique* item on a page. Use ID styles to identify an object (or an area of a page) that appears only once—like a Web site's logo, copyright notice, main navigation bar, or a banner. Designers frequently use IDs when creating CSS-based layouts like those presented in Chapter 9. An ID style is very similar to a class style, in that you supply the style's name and apply the style manually. However, while you can apply a class to many different elements on a page, you can apply an ID to only one tag per page. (It's okay to use multiple IDs on a single page, as long as each ID name is different.)

The other major type of CSS style is called a *tag style*, and applies globally to an individual HTML tag, as opposed to individual selections. Suppose you wanted to display every Heading 1 paragraph in the Arial font. Instead of creating a class style and applying it to every Heading 1 on the page, you could create an HTML tag style for the <h1> tag. In effect, you redefine the tag so that it's displayed in Arial.

The main benefit of redefining an HTML tag in this way is that you don't have to apply the style by hand. Since the new style says that *all* <h1> tags must use Arial, wherever a Web browser encounters an <h1> tag, it displays the text in Arial, the specified font.

These HTML tag styles are the easiest way to format a page. For one thing, there's no need to select the tag and apply the style; the page needs only to contain an instance of the tag—<h1>, for example—that you've redefined.

Nevertheless, sometimes only a class style will do, such as when you want to format just a few words in a paragraph. Simply redefining the <p> tag won't do the trick, since that would affect the entire paragraph. Instead, you have to create a class style and apply it to just the words you wish to style. In addition, class styles are handy when you want to format just one instance of a tag differently from others. If you want to format the introductory paragraph on a page differently from all other paragraphs on the page, then you create a class style and apply it to that first paragraph. (Another solution to that dilemma is a slightly more complicated, but more flexible, type of style called a *descendent selector*—you'll read about that type of style later on page 301.)

Note: In addition to classes and tag styles, other types of styles provide added control for particular situations. You can read about these more advanced styles starting on page 299.

Creating Styles

Dreamweaver CS4 provides several ways to create CSS styles. For text, you can use the Property inspector's CSS mode to create a style for setting fonts, font size, font color, font weight, and alignment. To create styles for elements besides text (like images or tables) or to tap into the dozens of other CSS properties not listed in the Property inspector, use the CSS Styles panel (see Figure 4-1). To get a complete overview of the style creation process, we'll look at both methods—starting with the more versatile CSS Styles panel, and then moving onto the Property inspector.

Phase 1: Set Up the CSS Type

Dreamweaver gives you many ways to create a new style: On the CSS Styles panel, click the new style button (see Figure 4-1); right-click anywhere in the CSS Styles panel, and then, from the menu that appears, select New; or choose Format → CSS Styles → New. The New CSS Rule dialog box appears (Figure 4-2), where you begin the process of creating your new style. (In the technical language of CSS, a style is actually called a *rule*, but for simplicity's sake this book just uses the term *style*. After all, *Cascading Rule Sheets* doesn't have much of a ring to it.)

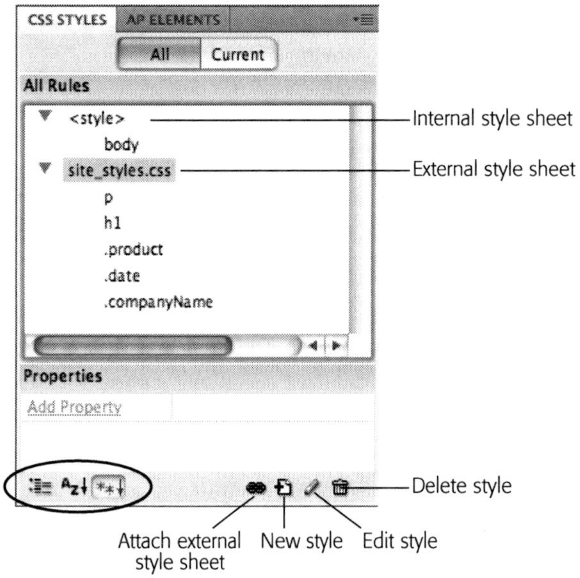

Figure 4-1:
With the "All" button selected, the CSS Styles panel lists the names of all styles available to the current page, including those in both external and internal style sheets. Here, one external style sheet–site_styles.css–contains five styles. The first two are tag styles (notice that the names match various HTML tags), while the next three are class styles (note the period at the beginning). You also see one tag style defined in an internal style sheet–the one listed below "<style>". Click the minus (–) icon (arrow on Mac) to the left of the style sheet to collapse the list of styles, hiding them from view. The "Properties" list in the bottom half of the panel lets you edit a style as described on page 305; the three buttons at the bottom left of the panel (circled) control how the Properties list is displayed.

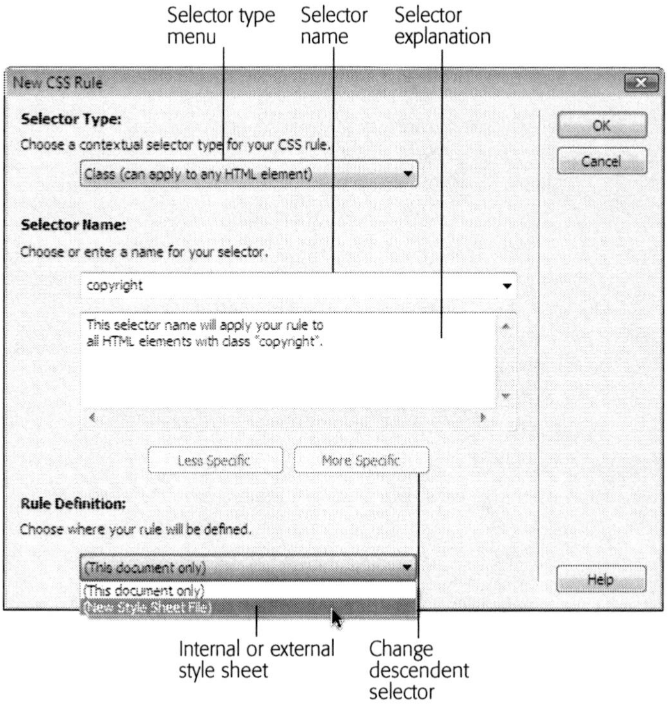

Figure 4-2:
In the New CSS Rule dialog box, you choose a type of style, give it a name, and decide whether to place the style in an internal or external style sheet. If you've used previous versions of Dreamweaver, then you'll notice that this dialog box has changed significantly in Dreamweaver CS4.

Here's a quick tour of your choices:

- **Selector Type.** From the Selector Type menu, choose the kind of style you wish to create: *Class* (to create a style that you must manually apply to page elements), *ID* (to create a style that may be used only once on the page), or *Tag* (to create an HTML tag style that Dreamweaver automatically applies to each occurrence of the tag). See the previous section (page 114) for a discussion of these three types.

  You'll want to use the fourth type, *Compound*, to create more advanced style types such as pseudo-classes, attribute selectors and descendent selectors. (You'll learn about these types in various parts of the book; you can find a detailed discussion of them starting on page 299.)

  In addition, if you've selected something on the page (such as a paragraph, an image, or a headline), then Dreamweaver highlights the Compound option and, in the Selector Name field, suggests what's called a *descendent selector*. You'll learn more about descendent selectors on page 301, but basically, they're a type of style that indicates how a particular element is nested within *other* HTML tags. For example, *div p* is a descendent selector that applies to any paragraph tag that appears within a <div> tag. So in cases where you want a descendent selector, use the Compound type.

- **Selector Name.** If you selected Class or ID from the Selector Type menu, enter a name for the new style. According to the rules of CSS, Class style names must begin with a period—*.copyright*, for example—and ID style names begin with a # symbol—*#banner*, for example. Dreamweaver automatically adds the proper symbol, if you forget.

  Another Class or ID style name rule: A letter must follow the period or # symbol. After that, you can use any combination of letters and numbers, but avoid unusual characters and spaces. For example, *.logo, #main_content, #column2* all work fine. Dreamweaver lets you know if you use any invalid characters for the name.

  If you chose Tag instead, then, from the Tag pop-up menu (which appears when you select Tag from the Selector Type menu), select the HTML tag you want to redefine.

Note: If you're an HTML guru, you may find it faster to skip the Tag pop-up menu and just type the tag (minus the brackets) in the Name box. For example, if you want to create a style for all unordered (bulleted) lists, type *ul*.

  If you selected the Compound option, then Dreamweaver lets you type any valid CSS selector type in the Selector field (you'll learn about more selectors on page 299). You'll use this feature for some advanced CSS tricks, but you can also use it just to create a tag or class style.

Note that when you add a Class, ID, tag, or other selector to the Selector Name field, Dreamweaver briefly explains to which HTML elements the particular selector will apply. For example, Figure 4-2 displays the New CSS Rule dialog box in the process of creating a new class style named *copyright*. The dialog box explains that this rule will apply to all HTML tags that have the *class* property set to copyright (in other words, all tags that have the class applied to them as described on page 122). For simple styles like class and tag styles, this explanation is pretty much like "Uh, yeah. Tell me something I don't know Dreamweaver." But for complex selectors such as the descendent selectors you'll learn about on page 301, this explanation box can help clarify which page element an otherwise confusing selector name will apply to.

- **Rule Definition.** The Rule Definition menu at the bottom of the dialog box lets you specify where the CSS code you're about to create gets stored. Choose "This document only" if you want the styles to apply only to the current Web page (creating an *internal* style sheet, as described on page 113). To create a new *external* style sheet, from the pop-up menu, choose New Style Sheet File. This option not only creates a new external CSS file (which you can save anywhere in your site folder), but also adds the necessary code in the current document to link it to that file.

If you've previously linked this document to an external style sheet (see page 113), then that style sheet's name appears in the pop-up menu, indicating that Dreamweaver is going to store the new style in this style sheet file.

Note: If you create a bunch of internal styles in a particular page, and later realize you'd like to turn them into an external style sheet that you can use in other pages, you're in luck. Dreamweaver includes many tools for managing your style sheets. You'll learn how to use them starting on page 308.

If you indicated that you want to create an external style sheet, clicking OK makes a Save Style Sheet As dialog box appear. Navigate to your site's folder, and then type a name for the new external CSS file. Just as HTML files end in .html, CSS files end in .css.

Note: If you'll be using this style sheet for all your site's pages, you may want to save it in your site's root folder, or in a folder specifically dedicated to style sheets, and give it a general name like *site_styles.css* or *global.css*. (You don't have to type the .css file name extension, by the way. In this case, Dreamweaver adds it.)

No matter what "Define in" option you selected, clicking OK eventually brings you to the CSS Rule Definition window.

Phase 2: Defining the Style

The CSS Rule Definition window provides access to all the available formatting for styling text and graphics (see Figure 4-3). You'll learn about each of the different properties throughout this book.

Once you've defined the style, at the bottom of the Rule Definition window, click OK. Dreamweaver adds the style to the specified style sheet, and displays it in the CSS Styles panel (Figure 4-1).

The real trick to creating a style is mastering all the different properties available, such as borders, margins, and background colors, and *then* learning which ones work reliably in the different browsers. You'll learn about different CSS properties starting on page 133.

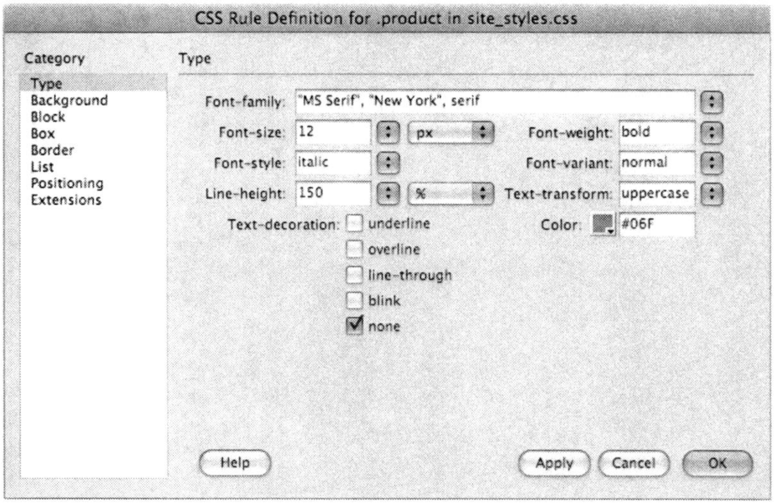

***Figure 4-3:** For ultimate formatting control, Dreamweaver lets you set dozens of different Cascading Style Sheet properties from the CSS Rule Definition window. You'll learn about these options throughout this book. For example, the Type properties are discussed on page 133.*

Creating a Style with the Property Inspector

The Property inspector's CSS mode lets you quickly create (or modify) styles for specific text formatting such as choosing a font or a font size (see Figure 4-4). In CSS mode, the Property inspector looks a lot like a formatting bar in a word processing program: dedicated buttons let you do things like make text bold or italics, control alignment, and set font type, size, and color. All these controls use CSS properties to achieve their effects.

To use the CSS mode, select some text on the page. For example, drag to select a portion of text, double-click to select a word, or triple-click to select an entire paragraph or headline. Then, from the Property inspector, select an option—for example, choose a selection of fonts from the font menu. If there's no style currently applied to the selection, you see <New CSS Rule> in the Targeted Rule menu on the Property inspector (see Figure 4-4, top). At that point Dreamweaver opens the New CSS Rule dialog box (Figure 4-2).

Now it's up to you to pick the type of style, name it, and decide where to store the style; just follow the same steps you'd use when creating a new style use the CSS Styles panel as described on page 115. You're free to create a class, tag, ID, or other style. After you create the new style, you return to the Property inspector (you skip the Rule Definition window). The Property inspector then lists the new style name in the Targeted Rule menu and displays the formatting you've selected (for example, the font you choose appears in the Font menu).

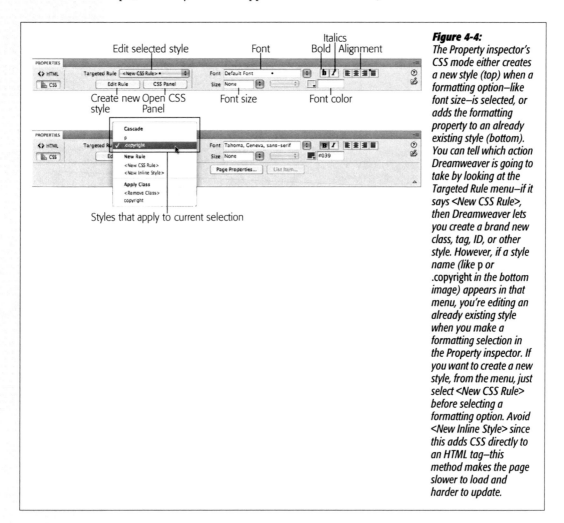

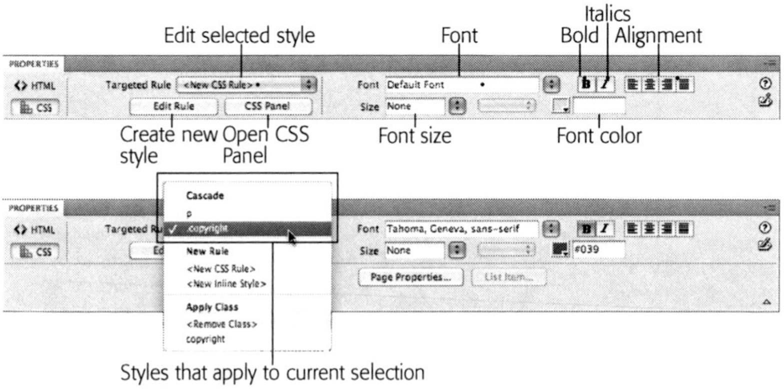

Figure 4-4: *The Property inspector's CSS mode either creates a new style (top) when a formatting option—like font size—is selected, or adds the formatting property to an already existing style (bottom). You can tell which action Dreamweaver is going to take by looking at the Targeted Rule menu—if it says <New CSS Rule>, then Dreamweaver lets you create a brand new class, tag, ID, or other style. However, if a style name (like* p *or* .copyright *in the bottom image) appears in that menu, you're editing an already existing style when you make a formatting selection in the Property inspector. If you want to create a new style, from the menu, just select <New CSS Rule> before selecting a formatting option. Avoid <New Inline Style> since this adds CSS directly to an HTML tag—this method makes the page slower to load and harder to update.*

Let's look at a basic example. Suppose you wanted to format a copyright notice at the bottom of the page in a way that's different from other text on the page. You would first triple-click the copyright paragraph to select the text, and then choose whatever formatting options you want from the CSS mode of the Property inspector—for example, select 12 from the Size menu to create small, 12-pixel type.

At this point the New CSS Rule dialog box opens and, from the Selector menu, you select Class, and then, in the Selector name field, type *copyright*. You could then store the file in either an external or internal style sheet as described on page 113. When you close the New CSS Rule window, a new class style named *copyright* is applied to the paragraph and the Size box in the Property inspector displays 12 pixels.

The Property inspector's CSS Mode behaves differently, however, if there's already a style created that applies to the selected text. In that case, the style appears in the Targeted Rule menu. For example, in Figure 4-4, bottom, the class style *copyright* is already applied to the selected text, so you see ".copyright" listed in that menu. At this point, choosing another formatting option from the Property inspector—for instance, clicking the bold button, or selecting a font from the font menu—doesn't create a new style. Instead it adds the new formatting choice to the already existing style.

For example, say you created a copyright class style with a font size setting of 12 pixels. At this point, if you select that copyright text again, and then select a font color, the copyright class style is updated—the CSS color property is added to the style. Making additional formatting choices also updates the style.

UP TO SPEED

Anatomy of a Style

Dreamweaver automatically handles the details of adding the proper CSS code to your pages, but if you're looking for a way to impress your neighbors, here's the behind-the-scenes scoop on how it works.

When you create an internal style sheet, Dreamweaver adds a pair of <style> tags to the head of the page (and a pair of HTML comment tags that hide the CSS from very old browsers). The opening <style> tag tells a Web browser that the following information isn't HTML—it's CSS code. When the Web browser encounters the closing </style> tag, it knows the CSS style information has ended.

Within the <style> tag, you see one or more styles (reminder: in CSS-speak, styles are also called "rules"). An HTML tag style for the Heading 1 tag (<h1>), for example, might look like this:

```
h1 {
font-size: 24px;
color: #003399;
}
```

The first part—h1—is called a *selector* (in CSS-speak) and indicates what the style applies to. In this case, wherever the <h1> (Heading 1) tag appears in the Web page's code, this style applies.

The information between the braces—{ }—states what formatting the browser should apply. The code above contains two formatting instructions for the <h1> tag. Each one is called a *declaration* and is composed of a *property* and a *value*. For instance, *font-size: 24px* is one declaration, with a property of *font-size* and a value of *24px*. In other words, this rule tells a Web browser that text inside an <h1> tag should be 24 pixels tall. The second declaration in the code makes the text of all <h1> tags show up in the color #003399.

A class style looks just like an HTML tag, except that instead of a tag, the selector is a name you've supplied, preceded by a dot, like this:

```
.company {
font-size: 24px;
color: #003399;
}
```

Styles stored in an external style sheet look exactly the same; the only difference is that external style sheets don't include the <style> tags and shouldn't include any HTML code. In Dreamweaver CS4 you can easily get a look at the raw style information of an external style sheet: Near the top of the document window, in the list of related files, just click the CSS file's name (see Figure 1-2).

Using Styles

Once you've created styles, you can easily apply them. In fact, if you created HTML tag styles, you don't need to do anything to apply them: Their selectors (see the box on page 121) automatically dictate which tags they affect.

Applying a Class Style

You can apply class styles to any selection in the document window, whether it's a word, an image, or an entire paragraph. In fact, you can apply a class style to *any* individual HTML tag, such as a <p> (paragraph), <td> (table cell), or <body> tag. You can even select just a single word within a paragraph and apply a style to it.

Applying a class style to text

Start out by selecting some words. Then, from the Property inspector, select the style name—you can do this either in HTML mode, in which case you select the name from the class menu (Figure 4-5, top), or in CSS mode, where you use the Targeted Rule menu (Figure 4-5, bottom).

To style an entire paragraph, triple-click within the paragraph (or heading) to select it, and then use the Property inspector to select the style. When you style an entire paragraph, you're actually telling Dreamweaver to apply the style to the <p> tag. In that case, Dreamweaver adds a special *class* property to the page's code, like this: <p class="company"> (for a class style named *.company*).

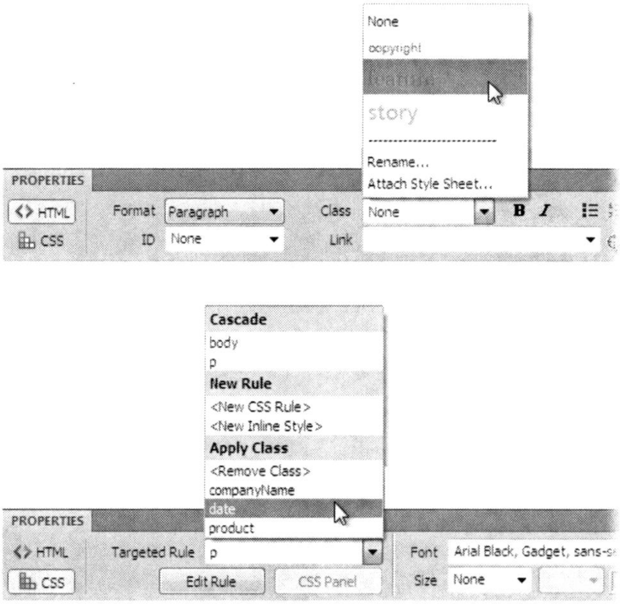

Figure 4-5:
The Property inspector gives you the easiest method of applying a class style. For non-text elements like images or tables, a Class menu appears in the top right of the Property inspector. For text, you apply class styles using either the Class menu if the Property inspector is in HTML mode (top) or the Targeted Rule Menu in CSS mode (bottom). Only the bottom section of the Targeted Rule Menu (the stuff below Apply Class) is used to add (or remove) a class from a text selection. The other items listed are for creating new styles, or viewing the styles that apply to the selection.

Tip: You can also add a class to an entire paragraph or heading simply by clicking anywhere inside the paragraph, and then, from the Property inspector, choosing the class name–just make sure you don't select *any* text, otherwise the style is applied just to the selected text and not the entire paragraph.

On the other hand, if you apply a class to a selection that isn't a tag—like a single word that you've double-clicked—Dreamweaver wraps the selection within a <span> tag like this: <span class="company">Chia Vet</span>. This tag, in other words, applies a style to a *span* of text that can't be identified by a single tag.

Applying a class style to objects

To apply a class style to an object (like an image or a table), start by selecting the object. As always, the Tag selector at the bottom of the document window is a great way to select a tag. Then, at the top right of the Property inspector, use the Class pop-up menu to select the style name.

Note: You can apply any class style to any element, although doing so doesn't always make sense. If you format a graphic with a style that specifies bold, red Courier type, it doesn't look any different.

Other class styling options

You can also apply a class style by selecting whatever element you wish to style, choosing Format → CSS Styles, and then, from the submenu, selecting the style. Or you can right-click (Control-click) the style's name in the CSS Styles panel, and then, from the pop-up menu, choose Apply. Finally, you can also apply a class from the document window's Tag selector, as shown in Figure 4-6.

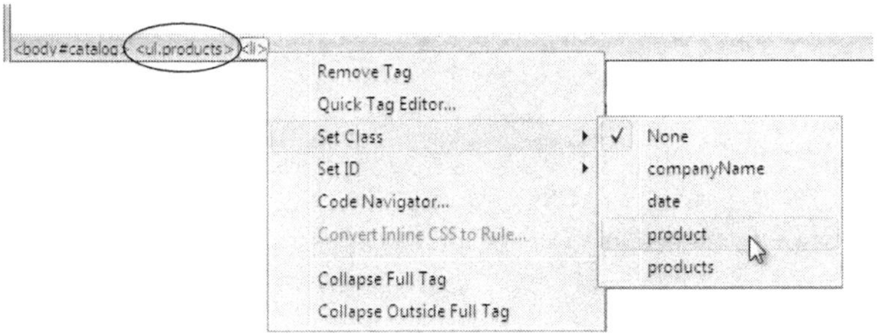

Figure 4-6: *You can apply a class style directly to a tag using the document window's Tag selector at the bottom of the window. Just right-click (Control-click) the tag you wish to format, and then, from the Set Class submenu, select the class style. In addition, the Tag selector lets you know if a tag has a class style applied to it. If so, the style's name is added at the end of the tag. For example, in this figure, a class style named .products has been applied to a bulleted list (the <ul> tag) on the page (circled).*

Removing a Class Style

To remove a class style from text on a Web page, simply select the text, and then, from the Property inspector (see Figure 4-5), choose None from the Class menu (HTML mode) or <Remove Class> from the Targeted Rule menu (CSS mode). To remove a class style from another object (like an image), select the object, and then, from the Property inspector's Class menu, choose None. You can also choose Format → CSS Styles → None to remove a style from any selection (even non-text elements like images or tables).

Tip: If you've applied a class style to a selection of text, then you don't actually have to select *all* the text to remove the style. Just click anywhere inside it, and then select None from the Property inspector's Class menu or <Remove Class> from the Targeted Rule menu. Dreamweaver is smart enough to realize you want to remove the style applied to the text. (If you applied the style to a tag, then Dreamweaver removes the Class property. If you applied the style using the <span> tag, then Dreamweaver removes the <span> tag.)

You can't, however, remove *tag* styles from HTML tags. For example, suppose you've redefined the <h2> tag using the steps outlined on page 115. If your page has three Heading 1 (<h2>) paragraphs, and you want the third heading to have a different style from the other two, you can't simply "remove" the <h2> style from the third paragraph. Instead, what you need to do is create a new *class* style with all the formatting options you want for that third heading, and then apply it directly to the <h2> tag. (By the magic of CSS, the class formatting options override any existing tag style options—see page 314 for more on this sleight of hand.)

Applying IDs to a Tag

To apply an ID to text, just select the text, and use the ID menu in the HTML mode of the Property inspector (see Figure 4-5, top). Since you can apply each ID name only once per page, this menu lists only IDs that exist in your style sheet but haven't yet been applied to a tag on the page.

For non-text elements, select the element, and then, in the Property inspector, type the ID name into the ID field. (For some elements the ID field is unlabelled, but you can always find it on the far left of the Property inspector.)

You can also use the Tag selector as outlined in Figure 4-6. Just use the Set ID menu in the contextual menu that appears when you right-click (Ctrl-click) the tag.

Tip: The Tag selector tells you if an ID is applied to a tag. An ID is indicated with a # symbol, so in Figure 4-6, for example, body#catalog indicates that the <body> tag has an ID named "catalog" applied to it.

Whenever you apply an ID to a tag, Dreamweaver adds a bit of HTML code to your page. For instance, an ID style named *#copyright* applied to a paragraph would look like this in the HTML: <p id="copyright"> (this is just like the "class" property that's added when you use class styles, as described on page 122).

To remove an ID from a text element, select the text, and then, from the Property inspector's ID menu, select None. For non-text elements, just select the element, and then, in the Property inspector's ID field, delete the ID name.

Linking to an External Style Sheet

Whenever you create an external style sheet, Dreamweaver automatically links it to the current document. To use its styles in a different Web page, however, you must *attach* it to the page.

To do so, open the Web page to which you wish to add the style sheet. Then, on the CSS Styles panel, click the Attach External Style Sheet button (see Figure 4-1). (If the CSS Styles panel isn't open, choose Window → CSS Styles or press Shift-F11.)

Tip: You can also use the Property inspector to attach a style sheet. Just select "Attach Style Sheet…" from the Class menu in HTML mode (see Figure 4-5, top).

The Attach External Style Sheet window appears (see Figure 4-7). Click Browse. In the Select Style Sheet File dialog box that appears, navigate to and double-click the CSS (.css) file you wish to attach to the document. If the style sheet you select is outside the current site—for example, you've selected a style sheet you like from another one of your Web sites—Dreamweaver offers to copy the style sheet file into your site's root folder; click Yes.

The Attach External Style Sheet window provides two other options: how to attach the style sheet, and what type of "media" you want the styles to apply to. The "media" setting is optional and dictates when the styles from the style sheet are applied (for example, you can apply a different set of styles when a page is printed vs. when it displays on a computer monitor). You'll find in-depth information on media types and how to use them on page 322.

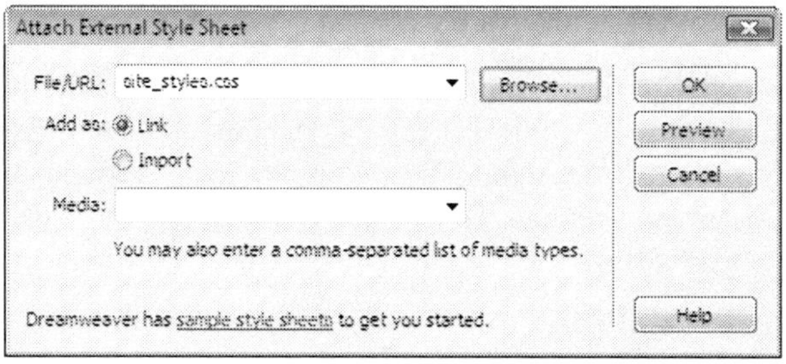

Figure 4-7: *Adding styles from an external style sheet is as simple as browsing for the file, and then clicking OK. Choosing a media type is optional.*

When attaching an external style sheet, you can either "link" it or "import" it. These two choices are nearly identical; they're simply two different methods of attaching an external style sheet to a Web page. To save you one extra click, just go with Dreamweaver's suggestion: link.

Tip: You can preview the effect of the style sheet on your page by clicking the Preview button in the Attach External Style Sheet window.

After choosing your options, click OK, and Dreamweaver adds the necessary HTML code to the head of the Web page, and automatically formats any tags in the document according to the style sheet's HTML tag styles. You see the formatting changes take place in the document window immediately after attaching the external style sheet.

If the style sheet contains *class* styles, on the other hand, then you don't see their formatting effects until you apply them to an element on the page, as described on page 122.

Manipulating Styles

As with anything in Dreamweaver, styles are easy enough to edit, delete, or duplicate; all you need is a map of the terrain.

Editing Styles

While building a Web site, you almost always continually refine your designs. That chartreuse color you assigned to the background of your pages may have looked great at 2 a.m., but it loses something in the light of day.

Fortunately, one of CSS's greatest selling points is how easy it makes updating the formatting on a Web site.

Tip: Although this section focuses mainly on how to style your text, you also use CSS styles to add background colors, background images, borders, and accurately position elements on page. The next few chapters show you how to style links, images, tables, forms, and other page elements with CSS.

Dreamweaver provides many ways to edit styles:

- In the CSS Styles panel, select a style (Figure 4-1), and then click the Edit Style button to open the Rule Definition window (Figure 4-3). (This is the same window you used when first creating the style.) Make your changes, and then click OK to return to the document window. Dreamweaver reformats the page to reflect any changes you made to styles used in the current document.
- Double-clicking the name of a style in the CSS panel also opens the Rule Definition window. Actually, depending on a preference setting—or a setting someone else may have tweaked while using your computer—double-clicking a style in the CSS panel may display the—eeck!—raw CSS code in Code view. To change this behavior, open the Preferences window (Ctrl+U [⌘-U]), click the CSS Styles category, and then select the "Edit using CSS dialog" button.

FREQUENTLY ASKED QUESTION

When Formatting Disappears

Sometimes when I copy text from one Web page and paste it into another Web page, all the formatting disappears. What's going on?

When you use Cascading Style Sheets, keep in mind that the actual style information is stored either in the <head> of the Web page (for internal style sheets) or in a separate CSS file (an external style sheet). If a page includes an internal style sheet, then when you copy text, graphics, or other page elements, Dreamweaver copies those elements and any class or ID style definitions used by that content. When you paste the HTML into another page, the styles are written into the <head> of that page. This feature can save you some time, but doesn't solve all of your woes. It doesn't, for example, copy any *tag styles* you've created, or most advanced styles you may create (see page 299 for more on advanced styles). So if you copy and paste some text—say, an <h1> tag styled with an h1 tag style—the <h1> tag and its contents paste into another page, but the tag style doesn't.

In addition, if a page uses an external style sheet, then when you copy and paste text, the styles themselves don't go along for the ride. If you copy a paragraph that has a class style applied to it, and paste it into another document, the code in the paragraph is pasted (<p class="company"> for instance), but the actual "company" style, with all its formatting properties, isn't.

The best solution is to use a common external style sheet for all pages on your site. That way, when you copy and paste HTML, all the pages share the same styles and formatting. So in the example above, if you copy a paragraph that includes a class style—class="company"—into another page that shares the same style sheet, the paragraphs look the same on both pages. See pages 118 and 125 for more on how to create one of these uber, sitewide external style sheets.

- In the CSS Styles panel, right-click (Control-click) the name of a style, and then, from the shortcut menu, choose Edit, which also opens the Rule Definition window. Make your changes to the style, and then click OK to return to the document window.

Tip: The properties pane in the CSS Styles panel offers yet another, faster method of editing a style. This advanced technique requires a bit of CSS savvy and is discussed on page 305.

Deleting a Style

At some point, you may find you've created a style that you don't need after all. Maybe you redefined the HTML <code> tag, and realize you haven't even used the tag in your site. You don't need to keep it around, taking up precious space in the style sheet.

To delete a style, make sure the CSS Styles panel is open (Window → CSS Styles), and the All button is highlighted (see Figure 4-1). Click the name of the style you wish to delete, and then press your keyboard's delete key (you can also click the Trash can icon at the bottom of the panel). You can also remove all the styles in an internal style sheet (as well as the style sheet itself) by selecting the style sheet—indicated by "<style>" in the CSS Styles panel (see Figure 4-1)—and pressing

FREQUENTLY ASKED QUESTION

When Undo Won't Do

Sometimes when I edit a style—say, to change the font color—I can undo that change. But sometimes, I'm unable to undo changes I've made to a style. What gives?

You can undo only changes made to a document you're currently working on. So say you've added an internal style sheet (see page 113) to a document. If you edit one of those styles, Dreamweaver lets you undo those changes. Because the styles in an internal style sheet are a part of the Web page you're working on, choosing Edit → Undo undoes the last change you've made to that style.

However, if you're using an external style sheet, you're actually working on two *different* files at the same time—the Web page you're building, and the style sheet file in which you add, delete, or edit styles. So if you're designing a Web page, and edit a style contained in the external style sheet, you're actually making a change to the style sheet file. In this case, choosing Edit → Undo undoes only the last change made to the *Web page*. If you want to undo the change you made to the external style sheet, you need to use the related files feature, new to Dreamweaver CS4. The name of the external style sheet appears on the Related Files toolbar, which appears below the title of the Web page file; click the file's name to move to its code, and then choose Edit → Undo. Click the Source Code button to return to the Web page (you'll learn more about the related files bar on page 410).

Delete (or clicking the Trash can icon). If you "trash" an *external* style sheet, however, you merely unlink it from the current document without actually deleting the .css file.

Unfortunately, deleting a class style *doesn't* delete any references to the style in your site's pages. For example, if you've created a style called *.company* and applied it throughout your site, and you then delete that style from the style sheet, Dreamweaver doesn't remove the <span> tags or class properties that refer to the style. Your pages are still littered with orphaned code like this—<span class="company"> CosmoFarmer</span>—even though the text loses the styling. (See how to solve this problem using Dreamweaver's powerful "Find and Replace" tool on page 792.)

Renaming a Class Style

You can rename any style by selecting it in the CSS Styles panel, pausing a second, and then clicking the name again. This makes the name editable, at which point you can type a new name in its place. Of course, if you change a style named *p* to a style named *h1*, you've essentially removed a p tag style and added an h1 tag style—in other words, all paragraphs would lose the style's formatting, and all <h1> tags would suddenly change appearance. Alternatively, you could open the .css file in Code view, and then edit the name. However, when it comes to class styles just changing the name doesn't do much good if you've already applied the style throughout your site. The *old* class name still appears in the HTML in each place you used it.

What you really need to do is rename the class style, and *then* perform a find-and-replace operation to change the name wherever it appears in your site. Dreamweaver includes a handy tool to simplify this process.

To rename a class style:

1. **On the Property inspector, in the Class menu (Figure 4-5), choose Rename.**

   The Rename Style window appears (Figure 4-8).

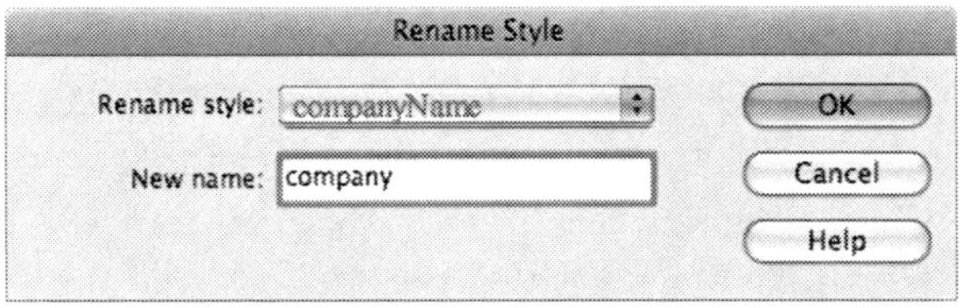

Figure 4-8: *The Rename Style tool is a fast and easy way to change the name of a class style even if you've already used the style hundreds of times throughout your site.*

2. **From the top menu, choose the name of the style you wish to rename.**

   This menu lists all class styles available on the current page, including external and internal styles.

3. **In the "New name" box, type the new style name.**

   You must follow the same rules for naming class styles described on page 117. But, just as when creating a new class, you don't need to precede the name with a period—Dreamweaver takes care of that.

4. **Click OK.**

   If the style whose name you're changing is an internal style, Dreamweaver makes the change. Your job is complete.

   However, if the style belongs to an external style sheet, Dreamweaver warns you that other pages on the site may also use this style. To successfully rename the style, Dreamweaver must use its "Find and Replace" tool to search the site and update all pages that use the old style name. In that case, continue to step 5.

5. **If you get cold feet, click Cancel to call off the name change, or click Yes to open the "Find and Replace" window, where you should click Replace All.**

   One last warning appears, reminding you that this action can't be undone.

Note: If you click No in the warning box that appears after step 4, Dreamweaver still renames the style in the external style sheet, but doesn't update your pages.

6. **Click Yes.**

   Dreamweaver goes through each page of your site, dutifully updating the name of the style in each place it appears.

Duplicating a Style

Dreamweaver makes it easy to duplicate a CSS style, which is handy when you've created, say, an HTML tag style, and then decide you'd rather make it a class style. Or you may want to use the formatting options from one style as a starting-off point for a new style. Either way, you start by duplicating an existing style.

You can duplicate a style in two ways. The easiest method is to open the CSS Styles panel (Window → CSS Styles), right-click (Control-click) the name of the style you wish to duplicate, and then, from the shortcut menu, choose Duplicate.

The Duplicate CSS Rule window appears (Figure 4-9), where you can give the duplicated style a new name, reassign its Type setting, use the "Define in" menu to move it from an internal to an external style sheet, and so on.

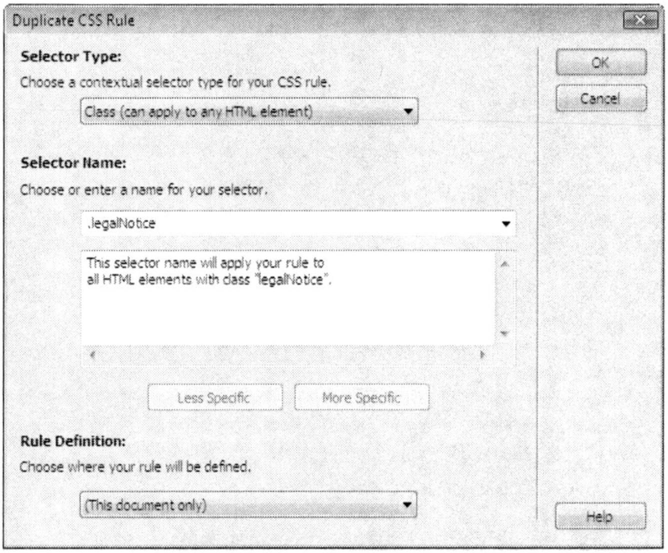

Figure 4-9:
The Duplicate CSS Rule dialog box looks and acts just like the New CSS Rule box (Figure 4-2). You can select a new style type, name it, and then add it to an external or internal style sheet. The only difference is that the duplicated style retains all the original style's CSS properties.

When you click OK, Dreamweaver adds the duplicate style to the page or external style sheet. You can then edit the new style just as you would any other, as described on page 126.

Checking Browser Compatibility

As if learning Dreamweaver, HTML, and CSS weren't big enough challenges, Web designers also have to contend with the fact that not all browsers display CSS in the same way. What looks great in Firefox may look terrible in Internet Explorer—and vice versa. Unfortunately, a lot of CSS display problems aren't the fault of the Web designer or CSS, but are caused by bugs in the browsers. This sad fact of browser life usually forces Web designers to spend lots of time testing Web pages in different browsers to identify and fix problems.

Fortunately for you, Dreamweaver includes a tool to help diagnose CSS problems, and advise you on the best way to fix them, saving you many hours of testing and troubleshooting. The Check Browser Compatibility tool scans a page's HTML and CSS, and determines if one or more browsers are likely to have trouble displaying your page. It actually checks two things: whether you've included any CSS properties or values that one or more browsers don't understand, and whether the particular combination of HTML and CSS you're using might trip up a particular browser.

For example, the *blink* value of the CSS Decoration property (page 143) isn't supported by Internet Explorer or Safari. If you place that value in a style on a page, and then use the Check Browser Compatibility tool, Dreamweaver lets you know those browsers won't do anything with the blink setting. These types of errors are straightforward: You either change the property (or remove it) so that the style works in all browsers, or live with the fact that the specified browser will ignore the particular style instruction.

The second type of problem is more nebulous. Dreamweaver also warns you of potential browser problems that might arise because of the way you've used HTML and CSS. The warning Dreamweaver gives in this case is not as clear-cut as, "*That* browser doesn't understand *that* CSS property;" it's more like, "That browser *does* understand that CSS property, but in this one instance, the browser may get it horribly wrong, and mess up your Web page."

For example, Internet Explorer knows what a bulleted list is; it also knows what the CSS *display* property is (see page 146). In most cases, Internet Explorer has no problem displaying both bulleted lists and items styled with a *block* value for the display property. But, in one case—when a link inside a list item has a display value of *block*—the list items appear with a mysterious extra space below them. The result: an unattractive white space between an otherwise orderly stack of navigation buttons...but this happens *only* with Internet Explorer. These are the types of obscure problems that make Web designers consider new careers.

Fortunately, the Check Browser Compatibility tool is aware of many of the most common, hair-pulling, browser bugs, and can save you lots of time by letting you know when a page might have a problem. To use the tool:

1. **Open a Web page that you'd like to test.**

   You can open any Web page; if the page has an external style sheet, Dreamweaver checks that as well. You can even open an external style sheet (.css) file and run this command on it to identify CSS properties and values that some browsers might not understand.

2. **Choose File → Check Page → Browser Compatibility.**

   Alternatively, from the Check Page menu at the top right of the document window, you can choose Check Browser Compatibility (see Figure 4-10). In either case, Dreamweaver analyses the HTML and CSS for the page, and spits out the results in the Results panel's Browser Compatibility tab (see Figure 4-11).

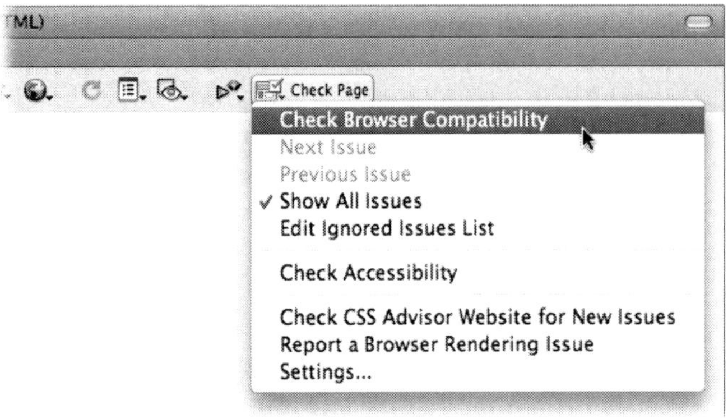

Figure 4-10: *The Check Page menu lets you examine a page and see how compatible its HTML and CSS are with a variety of Web browsers. To change the browsers Dreamweaver uses for its analysis, select the Settings option. A window listing the most common browsers appears, from which you specify the earliest version of the browser you wish to check against. For example, if you don't worry about Internet Explorer 5 any longer, choose 6 from the menu. Now Dreamweaver checks only for problems that occur in version 6 or later. Unless you're catering to some old Macs, uncheck the Internet Explorer for Mac checkbox–that browser is only rarely used anymore and hasn't even been available for years.*

Each issue that Dreamweaver discovers is displayed with an icon indicating the severity of the problem, the line number in the HTML code where the potential problem occurs, and a short description of the issue.

An icon in the far left column of the results panel indicates the type of issue and its likelihood of causing a browser problem. An ! mark indicates an error—a problem with the CSS such as a property or value that's either invalid or isn't understood by a particular browser. Problems identified by a red pie graph are warnings, and they indicate the likelihood of encountering a problem in a particular browser: A single slice means that yes, the page has something that might cause difficulty for a particular browser, but then again the browser may display the page just fine. You see this icon for an issue that's rare or crops up only when a very particular set of HTML and CSS are in place (and Jupiter's rising while Mars descends).

A fully red circle indicates that you're likely to see a problem in the specific browser. For example, the Internet Explorer problem related to links, lists, and the display property mentioned previously is nearly a sure thing. If you've set up your CSS and HTML in that way, you *will* see that problem in Internet Explorer.

You should always test any page that shows an error or warning, even if Dreamweaver thinks the problem is only slightly likely to occur.

3. **In the Results panel, select an issue (Figure 4-11).**

After selecting an issue in the Results panel, a detailed explanation of the problem appears in the right side of the panel; in addition, you see a list of which browsers this problem may affect, and the likelihood that the problem will crop up. In Figure 4-11, the issue "Three pixel text jog" is selected. You can see what causes it and see that it affects Internet Explorer 6.

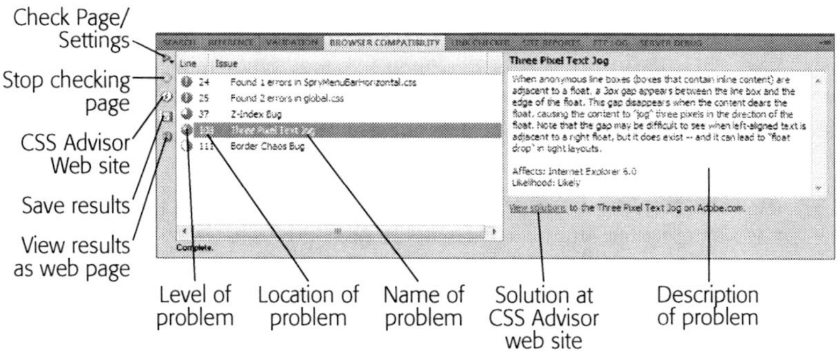

***Figure 4-11:** Don't bother with the Save Results button in the left edge of the Results panel. Clicking this button creates a hard-to-read and not so useful XML file that lists the same information you find in the Results panel. (That said, perhaps this file could come in handy if you want to report back to your pet robot about how your day went.)*

4. **Fix the problem.**

   Dreamweaver just identifies the problem; it doesn't, alas, fix it. However, Adobe hasn't left you totally in the lurch. When you select a problem in the Results panel, at the bottom right of the panel, a link ("View solutions") appears (see Figure 4-11). Clicking that link launches a Web browser, and opens a page on Adobe's CSS Advisor site. This Web site is an ever-evolving catalog of CSS browser problems and recommended solutions. Dreamweaver's Results panel integrates with this site, so the link on the panel takes you to a page that addresses the very problem you're trying to solve. Nice.

   In most cases the solution to an issue involves adding an additional style or editing an already created style. You shouldn't try to make too much sense out of the solutions—many don't make any technical sense. For example, the solution for the "Extra White Space in List Links" bug is to create two styles (both of which target the link tag inside the affected list), and apply two different display properties (see page 146): The first style uses the *inline-block* value, and the second applies the *block* value. It's not logical, but it does knock some sense into IE. Most of the solutions are the results of countless hours of trial and error by exasperated and industrious Web designers. Just be thankful the answers to these problems are just a click away.

Text Formatting with CSS

One of the best uses for Cascading Style Sheets is to convert the drab appearance of HTML text into lavishly designed prose. Or, if you like a somber, corporate style, CSS can help with that too. Whatever your design inclination, you can improve the look of your Web text using CSS.

You can access six different text-related CSS properties using the CSS mode of the Property inspector (see Figure 4-4), or use the full-blown CSS Rule Definition window to deploy over 64 different CSS properties. The most commonly used properties for text are stored in the Type (Figure 4-14) and Block categories, while the List category offers several options for formatting bulleted and numbered lists.

Note: You can apply nearly every CSS property to text. For example, you can use the border property to underline text, and the margin property to remove space between paragraphs. Those properties and others not listed in the Type or Block categories are introduced later in this book (don't want to blow your circuits too quickly). For now, you'll learn the most type-centric properties.

Choosing a Font

Formatting fonts for the Web is very much like using fonts in a word processor. Sadly, it carries some of the same drawbacks. For example, if you create some beautiful document in Microsoft Word, using fancy fonts you just bought from a small font company in Nome, Alaska, you're in for a rude surprise when you email the document to your boss. He won't see anything resembling what the memo looked like on *your* screen. Because he doesn't own the same fonts, he'll see some default font on his computer—Times, perhaps. Fonts show up in a distributed document only if each recipient has the same fonts installed.

On the Web, you're in the same predicament. You're free, as a Web designer, to specify *any* font you want in a Web page, but it doesn't show up on a viewer's computer unless she's installed the same font on her system. If she hasn't, your visitor's Web browser shows your text in a default font, which is usually some version of Times, Arial, or Courier.

You have several solutions to this dilemma. One is to convert your text into graphic images—unfortunately that process takes time and forces your Web visitors to download byte-hogging images just to read your Web page. Another option is to specify the font you'd *like* to use; if your viewer's computer has the specified font installed, that's what she'll see. You can specify secondary or tertiary font choices if the preferred font isn't available. In fact, Dreamweaver offers prepackaged lists of such "first choice, second choice, third choice" fonts, as you'll find out in the following section.

Applying font formatting

You can use either the Font menu in the Property inspector's CSS mode (Figure 4-4) or the CSS Rule Definition window's Font-family menu (Figure 4-14). In either case what you're actually doing is either creating a new style as described on page 115 or updating an already existing style.

You'll soon discover that Dreamweaver's font menus aren't quite what you're used to. When you apply a font to text, you have to choose from one of the prepackaged lists just described; a typical choice is something like "Arial, Helvetica, sans-serif". In other words, you can't just choose a single font, such as Helvetica.

UP TO SPEED

Knowing Your Font Types

You can find literally tens of thousands of different fonts to express your every thought: from bookish, staid, and classical typefaces to rounded, cartoonish squiggles.

Most fonts are divided into two categories: serif and sans-serif. Serif fonts are often used for long passages of text, as it's widely believed that serifs—small decorative strokes ("hands" and "feet") at the end of a letter's main strokes—gently lead the eye from letter to letter, making text easier to read. Examples of serif fonts are Times, Times New Roman, Georgia, and Minion, the font in the main body paragraphs of this book.

Sans-serif fonts, on the other hand, are often used for headlines, thanks to their clean and simple appearance. Examples of sans-serif fonts include Arial, Helvetica, Verdana, and Formata, which you're reading now. Some people believe that you should use only sans-serif fonts on Web pages because they think the delicate decorative strokes of serif fonts don't display well on the coarse resolution of a computer screen. This is an aesthetic judgment, so you should feel free to pick the fonts you think look best.

If the first font isn't installed on your visitor's computer, the browser looks down the list until it finds a font that is. Different operating systems use different fonts, so these lists include one font that's common on Windows and another, similar-looking font that's common on the Mac. Arial, for instance, is found on all Windows machines, while Helvetica is a similar font for Macs.

That's it. You've just selected one of Dreamweaver's preinstalled fonts, and any text formatted by the CSS style you just created will use the font you selected. If you'd like a greater degree of control of the fonts your page displays, read on.

Creating custom font lists

Dreamweaver CS4 comes with 13 preset "first choice, second choice, third choice" font lists, which incorporate fonts common to both Windows and Macs. But you can easily stray from the pack and create your own font lists for use in your Web pages. If you proceed with the custom approach, make sure you know what fonts your visitors have—easily done if you're designing a corporate intranet and know what computers are used in your company—and always specify one font that you *know* is installed. In this way, your page may not look exactly as you intended, but it'll at least be readable.

Here's how you create a new "first choice, second choice, third choice" font list.

Note: Technically, you can specify any number of fallback fonts in one of these lists, not just first, second, and third choices. Your list can range anywhere from just a single font to a long list arranged in order of preference.

1. **Open the Edit Font List dialog box.**

   From the Property inspector's Font menu (visible only in CSS mode), choose Edit Font List, or choose Format → Font → Edit Font List. Either way, the Edit Font List dialog box appears (Figure 4-12).

POWER USERS' CLINIC

Font Convergence

While Mac and Windows used to come with very different sets of preinstalled fonts, there's been some convergence in the past few years. These days, you can count on the average Mac or PC having the following fonts: Arial, Arial Black, Arial Narrow, Comic Sans MS, Courier, Courier New, Georgia, Times New Roman, Trebuchet MS, Verdana, and Webdings. In fact, Dreamweaver CS4, for the first time in the long history of the program, has added a bunch of additional combinations of fonts.

If your audience includes people running Unix or Linux, all bets are off. In that case, stick to these three fonts: Helvetica (make sure to also specify Arial for Windows owners), Times (Times New Roman for Windows), and Courier (Courier New for Windows).

You can find a concise comparison that lists fonts friendly to both Windows and Macs at *www.ampsoft.net/webdesign-l/WindowsMacFonts.html*. And another useful list at *http://dustinbrewer.com/fonts-on-the-web-and-a-list-of-web-safe-fonts*. You can find a great article on the subject at *http://24ways.org/2007/increase-your-font-stacks-with-font-matrix*.

To jump-start your adventures, here are a few font combinations that work relatively well for both Mac and Windows visitors:

- Marker Felt Wide, Comic Sans MS, fantasy
- Century Gothic, Gill Sans, Arial, sans-serif
- Franklin Gothic Medium, Arial Narrow, sans-serif
- Optima, Segoe UI, Arial, sans-serif

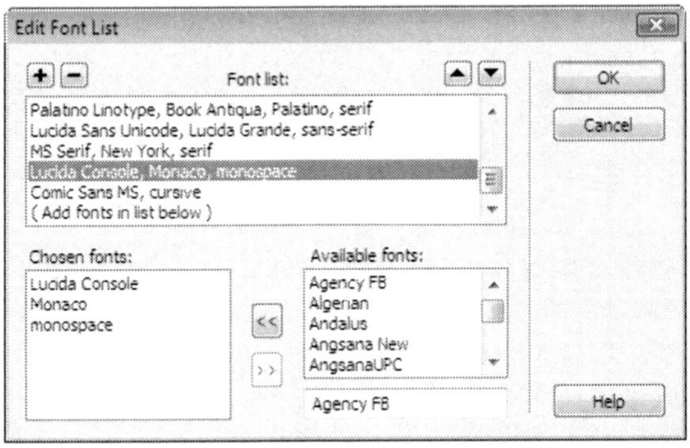

Figure 4-12: *Not only can you create your own font lists, but you can also edit, remove, or reorder the current lists in this dialog box. When you click a list in the "Font list" menu, the "first choice, second choice, third choice" fonts appear in the lower-left corner. To remove a font from that list, click the font name, and then click the >> button. To add a font to the list, select a font in the "Available fonts" menu, and then click the << button. Finally, to reorder the font lists as they appear in the Property inspector, the CSS Rule Definition window's Font menu, or the Format → Font menu, click the arrow keys near the upper-right corner of the dialog box.*

2. **Select a first-choice font from the list of "Available fonts", or type in the font name.**

   All fonts on your computer are listed in the "Available fonts" menu. Simply click to select the font you wish to add.

   Alternatively, you can type a font's name into the box that appears directly below the list of available fonts—a handy trick if you want to include a font that isn't installed on your computer (a Windows font when you're working on a Mac, for example).

3. **Add the font you've just specified to your new, custom font list by clicking the << button (or just double-clicking the font name).**

   Your first-choice font appears in the "Chosen fonts" list.

4. **Repeat steps 2 and 3 for each font you wish to include in your custom list.**

   The order in which you add the fonts is the order they appear in the list. These become the "first choice, second choice, third choice" fonts.

   Unfortunately, there's no way to change the order of the fonts once you've added them. So if you accidentally put the fonts in the wrong order, you must delete the list by clicking the minus (–) button (at the upper-left corner of the dialog box) and start over.

5. **Add a generic font family.**

   This last step isn't strictly necessary, but it's a good idea. If your Web page visitor is some kind of anti-font radical whose PC doesn't have *any* of the fonts you've chosen, his browser will substitute the generic font family you specify here.

   Generic fonts are listed at the bottom of the list of "Available fonts" and include "cursive", "fantasy", "monospace", "sans-serif", and "serif". On most systems, the monospaced font is Courier, the serif font is Times, and the sans-serif font is Arial or Helvetica. Select a generic font that's similar in appearance to the fonts in your list. For instance, choose "sans-serif" if your list consists of sans-serif fonts like Helvetica or Arial; choose "serif" if you specified fonts like Times or Georgia; or choose "monospace" for a font like Courier.

6. **Click OK.**

   Your new font package appears in the Property inspector's Font menu, ready to apply.

Changing the Font Size

Varying the sizes of fonts on a Web page is one way to direct a viewer's attention. Large type screams "Read Me!"—excellent for attention-grabbing headlines—while small type fades into the background—perfect for necessary but unexciting legal mumbo jumbo like copyright notices.

Unless you specifically define its size, text in a regular paragraph appears at the default size specified by your visitor's Web browser: In most browsers today that size is 16 pixels. However, not only can people change that default size (much to the eternal frustration of Web designers), but different operating systems have also been known to display text at different sizes. Bottom line: You can't really trust that text will appear the same size for all the different viewers of your site.

You can use either the Size menu in the Property inspector's CSS mode (Figure 4-13) or the CSS Rule Definition window's Font-size menu (Figure 4-14).

In either case you're either creating a new style as described on page 115 or updating an already existing style. The choices available from the Size menu break down into four groups:

- The *None* option removes any size information that you may have applied to the text. The text returns to its default size.
- The numeric choices—*9 through 36*—indicate how tall you wish to make the text, in pixels. Nine-pixel-tall text is nearly unreadable, while 36 pixels makes a bold statement. One benefit of pixel sizes is that text appears nearly the same across different browsers and different operating systems, overcoming the problems mentioned above.
- The options *xx-small* through *xx-large* indicate fixed sizes, replacing the sizes 1 through 7 used with the old HTML <font> tag. The *medium* size is usually the same as the default size.
- The last two choices—*smaller* and *larger*—are relative sizes, meaning that they shrink or enlarge the selected text based on the default size. These choices come in handy when you've defined a base font size for the entire page using the Page Properties window (see Figure 1-22 on page 55).

  Suppose the default size of text on a page is 12 pixels. If you apply a "larger" size to a selection of text, then it gets bigger (the exact amount varies by Web browser). If, later, you change the base size to 14 pixels (in Page Properties), all of that "larger" text will also increase proportionally.

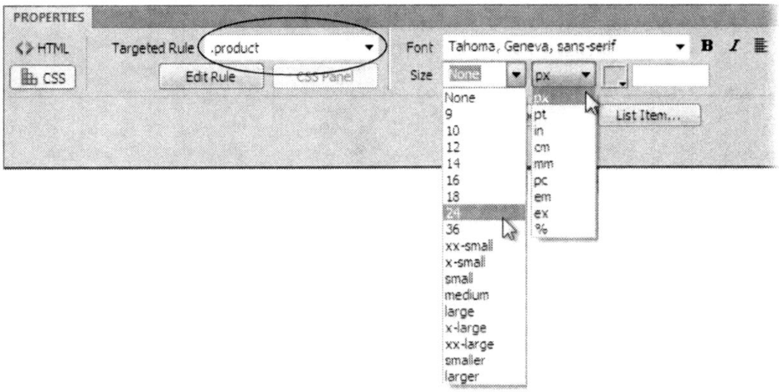

***Figure 4-13:** You can set a dizzying array of font sizes using CSS. When using the Property inspector's CSS mode to set the size of text, you either create a new style—in which case you see <New CSS Rule> listed in the Targeted Rule field (circled)—or you edit an already existing style, as shown here. In this case, the class style, .product, is listed, so picking a font size edits that CSS style.*

To change the size of text, simply select it, and then, from the Property inspector, choose a new size (Figure 4-13), or edit the appropriate CSS style as described on page 126. If you applied a number (that is, a pixel value), you have an additional option: If you don't like any of the sizes listed, you can type any number you wish.

In fact, unlike HTML, CSS can handle humongous text—hundreds of pixels tall, if that's what you're into.

You're not limited to pixels, either. The Units pop-up menu (to the right of the Size menu, shown in Figure 4-13) lets you specify pixels, points, inches, centimeters, millimeters, picas, ems, percentages, or exes (an *ex* is the width of the letter X in the current font). Most of these measurement systems aren't intended for onscreen display. The most popular options are:

- *Pixels* are great for ensuring that text looks the same size across different browsers and operating systems. The downside, however, is that Internet Explorer 6 and earlier for Windows doesn't let Web surfers adjust the pixel size. So people who can't see well, or whose monitors are set to very high resolutions, are stuck with your choice of pixel size. Make it too small, and they won't be able to read your text. (Fortunately, as Internet Explorer 7 becomes more popular, this becomes less of an issue.)

Note: This isn't entirely true. You *can* tweak Internet Explorer to allow resizing of pixel-sized text, but you have to change some of the default settings of the browser. That's something most people would never do.

- *Ems* are a relative measurement, meaning that the actual point size varies.

  One em is equal to the default font size. So suppose a Web browser's default font size is 14 pixels tall. In that case, 1 em would mean 14 pixels tall, 2 ems would be twice that (28 pixels), and 1.5 ems would be 21 pixels.

  The advantage of ems is that they let your Web visitors control the size of onscreen text. If it's too small, they can increase the base font size. (In Internet Explorer, you make this adjustment by choosing an option from the View → Text Size menu [View → Make Text Bigger on Safari on the Mac].) Any text measured in ems then changes according to the Web browser's new setting.

  You can use pixels and ems together. You could, for instance, set the base font size on your page to 16 pixels, and then use ems for other parts of the page. For example, you could set headlines to 2 ems, making them 32 pixels tall. If you later thought the overall text size of the page was too small or too large, you could simply change the base font size for the page, and the headlines and all other text would resize proportionally.

  Many Web experts advocate the use of ems, because they let visitors decide how big text should appear, thus making the site more widely accessible. Many designers, on the other hand, don't like the fact that other people can radically change the design of a page by simply changing a browser setting.

Note: As you get more advanced with CSS, you'll probably run into some weird problems with em or percentage text sizes due to an advanced concept known as the *cascade*. The gruesome details begin on page 314.

- *Percentages* (%) are another relative size measurement. When applied to text size, they're functionally equivalent to ems. If you're more comfortable with the notion of percentages than the typography-inspired ems, use percentage values instead.

The other measurement options, like inches and millimeters, don't make as much sense as pixels, ems, and percentages, because you can't consistently measure them on monitors. For example, Windows is set to 96 pixels to the inch, whereas Mac OS X is set to 72 pixels per inch—but even these settings can be changed, so there's no reliable way to measure an "inch" on a computer screen.

Picking a Font Color

Most color formatting in Dreamweaver, whether it's for text or for a table cell, makes use of Dreamweaver's *color box.*

To set the color of text, use the CSS Color property. You can use the Property inspector's CSS mode to choose a color, or assign a text color in the Text category of the CSS Rule Definition window (Figure 4-14). In both cases, you encounter Dreamweaver's color box as described on page 59. You can pick a color by clicking the color well and, from the pop-up color palette, selecting a color, or you can type a *hexadecimal number* (see page 59) of the color you want. (Clearly, this is the option for hard-core HTML geeks. After all, surely you've memorized the hex number of that light shade of blue you always use—#6699FF, isn't it?)

Adding Bold and Italics

You can use the Property inspector to make text bold or italics. However, depending on which mode the inspector is in—HTML or CSS—clicking the B or I button does different things. In HTML mode, the B button wraps selected text with the <strong> HTML tag, while the I button wraps the text with the <em> (for emphasis) tag. However, in CSS mode, the B button sets the CSS *Font-weight* property to bold, while the I button sets the CSS *Font-style* property to italic. In other words, those two buttons either insert HTML tags or add CSS properties to a style.

If you want to just change the appearance of text, use CSS mode, but if you actually want to emphasize some text because it's important for the sentence's meaning, then use HTML mode. For example, if you just want the word "Monday" to stand out visually on the page, use CSS. But for a sentence like "He *never* makes mistakes" the emphasis on "never" is important to understanding the sentence; in that case, use HTML mode. The people viewing your site might not notice the difference, but Google, other search engines, and screen reading software will.

Note: If you use the Property inspector's CSS mode, the B button only makes type bold or removes bold formatting you previously applied. In the case of headlines, which browsers automatically display as bold, clicking the B button has no effect. To remove the bold formatting from headlines you have to use the CSS Style Definition window, and, from the font-weight menu, select *normal* (see Figure 4-14).

Aligning Text

The alignment buttons in the Property inspector's CSS mode (Figure 4-4) set the CSS text-align property to either *left*, *right*, *center*, or *justify*. These same options are available under the Block category of the CSS Rule Definition window (Figure 4-17).

CSS Type Properties in the Rule Definition Window

As the name implies, the Rule Definition window's Type category lets you set formatting options that affect text (see Figure 4-14). Most of these settings are the same as those available from the Property inspector in CSS mode and have been discussed in depth starting on page 119. But to summarize, this category of CSS properties includes:

- **Font.** You choose a font for the style from the Font menu. As discussed on page 134, you choose from *groups* of fonts rather than the specific one you have your heart set on. Dreamweaver also lets you create your own "first-choice, second-choice..." font choices from this menu, exactly as described on page 135.

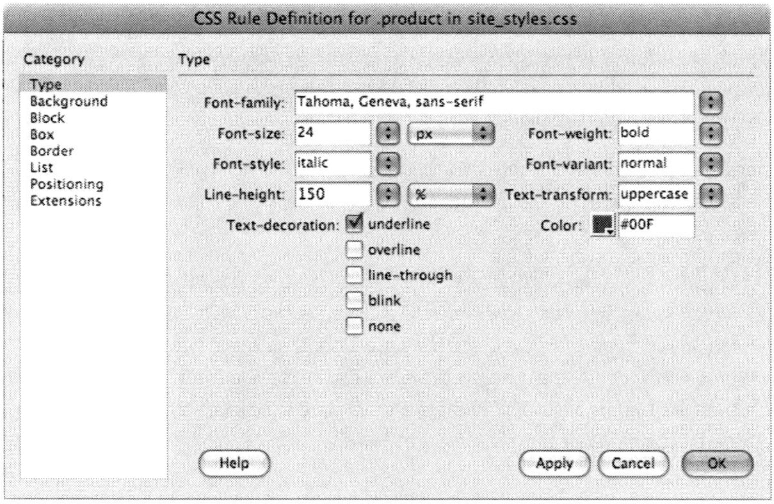

***Figure 4-14:** While you can set some text formatting using the Property inspector, the CSS Rule Definition window's Type category offers additional formatting options. For example, you get the ability to control the space between lines of text, and an option to change the case of text–make text upper or lowercase.*

- **Size.** As described on page 137, you can choose from among many different systems for sizing text, but the most common are pixels, ems, and percentages.
- **Weight.** Weight refers to the thickness of the font. The Weight menu offers 13 different choices. Normal and bold are the most common, and they work in all browsers that understand CSS. See Figure 4-15 for details.
- **Style.** In this peculiar instance, Style means italic, oblique, or normal. Technically, italic is a custom-designed, emphatic version of a typeface, *like this.* Oblique, on the other hand, is just a computerized adaptation of a normal font,

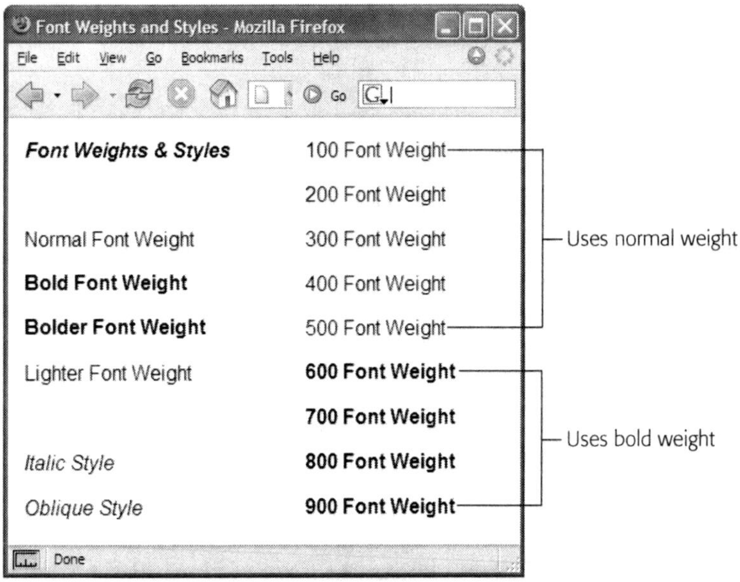

Figure 4-15:
CSS was designed so that each of the nine numeric weight values between 100 and 900 would tweak the thickness of fonts that have many different weights (ultrathin, thin, light, extra bold, and so on). 400 is normal; 700 is the same as bold. However, given the limitations of today's browsers, you'll notice no difference between the values 100 and 500 (top text in right column). Similarly, choosing any of the values from 600 to 900 just gets you bold text (bottom text in right column). You're better off keeping things simple and choosing either "normal" or "bold" when picking a font weight.

in which each letter is inclined a certain number of degrees to the right. In practical application, there's no visible difference between italic and oblique in Web browsers.

- **Variant.** This pop-up menu simply lets you specify small-caps type, if you like—a slightly formal, fancy-looking type style much favored by attorneys' offices.
- **Line Height.** Line height, otherwise known as *leading* (pronounced "LED-ing"), refers to the space between lines of text in a paragraph (see Figure 4-16). To create more space between lines, set the line height greater than the font size. (If you type a number without a % sign, Dreamweaver assumes you're specifying a line height in pixels. You can change the units of measurement using the pop-up menu to the right of the Line Height field.)

Tip: A good approach for line height is to type in a percentage measurement, such as *120%*, which is relative to the size of the text; if your text is 10 pixels tall, the space from the base of one line of text to the next is 12 pixels (120% of 10). Now, if you change the size of the text, the *relative* space between lines remains the same.

"Normal", the default setting (top paragraph in Figure 4-16), uses a line height that's slightly larger than the height of the text. You don't get access to the pop-up menu of measurement units (pixels, points, %, and so on) unless you choose "value" from this menu.

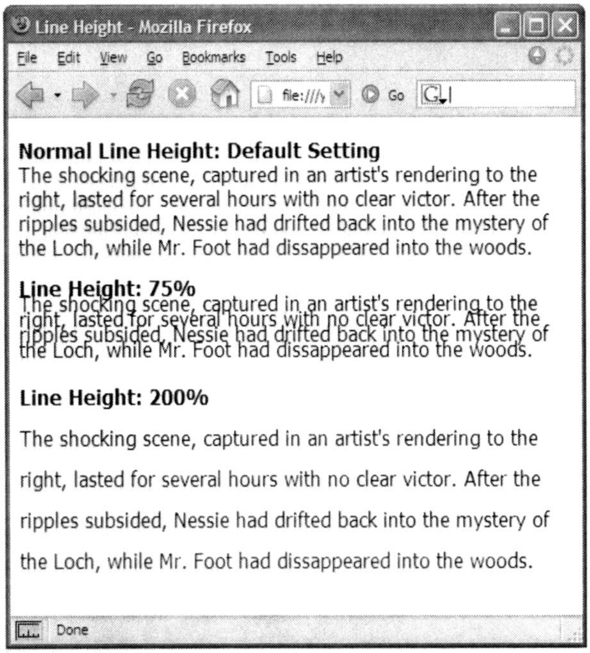

Figure 4-16:
Control the space between lines with the Line Height property in the CSS Rule Definition dialog box. In this example, each paragraph's text is set in 16-pixel Tahoma. With CSS, you can make lines bump into each other by setting a low line-height value (middle paragraph), or spread them far apart by using a larger value (bottom paragraph).

- **Case.** From this menu, you can automatically capitalize text. To capitalize the first letter of each word, choose "capitalize". The "uppercase" option gives you all-capitals typing, while "lowercase" makes all letters lowercase. The factory setting is "none", which has no effect on the text.
- **Decoration.** This strange assortment of five checkboxes lets you dress up your text, mostly in unattractive ways. "Underline", "overline", and "line-through" add horizontal lines below, above, or directly through the affected text, respectively. Turning on "blink" makes affected text blink on and off (but only in a few browsers); unless you want to appear on one of those "worst Web site of the week" lists, avoid it. You can apply any number of decorative types per style, except with "none", which, obviously, you can't choose along with any of the other options. The "none" setting is useful for hiding the underlines that normally appear below links (see page 181).
- **Color.** Set the color of the style's text using Dreamweaver's color box, which is described on page 59.

Block Properties

The Block Properties panel is a hodgepodge of CSS settings that affect how letters and words are displayed (see Figure 4-17).

Tip: To completely remove the space between paragraphs, set the Top and Bottom margin for paragraphs to 0 in the CSS Rule Definition window's Box category. This setting also helps to remove space that appears before and after headlines. To indent paragraphs, set the Left and Right margin properties.

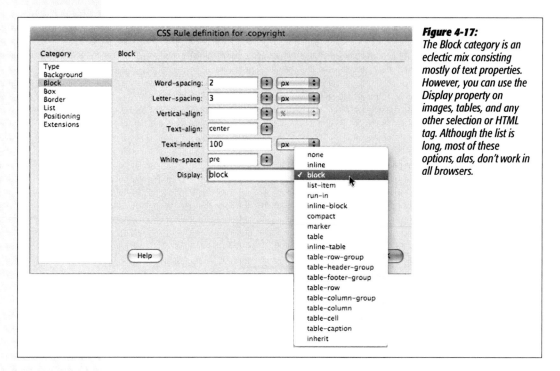

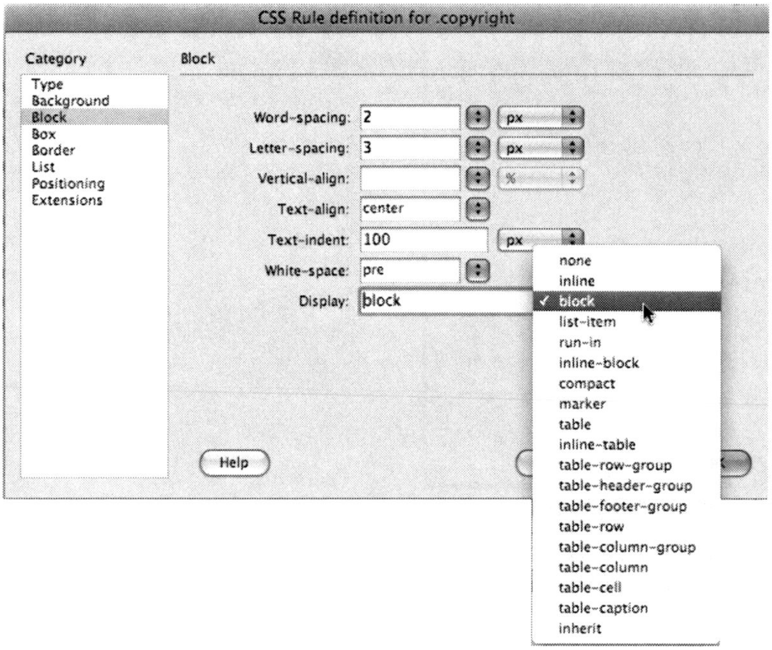

Figure 4-17: *The Block category is an eclectic mix consisting mostly of text properties. However, you can use the Display property on images, tables, and any other selection or HTML tag. Although the list is long, most of these options, alas, don't work in all browsers.*

Despite this category's name, these properties don't just apply to block-level elements (paragraphs, headlines, and so on). You can apply a style with these properties to even a single word or two. (The one exception is the Text Align property, which can apply only to paragraphs and other block-level elements.) Here are your choices:

- **Word spacing.** This property helps you clean up text by adding or removing space *between* words. The default value, "normal", leaves a normal, single space between words. If you want words in a sentence to be spaced   apart   like   this, then type a value of about 10 pixels. (Choose Value from the first pop-up menu, then the units you want from the second one.) The bigger the number, the larger the gap between words. You can also *remove* space between words by using a negative number—a great choice when you want to make your pages difficult to read.

- **Letter spacing.** This property works just like word spacing, but governs the space between *letters*. To add space l i k e t h i s, type a value of about 5 pixels. The result can make long passages of text hard to read, but a little space between letters can add a dramatic flair to short headlines and movie titles.

- **Vertical alignment.** With this property, you can change the vertical placement of an object—such as an image or text—relative to other items around it. For example, you could move text above or below surrounding text to format a trademark, copyright symbol, or footnote reference. The options—"sub" and "super"—can be used in this situation to create subscript and superscript styles. If you wanted to add the trademark symbol to, say, *Chia Pet*™, then you'd select the letters TM and set the vertical alignment to "super". In addition, for more accurate control, you can type a value (like 10%) to raise an object above its normal baseline, or a negative value (like –10% or –5 pixels) to move an object down.

  Vertical alignment also works with graphics, and designers often use the options top, bottom, and middle with HTML table cells to place content within a cell (see page 273 for details on how that works).

Note: The "sub" and "super" alignment options don't change text size. If you want to create true subscript or superscript (for chemical symbols, trademark or copyright symbols, and so on), you should also use a smaller font size in the style; 75% works great.

- **Text align.** This property controls the alignment of a block-level element like a paragraph or table. You can choose from among the usual suspects—"left", "center", "right", or even "justify". (Like the text in this paragraph, justified text has both the left and right edges of the text aligned.)

  Use the "justify" option with care, however. Because Web browsers don't have the advanced controls that page-layout software does, they usually do an awful job of justifying text on a computer screen. The results are often difficult to read, and ugly.

- **Text indent.** This useful option lets you indent the first line of a paragraph. If you enter 15 pixels, each paragraph gets an attractive first-line indent, exactly as in a real word processor.

  You can also use a *negative* number, which makes the first line extend past the *left* margin of the paragraph, creating a hanging indent (or *outdent*)—a nice effect for bulleted lists or glossary pages. If you use a negative number, it's a good idea to set a left-margin (page 343) for the paragraph that equals the value of the negative text indent, otherwise the first line might extend to the left, off the screen!

- **Whitespace.** This property controls how the browser displays extra white space (spaces, tabs, returns, and so on). Web browsers normally ignore extra spaces in the HTML of a page, reducing them to a single space character between words and other elements (see page 77). The "pre" option functions just like the HTML <pre> tag: Extra white space (like tabs, multiple spaces, and carriage returns) *in the HTML code* appear in the document window (see page 97 for more on this option). The "nowrap" option prevents lines from breaking (and wrapping to the next line) when they reach the end of the browser window.

- **Display** defines how a Web browser should display a particular element like a paragraph or a link. The range of choices for this property may overwhelm you—and you may be underwhelmed when you find out that all browsers don't support most of these options.

  The only three options that work reliably across browsers are "none", "inline", and "block". The "block" option treats any item styled with this property as a block—separated from other content by space above and below it. Paragraphs and headings normally appear this way. But you can apply this value to a link (which normally appears inside a block-level element like a paragraph) to turn it into its own block. Usually, you have to click directly on the text or image inside a link to jump to the linked page. But when you set a link's display to "block", its entire width—even areas where no text appears—is clickable.

  The "inline" option treats the item as though it's part of the current block or paragraph, so that any item styled with this property (like a picture) flows together with other items around it, as if it were part of the same paragraph. People frequently use this property to take a bulleted list of links and turn it into a horizontal navigation bar. The Spry Menu bar, discussed on page 184, uses this technique to create a horizontal menu. For a good tutorial on this topic, visit *http://css.maxdesign.com.au/listutorial/horizontal_introduction.htm.*

  The "none" option is the most fun: It turns off the display of an item. In other words, any text or item styled with this option doesn't appear on the page. You can use JavaScript programming to switch this property on and off, making items seem to appear and disappear. In fact, Dreamweaver's Change Property behavior gives you one simple way to do this (see page 593).

List Properties

To exercise greater control over bulleted and numbered lists, use the CSS options in the CSS Rule Definition window's List category (see Figure 4-18).

- **Type.** Select the type of bullet you'd like to use in front of a list item. Options include: "disc", "circle", "square", "decimal" (1., 2., 3.), "lower-roman" (i, ii, iii), "upper-roman" (I, II, III), "lower-alpha" (a, b, c), "upper-alpha" (A, B, C), and "none" (no bullet at all).

- **Bullet image.** For the ultimate control of your bullet icon, skip the boring options preprogrammed into a Web browser (like disc, circle, square, or decimal) and supply your own. Click the Browse button, and then, from your site folder, select a graphics file. Make sure the graphic is appropriate bullet material—in other words, small.

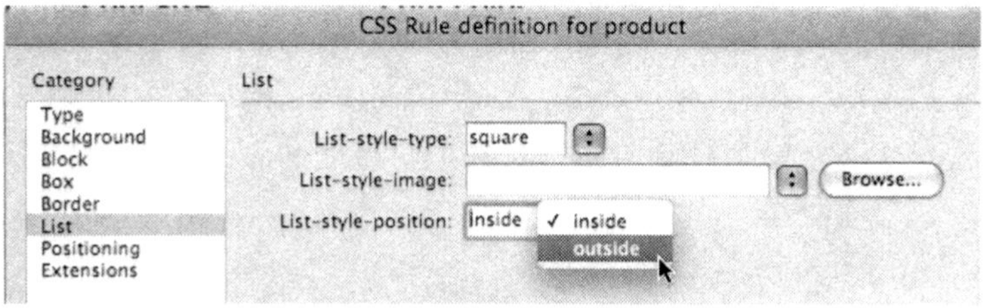

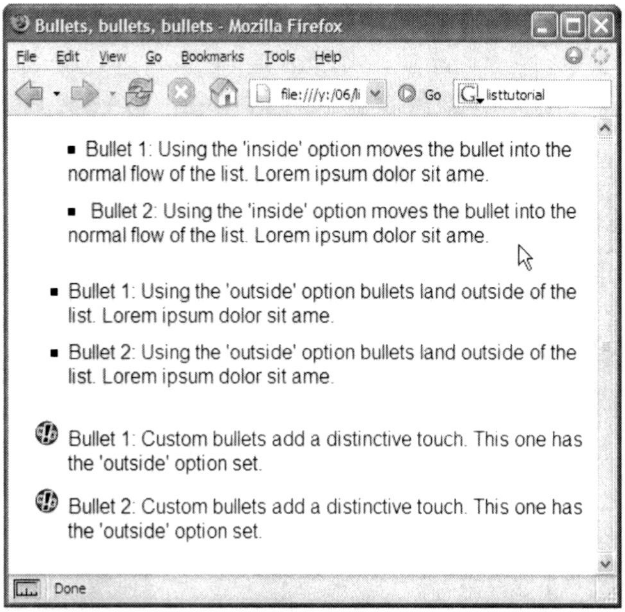

Figure 4-18:
Top: Take control of your bulleted and numbered lists using the CSS Rule Definition window's List category. With Cascading Style Sheets, you can even supply your own graphic bullets.

Bottom: A bullet-crazed Web page, for illustration purposes. Parading down the screen, you can see "inside" bullets, "outside" bullets, and bullets made from graphics.

Tip: The Background Image property (see page 233) is a more versatile solution to adding bullet images to a list. Since you can accurately position a background image, you can easily tweak the placement of your bullets. Here's how to do it: Create a style for the <li> tag (or a class style that you apply to each <li> tag); make sure you set the List property type to "none" (this hides the bullet); set the background image to your graphical bullet; and play with the background position values (page 235). Playing with the padding values (page 343) helps position the text relative to the image.

- **Position.** This property controls how the bullet is placed relative to the list item's text. The "outside" option places the bullet outside the margin of the text, exactly the way bulleted lists normally appear on a Web page. "Inside", on the other hand, displays the bullet within the text margin, so that the left edge of the *bullet* aligns with the left margin; Figure 4-18 should make the effect clearer.

Tip: If you want to adjust the amount of space Web browsers normally use to indent lists, set the left padding property (see page 343) to 0, and set the left margin (see page 48) to the amount of indent you'd like. Sometimes you want no indent at all–for example, if you're creating a list of links that should look like buttons, not bulleted items–set both the left padding and left margin to 0 (while you're at it, set the bullet type to "none" as described above).

Cascading Style Sheets Tutorial

In this tutorial, you'll practice the basic techniques required to create and edit styles. Make sure you grasp the fundamentals covered in the following pages: You'll be building lots of style sheets in the other tutorials throughout this book using these same methods. For this tutorial, you'll create an external style sheet for formatting pages on the Chia Vet Web site.

Note: Before getting started, download the tutorial files from *www.sawmac.com/dwcs4/*. See the Note on page 48 for more details.

Setting Up

Once you've downloaded the tutorial files and opened Dreamweaver, you need to define a site for this tutorial. In the first tutorial back in Chapter 1, you used Dreamweaver's Site Definition Wizard to step you through the process of defining a site. In this tutorial, you'll practice the advanced method that provides the fastest way to define a site and get started working.

1. **Choose Site → New Site.**

   The Site Definition window appears.

2. **Click the Advanced button and, for the Site Name, type *CSS Tutorial.***

   The only other step that's required to define the site is to tell Dreamweaver where the site's files are located on your computer.

3. **To the right of the "Local root folder" box, click the folder icon.**

   The Choose Local Root Folder window appears (see Figure 1-14 on page 41). This is just a window onto your computer's file system; navigate to the proper folder just as you would when working with other programs.

4. **Navigate to and select the Chapter04 folder located in the MM_DWCS4 folder. Click the Select (Choose on Macs) button to select this folder, and then, in the Site Definition window, click OK to complete the process of defining a site.**

   You should see two files—*about.html* and *services.html*—in the Files panel. (If you don't see the Files panel, choose Window → Files to open it.)

Creating an External Style Sheet

In this example, you'll create a collection of styles for the Chia Vet Web site.

1. **Choose File → Open; click the Site Root button (at the lower left of the open file window).**

   The Site Root button is a handy tool. It automatically takes you to the local root folder for the site you're currently working on, saving you the effort of having to manually navigate to that folder.

2. **Double-click the file named *services.html*.**

   The Web page contains a listing of services for the Chia Vet company. The page has a few headline tags and a bunch of paragraphs. The page's text is plain, boring-looking HTML, so you'll use CSS to spiff it up.

   To start, you'll create a style for the first headline.

Tip: You can also open a file by double-clicking its name in the Files panel.

---

3. **Triple-click the headline "Chia Vet Services".**

   This selects the entire headline. You'll now use the Property inspector to select a font.

4. **Make sure the CSS button is pressed in the Property inspector (see Figure 4-4), and then, from the Font menu, choose "Palatino Linotype, Book Antiqua, Palatino, serif".**

   Because you'll be creating a new style, the New CSS Rule window opens (see Figure 4-19). You'll first pick the type of style you wish to create.

5. **From the Selector Type menu at the top of the window, select Tag.**

   This step lets you create a style for a particular HTML tag—in this case, the <h1> tag. In other words, you're going to create a formatting rule that applies automatically to every heading 1 paragraph.

6. **The Selector Name field should have "h1" listed, but if it doesn't, use the middle drop-down menu to select "h1".**

   Next you'll choose where to store the CSS code for this new style—in this case, in an external style sheet.

7. **From the bottom menu, choose New Style Sheet File as pictured in Figure 4-19. Click OK.**

   The Save Style Sheet File As dialog box appears. You're about to create the file—an external style sheet—that stores the styles for this page.

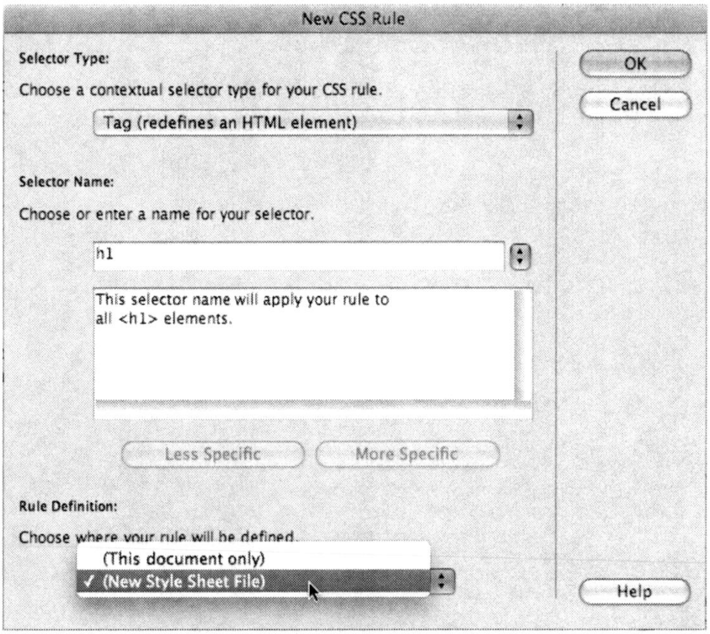

Figure 4-19:
The New CSS Rule window has changed a lot since the last version of Dreamweaver, but the three basic tasks it requires are the same: Pick the type of style you want to create; name the style; and pick where the CSS code should be stored. Notice how the large text box explains what Web page elements the style will apply to–in this case all <h1> tags.

8. **In the File Name box (the Save As field on the Mac), type *global.css,* and then click Save.**

   Cascading Style Sheet files always end in .css; that's how Web servers and browsers can tell what kind of files they are.

   Notice how the headline now uses the new font. You've created a style and added an external style sheet to your site in just a couple steps. Now, you'll add some color.

9. **Make sure the headline is still selected, and then, in the Property inspector's Color field, type *#779A00* (see Figure 4-20).**

   You can use the color box to select a color if you prefer.

   The New CSS Rule window doesn't appear this time, because now you're editing the h1 tag style you created previously. Time to change the size of the font.

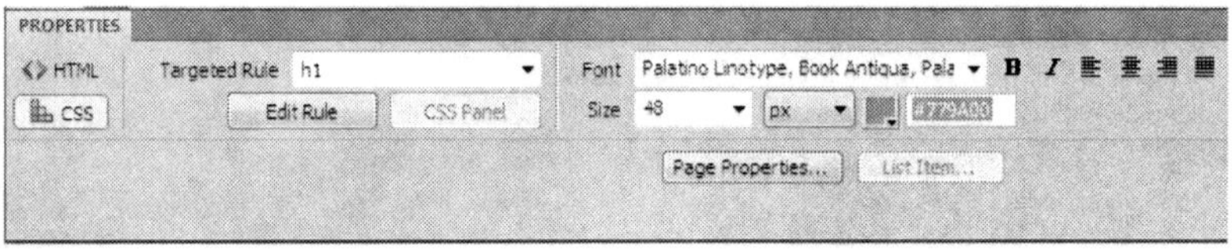

Figure 4-20:
Choosing properties for an element that already has a style applied to it–like the h1 tag style here–updates that style.

Note: If the New CSS Rule window appears again at either steps 9 or 10, something went wrong. Click the Cancel button. You must have accidentally selected some other text–maybe just part of the headline–before using the Property inspector. To get back on track, triple-click the top headline again, and then repeat step 9 or 10.

10. **In the Property inspector's Size box, type *48*.**

    The Property inspector should now look like Figure 4-20. You've just set the font size to 48 pixels tall. You've pretty much reached the limit of what the Property inspector is capable of, but you've barely scratched the surface of Cascading Styles Sheets. In the next part of this tutorial, you'll learn how to edit a style and access the wide range of formatting options that CSS offers.

Editing a Style

1. **Make sure the CSS Styles panel is open (Window → CSS Styles), and make sure the All button is selected at the top of the panel.**

   This displays all the style sheets attached to this page (in this case, just *global.css*).

2. **If it isn't already, expand the list of styles in the *global.css* style sheet by clicking the + icon (arrow on the Mac) to the left of "global.css".**

   This lists all the styles you've added to the external style sheet—just the one h1 tag style at this point.

3. **In the list, double-click "h1".**

   This action opens the CSS Rule Definition window where you can access a wide range of CSS properties (see Figure 4-21). First, you'll remove the bold formatting from the headline.

4. **From the Font-Weight menu, choose "normal", and then click the Apply button.**

   You can preview the look of a tag style without closing the CSS Rule Definition window by clicking the Apply button—just drag the window out of the way of the headline.

   When formatting text, you can use many other non-text related CSS properties. For example, you can add border lines to any element on a page.

5. **In the category list, click Border.**

   The CSS Rule Definition window now displays all the properties used to put a border around a style. You can control each border individually, or use the same line style for all four edges. In this case, you'll add lines to just the top and bottom of the headline.

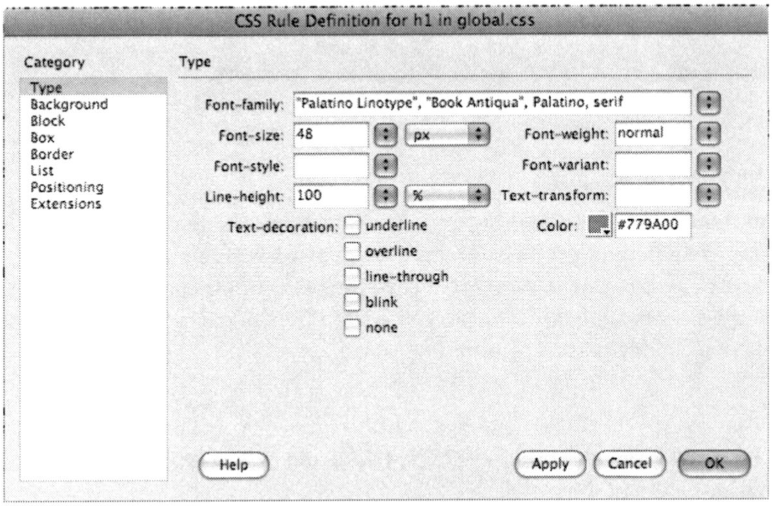

Figure 4-21: *The CSS Rule Definition window provides access to many more CSS properties than the Property inspector. In addition, you have to use the Font-weight menu to remove bold formatting from a heading tag–no matter how many times you click the B button on the Property inspector, you can't remove bold from headlines.*

6. **Click to turn off all three "Same for all" checkboxes. For the Top border, choose "solid" from the Style menu, type *7* in the Width box, and type *#F93* in the color box. For the Bottom border, choose "solid" from the Style menu, type *2* in the Width box, and type *#F93* in the color box.**

   The window should now look like Figure 4-22. As mentioned on page 59, #F93 is shorthand for #FF9933. If you click the Apply button now, you may notice that the top border is a little too close to the top of the headline. You can add a little breathing room using the CSS Padding property.

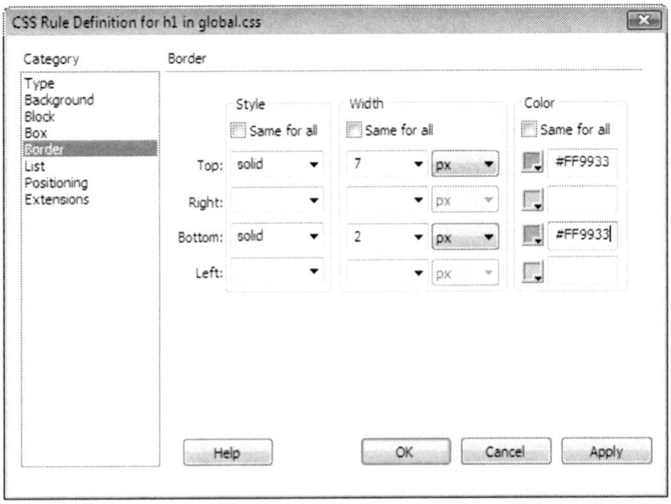

Figure 4-22: *Use the Border properties to add rules to any or all of the four edges of an object. You can emphasize a headline by underlining it, or give an image a stylish border around its edges.*

Note: When typing a hex color value for a CSS property (for example, *#779A00*), don't forget the # symbol. Without it, the color doesn't appear.

7. **In the Rule Definition window, click the Box category. Uncheck the "Same for all" box underneath Padding, and then, in the Top padding box, type** *5*.

   Padding is the space between the edge of an element (where the border appears) and the stuff inside the element (like text). In this case, adding 5 pixels of top padding adds 5 pixels of space between the top border line and the headline's text. You'll learn more about padding on page 343.

8. **Click OK to close the window and complete editing the style.**

   Now you have a distinctive looking headline. But you've just started building styles for this page.

9. **Choose File → Save All.**

   The Save All command can be a real lifesaver when working with external style sheets. Even though you're looking at and working on the Web page (*services.html*), each time you add a style, Dreamweaver updates the external style sheet file (*global.css*). So most of the work you've done so far in this tutorial has caused Dreamweaver to update the *global.css* file. Unfortunately, the regular keyboard shortcut to save a file, Ctrl+S (⌘-S), saves only changes to the Web page (the file currently visible to you). Make sure you invoke the Save All command frequently, otherwise if Dreamweaver or your computer crashes, you could lose all the changes you've made to an external style sheet. (You can even set your own keyboard command for the Save All command. See page 799 for details.)

Adding Another Style

The Property inspector isn't the only way to create a style—in fact, since it offers only a limited number of formatting options, it isn't even the best way to create a style. The CSS Styles panel provides a faster method with more comprehensive choices.

1. **At the bottom of the CSS Styles panel, click the New Style button (the + button pictured in Figure 4-1).**

   The New CSS Rule window appears. You'll be creating another tag style for the heading 2 tag.

2. **From the top menu, choose Tag; in the Selector Name field, type** *h2* **(or select "h2" from the menu); and, in the bottom menu, make sure "global.css" is selected. Click OK.**

   This action adds a new tag style to the *global.css* style sheet. You'll set a few text properties next.

3. **From the Font-family menu, choose "Palatino Linotype, Book Antiqua, Palatino, serif".**

   You'll use the same font as the heading 1, but you'll change its size and color.

4. **In the Size box, type *24* and, in the Color box, type *#EC6206*.**

   This action creates medium-sized, orange text. To make the headline stand out a bit, you'll make all the text uppercase. Fortunately, you don't have to hold down the caps-lock button and retype each headline to make them uppercase—there's a CSS property that can do that for you.

5. **From the Text-transform menu, choose uppercase.**

   One problem with this design is the large gap between the subheads and the paragraphs following them. The heading 2 paragraphs ("Preventative Care", for example) introduce the paragraph that follows. Removing the gap that appears between the heading and the following paragraph would visually tie the two together better. To make this change, you must first remove the margin below each headline.

6. **In the left hand list of CSS categories, select Box. In the Margin area, turn off the "Same for all" checkbox; in the Bottom box, type *0*.**

   This action should remove any space that appears below the heading 2 tags.

7. **Click OK to close the Rule Definition window and finish editing the style.**

   The space between the headlines and the paragraphs hasn't changed a bit. What gives? Paragraphs and headlines have space both above *and* below. The space you're seeing is actually the *top* margin of the paragraph tag.

   Top and bottom margins have a peculiar feature: They don't add up like 1+1=2. In other words, the bottom margin of the heading 2 isn't added to the top margin of the paragraph in order to calculate the total space between the two blocks of text. Instead, a Web browser uses the margin with the *largest* value to determine the space between paragraphs (a lot of text layout programs, including word processors, share this behavior).

   For example, say the <h2> tag has a bottom margin of 12 pixels, while the paragraph following has a top margin of 10 pixels. The total space between the two isn't 22 pixels (10+12)—it's 12 pixels (the value of the larger margin). So, if you remove the top margin of the paragraph, the gap between the two blocks of text is still 12 pixels (the h2's bottom margin). That's exactly what's happening here, so you need to modify the paragraphs' margins. You can do that by creating another style.

8. **In the CSS Styles Panel, click the New Style button.**

   The New CSS Rule window appears. You'll create a tag style to control the formatting of paragraphs.

9. **From the top menu, choose Tag; in the Selector Name box, type *p*, and then, in the bottom menu, make sure "global.css" is selected. Click OK to create the style.**

Before getting to that pesky margin, first set some basic type options.

10. **From the Font-family menu, choose "Trebuchet MS, Arial, Helvetica, sans-serif", and then, in the Font-size box, type *14*.**

CSS provides a lot of control over type, including the ability to adjust the leading, or space, between lines in a paragraph.

11. **In the Line-height box, type *150*, and then, from the pop-up menu to the right, choose %.**

The line-height property controls the space between lines of text. In this case, you've set that space to 150%, which means that each line will be 150% (or 1.5 times) the size of the font. A setting of 150% adds more space than usual between each line of text in a paragraph—the result is more white space and a more luxurious feel.

Now back to that margin problem.

12. **Click the Box category; in the Margin section, uncheck the "Same for all" box. Type *5* in the Top box, and *75* in the Left box.**

The window should now look like Figure 4-23. The 5 pixel top margin adds just a small amount of space between the paragraph and the <h2> tag above it—completely removing all space between the two would make them seem crowded together. The 75 pixel left margin is just for fun. This margin indents the paragraphs from the left edge of the page by 75 pixels, creating a distinctive look that makes the heading 2 paragraphs stand out more.

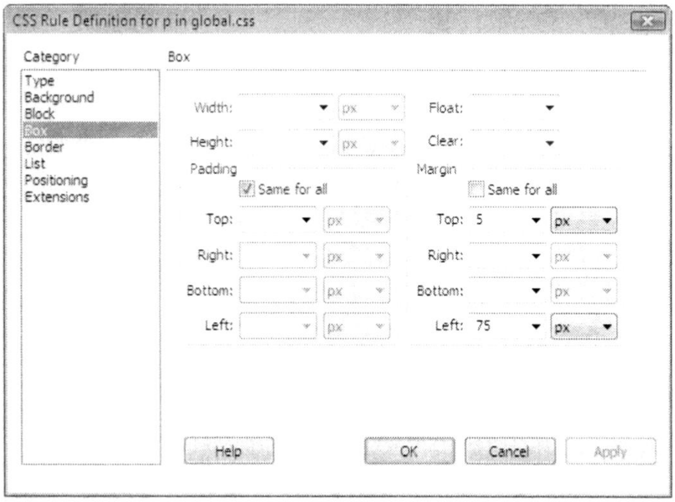

Figure 4-23:
To remove space that appears above a paragraph, a headline, or other block of text, set the top margin to 0. To completely remove the space that appears between paragraphs, set the bottom margin to 0 as well.

13. **Click OK; choose File → Save All.**

The page is nearly complete. Just one more style to create.

Creating a Class Style

Now you'll create a style to format the copyright notice at the bottom of the page. It's inside a regular paragraph (<p> tag), so it's getting all its formatting from the p tag style. Here's an instance where you'd like to style a single paragraph, without affecting the other paragraphs on the page. A class style is perfect for this kind of specific styling task.

1. **On the CSS Styles panel, click the New CSS Style button** (+).

   The New CSS Rule window opens. This time, you'll create a class style rather than an HTML tag style.

2. **From the top menu, select Class. In the Selector Name box, type *.copyright* (with a period before it).**

   Class styles always begin with a period—however, if you leave it out, Dreamweaver puts the period in there for you.

Note: Some beginners think that whenever you create a new style, you also need to create a new external Style Sheet. On the contrary, you can–and should–store more than one style in a single external style sheet. In fact, if you're creating a set of styles for an entire site, put them all in the same external style sheet.

---

3. **Make sure "global.css" is selected in the bottom menu, and then click OK.**

   You're adding yet another style to the external style sheet you created at the beginning of this tutorial. The CSS Rule Definition window appears. You'll add a few new properties to make this style look different from the rest of the text on the page.

4. **In the size box, type *12*; from the Font-weight menu, choose "bold"; and for the Color, type *#666666* or use the Color box to select a gray color.**

   The smaller text and lighter gray color make the copyright less prominent on the page; the bold setting makes it stand out from the other paragraphs. Finally, you'll add a line above the copyright to separate it from the page.

5. **In the category list, click Border.**

   The CSS Rule Definition window now displays all the properties used to put a border around a style. In this case, you'll add a line above the copyright notice.

6. **Click to turn off all three "Same for all" checkboxes. For the Top border, choose "dashed" from the Style menu, type *1* in the Width box, and type *#93BD00* in the color box.**

   You have several different styles of borderlines, including dashed (see page 231 for the different types of borders). Lastly, you'll add a little space between the border and the text.

7. **In the left hand list of CSS categories, click the Box category. Uncheck the "Same for all" box in the Padding area, and then, in the Top box, type *5*.**

   While margins control the space between elements (like the gap between paragraphs), *padding* controls the space from the content to the content's border. In other words, adding padding pushes a border further away from the text (or other content) you're styling.

   You'll change the copyright notice's margin settings as well.

8. **In the Margin area, uncheck the "Same for all" box, and then type *25* in the Top box and *0* in the Left box.**

   The window should look like Figure 4-24. The 25 pixels of top margin pushes the copyright notice away from the bottom of the paragraph of text above it. In addition, since all the paragraphs are indented 75 pixels from the left edge, you need to set the left margin of the copyright notice to 0. This action essentially overrides the 75 pixel margin from the p tag style and lets the copyright notice hug the left edge of the page.

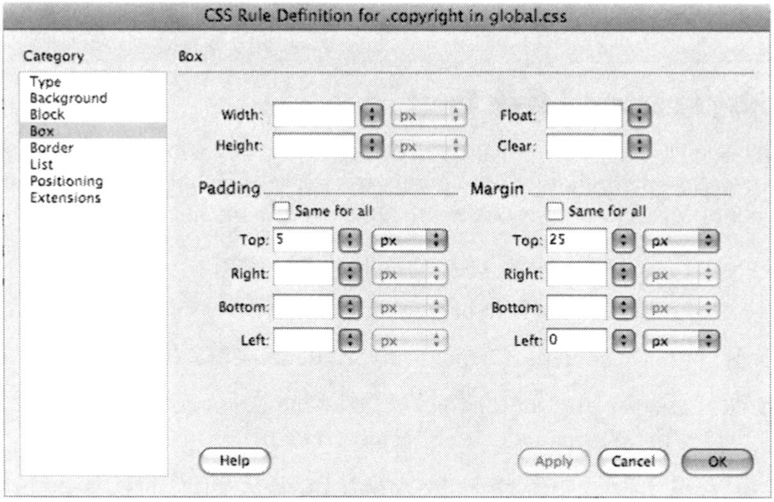

***Figure 4-24:** The difference between padding and margin is subtle, but important. Both properties add space around the content that's being styled. And if you don't have a background color, image, or border, both properties pretty much act the same. However, when you do have a background color, image, or border, padding adds space between the content and the edge of the backgrounds and borders. Margins add space outside the border and background.*

9. **Click OK.**

   The Rule Definition window closes, but this time, nothing's changed in the document window. Unlike HTML tag styles, class styles don't show up anywhere until you apply them by hand.

10. **Scroll to the bottom of the page, and select the last paragraph with the copyright notice.**

    This action sets you up for applying the style. You can also just click anywhere inside the paragraph (without selecting any text) to apply a class style to it.

11. **In the Property inspector, click the HTML button, and then, from the Class menu, choose "copyright" (see Figure 4-25).**

    Boom—the copyright notice suddenly changes size, color, and grows a line above it. Magic. You may also notice that the copyright still uses the same font as the other paragraphs. In fact, it has "inherited" that font type from the p tag style—you'll learn about inheritance, an advanced CSS concept, on page 312.

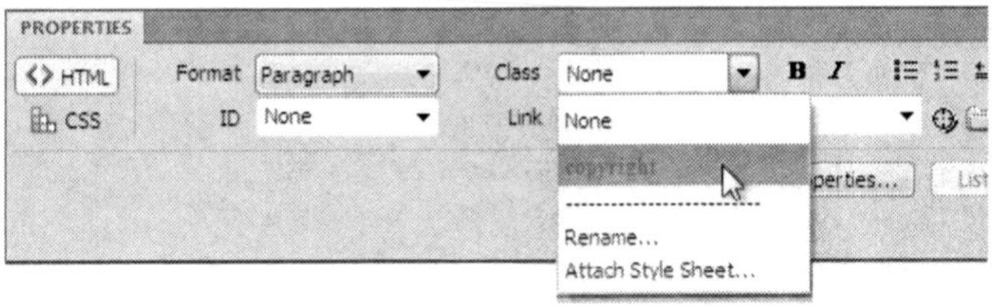

Figure 4-25: *The Class menu in the HTML mode of the Property inspector lists all class styles. It also displays the style name using the style's text formatting–in this case, bold, gray text. Notice that only class styles are listed; tag styles don't appear in this menu, since you don't apply them manually. You can also apply a class using the Property inspector's CSS Mode as described on page 122.*

Attaching an External Style Sheet

Now that you've created these styles, you may be wondering how you can use them on other pages—after all, that's the beauty of external style sheets. Once created, it's a simple process to add a style sheet to other pages in the site.

1. **Choose File → Save All; close the *services.html* Web page.**

   You'll need to open a new Web page to attach the external style sheet.

2. **Choose File → Open. In the Chapter04 folder, double-click the file *about.html*.**

   This file is another page for the Chia Vet Web site. It has no formatting yet, so you'll attach the external style sheet you just created.

3. **On the CSS Styles panel, click the Attach External Style Sheet button (see Figure 4-1).**

   The Link External Style Sheet window appears.

4. **Click the Browse button.**

   The Select Style Sheet dialog box appears.

5. **Navigate to the Chapter04 folder (or click the Site Root button), and then double-click the *global.css* file.**

   Don't forget the Site Root button. It appears on every window in which you need to save, open, or select a file. It's a great shortcut to make sure you're working in the correct folder for your site.

   You can ignore the other settings in the Attach External Style Sheet window for now (they're described on page 125).

6. **Click OK to attach the style sheet to the page.**

   Dreamweaver instantly formats the headlines and main text of the story. Pretty cool—and very efficient. You need to apply the *.copyright* class style only to the last paragraph on the page.

7. **Scroll to the bottom of the page, and then click anywhere inside the paragraph with the copyright notice.**

   Next you'll add a style to the tag.

8. **From the Class menu on the Property inspector, select "copyright" (see Figure 4-25).**

   This page is done. Time to view it.

9. **Press F12 (Option-F12 on Mac) to preview the page.**

   Dreamweaver probably prompts you to save your files; go ahead and do that. The finished page should look something like Figure 4-26. If you'd like to compare your finished product to the completed version, you'll find those pages in the Chapter04_finished folder in the tutorials folder.

Note: You may need to hit your browser's refresh button to see the most recent changes you made to the style sheet. This is one problem related to designing with external style sheets—they're often *cached* by a Web browser (see page 666). Normally that's a good thing—it means visitors to your site have to wait only once for the file to download. But when you're in the midst of a design, frantically switching back and forth between Dreamweaver and a Web browser preview, the browser might retrieve the older version of the external style sheet that's saved in its cache, rather than the newly updated file on your computer.

You can work around this problem: Open the Preferences window (Edit → Preferences [Dreamweaver → Preferences on Mac]); select the "Preview in Browser" category, and then turn on the "Preview using temporary file" box. Now, when you preview the page, Dreamweaver actually makes a temporary file on your computer that incorporates both the CSS and HTML of the page. This defeats a browser's cache so that now you're seeing the very latest changes. This setting has the added benefit of stopping Dreamweaver's annoying "You must save your file before previewing" dialog box each time you preview a page.

About Chia Vet - Windows Internet Explorer
About Chia Vet
Page
Tools
About Chia Vet
Vivamus in turpis ac nunc scelerisque dapibus. Lorem ipsum dolor sit amet, consectetuer adipiscing elit. Morbi commodo ante quis odio. Quisque auctor mauris id urna. Duis nec risus. Cras facilisis. Morbi fringilla consectetuer pede. Ut sodales sagittis sem. Sed dolor nibh, consectetuer vel, condimentum luctus, tempus ut, tellus. In erat. Nulla non odio non justo gravida fringilla. Cras vitae purus. Pellentesque a pede vitae ante tincidunt venenatis. Cras molestie. Nam sed libero. Curabitur facilisis, ligula elementum rhoncus vulputate, nulla massa facilisis purus, non laoreet felis neque sed ante.
OUR INCREDIBLE TRUE STORY
Vivamus in turpis ac nunc scelerisque dapibus. Lorem ipsum dolor sit amet, consectetuer adipiscing elit. Morbi commodo ante quis odio. Quisque auctor mauris id urna. Duis nec risus. Cras facilisis. Morbi fringilla consectetuer pede. Ut sodales sagittis sem. Sed dolor nibh, consectetuer vel, condimentum luctus, tempus ut, tellus. In erat. Nulla non odio non justo gravida fringilla. Cras vitae purus. Pellentesque a pede vitae ante tincidunt venenatis. Cras molestie. Nam sed libero. Curabitur facilisis, ligula elementum rhoncus vulputate, nulla massa facilisis purus, non laoreet felis neque sed ante.
THE EARLY YEARS
Vivamus in turpis ac nunc scelerisque dapibus. Lorem ipsum dolor sit amet, consectetuer adipiscing elit. Morbi commodo ante quis odio. Quisque auctor mauris id urna. Duis nec risus. Cras facilisis. Morbi fringilla consectetuer pede. Ut sodales sagittis sem. Sed dolor nibh, consectetuer vel, condimentum luctus, tempus ut, tellus. In erat. Nulla non odio non justo gravida fringilla. Cras vitae purus. Pellentesque a pede vitae ante tincidunt venenatis. Cras molestie. Nam sed libero. Curabitur facilisis, ligula elementum rhoncus vulputate, nulla massa facilisis purus, non laoreet felis neque sed ante.
A COPORATE DYNASTY
Ut sodales sagittis sem. Sed dolor nibh, consectetuer vel, condimentum luctus, tempus ut, tellus. In erat. Nulla non odio non justo gravida fringilla. Cras vitae purus. Pellentesque a pede vitae ante tincidunt venenatis. Cras molestie. Nam sed libero. Curabitur facilisis, ligula elementum rhoncus vulputate, nulla massa facilisis purus, non laoreet felis neque sed ante.
Done
Internet | Protected Mode: On
100%

Figure 4-26: *CSS offers a lot of design tools to produce beautiful typography for your Web pages. In addition, an external style sheet lets you quickly, easily and consistently add style to hundreds of pages without much work.*

CHAPTER

5

Links

The humble hyperlink may not raise eyebrows anymore, but the notion that you can navigate a whole sea of information, jumping from one island of content to another with a simple click, is a very recent and powerful invention. Interested in a particular band? Go to Google, type in the band's name, *click* to go to its Web site, *click* to go to the page that lists its upcoming gigs, *click* to go to the Web site for the club where the band is currently playing, and *click* to buy tickets.

Although links are a basic part of building pages, and although Dreamweaver—for the most part—shields you from their complexities, they can be tricky to understand. The following section provides a brief overview of links, including some of the technical distinctions between the different types. The rest of the chapter helps turn you into a link-crafting maestro, with sections on formatting the appearance of your links and on creating a navigation menu.

Note: If you already understand links, or are just eager to start using Dreamweaver, jump to "Adding a Link" on page 167.

Understanding Links

A link is a snippet of code that gives a Web browser directions for how to get from one page to another on the Web. What makes links powerful is that the distance covered by those directions doesn't matter. A link can just as easily lead to another page on the same site as to a page on a Web server halfway around the globe.

Behind the scenes, a simple HTML tag called the anchor (<a>) tag makes each and every link work. Links come in three different flavors: *absolute, document-relative,* and *root-relative*. See page 165 for some examples of each link type in practice.

Absolute Links

When people want to mail you a letter, they ask for your address. Suppose it's 123 Main St., Smithville, NY 12001. No matter where in the country your friends are, if they write *123 Main St., Smithville, NY 12001* on an envelope and mail it, their letters will get to you. That's because your address is unique—just like an absolute link.

Similarly, every Web page has a unique address, called a *URL* (most people pronounce it "you are el"), or Uniform Resource Locator. If you open a Web browser and type *http://www.sawmac.com/dwcs4/index.html* into the address bar, the home page for this book opens.

This URL is an *absolute link*—it's the complete, unique address for a single page. Absolute links always begin with *http://*, and you'll use them any time you link to a Web page *outside of your own site*. An absolute link always leads to the same page, whether the link to it is on a page in the current site or an entirely different site.

The bottom line: use absolute links when you want to link to a page on another Web site.

Document-Relative Links

Suppose you, the resident of 123 Main Street, drop in on a couple who just moved into the neighborhood. After letting them know about all the great restaurants nearby, you tell them about a party you're having at your place.

When they ask you where you live, you could say, "I live at 123 Main St., Smithville, NY 12001," but your neighbors would probably think you needed a little psychiatric help. Instead, you'd say something like, "Just go across the street and turn left. I'm the second house on the right." Of course, you can't use these instructions as your mailing address, because they only make sense from your neighbor's house.

When you want to create a link from one Web page to another within the same Web site, you can use similar shorthand: a *document-relative link*. In essence, a document-relative link—like the directions you give your neighbor—simply tells the browser where to find the linked page *relative* to the current page. If two pages are in the same folder, for instance, the path is as simple as "Go to that page over there." In this case, the link is simply the name of the file you wish to link to: *index.html*, for example. You can leave off all that *http://www.your_site.com/* business, because you're already there.

Document-relative links can be finicky, however, because they're completely dependent on the location of the page containing the link. If you move the page to another part of the site—filing it in a different folder, for example—the link won't work.

That's why working with document-relative links has traditionally been one of the most troublesome chores for Web designers, even though this kind of link is ideal for linking from one page to another in the same site.

Fortunately, Dreamweaver makes working with document-relative links so easy, you may forget what all the fuss is about. Whenever you save a page in a different folder—a maneuver that would normally shatter all document-relative links on the page—Dreamweaver quietly *rewrites* the links so they still work. Even better, using the program's site management tools, you can cavalierly reorganize your Web site, moving files and folders without harming the delicate connections between your site's files. Dreamweaver's site management features are discussed in depth in Part 4.

Root-Relative Links

Root-relative links describe how to get from one page to another within the same site, just like document-relative links. However, in this case, the path is described relative to the site's *root folder*—the folder that contains the home page and other pages, folders, and files that make up your site. (For a detailed description of the root folder and structuring a Web site, see Chapter 15.)

Imagine you work in a big office building. You need to get to a co-worker's office in the same building for a meeting, so you call her for directions. She may not know the precise directions from your office to hers, but she can tell you how to get from the building's entrance to her office. Since you both know where the building's front door is, these directions work well. In fact, she can give the same directions to anyone else in the building, and since they know where the entrance is, they'll be able to find her office, too. Think of the office building as your site, and its front door as the *root* of your site. Root-relative links always begins with a slash (/). This slash is a stand-in character for the root folder—the front door—of the site. The same root-relative link always leads to the same page, no matter where it is on your Web site.

If you use Dreamweaver for all your Web page development, you probably won't need root-relative links, but they can come in handy. For example, suppose you're asked to create a new page for an existing Web site. Your client gives you text, some graphics, and a list of the other pages on the site that this page needs to link to. The problem is, your client doesn't know where on the site the new page needs to go, and his Webmaster won't return your calls.

Fortunately, you can use root-relative links to solve this dilemma. Since these links work no matter where the page is on your site, you could complete the page and let the client put it where it belongs—the links will still work.

But there's one major drawback to using root-relative links in Dreamweaver: They don't work when you test them on your own computer. If you view a Web page sitting on your computer's hard drive, clicking a root-relative link in a Web browser either doesn't work, or produces only a "File not found" error. Such links work only after the files that contain them are moved to a Web server. Web servers understand root-relative links, but your personal computer doesn't.

UP TO SPEED

Parts of a URL

Each chunk of a URL helps a Web browser locate the proper Web page. Take the following URL, for instance: *http://www.sawmac.com/dwcs4/index.html*.

- **http://**. This portion specifies the *protocol*: the method the Web browser must use to communicate with the Web server. *HTTP* stands for *hypertext transfer protocol*. HTTP specifies a connection to a Web page, as opposed to protocols like *ftp* (for transferring files) and *mailto* (for email addresses).
- *www.sawmac.com*. This specifies the computer that's dishing out the Web site in question—that is, it's the address of the Web *server*. The www part identifies a Web site within the *domain* sawmac.com. It's possible to have multiple Web sites in a single domain, such as *news.sawmac.com*, *secret.sawmac.com*, and so on.
- **/dwcs4/**. This is the name of a folder (also called a directory) on the Web server.
- **index.html**. This is the name of the actual document or file that the Web browser is supposed to open—the Web page itself. These are the HTML documents that Dreamweaver creates.

One solution to this problem is to install a Web server on your computer and put your site files inside it. This is the approach you take when building the dynamic sites discussed in Part 6 of this book.

Note: There's one exception to the "root relative links don't preview correctly" dilemma. Dreamweaver provides two ways of previewing a Web page: *with* a temporary file or *without* one. The temporary-file option has a couple of advantages: You can preview a page without having to save it first, and you can preview—on your local computer—any root-relative links you've created. To turn this feature on, open Preferences (Edit → Preferences or, on a Mac, Dreamweaver → Preferences), click the "Preview in Browser" category, and turn on the Preview Using Temporary File checkbox. Behind the scenes, Dreamweaver secretly rewrites root-relative links as *document relative* links whenever it creates a temporary file. If you see files in your site with weird names like TMP2zlc3mvs10.htm, those are the temporary files Dreamweaver creates. Feel free to delete them.

Unless you have a specific reason to use root-relative links (like your IT department says you have to), it's best to stick to document-relative links for your pages, but keep this discussion in mind. You'll see later that Dreamweaver's site management features use root-relative paths to track your site's files behind the scenes.

Note: You can run into trouble with root-relative links if the site you're working on isn't located in the Web server root folder. For example, say your buddy gives you space on his Web server. He says you can put your site in a folder called *my_friend*, so your URL is *www.my_buddy.com/my_friend/*. In this case, your Web pages don't sit at the root of the site—they're in a folder *inside* the root. So a root-relative link to your home page would be */my_friend/index.html*. Dreamweaver can handle this situation, but only if you provide the correct URL of your site—*http://www.my_buddy.com/my_friend*—in either the first screen of the New Site wizard (see step 3 on page 39), or in the HTTP address box on the Advanced tab of the New Site window (see Figure 5-1).

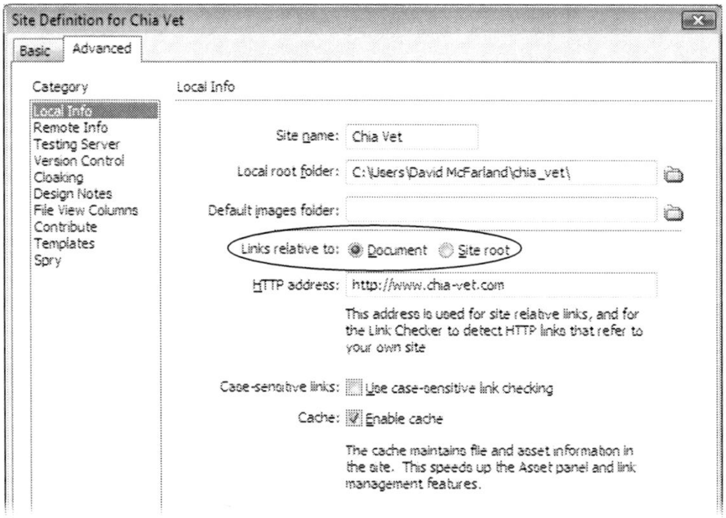

Figure 5-1: *When defining a site in Dreamweaver, you can identify the URL of the site you're working on–its actual address on the Internet–using the HTTP address box. You can also tell Dreamweaver which type of link–document-relative or site root-relative–it should use when creating a link to another page on your site (circled). You can always return to this window if you want to change this option: Choose Site → Manage Sites, select your site, and then click Edit.*

Link Types in Action

Figure 5-2 shows a Web site as it appears on a hard drive: folders filled with HTML documents and graphics. Here's a closer look at some links you might find on those pages, and how they might work.

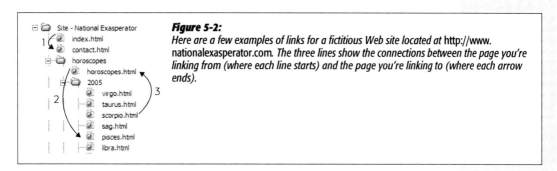

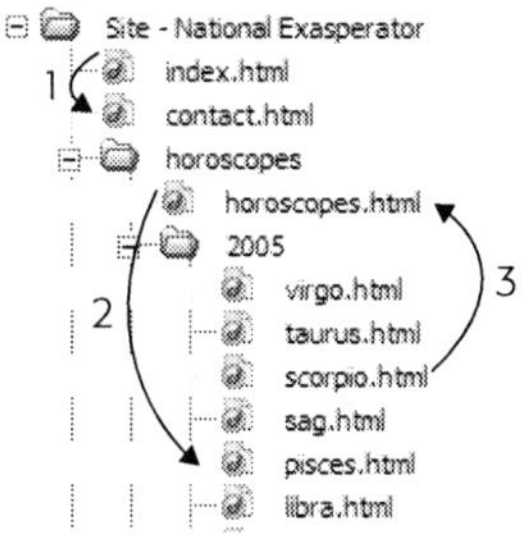

Figure 5-2: *Here are a few examples of links for a fictitious Web site located at* http://www.nationalexasperator.com*. The three lines show the connections between the page you're linking from (where each line starts) and the page you're linking to (where each arrow ends).*

Link from the Home page (index.html) to the Contact Us page (contact.html)

The home page document is usually called *index.html* or *index.htm*. (The exact name depends on the configuration of your Web server. Contact your Web host, or the person in charge of your Web server, to confirm the file name you need to use for your Web server.) You could create the link from it to the *contact.html* page—identified by the number 1 in Figure 5-2—using any of the three link types:

- **Absolute:** *http://www.nationalexasperator.com/contact.html*. What it means: Go to the Web site at *http://www.nationalexasperator.com* and download the page *contact.html*.

- **Document-Relative:** *contact.html*. What it means: Look in the same folder as the current page and download the page *contact.html*.
- **Root-Relative:** */contact.html*. What it means: Go to the top-level folder of this site and download *contact.html*.

Tip: If you can write an absolute URL, you can easily create a root-relative URL. Simply strip off the *http://* and the Web server name. In the example above, erasing the *http://www.nationalexasperator.com* in the absolute address leaves */contact.html*—the root-relative path.

Link from the Horoscopes page to the Pisces page

Now imagine you're building a Web page and you wish to link it to another page that's inside a subfolder on your site. Here's how you'd use each of the three link types to open a document that's nested in a subfolder (called 2005, in this case), as identified by the number 2 in Figure 5-2:

- **Absolute:** *http://www.nationalexasperator.com/horoscopes/2005/pisces.html*. What it means: Go to the Web site at *http://www.nationalexasperator.com*, look in the folder *horoscopes*, then in the folder *2005*, and download the page *pisces.html*.
- **Document-Relative:** *2005/pisces.html*. What it means: From the current page, look in the folder *2005* and download the page *pisces.html*.
- **Root-Relative:** */horoscopes/2005/pisces.html*. What it means: Go to the top-level folder of this site, look in the folder *horoscopes*, then in the folder *2005*, and download the page *pisces.html*.

Link from the Scorpio page to the Horoscopes page

Now suppose you're building a Web page that's in a deeply nested folder, and you want it to link to a document that's outside of its folder, like the link labeled 3 in Figure 5-2:

- **Absolute:** *http://www.nationalexasperator.com/horoscopes/horoscopes.html*. What it means: Go to the Web site at *http://www.nationalexasperator.com*, look in the folder *horoscopes*, and download the page *horoscopes.html*.
- **Document-Relative:** *../horoscopes.html*. What it means: Go up one level—outside of the current folder—and download the page *horoscopes.html*. In links, a slash / represents a folder or directory. The two dots (..) mean, "Go up one level," into the folder that *contains* the current folder. So to link to a page that's up two levels—for example, to link from the *scorpio.html* page to the home page (*index.html*)—you would use ../ twice, like this: *../../index.html*.
- **Root-Relative:** */horoscopes/horoscopes.html*. What it means: Go to the top-level folder of this site, look in the folder *horoscopes*, and download the page *horoscopes.html*.

Executive Summary

In short: Use absolute URLs to link *outside* your site, use document-relative links for links *within your site*, and, unless you know what you're doing (or your IT department tells you you have to), avoid using root-relative links altogether.

Adding a Link

If all that talk of links got you confused, don't worry. Links *are* confusing, and that's one of the best reasons to use Dreamweaver. If you can navigate to a document on your own computer or anywhere on the Web, you can create a link to it in Dreamweaver, even if you don't know the first thing about URLs and don't intend to learn the details of how they're configured.

Browsing for a File

To create a link from one page to another on your own Web site, use the Property inspector's "Browse for File" button (see Figure 5-3) or its keyboard shortcut, as described in the following steps.

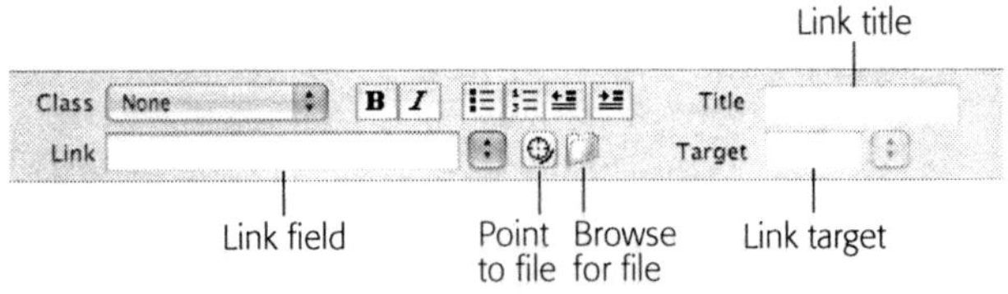

Figure 5-3: *The Property inspector provides three ways to add links to a Web page: the Link field, "Point to file" tool, and "Browse for file" button.*

To browse for a file in Dreamweaver, you use the same type of dialog box that you use to open or save a file, making "Browse for File" the easiest way to add a link. (To link to a page on *another* Web site, you'll need to type the Web address into the Property inspector. Turn to page 171 for instructions.)

1. **In the document window, select the text or image you want to use for the link.**

   You can select a single word, a sentence, or an entire paragraph. When this process is over, the selected words will show up blue and underlined (depending on your visitors' Web browser settings), like billions of links before them.

   In addition, you can turn a picture into a link—a great trick for adding attractive navigation buttons.

2. **In the Property inspector, click the folder icon—that's the "Browse for File" button.**

   Or, choose Modify → Make Link, or press Ctrl+L (⌘-L). In any case, the Select File dialog box opens (see Figure 5-4 for Windows, Figure 5-5 for Mac).

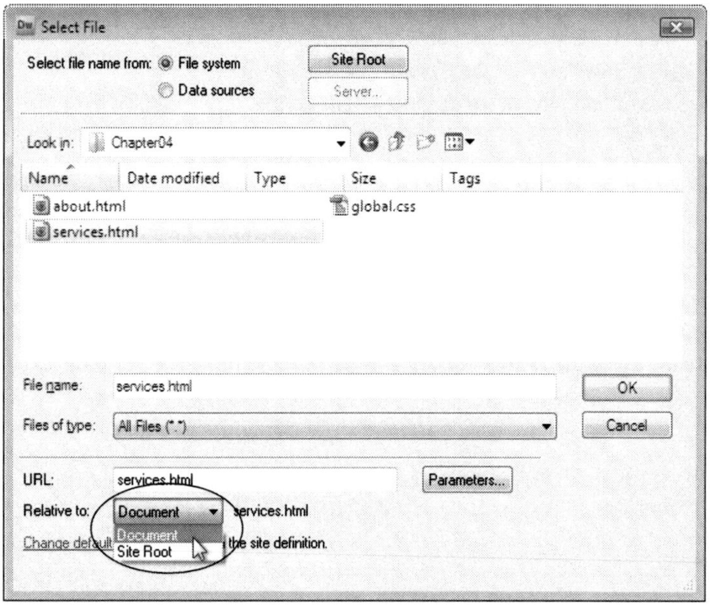

Figure 5-4: *In Windows, the Select File dialog box lets you browse your computer to select the file you wish to link to. From the "Relative to" pop-up menu (circled), you can choose what type of link to create: Document- or Site Root-relative. You tell Dreamweaver which type of link to use in the Site Definition window, as described in Figure 5-1. If you find that your links aren't working when you preview your pages, odds are you have the Site Root option set, or you've been selecting Site Root from the "Relative to" pop-up menu.*

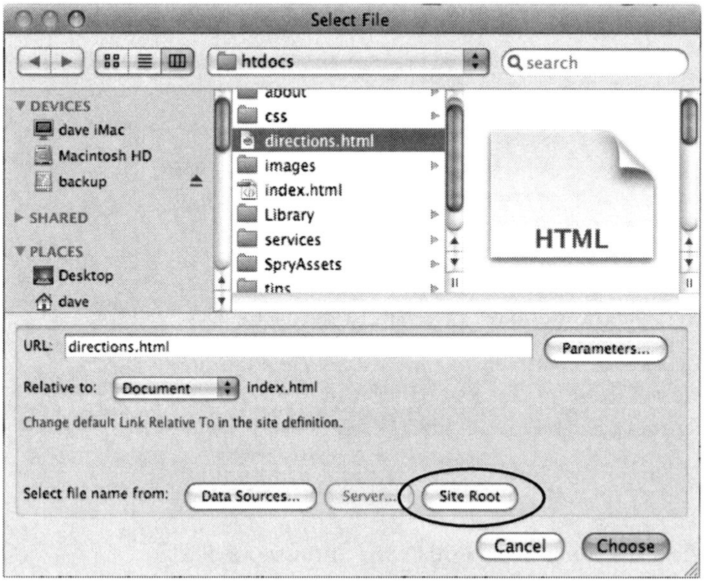

Figure 5-5: *Every file in a Web site needs to be somewhere inside what's called a local root folder (see the box on page 43). This master folder holds everything on the site, including other folders with other files. Because it's so central to your Web files, Dreamweaver includes a "Site Root" button (circled) to every window that requires selecting or saving a file. (This example shows what you see on a Mac; on Windows computers, the button's at the top of the window as shown in Figure 5-4.) Click this button and you jump straight to your site's root (which lets you know where you are on your hard drive), making it easy to navigate to the file you need.*

3. **Navigate to and select the file you want the link to open.**

   The file should be a Web page that's part of your Web site. In other words, it should be in the local root folder (see the box on page 43), or in a folder therein.

If you try to link to a file *outside* the root folder, Dreamweaver alerts you to this problem and offers to copy the file to the root folder. Accept the offer. Remember: To a Web site, the root folder is like the edges of the known universe—nothing exists outside it.

Tip: You can double-click the name of the file in the Select File dialog box and Dreamweaver selects the file *and* closes the Select File dialog in one step...or is that two clicks?

4. **Make sure the correct type of link—Document or Site Root—is selected from the "Relative to" menu.**

   As noted earlier in this chapter, document-relative links are usually the best choice. Root-relative links (which is actually short for *Site Root–relative links*) don't work when you preview the Web site on your own computer. (They do, however, work once you move them to your Web server.)

Note: You can skip step 4: Just set the type of link you want in the Site Definition window, and then forget about it. Dreamweaver always uses the link type you specified here. See Figure 5-1 for details.

FREQUENTLY ASKED QUESTION

The Mysterious Triple Slashes

Why do my links start with file:///?

Links that begin with *file:///* (*file:///D:/missingmanual/book_site/cosmo/subscribe.html*, for example) aren't valid links on the Web. Rather, they're temporary addresses that Dreamweaver creates as placeholders for links to be rewritten later. (A *file:///* path tells Dreamweaver where to look for the file on your computer.) You'll spot these addresses when you add document-relative links to a page that hasn't been saved, or when working with files that are outside of your site's local root folder.

Suppose you're working on a Web page that will contain your company's legal mumbo-jumbo, but you haven't yet saved it. After adding a document-relative link to your home page, you notice that the path displayed in the Property inspector's Link field begins with *file:///*. Since your legal page hasn't yet been saved and therefore doesn't yet have a folder location, Dreamweaver can't create a link telling a browser how to get from it to the home page. So Dreamweaver creates a temporary link, which helps it keep track of which page to link to. Once you save the page somewhere in the site, Dreamweaver rewrites the link in proper document-relative format, and the *file:///* disappears.

Likewise, when you work with files that are outside of the local root folder, Dreamweaver can't write a proper link. (Any folder outside of the local root folder isn't part of the Web site, and there's no way to write a correct link from nowhere to somewhere.) So, if you save a page *outside* of the local root folder, Dreamweaver writes all document-relative links on that page as file paths beginning with *file:///*. To avoid this invalid link problem, always save your Web pages inside the local root folder or in a folder *inside* of the local root folder. To learn more about root folders and Web sites, see Chapter 15.

When you *link to* a page—or add an image (Chapter 6)—that's stored outside of the local root folder, Dreamweaver has the same problem. However, in this instance, Dreamweaver gives you the option of copying the out-of-bounds file to a location of your choosing within the root folder.

5. **Click OK (Windows) or Choose (Mac) to apply the link.**

   The text or image now links to another Web page. If you haven't yet saved the other Web page into your site, Dreamweaver doesn't know how to write the document-relative link. Instead, it displays a dialog box saying that it will assign a temporary path for the link until you save the page—see the box on page 169.

After you apply a link, linked text appears underlined and colored (using the color defined by the Page Properties window, which is shown in Figure 1-24). Images have a blue borderline around them. If you want to take the link for a spin, press F12 (Option-F12 on a Mac) to preview the page in your browser, where you can click the link.

Note: To get rid of the ugly blue border around linked images, create a CSS style for the <img> tag (see page 115 if you're unsure about creating styles) and set its border style to "none" (see page 231). The tutorial at the end of this chapter has an example of this on page 195.

Using the Point-to-File Tool

You can also create links in Dreamweaver by dragging from the Property inspector to the Files panel (shown in Figure 5-6). If your site involves a lot of links, learning to use the Point-to-File tool will save you time and energy.

To use this trick effectively, position your document window and Files window side by side, as shown in Figure 5-6.

1. **In the document window, select the text or image you want to turn into a link.**

   Make sure that both the Property inspector and Files window are open. To open the Property inspector, choose Window → Properties. To open the Files window, choose Window → Files. (Before using the Files window, you need to create a local site, as described on page 37.)

2. **Drag the Point-to-File icon from the Property inspector onto a Web page in the Files window (see Figure 5-6).**

   Or you can Shift-drag the selected text or image in the document window to any Web page in the Files panel, bypassing the Property inspector altogether.

Tip: You can also drag a file from the Files panel into the Link box (in the Property inspector) to link to it.

3. **After dragging over the correct Web page, release the mouse button.**

   The selected text or image in your Web page turns into a link to the file you just pointed to.

Bizarre Bug Alert: If you're using *two monitors* the Point-to-File icon might not work. If your main monitor (the one with the Start menu for Windows, or the one where a program's menu bar appears on Macs) is on the right, and your second monitor is on the left, then the Point-to-File icon *may not* work, then again, it might! Strange, but true.

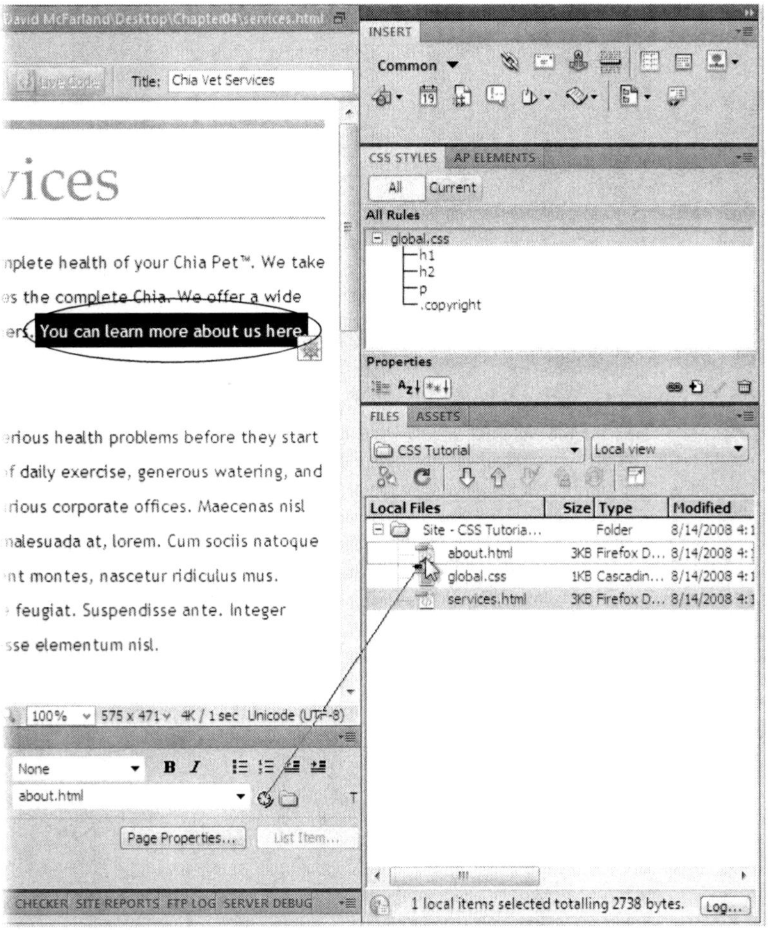

Figure 5-6: *In this figure, some text (circled) is selected in the document window; this is the text that's going to be turned into a link. To link to another page, drag from the Point-to-File icon (the bullseye icon in the Property inspector) to a Web page in the Files panel (right). In this example, Dreamweaver creates a link to the Web page called* about.html. *You could also Shift-drag from the selected text to the page* about.html *in the Files panel to create the same link.*

Typing (or Pasting) the URL or Path

If you need to link to another Web site, or you feel comfortable with how document-relative links work, you can also simply type the URL or path to the page into the Property inspector. Note that this manual insertion technique and the hyperlink object tool discussed next are the *only* ways to add links to pages outside the current Web site.

1. **In the document window, select the text or image you want to make into a link.**

2. **In the Property inspector, type the URL or path to the file into the Link field (see Figure 5-3).**

   If the link leads to another Web site, type an absolute URL—that is, a complete Web address, starting with *http://*.

Tip: An easier approach is to copy a complete URL–including the *http://*–from the address bar in your browser window and paste it into the Link field.

To link to another page on your own site, type a document-relative link (see page 165 for some examples). Letting Dreamweaver write the correct path using the browsing or point-to-file techniques described above is a good way to avoid typos. But typing the path can come in handy when, say, you want to create a link to a page you haven't yet created.

3. **Press Enter (Return) to apply the link.**

While you don't necessarily have to hit Enter (Return)—sometimes you can just click elsewhere on the page and keep working—Dreamweaver has been known to forget the link and not apply it. This is true for most fields in the Property Inspector—so if you type information directly into the Property inspector (to create a link, add a title property, and so on) get into the habit of hitting the Enter (Return) key to make sure your change sticks.

Tip: If you're adding an absolute link to a Web site without specifying a Web page, add a final forward slash (/) to the address. For example, to link to Yahoo, type *http://www.yahoo.com/*. The final slash tells the Web server that you're requesting the default page (home page) at Yahoo.com.

Although leaving out the slash works, too (*http://www.yahoo.com*), the server has to do a little extra work to figure out which page to send back, resulting in a slight and unnecessary delay.

Also include the final slash when you provide a link to the default page inside a folder on a site, like this: *http://www.sawmac.com/dwcs4/*.

Using the Hyperlink Object

Dreamweaver provides yet another way to add a link. The Hyperlink object on the Common category of the Insert panel (Figure 5-7) lets you insert a link with many optional properties. Its only real benefit is that it lets you add text and a link in one step (instead of adding text to the page, selecting it, and *then* applying a link). Unfortunately, this tool only works with text (not graphics) and some of the optional properties don't work in all browsers.

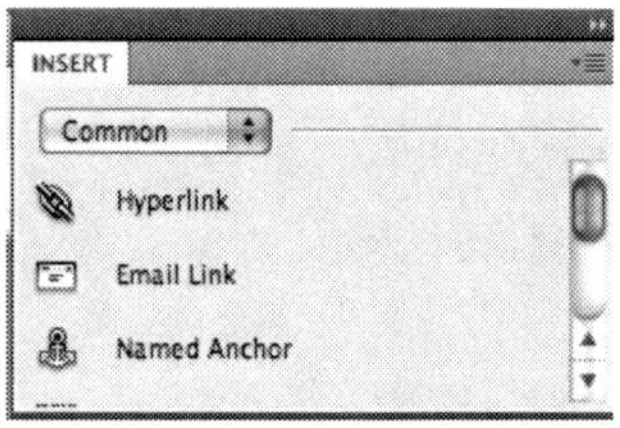

Figure 5-7:
The Common category of the Insert panel includes three link-related objects: the Hyperlink (for adding links), the Email link (for adding links for email addresses), and the Named anchor (for adding links within a page). You may not see these labels–just the icons–if you followed the advice in step 7 on page 51 and hid the labels.

FREQUENTLY ASKED QUESTION

Targeting and Titling Links

What's the Title box and Target menu in the Property inspector for?

A link's *Title* property is used to supply additional information about a link, usually to clearly indicate where the link leads. For example, if you linked "click here for more" to an article describing different types of termites, the link text alone doesn't clearly explain where this link goes—click for more of *what*? In this case, you could type "A complete list of Termite species" into the Title box on the Property inspector (see Figure 5-3). The title property is completely optional, and if the link text already clearly explains where the link leads, then you shouldn't bother setting the title property. In fact, you can avoid the title property altogether if you write text that explains where the link leads: "Click here for a complete list of Termite species," for example.

However, in the case of linked images (such as a logo that also acts as a link back to a site's home page), adding a title is a very good idea. Search engines like the title tag in this case, because it lets them know the purpose of the link; people who use screen readers (programs that help those with vision problems surf the Web) also benefit, since the title tag can be read out loud and the visitor will know where the link goes. The title property has one other unique feature: Web browsers display a pop-up tooltip window with the title's text when the mouse is moved over the link.

The *Target* menu has nothing to do with the accuracy of your links, nor with shooting ranges. It deals with how the destination page appears when you click a link.

The new page can appear (a) right in the browser window, just the way most links work; (b) in a new browser window (choose the *_blank* option); or (c) in a different *frame* on the same page (for details about this increasingly obsolete technology, see the online-only chapter about frames, located at *www.sawmac.com/missing/dw8/appc.pdf*).

_blank is pretty much the only option used these days, but be careful if your pages use the "Strict" forms of HTML 4.01 and XHTML 1.0 (see page 46): The Target attribute is not valid code for those types of documents.

If you're still interested, here's how it works. Start by clicking on the page where you wish to insert a link. Then:

1. **Choose Insert → Hyperlink or click the chain icon on the Insert bar.**

   The Hyperlink dialog box opens (see Figure 5-8). If you want to apply a link to text already on the page, select it first, then choose Insert → Hyperlink.

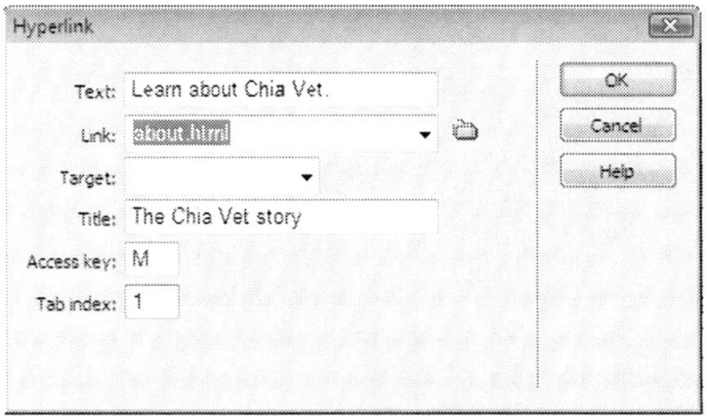

Figure 5-8: *You can apply everything except the "Access key" and "Tab index" properties shown in this dialog box to an image or existing text using the Property inspector. Also, keep in mind one somewhat special case: If you want to add an Access key and Tab index to an already existing link, you have a couple of options: go into Code view (as described in Chapter 10) and hand edit the HTML, or use the Tag inspector to access all the properties available to a particular link. (For details, see page 415.)*

2. **In the Text box, type the text you want to appear on the page.**

   Whatever you type here is what you'll see on the page, and what your audience will click to follow the link. If you previously selected some text on the page, it shows up in the Text box automatically.

3. **Click the folder icon and search for the page you want to link to.**

   Alternatively, you can type a URL in the Link box.

4. **Set the target for the link.**

   If you want the link to open in the same window—like most links—don't select anything. To make the page open in a new window, select the *_blank* option (see the box on page 173 for more on targeting a link).

   The last three options are more interesting.

5. **Type a title for the page you're linking to.**

   This property is optional. As described in the box on page 173, most Web browsers display this property in a small tooltip window when visitors move their mouse over the link.

6. **Type a key in the "Access key" box.**

   An *access key* lets you trigger a link from your keyboard. Internet Explorer, Safari, and Firefox understand this property in conjunction with the Alt key (Control key on a Mac). For example, if you type *h* in the "Access key" box, then a visitor to your page can press Alt+H (Control-H) to mouselessly open that link. Of course, unless people who visit your site are psychic, it's a good idea to provide instructions by adding the access key information next to the link itself: Home Page (Alt+H).

7. **In the "Tab index" box, type a number for the tab order.**

   In most browsers, you can press the Tab key to step through the links on a page (and boxes on a form). This feature not only provides useful keyboard control of your Web browser, but it's also important for people who can't use a mouse due to disabilities.

   Normally when you press Tab, Web browsers highlight links in the order in which they appear in the page's HTML. The Tab index, by contrast, lets *you* control the order in which links light up as visitors tab through them. For example, you can make your main navigation buttons the first things that are highlighted when someone presses Tab, even if they aren't the first links on the page.

   For the first link in order, type *1* here. Number other links in the order you want the Tab key to follow. If you aren't concerned about the order of a particular link, leave this option blank or type *0*. The Web browser will highlight that link after the visitor has tabbed through all links that *do* have a Tab index.

EXTENSION ALERT

QuickLink Is Quick Work

Dreamweaver makes it easy to add innovative commands and tools–including those written by independent, non-Adobe programmers–to your copy of the program. You can read a lot more about these add-on programs, called *extensions*, in Chapter 21.

When you're working with links, one extension that really comes in handy is called QuickLink. Created by renowned Dreamweaver guru Tom Muck, this extension instantly turns text into either a *mailto* or an *absolute* URL. You can find QuickLink at *www.tom-muck.com/extensions/help/quicklink/*. Amazingly, even though this extension hasn't been updated since Dreamweaver MX 2004, it still works in CS4.

Once you've installed this extension, here's how it works: Suppose you insert your cursor somewhere on a Web page in Dreamweaver and type the text, "You can download the free PDF viewer at *http://www.adobe.com*." To turn *http://www.adobe.com* into a real link, you can either select the text and then go to the Property inspector and type *http://www.adobe.com/*, or–with QuickLink–simply select the text and choose Commands → QuickLink. QuickLink writes the proper code in the Property inspector, including the initial (and mandatory) *http://*, even if those characters were missing from the original text. (Note that this extension has one small bug: After you install it, the QuickLink command will appear *twice* in the Commands menu. Either option works.)

QuickLink also converts email addresses to proper *mailto* links: Just select the email address (*missing@sawmac.com*, say), apply the QuickLink command, and watch as the extension automatically inserts the correct code (mailto: *missing@sawmac.com*) into your page.

For even faster action, create a keyboard shortcut for this command; Shift+Ctrl+L is a good one. (See page 809 for more on keyboard shortcuts.)

Adding an Email Link

If you want to invite your site visitors to email you, then an *email link* is the perfect solution. When someone clicks an email link, her email program launches automatically, and a new message opens with your email address already in the To field. She can then just type her message and send it off.

An email link looks like this: *mailto:vets@chia-vet.com*. The first part (*mailto*) indicates the type of link, while the second part (*vets@chia-vet.com*) specifies the email address.

Note: Email links work only if the person who clicks the link has an email program set up and running on his computer. If someone visits your site from a computer at the public library, for example, he might not be able to send email. If this drawback troubles you, you can also collect information using a *form* (as discussed in Chapter 11), a feedback method that has neither the limitations nor the easy setup of an email link.

You can create an email link much the way you'd create any other Dreamweaver link: by selecting some text or an image and typing the *mailto* address, as shown above, into the Link field in the Property inspector. To simplify this process, Dreamweaver has a quick method of inserting an email link:

1. **Under the Insert panel's Common category, click the Email link icon, which looks like an envelope (see Figure 5-7).**

   Alternatively, choose Insert → Email link. Either way, if you've already typed the text (*Email me!*) on your Web page, select it first. The Email Link dialog box opens (see Figure 5-9).

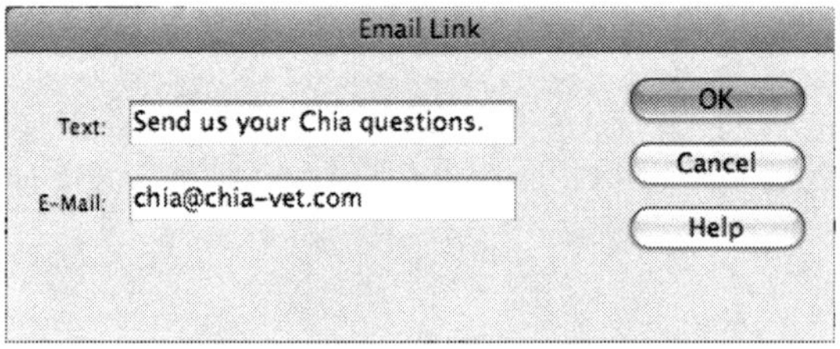

***Figure 5-9:** The Email Link dialog box lets you specify the text that appears on the Web page and the email address for a* mailto *link. You can also select some text you've already added to the document and click the Email Link icon on the Objects panel. The text you selected appears in the Text field in this dialog box.*

2. **In the Text field, type the text that you want to appear on the Web page.**

   This text can indicate the link's purpose, like *Email the Webmaster*. (If you select text in the document first, it automatically appears in the Text field.)

3. **Type an email address into the E-Mail field.**

   This is the address that appears in your visitors' email program when they click the link. (You don't have to type *mailto:*—Dreamweaver adds it automatically.)

4. **Click OK.**

   Dreamweaver adds the text to the page, complete with a *mailto* link.

Note: Some people don't add email links to their Web sites because they're afraid of spammers' automated programs that search the Web and collect email addresses. There are some tricks to fool these "spambots," but spammers have figured most of them out. The fact is, spammers can attack even "Contact Us" Web forms. If you're absolutely obsessed with never being spammed, then leave your email address off your site. However, many businesses rely on people contacting them for more information, and the harder you make it for a legitimate visitor to contact you, the fewer legitimate contacts you'll receive–after all, you wouldn't have much of a freelance design business if you never provided a way for someone to contact you. Your best bet is to let the spam come, but add a spam filter to your email program to separate the wheat from the chaff.

Linking Within a Web Page

Clicking a link usually loads a Web page into the browser window. But what if you want to link not only to a Web page, but to a specific *spot* on the page? See Figure 5-10 for an example. There are actually two methods for doing this: using the original *named-anchor* method or adding an ID. The named-anchor link is a special type of link that's designed to auto-scroll to a particular spot on a particular page—it's been around since the earliest days of the Web. All current Web browsers now support another method—adding an ID name to the spot on the page you wish to link to. You'll learn about both methods.

Method 1: Creating a Named Anchor

Creating a named-anchor link is a two-step process: First you add and name an anchor on the page that you're linking to, thus identifying the destination for the link; then you add a link that goes to that named anchor. For instance, in the Table of Contents page example shown in Figure 5-10, you would place a named anchor at the beginning of each chapter section.

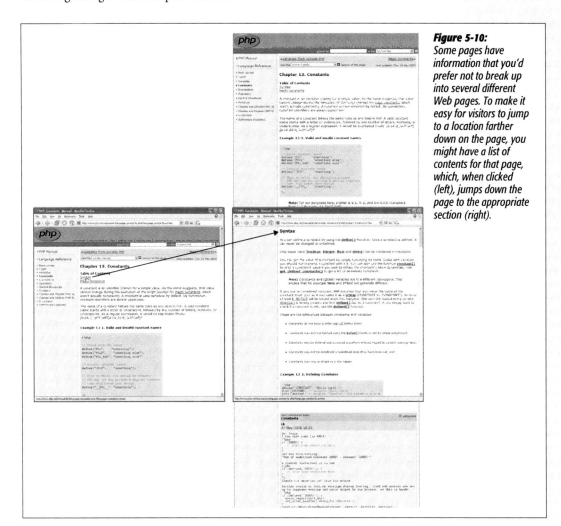

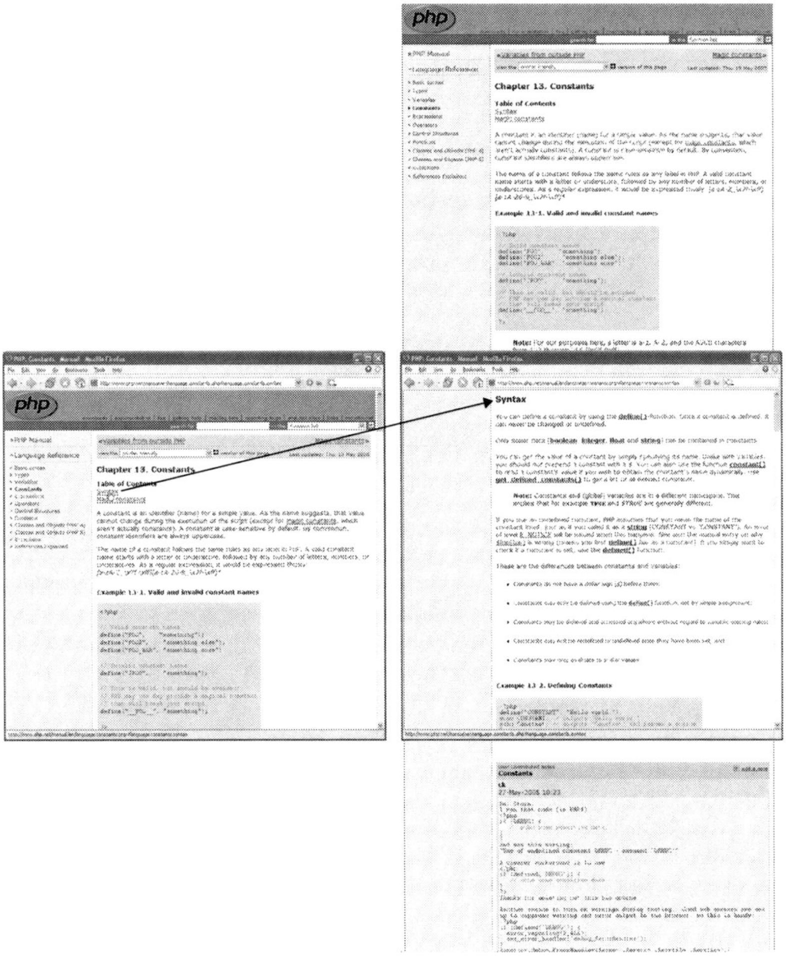

Figure 5-10: *Some pages have information that you'd prefer not to break up into several different Web pages. To make it easy for visitors to jump to a location farther down on the page, you might have a list of contents for that page, which, when clicked (left), jumps down the page to the appropriate section (right).*

To create a named anchor:

1. **In the document window, click where you want to insert the named anchor.**

   The named anchor is the place where you want the link to jump to.

2. **Insert a named anchor.**

   You can do so using any of three methods: Choose Insert → Named Anchor; press Ctrl+Alt+A (⌘-Option-A); or, from the Insert bar, select the Common category and click the Named Anchor icon (see Figure 5-7).

3. **Type the name of the anchor in the Insert Named Anchor dialog box.**

   Each anchor on a page should have a unique name, something short and easy to remember. No spaces or punctuation marks are allowed. If you violate any of these rules, Dreamweaver will remind you with an error message and strip out the offending characters.

4. **Click OK to insert the named anchor.**

   You'll see a gold shield with an anchor on it at the point where you created the anchor. Click this icon to show the name of the anchor in the Property inspector. (If you don't see it, see the opposite page for details on hiding and showing anchors.)

The Named Anchor icon (the gold shield) is the key to removing or editing the anchor later: just click the icon and press Delete to get rid of it, or click it and change its name in the Property inspector. (Deleting the name in the Property inspector deletes the anchor from the page.)

Method 2: Adding an ID

Instead of adding a named anchor to a page, you can simply assign an ID to the spot on the page you wish to link to. For example, if you want to link to a subhead way down on a page (for example a heading 2, or <h2> tag) then you can assign an ID to that heading. Often IDs are used in conjunction with ID *styles* in a style sheet (see page 114 for more on ID styles). However, you don't need a style to add an ID *name* to a tag. You can simply add an ID name to any tag and never create a style to control the formatting of that tag (of course, if you also want to style that tag, then you can create a style with the same ID name as well).

For text, you can add an ID by clicking anywhere inside a paragraph and, in the Property inspector's ID box, type the name you want to use. As with named anchors, the ID name shouldn't have spaces or punctuation marks.

For non text elements like images or tables, select the tag (the Tag selector discussed on page 24 is the best way), and type the ID name in the ID box on the left side of the Property inspector.

Linking to an Anchor or ID

Creating a link to a named anchor or ID isn't all that different from linking to a Web page. Once you've created and named an anchor or added an ID name to a tag, you can link to it from within the same Web page, or from a different page.

To link to an anchor or ID on the same page:

1. **In the document window, select the text or image you want to make into a link.**

   For example, drag across some text, or highlight a graphic.

2. **In the Property inspector's Link field, type #, followed by the anchor or ID name.**

   The # sign indicates that the link goes to a named anchor. In other words, if you wish to link to an anchor named *directions*, the link would be *#directions*.

You can also link from one Web page to a particular location on another Web page in your site. The process is the same as linking to an anchor on the same page, except that you have to specify both the path to the Web page and the name of the anchor:

1. **In the document window, select the text or image you want to turn into a link. In the Link field of the Property inspector, type or choose the URL or path of the page you wish to link to.**

   You can use any of the methods described above: browsing, Point-to-File, or typing the path. Unfortunately, if you browse to select the linked file, Dreamweaver doesn't display any anchors or IDs on that page, so you need to perform one extra step.

2. **Click at the end of the URL or path. Type # followed by the anchor or ID's name.**

   The Link field should look something like this: *contact.html#directions*.

Viewing and Hiding Anchors

A named anchor isn't visible in a Web browser; it appears in Dreamweaver as an anchor-on-a-gold-shield icon. Like other invisible elements—line breaks, for instance—you can hide named anchors in Dreamweaver by choosing View → Visual Aids → Invisible Elements, or choosing Visual Aids → Invisible Elements from the Visual Aids menu in the toolbar (see Figure 9-12 on page 345). (If anchors still don't appear, visit the Preferences window, pictured in Figure 1-14, and in the Invisible Elements category, make sure the Anchor box is turned on.)

ID names, however, never appear visibly on the page within Dreamweaver and there's no way to change that.

FREQUENTLY ASKED QUESTION

Anchors Away

When I click a link to an anchor or ID, the Web browser is supposed to go to the page and display the anchor or the tag with the specified ID at the top of the browser window. But sometimes the linked-to spot appears in the middle of the browser. What's that about?

Web browsers can't scroll beyond the bottom of a Web page, so an anchor or ID near the bottom of a page sometimes can't move to the top of the browser window. If one of your own Web pages exhibits this problem, the fix is simple: create a style for the <body> tag and add *bottom padding* (page 343). This adds space between the bottom of the page and the last bit of content on the page, so the browser can scroll the page all the way to the anchor.

Modifying a Link

At some point, you may need to change or edit a link. Perhaps the URL you were linking to has changed, or you simply no longer need that link.

Changing a Link's Destination

As you'll read in Part 4, Dreamweaver provides some amazing tools for automatically updating your links so that your site stays in working order, even if you move files around your site. But even Dreamweaver isn't smart enough to know when a page on someone *else's* Web site has been moved or deleted. And you may decide you simply need to change a link so that it points to a different page on your own site. In both of these cases, you'll need to change the links on your Web pages by hand:

1. **Select the text link or picture link.**

   The existing link path appears in the Link field in the Property inspector.

2. **Use any of the techniques described on page 167 for specifying the link's target.**

   For example, click the "Browse for File" button in the Property inspector and locate a different Web page in your site, or type a complete URL to point to another page outside your site. The destination of the link changes to the new URL, path, or anchor.

Removing a Link

Sometimes, you want to stop a link from linking—when the Web page you were pointing to no longer exists, for example. You want the text or image on your Web page to stay the same, but you want to remove the disabled link. In that case, just select the link text or image and then use one of these tactics:

- Choose Modify → Remove Link, or press Ctrl+Shift+L (⌘-Shift-L).
- Delete the text in the Link field of the Property inspector and press the Enter or Return key.

The text or image remains on your Web page, but it no longer links to anything. If it's a text link, the color changes from your site's link color to the normal text color for the page.

Of course, if you're feeling particularly destructive, you can also delete the link text or image itself; doing so also gets rid of the link.

Styling Links

You can control the basic look of links from the Links category of the Page Properties window (Figure 5-11). To open it, choose Modify → Page Properties, press Ctrl+J (⌘-J), or click the Page Properties button in the Property inspector (this button's only visible when either nothing is selected on the page or text is selected).

The top set of options—font, size, bold, italic—set basic formatting for every link on the page. The next group of options set the color of links under specific conditions. Web browsers keep track of how a visitor interacts with links on a page: for example, whether he's moving his mouse over the link. Each link can be in one of four different modes (called *states*): a plain unvisited link is just called a *link*; a link to a page the visitor has already been to (this is determined by the browser's pages-viewed history) is called a *visited* link; a link that the mouse is currently over is technically called a *hover* state (but Dreamweaver refers to it as a *rollover* link); and a link that's in the process of being clicked is known as an *active* link.

Each of these states provides useful information to a visitor, and you can style each one individually. In most Web browsers, a plain link normally appears blue until you visit the page it links to—then that link turns purple. This helpful color coding lets a visitor quickly determine whether to follow a link: "Hey, there's a page I haven't seen," or, "Been there, done that."

The rollover (or hover) link is particularly useful in instructing visitors that they can click the link, and it also provides a lot of creative design potential. For example, you can completely change the look of a link when a visitor mouses over it, including changing the color, adding a background image (page 233), or changing its background color (page 233). (However, to get neat effects like this, you'll need to go beyond the Page Properties window and set styles for your links as described in the next section.)

Finally, an *active* link is for that fleeting moment between when a visitor clicks a link and releases the mouse button. It happens so fast that it's usually not worth spending too much time formatting the active link state. (However, if someone is using the tab key to cycle through the links on a page, the active link style is applied when the person tabs to the link; the link stays "active" until the visitors hits the Enter key—to follow the link—or tabs off to the next link.)

The Page Properties (Figure 5-11) window lets you change the color for each of these different link states. In addition, the "Underline style" menu lets you control whether a line always appears beneath a link (this is normally how Web browsers display text links); never appears beneath links; only appears when you move your mouse over a link; or appears normally but disappears when the mouse is moved over the link. Since Web surfers are accustomed to thinking of underlined text as a big "CLICK ME" sign, think twice before removing underlines from links. Without some clear indication that the text is a link, visitors may never see (or click) the links on your page.

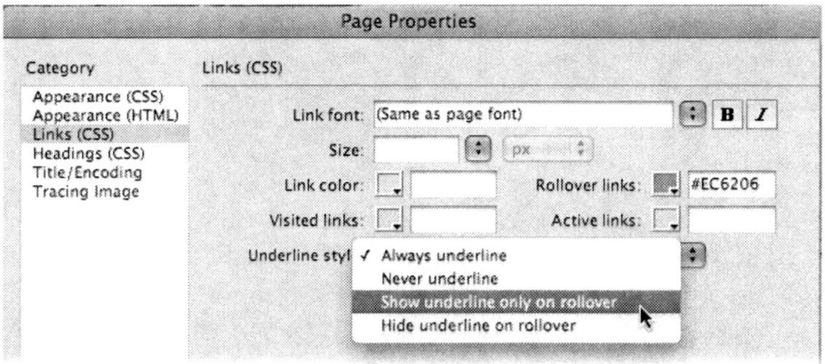

Figure 5-11:
The Page Properties window lets you set basic properties for a Web page, including the font, color, and size of links. This window is mainly a shortcut for creating CSS styles.

One problem with using the Page Properties window to set link properties is that those settings only apply to the current page. Fortunately, you don't need to set the Page Properties on every page of your site; you can move styles created by the Page Properties window to an external style sheet (see page 113 if you don't know what an external style sheet is). In fact, the Page Properties window actually creates CSS styles to format links; it's just that Dreamweaver creates those styles in the page itself using an internal style sheet. If you use the Page Properties window for one page, you can export those styles or even drag them into an external style sheet. (These style management techniques are discussed on page 308.) Another method is to bypass the Page Properties window altogether and create CSS link styles from scratch—a method you'll learn about in the next section.

CSS and Links

Using the CSS Styles panel to create styles for your links gives you access to many more formatting options besides font, color, and size. In fact, nearly every CSS property can be applied to links. For example, all of the text options discussed on page 133—font size, weight, variant, letter spacing, and so on—can be used to format a link. In addition, you can add a border (page 213) and a background color (page 233) to a link to make it look like a button.

To format the general look of all links, create a tag style (page 113) for the <a> tag (the tag used to create links) using the instructions starting on page 115. Alternatively, you might want a different look for a particular link. For example, you might want that "Buy Now!" link to be bigger and bolder than other links on the page. In that case, you can create a class style (page 113) and apply it directly to that link.

To control how a link looks for the different states (link, visited, hover, and active), you need to dip a little deeper into the CSS pool and use what's called a *pseudo-class*. As you've read, a selector is merely the part of a style that instructs a browser where to apply a style—*h1* is the selector for formatting every Heading 1 paragraph, for example. When you select Compound from the Selector Type menu at the top of New CSS Rule window, Dreamweaver lets you select one of four *pseudo-classes*, each of which refer to a different type of link, as shown in Figure 5-12. These four options (*a:link*, *a:visited*, *a:hover*, and *a:active*) correspond to the types of links in the Page Properties window.

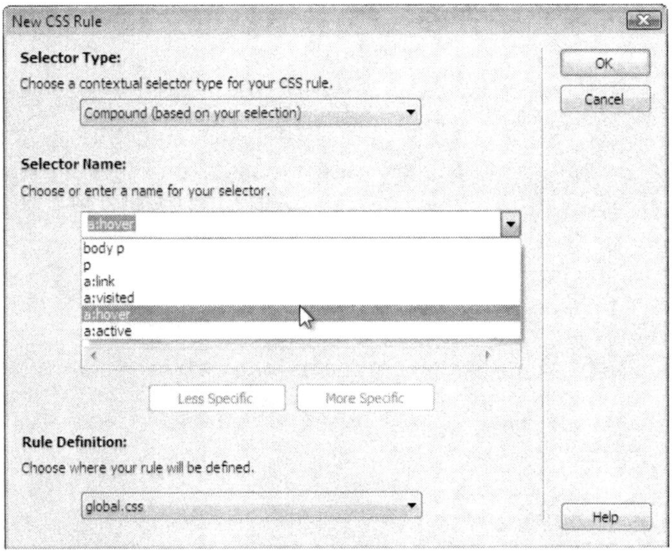

Figure 5-12: *The drop-down menu that appears when you select "Compound" as the selector type (from the top menu) lists the four link pseudo-classes. In addition, you may see one or more other names listed at the top of the list–for example "body p" and "p" in this menu. This menu lists possible other style names that would apply to whatever is currently selected on the page. In this case, the cursor was placed inside a paragraph before the New CSS Rule button was clicked–so Dreamweaver suggests creating a p style or a body p style. (This last style is called a descendent selector–you'll learn about them on page 301.)*

To use a pseudo-class, select Compound from the Selector Type menu at the top of the New CSS Rule window, and then choose the appropriate selector from the Selector Name drop-down menu. For example, to format how a link looks when the mouse moves over it, choose a:hover. You don't have to set all four pseudo-classes: If you're not interested in how your links look during the nano-second it's being clicked, then skip the a:active option. If you want to set more than one of these pseudo-classes, you must create them in the order that they appear in the menu. (A helpful mnemonic for remembering this rule is LoVe HAte—that is, *:link* comes before *:visited*, which comes before *:hover*, which comes before *:active*.)

Note: Firefox and Safari understand an additional pseudo-class related to links: *a:focus*. This selector applies when a visitor uses their keyboard to navigate to different links on a page. Pressing the Tab key highlights a link on a page. Each time you press the Tab key you jump to the next link–when a link is highlighted in this way it's given "focus." So if you want links to look different (at least in Firefox and Safari) when someone presses the Tab key to access them, use the *a:focus* selector.

Using these styles, you can make your link text appear red and underscored before it's clicked, twice as large when the mouse moves over it, purple boldface when clicked, and pale pink after it's been visited. (Granted, you might never be hired to do Martha Stewart's Web site, but you get the point.)

Note that these link pseudo-classes have one drawback: setting them affects *all* links on a page. In that respect, they're like tag styles.

If you want to apply a style to only certain links on a page, here's what to do: create a new style (click the + button in the Styles panel, for example); choose Compound from the Selector Type menu in the New CSS Rule window (Figure 5-12); and then, in the Selector Name box, type a class name followed by a colon and the appropriate link state. For example, to create a style that changes the look of a "Buy Now!" link, you could create a style called *.buyNow:link*; to make that link look different when someone mouses over it, the style would be named *.buyNow:hover*.

After naming the style (and saving it into an external style sheet), you then follow the steps on page 119 to create the look for that style (choose a font, select a color, and so on). After the style's created, simply apply the class to the specific link (or links) you wish to style, using any of the techniques described on page 122. (In the example above, the class name is *buyNow*, and that's what you'll see listed in the Property inspector's Class menu.)

Note: Descendent selectors provide a more efficient–but more complex–way of formatting specific links differently than others. This advanced CSS concept is discussed on page 301.

Creating a Navigation Menu

Every Web site should have a set of navigational links which let visitors quickly jump to the site's main areas. On a shopping site, those links might point to the categories of products for sale—books, DVDs, CDs, electronics, and so on. For a corporate intranet, links to human resources, office policies, company events, and each department might be important. Whatever the site, a Web designer should strive to get visitors where they want to go using the shortest route possible.

Dreamweaver CS4 inclues a powerful and easy navigation building tool—the Spry Menu Bar. With it, you can put all of your site's most important links into a compact horizontal or vertical menu (see Figure 5-13). Each menu button can even support two levels of pop-up submenus, so a visitor can quickly jump to a page buried deep within your site's structure.

The Spry Menu Bar is just one of the many "Spry" tools in Dreamweaver CS4. You'll learn a lot more about what Adobe calls the "Spry Framework" in Chapter 12, but in a nutshell, Spry is a collection of advanced JavaScript programming that lets you add lots of dynamic effects to your Web pages. (If you're familiar with the old Dreamweaver Behaviors, Spry is like those—on steroids.)

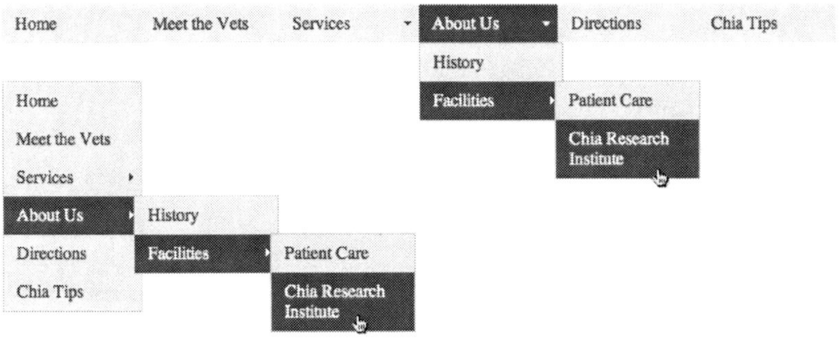

Figure 5-13: *Dreamweaver's Spry Menu Bar object lets you quickly add either a horizontal (top) or vertical (bottom) menu to your Web site. Pop-up submenus let you cram loads of links into a small space. The menu can hold up to three levels of links. However, navigating the rat maze to reach a link in a sub-submenu is sometimes a tiring test of hand-mouse coordination.*

Adding a Menu

The first step in inserting a Spry menu is deciding where on the page you wish to place it. A horizontal menu bar, with buttons sitting side by side, sits near the top of the page, either at the very top or below the area dedicated to the logo (often called the "banner"). A vertical menu bar, whose buttons are stacked one on top of the next, is usually positioned at the left edge of the page, below the banner area. To add a Spry menu:

1. **In the document window, click where you want to insert the menu.**

   When you learn more about Web page layout in Chapter 9, you'll discover that most elements on a page—like graphics, paragraphs, and menus—go inside of <div> tags which are used to lay out areas of the page. (If you've built sites in the past, you may have used HTML tables to lay out Web pages. If you're still using tables, you'd insert the menu in a table cell.)

2. **Click the Insert Spry menu button on the Layout category of the Insert panel (Figure 5-14).**

   The same button is on the Spry tab of the Insert Bar, and you can also choose Insert → Spry → Spry Menu Bar. In any case, the Spry Menu Bar window appears asking whether you want a horizontal or vertical menu bar.

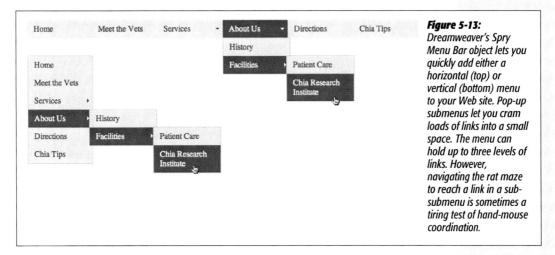

Figure 5-14: *The Insert Spry menu button appears in two places on the Insert Bar: in the Spry category (pictured here) and in the Layout category.*

3. **Depending on the type of menu you want, choose either the Horizontal or Vertical button and then click OK.**

   Dreamweaver inserts a "starter" menu containing a few links and pop-up menus (Figure 5-15). You can change and add links using the Property inspector, as described next.

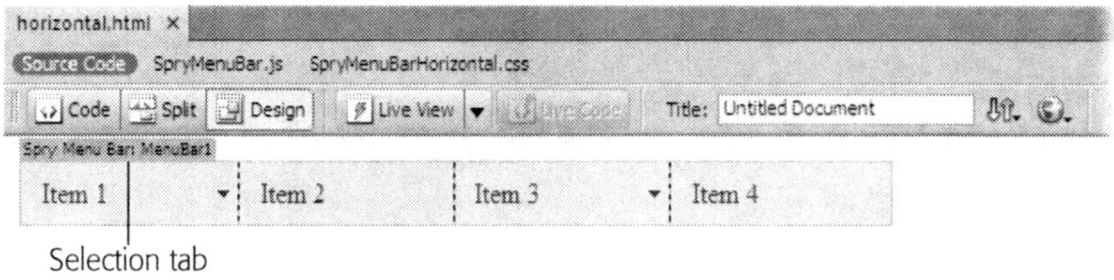

***Figure 5-15:** The Spry menu tab and the blue outline around the menu appear only when you move your mouse over the menu, or click anywhere inside it. Click the blue Selection tab to select the menu for editing. However, the blue tab still might not appear if the "show invisible elements" setting is turned off: Choose View → Visual Aids and make sure that Invisible Elements is checked and that Hide All is not checked.*

Adding, Editing, and Removing Links

The starter Spry menu that Dreamweaver inserts onto your page isn't very useful (unless you coincidentally have four sections on your site named Item 1, Item 2, Item 3, and Item 4). To make the menu your own you need to relabel the buttons Dreamweaver supplies and link them to pages on your site; you can also add more buttons and assign links to each of them. To edit the Spry menu, select it by clicking the blue Spry Selection tab (see Figure 5-15). Once selected, the menu's labels and links appear in the Property inspector (Figure 5-16).

A Spry menu supports up to three levels of menus. The main navigation buttons always appear on the page; each of those main buttons can have its own pop-up menu, which only appears when a visitor mouses over the particular button. Each button on the second level of menus (the pop-up menu), can have another pop-up menu. Dreamweaver represents each of these three menu levels with a column in the Property inspector (see Figure 5-16), and each column has its own set of widgets for adding, deleting, and moving menu buttons.

Note: The pop-up menu feature of a Spry menu depends on JavaScript. While most people surfing the Web use browsers with JavaScript turned on, some people either purposefully turn off JavaScript or use a browser that doesn't understand it. That means it's possible that someone visiting your site might *never* see the options in the pop-up menus. Because of this slightly irksome fact, always make sure the buttons on the main navigation menu link to a page that also provides links to the pages listed in the pop-up menus. If you don't, some people won't be able to visit some pages on your site.

To edit one of the main navigation buttons on a Spry menu, select the button's label (for example, Item 1) in the left-hand column of the Property inspector; in the Text box, change the label to the text you want to appear on the nav button ("Home" or "About Us," for example). Then add a link by using the "Browse for File" button or typing the URL in the Link box (see page 167 for more on setting links). You can leave the Title and Target boxes empty (see the box on page 173 for descriptions of these properties).

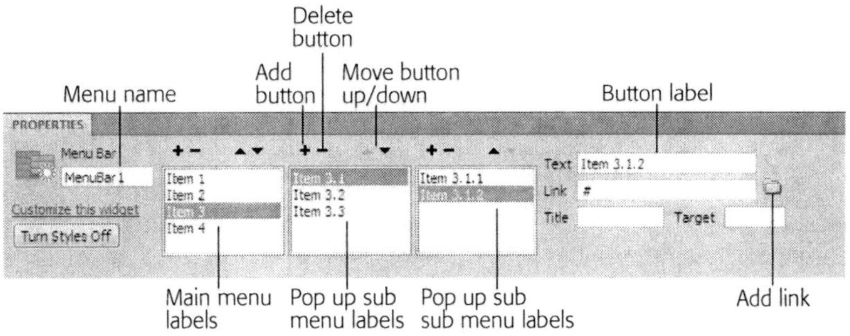

Figure 5-16: *Dreamweaver provides a generic name for each Spry menu it inserts—like MenuBar1. There's no harm in leaving that name (you'll never see it on the page), but feel free to change it to something more descriptive like* mainNavigation. *The only requirement is that you use only letters and numbers, and no spaces or punctuation (the naming rules are the same as for class styles, as described on page 117).*

To add a button to the main menu, click the + button above the left-hand column. Dreamweaver inserts a new "Untitled Item" in the list of links. Change the button's label in the text box, and then set a link using either method discussed in the previous paragraph.

To delete a button on the main nav bar, click its name in the left-hand column, and then click the – (minus) button at the top of the column. You can also rearrange the order of the buttons by selecting a name from the list and clicking the up or down arrow (on a horizontal menu bar the up arrow moves the button to the left, while the down arrow moves the button to the right).

Adding, editing, and arranging submenus is a similar process: First, select the Spry menu (click the blue menu tab [Figure 5-15]); and then, in the Property inspector, select the item you wish to add a submenu button to. For example, in Figure 5-16, to add another button to the pop-up menu that appears when a visitor mouses over the "Item 3" button, select Item 3 from the left-hand column, and then click the + button in the *middle* column. Once the pop-up menu is highlighted, you can delete and rearrange buttons on that menu using the minus and up and down arrow buttons at the top of that menu's column. To work with a sub-submenu (the third level of menus), first select an item from the left-hand column, and then click an item in the middle column.

Note: You can also edit a Spry menu's text and links in the document window. The main nav buttons are always visible, so you can click inside one to edit the text or change the link as described on page 180. To see a pop-up menu in the document window, select the Spry menu; in the Property inspector, select a menu item that has a pop-up menu; and then select one button in the pop-up menu list. That pop-up menu will now appear in the document window. In fact, the pop-up menu won't *disappear* (potentially covering other content on your page) until you select one of the main nav buttons from the left-hand column in the Property inspector.

When Dreamweaver inserts a Spry menu, it also adds a bunch of files to your site. Dreamweaver places those files in a folder named SpryAssets in your site's local root folder (a message listing the names of the files appears as soon as you save a page after inserting a menu). These files control the look and functionality of the menu: Dreamweaver adds one CSS file, one JavaScript file, and some image files for the arrows used to identify buttons with submenus. When you eventually move your Web pages to a Web server, make sure you upload these files as well.

Tip: If you don't like the folder name SpryAssets, or you'd like to store these supporting files in a different folder on your site, choose Site → Manage Sites to open the Manage Sites window; select your site from the list, and then click the Edit button. Doing so opens the Site Definition window (the one you used when you first defined the site). Click the Advanced Tab, select Spry from the left-hand list of categories, and then click the Folder icon to locate another folder on the site. If you select a new folder after you've already inserted a Spry object into a page, just drag the files from the SpryAssets folder to the new folder in the Files panel (the one you just told Dreamweaver to use for all Spry files). (See page 623 for more information on moving files using the Files panel.) You can then safely delete the empty SpryAssets folder from your site.

Changing the Look of the Menu

The "direct from the manufacturer" look of Spry menus leaves something to be desired. The battleship gray buttons and vibrant, "Hey, look at me, I'm purple!" rollovers aren't the most pleasing combination. Because all the menu formatting is accomplished with a collection of CSS styles, the power to improve the look of Spry menus is within your reach. Unfortunately, decoding the tangle of CSS used

POWER USERS' CLINIC

Spry Menus Behind the Scenes

A Spry menu might look like a fancy navigation bar made up of colorful buttons and interactive pop-up menus, but under the hood it's just a simple bulleted list of links. The stylish look and dynamic behavior are supplied by some pretty clever CSS (to make the cool looking buttons) and JavaScript (to make the pop-up menus pop).

Since the HTML behind a menu is so simple, it can be easier to edit a Spry menu without the fancy CSS applied. To do this, select the Spry menu by clicking its blue tab (Figure 5-15); then, in the Property inspector, click the Turn Styles Off button (Figure 5-16). Bam! You have an ugly bulleted list, just like the ones you learned about in Chapter 3. In fact, you can use the same techniques described on page 102 to add, edit, and delete bulleted items. The text you add to each bulleted item is what will appear on the navigation bar button: Select this text and add a link as described on page 104.

The main navigation buttons are represented by the primary set of bullets (the ones furthest to the left). The pop-up menus are just nested lists as described on page 122. Take this simple list:

```
* Home
* Our Services
    * Consultation
    * Garden Planning
        * Basic Apartment Plan
        * Deluxe Apartment Plan
* Contact Us
```

This list would produce a navigation bar with three buttons labeled "Home", "Our Services", and "Contact Us". Moving the mouse over the "Our Services" button would open a pop-up menu with two other buttons labeled "Consultation" and "Garden Planning". In other words, the bullets labeled "Consultation" and "Garden Planning" are a nested list inside the bulleted item named "Our Services," while the two bullet items "Basic Apartment Plan" and "Deluxe Apartment Plan" are a nested list inside the "Garden Planning" bulleted item.

If you decide to take this quick and dirty approach to editing a Spry menu, keep one thing in mind: Dreamweaver expects any bulleted item containing a nested list (a pop-up menu) to have a special CSS class applied to it: *MenuBarItemSubmenu*. In the example above, both the "Our Services" and "Garden Planning" list items would need this style applied to it. To apply this style, just click inside the bulleted item (the one containing the nested list), and use the Class menu in the Property inspector's HTML mode to apply the *MenuBarItemSubmenu* style (turn to page 126 for a refresher on applying class styles).

to format these menus requires a guidebook. Basically, the process involves identifying the name of the CSS style responsible for the formatting you want to change, then editing that style using the basic techniques you learned on page 305, or using one of the advanced methods discussed on page 553.

Tip: You can preview the Spry menu bar—complete with interactive pop-up menus—by using Dreamweaver CS4's new Live View (page 553). Click the Live View button at the top of the document window or choose View → Live View. Now you can mouse over the menu and see its buttons highlight and submenus pop up. In other words, its just like viewing the page in a Web browser. To leave Live View, click the Live View button a second time, or choose View → Live View again.

For example, if you want to change the font used for a menu, open the CSS Styles panel (Window → CSS Styles) and then click the All button to display all styles available for a page. The styles for menu bars are stored in their own style sheets (*SpryMenuBarVertical.css* for vertical menu bars and *SpryMenuBarHorizontal.css* for horizontal menu bars). Expand the list of styles (click the + symbol to the left of the style sheet name in the CSS Styles panel), then double-click *ul.MenuBarVertical a* (if you're working on a vertical menu) or *ul.MenuBarHorizontal a* (for a horizontal menu) style. This opens the Style Definition window for that style. You can then change the menu's font (see page 134).

Note: The strange style names used for Spry menus (*ul.MenuBarVertical a*, for example) are called *descendent selectors*. They're an advanced type of CSS selector used to pinpoint very specific elements contained in a particular part of the page. You can read about them on page 301. But for now, here's the ultra-quick cheat sheet for descendent selectors: Read them from right to left. The element on the far right is the element that will ultimately be styled. In this example, it's the <a> tag used for the links in the navigation bar. The "ul.MenuBarVertical" part specifies an unordered list that also has a class of *MenuBarVertical* applied to it. So running that selector through the universal translator produces this instruction: "Format every <a> tag that appears inside of a bulleted list with the class MenuBarVertical." In other words, only the links inside the Spry Menu Bar are affected by this style.

There are two different types of menu buttons on a Spry menu: a regular menu item, and a submenu item (see Figure 5-17). A regular menu item is a button that doesn't have a pop-up menu attached; it's just a simple button that the visitor clicks to go to a new page. A submenu button is any button that produces a pop-up menu when a visitor mouses over it. In addition, these two button types each have two looks: the button as it sits on the page, and the button when the mouse is moved over it (a rollover).

Formatting regular menu buttons

You can define the look of a regular menu button, and at the same time set the basic look for all buttons by editing the *ul.MenuBarHorizontal a* style (for a horizontal menu) or *ul.MenuBarVertical a* style (for a vertical menu). Just double-click the style's name in the CSS Styles panel to edit the style.

You can set any of the CSS text properties discussed on page 133, such as selecting a font, specifying a font size, and picking a font color. All text settings (except color) will be shared with the other types of buttons—the font color changes when the mouse rolls over any button.

In addition, the background color of both regular buttons and submenu buttons is controlled by this style. To change the background color, edit the appropriate style (for example, *ul.MenuBarVertical a* for a vertical menu) and change the background color option found under the Background category of the Rule Definition window.

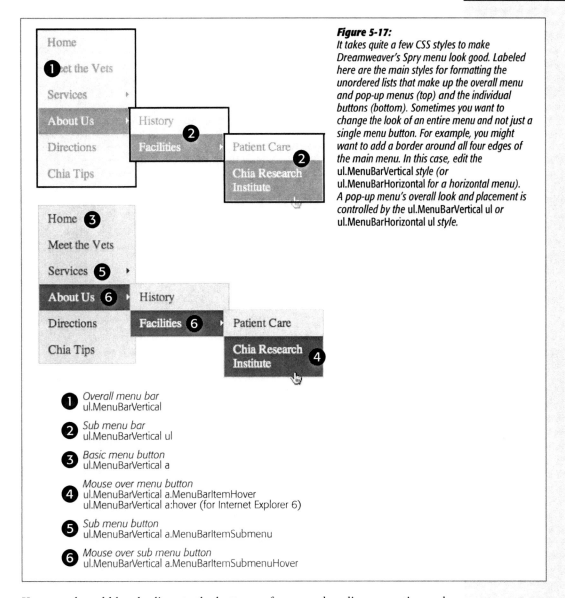

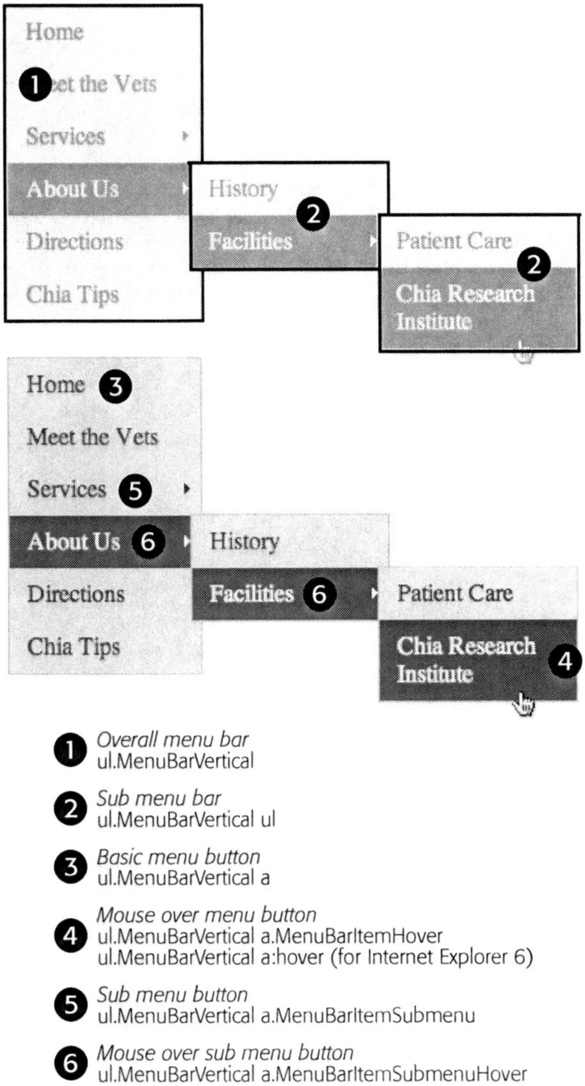

Figure 5-17:
It takes quite a few CSS styles to make Dreamweaver's Spry menu look good. Labeled here are the main styles for formatting the unordered lists that make up the overall menu and pop-up menus (top) and the individual buttons (bottom). Sometimes you want to change the look of an entire menu and not just a single menu button. For example, you might want to add a border around all four edges of the main menu. In this case, edit the ul.MenuBarVertical *style (or* ul.MenuBarHorizontal *for a horizontal menu). A pop-up menu's overall look and placement is controlled by the* ul.MenuBarVertical ul *or* ul.MenuBarHorizontal ul *style.*

You can also add border lines to the buttons—for example, a line separating each button—by setting the border properties for this style (see page 231 for more on CSS borders). Set the *padding* (page 343) to control the space between the text on a button and the edge of the button. To make the text appear close to the edges of the button, decrease the padding; to place empty space around the text, increase the padding.

Formatting rollover menu buttons

Visitors get instant feedback when they interact with a Spry menu on a Web page. Moving the mouse over a menu button changes the color of the button and its text, letting visitors know "Hey, I'm a link, click me!" The rollover buttons Dreamweaver creates have a purple background and white text, but you can change those settings by editing either the *ul.MenuBarVertical a.MenuBarItemHover* or the *ul.MenuBarHorizontal a.MenuBarItemHover* style (depending on whether you've inserted a vertical or horizontal menu). In addition, to make sure the rollovers work in Internet Explorer 6 for Windows, you must edit either the style *ul.MenuBarVertical a:hover*, or *ul.MenuBarHorizontal a:hover*.

Locate a style in the CSS Styles panel, and double-click it to open the style for editing. The Dreamweaver-created style only changes the text color and the background color, but you're free to change any CSS property. For example, if you added border lines between buttons in the menu bar, you could alter the color of those border lines for the rollover button. Or, you could make text appear bold when its button is hovered over.

Note: The name of the style used for rollover menu buttons is actually a combination of three different selectors and is so long that its full name doesn't even fit in the CSS Styles panel: *"ul.MenuBarHorizontal a.MenuBarItemHover, ul.MenuBarHorizontal a.MenuBarItemSubmenuHover, ul.MenuBarHorizontal a.MenuBarSubmenuVisible"* (the name will be slightly different for a vertical menu). This peculiar style is called a *group selector*. It's an efficient way to apply similar formatting rules to multiple elements on a page (see page 304 for an explanation of group selectors).

Formatting submenu buttons

Submenu buttons (the buttons that produce a pop-up menu when moused over) look nearly identical to other menu buttons. In fact, the two styles mentioned above that control a menu in its normal and rollover states define the basic formatting for submenu buttons as well. The only visible difference is the small arrow that appears on the right edge of a submenu button (see Figure 5-17). The arrow visually indicates the presence of a pop-up menu; it's a kind of "there's more this way" icon.

You can replace the graphics Dreamweaver uses for submenus: they're named SpryMenuBarDown.gif, SpryMenuBarDownHover.gif, SpryMenuBarRight.gif, and SpryMenuBarRightHover.gif. (The two "down" arrow graphics are only used for horizontal menu bars.) Create your own arrow graphics (in GIF format) with the same names and replace the original graphic files, which are located in the SpryAssets folder (unless you changed the name and location as described in the Tip on page 188). The graphics should be small enough to be visible in the menu buttons—the ones that Dreamweaver supplies are 4×7 pixels (right arrow) and 7×4 pixels (down arrow)—and there should be versions for both the normal and roll-over states of the submenu button.

Tip: You can *permanently* replace the arrow graphics supplied with Dreamweaver so that your own graphics are inserted each time you add a Spry menu. Just replace Dreamweaver's graphics with your own in the Dreamweaver configuration folder: In Windows this is located at C:\Program Files\Adobe\Adobe Dreamweaver CS4\configuration\Shared\Spry\Widgets\MenuBar; on Macs you'll find these images in Applications → Adobe Dreamweaver CS4 → configuration → Shared → Spry → Widgets → MenuBar. Make sure that your graphic files have the exact same names as those supplied by Dreamweaver.

If you want to further customize the submenu button appearance (for example, to change the font just for submenu buttons) edit either the *ul.MenuBarVertical a.MenuBarItemSubmenu* or *ul.MenuBarHorizontal a.MenuBarItemSubmenu* style. The rollover state for submenu buttons in vertical menus is controlled by the *ul.MenuBarVertical a.MenuBarItemSubmenuHover* style and, in horizontal menus, by the *ul.MenuBarHorizontal a.MenuBarItemSubmenuHover* style.

Changing the width of menus and buttons

Spry menu buttons have preset widths. The main navigation menu buttons are each 8ems wide, while the buttons on pop-up menus are 8.2ems (see page 139 for information on ems). If your navigation buttons have a lot of text on them, 8 ems may be too narrow to fit everything in. Or, 8 ems may be too much space if the menu text is small and made up of short words like "Home," "About," and "Contact." You can adjust the width of buttons and menus by opening the appropriate CSS Style (discussed next) and adjusting the style's *width* property. For example, double-click the style name in the CSS Styles panel, and then change the *width* property located in either the Box or Positioning categories of the CSS Rule Definition window. (The CSS Properties Pane provides an even quicker method, as discussed in Figure 5-18.) Here are the settings you can edit:

- **Main menu width.** The overall width of the menu is set by the *ul.MenuBarVertical* style. (Setting the width of a horizontal menu has no effect, since the width of a horizontal menu is determined by the number of buttons on the menu.) For a vertical menu bar, use the same width value for the menu as you do for the button width (discussed next).

- **Main menu button width.** The width of the buttons that appear on the main Spry menu are determined by the *ul.MenuBarVertical li* style or *ul.MenuBarHorizontal li* style. You may want the button to be just as wide as the text inside it—in other words, have the buttons be different widths based on the amount of text on the button's label. For this effect, set the width of this style to *auto*. Variable width buttons look good for horizontal menus, but not for vertical menus, where the staggered right edges of the stacked column of buttons looks uneven and distracting.

- **Pop-up menu width.** Control the overall width of pop-up menus with the *ul.MenuBarVertical ul* or *ul.MenuBarHorizontal ul* style. The width you set for this style should match the width for the pop-up menu buttons, covered next.

- **Pop-up menu button width.** The *ul.MenuBarVertical ul li* and *ul.MenuBarHorizontal ul li* styles control the width of pop-up menu buttons on the vertical and horizontal menu, respectively. Dreamweaver's normal setting is 8.2ems, but you can adjust this to create wider or narrower buttons.

Tip: If you want to add space between buttons in a horizontal menu bar, add some left or right margin to the *ul.MenuBarHorizontal li* style. You then have to set that same margin (left or right) for the *ul.MenuBarHorizontal ul li* style to 0. There's an example of this in the tutorial on page 206.

Positioning pop-up menus

The pop-up menus on vertical menu bars overlap the button that opened them (see Figure 5-17). This stacking appearance gives a 3-D look to the menu, as if the pop-up menu really were popping out of the page. However, you may want the pop-up menu to appear directly next to the menu button that opened it, or to make the pop-up menu overlap even more dramatically.

To change the position of a pop-up menu, edit the *ul.MenuBarVertical ul* (or *ul.MenuBarHorizontal ul*) style (see Figure 5-18). The CSS *margin* property controls the placement of the menu. For a vertical menu, the pop-up menu has a –5% top margin; this places the top of the pop-up menu a little *above* the submenu button that triggers it. The left margin is set to 95%, which moves the pop-up menu to the far right of the submenu button. To make the pop-up menu appear directly to the right and aligned with the top of the submenu button, change the top margin to 0 and the left margin to 100%. To make the pop-up menu overlap even more, you could change –5% to –10% for the top margin, and 95% to 85% for the left margin.

A horizontal menu's pop-up menu appears directly below the submenu button that triggers it. Its margin setting is 0. If you wished to make that menu overlap the submenu button, you could change the top margin to –5% and the left margin to 5%.

Note: The look of sub-submenus for the horizontal menu bar is controlled by a style named *ul.MenuBarHorizontal ul ul*. There is no sub-submenu style for vertical menus, but you could create one named *ul.MenuBarVertical ul ul*.

Removing a Spry menu

To get rid of a Spry menu, just select it (for example, click the blue tab shown in Figure 5-15), and then press the delete key. In addition to removing the HTML for the menu, Dreamweaver will also—as long as there are no other Spry menus on the page—remove the menu's linked external style sheet and JavaScript file.

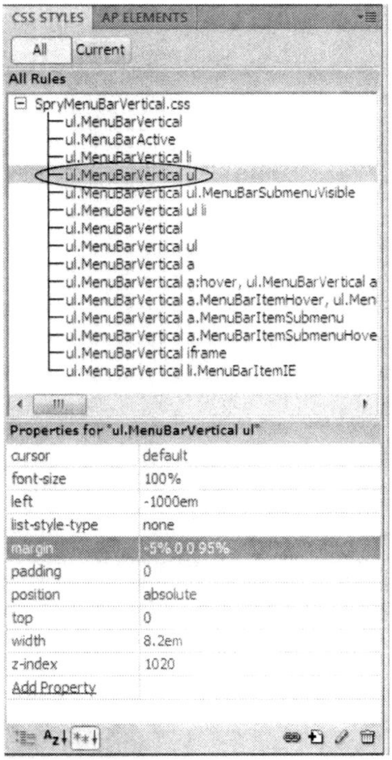

Figure 5-18:
Dreamweaver's CSS style sheet for Spry menus lists the pop-up menu style, ul.MenuBarVertical ul *in this case, twice. The first one listed (circled) controls the positioning of the pop-up menu. Double-clicking the style lets you edit its properties using the Rule Definition window. For a really quick edit like changing the positioning of a pop-up menu by adjusting its margin property, you can use the Properties pane of the CSS Styles panel (pictured in the bottom half of this image.) Just select the current value for the property and type in a new value. For example, in this image, clicking the "-5% 0 0 95%" value (which represent the top, right, bottom, and left margin values, respectively) to the right of the word "margin" lets you type in a new value:* 0 0 0 100%, *say. Editing with the Properties Pane is discussed in detail on page 305.*

Link Tutorial

In this tutorial, you'll put the lessons from this chapter to use. You'll learn how to link to other pages on your site, link to another site on the Web, and use Dreamweaver's Spry Menu Bar to create a great looking navigation bar—complete with fancy JavaScript-driven pop-up menus. The completed page will look like the one shown in Figure 5-28.

Note: You'll need to download the tutorial files from *www.sawmac.com/dwcs4/* to complete this tutorial. See the Note on page 49 for more details.

Linking to Other Pages and Web Sites

Once you've downloaded the tutorial files and opened Dreamweaver, define a new site as described on page 42: Name the site *Site Navigation,* and then select the Chapter05 folder (inside the MM_DWCS4 folder). In a nutshell: Choose Site → New Site. In the Site Definition window, click the Advanced tab, type *Site Navigation* into the Site Name field, click the folder icon next to the Local Root Folder field, navigate to and select the Chapter05 folder, and then click Choose or Select. Finally, click OK.

Once again, you'll be working on a page from Chia-Vet.com.

1. **Choose File → Open, and then, in the bottom left of the open file window, click the Site Root button.**

   The Site Root button is a handy tool. It automatically takes you to the local root folder for the site you're currently working on, saving you the effort of manually navigating to that folder.

2. **Double-click the file named *tips.html*.**

   You can also open the file by selecting its name, and then clicking the OK (Select on Macs) button to open the file; double-clicking, however, is a lot faster. You're now looking at a nearly completed Web page with multiple columns, but no navigation bar. (You'll learn how to create this kind of layout in Chapter 9.)

   If Dreamweaver opens the page in Split View, meaning the document window shows both the raw HTML code and the visual Design view, at the top left of the document window, click the Design button (or choose View → Design).

   In the upper-right corner of the page you can see the text "Sign up for our newsletter". You want that to link to a newsletter sign-up page on the site.

3. **Select the text "Sign up for our newsletter". In the Property inspector, to the right of the Link box, click the "Browse for File" button (see Figure 5-3).**

   The Select File window opens.

4. **In the site's root folder, double-click the file named *newsletter.html*.**

   The Select File window closes. That's it? Yup. You've just created a link. Now, you'll learn an even faster way.

5. **In the top left of the page, click the logo image to select it. Make sure the Files panel is open (Window → Files).**

   On many Web sites, you'll find that the site's logo is actually a clickable link to the site's home page. That's not the case here, so you'll turn the large Chia Vet logo into a direct route to the home page.

6. **In the Property inspector, drag the small Point-to-File icon (see Figure 5-6) into the Files panel; move your mouse over the file *index.html*, and then release the mouse button.**

   The link is added to your page. (Unless you have a particular configuration of double monitors as explained in the Note on page 170. In that case, just use the technique in steps 3 and 4 to link to the *index.html* file.) You'll also notice that the logo image now has a big blue outline—you'll fix that soon.

   Note that if you wanted to link the same text to a page on another Web site, then you couldn't use either of the last two methods. Instead, you'd need to type an absolute URL, as you'll see in the next two steps.

7. **Scroll to the bottom of the page. In the footer you see small gray type that reads "A division of CosmoFarmer.com". Select the text "CosmoFarmer.com".**

   You want this text to link to this site's parent company.

8. **In the Property inspector, in the Link box, type *http://www.cosmofarmer.com/*, and then press Enter or Return.**

   Now the text is linked to the CosmoFarmer Web site. Unfortunately the blue links don't fit in with the Chia Vet color palette, and the logo still has a big blue outline around it. You'll remedy that in the next section.

Formatting Links

You can change the look of links using a little CSS. First, you'll remove the clunky blue border from around the logo image.

1. **Make sure the CSS Styles panel is open (Window → CSS Styles); at the bottom of the panel, click the + button.**

   The New CSS Rule window opens. (For a refresher on creating CSS styles, see page 115.)

2. **From the top menu, select the Tag; in the Selector Name box, type *img* (or choose *img* from the menu); and make sure, at the bottom of the window, that the "Rule Definition" menu lists *global.css*. Click OK to create the style.**

   The CSS Rule Definition window opens. The blue line around the image is a border that's being applied to the graphic with the link (it's the equivalent to the blue underline used for text links). To remove it, you just turn off borders for this style.

3. **In the left hand list of CSS categories, select Border; in the Top style menu, select "none".**

   Make sure the "Same for all" checkbox is turned on (this removes the border from all four sides).

4. **Click OK.**

   The blue border around the image disappears. Now it's time to change the look of the links.

5. **Create a new tag style for the <a> tag.**

   You should be getting used to this routine by now but here's a recap: At the bottom of the CSS Style panel, click the + button; from the top menu, choose Tag; in the Selector Name box, type *a* (or select *a* from the menu), and then click OK. The New CSS Rule Definition window appears.

6. **For the Color property, type *#EC6206*; from the font-weight menu, select Bold, and then click OK.**

   The newsletter sign-up link in the top right of the page loses its bright blue color in favor of the orange color used in the Chia Vet logo. You'll now change how the links look when a mouse hovers over them.

7. **In the CSS Styles panel, click the + button; in the New CSS Rule window from the top menu, select Compound, and then, from the Selector Name pull-down menu, select *a:hover*. Click OK.**

   Again, the CSS Rule Definition window appears.

8. **From the CSS Rule Definition window's Type category, type *#779A00* in the Color field, and then, in the Decoration area, turn on the "none" checkbox (see Figure 5-19). Click OK to finish the style and return to the document window.**

   To see how this rollover style works, you'll use Dreamweaver CS4's new Live View.

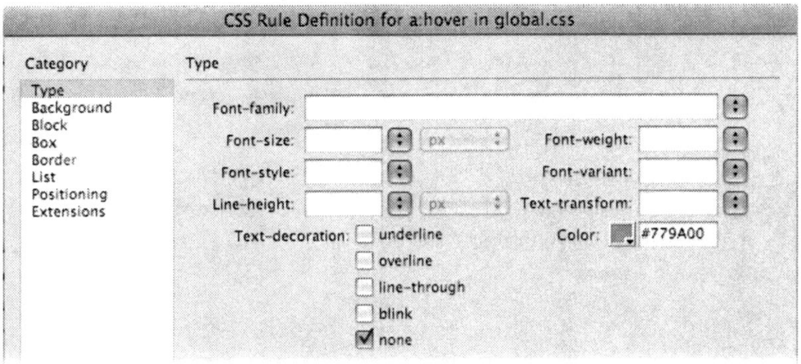

***Figure 5-19:** To completely remove an underline from a link, set the CSS Text-decoration property to "none". You can create a look similar to an underline (but with a lot more design choices) by turning this underline off, and then using the CSS border property to create a dotted, dashed, or different color underline.*

9. **At the top of the Document window (just to the right of the Design button), click the Live View button (or choose View → Live View).**

   Live View lets you preview the look (and functionality) of a Web page directly within Dreamweaver CS4. This latest version of Dreamweaver includes an embedded version of Apple's Webkit (pretty much the Safari Web browser). With Live View you can interact with JavaScript as well as view CSS hover effects: Move your mouse over the "Sign up for our newsletter" link, and you see the link change to green and the underline disappear. (Of course Safari isn't Internet Explorer or Firefox, so you still need to eventually preview the page in those browsers to make sure it looks good. Live View is discussed in more detail on page 553.)

10. **Click the Live View button (or choose View → Live View) a second time to leave Live View.**

    You can't edit a page when in Live View, so you always need to leave it when you're ready to work on your page again. Now you'll add a Spry Menu Bar.

Adding a Navigation Bar

One of the exciting tools in Dreamweaver CS4 is the Spry Menu Bar. This sophisticated combination of HTML, CSS, and JavaScript lets you create slick-looking navigation bars with rollover effects and drop-down menus. Since the Dreamweaver engineers have done all the complex programming for you, you just have to insert, modify, and format the menu to make it fit perfectly into your Web site design.

1. **Return to Dreamweaver and make sure the file *tips.html* is open; click right below the Chia Vet logo inside the grassy background image (circled in Figure 5-20).**

   You'll be inserting a horizontal menu bar that spans most of the page's width. Placing it near the top of the page, as part of the banner, lets site visitors easily find and use it.

Figure 5-20: *What's that strange ship steering wheel (to the right of the circled area), you ask? It's new in Dreamweaver CS4 and it's called the Code Navigator. You use it to navigate to the CSS code that formats the current selection. You'll learn about it on page 320.*

2. **Choose Insert → Spry → Spry Menu Bar.**

   Alternatively, you could click the Spry Menu Bar button on the Layout tab of the Insert bar (Figure 5-14). Either way, the Spry Menu Bar window appears.

3. **Choose the Horizontal option, and then click OK.**

   A gray menu appears at the top of the page with four buttons: Item 1, Item 2, Item 3, and Item 4 (see Figure 5-21).

Figure 5-21: *The Spry Menu Bar starts life with four plain-looking buttons. Item 1 and Item 3 each have a down-pointing arrow icon, indicating that a pop-up menu will appear when visitors mouse over either of them.*

4. **Choose File → Save.**

   A window appears letting you know that Dreamweaver just added six new files to your site. Click OK to dismiss this window. Dreamweaver places these files inside a new folder named SpryAssets. (You can see that folder listed in the Files panel as well—but you may need to press the "Refresh" button [the circle with an arrow tip] to see it.)

   The next step is to change the button labels, add new buttons, and create links.

5. **In the document window, click the blue Spry Menu Bar tab, which appears just above the new menu (circled in Figure 5-21).**

   If you don't see that tab, move your mouse over the menu until it appears. If you still can't see the tab, see Figure 5-15 for a solution.

   The Property inspector changes to display the properties for the menu bar.

6. **In the Property inspector, select Item 1 from the left column of button labels; in the Text box, type *Home* (see Figure 5-22), and then press Enter or Return.**

   Notice in the document window that the first button now says "Home". Now you'll add a link.

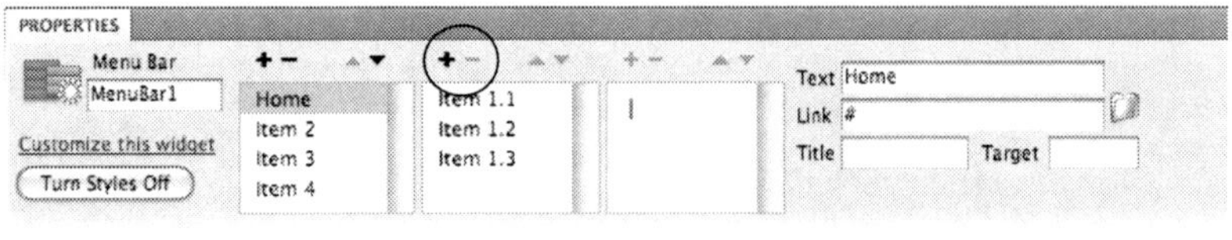

Figure 5-22: *Use the + and – buttons at the top of each column to add or remove buttons from a menu.*

7. **To the right of the Link box, click the "Browse for File" button (the folder icon).**

   This is the same process you followed earlier to add a link to one of the sidebar paragraphs.

8. **In the Select File window, click the Site Root button (top of window for Windows, bottom right on Macs); double-click the *index.html* file.**

   You've labeled your first button and created the first link on this menu bar. Unfortunately, Dreamweaver has added a pop-up menu to this button with three additional buttons. Since the Home button isn't really a "section" of the site with additional pages, you don't need that submenu.

9. **In the middle column in the Property inspector, select item 1.1 and press the – (minus) button at the top of that column (circled in Figure 5-22).**

   Dreamweaver removes the top button from the list. If you look in the document window, you'll see the pop-up menu. When you select an item inside one of the submenu columns in the Property inspector, Dreamweaver temporarily displays the pop-up menu. This is a great way to preview what the pop-up menu will look like in action.

Note: If the Property inspector no longer shows the properties for the Spry Menu Bar, just click the bar's blue tab in the document window to select it.

---

10. **Repeat step 9 for Item 1.2 and Item 1.3.**

    After removing Item 1.3, notice that the down-pointing arrow on the Home button in the document window disappears. Because there's no longer a pop-up menu associated with this link, Dreamweaver removes the arrow graphic. Now, you'll add another button.

11. **Repeat steps 6–8 for Item 2: Change its label to *Meet the Vets*, and then link to the *meet_vets.html* file located in the site root folder.**

    The button's text on the page changes. You'll also notice that it doesn't fit inside the button. That's OK for now; you'll change both the size of the text and the size of the buttons in a little bit. Next you'll edit another button and edit its pop-up menu.

12. **Repeat steps 6–8 for Item 3: Change its label to *Services*, and then link to the *index.html* file located inside the folder named services.**

    It's common to place Web pages for a particular section of the site into a folder just for that section. For example, all pages relating to the various services offered by Chia Vet go inside a folder named *services*. In this case, the main page for the section is usually stored in that folder and named *index.html*. The reasoning behind that is discussed in detail starting on page 618. But for this tutorial, just keep in mind that although you'll be instructed to link to an *index.html* page several times, each time you'll be linking to a *different* file inside a different folder on the site.

This button also has a pop-up menu, but instead of deleting it, you'll just change the pop-up menu buttons to match the Chia Vet site.

13. **In the middle column in the Property inspector, select Item 3.1; change its label to *Preventative Care,* and then, link it to the *preventative.html* file inside the services folder.**

    This button has its own pop-up menu (a sub-submenu). But you don't need it here.

14. **From the right column in the Property inspector, select and delete Item 3.1.1 and Item 3.1.2.**

    Use the same technique described in Step 9 (just select the item, and then click the – button at the top of its column).

15. **Repeat step 13 for Item 3.2 and Item 3.3: Label one *Boarding* and link it to *boarding.html* inside the services folder; label the other *Emergency Services* and link it to the *emergency.html* file in the services folder.**

    The menu's coming together. You just need to add a few more buttons and a couple of pop-up menus.

16. **Repeat steps 6–8 for Item 4: Change its label to *About Us,* and then link to the *index.html* file located inside the about folder.**

    This button requires a pop-up menu, but Dreamweaver hasn't supplied one. You'll have to create the buttons for it yourself.

17. **Make sure the Spry Menu bar is still selected (if not, click its blue tab) and that About Us is selected in the left column in the Property inspector; click the + button in the middle column to add a new button for a pop-up menu.**

    This adds a new pop-up menu and button. You just need to label and link it.

18. **In the Text field, type *History,* and add a link to the file *history.html* inside the about folder.**

    Now you'll add one more button to this pop-up menu.

19. **Click the + button in the middle column to add another button to the About Us pop-up menu. Label it *Facilities* and link to *facilities.html* in the about folder.**

    This button will have its own pop-up menu.

20. **Make sure Facilities is selected in the Property Inspector, and then, in the far right column, click the + button.**

    Dreamweaver adds "Untitled Item" to this column, creating another pop-up menu. Time to label and link.

21. **Repeat step 18: Use *Patient Care* for the label, and then link to the *patient.html* file inside the about folder.**

    By now you should be nearly an expert at adding, editing, and linking buttons and pop-up menus. Just a few more buttons to go.

22. **Repeat steps 20 and 21. Label the new button *Chia Research Institute,* and then link it to *research.html* in the about folder.**

    This adds one more button (thankfully the last one) to the sub-submenu. The Property inspector should now look like Figure 5-23. Now you have just two more buttons to add to the main navigation bar.

***Figure 5-23:** The highlighted items in the left and middle columns indicate which buttons a visitor would have to roll over in order to see the options in the right-hand column.*

23. **Click the + button in the far-left column to add another button to the main navigation menu. Label it *Directions,* and link to *directions.html* in the main site root folder.**

    Just one more button on the main menu.

24. **Repeat step 23: Name the button *Chia Tips* and link to *tips.html* in the main site root folder.**

    That's actually a link to this very page.

    You're done! Thankfully, once a navigation bar is complete, you can reuse it throughout your site, so you don't have to go through this laborious procedure for each page of your site. (Dreamweaver's Template feature can make the process even easier, as described in Chapter 19.)

    You can press the Live View button (see step 9 on page 198) to test the menu bar without leaving Dreamweaver. Make sure to click the Live View button again when you're done taking the menu bar for a spin.

Styling the Menu Bar

The basic look of a Spry menu probably doesn't fit the design of your site, so learning to edit the CSS that Dreamweaver supplies when it inserts a Spry menu is an important skill. In this part of the tutorial, you'll edit the look of the buttons and pop-up menus, as well as replace the premade arrow graphics with custom images.

Let's start with the basic look of the buttons.

1. **Make sure the CSS Styles panel is open (Window → CSS Styles) and the All button at the top of that panel is highlighted.**

   When you inserted the menu bar, Dreamweaver attached an external style sheet named SpryMenuBarHorizontal.css to the page. This style sheet contains all the styles you need to modify the look of the menu.

2. **Click the + button (arrow icon) to the left of SpryMenuBarHorizontal.css.**

   The list expands to display all the styles for this style sheet. While you're at it, hide the list of styles in both the *global.css* style sheet and the *twoColFixRtHds.css* style sheet by clicking the – (minus) button to their left. (The oddly named *twoColFixRtHdr.css* file is part of Dreamweaver's built-in CSS layouts. You'll learn how to work with these layouts in Chapter 9.)

3. **In the CSS Styles panel, double-click the style *ul.MenuBarHorizontal a* (it's about half way down the list of styles).**

   The CSS Rule Definition window opens, displaying the current settings for this style. This particular style is called a descendent selector. You'll learn about that type of style on page 301, but in a nutshell you read the style from right to left, with the rightmost element being the one that will be formatted. In this case, the style will apply to an <a> tag (a link), but only when the link is inside an unordered list (ul) that has the class *MenuBarHorizontal* applied to it. In other words, this style applies to every link inside the Spry Menu Bar. You'll make some type changes first.

4. **From the Font-family menu, select "Tahoma, Geneva, sans-serif"; in the font-size menu, type *11*; from the font-weight menu, choose "bold"; from the text-transform menu, choose "uppercase"; and change the color to #779A00.**

   The window should look like Figure 5-24. Next, you'll change the background color of the buttons to plain white.

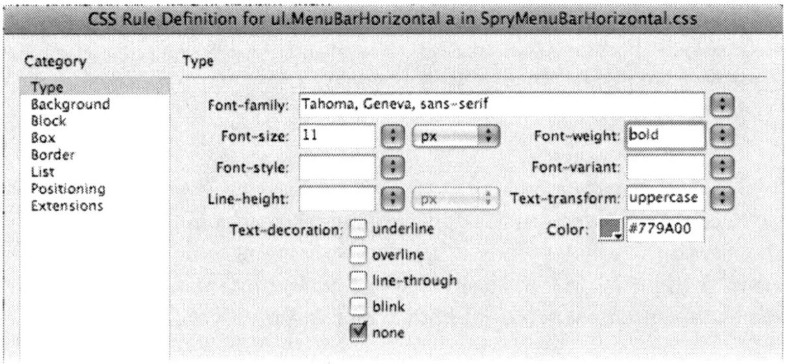

***Figure 5-24:** Changing the text properties for the* ul.MenuBarHorizontal a *style defines most of the basic styles for all menu buttons. Only the color property is different for rollover links. Make sure you don't uncheck the "none" option under Text-decoration, or a line appears underneath the text in each button.*

5. **Click the Background category, and select white for the background color.**

   You can also just type *#FFF* into the text field to the right of the color box. The text inside each button is aligned to the left edge; for a bit of variety (and more practice with Dreamweaver) you'll center align the text.

6. **Click the Block category, and select center for the text-align menu.**

   The buttons will look better with thick, distinctive borderlines drawn across the top of each button.

7. **Click the Border category; turn off all three "Same for all" checkboxes; for the top border, select "solid" from the Style menu, type *2* in the Width menu, and set the color to #EC6206.**

   Next, you'll give the text inside a little breathing room.

8. **Click the Box category; change the padding settings so that the Top and Bottom padding are both 5px and the Left and Right padding are 3px.**

   The window should now look like Figure 5-25. You can quickly set each of these values if you just type *5px* (or *3px* if you're setting the left or right padding), instead of typing 5 (or 3) in the first box, and then choosing px from the menu to the right.

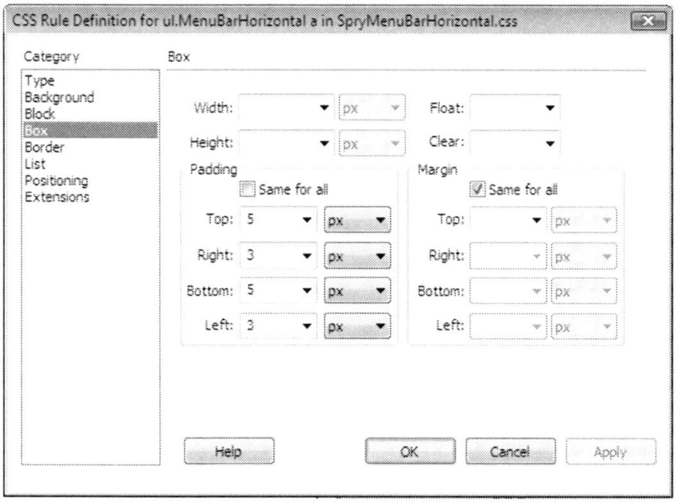

Figure 5-25: *Adding padding to the navigation buttons adds white space inside the button, separating the text inside the button from the button's edges. This process makes for a larger clickable target and more prominent buttons.*

9. **Click OK to finish editing the style.**

   The text on the buttons looks pretty good, but to fill up the banner area the buttons could be a little wider and spaced apart a bit.

10. **In the CSS Styles Panel, select the *ul.MenuBarHorizontal li* style (circled in Figure 5-26).**

    Don't double-click the style name. Here's another descendent selector style—it applies to every <li> tag (list item) inside the Spry Menu Bar. For a quick edit to an already defined property, in the CSS Styles panel, you can use the Properties pane. Notice that the style currently has a fixed width of 8em. You'll change that.

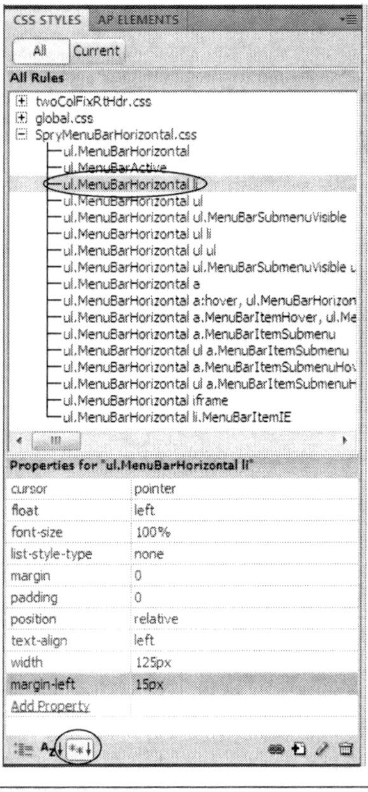

Figure 5-26: *When you select a style name in the Styles panel, all of its properties appear in the Properties pane in the bottom half of the panel. To see only the properties that are currently set for the style, make sure the "set properties" button (bottom circle) is pressed. Click any value (for example, "125px" in the width field here) to type a new value for a CSS property.*

11. **Click 8em to the right of "width" in the Properties pane, type *125* into the first box, and choose *px* from the second pull-down menu (or just type *125px* in the first box).**

    You can also *add* a CSS property using the Properties pane.

12. **At the bottom of the Properties Pane, click the Add Property link; either type *margin-left* in the box or click the menu button and select margin-left from the list of CSS properties; press the Tab key, and then type *15px*. Hit the Enter (or Return) key to make your edits take effect.**

    The CSS Properties pane should look like Figure 5-26. You've just added 15 pixels of space to the left side of each list item—this effectively spreads out the buttons, adding a bit of space between each. The main navigation buttons are all

125 pixels wide, but if you save and preview the page now (or press the Live View button at the top of the document window), you see that the pop-up menus look a bit weird—there's a strange border that doesn't fit the buttons. In addition, the pop-up menu buttons are wider than the main navigation buttons, and they don't sit directly under the main buttons.

Tip: When setting a measurement (like width or height) in the Properties pane, you don't have to type a value in the first field, and *then* use the measurements menu to select a value like px, em, or %. A faster method is to type the measurement value along with the number–for example, type *125px*–then hit Enter (or Return) to make the change stick.

---

13. **Repeat steps 10 and 11 for the *ul.MenuBarHorizontal ul* style (skip step 12 though—you don't change the left margin on this style).**

    You have two *ul.MenuBarHorizontal ul* styles; for this step, edit the first style (near the top of the list of styles). The second instance of that style adds a border around the pop-up menus, which doesn't look good, so you'll remove it.

14. **In the CSS Styles panel, select the second *ul.MenuBarHorizontal ul* (about half way down the list of styles), and click the Trash can icon (delete button) in the lower right of the CSS Styles panel.**

    Alternatively you can hit Delete to remove the style. Finally, you'll position the submenus so that they line up underneath the main buttons and resize them to match the main buttons. The reason the submenus are indented has to do with how nested lists work. A nested list is actually a bulleted list that's inside an item in another list—in other words, a nested list includes list items (the <li> tag) inside the <li> tag of the main list. In this example, the main navigation buttons are the main list and a submenu (for example the ones that appear under Services) is a series of list items contained inside a main navigation button. This means that in step 12, you added 15 pixels of left margin to every <li> item—so the main navigation button is indented 15 pixels, and then every button on the submenu is indented *another* 15 pixels. You just want that left margin on the main navigation buttons, but you don't want it on the submenus. So you need to edit a style that applies just to the submenu buttons.

15. **In the CSS Styles panel, select the style *ul.MenuBarHorizontal ul li.* Using the Properties pane, set the width to 125px, and add the margin-left property and set it to 0.**

    This style, another descendent selector, applies to list items (the <li> tag), but only to list items that appear inside a <ul> tag that is itself inside a <ul> tag with the class *MenuBarHorizontal* applied to it. In other words, this style affects only list items inside a nested list. You can review steps 10-12 to see how to make these changes. In this case, you're setting the left-margin to 0 in order to remove the indent you see on the submenus.

Submenus and Rollover Buttons

Overall, the menu bar is looking good and works well. There are just a few tweaks left. The rollover buttons don't look so great—electric purple just doesn't fit the look of Chia Vet. In addition, the sub-submenu (the one that appears when you rollover the Facilities button under the About Us menu) is positioned too far to the right of the button that triggers it. You'll tackle that problem first.

1. **In the CSS Styles panel, double-click the style *ul.MenuBarHorizontal ul ul.***

   This style is used to style a—take a deep breath—bulleted list that's inside a bulleted list that's inside a bulleted list with the class MenuBarHorizontal applied to it. Since, under the hood, the HTML for a Spry Menu Bar is just a bunch of nested lists (see page 104), this style affects the third level unordered list—or the sub-submenu of the navigation bar.

2. **In the CSS Rule Definition window, select the Box category. Change the top margin setting to –1px, and the left margin setting to 125px.**

   Make sure you change the % setting to px, so that the sub-submenu is positioned in a precise pixel location relative to the button that triggers it. In this case, the sub-submenu will be positioned directly to the right of the button.

3. **Click OK to close the CSS Rule Definition window and finish editing the style.**

   Now it's time to turn your attention to the appearance of the buttons when the mouse rolls over them. You actually need to edit several styles: one for regular buttons and two others for buttons that open pop-up menus.

4. **In the CSS Styles panel, select the style *ul.MenuBarHorizontal a.MenuBarItem-Hover* (a little over half of the way down the list of styles).**

   You may need to expand the width of the Styles panel to see the full name of the styles: Drag the gray bar separating the document window and panel groups to the left. Actually, it's a much longer group of styles named "*ul.MenuBarHorizontal a.MenuBarItemHover, ul.MenuBarHorizontal a.MenuBarItemSubmenuHover, ul.MenuBarHorizontal a.MenuBarSubmenuVisible*", but you'll probably only be able to see the first part. Notice that, in the Properties pane, a background color and text color are set; you'll change these.

5. **In the Properties pane, click the color box to the right of "background-color", and then type *#CAE0EC*; click the #FFF value next to the color property, and then type *#333*.**

   The style you just changed won't affect Internet Explorer 6; there's another style you have to change to get a rollover effect in that browser.

6. **In the Styles panel, select *ul.MenuBarHorizontal a:hover,* and then repeat step 5.**

   Again, the actual style name is a bit longer and includes an additional selector: "*ul.MenuBarHorizontal a:hover, ul.MenuBarHorizontal a:focus*".

For some strange reason, Internet Explorer 6 has its own style for the button rollovers, so whenever you update the rollover style used for the other browsers—*ul.MenuBarHorizontal a.MenuBarItemHover*—then you also have to update this style to match.

Now, you'll replace Dreamweaver's default arrow graphics with arrows custom made to match the Chia Vet site.

7. **Open the Files panel (Window → Files), and then expand the folder named NEW_NAV_IMAGES so you can see the four files inside that folder.**

   To expand the folder, click the + (arrow on a Mac) button. The four image files in this folder are named exactly the same as the ones Dreamweaver supplies. You can just drag these into the SpryAssets folder to replace the old ones.

8. **In the NEW_NAV_IMAGES folder, click one of the image files to select it; then hold down the control key (⌘ key) and click each of the remaining three files. Once selected, drag them into the SpryAssets folder (see Figure 5-27).**

   Dreamweaver lets you know that you're about to replace some existing files; that's what you want to do, so click the "Yes to All" button.

   You're almost there, but one bug crops up in Internet Explorer 6—the navigation bar has a huge space below it. This bug is one of the many you'll find in IE. The fix is pretty obscure, but it works.

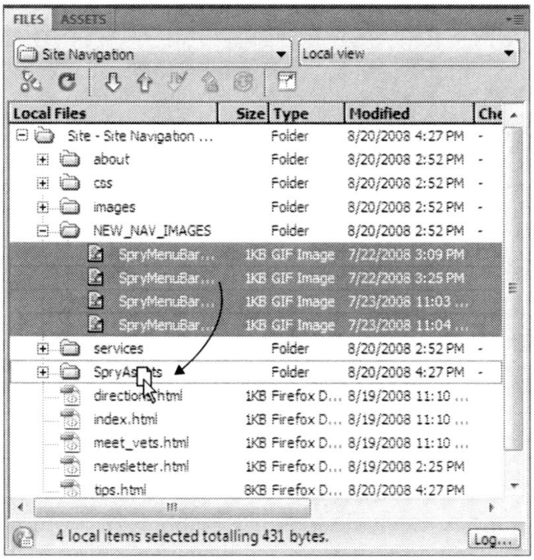

***Figure 5-27:** The Files panel offers more than just a list of files in a Web site. It also lets your rearrange, rename, and create Web page files. You'll learn how to get the most out of this useful tool on page 625.*

9. **In the Styles panel, select *ul.MenuBarHorizontal.* At the bottom the Properties Pane, click the Add Property button; type *zoom*; press Tab, and then type *1*.**

   This adds an IE-only CSS style named zoom to the menu bar style. This property lets you zoom into page content, but with a setting of 1 it has absolutely no visual impact on the page in any browser. However, it's a way of knocking IE 6 upside the head so that it correctly displays the menu. The reason it works is a bit of a mystery—you can find out more about this technique at *http://haslayout.net/haslayout*, and *CSS: The Missing Manual* has an in-depth discussion of Internet Explorer bugs and the use of zoom:1 to fix them.

   Fortunately, you won't always (and hopefully won't even usually) need to turn to this technique. However, if you do discover that IE 6 is displaying parts of a page completely differently from other browsers, including IE 7, slapping a zoom:1 on the offending element's style sometimes works. Dreamweaver's Check Browser Compatibility tool can help too (see page 130).

   Now, you can take the menu bar for a spin. However, you have one more step if you plan on previewing this page using either Internet Explorer 6 or 7 for Windows.

10. **Choose Commands → "Insert Mark of the Web".**

    This option probably sounds like some Adobe programmer's idea of a practical joke. Unfortunately it's not. Most versions of Internet Explorer 6 and 7 don't let you preview the cool pop-up menus without this step. For security reasons, IE doesn't let you preview any JavaScript effects (the pop-up menu, for example) on a page you open directly off your hard drive. Inserting the "Mark of the Web" (the cult conspiracy theories are already flying) stops IE from interfering with JavaScript. The whole story on this bizarre command is on page 250.

    Note that if you put this Web page on an actual Web server, then Internet Explorer doesn't have any problem with the JavaScript and the "Mark of the Web" isn't necessary. To remove the "mark," choose Commands → "Remove Mark of the Web".

    And if you're just testing on Firefox, Safari, or Opera, then you can skip this step.

Note: You may need to completely close Internet Explorer and preview the "marked" Web page to make sure the pop-up menus work.

11. **Choose File → Save All; Press the F12 (Option-F12) key to preview the finished product.**

    Move your mouse over the buttons. It should look like Figure 5-28. (You may need to press your browser's reload button to make it load the new graphics.)

    You'll also find a completed version of this tutorial in the Chapter05_finished folder that accompanies the downloaded tutorial files.

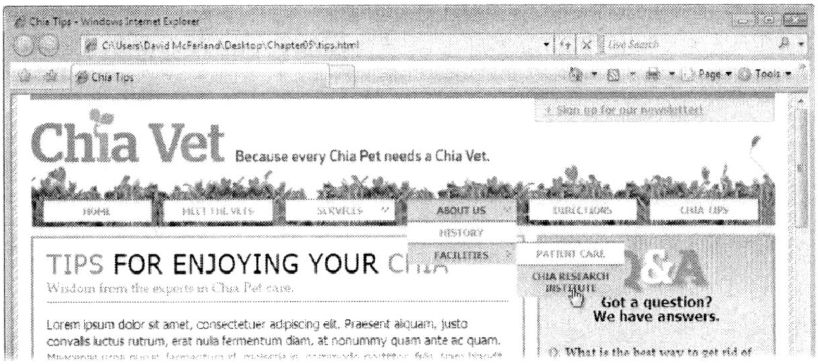

Figure 5-28: *Adding a Spry menu may take quite a few steps, but it delivers a high-quality dynamic navigation bar and saves you countless hours of JavaScript programming and browser testing.*

Note: When you preview an unsaved page, or a page that uses an external style sheet that's opened and unsaved, Dreamweaver pops up an annoying "save these files" window. You must click Yes to see the newest version of the page. If you're getting tired of this window, you can use the "Preview using temporary file" feature. It's described on page 159.

CHAPTER 6

Images

Nobody believes that a picture is worth a thousand words more than today's Web designers, as evidenced by the highly visual nature of the Internet. In fact, it's not difficult these days to stumble onto a home page composed almost entirely of graphics, as you can see in Figure 6-1.

Even if you don't want to go that far, understanding how to use graphics effectively is invaluable. Whether you want to plop a simple photo onto your page, cover it with clickable "hotspots," or design an interactive set of buttons that light up when the cursor passes over them, Dreamweaver makes the job easy.

Adding Images

If you were writing out the HTML instructions for your Web page by hand, you'd insert an image into a Web page using the image tag: <img>. For example, the HTML snippet <img src="images/george.jpg"> tells a browser to display a graphic file named *george.jpg*, which you can find in the *images* folder. (An image tag's primary property is called the *source* [src] property; it indicates the URL or path to the graphics file.)

Dreamweaver does all this coding for you automatically when you insert a picture into your fledgling Web page:

1. **Save the Web page that will contain the image.**

   To insert an image, Dreamweaver must determine the path from your Web page to that image, which could be anywhere on your hard drive. As with links, saving the page before you proceed lets Dreamweaver correctly determine the path from the page you just saved to the image.

Figure 6-1:
Some Web sites rely almost exclusively on graphics for both looks and function. The home page for the Curious George Web site at http://pbskids.org*, for instance, uses graphics not just for pictures of the main character, but also for the page's background and navigation buttons.*

2. **In the document window, click where you want to insert the image.**

   You can choose anywhere within a paragraph, a cell in a table (see Chapter 7), or a <div> tag (see page 333). To set a graphic apart from other text, press Enter (Return), creating a blank line, before inserting it so that it's inserted into its own paragraph.

3. **Choose Insert → Image.**

   Alternatively, from the Insert panel's Common category, you can click the Image button (see Figure 6-2). Or, if you're a keyboard shortcut fan, press Ctrl+Alt+I (⌘-Option-I).

   In any case, the Select Image Source dialog box opens. This box is identical to the Select File window that appears when adding a link to a page (see Figure 5-4). The only difference is a Preview Images checkbox—turning it on shows a thumbnail of any selected image in the Preview window.

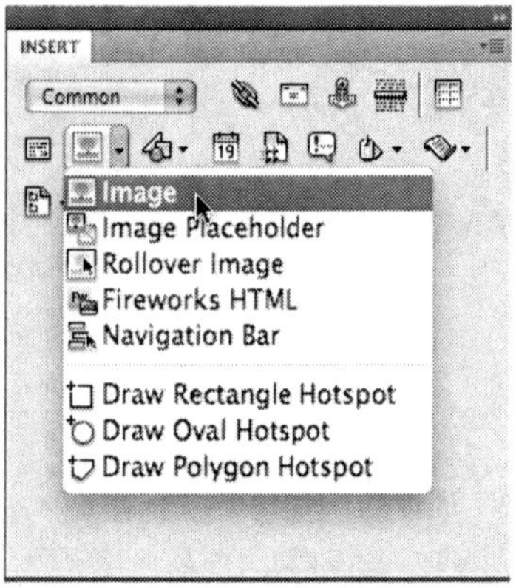

Figure 6-2:
The Image menu on the Insert panel's Common category provides tools for adding graphics to your pages.

4. **Browse to, and then select the graphics file you wish to add to the page.**

   The file must be in one of the formats that work on the Web: GIF, JPEG, or PNG.

   The file should be stored somewhere in the local root folder of your site (see page 43) or in one of its subfolders. If it isn't, Dreamweaver can't add the correct path to your Web page.

Note: The primary file format for Fireworks, Adobe's Web-friendly image-editing program, is PNG (just as Photoshop's format is PSD). However, a native Fireworks file contains additional data used by the program to keep track of fonts, layers, and other information. That extra data significantly increases file size. So always make sure you use the Export command from within Fireworks to properly compress the image into a GIF, JPEG, or PNG (without all the extra Firework info) file.

   That's why, if you select a graphic for insertion that's not already in your site folder, Dreamweaver offers to add a *copy* of it there. If you choose Yes, then a Copy File As dialog box opens, so that you can save the file in your local root folder, renaming it if you wish. If you choose No, then Dreamweaver uses a file-relative path (beginning with *file:///*) for the image's Src property (see page 213). But clicking No is a bad idea: while it allows the graphic to be displayed while you work with Dreamweaver on your computer, the graphic doesn't appear once you move the document to the Web (see the box on page 169).

Note: Dreamweaver lets you choose a Photoshop file when inserting an image. Dreamweaver doesn't insert the PSD file itself, but it opens a window letting you save a new GIF, JPEG, or PNG file with Web-appropriate optimization settings. Page 217 has the full story on this feature.

5. **Click OK (Windows) or Choose (Mac).**

   You should see an Image Tag Accessibility Attributes window, which lets you assign an "alternate" text description of the image (for the benefit of those visitors who can't see your images—those using screen reading software, for instance). If you don't see this window, somewhere along the line you or someone else turned off this option—you can turn it back on as described in the box on page 228.

6. **In the Alternate Text box, type a short, text description of the image, and then press OK.**

   Dreamweaver inserts the image. The options in the Image Tag Accessibility Attributes window are described in greater detail on page 225 and the box on page 228, but in a nutshell, you should add a short description for any image that adds meaning to a page. For example, if you're inserting a graphic of your company's logo, the alternative text should be your company's name. Use the second option—Long Description—to provide a link to another page with detailed information about an information-heavy graphic such as a chart or map. You'll almost always skip it, but for more details on how it works, see the box on page 228.

Tip: Dreamweaver also permits several drag-and-drop techniques for quickly adding images to your pages.

Make sure you've defined a site as described on page 37. Then open the Files window (press F8). You can drag any graphics file from that window right into an open Dreamweaver document. You can also drag graphics in from the Assets panel, as described on page 633.

Dreamweaver even lets you drag a graphic from your desktop onto a page. If you do this, Dreamweaver dutifully informs you that you must copy the file into your site folder (and provides a dialog box that lets you specify *which* folder), so that the image shows up properly on the Web page. (You can even define a default images folder for a site, so that when you drag an image onto a page, Dreamweaver automatically copies it into the correct folder; see page 620.)

Dreamweaver even lets you drag Photoshop files into a Dreamweaver document.

Adding an Image Placeholder

You'll often find yourself working on a Web site without all the pieces of the puzzle. You may start building a page, even when your client has yet to give you all the text she wants on the page. Or you may find that a photograph hasn't been shot, but you want to get the page ready for it. Other times, you may be responsible for building the Web pages while another designer is creating the banners and navigation buttons.

To help out in these kinds of situations, Dreamweaver includes the Image Placeholder button. It lets you insert a placeholder—called an *FPO* (For Placement Only) image in publishing lingo—so that you can stake out space on the page for a graphic that isn't ready yet. This way, you can lay out the basic structure of the page without having to wait for all the graphics to arrive in their final form.

To insert a placeholder, do one of the following:

- Choose Insert → Image Placeholder.
- On the Insert bar's Common category, from the Image menu, select the Image Placeholder icon (see Figure 6-2).

In the window that appears (see Figure 6-3), type a width and height for the image, which determines how much space the placeholder takes up on the page. This should match the dimensions you have planned for the final image. The Name and "Alternate text" fields are optional. (If you fill them out, then they appear in the Name and Alt boxes of the image's Property inspector, as discussed next.)

The Color box lets you specify a color for the placeholder—presumably to make the placeholder more colorful than the default gray color. Avoid this option: It inserts inline CSS code that isn't removed when you replace this placeholder with a real graphic, adding unnecessary code to the page. What's worse, if the image you eventually use has any transparency areas, the color defined here will show through the graphic!

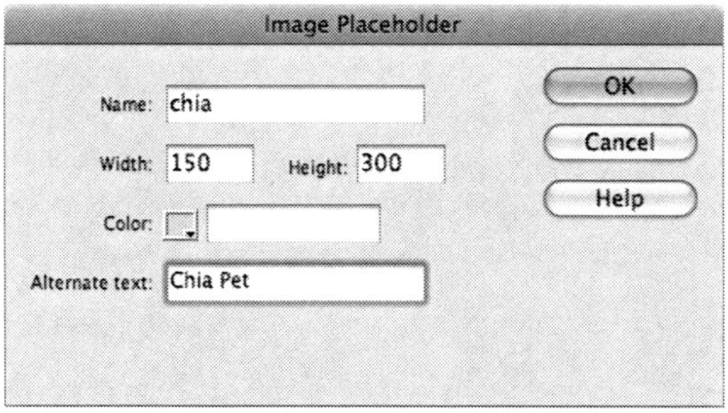

Figure 6-3:
The values you type for Name, Width, Height, and "Alternate text" appear in the Property inspector after you insert an image placeholder. The Color option just lets you choose a color for the placeholder.

Warning: Dreamweaver takes the name you provide for a placeholder image and uses it as an ID attribute to the <img> tag. IDs are used for both JavaScript and CSS. If the name you provide for the image placeholder is the same as an ID name for a CSS style you created, then you can run into some weird display problems. Bottom line: Unless you plan on using a CSS ID style to format the image or JavaScript to control the image, just leave the name field empty when you insert the placeholder.

Of course, using a placeholder doesn't do you any good if you don't eventually replace it with a real image. Once you've got the image that should finally appear on the page, on the Web page, just double-click the placeholder. The Select Image Source window appears. Follow steps 4 through 5 on page 215 to insert the new image.

If you also own Fireworks, Adobe's Web graphics companion program, there's an added benefit to the image placeholder. When an image placeholder is selected in the document window, the Property inspector includes a button called Create. Clicking this button launches Fireworks and opens a new, blank graphics document set to the exact dimensions you specified earlier. You can then create your graphic in Fireworks. After you save the file, Fireworks exports it to whatever folder you specify, and then automatically inserts it into your document—replacing the placeholder.

Inserting an Image from Photoshop

Since Adobe (the maker of Photoshop) bought Macromedia (the maker of Dreamweaver), it was only a matter of time before these two powerful programs were brought together. Dreamweaver CS4 builds on the tools added in Dreamweaver CS3 to streamline the process of getting images back and forth between Photoshop and Dreamweaver. You have two primary methods of adding a Photoshop document to a Web page: Insert a PSD file (Photoshop's native format), or copy an image from Photoshop, and then paste it into a Dreamweaver document.

UP TO SPEED

GIFs, JPEGs, and PNGs: The Graphics of the Web

Computer graphics come in hundreds of different file formats. The assorted acronyms can be mind numbing: JPEG, GIF, TIFF, PICT, BMP, EPS, and so on.

Fortunately, graphics on the Web are a bit simpler. All of today's Web browsers support only three graphics formats, each of which provides good *compression*; through clever computer manipulation, compression reduces the graphic's file size so it can travel more rapidly across the Internet. Which you choose depends on the image you wish to add to your page.

GIF (Graphics Interchange Format) files provide good compression for images that have areas of solid color: logos, text, simple banners, and so on. GIFs also offer single-color transparency, meaning that you can make one color in the graphic disappear, permitting the background of a Web page to show through part of the image. In addition, GIFs can include simple animations.

A GIF image can contain a maximum of only 256 shades, however, generally making photos look posterized (in other words, not completely realistic). That radiant sunset photo you took with your digital camera won't look so good as a GIF. (If you don't need to animate an image, the PNG8 format discussed below is a better choice than GIF.)

JPEG (Joint Photographic Experts Group) graphics, on the other hand, pick up where GIFs leave off. JPEG graphics can contain millions of different colors, making them ideal for photos. Not only do JPEGs do a better job on photos, they also compress multicolored images much better than GIFs, because the JPEG compression algorithm considers how the human eye perceives different adjacent color values. When your graphics software saves a JPEG file, it runs a complex color analysis to lower the amount of data required to accurately represent the image. On the downside, JPEG compression makes text, and large areas of solid color, look blotchy.

Finally, the **PNG** (Portable Network Graphics) includes the best features of GIFs and JPEGs, but you need to know which version of PNG to use for which situation. PNG8 is basically a replacement for GIF. Like GIF, it supports 256 colors and basic one-color transparency. However, PNG8 usually compresses images to a slightly smaller file size than GIF, so PNG8 images download a tiny bit faster than the same image saved in the GIF format.

PNG24 and PNG32 offer the expanded color palette of JPEG images, without any loss of quality. This means that photos saved as PNG24 or PNG32 tend to be higher quality than JPEGs. But before you jump on the PNG bandwagon, JPEG images do offer very good quality and a *much* smaller file size than either PNG24 or PNG32. In general, JPEG is a better choice for photos and other images that include lots of colors.

Finally, PNG32 offers one feature that no other format does: 256 levels of transparency (also called *alpha* transparency), which means that you can actually see the background of a Web page through a drop shadow on a graphic, or even make a graphic that has 50 percent opacity (meaning you can see through it) to create a ghostly translucent effect. Unfortunately, Internet Explorer 6 for Windows doesn't support PNG32's 256 levels of transparency—instead of seeing through the transparent areas, IE6 replaces the transparent areas with a hideous blue background. (Several JavaScript based techniques–see *http://24ways.org/2007/supersleight-transparent-png-in-ie6*, for example–help IE 6 display PNG transparency correctly.) Fortunately, the increasingly popular Internet Explorer 7 does support PNG transparency, as do Firefox, Safari, and Opera.

The first method—inserting a PSD file—now supports what Adobe calls *Smart Objects*, which lets Dreamweaver keep track of whether an original Photoshop file has been updated, and if so, gives you the option of updating the compressed,

Web-ready version of the image on a Web page. Nice. That's great news if you're the type who's constantly tweaking your artwork in Photoshop. The second method—copying and pasting from Photoshop—doesn't keep track of any changes to the original Photoshop file, and works just as it did in Dreamweaver CS3. Both methods are explained in the following pages.

Method 1: Using the Insert Image Object

You can insert a regular Photoshop file using the same steps described on page 213 for inserting GIF, JPEG, or PNG files. For example, use the Image button on the Insert panel (Figure 6-2), or choose Insert → Image. As when inserting a standard Web-ready image file, the Select Image Source window appears. You can then choose a Photoshop document (a .psd file), and click the OK (Choose on Mac) button. Instead of just inserting the image, however, Dreamweaver opens an Image Preview window that lets you choose how to optimize the graphic (see Figure 6-4).

Tip: You can also insert a PSD file by dragging it directly from the desktop (or any folder) and dropping onto a Dreamweaver document. If the PSD file is stored somewhere inside your local root folder, then you can also drag it from the Files panel and drop it onto the page.

Although Dreamweaver gives you lots of options, the decision-making process can be boiled down to three steps:

1. **From the Format menu (circled in Figure 6-4), choose the graphic format you want to use on the Web page.**

   You get to choose from among the three formats: GIF, JPEG, and PNG (see the box on page 218). In general, you'll want to choose PNG8 for images with solid colors and text, like logos; use JPEG for photos. Steer clear of the Animated GIF option; it has absolutely no effect. You can't import animated images using the Image Preview window; instead you need to export an animated GIF from the program in which it was created (like Fireworks or Photoshop). And if you really want to have 256 levels of transparency (great for drop shadow effects, but—as noted on page 218—not so great for Internet Explorer 6), then choose PNG32.

2. **Set your image's optimization settings.**

   The exact optimization choices depend on the graphic format you selected in step 1. Settings for each format are discussed in the sections that follow. Make your choices using the menus and buttons on the window's left side.

   In the right half of the Image Preview, the preview window shows what the final, optimized graphic will look like; you can even compare different optimization settings (see Figure 6-4). The preview window also displays information about the final optimized graphic, such as its file type, the quality or kind of compression used, the number of colors supported, the final size of the file, and how long the file will take to download over a 56K dialup modem.

Figure 6-4 shows what the image looks like when saved as a JPEG (top preview image) and as a PNG8 (bottom preview image). The JPEG version has a quality of 60 (see the oppositepage for a discussion of this property), supports millions of colors, and is 18.79 kilobytes (K) in size. The PNG8 version, on the other hand, is 103.50 K! Given the comparable image quality, JPEG is the obvious choice.

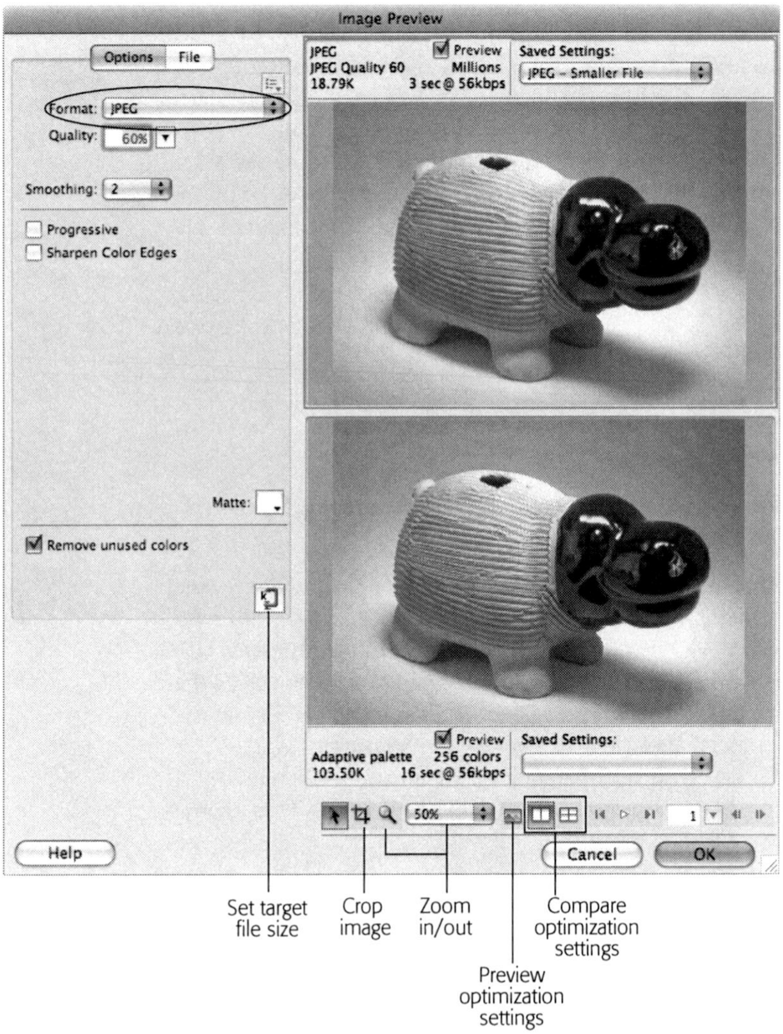

Figure 6-4: *Picking the proper optimization for any particular image is usually just a matter of trial and error, so you'll often want to see how an image looks and compresses as a JPEG and a PNG before deciding which format to choose. You can compare different file types and optimization settings side by side by clicking either the "two-up" or "four-up" buttons at the bottom of the window. Two-up lets you compare two different optimization settings, while the four-up shows four previews. This method is a great way to answer a question like "Would this graphic look better and be smaller as a JPEG, GIF, or PNG8?"*

3. **Click OK, and then name and save the file into your Web site.**

Dreamweaver saves the new image file and places it into your page—at this point it's a GIF, JPEG, or PNG file; however, Dreamweaver adds a small icon in the upper-left corner of the image on the page (see Figure 6-20). This icon indicates that the image is a *Smart Object* and retains a link to the original PSD file.

What makes it "smart" is that Dreamweaver tracks any changes to the PSD file—if you decide to open Photoshop and add some cool effect to the image, then save the image, then Dreamweaver knows you changed the original. At this point you can update the image on your Web page directly in Dreamweaver. Page 241 shows you how.

When you insert a Photoshop image in this manner, unfortunately, *slices* you've made in the Photoshop document are ignored. (Slices provide a way to take a larger Photoshop image and identify, or slice, smaller images out of it.) So if you're used to creating a giant Photoshop Web page mock-up—complete with button graphics, banner graphics, and individual icons—that you slice and individually export out of Photoshop, this technique isn't the best. Dreamweaver tries to insert the entire image, not the bits and pieces you're interested in.

You aren't, however, required to use the entire image when you import it. As pictured in Figure 6-4, you can use the Image Preview box's crop tool to extract just one rectangular area. Dreamweaver optimizes and imports only that part of the image. In addition, Dreamweaver remembers the crop you set, so you can update the image and retain just the cropped portion when you update the Photoshop document.

Tip: For ultra-precise cropping control, click the Image Preview box's File button (Figure 6-5, top left); check the "Export area" box; and then enter precise pixel values for where you want the crop to start, and how wide and tall the cropped area should be.

Cropping an image in this manner has no effect on the original PSD file—it remains its full size; cropping only affects which part of the larger image is turned into a Web graphic and added to the page you're working on. You can even have multiple Smart Objects based on the same Photoshop document (just follow the Insert → Image routine each time). When you update the original Photoshop document, you can update every Smart Object based on that document.

JPEG optimization options

Dreamweaver doesn't give you many choices for optimizing JPEG images. Basically, you can select a quality level that affects both how good the image looks and the size of the graphics file: the higher the quality, the larger the file; the worse the quality, the smaller the file. The Quality setting runs from 1 (low quality/small file) to 100 (high quality/large file). 80 is the normal choice for very good quality and fairly manageable file size; 60 is also a good choice, when you want to keep file size on the slim side. The exact setting depends on what the image looks like, so you should just preview different quality settings until you're satisfied both with how the image looks and the file size.

For most images, turning on the "Progressive" and "Remove unused colors" checkboxes trims down the file size without harming the image. In fact, progressive browser display lets the image appear on the page before the entire graphic file is downloaded, giving the appearance that your site is loading more quickly.

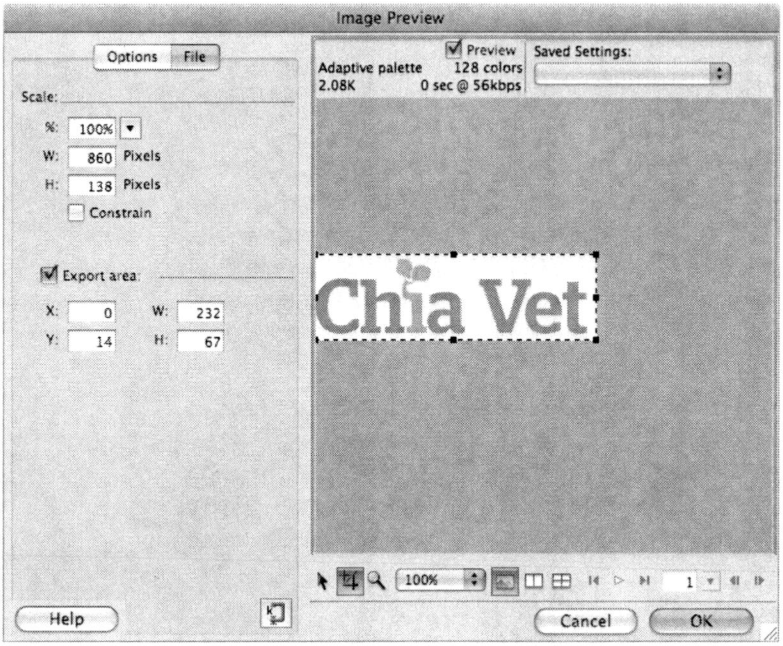

Figure 6-5: *In the Image Preview window, the File options let you precisely control the scale of the final image. For example, if the original Photoshop image is very large, you could type 25 in the Scale section's "%" field, to make the final, imported image 25 percent the size of the Photoshop image. This setting has no effect on the Photoshop document itself, just the final image. You can also import just a selected area of the image by turning on the "Export area" checkbox and then specifying which part of the image to import. You can insert the same Photoshop image several times, but set a different export area for each Smart Object. Doing so lets you preserve a large Web page mockup, while inserting separate bits of the document (such as individual icons, a banner, and so on).*

The Smoothing pull-down menu makes the image look out of focus, but does decrease file size. Turning on the "Sharpen color edges" checkbox can make an image look more in focus, but usually at a significantly higher file size. You might want to experiment with these options on different images, but you'll most probably skip these two settings.

GIF and PNG8 optimization options

GIF and PNG8 files have identical optimization settings; in most cases, you get a smaller file size from a PNG8 file than a GIF. The size of a GIF and PNG8 file is mainly controlled by the number of colors in it—the size of its *palette*. Fewer colors means a smaller file size. Most of the settings available for GIF and PNG8 images control the number and type of colors used (see Figure 6-6).

For optimal compression settings with a GIF or PNG8 image, follow these two steps:

1. **From the Palette menu, select Adaptive.**

   Since both these image types are limited to just 256 colors, this menu determines which colors your image will use. You have a lot of options here, but you can ignore all but Adaptive, which means that Dreamweaver picks the best 256 colors from the image file itself. (The other options select colors from palettes that aren't necessarily contained inside the image file. This ability used to be important when people had monitors that displayed only 256 colors—back when Duran Duran ruled the air waves; but today, these other palettes usually distort the look of the original image.)

Tip: To convert a color image into a black and white GIF or PNG8 file, from the Palette menu, choose Grayscale.

2. **In the "Number of Colors" menu, select a value (Figure 6-6).**

   This menu lets you select from 2 to 256 different colors (256 is the maximum for a GIF or PNG8 image). If the original Photoshop image starts out with only 64 colors, then choosing 256 doesn't add colors or quality to the image. However, you can often choose a *lower* number, eliminating colors from the graphic, and reduce the file size significantly without overly harming the quality of the final image. Again, each image is different, so you should use trial and error to see the minimum colors you need while still maintaining maximum image quality.

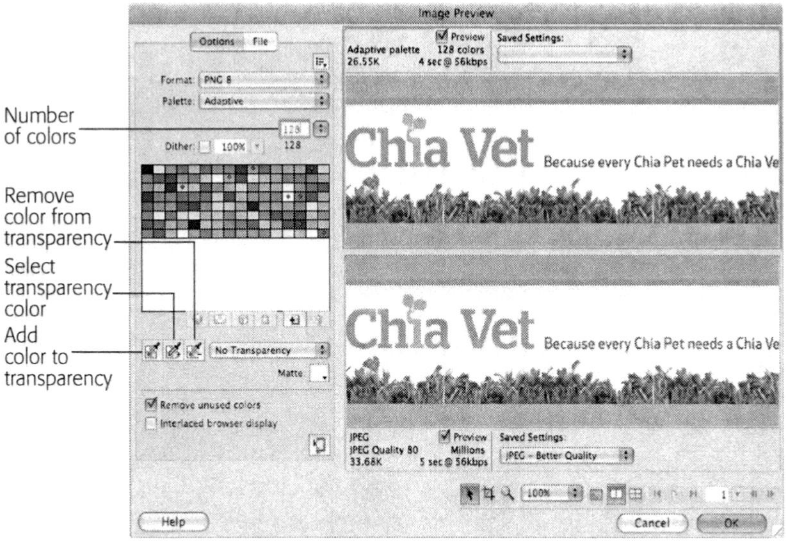

Figure 6-6: *The transparency tools for GIF and PNG8 images let you select one or more colors as "transparent"–that is, those colors disappear from the image, and the background of the page shows through. From the Transparency menu, just select Index Transparency; click the Select Transparency Color tool; then, on the preview image, click the color you wish to disappear (a white background, for example). To add additional colors, use the same process with the "Add Color to Transparency" tool.*

The Loss option (available only for GIF images) also decreases file size at the cost of image quality. In general, increasing the "loss" setting makes an image look spotted and windswept, so, unless you're going for a special effect, use a low loss setting or none at all. The Dither option is intended to make up for lost colors—for example, when you choose 32 from the "Number of Colors" menu, but the image is a vibrant sunset with millions of colors. Skip this setting: It makes images look blotchy and really increases a file's size. If you have an image with millions of colors, then save it as a JPEG file, not a GIF or PNG8.

PNG optimization options

If you're saving a file in the PNG8 format, you have the same options as GIF images (see the previous section). If you choose PNG24 or PNG32, your choices are simple...well, actually, you don't have any choices. In the Image Preview window, just click OK, and then save the file. But as mentioned in the box on page 218, while PNG24 and PNG32 can offer higher image quality than JPEGs, they usually produce significantly larger file sizes. However, PNG32 is the only format that lets you tap into 256 levels of alpha transparency.

Method 2: Copying and Pasting from Photoshop

You can also copy a selection (a layer, an entire image, or a "slice" created with the Web-oriented slicing tool) from Photoshop, and paste it into a Dreamweaver Web page. When you do this, the Image Preview window appears—the same window you use when inserting a Photoshop document. Follow the same steps described on page 219 for optimizing and saving the pasted image. However, unlike a Photoshop image inserted using the Insert panel or the Insert menu, a pasted image is not considered a Smart Object. Dreamweaver still keeps track of the *location* of the original PSD (useful for editing, as you'll see on page 244), but it doesn't notify you if someone updates the original PSD file.

Tip: To select all the layers in a Photoshop document, first select the entire image (Select → All), and then choose Edit → Copy Merged. This copies all layers for that selection to the clipboard. If you want to copy just a portion of the entire image, use the Marquee tool to make a rectangular selection, and then choose Edit → Copy Merged.

Modifying an Image

After inserting a graphic, you can work on it in several ways: Attach a link to the image, align it on the page, or add a border and margin to it, to name a few. Dreamweaver also includes some basic tools that let you crop, resize, optimize, sharpen, and adjust contrast and brightness (see page 238).

As with most objects on a Web page, you set image properties using the Property inspector (see Figure 6-7).

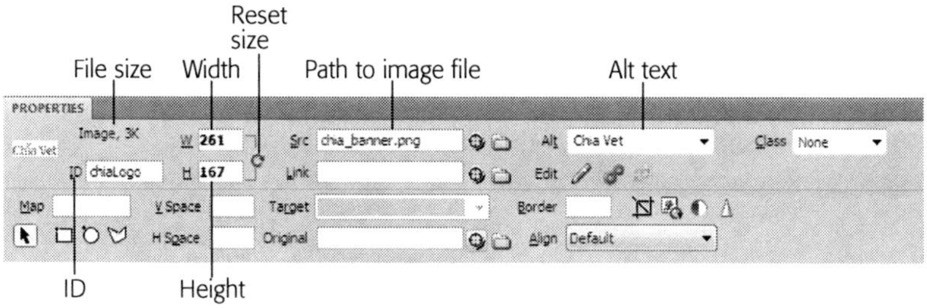

Figure 6-7: *The Property inspector shows the selected graphic's dimensions, source, alignment, border, and margins. To the left of the File size (3K), you see either Image (meaning a regular GIF, PNG, or JPEG file) or PS Image (meaning the image is coming from a Photoshop document).*

Adding an ID to an Image

On the Property inspector, just to the right of an image's thumbnail is a small field where you can type an ID for that image (see Figure 6-7). Most of the time, you'll leave this field blank.

However, if you plan to add interactive effects to it—like the rollover effect discussed on page 248—using Dreamweaver behaviors (see Chapter 13) or your own JavaScript programming, then you *must* add an ID. Whatever name you choose should use only letters and numbers—no spaces or other punctuation. Furthermore, since this adds an ID to the image (see page 114), the name must be unique on the page. Following this rule lets JavaScript "talk" to a specific image.

When you add an ID, Dreamweaver adds both a Name property and an ID property to the image tag. Most browsers still use the name tag, but the ID tag is JavaScript's standard way to identify an object on a page. (Cascading Style Sheets also use IDs, as described on page 114.)

Note: JavaScript uses the image name or ID that you type in the Image Placeholder box for its own reference; no one actually sees this name in a Web browser. In other words, this box isn't the place to give your graphic a text label that shows up when your reader has graphics turned off. For that purpose, read on.

Adding a Text Description to an Image

Not everyone who visits your Web site gets to see those stunning photos of your last summer vacation. Some people deliberately turn off graphics when they surf, enjoying the Web without the wait, since graphics-free Web pages appear almost instantly. Other people have vision impairments that prevent them from enjoying the Web's visual aspects. They rely on special software that reads Web page text aloud, including any labels you've given your graphics.

To assist Web surfers in both situations, make a habit of setting the image's Alt property. Short for *alternative text*, the Alt property is a text description that Web browsers use as a stand-in for the image (see Figure 6-8).

Figure 6-8: *The Alt property is an important aid for people who are surfing but can't see the graphics on your Web page.*

Top: Graphics are used for the site's logo (1), ads (2), sub-sections of the site (3), and to highlight stories (4).

Bottom: With graphics turned off, a lack of alt text makes the site's identity invisible (1). Good alt text–like the "Commarts store" text (2) clearly describes the graphic's message. Bad alt text is either misleading or not informative. For example, the Creative Hot List image (3) has the alt text "CHL Logo", which is pretty meaningless. A better description would simply be the text already in the image: "Creative Hot List." And the bizarre alt text "16793_13_LTE5MDQ0OTM4NDYtMTM1MTU3NDU1Nw" for the site's main story (4) won't help anyone, even a computer, understand what that image is.

Note: Dreamweaver normally reminds you to add an Alt property each time you add an image to a page, but this setting can get turned off. See the box on page 228.

To add a text description to an image, type it in the Property inspector's Alt field. If you're naming graphics that will be navigation buttons, you could just use the same text that appears on the button, such as *Home* or *Products*. For images that carry greater meaning—such as a photo of the product itself—you might use a more detailed description: "Photo of Sasquatch relaxing at his lodge in the Adirondacks."

Note: In some cases, however, a description is more of a distraction than a help. For example, you might insert an image of an intricate swirling line to act as a visual divider between two paragraphs. The image doesn't actually convey any meaningful information; it's just for decoration.

In this instance, you can use the pop-up menu that appears in the Property inspector, to the right of the Alt field. This menu lets you choose one option: <empty>. Use the <empty> Alt property for any images that don't add meaning to the page, like decorative elements. This trick helps your pages meet accessibility requirements without adding distracting and unnecessary descriptions.

Changing an Image's Size

A graphic's Width and Height properties do more than determine its screen size; they also help Web browsers load the graphic quickly and efficiently. Since the HTML of a Web page downloads before any graphics do, a Web browser displays the text on the page first, and then adds the images as they arrive. If width and height attributes are missing, then the browser doesn't know how much space on the page to give each image, so it has to redraw the page after each image is downloaded. The stuttering appearance of this redrawing is disconcerting, makes Web pages appear slowly, and does little for your reputation as a cool, competent Web designer.

Fortunately, you don't have to worry about specifying the picture's dimensions yourself: Whenever Dreamweaver inserts an image into a Web page, it automatically calculates its width and height, and then enters those values into the Property inspector's W and H fields (see Figure 6-7).

You can, if you like, shrink a graphic by typing smaller values into the W and H fields, but doing so doesn't do anything to speed up the download time. You make the picture *appear* smaller, but the Web browser still has to download the entire graphics file. To make your graphic smaller both in appearance and file size, shrink it in an image-editing program like Fireworks or Photoshop, or use the Resample Image tool described on page 238. Not only do you get an image that's exactly the size you want, but the image usually looks better and you also trim a few bytes off its file size, and maybe even save a second or two in download time.

On the other hand, setting width and height values that are *larger* than the actual dimensions of the graphic merely distorts the image by stretching it, creating an undesirable pixellated effect. If you want a larger image without distortion or pixellation, start with a larger original image. To do so, return to your digital camera or stock photo CD, or recreate the graphic at a larger size in Photoshop or Fireworks.

Some Properties to Avoid

You'll notice that the Property inspector includes a few other properties (see Figure 6-7) that seem intriguing and possibly useful—Align, V Space, H Space, and Border. These properties affect how an image is positioned inside a block of text (or next to another image), and the size of the margins and borders around an image. However, steer clear of these properties. Not only are these properties so

POWER USERS' CLINIC

Making Accessible Web Sites

Many people using the Web have disabilities that make reading, seeing, hearing, or using a mouse difficult. Visually impaired people, for example, may be unable to benefit from images on the screen, even if they have software that can read a Web page's text aloud.

Dreamweaver includes a number of features for making your Web sites more accessible. That's good news if you're building a Web site for the federal government or one of the many states that support Section 508 of the Workforce Investment Act. This law requires Web sites built for or funded by the government to offer equal or equivalent access to everyone. Throughout this book, you'll find tips for using Dreamweaver's accessibility features, and on page 660, you'll learn how to use a tool to find out if your site complies with recognized accessibility standards.

The Alt property described on page 225 is an important first step for assisting visually impaired Web surfers. For complex images, such as a graph that plots changes in utility rates over time, you can also supply a more detailed description on a separate Web page. The *Longdesc* (long description) property of an image lets you specify a link to a page containing a text description of the image. Some Web browsers understand this property, letting visually impaired visitors jump to a page with a text description that screen-reading software can read aloud.

While you can't find the *Longdesc* property in the Property inspector, you can turn on an accessibility option in Dreamweaver that lets you add it every time you insert a graphic. This option is already turned on in Dreamweaver, so you should be seeing it every time you insert an image. But if you don't see the Accessibility Options window when you insert an image, then you can turn it on by choosing Edit → Preferences (Dreamweaver → Preferences on the Mac) to open the Preferences window. Select the Accessibility category, and then turn on the Images checkbox.

Now whenever you insert a graphic, you can quickly set the Alt text, and select an HTML page containing a long description. (You can also use the Tag inspector described on page 415 to add a Longdesc property to a graphic you've already inserted into a page.)

Note that you're *not required* by Section 508 to use the long description property when inserting images. It's merely recommended if the image is particularly complex or includes information that can't be explained in the Alt property—for example, graphs or images that include a lot of text information. You'll probably rarely, if ever, find yourself adding a long description for an image. For an overview of Web accessibility and helpful tips on making accessible sites, visit *www.w3.org/WAI/gettingstarted/*.

Web-Design-Circa-1999, but they're on the way out and unsupported in the strict versions of HTML and XHTML. In addition, they offer very anemic design control. For example, you can't easily control the color of the border around the image, nor can you specify different margins for both the right *and* left or bottom *and* top edges of an image.

Fortunately, you'll find that Cascading Style Sheets once again come to the rescue, as discussed next.

Note: If you're not obsessed with building a Web site that meets the strictest HTML/XHTML standards, the Align menu's left and right options are useful. These choices move an image to either the left or right side of the page (or table cell, or <div>) and force other content like text to wrap around it. You can also achieve the same effect with the CSS float property as described below.

WORKAROUND WORKSHOP

Watch Those Resize Handles!

After you insert an image in the document window, a thin black border appears around it, indicating that it's selected. Three small black squares–the resize handles–appear on the right edge, bottom edge, and lower-right corner, as circled in the illustration.

Dragging these handles changes the graphic's width and height–or, rather, in the Property inspector, the Width and Height properties. Pressing Shift while dragging the corner handle keeps the proportions of the image the same. The graphic file itself remains unchanged.

However, dragging one of these handles to make the picture appear bigger is almost always unsuccessful, resulting in distortion and ugly pixellation.

But you can far too easily accidentally grab and drag those pesky resize handles. In fact, sometimes you may resize a graphic and not even know it. Perhaps you accidentally dragged the left resize handle a few pixels, making the graphic wider, but not enough to notice.

Fortunately, the Property inspector does give some subtle feedback to let you know if your graphic is distorted.

A boldfaced number in the W or H field tells you that the Width or Height property now differs from the actual dimensions of the graphic.

In the Property inspector, clicking the letter W or H resets the Width or Height property back to that of the original graphic file, undoing your little slip of the mouse. Clicking the "Reset size" icon (see Figure 6-7) resets both properties.

Controlling Images with CSS

Cascading Style Sheets aren't just for stylizing text. You can also use the design power of CSS to add borders to an image, force text to wrap around an image, and even add images to the background of other elements. For example, the CSS *background-image* property lets you place an image in the background of a Web page, or add a graphical background to a link, headline, or any HTML tag.

In general, you probably don't want to create a tag style (see page 114) for the <img> tag. That type of style applies across a site, and affects every image. And while you may want a bright red, 10-pixel border around each thumbnail in a photo gallery, you probably don't want that border around the site's logo or the graphical navigation buttons on that same page. You're more likely to create class styles that you manually apply to certain graphics. In this case, create a class style with the proper border setting, and then apply that class to each gallery image (you can be even more efficient method and use a *descendent selector* as described on page 301).

Wrapping Text Around an Image

When you add an image to a page, you might initially be staring at a bunch of empty white space surrounding the image (see Figure 6-9, top). Not only does this waste precious screen real estate, it's usually unattractive. Fortunately, using the CSS *float* property, you can wrap text around images (see Figure 6-9, bottom).

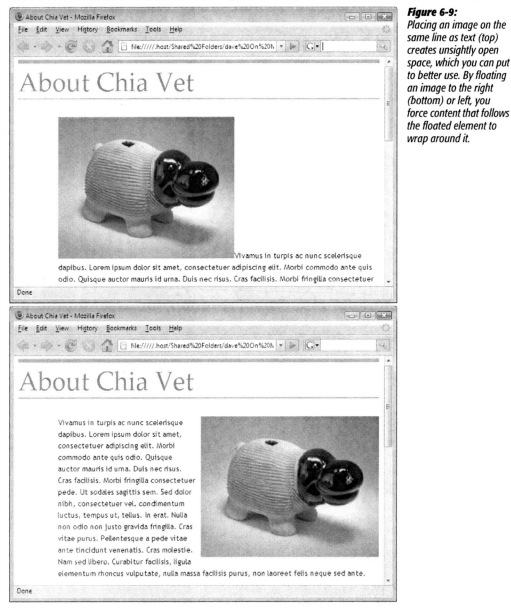

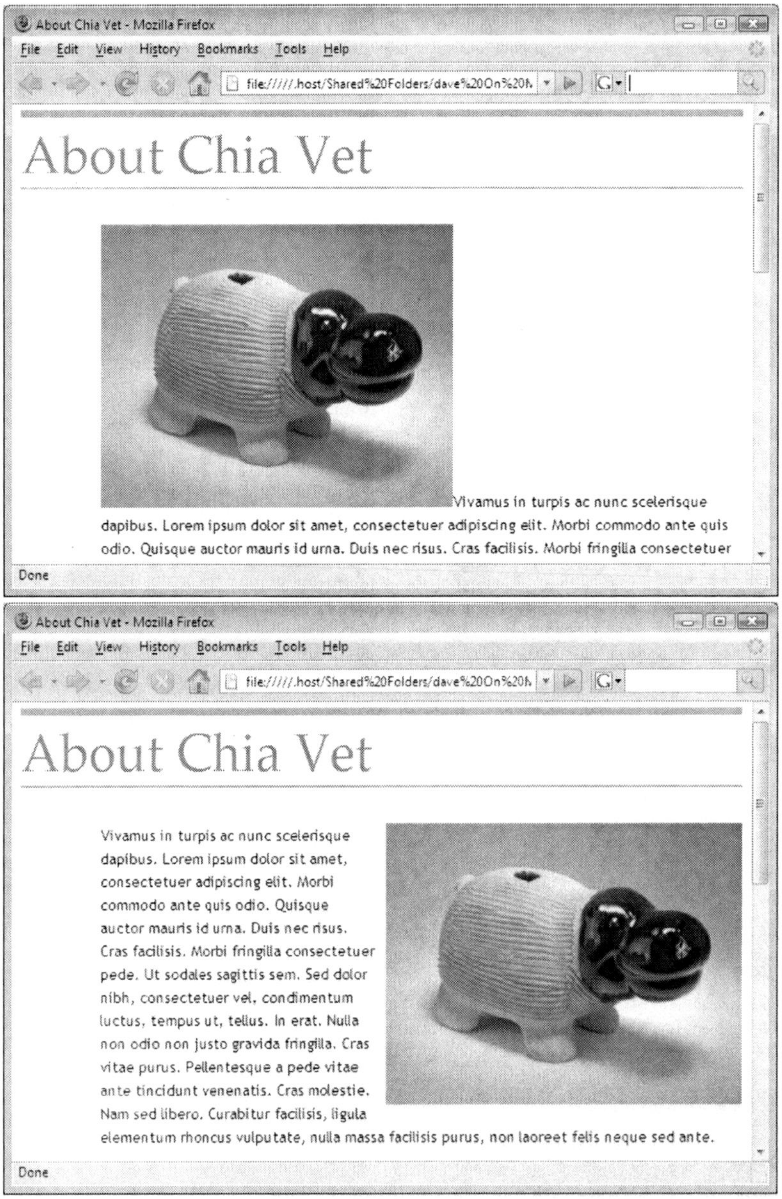
About Chia Vet - Mozilla Firefox
File Edit View History Bookmarks Tools Help
file:////.host/Shared%20Folders/dave%20On%20M
About Chia Vet
Vivamus in turpis ac nunc scelerisque dapibus. Lorem ipsum dolor sit amet, consectetuer adipiscing elit. Morbi commodo ante quis odio. Quisque auctor mauris id urna. Duis nec risus. Cras facilisis. Morbi fringilla consectetuer
Done
About Chia Vet - Mozilla Firefox
File Edit View History Bookmarks Tools Help
file:////.host/Shared%20Folders/dave%20On%20M
About Chia Vet
Vivamus in turpis ac nunc scelerisque dapibus. Lorem ipsum dolor sit amet, consectetuer adipiscing elit. Morbi commodo ante quis odio. Quisque auctor mauris id urna. Duis nec risus. Cras facilisis. Morbi fringilla consectetuer pede. Ut sodales sagittis sem. Sed dolor nibh, consectetuer vel, condimentum luctus, tempus ut, tellus. In erat. Nulla non odio non justo gravida fringilla. Cras vitae purus. Pellentesque a pede vitae ante tincidunt venenatis. Cras molestie. Nam sed libero. Curabitur facilisis, ligula elementum rhoncus vulputate, nulla massa facilisis purus, non laoreet felis neque sed ante.
Done

Figure 6-9: *Placing an image on the same line as text (top) creates unsightly open space, which you can put to better use. By floating an image to the right (bottom) or left, you force content that follows the floated element to wrap around it.*

To do so, in the CSS Rule Definition window's Box category, you set the *float* property (see Figure 6-10). An element can be floated *left* or *right*. If you want an image to appear at the right side of the page and have text flow around its left and bottom edges, from the Float menu, choose "right". The Float property behaves just like the right and left alignment options for images (see the following Note).

Note: The Float property has many uses, from positioning images on the right or left side of the page, to creating thumbnail photo galleries, to laying out entire Web pages. You'll learn about using it for layout in Chapter 9. For an excellent introduction and set of tutorials on the float property in general, visit *http://css.maxdesign.com.au/floatutorial/*; book lovers should pick up *CSS: The Missing Manual* for in-depth discussion, tutorials, and practical tips on using floats.

One thing to keep in mind with floats: The floated element must appear *before* anything that you wish to wrap around it. Say you have a paragraph of text that you'd like to wrap around a right-floated image. The image needs to be inserted before the text (a good spot is before the first letter in the paragraph). If you float an image to the right, but place the image after the text, then the image moves to the right, but the paragraph of text remains above the image.

You'll also frequently use the margin property with floats (see Figure 6-10). The margin is the outermost space surrounding an element. It lets you add space between one element and another. So for a right-floated image it's usually a good idea to add a little *left*, *bottom* and *top* margin. This method creates a bit of breathing room between the image and anything else that wraps around it; omitting a left margin on a right-floated image can cause text to butt right up against the image. You can use any of the measurement values—pixels, percentages, and so on—that CSS supports for a margin.

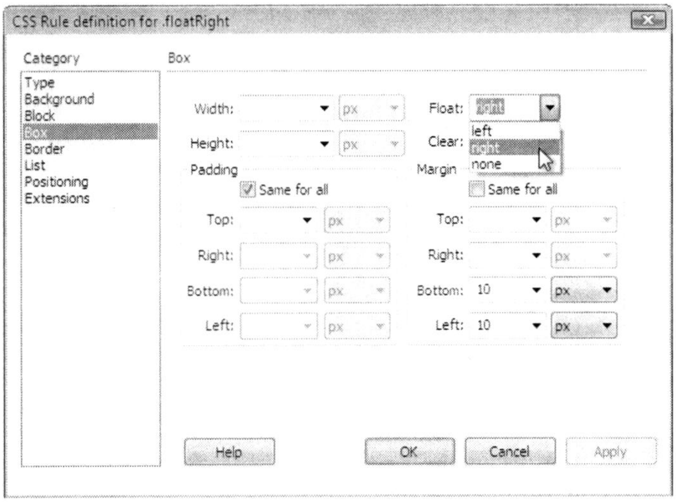

Figure 6-10:
The Box category contains some of the most used CSS properties: the Float property for aligning images and other page elements to the left or right; the Margin property for adding or removing space between elements (like adding space between the edge of a right floated image and the text that's wrapping around the image); and the Padding property for adding space between content and any borders around the element.

Adding Borders

As you saw in the tutorial for Chapter 4, you can add a border to any element on a page—a paragraph, or even a single word. But borders can really add to the impact of a photo on a Web page, by adding a polished "frame-like" appearance; and borders can help unify a page full of thumbnail images.

The border is controlled, logically enough, from the CSS Rule Definition window's Border category (see Figure 6-11). You can control each *side* of the border independently with its own width and color settings by specifying the three main border properties:

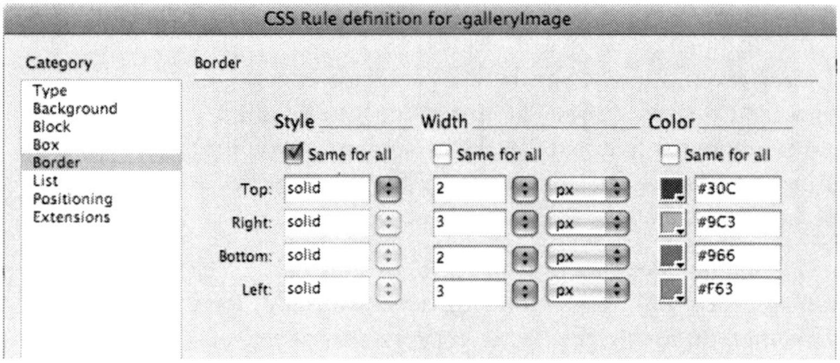

Figure 6-11: *Add colorful and stylish borders to paragraphs, images, tables, and links with the CSS Border properties. Turning on only the bottom border for a paragraph is a great way to add a horizontal rule between paragraphs. While HTML's Horizontal Rule object also does this, only CSS lets you control the rule's color.*

- **Style.** This menu lets you specify the type of line used for the border. Dreamweaver gives you more options than a frame shop: "none" (the default choice), "dotted", "dashed", "solid", "double", "groove", "ridge", "inset", and "outset" (see Figure 6-12). You can use a different style for each edge, or, from the top menu, select a style, and then turn on the "Same for all" box to apply the same style to all four borders.

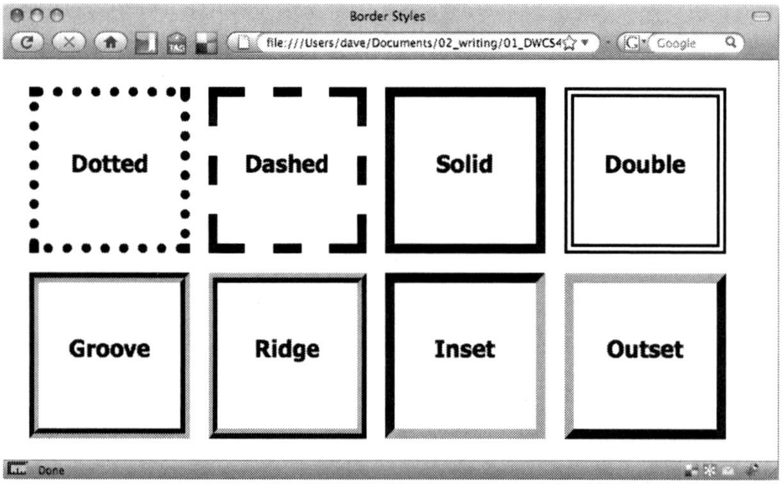

Figure 6-12: *CSS provides eight different border styles. Some, like double, ridge, and groove, look good only with a thick border (more than 1 pixel).*

Note: You have to select a style from the pop-up menu to see the borders. If you leave this option blank or select "none", then you don't see the borders even if you set the width and color.

- **Border Widths.** You can set the border separately around each side of a styled object. Choose one of the preset widths—"thin", "medium", "thick", or "auto"—or, if you choose "(value)" from the pop-up menu, you can type a value into the Width box, and then, from the pop-up menu to the right, select a unit of measurement. Again, you can choose from a wide range of types: pixels, percentage, inches, and so on (see page 59 for more on CSS measurement types). If you want to eliminate the border on one side, type *0* into the appropriate box (or, from the Style menu, choose *None*).
- **Border Colors.** You can color each of the four borders individually using the ubiquitous Dreamweaver color box. If you don't assign any colors, but do assign border *widths*, then the borders match the color of the surrounding text.

If you use borders to "frame" an image, you can also use the *padding* property to add space between the image and the border—this simulates the appearance of the cardboard mat used in professionally framed photographs. Padding is the gap that separates the style's content—such as a paragraph of text or an image—and its border.

You can control padding settings from the CSS Style Definition window's Box category (see Figure 6-10). If you put a 1-pixel border around an image and want to add 10 pixels of space between the image and the border, type *10* into the Top padding box, and then, from the pop-up menu, choose "pixels". Turn off the "Same for all" box if you wish to set the padding around each edge separately; then, type values into each of the four boxes.

Background Images

Inserting an image into a page as described on page 184 isn't the only way you can add graphical beauty to a Web page. CSS also provides a method of adding an image to the background of any tag. In this way you can put a graphic in the background of a page, enhance a headline with an icon, or add your own custom graphics to links (in fact, the arrow icons used for the Spry Menu Bar discussed on page 184 are images placed into a link's background).

You control background images by setting the following properties in the CSS Rule Definition window's Background category (see Figure 6-13):

Background image

Add a background image to the style by clicking the Browse button, and then selecting an image from your site. You can also type an absolute URL, starting with *http://*, to use an image off the Web.

To fill your entire page background with some repeating graphic, you could either redefine the <body> tag using this property, or create a class style with a Background Image property, and then apply it to the <body> tag as described on page 122 (the tutorial from Chapter 1 uses this technique—see page 56).

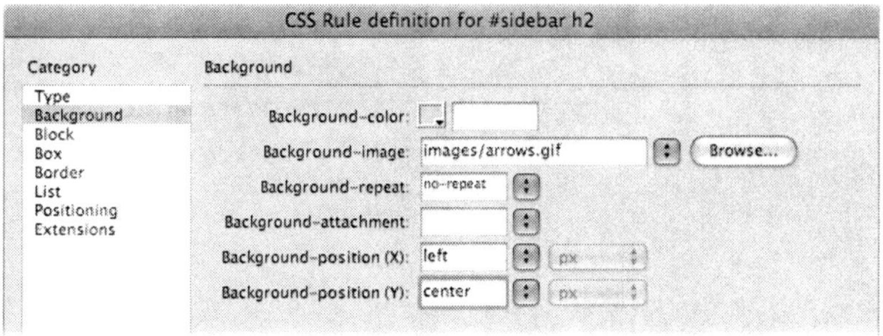

Figure 6-13: *The CSS Background category lets you specify a background color and image for a style. While you won't frequently apply a background color to an image (after all, the image would usually cover up anything behind it), it can come in handy when used with the padding property (see page 343): In this way you can create a customized "mat" color.*

You can even control how the image tiles (repeats) and where it's placed on the page (see the following sections). Furthermore, you can add background images to any *individual* element on your page: paragraphs, tables, layers, and so on.

Background images appear above any background color, so you can (and often will) combine the two. For example, you may want to position an interesting graphic on top of a colorful background.

Note: One common byte-saving technique is to create an image that looks like a button, and then use it for the background image of navigation links on a page. The links themselves include regular text—"Home", "About Us", and so on—but the background of each link looks like a graphical button. This technique's main benefit is that you don't need to create separate graphics for each button.

Background repeat

Background images—for example, the background of a page—normally fill the available space by tiling (that is, repeating over and over again) across and down. A small image of a carrot added to the background of a page appears as a field of carrots—one next to another, row after row.

But with CSS, you can control *how* the background image repeats. You can select from the following options:

- *repeat* tiles the image horizontally and vertically. This is how browsers normally display a background image.
- *repeat-x* and *repeat-y* display a horizontal and vertical band of images, respectively. So if you'd like to have a single row of images appear at the top of a page, use the repeat-x option; It's a good way to add a graphical background to a banner. *repeat-y*, on the other hand, is great for a graphical sidebar that appears down the left edge of a page.
- *no-repeat* displays the image only once (see the examples in Figure 6-14).

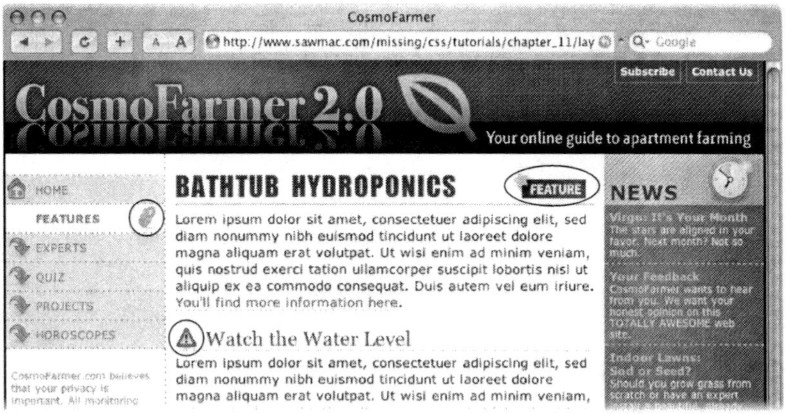

***Figure 6-14:** Background images aren't just for the body of a Web page. You can apply styles that include background images to any selection, including links, headlines, and paragraphs of text. The circled graphics in this image are just a few examples on this Web page of background images.*

Background attachment

By default, the background image on a page scrolls with the rest of the page, so that as you scroll down to read a long Web page, the image scrolls along with the text.

But using CSS, you can lock the image in place by choosing "fixed" from the Attachment menu. Say you added your company's logo to the background of a page, and set the Repeat property (described above) to "no-repeat". The logo now appears only once in the upper-left corner of the page. If you use the "fixed" option for this property, then when a visitor scrolls the page, the logo remains fixed in the upper-left corner. (Choosing "scroll" from the Attachment menu means, of course, that the background image scrolls with the page—this is the normal behavior so you needn't choose this option.) Note that using "fixed" really works only with an image that's applied to the body of a page—the image stays fixed when the rest of the content on the page scrolls.

Horizontal and vertical position

Using these controls, you can specify a position for the affected text or other Web page element. The Horizontal Position options are: "left", "center", and "right". You can also choose "(value)", type an exact number in the box, and then, from the menu to the right, select a unit of measurement. Similarly, the Vertical Position options include "top", "center", and "bottom", or you can enter a specific value.

These positioning options refer to the position of the styled object. Suppose you created a class style that included a background image with Horizontal and Vertical Position both set to *center*. Then say you applied that class style to a paragraph. The background image would appear in the center of that *paragraph*, not in the center of the Web page.

Likewise, if you set the horizontal position of the image to 10 pixels and the vertical position to 20 pixels, then the image would start 10 pixels from the left edge of the paragraph and 20 pixels from the top edge.

And if you wanted to place an image in the exact center of the page, you'd choose "center" from both the Horizontal and Vertical Position menus, set the Repeat property to "no-repeat", and then apply the style to the page's <body> tag.

Note: You can even use percentage values to position a background image. For information on how that works, visit *http://tinyurl.com/yt7eqt*.

Editing Graphics

Nothing's ever perfect, especially when you're building a Web site. Corrections are par for the course—not just to a Web page, but to the pictures on it, as well. Perhaps a picture is a tad too dark, or you'd like to crop out the rowdy coworker being escorted out by security from your company's holiday party photo.

In the hands of less capable software, you'd face quite a tedious switching-and-opening task each time you wanted to edit a graphic. You'd have to open Photoshop, Fireworks, or whatever graphics program you prefer; choose File → Open; navigate to your Web site folder; find the graphic that needs touching up (if you can even remember its name); and then open it to make your changes.

Dreamweaver includes tools for performing many basic editing tasks. For more complex work, like changing the text on a button from "Now Firing" to "Now Hiring", you need to switch to a different program. However, Dreamweaver is considerate of your time; it lets you access your favorite graphics program with just a couple of clicks.

The Built-In Editing Tools

Dreamweaver includes four tools for cropping, resizing, sharpening, and adjusting the brightness and contrast of images (see Figure 6-15). Suppose your boss emails you his portrait with instructions to put it on his "Meet the boss" page. Unfortunately, it's too big and too dark. Rather than launch a separate image-editing program, you can simply add the photo to the page, and then make the corrections within Dreamweaver.

But first, a warning: All these tools change the *original* GIF, PNG, or JPEG image in your site folder. If you shrink a graphic, and then later change your mind, you may be out of luck. It's a good idea, therefore, to make backups of all of your images before you use these tools. In addition, if you've inserted a Photoshop document and created a Smart Object (page 219), the tools discussed next break the link with the Photoshop file. That means, for Smart Objects, you're better off editing the original Photoshop document as discussed on page 241.

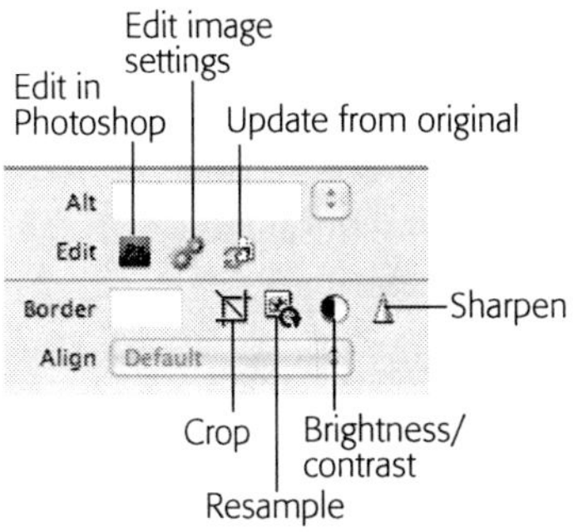

Figure 6-15:
The Property inspector includes tools for editing images directly inside Dreamweaver.

Furthermore, remember that if you use that same file on other pages, your modifications appear on those pages, too. For instance, if you decide you want to shrink your company logo to a smaller size on one page, you may find that *every* page on your site now has the smaller logo! What's worse, on the other pages, the image's width and height settings don't change, so on those pages, that logo looks unnaturally pixellated. If you want to change a graphic on only one page, make a copy of it first, insert the *copy* on the page you wish to change, and then modify just that image file. That way, the rest of your site keeps the original graphic.

Of course, if you discover right away that you've made a change you don't want, you can choose Edit → Undo or press Ctrl+Z (⌘-Z). Until you close the page, you can continue to undo multiple image changes.

EASTER EGG HUNT

Meet the Geeks Behind Dreamweaver

Want to see pictures of the engineers behind Dreamweaver? OK, maybe you don't, but you *can*, if you want, find these little snapshots hidden away in the Property inspector. Select an image in the document window. Then, in the left side of the Property inspector, simply Ctrl+double-click (or ⌘-double-click) the thumbnail of the graphic.

A picture of one of Dreamweaver's programmers appears, along with his or her name. Ctrl (⌘) double-click the thumbnail repeatedly to cycle through the names and pictures of other members of the Dreamweaver team.

Cropping an image

Dreamweaver's Crop tool can remove extraneous or distracting parts of an image. (You can use it to focus on a single person, or to get rid of those teenagers making faces in the corner.)

To do so, select the graphic you wish to crop, and then, on the Property inspector, click the Crop tool (see Figure 6-15). (Alternatively, choose Modify → Image → Crop.)

A rectangular box with eight handles appears inside the image; anything outside the box is cropped out. So just move this box (by dragging it), and resize it (by dragging the handles), until you've got just what you want inside the box.

When you're done, double-click inside the box, or click the Property inspector's Crop tool again. Dreamweaver crops the image, discarding the graphic's unwanted areas.

To undo a crop you don't like, simply press Ctrl+Z (⌘-Z). In fact, you can back out before you've used the Crop tool at all; clicking anywhere on the page outside the image makes the cropping box go away.

Resampling an image

If a photo is just too big to fit on a Web page, you could select the image, and then use one of the resize handles to alter its dimensions (see page 229). Unfortunately, graphics that you shrink this way give you the worst of both worlds: They look muddier than they were before, yet they still retain all the slow-downloading data of the larger image.

You can, however, use this resizing technique in conjunction with the Image Resample tool to resize the actual graphic file. You'll end up with a trimmed-down file with its appearance intact.

To use the Resample tool, select an image on a page, and then resize it using the resize handles. (Shift-drag to prevent distortion.) When you're done, on the Property inspector, click the Resample button (Figure 6-15). Dreamweaver resizes the image file.

You can even make an image *larger* than the original using this technique. The end result isn't perfect—even Dreamweaver can't create image information that was never there—but the program does its best to prevent the image from looking too pixellated. You don't want to enlarge images this way often, but in a pinch, it's a quick way to make a photo just a little bit larger.

Dreamweaver changes the graphic, altering the width and height of the actual file. If you change your mind about resampling the image, your only option is the old undo command, Ctrl+Z (⌘-Z).

Brightness and contrast

If an image on a page is too light, dark, or washed out, you can use Dreamweaver's Brightness/Contrast dialog box to fix it.

First, select the picture, and then, on the Property inspector, click the Brightness/Contrast icon (Figure 6-15) to open the Brightness/Contrast dialog box (Figure 6-16). Move the Brightness slider to the right to lighten the image (great for underexposed interior shots), or to the left to darken the image. The Contrast control works in the same way: right to increase contrast (making dark colors darker and light colors lighter); left to decrease contrast (moving all colors toward gray).

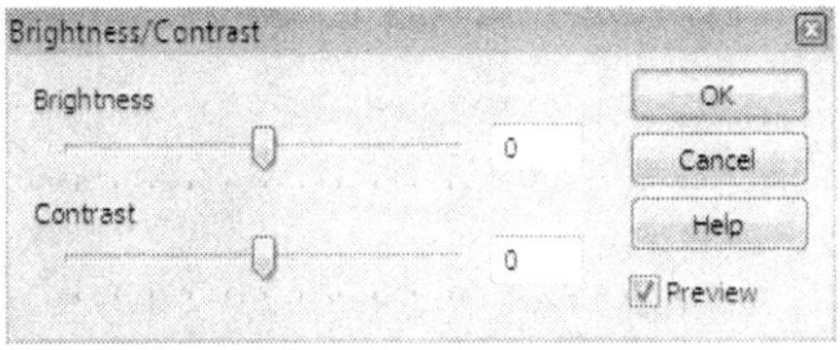

Figure 6-16:
If you've ever used image-editing software like Fireworks or Photoshop, this dialog box should look familiar. Make sure the Preview checkbox is turned on so that you can see your changes right in the document window before you click OK.

You'll often use the Brightness and Contrast sliders in conjunction. Brightening (lightening) an image also has a fading effect. By increasing contrast, you can restore some punch to a brightened image.

As with the other image-editing controls, if you're unhappy with the changes you've made, choose Edit → Undo or press Ctrl+Z (⌘-Z) to return the image to its previous glory.

Sharpening images

Sometimes graphics, even those from some scanners and digital cameras, look a little fuzzy, especially if you've resampled the image (see previous page). Dreamweaver's Sharpen tool on the Property inspector helps restore clarity and make such images "pop." It works like similar tools in graphic-editing programs: It increases the contrast between an image's pixels to create the illusion of sharper, more focused graphics. (Insert your own Sharper Image joke here.)

To use this tool, select the graphic, and then, on the Property inspector, click the Sharpen icon (Figure 6-15). The Sharpen window appears, as shown in Figure 6-17. Move the slider to the right to increase the amount of sharpening, or type a number in the box (10 is maximum sharpening; 0 is no change). You probably won't use the maximum setting unless you're going for a special effect, since it tends to highlight "noise" in the image, creating an unappealing halo effect around pixels. Once you've selected a level of sharpening that you like, click OK.

If you're unhappy with the results, just press Ctrl+Z (⌘-Z), or choose Edit → Undo.

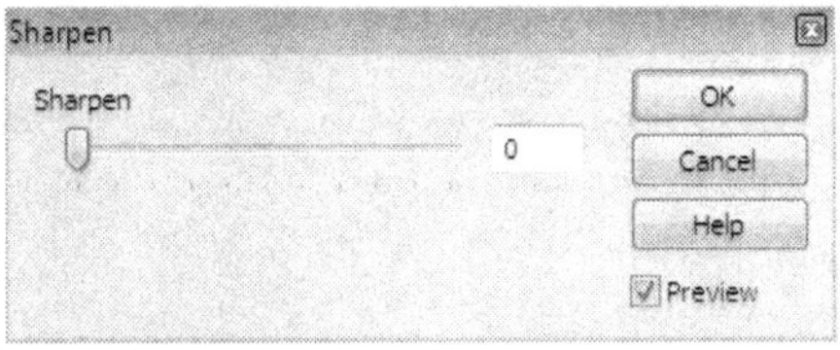

Figure 6-17:
The Sharpen box can make fuzzy pictures "pop." Make sure the Preview checkbox is turned on so you can see the effect on the image as you move the slider.

Setting Up an External Editor

When you double-click an image file in the Files panel, your favorite image editing program launches and opens the file, ready for you to edit. When you first install Dreamweaver, it tries to figure out which program to use by looking through the software installed on your computer. But if you want to use a program other than the one Dreamweaver assigns, then you need to tell Dreamweaver which graphics program you want to use.

1. **Choose Edit → Preferences (Dreamweaver → Preferences on the Mac).**

   The Preferences dialog box opens, as shown in Figure 6-18.

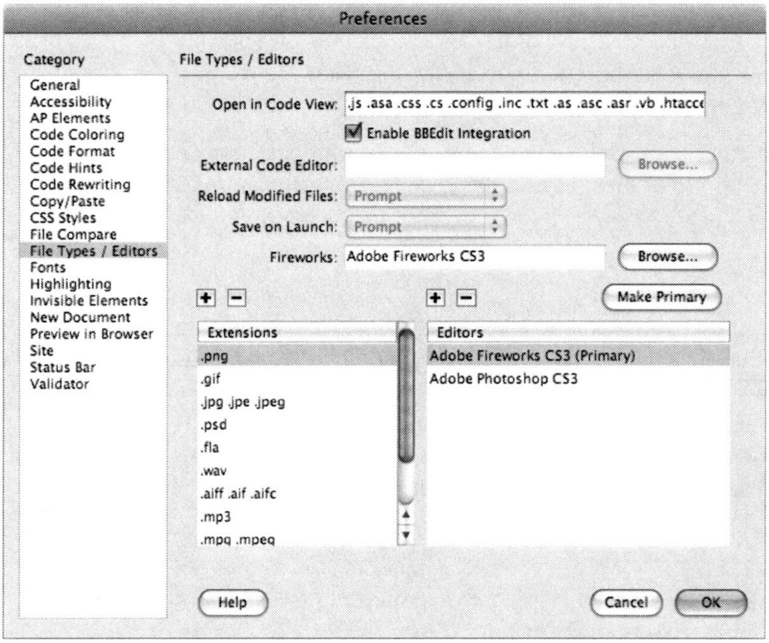

***Figure 6-18:** You can tell Dreamweaver to use certain programs for editing different types of files such as JPEG, GIF, or PNG files. If you have .fla (Flash files), .mp3 (music files) or other types of non-HTML files in your site, you can assign programs to those types as well—double-clicking the file in the Files panel launches the associated program for editing. The BBEdit integration box is just for Mac users, who might as well uncheck this box. Dreamweaver is also a powerful text editor, so you don't need to use BBEdit (see Chapter 10 for more on Dreamweaver's code-editing features).*

2. **In the left pane, click File Types/Editors.**

   The Preferences box now displays your current settings for the editing programs you prefer for editing different types of files. In the bottom half of the box, two columns appear: Extensions and Editors.

3. **From the Extensions list, select a graphic extension.**

   Three types of graphic files are listed: GIFs, JPEGs, and PNGs. You can choose a different editing program for each type of file, if you like. You can add filename extensions for file types not shown by clicking the + button above the Extensions list.

4. **Click the + button above the Editors list.**

   The Select External Editor dialog box opens.

5. **On your hard drive, find the program you wish to assign as an editor for the selected type of graphics file.**

   It can be Photoshop, Photoshop Elements, Fireworks, or whatever.

6. **If you wish to make this program the primary program for editing this type of file, click Make Primary.**

   This *primary* editor is the one Dreamweaver opens when you choose to edit the graphic. (You can define other, less frequently used editors, as well. See the Tip at the end of this list.)

7. **Repeat steps 3–6 for each type of graphics file you work with.**

   Dreamweaver treats GIFs, JPEGs, and PNGs as separate file types, so you need to assign an editor to each. Of course, most people choose the same program for all three file types.

8. **Click OK to close the Preferences dialog box.**

   From now on, whenever you need to touch up a graphic on your Web page, just select it, and then, on the Property inspector, click Edit (see Figure 6-7). Alternatively, in the Files panel, you can simply double-click the file, or Ctrl-double-click (⌘-double-click) the image on the page. In any case, your graphic now opens in the graphics program that you set as your primary editor in step 4.

Note: If you've inserted a Photoshop image using either the Insert method (page 218) or the copy and paste method (page 224), then clicking the Property inspector's Edit button launches Photoshop and opens the original PSD file—no matter what the image's file type.

Now you can edit the graphic and save changes to it. When you return to Dreamweaver, the modified image appears on the page. (If you're a Photoshop or Fireworks fan, you're in even better shape; read on.)

Tip: You aren't limited to just one external editor. For instance, if there's a Fireworks feature you need, even though Photoshop is your primary editor, you can still jump to Fireworks directly from Dreamweaver.

The trick is to right-click (Control-click) the image you want to edit, whether it's in the document window or the Site Files window. Choose the Edit With menu. If you've added the other image editor to your preferences (Figure 6-18), then the submenu lists that editor. Otherwise, from the contextual menu, select Browse, and then, in the resulting dialog box, choose the editing program you want to use. That program opens automatically, with the graphic you clicked open and ready to be edited.

Editing Smart Objects

Since Adobe makes the ubiquitous Photoshop as well as Dreamweaver, it makes sense that the two programs should work together. As you read on page 217, you have two ways to get a Photoshop image into a Web page in Dreamweaver. First, you can simply insert the PSD file. Second, you can copy a selection, layer, slice, or entire image in Photoshop, and then paste it into Dreamweaver. The first method creates a Smart Object (page 219), while the second simply lets you optimize the image to create and insert a GIF, JPEG, or PNG file. In both cases, Dreamweaver keeps track of the PSD file, and gives you a way to return to and edit the original Photoshop document. However, the editing process is different for each method, as explained in the following pages.

Smart Objects really are a, well, smart idea. They let you preserve an original high-resolution Photoshop file as the main source of one or more Web-ready graphics. Since producing Web graphics often entails reducing a file's size, any edits you make to the image are best made to the highest quality version of that image. For example, if you want to change the font of your company logo, you don't edit the GIF or PNG file used on a Web page. Instead, you edit the PSD version of the logo in Photoshop. Smart Objects make this process easy.

You can launch Photoshop, and then open the PSD file to work on it, or better yet, you can launch Photoshop directly from Dreamweaver—on the page, just select the Smart Object, and then click the Property inspector's "Edit in Photoshop" button (see Figure 6-19). This opens the PSD file in Photoshop where you can make the desired edits—modify the company logo, crop the image, use creative filters, and so on. When you're done, save and close the file.

Tip: You can also launch Photoshop to edit a Smart Object's original Photoshop document directly from the Files panel. Right-click (Ctrl-click) the Smart Object–which is a GIF, PNG, or JPEG file in the Files panel–and then, from the contextual menu that appears, choose "Edit Original with Photoshop".

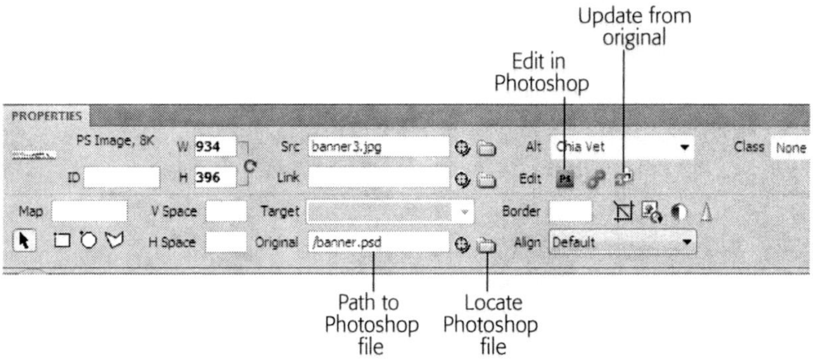

***Figure 6-19:** When using Smart Objects, the Property inspector includes an "Update from original" button, which lets you update an image whenever the image's original Photoshop source file is changed.*

Smart objects are "smart" because they keep track of any changes to the original PSD file. You can recognize a Smart Object by the recycling logo that appears in the upper left of the image in Dreamweaver's Design View (see Figure 6-20). Immediately after inserting a Photoshop image, the two arrows in the icon are green, meaning that the image on the page is based on the latest version of the Photoshop file (Figure 6-20, top). However, if you update the Photoshop document in Photoshop, the bottom arrow turns red (Figure 6-20, middle). This red arrow means the original Photoshop document has been modified. To bring the version on the Web page back in sync with the original, select the image, and then, in the Property inspector, click the Update From Original button (see Figure 6-19). You can also right-click (ctrl-click) the image, and then, from the contextual menu that appears, select Update From Original.

When you update an image in this way, Dreamweaver retains all the previous optimization settings—including the file format (JPEG, GIF or PNG), cropping, resizing, and file name.

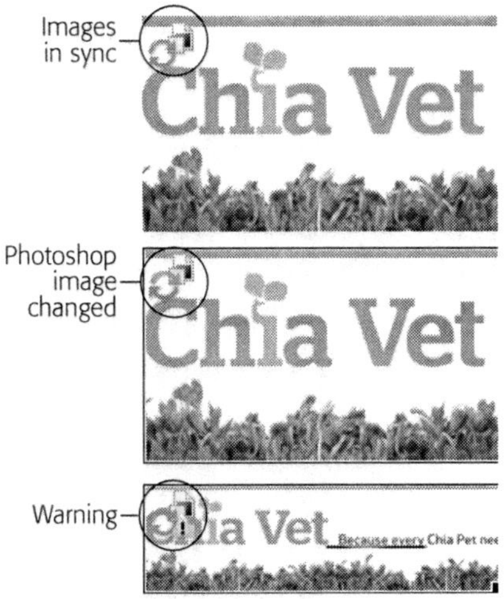

Figure 6-20:
A Smart Object is a GIF, PNG, or JPEG file that's been inserted from a Photoshop (PSD) file. In Dreamweaver's Design view, an icon appears at the top left of the image indicating that the image is a Smart Object. If one of the arrows in the icon is red, then the image doesn't match the Photoshop file. If the bottom arrow is red (middle), then the Photoshop file has changed since you inserted the image. In addition, a warning symbol (yellow triangle with exclamation mark) appears in a couple of situations described below.

Smart Object Warnings

Sometimes you see a warning symbol (a yellow triangle with an exclamation mark) as part of the Smart Object icon (see Figure 6-20, bottom). The warning symbol indicates either that Dreamweaver can't locate the original PSD file or that you've resized the inserted image in Dreamweaver—probably by dragging the resize handles as discussed on page 229.

If Dreamweaver loses track of the PSD file, simply select the Smart Object (you need to be in Design view), and then, in the Property inspector, click the folder icon (to the right of the Original box; see Figure 6-19). This action opens the Select Original File window—just a basic "pick a file on your computer" dialog box. Navigate to the PSD file, and then select it. Unfortunately, once Dreamweaver has lost track of the PSD file, it also loses all of the optimization information, such as the file format, name of the Web-ready file, and any cropping and optimization settings you made. You have to set all these options again as described on page 221.

You also see the yellow warning symbol when you resize the image in Dreamweaver. If you make the image on the page *smaller* than the original PSD file (for example, by dragging the resize handles, or by entering smaller width and height values in the Property inspector [see Figure 6-7]), then just click the Property inspector's "Update from Original" button (see Figure 6-19). Doing so re-exports the original image (using all your optimization settings) so that it matches the new size you set on the page. (This has no affect on the original PSD image. It always remains the same size and quality.)

However, if you resize the image on the page so that it's *larger* than the original PSD file, then the yellow warning icon remains, no matter what. In this case it indicates that the PSD file doesn't have enough pixels to make the image the size you want it, without hurting the quality of the image. In other words, you can't make the images on your page larger than the Photoshop file they come from without getting a worse quality image.

Tip: If you resize a Smart Object on the page, you can return it to its original size (that is, the size of the image in the original Photoshop file). In Design view, right-click (ctrl-click) the Smart Object, and then, from the menu that appears, choose "Reset size to original". Unfortunately, this option is useful only if you inserted the entire Photoshop image–if you cropped the image when you inserted it (see Figure 6-5 on page 222), and then you try to reset the image to the original size, Dreamweaver resizes (and distorts) the cropped image to the size of the entire Photoshop document.

Editing Images Pasted from Photoshop

When you add an image from Photoshop using the copy and paste method (see page 224), Dreamweaver keeps track of the original Photoshop document used to create the imported image. The path to the original PSD file is listed in the Property inspector (see Figure 6-19). Clicking the Property inspector's "Edit in Photoshop" button launches Photoshop, and then opens the original PSD file. At this point, you can make any edits you want to the image.

Unfortunately, Dreamweaver doesn't keep track of these edits. To get an edited image back *into* Dreamweaver, in this instance, is a bit clunky. There's no "I'm done, export this image back to Dreamweaver" button; instead, you need to copy the revised image and paste it back into Dreamweaver. Do so by copying the image (or portion of the image you wish to use) in Photoshop (see the Tip on page 224); then return to Dreamweaver, select the image you're replacing in Design view, and then choose Edit → Paste. Dreamweaver quickly replaces the old image with the new one. One nice thing: You don't have to revisit the Image Preview window (see Figure 6-4 on page 220). Dreamweaver remembers the optimization settings—including the file name—you set when you first inserted the image.

Tip: You may want to use different bits of one Photoshop document on a page. You might create a single-page mockup that includes icons, photos, and graphical navigation buttons. Use the Photoshop Slice tool to identify each individual graphic element; then use the Select Slice tool to select a slice. Choosing Edit → Copy then copies just that slice.

Optimizing an Image

You can optimize an image—compress its file size for faster download—by clicking the Optimize image button in the Property inspector. After clicking the button, the Image Preview window appears. This is the same window with all the same controls that appears when importing a Photoshop file (see Figure 6-4). While this feature does leave you with a smaller image file, you should usually avoid it. That's because when you optimize a GIF, JPEG or PNG image, you're compressing an already compressed file. Applying additional optimization to an image usually degrades the quality.

In addition, you shouldn't convert a JPEG file into a GIF, or vice versa. The image almost always ends up looking worse. If you have a JPEG file that you think should be a GIF instead (see page 218 for some guidelines), or you simply want to see if you can shave a few more bytes from a file by optimizing it again, it's best to return to the original Photoshop, Fireworks, or Illustrator file, if available, and use that program's export or "Save for Web" feature to generate a new GIF, JPEG, or PNG file. (Alternatively, use either of the techniques described on page 241 for editing Photoshop files.)

If you decide to ignore this warning (or you don't have the original image and really need to optimize the image further), then follow the directions on page 221. Once you've made your optimization changes, in the Preview Image window, click the OK button. The image is optimized again. You can choose Edit → Undo to back out of the change.

Note: Previous versions of Dreamweaver had two features–Flash text and Flash buttons–that let you insert simple Flash movie files designed to let you use any font on your computer and create interactive buttons. These tools were removed in Dreamweaver CS4, because the text and buttons weren't accessible by search engines or screen readers, produced slower-loading pages, and often caused unintended problems.

Image Maps

As Chapter 5 makes clear, you can easily turn a graphic into a clickable link. You can also add *multiple* links to a single image.

Suppose your company has offices all over the country, and you want to provide an easy way for visitors to locate the nearest state office. One approach would be simply to list all the state names, and link them to separate pages for each state. But that's boring! Instead, you could use a map of the United States—one image—and turn each state's outline into a hotspot that's linked to an appropriate page, listing all the offices in that state.

The array of invisible link buttons (called *hotspots*) responsible for this magic is called an *image map*. An image map contains one or more hotspots, each leading somewhere else.

Here's how to create an image map:

1. **Select the graphic you wish to make into an image map.**

   The Property inspector displays that image's properties and, in the lower-left corner, the image map tools, shown at the bottom in Figure 6-21. (These tools appear in the lower half of the Property inspector, which appears only if the Property inspector is fully expanded, as described on page 30.)

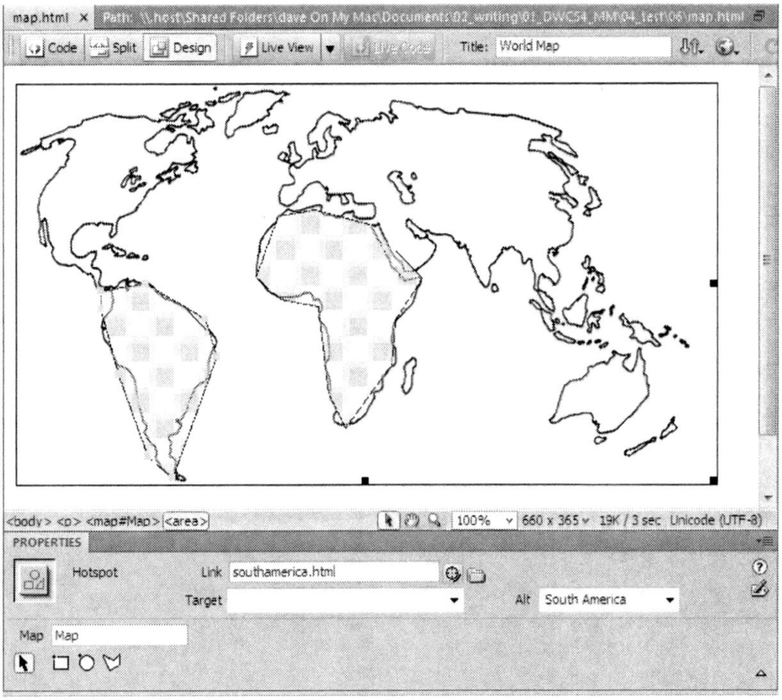

Figure 6-21: *Each link on an image map is called a hotspot. (Shown here are hotspots around South America and Africa.) When you select a hotspot, the Property inspector displays its Link, Target, and Alt properties. The lower half of the inspector displays the name of the map, as well as tools for selecting and drawing additional hotspots.*

2. **In the Property inspector's Map field, type a name for the map.**

   The name should contain only letters and numbers, and can't begin with a number. If you don't give the map a name, Dreamweaver automatically assigns the map the ingenious name *Map*. You don't really need to change the name; your visitors never see that name, the browser uses it just to correctly identify the image map. If you create additional image maps, then Dreamweaver calls them *Map2*, *Map3*, and so on.

3. **Select one of the image map tools.**

   Choose the rectangle tool, the circle tool, or the polygon tool, depending on the shape you have in mind for your hotspot. For instance, in the image in Figure 6-21, the polygon tool was used to draw each of the oddly shaped hotspots.

Note: If you have the image accessibility preference setting turned on (page 228), then you get a window reminding you to add an Alt property to the hotspot you're about to draw. Each hotspot can have its own Alt description.

4. **Draw the hotspot.**

   To use the rectangle and circle tools, click directly on your picture; drag diagonally to form a rectangle or circle. To make a perfect square, press Shift while dragging with the rectangle tool. (The circle tool always creates a perfect circle.)

   To draw an irregularly shaped hotspot using the polygon tool, click once to define one corner of the hotspot. Continue clicking until you've defined each corner of the hotspot. Dreamweaver automatically joins the corners to close the shape.

   Dreamweaver fills the inside of the hotspot with a light blue tint to make it easy to see. (Your Web visitors won't see the blue highlighting.)

   If you need to adjust the hotspot you've just drawn, on the Property inspector, click the arrow tool. You can drag the light blue square handles of your hotspot to reshape or resize the area, or drag inside the hotspot to move the whole thing. If you change your mind about the hotspot, press Delete to get rid of it altogether.

Note: After you draw a hotspot, the drawing tool is still active so that you can draw additional hotspots. In the Property inspector, click the arrow tool to deselect the hotspot drawing tool.

5. **Add a link to the hotspot.**

   After you draw a hotspot, that same hotspot is selected; its properties appear in the Property inspector (see Figure 6-21). Use any of the techniques discussed on page 167 to link this hotspot to another Web page or anchor.

6. **If necessary, set the Target property.**

   Most of the options in the Target pop-up menu are useful only when you're working with frames, as discussed on page 173, and in the online chapter about frames, which you can find at *www.sawmac.com/missing/dw8/appc.pdf*. The "_blank" option, however, is useful any time: It forces your visitor's Web browser to load the linked page into a *new* browser window. The original page remains open, underneath the new window.

7. **Set the hotspot's Alt property.**

   By typing a label into the Property inspector's Alt box, you provide a written name for this portion of the graphic. As noted on page 225, *alt* tags are extremely important to people who surf the Web with graphics turned off, or who use text-to-speech reading software.

8. **Repeat steps 2–7 for each hotspot you wish to add to an image.**

   As you work, you can see the light blue hotspots filling in your image map.

Editing a Hotspot's Properties

As noted in step 4, you can change a hotspot's shape by dragging its tiny square handles. But you can also change its other properties—like which Web page it links to.

To do so, click to select the image map. Using the black arrow tool—the hotspot selection tool— on the Property inspector's far left side (see Figure 6-21), click the hotspot you wish to edit. Then use the Property inspector controls to edit the Link, Target, and Alt properties.

If you're having a fit of frustration, you can also press Delete or Backspace to delete the hotspot altogether.

Rollover Images

Rollover images are common interactive elements on the Web. People frequently use them for navigation buttons (see Figure 6-22), but you can use them anytime you wish to dramatically swap one image for another. Say you've placed a photo of a product you're selling on a Web page. The photo links to a page that describes the product, and lets the visitor purchase it. To add emphasis to the image, you could add a rollover image so that when the visitor moves his mouse over the photo, *another* image—for example, the same image but with "Buy Now!" or "Learn more" printed across it—appears. You've almost certainly seen rollovers in action, when your mouse moves over a button on some Web page, and the image lights up, or glows, or turns into a frog.

Figure 6-22:
Rollover graphics appear frequently in navigation bars. Before your cursor touches a rollover button like the Horoscopes link (top), it just sits there blankly. But when your cursor arrives, the button changes appearance (bottom) to indicate that the graphic has a functional purpose–in this case, "I'm a link. Click me."

This simple change in appearance is a powerful way to inform a visitor that the graphic is more than just a pretty picture—it's a button that actually does something. Rollovers usually announce that the image is a link. (Though you can use them for other creative effects, as described on page 584.)

Behind the scenes, you create a rollover by preparing *two different* graphics—a "before" version and an "after" version. One graphic appears when the Web page first loads, and the other appears when your visitor's mouse moves over the first. If the cursor then rolls away without clicking, the original image pops back into place.

You achieve this dynamic effect by using *JavaScript*, a programming language that lets you add interactivity to Web pages. You saw JavaScript in action with the Spry Menu Bar (page 184). Aside from Spry objects, Dreamweaver includes many prewritten JavaScript programs, called *behaviors*, that let you add rollover images and other interactivity to your pages. (You can find more about behaviors in Chapter 13.)

To insert a rollover image, start by using a graphics program to prepare the "before" and "after" button images. Unless you're going for a bizarre distortion effect, both images should be exactly the same size. Store them somewhere in your Web site folder.

Then, in the document window, click where you want to insert the rollover image. If you're building a navigation bar, you might place several images (the buttons) side by side.

Choose Insert → Image Objects → Rollover Image (or, on the Insert panel's Common category, click the Rollover Image button). Either way, the Insert Rollover Image dialog box appears (see Figure 6-23). Fill in the blanks like this:

- **Image name.** Type a name for the graphic, if you like. JavaScript requires *some* name for the rollover effect. If you leave this blank, Dreamweaver gives the image an unimaginative name—like Image2—when you insert a rollover. However, if you plan to later add additional interactive effects (Chapter 13), you may want to change it to something more descriptive, to make it easier to identify the graphic.

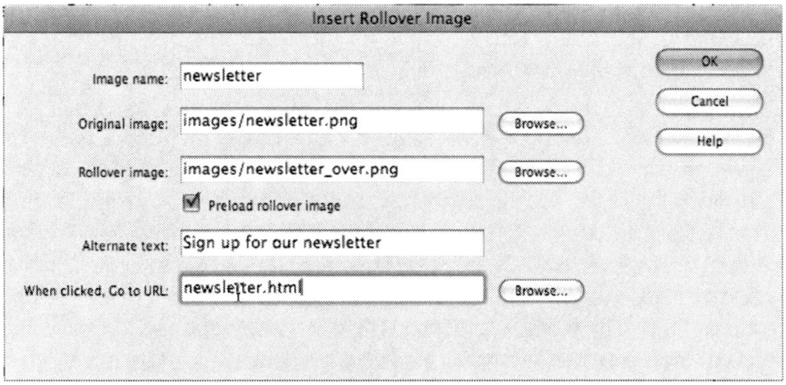

Figure 6-23:
This box lets you specify the name, link, and image files to use for the rollover effect. "Preload rollover image" forces the browser to download the rollover image file along with the rest of the page, avoiding a delay when the mouse moves over the rollover image for the first time.

- **Original image.** When you click the top Browse button, a dialog box appears, prompting you to choose the graphic you want to use as the "before" button—the one that first appears when the Web page loads. (See step 4 on page 215 for more on choosing graphics.)
- **Rollover image.** When you click the second Browse button, Dreamweaver prompts you to choose the "after" graphic image—the one that appears when your visitor's mouse rolls over the first one.
- **Alternate text.** You can give a text description for a rollover button just as you would for any graphic, as described on page 225.
- **When clicked, go to URL.** Rollover images are most commonly used for navigation elements that, when clicked, take the surfer to another Web page. In this box, you specify what happens when your visitor actually falls for the animated bait and *clicks* the rollover button. Click the Browse button to select a Web page from your site (see page 167 if you're not sure how to set a link), or, if you wish to link to another Web site, type an absolute URL (see page 162) beginning with *http://*.

When you click OK, you return to your document window, where only the "before" button image appears. You can select and modify it just as you would any image. In fact, it's just a regular image with a link and a Dreamweaver behavior attached.

You can see the rollover in action directly in Dreamweaver CS4: Click the Live View button near the top of the Document window—this turns on the embedded Webkit browser so you can actually see the JavaScript in action as it appears in a Web browser (or at least as it appears in Apple's Safari browser which uses Webkit). When you're done, click the Live View button again to return to the page for editing. To see how the rollover works in other browsers, press the F12 key (Option-F12 on a Mac) or use the File → "Preview in Browser" command.

You can achieve the same effect as the rollover behavior, with a little more effort, using Dreamweaver's Swap Image behavior, discussed on page 583. In fact, this versatile behavior lets you create multiple, simultaneous image swaps where several images change at the same time.

Note: If you're previewing a page with rollover images in Internet Explorer for Windows, you may have trouble previewing your rollover images. If, when previewing your page, you see a yellow banner with the ominous statement that begins "To help protect your security…", then you'll notice that the rollover image doesn't appear until you click the yellow banner and jump through a couple of hoops. Fortunately, this glitch affects only pages viewed locally–off your hard drive–and doesn't affect any of the thousands of visitors who come to your live site on the Internet. But if this still drives you crazy, Dreamweaver provides a simple solution: Choose Commands → "Insert Mark of the Web". Selecting this adds a little code to your page, which stops Internet Explorer from butting into your rollover business. When you're ready to move the page to the Web, you can remove this extra code by choosing Commands → "Remove Mark of the Web".

Tutorial: Inserting and Formatting Graphics

In this tutorial, you'll learn how to insert a photo, add a rollover image, and apply CSS to improve the look of a Web page. You'll also learn how to use background images to enhance the look of headlines.

Note: You'll need to download the tutorial files from *www.sawmac.com/dwcs4/* to complete this tutorial. See the Note on page 48 for more details.

Setting Up

Once you've downloaded the tutorial files and opened Dreamweaver, define a new site as described on page 42. You should be pretty good at this routine by now, but here's a quick recap as well as the introduction of another setting that's helpful when working with images.

1. **Choose Site → New Site.**

   The Site Definition window appears.

2. **Click the Advanced button, and, for the Site Name, type *Images*. To the right of the "Local root folder" box, click the folder icon.**

   The Choose Local Root Folder window appears. This is just a window onto your computer's file system; navigate to the proper folder just as you would when working with other programs.

3. **Navigate to MM_DWCS4 folder, and then select Chapter06. Click the Select (Windows) or Choose (Mac) button to identify this folder as the local root folder.**

   The just completed steps are the only ones required to define the site; however, one other setting is useful when working with images.

4. **To the right of the "Default images folder" box, click the folder icon. Inside the Chapter06 folder, double-click the images folder, and then click the Select (or Choose) button. In the Site Definition window, click OK to complete the process of defining a site.**

   By defining a default location for image files, certain operations, like dragging an image from the desktop or inserting a Photoshop image go faster—Dreamweaver already knows where in your site you want those images to go.

Adding an Image

Once again, you'll be working on a page from the Chia Vet site.

1. **Choose File → Open; click the Site Root button (bottom left of the Open File window). Double-click the file named *about.html*. Click directly after the letter "t" at the end of the "About Chia Vet" headline at the top of the page.**

   You'll add an image after the headline text advertising the Chia Vet newsletter.

2. **Choose Insert → Image. Navigate to the *images* folder, and then double-click the file *newsletter.png*.**

   The Image Tag Accessibility Attributes window appears. (If it doesn't, that's OK, just fill out the Property inspector's ALT box with the text "Sign up for our newsletter", and skip the next step.)

3. **In the Alternate text box, type *Sign up for our newsletter,* and then click OK.**

   A small icon advertising the Chia Vet newsletter appears. A black outline and three black boxes (resize handles) indicate that the image is selected—if you don't see these boxes, then just click the image on the page to select it.

   Next you'll link this image to the newsletter page.

4. **In the Property inspector, to the right of the Link box, click the folder icon. In the Chapter06 (the local root) folder, double-click the *newsletter.html* page.**

   If you need a recap on linking, check out page 167.

   You've added a link to the graphic, which causes an ugly blue line to appear around the image (you actually don't see this line until you deselect the image); in addition, the image is a bit too close to the headline text. You can fix both problems with a little CSS.

5. **Make sure the CSS Styles panel is open (Window → CSS Styles); in the panel's bottom right, click the Create New Style button (the + button).**

   The New CSS Rule window appears. You'll create a class style to apply to the image, and store the CSS information into an already attached external style sheet.

6. **From the top menu, select Class; in the Selector Name box, type *.newsImage*; in the bottom menu, select *global.css*, and then click OK.**

   The CSS Rule Definition window appears. First, you'll get rid of the blue border.

7. **From the Rule Definition window, select the Border category, and then, from the Top style menu, choose None.**

   This routine is the same as step 3 on page 197 in the last chapter. Next you'll add a bit of space to the left of the image.

8. **Select the Box category. Under Margin, uncheck the "Same for all" box and then, in the Left margin box, type *50*. Click OK to complete the style.**

   Nothing happens, yet. You have to apply the class style.

9. **Click on the image to select it. In the Property inspector, from the Class menu, choose *newsImage*.**

   The blue border disappears and the image moves 50 pixels to the right.

Inserting a Photoshop File

Dreamweaver makes it easy to insert and optimize files from Photoshop.

1. **In the word Vivamus in the first paragraph, click just to the left of the letter V. Choose Insert → Image.**

   In the Insert Panel's Common category, you can also use the Insert Image button (see Figure 6-2). Either way, the Select Image Source window appears. Now you'll select a PSD file.

2. **Click the Site Root button, and then double-click the *hippo.psd* file.**

   The Image Preview window appears. Dreamweaver suggests converting the PSD file to a JPEG image with a quality setting of 80%. Since this is a photo, JPEG is a good choice, but you can still squeeze a few precious bytes from the file by reducing the quality slightly.

3. **In the top left of the window, type *70* in the quality box.**

   The image is also a bit too big. You can make the Web-ready version of the image smaller when you insert it (without affecting the original Photoshop file).

4. **In the top left of the window, click the File tab (circled in Figure 6-24). In the Scale percentage box, type *50*; click OK to optimize the image. Click the Save button to save the file as *hippo.jpg*.**

   Notice that when the Save Web Image window appeared, the *images* folder was selected—that's because of step 4 on page 251 above when you specified the default images folder.

5. **In the Image Tag Accessibility Attributes window's Alternate Text box, type Chia Hippo, and then click OK.**

   A big photo appears on the page (see Figure 6-25). You'll notice the Smart Object logo in the top-left corner (circled in Figure 6-25), and three resize handles (black squares that appear on the bottom right corner, bottom edge, and right edge of the photo). The photo's still a bit large, but you can resize it in Dreamweaver.

6. **Hold down the Shift key, and then drag the image's resize handle up and to the left until the image is about 1/4 its original size.**

   If you don't see the resize handles, click the image to select it. The Shift key makes sure the image scales proportionally, and also makes sure you don't accidentally distort the image. The exact dimensions don't matter; just resize the image to a smaller size that you like.

   Now you see a yellow warning sign in the image's upper-left corner (see Figure 6-26). This sign means that the actual dimensions of the image no longer match the width and height specified in the HTML—by resizing the image this way you just change the HTML and not the actual image file. As mentioned in

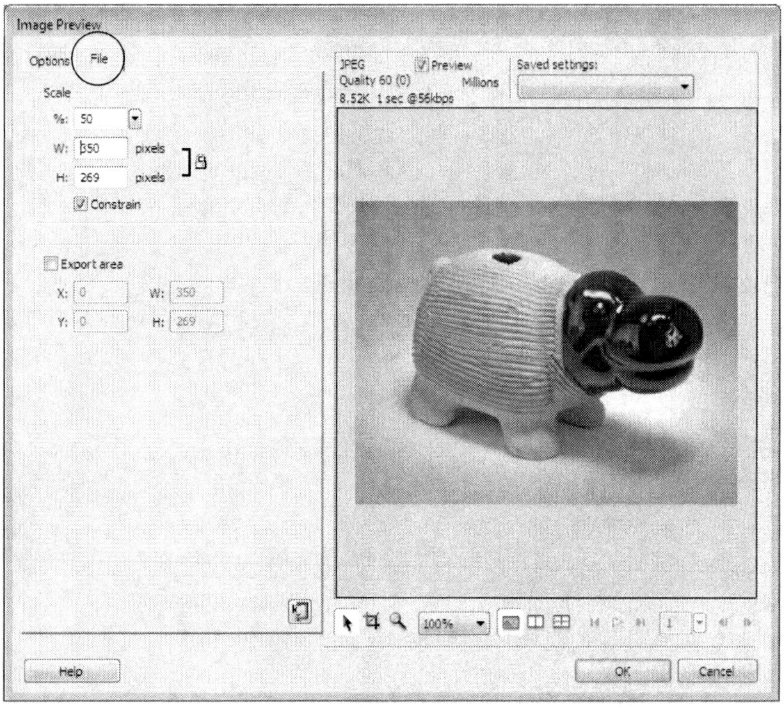

Figure 6-24: *When importing an image from a Photoshop document, you can generate a file that's much leaner, size-wise, than the original Photoshop image. The File tab of the window lets you specify a percentage value so you can resize the imported image's physical dimensions (and also create a smaller file)—this action doesn't change the original Photoshop file at all. In addition, you can import a specific area of the image by checking the "Export area" box, and then specifying a width, height, and starting position for the portion of the image you wish to extract. Use the X box to specify how many pixels from the left edge of the cropped/exported image you want to exclude, and Y to specify the number of pixels from the top. For example, if you type* 100 *in the X box and* 50 *in the Y, then the exported image crops out the left 100 pixels of the image, and the top 50 pixels.*

the box on page 229, this isn't a good idea—the image doesn't look as good and the file is larger than it needs to be (meaning it will download more slowly). Fortunately, because this is a Smart Object, you can easily recreate a JPEG file that matches the smaller dimensions you just specified while maintaining the image's original quality.

7. **In the Property inspector, click the "Update from Original" button (circled in Figure 6-26).**

   Dreamweaver re-optimizes the image based on the Photoshop file. This means that, behind the scenes, Dreamweaver creates a new JPEG image—complete with all your original optimization settings (except of course the 50% size you

about.html (XHTML)
Code
Split
Design
Live View
Live Code
Title:
About Chia Vet
Source Code
global.css
About Chia Vet
Chia Vet
NEWSLETTER
Vivamus in turpis ac nunc scelerisqu
Lorem ipsum dolor sit amet, consectetuer adipiscing elit. Morbi commodo ante quis odio.
mauris id urna. Duis nec risus. Cras facilisis. Morbi fringilla consectetuer pede. Ut sodales
dolor nibh, consectetuer vel, condimentum luctus, tempus ut, tellus. In erat. Nulla non odi
gravida fringilla. Cras vitae purus. Pellentesque a pede vitae ante tincidunt venenatis. Cras

Figure 6-25: *An image positioned like this one is called an "inline" element in HTML—this just means it can sit right next to letters on a line of text. In other words, an image acts sort of like a really, really tall letter. Unfortunately, that phenomenon usually leaves large areas of white space on the page.*

set in step 4). Modifying an image using Smart Objects, aside from being very fast, is the best way to assure a high quality Web image.

If you own Photoshop, launch it now (if you don't have Photoshop, just skip to the next paragraph); then, in the Chapter06 folder, open the *hippo.psd* file, and edit it—apply a filter, add some text, or whatever. Save the file, and then return to Dreamweaver. You'll see that a red "out-of-sync" arrow appears. Select the image, press the "Update from Original" button again, and the image is updated from the original PSD file. Very cool.

You still have a few things to do with this image. For example, all the story's text appears below the image, leaving a large and unattractive white space to the image's right. To fix this, you'll create a style to move the photo to the right side of the page, and allow text to wrap around it.

8. **In the CSS Styles panel, click the Create New Style button (the + button) in the panel's bottom right.**

   The New CSS Rule window appears. You'll create a class style to apply to the image, and store the CSS information into the already attached *global.css* style sheet.

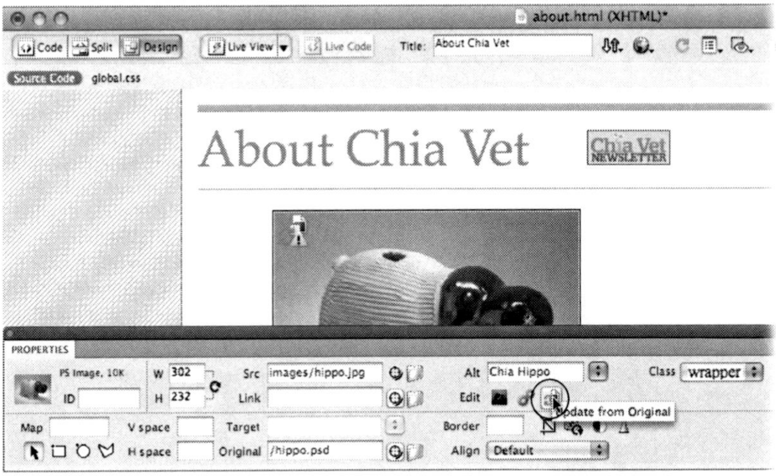

Figure 6-26: *When a warning icon (the yellow triangle) appears on a Smart Object, it usually means that you've resized the image on the page. The "Update from Original" button lets you recreate the Web graphic file to match the dimensions you're after.*

9. **From the top menu, select Class; in the Selector Name box, type *.photoRight*; in the bottom menu, select *global.css*, and then click OK.**

   Class names should be descriptive; in this case, photoRight is a good name to identify a style that aligns a photo to the right.

   The CSS Rule Definition window appears. Time to add a decorative border.

10. **From the left-hand list of categories, Select Border; from the top Style menu, choose "solid"; in the Width box, type *2*; from the Color box, select black (or any color you like).**

    Leave all three "Same for all" checkboxes turned on to make sure the border is applied to all four sides of the photo. Next, you'll move the photo to the right and force the text to wrap around it.

11. **Click the Box category; from the Float menu, select Right; uncheck the "Same for all" box for the Margin settings, in the Bottom margin box, type *10;* and in the Left margin box, type *15*. In the top padding box, type *10*.**

    The window should look like Figure 6-27. Now it's time to finish and apply the style.

12. **Click OK to finish the style.**

    Because you just created a class style, its formatting power won't take affect until you've applied it to the image.

13. **Select the photo on the page, and then, from the Property inspector's Class menu, choose *photoRight*.**

    The newly inserted image moves to the right, the text wraps around it, and a border appears (see Figure 6-28).

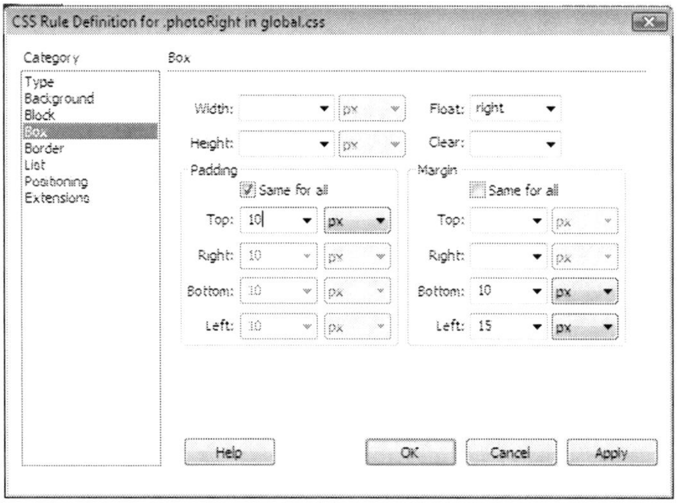

***Figure 6-27:** When you float an image to the right (or left), it's a good idea to add some margin to the side of the image around which text will wrap. This adds white space between the text and graphic, making the design feel less cramped and cluttered.*

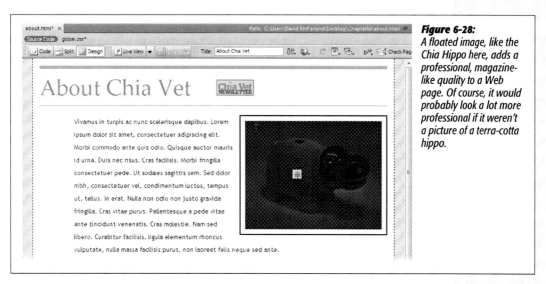

***Figure 6-28:** A floated image, like the Chia Hippo here, adds a professional, magazine-like quality to a Web page. Of course, it would probably look a lot more professional if it weren't a picture of a terra-cotta hippo.*

Inserting a Rollover Image

The Chia Vet Newsletter logo you added is intended to get visitors to sign up for the company's monthly newsletter. A rollover image would more effectively grab people's attention.

1. **At the top of the Web page, select the Chia Vet newsletter icon. Hit Delete to remove the image.**

   Oh, your hard work is gone! Hey, it was good practice, and now you'll add a much more interesting rollover image.

2. **Choose Insert → Image Objects → Rollover Image.**

   The Insert Rollover Image window appears (see Figure 6-29).

3. **In the name box, type *newsletter*.**

   The name you give here won't appear anywhere on the page. It's just an internal name—a way for the JavaScript programming that triggers the image rollover to identify and "talk" to this graphic.

4. **Click the first Browse button, and then, in the images folder, double-click the *newsletter.png* file; click the second Browse button, and then double-click the *newsletter_over.png* file.**

   You've just selected the two files used for the rollover effect—the first appears when the page loads, and the second when a visitor moves her mouse over the image. In order for the rollover to work, you need to supply a link (and while you're at it, some alt text is a good idea, too).

5. **In the Alternate text box, type *Signup for our newsletter*; at the bottom of the window, click the Browse button; in the file selection window that appears, click the Site Root button, and then double-click the *newsletter.html* file.**

   The window should now look like Figure 6-29. Time to finish inserting the rollover image and apply the class style you created earlier.

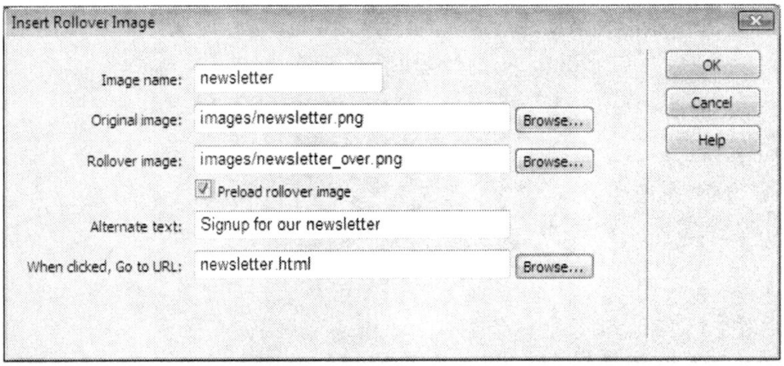

Figure 6-29: *In one window, you can set up everything you need to add dynamic rollover images to a page. Dreamweaver handles all the messy JavaScript programming that makes the whole thing work.*

6. **Click OK to insert the Rollover image. In the Document window, click the image, and then, from the Property inspector's Class menu, choose "newsImage".**

   The image moves to the right about 50 pixels. Time to check out the rollover.

7. **At the top of the Document window, click the Live View button.**

   Move your mouse over the newsletter icon and see it change. Magic! When you're done having fun, click the Live View button again to return to editing the page.

Using Background Images

The HTML <img> tag isn't the only way to add an image to a Web page. You can also use the CSS *background-image* property to give any HTML tag a graphical backdrop. You added a background image to the body of a Web page in the first tutorial (page 56). In fact, this page already has a background image applied to it (the blue and white cross-hatched pattern). But you can also add a background image to other HTML tags as well. Next, you'll add a background image to each of the second-level headings on the page.

1. **Make sure the CSS Styles panel is open (Window → CSS Styles), and that the All button at the top of the panel is selected.**

   The All button lets you view all the styles attached to a page. In this case, you see one style sheet—*global.css*. You're going to edit an already existing style in that external style sheet file.

2. **If you can't see any styles listed under *global.css* in the Styles panel, click the + (flippy triangle on Mac) to the left of *global.css* to expand the list. Double-click the style named *h2*.**

   This tag style formats all heading 2 headlines on the page. The CSS Rule Definition window opens.

3. **In the Rule Definition window, select the *Background* category; click the Browse button, navigate to the *images* folder, and then double-click the file *vet_logo.png*.**

   The image is a simple icon for the veterinary profession (of which Chia Vet is a member, of course). It should appear only once at the left side of the headline; because the normal behavior of a background image is to repeat indefinitely, you need to make sure the graphic appears only once.

4. **From the Background-repeat menu, choose "no-repeat".**

   Normally a background image is placed in the top left corner of whatever the image is added to—for example, the top left corner of the Web page, or in this case, the top left corner of the *h2* tag. For precise placement of the background image, you can specify both a horizontal and vertical position. You can use either pixels, percentages or predefined placement options. In this case, the image should appear on the far left, and centered vertically in the middle of the headline.

5. **Choose "left" from the "Background-position (X)" menu, and "center" from the "Background-position (Y)" menu.**

   The window should look like Figure 6-30.

6. **Click the Apply button to see the effect.**

   The Apply button lets you see how the style is shaping up. (If nothing happens when you press Apply, you may still be in Live View from step 7 on page 258.

That's OK, just read the following description of what the page should now look like.) You'll see that the headline text overlaps the image. In addition, because the graphic is taller than the text, the top and bottom part of the image are clipped off. You can fix both these problems by adding a little padding.

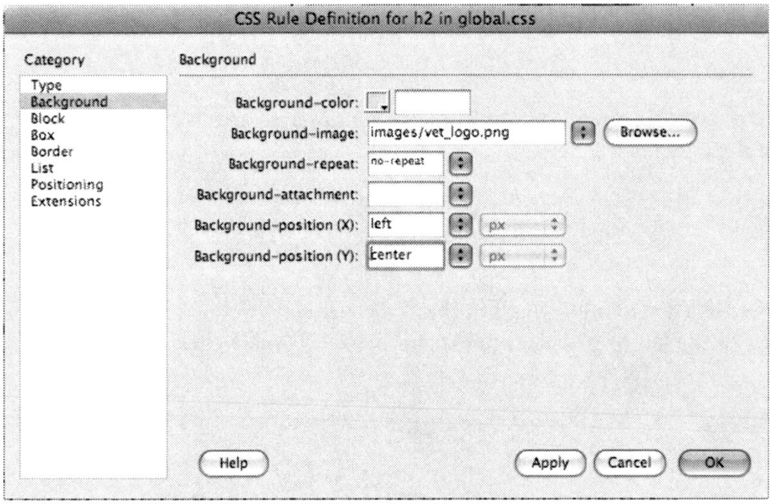

Figure 6-30: *Selecting "no-repeat" from the Repeat menu displays the image just once in the background instead of tiling it. The Horizontal and Vertical position options work well for this situation, since they let you accurately place that single image.*

7. **Click the Box category; under the Padding area, uncheck the "Same for All" box, type *10* in the Top box, type *0* in the right box, type *10* in the bottom box, and type *55* in the left box.**

   Padding is the space between the content inside a tag (like the text in the heading) and the outer edge of the tag. (See Figure 9-11 on page 344 for a visual of how this works.) It lets you add space between a borderline and text; and, here, the padding makes room for the background image. (Padding settings don't affect background images.)

   Finally, you'll scoot the whole headline (including the background image) over just a little bit to the right.

8. **Type *20* in the left margin box, and then click OK to finish the style.**

   The margin property adds space around the edges of an element, and moves not just the text but also the borderline and background images as well.

9. **Hit F12 (option-F12) to preview the page in a Web browser.**

   Your finished design should look like Figure 6-31. You may have trouble previewing the rollover image in Internet Explorer—see page 250 for how to handle this. You'll find a completed version of this tutorial in the Chapter06_finished folder that accompanies the downloaded tutorial files.

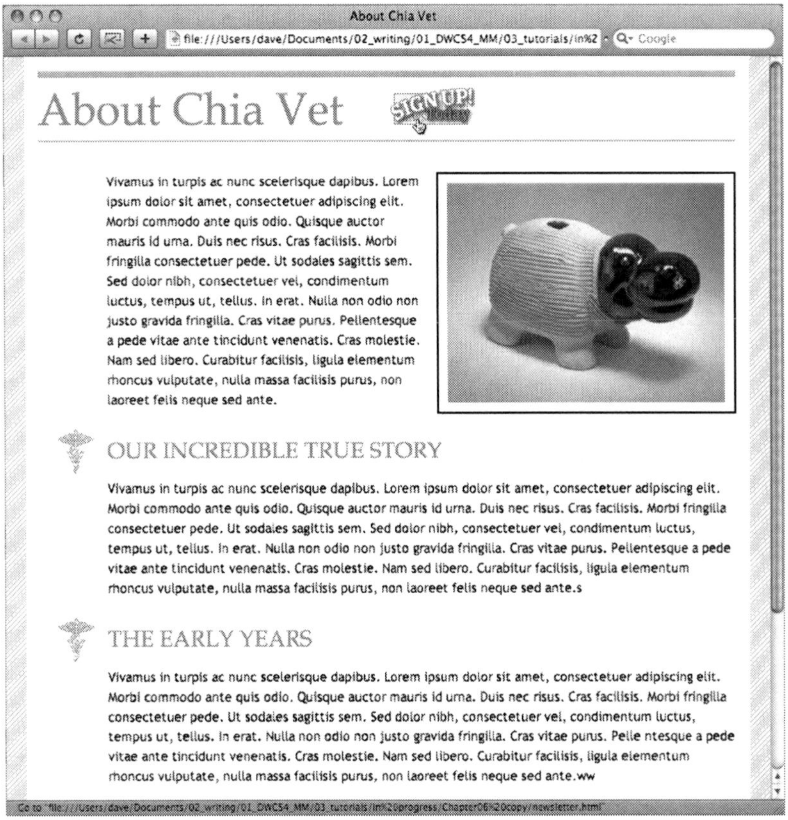

About Chia Vet
file:///Users/dave/Documents/02_writing/01_DWCS4_MM/03_tutorials/in%2
Google
About Chia Vet
SIGN UP! Today
Vivamus in turpis ac nunc scelerisque dapibus. Lorem ipsum dolor sit amet, consectetuer adipiscing elit. Morbi commodo ante quis odio. Quisque auctor mauris id urna. Duis nec risus. Cras facilisis. Morbi fringilla consectetuer pede. Ut sodales sagittis sem. Sed dolor nibh, consectetuer vel, condimentum luctus, tempus ut, tellus. In erat. Nulla non odio non justo gravida fringilla. Cras vitae purus. Pellentesque a pede vitae ante tincidunt venenatis. Cras molestie. Nam sed libero. Curabitur facilisis, ligula elementum rhoncus vulputate, nulla massa facilisis purus, non laoreet felis neque sed ante.
OUR INCREDIBLE TRUE STORY
Vivamus in turpis ac nunc scelerisque dapibus. Lorem ipsum dolor sit amet, consectetuer adipiscing elit. Morbi commodo ante quis odio. Quisque auctor mauris id urna. Duis nec risus. Cras facilisis. Morbi fringilla consectetuer pede. Ut sodales sagittis sem. Sed dolor nibh, consectetuer vel, condimentum luctus, tempus ut, tellus. In erat. Nulla non odio non justo gravida fringilla. Cras vitae purus. Pellentesque a pede vitae ante tincidunt venenatis. Cras molestie. Nam sed libero. Curabitur facilisis, ligula elementum rhoncus vulputate, nulla massa facilisis purus, non laoreet felis neque sed ante.s
THE EARLY YEARS
Vivamus in turpis ac nunc scelerisque dapibus. Lorem ipsum dolor sit amet, consectetuer adipiscing elit. Morbi commodo ante quis odio. Quisque auctor mauris id urna. Duis nec risus. Cras facilisis. Morbi fringilla consectetuer pede. Ut sodales sagittis sem. Sed dolor nibh, consectetuer vel, condimentum luctus, tempus ut, tellus. In erat. Nulla non odio non justo gravida fringilla. Cras vitae purus. Pelle ntesque a pede vitae ante tincidunt venenatis. Cras molestie. Nam sed libero. Curabitur facilisis, ligula elementum rhoncus vulputate, nulla massa facilisis purus, non laoreet felis neque sed ante.ww

Figure 6-31: *Photos, icons, and other graphic elements add visual interest to any Web page, while rollover images (the "Sign Up!" button at top) add interactivity and a sense of fun.*

CHAPTER

7

Tables

The HTML <table> tag has had a somewhat infamous existence in the world of Web design. It was originally intended to present scientific research in a spreadsheet-like manner. But as the Web grew, graphic designers got into the Web design game. They wanted to recreate the types of layouts seen in magazines, books, and newspapers (in other words, they wanted to make good-looking Web sites). The most reliable tool at the time was the <table> tag, which designers morphed into a method for creating columns, sidebars, and, in general, precisely positioning elements on a page.

The wheel has turned again. Today, with nearly everyone on the planet using advanced Web browsers like Internet Explorer, Firefox, Safari, and Opera, a newer method—CSS-based layout—is now the most common technique for professional Web design. Table-based layout is an aging dinosaur that produces pages heavy with code (meaning they download slower), are hard to update, and are hostile to search engines and alternative browsers such as screen readers, mobile phones, and text-only Web browsers.

This chapter shows you how to use tables for their intended purpose: displaying data and other information that's best presented in rows and columns (see Figure 7-1). If you're a long-time Web designer who still uses tables for page layout, you can still use Dreamweaver and the instructions in this chapter to continue that technique. However, you're better off in the long run making the switch to CSS-based layout. Dreamweaver's advanced CSS tools and its CSS Layouts can make building these types of pages much simpler. You'll learn all about CSS layout in Chapter 9.

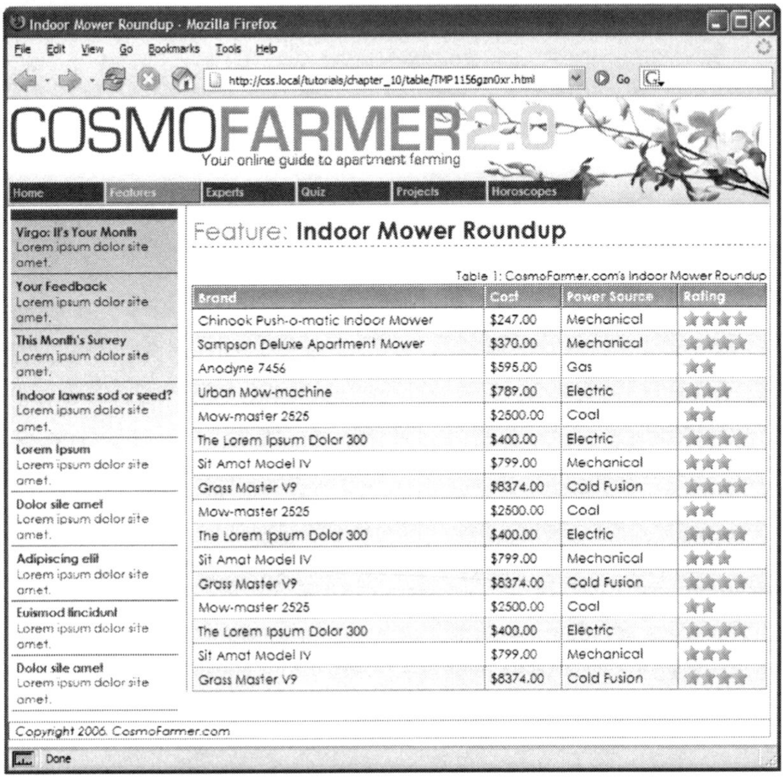

Figure 7-1: *You can do all your page layout and design with CSS, and use tables for what they're intended–displaying rows and columns of information. The list of products in the center of this page is nestled inside a basic <table> tag, while the rest of the page is laid out using CSS.*

Table Basics

A table is a grid of rows and columns that intersect to form *cells*, as shown in Figure 7-2. If you've used a spreadsheet before, an HTML table should feel familiar. A row usually represents a collection of data for a single item. In Figure 7-1, each row holds data for one particular mower. A column represents data of a particular type. The first column contains the name of each mower, while the second column displays a mower's cost. A cell, then, holds one piece of data for a particular row: like the exact price of the Chinook Push-O-Matic Lawn Mower.

Two different types of cells exist, each represented by a different HTML tag. A table cell that contains data—$247.00, for instance—is created with the <td> or *table data* tag. Browsers display text inside a <td> aligned to the left edge of the cell. A cell that holds a label announcing the type of information in a row or column is called a <th> or *table head* tag. Text inside a <th> tag appears centered and in boldface. The overall table itself is created using the <table> tag, In Figure 7-1, all the cells in the table's top row are table headers, since they identify what type of data appears in the cells below: Brand, Cost, and so on.

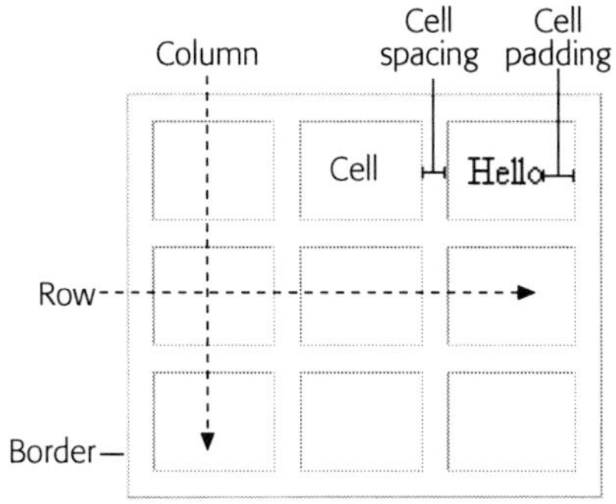

Figure 7-2:
Rows, columns, and cells make up a table. Cell spacing specifies how many pixels of space appear between cells. Cell padding, on the other hand, provides a space between the four sides of the cell and the cell's content.

Inserting a Table

One of the main problems with an HTML table is that it takes a lot of HTML code to make one. Not only is this one reason why CSS is a better page layout method, it's also a good reason to use Dreamweaver to create a table. If you've ever hand-coded an HTML table, you know what a tangled mess of code it requires: One typo in your HTML can sink your whole page. Fortunately, Dreamweaver makes creating an HTML table a simple process.

1. **Place the insertion point in the document window where you'd like to insert a table.**

   You can add a table anywhere you can add a paragraph of text. You can even add a table inside *another* table, by clicking inside a table cell.

2. **Choose Insert → Table.**

   You can also click the Table button on the Insert panel. It appears under both the Common category and the Layout category. You can also press Ctrl+Alt+T (⌘-Option-T). Either way, the Table dialog box opens (see Figure 7-3).

3. **Using the Rows and Columns fields, specify how many rows and columns you want in your table.**

   Don't fret too much over your estimate, since you can always add or remove rows or columns later.

4. **Type the amount of cell padding, in pixels, you want for the table.**

   Cell padding is the margin inside the cell—the space from the edge of a cell to its contents (see Figure 7-2). Unfortunately, this property applies to *every* cell in a table (it also applies equally to all four sides of the cell). You can't add this space to an individual cell in a table, or have different amounts of padding (for example, 10 pixels of space on the left side of the cell, but only 5 pixels at the top) unless you use the CSS *padding* property as described on page 343. People often either type 0 or leave this box empty, and then use the CSS *padding* property to control padding on individual table cells (via the <td> and <th> tags).

5. **Type the amount of cell spacing, in pixels, you want for the table.**

   Cell spacing specifies how many pixels of space separate one cell from another (see Figure 7-2). Again, this property applies to every cell in a table, but, unlike padding, there's no effective CSS equivalent. So if you do wish to insert space between each cell, then you should add a value here (you can change this later, as described on page 273). Type *0* to remove any space between cells. (Note that leaving these fields empty isn't the same as setting them to zero; see Figure 7-3.)

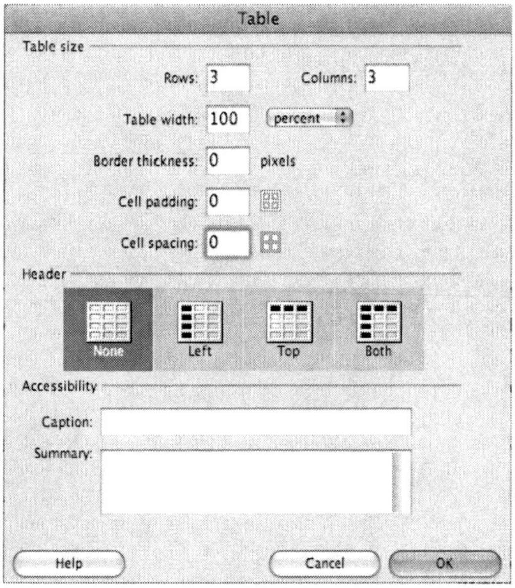

Figure 7-3:
The Table dialog box lets you control a table's appearance. Leaving the Cell Padding and Cell Spacing fields empty isn't the same as setting them to 0. If these properties are empty, most Web browsers insert 1 pixel of cell padding and 2 pixels of cell spacing. If you notice unwanted gaps between cells in a table or between content in a table and the cell's edges, empty settings here are the likeliest culprit. To truly leave zero space, set Cell Padding and Cell Spacing to 0. (Dreamweaver remembers the settings you use. When you use the Insert Table dialog box again, it starts with the same settings you entered previously.)

6. **Using the "Table width" field, specify how wide you want the table to be** (**in units that you specify using the pop-up menu**).

   Tables can have either a specified, fixed minimum width, or they can take up a specified percentage of the space available on the page. To set a fixed width, choose Pixels as the unit of measurement, and then, in the "Table width" field, type a pixel amount. Fixed-width tables remain the same size regardless of the browser window's size.

   Percentage widths let tables grow or shrink relative to the space available. In other words, if you place a 100% wide table on a blank Web page, the table stretches all the way across your visitor's browser window, no matter how wide or narrow it is. But the percentage isn't always based on the overall browser window width. If you place a table *inside* another object—either another table cell, or a <div> tag—that has a set width, Dreamweaver calculates the percentage based on that object. Say you have a sidebar on a page, and the sidebar is 300 pixels wide; if you insert an 80% wide table inside the sidebar, then the table takes up 80 percent of 300 pixels, or 240 pixels.

Note: Sometimes Internet Explorer 6 for Windows treats 100% as a little bigger than 100%. This confounding behavior can cause 100% wide tables in CSS layouts to not fit (usually forcing the table to jump down below most of the page design). Using a slightly smaller percentage like 99% or 98% usually fixes this glitch.

7. **In the "Border thickness" box, type a number, in pixels, for the border.**

   If you don't want a border, type *0*. Dreamweaver uses dotted lines in Design view to help you identify rows, columns, and cells whose border is 0. (The dotted lines won't appear on the finished Web page.) Again, CSS offers a much better method of adding borders (see page 231).

8. **Using the buttons in the middle of the dialog box, select a Header option.**

   The Header property inserts the <th> tag to create the cells in the top row or left-hand column. <th> is a table header tag; it indicates that a cell is a *headline* for a column or row of data, and identifies the kind of content that appears in the cells below the column headline or to the right of the row headline. A table that displays a company's yearly sales figures, broken down by region, might have a top row of headers for each year ("2005," "2006," "2007"), while the left column would have table headers identifying each region ("Northwest," "West," "South," and so on).

   The only visible change you get with a <th> tag is that Web browsers display header cell text in bold type and center aligned. However, this option also makes the table more accessible by telling screen readers (used by the visually impaired) that the cell serves as a header for the information in the column. (You can always change the look of these cells using CSS; just create a style for the <th> tag as described on page 115.)

9. **In the bottom section of the Table dialog box, add any Accessibility settings you wish to use.**

   In the Caption box, type information identifying the table; it appears centered, above the table. Use the Summary box when you want to explain a particularly complex data table. This information doesn't show up in a browser window; it's intended to clarify the contents of a table to search engines and screen readers. Basic data tables (just simple rows and columns) don't need a summary; search engines and screen readers can understand them just fine. It's only when you create a complex table with merged cells (see page 280) and multiple levels of headers that you might want to fill out the summary.

   For more information on these options and to get a complete rundown on table accessibility, visit *www.w3.org/TR/WCAG10-HTML-TECHS/#tables*.

10. **Click OK to insert the table.**

Once you've added a table to a page, you can begin filling the table's cells. A cell works like a small document window; you can click inside it and add text, images, and links using the techniques you've already learned. You can even insert a table inside a cell (a common technique in the bad old days of table-based layout).

To move the insertion point from one cell to the next, press Tab. When you reach the last cell in a row, the Tab key moves the insertion point to the first cell in the row below. And if the insertion point is in the last *cell* of the last row, pressing Tab creates a new row at the bottom of the table.

Shift+Tab moves the cursor in the *opposite* direction—from the current cell to a cell to the left.

Selecting Parts of a Table

Tables and their cells have independent properties. For example, a table and a cell can have different alignment properties. But before you can change any of these properties, you must first *select* the tables, rows, columns, or cells you want to affect.

Selecting a Table

You can select a table in the document window in a number of ways:

- Click the upper-left corner of the table, or anywhere on the bottom edge. (Be careful using the latter technique, however. It's easy to accidentally *drag* the border, adding a height property to the table in the process—an attribute that isn't valid HTML.)
- Click anywhere inside the table, and then select the <table> tag in the document window's status bar (see page 24 to learn about the Tag selector).
- Click anywhere inside the table, and then choose Modify → Table → Select Table.
- Right-click (Control-click) inside a table, and then, from the shortcut menu, choose Table → Select Table.
- If the insertion point is in any cell inside the table, pressing Ctrl+A (⌘-A) twice selects the table.

Once selected, a table appears with a thick black border and three tiny, square resize handles—at the right edge, bottom edge, and lower-right corner.

Selecting Rows or Columns

You can also select an entire row or column of cells by doing one of the following:

- Move the cursor to the left edge of a row or the top edge of a column. When it changes to a right- or down-pointing arrow, click, as explained in Figure 7-4.
- Click a cell at either end of a row, or the first or last cell of a column, and then drag across the cells in the row or column to select them.

- Click any cell in the row you wish to select, and then click the <tr> tag in the Tag selector. (The <tr> tag is how HTML indicates a table row.) This method doesn't work for columns.

When a cell is selected, it has a dark border around it. When multiple cells are selected, each has a dark border (see Figure 7-4).

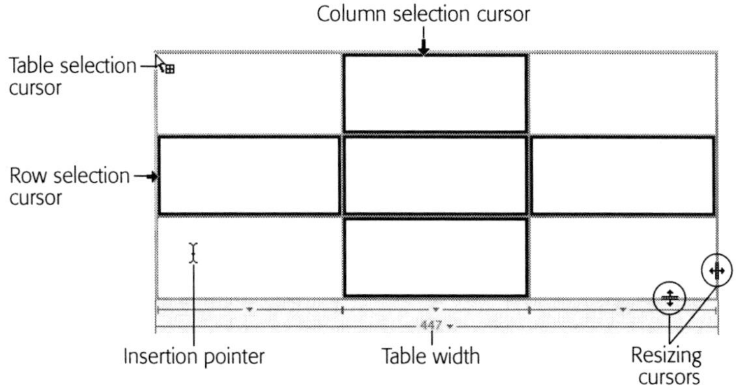

Figure 7-4: *When you're working with tables, the cursor can take on many different roles. The Table selection cursor lets you select the entire table. When the cursor turns into an arrow (pointing either down or to the right), you can click to select a column or row of cells. The insertion-point cursor lets you click to insert content into a cell. When you pass the cursor over a resize handle, it becomes a resize icon, which you can drag to resize rows, columns, or the entire table.*

Selecting Cells

To select one or more cells:

- Drag over adjoining cells. A solid black border appears around a cell when it's selected.
- To select several cells that aren't necessarily adjacent, Ctrl-click (⌘-click) them one at a time. (You can also Ctrl-click [⌘-click] an already selected cell to deselect it.)
- Click a cell, and then Shift-click another cell. Your two clicks form diagonally opposite corners of an imaginary rectangle; Dreamweaver highlights all cells within it.
- Use the Tag selector (see page 24) to select a cell. Click inside the cell you wish to select, and then click the <td> tag in the Tag selector.
- If the insertion point is inside the cell you wish to select, press Ctrl+A (⌘-A).

Expanded Table Mode

If you remove all padding, cell spacing, and borders from a table, it can be difficult to select tables and individual cells. This phenomenon is especially true if you nest tables within table cells (a common table-layout technique). To help you out in this situation, Dreamweaver offers an Expanded Table mode. Clicking the Expanded button on the Layout category of the Insert panel adds visible borders to every table and cell, and increases onscreen cell padding. (Choosing View → Table Mode → Expanded Tables does the same thing.) Expanded Table mode never changes the actual page code; it merely affects how the page is displayed in Design view. The guideline borders and extra spacing that appear in Design view don't appear in a Web browser.

If you simply use tables to display data, you'll probably never need Expanded Table mode, but if you have to edit old Web pages built with complicated table layouts, Expanded mode is a big help.

To return to Standard view, click the Standard button on the Layout catory of the Insert panel, or choose View → Table Mode → Standard Mode.

Formatting Tables

When you first insert a table, you set the number of rows and columns, as well as the table's cell padding, cell spacing, width, and borders. You're not stuck, however, with the properties you first give the table; you can change any or all of these properties, and set a few additional ones, using the Property inspector.

When you select a table, the Property inspector changes to reflect that table's settings (see Figure 7-5). You can adjust the table by entering different values for height, width, rows, columns, and so on in the appropriate fields.

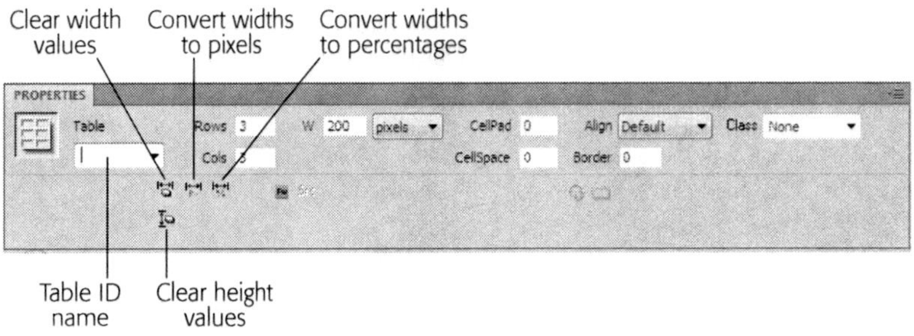

Figure 7-5: *When you select a table, you can do everything in the Property inspector, from adjusting its basic structure to fine-tuning its appearance. Dreamweaver includes two menus–Table on the far left and Class on the far right–which let you apply a CSS ID selector (see page 114) or a class style (page 114) to a table.*

In addition, the Property inspector lets you set alignment options, and add colors or a background image, as described next.

Aligning Tables

In the normal flow of a Web page, a table acts like a paragraph, header, or any other HTML block-level element. It's aligned to the left of the page, with other elements placed either above it or below it.

But you can make several useful changes to the way a table interacts with the text and other elements around it. After selecting the table, use one of the three alignment options in the pop-up menu at the right of the Property inspector:

- The Left and Right options align the table with the left or right page margins. Anything you then add to the page—including paragraphs, images, or other tables—wraps around the right or left side of the table. You can also apply the CSS Float property to a table (just as with images) to achieve the same effect (see page 229).
- The Center option makes the table sit in the center of the page, interrupting the flow of the elements around it. Nothing wraps around the table.

Note: Some of the properties Dreamweaver lets you adjust to make tables look better aren't technically valid for some of the different HTML "document types" Dreamweaver can create. As you read on page 46, Dreamweaver can create HTML 4.01 Transitional, XHTML 1.0 Transitional, and several other types of HTML documents. In general, HTML 4.01 Transitional and XHTML 1.0 Transitional are commonly used document types–XHTML 1.0 Transitional is the "out of box" setting in Dreamweaver. However, the more "strict" types, like HTML 4.01 Strict and XHTML 1.0 Strict, don't support some table properties–the *align* property discussed above, for example.

This discrepancy is more a technicality than a design nuisance; most Web browsers still display the alignment you select, even when used with these types of documents. The newer and recommended method is to use CSS properties to accomplish the same display goals; for example, using CSS to set the left and right margins of a table to "auto" centers the table on the page (see page 343), while applying a CSS Left Float and Right Float to a table is the same as the Left and Right align options. See page 651 for more on "valid" HTML.

Clearing Height and Width Values

When creating complex table designs, it's easy to get yourself into a situation where width and height measurements conflict and produce unreliable results. For example, it's possible to set one cell to 300 pixels wide, and later set another cell *in the same column* to 400 pixels wide. Since a Web browser can't do both (how can one column be both 300 *and* 400 pixels wide?), you might not get the results you want.

In tables with many cells, these kinds of problems are tough to ferret out. That's when you'll find the following timesaving tools—located behind the obscure-looking buttons in the Property inspector's bottom half (see Figure 7-5)—handy. They let you delete the width and height measurements and start from scratch (see "Tips for Surviving Table Making" on page 276).

- Clicking the Clear Height Values button removes the height properties of the table and each cell. Doing so doesn't set the heights to zero; it simply deletes the property altogether.

- Clicking the Clear Width Values button accomplishes the same purpose for the width properties of a table and its cells (see "Setting Cell Dimensions" on page 276).

Two additional buttons let you convert pixel-based table widths to percentage measurements, and vice versa. In other words, if a table is 600 pixels wide and you click the "Convert Widths to Percentages" button, then Dreamweaver assigns percentages to the table and each cell whose width is specified using pixels.

These percentages depend on how much of the document window your table takes up when you click the button. If the document window is 1200 pixels wide, that 600-pixel-wide table changes to a 50% width. Because you'll rarely do this, don't waste your brain cells memorizing such tools.

Note: Dreamweaver CS4 has removed the outdated *border color, background color,* and *background image* HTML properties from the Property inspector. Instead, you should use the CSS equivalents: *border* (page 231), *background-image* (page 233), and *background-color* (page 233). You'll find examples of how to use CSS to add background images, colors, and borders to a table in the tutorial at the end of this chapter. In addition, you'll learn how to use the very valuable *border-collapse* property on page 295.

Resizing a Table

While you define the width of a table when you first insert it, you can always change your mind later. To do so, first select the table, and then take either of these steps:

- Type a value into the W (width) box on the Property inspector, and then choose a unit of measurement, either pixels or percentages, from the pop-up menu.
- Drag one of the resize handles on the right edge. (Avoid the handle in the right corner of the table—this adds an invalid *height* property to the table tag. If you do add a *height* property this way, you can easily remove it using the "Clear Height Values" button in the Property inspector—see Figure 7-5.)

In theory, you can also convert a table from a fixed unit of measurement, such as pixels, to the stretchy, percentage-style width setting—or vice versa—using the two "Convert table width" buttons at the bottom of the Property inspector (see Figure 7-5). What these buttons do depends on the size of the current document window in Dreamweaver. For example, suppose the document window is 700 pixels wide, and you've inserted a table that's 100% wide. Clicking the "Convert Widths to Pixels" button sets the table's width to around 700 pixels (the exact value depends on the margins of the page). However, if your document window were 500 pixels wide, clicking the same button would produce a fixed-width table around 500 pixels wide.

Note: The HTML <table> tag doesn't officially have a Height property. Dreamweaver, however, adds a Height property if you drag the bottom of the table to resize it. Most Web browsers understand this Height property and obey your wishes. But since it's not standard code, there's no guarantee that newer browsers will support this maneuver.

You have several alternatives: First, you could decide not to worry about height. After all, it's difficult to control the height of a table precisely, especially if there's text in it. Since text sizes appear differently on different operating systems and browsers, the table may grow taller if the text is larger, no matter where you set the height. Or you could use the CSS *height* property (page 341) to set a height for a table. Finally, you can always insert a transparent graphic in a table cell to pop it up to the height you want. (See "The contents take priority" on page 276.)

The "Convert Width to Percentages" buttons take the opposite tack. They set the width or height of a table and its cells to percentages based on the amount of the document window's width and height they cover at the moment. The bigger the window, the smaller the percentage.

Because the effects of these buttons depends upon the document window's size, you'll find yourself rarely, if ever, using these two tools.

Modifying Cell and Row Properties

Cells have their own properties, separate from the properties of the table itself. So do table *rows*—but not columns (see the box on page 275).

When you click inside a cell, the top half of the Property inspector displays the cell's text formatting properties; the bottom half shows the properties for that particular cell (see Figure 7-6).

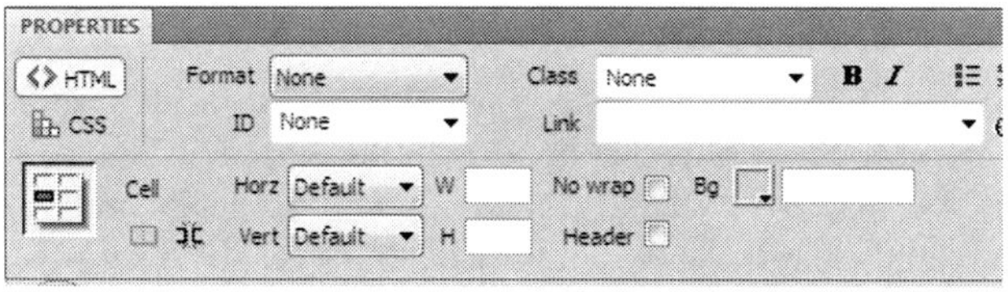

Figure 7-6: *The Property inspector displays the properties of a cell. If you select an entire row of cells, or select <tr> in the Tag selector, however, the background color property (listed as Bg on the Property inspector shown here) applies to the <tr> tag. Still, when a row is selected, the Width, Height, No Wrap, or Header options affect the individual cells in the row.*

Alignment Properties

At the outset, a cell's contents hug the left wall of the cell and float halfway between the top and bottom of the cell. After selecting a row, a cell, or several cells, you can change these alignments using the Property inspector. For example, the Horz (Horizontal) menu in the Property inspector (see Figure 7-6) offers Left, Center, Right, and Default alignment options. (Default produces the same effect as Left without adding any extra HTML code.)

Note that these options are distinct from the *paragraph* alignment options discussed in Chapter 3. In fact, you can mix and match the two. Suppose you have a table cell containing four paragraphs. You want all but one paragraph to be center aligned; you want the last paragraph to be right aligned. To do so, you could set the alignment of the *cell* to Center, and then select just the last paragraph and set its alignment to Right. The paragraph's alignment overrides the alignment applied by the cell.

You can set the vertical alignment property in the same manner. Select the cells, and then use one of the five options available in the Property inspector's Vert (Vertical) menu: Default (the same as Middle), Top, Middle, Bottom, or Baseline.

Note: The CSS *text-align* property (located in the Block category of the CSS Rule Definition window) provides the same effect as Horizontal cell alignment; the *vertical-align* property (in the Block category of the CSS Rule Definition window) is the CSS replacement for a cell's vertical alignment.

(Skip the Baseline option; although it's supposed to align the bottom of the first line of text in the cell to the baseline of text in all the other cells in the row, only Internet Explorer actually gets this setting right.)

Table Header

The Table Header option lets you convert a <td> tag to a <th> tag, which is useful when you want to turn, say, the row at the top of a table into a header. It's a similar scheme to the column or row headers available in the Table dialog box, described on page 267.

Tip: You can also uncheck the Table Header box to turn a table header into a regular table cell. This is handy when you insert a table that shouldn't have headers, but you forgot to unselect the header option in the Table dialog box (see Figure 7-3).

You'll usually use this option for tables that include actual tabular data, like a spreadsheet, to indicate the meaning of the data that appears in the other cells in a row or column. For example, you may have a table containing data from different years; each cell in the top row could identify the year of the data in the cells below it.

While Dreamweaver lets you change a single cell into a header, you'll most likely apply this to a row of cells or the left column of cells.

A Property to Forget

The No Wrap option is of such little value that you'll probably go your entire Web career without using it.

But for the sake of thoroughness—and in case you actually find a use for it—here's a description. The No Wrap property prevents a Web browser from wrapping a line of text within a cell onto multiple lines. The browser widens the cell instead, so

POWER USERS' CLINIC

The Dawn of Columns

As far as the standard HTML language is concerned, there really isn't any such entity as a column. Tables are created with the <table> tag, rows with the <tr> tag, and cells with the <td> tag—but there's no column tag. Dreamweaver calculates the columns based on the number of cells in a row. If there are seven rows in a table, each with four cells, then the table has four columns. In other words, the number of cells in each row determines the number of columns.

Two tags introduced in HTML 4—the <colgroup> and <col> tags—let you control various attributes of columns in a table. Unfortunately, Dreamweaver provides no easy way to add them. You can find out more about them, however, by checking out Dreamweaver's built-in HTML reference (see page 422).

that it can include the line without line breaks. The result is almost never useful or attractive. Furthermore, if you specify a width for the cell, this property doesn't work at all!

Cell Decoration

Cells needn't be drab. As with tables, you can give individual cells background colors, or even background graphics. However, just as with tables, you should avoid the decorative table cell options available in the Property inspector. Instead, use CSS—the *background-color* property (page 233) to add a color to a cell, the *background-image* property (page 233) to add a graphic to the background of a cell, and the *border* property (page 231) to add color borders around cells.

Note: Dreamweaver CS4 has removed most of the outdated HTML properties used to format table cells from the Property inspector—the one exception being *background color*. As with tables, you should use the CSS equivalents: *border* (page 231), *background-image* (page 233), and *background-color* (page 233).

FREQUENTLY ASKED QUESTION

Suddenly Jumbo Cells

When I added some text to a cell, it suddenly got much wider than the other cells in the row. What gives?

It isn't Dreamweaver's fault. This is how HTML works.

Web browsers (and Dreamweaver) display cells to match the content inside. For example, say you add a three-column table to a page. In the first cell of the first row, you type in two words, you leave the second cell empty, and add a 125-pixel wide image in the third cell of that row. Since the image is the biggest item, its cell is wider than the other two. The middle cell, with nothing in it, is given the least amount of space.

Usually, you don't want a Web browser making these kinds of decisions. By specifying a width for a cell (page 276), you can force a Web browser to display a cell with the dimension you want, but keep in mind that there are exceptions to this rule; see "The contents take priority" on page 276.

Setting Cell Dimensions

Specifying the width or height of a particular cell is simple: Select one or more cells, and then type a value in the Property inspector's W (width) or H (height) field. This value can be in either pixels or percentage. For instance, if you want a particular cell to be 50 pixels wide, type *50*. For a cell that you want to be 50% of the total table width, type *50%*. Read the next section for details on the tricky business of controlling cell and table dimensions.

You can also resize a column or row of cells by dragging a cell border. As your cursor approaches the cell's border, it changes shape to indicate that you can begin dragging. Dreamweaver also provides an interactive display of cell widths (circled in Figure 7-7) when you use this method. This helpful feature lets you know exactly what width your cells are at all times, so you can drag a cell to the exact width you're seeking.

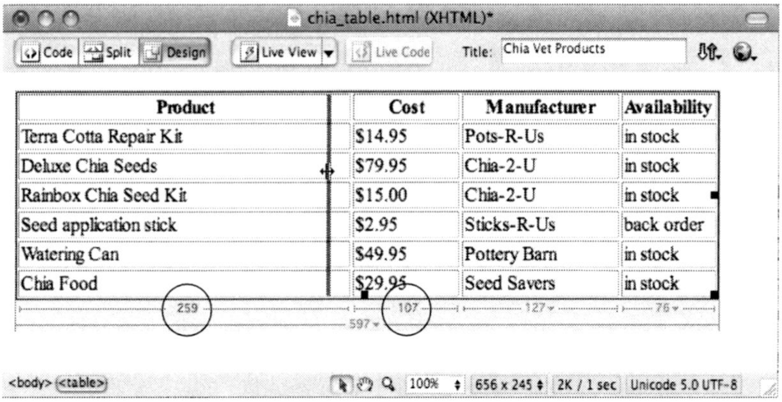

Figure 7-7:
As you drag the border between cells, Dreamweaver shows you the changing widths of the two adjacent cells in real time. The width values change to blue and update themselves as you move your mouse.

Tips for Surviving Table Making

Nothing is more confounding than trying to get your tables laid out exactly as you want them. Many beginning Web designers throw their hands up in despair when working with tables, which often seem to have minds of their own. Here are a few problems that often confuse designers—and some tips to make working with tables more straightforward.

The contents take priority

Say you've created a 300-pixel-wide table and set each cell in the first row to 100 pixels wide. You insert a larger graphic into the first cell, and suddenly—Kablooie! Even though you set each cell to 100 pixels wide, as shown in Figure 7-8, the column with the graphic is much wider than the other two.

That's because a cell can't be smaller than the largest piece of content inside it. In this case, although you told the cell to be 100 pixels wide, the image is 120 pixels wide, which forces the first column to grow (and the others to shrink) accordingly.

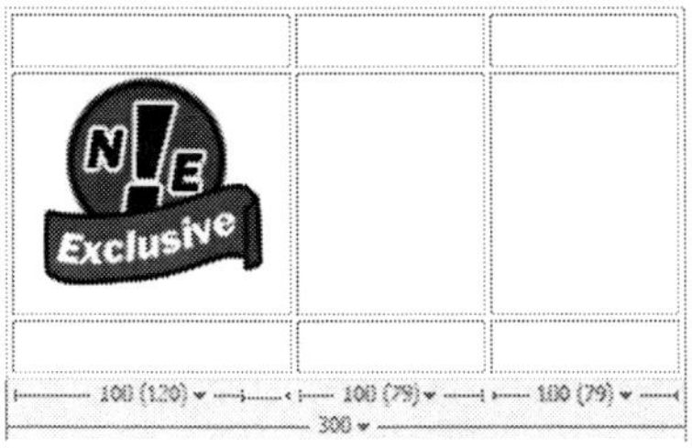

Figure 7-8:
Because a Web browser can't shrink the image or hide part of it, the cell has to grow to fit it. That first column of cells is now 120 pixels wide; the other two columns must shrink in order to keep the table 300 pixels wide. The numbers at the bottom of each cell indicate its width as set in the HTML–100–and the actual width as displayed in Dreamweaver in parentheses (120, 79, and 79).

There's no such thing as column width–only cell width

To set the width of a column of cells, you have to set the width of only *one* cell in that column. Say you have a table with three rows and three columns. You need to set only the width for the top row of cells; you can (and should) leave the cell widths for the remaining cells in the two bottom rows empty. (You can do this with any row of cells, not just the top row.)

This principle can save a lot of time and, because it reduces the amount of code on a Web page, makes your pages load and appear faster. For consistency, it's a good idea to pick either the first or last row of a table for width-setting.

The same holds true for the height of a row. You need only to set the height of a single cell to define the height for its entire row.

Fortunately, Dreamweaver is smart. When you resize one or more cells, it adds width and height values only where they're needed, without filling every cell with needless height and width values.

Do the math

Calculators are really useful when you're building tables. Although you *could* create a 400-pixel-wide table with three 700-pixel-wide columns, the results you'd get on the screen could be unpredictable ($700 + 700 + 700 \neq 400$).

As it turns out, Web browsers' loyalty is to *table* width first, and then column widths. If you make the widths of your columns add up to the width of your table, you'll save yourself a lot of headaches.

You'll need to account for a few other factors if you add borders, cell padding, and cell spacing. For example, say you create a 500-pixel-wide table with two columns and 10 pixels of padding. If you want the first column to be 100 pixels wide, you would set the width value to 80 pixels: 10 pixels left padding + 80 pixels of cell space + 10 pixels of right padding = 100 pixels total width.

WORKAROUND WORKSHOP

Beware the Resize Handles

Dreamweaver provides several techniques for resizing tables and cells while in Design view. Unfortunately, the easiest method–dragging a cell or table border–is also the easiest to do by mistake. Because moving the cursor over any border turns it into the Resize tool, almost every Dreamweaver practitioner drags a border accidentally at least once, overwriting carefully calculated table and cell widths and heights.

On occasions like these, don't forget the undo feature, Ctrl+Z (⌘-Z). And if all is lost, you can always clear the widths and heights of every cell in a table (using the Property inspector's buttons) and start over by typing new cell dimensions (see Figure 7-5).

Adding and Removing Cells

Even after inserting a table into a Web page, you can add and subtract rows and columns from your table. The text or images in the columns move right or down to accommodate their new next-door neighbor.

Adding One Row or Column

To add a single row to the table, you can use any of these approaches:

- Click inside a cell. On the Insert panel's Layout category, click the Insert Row Above button (see Figure 7-9) to add a row above the current row. Click the Insert Row Below button to add a row below the current row.
- Click inside a cell. Choose Modify → Table → Insert Row, or press Ctrl+M (⌘-M), to insert a new row of cells above the current row. Alternatively, you can right-click (Control-click) a cell, and then, from the shortcut menu, choose Table → Insert Row.
- To add a new row at the end of a table, click inside the last cell in the table, and then press Tab.

The new rows inherit all the properties (except width) of the row you originally clicked.

To add a single *column* of cells:

- Click inside a cell. On the Insert bar's Layout tab, click the "Insert Column to the Left" button (see Figure 7-9) to add a column to the left of the current column. Click the "Insert Column to the Right" button to add a column to the right of the current column.
- Click inside a cell, and then choose Modify → Table → Insert Column.
- Click inside a cell, and then press Ctrl+Shift+A (⌘-Shift-A).

- Right-click (Control-click) a cell, and then, from the shortcut menu that appears, choose Table → Insert Column.

In each case, a new column appears to the left of the current column.

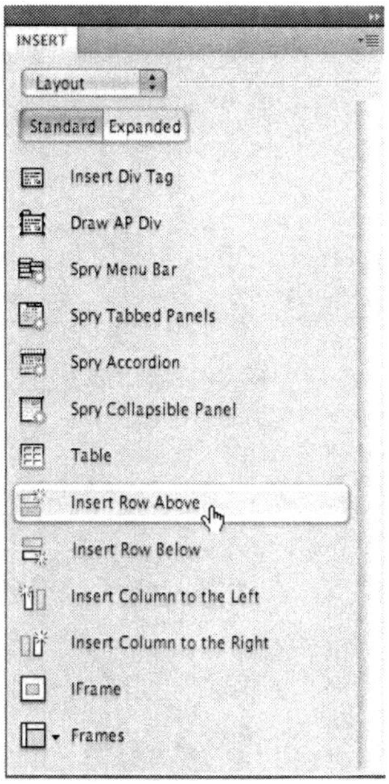

Figure 7-9:
Four buttons in the Layout category of the Insert panel make it easy to add new columns and rows. They also make it easy to control where the new row or column goes—a feat not possible with a simple keyboard shortcut. On a side note, the IFrame button on the Insert panel is less than helpful—it merely jumps to Code view and inserts the HTML <iframe> tag. There's no WYSIWYG method of adding iframes. (iframes provide a way of embedding an HTML page within another page. You can read up on this technology at www.cs.tut.fi/~jkorpela/html/iframe.html*.)*

Adding Multiple Rows or Columns

When you need to expand your table more rapidly, you can use a special dialog box that lets you add many rows or columns at once.

1. **Click inside a cell. Choose Modify → Table → "Insert Rows or Columns".**

   The "Insert Rows or Columns" dialog box appears (see Figure 7-10).

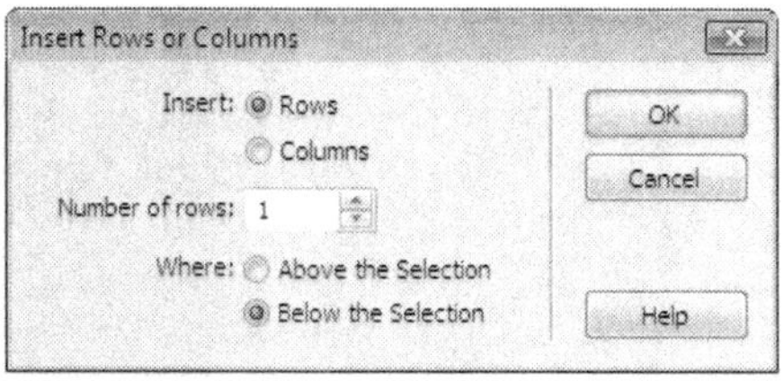

Figure 7-10:
The "Insert Rows or Columns" dialog box lets you add multiple rows or columns to a table. The wording of the options changes depending on whether you're inserting rows or columns.

2. **Click either Rows or Columns. Type the number of rows or columns you wish to add.**

   Windows users can also click the tiny up and down arrow buttons next to the "Number of rows" (or columns) field.

3. **Indicate where you wish the new rows or columns to appear, relative to the cell you selected, by clicking Above or Below (for rows) or Before or After (for columns). Click OK to insert them.**

Using the dialog box gives you the advantage of choosing whether you want the new row or column to come *before* or *after* the selected information in your table, as shown in Figure 7-10.

Deleting Rows and Columns

To delete a row from your table, you can use one of the following techniques.

Tip: When you remove a row or column, Dreamweaver also eliminates everything inside. So before you start hacking away, it's a good idea to save a copy of the page with the table.

- Select the row (see page 268); press Delete to delete all of the cells—and everything in them—for the selected row.
- Click a cell. Choose Modify → Table → Delete Row, or use the keyboard shortcut Ctrl+Shift+M (⌘-Shift-M).
- Right-click (Control-click) inside a cell, and then, from the shortcut menu, choose Table → Delete Row.

Deleting a column is equally straightforward.

- Select the column (page 268), and then press Delete. You've just eliminated all the selected cells and everything in them.
- Click a cell, and then choose Modify → Table → Delete Column, or use the keyboard shortcut Ctrl+Shift+Hyphen (⌘-Shift-Hyphen).
- Right-click (Control-click) inside a cell, and then choose Table → Delete Column from the shortcut menu.

Note: Dreamweaver doesn't let you delete a row if one of its cells is *merged* with a cell in another row. Nor can you delete a column if it contains a cell that's merged with a cell in an adjacent *column*. (Merged cells are discussed in the next section.)

Deleting a column in this way is actually quite a feat. Since there's no column tag in HTML, Dreamweaver, behind the scenes, has to select individual cells in multiple rows—a task you wouldn't wish on your worst enemy if you had to do it by editing the raw HTML code.

Merging and Splitting Cells

Cells are very basic creatures with some severe limitations. For example, all the cells in a row share the same height. A cell can't be taller than the cell next to it, which can pose some serious design problems. In table-based design, designers solved this problem by combining multiple cells to form, for example, one wide banner area that spans three table columns.

Note: If you're still using tables for page layout, be careful when merging cells; as a technique for managing a page layout, merged cells can be big trouble. For more information, go to *www.apptools.com/rants/spans.php*. (P.S. You really don't have to use tables for layout anymore. Turn to Chapter 9 and learn how to use CSS for page layout.)

But even when using tables for data, there are times when you need to combine multiple cells. In Figure 7-11, data for a single year—like 2006—is broken down into two demographic groups—men and women. Since the data in the two sets of "men" and "women" columns pertain to particular years, two table cells are merged to identify the first year, 2006, and two additional cells are merged for the year 2007. In such situations, Dreamweaver provides several ways of persuading cells to work well together. The trick is to *merge* cells—combine their area—to create a larger cell that spans two or more rows or columns.

CosmoFarmer Subscriber Information by Year

Year	2006		2007	
Gender	Men	Women	Men	Women
Number	10,000	15,000	25,000	27,000
Average Age	39	34	33	30
Avg Yearly Income	$65K	$66K	$100K	$100K

Figure 7-11: *You can create larger cells that span multiple rows and columns by merging adjacent cells. This is one way to represent multiple related rows or columns of information with a single table header.*

To merge cells, start by selecting the cells you wish to merge, using any of the methods described on page 268. (You can only merge cells that form a rectangle or square. You can't, for instance, select three cells in a column, and only one in the adjacent row, to create an L shape. Nor can you merge cells that aren't adjacent; in other words, you can't merge a cell in one corner of the table with a cell in the opposite corner.)

Then, on the Property inspector, click the Merge Cells button (Figure 7-12), or choose Modify → Table → Merge Cells. Dreamweaver joins the selected cells, forming a single new super cell.

Figure 7-12: *The Merge Cells button is active only when you've selected multiple cells. The Split Cells button appears only when you select a single cell, or you've clicked inside a cell.*

Tip: Better yet, use this undocumented keyboard shortcut: the M key. Just select two or more cells, and then press M. It's much easier than the keyboard shortcut listed in the online help: Ctrl+Alt+M (⌘-Option-M).

You may also find yourself in the opposite situation: You have one cell that you want to *divide* into multiple cells. To split a cell, click, or select, a single cell. In the Property inspector, click the Split Cells button. (Once again, you can trigger this command in several alternative ways. You can choose Modify → Table → Split Cell. And if you prefer keyboard shortcuts, you can press Ctrl+Alt+S [⌘-Option-S]. You can even right-click [Control-click] the selected cell, and then, from the shortcut menu, choose Table → Split Cell.)

When the Split Cell dialog box opens (see Figure 7-13), click one of the buttons to indicate whether you want to split the cell into rows or columns. Then type the number of rows or columns you wish to create; click OK.

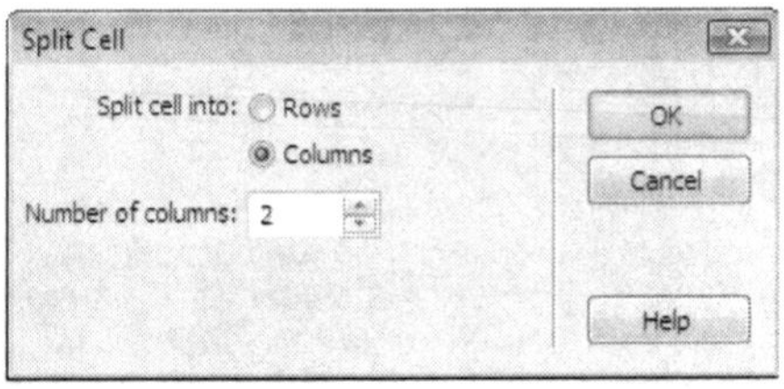

Figure 7-13: *The Split Cell dialog box lets you divide a single cell into multiple cells. You can choose whether to divide the cell into rows (multiple cells on top of one another) or columns (multiple cells side by side).*

If you split a cell into columns, everything in the cell winds up in the left column, with the new, empty column or columns to the left. When you split a cell into rows, the contents end up in the top row.

Tabular Data

Since tables are meant to display data, Dreamweaver provides useful tools to import and work with data.

Importing Data into a Table

Say your boss emails you your company's yearly sales information, which includes data on sales, profits, and expenses organized by quarter. She asks you to get this up on the Web for a board meeting she's having in half an hour.

This assignment could require a fair amount of work: building a table and then copying and pasting the correct information into each cell of the table, one at a time. Dreamweaver makes your task much easier, because you can create a table and import data into the table's rows and columns, all in one pass.

For this to work, the table data you want to display must begin life in a *delimited* format—a task that most spreadsheet programs, including Excel, or database programs, such as Access or FileMaker Pro, can do easily. (In most programs, you can do this by choosing File → Export or File → Save As; then choose a tab-delimited or comma-separated text file format.)

Note: Windows users don't need to create a delimited format file, if they have data in an Excel file. You can directly import Excel files into Dreamweaver for Windows, which converts the data into a well-organized table. See page 85 for details.

In a delimited file, each line of text represents one table row. Each line is divided into smaller units using a special character called a delimiter—most often a tab, but possibly a comma or colon. Each unit represents a single cell in the row. In a colon-delimited file, for example, the line *Sales:$1,000,000:$2,000,000:$567,000:$12,500* would be converted by Dreamweaver into a row of five cells, with the first cell containing the word *Sales*.

Once you've saved your boss's spreadsheet as a delimited file, you're ready to import it into a Dreamweaver table:

1. **Choose File → Import → Tabular Data.**

   The Import Tabular Data dialog box appears (Figure 7-14).

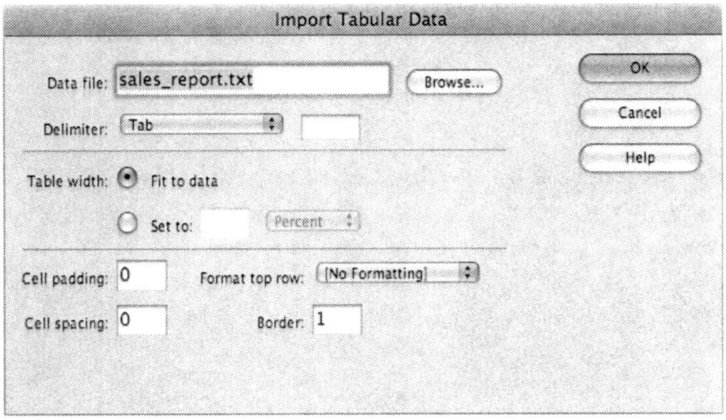

Figure 7-14: *The Import Tabular Data dialog box lets you select a text file of data to import and choose formatting options for the table.*

2. **Click Browse. In the Insert Tabular Data dialog box, find and select the delimited text file you wish to import.**

   A delimited file is no longer a spreadsheet, but a plain text file. Navigate to and double-click the file in the dialog box.

3. **From the pop-up menu, select the delimiter that was used to separate the data in the text file.**

   The choices are Tab, Comma, Colon, Semicolon, or Other. If you select Other, an additional field appears, where you can type the character you used as the delimiter.

4. **Select a table width.**

   Choose "Fit to data" if you want the table to fit itself to the information you're importing—an excellent idea when you aren't completely sure how much information the file contains. (You can always modify the table, if necessary, after importing the data.)

   On the other hand, if your Web page needs a table of a certain size, you can specify it by selecting the Set button, and then typing a value in the field next to it. Select pixel or percentage value (see page 266).

5. **Set Cell padding, Cell spacing, and Border, if you like.**

   See page 265 for details.

6. **Select a formatting option for the top row of data.**

   If the first line in the text file has column headings—Quarter 1 Sales, Quarter 2 Sales, and so on—Dreamweaver lets you choose Bold, Italic, or Bold Italic to set this header row apart from the rest of the table. Unfortunately, this option doesn't turn the cells in this first row into table header (<th>) tags, which is what they should be. It's best to choose no formatting, manually select the cells, and then turn them into table header (<th>) tags as described on page 274.

7. **Click OK to import the data and create the table.**

   The table is added to your Web page. It's a regular HTML table at this point and you can edit the contents as you normally would, or modify the table (add rows and columns, for example) using any of the techniques discussed in this chapter.

Sorting Data in a Table

If you have a table that lists employee names, you probably want to present that list in alphabetical order—or alphabetically *and* by department. Dreamweaver's Sort Table command takes a lot of the drudgery out of this task.

1. **Select the table you wish to sort.**

   See page 268 for some table-selection techniques.

2. **Choose Commands → Sort Table.**

   The Sort Table dialog box appears (Figure 7-15).

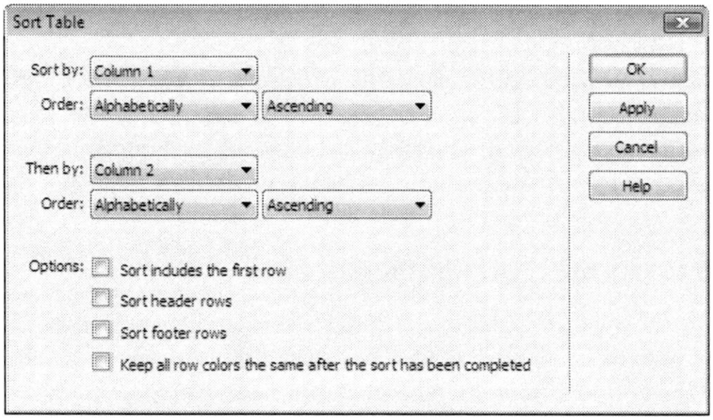

Figure 7-15: *The Sort Table command works well with Dreamweaver's Import Tabular Data feature. Imagine you're given a text file listing all your company's employees. You import the data into a table, but realize that the names aren't in any particular order.*

3. **Using the "Sort by" pop-up menu, choose the column by which you wish to sort.**

   You can choose any column in the table. Suppose you have a table listing a bunch of products. Each row has the product name, number, and price. If you want to see the products listed from least to most expensive, you could sort by the column with the product prices.

Note: The Spry Data Set tools let you create a table that can be sorted *interactively* by the visitor viewing the Web page. This cool tool is covered on page 518.

4. **Use the next two pop-up menus to specify how you want the data sorted.**

   Data can be sorted alphabetically or numerically. To order the product list by price, from the Order pop-up menu, choose Numerically. However, if you're sorting a Name column, choose Alphabetically.

   Use the second pop-up menu to specify whether you want an Ascending sort (A–Z, 1–100) or Descending (Z–A, 100–1).

5. **If you like, choose an additional column to sort by, using the "Then by" pop-up menu.**

   This secondary sort can come in handy when several cells in the *first* sorting column have the same value. If several items in your product list are all priced at $100, a sort by price would place them consecutively in the table; you could then specify a secondary sort that would place the products in alphabetical order within each price group. In this way, all the products would be listed from least to most expensive, *and* products that are the same price would be listed alphabetically within their group.

6. **If the first row of the table contains data to be sorted, turn on "Sort includes the first row."**

   If, however, the first row of the table contains *headings* for each column, don't turn on this box.

7. **Choose whether to sort header rows and footer rows as well.**

   The Sort Header Row option isn't referring to cells that have the "header" property set (see page 274). This option, and the next one, refer to the <thead> (table header) and <tfoot> (table footer) tags, which are intended to let you turn one or more rows into repeating headers and footers for long tables. Since Dreamweaver doesn't insert these tags for you, you'll most likely never use these options.

8. **Choose whether to keep row colors with the sorted row.**

   One way to visually organize a table is to add color to alternate rows. This every-other-row pattern helps readers to stay focused on one row of information at a time. However, if you sort a table that you had formatted in this way, you'd wind up with some crazy pattern of colored and uncolored rows. The bottom line: If you've applied colors to your rows, and you'd like to keep those colors in the same order, leave this checkbox off.

   Dreamweaver is even in step with current Web design practices, which don't assign a background color to table rows (using the outmoded *bgcolor* HTML property), but instead use CSS. A common approach to coloring table rows is to apply a CSS class style to every *other* row in a table. That class style might have the *background-color* property set so that alternating rows are colored. When you use the Sort Table command, Dreamweaver keeps the class names in the proper order. That is, it keeps the classes applied to every other row, even when you re-organize the data with the Sort Table command. This only works if you *don't* check the "Keep all row colors the same" box—so don't check it!

9. **Click Apply to see the effect of the sort without closing the dialog box.**

   If the table meets with your satisfaction, click OK to sort the table and return to the document window. (Clicking Cancel, however, doesn't then undo the sort. If you want to return the table to its previous sort order, choose Edit → Undo Sort Table after closing the sort window.)

Exporting Table Data

Getting data out of a table in Dreamweaver is simple. Just select the table, and then choose File → Export → Table. In the Export Table dialog box that appears, select the type of delimiter (tab, comma, space, colon, or semicolon) and the operating system where the file will be used (Mac, Windows, or Unix), and then click OK. Give the file a name and save it on your computer. You can then import this delimited file into your spreadsheet or database program.

Tables Tutorial

In this tutorial, you'll create a data table containing product information. In addition, you'll use some Cascading Style Sheet magic to make the table look great (see Figure 7-25).

Note: You'll need to download the tutorial files from *www.sawmac.com/dwcs4/* to complete this tutorial. See the Note on page 48 for more details.

Once you've downloaded the tutorial files and opened Dreamweaver, define a new site as described on page 42: Name the site *Tables*, and select the Chapter07 folder (inside the MM_DWCS4 folder). (In a nutshell: choose Site → New Site. In the Site Definition window, click the Advanced tab, type *Tables* into the Site Name field, click the folder icon next to the Local Root Folder field, navigate to and select the Chapter07 folder, and then click Choose or Select. Finally, click OK.)

Adding a Table and Data

Once again, you'll be working on a page for the good people who run *Chia Vet.*

1. **Choose File → Open; click the Site Root button (bottom left of the open file window).**

   You'll be working on a page similar to the ones you've been building so far.

2. **Double-click the file named *recommend.html.* Click in the empty space, below the orange line, beneath the text "Quality products that we use ourselves."**

   You'll insert a table into this space.

3. **Choose Insert → Table.**

   You can also click the table button on the Insert panel's Common category. Either way, the Table window appears (see Figure 7-16). You need to define the table's basic characteristics.

4. **Type *3* in the Rows box and type *3* in the Columns box.**

   You'll start with a basic 3×3 table, but as the tutorial progresses, you'll add additional rows and columns. Time to set the width, spacing, and padding properties.

5. **In the Table width box, type *100,* and select "percent" from the pull-down menu. Type *0* in the Border thickness, Cell padding, and Cell spacing boxes.**

   Setting the width to 100% size means the table will fill the width of the main content area—the part of the page where the headline currently sits. Setting the other three properties here to 0 is common. You have greater control of borders and cell padding using CSS.

6. **In the window's Header section, select the "Top" option.**

   The header setting indicates which cells should be marked as "table headers"—these cells contain labels that describe what kind of information is in the column cells below (when "top" is selected), or the kind of information in the cells of a row (when "left" is selected). Now that you've picked "Top," the top row of cells will hold labels like "Product," "Cost," and "Manufacturer."

   You can skip the caption. It's not a requirement and the page's titles makes clear what the table is all about. The window should now look like Figure 7-16.

7. **Click OK.**

   A new table appears on the page. Next, you'll add some headers to the table

8. **Click the first table cell in the top-left corner of the table, and then type *Product*.**

   The word appears bold and centered in the cell. That's how table header cells normally appear. You'll be able to change that look in a moment. Now add two more labels.

9. **Press Tab to jump to the next cell to the right, and then type *Cost*. Press Tab again, and then type *Manufacturer*.**

   Now it's time to add some actual data.

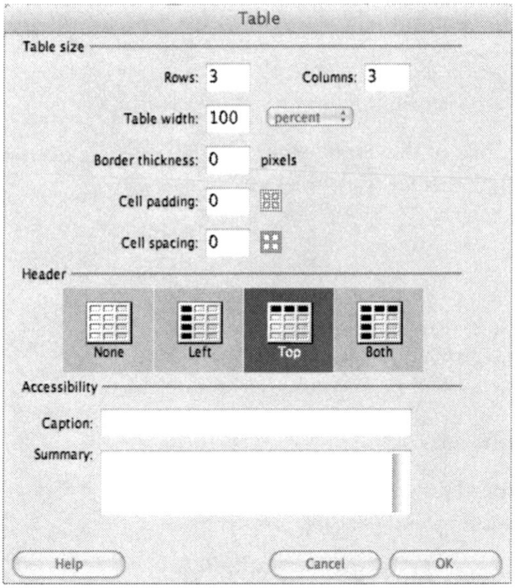

***Figure 7-16:** Inserting a table into a Web page is just a matter of making a few choices in the Table dialog box. Any text you type into the Summary box doesn't appear in the Web browser window, so you probably won't use this option frequently. It's intended to explain a particularly complicated table to non-visual Web browsers (like Google's spidering software or a screen reader used by the visually impaired).*

10. **Press Tab, and then type *Watering Can* in the first cell of the second row; press Tab again, and then type *$49.95*; press Tab to jump to the last cell in the second row and type *Pottery Barn*.**

    You've just added the first item to the table; time for another.

11. **Press Tab to move to the first cell of the last row. Follow step 10 using the following information: *Deluxe Chia Seeds, $79.95*, and *Chia-2-U*.**

    At this point, you've filled up the entire table—there aren't any more rows for information. No problem; it's easy to add more.

Note: A table cell isn't limited to just a few words or numbers, as in this tutorial. You can place any HTML inside a table cell, including headlines, multiple paragraphs, images, and so on.

12. **Click in the last cell of the table (bottom right), and then press the Tab key.**

    When you've reached a table's last cell, pressing the Tab key creates another row of cells. Just a little more typing to go.

13. **Using the same techniques as above (steps 11-12), create the table pictured in Figure 7-17.**

    You don't need to complete the entire table if you don't want. If you've learned the technique and your fingers are tired, just add as many rows as you'd like.

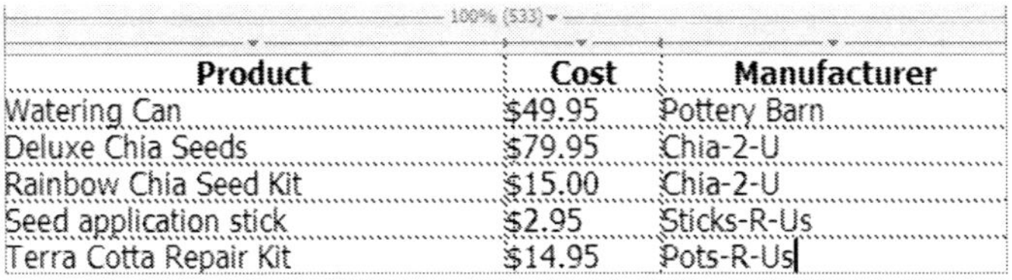

Product	Cost	Manufacturer
Watering Can	$49.95	Pottery Barn
Deluxe Chia Seeds	$79.95	Chia-2-U
Rainbow Chia Seed Kit	$15.00	Chia-2-U
Seed application stick	$2.95	Sticks-R-Us
Terra Cotta Repair Kit	$14.95	Pots-R-Us

Figure 7-17: *Inputting data like this by hand gets the job done, but can be tedious and time-consuming. If you've already got the data in a spreadsheet or a text file, you can probably use Dreamweaver's Import Tabular Data tool, described on page 282, to save your data-entering tendons.*

Modifying the Table

Just as you type the last row of information, Chia Vet headquarters calls and says they need an additional column of information added to the table. For HTML hand-coders, this would be a challenging and time-consuming task, but Dreamweaver makes the process easy.

1. **Click any cell in the third column.**

   For example, click the cell with the word "Manufacturer." You'll now add a column to the table.

2. **Make sure the Layout category is selected in the Insert Panel; click the "Insert Column to the Right" button (see Figure 7-18).**

   Dreamweaver adds a thin column at the far right of the table. This column identifies an item's availability status.

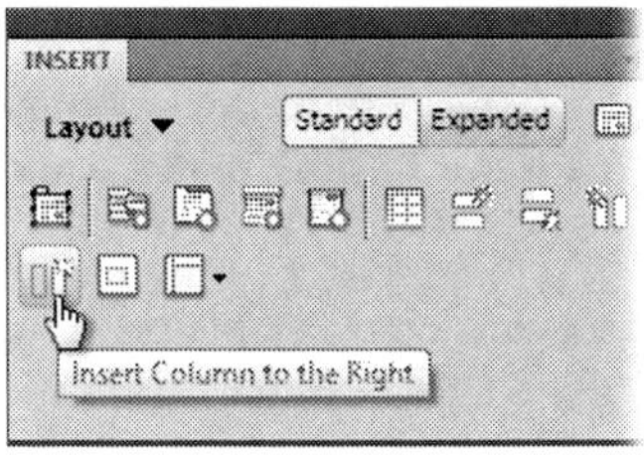

Figure 7-18: *As described in Figure 1-3 on page 26, you can either show or hide text labels next to the buttons in the Insert panel. Here, the labels are hidden to save screen space.*

3. **Click the top cell of the new column, and then type *Availability*.**

   This is a <th> (table header) tag, so it's bold and centered. The actual data goes in the cells below.

4. **Click the cell below Availability, and then type *In stock*.**

   You can also press Tab four times to jump from the table header to this cell.

5. **Fill out the remaining cells in the column with either "In stock," "Back order," or "Silly tutorial."**

   And that's pretty much all there is to building a data table. Of course, making it look good is another story. For that, you'll turn to CSS.

Formatting the Table

Tables, like everything HTML, are drab by themselves. To make data really stand out, you need to turn to the power of Cascading Style Sheets. In this section you'll format the basic font attributes of the table, make the table headers stand out, and add lines around the cells.

1. **Make sure the CSS Styles panel is open (Window → CSS Styles); in the bottom right of the panel, click the Create New Style button (the + button).**

   The New CSS Rule window appears. You'll create a class style that you'll apply to the table tag and store the CSS information into an already attached external style sheet. (For a recap on creating styles, turn to page 115.)

2. **Choose Class from the top menu; type *.products* in the Selector Name box; select *global.css* in the bottom menu, and then click OK.**

   The CSS Rule Definition window appears. Instead of creating a tag style named *table*, you're creating a class. Tag styles apply globally to every instance of the HTML tag. If this site still had some tables used for layout purposes, a table tag style would probably ruin their look; in addition, by using a class style, you have the flexibility to create different designs for different types of data tables.

3. **From the Font-family menu select "Trebuchet MS, Arial, Helvetica, sans-serif". In the Font-size box, type *13*. Click OK.**

   This class style doesn't take effect until you apply it.

4. **Click the bottom border of the table to select it (or use any of the techniques described on page 268). From the Property inspector's Class menu, choose *products*.**

   Notice how the font changes for the table headers, and regular table cells. Even though you applied these font settings to the <table> tag, the other tags inside it (<td>, <th>) use the *same* settings. This step demonstrates a useful CSS concept known as *inheritance* (you'll learn about inheritance in the next chapter on page 312).

The table headers don't really command enough attention. You'll make them stand out by using a background graphic and increasing the space inside each cell.

5. **Click the Create New Style button. In the CSS Rule Definition window, choose Compound from the top menu (see Figure 7-19).**

   A "compound" style is usually what CSS veterans know as a descendent selector—a style name composed of two or more CSS selectors. You'll learn more about this setting in the next chapter, but for now, just keep in mind that you want to create a style that affects only table headers that appear inside the table on this page—in other words, <th> tags that appear inside a table that's styled with the *products* class.

6. **Replace whatever's currently listed in the Selector Name box with *.products th* and make sure *global.css* is selected in the bottom menu (see Figure 7-19). Click OK to create the style.**

   Here's a descendent selector: this time defining the look of every <th> tag inside another tag with a class of *products*. You'll make the text white on an orange background.

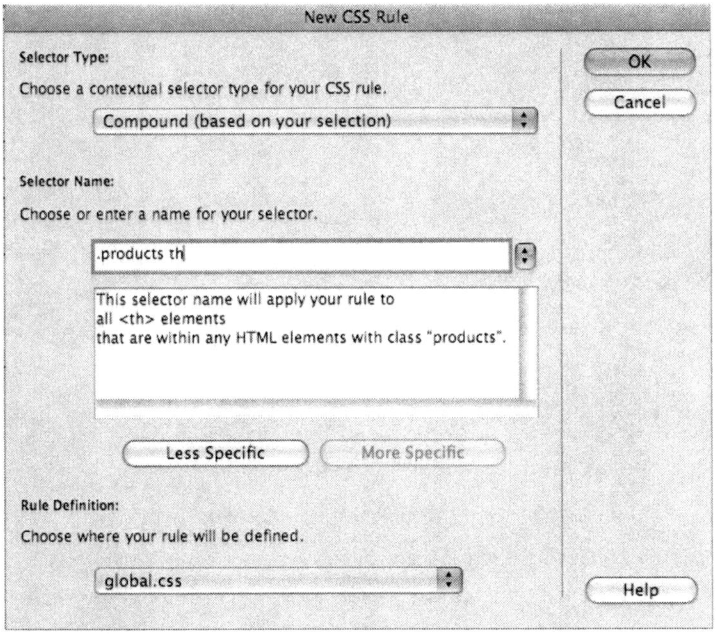

Figure 7-19: *What Dreamweaver calls a "compound" style is really just a catch-all term for any type of style including class, tag, or ID styles. More significantly, Dreamweaver uses it to create one of the most important types of CSS styles: descendent selectors, like the* .products th *selector pictured here. This selector homes in on a very specific group of tags: <th> tags that are inside any other tag that has the class products applied to it.*

7. **In the Type category, select white from the color box; select *uppercase* from the Text-transform menu. From the Color box select white.**

   This makes the text white and all the letters uppercased. You'll use a graphic for the background.

8. **Click the Background category; set the Background color to *#EC6206* (a bright orange color). Click the Browse button, and then, in the *images* folder, select the file *bgTh.jpg*.**

   Why add a background color, when you're already using a background image? Remember that in the last step, you made the text white. If you don't also specify a darker background color, the column headers might be invisible. For example, if for some reason the graphic doesn't appear (the visitor has turned off graphics, or the image doesn't download properly), then the table headers appear as white text on a white background. However, by setting a dark background color too, you're covered. If the image doesn't download, then the text is still readable—white text on an orange background.

   Currently, the column headers are centered in their cells. To match the appearance of the other cells, you'll align them to the left.

9. **Click the Block category, and then, from the "Text align" menu, choose *left*.**

   You could also set the horizontal alignment of each table header cell to "left": select each cell, and then use the Property inspector. But not only is that more work, it also adds extra HTML code to your page. The CSS method is easier and makes for faster-loading Web pages.

   If you click the Apply button now, you see how this style is shaping up. The text is a bit cramped inside each cell. To add some breathing room between the edges of each cell and the text inside, you'll use the CSS padding property.

Note: If you accidentally press the OK button before completing the style, just double-click the style's name in the CSS Styles panel to re-open the Style Definition window (see page 126 for detailed instructions).

---

10. **Click the Box category; turn off the "Same for all" checkbox under the Padding category; type *4* in the Top box; *5* in the Right box; *2* in the Bottom box; *10* in the Left box.**

    The window should look like Figure 7-20. One last touch: a border to separate each table header cell.

11. **Click the Border category; choose *solid* for the style, type *1* in the width box and make the color orange—#EC6206. Click the OK button to complete the style.**

    This action adds a border around each table header. Now you'll format the regular table cells.

12. **Click the Create New Style button. In the CSS Rule Definition window, choose Compound from the top menu, type *.products td* in the Selector Name box; make sure *global.css* is selected in the bottom menu, and then click OK.**

    You should be getting the hang of these descendent selectors by now: this style will apply to every <td> tag (that's an individual table cell) that's within another tag that has the class named *products* applied to it. You'll add padding and border lines to clearly indicate each cell.

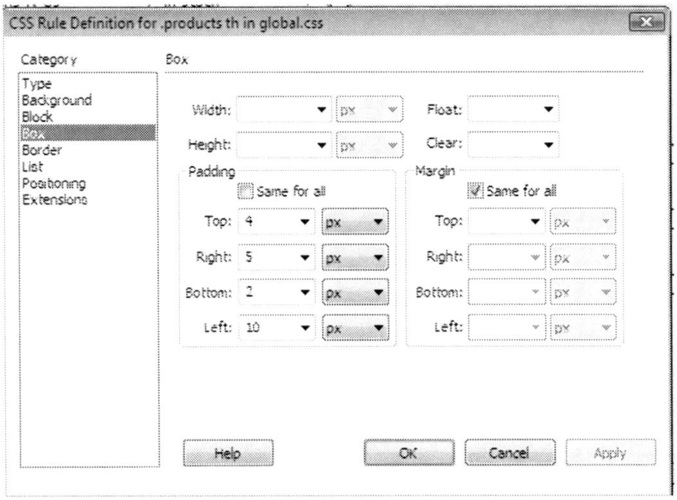

Figure 7-20:
The CSS padding property has a lot of benefits over a table's cell padding property. Not only does it eliminate unnecessary HTML for every table on your site, it also lets you precisely control the amount of space around each of a cell's four sides.

13. **Click the Box category; turn off the "Same for all" checkbox under the Padding category; type *2* in the Top box; *2* in the Right box; *2* in the Bottom box; *10* in the Left box.**

    Time to add some borders.

14. **Click the Border category; leave the "Same for all" checkboxes turned on; choose *solid* for the style, type *1* in the Width box, and make the color orange—#EC6206. Click OK to complete the style.**

    If you preview the page in a Web browser (F12 [Option-F12]), or click the Live View button at the top of the Document window, you'll notice that where two cells touch, the borders are a bit thick (see Figure 7-21). Because you've added a border around all four sides of each cell, the border is twice as thick and looks a little chunky where two cells meet. You could edit the style and add a border to only some sides of the cell (like the left and bottom sides) so that the borders don't double up, but CSS gives you an easier way.

Note: Make sure to exit Live View when you're done viewing your page—just click the Live View button a second time. If you don't leave Live View you can't edit your page.

PRODUCT	COST	MANUFACTURER	AVAILABILITY
Watering Can	$49.95	Pottery Barn	In stock
Deluxe Chia Seeds	$79.95	Chia-2-U	In stock
Rainbow Chia Seed Kit	$15.00	Chia-2-U	Back order
Seed application stick	$2.95	Sticks-R-Us	In stock
Terra Cotta Repair Kit	$14.95	Pots-R-Us	Back order

Figure 7-21:
Adding a border to table cells creates a slightly chunky double-border where cells touch each other. Fortunately, with a little-known CSS property you can overcome that aesthetic nuisance.

Final Improvements

To finish this tutorial, you'll get rid of the double-border problem, and make the table rows easier to read by coloring every other row.

1. **Make sure the CSS Styles panel is open (Window → CSS Styles), and that the All button at the top of the panel is selected.**

   The All button lets you view all the styles attached to a page. In this case, there are three external style sheets—*twoColFixRtHdr.css, global.css* and *SpryMenuBarHorizontal.css*. You're going to edit an already existing style in the *global.css* file.

2. **If you can't see any styles listed under *global.css* in the Styles panel, click the + (flippy triangle on Mac) to the left of *global.css* to expand the list. Locate the style named *.products*, and then select it.**

   Don't double-click the style name—that opens the CSS Rule Definition window again. You're about to add a CSS property that Dreamweaver doesn't make available in that window. Instead, you need to use another technique for adding properties to a style—the Properties pane.

   The Properties pane is located at the bottom of the CSS styles panel. It should look like Figure 7-22.

Note: If your Properties pane only has one property listed–*"font 13px 'Trebuchet MS', Arial, Helvetica, sans-serif"*–Dreamweaver is using CSS shorthand properties (see page 308). This doesn't affect the performance of your CSS, just the way it's written. You control this setting from the Preferences window's CSS Style category.

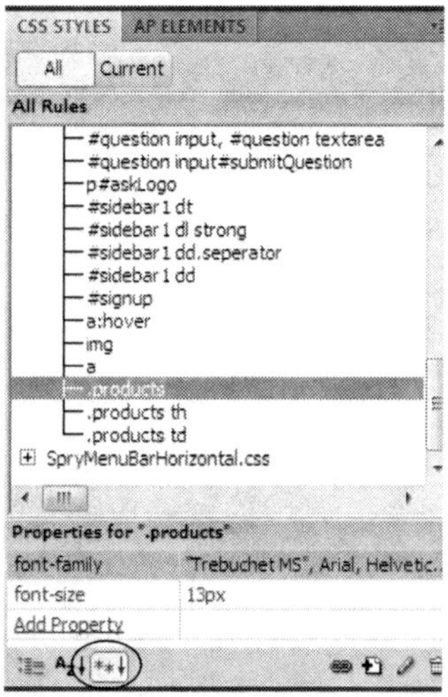

Figure 7-22:
When you select a style in the "All" view of the CSS Styles panel, the properties for that style appear in the Properties pane below. In this case, the style .products *is selected and its two properties (font-family and font-size) appear. You can add more properties by clicking the Add Property link. There are actually three different views to the Properties pane, but it's most useful to see just the currently set properties. Click the "Show only set properties" button (circled) for this view. (The Properties pane is discussed in depth on page 305.)*

3. **Click the Add Property link, and then, in the box, type *border-collapse*.**

   Border-collapse is a special CSS property that forces adjoining cells to "collapse" onto each other: Essentially it removes space between cells and prevents this double-border problem.

4. **From the menu to the right of the *border-collapse* property you just added, select *collapse* (see Figure 7-23).**

   That removes the double-border between adjacent cells (you don't see this effect in Dreamweaver's Design view; but if you click the Live View button, or preview the page in a Web browser, you will). Now you'll highlight alternating table rows. This technique makes tables easier to scan, since your eye can easily identify all the cells in a row. To do this, you'll create two new class styles.

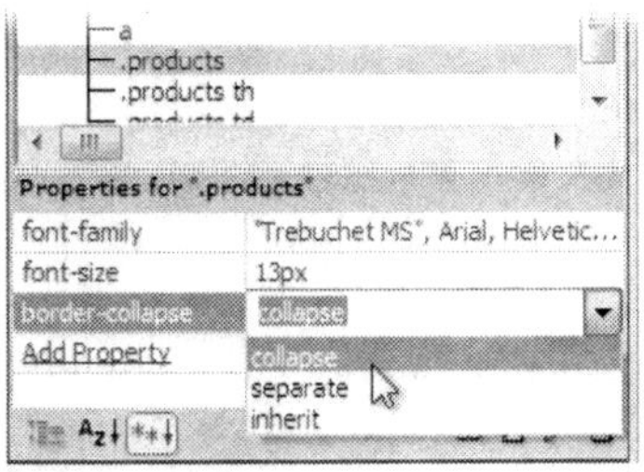

Figure 7-23: *The border-collapse property is an official CSS property, even though it doesn't appear in Dreamweaver's CSS Rule Definition window. You can, however, add it by hand using the Properties pane.*

5. **Click the Create New Style button. In the CSS Rule Definition window, choose Class from the top menu, and then type *.odd* in the Selector Name box; make sure *global.css* is selected in the bottom menu, and then click OK.**

   All you need to do now is define a background color.

6. **In the CSS Rule Definition window, select the Background category; set the background color to #ECF4F9 (light blue). Click OK to complete the style.**

   Now you'll apply this to every other row.

7. **Move your mouse just to the left of the cell with the text "Watering Can". When the mouse pointer changes to a right-pointing arrow, click to select the row of cells (see Figure 7-24).**

   The row is selected—you can also use any of the other techniques discussed on page 268 for selecting a table row. Now just apply the class style.

8. **Make sure the HTML button is selected in the Property inspector and then choose *odd* from the Class menu.**

   Every cell background in the row changes to light blue. Now for the rest of the table.

9. **Repeat steps 7 and 8 for the remaining alternating rows in the table.**

   Use Figure 7-25 for reference. You can do the same for every even row as well.

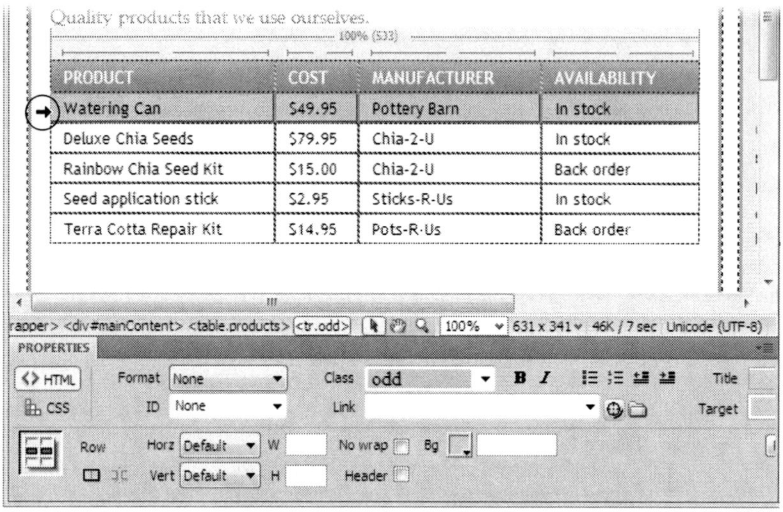

Figure 7-24: *When the cursor changes to a right pointing arrow (circled), click to select the table row. You can achieve the same thing by clicking inside any cell inside the row you wish to select, and then, at the bottom of the document window, clicking the <tr> tag listed in the Tag selector.*

10. **Repeat steps 5-9; create a class style named *.even* with a background color of *#F4FBD9* (a light green color), and apply the *even* class to the unstyled, even table rows.**

    Now you have a table where every odd row has a blue background and every even row a green background, making it very easy to scan across a row of data.

11. **Press the F12 (Option-F12) key to preview your hard work in a Web browser.**

    The complete page should look like Figure 7-25. You'll find a completed version of this tutorial in the Chapter07_finished folder that accompanies the downloaded tutorial files.

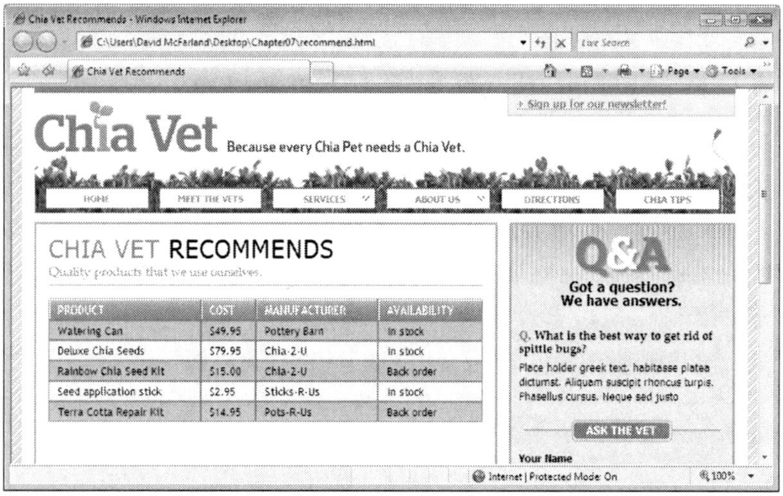

Figure 7-25: *With Dreamweaver and a little CSS, you can make elegant HTML tables.*

2

Part Two: Building a Better Web Page

CHAPTER
8

Advanced CSS

Chapter 4 introduced the basics of Cascading Style Sheets. In other chapters, you learned how to use CSS to style links, navigation bars, text, and tables. You can go a long way in Web design with just those basic techniques (many people do). However, to really become a Web design expert, there are a handful of advanced CSS concepts you should grasp. Fortunately, Dreamweaver also includes tools to help you with these concepts so you can work more efficiently and avoid those head-scratching "Why the heck does my design look like that?!" moments.

Note: This chapter will definitely help you on your journey from CSS novice to master. But keep in mind that it's the rare mortal who understands everything about CSS from reading a single chapter. If you really want to know the ins and outs of CSS, you owe it to yourself to pick up a friendly, real-world tested guide. *CSS: The Missing Manual* has gotten rave reviews on that front, and that's not marketing-speak: it's honest-to-goodness advice.

Compound Selectors

Tag, class, and ID styles are relatively easy to learn and use. To be technically accurate, all these styles aren't really styles per se. In CSS lingo, they're known as different types of *selectors*. A CSS selector is an instruction that tells a Web browser *what* it should apply the CSS formatting rules to. For example, a tag selector (not to be mistaken with Dreamweaver's time-saving selection tool, *the* Tag selector) tells a browser to apply the formatting to *any* instance of a particular tag on the page. Thus, an *h1* tag style applies to *all* <h1> tags on a page. A class selector, on the other hand, applies only when the browser encounters the class name attached to an element on a page. Similarly, an ID selector applies to a tag on the page with a matching ID name: for example, <body id="home">. (Flip back to page 114 for a review of key differences between class and ID selectors.)

Note: For a detailed discussion of selectors, visit *http://css.maxdesign.com.au/selectutorial/*.

But tag, ID, and class selectors are just the tip of the selector iceberg. CSS offers many other selector types that provide more detailed ways of specifying which page element to format; Dreamweaver lumps them together under the term *compound selectors*. "Compound selector" is just a Dreamweaver term, not a CSS term, so don't go using it at your weekly Web designer get togethers. It's intended to describe more advanced types of selectors such as the "pseudo-class" styles used for formatting the different link states (*a:link*, *a:visited*, *a:hover*, and *a:active*, as described on page 181), or the descendent selectors used in the Spry menu bar (page 184).

There are a variety of these advanced selectors in the CSS arsenal (a few of the most common and useful are mentioned below), but in Dreamweaver, you go about creating all of them the same way: Start by creating a CSS style, following the instructions on page 115. But when you get to the New CSS Rule window (Figure 8-1), instead of selecting the Class, ID, or Tag selector type, choose the Compound option.

With the exception of the four link state options in the drop-down menu, you must type the selector name of any advanced selector in the Selector Name box (see Figure 8-1). As described in the following sections, you'll need to use a different syntax (naming protocol) for each type of selector. (The rest of the process for creating the style works just like creating a tag or class style, and the process of editing or deleting these styles is also identical.)

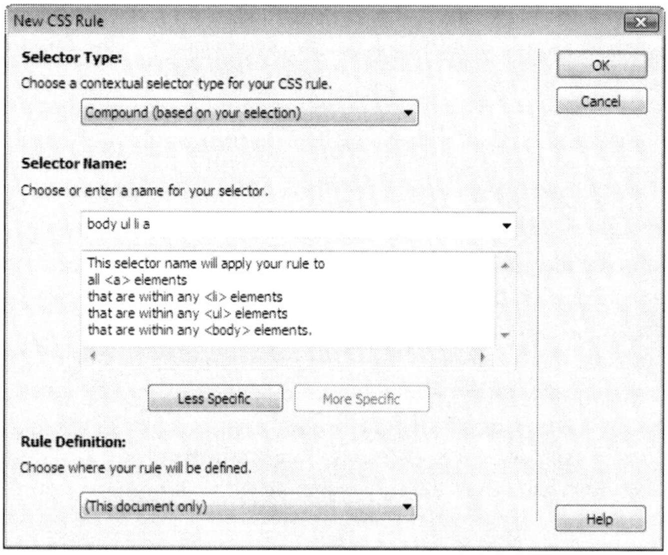

Figure 8-1:
The Compound selector option lets you type any valid CSS selector in the Selector Name box. You can even create class, tag, and ID styles after choosing the Compound selector option. For a new class, just type the name of the class preceded by a period, like this: .copyright *To create a tag style, just type the tag name without brackets:* p *for the* <p> *or paragraph tag, for instance. And, to create a new ID style, just type the # symbol followed by the ID name:* #mainContent, *for example.*

Descendent Selectors

Tag styles have their drawbacks. While a tag style for the <p> tag makes simple work of formatting every paragraph on a page, it's also indiscriminate. You may not *want* every paragraph to look the same.

Suppose you want to divide a Web page into different sections—a sidebar and a main content area—using smaller size text for the sidebar's paragraphs and headings. You *could* create two class styles—such as *sidebarText* and *mainText*—and then apply them to the appropriate paragraphs (<p class="sidebarText"> for sidebar paragraphs and <p class="mainText"> for body text). But who has that kind of time?

What you really need is a "smart" tag style, one that can adapt to its surroundings like a chameleon, and use the appropriate formatting depending on where the style is located on the page. Enter *descendent selectors.*

Essentially, you'll use descendent selectors to format every instance of a particular tag in a similar manner (just like tag selectors)—but only when they're in a particular part of a Web page. In effect, it's like saying, "Hey, you <a> tags in the navigation bar, listen up. I've got some formatting for you. All you other <a> tags, just move along; there's nothing to see here." In other words, a descendent selector lets you format a tag based on its relationship to other tags. To understand how it works, you need to delve a little more deeply into HTML.

Think of the HTML that forms any Web page as a kind of "family tree", like the one shown in Figure 8-2. The first HTML tag you use on a page—the <html> tag—is like the grandpappy of all other tags. In essence, if a tag is *inside* another tag, it's a *descendent* of that tag. In Figure 8-2, the text "wide range of topics" is bolded in the long paragraph of text. That's achieved by applying a <strong> tag to that text. Because that bolded text is inside the paragraph, that particular <strong> tag is a descendent of that paragraph.

Note: The tutorial in the previous chapter includes an example of the power of descendent selectors. See steps 5 and 6 on page 291.

Descendent selectors let you take advantage of the HTML family tree by formatting tags differently when they appear inside certain other tags or styles. For example, say you have an <h1> tag on your Web page, and want to emphasize a word within that heading. One option is to select the word and press the B button on the Property inspector—this applies the <strong> tag to that word. The trouble is, most browsers display both heading tags and the <strong> tag in bold, so anyone viewing the page can't see any difference between the emphasized word and the other words in the headline. Creating a tag selector to change the <strong> tag's color and make it stand out from the headline isn't much of a solution: you end up changing the color of *every* <strong> tag on the page, like it or not. A descendent selector lets you do what you really want: change the color of the <strong> tag *only when* it appears inside of an <h1> tag.

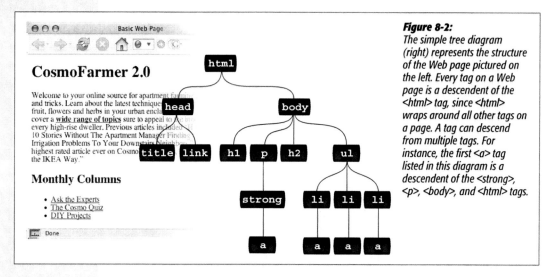

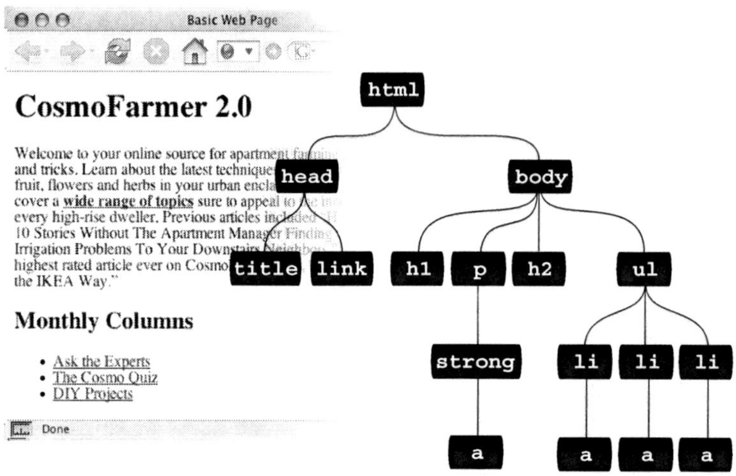

Figure 8-2: *The simple tree diagram (right) represents the structure of the Web page pictured on the left. Every tag on a Web page is a descendent of the <html> tag, since <html> wraps around all other tags on a page. A tag can descend from multiple tags. For instance, the first <a> tag listed in this diagram is a descendent of the <strong>, <p>, <body>, and <html> tags.*

Creating descendent selectors isn't much more difficult than creating any other type of style. You follow the same process as described on page 115 for creating a style—but in the New CSS Rule window, select Compound from the Selector Type menu. You then type the descendent selector's name in the Selector Name box. Figuring out how to name the selector is the tricky part.

You name a descendent selector by tacking together a series of selectors (separated by spaces) that identify the location in the family tree of the element you want to style. The most distant ancestor is on the far left and the element you wish to style is on the far right. Consider the example of the bolded word inside the headline discussed above. To style that bolded text (but leave any other bold text as it is), the descendent selector is *h1 strong*. Strong is the actual tag you're formatting, but only when it's inside an h1 tag.

Figure 8-2 shows another example. There are four links (<a> tags) on the page. Three of the links are inside bulleted list items (that's the <li> tag). If you wanted to create a style that would only apply to those three links and leave the fourth link untouched, you'd create a descendent selector like this: *li a*. Again, the actual tag you wish to format—the link—appears on the far right, while the tag that wraps around the link—the <li> tag—appears to the left.

A descendent selector can contain more than just two elements as well. The following are all valid selectors for the <a> tags inside the bulleted lists in Figure 8-2.

- ul li a
- body li a
- html li a
- html body ul li a

These four selectors—all of which do the same thing—demonstrate that you don't have to describe the entire lineage of the tag you want to format. For instance, in the second example—*body li a*—*ul* isn't needed. This selector works as long as there's an <a> tag that's a descendent (somewhere up the line) of an <li> tag (which is also a descendent of the <body> tag). This selector can just as easily apply to an <a> that's inside of an <em> tag, that's inside of a <strong> tag, that's inside a <li> tag, and so on.

Note: One reason you might make a descendent selector longer by tacking on additional selectors is if you've written several different rules that simultaneously format a tag. The more selectors that appear in a style name, the more powerful that style is and the more likely it is to override any conflicts with other styles. More on this concept on page 314.

When you choose Compound from the Selector Type menu in the New CSS Rule window, Dreamweaver suggests a descendent selector based on what's currently selected on the page (or where the cursor is, if nothing's selected.) For example, say you had the page pictured in Figure 8-2 open in Dreamweaver. If you selected the link with the text "Ask the Experts", created a new style (for example, by clicking the New CSS Rule button on the CSS Styles panel), and then selected Compound from the Selector Type menu, you'd see something like Figure 8-1. Having Dreamweaver compose the selector for you, as you can imagine, is a brain cell-saver. In this case, Dreamweaver suggests "body ul li a". In other words, a descendent selector style that translates to format every link (a) which is inside a list item (li), which is part of an unordered list (ul) that is itself inside the body of the page (body).

Tip: When writing your own descendent selectors, Dreamweaver CS4's new selector explanation box (the text box that appears below the Selector Name field) is a big help. It explains, in plain English, what elements that descendent selector will apply to (see the box below the *body ul li a* selector name in Figure 8-1, for an example).

That's a pretty long-winded style name and, as mentioned above, you don't have to have all that information to accurately target the elements on the page you wish to style. For example, a simpler style, *li a*, would also get the job done. Dreamweaver generally suggests the most complete descendent selector, including the tag you want to format as well as every ancestor tag (every tag that's wrapped around the selected element). In most cases, you won't need such complicated descendent selector names. You can simply replace Dreamweaver's suggestion with a simpler descendent selector of your own. (Just delete what Dreamweaver provides and type your own descendent selector name.) You can also click the Less Specific button on the New CSS Rule window (see Figure 8-1). Each click of that button removes the ancestor on the far left of the list. For example, in Figure 8-1, clicking the Less Specific button once, changes the descendent selector to *ul li a*; clicking it a second time makes it *li a*.

Descendent selectors with Class and ID styles

You're not limited to just using tag selectors in your descendent selector names, either. You can build complex descendent selectors by combining different types of selectors. Suppose you want your links to appear in yellow only when they're in introductory paragraphs (which you've designated with a class style named *intro*). The following selector does the trick: *.intro a*. This descendent selector will format any link (a) that's inside any other tag that has the *intro* class applied to it.

This is a very common approach when working with the CSS-based layouts discussed in the next chapter. For instance, you'll frequently want paragraphs in the main content area of the page to look different than paragraphs in sidebars (for example, the sidebar paragraphs might use a different font and a smaller font size). Each section of a CSS layout is usually wrapped inside a <div> tag that has an ID style applied to it. For example, the main content area might be wrapped in a div that has an ID style named *#mainContent* applied to it. To format just the paragraphs inside that area, the descendent selector you'd use would be *#mainContent p* (don't leave out the # symbol).

Tip: When working with descendent selectors, it helps to read the selector name *backwards, from right to left*. Take, for example, the selector *#mainContent td li*. The *li* means "This style applies to the <li> tag"; the *td* means "But only when it's inside a <td> tag"; and *#mainContent* means "And only when that <td> tag is inside another tag that has the ID mainContent applied to it."

Likewise, if you wanted to define the look of bulleted lists wherever they appear inside a tag with an ID named *#banner*, you'd type *#banner ul* in the Selector box.

After you name the descendent selector, select where to store the style's code. (In other words, select either an internal or external style sheet as described on page 113.) Then click OK in the New CSS Rule window. You're ready to start adding the CSS properties that define the formatting of your descendent selector style. So proceed as you normally would when creating *any* type of style (see page 115 for a refresher).

Styling Groups of Tags

Sometimes you need a quick way to apply the same formatting to several different elements. Say you'd like all headers on a page to share the same color and font. Creating a separate style for each header—*h1, h2, h3, h4, h5, h6*—is way too much work, and if you later want to change the color of all of the headers, you have six different styles to update. A better approach is to use a *group* selector. Group selectors let you apply a style to multiple selectors at the same time.

To create a style that applies to several different elements at once, follow the steps on page 115 to create a new style, and then choose Compound from the top menu in the New CSS Rule window (see Figure 8-3). In the Selector Name box, type a list of selectors separated by commas. To style all heading tags with the same formatting options, you'd create the following selector: *h1, h2, h3, h4, h5, h6*.

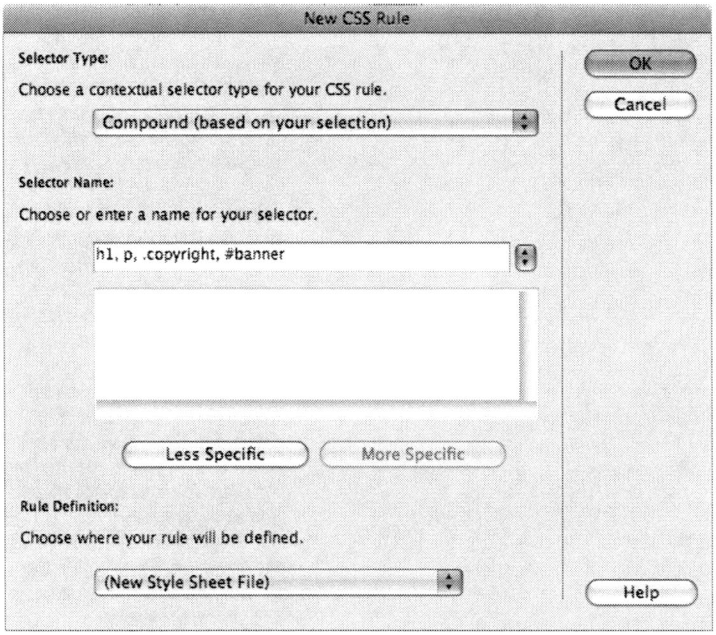

Figure 8-3: *Group selectors aren't limited to tag styles. You can use any valid selector (or combination of selector types) in a group selector. For example, the selector listed here applies to the <h1> tag, the <p> tag, any tag styled with the* .copyright *class, and the tag with the* #banner *ID.*

Tip: At times you may want a bunch of page elements to share *some*—but not all—of the same formatting properties. Suppose you want to use the same font for several tags, but apply different font colors to each of those tags. You can create a single style using a group selector with the shared formatting options, and separate styles with unique formatting for each individual tag.

Fast Style Editing With the Properties Pane

The CSS Rule Definition window (Figure 4-3) can be a rather tedious way of editing CSS properties. It's easy to use, but opening the window and jumping around the categories and menus may slow down experienced CSS jockeys. Fortunately, Dreamweaver offers the Properties pane (Figure 8-4) for fast CSS editing. This pane displays a selected style's currently defined properties, as well as a list of other not-yet-set CSS properties.

Start by selecting the style you wish to edit in the CSS Styles panel. The Properties pane (found in the bottom third of the Styles panel) displays CSS properties in one of three different views: a "set properties" view, which displays only the properties that have been defined for the selected style (Figure 8-4); a Category view, which groups the different CSS properties into the same seven categories used in the Rule Definition window (Figure 8-5, left); and a List view, which provides an alphabetical listing of *all* CSS properties (Figure 8-5, right). Clicking the view buttons at the bottom-left corner of the CSS Styles panel switches between these three displays (see the circled buttons in Figure 8-4 and Figure 8-5).

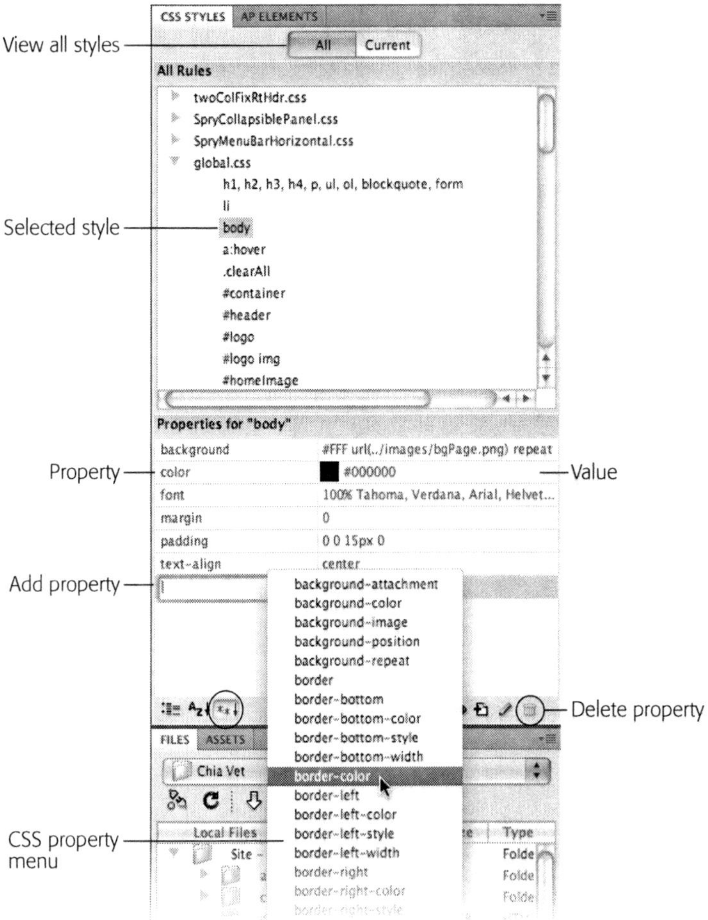

Figure 8-4:
The CSS Styles panel has two views: All (shown here) and Current. The Properties pane is available in both views, but you access it slightly differently when in Current view (see Figure 8-9). In this figure, with the All button selected, you can click any style from the list of CSS styles (body in this case) and use the Properties pane to add and edit properties. The "show only set properties" view of the Properties pane, accessed by clicking the icon circled in this figure, provides a clear view of a particular style's properties. You can quickly see which CSS properties are used by the style, delete or edit them, and add a new property by clicking the Add Property link (hidden behind the pop-up menu) and selecting the new property's name from the CSS property menu.

Property names are listed on the left, and their values are on the right. Figure 8-4 shows an example of a style for the <body> tag, which lists six properties (such as *background-color* and *margin*) and their corresponding settings (#333333, 0px, and so on).

To add a new property, click the Add Property link below the list of properties on the Properties pane, and then select the property name from the pop-up menu. You set (and can edit) the value of a particular property in the space to the right of the property name. Most of the time, you don't have to type in the value. Dreamweaver provides the tools you're likely to need for each property: the ubiquitous color box (see page 59) for any property that requires a color, like font color; a pop-up menu for properties that have a limited list of possible values, like "Repeat-y" for the *background-repeat* property shown in Figure 8-4; and the familiar "Browse for File" folder icon for properties that require a path to a file, such as the *background-image* property.

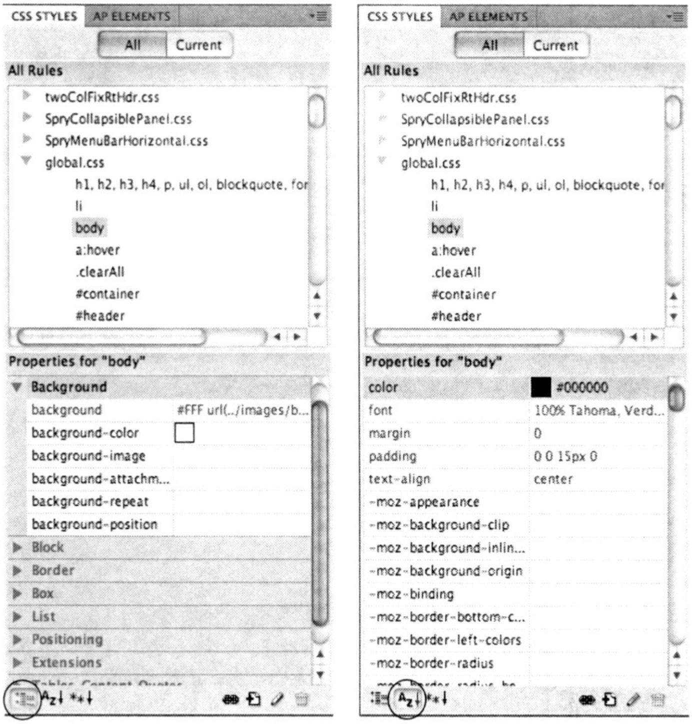

Figure 8-5:
The Properties pane's two other views aren't as streamlined or as easy to use as the "show only set properties" view pictured in Figure 8-4. Add new properties in these views by simply typing a value in the empty box to the right of the property name–in the left view, in the empty box to the right of "background-color," for example. However, since these views aren't the fastest way to edit CSS with the Properties pane, you're better off not using them.

Some other properties, however, require you to know enough CSS to enter them manually, in the correct format. That's what makes the Properties pane a good advanced option for experienced CSS gurus. (If your goal is to become one, Dreamweaver includes a built-in CSS reference so you can sharpen your knowledge of this powerful but slightly daunting technology, as discussed on page 422.)

But even those not so experienced with CSS should find the Properties pane helpful. First, it's the best way to get a bird's-eye view of a style's properties. Second, for really basic editing such as changing the colors used in a style or assigning it a different font, the Properties pane is as fast as it gets.

To remove a property from a style, just delete its value in the right column. Dreamweaver not only removes the value from the style sheet, but the property name as well. In addition, you can right-click (Control-click) a property name and then select "delete" from the pop-up menu, or simply click a property name and either press the Delete key or click the Trash can icon to banish it from your style sheet (see Figure 8-4).

FREQUENTLY ASKED QUESTION

CSS Shorthand

In the CSS Properties pane, sometimes I'll see all the font properties grouped into a single property named font*; other times, font properties are listed individually, like* font-family, font-size, *and so on. Why is that?*

Some CSS properties seem to go together: font properties, background properties (like *background-color, background-image, background-repeat,* and so on), margin, border, padding and list-style properties. CSS provides a shorthand method that combines related properties into a single property name. For example, the *font-family, font-size, font-weight, font-style,* and *line-height* properties can be combined into a single font property. This shorthand makes writing CSS by hand faster. For example, instead of typing all of the above font properties—one line of CSS code per property—you could combine them into a single line like this:

```
font: italic bold 16px/150% Tahoma,
Verdana, Arial, Helvetica, sans-serif;
```

Dreamweaver will use either the shorthand or longhand method depending upon your preference settings. Choose Edit → Preferences (Dreamweaver → Preferences on Macs) to open the Preferences window (or use the keyboard shortcut Ctrl-U [⌘-U]); click the CSS Styles category to view the settings Dreamweaver uses when it writes CSS code. The top group of checkboxes lets you turn on and off shorthand mode.

If you do hand edit your CSS then you might want to leave the shorthand boxes checked. However, if Dreamweaver is writing all your CSS code you should uncheck these boxes, for two reasons. First, unless you know your CSS well, shorthand versions of CSS properties are harder to edit in the Properties Pane—it's very easy to make a typo, and many of the friendly pop-up menus (like a list of fonts to apply to text) that Dreamweaver displays for "longhand" versions of properties don't appear for shorthand versions. In addition, with the *background* shorthand property, you can sometimes find yourself in a weird mess, where background colors and images disappear from elements on a page.

Moving and Managing Styles

In the old days, when CSS support in Web browsers was new, Web designers would create just a handful of styles to format headlines and text. Keeping track of a site's styles back then wasn't too hard. Today, with great CSS support in Web browsers and CSS-based layout becoming the norm, it's not uncommon to create a style sheet with hundreds of styles.

You might want to take a really long, complicated style sheet and split it up into several smaller, easier to read external style sheets. One common Web design practice is to store styles that serve a related function in a separate style sheet—for example, all the styles related to formatting forms in one style sheet, styles for text in another, and styles for page layout in yet another. You can then link each of the external style sheets to your site's pages as described on page 125.

Even if you don't have enough styles to warrant multiple style sheets, it's still useful to organize the styles *within* a style sheet. To keep track of their CSS, Web designers frequently group related styles together in a style sheet; for example, all the styles for basic layout in one section of the style sheet, basic tag selectors in another section, and specific styles for text, images, and other content grouped according to the part of the page where they're used (sidebar, banner, and so on).

By grouping related styles, it's a lot easier to find any particular style when it comes time to edit it.

Fortunately, you don't need to venture into Code view to move styles around in your style sheets. Dreamweaver provides a simple and logical way to move styles within a style sheet and to move styles from one style sheet to another.

- **To move a style from one place to another in the same style sheet**, drag the style in the CSS Styles panel (see Figure 8-6, left). The order the styles are listed in the CSS Styles panel represents their order in the actual CSS code—so dragging one style below another repositions the CSS code in the style sheet. (Order is important in CSS for reasons you'll learn more about starting on page 314; in a nutshell, styles listed lower in a style sheet are given greater priority in case of conflicts.) You can select and move more than one style at a time by Ctrl-clicking (⌘-clicking) each style you wish to select and then dragging the highlighted group of styles (Ctrl-click [⌘-click] a selected style to deselect it). Select a range of styles by clicking one style and then Shift-clicking another style: every style between the two is also selected.

Note: You'll see the full list of styles in a style sheet (and be able to rearrange those styles) only when the All button (circled in Figure 8-6, left) is selected in the CSS Styles panel.

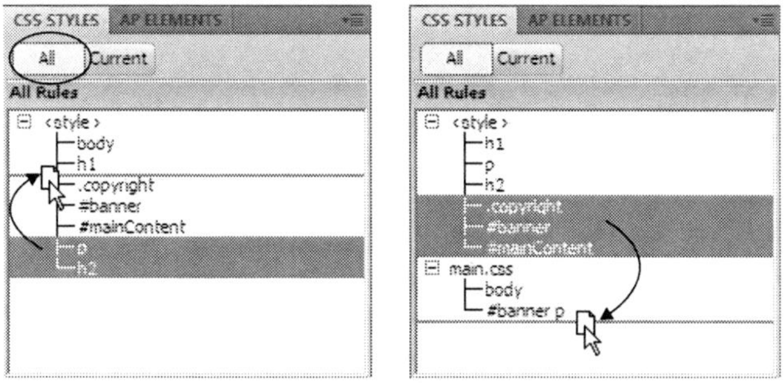

Figure 8-6:
In the CSS Styles panel you can drag styles to different locations within a style sheet (left). In this case, dragging the styles below the h1 style groups all the basic tag selectors (body, h1, p, and h2) together. You can also drag styles between style sheets to move a style from one style sheet to another. In the Styles panel on the right, three styles are being moved from an internal style sheet to a CSS file named main.css.

- **To move one or more styles between two style sheets**, drag the style from one style sheet to another in the CSS Styles panel. This works both for moving a style from an internal style sheet to an external style sheet, and for moving a style from one external style sheet to another. Say you've created an internal style sheet (page 113) for the current page and also attached an external style sheet (page 113) to the same page. Dragging a style from the internal style sheet (represented by <style> in the CSS Styles panel) to the external style sheet (represented by the file name—*main.css*, for example) moves the style *out* of the internal style sheet and *into* the external style sheet (Figure 8-6, right). Dreamweaver then deletes the CSS code for the style from the first style sheet. You can also use this method to move a style between two attached external style sheets as well.

If you drag a style into another style sheet and the destination style sheet already contains a style with the same name, you can run into some confusion. For example, say you've got a tag style for the <body> tag defined in an internal style sheet; in addition, you've got an external style sheet attached to the same page and it also has a body tag style (perhaps with different properties). If you drag the body tag style from one style sheet into another, you're suddenly trying to add the same named style a second time. When this happens, Dreamweaver informs you of the potential problem (see Figure 8-7).

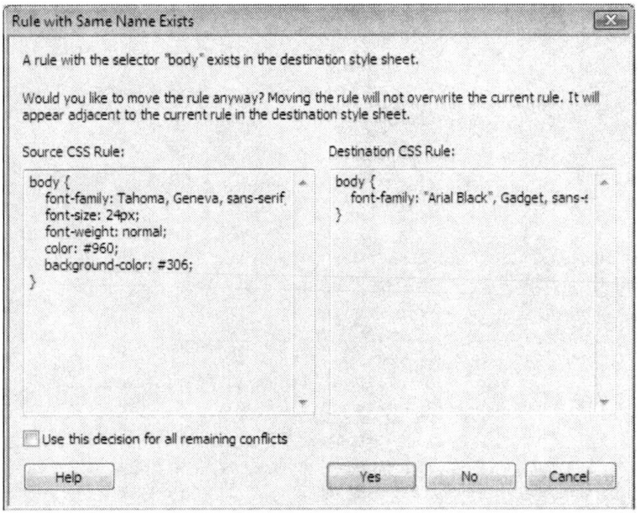

Figure 8-7: *When dragging a style from one style sheet to another, it's possible that a style by the same name already exists in the destination style sheet. When that happens, this dialog box appears, letting you either cancel the move or move the style anyway. To help you figure out what to do, Dreamweaver lists the properties in both the style you're trying to move and the one that's present in the style sheet you're dragging into. You can use this information to determine which of the two styles you wish to keep, or to note which properties from each style are most important.*

Note: Unfortunately, Dreamweaver doesn't provide a way to reorder the sequence of internal and external style sheets on a page. They're attached to the page in the order in which you add them. For example, if you attached an external style sheet to a Web page and then created an internal style sheet, the internal style sheet's code appears *after* the link to the external style sheet. This can have some serious effects on how the cascade works (see page 314). To change the order of the style sheets in the HTML, you have to go to Code view (see page 395) and cut and paste the code.

You have two choices at this point. You can decide not to move the style; click the No button (the Cancel button has the same effect) and the window closes and no styles are moved. Or, click the Yes button and Dreamweaver moves the style to the style sheet. It doesn't replace the old style; nor does it try to merge the properties from the two styles into a single style with the same name. Instead, it just places the new style along with the old style in the same style sheet—in other words, you end up with one style sheet containing two separate styles with the same name. Even though this is perfectly valid CSS, it's very confusing to have the same style twice in one style sheet. You should delete one of the styles, and, if necessary, edit the remaining style to match any properties from the deleted style.

Note: Dreamweaver says that it will place a style adjacent to the style with the same name when moving like-named styles (see Figure 8-7), but it doesn't. Dreamweaver places the moved style wherever you drop it in the list of styles in the destination style sheet.

- You can also **move one or more styles into an external style sheet** that's not attached to the current page. As discussed on page 113, external style sheets are the most efficient way of styling a Web site's collection of pages. However, it's often easier to use an internal style sheet when you're first starting a design. This way, as you tweak your CSS, you only have to edit the one file (the Web page with the internal style sheet) instead of two (the Web page *and* the external CSS file). But once you've completed the design, it's best to move the styles from the internal style sheet to an external style sheet. This process is as easy as a right-click (Ctrl-click).

  In the CSS Styles panel, select the styles you wish to move to an external style sheet (Ctrl-click [⌘-click] each style name to select it). Right-click (Ctrl-click) the selected styles and choose "Move CSS Rules" (see Figure 8-8, top). The "Move to External Style Sheet" window opens (Figure 8-8, bottom). You can then either add the rules to an existing external style sheet by clicking the browse button and selecting an external CSS file in the site, or turn on the "A new style sheet…" radio button to create a new CSS file and move the styles there. When you click OK, the styles are either moved to an existing CSS file, or a dialog box appears letting you name and save a new CSS file. Either way, Dreamweaver removes the styles from the internal style sheet and places them into an external style sheet; even better, if the external CSS file isn't already attached to the current page, Dreamweaver attaches it for you, which lets you skip the manual process of attaching the style sheet, described on page 125.

Tip: If you move all the styles from an internal style sheet to an external style sheet, Dreamweaver still leaves some useless <style> tags in the Web page. To remove those, just select <style> from the list of styles in the CSS Styles panel, then press the Delete key, or click the trash can icon in the lower-right corner of the Styles panel.

More about CSS

As you begin to pile more and more styles onto your pages, you may notice that a page might not look exactly as you expect. A paragraph of text might be green even though you didn't create a style for a green paragraph. Or you've styled a particular paragraph to appear with green text, but it refuses to change color. Most peculiar behaviors like these occur when multiple styles collide. The rules governing these interactions can be complex, but they boil down to two main concepts: *inheritance* and *the cascade*.

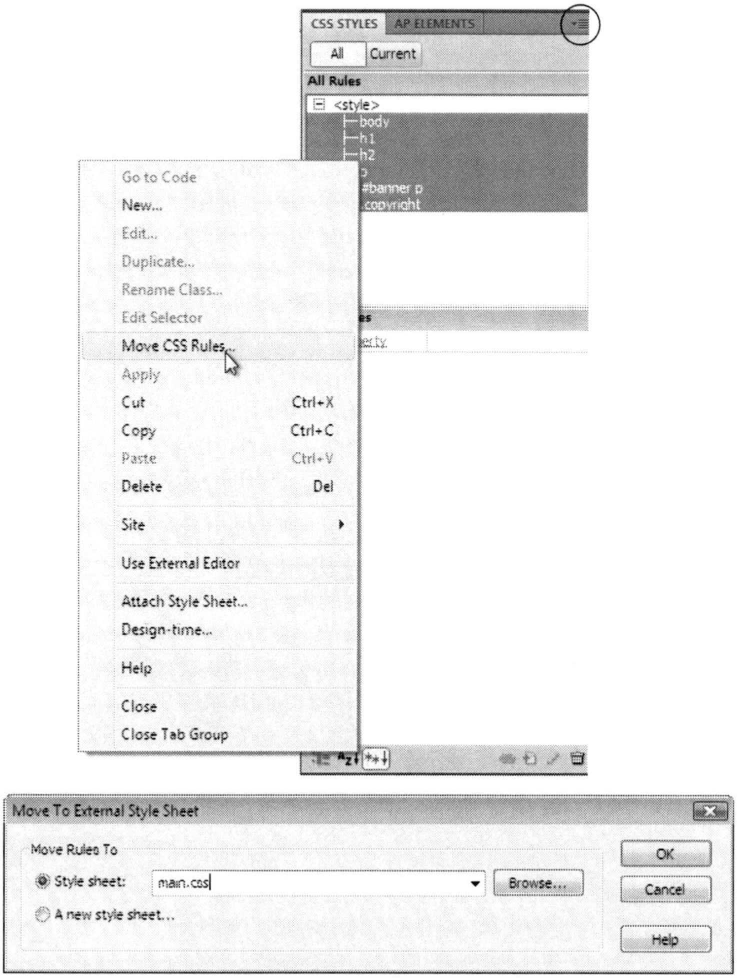

Figure 8-8: *Moving internal styles to an external style sheet is a two-step process. First, select the styles you wish to move and right-click to select "Move CSS Rules". Second, tell Dreamweaver which style sheet to move the style to. You can also access the "Move CSS Rules" option from the Option menu on the CSS Styles panel (circled). This technique is also a good way to take one really long external style sheet file and move related styles into several, smaller CSS files.*

Inheritance

Imagine that you've created a new style by redefining the paragraph tag (<p>). This style uses Arial font, is red, and is 24 pixels tall. Then you select a single word in a paragraph and apply bold formatting to it. When you use the Property inspector's bold button to do this, Dreamweaver wraps that word in a pair of <strong> HTML tags.

When a browser loads the page, it formats all paragraphs in red Arial text, with a font size of 24 pixels, because that's how you defined the <p> tag. But what happens when the browser suddenly encounters the <strong> tag inside that paragraph? Since you didn't redefine the <strong> tag in red, Arial, 24 pixels, the browser scratches its little silicon head: Should the browser just resort to the *default* font, size, and color when it gets to the <strong> tag?

No, of course not. The bolded word should look just like the rest of the paragraph—Arial, red, 24 pixels—but be bold, *too*. And indeed, that's how CSS works: The <strong> tag *inherits* the formatting of the surrounding <p> tag.

Just as human babies inherit traits like eye color from their biological parents, nested HTML tags inherit the properties of tags that surround them. A tag that's nested inside another tag—such as that <strong> tag inside the <p> tag—is called a *child*, while the enclosing tag is called the *parent*.

Note: As you read on page 310, a tag inside another tag is also called a *descendent*, while a tag that surrounds another tag is called an *ancestor*.

Inheritance passes from parent to child and ancestor to descendent. So in this example, the <p> tag (the parent) passes on the Arial font, red color, and 24 pixel size to the <strong> tag (the child). But just as children have their own unique qualities, the <strong> tag adds its own quality—boldness—to the properties it inherits from its parent.

Note: Inheritance applies to all styles, not just HTML tag styles. For example, if you apply a class style, to the <body> tag, then all tags inside the body–paragraphs, images, and so on–inherit the properties of the class style.

Inheritance comes in quite handy at times. Say you want to display *all* text on a page (paragraphs, headings, unordered lists, and links) using the Verdana font. You could dedicate yourself to a lengthy tagging extravaganza and redefine *every* HTML tag used to format text—<h1>, <h2>, <p>, <a>, <ul>, and so on—or create a class style and then manually apply it to all text on the page.

However, a better and faster technique is to take advantage of inheritance. Every Web page contains a <body> tag, which contains *all* the elements of your page. The <body> tag, therefore, is an ancestor of *all* the HTML you see in a page—images, paragraphs, headings, and so on. To quickly format all text, you could create an HTML tag style for the <body> tag and set the font to Verdana, or create a class style using that font and apply it to the <body> tag. Every bit of text inside the body—all children—then inherit the Verdana font property.

Note: Actually, not all CSS properties are inherited. For the most part, these are logical exclusions. For example, say you created a border around an unordered list to visually set it off in its own box. If the border property were inherited, then all the elements *inside* the unordered list–like list items, links, or bolded words–would each have their own box drawn around them as well. Padding and margin are two other common properties that are not inherited. Dreamweaver's built-in CSS Reference provides a complete list of the properties which *aren't* inherited (see page 422).

The Cascade

At times, styles can conflict. Let's say you redefine the <h1> tag in an external style sheet, so that all <h1> tags show up in red, Arial font. But now you attach this external style sheet to a Web page that already has an *internal* style sheet whose <h1> tag style has been set to Times, 24 pixels.

When a Web browser has to display any of this Heading 1 formatted text, it runs into a little dilemma. The page has two different styles—two sets of formatting rules—for the *same tag*. To make matters even more confusing, suppose one particular <h1> tag has a class named *.highlight* applied to it. The *.highlight* class style sets the font family to Trebuchet MS and makes all of the text uppercase. So which style does the browser choose: the style from the internal style sheet, the style from the external style sheet, or the class style?

The answer is all of them. The browser merges the three styles into a sort of hybrid, following these rules:

- **Properties that don't conflict are applied as usual.** In the previous example, the red color property exists only in the external style, while only the internal style specifies a font *size*. And the class is the only style to specify uppercase text. So far, the browser knows that, for this page, text inside <h1> tags should be red, 24 pixels tall, and uppercase.

- **When properties *do* conflict, the Web browser uses the property from the style with the greatest *specificity*.** Specificity is just CSS jargon meaning the style with the most authority. The type of selector is one way to affect specificity: ID selectors are considered more specific than class styles, which are more specific than tag styles. In general, this means that properties from an ID style override properties from a class style, and properties from a class style override any conflicts with a tag style. For an amusing—but accurate—description of specificity, read this article: *www.stuffandnonsense.co.uk/archives/css_specificity_wars.html*. Make sure you print out the accompanying Star Wars-themed chart which visually explains specificity by equating class selectors with Darth Vader, and IDs with the Dark Emperor himself: *www.stuffandnonsense.co.uk/archives/images/specificitywars-05v2.jpg*. May the force be with you.

- **If two styles with the same specificity conflict**—like the h1 style in the external style sheet and the h1 style in the internal style sheet in this example—**the browser chooses the properties from the styles that were added to the page *last*.** Say you first created an internal style sheet (at which point Dreamweaver inserted the appropriate HTML and CSS code into the Web page) and *then* attached an external style sheet. That means the link to the external style sheet appears *after* the internal style sheet in the Web page. In that case, a style from the external style sheet with the same name as a style from the internal style sheet wins out in the case of any conflicts. Similarly, if you attach the external style sheet first and then create the internal style sheet, the internal style sheet wins.

To summarize this example, then: the Web browser determines that text inside an <h1> tag on this Web page should be Trebuchet MS and uppercase (from the class style), red (from the h1 style in the external style sheet), and 24 pixels (the h1 style in the internal style sheet).

Note: Descendent selectors, which include combinations of tag, class, and ID names–such as *#banner h1*, *.main p*, or *h1 strong*–have even more force since the specificity adds up. Say you create a *p* tag style with a bright-red text color, and a descendent selector, *.sidebar p*, with purple text. Any paragraphs inside another element (like a <div> tag) that use the *.sidebar* style are purple–*not* red. Fortunately, Dreamweaver provides several methods for deciphering this confusing jumble of conflicting styles for you (described in the next section).

Inherited properties, however, have no specificity, so when child elements inherit properties from parent elements (as described on page 312), any style applied directly to the child element will overrule properties from the parent element—no matter what the specificity of the parent tag's style. Suppose you create an ID style named *#homepage* with the following properties: purple text and the Arial font. If you apply the *#homepage* id to the <body> tag, then the child elements (anything within the <body> tag) inherit those properties. If you then redefine the paragraph tag so that paragraph text is green, paragraph text inherits the Arial font from the body, but ignores the purple color in favor of the green. Even though an ID style like *#homepage* has greater authority than a simple *p* tag selector, the inherited properties don't beat out properties applied specifically to the paragraph through the p tag style.

To learn more than you probably ever wanted to know about the cascade, visit the following Web pages:

- *www.blooberry.com/indexdot/css/topics/cascade.htm*
- *www.w3.org/TR/CSS2/cascade.html*

Note: For a really in-depth but super-illuminating explanation of confusing CSS concepts check out *CSS: The Missing Manual*. In that book, you'll find chapters dedicated to both inheritance and the cascade.

The Other Side of the CSS Styles Panel

If you haven't yet put this book down in hopes that the swelling in your brain will subside, you've probably absorbed the notion that the application of style properties is quite complex. With all this inheritance and cascading going on, it's very easy for styles to collide in hard-to-predict ways. To help you discern how styles interact and ferret out possible style conflicts, Dreamweaver includes another view for the CSS Styles panel (see Figure 8-9). By clicking the Current button, the panel switches to Current Selection mode, which provides insight into how a selected item on a page—such as an image, a paragraph, a table, or a div tag—is affected by the page's styles.

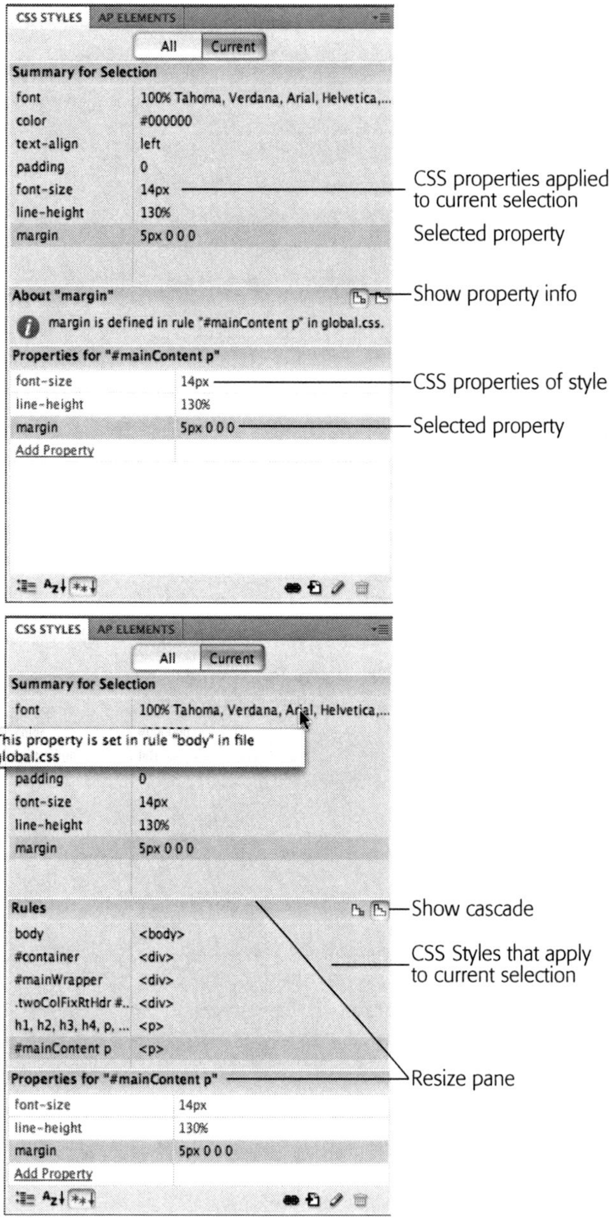

Figure 8-9:
The two views of the Styles panel–Property Information (top) and Cascade (bottom)–are mostly the same. Both show a summary of properties that apply to the current selection, and both display, at bottom, the Property list pane (see page 305) used to edit those properties. Property Information view shows where a selected property "comes from"–that is, which style and which style sheets were used in defining a property. Cascade view, however, is by far the more useful option. You can get the same information as in Property Information view simply by mousing over a CSS property in the Summary pane. For example, in the bottom image, hovering the mouse over the font property opens a pop-up tooltip that explains that this particular property is set in a body tag style that's defined in an external style sheet named global.css. *In addition, Cascade view lists all styles that apply to the currently selected tag: in this case, six different styles help format the text currently selected in the document.*

Current Selection mode is really an incredible tool that's invaluable in diagnosing weird CSS behavior associated with inheritance and cascading. But like any incredible tool, it requires a good user's manual to learn how it works. The panel crams in a lot of information; here's a quick overview of what it provides:

- **A summary of style properties for the currently selected item is in the "Summary for Selection" pane.** Remember that whole thing about how parents pass on attributes to child tags, and how as styles cascade through a page, they accumulate (which means, for example, it's possible to have an <h1> tag formatted by multiple styles from multiple style sheets)? The "Summary for Selection" pane is like the grand total at the bottom of a spreadsheet. It tells you, in essence, what the selected element—a paragraph, a picture, and so on—looks like when a Web browser tallies up all of the styles and displays the page. For serious CSS fans, this pane is almost worth the entire price of Dreamweaver.
- **The origin of a particular property is displayed in the About pane** (Figure 8-9, top). If a headline is orange, but you never created an <h1> tag with an orange color, you can find out which style from which style sheet is passing its hideous orangeness to the heading. You can get the same information by mousing over any property listed in the Summary section; in addition, when the About pane is visible you can't see the much more useful Rules pane, discussed next. So you're better off skipping this pane.
- **A list of styles that apply to the current selection appears in the Rules pane** (Figure 8-9, bottom). Since any element can be on the receiving end of countless CSS properties handed down by parent tags, it's helpful to see a list of all the styles contributing to the current appearance of the selected object on the page.
- **The order of the cascade is in the Rules pane** (Figure 8-9, bottom). Not only are styles that apply to the current selection listed here, they're also listed in a particular order, with the most general style at the top and the most specific ones at the bottom. This means that when the same property exists in two (or more) styles, the style listed last (farthest down the list) wins.

A few examples can help demonstrate how to read the CSS Style panel when it's in Current Selection mode. Figure 8-9 shows the CSS properties affecting a selection of text (in this case, a paragraph within the main content area) on a Web page. The "Summary for Selection" pane lets you know that if you viewed this page in a Web browser, this paragraph would be displayed using the Tahoma typeface, in black (#000000), left-aligned, with no padding, at a font size of 14 pixels, with a 130% line height (space between each line of text), and with 5 pixels of space for the top margin. When you select a property from the "Summary for Selection" pane and then click the Show Property Information button (Figure 8-9, top), the About pane displays where the property comes from—in this case, that the margin property settings belong to a descendent selector—*#mainContent p*—which is defined in an external style sheet named *global.css.*

You've seen the bottom part of this pane before. It's the Properties pane, and it's used to delete, add, and edit the properties of a style. Simply click in the area to the right of the property's name to change its value, or click the Add Property link to select a new property for the style. Notice that in this example, the Properties pane contains fewer properties than the summary view. That's because it only displays properties of a single style (the *#mainContent p* descendent selector), while the Summary view shows all properties inherited by the current selection.

Note: Sometimes one or more of the three panes are too small for you to see all the information displayed. You can use the gray bars containing the panes' names as handles and drag them up or down to reveal more or less of each pane.

Clicking the Show Cascade button (Figure 8-9, bottom) reveals a list of all styles that affect the current selection. In this case, you can see that six different styles—the body tag style, two ID styles (*#container* and *#mainWrapper*), a descendent selector, a group selector (*h1, h2, h3, h4, p*) and, finally, the descendent selector *#mainContent p*—contribute to styling the selected paragraph of text. In addition, as mentioned above, the order in which the styles are listed is important. The lower the name appears in the list, the more "specific" that style is—in other words, when several styles contain the same property, the property belonging to the style *lower* on the list wins out. (See page 314 for more on conflicts caused by cascading styles.)

Tip: You can also see the cascade of rules listed in the Property inspector. On the document, select the text you want to analyze; click the CSS button on the Property inspector, and then select the Targeted Rule menu–the top group of items in the menu is a listing of the Cascade exactly as it appears in the Rules pane of the CSS Styles panel.

Clicking a style name in the Rules pane reveals that style's properties in the Properties pane below. This pane not only lists the style's properties but also crosses out any properties that don't apply to the selected tag. A property doesn't apply to a selection for one of two reasons: either because the property is overridden by a more specific style, or because that property isn't inherited by the selected tag.

For example, Figure 8-10 shows that four styles affect the formatting of a single headline: three tag styles (<body>, <h2>, and <h2>) and one class style (*.highlight*). In the left-hand image, the color and font-size properties for the h2 style are crossed out—meaning those properties don't apply to the current selection. The font-family property, on the other hand, isn't crossed out, indicating that the current selection is displayed using the font Trebuchet MS. Because that h2 appears near the top of the list of styles in the Rules pane, you can determine that that style is less "specific" (less powerful) than styles listed later. The style that appears last on the list—*.highlight* in this example—is most "specific" and its properties override conflicts from any other style. Selecting *.highlight* in the Rules pane (Figure 8-10, bottom right) demonstrates that, yes indeed, its font size and color properties "win" in the battle of cascading style properties.

Tip: If you mouse over a property that's crossed out in the Properties pane, Dreamweaver pops up a tooltip explaining why a browser won't apply that property. If the property is crossed out because it's overruled by a more specific style, Dreamweaver also tells you which style won out.

If your Web pages are elegantly simple and use only a couple of styles, you may not find much need for this aspect of the CSS Styles panel. But as you become more proficient (and adventurous) with CSS, you'll find that this panel is a great way to untangle masses of colliding and conflicting styles.

Tip: One way to make a style more "powerful"—so that its properties override properties from conflicting styles—is to use a descendent selector (see the note on page 303). For example a *body p* descendent selector has more authority than just a plain *p* tag style, even though both styles target the exact same tags. You can quickly rename a style or create a more longwinded and powerful descendent selector using the CSS Styles panel: Select the name of the style in the CSS Styles panel (use the "All" view); click the style name a second time to edit it.

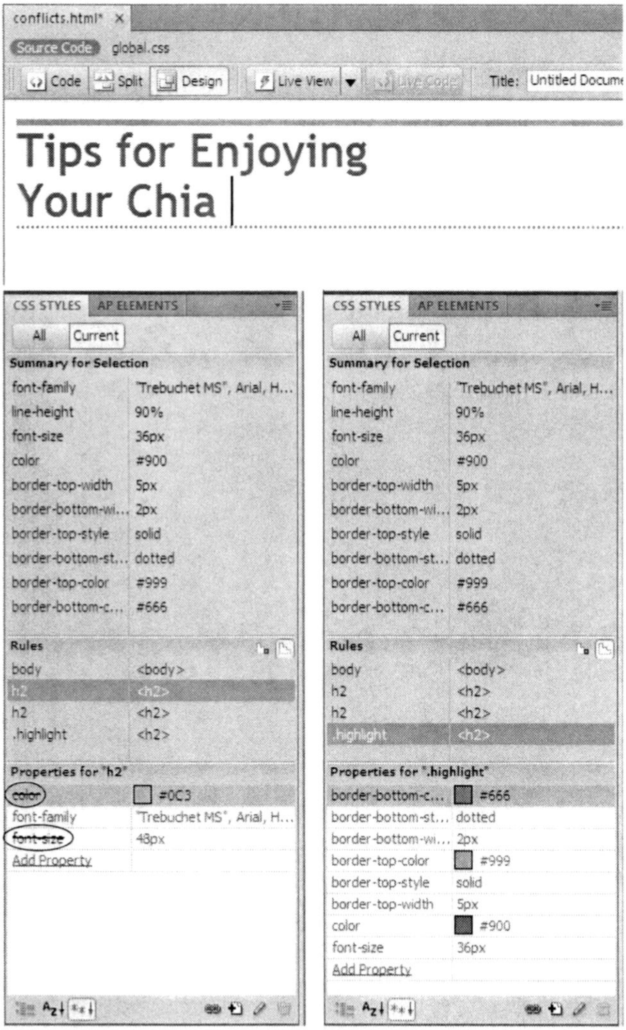

Figure 8-10:
Selecting the Current view of the CSS Styles panel lets you easily view all the properties that apply to the currently selected item—in this example it's the headline (an <h2> tag) pictured at top. A line (circled in the left corner of the panel below) strikes out properties from a style that don't apply to the headline. In this case, the font-size and color in the first <h2> style is overridden by the same properties in the more specific .highlight *class style (bottom right).*

Using the Code Navigator

Dreamweaver CS4 introduces a new tool for CSS pros: Code Navigator, which provides a quick way to view all CSS styles that apply to any element you click on. In this way, it's kind of like the Rules Pane of the CSS Styles panel (discussed in the previous section). However, Code Navigator is a pop-up window that appears directly in the document window (see Figure 8-11).

To access the Code Navigator, hold down the Alt key and click an element on the page (for Macs, you need to press ⌘-Option and click). You can click any element whose CSS you wish to examine: for example, an image, a heading, a paragraph, a table, and so on. For example, in Figure 8-11, ⌘-Option clicking the "Tips" headline (that would be Alt-Click for Windows) opens the Code Navigator which lists the styles that apply to that headline.

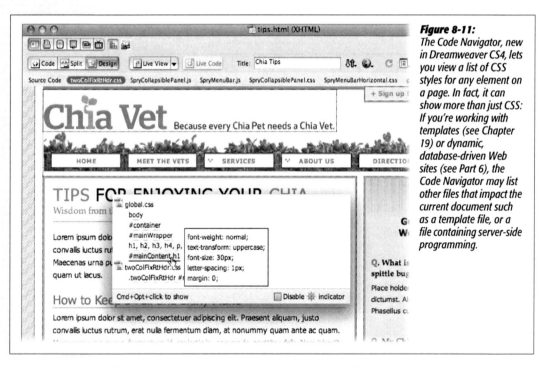

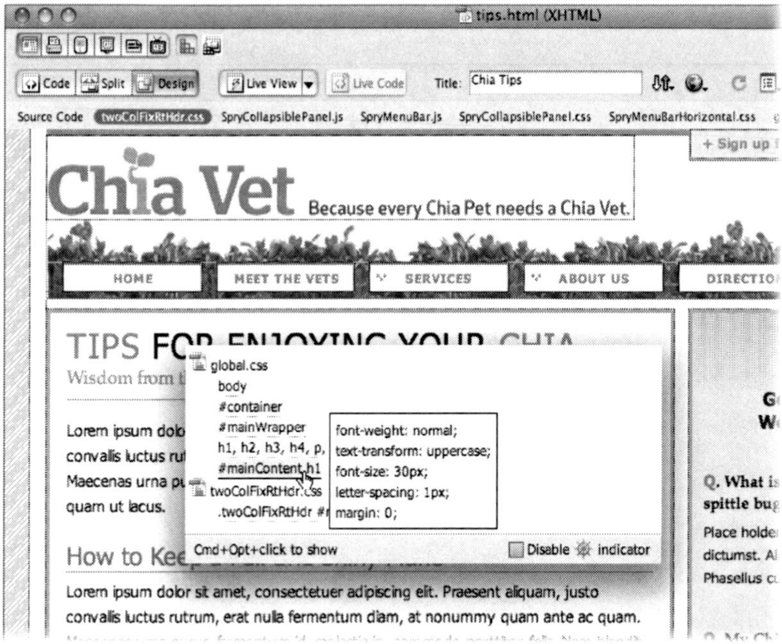

Figure 8-11: *The Code Navigator, new in Dreamweaver CS4, lets you view a list of CSS styles for any element on a page. In fact, it can show more than just CSS: If you're working with templates (see Chapter 19) or dynamic, database-driven Web sites (see Part 6), the Code Navigator may list other files that impact the current document such as a template file, or a file containing server-side programming.*

There are several other ways to access the Code Navigator window, as well:

- Click the Code Navigator icon (circled in Figure 8-12). This ship steering wheel icon appears above an element that you've selected on the page (or above the element where the cursor is currently placed). It usually takes a second or so to appear, so you may want to stick with the keyboard shortcut (Alt-click or ⌘-option-click).
- Right-click any item on the page, and choose Code Navigator from the pop-up shortcut menu.

- Select an item on a page (a table, image, paragraph, and so on) and choose View → Code Navigator, or press Ctrl-Alt-N (Windows) or ⌘-Option-N (Mac).

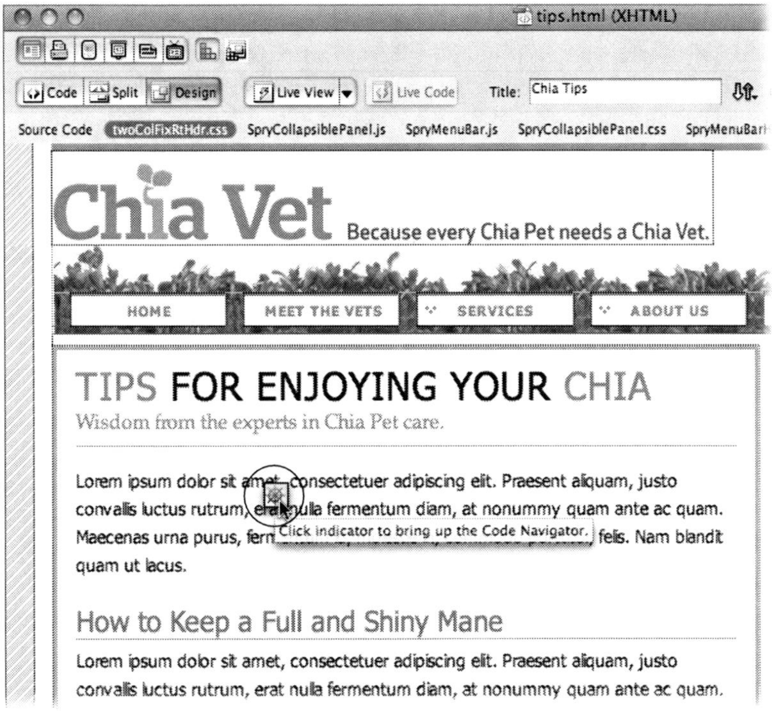

Figure 8-12: *If the Code Navigator's ever present steering wheel icon bothers you, turn it off by putting a checkmark in the disable box in the Code Navigator window (see Figure 8-11). At that point, you need to use the keyboard shortcut or one of the other methods discussed in this chapter for opening the Code Navigator.*

Once the Code Navigator window opens, you'll see all CSS styles that affect the current item. In Figure 8-11, for example, the Code Navigator lists six styles which impact the formatting of the headline "Tips for Enjoying Your Chia"—five styles are in the *global.css* external style sheet and one is in the *twoColFixRtHdr.css* external style sheet. If you move your mouse over one of the styles, you'll see a list of that style's CSS properties.

Code Navigator provides a quick way to see properties for all styles that affect the page element as well. In Figure 8-11, hovering over the *#mainContent h1* style, lists that styles properties: a *font-size* of 30 pixels, 1 pixel of *letter-spacing,* and so on. Although this is a quick way to view styles and their properties it isn't as useful as the Current view of the CSS Styles panel (page 315), which shows exactly which *properties* (not just which styles) apply to the current selection. In addition, the Code Navigator window doesn't always accurately display the CSS Cascade (page 314)—it does list the styles in order of specificity, but it splits up the list of styles by style sheet, so if a page has more than one style sheet you may not get a clear picture of the cascade. The CSS Rules Pane (page 315), on the other hand, shows a complete list of styles from least to most specific, regardless of how many style sheets you use.

If you're a code jockey who prefers to type CSS code instead of relying on Dreamweaver's windows and panels, the Code Navigator lets you jump immediately to CSS code. Once the Code Navigator window is open, just click any style listed. Dreamweaver will jump into Split mode (a view of raw code and the page's Design view) and display the CSS code for the selected style (Split mode is discussed on page 395). Of course, you need to know how to write your own CSS code for this to be useful. If you're not comfortable with that, you should stick with the CSS Styles panel and the methods discussed on pages 126 and 305 for editing styles.

Styling for Print

You may be surprised to see a section on print design in a book dedicated to creating beautiful onscreen presentations. However, it's common to see people print out Web pages: printed directions to get to a concert, a list of product names and ratings to review while out shopping, or a longwinded Web treatise that's easier to read on paper while reclining in a favorite chair.

Unfortunately, some Web pages just don't print well. Sometimes the banner's too big to fit on one sheet, so it spans two printed pages; or the heavy use of ads wastes toner when printed. And some CSS-based layouts simply print as jumbled messes. Fortunately, CSS has an answer: *printer style sheets*. The creators of CSS realized that Web pages might be presented in different ways, such as printed on paper. In fact, they went so far as to define a large group of potential "media types" so that Web designers could customize the display of a page for different output devices including teletype machines, Braille readers, and more.

Basically, by specifying a media type, you can attach an external style sheet that's *only* applied when the page is output to a particular type of device. For instance, you could have a style sheet that only works when the Web page is viewed on a monitor, and another that only applies when the page is printed. In this way you can tweak the styles so the page looks better when printed, without affecting the page's appearance onscreen. Figure 8-13 shows the concept in action.

The basic process involves creating an external style sheet that contains styles for the particular media type, and then attaching the style sheet to a Web page and assigning the appropriate media type.

Attaching an external style sheet is discussed on page 125, but in a nutshell you simply click the Attach External Style Sheet button on the CSS Styles panel (see Figure 4-1). Doing so opens the Attach External Style Sheet window (see Figure 8-14). Click the browse button and locate the proper CSS file, select the media type from the Media menu, and then click OK.

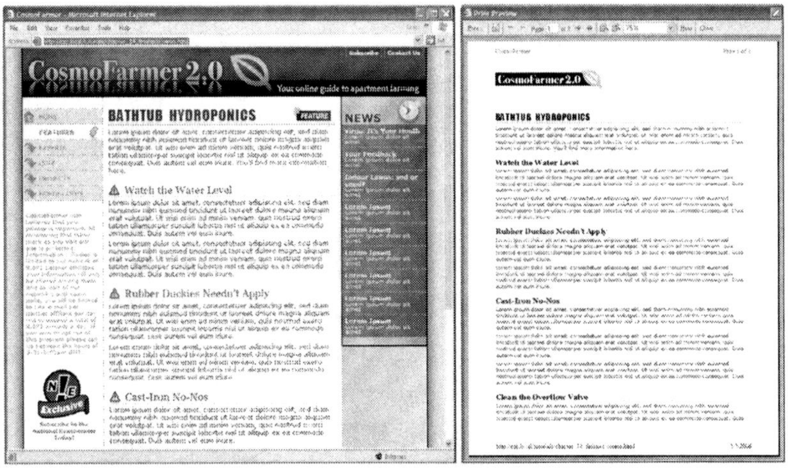

Figure 8-13: *When printing a Web page, you really don't need navigation links or information that's not related to the topic at hand (left). Use a print style sheet to eliminate unnecessary content and format the page so it prints well (right).*

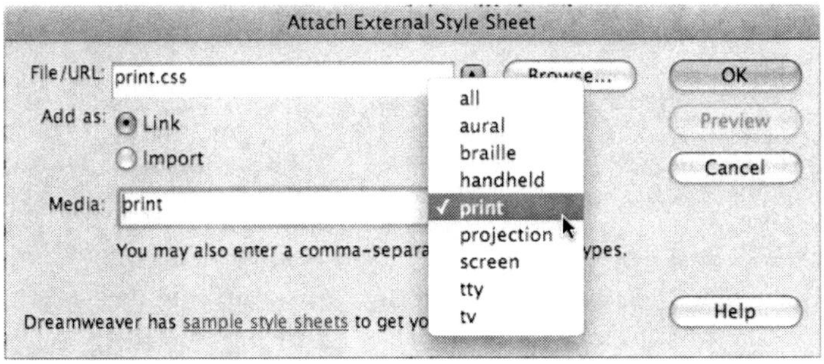

Figure 8-14: *When attaching an external style sheet, you can indicate that the style sheet should be used only when the Web page is printed (print), when it's viewed on a monitor (screen), or at all times for all media (all). Leaving this option blank is the same as selecting "all".*

Tip: If you attach an external style sheet and select one of the media type options, Dreamweaver displays the media type name on the CSS Styles panel. For example, if you attach an external style sheet file named *print.css* and specify the print media type, then "print.css (print)" appears in the CSS Style Panel.

Although Dreamweaver lists many different media types (aural, Braille, handheld, and so on), only three options are widely supported: *print, screen*, and *all*. "Print" specifies that the styles only apply when the page is printed; "screen" indicates a style sheet that only takes effect when the page is viewed on a monitor; and "all" is the same as not selecting anything—the style sheet applies when printed, viewed on a monitor, felt on a Braille reader, and so on. This option comes in handy when you want to create a style sheet that defines the basic look of your Web site—such as the font, line height, and text alignment—and applies both when printed and viewed on the screen. You can then create two additional style sheets (one for onscreen and one for print) that tweak that basic design for presentation on a monitor and on a piece of paper.

Note: Dreamweaver CS4 doesn't provide a way to create a new external style sheet *and* define its media type at the same time. So to create and use a new printer-only style sheet, you need to follow the steps on page 118 to create the external style sheet, then unlink that style sheet from the page (page 127) and then reattach the external style sheet and select the print option from the Media menu. Alternatively, you could just create a CSS style sheet file by choosing File → New and selecting CSS from the Blank Page category of the New Document window; save the file (don't forget the .css extensions), and then add styles to the file using the same methods you use when adding styles to a Web page (see page 115). You can then attach this style sheet to a Web page and specify a media type as described on page 322.

Previewing Media Styles in Dreamweaver

Dreamweaver is mainly used to create Web pages that people view onscreen. Because of that, the program normally shows only styles that are attached when either no media type is selected or when the "all" or "screen" type is specified. So how can you see what the printed version will look like when designing a print style sheet? Dreamweaver sports a fancy toolbar just for this purpose: the Style Rendering toolbar (Figure 8-15). To turn it on, choose View → Toolbars → Style Rendering, or right-click (Control-click) the document toolbar, and then choose Style Rendering.

Note: If you're in Live View (page 553) then the Style Rendering toolbar has no effect. In Live View, Dreamweaver displays only what the page will look like when displayed in a Web browser.

Each button in the toolbar lets you view the page as it will look on screen, in print, or through one of the other media types. Click the Screen button to see how Dreamweaver (and a Web browser) normally display the page. Click the Print button and any styles attached using the "print" and "all" media types appear; in other words, when designing the page for print, click the Print button.

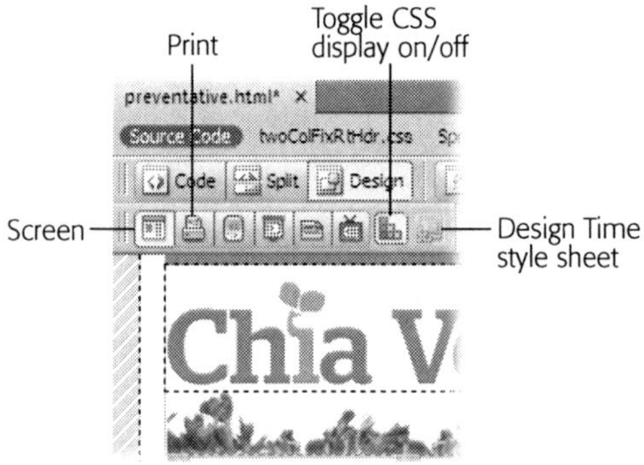

Figure 8-15: *The Style Rendering toolbar lets you show styles that match the media type you selected when you attached the style sheet to the page. The toolbar also includes buttons to attach a Design Time style sheet (see the box on page 327) and to completely hide all styles. This last option is particularly good when creating complex CSS-based designs, which can sometimes make selecting and editing HTML difficult. Click the "toggle CSS display" button to temporarily hide the styles and just display the simple, unadorned HTML.*

Note: If your CSS styles don't seem to have any affect on a page, you either have the wrong media type selected in the Style Rendering toolbar, or you might have turned off the display of CSS by clicking the Toggle CSS Display button (see Figure 8-15). Click the Toggle CSS Display again to display the CSS-styled page.

Tips for Printer Style Sheets

A printer style sheet can redefine the look of any element of a page when it's printed. You can change fonts, adjust type size, increase leading (space) between lines of text, and so on. You can use any CSS property you want and modify any style to your liking, but there are a few common tasks that most printer style sheets perform.

- **Override properties from another style sheet.** If you've attached an external style sheet with the "all" media type or you didn't specify any type at all, the printed page will use styles from that style sheet. The print style sheet may need to override some of the settings present in those style sheets. The best way to do this is to simply create styles with names that match the style you wish to override. For example, if a style sheet attached to the page has a *p* tag style that specifies the font size as 12 pixels, you can create another *p* tag style in the print style sheet that changes the font size to 12 points. (Due to the rules of the Cascade [page 314], the printer style sheet needs to be attached *last* to the Web page in order for its styles to overrule similarly named styles in another style sheet.)

  Another solution to this problem is to simply create two separate style sheets—one for print and one for screen—and attach each with its respective media type. This way there won't be any overlap between styles in the two style sheets.

- **Text size and color.** For screen display, you'll use either pixels, ems, or percentages to size text (see page 137). Unfortunately, these measurement units don't make a lot of sense to an inkjet printer. If you've used Microsoft Word, you probably know the measurement of choice for printed text is points. If you don't like the size of type when a page is printed, redefine font sizes using a printer-friendly size. In addition, while bright yellow type on a black background may look cool onscreen, black type on white paper is the easiest to read. If you colored your text, it may print out as a shade of gray on a black and white printer. Setting text to black in a print style sheet can help your visitors' weary eyes.

- **Hide unnecessary page elements.** Some parts of a Web page don't really need to print. Why, for example, do you need to see the site's navigation bar or a sidebar of links on a printed page? After all, you can't click them! Fortunately, CSS provides a property that will let you completely hide unwanted page elements. Just create a style that applies to the part of the page you wish to hide—for instance, with CSS-based layouts you typically divide sections of a page into separate <div> tags, each with its own unique ID. Say the site's navigation is contained inside a tag that has an ID named *#navbar* applied to it. To hide the nav bar, create an advanced style named *#navbar* in your print style sheet. In the CSS Rule Definition window (see Figure 4-3), click the Block category and then choose "None" from the Display property menu. (In Figure 8-13, right, for example, the banner and both sidebars are hidden in the printed version of the page.)

- **Adjust margins and widths.** To make a design look more elegant, you might increase the margins around the edges of a page. But this extra space only wastes paper when printed. Remove any margins you've applied to the body tag. In addition, if you hide parts of a page when printing, it's possible that the remaining page elements won't fill the printed page. In this case, add a style to the print style sheet that changes the widths of the printed elements. For example, if you have a two-column design—a sidebar with links and other site-specific info, and a main column filled with all the useful info that should appear on a printed page—and you hide one column (the sidebar), you'd then set the width of the remaining column to 100% and remove any margins on its left and right side. That way, the printed information will fill the entire width of the page.

- **Take advantage of *!important*.** As mentioned earlier, sometimes the printer style sheet needs to override certain CSS properties from another style sheet. Thanks to the Cascade (page 314) a style must have greater "specificity" to overrule conflicts with another style. If you're trying to override, say, the font color used for a descendent selector named *body #wrapper #maincontent p*, then you have to add the same longwinded style name to your print style sheet. Fortunately, CSS provides a simpler method: the *!important* directive. Adding *!important* to a property in a CSS style lets that property overrule any conflicting property values from other styles, even if those other styles are more specific.

  Unfortunately, Dreamweaver doesn't give you a way to easily add this option. You have to manually edit the style sheet in Code view. Say you want the text of all paragraph tags to print black. Create a *p* tag style in the print style sheet and set the *color* property to "black". Then open the print style sheet in Code view and add *!important* after the color value and before the semicolon character. Here's what that would look like in Code view:

  ```
  p {
  color: #000000 !important;
  }
  ```

  This style in the print style sheet will now override any color settings for any paragraph tags in a competing style sheet—even a much more specific style.

GEM IN THE ROUGH

A Time to Design

A Dreamweaver feature called *Design Time style sheets* lets you quickly try different CSS style sheets while developing your Web page. You can hide the (external) style sheets you've attached to a Web page and substitute new ones.

Design Time style sheets come in handy when working on HTML that, later on, you intend to make part of a complete Web page. Dreamweaver Library items are a good example; this feature (discussed in Chapter 18) lets you create a chunk of HTML that can be used by any number of pages on your site. When you update the Library item, every page that uses it is updated. A timesaving feature, for sure, but since a Library item is only *part* of a page, it doesn't include the <head> portion needed to either store styles or attach an external style sheet. So when designing a Library item, you're working in the dark (or at least, without any style). But by using Design Time style sheets, you can access all the styles in an external style sheet and even preview the effects directly in Design view.

You'll also turn to this feature when working with Dreamweaver's server-side XML tools (see Chapter 26), which let you add an "XSLT fragment" to a complete Web page—essentially letting you convert XML (like you'd find in an RSS news feed) into a chunk of HTML. But to accurately design these components, you'll need to use Design Time style sheets.

You can apply a Design Time style sheet by clicking the Design Time style sheet button in the Style Rendering toolbar (see Figure 8-15) or by choosing Format → CSS Styles → Design Time; the Design Time Style Sheets window appears. Click the top + button to select an external style sheet to display in Dreamweaver. Note that clicking this button doesn't attach the style sheet to the page; it merely selects a .css file to use when viewing the page inside Dreamweaver.

To properly view your page with this new style sheet, you may need to get an attached external style sheet out of the way. To do that, use the bottom + button to add it to the Hide list.

Design Time style sheets apply only when you're working in Dreamweaver. They have no effect on how the page looks in an actual Web browser. That's both the good news and the bad news. Although Dreamweaver lets you apply class styles that you take from a Design Time style sheet to your Web page, it doesn't actually attach the external style sheet to the appropriate page. For example, if you use a Design Time style sheet to help design a Library item, Dreamweaver doesn't guarantee that the Web page using the Library item has the style sheet attached to it. You have to attach it yourself, or else your visitors will never see your intended result.

CHAPTER

9

Page Layout

Web design, unfortunately, isn't like most other forms of graphic design. For magazine and book projects, software like InDesign let you place text and images anywhere you want—even rotate and overlap them. But Web designers are stuck with the basic technology of HTML which just wants to flow from the top of the window to the bottom, in one long column. In order to place elements around the page and create multiple columns of content, you need to resort to some fancy footwork.

For much of the Web's short life, designers have used the HTML <table> tag to control the positioning of elements on a page—to create columns, sidebars, banners, and so on. Unfortunately, since the <table> tag was intended to display information in a spreadsheet-like format, bending it to a Web designer's will often resulted in complex HTML that downloaded slowly, displayed sluggishly, and was very difficult to modify.

But now that CSS-friendly Web browsers like Internet Explorer, Firefox, Safari, and Opera rule the Web, designers can safely rely on a much better (though often frustrating) method: Cascading Style Sheets. That's right; not only is CSS great for formatting text, navigation bars, images, and other bits of a Web page, it also has all the tools needed to create sophisticated designs, like the ones shown in Figure 9-1.

CSS provides two methods for laying out a Web page—*absolute positioning* and *floats*. Absolute positioning lets you position an element anywhere on the page with pixel level accuracy—or so the theory goes. This kind of total control is exciting, but actually very difficult to achieve. That's why the vast majority of Web pages use float-based layouts—a method that lets you create great looking multi-column designs.

Dreamweaver can produce both types of layouts and includes a starter set of 32 CSS Layouts (only two use Absolute Positioning). These CSS Layouts provide Web designers with the files for building the most commonly used page layouts. These layout files aren't complete Web page designs as much as a basic scaffolding that you can modify to match your own design sensibility. Best of all, the complex part of getting the designs to work in all current Web browsers has been done for you.

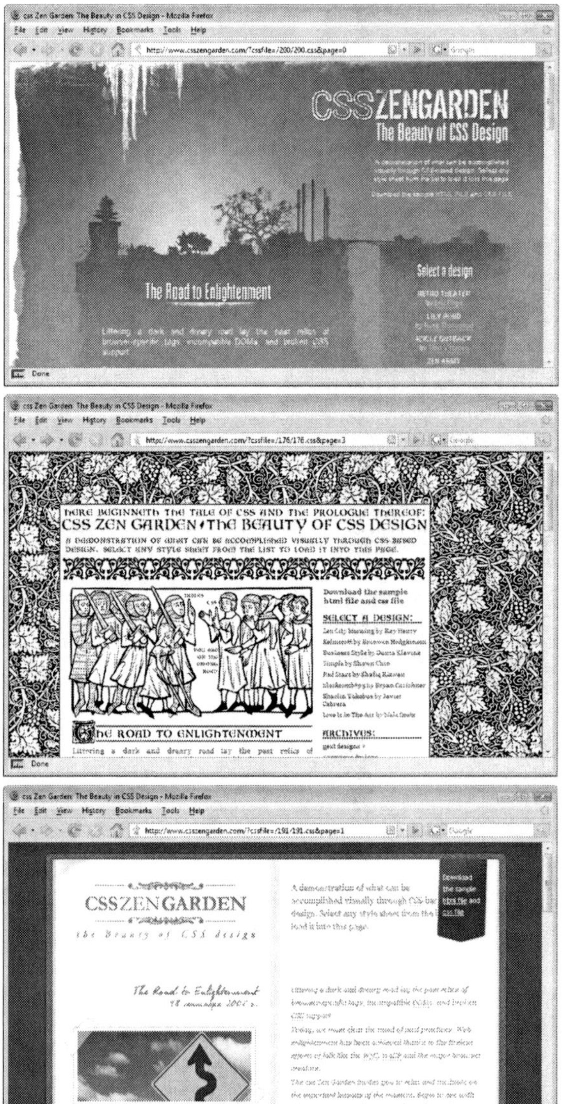

Figure 9-1:
*CSS Zen Garden (*www.csszengarden.com*) is the original showcase for CSS layout. It has caused many a Web designer to bow down and proclaim, "I'm not worthy. I'm not worthy." The site is interesting not only for the great design work it showcases, but because each page includes the same content, but is formatted in radically different ways using CSS. The exact same HTML is shared by these three pages–only the external style sheet and graphics used in the style sheet differ. Making drastic visual changes to a table-based layout requires a lot of tinkering with the underlying HTML. CSS, by contrast, lets you redesign sites without rewriting any HTML.*

Note: CSS Layout is one of those complex topics that is sometimes better learned by doing instead of reading. To get a taste of how CSS Layout works, try the tutorial on page 375 first, then flip back to the beginning of this chapter for all the messy details.

This chapter introduces the basic concepts behind float-based layouts—what they are, how they work, and how to create one; it also provides instructions for modifying Dreamweaver's CSS designs. In addition, you'll learn about absolute positioning, and how to use it for placing selected elements where you want them on a Web page.

Types of Web Page Layouts

Being a Web designer means dealing with the unknown. What kind of browsers do your visitors use? Do they have the latest Flash Player plug-in installed? But perhaps the biggest issue designers face is creating attractive designs for different display sizes. Monitors vary in size and resolution: from petite 15-inch 640×480 pixel displays to 30-inch monstrosities displaying, oh, about 5,000,000×4,300,000 pixels.

Float-based layouts offer three basic approaches to this problem, two of which power most of the best-looking sites you see today: *fixed width* or *liquid* (also called *fluid layouts*). A fixed width gives you the most control over how your design looks, but can inconvenience some of your visitors. Folks with really small monitors have to scroll to the right to see everything, and those with large monitors have wasted space that could be showing more of your excellent content. Liquid designs make controlling the design of the page more challenging for you, but make the most effective use of the browser window. There's also a third type, elastic design, which combines some advantages of both.

- **Fixed Width.** Many designers prefer the consistency of a set width, like the page shown in Figure 9-2, top. Regardless of the browser window's width, the page content's width remains the same. In some cases, the design clings to the left edge of the browser window, or, more often, it's centered in the middle. With the fixed-width approach, you don't have to worry about what happens to your design on a very wide (or small) monitor.

  Many fixed-width designs are about 760 pixels wide—a good size for a fully maximized browser window on a 800×600 screen. It's only 760 pixels since even a browser that's set to fill an 800 pixel-wide monitor still needs a little room for scroll bars and other parts of the browser's "chrome". For the past few years, the prevailing wisdom has been that you can count on most visitors having a minimum screen resolution of 800×600. However, more and more sites (especially ones aimed at a more tech-savvy crowd) are about 950 pixels wide, on the assumption that visitors have at least 1024×768 monitors and expand their brower windows to fill that space.

Tip: For examples of fixed-width designs aimed at larger monitors, visit *www.alistapart.com*, *www.espn.com*, or *www.nytimes.com*.

- **Liquid.** Sometimes it's easier to roll with the tide instead of fighting it. A liquid design adjusts to fit the browser's width—whatever it may be. Your page gets wider or narrower as your visitor resizes the window (Figure 9-2, middle). While this type of design makes the best use of the available browser window real estate, it's more work to make sure your design looks good at different window sizes. On very large monitors, these types of designs can look ridiculously wide.
- **Elastic.** An elastic design is really just a fixed-width design with a twist—type size flexibility. With this kind of design, you define the page's width using *em values*. An em changes size when the browser's font size changes, so the design's width is ultimately based on the browser's base font size (see page 139). If a visitor increases the size of the browser's display font (by pressing Ctrl-+ in Firefox, for example), the page's width grows as well.

  Figure 9-2, bottom, shows an elastic page with the browser's normal font size (left) and several font sizes larger (right). Increasing the font size widens all page elements as well. Elastic designs keep everything on your page in the same relative proportions, and make sure that when someone with poor vision has to pump up the text size, the columns holding the text grow as well. However, newer browsers (IE7, Opera, and Firefox 3) include a "zoom" function which zooms in or out of the page, essentially scaling the page either larger or smaller—in other words, you can create either a fixed width or liquid layout and still achieve the benefit of elastic layouts.

Fixed width designs are probably the most common layout type on the Web, followed by liquid designs and then elastic. Most likely you'll choose between either a fixed width or liquid design, since the benefits of an elastic design aren't useful to most people and are quickly becoming obsolete due to new browser features.

Float Layout Basics

Float-based layouts take advantage of the CSS *float* property to position elements side by side, and create columns on a Web page. As you read on page 229, you can float an image to make text wrap around a photograph. But it's also a powerful layout tool to move a bunch of related page elements (like a list of links that you want to appear in a left-hand column) to one side of the page or the other. In essence, the *float* property moves a page element to the left or the right. Any HTML that appears *after* the floated element moves up on the page, and hugs up against the side of the float.

Float is a CSS property, available when you create a CSS style (see page 115 for instructions on creating a style). It's listed in the CSS Rule Definition window's Box category (see Figure 9-3). Choose the "left" option, and the styled element floats to the left, choose the "right" option and the element moves to the right. For example, if you want to position a sidebar on the left side of a page, then you float it to the left.

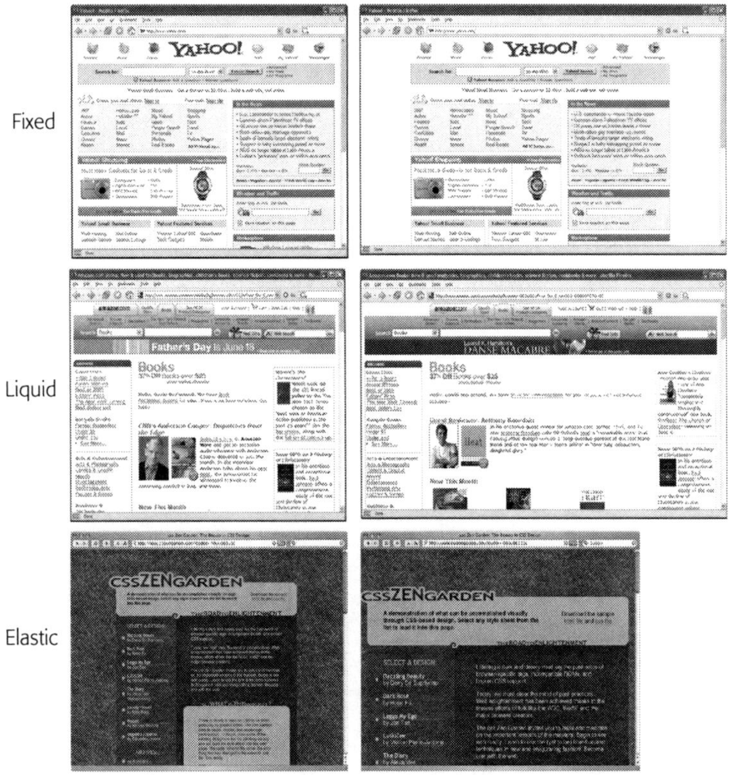

Figure 9-2:
CSS gives you several ways to deal with the uncertain widths of Web browser windows and browser font sizes. You could simply ignore the fact that your site's visitors have different resolution monitors and force a single, unchanging width for your page (top). Or you could create a liquid design that flows to fill whatever width window the page encounters (middle). An elastic design (bottom) changes width only when the font size–not the window width–changes.

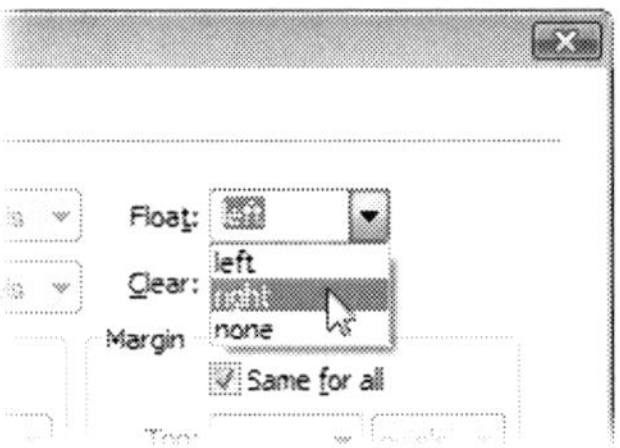

Figure 9-3:
There are just three options when you want to float an element: left, right, and none. You might never need the "none" option–it simply positions an element like a normal, unfloated element. Since this is the regular behavior of any element, you'd need this option only if you wanted to turn off a float applied by another style (see page 314 for more on how multiple styles can affect the same element).

The Mighty <div> Tag

Whether you're using tables or CSS, Web page layout involves putting chunks of content into different regions of the page. With CSS, the most common element for organizing content is the <div> tag. The <div> tag is an HTML element that has no inherent formatting properties (besides the fact that browsers treat the tag as a block with a line break before and after it); you use it to mark a logical grouping of elements, or a *division*, on the page.

You'll typically wrap a <div> tag around a chunk of HTML that belongs together. For example, the elements comprising the logo and navigation bar in Figure 9-4 occupy the top of the page, so it makes sense to wrap a <div> tag around them (labeled "banner div" in the figure). At the very least, you would include <div> tags for all the major regions of your page, such as the banner, main content area, sidebar, footer, and so on. But it's also possible to wrap a <div> tag around one or more *other* divs. People often wrap the HTML inside the <body> tag in another <div>. This tag, then, wraps around all the other divs on the page: You can set some basic page properties by applying CSS to this *wrapper* <div>. You can set an overall width for the page's content, for example, set left and right margins, or center all of the page's content in the middle of the screen.

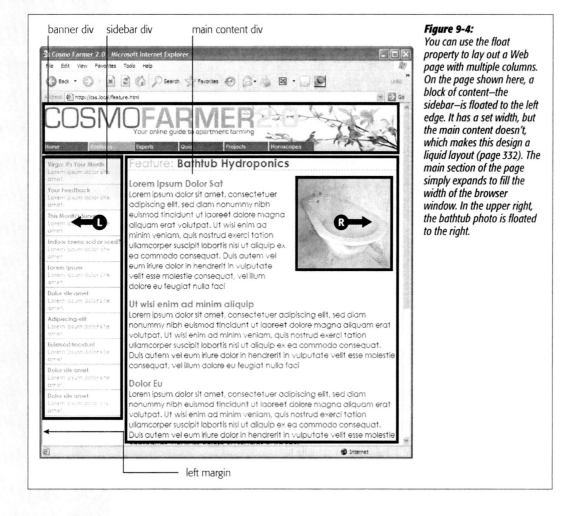

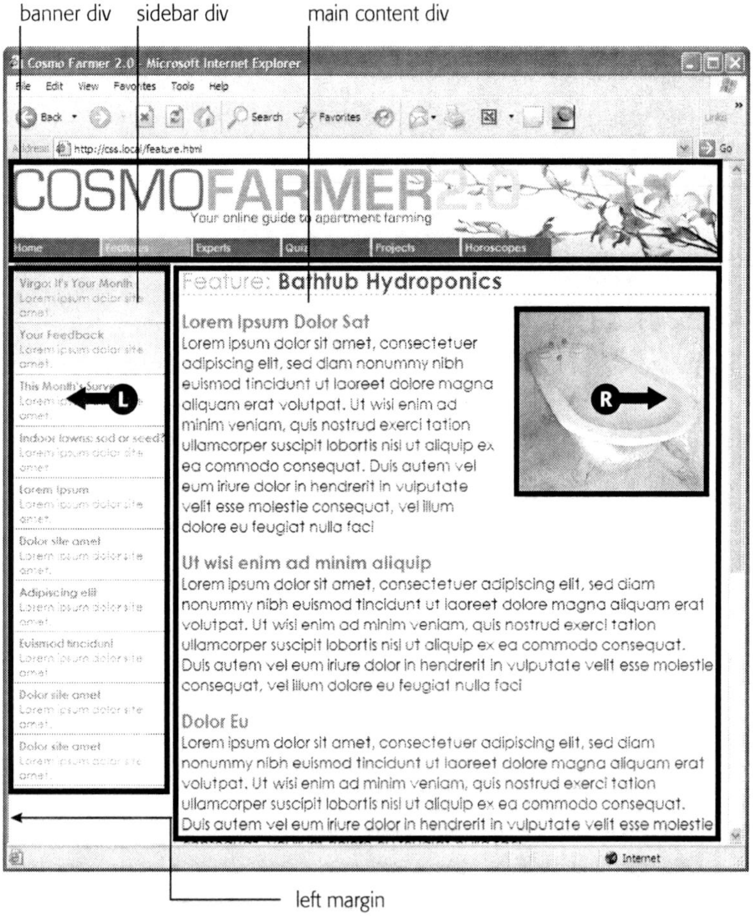

Figure 9-4: *You can use the float property to lay out a Web page with multiple columns. On the page shown here, a block of content–the sidebar–is floated to the left edge. It has a set width, but the main content doesn't, which makes this design a liquid layout (page 332). The main section of the page simply expands to fill the width of the browser window. In the upper right, the bathtub photo is floated to the right.*

Note: If you're a long time <table> tag jockey, you need to develop a new mindset when you begin to use CSS for layout. First, forget about rows and columns (a notion that's important when working with tables). With CSS, there are no column spans or row spans, and the grid-like structure of a table is nowhere to be found. You can, however, think of a <div> tag as a table cell. As with table cells, a <div> tag is the logical place to put content that you want to position in one area of the page. In addition, as you'll see, CSS designs often nest a div inside another div, much like you'd nest tables within tables to get certain effects–but, fortunately, the CSS method uses a *lot* less HTML code.

Once you've got your <div> tags in place, you add either a class or ID style to each one, which becomes your handle for styling each <div> separately. For parts of the page that appear only once and form the basic building blocks of the page, designers usually use an ID (see page 114). For example, the <div> tag for a page's banner area might look like this: *<div id="banner">*. Recall that you can use an ID only once per page, so if you have an element that appears multiple times, use a class instead. If you have several divs that position photos and their captions, you can create a style like this: *<div class="photoBox">*.

Note: If you select a <div> tag in the document window, the Property inspector provides two menus: one to apply an ID to the div, and another to apply a class style to the div.

The Insert Div Tag Tool

Because grouping parts of a page using <div> tags is such an important part of CSS layout, Dreamweaver includes a tool to simplify the process. The Insert Div Tag tool lets you wrap a <div> tag around a selection of page content, or simply drop an empty div onto a page for you to fill with images, links, paragraphs of text, or whatever.

To use this tool, either select the content you wish to wrap with a div (for example, click at the beginning of the selection and drag to the end of the selection) or click on the page where you wish to insert an empty <div> tag. Then click the Insert Div Tag button on the Layout category of the Insert panel (see Figure 9-5). That button is also listed in the Common category, and you can also insert a div by choosing Insert → Layout Objects → Div Tag. In either case, the Insert Div Tag window appears (Figure 9-6).

If you click OK, Dreamweaver will wrap any selected content in a <div> tag, or, if you didn't select anything on the page, just drop a new <div> tag onto the page with the text "Content for New Div Tag Goes Here" (of course, you'll replace that text with your own content). But usually you'll take an additional step: applying either a class or ID to the div. You can do this in a couple of ways:

- **Choose a class from the Class menu or choose an ID from the ID menu.** The Class menu on the Insert Div Tag window lists all the class styles available to the current page. You'd usually select a class if you're inserting a div tag that's formatted the same as other divs on the page. You might use a div tag to position an image and a caption on a page, or to create a pull-quote in the middle of an

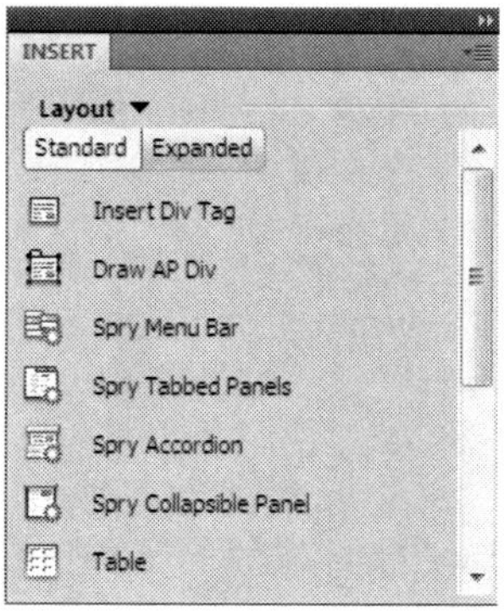

Figure 9-5:
The Layout category of the Insert panel contains buttons for adding both <div> tags and absolutely positioned divs (see page 358).

article; if you had multiple instances of photos with captions, you could create a class style (like .figure) to format each photo-caption pair. You could then select a photo and caption on the page, use the Insert Div Tag tool, and then select the class name (.figure in this example) from the class menu. You could repeat this procedure multiple times on a single page.

The ID menu on the Insert Div Tag window behaves a bit differently. Since you can only use an ID once per page (see page 114 for the reason) the ID menu lists only IDs that exist in your style sheet, but which haven't yet been applied to any tags. Say you created an ID style named *#banner* that you plan on applying to a <div> tag to define the banner area of your page. You could select the banner content (like the site logo and navigation bar), and then click the Insert Div Tag button. At this point, you'd select #banner from the ID menu. If you then inserted a second div on the page using the Insert Div Tag tool, *#banner* would no longer appear in the ID menu.

- **Create a new class or ID.** If you haven't yet created a style to apply to the new div tag, you can click the New CSS Rule button (see Figure 9-6). This button opens the familiar New Style Rule window, so you can create a new style. The process is the same as creating any style, as described on page 115. Once you've completed the style, you'll return to the Insert Div Tag window, and the name of the style you just created appears in the appropriate box. (In other words, if you created a class style, the name of the new class appears in the Class box; similarly, a new ID name appears in the ID box.)

After you apply a class or ID, and then click the OK button, Dreamweaver inserts the new <div> tag complete with the appropriate HTML to apply the style: for example, <div id="banner">. (Note that when creating an ID style, you add a # sign—for example, *#banner*—but when the ID name is used in the HTML the # sign is omitted.) In addition, Dreamweaver takes any styling you created for the class or ID and applies it to the div. In the case of CSS layout, that could mean sizing the div and positioning it on the page, as well as adding a background color, changing the size of text, or any of the other effects possible with CSS. You can add new content inside the div, edit what's there, or completely delete the contents of the div.

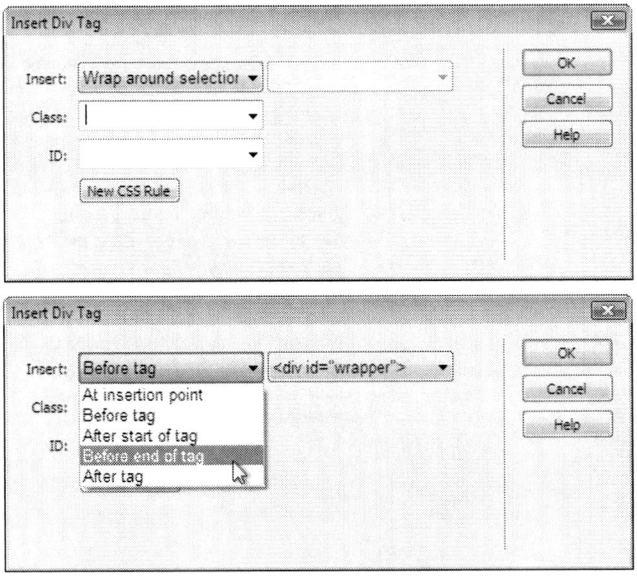

Figure 9-6:
The Insert Div Tag tool can help you precisely place the div in relation to other tags on the page (see your choices listed in the left-hand Insert menu). The right-hand Insert menu lets you choose the tag the new div will be placed in relation to. That menu lists tags that have an ID applied to them, or, if you've chosen the "after start of tag" or "before end of tag" options (from the left-hand menu), it lists the <body> tag. Suppose, for example, you want to insert a <div> tag to display a footer at the bottom of a page. Because you know the footer will go last on the page, you click the Insert Div Tag button, select "Before end of tag" from the Insert's left menu, and <body> from the right menu. The <div> tag then appears at the very end of the page's content, just before the closing </body> tag.

Note: CSS-based layout is a big topic, worthy of a book or two by itself. For more in-depth coverage of CSS layout, including solutions to common float problems, pick up a copy of *CSS: The Missing Manual*.

A Simple Example

To get a better idea of how using a div to help with page layout actually works, look at the layout shown in Figure 9-4. This design has a banner (logo and navigation bar), a left-hand sidebar (list of story titles and links), and the main story. Figure 9-7, left, shows the order in which the HTML appears in the page: The banner elements come first, the sidebar links second, and the main story (headlines, paragraphs, photo and so on) appear last. (Remember, what you're seeing in Figure 9-7 demonstrates the power and the beauty of the HTML/CSS tango: Your HTML file contains your structured chunks of content, while your CSS controls how that content gets displayed.) Viewed in a Web browser, without any CSS styling, these different HTML sections would all appear stacked one on top of the other.

Note: You don't have to use this particular technique to get started with CSS layout. Dreamweaver ships with 32 premade layout designs called CSS Layouts. You can read about these starting on page 345.

To create a two-column design, you could follow these easy steps:

1. **Select the contents of the banner. Then, on the Layout category of the Insert panel, click the Insert Div Tag button (Figure 9-5).**

   For example, click before the logo image and drag to select the navigation bar. With this HTML selected, you can then wrap it in a <div> tag.

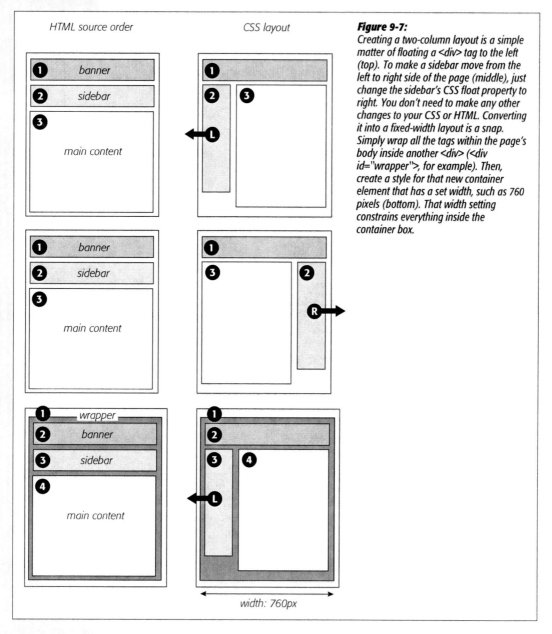

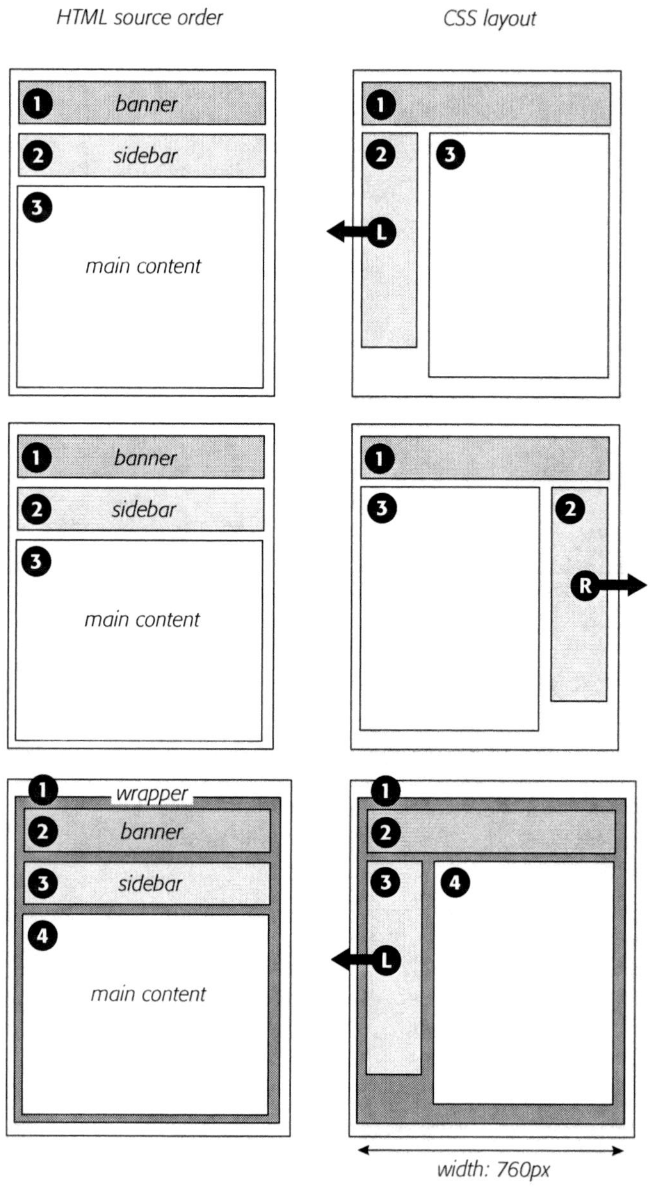

Figure 9-7:
Creating a two-column layout is a simple matter of floating a <div> tag to the left (top). To make a sidebar move from the left to right side of the page (middle), just change the sidebar's CSS float property to right. You don't need to make any other changes to your CSS or HTML. Converting it into a fixed-width layout is a snap. Simply wrap all the tags within the page's body inside another <div> (<div id="wrapper">, for example). Then, create a style for that new container element that has a set width, such as 760 pixels (bottom). That width setting constrains everything inside the container box.

2. **In the ID box, add an ID name.**

   You can add the name in several ways, depending upon whether you want to create an ID style immediately, have already created an ID, or want to create the style later on.

- **To create an ID style, click the New CSS Style button.** The process at this point is the same as creating any new style, as described on page 115. You could create a class style, but for the main sections of a page, Web designers usually create an ID. In this case, the name of the style might be *#banner*. You can set any CSS properties you'd like for the banner: You can add a border around all four sides, color the background of the banner, or even set a width for it.

Note: When you create an ID style using the New CSS Rule box, the ID's name must begin with a # symbol, like this: *#banner*. However, when identifying the ID in the Insert Div Tag window, you omit the # symbol. In the ID box, you'd just type *banner*. The same applies to class styles–use a period when creating a style (*.pullquote*, for example), but omit the period in the Insert Div dialog box.

- **Select an ID name from the ID menu.** The Web page may already have an external style sheet attached, which contains all the necessary styles for the layout. Just select the ID name for the div you're inserting (for example, *banner*).

- **Type a name in the ID box.** If you don't want to create a style, you could just type *banner* in the ID box, and create the style later.

3. **Click OK to close the Insert Div Tag window.**

   Dreamweaver wraps the selected HTML with a <div> tag, and (if you created a new style) formats the banner region.

4. **Select the contents of the sidebar, and then, in the Insert bar, click the Insert Div Tag button. Click the New CSS Style button, and create a new ID style named *#storyLinks* (or whatever you'd like to name the ID).**

   This style formats and positions the left sidebar. We're finally getting to the "float" part of this design.

5. **In the CSS Rule Definition window, click the Box category, and then, from the float menu, select "left" (see Figure 9-8).**

   When you work with floats, the source order (the order in which you add HTML to a file) is important. The HTML for the floated element must appear *before* the HTML for the element that wraps around it.

   Figure 9-7 shows three different two-column layouts. The diagrams on the left show the page's HTML source order: a <div> for the banner, followed by a <div> for the sidebar and, lastly, a <div> for the main content. On the right, you see the actual page layout. The sidebar comes *before* the main content in the HTML, so it can float either left (top, bottom) or right (middle). The main text area then moves up the page and wraps around the floated element.

6. **Type a value in the Width box (circled in Figure 9-8).**

   Unless you're floating an image with a predefined width, you should always give your floats a width. In this way, you create a set size for the floated element, letting the browser make room for other content to wrap into position.

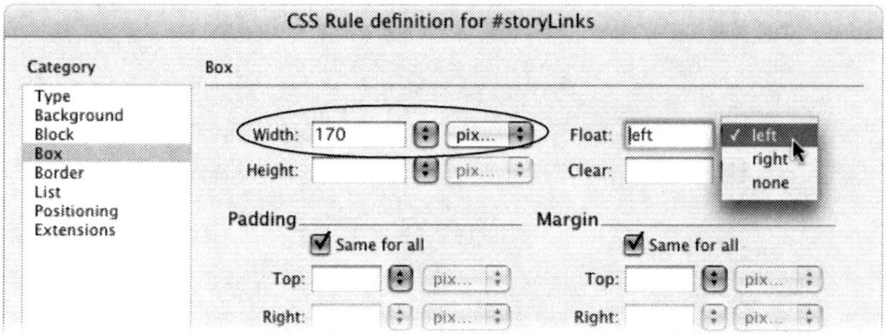

Figure 9-8: *Whenever you float an element (other than an image), always set a width as well. The width constrains the floated element so that other content has room to move next to it.*

The width could be a fixed size like, say, *170px* or *10em*. You can also use percentages for a flexible design that's based on the width of the browser window (see page 137 for more about the pros and cons of the different measurement units). If the sidebar is 20% wide and the browser window is 700 pixels wide, the sidebar will be 140 pixels wide. But if your visitor stretches the window to 1000 pixels wide, then the sidebar grows to 200 pixels. Fixed-width sidebars are easier to design for, since you don't have to consider all the different widths the sidebar might stretch to.

Note: If the overall page design is a fixed width (as described on page 331), percentage width values for the sidebar are based on the fixed width containing element. The width isn't based on the window size, and doesn't change when the browser window changes size. This is actually true of any element whose width is specified using percentage values: the percentage is based on the width of the tag that surrounds the element.

7. **Complete the style, and then insert the div.**

   At this point you can continue to style the sidebar: You could add a background color, set a font family, that, thanks to inheritance (see page 312), will apply to all of the text inside the div, and so on. When you're done, just click the OK button in the Style Definition window; you return to the Insert Div Tag window with the ID box filled out with your freshly created style's name. Click OK to insert the div, and then watch the sidebar float.

   Now it's time to style the main column.

8. **Follow the same steps for the main content div: Select the page elements that form that main content on the page, click the Insert Div Tag button, and then create a new ID style for the page's main content region.**

   In this instance, you don't need to float anything. You merely have to add a left margin to the main content so that it won't try to wrap *underneath* the sidebar. If the sidebar is shorter than the other content on the page, the text from the main column wraps underneath the sidebar. It's much like how the main text interacts with the right-floated photo in Figure 9-4. If the main content wrapped underneath the sidebar, the appearance of two side-by-side columns would be ruined. Adding a left margin that's equal to or greater than the width of the sidebar indents the main content of the page, creating the illusion of a second column.

By the way, it's usually a good idea to make the left margin a little bigger than the width of the sidebar: This action creates some empty space—a gutter—between the two elements. So if the sidebar is 170 pixels wide, adding a left margin of 185 pixels for the main content div adds 15 pixels of space between the two columns. If you use percentages to set the width of the sidebar, use a slightly larger percentage value for the left margin.

In addition, avoid setting a width for the main content div. It's not necessary, since browsers simply expand it to fit the available space. Even if you want a fixed-width design, you don't need to set a width for the main content div, as described in Figure 9-7.

Expanding the two-column design into a three-column design isn't difficult either (Figure 9-9). First, add another <div> *between* the two columns, and float it to the right. Then add a right margin to the middle column, so that if the text in the middle column runs longer than the new right sidebar, it won't wrap underneath the sidebar.

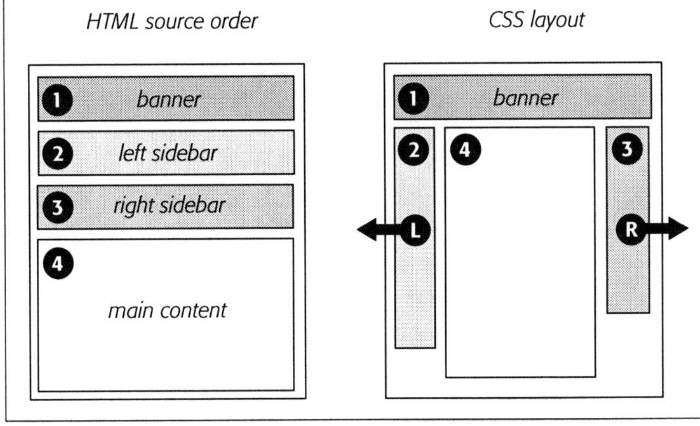

Figure 9-9:
A three-column design uses the same concepts used to create a two-column design. In this case, you float both the left and right sidebars, and add both left and right margins to the center column. The left-hand diagram shows the order of the HTML, the right side shows what the Web page looks like.

Understanding the Box Model

It's no coincidence that the float property is located under the "Box" category of the CSS Rule Definition window (Figure 9-10). To fully understand CSS layouts and how to make the most of using floats, you also need to understand the other CSS properties located within this category: width, height, padding, margin, and clear.

- **Width and height.** You can specify the width and height for any styled object using these properties. If you want a paragraph to be 100 pixels wide, create a class style with the Width property set to 100 pixels, and then apply it to the paragraph. You'll often use the Width property in conjunction with the Float property (see the following paragraph) to do things like create a box with a set width that floats to either the left or right side of the page—a common format for pull-quotes, message boxes, and sidebars.

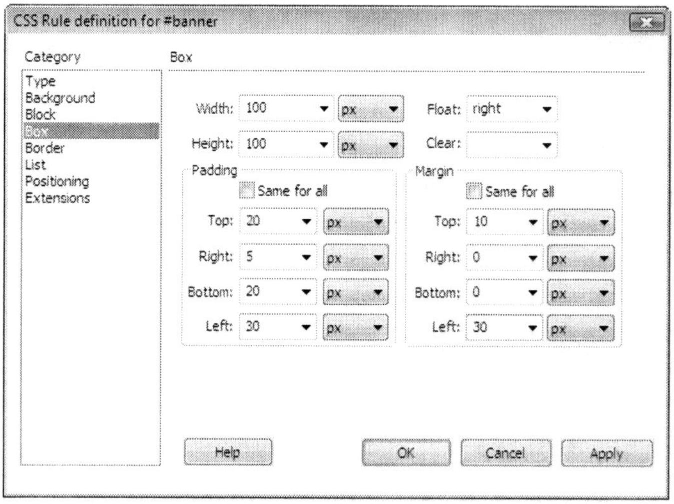

Figure 9-10: *Use the Box category to define the dimensions of a style, to position an object on the page, and to add space between the styled object and other objects around it.*

Be careful with the height property. Many designers turn to this property to provide precise control over page elements. Unfortunately, height is tricky to control. If you've set a specific height for a sidebar that contains text, and you later add more text, you can end up with text spilling outside the sidebar—this can also happen if a visitor increases the text size in his browser. Because Internet Explorer 6 (and earlier versions) handles these instructions differently than other browsers, you can end up with inconsistent and strange results in different browsers. In other words, set the height of an object only if you're *sure* the content inside will never get taller—for example, if the contents are images only.

- **Float.** If you want to move an object to the left or right side of a page and have other content wrap around it, use the Float property. Of course, that's been most of the point of this chapter, so you probably understand this property by now. However, there's one important point to keep in mind: Floating an object doesn't necessarily move it to the side of the page or the browser window. A floated object merely goes to the left or right edge of what's called its "containing block." If you float a div to the left of the page to create a sidebar, and then insert an image into the sidebar and float that image right, the image goes to the right edge of the sidebar, *not* the right edge of the page. In addition, if you float multiple elements, they can often end up sitting beside each other—this technique is used to create four-column layouts, where each column is floated next to the other.

- **Clear.** Clear *prevents* an element from wrapping around any object with a right or left Float property. This property can come in handy when you want to force an element to appear *below* a floated object instead of wrapping around it. The classic example with float layouts is a page's footer (the area at the bottom of the page usually containing contact information and a copyright notice). If a page has a particularly long left-floated sidebar, the footer can move up the page and wrap around the sidebar. In this case, the bottom of the sidebar is at the bottom of the page, and the footer is somewhere in the middle. To fix this problem, simply create a style for the footer that includes a value of *both* for the clear property. This style forces the footer to drop below both left-floated and right-floated elements. (If you merely want something to drop below a left-floated element, but still wrap around anything floated right, choose the *left* option; to clear a right-floated element, choose *right*.) In other words, if you ever see page content appear next to a floated element instead of underneath it, use the *clear* property on that content to make it go beneath the float.

- **Padding.** Padding is the gap that separates the content of the styled tag—such as a paragraph of text or an image—and its border (see page 231). If you put a 1-pixel border around an image and want to add 10 pixels of space between the image and the border, type *10* into the top padding box, and then choose "pixels" from the pop-up menu. Turn off the "Same for all" box if you wish to set the padding around each edge separately; then, type values into each of the four boxes.

Warning: Unfortunately, Internet Explorer 5 for Windows doesn't handle the "Box" model correctly. If you set the padding or borders of a style, Internet Explorer displays the element smaller than other browsers, ruining your Web page's layout. Although IE 5 is nearly extinct (thank goodness), if you still have visitors using IE 5 to view your site, you can find more information on this problem and a clever workaround. Visit *http://css-discuss.incutio.com/?page=BoxModelHack*.

- **Margin.** The margin is the outermost space surrounding an element (Figure 9-11). It surrounds the border and padding properties of the style, and lets you add space between elements. Use any of the values—pixels, percentages, and so on—that CSS supports.

Padding, margins, borders, and the content inside the styled tag make up what's called the CSS Box Model, as described in Figure 9-11. Margins and padding are invisible. They also have similar effects: 5 pixels of left padding adds 5 pixels of space to the left edge of a style; the same happens when you add a 5-pixel left margin. Most people use margins to put space between elements (for example, between the right edge of one column and left edge of an adjacent column), and padding to put space between an element's border and its content (like moving text within a column away from a borderline surrounding the column). Because you can't see padding or margins (just the empty space they make), it's often difficult to know if the gap between, say, the banner at the top of your page and the main area of content is caused by the style applied to the banner or the main area.

You also can't always tell if any extra space is caused by a padding or a margin setting. Dreamweaver includes a helpful diagnostic tool (see Figure 9-12) that lets you clearly see these invisible properties.

When you select a <div> tag that has margin or padding properties set, Dreamweaver draws a box around that div, and adds slanting lines to indicate the space occupied by margins and padding (Figure 9-12 shows this box and lines in action).

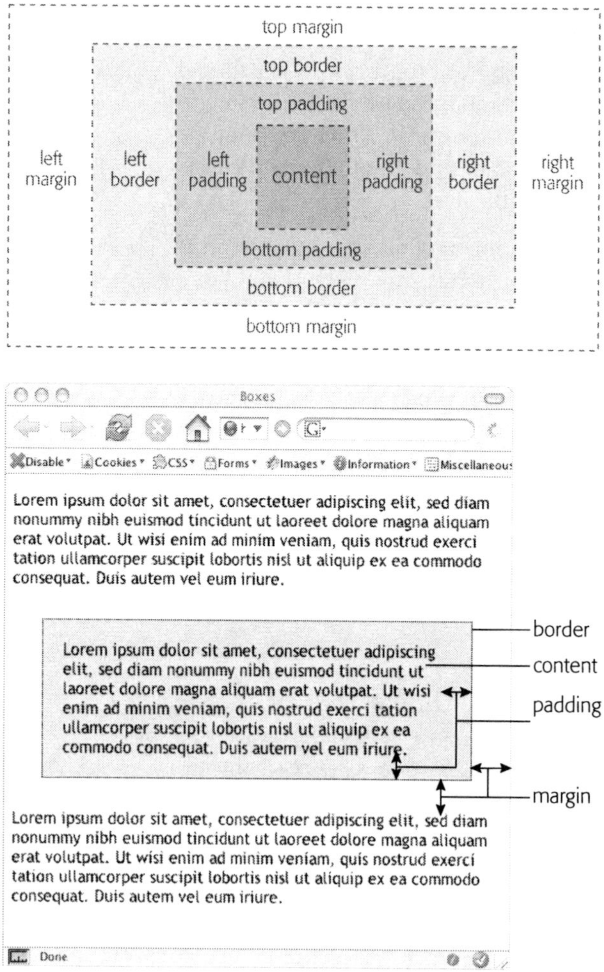

Figure 9-11:
In the CSS Box Model, every style is composed of multiple boxes, one inside the other. Each box controls certain display properties of the style. The outermost box of a style is called the margin. It controls the space between the border of the style and any other objects around the styled object, such as images, paragraphs, or tables; padding is the space between the border and the content itself (the innermost box). The area within the border, which includes the content and padding, may also have a background color. Actually, the background color is drawn underneath the border, so if you assign a dashed or dotted border, the background color appears in the gaps between the dots or dashes.

Margins appear outside padding, and are represented by lines that slant *downward* from left to right; padding appears inside the margin, and is represented by lines that go *upward* from left to right. In Figure 9-12, the area that contains the main information is enclosed in a <div> tag with an ID style named *mainContent* applied to it. When that div is selected (the tag selector in the lower-left corner of the document window is great for this), Dreamweaver highlights the margins and padding values that are defined in that ID style. As you can see, there's a considerable amount of margin on the right edge, a smaller amount of margin at the top edge, and a small amount of padding (20 pixels) applied to the top, left, and right edges.

If you find these visual aids confusing, you can turn them off via the Visual Aids menu in the document window (see Figure 9-12), or by choosing View → Visual Aids → Layout Box Model. These same steps turn the margin and padding visual aids back on.

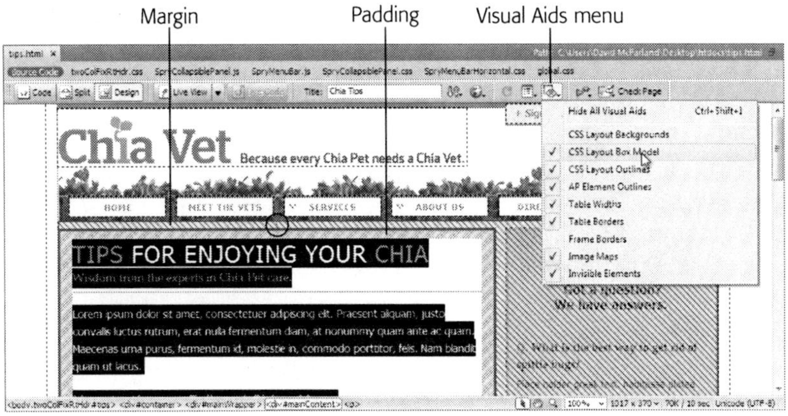

***Figure 9-12:** In addition to displaying the space occupied by margins and padding, the CSS Layout Box Model's visual aids indicate the vertical and horizontal center point (circled in this figure) of the <div> tag.*

Dreamweaver's CSS Layouts

You'll find yourself contending with many details when building CSS-based layouts. You need to understand the intricacies of the CSS Box Model, as well as the sometimes bizarre behavior of floats. In addition, different browsers handle some CSS properties in different ways, which sometimes means a design that looks great in Firefox completely falls apart in Internet Explorer 6. (Remember, even though much of the Windows-loving world has upgraded to IE7, there are still plenty of folks cruising around the Web in IE6 jalopies.) Fortunately, Dreamweaver is ready to give you a helping hand with 32 "CSS Layouts" to get you started.

CSS Layouts aren't finished Web page designs. They don't have graphics, fancy text, drop-down menus or any whiz bang features. They're simply basic designs that are intended to lay the foundation for your design talents. Each layout is a simple HTML file and a (not quite so simple) style sheet. Each design works in all current browsers and each design's hand-crafted CSS code irons out the many wrinkles presented by troublesome browsers (most notably Internet Explorer 6). In other words, instead of spending a day stretching and sizing your own canvas, a Dreamweaver CSS layout is like going to the art store and buying a ready-made and primed canvas so you can get busy painting.

Creating a new CSS layout page takes just a few steps:

1. **Choose File → New.**

   This is the same first step you take when creating any new Web page. The New Document window appears (Figure 9-13). You can also use the Ctrl+N (⌘-N) keyboard shortcut to open this window (however, it's possible to disable this keyboard shortcut as described on page 46; you might want to do that if you'd rather skip this clunky window whenever you just want a new, blank Web page).

2. **Choose Blank Page from the left column, and the type of page you wish to create in the Page Type column.**

   Usually, you'll select HTML from the page type category, since most of the time you'll be creating regular Web pages. However, if you're creating one of the database-driven pages described in Part 6 of this book, choose one of the page types listed in the bottom half of this column (PHP, ColdFusion, and so on).

Note: The Page From Sample category in the left column of the New Document window (see Figure 9-13) isn't very useful. In Dreamweaver CS4, Adobe removed most of the page designs since they used outmoded Web design techniques. All that's left in that category are a few CSS style sheets (you can do better), and a few designs for frame pages—a technology that you're better off avoiding.

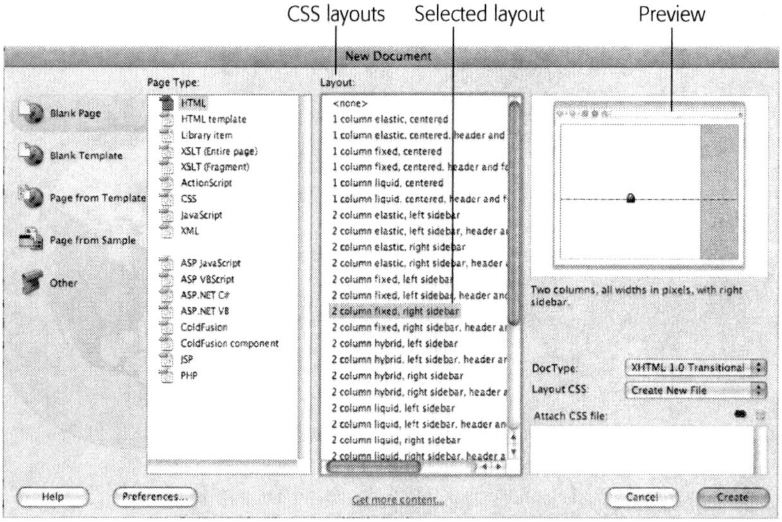

***Figure 9-13:** This dialog box lists Dreamweaver's different types of ready-made CSS Layouts. For example, "2 column fixed, right sidebar" indicates a design with 2 columns: the main content column on the left, and a thinner sidebar (for supplementary info like links) on the right. The design also sports a fixed width and has no header or footer. A preview of the selected layout appears in the top right of the window; a short description below the preview provides more detail on how the layout works.*

3. **From the Layout column, select a page layout.**

   This is where the fun begins. As you've read before, choose <none> here to create an empty Web page. The other options, however, let you choose one of 32 different CSS-based layouts. Basically, you decide how many columns you want (1, 2 or 3), whether there should be a header and footer on the page (like a banner at the top or a copyright notice at the bottom), and the type of Web page layout (fixed width, liquid, or elastic).

   This last choice relates to the kinds of Web page layouts discussed on page 331. For example, a fixed width design maintains a constant overall width no matter what the width of the visitor's browser window. Dreamweaver refers to some layouts as "hybrid"—meaning that the different columns use different width types. For the layouts Dreamweaver supplies, this means the main column is "liquid" (it resizes as the browser window resizes), while any sidebars are "elastic" (meaning the sidebars change width only when a visitor changes the font size of her browser). A preview in the top right of the New Document window contains a set of visual codes to help you understand how the different layouts behave, as explained in Figure 9-14.

4. **Choose a DocType from the DocType menu.**

   Here's where you decide which type of HTML/XHTML you wish to use for the page. It's the same option you faced when creating a new, blank Web page, as described on page 44. You're safe going with the default option of XHTML 1.0 Transitional.

5. **From the Layout CSS menu, select where to store the layout's CSS code.**

   Each Dreamweaver CSS Layout requires its own style sheet containing all of the styles you need to make the layout work. When creating a new page from a CSS layout, you have several options for where to store that style sheet. The "Add to Head" option creates an internal style sheet in the HTML file that Dreamweaver's about to create. Most of the time, you don't want this option, since external style sheets are more efficient (see page 113 for an explanation).

   You can also store the CSS layout styles in a new, external style sheet. Choose Create New File to let Dreamweaver create a new external CSS file and store the necessary CSS rules there. You'll choose this option when you're first using one of Dreamweaver's CSS layouts to create a new page. This will create a separate file with all the necessary CSS to control the layout of the page. If you want to add another page to your site using a layout (for example, a 2-column fixed design with a header and footer) you've already used, then read on.

   The "Link to Existing File" option sidesteps the entire process of creating new CSS styles. This option assumes you already have the appropriate styles defined in another external style sheet. Choose this option if you've previously created a Web page using the same type of CSS layout. Say you've earlier created a two-column fixed layout using a Dreamweaver CSS Layout. At that time, you saved

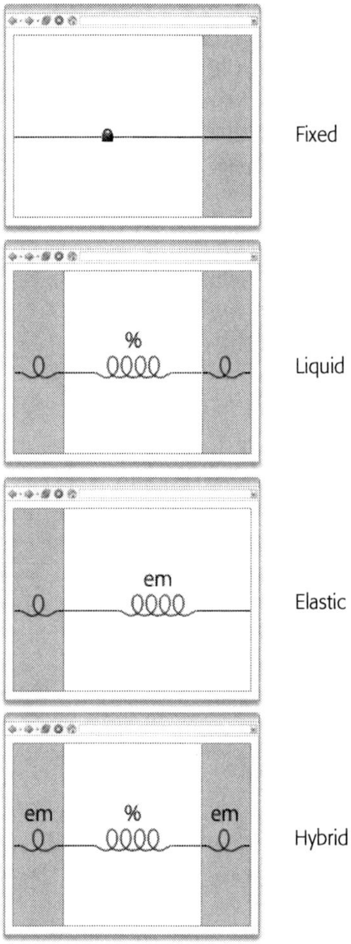

Figure 9-14:
The layout preview displayed in the New Document window visually identifies the type of CSS layout you've selected. A small lock icon indicates a design that's "fixed" (top): The width of each column is set using pixel values, and doesn't change when the browser window is resized. The % symbol indicates a liquid design (second from top): Column widths are defined using percentage values that change based on the width of the browser; a wider browser window means wider columns. These designs fill the entire width of the browser. The word "em" in the preview window identifies an elastic layout, where column widths are defined with ems (second from bottom). Elastic designs are very much like fixed width designs: Their widths don't change when you resize the browser window. However, if a visitor changes the size of his browser's font size, the width of each column changes (columns get wider if the font size is increased, thinner if the font size is decreased). With a hybrid design (bottom), the center column is liquid, but the sidebars remain a set width, defined in ems.

the necessary styles into an external style sheet, and saved that style sheet to your site. Now, you want to create a *new* two-column fixed layout page, so you follow steps 1-4 above. At this point, an external style sheet with the styles you need already exists, so you can choose "Link to Existing File", and then proceed to step 6 to link the external style sheet already on your site.

Keep in mind, however, that each CSS Layout has its *own* style sheet. So if you create a two-column fixed layout page, and then you want to create a three-column liquid layout page, you can't just link to the style sheet Dreamweaver created for the two-column layout. In other words, whenever you create a new *type* of CSS layout (two-column fixed, three-column liquid, and so on), choose the Create New File option, so Dreamweaver can create the appropriate styles in a new external style sheet.

Tip: You don't need to go through these steps each time you want to create a new page using a CSS layout you've used before. Suppose you want to build a site that's got 40 Web pages and each Web page has a two-column fixed layout. Instead of going through the New Document dialog box (and the steps listed here) for *each* of those pages, just use the New Document dialog box once to create the initial page, and then choose File → Save As, to save a copy of that design for the next two-column page you wish to create. Better yet, use Dreamweaver's Template tool described in Chapter 19 to manage pages with the same layout.

6. **Click the "Attach Style Sheet" button to attach any external style sheets to the page (see Figure 9-15).**

   This is an optional step, but if you've already got an external style sheet that you're using to format the pages of your site, now's the time to link to it. In addition, if you chose "Link to Existing File" in the previous step, you have to link to the external style sheet containing the styles to create the particular layout type. The process of linking to the external style sheet is the same as with any Web page, as described on page 125.

Note: If, when creating a new Web page, you link to an external style sheet as described in step 6, Dreamweaver may pop-up a warning message box that says something about needing to save your Web page in order to correctly attach the style sheet. You can safely ignore this message. In fact, turn on the "Don't show me this message again" checkbox, so that you can skip this annoying message in the future.

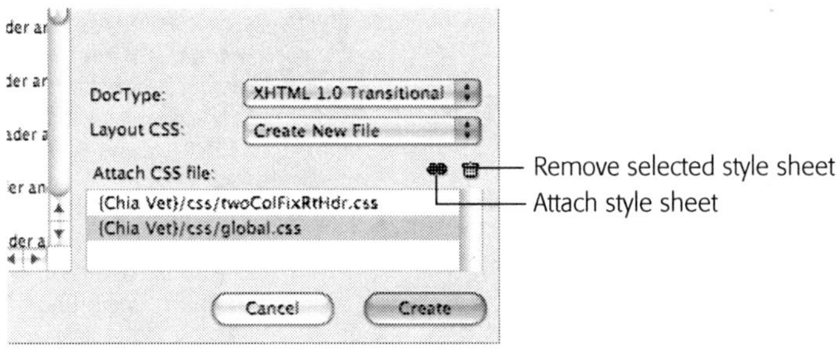

Figure 9-15: *You can attach more than one external style sheet when creating a CSS-based layout page: You might have one that defines the basic look of headlines, text, images, and other elements on your site, another that controls the layout of columns, and a third "printer" style sheet to dictate how the page will look when printed (see page 322).*

7. **Click the Create button to bring your new Web page to life.**

   If you selected the Create New File option in step 5, Dreamweaver now asks you to name the new style sheet, and select where in the site you wish to save it (this is just like when you create a new external style sheet, as described on page 125). Dreamweaver suggests names for the CSS files for each of its layouts—such as *twoColFixRtHdr.css* for a two column, fixed design with a right sidebar and a header and footer. You can change the name if you like, but the name Dreamweaver suggests is descriptive.

After all of that, you end up with a page with basic structure, and some "dummy" text to fill in the different areas of the page (see Figure 9-16). Don't forget to save and then title the page (see page 44 if that's news to you).

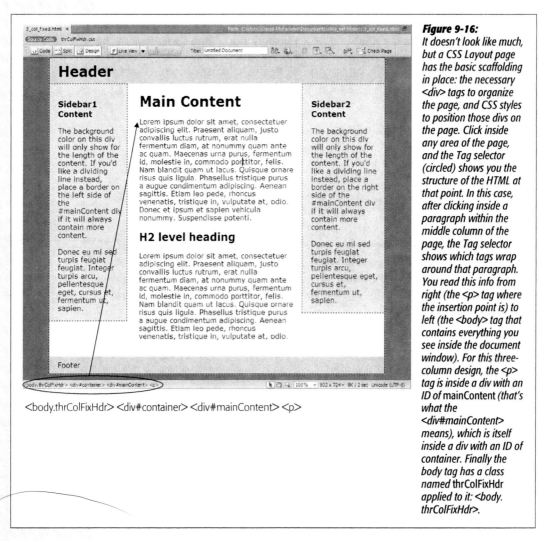

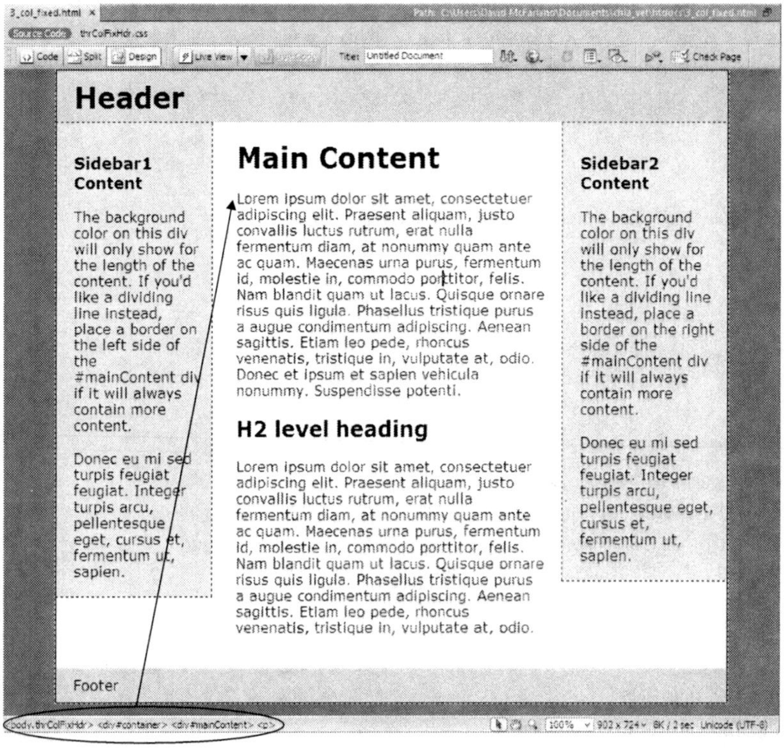

<body.thrColFixHdr> <div#container> <div#mainContent> <p>

Figure 9-16: *It doesn't look like much, but a CSS Layout page has the basic scaffolding in place: the necessary <div> tags to organize the page, and CSS styles to position those divs on the page. Click inside any area of the page, and the Tag selector (circled) shows you the structure of the HTML at that point. In this case, after clicking inside a paragraph within the middle column of the page, the Tag selector shows which tags wrap around that paragraph. You read this info from right (the <p> tag where the insertion point is) to left (the <body> tag that contains everything you see inside the document window). For this three-column design, the <p> tag is inside a div with an ID of* mainContent *(that's what the <div#mainContent> means), which is itself inside a div with an ID of container. Finally the body tag has a class named* thrColFixHdr *applied to it: <body.thrColFixHdr>.*

The Structure of Dreamweaver's CSS Layouts

Dreamweaver's CSS Layouts are made up of a handful of page elements: Some pages have a header and a footer, some have one or two sidebars, and all of them have an area for your page's main content. Each section is represented by a <div> tag, and each div has its own ID applied to it. A layout's accompanying style sheet has predefined ID styles that control where the different divs are placed on the page.

To keep the CSS layouts consistent, Dreamweaver uses the same ID names for every layout (see Figure 9-17). The ID for the <div> tag containing the main content on the page is *mainContent*; if the layout has a sidebar, its ID is *sidebar1*; if there's a second sidebar, it's called *sidebar2*. The header div is ID'ed with *header*, while the div at the bottom of the page is *footer*. There's one more <div> that surrounds all the other divs: Its ID is *container*.

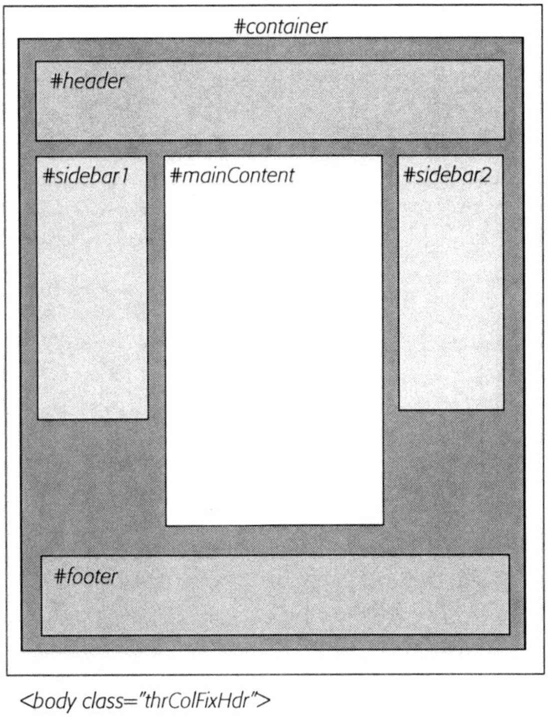

Figure 9-17:
Each Dreamweaver CSS Layout's basic structure is the same. Several <div> tags identify the various layout regions of a page. Each div has its own unique ID name, which is then controlled by an ID style in the design's style sheet.

You may be wondering: If all the CSS layouts share the same names for their layout divs, how do we end up with different types of designs like fixed, liquid, or elastic? That's determined by the <body> tag. The <body> tag of each CSS layout has a class applied to it: This class defines the basic type of page (two-column fixed, three-column liquid, and so on). For example, the page pictured in Figure 9-16 is a fixed-width, three-column design with a header and footer. The class applied to the <body> tag defines that page's style: In this example (just look at the tag selector in the image), the class is named *thrColFixHdr*.

The first sidebar in Figure 9-16 "knows" it's 150 pixels fixed width and floated to the left because a descendent selector in the layout's style sheet tells it so. You'll recall from page 301 that a descendent selector lets you format a particular tag based on the tags it's nested inside. In this case, the descendent selector *.thrColFixHdr #sidebar1* applies to the tag that has the *sidebar1* ID applied to it, but only when that tag is inside *another* tag with the class *thrColFixHdr*. In other words, this style applies only to a sidebar for a three column, fixed-width layout with a header and footer. How's that for precision?

This well-thought out structure has several benefits. First, since all of these layouts—regardless of whether you're using a single column or two columns, with or without a footer, and so on—share the same ID names, you can create a single style that will format all of those particular page areas on any CSS layout page. For example, say you want the header region on your site to have a baby-blue background color. All you need to do is create a style named *#header* with the desired background color and add it to a stylesheet that's shared by the other pages in the site. Regardless of whether the page is a two-column fixed design or a three-column liquid design, the header area will be baby blue.

Tip: When using more than one Dreamweaver CSS layout design, create a sitewide stylesheet–name it *global.css* or *site.css*–and attach that stylesheet to every page on your site. Then add all of the styles that are common between your pages to that style sheet.

In addition, you can target styles that apply only to one type of layout by creating a descendent selector that uses the class name applied to that layout. For example, for a two-column liquid layout with a left sidebar, the body tag has the class *twoColLiqLt* applied to it. If you wanted to create a style that only applied to the sidebar for that type of layout, you could create a descendent selector named *.twoColLiqLt #sidebar1*. That style will now only apply to the sidebar for that type of layout.

Modifying Dreamweaver's CSS Layouts

The basic look of a freshly minted Dreamweaver CSS Layout doesn't have much to recommend it: grey sidebars, header, footer, a dark grey page background, and overly large text. One of the first things you want to do with a new layout is remove some of the Dreamweaver formatting. In addition, you might want to tweak some of the basic layout properties, like the width of a fixed-width design, or the width of sidebars and main columns.

Making General Changes

One of your first tasks should be to remove (or change) the gray background colors for the sidebar and other page elements (unless you really like gray, in which case your job is a lot easier). This task generally means editing the style defined in the Dreamweaver-supplied style sheet. You've already learned several methods for editing styles—like double-clicking the style's name in the CSS Styles panel (page 126), or using the Properties Pane (page 305). The real trick is locating the correct style to edit. Here's the fast method:

FREQUENTLY ASKED QUESTION

Paying Attention to Conditionals

I've noticed that when I create a page using a Dreamweaver CSS Layout, the page has some weird-looking code just above the beginning <body> tag. What's that about?

If you go into Code view of a CSS Layout page, you'll notice some grayed-out HTML that begins with *<!--[if IE 5]>* and ends with *<![endif]-->*. It's grayed out because Dreamweaver treats this code like an HTML comment. HTML comments are mostly used by those who code their pages by hand. Their purpose is to let a Web designer leave notes about the page—like an explanation for why a chunk of HTML was added, a note to identify which div a particular closing </div> tag belongs to. Dreamweaver and other browsers ignore HTML comments.

However, this particular HTML comment, while ignored by every other browser, has special significance for Internet Explorer. HTML comments that begin like this *<!--[if IE]>* are actually secret messages, called *conditional comments*, intended just for Internet Explorer. Conditional comments are a way of sending HTML, CSS, and JavaScript to Internet Explorer only; you can even send special HTML to particular versions of Internet Explorer (for example, *<!--[if IE 5]>* sends HTML to just version 5 of Internet Explorer.

In the case of Dreamweaver CSS Layouts, these conditional comments provide additional CSS styles that make sure Internet Explorer correctly displays the layout (in other words, Dreamweaver is saving you the hair-pulling experience of creating a design that looks great in Firefox, but breaks in Internet Explorer). In fact, in a Dreamweaver CSS Layout there are two conditional comments: one that targets IE 5 and another for other versions of IE. If you don't care about IE5, which is almost gone from the planet, then remove everything from *<!--[if IE 5]>* to the first *<![endif]-->*.

However, don't remove the second conditional comment—it begins with <!--[if IE]>— which ensures that the layout works in IE 6 and IE 7. In addition, you'll see that for layouts that include a sidebar, these comments include CSS code which sets a top padding for each sidebar. If you adjust the padding in the main CSS file as described next, then make sure you change the padding in this conditional comment—see the box on page 356 for more on this.

For a short tutorial on conditional comments, visit: *www.javascriptkit.com/howto/cc2.shtml*.

1. **On the CSS Styles panel, click the Current button** (see Figure 9-18, right).

   If the Styles panel isn't open, choose Window → CSS Styles. The Current view in this panel shows the styles and properties that affect whatever's selected in the Document window.

2. **Make sure that, in the Rules Pane, the Show Cascade button is selected** (see Figure 9-18).

   The Show Cascade option lists all styles that affect the current selection in the order of the "cascade"—most specific style at the bottom, least specific at the top of the list (see page 314 for a refresher on the cascade and specificity).

3. **Highlight the div you want to format.**

   For example, if you want to reformat the header region, select the div with the headline text Header. You can select a div in a couple of ways:

   - Click inside the div, and then click the corresponding <div> in the Tag selector at the bottom left of the Document window (see Figure 9-18, left). For example, click inside the header and then click <div#header> in the Tag selector. This selects the div tag.

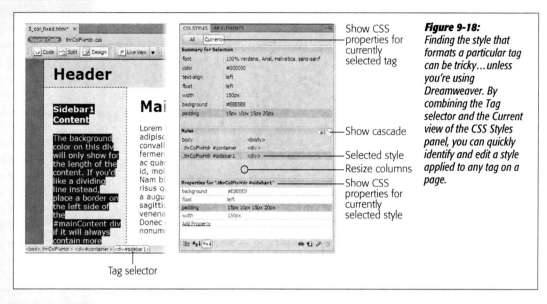

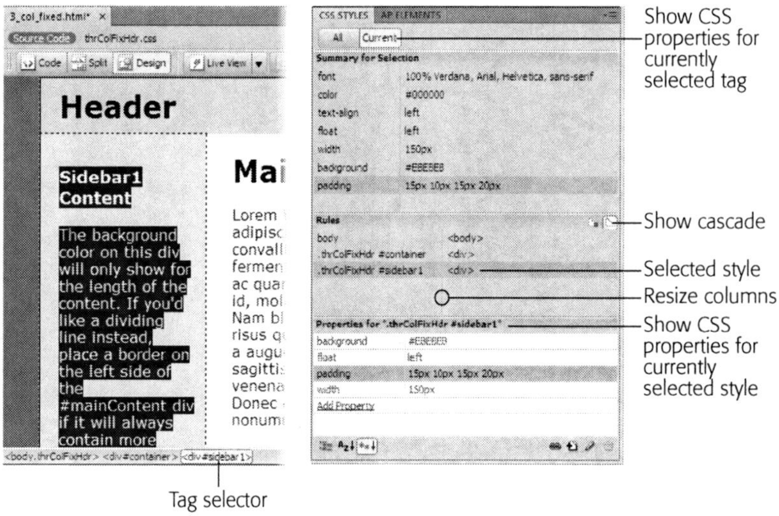

Figure 9-18: *Finding the style that formats a particular tag can be tricky...unless you're using Dreamweaver. By combining the Tag selector and the Current view of the CSS Styles panel, you can quickly identify and edit a style applied to any tag on a page.*

- Click inside the div, and then press Ctrl+A (⌘-A), or choose Edit → Select All. This selects the contents of the div, and highlights the div in the Tag selector. (Pressing Ctrl+A twice selects the <div> tag itself). To highlight a <div> tag that wraps around the div you clicked into, press Ctrl+A (⌘-A) more than once. To highlight the *container* div that surrounds the header, sidebars, main content, and footer, you can click the header region, press Ctrl+A twice to select the header, and then press Ctrl+A once more to highlight the *container* div.

After you highlight the div, its style appears in the CSS Styles panel's Rules pane. In Figure 9-18, selecting the sidebar div—*<div#sidebar1>*—from the Tag selector (left) selects that div's style—*.thrColFixHdr #sidebar1* in this instance—in the Rules pane (right). At this point you can use the Properties pane (directly below the Rules pane) to edit the style as described on page 305, or simply double-click the style name in the Rules pane to open the user-friendly Style Definition window.

Tip: The styles for Dreamweaver CSS Layouts use what's called CSS "shorthand properties." These combine several CSS properties under a single property name. For example, the values for *background-color* and *background-image* can be combined into a single property named *background*, while all four margins (top, right, bottom, and left) can be specified with just one property: *margin*. This makes for more compact styles, but it also means that in order to edit a shorthand property in the Properties pane, you need to know how to write the values yourself: Dreamweaver doesn't provide a color box, link button, or any of the other helpful tools used to set the values of a "longhand" property like *background-color*. In other words, unless you know CSS well, if you want to really make changes to a style, you're better off double-clicking the style's name in the Rules pane to access the much more user-friendly Rule Definition window.

Once you've selected a layout region on the page (header, sidebar, and so on), there are a few common changes you'll probably make:

- **Background colors.** To completely remove the gray background of a div, just delete the value next to the *background* property in the Properties pane. You can also double-click the style's name in the CSS Styles panel to open it for editing, and then select the Background category of the Rule Definition window, as described on page 233, to edit the color.
- **Padding.** The header, sidebars, and footer of a Dreamweaver CSS Layout include padding to add space from the edges of the layout region and the content inside. In many cases, this is a good thing: Designs can look cramped if text runs from edge to edge in a box. But if you want to completely fill the div, you must remove the padding. You might want to insert an image that fills the entire header region—say, a banner graphic that spans from side to side. Padding adds space between the graphic and the edge. Use the Properties pane to remove the padding (just delete the values that are listed), or double-click the style in the Rules pane to use the Rule Definition window. (Note that you may encounter some differences in the space given for the top padding in Internet Explorer vs. Firefox, Safari, or Opera. See the box on page 356 for the explanation.)
- **Text formatting.** You can modify the text and other content of the page to your heart's content. The earlier chapters in this book cover the techniques for formatting headlines, paragraphs, images, and links. However, when creating styles for these elements, use an external style sheet other than the one Dreamweaver uses for the layout styles. You can store these types of styles in a generic style sheet like *global.css*, instead of the layout-specific style sheet such as *twoColFixLtHdr.css*. See step 5 on page 347 for the reason.

Modifying Fixed Layouts

The width of any Dreamweaver fixed layout is 780 pixels. That width may be too wide or too narrow for your tastes. If you're designing for the cinema-screen audience, you might want a page that takes advantage of the wider screen, so you might bump the width to 900 pixels or more. In addition, you may want to change the widths of columns on the page. Here are a few key layout changes you may wish to make:

- **Page width.** The area of the page that includes the header, sidebars, and main content is fixed at 780 pixels. This setting is defined in the *container* div. Just select the div, and then change 780 to whatever width you want.
- **Column width.** The sidebar columns have a fixed width setting. Depending on the number of columns in the design, sidebars range in width from 150 to 200 pixels. Select the sidebar you wish to make wider or narrower, and then adjust its *width* property. The main content column—a div with the ID *mainContent*—doesn't have a set width; rather, its width is determined by its

FREQUENTLY ASKED QUESTION

Spacing Differences with IE

I've created a two-column layout. Why is the space between the top of the sidebar and the first paragraph of text different in Internet Explorer and Firefox?

Yes, Firefox and most other browsers can insert space above the first paragraph of text inside a div. That same space, however, doesn't appear in Internet Explorer. The fault lies with the paragraph's top margin (the same applies to headlines or any tag with a top margin). If the paragraph is at the top of the div, IE ignores its top margin. It figures you don't want the space there. Firefox and Safari, however, say, "Hey, there's a top margin. I'd better insert some extra space." The upshot is you get inconsistent spacing.

The easiest way to deal with this problem is to simply remove the top margin for headings and paragraphs. You could do this by creating a tag style for the <p> and headline tags that sets their top margin to 0 (see page 343 for more on setting margins). You can adjust the style's bottom margin to provide space between paragraphs or between a paragraph and whatever tag follows it.

Another approach is to create a class style that has 0 top margin and apply it to the first tag in the div. This style removes the top margin for just that tag, and eliminates the difference between the browsers. (For this trick to work, you need to make sure the class is more *specific* than any other style affecting the tag. See page 314 for more on the gory details of specificity.)

Some of Dreamweaver's CSS Layouts introduce another wrinkle. In some cases, Dreamweaver inserts CSS code using an IE Conditional Comment which adds extra padding to the top of sidebars (see the box on page 353 for information on conditional comments).

For example, if you look into the HTML that Dreamweaver creates for a two column fixed design, you'll see this:

```
<!--[if IE]>
<style type="text/css">
/* place css fixes for all versions of IE
in this conditional comment */
.twoColFixLtHdr #sidebar1 { padding-top:
30px; }
.twoColFixLtHdr #mainContent { zoom: 1; }
/* the above proprietary zoom property
gives IE the hasLayout it needs to avoid
several bugs */
</style>
<![endif]-->
```

The highlighted code above (the line with *.twoColFixLtHdr #sidebar1*) includes an instruction to add 30 pixels of space between the top of the first sidebar and the top of the first tag inside the sidebar. If you adjust the sidebar's padding in the main style sheet (as recommended on page 355), you'll probably find that the space at the top of the sidebar is different in IE and Firefox. You can either delete this line entirely and use one of the methods suggested above (like removing the top margin from the first element in the sidebar) or edit the code inside this conditional comment until the design looks good. For example, if you see more space in IE than Firefox, change *padding-top: 30px* to something smaller like *padding-top: 20px* until the display matches up between the browsers.

left and right margin values. A left value is used to indent the main content div from a left sidebar, while a right margin value indents the div from a right sidebar. Don't set a width value for this div—it can lead to some weird cross-browser display problems. Instead, adjust the left and right margins until the main content area is the width you wish.

Tip: If you often use Dreamweaver CSS layouts, you may frequently make the same adjustments. For example, you might always remove the padding and background color and adjust the column widths of your designs. Instead of doing that over and over, you can edit the default HTML and CSS files Dreamweaver uses when creating a new blank CSS layout page. You'll find them on Windows in the C:\Program Files\Adobe\Adobe Dreamweaver CS4\configuration\BuiltIn\Layouts folder, and on the Mac in the Applications → Adobe Dreamweaver CS4 → configuration → BuiltIn → Layouts folder. You can also clean up this folder by deleting designs you don't use. *Just make sure you back up the folder before you do anything to the files inside. And then, back up your new designs so that if you ever have to reinstall Dreamweaver, you have a backup of your modified templates.*

Modifying Liquid Layouts

Liquid layouts adjust to the width of the browser window. Columns grow wider as visitors widen the browser window, and shrink when the browser window shrinks. However, you can still control the relative widths of the page:

- **Page width.** Although the page content adjusts its width with a liquid layout, Dreamweaver's default styles make the page content 80 percent of the window width. In other words, there's always some empty space on either side of the container div (10 percent, to be precise). If you want to remove this space to make the page fill the entire width of the browser window, edit the *#container* style: Just delete the width entirely, don't set its width to 100 percent. (Doing so can cause the page to appear a little *wider* than the browser window, forcing visitors to scroll right to see all of the page's content. See the box on page 360 for an explanation.)
- **Column width.** As with fixed layouts, the sidebar widths are set using the width property, and the main content area is controlled by the left and right margin properties of the *#mainContent* style. The only difference is that the width and margin values are set using percentages. So to make the left sidebar wider, change its style's width from 24% to 28%, for instance.

Modifying Elastic Layouts

Elastic layouts are put together very much like fixed width layouts, but instead of using pixels to define the width of the page content and columns, they use ems (see page 139 for a discussion of ems). Use the same instructions on page 355 for adjusting the widths on fixed layouts.

You need to keep one thing in mind when working with elastic layouts, however. The actual onscreen width of an em depends not only on the visitor's browser settings, but also on the font size defined for the <body> tag on the page. The normal style sheet Dreamweaver spits out for elastic designs sets the font to 100%. If you make this smaller, the page width and columns get thinner. Make the <body> tag's font size larger, and the page and columns get wider.

In addition, the width of a column also changes if you set a font size for the column's style. Suppose you want all the text inside the left sidebar to be 80% the size of other text on the page: One technique would be to define the font size for the *#sidebar1* style to 80%; then the tags inside this div will inherit that size (see page 312 for how this works). Unfortunately, that action also defines the size of the em for that div, so its width gets smaller. To get around this, set font sizes for the styles formatting the tags *inside* the <div>.

Absolute Positioning

Beyond float-based layouts, CSS's other main technique for placing elements on a page, absolute positioning, lets you specify an exact position on a page for any element. But before you start thinking you've found page layout heaven, keep in mind that the Web is a fluid environment that's difficult to control with pixel level precision. If a visitor increases the font size in her browser, the enlarged text may spill out of your carefully crafted layout. In addition, it's nearly impossible to force a footer to the bottom of a page that's laid out using absolute positioning (a trivial task with float-based layouts). That's why most CSS layouts use floats and the techniques discussed at the beginning of this chapter.

Note: In versions of Dreamweaver prior to CS3, absolutely positioned elements were called *layers*; Dreamweaver now refers to them as either AP Divs or AP Elements: *AP* meaning ***absolutely positioned***. Any tag can take advantage of CSS positioning, but most often you'll apply positioning to a <div> tag that contains text, images, or other content. In this book, the term AP Div refers to any absolutely positioned div. However, because any tag (a link, unordered list, or just a simple paragraph) can be absolutely positioned, you'll see the term AP Element used to describe any tag that's absolutely positioned.

That's not to say you shouldn't use absolute positioning. It's great for moving small elements, like a logo, image, or short set of links to a position on the page; and it's the only way to have one element overlap another element on a page (see the circled image in Figure 9-19). As long as you don't try to dictate the exact width, height, and position of every design element, you'll find absolute positioning powerful and helpful.

The CSS Positioning Properties

Several CSS properties are specifically meant for positioning elements on a screen. You'll find them under the Positioning category of the CSS Rule Definition window (Figure 9-20).

Positioning type

Normally, tags are positioned on the screen in the order they appear in the HTML: What appears first in the HTML appears at the top of the browser window. Similarly, HTML at the end of Web page files appears at the bottom of the browser

Figure 9-19:
One unique aspect of CSS positioning is its ability to place an element on top of other page content. In this example, a small button with a Chia Kitten sits above the page to the left of the headline–it even appears to be hanging off the left edge of the page.

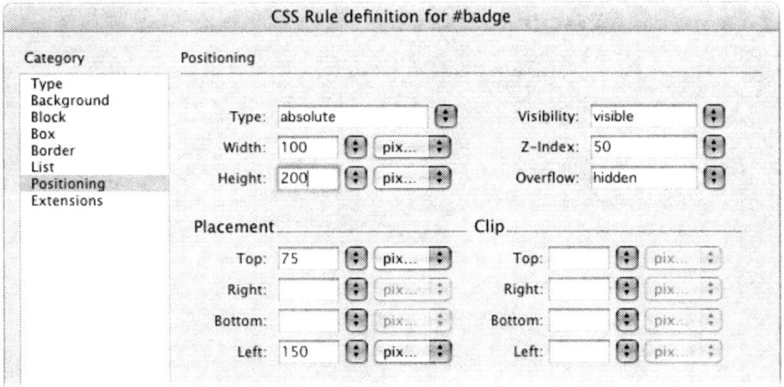

Figure 9-20:
Dreamweaver gives you easy access to the many CSS Positioning properties available. You'll never need to set all of them, and a few, like the settings found in the Clip section of this dialog box, aren't often used by most Web designers. (See page 365 for details on the Clip section's woeful lot in life.)

window. In Figure 9-21, the top left image shows a headline, followed by a paragraph of text, followed by a headline, an image, and another paragraph. The order in which they appear in the HTML is the order displayed by the browser: top to bottom.

The CSS *position* property, however, lets you alter how a styled element appears on the screen by assigning one of four available position types: *absolute, relative, static,* and *fixed.*

- **Absolute is the most common option.** It lets you place a tag anywhere on a page, regardless of where the HTML code for the tag is positioned within the Web page's HTML. The top-right image in Figure 9-21 shows a graphic of a sticky note. The graphic is absolutely positioned. Even though in the HTML the

FREQUENTLY ASKED QUESTION

When Width Doesn't Equal Width

In my style sheet, the CSS width *property of one of my styles is set to 150 pixels. But when I preview the page in a Web browser, the <div> tag I applied the style to is much wider than 150 pixels. Is this a bug with my browser?*

No, you're browser's fine. The problem lies with the difference between the CSS *width* property and the final calculated width of an element onscreen. The width you see onscreen is the sum total of several separate CSS properties, not just the *width* property. The *width* property merely defines the width of the content area of the style—the place where the text, images, or other nested tags sit.

The actual width—that is, the amount of screen real estate given by the Web browser—is the *total* of the widths of the left and right margins, left and right padding, left and right borders, and the *width* property. So say you've created a style that has a width of 100 pixels, 10 pixels of padding on all four sides, a 2 pixel border, and 20 pixels space on the left margin. While the space dedicated to the content inside the style is 100 pixels, any tag with this style will have an onscreen width of 144 pixels: 100 (width) + 10 (left padding) + 10 (right padding) + 2 (left border) + 2 (right border) + 20 (left margin).

To make matters just a bit more confusing, Internet Explorer 5 on Windows gets the whole thing wrong. That browser includes left and right padding and borders as *part* of the width property. In other words, page elements can appear a lot thinner in that browser than in others. Fortunately, Internet Explorer 5 is pretty rare these days, and you may find that none of your site's visitors even use that browser any more. But if you're one of the unlucky ones who still has to build Web pages to support IE 5, you can find out how to solve this dilemma here: *www.communitymx.com/content/article.cfm?cid=E0989953B6F20B41*.

The CSS height property and the final height of a style behave the same way. The onscreen height of an element is a combination of the height, plus top and bottom margins, padding, and borders (and yes, IE 5 gets this one wrong, too).

code for that image falls after the "Malorum Gipsum" headline, its visual placement is at the top (and even a little bit off the top) of the page. The space where the graphic appeared prior to positioning (top-left image) is now filled by the paragraph of text beneath the second headline.

In other words, the actual HTML code can go *anywhere* inside the <body> tag and still appear *anywhere* on the page—its location in the code has nothing to do with the positioning of the element on the screen. In addition, any element that's absolutely positioned is removed from the normal flow of the page—other tags on the page aren't even "aware" the AP element exists.

After you select this option, use the Placement properties (see page 364) to specify a specific position.

- **The relative option lets you position a tag relative to its position in the HTML.** When you choose this option and then assign, say, a left and top placement, the positioned element appears relative to where it appeared prior to any positioning. The bottom left image in Figure 9-21 shows the same sticky note graphic positioned using the relative property. The top and left placement values (page 364) are the same as for the top-right image; in this case, however, the graphic is placed relative to its old position below the second headline. Another side effect is that the space formerly taken up by the image remains: Notice that the last paragraph doesn't try to fill up the space where the graphic was. There's still a big empty area.

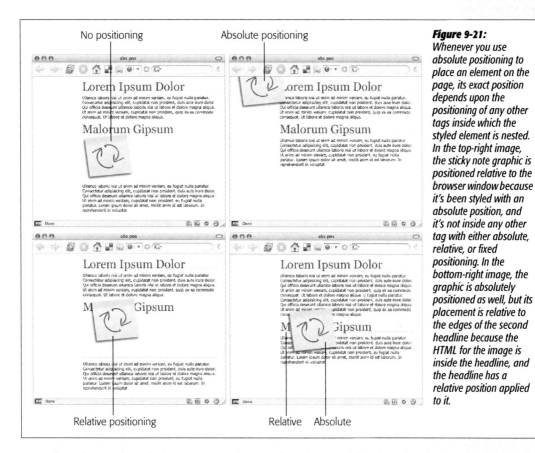

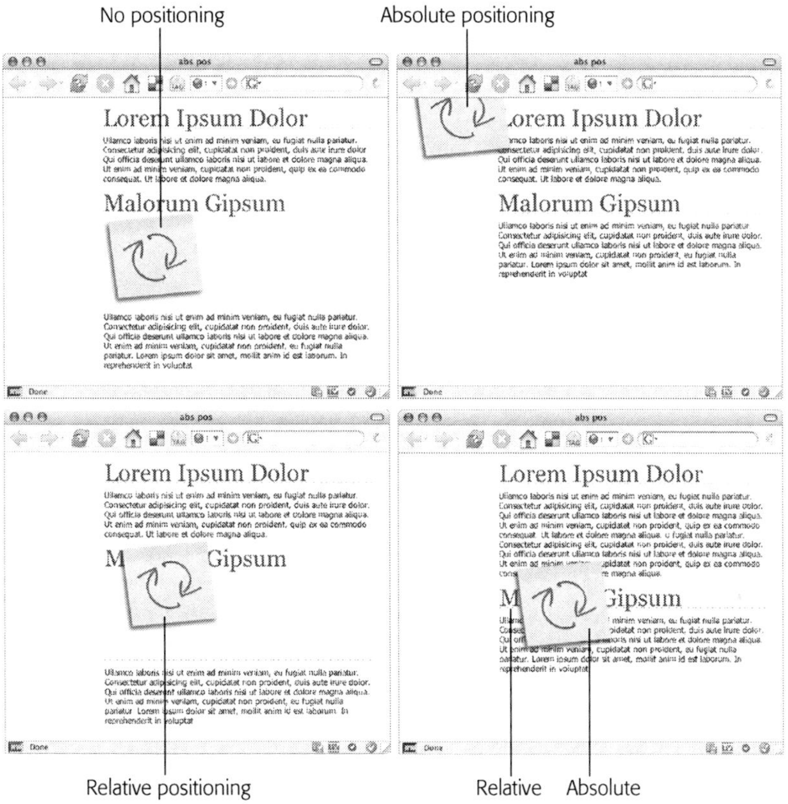

Figure 9-21: *Whenever you use absolute positioning to place an element on the page, its exact position depends upon the positioning of any other tags inside which the styled element is nested. In the top-right image, the sticky note graphic is positioned relative to the browser window because it's been styled with an absolute position, and it's not inside any other tag with either absolute, relative, or fixed positioning. In the bottom-right image, the graphic is absolutely positioned as well, but its placement is relative to the edges of the second headline because the HTML for the image is inside the headline, and the headline has a relative position applied to it.*

At first glance, the *relative* option might seem less than useful. After all, what's the point of positioning something on the page, just to leave a big empty ("I *was* here") space? In many cases, you don't actually apply relative positioning to the element you want to position. You apply it to a tag that wraps *around* the element you wish to position, in order to create a new set of coordinates for an absolutely positioned element to use.

Say you placed an image inside a headline, and you want the image to appear on the left edge of that headline. If you simply position the image in an exact spot in the browser window on the left edge of the headline tag, you're taking your chances. If the headline moves (say you add some new body text), the absolutely positioned image stays glued to its assigned spot. Instead, what you want to do is position the image *relative* to the headline tag, so that when the headline moves, the image moves with it. Look at the bottom right image of Figure 9-21. In this case, the headline (Malorum Gipsum) has a relative position applied to it, and the sticky note graphic (which is inside the headline tag) has an absolute position. Even when, later on, you add a little more text to the top of the page (thereby forcing the headline to move down), the sticky note travels along for the ride.

- **Static positioning is the normal behavior of HTML.** Static simply means the content follows the normal top-down flow of HTML. Why would you want to assign an element static positioning? The short answer: You probably never will.
- **Fixed is similar to the "fixed" value of the CSS *attachment* property used to lock a background image in place** (see page 235). This option "fixes" the AP div in place in the browser window. When you scroll down the page, the AP div doesn't move, but remains in an exact position in the browser window. It's a cool option with exciting possibilities...and absolutely *no* support in Internet Explorer 6 and earlier versions. You may want to experiment with the "fixed" option in Internet Explorer 7 or Firefox, but when building a Web site you actually want the whole world to see, skip it.

Width and height

These properties, logically enough, set the width and height of the element. You can use any of the available CSS measurement systems like pixels, ems, and percentages. In most cases, when you want precise control over the dimensions of your tags—that is, a page element that's *exactly* 200 pixels wide and won't change even if the visitor changes the size of her browser window—use pixels. However, if you want the element to resize as the visitor resizes her browser window, use percentages. In this way, you can make a style that's 50 percent the width of the browser window, no matter the size of the window.

Note: The Width and Height properties available under the Positioning category of the CSS Rule Definition window are identical to the options with the same name under the Box category (see Figure 9-10). Also note that CSS calculates the total width of a style as the Width value *plus* any borders, margins, or padding (see the box on page 360 for more). Same is true for the height of an element.

Visibility

If left to its own devices, Dreamweaver makes the contents of all tags visible on the page, so you'll usually leave this property blank. After all, if you put something on your page, it's usually because you want people to see it. But there are situations in which you may want to make a certain tag (and its contents) invisible in your visitors' Web browsers.

The power of the Visibility property becomes clear when you start using Dreamweaver behaviors or your own JavaScript programming; in these instances, you can make previously hidden tags visible again, on cue. Imagine a Web page where you've superimposed many hidden divs on a diagram of a car engine. Moving the mouse over a part of the image makes the div visible, revealing text that describes the corresponding engine part. (Page 590 shows you how to create this effect.)

Tip: The CSS *display* property also has an option to hide an element: *none* (see page 146). The benefit of using the *display* property over the *visibility* property is that an element whose display is set to none literally disappears from the page; whereas an element with visibility of *hidden* can still take up space on the page–it just leaves a hole where it normally would appear. After hiding an element by setting its display property to *none*, you can make it visible again by changing the display property to *block* (for example, using the Change Property behavior discussed on page 595). That property makes the element visible again.

The options for this property let you make the AP div "visible" (which is how all tags start out anyway); make it "hidden," so it doesn't appear until you make it visible; or make it "inherit" the visibility of another AP div. (The inheritance option can be useful with nested AP divs, as discussed on page 374.)

Z-index

Welcome to the third dimension. Absolutely positioned tags are unique in the world of Web elements, because they "float" above (or even behind) a Web page, and can overlap each other, completely or partially.

If you were awake in high school algebra, you may remember the graphing system in which the X axis specified where a point was in space from left to right and the Y axis specified where the point was vertically from top to bottom. And if you were awake *and* paying attention, you may remember that the Z axis denoted a point's position in *front-to-back* space. When you draw a three-dimensional object on this type of graph, you need to use all three axes: X, Y, and Z.

The Z-index of an absolutely positioned element doesn't make your Web page *appear* three-dimensional; it simply specifies the "front-to-backness" of overlapping AP elements. In other words, the Z-index, represented by a number in the Z-index field, controls the stacking order of AP elements on a page.

Note: The Z-index setting doesn't always work when you try to overlap certain kinds of content, like pull-down menus, radio buttons, or other form elements. It also may not work with plug-in content like Flash or Java applets. This is because Web browsers let other programs control the display of these items.

The page itself lies behind all AP elements, and the AP elements stack up from there. In other words, the higher the Z-index number, the higher the AP elements, so that an AP element with a Z-index of 4 appears *behind* an overlapping AP div with a Z-index of, say, 7.

Z-index numbers have no relation to the actual number of absolutely positioned items on a page. You can have three AP elements with Z-indexes of, say, 2, 499, and 2000, if you choose. You'd still just have three AP elements, one on top of the other in ascending order. Spacing your Z-index numbers in this somewhat arbitrary manner is helpful, since it lets you insert divs between already positioned divs as you develop your page without having to renumber the Z-indexes of all your AP divs.

Overflow

Suppose you create a square AP div that's 100 × 100 pixels. Then you fill it with a graphic that's 150 × 162 pixels—that is, larger than the AP div itself.

You've already seen how a table cell reacts to this situation: It simply grows to fit the content inside it. AP divs, however, are more (or less) flexible, depending on your choice of Overflow option in the Property inspector. The following choices let you decide how browsers handle the excess part of the image:

- **Visible** makes the AP div grow to accommodate its contents. If you don't choose another setting, then AP divs grow to fit automatically.
- **Hidden** chops off the excess. In the example above, only the top-left 100 × 100 pixels of the image would be visible.
- **Scroll** adds scroll bars to the AP div, so that a visitor can scroll to see all of the AP div's contents. It's like having a miniature browser window embedded in the page. This feature offers an interesting way to add a small, scrollable window within a Web page: Imagine a small "Latest Company News" box, which visitors can scroll to read the text inside without disturbing anything else on the page.
- **Auto** adds scroll bars to an AP element *only* if necessary to accommodate its oversize contents.

In Design view, if you've selected any option besides "Visible", you see the AP div's set dimensions—for example, 100 pixels by 100 pixels. Any content outside that area—the overflow—isn't displayed.

You may have content you'd like to edit that's part of the overflow—like the "Latest Company News" box example above. Dreamweaver does give you an easy way to edit any of that hidden content—just double-click the AP div. Doing so expands the AP div (just as if you'd selected the visible option) so you can edit it. To reset the AP div back to its original dimensions, right-click (Control-click) the AP div and, from the shortcut menu that appears, select Element View → Hidden.

Placement

These properties let you specify an absolutely positioned element's position, which is, after all, the whole point of AP divs. The four properties control where each of the four edges of the AP div begin. Setting the Top box to 200 pixels places the top of the AP div 200 pixels down the screen, whereas the Bottom option identifies where the bottom of the AP div starts. Similarly, the Left and Right properties set where the left edge and right edge of the AP div should appear.

Frequently, you'll use a combination of the Width property (page 362) with the Top and Left or Right properties. To place a 150-pixel-wide sidebar 200 pixels from the top of the page and 15 pixels in from the left side of the page, you'd set the Width property to 150 pixels, the Top property to 200, and the Left property to 15 pixels. The Right property is also handy. Say you want to put a 200-pixel-wide sidebar at the right side of the page. Since you don't know the exact width of a visitor's browser window—580 pixels, 1200 pixels?—you can't know ahead of time how far the AP div needs to be from the left edge of the window. Instead, you can set the Right property to 0—if you want the sidebar to touch the right edge of the page. If you want to indent the AP div 20 pixels from the right edge of the window, type *20*.

While it's technically possible to use Left and Right positioning simultaneously—say, placing an AP div 50 pixels from the left edge and 20 from the right—Internet Explorer doesn't support this combination. Instead, use absolute positioning with one edge of the AP div and a margin setting (see page 343) for the other edge.

Positioning isn't quite as straightforward as it may seem. The exact position of a positioned div is a combination of not only these position values, but also what type of placement you choose for the AP div—absolute or relative. As noted earlier, with relative positioning, the numbers you type for Top or Left, for instance, are calculated based on where the AP div already appears in the HTML code and on the screen. So setting the Top property to 100 pixels doesn't place the AP div 100 pixels from the top of the browser window; it places it 100 pixels from where it would appear on the screen based on the HTML code.

Absolute positioning, however, lets you place an AP div at an exact spot on a page. So setting the Top and Left properties for an absolutely positioned AP div to 100 and 150 pixels *will* place that AP div 100 pixels from the top of the browser window and 150 pixels from the left edge.

Note: There's one additional wrinkle to absolute positioning. For a div that's nested inside another div that has either a "relative" or "absolute" position setting, position values are calculated based on the position of the *parent* div. If you have one AP div that's located 300 pixels from the top of the page, an absolutely positioned AP div nested inside *that* AP div with a Top position setting of 20 doesn't appear 20 pixels from the top of the page. Instead, it appears 20 pixels from the top of the parent AP div, or, here, 320 pixels from the top of the page.

Clip

The Clip property can hide all but a rectangular piece of an AP div. In most cases, you should avoid this property, since it's rarely useful, and it's also a waste of precious bandwidth.

Suppose you put a large graphic into an AP div, but you want to display only one small area. You *could* use the Clip property, but the Web browser still has to download the *entire* graphic, not just the clipped area. You're much better off just preparing the smaller graphic at the right size to begin with (see Chapter 6). The kilobytes you save may be your own.

You can use JavaScript to *move* the clipping area, creating an effect like a spotlight traveling across the AP div. Although that may be a more useful purpose for the Clip property, Dreamweaver unfortunately offers no tools for performing this maneuver.

The four clipping settings—top, right, bottom, and left—specify the positions of the clipping box's four edges. In other words, these indicate the borders of the visible area of the AP div.

Adding an AP Div to Your Page

In most cases, you'll position a <div> tag that contains a variety of HTML elements—images, paragraphs, headlines, and so on. For example, to place a series of links on top of the banner at the top of the page, you could wrap those links in a div tag and position that div. Dreamweaver gives you a couple of ways to insert an absolutely positioned div:

- **Use the Insert Div Tag tool** discussed on page 335. You can start out by selecting already existing content on the page, or just click where you wish to add a new absolutely positioned div. Either way, you either need to create an ID style first (with the positioning properties discussed above), and then select that style from the ID menu of the Insert Div Tag window (Figure 9-6); or, alternatively, create the ID style by clicking the New CSS Style button on the Insert Div Tag window (Figure 9-6).
- **Use the Draw AP Div tool.** Dreamweaver provides a tool to draw a div tag directly onto the document window. Page 369 shows you how this tool works.

Unless you add a background color or border to your AP div, it's difficult to identify its boundaries. To make working with AP divs easier, Dreamweaver provides visual cues in Design view, as shown in Figure 9-22, and explained in the following list:

- **AP element marker.** The gold shield with the letter C (huh?) represents the position in the underlying HTML where the code for the AP div actually appears.

  These markers aren't normally visible. To see them, you must turn them on in the Preferences window: Press Ctrl+U (⌘-U) to open the window, click the Invisible Elements category, and make sure the "Anchor points for AP elements" option is turned on.

  While HTML objects generally appear in the document window in a top-to-bottom sequence that mirrors their order in the HTML source code, the position of AP divs *doesn't* depend on where the AP div-creating code appears in the page's HTML. In other words, it's possible to have an AP div appear near the bottom of the final Web page, whereas the actual code may be the first line in the body of the HTML page (see Figure 9-22 for more detail).

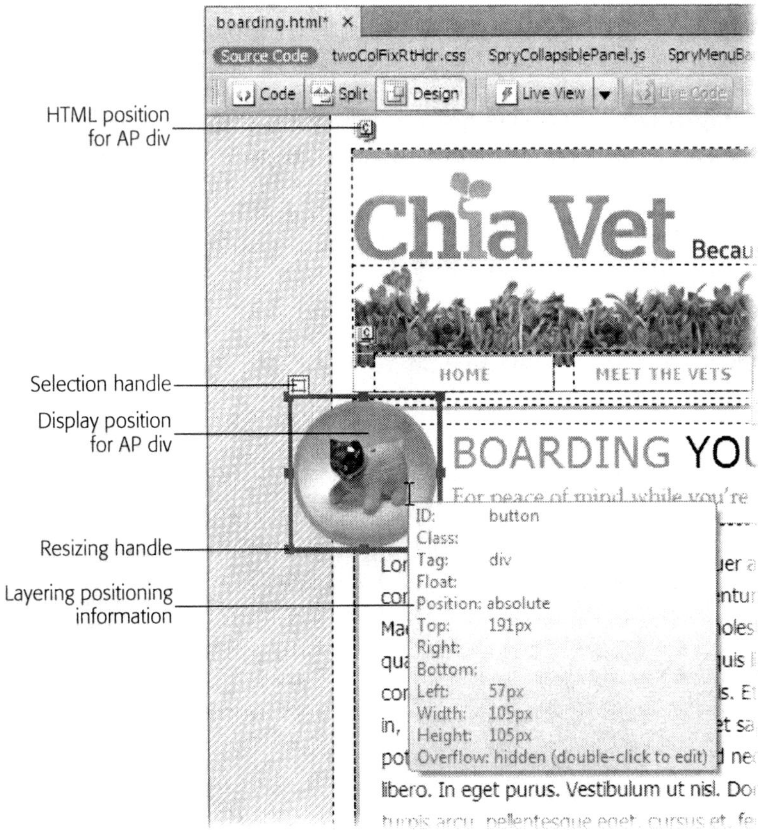

***Figure 9-22:** Unlike other page elements, AP elements don't appear in the same place on the page as their HTML code. Here, a div containing the Chia Kitten button, hovers over a headline, and several hundred pixels below the top of the page. The HTML for the div, however, is the first bit of HTML on the page (and is therefore represented by the AP element marker in the top-left corner of the page).*

If you want to move the HTML of the AP div, drag the shield icon. Since it's absolutely positioned, this element appears in the same place on the page, but its code moves to a new location within the page's HTML. Note, however, that dragging the selection handle (described next) visually moves the div, but leaves the HTML in the same location.

That distinction often confuses Dreamweaver users. For instance, be careful not to drag an AP div marker (the gold shield which represents the HTML code) into a table. Putting an AP div inside a table can cause major display problems in some browsers.

That said, an AP div can *visually overlap* a table, or even appear to be inside a cell; just make sure the gold AP div marker itself isn't inside a cell.

Tip: The AP div marker (shield icon) takes up room on the screen and can push text, graphics, and other items out of the way. In fact, even the thin borders that Dreamweaver adds to divs take up space in the document window, and the space they occupy may make it difficult to place AP divs precisely. The keyboard shortcut Ctrl+Shift+I (⌘-Shift-I) hides or shows invisible items like AP div markers. The Hide All Visual Aids option from the Document toolbar does the same thing (see Figure 9-23).

- **Selection handle.** The selection handle provides a convenient way to grab and move an AP div around the page. The handle appears when you select the AP div, or when you click inside the AP div to add material to it. The handle lets you move the position of the AP div without changing the position of its code (see "Moving AP Elements" on page 372). Behind the scenes, Dreamweaver updates the CSS code (the left and top position properties described on page 364) automatically…pretty nifty.

- **AP element outline.** When an absolutely positioned element isn't selected, a thin, gray, 3-D border outlines each AP element. Like the AP div marker and selection handle, it's there only to help you see the boundaries of the AP element, and doesn't show up in Web browsers. You can turn it on and off, but to turn it off, you need to make sure two options in the View → Visual Aids menu don't have checkmarks next to their names: AP Element Outlines and Layout Outlines. You can also use the Visual Aids menu in the document window (see Figure 9-23).

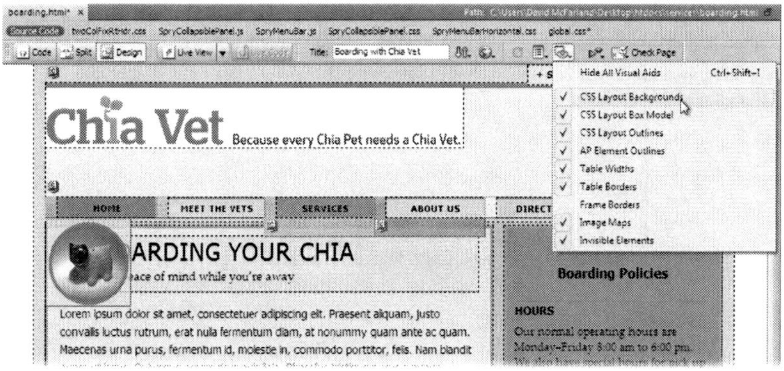

***Figure 9-23:** Choices 2–5 in the Visual Aids menu provide visual cues to help you with CSS layouts in Design view. The CSS Layout Backgrounds option—selected here—lights up each <div> tag on a page with a hideous, randomly selected background color. It also highlights any element whose display property is set to "block," (see page 146) or that uses either absolute or relative positioning (see page 358). Both the CSS Layout Outlines and AP Element Outlines options draw a gray line around positioned elements. In addition, the Layout Outlines option draws a black border around <div> tags that aren't absolutely positioned. The CSS Layout Box model option is discussed on page 344.*

Note: If one AP element overlaps another, the top AP element–the one with the higher Z-index, as described on page 363–has a solid outline; the lower absolutely positioned element's outline appears as a dashed line where the top AP element overlaps it.

- **AP div positioning summary.** If you select an AP div and hover your mouse over that div, Dreamweaver pops up a box with information about how that AP div is positioned (see Figure 9-22), including the name of the ID style or class style, what type of positioning is used, the dimensions of the AP div, and so on. This box provides a quick summary of relevant positioning information, and gives you a bird's-eye view of the CSS properties defining the AP div's placement on the page.

Drawing AP Divs

Dreamweaver wouldn't be Dreamweaver if it didn't give you several ways to perform a certain task, like creating an absolutely positioned div. You can create an AP div as described above, or turn to two methods designed specifically for adding AP divs to a page: You can drag to create an AP div freehand, or use a menu command to insert a full-blown, complete AP div. Your choices are:

- **Use the Draw AP div tool.** The Draw AP div tool is on the Insert panel, in the Layout category (see Figure 9-5). Click the AP div button, and then drag the + cursor diagonally in the document window to create a box—the outline of the AP div.

Tip: For accurate drawing, you should hide Dreamweaver's visual aids (like the AP div border and selection handles), which take up space and move AP divs slightly out of position in Design view. Ctrl+Shift+I (⌘-Shift-I) does the trick.

- **Use a menu command.** To insert an AP div at the insertion point, choose Insert → Layout Objects → AP Div.

  If you don't like the looks of the default AP div that Dreamweaver inserts, choose Edit → Preferences (Dreamweaver → Preferences), select the AP Elements category, and then adjust the default properties there. Add a background color, for example, or increase the AP div's size. From then on, you can instantly create your favorite kind of AP div using the Insert → AP div command.

However, Dreamweaver's AP div tools have one drawback: They create internal ID styles with generic names like apDiv1, apDiv2, and so on. So you don't get to take advantage of the byte-saving virtues of an external style sheet until you move the styles to an external style sheet. Fortunately, Dreamweaver's CSS management options make this maneuver simple, as described on page 308. In addition, you have to take a second to rename these AP divs to something a little more understandable—like changing apDiv1 to *button*. (Your new friend, the AP Elements panel, makes this easy to do, as shown in Figure 9-24, and explained in the next section.)

The AP Elements Panel

The AP Elements panel (Figure 9-24) helps you manage absolutely positioned elements in a document. To open it, choose Window → AP Elements, or press F2. It's called the AP Elements panel instead of the AP Divs panel because any tag that has an ID style and which has its position property set to absolute (see page 358) appears here. So if you absolutely position a single paragraph, its ID appears in this panel. The panel's three columns provide information on each element:

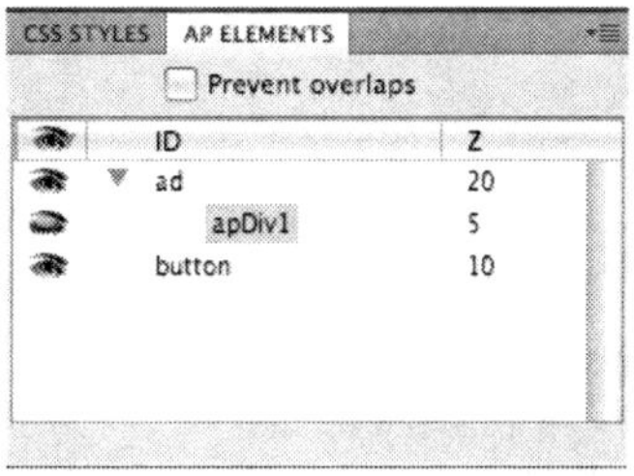

Figure 9-24:
The AP Elements panel lets you name, reorder, and change the visibility of AP elements. Turning on the "Prevent overlaps" checkbox ensures you can't position or drag an AP div on top of another. This feature is intended to make it easy to convert an AP div layout to a table-based layout using the Modify → Convert → "AP divs to Table". Don't do it! This creates horribly bloated HTML that easily falls apart as you add, edit, and adjust content on the page.

- **Visibility.** To change an absolutely positioned element's visibility property (page 362), click in the column with the eye icon next to the element's name. An open eye indicates that the property is set to visible; a closed eye, hidden. No eye icon at all represents the factory setting: The element is still visible on the page, it's just that the CSS visibility property isn't set.

- **AP element ID.** If you use Dreamweaver's Draw AP div tool, Dreamweaver gives the AP div a generic ID name—like apDiv1. If you created the div yourself, you probably already came up with a pretty good ID like *siteTools* or *navBar*. But if you want to change that name (or provide a more descriptive name for a Dreamweaver-created AP div), double-click the AP element ID name, and then type a new name. (AP element names are just ID names, so they must start with a letter, and can contain only letters and numbers. As Dreamweaver is quick to remind you, spaces and other punctuation aren't allowed.)

  Clicking an item in the AP Elements panel, by the way, is another way to select that element in the document window.

Warning: Don't rename an AP element's ID if you've already used it in a Dreamweaver behavior like the Show/Hide Elements action (see page 592). JavaScript uses those names to "talk to" the absolutely positioned elements. If you change its ID in the AP Elements panel, Dreamweaver doesn't automatically update the name in the JavaScript code in your page. The behavior, therefore, no longer works. In that case, you need to edit the behavior using the new ID name.

- **Z-index.** As you read about back on page 363, the Z-index provides a third dimension to absolutely positioned elements, letting them overlap one another. To change the Z-index of an element, click the number in the Z column, and then type another number. Software veterans will find that Dreamweaver's AP

Elements panel works just as it does in Photoshop or Fireworks: You can drag the name up or down the list to the desired position. The AP element at the top of the list (highest number) is in front of all other AP elements, while the AP element at the bottom of the list (lowest number) appears behind all other AP elements.

However, keep in mind the following slightly quirky behavior: When you place an AP element inside another AP element (page 374), the nested element shares the same z-index as the AP element it's inside. For example, in Figure 9-24 the HTML for the div with the ID *apDiv1* is placed inside the div tag with the ID *ad*. (You can tell this is the case because *apDiv1* is indented underneath the *ad* element in the panel.) The z-index for the *apDiv1* element is only 5, but it will still appear *above* the *button* element with the z-index 10. That's because the *ad* element has a z-index of 20, and, since the *apDiv1* element's HTML is *inside* the ad element, it's z-index is also 20, relative to other elements on the page. So why does the nested element have a z-index at all? It doesn't have to, but if you have multiple absolutely positioned elements nested inside another AP element, the z-index determines how those nested elements are stacked relative to each other.

Modifying AP Element Properties

Once you've added an AP div, you don't need to go back to the CSS Rule Definition window to edit most of the AP div's positioning properties. Using the Property inspector, you can rename it, resize it, move it, align it with other AP divs, and set many other properties.

But first, you have to select the AP div using one of these methods:

- Click the AP div's name in the AP Elements panel (Figure 9-24).
- Click the AP div's selection handle (Figure 9-22).
- Click the AP div's border. The border turns red when you've moved your mouse into the proper position.
- Click the AP element marker that indicates the HTML code for the absolutely positioned item (Figure 9-22). (Out of the box Dreamweaver hides these markers, since they can get in the way of your design work; to show them, see page 367.)

And if those aren't enough ways to select an AP div—Adobe's programmers never sleep—you can also Shift-click an absolutely positioned element. This technique also lets you select multiple AP divs, so that you can set the properties of (or align) many AP divs at once. If you're working in an AP div or have an AP div selected, Shift-clicking another AP div selects them both. You can continue to Shift-click to select additional AP divs. (Shift-click a second time to deselect a selected absolutely positioned element.)

Resizing Absolutely Positioned Elements

When you select an AP element, eight handles appear around the edges of the AP div (see Figure 9-22). You can drag any of these handles to change the AP div's dimensions. The corner handles resize both the width and height simultaneously.

You can also use the keyboard to resize an absolutely positioned element. First, select the AP element, and then do one of the following:

- Press the Ctrl (⌘) key, and then press the arrow keys to change the AP element's size by one pixel. The up and down arrow keys adjust the AP div's height; the left and right arrows affect its width.
- To change the size *10* pixels at a time, press Ctrl+Shift (⌘-Shift), and then press the arrow keys.

For better precision, use the Property inspector to set an exact width and height for the AP element (see Figure 9-25). Type values in the W and H boxes to change the width and height of the AP element, respectively. You can specify any unit of measurement that CSS understands: px (pixels), pc (picas), pt (points), in (inches), mm (millimeters), cm (centimeters), em (height of the current font), ex (height of the current font's x character), or % (percentage)—see page 137 for more on CSS measurement units. To pick your measurement unit, type a number *immediately* followed by the abbreviation for the unit. For example, type *100px* into the W box to make the AP div 100 pixels wide. Don't leave out the measurement unit—px, em, or %, for example—or browsers won't display the correct dimensions of the AP element.

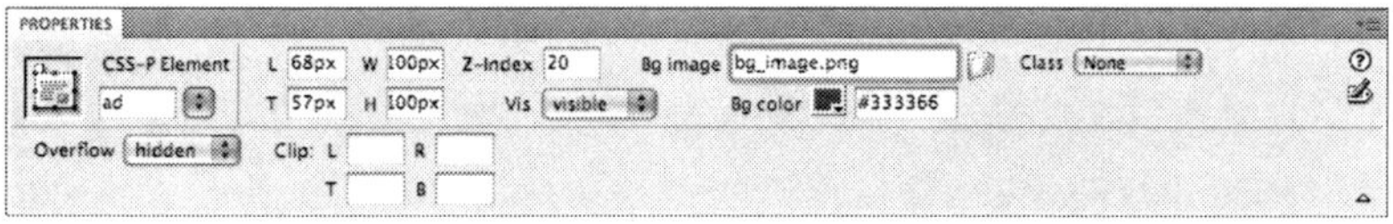

Figure 9-25: *The Property inspector controls many AP element properties (although some require editing CSS styles).*

Another benefit of using the Property inspector is that Dreamweaver lets you resize multiple AP divs at once. Shift-click two or more AP divs to select them, and then type new widths and heights. Dreamweaver sets all selected AP divs to these same dimensions.

Moving AP Elements

Moving an absolutely positioned element is just as simple as resizing it. Drag any border of the element, or the AP element's selection handle (shown in Figure 9-22). (Avoid the eight resize handles, which change the size of the AP div when dragged.)

For less speed but greater precision, you can move an AP element using the keyboard. First select the element and then do one of the following:

- To move an AP element one pixel at a time, press the corresponding keyboard arrow key.

- Press Shift while using an arrow key to move the element 10 pixels at a time.

As you'd guess, you can also control an AP element's placement by using the Property inspector (see Figure 9-25). Dreamweaver measures an AP div's position relative to the left and top edges of the page (or, for nested AP divs, from the left and top edges of a parent div with a position property set to either absolute or relative). The Property inspector provides two boxes for these values: L specifies the distance from the left edge of the page to the left edge of the selected AP div; T specifies the distance from the top edge of the page to the top of the selected AP div.

Note: You can't edit an AP div's Right or Bottom positioning properties from the Property inspector. For these properties, edit the style using one of the methods discussed on page 364.

To position an AP div using the Property inspector, select the div (for example, by clicking the div's border or selecting its name in the AP Elements panel), and then type distances in the L and T boxes. You can use any of the units of measurement mentioned previously. You can even use negative values to move part or all of an AP div off the page entirely (offstage, you might say), which is something you'd do if you intended a subsequent animation to bring it *onstage*, into the document window (Dreamweaver no longer has tools for creating animations, but with a little bit of JavaScript you can add your own animations. For example visit *www.viget.com/inspire/fun-with-jquerys-animation-function/* for a few examples).

If you draw a 100-pixel-tall and 50-pixel-wide AP div, you can move it to the very top-left corner of the page by selecting it, and then typing *0* in both the L and T boxes. To position that same AP div so that it's just off the left edge of the page, type *–50px* in the L box.

Aligning AP Elements

At times, you may want to align several AP elements so that their left, top, bottom, or right edges line up with each other. Dreamweaver's Align command does just that; it can even make the width and height of selected AP elements the same.

To use this feature, select two or more AP divs (by Shift-clicking them), choose Modify → Arrange, and then select one of the following options from the submenu:

- **Align Left** aligns the left edges of all selected AP divs. In other words, it gives each AP div the same L property.
- **Align Right** aligns the right edges.
- **Align Top** aligns the top edges, so that the T properties are all set the same.
- **Align Bottom** aligns the bottom edges of the AP divs.
- **Make Same Width** sets the same width for all selected AP divs (in the W box in the Property inspector). **Make Same Height** does the same for the height of the AP divs.

The AP div you select *last* dictates how Dreamweaver aligns the AP divs. Say you have three AP divs—A, B, and C—and select them in order from A to C. You then align them to Left. Dreamweaver uses the left edge of AP div C (the last one you selected) as the value for the other AP divs.

Background Image and Color

To add a background image to the AP div, click the folder icon next to the Bg Image field, and then select an image from your site folder. As usual, Dreamweaver tiles the image, if necessary, until the entire AP div's filled with repeating copies of the graphic. (To adjust how or whether the image tiles, you'll need to edit the style using the normal CSS-style editing techniques; see page 233.)

Setting a background color is even easier. Just use the Bg Color box to select a color or sample a color off the screen.

Nesting AP Divs

Nesting doesn't necessarily mean that one AP div appears inside another AP div; rather, it means that the HTML for one AP div is written inside the code for another. The nested AP div itself can appear anywhere on the page. The main benefit of nested AP divs is that the *parent* AP div—the AP div containing the HTML of one or more other AP divs—can control the behavior of its *child AP divs.*

Suppose you create one AP div, and nest two AP divs inside it. If you move the parent AP div on the screen, the two child AP divs follow it, which gives you an easy way to move several AP divs in unison. Furthermore, the parent AP div can control its children's visibility. When you hide the parent AP div (see page 370), the nested AP divs also disappear (unless you've specifically set the nested AP divs' visibility property to *visible*).

Tip: Dreamweaver's factory settings hide a useful visual cue—"AP element" markers (see the "HTML position for AP div" marker in Figure 9-22). These markers identify where in the code the HTML for the AP div appears. Since a nested absolutely positioned element is a tag whose code appears inside another absolutely positioned element—like inside the parent's <div> tag—an AP element marker appears inside the parent AP div for each nested AP div. To turn on the AP element marker feature, press Ctrl+U (⌘-U) to open the Preferences window, click the Invisible Elements category, and then turn on the "Anchor Points for AP Elements" checkbox. You also need to make sure visual aids are turned on (as explained in Figure 9-23).

Here's how to create a nested AP div:

- While pressing the Ctrl (⌘) key, drag one AP div in the AP divs panel (see Figure 9-24) onto another AP div. The dragged AP div becomes the child of the AP div you drop it on, and its name appears indented in the AP divs panel, also shown in Figure 9-24.

To un-nest an AP div, drag it above or below the parent AP div in the AP divs panel. (Doing so places the code for the nested AP div directly before the opening <div> tag of the parent AP div.)

Tip: You can also un-nest an AP div, and gain more control over where the HTML for that AP div is written in the document, by dragging the AP element marker to a new spot in the document window. (This AP element marker isn't always immediately visible, however; see the preceding Tip.)

- Use the Insert Div Tag button on either the Common or Layout category of the Insert panel, or choose Insert → Layout Objects → Div Tag. In either case, the Insert Div Tag window appears (Figure 9-6). Select the name of the AP div you wish to nest inside another AP div; choose either "After start of tag" or "Before end of tag" from the first Insert menu; then choose the name of the parent AP div from the second menu.
- Click inside an AP div, and then choose Insert → Layout Objects → AP div. You get a new, nested AP div inside it.
- Drag the Draw AP Div *button* (see Figure 9-5) from the Insert panel's Layout category, and drop it inside an AP div on the page.

CSS Layout Tutorial

In this tutorial, you'll create a page using one of Dreamweaver's CSS Layouts. You'll then add content to the page, apply styles, and modify the design to meet the exacting standards of Chia Vet (see Figure 9-36).

Note: You need to download the tutorial files from *www.sawmac.com/dwcs4/* to complete this tutorial. See the Note on page 48 for more details.

Once you've downloaded the tutorial files and opened Dreamweaver, define a new site as described on page 42. Name the site *CSS Layout*, and select the Chapter09 folder (inside the MM_DWCS4 folder). (In a nutshell: choose Site → New Site. In the Site Definition window, click the Advanced tab, type *CSS Layout* into the Site Name field, click the folder icon next to the Local Root Folder field, navigate to and select the Chapter09 folder, and then click Choose or Select. Finally, click OK.)

1. **Choose File → New.**

   The New Document Window opens (see Figure 9-26).

2. **Select the "Blank Page" category in the left column; select HTML from the Page Type column, and select "2 column fixed, right sidebar, header and footer" from the Layout column.**

   You've selected a design that has two columns, a right-hand sidebar and a main content area on the left, with areas at the top and bottom of the page to hold a banner and copyright notice.

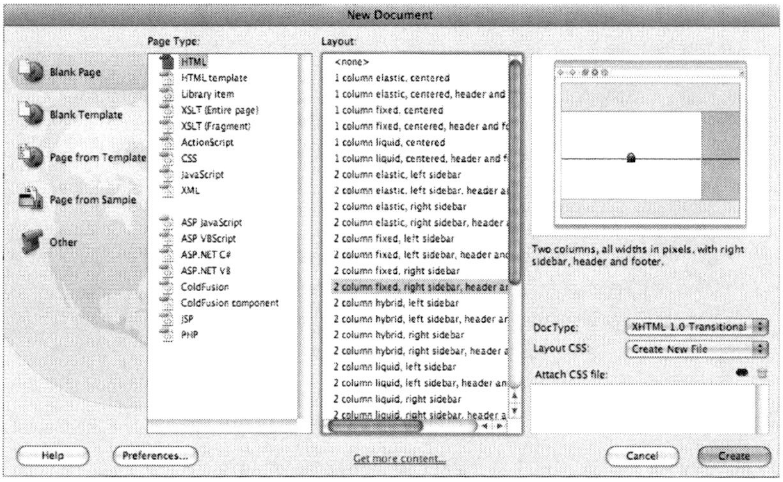

Figure 9-26: *Dreamweaver provides 32 CSS layouts organized by the number of columns each layout has.*

Next you need to tell Dreamweaver where to store the CSS required to make this design work.

3. **Make sure Create New File is selected in the Layout CSS menu.**

   This option tells Dreamweaver to create a new external style sheet with the required styles, and to link it to the new page Dreamweaver is about to create.

4. **Click the Create button.**

   The Save Style Sheet File As window appears. Before Dreamweaver creates a new Web page, you first have to save the external style sheet. Dreamweaver recommends a file name—*twoColFixRtHdr.css* in this instance. You can rename this file to anything you'd like, but the name Dreamweaver suggests is descriptive, if not particularly elegant.

5. **Click the Site Root button to navigate to this site's main folder, and then double-click the *css* folder to open it. Click Save.**

   Dreamweaver saves the file, and creates a new document. It's not much to look at yet, but you'll add your own design touches to this page in the steps ahead.

6. **Choose File → Save; click the Site Root button to move to the main folder for the site, and then save the file as *tips.html*.**

   Every page needs a title and the one Dreamweaver supplies—"Untitled Document"—isn't very helpful.

7. **Select and delete "Untitled document" in the Title box at the top of the Document window, and then type *Chia Tips*.**

   The first step after creating a page based on a Dreamweaver CSS Layout is to remove some of the formatting that Dreamweaver supplies. For example, to help you easily identify the header, sidebar, and footer, Dreamweaver adds a gray background to each of these elements. Unless you're designing a battleship tribute site, you should remove these colors (or at least change them to colors you like).

8. **Make sure the CSS Styles panel is open (Window → CSS Styles), and the Current button is selected at the top of the panel (see Figure 9-27).**

   Dreamweaver's CSS Panel provides a quick and easy way to identify and edit a style applied to a part of the page. The panel's Current view displays the styles affecting the current selection. Also make sure the Cascade button (labelled in Figure 9-27) is pressed.

9. **In the document window, click inside the word "Header" at the top of the page, and then choose Edit → Select All (Ctrl+A or ⌘-A for Macs works just as well).**

   Clicking inside the headline places the insertion point inside the <h1> tag, and inside the <div> tag used to define the header portion of the page. The Select All command works slightly differently when the cursor's inside a <div>. Instead of selecting *everything* on the page (probably what you'd think Select All would do), it selects all of the div's contents. Now, if you look at the CSS Styles panel, you see a style named *.twoColFixRtHdr #header* listed in the Rules pane (see Figure 9-27).

Note: When you click inside a <div> tag and choose Edit → Select All Dreamweaver highlights the <div> tag in the Tag selector at the bottom of the document window. A highlighted tag in the Tag selector usually means that the *entire tag* (meaning the opening <div> and closing </div> tags) is selected. In this situation, however, only the *contents* inside the div tag are selected; you must choose Edit → Select All a second time to actually select the tag.

---

10. **Make sure *.twoColFixRtHdr #header* is selected in the Rules pane (see Figure 9-27). In the Properties pane, click the Background property value—#DDDDDD—press Delete, and then hit the Enter (Return) key.**

    This removes the background color and, at the same time, deletes the background property from the style sheet. You could also have changed the color to something more appropriate for the site.

    Next, you'll remove the space that surrounds the headline inside the header area.

11. **In the Properties pane, click the padding values—"0 10px 0 20px"—to select them. Type *0*, and then Enter (or Return).**

    This action removes any padding inside the header div—in other words, it removes the space between the div's edge in the content inside. In some cases, you may want to keep or adjust the padding if you want to keep text or images inside the div from running to the very edge of the div.

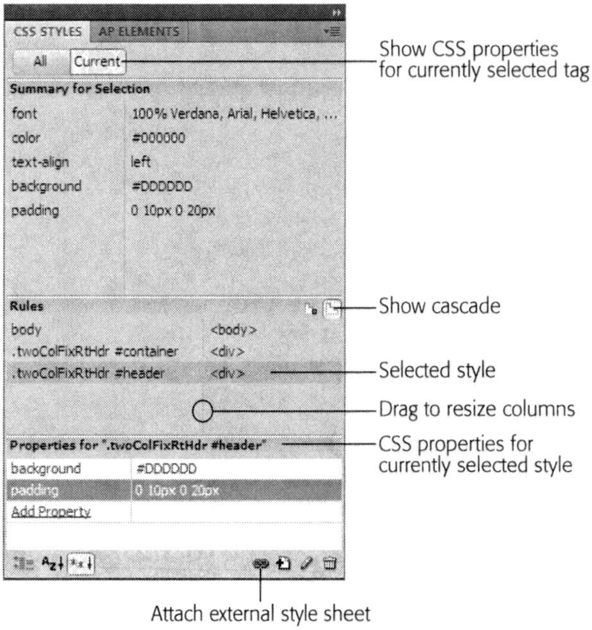

Figure 9-27:
The Current View of the CSS Styles Panel is one of Dreamweaver's greatest CSS productivity tools. It shows properties and styles that apply to any element you select in the Document window. It's most useful when you click the Show Cascade button (labeled), which displays every style that might affect the current selection, and displays those style names in the order of their importance, with the style that has the greatest impact on the selected page element listed at the bottom. *Turn to page 315 to learn more about using the CSS Styles panel.*

12. **Repeat steps 9–10 to remove the background color, for the sidebar and footer.**

    For example, click inside the text "Sidebar1 Content," press Ctrl+A (⌘-A), and edit the *.twoColFixRtHdr #sidebar1* style. The name of the style controlling the footer is *.twoColFixRtHdr #footer*. You can leave the padding values for these styles alone, since you want a bit of space inside them to keep the content from touching the edges of the divs.

    If you preview the page now (or click the Live View button at the top of the document window), you'll notice a black border framing the header, sidebar, main content, and footer areas. This border is applied to a <div> tag that wraps all of the other tags. You'll remove that border now.

13. **In the Tag selector at the bottom left of the document window, click <div#container> to select the div. In the Properties pane of the CSS Style panel, delete the value "1px solid #000000" from the *border* property.**

    In other words, click "1px solid #000000", and then press Delete. (If you don't see <div#container> in the Tag selector, click inside any of the areas with text on the page.)

    Finally, you'll remove the background color for the page.

14. **In the Tag selector click <body.twoColFixRtHdr> to select the page's <body> tag. In the Properties pane of the CSS Style panel, remove the gray background color.**

    This is the same as step 10 above. At this point, you've removed some of the visual formatting to start with a clean slate. In the next section you'll add actual content.

Adding Content

Now it's time to add the real content to this page...OK, it's not "real" content, since *Chia-Vet.com* doesn't really exist, but you get the idea.

1. **Select and delete the text "Header" at the top of the page; choose "Paragraph" from the Property inspector's Format menu.**

   You'll replace that text with a banner image.

Note: If you find that you can't edit the content on the page, you may be in Live View—meaning you clicked the Live View button at the top of the document window and are seeing the page as it would look in a Web browser. In this state, the page's contents can't be edited. Just click the Live View button again to return to editing mode.

---

2. **Choose Insert → Image; navigate to the *images* folder, and then double-click the file *logo.png*.**

   If the Image Tag Accessibility window appears, type *Chia Vet* in the Alternate text box, and then click OK.

   The sidebar lists links to other pages related to this one. The content for that sidebar is located in another HTML file in this tutorial.

3. **In the files panel, locate the file *sidebar_content.html* in the content folder, and double-click it to open it.**

   You could also choose File → Open, navigate to the content folder in the site, and then double-click the *sidebar_content.html* file to open it. Either way, a Web page opens with a headline, some text and a form. You'll copy the contents of this page and paste it into the new layout.

4. **Choose Edit → Select All, then Edit → Copy; at the top of the document window, click the tab for *tips.html* to switch to that page. Click anywhere inside the sidebar, and then choose Edit → Select All and Edit → Paste.**

   The sidebar's dummy text supplied with the layout page is replaced with not much smarter text from *Chia Vet*. You'll do the same for the main content area.

5. **Repeat steps 3 and 4 with the *main_content.html* file and the main content region of the page.**

   In other words, open *main_content.html*, and then paste its contents into the div with the big headline "Main Content." You'll just type the copyright notice into the footer.

6. **Repeat steps 3 and 4 with the *footer.html* page and the footer region at the bottom of the page.**

   The page should look like Figure 9-28. Now it's time to add adjust the layout a bit.

Figure 9-28: *The dotted lines that run around the different layout regions on the page represent the <div> tags that are positioned to create this two-column layout. The right-hand sidebar is a right floated div with a set width.*

Fine-Tuning the Layout

Now it's time to tune the CSS layout to make it your own. First, you'll tackle all the main components of the page: the body, the header, the sidebar, and so on.

1. **At the top of the CSS Styles panel, click the All button.**

   You should now see a list of the styles in the attached *twoColFixRtHdr.css* style sheet. If you don't see the names of the styles, you need to expand the style sheet listing by clicking the + sign (flippy triangle on Mac) in the CSS Styles panel, to the left of the style sheet name.

   At the top of the list is a tag style for the <body> tag. You'll edit that style first.

2. **Double-click *body* in the list.**

   The CSS Rule Definition window opens. You'll change the font and a few other properties.

3. **From the Font-family menu, select "Tahoma, Geneva, sans-serif".**

   Now you'll add a background image and color to the page.

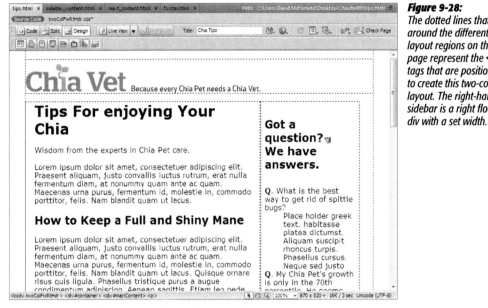

4. **Click the Background category, and then type *#CAE0EC* in the "Background-color" box; click the Browse button, and then from the *images* folder, select the file *bgPage.png* (see Figure 9-29).**

   In this case, the *bgPage.png* file is a graphic that will tile seamlessly in the background.

Tip: Don't forget the # when typing a color value in the color box. If you leave off the # symbol, then Dreamweaver displays the color correctly, but browsers don't.

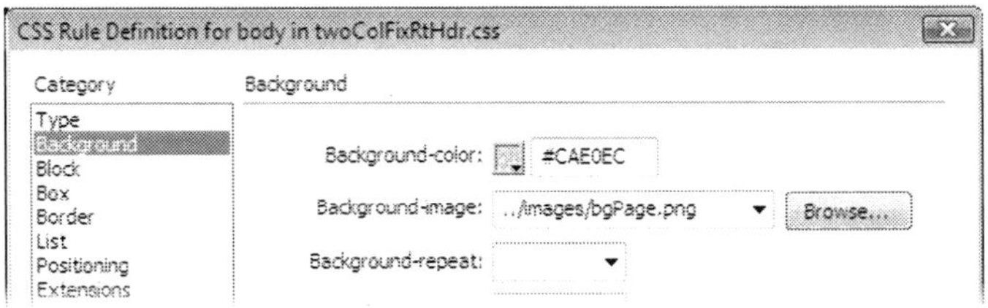

Figure 9-29: *It's a good idea to set a background color even when assigning a background image to a page. The background color should match the general tone of the image. That way, if a visitor has graphics turned off, or for some reason the background image fails to load, you still have background color.*

5. **Click OK to complete the style.**

   Now it's time to readjust the overall page width. Dreamweaver's fixed-width CSS layouts are a mere 780 pixels wide. In this day and age, most Web surfers have monitors capable of handling a much wider page size.

6. **In the CSS Styles panel, double-click the style named *.twoColFixRtHdr #container*.**

   The CSS Rule Definition window opens. The container div wraps around all other <div> tags on the page and provides the overall width of the page's content area. You'll change the width and add some padding to add some white space around the inside of this div.

7. **Click the Box category. Type *860* in the Width box; under Padding, turn off the "Same for all" checkbox, and then type *0* for the top, *15* for the right, *3* for the bottom and *15* for the left.**

   The Rule Definition window should look like Figure 9-30.

8. **Click OK to finish editing the style.**

   Next you'll add a few distinctive touches for the header of the page.

9. **In the CSS styles panel, double-click the style named *.twoColFixRtHdr #header*.**

   The Rule Definition window opens once again. First, you'll add a distinctive graphic to the background of the header.

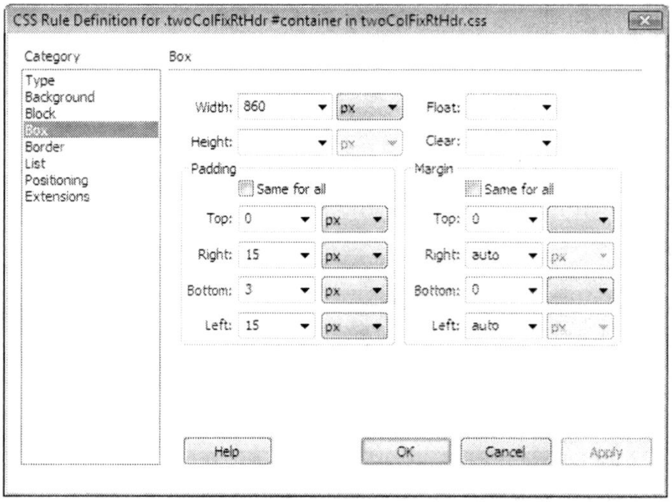

Figure 9-30:
The Rule Definition window's Box category provides the basic properties for controlling the width of an element. It also lets you control the space that surrounds the element (margin) and the space inside the element (padding).

10. **In the Rule Definition window, click the Background category. Click the Browse button, and then in the *images* folder, locate and double-click the file named *bgGrass.jpg*. From the "Background-repeat" menu, select "no-repeat"; from the "Background-position (X)" menu, choose "left", and from the "Background-position (Y)" menu, choose "bottom".**

    The window should now look like Figure 9-31. Now you'll control the size and margins for this style.

11. **Click the Box category, and then, in the Height box, type *142*; under Margin, uncheck the "Same for all" box, and then type *0* for the top, *0* for the right, *10* for the bottom, and *0* for the left margins.**

    As mentioned on page 342, you should set the height of an element only if you're sure that the content inside the element won't be taller than the height you specify. Otherwise content spills out of the element, and since browsers handle this situation in different ways, you end up with some weird display problems. In this case, however, there's only the logo image and a single line navigation bar (which you'll add soon), so you know how tall the style needs to be.

    Finally, you'll add a bold border to the top of the header.

12. **Click the Border category, and then uncheck all three "Same for all" boxes. From the top style menu, choose solid, type *6* in the top width box, and type *#F63* in the top color box. Click OK to complete the style.**

    You should now see a bright orange border at the top of the header, as well as a green grass-like image at the bottom.

    Since you made the page wider in step 7 above, you have plenty of room to make the sidebar wider; while you're at it you'll color the background of the sidebar as well.

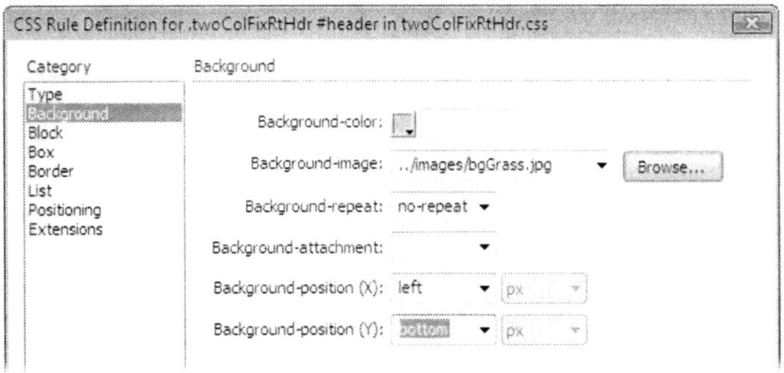

Figure 9-31:
You can use CSS to control the placement of background images as well as whether the image tiles (repeats). In this example, the image bgGrass.png *appears in the background of this style. The image appears only once (no-repeat), and it's placed at the bottom-left corner of the element.*

13. **In the CSS Styles panel, double-click *.twoColFixRtHdr #sidebar1*. Click the box category, and then change the width from 200 to 250 pixels. Change the Top padding settings from 15px to 65px.**

    The 65 pixel top padding is there to add enough empty space at the top of the sidebar to accommodate the graphic you'll add next.

14. **Click the Background category, and then, in the Background-color box, type *#EAEBE4*; click the Browse button, and then select the file *bgQnA.png*, which is located in the images folder. Finally, from the Background-repeat menu, choose no-repeat; and then position the image in the center and top using the Background-position menus. Click OK to finish the style.**

    Since you just expanded the sidebar to make it wider, you'll next need to make the main content area thinner—you do this by increasing the right margin for that div.

15. **In the CSS Styles panel, double-click *.twoColFixRtHdr #mainContent*. Click the box category and change the right margin from 250 to 290 pixels. Change the padding settings to: top *10px*, right *15px*, bottom *60px*, and left *15px*.**

    The Rule Definition window should now look like Figure 9-32. You're just about done with this page.

16. **Click OK to finish the style.**

    At this point the page should look like Figure 9-33.

Adding Styles and Navigation

At this point, you could create new styles to format this page using the techniques you've read about earlier in this book—change the fonts and font sizes, add underlines to headlines, change the look of links, and so on. For the sake of keeping this book from rivaling the length of *War and Peace*, we assume you've already got those skills under your belt, so you'll attach a style sheet with some already created styles.

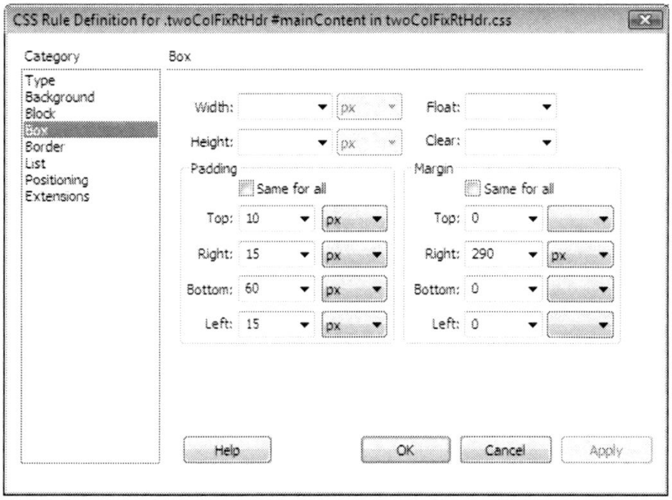

***Figure 9-32:** When adjusting the padding and margin settings on some of Dreamweaver's CSS Layouts, make sure you specify a measurement unit–px, ems, or %–that you want. You can do this by typing a value, and then selecting a measurement type (px, ems, %, and so on) from the menu to the right, or by typing the value and measurement type all at once: For example, type 10px to specify 10 pixels. This method is especially important when the value of any setting is 0. If you simply change 0 to 10–because, say, you want 10 pixels of padding–Dreamweaver doesn't automatically set any measurement value, and browsers won't display that padding setting at all.*

***Figure 9-33:** It takes only a few steps to modify a stock Dreamweaver CSS layout. A few tweaks to the CSS lets you adjust the width of the page and the size of the columns. Most of the hard work lies in developing the individual styles to format your paragraphs, headlines, tables, lists, and so on… but that's the fun and creative part.*

1. **In the CSS Style panel, click the Attach External Style Sheet button (see Figure 9-27).**

   The Attach External Style Sheet window opens. It's a good idea to place any styles that don't directly affect the layout of one of Dreamweaver's CSS Layout pages in a separate CSS file, like the one you're about to attach. That way you can have one CSS file that controls style elements that apply to every type of page on your site—the background color of the body, the look of headings and text, and so on. Then you can attach this global style sheet so that it shares these same styles with other pages using different types of CSS layouts—1 column, 3 column, liquid, and so on.

2. **Click the Browse button, and then navigate to the *css* folder; double-click the file *global.css*. In the Attach External Style Sheet window, click OK.**

   Dreamweaver links the style sheet to the page, and styles the page content. The page is missing a navigation bar in the header. You could, of course, build that from scratch with a Spry Menu Bar (see page 184). But to save some time, a basic navigation bar has already been created for you.

3. **In the Files panel, double-click the file *menubar.html*.**

   Alternatively, you can choose File → Open, and then, in the site's local root folder, select the *menubar.html* file. In either case, a Web page with a simple bulleted list of links appears.

4. **Click anywhere in the page, and then choose Edit → Select All; choose Edit → Copy.**

   You've just copied the links. Now you'll paste them into the page you've been working on.

5. **At the top of the Document window, click the tips.html tab to return to the tutorial page. Click in the space below the logo (inside the grass image, for example) and then choose Edit → Paste.**

   A new navigation bar appears. You may be wondering where the bulleted list went. It's still there—it's just been transformed by the CSS stored in the *global.css*. If you want to learn how to make a navigation bar look like that, just turn to the tutorial on page 199.

   Now you'll apply a class style from the style sheet you attached in step 2.

6. **Click inside the paragraph, below the headline "Tips For Enjoying Your Chia". In the Property inspector, make sure the HTML button is selected, and then, from the Class menu, choose *tagline*.**

   Alternatively, you can right-click (ctrl-click) inside that paragraph, and then, from the contextual menu that appears, choose Styles → "tagline".

Fiddling with the Footer

The page is pretty much complete. However, the footer at the bottom of the page could use a little TLC. In addition, you have a good opportunity to get a taste of using the CSS *float* property to craft the design of a page. In this case, you'll be creating two mini columns—one to hold the phone number and copyright notice, and another for the mailing address.

1. **Scroll to the bottom of the page, and then click anywhere inside the footer. Choose Edit → Select All to select the div.**

   You'll start by getting rid of the padding in the footer section.

2. **At the top of the CSS Styles panel, click the Current button.**

   You'll see the Current view's three panes.

3. **In the middle pane—the rules pane—click the *.twoColFxRtHdr #footer* style. In the Properties pane, change the padding values from *0 10px 0 20px* to *10px 0 10px 0*.**

   You can also use the Rule Definition window for this—just double-click the *.twoColFxRtHdr #footer* style, and then, in the Box category, change the padding values. These new padding settings remove space from the left and right, and add some space to the top and bottom of the footer.

   The text looks a little big for the footer, so you'll create a style to format the paragraph tag inside the footer.

4. **Click inside any of the text in the footer. On the CSS Styles panel, click the "Create new style" button.**

   The New CSS Rule window appears. Dreamweaver suggests a long-winded style based upon where the cursor was. But this descendent selector is needlessly complex—you can simplify it, using the Less Specific button.

5. **Click the Less Specific button twice.**

   Depending upon which text you clicked inside before creating the style, in the Selector Name box you see either *#footer p* or *#footer p strong* (see Figure 9-34). Delete the strong part if you see that, so that you're just left with *#footer p*. This descendent selector affects only paragraph tags within another element (in this case a <div> tag) that has an ID of footer.

6. **At the bottom of the New CSS Rule window, from the Menu, select *global.css*, and then click OK.**

   The CSS Rule Definition window appears. You'll make the text smaller but spread out the line using the line-height property.

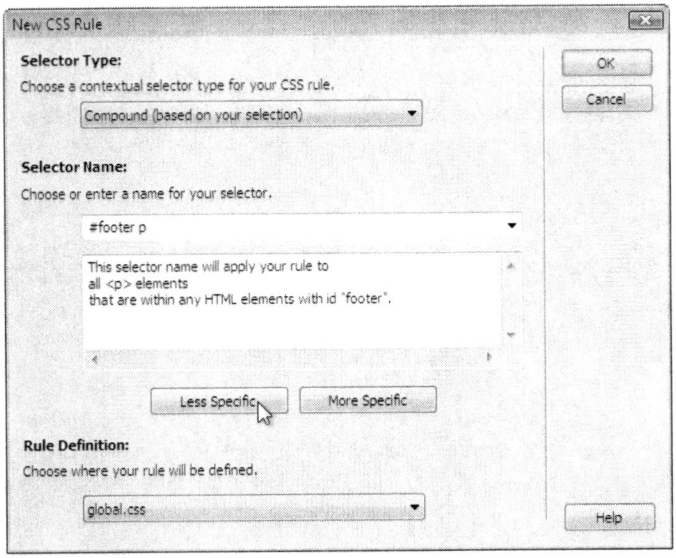

Figure 9-34: *When you have more than one style sheet attached to a page–in this case,* global.css *and* twoColFixRtHdr.css*–make sure to pay attention to the Rule Definition menu at the bottom of this window. You could easily accidentally store a style in the wrong style sheet.*

7. **In the Font-size box, type *12*; in the Line-height box, type *150,* and then, from the menu directly to the right, choose %. Click OK to complete the style.**

   The text in the footer shrinks and the new line-height setting increases the leading—or space between—the lines. Now you'll create a column to position some of the footer text.

8. **Click just before the M in "Make an appointment", and then drag down and to the right until you've selected the first five lines (stop just after "Inc.").**

   You may find it easier to click just to the right of "Inc." and drag *up* until you've selected the five lines of text. Next, you'll wrap this text in a div and create a style to position it.

9. **Choose Insert → Layout Objects → Div Tag.**

   This is the now-familiar Insert Div Tag you read about on page 335. Not only will you create a div, but you'll create an ID style while you're at it.

10. **Click the New CSS Rule button. From the top menu, select ID; in the Selector Name box, type *#footerCol1*; from the Rule Definition menu at the bottom of the window, choose *global.css*, and then click OK to begin creating the style.**

    The CSS Rule Definition window appears. To start, you'll add a background image to spice up the look of this div.

11. **Select the Background category; click the Browse button, and then, in the images folder, select the file *vetLogo.png*. From the Background-repeat menu, choose no-repeat.**

    Now it's time to position the div using the float technique you learned about starting on page 332. In essence, you're creating the first column of a mini-two column layout within the footer div itself.

12. **Click the Box category; in the Width box, type *475*; from the Float menu, select Left.**

    The two basic requirements for creating a multicolumn layout: giving a set width to the div, and then floating it to the left so the content that appears after it, wraps up around the right side of the div—creating a second column. You'll add a bit of padding to make room for the background image.

13. **Uncheck the Padding "Same for all" box. Type *0* in the Top box, *0* in the Right box, *10* in the Bottom box, and *70* in the Left box. Click OK to create the style.**

    You're returned to the Insert Div Tag window. Notice that the ID you just created—*footerCol1*—is listed in the ID box.

14. **Click OK to wrap the selected text in a div, and apply an ID to it.**

    The first chunk of text floats to the left and the Chia Vet address wraps around the right edge...voilà, 2 columns! There's one small problem—notice that the last line of this new column appears to pop out of the bottom of the main page area and overlaps the page's background image—you'll deal with this weird situation in a moment. But first, let's spiffy up the address in the footer. The address would look better slightly farther to the right, so you'll wrap it in a div as well.

15. **Click just before the C in "Chia-Vet.com", and then drag down and to the right until you've selected the first four lines. Stop just after the phone number. Repeat steps 9 and 10. Create a new ID style named *#footerCol2*.**

    You don't need to float this div. To position it to the right of the first div, you merely need to add enough of a left margin to clear the right edge of the floated div.

16. **In the CSS Rule Definition window, click the Box category. Uncheck the Margin properties "Same for All" box, and then, in the Left margin box, type *590*. Click OK once to complete the style, and then, in the Insert Div Tag window, click OK to add the <div> tag.**

    Now you have two precisely positioned side-by-side columns. However, there's still the little problem of the text popping out the bottom of the page on the left column. This problem is common with floats. When an element is floated, the element containing it acts as if the floated element isn't actually there! So the main footer region grows only as large as the content it's aware of—which happens to be the second, non-floated column (the one with the address). Fortunately, you have an easy fix to this problem.

17. **Click anywhere inside the footer, and then, in the Tag selector at the bottom of the document window, click <div#footer>.**

    This selects the div. You can quickly access its style from the Styles panel.

18. **At the top of the CSS Styles panel, click the Current button. In the Properties pane, click the Add Property link (see Figure 9-35). From the first column menu, choose Overflow. Click into the second column, and then, from the menu, choose "hidden".**

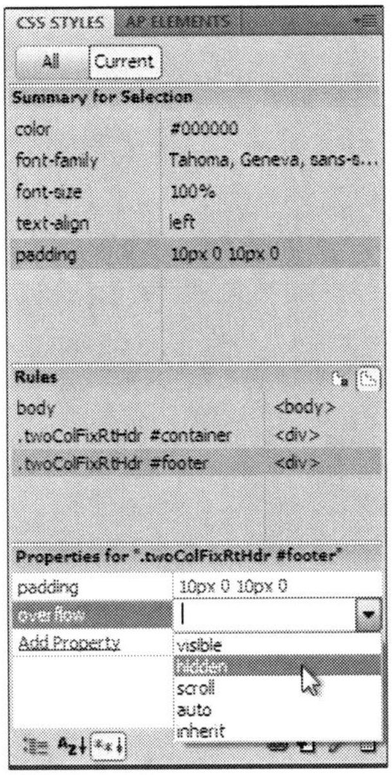

Figure 9-35:
A floated element can sometimes appear to pop out of the bottom of a tag it's inside–this phenomenon can lead to display problems like the one mentioned in step 14. You have several ways to fix this. One obscure method is to simply add an overflow property to the tag that wraps around the floated element, and set that overflow to "hidden". You can read more about this weird solution by going to: www.quirksmode.org/css/clearing.html.

19. **Save the page, and then preview it in a Web browser.**

    The finished page should look like Figure 9-36. A completed version of this tutorial is in the Chapter09_finished folder that's included with the downloaded tutorial files.

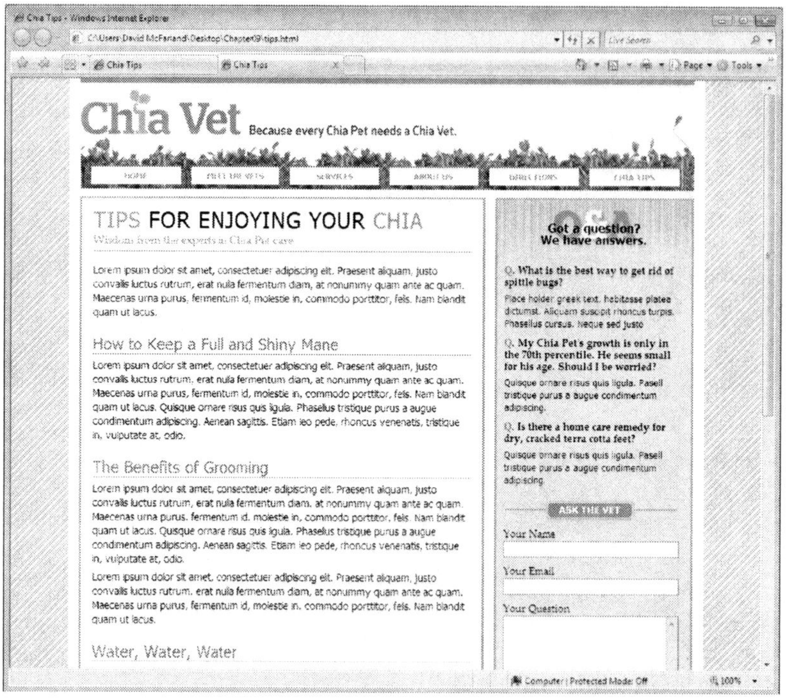

Figure 9-36:
Using Dreamweaver CS4's CSS Layouts as a starting point, you can quickly build a multicolumn Web page.

CHAPTER

10

Under the Hood: HTML

While Dreamweaver started life primarily as a visual Web page editor, it also hosts powerful code-editing tools that let you work on your pages' HTML, CSS, and JavaScript code directly. In fact, in recognition of the ever-multiplying types of files used to create Web sites, Dreamweaver lets you edit all text-based files, including XML, Java, ActionScript, and just plain text files. The code editor includes professional features like customizable syntax highlighting, auto indenting, line numbering, and code hints; code collapse, so you can concentrate on just the code you want; and the Code view toolbar, which provides one-click access to frequent hand-coding tasks. Dreamweaver may be the only Web page creation program even hard-core code junkies ever need. In fact, many of the new features in Dreamweaver CS4 are aimed specifically at helping those who work in Code view for editing HTML, CSS, and JavaScript.

Roundtrip HTML

Unlike many other visual HTML editors, Dreamweaver has always graciously accepted HTML written by hand (and even by other programs). In fact, Dreamweaver has always made it easy to jump between itself and text-editing programs like the much loved, but retired, HomeSite (for Windows) and BBEdit (for the Mac).

This ability, which Adobe calls *Roundtrip HTML*, lets Web developers write code the way they want, without worrying that Dreamweaver will change it. For example, suppose you have a particular way of formatting your handwritten code. Maybe you insert an extra carriage return for spacing after every <td> (table cell) tag, or you like to use multiple tabs to indent nested tags. In such cases, Dreamweaver doesn't try to rewrite your work to fit its own style—unless you ask it to.

Auto-Fixing Your Code

That's not to say that Dreamweaver doesn't ever change your code. In fact, the program can automatically fix errors when you open a page that was created in another program, including:

- **Overlapping tags.** Take a look at this example:

```
<p><strong>Fix your tags!</p></strong>
```

  This HTML is invalid, because the opening and closing <strong> tags should appear *inside* the <p> tag. Dreamweaver rewrites this snippet correctly:

```
<p><strong>Fix your tags!</strong></p>
```

- **Unclosed tags.** Tags usually come in pairs, like this:

```
<em>This text is in italics</em>
```

  But if a page is missing the ending tag (<em>*This text is in italics*), then Dreamweaver adds the closing tag.

- **Extra closing tags.** If a page has an *extra* closing tag (<strong>bold text</strong> </strong>), then Dreamweaver helpfully removes it.

This auto-fix feature comes turned *off* in Dreamweaver. If you're working on a site that was hand coded or created by another, less capable Web-editing program, it's wise to turn this feature on, since all those errors are improper HTML that can cause problems for browsers. (Once upon a time, some Web developers, for example, deliberately omitted closing tags just to save a few kilobytes in file size. While most browsers can still interpret this kind of sloppy code, it's poor practice.)

You can turn auto-fixing on in the Preferences window (see Figure 10-1); just turn on "Fix invalidly nested and unclosed tags" and "Remove extra closing tags". If you don't have these preference options turned on, then Dreamweaver doesn't fix the HTML, and there's no command you can run to fix these kinds of problems. Instead, Dreamweaver highlights these mistakes in Document view and Code view (skip ahead to Figure 10-5 to get a glimpse of what that looks like).

Note: The "Warn when fixing or removing tags" option doesn't really warn you as much as it reports code that Dreamweaver has gone ahead and fixed. By the time you see the "Warning" message, Dreamweaver's already rewritten the code in your page. You can't undo these changes, but you can close the file without saving the changes, to retain the old (improperly formatted) HTML.

Dreamweaver can also change the capitalization (case) of HTML tags and properties, if you want. For example, if you prefer lowercase letters for tags and properties, like this:

```
<a href="nextpage.html">Click here</a>
```

Dreamweaver can convert uppercase tags (<A HREF="next.html">) to lowercase, or vice versa, when it finds them in pages created by other programs. (You can turn on this feature, as described on page 408.)

Note: If you're creating XHTML pages (see page 10), then you don't get the option to choose between cases–tags must always be lowercase in XHTML files.

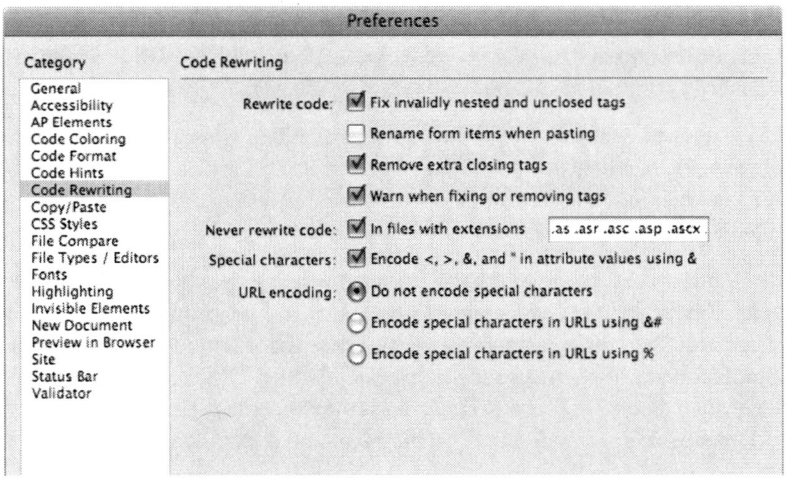

Figure 10-1: *To specify particular types of files (Active Server Pages, for instance) whose code you never want Dreamweaver to touch, choose Edit → Preferences. Then, in the Category list, choose Code Rewriting, and, in the extensions field, type a new file extension. (Make sure the "Never rewrite code" checkbox is turned on, as well.)*

Web Application Server Pages

Dreamweaver can leave pages with certain file name extensions untouched—pages created for Web application servers, for example. (Web application servers, covered in Part 6 of this book, process Web pages that access databases and other services like shopping cart programs and form-processing programs.) Many of these systems rely on special code within the HTML of a page—code that Dreamweaver might "fix," interpreting the portions as HTML errors.

Unless you change its settings, Dreamweaver doesn't rewrite code in pages that are designed for the leading application-server technologies—that is, files whose names end in .asp (Active Server Pages that run on Microsoft's IIS Web Server), .aspx (Microsoft's .NET technology), .cfm and .cfml (ColdFusion Markup Language pages that run on Adobe's ColdFusion Server), .jsp (JavaServer Pages that run on any Java Server), or .php (PHP pages), among others. Nor does it rewrite any code inside an external JavaScript file (a .js file), since it's common practice to write JavaScript that creates HTML on the fly—many time this means JavaScript coders add HTML fragments (incomplete tags and code) to their JavaScript. If you edit other types of files with Dreamweaver, but don't want Dreamweaver interfering with them, you can add those file types' extensions to the list in the Preferences window as shown in Figure 10-1.

Special Characters and Encoding

The Code Rewriting Preferences window also lets you control how Dreamweaver handles special characters like <, >, and ", whenever you enter them into the Property inspector or a dialog box. (This ability doesn't apply, however, when typing these characters into Code view or into the document window while in Design view. Dreamweaver always encodes [page 86] special characters you type directly into a page while in Design view; and, conversely, it never encodes special characters you type while in Code view.) Some characters have special meaning. The "less than" symbol (<), for example, indicates the beginning of an HTML tag, so you can't just link to a page named *bob<zero.html*. If you did, a Web browser would think a new HTML tag (called *zero*) was starting after the < symbol.

You have several ways to avoid this problem. First, whenever possible, avoid strange characters when you name pages, graphics, CSS styles, or any other object in your site. Sticking to letters, numbers, hyphens, and underscores (_) makes your life much easier.

Another option is to let Dreamweaver *encode* those special characters. Encoding a character simply means using a code to represent it. For example, you can represent a space as *%20*, or a < symbol as *<*. Thus, the infamous *bob<zero.html* file becomes *bob%<.html*, and your link works just fine. Other characters like ™ or © are encoded as *™* and *©*. To set up encoding, choose Edit → Preferences (Dreamweaver → Preferences on the Mac) and select the Code Rewriting category. Your options are as follows:

- **Special characters**. Turning on this checkbox means that Dreamweaver converts the less than, greater than, &, and * characters to the specially encoded format mentioned above. (This feature has no effect on code you type in Code view, nor on text you type into the document window while in Design view.)
- **Do not encode special characters**. Selecting this option, the first of three under "URL encoding", tells Dreamweaver not to touch any Web addresses you enter (in the Property inspector's Link box, say). (Again, selecting this option has no effect on any links you type in Code view.)
- **Encode special characters in URLs using &#** is the safest choice. It's especially helpful if you use a language that has a non-Latin alphabet. If you name your files using Japanese characters, for example, choosing this option can translate them into code that successfully transmits over the Internet.
- **Encode special characters in URLs using %** is intended for use with older browsers (and we're talking *old*, as in pre-Internet Explorer 4), so unless you've got a time machine and plan on going back to 1998 to build Web sites, skip this option.

Code View

Dreamweaver provides several different ways to view a page's HTML code:

- **Code view.** In Code view, Dreamweaver displays your page's raw code.
- **Split view.** This view shows the HTML code and the "regular" Design view simultaneously. Coders with big, wide monitors, rejoice: Dreamweaver CS4 finally lets you control where the two split views—Code and Design—are positioned. Just select "Split vertically" from the Code/Design View menu on the Application bar (Figure 10-2 has more on why this option is so welcome).
- **Split code view.** This option is new in Dreamweaver CS4 and is for serious coding junkies. It lets you view the code *twice*, so you can work on two sections of a page at the same time. This option is really only useful for pages with lots of HTML, and can come in handy when you want to edit the CSS in the <head> region of a page, while crafting HTML in the <body> of the page.
- **Code inspector.** The Code inspector is a floating code window that lets you use Design view in its full glory (not cut in half as in Split view), while still providing access to the code. (To open the Code inspector, choose Window → Code Inspector, or press F10 [Option-F10].) Code warriors who are into serious multitasking can also use the Code inspector to look at one area of code, while using the main document window to work on another area of code (though the new Split Code view works well for that too).

The rest of this chapter assumes that you're using Code view for HTML editing.

Dreamweaver gives you three ways to move between its different viewing options: Choose a name from the View menu: Code, Design, or "Code and Design" (Split view); use the buttons in the Document toolbar; or use the menu in the Application bar at the top of Dreamweaver. (The latter two options are shown in Figure 10-2.)

Tip: You can quickly jump between Code and Design view by pressing Control+` (on both Windows and the Mac). In Split view, this shortcut jumps between the two views, so you can insert an image in the design half of Split view, and then press Control+` to jump right into the HTML for that image in the Code half of the window.

Code view functions much like a text editor (only better, as you'll soon see). You can click anywhere inside the window, and then start typing HTML, JavaScript, CSS, or any other programming code (such as ASP, ColdFusion, or PHP).

You don't have to type out *everything* by hand; the Insert panel, Insert menu, and Property inspector also function in Code view. Using these sources of canned HTML blobs, you can combine hands-on HTML work with the easy-to-use, rapid action of Dreamweaver's objects. This trick can be a real timesaver when you need to add a table, which would otherwise be a multiline exercise in typing accuracy.

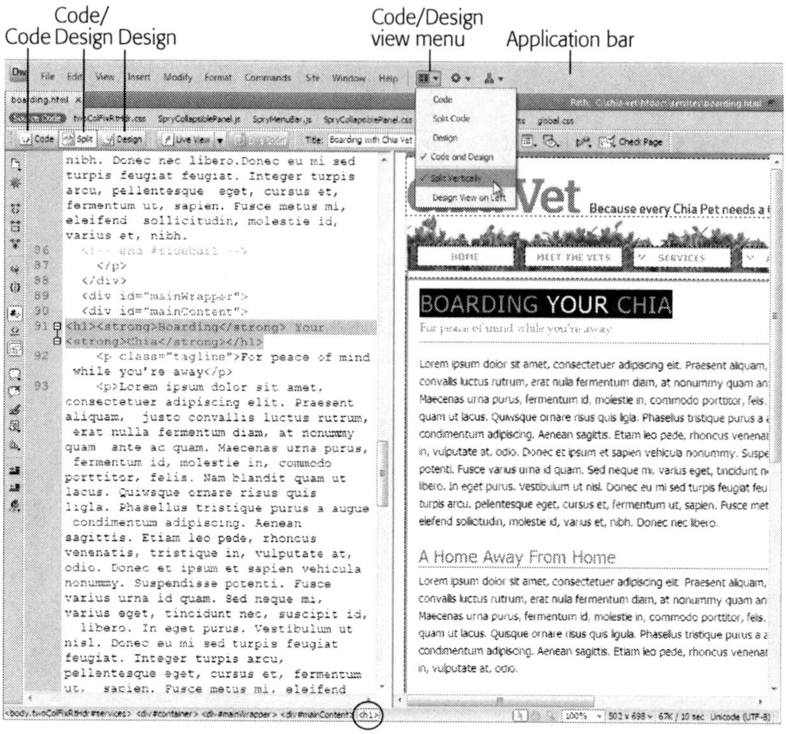

Figure 10-2: *In Split view (also called "Code and Design" view), you can display raw code side by side with the visual Design view. Normally, Dreamweaver displays the code above the design; however, from the Code/Design view menu, you can select Split Vertically. If you have a wide monitor, this is your best option, since stacking the two views on top of each other doesn't leave much space to work on either code or design. In Split view, when you select an object in the visual half (the selected "Boarding Your Chia" headline, for example) Dreamweaver selects the corresponding HTML in the code half (the highlighted <h1> tag in Code view in this figure)—a great way to identify an object in your HTML. As you work in one half of the Split view, Dreamweaver updates the other half. Use the buttons (labeled) in the Document toolbar to jump between the different views. (Notice that the Tag selector at the bottom of the document window [circled] also identifies the selected tag.)*

You can also select a tag (like an image's <img> tag) in Code view, and use the Property inspector to modify it.

Note: When you add HTML to Code view, Dreamweaver doesn't automatically update Design view, which can be disconcerting when you're working in Split view. (After all, how would Dreamweaver display a half-finished tag like this: *<table border="*?) In the Property inspector, click the Refresh button (see Figure 10-3), or press F5, to update the visual display.

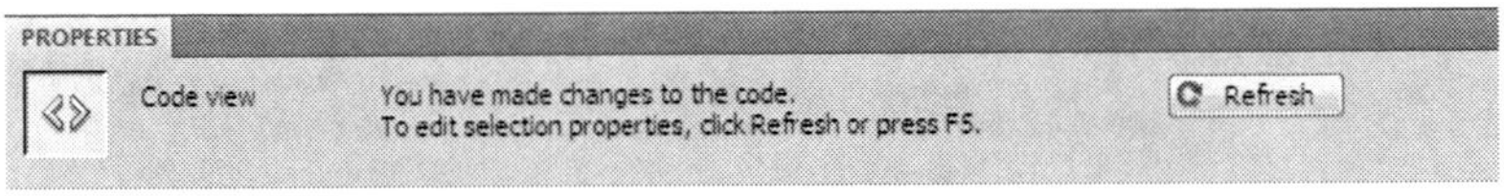

Figure 10-3: *After changing code in Split view, on the Property inspector, click Refresh to update Dreamweaver's visual display.*

To help you navigate your code, Code view provides several visual cues. They include:

- **Syntax coloring.** Dreamweaver displays different elements in different colors. Comments, for example, are gray. Text is black, HTML tags appear in dark blue, and HTML properties show up in a brighter blue. You can change any of these colors, and even specify unique colors for different types of tags, using the Preferences window (see Figure 10-4).

  To really make a tag stand out, you can underline it, make it bold, italicize it, and even give it a background color. Dreamweaver has separate color schemes for 24 different types of documents, such as ASP, CSS, and XML files. (But do you really need different colors for HTML forms in ASP pages, HTML pages, and PHP pages? You be the judge.)

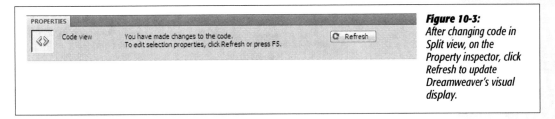

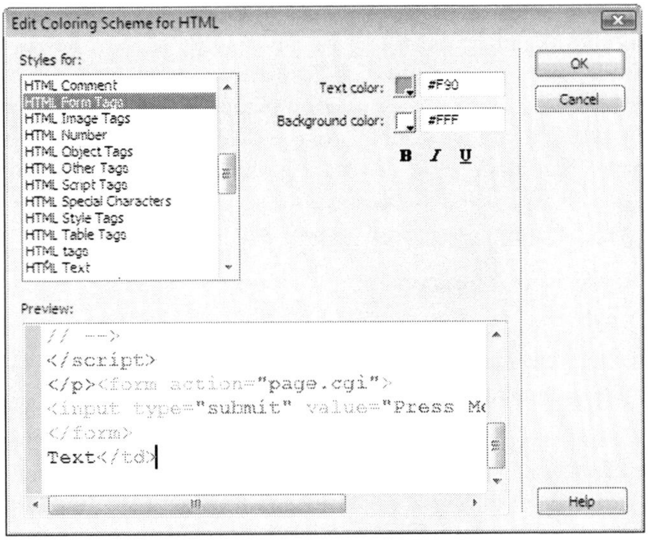

Figure 10-4: *From the Preferences window, you can control the color that Dreamweaver uses to display HTML and script code while in Code view. To do so, select the Code Coloring Category. Then select the type of document–HTML, ASP, CSS, or whatever–and click Edit Coloring Scheme. In the Edit Coloring Scheme window (shown here), select an item whose color you wish to change–Library Item or HTML Form Tags, for example–and set a text and/or background color using the color boxes. You can also make the code bold, italic, or underlined using the appropriate formatting buttons.*

- **Bad code highlighting.** When you type incorrect code (an opening tag without a closing tag, say), it's highlighted in yellow (see Figure 10-5). However, you'll see this highlighting only if you turn on the Highlight Invalid Code option from the Document toolbar's View Options menu (see Figure 10-6). That setting is turned off when you first install Dreamweaver.

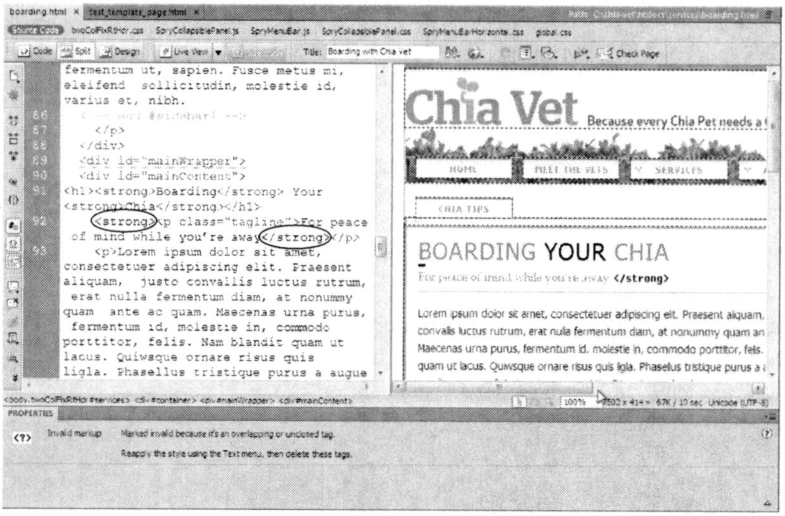

***Figure 10-5:** Dreamweaver highlights incorrect HTML code with bright yellow highlighting in Code view (like the <strong> tags in this figure). If you click the yellow area, then the Property inspector reveals the mistake. In this case, a tag is improperly nested–part of it is outside the <p> tag. (In Design view, on the other hand, Dreamweaver indicates mistakes by showing the HTML tag–</strong> for example–in front of a bright yellow background.)*

- **Templates.** Uneditable regions in pages built from templates appear in light gray. You can't actually change this code in Code view. This coloring scheme is a little confusing since HTML comments (see page 401) are also displayed in gray, and you *can* edit those. (For more on templates, see Chapter 19.)

- **Browser compatibility highlighting.** Much to the anguish of Web designers, browsers sometimes react differently to CSS formatting. What looks great in Firefox may crumble in Internet Explorer 6. Dreamweaver's new Browser Compatibility Checker can alert you to possible cross-browser CSS problems. When you see a squiggly line underneath code—like underneath the tag <div id="mainWrapper"> in Figure 10-5—Dreamweaver is alerting you to a potential problem. This cool feature is described on page 130.

- **Library Items.** Code from Library items (Chapter 18) has a light yellow background.

You can also control the following Code view display features by using the toolbar's View Options pop-up menu (see Figure 10-6), or by using the View → Code Options submenu:

- **Word Wrap.** This option makes long lines of code wrap (at the window's edge) to the next line, so you don't have to scroll horizontally to see it all. This option affects only how Dreamweaver displays the line in the document window; it doesn't actually change your code by introducing line breaks.

- **Line Numbers.** This automatic line numbering can come in handy when you're using Dreamweaver's Browser Compatibility Checker (see page 130), or when you encounter an error in a page containing server-side code (such as the code you create in Part 6 of this book). In Code view, you can also click a line number to select the entire line, which is a great way to delete or cut a line of code.

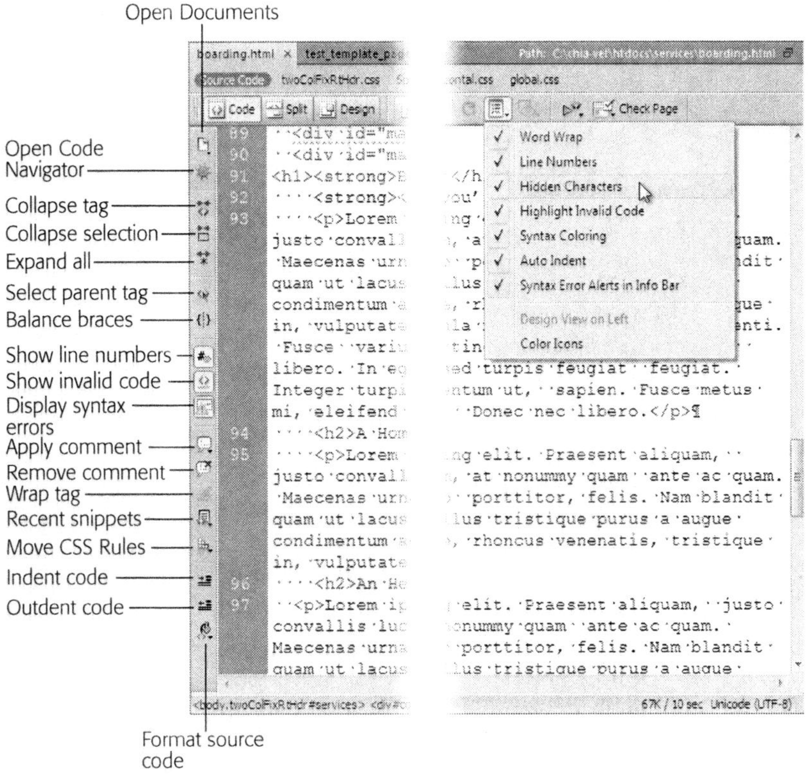

Figure 10-6: *Code view provides easy access to common code writing tasks with the Coding toolbar (left edge) and the View Options menu (top right), both of which let you modify how Dreamweaver displays the code. The Word Wrap option, for example, forces all code to fit inside the width of the window. If a line of code extends off the page, then Dreamweaver wraps it to the next line. Your only clue that you're looking at one long line is that the entire glob of text has only a single line number.*

- **Hidden Characters.** Some characters that you can type on the keyboard aren't visible on the screen: the end of a line, created by hitting the Enter or Return key, for example. Occasionally, these hidden characters can cause big trouble. When working with dynamic, server-side Web pages (described in Part 6), for example, you might find some cool code on the Web, and copy it to your own page. Sometimes copying and pasting code from a Web page introduces hidden characters that prevent the code from working. Turning on the Hidden Characters option can help ferret out these problem characters and eliminate them. Spaces appear as dots, tabs as a strange, lowercase *a* character, and paragraphs as a paragraph symbol (see Figure 10-6).

- **Highlight Invalid Code.** This option is the on/off switch for Dreamweaver's friendly tendency to highlight bad HTML in Code view (see Figure 10-5).

- **Syntax Coloring.** This option turns tags, comments, and text into colorful (and informative) text (see Figure 10-4).

- **Auto Indent.** When you're working with nested HTML tags, it's often helpful to press Tab to indent each level of nested tags, making it easier to identify large blocks of HTML (like a table and all its contents). The Auto Indent option carries the same size indent onto the next line when you hit Return or Enter.

Suppose you hit the Tab key twice, type a line of code, and then hit Return. Dreamweaver would place the insertion point on the next line, indented using two tabs. To un-indent, just press Backspace.

- **Syntax Error Alerts in Info Bar**. This new feature in Dreamweaver CS4 is aimed at JavaScript programmers. Dreamweaver can now keep track of potential syntax errors in your JavaScript programs (meaning typos or improper code). With this feature turned on, Dreamweaver puts a yellow info bar at the top of the document window alerting you to any JavaScript syntax errors.
- **Color Icons**. If you're a long-time Dreamweaver user, the new, somber gray tone of CS4's interface may trigger Seasonal Affective Disorder. If you miss the bright colors, choose Color Icons to change the icons that appear in the Document toolbar (as well as in other places in the program, such as the Insert Bar) from drab to fab.

Coding Toolbar

Dreamweaver includes a handy toolbar that makes many basic hand coding tasks go much more quickly. While working in Code view, the Coding toolbar appears on the left edge of the document window (see Figure 10-6). If you don't see it, you can turn it on by choosing View → Toolbars → Coding, or by right-clicking (Control-clicking) on another toolbar such as the Insert or Document toolbar, and then, in the pop-up menu, turning on the Coding option. Use the same technique to close the toolbar, if you don't use it.

The toolbar contains buttons that duplicate tasks and preference settings you can control from other parts of Dreamweaver. Here's a quick rundown of the buttons listed in Figure 10-6, with a brief explanation of what they do and, when applicable, a cross-reference to a more detailed description of the tool or action:

- **Open Documents**. This button gives you a pull-down menu, displaying all open documents. It lets you switch among the different documents you're currently working on, but it's actually more work than just clicking a document's tab at the top of the document window, so you'll probably want to skip it.
- **Collapse Full Tag/Collapse Selection/Expand All**. These three buttons work with Dreamweaver's Code Collapse feature described on page 404. They let you collapse (and expand) multiple lines of code, essentially hiding it so you can concentrate on the code you're currently working on.
- **Select Parent Tag**. This handy feature lets you quickly select the tag that surrounds your current selection. Say you've selected the text inside a link (<a>) tag, or just clicked inside that tag, and your cursor's blinking happily. Click this button, and the entire <a> tag is selected. Click it again, and that link's parent tag is selected. This button gives you a quick way to select the tag you're currently working on. If you really want to be productive, the keyboard shortcut Ctrl+[(⌘-[) is quicker.

- **Balance Braces.** If you do a lot of programming using JavaScript or one of the server languages like PHP, ColdFusion, or ASP, this button can help you find the matching brace ({ or }) character in a chunk of programming code—actually this tool selects *all* of the code between an opening and closing brace, but doing so lets you identify where the braces begin and end. Just click to the right of an opening brace ({), and then click this button to find the closing brace. To find a closing brace's mate, click to the left of the brace, and then click this button. The button also finds matching parentheses characters. The keyboard shortcut—Ctrl+' (⌘-')—is even faster.

- **Apply/Remove Comments.** Comments let you include helpful notes in your code, which don't appear on the page when it's displayed in a browser. You may want to leave some explanatory notes in your HTML page to help future generations of Web developers understand what you were doing. Or you might put a comment before a <div> tag (see page 333) that explains what should go inside it—"Put corporate logo and navigation bar here." People also frequently use comments to mark the end of a page section— "End of navigation bar." These buttons let you add or remove comments to HTML, CSS, JavaScript, PHP, and VBScript code, as demonstrated in Figure 10-7.

Note: Comments are very useful with Cascading Style Sheets. You can open a CSS file, select a property inside a style, and stick a pair of comment tags around this property. When you preview a page that uses the style, you see the style minus the property you've commented (or "commented out," as some programmers say). This maneuver lets you preview a style, temporarily hiding the effect of one or more styling properties without permanently deleting the property. It's a great help in debugging problematic styles.

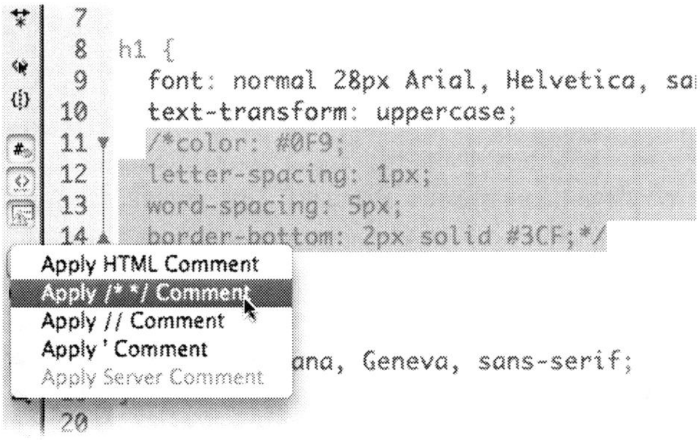

Figure 10-7:
The Coding toolbar lets you wrap HTML, CSS, JavaScript, or other programming code within comment characters. Just select the code you wish to turn into comments, click the Add comment button, and then select the type of comment you wish to add. Use the HTML comment option to hide HTML code; the / */ option to hide multiple lines of CSS, JavaScript, or PHP code; the // option to hide each line of JavaScript, or PHP code; the ' option to hide VBScript code; and, if you're working on a server-side page as described in Part 6, use the last option to hide code in those pages. To remove a comment, select all of the code (including the comment), and then click the Remove comment button (hidden in this figure; it's just below the Apply Comment button).*

- **Wrap tag.** Works the same as the Quick Tag editor described on page 707.
- **Recent Snippets.** This pop-up menu lists all the snippets (see page 309) you've recently used. Selecting an item from the menu inserts that snippet's code into your Web page.
- **Move CSS Rule.** This pop-up menu lets you move an inline CSS style to either an internal or external style sheet, or lets you move a rule from an internal to an external style sheet. You'll find more details on page 406.
- **Indent/Outdent.** These buttons indent or outdent lines of selected code, using the settings you've defined in the Code Formatting preferences (see page 406).
- **Apply Source formatting.** This button lets you apply specific formatting to an entire Web page, or just a selection of code, using the code-formatting options you've set up in the Code Formatting preferences window (see page 409) and the rules defined in the type-A-uber-geek-what-a-lot-of-work Tag Library described in the box on page 409.

Code Hints

Typing code can be a chore, which is why even longtime hand coders take advantage of anything that helps speed up the process. A perfect example is Dreamweaver's Code Hints feature (shown in Figure 10-8). It lets you select tags, attributes, and even Cascading Style Sheet styles from a pop-up menu as you type.

Note: Code Hints work with other tags as well as scripting languages like ASP.NET, ColdFusion, and PHP. In addition, Dreamweaver includes CSS Code Hints, so if you write your style sheets by hand, then you can take advantage of the auto-completion features of Code Hints to quickly type out CSS style properties. Dreamweaver CS4 has added code hints for JavaScript as well.

Here's how it works. After you begin a new tag by typing an opening bracket (<), a menu pops up, listing all available HTML tags. Use your mouse or arrow keys to select a tag, or type the first few letters of the tag, and let Dreamweaver select the closest matching item. When you press Enter (Return), Dreamweaver automatically fills in the tag name. Even better, a second menu now pops up, listing all the properties of that tag.

Note: You can also open the Code Hints menu by pressing Ctrl+Space bar (in both Mac and Windows). This shortcut's very useful when you're editing code and want to add a property or edit a property of a tag you've already created. For example, you could click inside the name of a class style applied to a tag–click inside the word "copyright" in the code *class="copyright"*, for instance–and then press Ctrl+space bar. This action not only selects the name so you can change it, but also opens a menu listing all of the classes available to the page. Then you can use the up and down arrow keys (or even your mouse) to select a different CSS style.

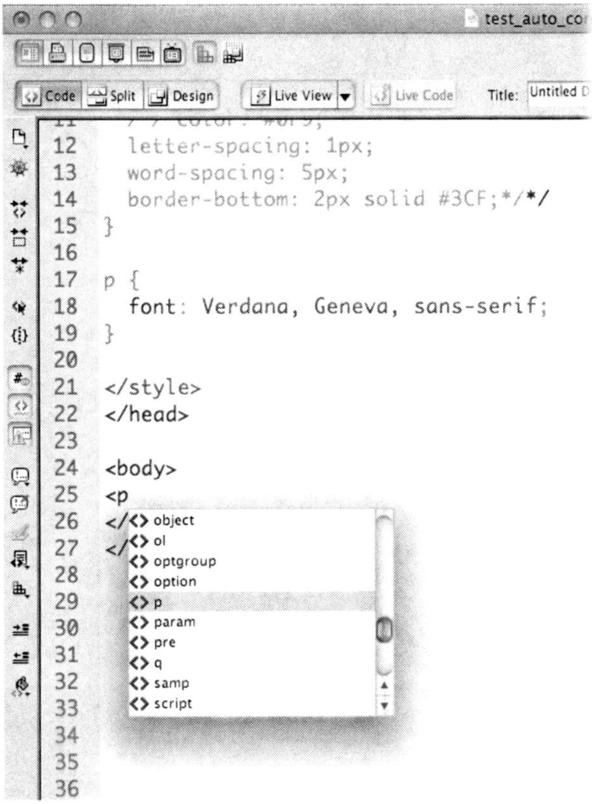

Figure 10-8:
The Code Hints feature saves your tired fingers from typing tags and tag properties. From a pop-up list, just select the appropriate item, and then let Dreamweaver type it for you. Dreamweaver's even thoughtful enough to show you all available CSS styles when you insert a class attribute in a tag.

If the feature annoys you, you can get it out of your way. You can turn off Code Hints completely, rein it in by setting a delay (so that pop-up lists don't appear immediately), or turn off Code Hints only for selected types of elements (such as tag properties). To make any of these adjustments, open the Preferences window by pressing Ctrl+U (⌘-U), and then select the Code Hints category. Make your desired changes to the Code Hints Preferences, and then click OK.

Dreamweaver also simplifies the writing of the closing tag: As soon as you type </ (the first two characters for any closing tag), Dreamweaver automatically finishes off your thought by closing the tag for you. For example, after you've typed an opening <p> tag, followed by the content in this new paragraph, Dreamweaver finishes the closing tag—</p>—the moment you type </. For a longer tag like the <address> tag, this feature saves your fingers a lot of work. (You can also change this behavior to make Dreamweaver automatically insert the closing tag immediately after you finish typing the opening tag [the way Dreamweaver 8 and earlier versions worked]; or, if you just can't stand the feature at all, you can make your wishes felt the Preferences window's Code Hints category mentioned in the previous paragraph.)

Note: If you like Code Hints, you'll love the Snippets panel, which makes reusing code a snap. See Chapter 18 for details.

POWER USERS' CLINIC

JavaScript Code Hints

Earlier versions of Dreamweaver didn't give JavaScript programmers the timesaving Code Hints feature available when typing HTML, CSS, or PHP. That's no longer true in Dreamweaver CS4. Now JavaScript programmers have access to a wide array of code hinting features that make JavaScript programming go faster.

In general, JavaScript code hints work just like regular HTML code hints. As you type JavaScript, Dreamweaver can pop up a box with suggestions that match what you're typing. However, JavaScript code hints go much farther than simply providing a list of JavaScript key words. Dreamweaver can provide hints for basic JavaScript objects like arrays, dates, numbers and strings. For example, say you create an array...gentle reader, if you have no idea what a JavaScript array is, feel free to skip this box. If you then write the array's name in your code, a hint box pops up listing all the various methods and properties of JavaScript array objects.

In addition, Dreamweaver can even keep track of JavaScript functions you've created, and provide code hints using your own function names, as well as custom created classes. Even better, Dreamweaver is aware of DOM (document object model) properties, and provides hints for all the properties and methods of DOM objects. Finally, if you use either the Spry or Prototype JavaScript library, Dreamweaver has built-in code-hinting support for those as well.

Code Collapse

One problem with raw HTML, CSS, JavaScript, or PHP is, well, it's raw—a bunch of letters, numbers, and symbols that tend to blend together into a mind-numbing sea of code. This can make locating a particular bit of code needle-in-a-haystack tough. On large pages, with lots of code, you can easily get lost as you scroll up and down to make a change. In many cases, you don't need to see all the code, because you're not likely to change it—for example, the top portion of a page containing the *DOCTYPE* and *html* declarations (see page 46)—or because you can't change it—like the HTML embedded in template-based pages (Chapter 19), or containing Dreamweaver Library items (Chapter 18).

Fortunately, Dreamweaver lets you get that in-your-way code out of your face. The Code Collapse feature condenses multiple lines of code into a single highlighted box of 10 characters (Figure 10-9). The basic process is simple: Select the code you want to collapse—like all the code above the <body> tag—and then click the icon (Figure 10-9, top) that appears just to the left of both the first and last line you wish to collapse. In Windows, this icon is a small box with a minus sign (–); on a Mac, it's a down-pointing arrow (at the beginning of the selection) and an up-pointing arrow (at the end). The code collapses into a gray outlined box. To expand the code, just select it, and then click the icon (a plus sign [+] in Windows, a right-pointing arrow on the Mac).

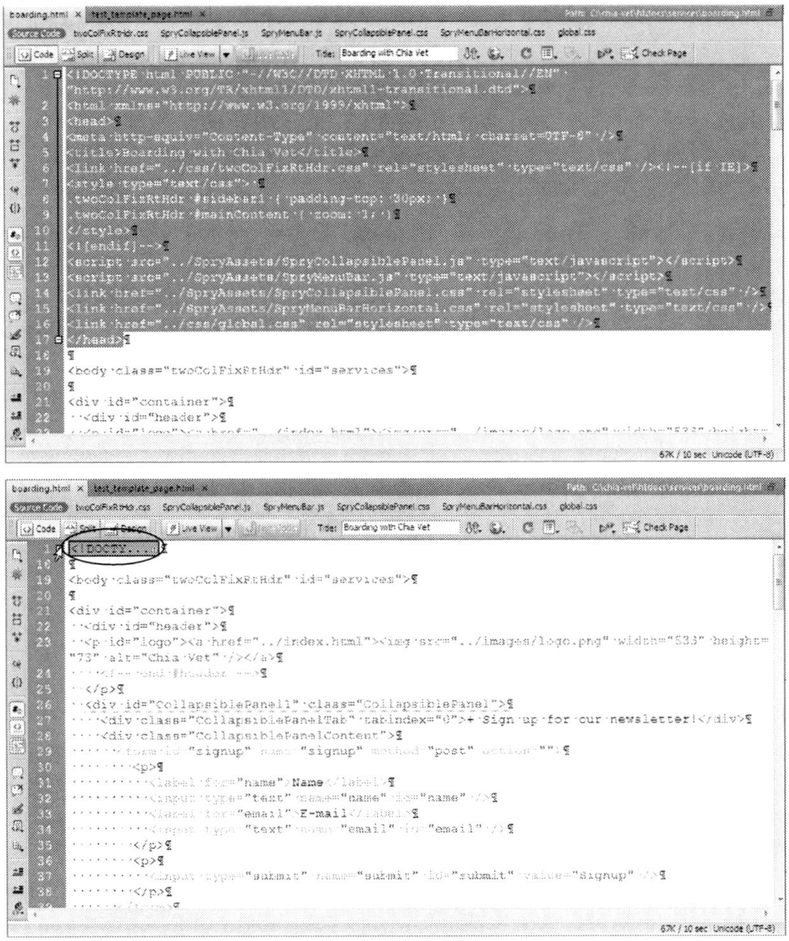

Figure 10-9: *Now you see it, now you don't. You can collapse a multiline selection of HTML code (top) into a compact little gray box (circled in the bottom image). The collapsed code is still there in your page—you haven't deleted it—but now it's conveniently tucked out of sight. If you need a reminder of what code you've collapsed, move your mouse over the gray box, and a yellow tooltip window appears displaying the HTML code.*

Tip: To quickly select multiple lines of HTML, click in the line-number area to the left of the code, indicating where you wish to begin the selection, and then drag to the line where you want to end the selection. (If you don't see any line numbers, you can turn them on using the Coding toolbar or View Options menu [see Figure 10-6].)

Dreamweaver includes a few more nuanced methods of collapsing code. You can:

- **Collapse an individual tag.** Say you want to hide a long paragraph of text. Instead of selecting it, just click anywhere inside the paragraph (<p>) tag, and then either click the Coding toolbar's Collapse Tag button (Figure 10-6), choose Edit → Code Collapse → Collapse Full Tag, or press Ctrl+Shift+J (⌘-Shift-J).

  This feature works on the tag the cursor is nearest. Say you have a paragraph of text, and, inside it, a link. If you click inside the <a> tag and use this feature, then the <a> tag collapses. But if you click anywhere else inside the paragraph, then the paragraph or <p> tag collapses. This behavior is a little confusing, but can be really useful. Say you want to hide everything inside a page's <head> tags. Instead of having to select all the lines inside the <head> tag, just click anywhere between the two <head> tags (but make sure you're not inside *another* tag like the <title> tag), and then use any of the commands mentioned in the previous paragraph.

- **Collapse the code outside an individual tag.** This is a quick way to hide everything *except* the code you want to work on. Suppose you want to see only the code inside the body tag. Click immediately after the opening <body> tag (in other words, inside the <body> tag, but not inside any other tags within the <body> tag), press the Alt (Option) key and then, on the Coding toolbar, click the Collapse Tag button (Figure 10-6). Choosing Edit → Code Collapse → Collapse Outside Full Tag, or pressing Ctrl+Alt+J (⌘-Option-J) also works.
- **Collapse the code outside the current selection.** This is another way to view only the code you wish to work on. Select the code, and then either press the Alt (Option) key and click the Coding toolbar's Collapse Selection button (Figure 10-6), choose Edit → Code Collapse → Collapse Outside Selection, or press Ctrl+Alt+C (⌘-Option-C).
- **Expand All.** If you miss all that hidden code, you can quickly restore it to its full glory by clicking the Coding toolbar's Expand All button (Figure 10-6), choosing Edit → Code Collapse → Expand All, or pressing Ctrl+Alt+E (⌘-Option-E).

You can hide any number of different regions in a page—for example, the top portion of a page, a navigation sidebar that never gets edited, and the copyright notice at the bottom of the page—so you can easily identify the code that you're really interested in working on. Dreamweaver even remembers the state of these sections, which means that if you close a document and then reopen it, the collapsed sections are still collapsed, so you don't have to continually hide code in that page each time you open it for editing.

Setting Code Formatting

Whenever you use the Insert panel, Dreamweaver adds a chunk of HTML that's pre-formatted for easier reading. The code for table rows, for instance, comes indented using two spaces; the code for table *cells*, meanwhile, is indented four spaces. If you're particular about how your HTML is written, Dreamweaver gives you plenty of control over these settings.

Note: If you don't work in Code view frequently, you may not care a whit how your HTML is formatted in the file—and that's fine. As long as the underlying HTML is valid (and Dreamweaver writes valid HTML), Web browsers can display HTML that's been formatted in many different ways. In fact, Web browsers simply ignore multiple spaces, empty lines, and other "white space" characters used to make HTML code more readable.

Dreamweaver provides several ways to control the formatting of the code it produces. Basic settings are available in the Preferences window; advanced settings for obsessive coders even let you control the formatting of individual tags (see the box on page 409). For basic formatting settings, open the Preferences window (Edit → Preferences or Ctrl+U [⌘-U]), and then click the Code Format category (see Figure 10-10). While Dreamweaver's standard settings work fine, you can still configure a number of options.

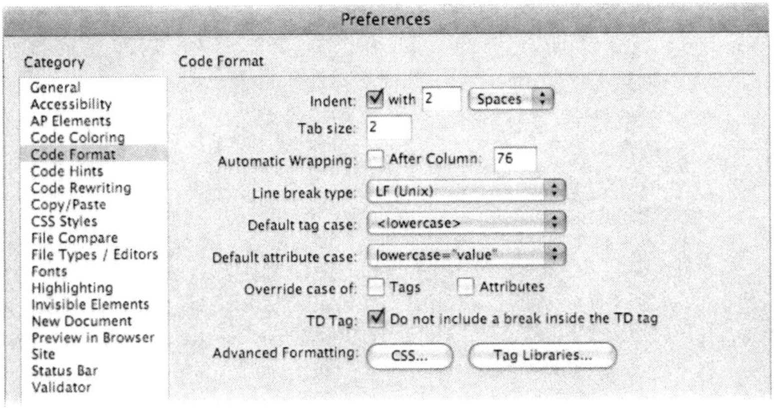

Figure 10-10: *For general control of HTML code, Dreamweaver offers the Code Format category in the Preferences window. For most people, this degree of control is overkill, but if the way HTML code appears in a page's file matters to you, go wild. (These settings don't affect how the page looks in a Web browser—only how the code appears when viewed in Dreamweaver's Code view or another text editor.)*

Indents

To make your code easier to read, it helps to indent nested tags and other block-level elements. But if you'd prefer that Dreamweaver quit auto-indenting such elements, turn off the Indent checkbox. This is also your opportunity to request tabs instead of spaces for indenting lines of code; from the pop-up menu, just choose Tabs.

You can also set the amount of indentation, like this:

- If Spaces is selected in the Indent menu, type the number of spaces you want into the Indent size field. The default setting is two, meaning each indent will be two spaces in the code.
- If you selected Tabs in the Indent menu, the number in the "Tab size" field indicates the size of each tab, measured in spaces. (The size you specify here affects only the display in Code view. In the code itself, Dreamweaver simply inserts a plain tab character.)

Text wrapping

When a line gets long, Dreamweaver can break it into two or more lines by inserting a hard return. This can make your HTML more readable in Code view, and free you from having to scroll to see all of your code. If that's the way you like it, turn on Automatic Wrapping, and then, in the After Column field, type a number. The number specifies how many characters long a line must be before Dreamweaver attempts to break it up.

This option doesn't affect how the page will look to your visitors, only how it looks in a text editor. But unlike Code view's simulated word-wrap option shown in Figure 10-6, this option adds real line-break characters to split your code into multiple, shorter lines. If you use the Code view's word wrap, then you can skip this more intrusive form of text wrapping.

Note: Although Dreamweaver can shorten lines by inserting returns after a specified number of characters, it never does so if the final effect will change the appearance of the Web page. The program is smart enough not to sacrifice the quality of a page just to make the code look better in Code view. That's why some lines of HTML may be considerably longer than the limit you specify here.

Line breaks

Windows, Mac OS, and Unix each look for a different invisible character at the end of each line of code. This expectation can cause problems when you use one kind of computer to create a page, while another OS runs the remote server that dishes out the page. Fortunately, Dreamweaver fixes the problem when it transfers a file to a Web server.

If you plan to use another text editor to edit your Dreamweaver pages, you should select your operating system from the "Line break type" pop-up menu. Doing so assures that the program on the receiving end will properly read the line breaks in Dreamweaver-produced pages.

Case for tags and attributes

You can write tag and property names using either uppercase letters (<B>bold</B>) or lowercase (<b>bold</b>); Web browsers don't care. However, *you* may care how they appear in your HTML display. If so, choose your preference from the two Case pop-up menus. Select either the lowercase or uppercase option from the two menus.

Note: HTML may treat capital and lowercase letters in its tags identically, but XML does not. Both it and the hybrid language *XHTML* require all-lowercase tag and property names.

That's why many Web developers now strictly use lowercase characters, even in their HTML. And that's why, if you select the XHTML option when creating a new page, Dreamweaver ignores an uppercase setting in the Preferences panel—even if you turn on either of the "Override case of" checkboxes.

If you also turn on the "Override case of" checkboxes, then you can make Dreamweaver scan tags and properties when opening a page created by someone else (or some other program). If the case doesn't match your preferences, then Dreamweaver rewrites the code to fit the wishes of you, its master.

TD tag

Adding a line break after an opening <td> (table cell) tag may look good in Code view, but in some browsers it adds an unwanted extra space character in the table cell. The extra space can wreak havoc on your design, so make sure this box is always turned on.

POWER USERS' CLINIC

Take Control of Code Formatting

For ultimate control over tag formatting, Dreamweaver includes the Tag Library Editor. Not only does it let you control *exactly* how Dreamweaver formats every HTML tag it inserts into a page, it also lets you dictate the formatting for nine other Tag Libraries, such as ASP, PHP, JSP, and ColdFusion tags.

Even if you're using some new bleeding-edge tag language unfamiliar to Dreamweaver, you're not out of luck. You can create additional Tag Libraries, and even import custom ASP.NET and JSP tags, as well as DTD Schemas for XML. You can also add additional tags to any Library; so if the HTML standard suddenly changes, you can add new or remove obsolete tags.

To control the formatting of tags in a Library, choose Edit → Tag Libraries to open the Tag Library Editor window. A list of all Tag Libraries appears. Click the + symbol to the left of a Tag Library name to see a list of tags for that Library. Select a tag, and then, from the Tag Format area in the bottom half of the window, select formatting options. Here's a shortcut for quickly reformatting a particular tag already present on a page: Select the tag in the Tag selector first, and then choose Edit → Tag Libraries; Dreamweaver then preselects that tag for you.

You can control where a line breaks in relation to the tag. Your choices are: no line breaks after the tag; no breaks before and after the tag; or no breaks before, inside, *and* after the tag. In addition, you can choose whether any formatting rules are applied to the contents of a tag, and choose the case—upper, lower, mixed—Dreamweaver uses when it adds the tags to the code.

Advanced formatting options

For real sticklers, two advanced formatting buttons let you instruct Dreamweaver how to format every aspect of your CSS and HTML code. The Tag Libraries button opens the Tag Library, discussed in the box above. The CSS button opens the CSS Source Format Options window, which lets you dictate how the CSS code Dreamweaver creates should be written: whether properties get indented; whether CSS properties should appear one per line; the placement of the opening brace used in the CSS rule; and whether there should be a blank line between rules to make the CSS more readable. All these options are matters of personal preference, and don't affect the performance of your Web pages or CSS.

If you find yourself wading through lots of HTML and CSS code, you might want to experiment with these settings to see if you can make the code Dreamweaver produces more readable. Both the Tag Library Editor and Source Format Options windows provide previews of what the formatted HTML and CSS code will look like with the settings you select. Keep in mind that these settings aren't going to affect how *you* write your code. But if you do find that your own HTML or CSS hand coding doesn't look as elegant as Dreamweaver's, you can turn to the Apply

Source Formatting command (Commands → Apply Source Formatting) to make Dreamweaver clean up your code. That command changes a page's code—adds indents, line breaks, and so on—based on the instructions defined by these two options.

Note: Another set of preference settings affect how Dreamweaver creates its CSS code. The Preferences window's CSS Styles category tells Dreamweaver whether or not to use CSS shorthand properties. See page 308 for more on CSS shorthand properties.

Related Files

With external style sheets, JavaScript libraries like the Spry framework (Chapter 12), and server-side programming (see Part 6 of this book) becoming more and more a part of the average Web designer's toolbox, Dreamweaver CS4 includes a new feature to make it easier for code jockeys to jump around the vast collection of files required to make a single Web page work. The Related Files toolbar (see Figure 10-11) shows all files that are included in the current Web page. This includes external style sheets, external JavaScript files (like those used to create the Spry navigation bar), and included server-side files such as server-side includes or other server programming files.

When you open a Web page that includes external style sheets or files with JavaScript or server-side programming, Dreamweaver CS4 displays the names of those files in the Related Files toolbar (Figure 10-11). The first item in the toolbar—Source Code—refers to the Web page itself. The other items represent style sheets or other linked programming files. For example, in Figure 10-11 there are six related files—four external style sheets and two JavaScript files.

Note: If you don't see the Related Files toolbar, it may have gotten turned off. To turn it back on, choose Edit → Preferences (Dreamweaver → Preferences on Macs), click the General Category, and then make sure the "Enable Related Files" box is checked.

When you click the name of a related file in the toolbar, Dreamweaver displays that file's code. How Dreamweaver displays the code depends on which view you're in: If you're in Design (or Split) view, then Dreamweaver displays the Web page design in the Design view and the code for the related file in the other pane. If you're in Code view, then Dreamweaver simply switches from the HTML of the Web page to the CSS, JavaScript, or server-side code of the related file.

When you're working in the related file, all the normal file operations apply to that file. For example, from the Related Files toolbar, if you select a CSS file, and edit the CSS, when you choose File → Save, only that CSS file is saved; changes you made to the Web page's code, or any other related files, aren't yet saved (see the Tip on this page). Likewise, if you choose Site → Put to move a file to the Web server as described on page 678, that CSS file gets whisked off to the server, but not the Web page itself. This sequence gets a little confusing when working in Split view since the Web page design is in one half of the Dreamweaver window, and the code for another file is in the other half. When working on the Web page in the Design view half, all file operations apply to the Web page document.

Tip: When working with the related files feature, you may be editing multiple files (for instance, the Web page, CSS, and JavaScript) at the same time. To make sure you save the changes to *all* the files, use the File → Save All command, which saves all opened and edited files. Better yet, create a keyboard shortcut (see page 799) for this useful command.

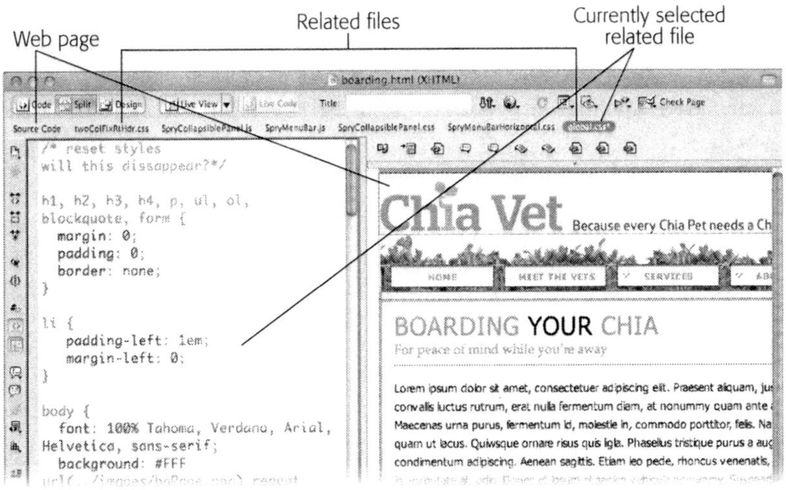

Figure 10-11: *The new Related Files toolbar is a big help for JavaScript programmers and those who like to code their CSS by hand. The toolbar gives you instant access to any CSS or programming file included on the current Web page, so that you can quickly summon and edit CSS, JavaScript, or server-side programming. That saves you a trip to the Open File dialog box and the need to hunt and peck through your file system to find the correct file. To get the side-by-side view pictured here, from the View menu, select "Code and Design", pictured back in Figure 10-2.*

Note: Server-side programming often includes several levels of programming files. For example, to add some PHP programming code to a Web page, you might "include" a single PHP file (kind of like using an external JavaScript file). A common technique is to have that file include *other* PHP files (this way, you can easily reuse common programs throughout a site). Unfortunately, Dreamweaver CS4 doesn't track included server-side files deeper than one level–in other words, Dreamweaver "sees" only files linked to the Web page you're working on, not files further down the link chain. So those files don't show up in the Related Files toolbar. So if you need to edit a file that's linked more than one level deep, then you have to open it from the Files panel, or choose File → Open, and then locate the file yourself. Fortunately, this doesn't apply to CSS, which lets you link an external CSS style sheet to another external style sheet. In that case, Dreamweaver sees all levels of linked external style sheets.

The related files feature works hand-in-hand with the Code Navigator that was also added to Dreamweaver CS4. As described on page 320, the Code Navigator (which appears as a small ship steering wheel icon floating above page elements) lets you see a list of all CSS styles that affect a page element. In the Code Navigator's pop-up list, if you click one of the styles, and that style is in an external style sheet, then Dreamweaver switches to Split view, opens the CSS file, and positions the cursor at the appropriate CSS style so you can edit it. (That said, you might find the other methods of editing CSS, described on page 126 and page 305, easier and more error-free.)

Live Code

Live Code is another new addition to Dreamweaver CS4. This feature works in conjunction with the Live View option introduced on page 189, and discussed in depth on page 553. (The short version: Live View lets you see what an in-progress Web page actually looks like in a Web browser…right within Dreamweaver.)

The Live Code button (see Figure 10-12) makes Dreamweaver jump into Split view, with the page's Design view in one half of the window, and the underlying HTML in the other half. When in Live Code view, the HTML appears atop a yellow background, and, as with Live View in general, you can't edit any of the HTML of the page. So what is Live Code *for*? Or, more accurately, *who* is it for?

Hear ye! Hear ye! Calling all JavaScript programmers.

Much of today's JavaScript programming is aimed at manipulating the HTML of a page by making elements appear or disappear. For example, people often make forms more useable by adjusting the options on the form based on selections the visitor makes. If someone checks the "married" button on a form under a question about marital status, it's possible, using JavaScript, to make a *new* set of questions (ones that, say, apply just to a married person) appear. In other words, JavaScript is actually changing the HTML that the page started with.

Live Code gives JavaScript programmers a glimpse into those changes. It lets you see if a JavaScript program is correctly changing how the page looks. If you're a JavaScript programming type, then you probably know about the DOM (or Document Object Model). Live Code is a view directly into the DOM—in other words, how the browser currently sees the HTML it's displaying. This view is useful when a JavaScript program doesn't seem to be changing the page in the way you think it should.

Activating Live Code is pretty straightforward. First, get yourself into Live View by going to the Document toolbar, and then clicking the button of the same name. Next, turn on its neighboring Live Code button. Now you're ready to see how the HTML changes based on your interactions with the page. Unfortunately, Dreamweaver doesn't highlight *what's* changed, so you have to hunt and peck around the code to see how the JavaScript program has affected the HTML.

And if you're not a JavaScript programmer? Skip Live Code, you don't need it.

Tip: The F6 key freezes any currently running JavaScript. So you can make a drop-down menu "stick" in place after mousing over it. It's like freezing the entire page, and it's great for working with Live Code, since you can freeze a dynamic, rollover effect, and see how the JavaScript programming has affected the HTML of the page. You can also use the Live View menu to freeze JavaScript as pictured in Figure 10-12.

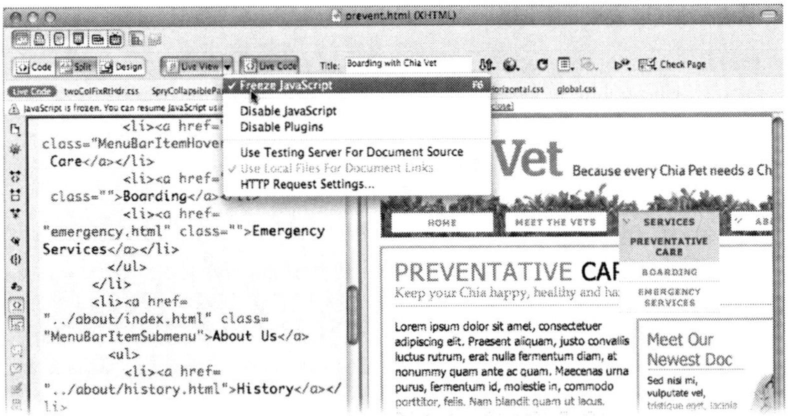

Figure 10-12: *Dreamweaver CS4's new Live View lets you preview interactive effects, such as the Spry-driven Services menu pictured here. In Live View, mousing over a menu item shows how the menu will behave in a real Web browser. If you want to inspect the HTML created by this mouseover, then choose Freeze JavaScript–in this example, the drop-down menu sticks in place, and you can inspect the HTML using Live Code.*

Quick Tag Editor

Code view is great when you really need (or want) to jump into the trenches and fine-tune your HTML. But if you're a visually-oriented person, you probably spend most of your time in Dreamweaver's Design view, enjoying the pleasures of its visual authoring environment.

Occasionally, however, you'll want to dip momentarily into the HTML pond, especially when you need to use some HTML that's not available from the Insert panel. You might wish you could type out a quick HTML tag on the spot, right there in Design view, without having to make the mental and visual shift required for a switch into Code view.

That's what the Quick Tag Editor is all about. To access the Quick Tag Editor, press Ctrl+T (⌘-T)—or, if you're feeling especially mouse-driven, in the Property inspector, click the Quick Tag Editor button (see Figure 10-13). Depending on what you've selected in the document window, the Quick Tag Editor opens in one of the following three modes (see Figure 10-13):

- **Insert new tag.** Inserts a new tag in the page. You get this mode if nothing is currently selected in your document window.
- **Edit tag.** Lets you edit the tag for whatever is selected in the document window (a graphic, for example), and all its properties.

- **Wrap tag.** If you've selected a swath of text or other objects (like two images), the editor opens in this mode, which lets you easily wrap a new tag around the current selection.

Tip: You can cycle through the modes by repeatedly pressing Ctrl+T (⌘-T).

Using the Quick Tag Editor

You can type tag names, properties, and property values directly into the Quick Tag Editor window. If you're editing a selected tag, you can change any of the properties listed, and even add new ones. When you're done, press Enter (Return). The Quick Tag Editor closes, and the changes take effect.

To make all this even easier, the Quick Tag Editor sports a helpful list—called *Tag Hints*—of HTML tags and properties, for your selection pleasure. It's much like Code view's Code Hints feature (in fact, in the Preferences window, the Code Hints category also controls Tag Hints). When you insert a tag, for example, a menu of available tags appears (top right in Figure 10-13). Use the up and down arrow keys or the scroll bar to move through the list. And when you type the first few letters of a tag or property, Dreamweaver jumps to the nearest match in the list.

To choose the highlighted name, press Enter or Return. Dreamweaver adds that tag or property name to the Quick Tag Editor window. If you've selected a tag property, then Dreamweaver adds the proper punctuation (href=" ", for example). The insertion point appears between the quotation marks, waiting for you to type the property's value.

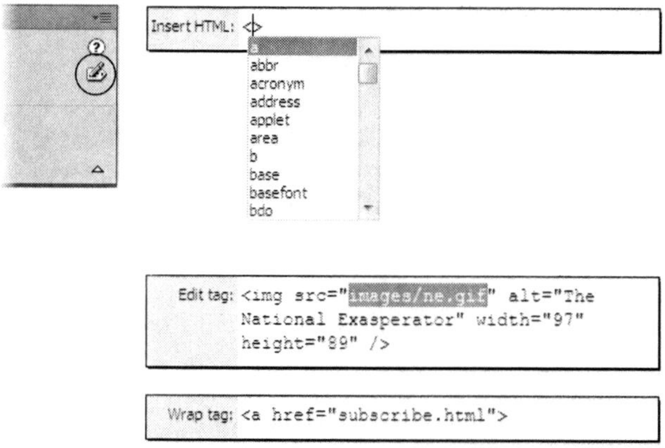

Figure 10-13:
Left: You can open the Quick Tag Editor by clicking the corresponding button in the Property inspector's upper-right corner (circled). (This button is visible only in Design view.)

Right: The three modes of the Quick Tag Editor let you insert new tags, edit old tags, or wrap a new tag around a selection. The Quick Tag Editor is mobile: Drag the window by its handle (the mode name) anywhere on the screen–ideal when you want to see the part of the page you're modifying.

Tip: When editing an existing tag in the Quick Tag Editor, press Tab to select the next property or property value. You can then type a new property or value. Shift+Tab selects the *previous* property or value.

Tag Inspector

The Property inspector is a handy tool. It lets you adjust properties for all sorts of HTML tags, like a table's width or a paragraph's font. But even the Property inspector doesn't tell the whole story: Some HTML tags have additional properties that don't appear there, such as the <a> tag's *tabindex* property, which lets you control the order in which links are highlighted as visitors press Tab.

For these hard-to-reach properties, turn to the *Tag inspector* (see Figure 10-14). Think of it as the uber–Property inspector. For hard-core HTML fanatics, it's the best way to set properties for every HTML tag. To display it, press the F9 key, or choose Window → Tag inspector (the same procedure also hides this panel).

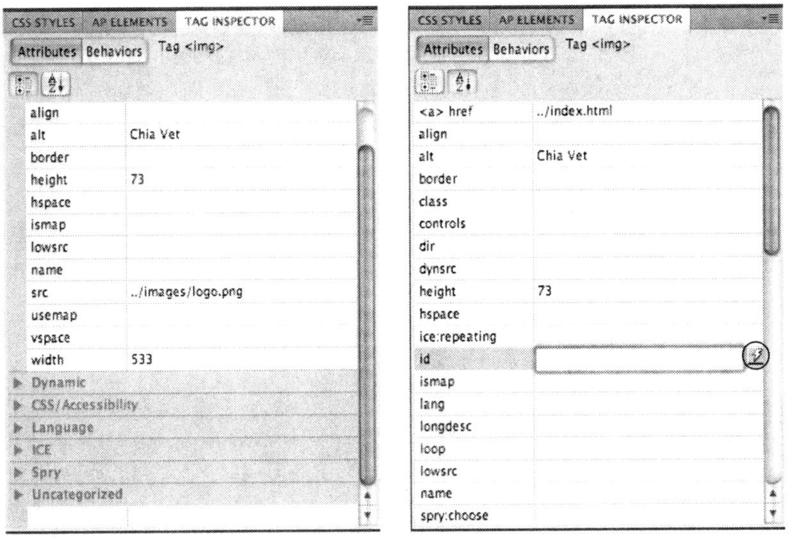

***Figure 10-14:** Dreamweaver's Tag inspector lets you edit every property of every tag on a page. What it lacks in user-friendliness–you need to know a lot about HTML to use it correctly–it makes up for in comprehensiveness. It has two faces: Category view (left) and List view (right). The List view is just that: a list of all properties for the selected tag. The Category view imposes a bit of order on this mess, by organizing the different properties into related categories. You can even set a property value dynamically, based on information retrieved from a database, using the lightning bolt button (circled). (Of course, you must first learn how to build dynamic Web sites by reading Part 6 of this book.)*

When you select a tag on the page (in either Code or Design view), *all* of its properties appear in the panel (see Figure 10-14). You can edit any of these properties by clicking in the space to the right of the property name. You can type a new value or, for certain properties, use a pop-up menu to choose from a list of property values. For color properties, use Dreamweaver's ubiquitous color box to select the particular shade you want.

Unfortunately, you need to understand HTML fairly well to set the correct values; Dreamweaver doesn't make the process foolproof, leaving open the possibility that you could enter an invalid property. (To learn more about HTML tags and their properties, turn to Dreamweaver's built-in HTML reference, described on page 422.)

Comparing Versions of a Web Page

Sometimes you make a change to a page, save it, preview it, close it, and move along to the next assignment for the day. Only later, when you're taking a second look at your day's changes, just before moving them up to the Web server, you notice that one of the pages you changed has some problem you didn't notice at first: Perhaps the left sidebar is suddenly wider than it was before. Since you've already closed the file, you can't use the Undo feature to remove whatever pesky mistake you made. You could, of course, retrieve the current version of the page from the Web server (see page 678), thus overwriting your changes. But what if you did a lot of good work on the page—adding text, graphics, and links—that you don't want to lose? Ideally, you'd like to see all the changes you made to the page, and selectively undo the mistake you accidentally introduced to the sidebar.

Enter the Compare File command. Dreamweaver includes a command that lets you compare two files, and see what lines of code are different between the two. This tool is a perfect solution for problems like the unintentionally botched sidebar. With it, you can compare the local file (the one with the messed-up sidebar) with the remote file (the live version of the Web site that works, but is missing the fine new pictures and words you added). You can then identify any changes you made, and smoke out your mistake.

Dreamweaver doesn't actually have this tool built into it. Instead, Dreamweaver just passes the files you wish to compare to a separate file-comparison utility (often called a "diff" tool, since it identifies *differences* between files). You need to download this utility, and you have a lot of different ones to choose from. Fortunately, you can download several free utilities for both Windows and Mac (see the following boxes).

After downloading and installing the file-comparison utility, you need to tell Dreamweaver where to find your new helper:

1. **Open the Preferences panel, by choosing Edit → Preferences (Dreamweaver → Preferences on the Mac), or pressing Ctrl+U (⌘-U), and then click the File Compare category.**

   There's not much to this Preferences category, just a single box and a Browse button.

2. **Click the Browse button, and then navigate to and select the file-comparison utility.**

   For example, on Windows you might find your utility here: *C:\Program Files\WinMerge\WinMergeU.exe.*

WINDOWS ONLY

Getting Your Hands on the Goodies

You can find lots of file-comparison tools for Windows. Beyond Compare from Scooter Software (*www.scootersoftware.com*) is a commercial product ($30) that offers a wide range of comparison options. For a free alternative, check out WinMerge (*www.winmerge.org*). This open source software provides all the basic options you'll need. Here's how you get it. Go to *www.winmerge.org*. Click the "Download Now" button. At this point you're asked to save the file to your computer—of course, if you're using Internet Explorer, one of those yellow "Warning, warning, enemy attack" banners appears at the top of the page—you need to click that, and then choose "Download File" to actually download the file to your computer.

Once you've downloaded the program, the process for installing it is like most other Windows programs. Just double-click the file to launch an installer, and follow the step-by-step instructions. You have several options along the way, but just accept the suggested settings and you'll be fine. Once it's installed, you're ready to proceed as described below.

On the Mac, it's slightly different. Instead of selecting the text-editing program Text Wrangler or BBEdit, you need to specify the proper "diff" tool, which is stored in a special location on your computer. Navigate to the */usr/bin* folder—something like this: *Macintosh HD:usr:bin*—and select the correct file. For Text Wrangler, it's *twdiff*; for BBEdit, it's *bbdiff*; and for FileMerge, it's *opendiff*.

3. **Click OK to close the Preferences window.**

   Dreamweaver's been notified of the location of the utility, so you're ready to begin comparing files.

MACS ONLY

What Difference Does It Make?

The Mac version of Dreamweaver supports only three file comparison tools: File Merge (which is a Mac developer program that comes with the XCode tools on your Mac OS X installation disc), BBEdit (the powerful, $125 commercial text editor), and Text Wrangler (the free little brother of BBEdit). Bare Bones Software (*www.barebones.com*) produces both BBEdit and Text Wrangler, but since Text Wrangler's free, it's the best place to begin.

Point your Web browser to *www.barebones.com/products/textwrangler/download.shtml*, and click any of the download links to get the program onto your computer. As with many Mac applications, this download opens a disk image—just like a folder—with the program inside it. Just drag it to your Applications folder to install it.

The Compare File command works with a local file and a remote file, so you need to have already defined a site with both local and remote root folders (see Chapter 17 for details on how to do this). In addition, since you're comparing two files, you need to make sure you've got a version of the same file on your local computer and another version on your remote site—for example, your home page, or one of the other pages in your site. To compare the files, follow these steps:

1. **In the Files panel, locate the file you wish to compare.**

   This file can be listed either in the Local View or Remote View of the Files panel (see page 678).

2. **Right-click (Control-click) the file, and then, from the pop-up menu that appears, select "Compare with Remote".**

   This menu says, "Compare with Local" if you're in the Remote view of the files panel.

   Dreamweaver does a little behind-the-scenes trickery before passing the files off to the file comparison program. It first creates a folder (if it's not already created) named *_compareTemp* in the local root folder of your site. Dreamweaver then creates a temporary file with all of the code from the remote-site file, and stores that in the new folder. In other words, you don't actually compare the file on the live Web server with the local file on your computer; you compare a copy of the remote file with the local file. This distinction is important to keep in mind if you want to incorporate changes between the files, as described in step 3.

   At any rate, your selected file-comparison program—for example, WinMerge or Text Wrangler—starts and compares the two files. If it finds no differences—they're *exactly* the same files—then you'll most likely get a message saying something to the effect of "The Selected Files are Identical." So if no differences are found between the files, your work is done. If there is a difference, then the file-comparison program displays the two files, and identifies the code that differs between the two files (see Figure 10-15 and Figure 10-14).

3. **Evaluate the differences, and incorporate any changes into your local file.**

   File-comparison programs generally work the same way. When comparing two files, you see the code for the two files side by side. In addition, the program has some way of notifying you of any differences. You can then review the differences in the code, and merge the changes into one file or the other. For example, say you accidentally deleted a table from your local file; a comparison of this file with the remote file shows the table intact in the remote file, and indicates that it's missing in the local file. You can then copy the table code from the remote file into the local file. If, however, you deleted the table purposefully, then do nothing, and move on to evaluate the next difference.

   Here's where Dreamweaver's little bait-and-switch mentioned in step 2 becomes important. You're not actually comparing the remote file with the local file; you're comparing a *copy* of the remote file saved locally in the *_compare Temp* folder. As a result, you want to move changes only in one direction—from the temporary file to your local file. Changes in the temporary file have no effect on the actual live file on your Web server. So how do you update the remote file? Move any changes you want made *from* the temporary file to your local file. Once you're satisfied with the changes, you can save them, return to Dreamweaver, and then upload them to your remote site folder. Then pour yourself a cup of tea and be thankful you don't have to do *that* very often.

4. **Save any changes, return to Dreamweaver, and then move your newly updated local file to your Web server.**

   The exact process varies from program to program, but see the next two sections for examples using WinMerge and Text Wrangler.

Tip: Dreamweaver lets you compare two files on your local hard drive (the home page of the site you're working on vs. a backup of that page you made last week, for example). To do this, go to the Files panel, and then, from the site list, select your hard drive (instead of a defined site). In this mode, the Files panel acts just like Windows Explorer or the Mac Finder. You just need to wade through all of the folders until you can see both files at once. Ctrl-click (⌘-click) each file to select them both, right-click (ctrl-click) one of the files, and then, from the pop-up menu, choose Compare Local Files. The process from that point on is the same as comparing a local and remote file.

Using WinMerge to Compare Files

If you've got a Windows PC and you're interested in taking Dreamweaver's Compare Files command for a test drive, see the box on page 417 for instructions on how to download WinMerge, and then follow these steps:

1. **Once you've downloaded and installed WinMerge, follow the steps on page 416 to set up Dreamweaver's preferences for working with WinMerge.**

   First you need to make sure Dreamweaver knows to use WinMerge for file comparison.

2. **Follow steps 1 and 2 on the opposite page to select a file and tell Dreamweaver to compare it with its sibling on the remote Web server.**

   WinMerge launches, and if there are any differences between the files, the program shows the code for the two files side by side, with all differences highlighted (see Figure 10-15).

   In WinMerge, differences are highlighted by one or more yellow bars in the left Location pane (circled in Figure 10-15), and the code is highlighted either in yellow (meaning there's content present in one file that's missing in the other file) or gray (meaning there's content missing in one file that's present in the other file).

3. **Click anywhere in the page, and then click any of the "diff" navigation buttons—next diff, previous diff, first diff, or last diff (see Figure 10-15).**

   "Diff" stands for difference, so clicking these buttons takes you to the locations in the files where the code differs. Doing so also selects the differing code and highlights it in red. You can now see which code you wish to keep.

4. **If the code in the remote file looks correct, click the Copy Right or Copy Left button.**

   Which button you click depends on whether the remote file is on the left or right side of the window. A file name beginning with TMP in a folder named

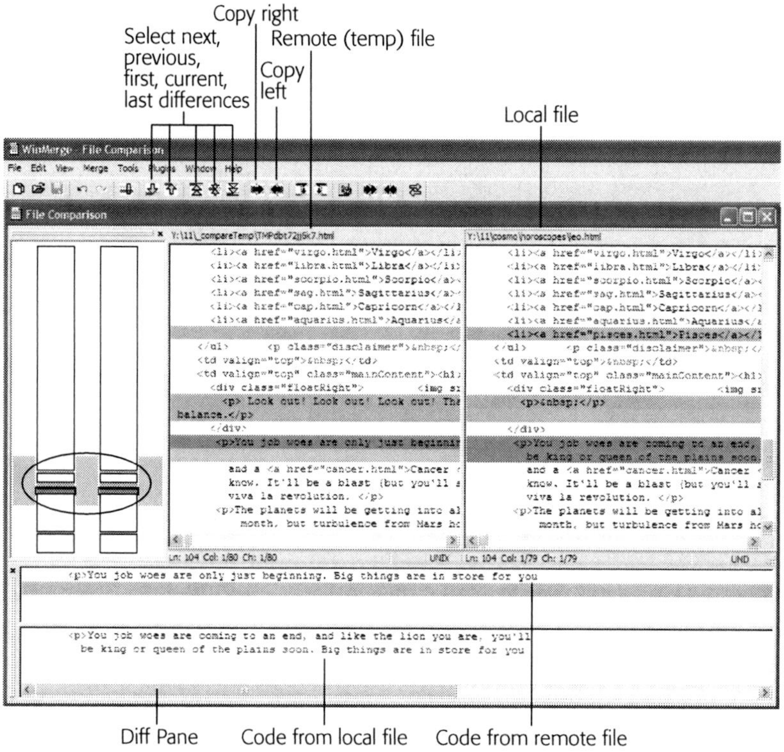

***Figure 10-15:** WinMerge includes a kind of bird's-eye view of code differences in the far-left Location pane. Click near any yellow bands (circled) to jump to code that differs between the two files. You can also tell which file is the temp (remote) file, by looking at the file path just above the page's code, and locating the file with _compareTemp in the name. In this example, the left page's path is* Y:\11_compareTemp\TMPdbt72jj6k7.htm; *it's the code from the remote file.*

_compareTemp is the remote file (for example, in Figure 10-15 the remote file is on the left). If the remote code is on the left, then click the Copy Right button. This button moves the code over to the page on the right—your local file.

You don't need to do anything if the code in the local file looks OK.

Note: The "diff" pane gives a clear picture of how the code differs between the files. To view it, choose View → Diff Pane.

5. **Continue with steps 3 and 4 until you've evaluated all the differing code in the two pages.**

   At this point, the "perfect" copy is your local file. It has all the correct code from the remote file, and all the correct code from the local file. You just need to move it to your Web server.

6. **Move your local file to your Web server, using one of the techniques described on page 678.**

Using Text Wrangler to Compare Files

Mac owners can download the free Text Wrangler if they want to compare files (see the box on page 417). And since BBEdit is a more powerful version of Text Wrangler, these steps work for that program as well:

1. **Once you've installed Text Wrangler, follow the steps on page 416 to set up Dreamweaver's preferences.**

   First you need to make sure Dreamweaver knows to use Text Wrangler for file comparison.

2. **Follow steps 1 and 2 on page 418 to select a file and tell Dreamweaver to compare it with its sibling on the remote Web server.**

   Text Wrangler launches, and if there are any differences between the files, it shows the code for the two files side by side (see Figure 10-16). Where lines of code differ, Text Wrangler identifies them in the Differences panel below the two pages. The program also gives some indication of how the lines differ: For example, "Nonmatching lines" means the lines are similar (some of the code is the same) but not identical, while "Extra lines before line 678" means that completely different lines of code are in one file but not the other.

   If the files are identical, then Dreamweaver pops up a "No difference found between these files" message (although sometimes, if there's no difference, you don't see any message at all).

3. **In the Differences panel, double-click the difference you wish to inspect.**

   It's a good strategy to just start at the top of the list and work your way down.

4. **If the code in the remote file looks correct, then in the Differences panel, click one of the Apply buttons.**

   Which button you click depends on whether the remote file is on the left or right side of the window (see Figure 10-16 for instructions on figuring this out).

   If the remote code is on the left, click the "Apply to Old" button. Doing so moves the code over to the page on the right, your local file.

   You don't need to do anything if the code in the local file looks OK.

5. **Continue with steps 3 and 4 until you've evaluated all the differing code in the two pages.**

   At this point, the "perfect" copy is your local file. It has all the correct code from the remote file, and all the correct code from the local file. You just need to move it to your Web server.

6. **Move your local file to your Web server, using one of the techniques described on page 678.**

You can quickly and easily compare a local file to a remote file with Dreamweaver. You can also access the file-compare feature to compare two local files, or two

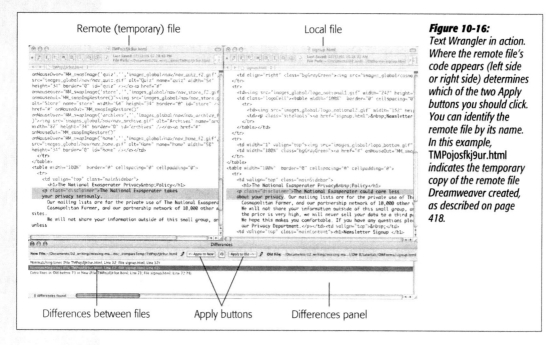

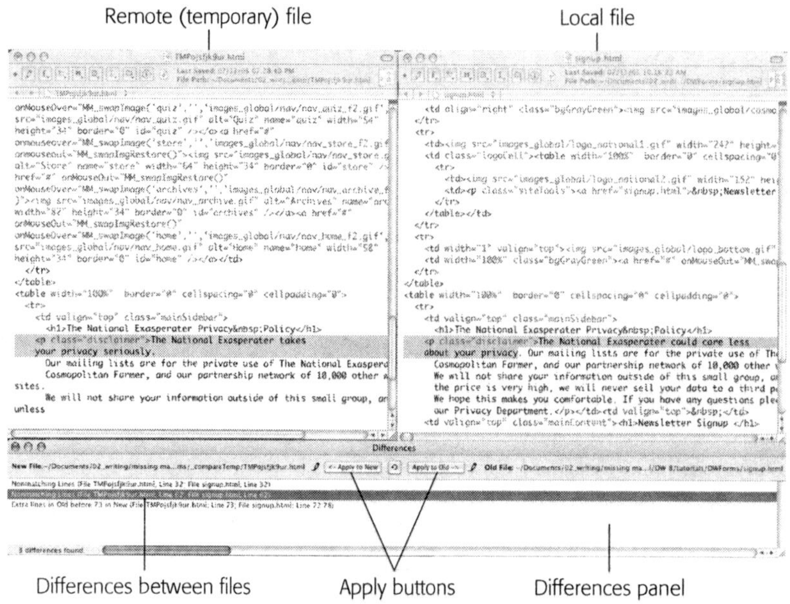

Figure 10-16: *Text Wrangler in action. Where the remote file's code appears (left side or right side) determines which of the two Apply buttons you should click. You can identify the remote file by its name. In this example,* TMPojosfkj9ur.html *indicates the temporary copy of the remote file Dreamweaver created, as described on page 418.*

remote files, but the steps are so convoluted that it's a lot easier just to bypass Dreamweaver and go directly to WinMerge, Text Wrangler, or the file-comparison utility of your choice. In the case of two remote files, download them first, and then conduct the comparison.

Reference Panel

When it comes to building Web sites, there's a lot to know. After all, Cascading Style Sheets, HTML, and JavaScript are filled with cryptic terms and subtle nuances. Fortunately, Dreamweaver's Reference panel makes your search for knowledge a little bit easier. It gives you quick access to reference excerpts on 13 Web topics from a variety of authoritative sources, including:

- *O'Reilly CSS Reference.* In-depth information on Cascading Style Sheets.
- *O'Reilly HTML Reference.* Complete guide to HTML tags and properties.
- *O'Reilly JavaScript Reference.* A not-so-well-organized reference to JavaScript topics, concepts, and commands.
- *O'Reilly PHP Pocket Reference.* A less-than-user-friendly reference to PHP. For seasoned programmers.
- *O'Reilly SQL Language Reference.* If you plan to go deeper into database-driven Web development, this great reference can help you figure out how to write the perfect database query.

- *O'Reilly ASP Reference.* Look up commands for Active Server Pages, one of Microsoft's server-side programming technologies.
- *O'Reilly ASP.NET Reference.* More server-side commands, but this time for ASP's more powerful successor, .NET. That said, the information here is out of date and doesn't apply to the current version of .NET.
- *UsableNet Accessibility Reference.* Guidelines for making Web pages more accessible to the disabled.
- *Adobe CFML Reference.* Complete reference to tags used in the ColdFusion Markup Language (used with Adobe's ColdFusion application server).
- *Adobe CF Function Reference.* A reference of different functions (commands) built into ColdFusion functions. Includes helpful examples of how to use each function.
- *O'Reilly JSP Reference.* Java got you down? Quickly look up Java Server Page commands here.
- *O'Reilly XML Reference.* Dreamweaver offers some interesting XML features (see Chapter 26), but this general dictionary of XML terms and properties isn't the place to start your education.
- *O'Reilly XSLT Reference.* To turn XML into readable XHTML, you'll turn to XSLT (and Chapter 26, where you'll learn how to use it). This reference describes the various XSLT functions.

To open the Reference panel, choose Help → Reference, or press Shift+F1. The Reference panel appears at the bottom of the screen, docked with the Results panel group (see Figure 10-17). The first menu at the top of the panel lets you choose the "book" you want. Once you've selected a reference, choose a particular HTML tag, CSS style, JavaScript object, or appropriate reference topic from the menu to the right of the Book menu. A description of that item appears in the main window. Depending on the reference, there may be sample usage and browser-support details. A secondary menu to the right lets you access additional information about a particular property or details of the selected tag, style, object, or topic. For example, in Figure 10-17, to display information about the <a> tag's *tabindex* property, from the Tag menu, you'd choose "a", and, from the Attribute menu, "tabindex".

Tip: You can quickly see reference information for a tag by either clicking or selecting a tag, and then pressing Shift+F1. The Reference panel opens, and information for that particular tag appears.

While you don't spend much time in the Reference panel, it's a good way to keep your HTML and CSS chops sharp.

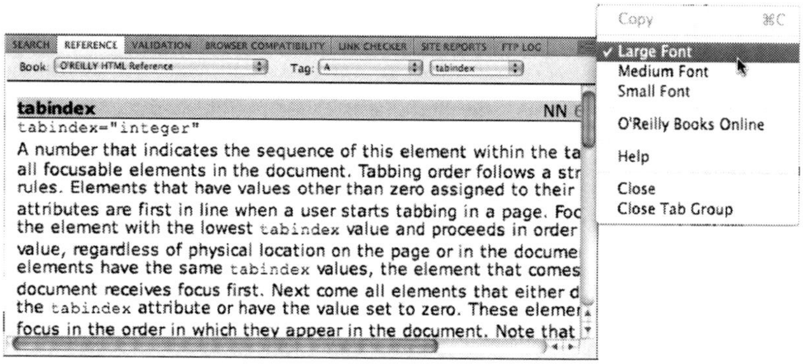

Figure 10-17:
If the print in the Reference panel is too small or too large, use the panel's shortcut menu (click the arrow in the panel's upper-right corner), as shown here, and select a different size. When perusing the reference panel, Dreamweaver lets you copy examples of tags and code, so you can paste them into a page, but it doesn't let you copy the reference information that explains the tag or code. Oh well. You'll just have to type your own "Plagiarist's Guide to Web Design."

Inserting JavaScript

Dreamweaver includes many fun and useful interactive effects—Spry Menus, Spry Form Validation, Spry Effects, Dreamweaver behaviors, and so on. All these effects are achieved with JavaScript programming. Of course, you can do a lot of other cool things with JavaScript that Dreamweaver isn't programmed for. In these cases, you need to wade into the depths of JavaScript programming yourself.

The most straightforward approach, especially if you're already familiar with JavaScript, is to simply switch into Code view (Ctrl+` [Option-`]), and then type away. Or, if you prefer, you can use Dreamweaver's Script window to add your JavaScript code (see Figure 10-18).

To add your JavaScript code, click in either the head or body section of the page, and then choose Insert → HTML → Script Objects → Script. In the Script window that appears (Figure 10-18), from the Type menu, choose "text/javascript" (you have a bewildering selection of options, but for straightforward JavaScript, choose "text/javascript").

Tip: You can use the Insert Script command in Design view also, but to add a script to the <head> of the page, first chose View → Head Content, which opens a small bar below the Document toolbar that lists all the different tags like <title>, <script>, and <meta> that appear in the head of a page. Click here, and then follow the above recipe for inserting a script.

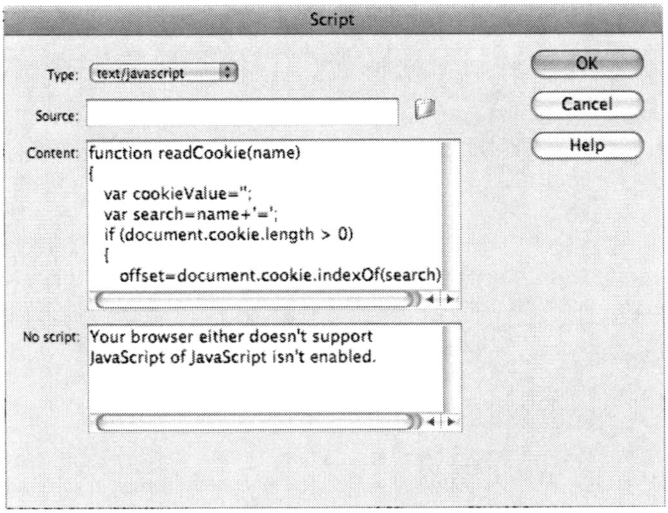

Figure 10-18:
Unlike Code view, the Script window doesn't respond to the Tab key; if you're accustomed to indenting your code, you need to use spaces. You can also insert a message in the "No script" box; the note appears if the Web browser doesn't understand JavaScript.

In the Content section, just type your script (no need to include <script> tags, as Dreamweaver handles that part), and then click OK. If you inserted the script in the body of the document, then you see a small gold icon (indicating an invisible element on the page) to mark its location.

You can edit your script in Code view, of course. In Design view, select the script icon, and then, in the Property inspector, click Edit.

If you use external JavaScript files, you can link to them directly in the Script window (see Figure 10-18). Instead of typing any code, click the familiar "Browse for File" icon (to the right of the Source box), locate the external JavaScript file, and then click OK. Dreamweaver adds the appropriate code to link the script file to the Web page.

Dreamweaver also lets you open and work on external JavaScript files (.js files) right in Code view and with the new Related Files toolbar discussed on page 410, you can easily jump right to the JavaScript code in an external JavaScript file. You can use the built-in text-editing capabilities of Code view to write your JavaScript programs.

Note: JavaScript programming is no walk in the park. While it's certainly easier to learn than full-featured languages like Java or C++, it can still be challenging. If you want to get your feet wet, here's a great resource for basic tutorials and information on JavaScript: *www.w3school.com/js/*. For a more in-depth coverage, check out *JavaScript: The Missing Manual*.

GEM IN THE ROUGH

JavaScript Extractor

For JavaScript programmers it's generally considered best practice to put as much of your JavaScript code as possible into an external file. An external JavaScript file has the same benefits as an external CSS file. First, you need to download the code only once, so overall download speed for your site is faster. Second, with most of the code in an external file, you can easily make sitewide changes to your programs by editing just a single file.

Unfortunately, Dreamweaver doesn't follow this philosophy when it comes to much of the code it creates. Dreamweaver behaviors (covered in Chapter 13), for example, insert their JavaScript code directly into a Web page. If you use the same behavior throughout your site, then you're unnecessarily repeating code in every page, when it would be much more efficient to store that code in a separate file, and then just attach that file to each Web page.

Dreamweaver CS4 introduces a new tool—the JavaScript Extractor—that lets you strip out chunks of JavaScript from your Web pages, and store it in an external JavaScript file. To use it, open a page with JavaScript code in it—for example, a page with a Spry menu (page 184), or one that uses Dreamweaver's image rollover tool (page 248). Then choose Commands → Externalize JavaScript. The Externalize JavaScript window appears, listing all the changes Dreamweaver will make. You can uncheck the box next to a proposed change to prevent Dreamweaver from making that particular change.

You can also choose how Dreamweaver moves the code from the page: The "Only externalize JavaScript" option leaves what are called inline event handlers in place (this is code embedded in a tag, like an <a> tag which triggers the JavaScript); while the "attach unobtrusively" option removes that code. The first option is good if you're just using the Dreamweaver behaviors described in Chapter 13 (but not the Spry effects). In that case, Dreamweaver removes the JavaScript, but you can still edit the behaviors as you normally would (page 564).

The second option isn't very useful, so skip it. It's intended to achieve one of the goals of a good JavaScript program—keeping JavaScript out of your HTML—but it doesn't achieve any of the other goals of unobtrusive JavaScript (like making sure your page works even with JavaScript turned off). To learn more about unobtrusive JavaScript, visit *www.onlinetools.org/articles/unobtrusivejavascript/*.

Unfortunately, either option makes any Spry effects, widgets, or datasets you've added to a page uneditable. Well, actually, they're still editable, but you have to do it yourself in Code view! In other words, if you use the JavaScript Extractor, you can't use Dreamweaver's friendly interface for changing your Spry widgets. In addition, if you choose the second export option—"attach unobtrusively"—even normal Dreamweaver behaviors become uneditable. The bottom line: If you ever want to update a Spry widget or Dreamweaver behavior you've added to a page, you're better off skipping this tool.

3

Part Three: Bringing Your Pages to Life

CHAPTER 11

Forms

A Web site is a great way to broadcast a message, announce a new product, post late-breaking news, or just rant about the state of the world. But that's all *one-way* communication, which you may find a bit limiting. You may be curious to get some feedback from your audience. Or you may want to build your business by selling your product online, and you need a way to gather vital stats from customers. If you want to receive information as well as deliver it, it's time to add *forms* to your Web design repertoire (see Figure 11-1 for a simple example). Whatever type of information you need to collect on your site, Dreamweaver's *form objects* make the task easy.

Form Basics

A form begins and ends with the HTML <form> tag. The opening <form> tag indicates the beginning of the form, and sets its properties; the closing </form> tag, of course, marks the form's end.

In between these tags, different objects provide the basic user-interface elements of the form. Radio buttons, text fields, and pull-down menus are just a few of the ways you can gather input. It's perfectly OK to include other HTML elements inside a form, too. In fact, your site's visitors would be lost if you couldn't also add (and format) text that explains each form object's purpose. And if you don't use a table or Cascading Style Sheets to lay out a form in an organized way, it can quickly become an unreadable mess (see the box on page 448).

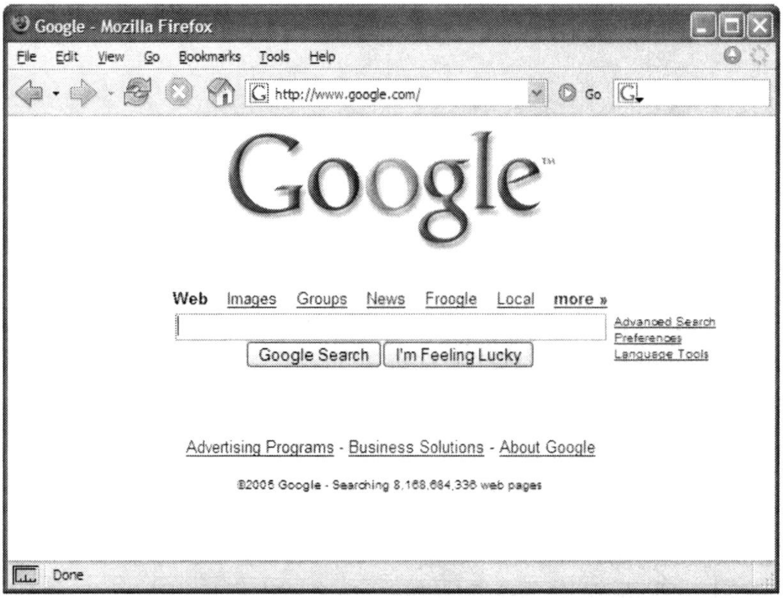

Figure 11-1: *A form can be as simple as a single empty text box (a field) and a button, or as complex as a 100-question survey composed of fill-in-the-blank and multiple-choice questions.*

Every form element, whether it's a text field or a checkbox, has a *name* and a *value*. The name is something you supply and indicates what information the element is intended to collect. If you want visitors to type their email addresses into a text field, you might name that field *email*. The value, on the other hand, is the visitors' actual input—what they type into the text field, for example, or the selections they make from a pull-down menu.

After your visitors fill out the form, and click the Submit button to transmit their responses, each form element is transmitted as a name/value pair like this: *email=bob@bobville.com*. Submitting both pieces of information helps the program that processes the form figure out what the input means. After all, without a name, a value of 39 doesn't mean much (39 what? Potatoes, steps, days until Christmas?). The name/value pair (age=39) provides context for a visitor's input.

The Code Backstage

Creating a form is just the first step in collecting information from your Web site's visitors. You also need to connect the form to a computer program that actually *does* something with the information. The program may simply take the data from the form and email it to you. However, it could do something as complex as contacting a bank, processing a credit card payment, creating an invoice item, or notifying a shipping department to deliver the latest Stephen King novel to someone in Nova Scotia.

A form, in other words, is pretty useless without a form-processing program running on the Web server. These information-crunching programs come in a variety of languages—Perl, C, C#, Visual Basic, VBScript, Java, ColdFusion Markup Language, PHP—and may be part of a dedicated application server like Macromedia's ColdFusion Server or Microsoft's .NET technology.

Writing the necessary behind-the-scenes processing software can be complex, but the concepts behind forms are straightforward:

1. **First, someone fills out a form on your Web page, and then clicks the Submit button (or the Search, Buy, or whatever you've actually labeled the submit button).**
2. **Next, the Web browser transmits the form data over the Internet to a program on your Web server.**
3. **The program collects the data and does something with it—whatever you and the programmer decide it should do: For example, send the data off as an email to you, search a vast database of information, or store the information in a database.**
4. **Finally, the Web server returns a page to the Web visitor. It may be a standard Web page with a message like "Thanks for the info", or a page dynamically generated by the program itself—like a detailed invoice page, or the results of a search.**

So how do you create the processing half of the forms equation if you're not a programmer? You can use Dreamweaver, of course. Part 6 of this book describes Dreamweaver's dynamic Web building tools for creating pages that use information collected from forms. If your Web server accommodates Active Server Pages, ColdFusion, or PHP, Dreamweaver can create form-processing programs for you. If you're part of a Web development team in a company, then you may already have programmers on staff who can help create the processing program.

Furthermore, even if your Web hosting company doesn't tolerate any of the application servers that work with Dreamweaver, they probably offer free form-processing programs as part of their services. Contact your Web host and ask about this; most companies provide basic instructions on how to use these programs.

Finally, if you feel adventurous, many form-processing programs are available free on the Web. For a thorough sampling, see the CGI Resource Index at *http://cgi.resourceindex.com*. Using these free programs can be tricky, however, because you need to download the appropriate program, and then install it on your Web server.

Creating a Form

In Dreamweaver, you can build forms with one-click ease using the Insert panel's Forms category (see Figure 11-2).

To begin, you need to insert a <form> tag on your Web page to indicate the boundaries of a form:

1. **In the document window, click where you'd like to insert the form.**

   You might decide to place it after a regular paragraph of introductory text, for example.

2. **On the Insert panel, select the Forms category.**

   The tab reveals 22 form-building tool icons.

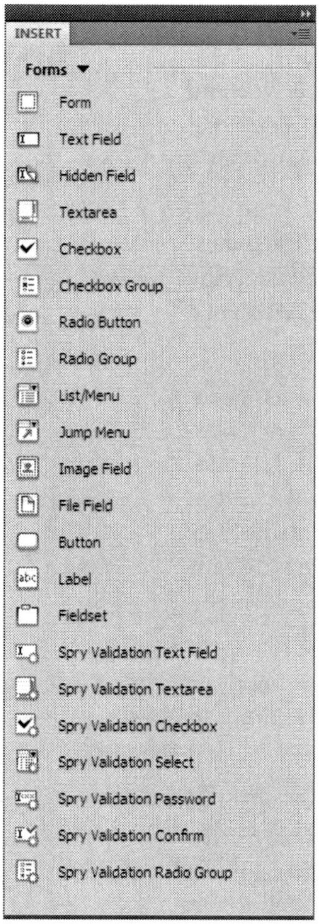

Figure 11-2:
The Insert panel's Forms category gives you one-click access to all the different form elements–buttons, text fields, checkboxes, and more. Dreamweaver CS4 has added 3 new Spry validation fields (page 454) and a new Checkbox Group tool (page 442). Since the Forms category has so many buttons, you might want to turn off the labels that appear next to each icon as described on page 26. This step lets you see all the form buttons without taking up your monitor's entire height.

3. **Click the Form icon (the very first square in the 22-icon list—or the far-left square if you're in the "Hide Labels" mode described on page 26).**

   Alternatively, if you're a menu-driven person, choose Insert → Form → Form.

Either way, a red, dashed-line rectangle appears in the document window, indicating the form's boundaries. (If you don't see it, then choose View → Visual Aids → Invisible Elements.) The top line represents the opening <form> tag; the bottom represents the closing tag. Make sure you always insert form objects, like buttons and menus, *inside* these lines. Otherwise, Dreamweaver thinks you're trying to create a second form on the page. (It's perfectly valid to include more than one form per page [as long as you don't try to insert a form inside *another* form], but your visitor can submit only one form—and its data—at a time.)

Tip: An even faster way to insert a <form> tag is to bypass step 3 and just insert a form element–like a text field or radio button–and Dreamweaver will ask if you want to add the <form> tag at the same time.

Since you can place so many other HTML elements inside a form, you'll often find it easier to insert the form first, and add tables, graphics, text, and form objects later.

4. **If it isn't already selected, click the dotted red line to select the form.**

   This step not only selects the form, but highlights everything inside the red lines. The Property inspector then displays the "Form ID" label at the upper-left corner, as shown in Figure 11-3.

5. **If you like, type a name for your form into the "Form ID" field.**

   This step is optional. Dreamweaver supplies a generic ID name—*form1*, but a form doesn't even actually need a name to work. However, a name is useful if you use JavaScript or the Spry form validation tools discussed later in this chapter to interact with the form or any of its fields.

6. **Into the Action field, type a URL, or select a file by clicking the tiny folder icon.**

   Your mission here is to specify the location of the program that will process the form. If someone else is responsible for the programming, ask that person what to enter here. It's a standard Web address—either an absolute URL (one that begins with *http://*) or just the path to the server's form-processing program. (See page 161 for more on these different kinds of links.) If you're using Dreamweaver's dynamic page-building tools, then you usually leave this field blank. When you apply a server behavior—the programming code that makes the page "dynamic"—Dreamweaver inserts the correct URL.

   Either way, the file name you add to the Action field *doesn't* end in .html. The path might be, for example, *../cgi-bin/forms.pl*. In this case, .pl is the extension used to indicate a program written in the Perl programming language. Other common file extensions for Web programs include .asp (for Active Server Pages), .cfm (for ColdFusion Markup Language pages), .aspx (for .NET pages), .php (for PHP pages), or .cgi (for CGI programs).

7. **Using the Method pop-up menu, specify how you want the form data transmitted to the processing program (see Figure 11-3).**

   Basically, forms can transmit data to a Web server in either of two ways. You'll use the more common method, called POST, most often. It sends the form data in two steps: First, the browser contacts the form program at the URL you specified in the previous step; then, it sends the data to the server. This method gives your data a bit more security, and it can easily handle forms with lots of information.

   The GET method, on the other hand, transmits the form data in the URL itself, like this: *http://search.yahoo.com/bin/search?p=dogs*. (Even though the GET method *sends* data, it's named GET. That's because its purpose in life is to *receive* information—such as the results of a search.) The characters following the ? in the address represent the form data. This code submits a single form field—named *p*, with the value *dogs*—to the server. If a form has lots of fields and accepts lots of user input, such a URL could get extremely long. Some servers can't handle very long URLs, so the GET method is inappropriate for forms that collect a lot of data.

Tip: The GET method has one big benefit: You can bookmark it. This ability is great if you want to save and reuse a common search request for Google, or want to send someone Google Maps driving directions. That's why search engines use the GET method for form submissions.

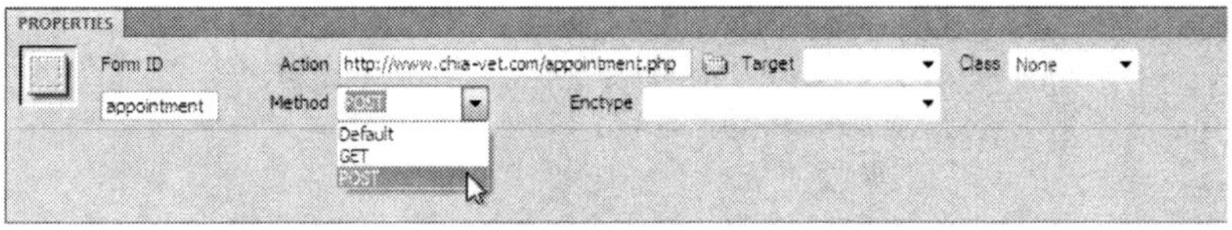

Figure 11-3: *You'll generally want to use the POST method of sending data to the server. See step 7 for more details.*

8. **If you're using frames, select a Target option.**

   You'll most likely skip this menu. Frames are so 1998 Web design, and pose serious problems for Web designers and search engines. However, you can choose the "_blank" option to open a new browser window to display the results. (See page 173 for more on the Target property.)

9. **Select an encoding type, if you like.**

   You usually don't have to select anything from the Enctype menu. Leaving this box empty is almost always correct, and is the same as selecting the much more long-winded "application/x-www-form-urlencoded" option.

   But if you're using the File Field button (see page 449) to let visitors upload files to your site, then you should use the "multipart/form-data" option. In fact, Dreamweaver automatically selects this option when you add a File Field to a form. See the box on the opposite page for more info on potential problems with File Fields.

You've laid the foundation for your form. Now you're ready to add the input controls—menus, checkboxes, and so on—to it, as described in the next section.

FREQUENTLY ASKED QUESTION

Using a Form to Upload Files

I want to let visitors upload photos to my site, but when I add a Form Field button to one of my forms, I get an error from the server whenever the form is submitted. Why?

In order to upload files from a Web page you need to do two things: Change the encoding method (see step 9 on the opposite page) to "multipart/form-data", and set up your server for receiving files. Dreamweaver automatically takes care of the first part: Whenever you insert a form field, the form's encoding method is changed to "multipart/form-data".

The second part is up to you (or your Web hosting company). Many Web servers have this option turned off for security reasons. Check to see if your Web hosting company lets you use forms for uploading files to your server. If it doesn't, then find a new Web hosting company that does.

In addition, the form processing script must be programmed to accept data in the "multipart/form-data" format. Since this task is challenging, you might want to enlist some help. The box on page 451 provides several resources for commercial Dreamweaver extensions that can help with this task.

If you decide that's too much trouble, and you simply choose to delete the Form Field button, you're still in trouble. Dreamweaver doesn't reset the encoding method to the original setting of "application/x-www-form-urlencoded". When visitors try to submit the form (even without the Form Field), they'll get a nasty error message from the server. You must remedy the situation manually by selecting the form, and then using the Property inspector to change the encoding method back to "application/x-www-form-urlencoded".

Adding Form Elements

Unless you've never used a computer before, the different user interface elements available for HTML forms should look familiar (Figure 11-4): text fields where people can type in information (their names, addresses, phone numbers, and so on); checkboxes for making multiple-choice selections; and menus for picking items from a list. The Insert panel's Forms category (Figure 11-2) lets you create all of these elements and more.

Dreamweaver includes some special form elements, called Spry Validation widgets. They're like the regular form elements discussed below, but have the added ability to *verify* the contents of a form field, and prevent a form from being submitted if it's not filled out correctly. Dreamweaver CS4 adds three new Spry validation widgets as well. The Spry Validation widgets are discussed starting on page 454.

What All Form Elements Have in Common

Adding form elements to your document always follows the same pattern:

1. **In the document window, insert a form (see page 431).**

   Or, if the page already has a form, click inside its red border.

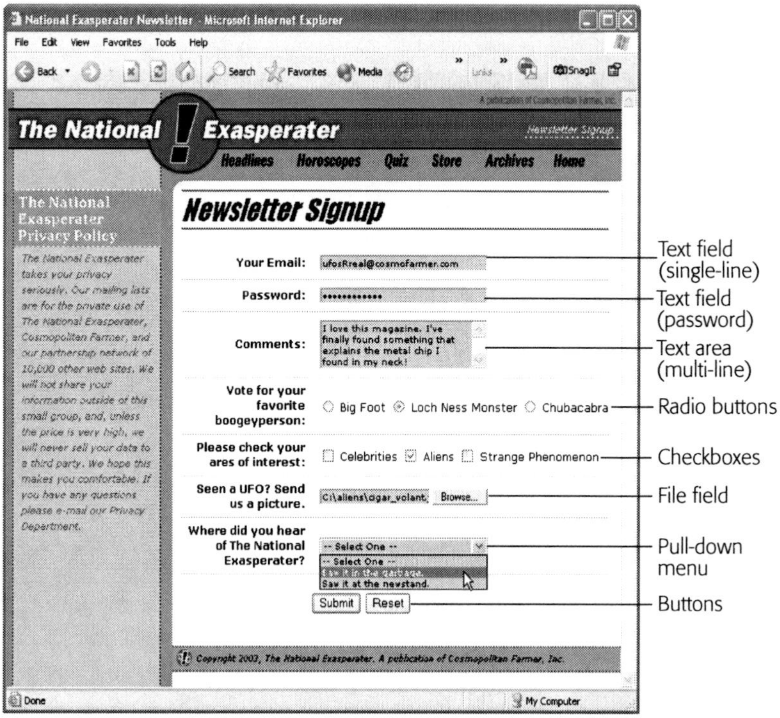

Figure 11-4: *Forms collect information using a variety of different interface elements like text boxes, password fields, and pull-down menus. You can even add a File Field to let visitors select and upload a file to your site.*

Tip: You can skip step 1 and have Dreamweaver add the form element when you first add a form field to a page. When you insert a field (step 2) and there's no form yet, Dreamweaver asks if you'd like to add the proper <form> tag. Click the Yes button, and Dreamweaver automatically creates the red, dotted-line form boundaries (and, behind the scenes, the corresponding <form> tags). You should *always* click the Yes button. A form field that isn't surrounded by the proper form tag doesn't work in all browsers.

2. **Of the Insert panel's Forms category, click the appropriate button** (see Figure 11-2).

   Alternatively, use the Insert → Form submenu. You'll soon discover that every form object on the Insert panel is also represented by a command on the Insert menu (for example, Insert → Form → Text Field).

3. **In the Input Tag Accessibility Attributes window, type an ID (see Figure 11-5).**

   This window serves a couple of functions. It lets you assign an ID (this step), and set a few accessibility options. These options add information and tools for the benefit of those who surf using *assistive technologies*—like screen readers—or those who use their keyboard (rather than their mouses) to jump from form field to form field.

The ID you type in this field also determines the *name* of the field. Remember, each field has a name so that the form processing program can identify what the information it's receiving is for (see page 429). Say you're adding a text field to a page that collects a visitor's town name. In the ID box, if you type *town*, then when Dreamweaver inserts the text field onto the page, the underlying HTML that Dreamweaver writes looks like this: <input type="text" name="town" id="town">.

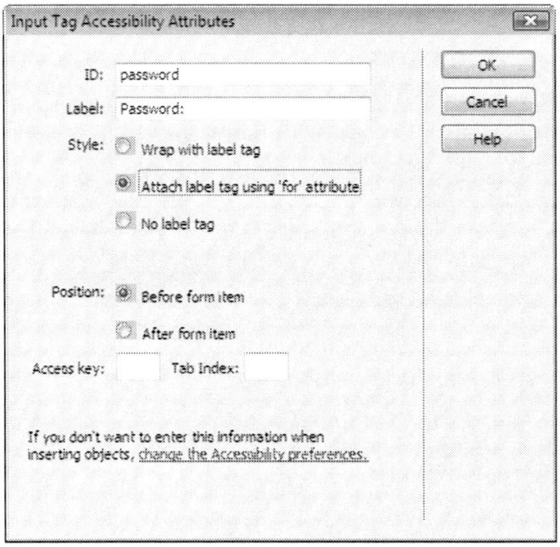

Figure 11-5: *This window appears when you're inserting a form element. If you don't see it, you or someone else has turned off Dreamweaver's factory setting to automatically launch this window. To summon it, choose Edit → Preferences (Dreamweaver → Preferences), click the Accessibility category, and then turn on the Form Objects checkbox.*

Be sure to follow the same naming conventions you'd use for CSS ID names: Begin with a letter, use only numbers, letters, hyphens, or underscores, and skip spaces, punctuation, and other characters. (Keep in mind that adding an ID to an HTML tag doesn't create a CSS ID style—but if you want to create a special look just for that one field, you *can* create an ID style.)

Note: The ID value you type in step 3 has a slightly different effect when adding radio buttons. Radio buttons that are part of the same group (like answers to a multiple-choice question) must have the same name: This characteristic lets only one button in the group be selected at a time (see page 445). Because all radio buttons in a group share the *same* name, and because you can apply each ID only once per page (see page 114), each radio button must have its own unique ID. So Dreamweaver takes the ID you enter, and adds it to the radio tag, but then sets that radio button's name to the generic "radio". Therefore, make sure you rename your radio button using the Property inspector as described on page 445.

4. **Type a label, and then select label options (see Figure 11-5).**

The label option lets you add text that identifies the form element's purpose. In fact, Dreamweaver wraps whatever text you type in an HTML tag, named, logically enough, the <label> tag. This tag is designed to identify the form field's purpose, and the text you supply is visible to the person filling out the form.

The label usually appears either to the left or right of the form field. If you add a text field to collect someone's name, the label might be *Name:*. Someone filling out the form then sees the text "Name:" followed by a box for typing a name. It's always a good idea to add a label. (You can read more about the <label> tag on page 453.)

Tip: Sometimes you don't need or want a label. For example, buttons already have a label—like Submit or Reset—so you don't need to add another. In this case, either click the Cancel button, which just adds the form field without any of these *accessibility* properties, or leave the label box empty, and select the "No label tag" radio button.

You have two ways to attach a label to a form element. The first method, indicated by the radio button labeled "Wrap with label tag" (as shown in Figure 11-5), wraps the <label> tag around both the text you type and the form element itself. This method keeps the two together and easily identifies which label goes with each form field. However, although wrapping a field with the <label> tag produces valid HTML, it isn't considered as accessible (to screen readers, for example) so the method described next is becoming standard industry practice.

The second method, "Attach label tag using 'for' attribute", also wraps the text you type inside a <label> tag. However, it places the form field *outside* the <label> tag. This method is useful if the label and form field don't appear directly next to each other in the HTML code. For example, Web designers often use a table to visually organize forms (see the box on page 448). By placing text labels in one table column and form fields in an adjacent column, you can neatly align the labels and their corresponding fields. However, organizing your page like this puts the labels and form fields into separate table cells, and "breaks" the connection between the label and the field. Those visitors who use a screen reader to read your form may not understand which label applies to which form field. Fortunately, Dreamweaver can add a *for* property to the <label> tag, which tells a Web browser which form element the label is "for."

Here's an example that might make this all more clear: Say you add a text field that lets someone enter her email address to register for your site's email newsletter. If, when you inserted the field, you used the ID *email*, the label "Your email address:", and the "Attach label tag using the 'for' attribute" option, then you end up with this HTML code:

```
<label for="email">Your email address:</label>
<input type="text" name="email" id="email" />
   <label for="email">Your email address: </label>
   <input type="text" name="email" id="email" />
```

At this point, you can move the <label> tag (or the text field) to any other location on your Web page, and the label remains related to the field. Of course, if you place the label at the top of the page and the field at the bottom, your visitors don't know they're related, so it makes sense to keep the two tags in close visual proximity. However, people often put the <label> tag in one table cell of a row, and the field in a table cell to the right (this technique is one way of visually organizing a form, as described in the box on page 448).

5. **Type an "Access key" and a Tab Index number, and then press OK.**

   These optional steps let visitors access the form field using the keyboard. The "Access key" option lets visitors use a keyboard shortcut to jump immediately into or select a field. If you enter *M*, for example, for a form element's access key, visitors can jump to that element using Alt+M (Windows) or Control-M (Mac). While this feature seems to be a great way to make your forms more usable, it has a couple of drawbacks. First, not all browsers support this feature. In addition, since it's not at all obvious to your site's visitors what keyboard shortcuts you've added to your form, you need to list the shortcut next to the form element, or create a "user's manual" of sorts that explains the shortcuts in your forms.

   Browsers support the Tab Index more often than the "Access key" property. The Tab Index lets you number each form field and, in the process, set the order in which the fields will be selected as a visitor presses the Tab key. Number 1 indicates the first field to be selected when a visitor presses the Tab key, and each number after that—2, 3, 4, and so on—dictates the order of selection when the Tab key is pressed. You don't usually need to go to this extreme, since most browsers jump to the next form field when you press the Tab key, but it sometimes comes in handy when you have a particularly complex form, and you use either tables or CSS to lay it out. In some cases, the order in which the fields are selected by default doesn't match the visual presentation of the form (in other words, when you press the Tab key, you actually jump to a different field than the one you expect). If this is the case, setting the Tab Index lets you correctly specify the tab order.

6. **In the Property inspector, set the form element's properties (Figure 11-6).**

   For instance, some elements let you specify things like width, height, and other variables. The following descriptions indicate the options available for each form element.

Text Fields

When you need to collect a specific piece of information like a person's name, phone number, or address, use a text field (shown in Figure 11-4). Text fields accept typed responses, and they're great for open-ended questions. They come in three different flavors: *single-line* fields for short responses, *password* fields to hide people's input from snooping eyes, and *multiline* fields for longer typed replies.

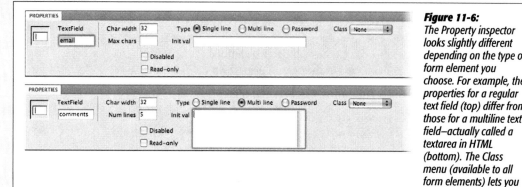

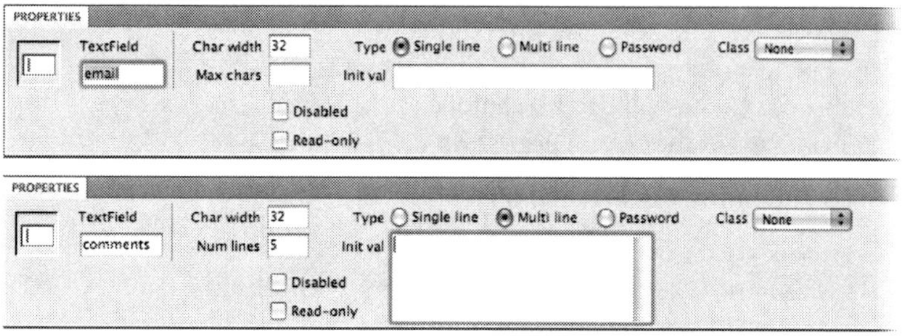

Figure 11-6: *The Property inspector looks slightly different depending on the type of form element you choose. For example, the properties for a regular text field (top) differ from those for a multiline text field–actually called a textarea in HTML (bottom). The Class menu (available to all form elements) lets you apply a Cascading Style Sheet class style (see page 122) to the selected form field.*

Once you've inserted the text field, in the Property inspector, you can adjust the following settings (see Figure 11-6):

- **Char Width.** The width of a text field is measured in characters; so if you type *20* for the Char Width (character width), then the text field is as wide as necessary to hold 20 typed letters. Be aware that the exact size can vary from browser to browser. (You can use Cascading Style Sheets to set an exact width using the *width* property described on page 341.)

- **Type.** You can choose from three different types of text fields:

  —A *single-line* text field, of course, holds just one line of text. This kind of text field is the most common; use it for collecting small pieces of information, like a last name, Social Security number, or credit card number.

  —*Multiline* fields provide a larger area for adding multiple lines of text. You need to use this kind of text field when offering a place to type longer comments, such as a "Let us know what you think!" or "Nature of problem:" field.

Note: Dreamweaver includes a separate button for adding a multiline text field–called *Textarea* in HTML (see Figure 11-2).

  —*Password* fields hide a password being typed from the prying eyes of passing spies. Whatever your Web visitor types appears as asterisks *** (Windows) or bullets •••• (Mac) on the screen. (Of course, the information in the password field is still transmitted as plain text, just like any other form field. The masking action takes place only in your visitor's browser.)

- **Max Chars/Num Lines.** Max Chars (maximum characters) lets you limit the number of characters the field accepts. It's a good way to help ensure that guests type the right information in the right place. For instance, if you use a field to collect the visitor's age, odds are you don't need more than three characters to do it; very few 1,000-year-olds surf the Web these days (and those who do don't like to reveal their ages).

When you've specified a multiline text field, the Max Chars box morphs into the Num Lines box. In this case, you can't limit the amount of text someone types into the field. Instead, this field lets you specify the height of the text field on the screen. (You can, however, use Spry Text Area to limit the number of characters typed into a multiline text field, as described on page 468.)

Note: The limit you specify here affects only how tall the field is *onscreen*. Your visitors can type as many lines of information as they want. (A scroll bar appears if the typing exceeds the size of the box you've specified with the Num Lines option.)

- **Init val.** Here, you can specify the Initial Value of the field—starter text that automatically appears in the field, so that it isn't empty when the visitor begins completing the form. You can use this feature to include explanatory text inside the field itself, such as "Type your name in this box" or "Example: (212) 555-1212". Another common use for the "Init val" box: When you've created an *update form*—a form for editing previously entered information. For example, if you want to update your Facebook profile, then you go to a page that presents a form containing all the information you've previously entered. You can change the information, and submit the form to update your profile. An update form requires a database and some server-side programming—you'll learn how to build this type of form in Chapter 24.

Note: If your form page is one of the dynamic file types with which Dreamweaver works–ASP, PHP, or ColdFusion–you also see a small lightning bolt to the right of the "Init val" box. This button lets you add *dynamic data*–information drawn from a database–to the text field. (In-depth coverage of this feature starts on page 920.)

- **Disabled** and **Read-only**. You probably won't ever have any reason to use these two options. These options were added in Dreamweaver CS4, and both make the text field uneditable. The disabled option grays out the text field, and prevents visitors from clicking into the field, or even selecting any text that's already there (the init val property discussed above). In addition, when a field is disabled, any data in it isn't submitted when the form is submitted.

  The Read-only option lets a visitor select and copy anything in the text field but doesn't let him change it. Since forms are meant to collect information from visitors, not taunt them with uneditable text fields, you should leave both these options alone. So why do they exist? People usually use these options in conjunction with JavaScript programming—for example, a text field might be disabled until a visitor selects another option.

FREQUENTLY ASKED QUESTION

Using the Password Field for Credit Card Numbers

Can I use the Password field type for credit card numbers and other sensitive information?

Yes, but it doesn't give the information any extra security.

The Password field does one thing: It hides people's input on the screen. Someone looking over your visitor's shoulder can't read what's being typed–it looks like a bunch of dots–but once that information is submitted over the Internet, it's just as visible as a regular text field.

To provide real security for form information, you need an encrypted connection between the Web server and the visitor's computer. Most Web site creators use SSL (Secure Socket Layer) technology for this purpose. Web browsers understand this technology, but your Web server must be specially configured to work in this mode. Contact your Web host to see if you can use SSL on your server (the answer is usually yes). If so, they can tell you how to set it up. You don't have to make any special changes to your Web pages to take advantage of SSL; once the server is set up, you put your Web pages on it as you would for a non-secure Web site (Chapter 17 covers moving your Web files onto the Web).

Checkboxes and Checkbox Groups

Checkboxes (see Figure 11-4) are simple and to the point; they're either turned on or not. They're great for questions in which your visitor can select more than one item in a group. Suppose you produce three different email newsletters that you send out each month. In your form, you might include some text—"Check the boxes for the newsletters you'd like to receive"—and three corresponding checkboxes, so that each visitor can sign up for only the newsletters he wants.

Once you've added a checkbox to a form, in the Property inspector, you can set up these options (Figure 11-7):

- **Checked value.** If your visitor turns on the checkbox, here's where you're specifying the information that's submitted when the form data goes to your processing program. It doesn't necessarily have to match the checkbox's label (which you create when you insert the checkbox [step 3 on page 444]); it could, instead, transmit some special coded response to your processing application. Your visitors never actually see this information.
- **Initial state.** If you like, your checkbox can already be filled when your Web page first appears. You may have seen this setup on sites that require you to sign up for some service. Usually there's a checkbox—already checked—down near the bottom of the form, with fine print like this: "Check here if you want to get daily, unsolicited email from our marketing department."

Note: As with many form elements, your checkbox can respond to information it retrieves from a database. The Property inspector's Dynamic button–available only when you're working on a dynamic page (ASP, PHP, or ColdFusion)–lets you set the checkbox state (Checked or Unchecked) based on data in a database. (See page 922 for details.)

After adjusting the Property inspector, if you don't use Dreamweaver's accessibility options discussed on page 436, make sure you return to the document window to add a text label next to the field. Let people know what the checkbox is for: "Yes, sign me up!" for example. Finally, you may want to insert another checkbox. Checkboxes don't have to come in groups, but they often do, as in "yes" and "no" boxes. Dreamweaver CS4 adds a tool to make inserting multiple checkboxes easier as discussed next.

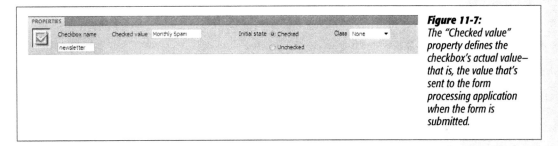

Figure 11-7: *The "Checked value" property defines the checkbox's actual value–that is, the value that's sent to the form processing application when the form is submitted.*

Checkbox Groups

Frequently checkboxes travel in groups—"What activities do you like? Check all that apply."

1. **On the Insert panel, click the Checkbox Group button.**

   The Checkbox Group window appears (see Figure 11-8).

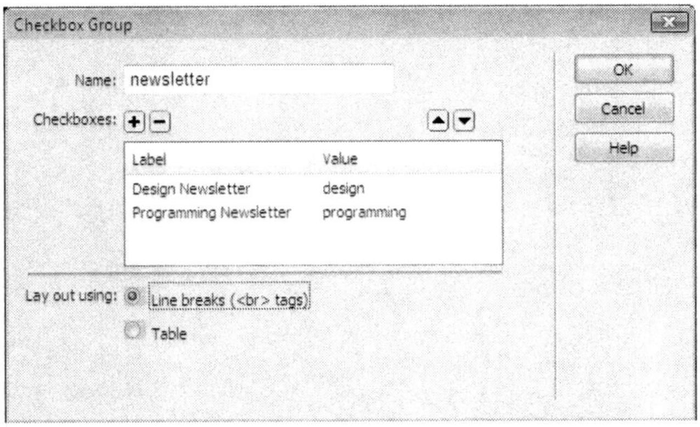

Figure 11-8: *The Checkbox Group dialog box lets you quickly add multiple checkboxes to a page. The boxes form a group of related answers to which someone filling out the form can add checkmarks.*

2. **In the Name field, type a name.**

   This name covers all the checkboxes in the group, saving you the trouble of typing the name for each checkbox yourself. The name you type is the name that's submitted to the Web server, so follow the naming rules that apply to all form fields: letter and numbers, no spaces or other funny characters except an underscore or a hyphen. Each checkbox shares the same name, but if someone filling out the form selects multiple checkboxes, then the data from *all* checked boxes is sent to the Web server.

3. **In the Label column, click the top Checkbox label. Type a label for the first button.**

   For example, if you're adding a set of checkboxes so that visitors can choose to sign up for one or more email newsletters, you might type the name of a newsletter—like "Our Design Newsletter". This label appears onscreen next to the checkbox.

Note: If you use the Checkbox group tool, then Dreamweaver skips the Accessibility Attributes window (Figure 11-5). You don't have any control over how the <label> tag is inserted; Dreamweaver just wraps the tag around the checkbox.

4. **Hit the Tab key to jump to the Value column for that checkbox, and then type a value for the first checkbox.**

   This value is the checkbox's "checked value." Type what you want passed to the Web server when somebody selects this checkbox and submits the form—for example, "design" for the "Design Newsletter" option.

5. **Repeat steps 3 and 4 for the second checkbox in the group.**

   You can create additional checkboxes by clicking the + button. Follow steps 3 and 4 for each additional button you add in this way.

6. **Select a layout option for the group.**

   Dreamweaver puts each radio button in the group on its own line. You can choose whether Dreamweaver uses a line break (
 tag) to separate each line, or whether it uses a table—one radio button per row.

   Don't care for either of these options? Pick the "Line breaks" option—it's the easiest to modify.

Tip: If you want a group of checkboxes to appear side by side instead of stacked one on top of the other, then, in the Checkbox Group dialog box, choose the "Line breaks" option. Then make sure Dreamweaver is set to display the invisible line break character (see page 76). Click the line break's gold shield, and then hit Backspace or Delete to move the lower checkbox onto the same line as another checkbox.

7. **Click OK to add the group of checkboxes to your page.**

   The checkboxes and their labels are essentially text and buttons on the screen. You can move the checkboxes around, change their labels, and, in the Property inspector, alter each checkbox's properties.

Note: When you insert checkboxes using the Checkbox Group tool, Dreamweaver inserts all the checkboxes with the same name, but gives each a unique ID. For example, if you insert two checkboxes with this tool, you might end up with HTML like this:

```
<label>
<input type="checkbox" name="newsletter" value="design" id="newsletter_0" />
Design newsletter</label>
<br />
<label><input type="checkbox" name="newsletter" value="programming"
id="newsletter_1" /> Programming newsletter
</label>
```

Notice that the two boxes have the same name—newsletter—but, since ID names must be unique, Dreamweaver creates IDs by tacking _0, _1, and so on to the end of each checkbox ID.

It's perfectly valid to use the same name for more than one checkbox—however, just keep in mind (and tell your programmer) that the data is submitted as an *array*—a data format common to programming languages that lets you store multiple items under a single name. In other words, the values of every checked box are sent together in one group using the name you supplied in step 2.

Radio Buttons and Radio Groups

Radio buttons, like checkboxes, are very simple (see Figure 11-4); they're either selected (represented on screen as a solid circle) or not (an empty circle).

But unlike checkboxes, radio buttons restrict your visitor to making only one choice from a group, just like the radio buttons on an old-style automobile dashboard (or, if you're too young to remember those car radios, like the buttons on a blender). Radio buttons are ideal for multiple-choice questions that require just a single answer, like, "What is your income: A. $10–35,000, B. $35–70,000, C. $70–100,000, D. None of your business."

In the Property inspector, you can set up the following options for a radio button (Figure 11-9):

- **Name.** Dreamweaver supplies the generic name *radio* (or radio2, radio3, and so on) when you insert a radio button. Make sure you change it to something more descriptive, and, when you insert a group of related radio buttons, give them all the *same name*. Given a group of radio buttons, your visitors should be able to select only one button in the group. To make sure that's the case, every button in the same group needs to share the same name (although they should have different "Checked values"; see the next bullet point).

  If, when testing your page, you notice that you can select more than one radio button at a time, you must have given them different names. (Consider using Dreamweaver's Radio Group object, described next. It acts as a wizard that simplifies the process of creating a group of radio buttons.)

- **Checked value**. This value is the information that the form submits when your visitor selects this button. Once again, it doesn't necessarily have to match the radio button's onscreen label. If you filled out the accessibility window's ID box (see Figure 11-5), then Dreamweaver uses the ID you supplied as the checked value. Change the value Dreamweaver supplies if it doesn't match the value you want.

- **Initial state**. Often, when a form page first loads, one radio button in each set is preselected. To do your visitors this timesaving courtesy, turn on Checked for the button that holds the default value—the one they'll choose most often.

  Of course, if making a choice here is optional, then you can leave all the buttons unselected by setting their initial states to Unchecked. However, once somebody *does* select a radio button, only the Reset button (if you add one) can make them *all* unselected again (see page 451 for information on creating a Reset button).

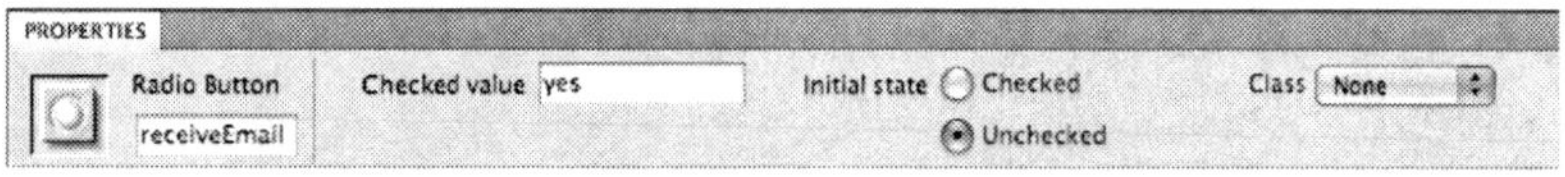

***Figure 11-9:** Radio buttons offer answers to a single multiple-choice question.*

Finally, you need to add text labels for the entire group. If you have the accessibility features turned on (see page 436), you'll have already added labels to each button. If not, simply click the document window and type, just as you'd add any text to the page. Your whole-group-of-buttons label may take the form of a question ("How would you like to pay?"); the labels for the individual buttons might say, "Visa", "MasterCard", and "I.O.U."

Radio Group

Although you can easily create a group of radio buttons using the Radio Button object, Dreamweaver includes the Radio Group object to make it even simpler. The Radio Group object provides a single dialog box for creating a group of radio buttons and their labels in one fell swoop. It works the same as the Checkbox group tool discussed on page 442—the only difference is that Dreamweaver inserts radio button form objects instead of checkboxes.

Pull-Down Menus and Lists

While checkboxes and radio buttons both provide ways to offer multiple choices, you should consider them only when you have relatively few choices. A form can quickly become overcrowded with buttons and boxes if people have too many options to choose from. The beauty of lists and pull-down menus (usually called *pop-up menus* on the Mac) is that they offer many choices without taking up a lot of screen space. (Figure 11-10 shows an example.)

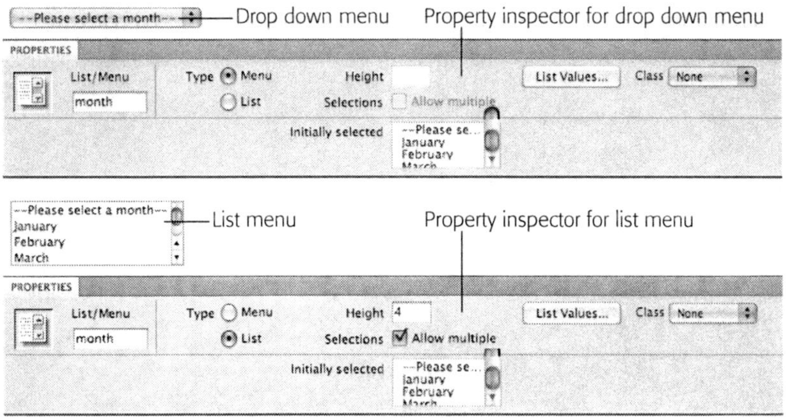

Figure 11-10: *A menu (top) is a single compact line; a list (bottom) can take up any number of lines on the page. Use the first menu or list item to tell visitors what to do. For example, "--Please select a month--" or "--Select One--."*

Once you've inserted a menu or list object into your document window, here's how to adjust the Property inspector settings:

- **Type.** Menus and lists differ both in appearance (see Figure 11-10) and function, as described in a moment. Click the one you want (Menu or List).
- **Height.** The number you type into the Height box (available only for lists) should reflect the amount of space you wish the list to take up on the page. A list can be a single line tall (in which case you might as well use a menu) or many lines (letting your visitors see a number of choices at once). A vertical scroll bar appears automatically if the height you specify here is smaller than the number of items in the list.
- **Allow multiple.** Here's a key difference between menus and lists: If you turn on this option, then a visitor can select more than one item from a list, just by pressing the Ctrl (⌘) key while clicking different options in the list. (If you do choose this option, you probably want to add some text that explains to visitors how they can select multiple items.)
- **List Values.** This button opens the List Values dialog box (see Figure 11-11), where you build the actual list of options in your list or menu. Each item is composed of two parts: a *label* (the text that actually appears in the menu or list on the Web page) and the *value* (the information that gets submitted with the form, which isn't necessarily the same thing as the label).

  To use this dialog box, type an item label. Press Tab (or click in the Value column), and then type the value, if you like. (See Figure 11-11 for details.)

  Including a value is optional; if you don't specify one, then your form submits the item's label *as* the value. Still, you'll often find that setting up a separate value is useful. Imagine that you've designed a pull-down menu on an e-commerce site so that your visitors can select their credit cards' expiration months.

Figure 11-11 shows what the items for such a pull-down menu might look like: The names of the months appear on the menu, but when a visitor selects, say, April, the form actually transmits the number 4 to your form processing program.

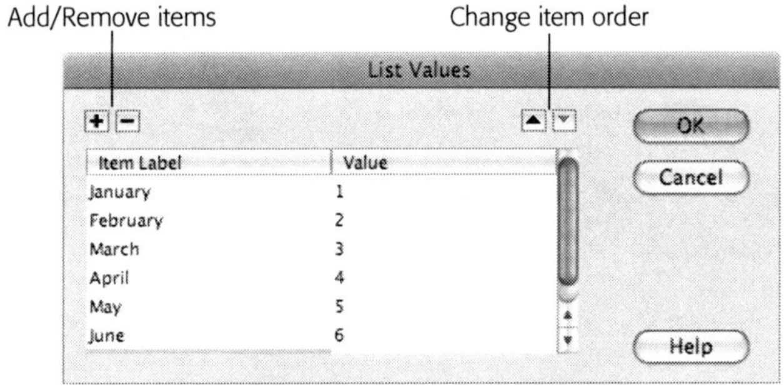

Figure 11-11: *Using the + button, you can add an item to the end of a list; when you click in the list's last item's Value column, pressing Tab creates a new list item. To delete an item, select it, and then click the minus sign (–) button. You can move an item higher or lower in the list of options by selecting the option, and then clicking the up or down arrow buttons. Like radio buttons, pop-up menu and list items always flock together—nobody ever creates just one.*

Since computer programs are often more comfortable with numbers than names—and humans are often the exact opposite—it makes more sense to use numbers for list values in this case.

When offering your visitors a pop-up menu of products from which to choose, the label might be the human-friendly name of the product, like "Blue Wool Cap". The value would be the model number that your form processing program can understand, like XSD1278.

- **Dynamic values.** Dreamweaver can also create a *dynamic menu*, where the menu's labels and values come from a database. This option—available only when you insert a menu into one of the dynamic page types, as described in Part 6 of this book—is great when the menu items change frequently, as they would in a list of employee or product names. This feature is described on page 925.

Click OK when you're finished building your menu or list. You can always return to this screen, and edit the list of options. To do so, in the document window, click the menu or list, and then, in the Property inspector, click the List Values button. You return to the dialog box shown in Figure 11-11.

As with other form elements, you can, and probably should, add some explanatory text alongside the list or menu in the document window. One easy method: You can automatically add a label to a menu or list using Dreamweaver's accessibility features as described on page 436.

Note: Styling form fields with CSS can be frustrating. Not all browsers format form fields in the same way, and some browsers limit what kind of styling you can apply to a form field. For a good introduction to styling form fields, visit *www.456bereastreet.com/archive/200701/styling_form_controls_with_css_revisited*.

POWER USERS' CLINIC

Giving Order to Your Forms

If you're not careful, creating forms can quickly lead to visual chaos. The different shapes and sizes of text boxes, radio buttons, and other form objects don't naturally align well with text. One solution: Use tables to control your forms' appearance.

In the left-hand form below, form elements were added next to the label text on each line, forcing your eye to follow an ungainly zigzag pattern created by the form's text boxes. The result is not only ugly, but also hard to read.

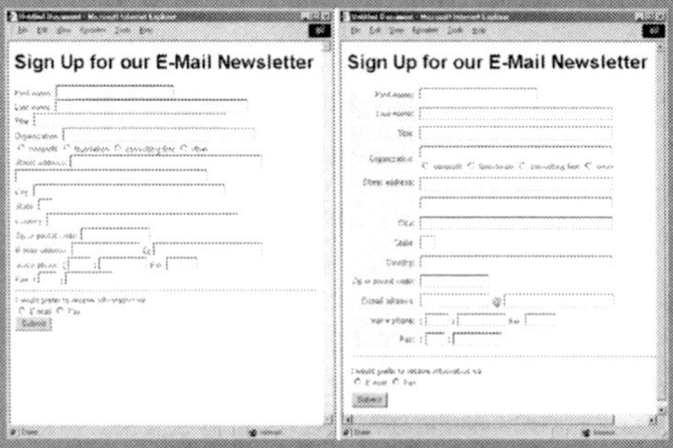

In the form on the right, a table made of two columns and 13 rows (one row for each question) organizes the text and form elements into two columns. Notice that the text next to each form element aligns to the right, creating a clean edge that effectively mirrors the edge created by the form fields.

To make this table-based solution work most effectively, set each text field to the same width, using the *Char Width* property or Cascading Style Sheets.

When using this technique, add the <form> tag first, insert the table inside the form's dotted red boundaries, and then add form elements inside the table. If you make a table first and then try to insert a form, then Dreamweaver lets you add it to only a single cell of the table. See Chapter 7 for more on creating tables.

You can also use CSS to lay out a form. This technique is a bit more complex, but if you're interested, you can find a good demonstration of CSS-based form layout at: *http://jeffhowden.com/code/css/forms/*.

File Field

Receiving responses to checkboxes, radio buttons, and pull-down menus is all well and good, but what if you'd like your visitors to submit something a little meatier—like an entire file? Imagine a bulletin board system that lets guests post JPEG images of themselves, or upload word processing documents to share with others. They can do just that, thanks to File Field (see Figure 11-4)—and a little magic from your Web server.

Before you get carried away with the possibilities the File Field offers, you need to do a little research to see whether you can use it on your Web site. Although Dreamweaver lets you easily *add* a field for uploading image files, text files, and other documents, you need to check your Web server administrator to see if anonymous file uploads are permitted (some servers don't allow this kind of activity for fear of receiving viruses or overly large files). Then, of course, you'll have to ensure that the program that processes the form is programmed to *do* something with the incoming file—store it somewhere on the server, for instance. Dreamweaver doesn't have anything built in that helps with this, but you can enlist some third-party solutions as described in the box on page 451.

When you click the File Field button on the Insert panel's Forms category (or choose Insert → Form Objects → File Field), Dreamweaver inserts a text field *and* a Browse button; together, they constitute a single File Field. When you click either one, you highlight both.

The Browse button, once it's posted on the Web and visible in somebody's browser, opens up the standard Windows or Macintosh Open File dialog box, letting your visitor navigate to and select a file for uploading.

The Property inspector offers only two settings to change (other than specifying a more creative name):

- **Char width.** The width of a text field is measured in characters; if you type *20* for the character width, the field is 20 characters wide.
- **Max chars.** Leave this blank, as explained in Figure 11-12.

Your File Field isn't finished until you've added a label to it in the document window, something like "Click the Browse button to select a file for uploading" (again, a task that Dreamweaver simplifies with the Label option in the form's Accessibility window described on page 436).

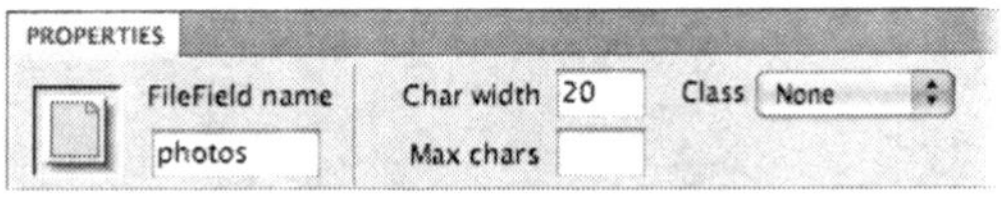

Figure 11-12: *Avoid the "Max chars" field. It's intended to limit the number of characters that the field accepts, but doesn't have any effect on the File Field, which selects the full path to the file regardless of how many characters long it is.*

Hidden Field

Most form elements are designed to accept input from your visitors: clicking radio buttons, typing into text fields, and making choices from menus, for example. But visitors don't even know about, and don't ever see, one kind of form field: the *hidden* field.

Note: Hidden fields aren't exactly hidden–visitors don't see the hidden field when looking at the page in a browser, but if a visitor checks the page's HTML (using the browser's View → View Source or View Page Source command), then the hidden field and it's data are visible. In other words, hidden fields aren't for data to which you don't want anyone to have access.

Why, you're probably asking, would you need to submit a value you already know? Hidden fields supply information to the programs that process forms—information that the program has no other way of knowing. For example, most Web hosting services offer a generic form-processing program that collects information submitted with a form, and emails it to a selected person. But how does the program know where to email the data? After all, it's a *generic* program that hundreds of other people use. The solution: A hidden field that stores the information required for the program to properly process the form—like *email=me@mydomain.com.*

To insert a hidden field, click the Insert panel's Hidden Field button (under the Forms category), or choose Insert → Form → Hidden Field. A gold shield icon appears on the page (this is Dreamweaver's symbol for HTML that you can't see in Web browsers). Use the Property inspector to give the field a name and a *value*—that is, the value that gets submitted to your form processing program (in the example above, your email address).

Note: The gold shield indicating a hidden field appears only if, in the Preferences window's Invisible Elements category, the Hidden Form Fields box is turned on (see page 76), and, in the View menu, Invisible Elements is turned on (View → Visual Aids → Invisible Elements).

EXTENSION ALERT

Adding File Upload Ability to Your Site

Imagine adding a "Job Application" page to your site, where applicants can upload their resumes for review. Or a Web-based way for clients to submit their graphic files and word processing documents.

Dreamweaver lets you add a File Field to a form, but doesn't provide the tools to make this useful feature function on your Web site. To compensate for that glaring omission, you can turn to extensions that add this missing power to Dreamweaver when building a dynamic Web site (as described in Part 6 of this book). But before you shell out any hard-earned cash on the extensions listed next, make sure your Web hosting company allows anonymous file uploads from a Web form—some don't.

DMXZone (*www.dmxzone.com/index.asp?TypeId=3&CatId=862*) offers two fee-based extensions for ASP and PHP. The Pure Upload extension offers many different settings to manage the process of uploading files to a Web site, including the ability to rename duplicate files, and add file information to databases.

WebAssist (one of the big players in the Dreamweaver Extensions market) offers a commercial product, Digital File Pro, for uploading *and* downloading files from a server (*www.webassist.com/professional/products/ProductDetails.asp?PID=112*). This extension works for PHP.

Buttons

No form is complete without a Submit button for your Web visitors to click as a final step (see Figure 11-4). Only then do their responses set out on their way to your form-processing application. People sometimes add a Reset button, which visitors can click when they've filled out a form and realize they've made an error. The Reset button clears all the form entries, and resets all the form fields to their original values.

Use the Insert panel's Forms category (see Figure 11-2), or choose Insert → Form → Button. If the Accessibility window appears (see page 436), then you don't need to add a label, since the button itself has "Submit", "Reset", or whatever text you wish emblazoned across its face, so just click the Cancel button.

The Property inspector controls (Figure 11-13) for a freshly inserted button are:

- **Button name.** The button's name provides the first half of the "name/value" pair that's sent when the form is submitted (see page 429).

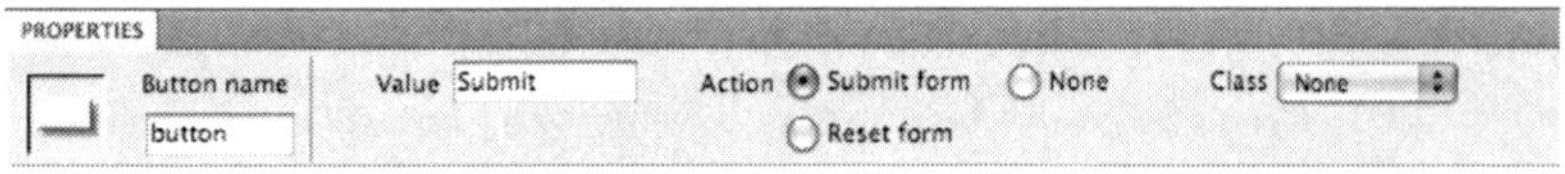

***Figure 11-13:** Buttons have just three properties: Name, Value, and Action. Like other form elements and HTML tags, Dreamweaver also lets you apply a CSS class style to improve your forms' design.*

- **Value.** The value is the label that appears on the button. Dreamweaver proposes *Submit*, but you're free to substitute *Do It, Make It So*, or *Send my data on its merry way*.

  So what your visitors see printed on the button—for example, "Click Me"—is also the value that's transmitted along with the button's name when the form is submitted. This characteristic opens up some interesting possibilities. You could, for example, include *several* Submit buttons, each with a different label. Maybe you're creating a form for a database application; one button might say Delete, while another says Edit. Depending on which button your visitor clicks, the program processing the form either deletes the record from the database or modifies it.

- **Action.** These three buttons govern what happens when somebody clicks your button. A "Submit form" button transmits the form data over the Internet to the form-processing program. A "Reset form" button sets all the fields back to their original values. (The fields, checkboxes, or menu items aren't left blank, unchecked, or unselected. Instead, they return to their *initial* values, which you specified when you created these various controls. For example, if you set the Initial State property of a checkbox to Checked, and your visitor unchecks the box, and then clicks the Reset button, then a checkmark reappears in the box.)

  The Reset button used to appear on nearly every form on the Web; these days it's much less frequent, mainly because it's unlikely that anyone would want to *completely* erase *everything* she's typed into the form. In addition, its presence offers the unfortunate possibility that a visitor, after painstakingly filling out a form, will mistake the Reset button for the Submit button, and click it—erasing everything she's typed. If you do add a Reset button, make sure you don't put it right next to a Submit button.

Note: A Reset button can come in handy on a page intended to *update* information. An update form contains previously recorded information (like your shipping address for your Amazon.com account). In this case, a Reset button lets the visitor erase any mistakes he made when updating his account information. Clicking a Reset button, in this case, sets the form back to display the original information. You'll learn how to create an update form for a database-driven site in Chapter 24.

Setting the button's action to None means that clicking on the button has no effect on the form. "Gee *that's* useful," you're probably thinking. But although the button doesn't submit the data or reset the form's fields, you need to choose the None option if you want to add interactivity to the button using Dreamweaver's built-in behaviors (see the Chapter 13). In this way, you can use a common user interface element—the 3-D beveled look of a form button—to trigger any of many different actions, like opening a new browser window, starting or stopping a Flash movie, or popping up a message on the screen. If you're a JavaScript programmer, then you can use the button to activate your own programs.

Tip: You can also use a graphic as a Submit button, thanks to something called an Image Field, thus freeing you to be more creative with the look of the button itself. On the Insert panel, click the Image Field button, or choose Insert → Form → Image Field, to select a graphic you want to use as a button. When a Web visitor clicks the image, it submits the form and all its data. (Unfortunately, Image Fields do only one thing: Submit form data. You can't use them as form Reset buttons.)

<label> Tag

As discussed on page 437, the <label> tag lets you associate a label with a particular form element, like a checkbox or text field. Of course, you can always place plain text next to a form element on the page. But because a <label> tag is "attached" to a particular form element, it's more helpful in explaining the function and layout of your form to people who use assistive technologies like screen-reading software for the blind.

On the Insert panel's Forms category, the Label tag button (see Figure 11-2) doesn't do much more than switch you into Code view, and drop the <label> tag into your HTML. You're much better off inserting labels with Dreamweaver's form accessibility option, as described on page 436. However, there are some cases where you don't want to put the label directly next to the form field; for example, when using tables to lay out a form, you usually put the label in one table cell, and the form element in another. In this case, you need to jump into Code view to add a label anyway, and this button can save you a little typing.

<fieldset> Tag

The <fieldset> tag is a form organization tool, intended to let you group related form fields. For example, if you're creating an online ordering form, you can organize all the "ship to" information—address, city, state, Zip code, and so on—into a single set. Again, this arrangement can help those using assistive technology to understand the organization and intent of a form.

In most of the latest browsers, the <fieldset> tag also has a visual benefit. Browsers display an attractive border around fieldsets. In addition, the Legend tag (which Dreamweaver automatically adds whenever you insert a fieldset) let's you supply a descriptive label to identify the fields grouped inside a fieldset. The legend appears at the top of the fieldset.

To use this tag, select the related form fields. The form fields must be next to each other onscreen, and can be organized within other HTML elements like a table. Then, on the Insert panel's Forms category, click the Fieldset button (see Figure 11-2). In the Label window that appears, type a label (called, somewhat dramatically, a "Legend") for the fieldset, and then click OK.

Dreamweaver, in addition to displaying the label you type, displays a simple border around the group of fields you select. Because different browsers display this border differently, make sure to preview the page (F12, or Option-F12 on a Mac) in a recent version of Internet Explorer, Firefox, Opera, or Safari to see both the label and the border surrounding the form elements in the set.

FREQUENTLY ASKED QUESTION

Emailing the Results of a Form

I don't want to store form submissions in a database or anything fancy like that. I just want to receive an email with the information from each form submitted on my site. How do I do that?

This common function—available on countless Web sites—may seem like an easy task, but Dreamweaver doesn't supply a tool for automating the process. Basically, you need a program to collect the data, and then send it off in an email. Most Web hosting companies provide just such programs. They generally work like this: You build a form, set the form's Action property (see page 433) to point to the URL of the form-emailing program, and then add one or more hidden fields. The hidden fields contain information for the program to use—such as the email address the results should go to, and the page the visitor should end up at after she submits the form. Since this form-emailing program varies from server to server, you need to contact your Web hosting company for details.

Many commercial extensions can help you. For basic form mailing, the Mail Form extension for ASP and PHP is available from Felix One (*www.felixone.it/extensions/dwextensionsen.asp*). Two other extensions offer much more advanced emailing features, including the ability to mass-email newsletters to email addresses stored in a database: WA Universal Email from WebAssist (*www.webassist.com/professional/products/ProductDetails.asp?PID=134*) works for PHP pages, and DMXZone (*www.dmxzone.com*) sells both an ASP and a PHP version of its Smart Mailer extension.

For all these extensions, however, you need to install some programming on your Web server, and your Web server needs to support the programming language (ASP or PHP)—Part 6 of this book has more details on server-side programming.

Validating Forms

You might get frustrated when you look over feedback that's been submitted via a form on your Web page, only to notice that your visitor failed to provide a name, email address, or some other piece of critical information. That's why, depending on the type of form you create, you might want to make certain information *mandatory*.

For instance, a form used for subscribing to an email newsletter isn't much use if the would-be reader doesn't type in an email address for receiving it. Likewise, if you need a shipping address to deliver a brochure or product, you want to be sure that the visitor included his address on the form.

Luckily, Dreamweaver includes a set of validation options that accomplish this exact task: Spry Form validation "widgets." (The term *widget* refers to any of the Web page elements Spry helps you create, such as the Spry Menu Bar, Spry Validation Text Field, and Spry tabbed panels.) With a Spry validation widget you can display a friendly "Hey, please fill this box out" message when someone tries to submit a form that's missing important information. You can specify that a particular field can't be left blank, or that it must contain information in a specific format, such as a phone number, email address or credit card number. If someone attempts to submit the form without the correct information or with the incorrect type of information, she's notified. And instead of popping up an annoying and amateurish JavaScript error window, Spry form validation displays error messages right on the Web page, directly next to the faulty form field. You can even change the field's look (add a red background to the field, for example) to further highlight the problem.

Note: Spry validation widgets are much more useful than Dreamweaver's old Validate Form behavior. The validation tools provide professional-looking error messages and a wider range of validation options. If you've used the Validate Form behavior in the past, then switch to the Spry validation widgets, and prepare to be pleased.

Spry Validation Basics

The Spry validation widgets let you validate input received via a text field, a text area, a pull-down menu, a checkbox, or a group of radio buttons. You can make sure a field is filled out, a checkbox turned on, a selection's been made from a pull-down menu, or a button amongst a group of radio buttons is selected. You can require a specific type of information such as a date or a phone number, and even limit the number of letters someone can type into a text box.

The basic process for all form validation widgets is the same:

1. **Insert the Spry widget.**

   Buttons for inserting the seven types of Spry validation form fields are on the Insert panel's Forms (see Figure 11-2) and Spry categories (Figure 12-2). You can also insert a Spry form field from the Insert → Form submenu. The initial steps are just like inserting any form field. The Input Tag Accessibility window appears (Figure 11-5), and you follow steps 3, 4, and 5 on page 436.

   If you've already inserted a text field, multiline text box, checkbox, or pull-down menu, then you can add Spry validation to it by selecting the form element on the page, and then, on the Insert panel, clicking the appropriate Spry form button. If you want to add validation to a text field, select the text field, and then click the Spry Validation Text Field button. You can't add validation to a group of already placed radio buttons, however. If you want to validate a group of radio buttons, then you have to create them as part of the Spry Validation Radio Group widget (page 476).

When you insert one of these widgets, Dreamweaver adds more than just the HTML needed for the form field: It also inserts a <span> tag that surrounds the form field, a label, and additional HTML for displaying one or more error messages. A Spry validation widget also adds JavaScript programming (to make sure the form field receives valid information), and CSS (to style the appearance of the field and the validation error messages).

Note: When you save a Web page after inserting a Spry widget, Dreamweaver pops up a window letting you know that it's added JavaScript and CSS files to a SpryAssets folder in the site's root folder (see the Tip on page 188).

---

2. **Rename the widget (optional).**

   Once inserted, you can customize the form widget using the Property inspector (see Figure 11-14). Every Spry widget is assigned a generic ID like *sprytextfield1*, *sprytextfield2*, and so on. You can change this, if you wish, to something more descriptive, but for clarity's sake leave "spry" in the ID name. If you inserted a Spry text field for collecting a person's email address, then you might name the widget spryEmail. Dreamweaver applies this ID to a <span> tag that wraps around the actual form field, form label, and error messages that Spry creates. Don't get this ID confused with the ID you assigned to the form field—that's a different tag that requires its own ID. That's why it's a good idea to include "spry" in the new ID you assign to the widget. If this all sounds confusing, then do yourself a favor and don't bother renaming the widget. Dreamweaver can track the IDs just fine, and since the generic name assigned by Dreamweaver is never visible on the form, no one visiting your site knows the difference.

3. **Assign a validation requirement.**

   Use the Property inspector to assign the type of validation you'd like to apply to the field. The most basic form of validation is simply requiring input from the form field. That is, ensuring that *something's* been typed in the text box or text area, a selection has been made from a pull-down menu, a checkbox has been turned on, or a radio button selected. But each type of form field has additional validation options. For example, you can make sure a text field is filled with numbers in the correct format for a credit card. The specific options for each type of form field are discussed below.

Note: Properties for a Spry widget appear in the Property inspector only when you've selected the widget (as opposed to selecting the form field itself). To select the widget, mouse anywhere over the form field until a blue Spry tab appears (see Figure 11-15); then click the tab to select the Spry widget.

---

4. **Select *when* validation occurs.**

   A browser validates form fields as soon as the visitor submits the form. In other words, when someone clicks the Submit button on the form, the JavaScript code in the Web page checks to make sure everything was filled out correctly.

If it's not, the form does not pass Go and one or more error messages appear, letting the visitor know what went wrong. In fact, Spry validation always works when the form is submitted, and you can't turn this behavior off (that's why, in the Property inspector, the Submit checkbox is checked and grayed out [see Figure 11-14]).

However, to provide more responsive feedback, you can also check to make sure the form has the right info immediately after the visitor interacts with it. Say you've added a text field to collect a visitor's email address, and some wisenheimer types, "I'm not telling" instead of his email address. You could present an error message—like "This is not a valid email address"—when the form is submitted. Or you could display an error message the moment he moves onto the next form field. This kind of instant feedback can make it easier for your site visitors: They can immediately see and fix their mistakes, and they don't have to wait until their forms are submitted to see (and fix) all the errors they may have made.

You dictate *when* a field is validated by turning on one or both of the Property inspector's "Validate on" checkboxes (circled in Figure 11-14). Dreamweaver lets you validate a form field when the field is "blurred," "changed," or both. "Blur" doesn't mean the form field suddenly gets fuzzy; it simply refers to the moment when the visitor clicks on another form field or another part of the page. If you type something into a text box, and then click the Tab key to jump to another form field, the text box is considered "blurred." Or if you type into a text box, and then click somewhere else on the page, that text box also becomes blurred. This blurred state is a great time to validate a text field, because you know the visitor is done providing input into that field the moment he tabs to the next field.

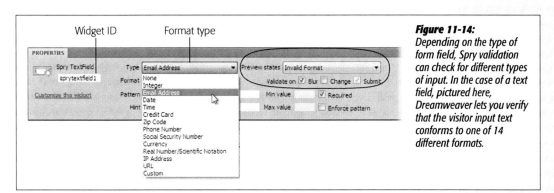

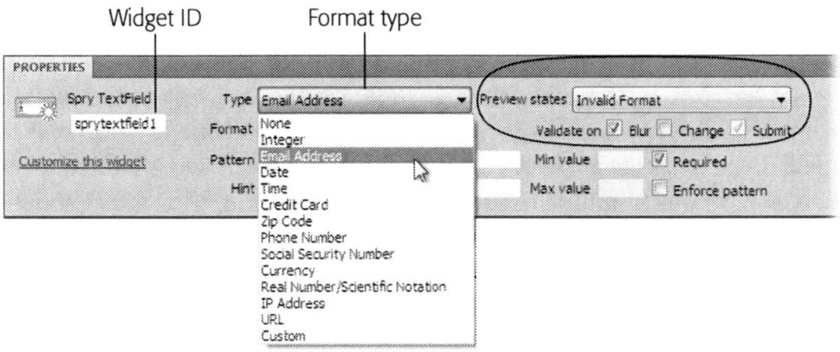

Figure 11-14: *Depending on the type of form field, Spry validation can check for different types of input. In the case of a text field, pictured here, Dreamweaver lets you verify that the visitor input text conforms to one of 14 different formats.*

You can also validate a field when it's changed. This change happens when someone types into a text field, for example. In fact, each letter the person types is a "change" to the field, so the field is validated following each keystroke. This quality can be a bit annoying, since an error message might appear the moment you start typing. With email address validation, the JavaScript that validates user input is looking for text in the form of *bob@somewhere.com*. So say Bob clicks into the field and starts to type. The moment he hits the 'b' key, the field is changed, and its contents are validated. Since 'b' isn't a proper email address format, an "Invalid Format" message appears on the page. That's a bit rude. In this case, the "blur" option is better, since it waits until the visitor has finished filling out the field.

On the other hand, validating a pull-down menu field when it changes can be quite useful. Say you've added a pull-down field to a form, and the first option is "Please make a selection". Obviously, you want people filling out the form to select something other than that initial "Please make a selection" option. Imagine that someone starts to fill out the form, and selects an item on the pull-down menu; then, for whatever reason, she goes back to the menu and chooses "Please make a selection". This option isn't valid, and the visitor should be notified immediately. If you validate the form when it changes, an error message pops up the moment she chooses "Please make a selection". On the other hand, if validation occurs when the menu is "blurred," the visitor is notified only after she's clicked somewhere else on the page—in other words, a few moments later, rather than immediately.

In general, "blur" works best for text fields and text areas, while "change" is better for checkboxes, radio buttons and pull-down menus.

5. **Set other options for the widget.**

   Some widgets have other settings that can come in handy. For instance, you can limit the number of letters someone can type into a text area validation widget; and in text field widgets, you can add a helpful "hint" (like "Type your name in this box", which would appear inside the text field). These options are discussed below.

6. **Modify the error messages.**

   Preventing incomplete visitor input solves only part of the problem. When a visitor leaves a required field blank, or types incorrect information into a field, you need to let him know what went wrong, so he can fix it. Every form validation widget includes one or more error messages. An error message appears next to a form field if the contents of the field aren't successfully validated: Different error messages appear under different circumstances. For example, a Spry validation text field displays the message "A value is required" if the field is left blank, or "Invalid format" if the field isn't empty but has the wrong type of response—a word instead of a year in a "What year were you born?" field, for instance.

   You can customize each of these error messages by selecting, from the Property inspector, the proper "preview state" (see Figure 11-15). After selecting a preview state, Dreamweaver changes the display of the page in Design view. In Figure 11-15, selecting "required" displays the error message that appears if the form is submitted but this field is left blank.

   To change the message, in Design view, select the text, and then type a new error message. It's generally a good idea to come up with a friendly and descriptive

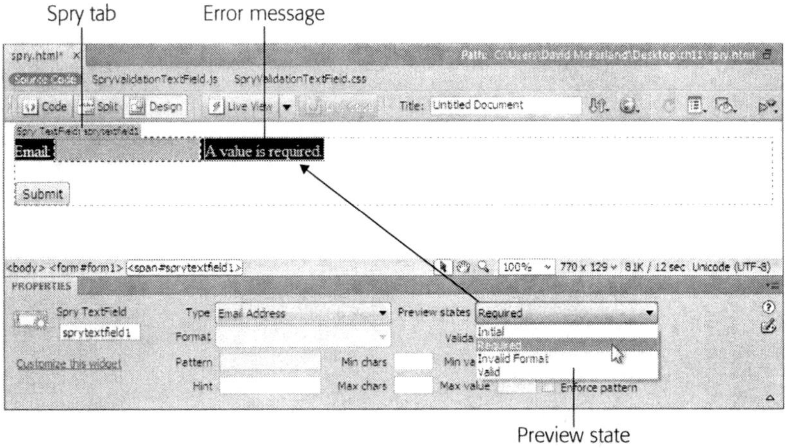

Figure 11-15: *Click the blue Spry tab to select a Spry validation widget. This way is the only way to display the widget's properties in the Property inspector. If you click the form field (text box, checkbox, or pull-down menu), you see just the regular form field properties, discussed on page 439.*

message. If a text field is programmed to accept a date in a particular format, you might change the "invalid format" error message to something like "Please enter a date in this format: 02/27/2009."

Warning: When changing the error message for a Spry form field, do not simply delete the error message that's there, and then type a new message. When you delete the current message, you also delete the <span> tag responsible for displaying the error message. Instead, select the old message, and then immediately type the new message. This action leaves the <span> in place so that the error message appears when it's supposed to.

Most validation widgets have more than one error message, so make sure you preview each of the different "states." Some preview states have no error message, so you're just previewing the page in the selected state. For example, no error message appears when the form first loads, so the "Initial" option in the preview state menu just shows what the form field looks like when the form page is first visited. Every other widget except for the checkbox widget also includes a "valid" preview state. This is how the form field looks when input is received. There's no error message in this instance, but the form field's background changes to green. You create this green formatting with CSS, which you'll learn to modify next.

Tip: You can change the placement of a Spry form field error message by going into Code view, and then moving the <span> containing the error message–it'll look something like <span cass=textfieldInvalidFormatMsg>Invalid format</span>. Because each form field can have multiple error messages (for required, invalid format, and so on), there may be more than one <span>. However, keep in mind that each Spry form widget has *another* <span> that surrounds the label, the field, and the error messages–it looks something like <span id="sprytextfield1">. You can move the <span> tags only for the error messages to another location *within* the surrounding widget's <span> tag. If you move them outside that, then the error messages no longer work.

Formatting Spry Error Messages and Fields

Spry's error messages appear on the Web page in red with a red outline. Fortunately, you're not stuck with this factory setting. CSS controls the display of Spry widgets; a single style, for example, controls the "invalid" error message's formatting. When you insert a Spry validation widget, Dreamweaver adds the style sheet to the SpryAssets folder in your site's root folder (see page 188). Each Spry validation widget (text boxes, text areas, menus, and checkboxes) has its own external style sheet. The style sheet is named after the type of widget: For example, the style sheet for a Spry validation text field is named SpryValidationTextField.css. If you add several different types of Spry validation fields, then you have to edit several different style sheets to change the look of the error messages.

Fortunately, you don't have to hunt and peck through the .css file to modify an error message's style. By using Dreamweaver's CSS Styles panel's Current view, you can easily identify the proper style, and then edit it. Here's how:

1. **Open the CSS Styles panel (see Figure 11-16).**

   For example, choose Window → CSS Styles, or Shift-F11 on Windows.

2. **At the top of the panel, click the Current button.**

   The Current view shows the styles and properties that apply to a given selection in the document window.

3. **Make sure the Cascade button is pressed (circled in Figure 11-16).**

   The Cascade button activates the Rules pane in the middle of the CSS Styles panel. It displays all CSS styles that apply to the selection in the order of their specificity—least specific on top, most specific at the bottom (see page 312 for a specificity refresher). The style that most directly applies to the given selection is listed last.

4. **Select the Spry validation widget.**

   To select the widget, mouse anywhere over the form field until a blue Spry tab appears (see Figure 11-15); click the tab to select the Spry widget.

5. **From the Property inspector's "Preview states" menu, select the preview state you wish to format.**

   The error message for the selected state appears. In addition, the preview state may also include formatting for the form field itself; for example, a text field in its "valid" state has a green background. You can adjust the formatting of that field as well.

6. **In the document window, click inside the error message or select the form field you wish to format.**

   The style appears in the CSS Styles panel's Rules pane (see Figure 11-16). The style's name is a rather long-winded descendent selector (like *.textfield-RequiredState .textfieldRequiredMsg*). In addition, several descendent selectors are usually lumped together in a group style (see page 304 for details on group styles). You don't really need to pay attention to the name, however, since you've already identified the style you're going to edit.

Note: When formatting an error message, just click inside the text. Don't try to select the entire message—if you do, you might select more than the error message, and the CSS Styles panel doesn't reflect the correct style.

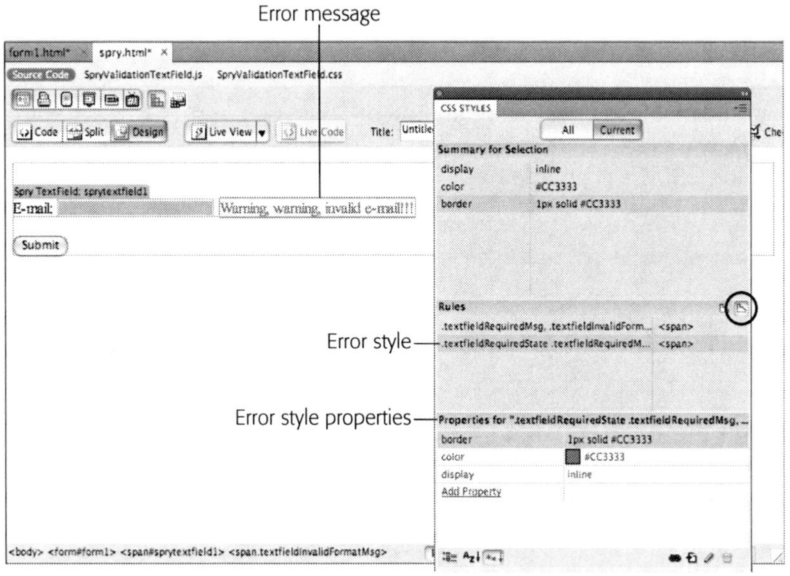

***Figure 11-16:** You can adjust the formatting of a Spry validation error message easily by clicking inside the error message, identifying the style in the Rules pane, and, in the Properties pane, editing the style properties. Or, just double-click the style name to open the friendly CSS Rule Definition window.*

7. **Edit the style's properties.**

   You can do this most easily by double-clicking the style's name in the Rules pane; this action opens the CSS Rule Definition window, where you can edit CSS properties as with any other style (see page 126). You can also use the Properties pane for a more rapid edit: To quickly change the text color, for instance (see page 305 for more on how to use the Properties pane to edit and set CSS properties).

Note: Spry error messages are presented inside <span> tags, which are displayed inline (meaning on the same line as the form field). If you want to put the error message on its own line, change the *display* property from *inline* to *block* (the chapter-ending tutorial includes an example of this trick on page 481).

In addition, you can move the <span> tags containing the error messages, and even change them from a <span> to a <div> or <p> tag. The exact tag type doesn't matter—but if you do change the tag type (from <span> to <p>, for instance), make sure the class name remains the same. Spry depends on the proper class name to identify the error message. If you move the error message, then it must remain inside the outer <span> tag that forms the Spry validation widget.

A few other styles affect the appearance of Spry form fields, but you can't preview or adjust them using the method just described. For example, when you click into a Spry-enabled text field, its background color changes to yellow; when you click a Spry menu, its background also changes to yellow (in all browsers except Safari). These different colors are applied to what's called the field's "focus state"—the moment a visitor interacts with the field. The styles to control these focus states are:

- **Text field focus style**: *.textfieldFocusState input, input.textfieldFocusState*. This style is located in the SpryValidationTextField.css file.
- **Text area focus style**: *.textareaFocusState textarea, textarea.textareaFocusState*. Located in the SpryValidationTextarea.css file.
- **Menu focus style**: *.selectFocusState select, select.selectFocusState*. Located in the SpryValidationSelect.css file. While Internet Explorer and Firefox let you use nearly any CSS style to format a menu, Safari lets you change only the font family, color, and size of pull-down menus.

In addition, another special style formats text fields and text area boxes when a visitor presses an invalid key on the keyboard (see the Tip on page 467).

Note: Dreamweaver CS4's new Live View can also help with CSS styling of elements controlled by JavaScript (like the Spry Validation widgets). Page 553 has more information.

Spry Text Field

Spry text fields have the most options of any Spry form validation widget. Dreamweaver gives you 14 different validation types as well as several other settings, such as an option to limit the minimum and maximum number of characters.

First you should decide whether the field is required, and if it is, then, in the Property inspector, turn on the Required box (circled in Figure 11-17). A form frequently has some fields that are required (an email address to sign up for a newsletter, for instance). Sometimes a response is optional, such as when you add a field for someone to add a phone number. In this case, you don't turn on the Required box. But you still want to use a Spry field, so that you can make sure any phone number that *is* submitted is formatted accurately.

Validation types

To make sure your visitors supply the appropriate information for your forms, you frequently validate the contents of a field to make sure the data is kosher: that a required zip code isn't just a series of letters, for instance. In the Property inspector, use the Type menu (see Figure 11-17) to assign one of 14 possible validation options:

- **None.** This option is the default setting: no validation. The contents of the field aren't inspected to make sure they match any particular format. You use this setting, in combination with the "Required" checkbox, when you don't care what someone types, just that they enter something: like a field used to capture visitor comments.

Note: When you assign any validation option other than "None", Dreamweaver adds an "Invalid Format" error message to the page. You can change this error message, as described in step 6 on page 458.

- **Integer.** Use this option to verify that a whole number was typed into the field, like a field asking for someone's age or a year of birth. The integer option checks for a whole number, so if someone types 1.25 into the field, then it doesn't validate: The form doesn't submit, and an "Invalid format" error appears. (If you *do* want to allow decimal values, then use the Real Number option discussed below.)

  If you specify integer validation, you can also assign minimum and maximum allowed values as discussed on page 467.

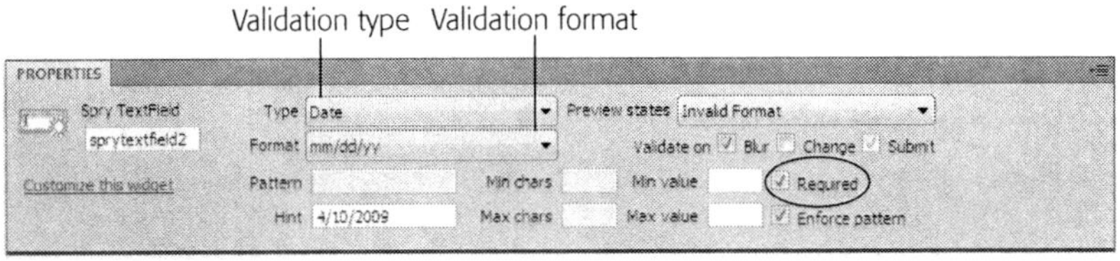

Figure 11-17: *Spry validation text fields provide multiple options for managing user input.*

- **Email.** This option looks for a validly formatted email address (like *missing@sawmac.com*). It can't actually make sure that the email address itself is real, however. Someone could still enter a fake email address like *nobody@nowhere.com*; but this option at least makes sure an honest visitor doesn't make a typo.

- **Date.** When you require a specific date, use this option. If you created a form for scheduling the use of a meeting room at the office, then you could add a "Date needed" field to the form. A date is composed of the month, day of the month, and the year, which can be formatted in many different ways: 12-02-2009, 12/02/09, 02.12.09, and so on. To specify the format you want, use the Property inspector's Format menu (see Figure 11-17).

Note: With data validation, the option *yyyy* means the field must have the full year (2009) to be valid. However, *mm* and *dd* both allow single digit values–for example, 1 for January, or 2 for the second day of the month. An initial zero (01 or 02) isn't required.

A month is indicated by *mm*, the day by *dd*, and the year by *yy* (for just the last two digits of the year: 09) or *yyyy* (for a complete year: 2009). Separators like / and the hyphen (–) are also used to separate the month, day, and year values. So, for example, the option *mm/dd/yyyy* means that 1/2/2009 and 12/15/2009 would both be valid inputs, but 1-2-2009 or 12/15/09 would not.

Note: If data from a date form field will eventually be stored in a MySQL database in a MySQL DATE field, then choose yyyy-mm-dd as the format option. That format matches the date format for MySQL.

- **Time.** This option validates a time in one of several different formats such as 12:15 PM or 23:15. You could use it along with a date field to capture the exact time of an event: A meeting room scheduling form might include a "What time does the meeting begin?" field, and another field to specify an ending time. As with the Date format, Time validation requires that you specify a particular time format using the Property inspector's Format menu. *HH* indicates the hour specified using 24-hour time: 13 for 1 p.m., for example; *hh* is the hour; *mm* is minutes; *ss* indicates seconds; *tt* is before noon and afternoon notation (that is, a.m. or p.m.); *t* indicates time of day using just a single letter, A or P.

  For example, the HH:MM option would validate 13:35, but not 01:35 PM (a zero is required for single digit hours, minutes, and seconds). The hh:mm:ss tt option requires a time to be formatted like this: 01:35:48 PM.

Note: Whenever you require a visitor to type information in a specific format—12:45 PM, for instance—be sure to include clear instructions on how to fill out the form. Something like, "Please enter the time you'd like to reserve, using this format: 12:45 PM." You can also take advantage of a Spry text field's Hint setting, as described on page 467.

- **Credit Card.** An e-commerce site isn't much good if you don't give people a way to pay for your products. To make sure a validly formatted credit card number is entered into a field, choose this option. If you accept only one type of credit card—like Visa or MasterCard—you can specify the acceptable type of card using the Property inspector's Format menu. As with email addresses, this validation format checks only to make sure the number is formatted correctly—it can't actually check to see if this is a real (and not stolen!) credit card.

Note: Be careful accepting credit card numbers online. An awful lot of responsibility goes along with taking someone's credit card number, as well as potential liability if the card was stolen, or someone manages to steal credit card numbers you collect. For an introduction to online payment processing, check out *http://particletree.com/notebook/processing-online-credit-card-transactions/*.

- **Zip Code.** To mail a brochure, t-shirt, book, or any product your site distributes, you need a Zip code. Use the Zip Code validation format to make sure the Zip code you receive is formatted correctly. The Format menu lets you specify a type and country. For example, US-5 means a 5 digit US Zip code like 97213, whereas US-9 is the 9 digit format composed of 5 digits, a hyphen, and 4 more numbers: 97213-1234. Dreamweaver also lets you select either Canadian or UK Zip code formats. You can even create your own Zip code format by specifying a custom pattern (see the opposite page).

- **Phone Number.** Use the Format menu to choose a US/Canada phone number format, or select Custom Pattern, which you then define in the Pattern field as described on page 466. The US/Canada phone format has to be entered like this: (555) 555-1234. The parentheses, space, and hyphen are required. For an alternative style, see page 466.

- **Social Security Number.** This option requires three numbers, a hyphen, two numbers, a hyphen, and three more numbers, like this: 555-12-4888. You might want to avoid requesting Social Security numbers: For reasons of privacy and fear of identity theft, many people are reluctant to disclose their Social Security numbers, and by law, they don't have to share these numbers with anyone.
- **Currency.** If you require someone to specify a monetary amount in a field—"How much money would you like to contribute to the home for wayward Web designers?"—then choose the currency option to validate their responses. You can choose between US and European formatting. US format is like 1,000.00, while in Europe the same value is expressed as 1.000,00. The comma (period for European value) that indicates a thousands position—1,000—is optional. Both 1000.00 and 1,000.00 are considered valid. However, an opening $ or € sign won't be accepted; so if a visitor enters $1,000.00 into a currency field, she gets an "Invalid format" error message.
- **Real number/Scientific Notation.** To allow decimal points in a field intended to capture numeric values, use this option. For a serious, scientific audience, numbers can even be entered using scientific notation: 1.231e10.
- **IP Address.** Since we all like having people type the unique set of numbers that identify a computer on the Internet, you can make sure only properly formatted IP addresses (like 192.168.1.1) are accepted. The Format menu lets you choose between the current IPv4 and (the newer, not yet fully implemented) IPv6, or both—oh, please…
- **URL.** Make sure visitors enter proper Web addresses using this option. For example, use this option for a form field requesting the address of a favorite Web site. The address has to include the protocol (http://) as well. So *http://www.sawmac.com/* is valid, but *www.sawmac.com* isn't.
- **Custom.** If you're unhappy with the validation options Dreamweaver offers, you can create your own as described next.

Custom validation

If you need to make sure information is entered in a very precise way, and none of Dreamweaver's predefined validation types fit the bill, you can create your own custom validation format. Say your company has an internal ID system for employees. Each employee is assigned an ID composed of three numbers, a hyphen, and the first three letters (in uppercase) of the person's last name: like 348-MCF. You can create your own custom validation "pattern" to enforce this format. If a visitor's input matches the pattern, the data is considered valid and the form can be submitted. If the input doesn't match the pattern, then an error message appears.

A pattern is just a series of symbols that indicate acceptable input; each letter in the pattern has a special meaning that defines the valid character type. AAA means "Accept three uppercase letters in a row as valid." To create your own custom validation, select a Spry text field widget, from the Property inspector's Type menu, choose Custom, and then into the Pattern field, type the pattern (see Figure 11-18). Here's a key to the symbols you use to create a pattern:

- **0** means a whole number between 0 and 9. If you want to make sure that someone enters five digits, type *00000* in the Property inspector's Pattern field. This pattern is the same as a five-digit Zip code.
- Type **A** to indicate a single uppercase alphabetic character. The pattern, A0A, for instance, is good for an uppercase letter, followed by a number, followed by another uppercase letter, like U5U.
- A lowercase **a** identifies a lowercase alphabetic character. The pattern *aaa*, then, matches *abc*, but not *ABC*.
- To accept either an uppercase or lowercase letter, use **B**. The pattern *BBB* matches both *abc* and *ABC*.
- To include numbers along with uppercase letters, use **X**; the letter **x** matches both numbers and lowercase alphabetical characters. Use **Y** for a case-insensitive match for numbers and letters. *XXX* matches *B2B, BBB* and *123*, but not *b2b* or *bbb*.

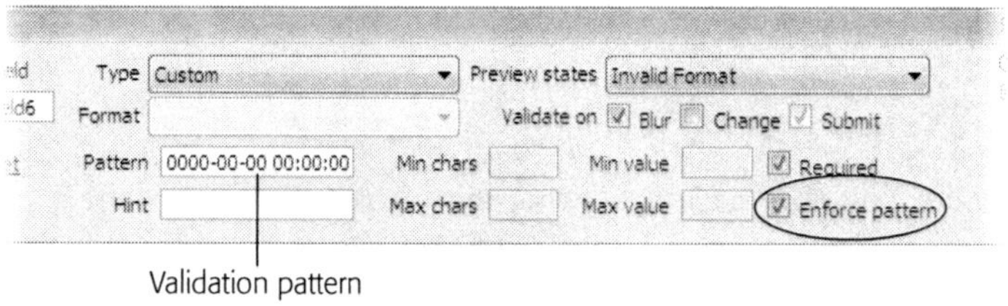

***Figure 11-18:** Are Spry's validation types not enough for you? Create your own by creating a pattern that a form field's input must match in order to validate.*

- Finally, use **?** as a kind of wild card. It stands in for any character whatsoever, and you should use it when a character other than a letter or number (like a period, !, or $ symbol) is also valid.

You can include any required symbol, like a period, comma, or hyphen, as part of the pattern. In the employee ID example discussed at the beginning of this section, the pattern to match that format would be 000-AAA. In other words, three numbers, a hyphen, and three uppercase letters. The pattern to match a phone number entered in this format (503-555-1234) is 000-000-0000. And the pattern to match the MySQL DATETIME format is 0000-00-00 00:00:00.

Enforcing a pattern

You can make sure incorrect characters aren't even allowed into a form field by turning on, in the Property inspector, the "Enforce pattern" checkbox (circled in Figure 11-18). When this option is selected, the form field blocks the input of invalid characters.

For example, suppose you added a Spry text field, and then set its validation type to Zip code using the US-Zip5 format. That box can accept only digits, and only five digits at that. If the "Enforce pattern" option were turned on for this field, then a visitor could type only five numbers into the field. If a visitor clicks into the field, and types the letter A, nothing happens. If the visitor types five numbers, and then any other character (like another number or even a letter), then that sixth character never appears.

You can choose the "Enforce pattern" option for any validation type except *None*. It even works with custom patterns that you create.

Tip: When someone types invalid characters into a form field that has the "Enforce pattern" option set, any text inside the box flashes bright red to indicate a problem. If you want to change that color, you can edit the styles responsible. For text fields, in the *SpryValidateTextField.css* file, the style is a group selector named "*.textfieldFlashText input, input.textfieldFlashText*". In the SpryValidationTextarea.css file, a similar style named "*.textareaFlashState textarea, textarea.textareaFlashState*" applies to text area fields.

Supplying a hint

As mentioned in the Tip on page 464, when you require a very specific format for a form field, you should provide clear instructions on how visitors should fill out the field. These instructions might appear next to the label or below the form field.

Dreamweaver also lets you add a short "hint" inside a Spry text field. This hint appears when the form first loads, but the moment a visitor clicks into the field, the hint disappears; visitors are then free to type a response.

To add a hint, select the Spry widget, and then, in the Property inspector's Hint field, enter what you want to appear (see Figure 11-17).

Since text fields are relatively short, the hint shouldn't really be instructions on what to type. Instead, hints work best if they're examples of the format the field requires. If the form field is intended to collect an email address, the hint might be *your_email@your_site.com*. If you're looking for a phone number and use the phone number validation type (page 464), you should add a sample phone number like this: (555) 555-1234. This lets visitors know that they should include the parentheses and hyphen.

Limiting characters and enforcing a range of values

At times you may want to control how much or how little text someone types into a form field. If you've created a form to create a member profile as part of your "members-only" Web site, you might want to collect a person's age—so you'll want an integer that's at least two numbers (no babies allowed!) but no more than three numbers long (and immortals must stay out as well!). As you've read, you can control the maximum number of characters entered into a text field with a text field's "Max chars" property (see page 440). However, HTML gives you no way to require *at least* a certain number of characters; setting the "Max chars" property doesn't alert a visitor when she's typed the maximum number of allowable characters.

With Spry text fields, you can set both, using the Property inspector's "Min chars" and "Max chars" fields (see Figure 11-19). Select the Spry widget by clicking the blue Spry tab that appears when you mouse over a Spry text field; then, in the "Min chars" field, type the minimum number of allowable characters, and, in the "Max chars", field, the maximum number of allowable characters. You can fill in either field, both, or neither. In the age example from the previous paragraph, in the "Min chars" box, you'd type *2;* and in the "Max chars" box, *3.*

Each setting has its own error message that you can view and edit by choosing the appropriate state from the Preview States menu (see step 6 on page 458). The error message for the minimum number of characters is "Minimum number of characters not met". You should change the error message to something more descriptive like "You're too young to join our club."

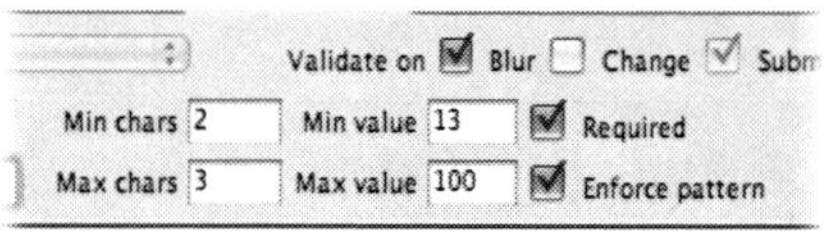

Figure 11-19:
Go ahead, be a dictator. The Spry text field validation widget even lets you control how many characters someone can type into a field.

Some types of validation also let you enforce a range of values. If you select the Integer validation type (see page 463), then, in the Property inspector, the "Min value" and "Max value" boxes (see Figure 11-19) become active. Say you include a question on a form that reads, "Please rate our service quality from 1 to 10," and supplies a text box for a response. In this case, set the "Min value" to 1 and the "Max value" to 10; that way answers like 100, or –10 aren't allowed.

You can also set Min and Max values for other numeric validation types like currency (page 465) and real numbers (page 465). These two settings even work with the date and time validation types (page 463). Say you're offering rebates to anyone who bought your product before a certain date—08/05/2007, for instance; the online rebate form includes a "Date purchased" field. In this instance, you can choose the Date validation type, from the Format menu, select mm/dd/yyyy, and then, into the "Max value" field, type *08/05/2007.* If someone who bought the product on 09/15/2007 tries to claim the rebate, he gets an error when he fills out the form.

Note: Setting a Min and Max value for a text field that uses Time validation works reliably only if you use 24-hour time (like 18:00 for 6:00 PM). If you use one of the formats that requires a.m. or p.m., then you can end up with inaccurate results. Spry treats 12:00 PM (noon) as later than 5:00 PM, and 8:00 AM as earlier than 12:00 AM (midnight).

Spry Text Area

A Spry text area has far fewer validation options than a normal text field. You can't select a type of validation or enforce a pattern on the text box's contents. However, the Property inspector for a Spry text area widget does let you specify whether content is required; dictate the minimum and maximum number of characters allowed; and supply a "hint" that appears inside the text area box when the form page first loads (see Figure 11-20). (These options works just like those for a text field, as described on page 439.)

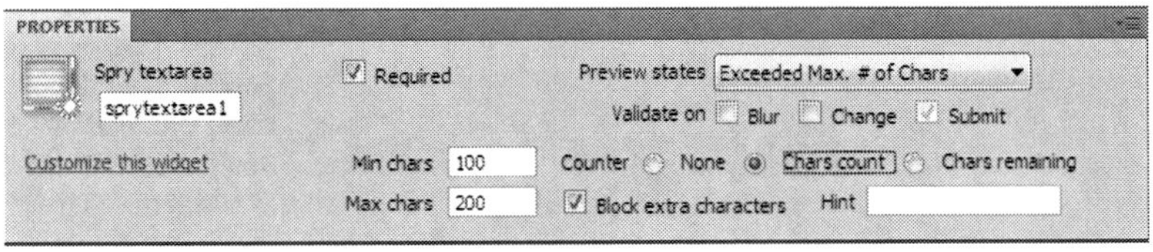

***Figure 11-20:** If you turn on the "Block extra characters" checkbox after you set a value in the "Max chars" field, anything someone types beyond the maximum character limit doesn't appear. HTML gives you no way to limit the amount someone can type into a multiline text box, so this Spry feature offers a nice workaround. (Also note that someone filling out the form never sees the error message that normally appears when someone exceeds the maximum number of characters if the "Block extra characters" option is turned on.)*

In addition, you can include a counter alongside the text area that indicates the total number of characters typed into the box. Maybe you want to limit the amount of feedback a visitor can type into a multiline text box, so you add a message like "Please limit your feedback to under 300 letters." If you select the "Chars count" radio button, then when the Web form is viewed in a Web browser, a counter appears next to the text area. As letters are typed into the box, the counter value increases to show the number of letters typed (Figure 11-21, top text box).

If you specify a maximum number of allowable characters in the "Max chars" field, then you can instead select the "Chars remaining" button (see Figure 11-20). Instead of displaying the number of characters inside the text area, it displays how many characters are still allowed (see Figure 11-21, bottom text box).

Both of these counters are helpful, but unfortunately, there's no context provided for the numbers: 128? 128 what? Letters remaining, or letters already typed into the box? To add a message that appears next to the number, you have to go into Code view. The best method is to select the text area field in Design view; click the Code or Split view button; then look for a <span> tag that looks something like: <span id="countsprytextarea2"> </span>. In this example, "sprytextarea2" is the Spry widget's name. You must add your message either before or after the <span>

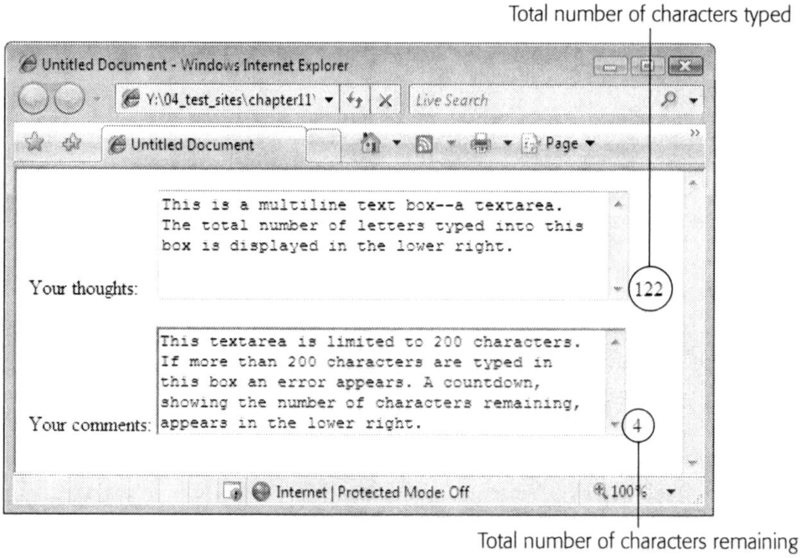

Figure 11-21: *A Spry text area can include feedback regarding how many letters have been typed into a multiline text box (top). It's also possible to display a countdown that shows how many letters are still allowed before the limit is reached (bottom).*

tag, but not *inside* the span. The code above could be changed to "<span id="countsprytextarea2"> </span> characters remaining" for a text area with the "Chars remaining" option turned on. In this way, a visitor would see something like "128 characters remaining".

Spry Checkbox

The Spry validation checkbox lets you make sure a particular checkbox has been selected. This checkbox is useful for those ubiquitous "I agree to your rules and conditions" checkboxes. In addition, you can add several checkboxes as a group, and require that the person filling out the form selects a minimum number ("Please make at least two choices") or a maximum number ("Please choose no more than two") of options.

To add a single Spry checkbox, choose Insert → Form → Spry Validation Checkbox, or, on the Insert panel's Forms category, click the Spry Validation Checkbox button (Figure 11-2). The Spry checkbox that appears on the page already has the "Required" option selected in the Property inspector (see Figure 11-22). If you want just a single checkbox that visitors must check in order to submit the form, you're done. But beyond the kind of "You must turn on this checkbox to free us from all legal responsibility" scenario, a single, required checkbox isn't so useful. After all, checkboxes more commonly come in groups as part of a multiple-choice question.

Unfortunately, Dreamweaver doesn't include a simple "Add a group of checkboxes" tool. If you insert several Spry checkboxes in a row, then each is inside its own Spry widget, and each is separately validated. Nor can you insert a bunch of regular checkboxes, select them, and then apply the Spry validation checkbox to them.

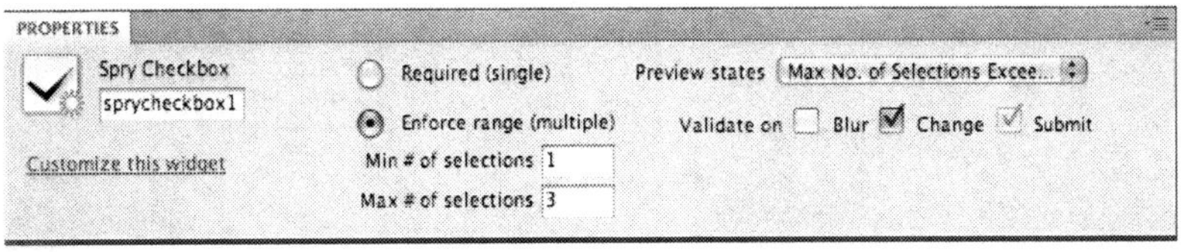

***Figure 11-22:** Use the Spry validation checkbox widget to make sure your site visitors turn on a checkbox (in cases where you want this to happen, of course).*

To create a group of related Spry checkboxes, therefore, you need to either go into Code view or do a delicate keyboard dance to insert all the necessary code just right. If you want to stay in Design view, here's a method for inserting a group of checkboxes that are validated together:

1. **Insert a Spry checkbox.**

   Use either the Insert → Form menu or the Insert bar. Dreamweaver inserts a checkbox, and the familiar blue Spry tab appears. Assume you added a label to the right of the checkbox, and you want to add another checkbox to the right of the one you just inserted.

2. **Click the label text (see top image in Figure 11-23).**

   Assuming you added a label (see page 436), your goal is to move the cursor *outside* the <label> tag for the current checkbox. If you simply click to the right of the label to insert the next checkbox, one of two (bad) things can happen: You insert another checkbox inside the first checkbox's <label> tag—when this happens, Dreamweaver gets really confused and omits a <label> tag for the new checkbox. Or, you insert the checkbox outside the Spry widget, meaning the new checkbox won't be validated along with the first checkbox.

3. **Press the right arrow key until the <label> tag disappears from the Tag selector, but you still want to see something like <span#sprycheckbox1> (Figure 11-23, bottom image).**

   Once again, the Tag selector comes to the rescue. When you no longer see <label> in the Tag selector, the cursor is outside the label, and you can now insert another checkbox. The <span#sprycheckbox1> identifies the tag responsible for the Spry checkbox widget. As long as you still see that in the Tag selector, the next checkbox you insert receives Spry validation.

4. **Insert a *regular (non-Spry)* checkbox as described on page 442.**

   The cursor is already inside a Spry checkbox widget, so don't insert a Spry checkbox.

5. **Repeat steps 2–4 to insert as many additional checkboxes as needed.**

   You can add as many checkboxes as you want. As long as they're inserted inside the Spry widget, they'll be part of the validation process.

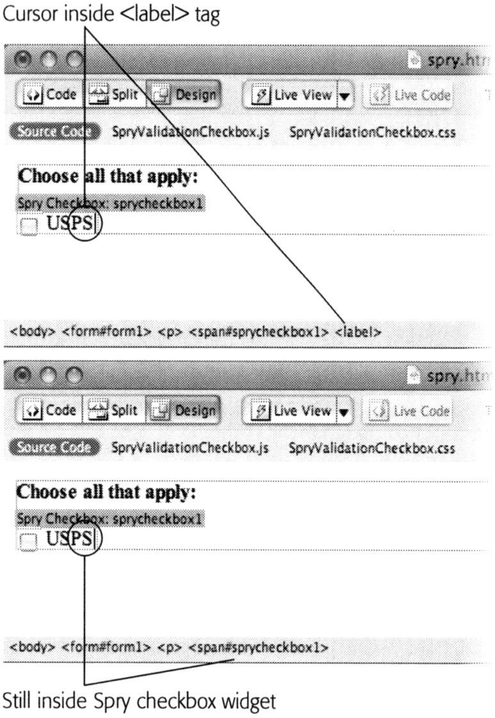

Figure 11-23: *If you want to include multiple checkboxes in a single Spry checkbox validation widget, you need to first insert a Spry checkbox, and then insert additional regular (non-Spry) checkboxes. The trick is making sure you don't insert the new checkbox inside the <label> tag of another checkbox (top), but still insert the new checkbox inside the Spry validation widget's code (bottom).*

Note: If you want to place each checkbox in its own paragraph, you must change the <span> tag used for the Spry checkbox validation widget to a <div> tag. According to the rules of HTML, a <span> tag can't be wrapped around block level elements such as paragraphs. Just go into Code view, locate the <span> (which should look something like <span id="sprycheckbox1">), and then change *span* to *div*. Then locate the closing </span> tag, and change it to </div>.

6. **Click the blue Spry tab to select the widget; in the Property inspector, select the "Enforce range" button, and then, in the "Min # of selections" and the "Max # of selections" fields, type numbers (see Figure 11-22).**

   You don't have to fill out both the Min and Max fields. If you have a question like "What type of food do you like (select as many as apply)", you might choose 1 for "Min # of selections" but leave the Max field blank. This way, you require at least one choice, but the visitor is free to choose as many other options as she wants.

   Or, you might have a question like "Select your four favorite foods". In this case, you'd type *4* in the Max field, since you don't want more than four answers. (You could also type *4* in the Min field if you want to make sure you get no more or less than four choices.)

Spry Select

The Spry validation select widget validates the selection of pull-down menus, and has two options to determine whether or not a selection in the menu is valid (see Figure 11-24). Remember that a pull-down menu (created with the <select> tag) consists of a label and a value (see page 446). The label is what someone sees when he makes a selection from the menu, and the value is what's sent over the Internet when the form is submitted.

With a Spry menu, you can prevent a form from submitting, and instead display an error message if the current menu selection has no value set or has a particular "invalid" value set. Say you have a menu listing all the months of the year. The label is the month's name and its value is a number (see Figure 11-11). Suppose you added "Please select a month" as the first item on the menu. This common technique lets visitors know what's listed on the menu and what they should select from the menu. Of course, when the form is submitted, you want to make sure a month and *not* "Please select a month" is selected.

Note: Although Dreamweaver inserts a pull-down menu when you insert a Spry validation select widget, you can convert the menu to a list, as described on page 446. The same validation options apply.

To prevent a visitor from submitting the form without selecting a month in this scenario, just leave the value for the "Please select a month" label blank, and turn on the "Blank value" checkbox for the Property inspector's "Do not allow" option (see Figure 11-24). With this setting, if the visitor selects a month (say February), there's a set value (2, for instance), and the menu validates. However, if she doesn't make a selection, the "Please select a month" choice (which has no value) invalidates the menu, and prevents the form from submitting.

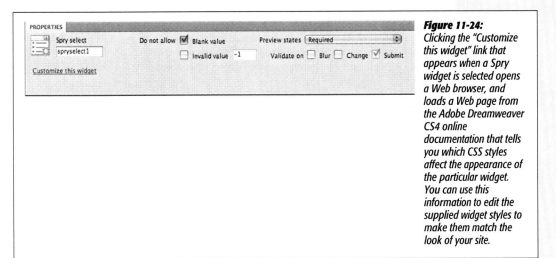

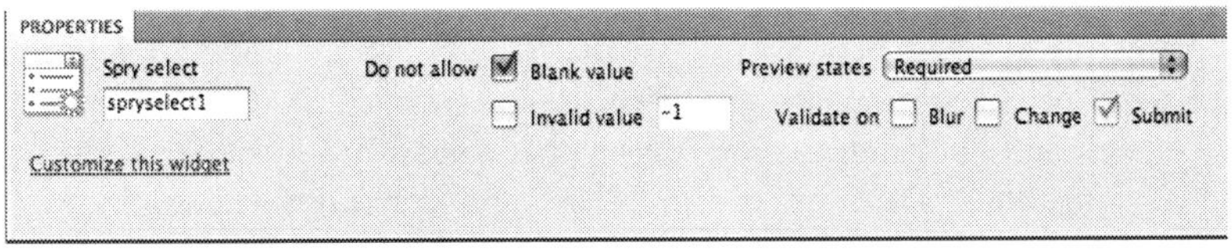

Figure 11-24: *Clicking the "Customize this widget" link that appears when a Spry widget is selected opens a Web browser, and loads a Web page from the Adobe Dreamweaver CS4 online documentation that tells you which CSS styles affect the appearance of the particular widget. You can use this information to edit the supplied widget styles to make them match the look of your site.*

Sometimes the label and the value are the same. On a menu with a list of years ("What year were you born?"), for example, the label ("1967") is the same as the value ("1967") and it would be a bit redundant to set both the label and value for each menu item. Fortunately, you don't have to double your effort in this case. As you read on page 446, a label doesn't require a value. If no value is specified, then the label is submitted as the value.

When there are no assigned labels, the "Blank value" validation option doesn't work. After all, even valid selections don't have a value explicitly set—just a label. In this case, use the "Invalid value" option. To use this option, just assign an arbitrary value to an illegitimate menu selection, and specify that value to the right of the Property inspector's "Invalid value" text, in the text box (Figure 11-24). For example, the first menu option on the list of years might be "Please select a year". Just assign a value (like –1) to that menu option in the List Values window (Figure 11-11). Then select the Spry widget, and specify the same value in the Property inspector's "Invalid value" field. (See page 446 for more on assigning labels and values to form menus.)

Tip: If your form menu has a long list of options, then you might add a separator (like a row of hyphens, ---------) as a label, in order to divide groups of options. You could either forego assigning a value to that separator and use the "Blank value" validation option, or assign it an invalid value (like -1) and use the "Invalid value" setting. In this way, if someone accidentally selects the separator, she can't submit the form.

Spry Password

A password like "sesame," "password," or "bob" isn't very secure. Any hacker with a dictionary (or access to an infinite number of monkeys) can easily infiltrate a password-protected Web page, or gain access to someone's private information. If you ever add a sign-up form that requires someone to come up with a password, use Dreamweaver CS4's new Spry Password widget. This helpful tool lets you enforce a set of rules for naming passwords so that visitors don't create easily hacked credentials. For example, you can say that a password must be at least eight characters long, have at least three numbers, and contain a minimum of two uppercase letters. This kind of password naming strategy means visitors have to come up with hard-to-hack passwords like AB3859kirI.

Note: Use the Spry Password widget only for forms where a visitor *creates* a password. Don't use it for a form field where a visitor must log in with an already created password. After all, there's no point in telling a visitor that she needs a certain number of letters or numbers in her password, if she already has a valid password.

Unlike some of the other validation widgets, like the Spry Text Field or Spry Textarea, you can't add password validation to an already inserted text field. You need to click in the area of the form where you want to add the Spry Password field, and then, on the Insert Panel's Forms category, use the Spry Validation Password button (Figure 11-2), or choose Insert → Form → Spry Validation Password. Then, just as when inserting any form field, the Input Tag Accessibility window opens (Figure 11-5); follow steps 3-5 on page 436 to insert the field.

Once inserted, the password field has a blue Spry Password tab, and the Property inspector shows the options for validating the field (see Figure 11-25). Since one of the goals of a good password is to make it hard to figure out, the validation options for the password widget help try to enforce a pattern that's essentially a random collection of numbers, letter, and characters. The Min and Max chars options let you specify that a password must be at least a certain number of characters and no more than a certain number of characters. You can set either or both of these options, but, at the very least, you should specify a minimum number of characters—8 is a solid amount—so that no one creates an easily hacked password like 1, A, or A1.

In addition, you can specify the *types* of characters that must be in the password for it to be valid. For example, you might decide that there need to be at least four letters, two numbers, and one special character. That rule would make a password like ABCDE38! valid, but wouldn't let someone create a password like ABCDEFGH, or 12345678. You can even make sure that a password has a certain number of uppercase letters as well, just to mix things up. For example, say you type 6 in the Min letters box; this rule means the password someone enters needs at least six letters in it. But to make sure there's a good mix of upper and lowercase letters, you could set the Min uppercase value to 2, and the max uppercase value to 4. This would mean that the visitor has to include at least a few uppercase and lowercase letters in the password.

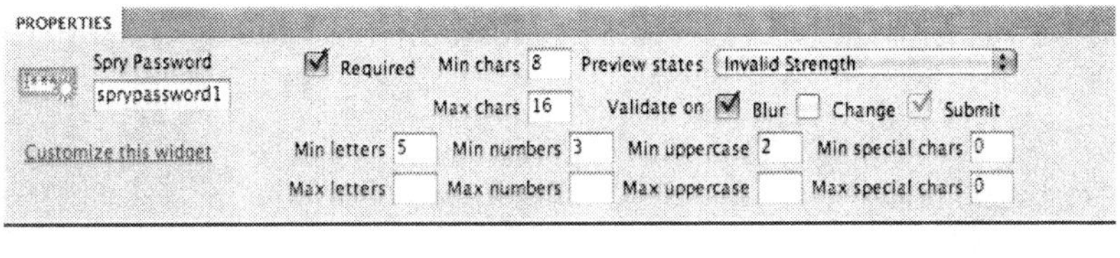

***Figure 11-25:** Use Dreamweaver CS4's new Spry password validation widget to make sure that new visitors creating a password for your site make it suitably random and difficult to crack.*

Depending upon which validation options you select for the password widget, you can customize up to four different error messages: the required message, displayed when a visitor simply leaves the password field blank when submitting the form; the "Min # of characters" message that appears when you've specified a value in the "Min chars" box and the user creates a password with less than those number of characters; the "Max # of characters" that appears when the visitor exceeds the number of characters you typed in the Max chars box; and, finally, if you set values for any of the other options ("Min letters" or "Min numbers" for example), an "Invalid Strength" message that appears if the visitor types a password that doesn't match the options you set.

The error message supplied by Dreamweaver—"The password doesn't meet the specified strength"—doesn't really tell your visitor what he did wrong. You should either change this message to something like "Please type a password that's at least 8 characters long and which contains letters, numbers, and at least one special character like ., ?, or !" or, even better, provide those instructions on the form to begin with. That way a visitor won't waste his time trying to figure out what characters he needs to type. (See step 6 on page 458 for instructions on editing Spry form validation error messages.)

Spry Confirm

Another new addition in Dreamweaver CS4, the Spry Confirm validation widget, comes in handy when you want to make sure someone correctly enters important information. For example, if you create a form for people to sign up for your email newsletter, you want to make sure they give you their correct email addresses. One way to do this is to have a visitor enter the information twice, by adding a second field that asks her to confirm her address by typing it again.

Tip: You can also use this double-checking maneuver in conjunction with a "Create a password" field. Remember, a password field (see page 440) displays what the visitor types as dots or asterisks. So it's easy, when creating a new password, to make a typo and create a password that's different from what you think you typed.

The Spry Confirm widget works only with text fields, and pops up an error message if the value in the text field doesn't match the value in another text field on the page. To use this widget, you should first add a text field—either a Spry text field, a Spry password field, or just a regular text field. That field is the original "Type your email" or "Create a password" box. Next, from the Insert Panel's Forms category, add the Spry Confirm widget (Figure 11-2), or choose Insert → Form → Spry Validation Confirm. (It's best to put this field directly after the original field, and use a label like "Please confirm your password".)

The options for a Spry Confirm widget are simple (see Figure 11-26). From the "Validate against" menu, simply select the name of the field you're comparing. For example, say you've added a Spry Password validation widget, and you named that field *password1*. When you insert the Spry Confirm field, in the Property inspector's "Validate against" menu, you select *password1*. Then, when someone fills out the form, she must type a password in the password1 field, and then, in the confirmation field, type the exact same password. If the two fields have different values, then an error message appears, letting the visitor know she made a typo.

Spry Radio Group

Sometimes you want to make sure a radio button is selected before a form is submitted. For example, say you have an e-commerce site, and you're collecting shipping information from a customer. For the shipping method, you want the customer to select either USPS, FedEx, or UPS. Since visitors have to choose a delivery method

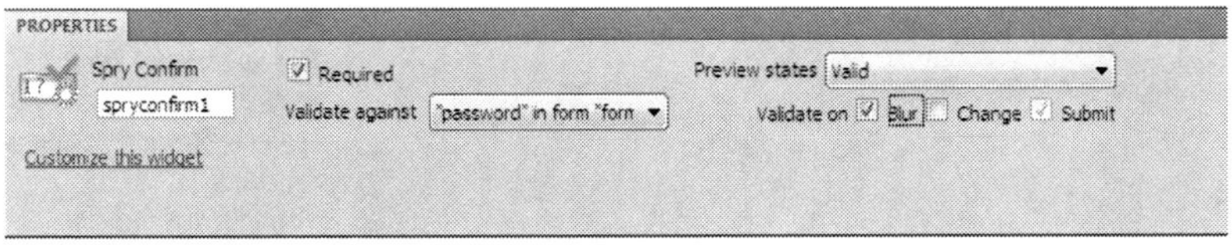

***Figure 11-26:** If the field you're comparing against is required, then make sure the "Required" box is turned on for the confirmation field as well. Since the information is so important that you need a second field to confirm it, odds are that it's required anyway, so you almost always leave the Required box checked.*

in order for you to ship a package, it's a good idea to make sure they click one of the radio buttons before submitting the form. This is where the Spry Radio Group comes in handy. Essentially, it's just like the radio group described on page 445, with the added feature of supplying an error message if no button is selected when the form is submitted.

To add a Spry Radio Group, use the Insert panel's Forms category or Insert → Form → Spry Validation Radio Group. The process is the same as inserting a regular radio group or a checkbox group. Once the group of buttons is added to the page, use the Property inspector to set up the validation options (see Figure 11-27). Dreamweaver gives you several ways of validating a radio group, but only one is really useful: The "Required" checkbox simply means that a radio button must be checked—doesn't matter which radio button, as long as one of the buttons in the group is selected.

The other two options—Empty Value and Invalid Value—produce error messages when a particular radio button *is* selected. In either of these boxes, enter the value you assigned when you first created the radio button. Selecting the radio button with the specified value produces one of two errors when the form is submitted. In the case of Empty Value, if the button is selected, then an error appears informing the visitor that he *hasn't* made a selection (huh?); and for the Invalid Value, an error appears announcing that the choice he made was invalid. Neither of these options seem like they would ever be useful: After all, do you really want to display an error message when a radio button is clicked, saying, in effect, "Ha, ha, you fool, you just released the hounds!"

Forms Tutorial

In this tutorial, you'll build a simple appointment sign-up form for *the Chia-Vet.com* Web site (see Figure 11-37). To make sure the folks at Chia Vet receive the right information, you'll also use the Spry form validation tools.

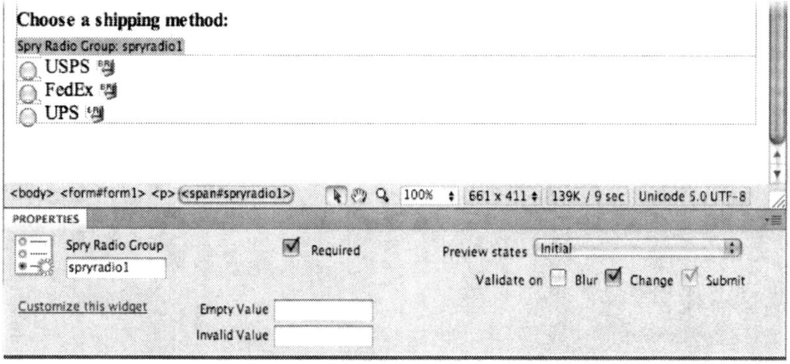

Figure 11-27: *The Spry Radio Group's Property inspector's only useful validation option is Required, which makes sure that site visitors select a button within a group of radio buttons. The Empty and Invalid Value boxes are just plain silly—even Adobe's online documentation doesn't provide a good use for these options. If you come up with one, send an email to* missing@sawmac.com.

Note: You'll need to download the tutorial files from *www.sawmac.com/dwcs4/* to complete this tutorial. See the Note on page 48 for more details.

Once you've downloaded the tutorial files, and then opened Dreamweaver, define a new site as described on page 42: Name the site *Forms*, and then select the Chapter11 folder (inside the MM_DWCS4 folder). (In a nutshell: Choose Site → New Site. In the Site Definition window, click the Advanced tab, type *Forms* into the Site Name field, click the folder icon next to the Local Root Folder field, navigate to and select the Chapter11 folder, and then click Choose or Select. Finally, click OK.)

Inserting a Form and Adding a Form Field

The first step to building a form is inserting a <form> tag. This tag encloses all the different fields in the form, and indicates where the form begins and ends. As noted earlier in this chapter, you can also insert other HTML elements, like text and <div> tags within the form.

1. **Choose File → Open; click the Site Root button (at the bottom left of the open file window). Double-click the file *appointment.html* to open it.**

   (If you have the Files panel open [Window → Files], then you can also just double-click *appointment.html* in the panel to open it.) The page is partly designed already with a banner, sidebar, and footer.

2. **Click the empty white space directly below the paragraph that begins with "Make an appointment with Chia-Vet.com 24 hours a day." On the Insert panel, select the Forms category (see Figure 11-2).**

   The Insert panel now shows you the Forms icons you need.

3. **Click the Insert panel's Form button (see Figure 11-2), or choose Insert → Form → Form.**

   A red, dashed rectangle appears in the document window, indicating the boundaries of the form.

4. **In the Property inspector, in the "Form ID" field, replace form1 with *appointment* (Figure 11-28).**

   You've just added an ID to your form.

5. **In the Action field, type *http://www.chia-vet.com/make.php*.**

   (Leave off the final period, as shown in Figure 11-28.)

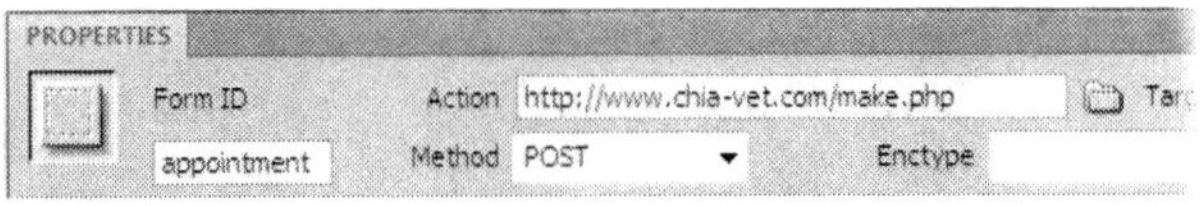

Figure 11-28:
The Action property of a form is simply a URL pointing to the program that processes the form.

   A form's Action property identifies the address of the program that processes the form's submitted data. In this case, you've been spared the effort of writing (or hiring a programmer to write) the required form-processing software. Such a program already exists on the Web site whose address you've just specified, and it's waiting to process the form you're about to design.

   You may be creating your own form-processing programs if you're using Dreamweaver's dynamic Web-building tools described in Part 6. See the tutorial on page 932 for an example.

6. **In the Method menu, make sure POST is selected. Leave the Target and Enctype fields blank.**

   The Method indicates how the form sends information to the form-processing program (see page 434).

   Now you're ready to insert a text field.

7. **In the document window, click in the form—anywhere inside the red, dashed lines. On the Insert panel, click the Text Field button (see Figure 11-2) or choose Insert → Form → Text Field.**

   The Input Tag Accessibility window appears (see Figure 11-29). If you don't see this window, choose Edit → Undo to remove the Text Field you just entered; use the Preferences window to turn on the accessibility options for form objects as described in Figure 11-5, and then repeat step 7.

8. **In the ID box, type *clientName*.**

   The name you type into the ID box is added as both the *name* and *ID* property of the field's HTML. The form processing program that receives the form input uses the name property: It's how that program knows what the visitor feedback means. In this case, clients type their names into this form field, so the form processing program receives information (*clientName=Bob*, for instance) in what's called a name/value pair (see page 429).

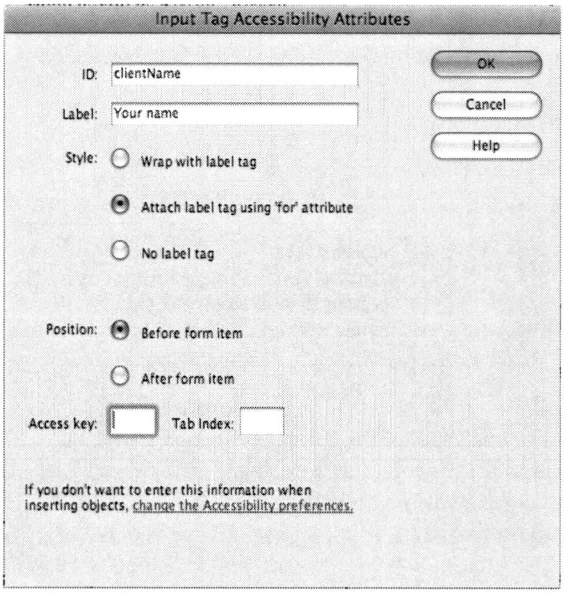

Figure 11-29: *The Input Tag Accessibility Attributes window gives you a great way to quickly insert a bunch of form-related HTML.*

The ID uniquely identifies the form element. If you want, you can create an ID style to format this particular form field—for example, to assign a width or background color to this one field. Next you'll add the text label that appears along with the text field on the Web page.

9. **In the Label box, type *Your name*; select the "Attach label tag using 'for' attribute"; and then select the "Before form item" button.**

   The window should now look like Figure 11-29.

10. **Click OK to insert the text field.**

    The label and text field appear side by side on the page. The label's text is wrapped inside the HTML <label> tag (page 453). Your first order of business is to set the width of the form field.

11. **Click the newly inserted field (the box on the page); in the Property inspector's "Char width" field, type *35*.**

    This action defines, in characters, the box's width. In other words, the box displays up to 35 letters (this step sets only the visible width of the field; a visitor can actually type more letters than this into the field, as described on page 440).

    Now it's time to add some style.

12. **Make sure the CSS Styles panel is open (choose Window → CSS Styles); on the Styles panel, click the + button to create a new style.**

    Alternatively, you can choose Text → CSS Styles → New Style. Either way, the New CSS Style window opens. (For a refresher on creating styles, see page 115.)

13. **If it's not already selected, from the top menu, choose Compound. Delete whatever is currently in the Selector Name box, type *#appointment .question*, and then, from the bottom menu, select *global.css*; click OK.**

    The CSS Rule Definition window opens. You've just created a descendent selector containing a new class style named *.question*. You'll use this style to make each form field's label stand out, and visually separate different questions on the form. But the formatting you're about to assign applies only to an element with the *question* class applied to it that also happens to be inside *another* tag with an ID of *appointment*. In step 4 above, you gave the form itself the ID *appointment*, so this style applies only to tags with the question class that are inside this form. If you want to use this style on other forms, you can simply create a class style named *.question*, and then use it throughout the site. But in this instance, you want to create a distinct look for just this form (and you also want to get some practice creating descendent selectors).

14. **In the Rule Definition window's Type category, from the Font-weight menu, choose *bold*; select the Block category, and, from the Display menu near the bottom of the window, choose *block*.**

    The block option for the CSS Display property formats a tag like a block-level element—in other words, there's a line break above and below the element. You use this option to change the display of a tag that would normally appear "inline" (side by side) with other elements. For example, the <label> tag is an inline element and, in the form you're working on, the label "Your Name" appears directly to the left of the text field. By applying this style with its *block* display to that label, you force the label to appear above the field. Positioning the label in this manner isn't any kind of requirement for forms; it's just a design choice to make the form more readable.

    Next you'll add a border above the label to visually separate it from an element above it.

15. **Select the Border category, and turn off the three "Same for all" checkboxes. From the Top Style menu, choose dashed; in the top Width box, type *1*; and then, in the top Color box, type *#9BBF13*.**

    Finally, you'll just add a bit of padding to separate the border and the label. You'll also add some top margin to create a bit more space between form elements.

16. **Select the Box category. Turn off the two "Same for all" checkboxes and, in the Padding's Top box, type *5*; in the Top Margin box, type *15*. Click OK to complete the style.**

    Because this is a class style, you must apply it manually.

17. **In the document window, click anywhere inside the label text "Your name". In the Tag selector, click <label> (circled in Figure 11-30) to select the label tag; in the Property inspector, make sure the HTML button is selected, and then, from the Class menu, choose *question* (see Figure 11-30).**

    The form field drops below the label. Next you'll add a field to collect the patient's name.

Note: You might be wondering after step 17 why you didn't just create a tag style for the <label> tag, instead of a class style that you had to manually apply to the tag. Good question. In some cases you can, but if you add checkboxes or radio buttons to a form, then you can't always go that route. For those type of form fields, each button or box has its own label (the text that appears next to it). Usually, other text introduces those groups of elements–for example, "Select a shipping method" or "Pick your 4 favorite fruits." That isn't in a <label> tag since it's not associated with any single form field. So creating a class style–*.question*–lets you apply that style to different types of tags and get the same formatting.

---

18. **In the document window, click to the right of the text field you added in the last part of this tutorial. Hit Enter (Return) to create a new paragraph.**

    The form field drops below the label. Next, you'll add a Spry form field to make sure the form submits the information you're looking for.

19. **On the Insert panel, click the Text Field button (see Figure 11-2) or choose Insert → Form → Text Field. Repeat steps 8-11 to add another field. Type *patient* for the field ID, and *Your Chia Pet's Name* for the label.**

    You've added a second text field—now it's time to add a little style.

20. **Repeat step 17 to apply the question class to the new field's label.**

    So much for regular text fields; now it's time to add a little Spry validation.

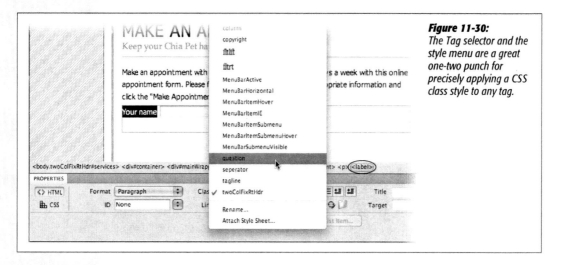

Figure 11-30: *The Tag selector and the style menu are a great one-two punch for precisely applying a CSS class style to any tag.*

Adding a Spry Validation Text Field

Next up for this form: a phone number field. The vets at Chia Vet need a way of contacting patients if an appointment needs to be rescheduled, so it's important that this field not be left blank. In addition, you'll want to make sure the patient doesn't make a typo, and enter too few or too many numbers. A Spry validation text field is the perfect solution.

1. **In the document window, click to the right of the text field you added in the last part of this tutorial. Hit Enter (Return) to create a new paragraph. On the Insert panel's Forms tab, click the Spry Validation Text Field button (see Figure 11-2).**

   Alternatively, you could choose Insert → Form → Spry Validation Text Field. Either way, the Input Tag Accessibility window appears just as it does when you're inserting a regular text field. You fill it out the same way, too.

2. **In the ID field, type *phone*; in the Label field, type *Your phone number*; make sure the "Attach label tag using 'for' attribute" and the "Before form item" radio buttons are selected; and then click OK to insert the text field.**

   A new text field and label appear. A blue tab also appears, identifying this field as a Spry widget. If you look at the Property inspector, you see all the properties available for Spry Text Fields. You'll choose a few options in a minute, but first you'll format this field like the one you inserted earlier.

3. **Repeat step 11 on page 480 to set the Char width of the new field to 35.**

   The label also needs some formatting.

4. **Repeat step 17 on the opposite page to format the "Your phone number" label.**

   When you use the Property inspector's style menu to apply the *question* class, you see a whole bunch of new classes listed. Those classes come from another external style sheet that Dreamweaver quietly attached to this page after you inserted the Spry form field.

5. **Choose File → Save.**

   Dreamweaver opens the Copy Dependent Files dialog box, letting you know the page now requires both a style sheet file and a JavaScript file for the new Spry validation field.

6. **Click OK to close the Copy Dependent Files window.**

   If you look at the Files panel (Window → Files), then you see a folder named SpryAssets where Dreamweaver just saved the two new files (see he Note on page 456 for an explanation). You see other files in there as well, for two other Spry widgets on this page—a Spry menu (page 184) and a Spry Collapsible panel (discussed in the next chapter on page 508).

7. **Move your mouse over the phone form field; click the blue Spry tab when it appears.**

   The Property inspector displays the Spry field's properties (see Figure 11-31). First you'll assign a validation type to this widget.

Note: Dreamweaver automatically creates an ID for the Spry widget. The Spry widget you just inserted has an ID *sprytextfield1*. You can change the ID to something more descriptive like *spryPhone*, but you don't have to. The name doesn't ever appear on the Web page; the Spry programming uses it to identify the particular validation widget.

---

8. **From the Property inspector's Type menu , select Phone Number, and then turn on the Blur checkbox (see Figure 11-31).**

   The Type menu defines what type of information should be allowed in the field. In this case, only a validly formatted U.S. or Canadian phone number works. The Blur box determines when the contents of the field get validated. For example, if a visitor types "not telling" into the field, and then presses the Tab key to jump to the next form field, he receives an error message.

   If you look at the document window now, you see that the email field has a red background color and a red "Invalid format" message to the right of it. Every Spry validation field has several "preview" states. You can preview the field as it looks at various points when a visitor to your Web site interacts with the field—for example, when she's typed invalid information, or simply left a required field blank. You'll tweak this error message now.

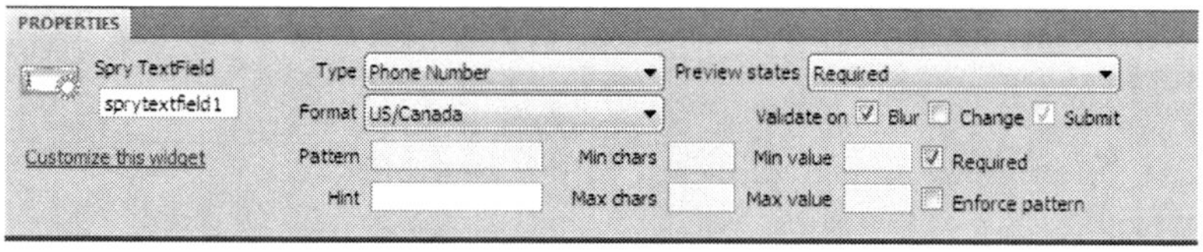

Figure 11-31: *Select a Spry validation widget in the document window, and then use the Property inspector to assign validation options.*

9. **In the document window, replace the text "Invalid format", and type *Please enter a valid phone number.***

   Now when some wise guy types "xxxxxxxxx," he gets an error message informing him he has to enter a validly formatted phone number. An error message also appears if this field is just left blank. You can adjust this message as well, but first you must switch to a different "preview state."

Warning: When replacing the error message in step 9, don't delete the "Invalid format" message before typing the new error message. If you do, then you actually delete the <span> responsible for making the error message work. Just select the text "Invalid format", and then immediately type the new error message.

---

10. **Click the blue Spry tab again; from the Property inspector's "Preview states" menu, select Required.**

    A new error message appears: "A value is required." This message appears when nothing is entered into a required answer field, and the visitor tries to submit the form.

11. **Repeat step 9, replacing the "A value is required" with "We need your number to contact you."**

    The red outline surrounding the error message doesn't fit the look of Chia-Vet.com. Fortunately, you can easily update the look of a Spry widget.

12. **Click anywhere inside the error message text you added in the last step; make sure the CSS Styles panel is open (Window → CSS Styles). At the top of the panel, select the Current button, and make sure the Cascade button is selected (circled in Figure 11-32).**

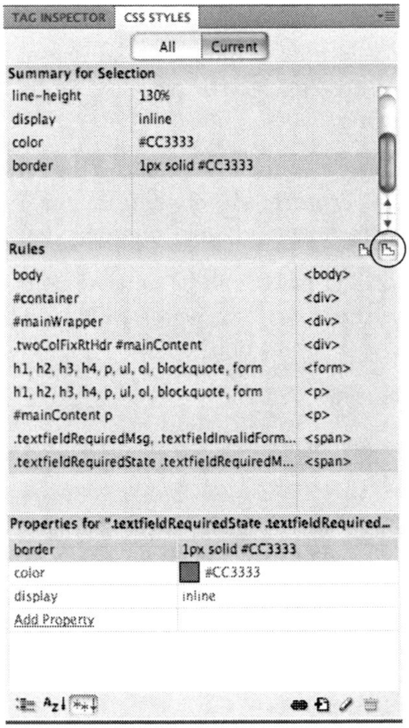

Figure 11-32:
When formatting Spry widgets, you can most easily use the CSS Styles panel's Current view. If the Cascade button is selected (circled), then you merely need to click the element whose style you want to change. In this case, selecting the error message for a Spry Validation Text field highlights the appropriate style's name. Double-click the name to open the CSS Rule Definition window, and style away!

A descendent selector named *.textfieldRequiredState .textfieldRequiredMsg* controls the error message's styling. This style is the last style listed in the Styles panel's Rules pane (the middle pane in Figure 11-32).

13. **In the Rules pane, double-click the style *.textfieldRequiredState .textfield-RequiredMsg* to open the CSS Rule Definition window.**

    You'll make the error message bold and remove the border.

14. **In the Rule Definition window, from the Font-weight menu, choose "Bold". Click the Border category, and then delete the contents of the top row of boxes.**

    Deleting the contents of the type, width, and color boxes removes the border entirely.

15. **Click OK to complete the style.**

    Notice that the error message next to the Spry form field is bold, but no longer has a border. Time to insert another form field.

16. **Repeat steps 1–4 to add another Spry text validation field. Use the ID *date*, and, for the label, type "Please specify the date you'd like."**

    Make sure you click to the right of the phone number widget's error message, before hitting Return to insert a new field.

    This new field you just added is used to collect the day, month, and year of the appointment. Since you want to make sure you receive properly formatted dates, you'll choose that validation option next.

17. **Select the Spry widget by moving your mouse over the new field, and then clicking the blue "Spry TextField" tab. In the Property inspector, from the Type menu, choose Date, and then, from the Format menu, choose "mm/dd/yyyy".**

    You've just specified that a date like 9/22/2009 needs to be entered into this field. If it's not, then an error message appears. Of course, people filling out this form might not know that, so you should give them a hint.

18. **In the Property inspector, in the Hint box, type *3/22/2009*.**

    The Property inspector should now look like Figure 11-33. Time to change the error message.

19. **In the Property inspector, from the "Preview states" menu, select "Invalid Format". On the Web page, change the text "Invalid format" to "Please enter a date."**

    Notice that the error message shares the same style as the one you added for the phone number; that's because you modified the look of error messages for all Spry text fields in step 14. Dreamweaver supplies Spry widgets for other types of form fields as well. You'll add a Spry Form Menu next.

Adding a Spry Form Menu

Text boxes aren't the only form fields you can validate. You can also make sure someone's made a selection from a pull-down menu, by adding a Spry menu to a form.

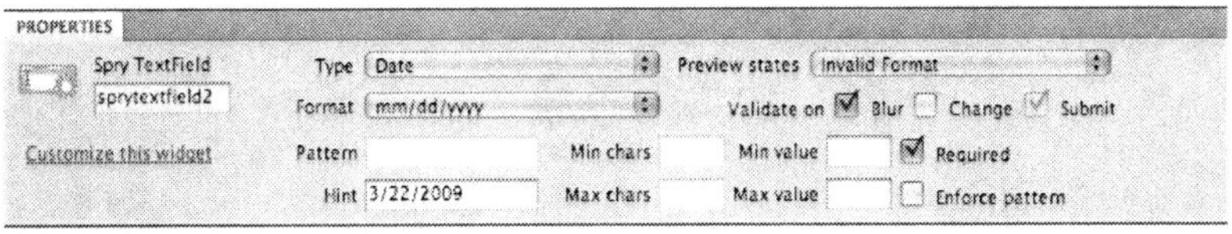

Figure 11-33: *You have many different ways to type a date–12/31/2009 or 12.31.2009, for example–so if you use the Spry text validation widget to collect a date, you should always provide a hint or other instruction that tells visitors how they should correctly type that date.*

1. **Click to the right of the error message you just added (after "Please enter a date."), and then press Enter or Return to insert a new empty paragraph.**

   Make sure you click to the right of the Spry widget's blue outline, before pressing return. If you hit Return immediately after typing in the error message (step 19 in the previous section of this tutorial), you're still inside the Spry Text Field widget, and the next steps don't work.

2. **Choose Insert → Form → Spry Validation Select, or, on the Insert panel, click the Spry Validation Select button** (see Figure 11-2).

   As with any form field, the Input Tag Accessibility window appears.

3. **In the ID field, type *time*; in the label box, type "Time of Appointment"; click OK to insert the menu.**

   A form menu appears on the page.

4. **Choose File → Save.**

   Another window appears, letting you know that an additional JavaScript file and CSS file are necessary to make this new Spry validation widget work. Click OK to dismiss that window. Time to style the label.

5. **Repeat step 17 on page 482 to format the "Time of Appointment" label.**

   At this point, the pull-down form menu is empty, so your next step is to add a few options.

6. **In the document window, click the newly inserted menu to select it. In the Property inspector, click the List Values button.**

   The List Values window opens (see Figure 11-34). Here you can add options for the menu.

7. **Type "-- *Select a Time* --"; press the Tab key, and then type *–1*.**

   The text ("Select a Time") appears at the top of the menu. It's an instruction for the person filling out the form, letting him know what he should do. Of course, you want someone to choose an option *other* than this one when submitting the form. The –1 is the value transmitted over the Internet when this option is selected and the form gets submitted—in this case, –1 is kind of a secret message that you use to notify the Spry validation program that this option isn't valid. Before you get to that, though, add the valid selections for this form.

8. **Press the Tab key, and then type *8:00am*; press the Tab key twice to create another list option, and then type *9:00am*. Continue adding options in this way until you've added *5:00pm* (or until you've got the hang of adding menu items).**

   The List Values window should look like Figure 11-34.

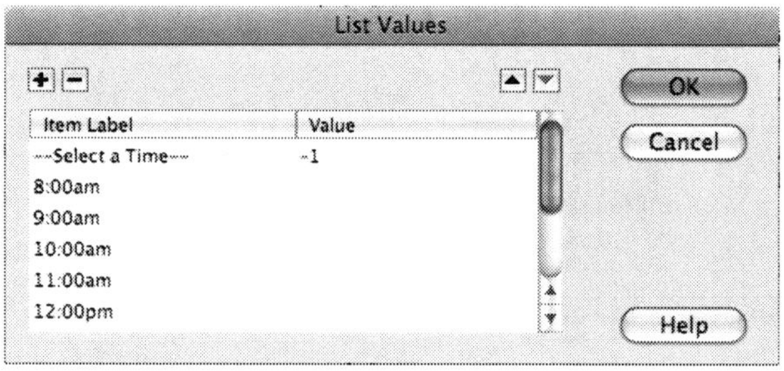

Figure 11-34: *The Item Label column displays what appears in the menu on the Web page, while the Value column contains the value that's actually submitted (–1 in the first row, for example). If you don't specify a value (as with all of the time ranges here), then the label's text is submitted as the value.*

9. **Click OK to insert the menu. Move your mouse over the menu, and then click the blue Spry tab to select it.**

   You need to specify what type of menu selection should be considered invalid.

10. **In the Property inspector, turn off the "Blank value" box; turn on the "Invalid value" box, and then make sure –1 appears in the field; turn on the Change checkbox.**

    The Property inspector should look like Figure 11-35. Make sure, in the "Preview states" menu, "Invalid" is selected. In the document window, to the right of the form menu, you should see a red error message, "Please select a valid item." You'll change this message and its style next.

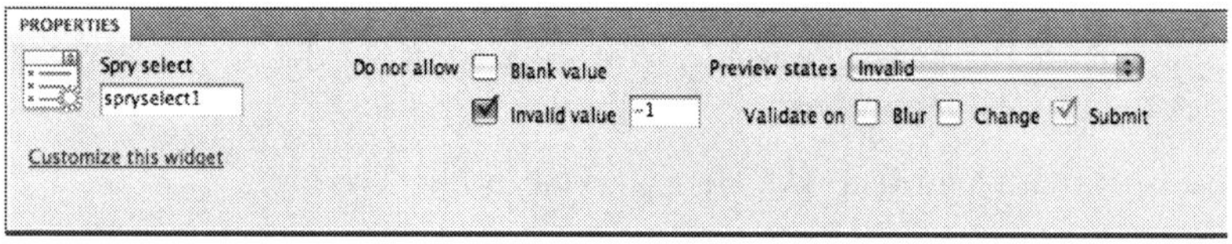

Figure 11-35: *You can assign an arbitrary value (like –1) to any menu item that you want to prevent from being submitted.*

11. **Replace the text "Please select a valid item" with "Please select a time." Repeat steps 12-15 on page 485 to make the error message bold and remove the borderline.**

    Each type of Spry validation widget (text field, menu, checkbox, text area) has its own CSS styles to format error messages. In the case of a pull-down menu error message, the style is named *.selectRequiredState .selectRequiredMsg*, and it's in an external style sheet named SpryValidationSelect.css.

Adding a Spry Radio Group

Just a couple more form fields and you'll be done. Now it's time to ask a multiple-choice question that requires a single response. This task is perfect for a group of radio buttons, but since an answer is required, you'll use Spry validation as well.

1. **Click to the right of the error message you just formatted (after "select a time"), and then press Enter (Return) to insert a new empty paragraph. Type *Please select a reason for this appointment.***

   If you no longer see the error message you created in step 11 in the previous section, then you probably just clicked somewhere else on the page, and deselected the Spry widget. Time to format the question.

2. **From the Property inspector's Class menu, select "question".**

   If you don't see the Class menu, make sure, in the Property inspector, the HTML button is selected. This selection formats the paragraph so that it looks like the labels for other questions on the form. Next you'll add a few checkboxes.

3. **Press the Enter (Return) key to create a blank paragraph.**

   The new paragraph also has the *question* class applied to it. You need to remove that style.

4. **From the Property inspector's Class menu, choose None. Choose Insert → Form → Spry Validation Radio Group.**

   Under the Insert panel's Forms category, you can also click the Spry Radio Group button (see Figure 11-2). Either way, the Spry Validation Radio Group window appears (Figure 11-36).

5. **In the Name field, type *appointmentType.***

   This names the group of radio buttons—each button shares the same name, but obviously the label and value of each button should be unique. You'll add those next.

6. **In the Label column, click the first instance of the word Radio; type *Routine check up.* Press Tab to jump to the value column, and then type *cv767.***

   The label is the text that appears next to the button, while the value is the data that's transmitted when the form is submitted—in this case, cv767 is Chia Vet's internal code for "Routine check up" (yeah, sure it is).

7. **Press Tab again to jump to the label column for the second radio button; type *Weed dip*; press Tab, and then type *cv524*.**

   You've changed the labels and values for the two generic buttons supplied in this window. To add another, you need to use the + button.

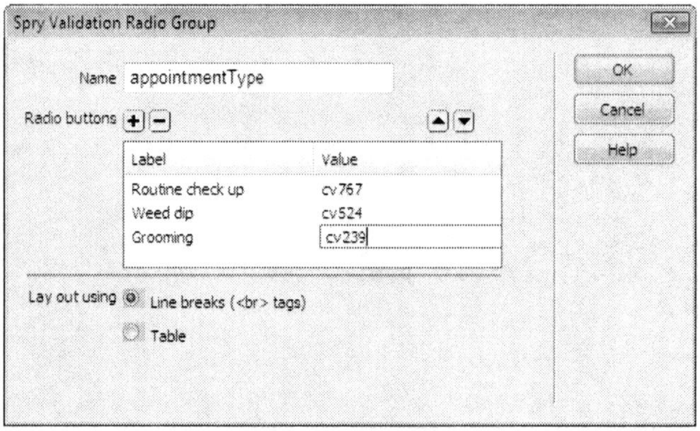

Figure 11-36: *When you insert a Spry Form Validation widget, you encounter the same Input Tag Accessibility Options window that appears when you insert regular form fields.*

8. **Press the + button to add another pair of label and value options. Type *Grooming* for the label, and *cv239* for the value.**

   The window should now look like Figure 11-36.

9. **Make sure the "Line breaks" button is selected, and then click OK to insert the group of three radio buttons.**

   Three rows of radio buttons appear on the page, and the now-familiar blue Spry tab appears. In the Property inspector, you don't have to make any validation choices because you always want the default option "required"—in other words, someone requesting an appointment can't submit this form until she's clicked one of the three radio buttons.

   You should, however, make sure the style of the error message matches the others on the page.

10. **In the Property inspector, from the Preview States menu, choose Required. Repeat steps 12-15 on page 485 to format the "Please make a selection" error message.**

11. **Choose File → Save.**

    Another window appears, letting you know that you need an additional JavaScript file and a CSS file to make this new Spry validation widget work (click OK to close that window).

Completing and Testing the Form

At this point, nobody can submit the form after it's filled out. You need to add a submit button.

1. **Click to the right of the "Please make a selection" message for the radio group. Hit Return to create a new paragraph. From the Property inspector's Class menu, choose *question*.**

   A green line and a little extra space appear above the paragraph. This look matches the look of the other parts of the form.

2. **Choose Insert → Form → Button or, on the Insert panel, click the Button icon (Figure 11-2).**

   Your old friend the Input Tag Accessibility window appears again. This time, however, you don't need an ID or label. Buttons (like Submit) already have a message printed on them, so you don't need to add a label.

3. **Click the Cancel button.**

   In the Input Tag Accessibility window, clicking Cancel doesn't actually cancel the process of inserting a form field—it just skips the steps of providing an ID and label for the field. A submit button appears on the page. You can change the generic "Submit" message to something more reflective of the form's purpose.

4. **Click the button on the page; in the Property inspector's Value field, type *Make appointment.***

   The form is done. Now take it for a test drive.

5. **Choose File → Save All, and then press the F12 (Option-F12) key.**

   A Web browser opens with the new form.

Note: If you preview this in Internet Explorer for Windows, then you may see a security warning. This problem and a solution are discussed on page 250.

6. **Click the Submit button.**

   The form doesn't submit (see Figure 11-37). Instead, several error messages appear. Fill out the form correctly, and try to submit it again.

Figure 11-37: *Dreamweaver's Spry Validation Form widgets can help ensure that your forms collect the information you want. Professional looking error messages, placed next to the offending responses, give visitors clear feedback.*

CHAPTER 12

Spry: Creating Interactive Web Pages

As a Web designer, you can count on one thing: The Web is always changing. Yesterday's technology is yesterday's news—remember Java applets, frames, and messages that scroll in your browser's status bar? You can see the most recent Web design innovations on Web sites like Google Maps, Flickr, and Facebook, all of which offer a high degree of interactivity without resorting to multimedia plug-ins like Flash. Google Maps, for example, lets you zoom in, zoom out, and scroll across a map of the world without loading a new Web page. Many of the most cutting-edge Web sites almost feel like the kinds of complex software you run right on your computer.

JavaScript—which has grown from a simple little language that helped create pop-up windows and image rollovers to a full-blown programming tool that can change the content of a Web page as you look at it—is the key to this interactivity. JavaScript can even update a page with new data that gets downloaded behind the scenes (that's what's happening when you scroll to new sections of that Google Map). Dreamweaver, which has always tried to provide tools to meet Web designers' current needs, includes a set of JavaScript tools that let you add interactive page elements like drop-down navigation menus, tabbed panels, pop-up tooltips, and data-driven, sortable tables. That's what this chapter is all about.

What is Spry?

You've already seen Spry in action in Chapter 5 and Chapter 11, where you learned about the Spry Menu Bar and Spry validation widgets. But what exactly is Spry? Spry isn't just a Dreamweaver tool; it's a technology developed by Adobe, and distributed freely and independently on the Adobe Labs Web site (*http://labs.adobe.com/technologies/spry/*).

It's officially called the "Spry framework for Ajax" and it's a collection of JavaScript programs that let you, the Web designer, offer sophisticated control of a Web page to your visitors through *widgets*, *effects*, and *data sets*. A widget is an interface element like a menu bar, form validation message, or set of tabbed panels that generally makes a site easier to use. For example, the Spry Menu Bar adds a lot of links to a compact navigation bar, so you can easily find your way around a Web site.

An effect is a visual treat that doesn't necessarily improve how a Web page works, but adds cool eye candy. You can use a Spry effect to fade page elements in and out of view (effects are discussed in the next chapter). Finally, a Spry data set is a data presentation format that's more interactive than a standard HTML table. Imagine you have a table listing products your company sells. Each product is presented in its own row with columns for product name, price, and availability. A visitor can sort a Spry data table by any of those columns, simply by clicking the name of a column. And it all happens without the browser ever having to reload a Web page.

In addition, a Spry data set can suck down the contents of an XML file or even just a garden-variety HTML table, and then update a Web page with the file's content; see page 522 for the full scoop on XML, an increasingly popular and extremely flexible data format. But because XML isn't used by all Web designers, Dreamweaver CS4 lets you put data into a common HTML table and use that as the basis for an interactive presentation of data. This Spry data set tango is the "Ajax" part of the "Spry framework for Ajax." Ajax is a term coined in 2005 to describe a time-saving system for transferring information from a Web server to a Web page (and vice versa). The revolutionary advantage of Ajax, as highlighted in the Google Maps example, is that it lets a page's contents change quickly without having to reload a new page from the server.

Note: Ajax originally stood for "Asynchronous JavaScript and XML," since most original Ajax examples used XML. Nowadays the term more commonly describes the use of JavaScript to send and receive data (XML or any other text format) to and from a Web server, and update the contents of a page based on that data.

Tabbed Panels

Some Web site visitors are loath to scroll; if they don't see what they want when a page first loads, they move on. Because of this attitude, some Web designers divide long passages of information into multiple pages so that each page presents small, easy-to-digest chunks. Of course that means building several pages instead of just one, and forces the visitor to click through (and wait for) a series of pages. Spry Tabbed Panels provides an alternative (see Figure 12-1). Instead of creating one long page, or several smaller pages, you can organize information into separate tabbed panels. That way your content is always front and center, and your visitors can easily access different sections by clicking a tab above each panel.

Adding a Tabbed Panel

You can place Spry tabbed panels anywhere on a Web page. But since the tabs form a single row at the top of the group of panels, you'll need enough horizontal space to accommodate all the tabs (see the box on page 502 for an exception to this limitation). Unless you have only a couple of tabs with one-word text labels, you should place the tabbed panels in a fairly wide space, such as the main column of a Web page, or across the entire width of the page. Just follow these steps:

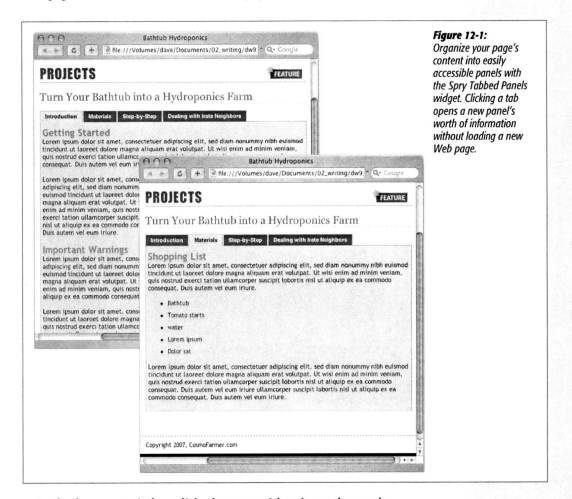

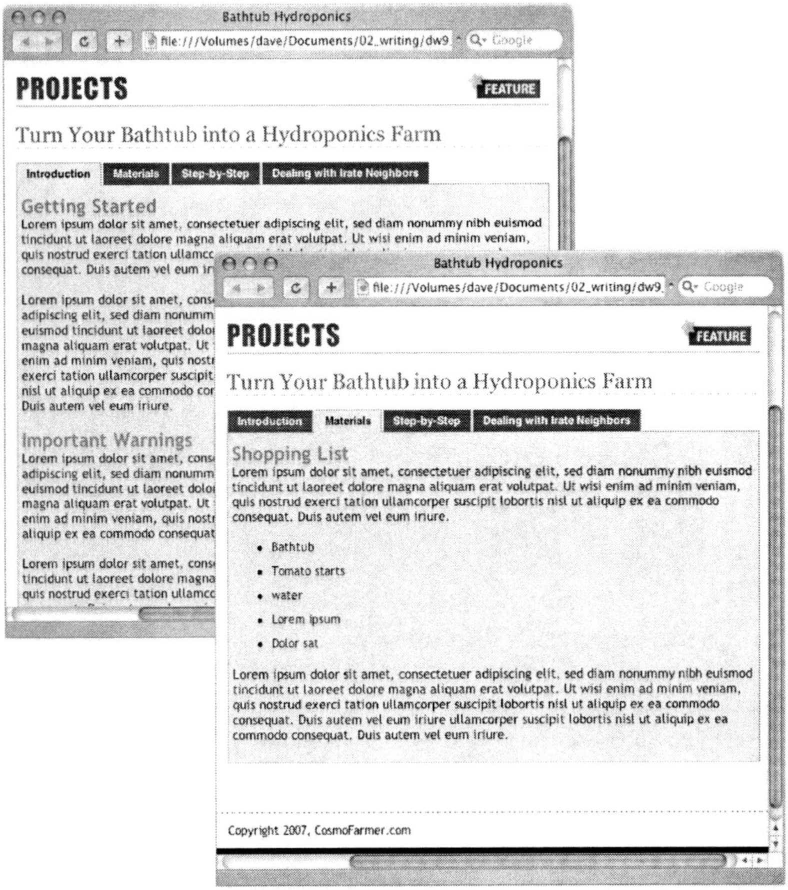

Figure 12-1: *Organize your page's content into easily accessible panels with the Spry Tabbed Panels widget. Clicking a tab opens a new panel's worth of information without loading a new Web page.*

1. **In the document window, click where you wish to insert the panels.**

   For example, inside a div tag (page 333).

2. **Choose Insert → Spry → Spry Tabbed Panels, or, on the Insert panel's Spry category, click one of the Spry Tabbed Panels buttons (see Figure 12-2).**

   You can find all the Spry goodies on the Insert panel's Spry category (Figure 12-2, left); several Spry widgets (including tabbed panels) are also listed under the Layout category (Figure 12-2, right); and other Spry buttons are grouped under other tabs (form validation Spry widgets appear under the forms tab, for example).

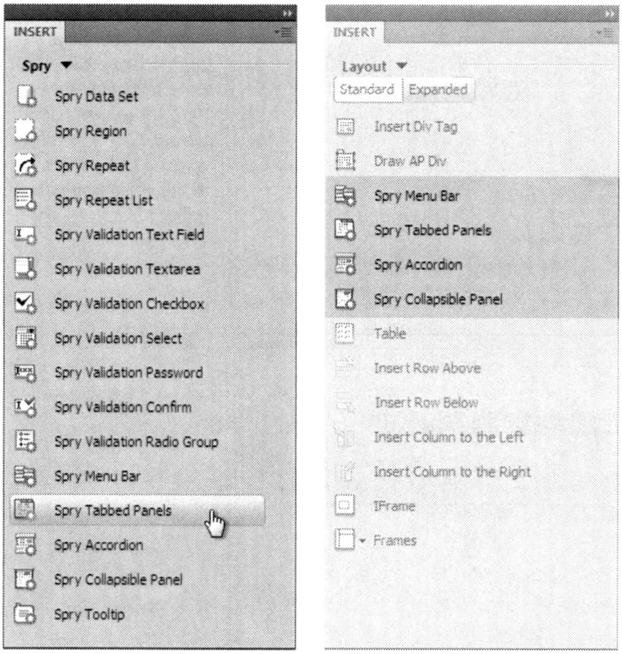

Figure 12-2:
In the Insert panel, you can identify a Spry icon by the starburst in the button's lower-right corner. It's even easier to distinguish them from other buttons if, from the Insert Panel's category menu, you choose Color Icons—this changes the drab gray starburst to a bright orange.

After inserting a tabbed panel, you see two tabs and two panels on the page (Figure 12-3); in addition, a blue tab appears above the panels indicating the Spry widget. The blue tab appears only in Dreamweaver's Design view, not when the page is viewed in a Web browser. The blue Spry tab provides an easy way to select the Spry widget and access its properties in the Property inspector.

Note: When you save a page after inserting a Spry Tabbed Panel, Dreamweaver notifies you that it has added two files to the site: a CSS file (SpryTabbedPanels.css) for formatting the panel group, and a JavaScript file (SpryTabbedPanels.js) to make the panels appear and disappear when the tabs are clicked. Dreamweaver saves both files in the SpryAssets folder in your site's root folder (see page 188). Make sure you upload this folder when moving your site onto your Web server.

3. **In the Property inspector, name the panel group (Figure 12-3).**

   This step is optional. Dreamweaver provides a generic name (TabbedPanels1, for example) for the group of panels. You don't really have to change this name; the name never appears in a browser window. However, if you take the plunge into manually modifying your Spry widgets in Code view, you may wish to change the Spry panel group's name to something more descriptive. If you create a group of tabbed panels to house information about a product, you might name the panel group, *productPanels*. A descriptive name helps you identify code related to this particular panel group if you ever want to dive into Code view, and enhance or change the functionality of the panels (see the box on page 508).

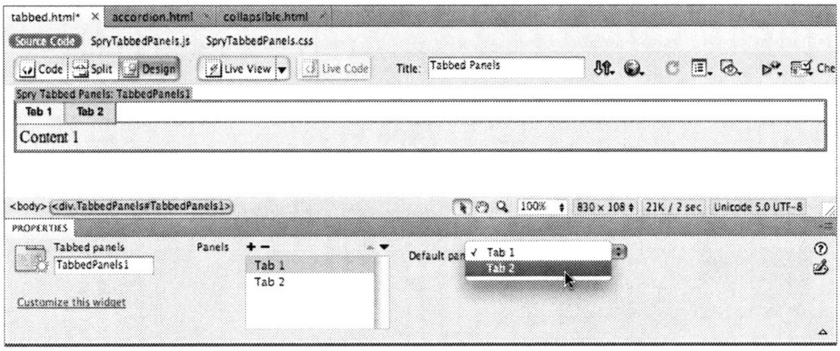

***Figure 12-3:** Normally, when a Web browser downloads a page containing Spry panels, the first tab and panel are highlighted. However, if you'd rather open another panel when the page loads, then, in the Property inspector's "Default panel" menu, select the tab's name.*

4. **Add additional panels.**

   If two panels aren't enough for your needs, use the Property inspector to add more. Above the list of tab names, click the + button (see Figure 12-3) to add a new panel. To remove a panel, in this list, click the name of a tab, and then click the minus (–) button. (You can also reorder the panels by selecting a tab from the list, and then clicking the up or down arrow button. The up arrow moves a panel to the left, while the down arrow moves a panel to the right.)

Note: A Spry widget's properties appear in the Property inspector only when you've selected the widget. To select the widget, click the blue tab that appears above the elements inside the widget (see Figure 12-3).

Adding and Editing Panel Content

Each tabbed panel has two parts: a labeled tab, and a panel containing content associated with the tab. In Figure 12-1, "Introduction", "Materials," "Step-by-Step", and "Dealing with Irate Neighbors" are each tabs, while the area of the page beginning with the "Shopping List" headline is the panel for the "Materials" tab.

To change the label on a tab, in Design view, just select and replace the tab's text. The label is normal HTML text, so you can just triple-click to select it as you would any block of text.

Text for the panel itself is contained inside a <div> tag, so you can select it by clicking anywhere inside the panel, and then choosing Edit → Select All (or Ctrl+A [⌘-A]). You can place any combination of HTML inside a panel: headlines, paragraphs, bulleted lists, forms, images, and Flash movies (you can even insert *another* Spry Tabbed Panel if you like that kind of Circus-Sideshow-hall-of-mirrors effect).

If you want to edit a panel's contents, you do need to make the panel visible first. Since the entire point of the Spry Tabbed Panels is to present a lot of information within overlapping panels, you see only one panel at a time. Fortunately, Dreamweaver offers a simple way to close the current panel and open another panel for editing: Move your mouse over the tab for a hidden panel, and an eye icon appears at the tab's right edge (see Figure 12-4). Click the eye to open the tab's panel for editing.

Figure 12-4:
Dreamweaver displays an eye icon for all Spry widgets that include tabs and panels. Clicking the eye makes a currently hidden panel visible and ready to edit.

Formatting Tabbed Panels

The tabbed panels and the content inside them are just basic HTML, made to look good with a generous dose of CSS. The tab buttons are a simple bulleted list, while each panel is a separate div; all the panels are wrapped together in another div. All the fancy formatting—tab buttons sitting side by side, borders, and background colors—is controlled by an external style sheet named SpryTabbedPanels.css, which is in the site root folder's SpryAssets folder.

Tip: Dreamweaver stores the Spry support files (the external CSS and JavaScript files that make Spry so spry) in a folder named SpryAssets in your site's root folder. If you don't like the name of that folder or would prefer to store those files elsewhere on your site, you can do that as described on page 188.

Dreamweaver supplies different CSS styles to format the panels, the currently selected tab, and the tabs whose panels aren't currently visible. The general process of modifying the look of any element in a panel group is simple: Identify the element you want to modify (like the panel or a selected tab), locate the style that controls that element, and then edit that style. If you want to change the text color of the currently selected tab, for example, in the SpryTabbedPanels.css file, you need to open the *.TabbedPanelsTabSelected* class style. The basic steps are as follows:

1. **Open the CSS Styles panel (Window → CSS Styles).**

   At the top of the Styles panel, make sure the All button is selected.

2. **Expand the list of styles for the SpryTabbedPanels.css style sheet.**

   Just click the + (arrow on a Mac) symbol next to the file's name to reveal all the styles for tabbed panels.

3. **In the Styles panel, double-click the style's name.**

   The Style Definition window for that style opens.

4. **Make the changes, and then, in the Style Definition window, click OK to finish editing the style.**

   You can use the CSS Properties pane (page 305) to edit the styles as well. For a recap on editing CSS styles, see page 126.

To help guide you in the process of modifying Spry panels, here's a list of panel elements and the styles that control them:

- **Spry Tabbed Panel group: *.TabbedPanels***

  Normally, the width of a collection of panels and tabs stretches to fit the available space. So if you place a panel group on an empty page, then it stretches to fit the entire width of the browser window. Placed inside a div with a set width, the group of panels stretches to match the div's width. If you wish to make the group of panels thinner, change the width property of the *.TabbedPanels* style. Normally it's set to 100%, but you could change this to 50% or a set pixel amount. The entire group of panels and tabs is floated to the left, so any content that appears after the panel group wraps around the right side of the panels (see page 332 for more on floats). (To adjust the height of a group of panels, see the "Panels" bullet point, below.)

- **All tabs: *.TabbedPanelsTab***

  There are two types of tabs: the one for the currently displayed panel, and the tabs that aren't active. The *.TabbedPanelsTab* style controls both types of tabs. If you want to change the font used on all tabs, edit the *.TabbedPanelsTab* style, and then choose a new font family. In addition, if you wish to change the borders that appear around the tabs, then edit this style. To adjust the amount of space between the edge of the tab and the text label inside, edit the style's padding property (page 343); to change the space between tabs, edit the style's margin property (page 343).

- **Not selected tab: *.TabbedPanelsTab* and *.TabbedPanelsTabHover***

  The *.TabbedPanelsTab* also dictates the basic look of an unselected tab, things like its background color. In addition, a non-selected tab has a hover style—*.TabbedPanelsTabHover*—so that when the mouse moves over the tab, it highlights to indicate that you can click it. The basic style sheet supplied with Dreamweaver merely changes the tab's background color when the mouse moves over it, but you're free to change other settings, such as the font color.

Tip: Dreamweaver CS4's new Live View lets you instantly preview style changes without leaving Dreamweaver. For example, with the CSS Styles panel open, and your Web page in Live view, you can make changes to the *.TabbedPanelsTabHover* style (change the background color, for instance) and immediately test that change by moving your mouse over the tab in Design view. See page 553 for more on Live View.

- **Currently selected tab: *.TabbedPanelsTabSelected***

  The *.TabbedPanelsTabSelected* style applies to the tab associated with the currently displayed panel. This style essentially overwrites style properties inherited from the *.TabbedPanelsTab* style that all tabs share. The background color and text color differ from the other tab style, but, again, you're free to modify this style (by picking a new font, for instance).

  With this style, be aware of a couple of things. First, the style has a set bottom border. You shouldn't eliminate it, unless you eliminate bottom borders on the *.TabbedPanelsTab* as well. Otherwise, you see a noticeable line separating the tab from its panel. In addition, if you change the background color of the tab and the panel (they're usually set to the same color to make it appear that they form one unified element), then set the color of the bottom border for this style to match. If you don't, then you end up with a line separating the tab from the panel.

Tip: If you make the text size for one type of tab larger or smaller than the other tab type, you end up with different heights for the different tabs. What's worse, the shorter tab no longer touches the top of the panel group. To fix this, add a *line-height* property (page 142) to the *.TabbedPanelsTab* style that's large enough to force the two tabs to occupy the same height–use a pixel value so that you can guarantee the different tabs will be the same height. You'll probably need to conduct some trial and error testing to get this right.

- **Panels: *.TabbedPanelsContentGroup* or *.TabbedPanelsContent***

  Two styles affect the panels. The first, *.TabbedPanelsContentGroup*, is applied to a <div> tag that wraps around the HTML of *all* of the panels. Second, the content of each panel is itself wrapped in a <div> tag with the *.TabbedPanelsContent* class applied to it. You can edit either style to adjust basic properties like font color, size, and so on. However, the *.TabbedPanelsContentGroup* controls the borders and background color for the panels; edit that style if you wish to change the panels' borders or backgrounds. Out of the box, the *.TabbedPanelsContent* style sheet just has padding set on it—the padding property (page 343) adds space inside each panel so its contents don't butt right up against the borders of the panel.

  Each panel is only as tall as the content inside it. If one panel has a lot of information and another just a little, then the panels grow or shrink wildly as you switch among the different tabs and panels. If you're a stickler for consistency, you can set a height for all panels: Edit the *.TabbedPanelsContent* style, and add a *height* property (see page 341). Be careful with height, however; before building a Web page, it's difficult to judge how much content a panel will have (and thus how tall it needs to be). If the content inside a panel grows taller than the panel's height setting, you get some weird display problems, as explained on page 342.

Tip: In Firefox, when you click a tab, it gains a fuzzy, dotted outline around it. This outline is applied by a "focus" state (see page 183). To remove it, you need to create a compound style named *.TabbedPanelsTab:focus*. Then you need to set the CSS *outline* property to *none*. Unfortunately, you can't do this setting with Dreamweaver's Rule Definition Window. To add this property, first create the *.TabbedPanelsTab:focus* style (make sure to save this new style in the SpryTabbedPanels.css style sheet); when the CSS Rule Definition window appears, just click OK. This action creates a style with no properties. Next, in the CSS Styles panel, find the style, and then select it; then, in the Properties Pane (see page 305), click the Add Property link, type *outline*, hit Tab, and then type *none*. You're done.

- **Content inside the panel**

  Dreamweaver doesn't start you off with any styles that control specific tags inside a panel. Although headlines and paragraphs inherit (see page 312) any text properties added to the panel styles, you might want to define a different look for headlines, paragraphs, lists, and other tags inside a panel. This situation is perfect for a descendent selector. A descendent selector, as you read on page 301, lets you specify the look of a tag when it's inside another tag, and thus lets you pinpoint the look of page elements based on where they appear on the page. In this case, say you want paragraphs inside a panel to look different from other paragraphs on the page: Create a descendent selector style named *.TabbedPanelsContent p*, and then add any CSS properties you'd like. Or, to format the look of heading 2 tags inside a panel, create a style named *.TabbedPanelsContent h2*. In other words, to control the look of any particular tag inside a panel, create an advanced style, and then tack on *.TabbedPanelsContent*, followed by a space before the name of any tag you want to look different when it appears inside a panel (see page 115 for more on creating styles).

Accordions

A Spry Accordion is another space-saving widget for stuffing lots of content into a multi-paneled display (Figure 12-5). Like Spry Tabbed Panels, a Spry Accordion contains panels of information, each with a labeled tab. However, the tabs are stacked on top of each other instead of side by side. When you click the tab of a panel that's not currently visible, that panel rises with a smooth animated effect. In addition, you must set each panel's height, so if the content inside a panel is taller than the panel itself, then, on the panel's right edge, a scroll bar appears: It's kind of like having a browser window inside a browser window. Dreamweaver's stock style sheet sets the height of each panel to 200 pixels, but you can change that (see the bullet point "Panels" on page 507).

FREQUENTLY ASKED QUESTION

.VTabbedPanels Explained

In the SpryTabbedPanels.css style sheet, what do all the styles whose names begin with .VTabbedPanels *do?*

The short answer: They don't do anything. The longer answer: unless you want to have vertical tabbed panels. A vertical tabbed panel displays the tabs one on top of the other along the left edge of the groups of panels. In other words, the panels appear to the right instead of the tabs. They don't look particularly good, and if that weren't reason enough to avoid them, they're difficult to manage. To see one in action, visit: *http://labs.adobe.com/technologies/spry/samples/tabbedpanels/tabbed_panel_sample.htm*.

If you feel like experimenting, you can turn a regular tabbed group of panels into vertical tabs by applying a *.VTabbedPanels* class to the <div> tag that surrounds the entire Spry Tabbed Panel group. (This <div> tag looks something like <div.TabbedPanels#TabbedPanels1> in the Tag selector). The exact ID—*#TabbedPanels1* in this example—depends on the ID you (or Dreamweaver) set on step 3 on page 497. You can most easily change this div's ID with the Tag selector method described on page 124.

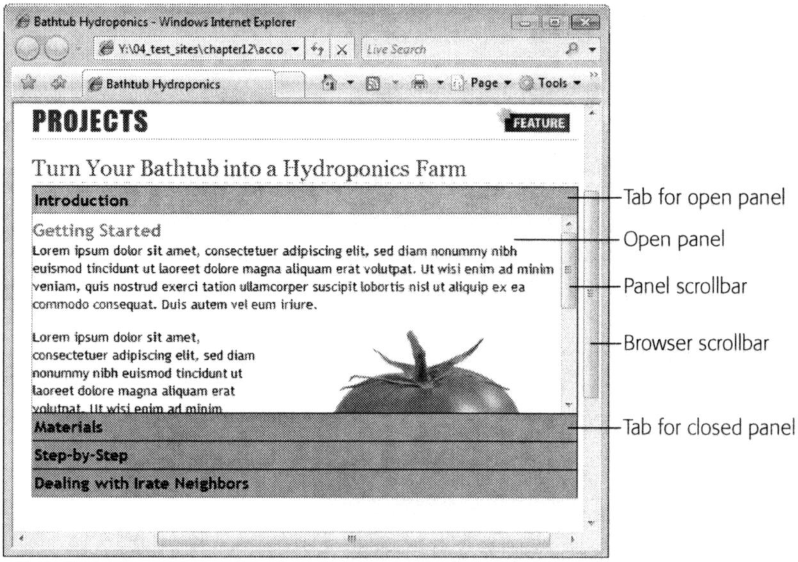

***Figure 12-5:** Accordion panels must have a set height, so you always know how much room they take up on a page. Panels that have lots of content automatically get scroll bars added to them. The content in the "Introduction" panel in this image doesn't fit within the height of the panel, so to read all the information, a visitor must use the small scroll bar. Depending on how you look at it, the additional scroll bar provides a great space-saving device or an annoying inconvenience that forces visitors to scroll unnecessarily.*

Adding an Accordion

You can place a Spry Accordion anywhere on a Web page—on an empty page, inside a div tag, and so on.

1. **In the document window, click where you wish to insert the accordion.**

   For example, inside a <div> tag.

2. **Choose Insert → Spry → Spry Accordion, or, on the Insert panel, click one of the Spry Accordion buttons (see Figure 12-2).**

   After inserting an accordion, you see a tab (labeled "Label 1"), an open panel (with "Content 1" inside) and another tab ("Label 2") at the bottom (see Figure 12-6); in addition, a blue Spry tab appears above the top tab, and the Property inspector displays the accordion's properties (Figure 12-6).

Tip: You can insert any Spry widget by dragging its icon from the Insert panel to anywhere on a Web page.

3. **In the Property inspector, name the accordion.**

   As with Spry Tabbed Panels, this step is optional (see step 3 on page 497).

4. **Add additional tabs and panels to the accordion.**

   If two panels aren't enough for your needs, use the Property inspector to add more. Click the + button above the list of tab names (see Figure 12-6) to add a new tab and panel. To remove a panel, in the panels list, click the name of the tab, and then click the minus (–) button. (You can also reorder the panels by selecting a tab from the list, and then, in the Property inspector, clicking the up or down arrow button.)

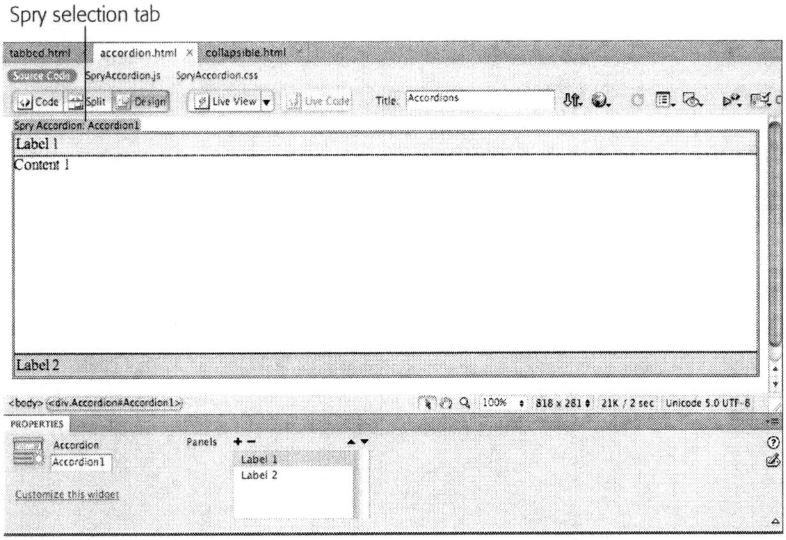

Figure 12-6: *To edit a Spry Widget's properties, select it: In Design view, on top of the widget, click the blue Spry tab. The blue tab is an internal Dreamweaver control, and doesn't appear in a Web browser.*

Adding and Editing Accordion Content

An accordion is divided into sections, composed of a labeled tab and a content panel associated with the tab. Each tab is embedded in its own <div> tag; content for a panel appears inside another <div> tag. Each tab-panel pair is enclosed by yet another div (and the entire accordion [all tab-panel groups] is wrapped in one final div).

To edit a tab's label, in Design view, just select its text, and then type a new label. (Since the label is enclosed in a <div> tag, you can also just click the tab, and then press Ctrl+A [⌘-A] to select all the label's text.) Since accordion widget tabs span the entire width of the accordion, you can put a lot more words on an accordion tab than on the tabbed panels you read about earlier in the chapter.

As with those Spry Tabbed Panels, you have to make a panel visible to edit it: Mouse over the tab whose panel is hidden, and then, at the right edge of the tab, click the eye icon to open the panel for editing. It's the same procedure (and same eye icon) as with tabbed panels (see Figure 12-4). To select all the text inside a panel, click the panel, and then choose Edit → Select All (or Ctrl+A [⌘-A]). You can place any combination of HTML inside a panel: headlines, paragraphs, bulleted lists, forms, images, and Flash movies.

You'll run into one big problem if you add more content than you can fit inside an accordion panel's height: You can't see all the content in Dreamweaver! Remember, accordion panels occupy a fixed height: When the accordion is viewed in a browser, you can just scroll inside the panel to see any content that doesn't fit (see Figure 12-5). But you don't get any scroll bars in Dreamweaver's Design view, so when you add more content than you can fit into the height of the panel, you can't edit it. You can work around this problem in two ways:

- Double-click the panel.
- Right-click (control-click) the panel, and then, from the contextual menu, choose Element View → Full (see Figure 12-7).

Either way, the panel fully expands so you can now see and edit all the content inside. In fact, all the panels in the accordion expand when you do either of these things. This "full" view is visible in Dreamweaver only in order to make it easier to edit content in the accordion panels: When someone views the page in a Web browser, he sees only the top panel, and he must click another tab to view another panel's content.

Formatting a Spry Accordion

When you add a Spry Accordion to a Web page, Dreamweaver links an external style sheet named SpryAccordion.css to the page. This CSS file contains all the styles that control the look of the accordion's tabs and panels. The process for modifying the appearance of those tabs follows the same general sequence described on page 498 for Spry Tabbed Panels: Identify the element you wish to format, and then open and edit that element's style to match your page's overall design.

To help guide you in the process of modifying Spry Accordions, here's a list of accordion elements and the styles that control them:

- **The Accordion (all tabs and panels):** ***.Accordion***

  The *.Accordion* class style controls the overall settings for the accordion. This class is applied to the <div> that surrounds the tabs and panels. If you add basic font formatting to this style, such as font color, size, and font family, the other tabs and panels inherit (see page 312) these same settings.

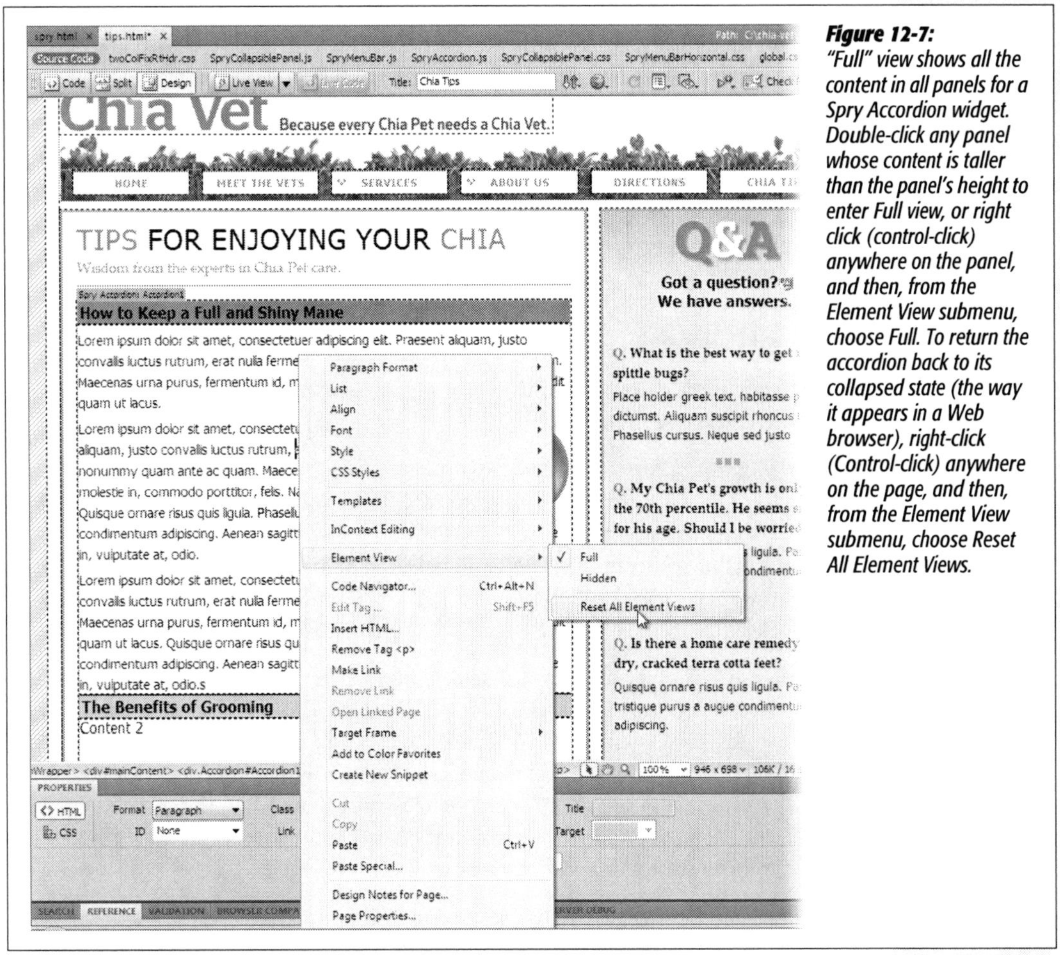

Figure 12-7: *"Full" view shows all the content in all panels for a Spry Accordion widget. Double-click any panel whose content is taller than the panel's height to enter Full view, or right click (control-click) anywhere on the panel, and then, from the Element View submenu, choose Full. To return the accordion back to its collapsed state (the way it appears in a Web browser), right-click (Control-click) anywhere on the page, and then, from the Element View submenu, choose Reset All Element Views.*

In addition, the left, right, and bottom borders that appear around the accordion are set in this style.

- **All tabs:** ***.AccordionPanelTab***

  Tabs inside a Spry Accordion are displayed in four possible ways (some design-inspired Adobe engineer got a little wild): As with a Spry tabbed panel, you see both a selected tab (the tab for the currently displayed panel) and a non-selected tab (the tab eagerly waiting to be clicked to reveal the hidden contents of its panel).

  In addition, both the selected and non-selected tabs have "focus" states that kick into action to format *all* tabs when you click any *one* tab (*.AccordionFocused .AccordionPanelTab*, and *.AccordionFocused .AccordionPanelOpen .AccordionPanelTab*). In other words, click a single tab, and all tabs change appearance—"Yes sir, my tabs-in-arms and I are ready for your command!" Overall, the focus tabs are visually distracting (especially since the background colors are two shades of electric blue). They aim to aid someone who is using a keyboard instead of a mouse to navigate the accordion panels (you can actually tab to the accordion, and then use the up and down arrow keys to hide and reveal panels).

Note: You can only see the "focus" state for tabs in Firefox, Internet Explorer, and Opera. Safari does not display the effects of the focus styles discussed here.

To alter the basic appearance of all tabs, edit the .AccordionPanelTab style. If you define a font family for this style, then all tabs use that font. In addition, the padding inside each tab, and the borders that appear around each tab, are defined in this style.

- **Not selected tab: *.AccordionPanelTab, .AccordionPanelTabHover,* and *.AccordionFocused .AccordionPanelTab***

The *.AccordionPanelTab* style also dictates the background color for a non-selected tab. In addition, a non-selected tab has a hover style—*.AccordionPanelTabHover*—so that when a visitor's mouse moves over the tab, the tab highlights to indicate that she can click it. The basic style sheet supplied with Dreamweaver merely changes the tab's text color when the mouse moves over it, but you're free to change other settings as well.

When any tab is clicked, all non-selected tags also change appearance, thanks to the *.AccordionFocused .AccordionPanelTab.* Tabs also use this style when a visitor presses his keyboard's Tab key to access the accordion panels. The stock style sheet changes the background color to a bright blue. You can delete the style completely if you don't want the tabs to change when clicked. (At the very least, for the sake of all who care about beauty in this world, change the electric blue color to something less obnoxious.)

Tip: The same Tip on page 501, regarding the fuzzy line that Firefox places around focused tabs, applies to the Spry accordion. In this case, the fuzzy line appears around the entire accordion. To remove this outline, create an advanced style called *.Accordion:focus*, and then set that style's *outline* property to *none*.

- **Currently selected tab: *.AccordionPanelOpen .AccordionPanelTab, .AccordionPanelOpen .AccordionPanelTabHover,* and *.AccordionFocused .AccordionPanelTab***

The *.AccordionPanelOpen .AccordionPanelTab* style applies to the tab associated with the currently opened panel. This style essentially overwrites style properties inherited from the *.AccordionPanelTab* style that all tabs share. In the stock style sheet, only the background color differs from the other tab style, but, again, you're free to modify this style. In addition, the text on a selected tab also changes color when a visitor's mouse moves over it, thanks to the *.AccordionPanelOpen .AccordionPanelTabHover* style. This subtle "you can click me" cue is useful for a non-selected tab (since clicking one of those tabs actually does something). But since clicking an already opened tab doesn't do anything, this hover style is actually a needless distraction.

A selected tab also changes color when you click its tab, or press the keyboard's Tab key to access the accordion (again, you see that hideous electric blue). The *.AccordionFocused .AccordionPanelTab* style is the culprit.

- **Panels: *.AccordionPanelContent***

  The *.AccordionPanelContent* class is applied to the <div> tag that surrounds the HTML contained in an accordion panel. You can adjust font settings for this style to affect only the text inside the panel.

  In addition, this style defines each panel's height. The CSS *height* property is set to 200 pixels at first, but you can make this value larger to display a bigger panel, or smaller for a shorter panel. Unfortunately, you can't make the panels automatically adjust to fit whatever content is inside them; you must have a set height for the accordion panels to work.

- **Content inside the panel**

  Dreamweaver supplies you with no specific styles for controlling specific tags inside an accordion panel. You can use the same general process described for Spry Tabbed Panels (under the bullet point "Content inside the panel" on page 501) to create descendent selectors that affect only tags inside accordion panels. Just use *.Accordion* as the first part of the selector. For example, *.Accordion p* is a descendent selector for formatting paragraphs inside an accordion panel.

  Also note that content inside an accordion panel butts directly up against the panel's left and right edges. If you apply padding directly to the panel (the *.AccordionPanelContent* style), then the opening and closing panel animation is not very smooth. It's a bit more work, but it's better to add padding to the tags that appear inside the panel. For example, if you want all heading 2 tags to indent 5 pixels from both the left and right sides of the panel, then create a descendent selector like *.Accordion h2*, and then set the left and right margin properties to 5 pixels.

Note: When creating descendent selectors, always keep in mind the *cascade* (page 314). This CSS concept provides a set of rules for handling styles that conflict. You can easily create some confusing conflicts as you add multiple descendent selectors to a page. For example, say that the main content region of a page is created by a div with an ID named *mainContent*. If you want to create a descendent selector for formatting paragraphs *inside* that main content region, you might name it *#mainContent p*. Now, say you insert a Spry Accordion, and you wanted to create a unique look for paragraphs inside it. You could then create a style named *.Accordion p*. Unfortunately, since the *#mainContent p* style is more specific (has greater power) than the *.Accordion p* style, if you pick a font size for both, then the size in the *#mainContent p* wins. In other words, it would be impossible to change the size of paragraphs inside the accordion... unless you create a more specific style. To overcome this problem, you could create an even more specific style for the accordion: *#mainContent .Accordion p*. All the messy details of this kind of problem (and how to fix it) are described on page 314.

POWER USERS' CLINIC

Get the Most from Spry

Spry isn't just a Dreamweaver tool; it's a separate JavaScript-based toolset that has a lot of bells and whistles beyond what's available from Dreamweaver's Insert bar and Property inspector. You can do things like change the speed of most effects (like how fast collapsible panels open and close). You can even program other ways to make an accordion panel open—by clicking another link on a page, or simply mousing over a tab. You can even change the underlying HTML for most Spry widgets. For example, you could change the <span> tags usually used for Spry Validation error messages to a <p> tag.

To modify the Spry widgets that Dreamweaver inserts into a Web page, you need to dip into Code view, and make some changes. This activity sounds scarier than it actually is. Adobe made Spry easy for non-programmers to learn and use. The complex programming that makes Spry work its magic is hidden; you need to learn only a few basic concepts, and have a handy guidebook nearby, to take control of your Spry widgets.

To learn more about Spry and how to modify it, check out the online manual at *http://livedocs.adobe.com/en_US/Spry/SDG/index.html.*

Collapsible Panels

A Spry Collapsible Panel is a single tab and panel (see Figure 12-8). The tab toggles the panel's display; each click of the tab either opens or closes the panel. You decide whether the panel is opened or closed when the Web page first loads. A closed collapsible panel is great for keeping information out of a visitor's face until she wants it—like a form for signing up for an email newsletter, or driving directions to your business. Add an opened panel to your page when you want to present an important announcement that, once read, can be quickly hidden with a click of the mouse.

Adding a Collapsible Panel

You can place a Spry Collapsible Panel anywhere on a Web page—on an empty page, inside a <div> tag, and so on.

1. **In the document window, click where you wish to insert the collapsible panel.**

   For example, inside a <div> tag.

2. **Choose Insert → Spry → Spry Collapsible Panel, or, on the Insert panel, click one of the Spry Collapsible Panel buttons (see Figure 12-2).**

   After inserting a collapsible panel, in the document window, you see a tab (labeled "Tab"), and an open panel with "Content"; in addition, a blue Spry tab appears above the top tab, and the Property inspector displays the properties for the collapsible panel (Figure 12-9).

3. **In the Property inspector, name the collapsible panel.**

   As with Spry Tabbed Panels, this step is optional (see step 3 on page 358).

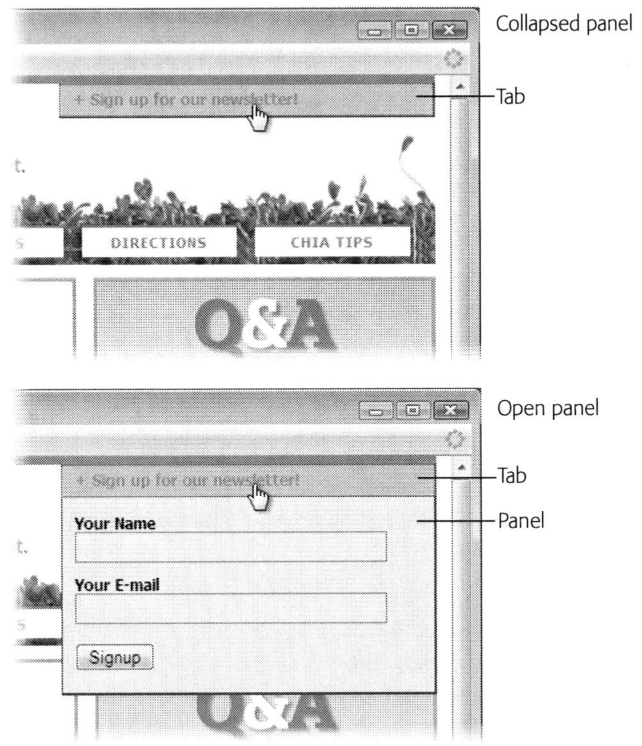

Figure 12-8:
Collapsible panels work especially well as absolutely positioned divs (page 497). Here, the collapsible panel is positioned at the top of the page overlapping an empty area on the page's banner (top). Since the panel is absolutely positioned, it floats above other content on the page. When a visitor clicks the tab, and the panel expands (bottom), it doesn't push other page content out of the way; it merely sits above the page, like a sheet of paper on a desktop. Clicking the tab above the panel once again hides the panel.

Unlike tabbed panels and accordions, a collapsible panel is just a single tab/panel pair. You can't add additional tabs or panels. You can, however, place multiple collapsible panels on a page, stacked one on top of the next. This method has two distinct advantages over an accordion. First, you don't have to have a panel open when the page loads. You can have three collapsible panels on a page with all three closed. A visitor clicks the tab of one panel, and it opens, leaving the other collapsible panels unaffected.

In addition, because each collapsible panel is independent, a visitor can have all of the panels open at once.

4. **From the Property inspector's Display menu, choose either Open or Closed (see Figure 12-9).**

   The Display menu controls only whether the panel is opened or closed in *Design view*. In other words, this setting is just to help you while working within Dreamweaver; it doesn't affect how the panel appears when the page is viewed in a Web browser.

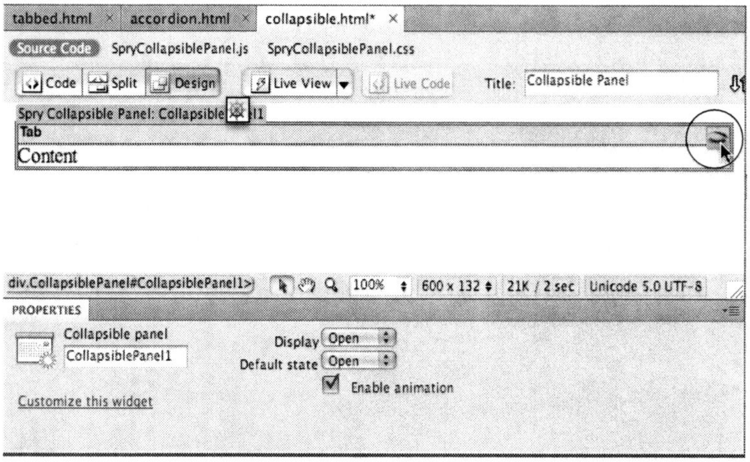

Figure 12-9: *In the Property inspector, you can skip the Display menu, and open and close the panel by clicking the eye icon (to open a closed panel) or the shut-eye icon (circled–to hide an open panel). Like the Display menu options, this action controls only whether the panel is opened or closed in Dreamweaver's Design view as you work on the page.*

5. **From the Property inspector's "Default state" menu, choose either Open or Closed (see Figure 12-9).**

   This menu controls how the panel appears—open or closed—when a Web browser first loads the page. In other words, a visitor sees the panel this way when she visits the page: Either the panel is open and visible, or closed and hidden. Of course, a visitor can change that view simply by clicking the tab when he views the page.

   If you start with the panel closed, you should somehow inform visitors that they need to click the tab to see the panel's content. For example, you could simply add a + sign to the tab text like this "+ Sign up for our newsletter". The + sign is commonly used to indicate that there's more information. Or you could just use text to let the visitor know what to do: "Click here to sign up for our newsletter."

6. **Enable or disable animation.**

   Turn on the Property inspector's "Enable animation" checkbox (see Figure 12-9) if you want the panel to move in and out of view in a smooth "window-blind" effect. Uncheck this box if you simply want the panel to instantly appear and disappear from view each time the tab is clicked. The choice is purely aesthetic, so choose according to your design preferences.

Adding Content to a Collapsible Panel

A collapsible panel consists of a simple combination of <div> tags: one <div> tag (marking the beginning and end of the widget) that wraps around two other <div> tags (one tag for the tab, followed by another div for the panel).

To edit a tab's label, in Design view, just select its text, and then type a new label. Since the label is enclosed in a <div> tag, you can also just click inside the tab, and then press Ctrl+A (⌘-A) to select all of the label's text.

To edit the panel's content, the panel must be visible, and you control it either with the Property inspector's Display menu (step 4 on page 509) or, on the panel's tab, by clicking the eye icon (Figure 12-9). To select all the text inside a panel, click anywhere inside the panel, and then choose Edit → Select All (or Ctrl+A [⌘-A]). You can place any combination of HTML inside a panel: headlines, paragraphs, bulleted lists, forms, images, and Flash movies.

Formatting a Collapsible Panel

When you add a Spry Collapsible Panel to a Web page, Dreamweaver links the page to an external style sheet file named *SpryCollapsiblePanel.css*, which contains all the styles that control the look of the tab and the panel. The process for modifying the appearance of those elements follows the same general sequence described on page 498 for Spry Tabbed Panels: namely, identify the element you wish to format, and then open and edit that element's style to match your page's overall design.

To help guide you in the process of modifying Spry Collapsible Panel styles, here's a list of the panel elements and the styles that control them:

- **The Collapsible Panel: *.CollapsiblePanel***

  This style controls the border that appears around a collapsible panel. Alter the color or style of the border, or completely remove it.

- **All tabs: *.CollapsiblePanelTab***

  Four styles control how a collapsible panel's tab is displayed. Each style applies to the tab under different circumstances: when the panel is open, when the panel is closed, when the mouse moves over the tab, and when the tab is clicked (this last action gives the tab "focus").

  To alter the basic appearance of all tabs, edit the *.CollapsiblePanelTab* style. For example, define a font family for this style, and all tabs use that font. In addition, this style dictates the padding inside each tab, and the border that separates the tab and the panel beneath it.

- **Tab when panel is closed: *.CollapsiblePanelTab***

  The *.CollapsiblePanelTab* style also dictates the properties, such as the background color, for the tab when the panel is closed.

Tip: The same Tip on page 501, regarding the fuzzy line that Firefox places around focused tabs, applies to the Spry Collapsible Panel. To remove this outline, create an advanced style called *.CollapsiblePanel:focus*, and then set that style's *outline* property to *none*.

- **Tab when moused over: *.CollapsiblePanelTabHover, .CollapsiblePanelOpen .CollapsiblePanelTabHover***

  This long group selector applies to the hover state for tabs—both when the panel is open and when it's closed. If you want to define a different hover appearance for a tab when the panel is open, create two styles: *.CollapsiblePanelTabHover* for a tab when the panel is closed, and *.CollapsiblePanelOpen .CollapsiblePanelTabHover* for a tab that's moused over when the panel is closed. (If you go this route, you should either delete the supplied group selector style—"*.CollapsiblePanelTabHover, .CollapsiblePanelOpen .CollapsiblePanelTabHover*"—or change its name as described on page 128 so that it applies only to one of the tab states.)

- **Tab when panel is opened: "*.CollapsiblePanelOpen .CollapsiblePanelTab, .CollapsiblePanelFocused .CollapsiblePanelTab*"**

  The *.CollapsiblePanelOpen .CollapsiblePanelTab* descendent selector style applies to the tab when the panel is opened. This style overwrites style properties inherited from the *.CollapsiblePanelTab* style. In the stock style sheet, only the background color differs from the other tab style, but, again, you're free to modify this style.

  A tab also changes color when a visitor clicks it, or presses the Tab key to access it (but not in Safari, as described in the Note on page 506). The *.CollapsiblePanelFocused .CollapsiblePanelTab* style is the culprit here, so you want to edit this style if you don't want this color change.

- **Panel: *.CollapsiblePanelContent***

  The *.CollapsiblePanelContent* class is applied to the <div> tag that surrounds the HTML contained in an accordion panel. You can adjust font settings for this style to affect only the text inside the panel, or add a background color to make the panel stand out from other page content.

- **Content inside the panel**

  As with the panels for Spry Tabbed Panels and Spry Accordions, Dreamweaver doesn't start you out with any styles that control specific tags inside a collapsible panel. You can use the same general process described for Spry Tabbed Panels (under the bullet point "Content inside the panels" on page 501) to create descendent selectors that affect only tags inside a collapsible panel. Just use *.CollapsiblePanel*, followed by a space as the first part of the selector: For example, *.CollapsiblePanel p* is a descendent selector for formatting paragraphs inside an accordion panel.

  Also note that content inside a collapsible panel butts directly up against the panel's left and right edges. Avoid adding padding directly to the panel (the *.CollapsiblePanelContent* style), since the animation of the opening and closing is not very smooth and the second time the panel is opened it's actually taller than when it started. Instead, add padding to the tags inside the panel. For example, if you want all heading 2 tags to indent 5 pixels from both the left and right sides of the panel, create a descendent selector (like *.CollapsiblePanelContent h2*), and then set the left and right margin properties to 5 pixels.

Spry Tooltips

Pop-up tooltips are a great way to provide supplementary information without visually overloading a Web page (see Figure 12-10.) A tooltip waits in hiding, until a visitor mouses over a word, sentence, or image, then...bam!...the tooltip appears. You can use a tooltip as a way of providing a definition, to display pictures and text, or even to point to a Web link containing extra information. Netflix.com, for example, provides simple listings of the DVDs they rent—just pictures, ratings, and a way to quickly add the DVD to a "to rent" list. However, when you mouse over the DVD listing, a tooltip appears featuring a detailed summary of the DVD. Dreamweaver CS4 includes a new Spry tool for creating these kinds of useful pop-up boxes.

Adding a Spry Tooltip

A Spry tooltip widget consists of a *trigger*—text or an image that your visitor mouses over—and the *tooltip* itself—the pop-up box. To add one:

1. **Select a word, sentence, image, or block-level element (like a headline paragraph or <div> tag).**

   You can turn any block-level element into a trigger, such as a paragraph, a headline or an entire <div> tag; or you can turn a single word, sentence or image into a trigger. Which way you go depends on the tooltip's purpose: For example, if you want to use tooltips to provide definitions of important words, then you would select a single word.

2. **Choose Insert → Spry → Spry Tooltip or, on the Insert panel, click the Spry Tooltip icon (Figure 12-2).**

   When you insert a tooltip, Dreamweaver first adds an ID to the trigger—if you select an entire paragraph, for example, the ID name is added to the <p> tag like this: <p id="spryTrigger1">. If you selected just a single word, then Dreamweaver wraps the word in a <span> tag with the proper ID name: <span id="spryTrigger1">Word</span>. The exact name used depends on whether you've already added tooltips to the page, so you might have various IDs on the page—spryTrigger1, spryTrigger2, and so on.

Note: You don't have to select anything to insert a tooltip. You can just place the cursor anywhere on a page, and complete step 2 here. Dreamweaver then inserts a <span> tag into the document at the location of the cursor with the text "Tooltip trigger goes here." You can then change the text to something more appropriate–"move your mouse here for a pop-up list of directions"–and even move the span to another location on the page (just cut and paste the tag). You can even delete the <span> tag entirely. This action lets you assign the tooltip to another tag as described in step 4 on page 515.

Figure 12-10:
Now you don't see it, now you do. A Spry tooltip lets you add an informative pop-up bubble that appears when a visitor mouses over a particular word, picture, or chunk of HTML.

Dreamweaver also inserts a new <div> tag containing some placeholder text—"Tooltip content goes here." This is the tooltip itself and, depending on how big your Web page is, you may not actually see it at first. That's because Dreamweaver adds tooltips to the very end of the Web page, after all other content. So, if you have many paragraphs of text, images, and so on, then you may need to scroll down to the bottom of the page to see and edit the tooltip text. By default, the tooltip has a light yellow background, but you'll be able to change that as described in the next section.

Note: In order to edit a tooltip's content, tooltips are always visible in Dreamweaver. However, when you view the page in a Web browser (or click the Live View button [page 553]), the tooltips are invisible until you hover over a tooltip trigger.

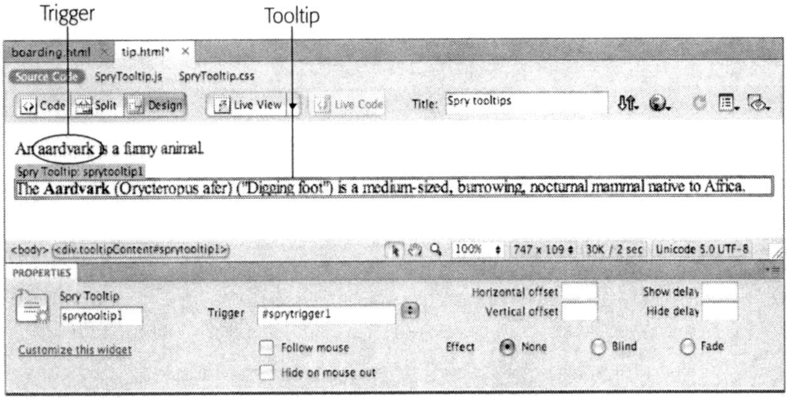

***Figure 12-11:** Spry tooltips can be confusing. Unlike a lot of other Spry elements, nothing on a page identifies a tooltip trigger. The telltale blue Spry tab you see with all other Spry widgets appears only above the tooltip box itself. In this figure, for example, the word "aardvark" in the top paragraph is the trigger—mousing over it pops open the tooltip below. But unless you remember that you tooltip-ified that word, simply scanning the page doesn't make you aware of its existence. In addition, in the Property inspector, to make any changes to the tooltip's settings, you have to click the blue tab above the tooltip <div>. You can't access the tooltip settings from the tooltip trigger text.*

3. **In the Property inspector, name the tooltip.**

   As with the other Spry widgets, this step is optional (see step 3 on page 497). Changing the name alters the ID applied to the tooltip <div> tag. Unfortunately, you can't use the Property inspector to change the ID name used for the trigger. To change the trigger's ID name, you must go into Code view and change it manually (change id="sprytrigger1" to id="defineWord", for example). Since that's a big pain, you're better off just letting Dreamweaver handle the naming. But if you do go to this trouble, make sure you follow the next step.

4. **If you want to change the HTML used as the trigger, then, from the Property inspector's Trigger menu, select an ID name.**

   In most cases, you'll skip this step. When you insert a tooltip, Dreamweaver correctly prepares all the HTML you need. However, if you changed the ID applied to the trigger's HTML, you can then select the ID from this menu. In fact, the Trigger menu lists *every* ID used on the page—even ID names applied to layout elements. This characteristic can come in handy if you actually want to use an already existing tag as the trigger.

For example, say you used one of Dreamweaver's CSS Layouts (see Chapter 7), and you want to have a tooltip appear when a visitor mouses over the banner region at the top of the page. In this case, *you* could just insert a tooltip (without first selecting any text as described in the Note on page 513), and then, from the Property inspector's Trigger menu, select *#header*. (Don't forget to delete the original trigger <span> that Dreamweaver inserted.)

5. **In the Property inspector, set one or more of the display options (Figure 12-11).**

The placement of the tooltip on your final Web page is dependent upon where the visitor's mouse is when moved over the trigger element. That is, if the trigger is an entire paragraph of text and a visitor moves his mouse into the top line of the paragraph, then the tooltip appears near the top of the paragraph; if he mouses up into the paragraph, then the tooltip appears near the bottom of the paragraph. You can fine-tune these settings in the Property inspector, with the additional tooltip options. Here's how they work:

- **Follow mouse.** With this option selected, the tooltip moves around following the mouse if it's moved around the trigger element. For example, say a particular tooltip is triggered when a visitor mouses over a large picture of the Eiffel Tower. If the visitor moves the mouse around the picture, then the tooltip follows along. Since this can induce sea-sickness, you might want to leave this box unchecked, in which case, once the tooltip appears, it doesn't move.

- **Hide on mouse out.** This confusingly-named option lets you keep the tooltip open as long as the mouse is over *either* the trigger element or the tooltip box itself. Normally, a tooltip disappears when you mouse off the trigger element. In general, this is a good idea, since you don't want tooltips cluttering the page. However, if the tooltip has content that the visitor might click on—such as a set of links—then turn this option on. If you don't, as soon as someone moves her mouse toward one of the links in the tooltips—at the same time moving the mouse off the trigger element—the tooltip disappears, and the visitor can never click the link! Turn on this option, and the tooltip remains visible while the mouse is over the trigger element or the tooltip; it disappears only when the mouse is no longer over either.

- **Horizontal and Vertical Offset.** Dreamweaver normally places tooltips 20 pixels to the right and 20 pixels down from the position where the mouse moves over the trigger element. If you want the tooltip to appear in a different location, you can type either a pixel or percentage value in the "Horizontal offset" box (to control the placement from left and right) or the "Vertical offset" box (to control the placement from top to bottom). You can even use a negative value. For example, in Figure 12-10 the tooltip's vertical offset is set to –60%. This places a little more than half of the tooltip above the mouse's position. By using a negative value for both offsets, you can make a tooltip appear directly over the trigger element.

- **Delay.** If you don't want a tooltip to appear immediately, then, in the "Show delay" box, type a number. The value you type is counted in milliseconds, so if you type *1000*, then the tooltip appears 1 second after the visitor mouses over the trigger. This ability may not seem very useful—after all, by the time one second passes a visitor has probably moved her mouse off the trigger, and the tooltip never appears. However, a small value like 100 prevents a tooltip from appearing if the mouse momentarily travels over a trigger. This setting keeps your tooltips from suddenly flashing on and then off as someone mouses to click a link.

  The "Hide delay" option determines how long the tooltip hangs around *after* the mouse moves off the trigger.

- **Effect.** You can also add visual effects to the appearance and disappearance of the tooltip. Check the None button if you just want the tooltip to appear or disappear in a blink. But for a fancier display, choose Blind (the tooltip wipes into and out of existence like a window shade) or Fade (the tooltip fades in and out like a ghost).

Adding Content to a Tooltip

The HTML for a tooltip is very basic: It's just a single <div> tag placed at the end of your page's HTML. After inserting a tooltip, just click inside the div, and then press Ctrl-A (⌘-A) to select the dummy text supplied by Dreamweaver; then add your own content. You can insert a simple paragraph, or a complex combination of HTML, including images, Flash movies, and other divs. If you want, you can even turn a tooltip into a mini–Web page—just make sure you don't add so much content that the tooltip doesn't fit in the browser window.

Note: Dreamweaver inserts the tooltip HTML at the end of a page–if you have a lot of content on a Web page, then you may not see the tooltip after inserting it. Scroll down until you reach the bottom of the page, and then you see the tooltip's text.

You can also edit the tooltip's trigger element—the text, paragraph, div, or image you selected before adding the tooltip. As mentioned above, Dreamweaver adds an ID to the trigger HTML (or, if you selected just a word or two, wraps the selection in a <span> tag, and then adds an ID to that span). Unfortunately, you have no immediate way to identify a particular tooltip's trigger element—it doesn't highlight, for example, when you select the tooltip. You need to either remember where the trigger is, or select the tooltip and then, in the Property inspector, look for the ID name applied to the trigger (see Figure 12-11). Once you know the ID, perform a search for that name using Dreamweaver's excellent "Find and Replace" tool described on page 782.

Formatting a Tooltip

When you add a Spry Tooltip to a Web page, Dreamweaver links the page to an external style sheet named SpryTooltip.css, which contains only two styles. Leave the first one—*.iframeTooltip*—alone. That style is used to overcome some browser display bugs related to the tooltip. The second style—*.toolTipContent*—defines the look of the pop-up tooltip. Out of the box, the style has just a single property—a light yellow background color. However, you'll probably want to modify this to change the background color, add some padding (page 343) to move the content away from the edges of the tooltip, and so on.

In addition, you may want to create styles that apply just to tags inside the tooltip—for example, to provide a unique look just for paragraphs or a heading inside a tooltip. Here, again, is a great place to use descendent selectors (see page 301). Since all tooltip content goes inside a <div> tag with the class *tooltipContent* applied to it, you can create special styles that apply only to the content. For example, the descendent selector *.tooltipContent p* affects only paragraphs inside a tooltip.

You might also want to create a style to format a tooltip trigger. Dreamweaver doesn't help you out with this—the program doesn't supply a style to make a tooltip trigger stand out. In fact, unless you do something to alter the look of a trigger element, it's difficult for anyone to figure out that any particular element has a tooltip attached to it! For example, say you select a single word on a page, and then add a tooltip to it—perhaps the tooltip provides a definition of the word. When viewed in a Web browser, that word doesn't look any different from any other word, so the visitor has no way of knowing that she should mouse over it.

One way to solve this problem is to create a class style—*.trigger*, for example—and then apply it to the HTML tag for the trigger (see page 122 for instructions on applying a class to a tag). If you add tooltips to single words (as in the definition example), then you might want to add a light background color to highlight the word. You could also change the cursor style used for that class. For example, if you set the *cursor* property to "Help", then the cursor changes to a question mark when a visitor mouses over the particular trigger.

Of course if the trigger is obvious—for example, it has the text "mouse over me to see..."—you might not want or need to create any special style for the trigger element.

Spry Data Sets

Dreamweaver includes a way to display data more dynamically than the plain-vanilla HTML table. Spry data sets provide several ways to display data from a variety of different sources, including basic HTML tables or XML files. With a Spry data set, for example, you can create an interactive table that visitors can sort just by clicking the top of a table column (Figure 12-12). Say a page has a table that lists all the employees in a company. Each employee's name, the region of the country in which he or she works, the phone number, and other important data is included. Sometimes you probably want to see the list of employees alphabetized by last name; other times you want to sort the list by the regions in which they work (Northeast, Southeast, and so on). Normally, this requires creating two pages: one with a table of employees listed by last name, and another with employees listed by their regions.

With a Spry data set, you need only one page and one table, no matter how many columns you wish to sort by. That's because a Spry table is interactive, just like a regular old Excel spreadsheet. Want to see employees organized by last name? Click the "Name" column. To group employees by region, just click the "Region" column. A Spry table is interactive, instantaneous, and doesn't require loading another Web page.

In addition, Spry data sets let you display detailed data on a single item contained within the table. Suppose you have a simple table that just lists employees' names and the regions in which they work. With Spry you can add an "Up Close and Personal" section to the page, so that when an employee name is clicked in a table row, detailed information such as the employee's phone number, photo, and email address appear in another part of the page. Once again, this little trick doesn't require the visitor to download a different Web page. All this information appears on the same Web page with a simple mouse click.

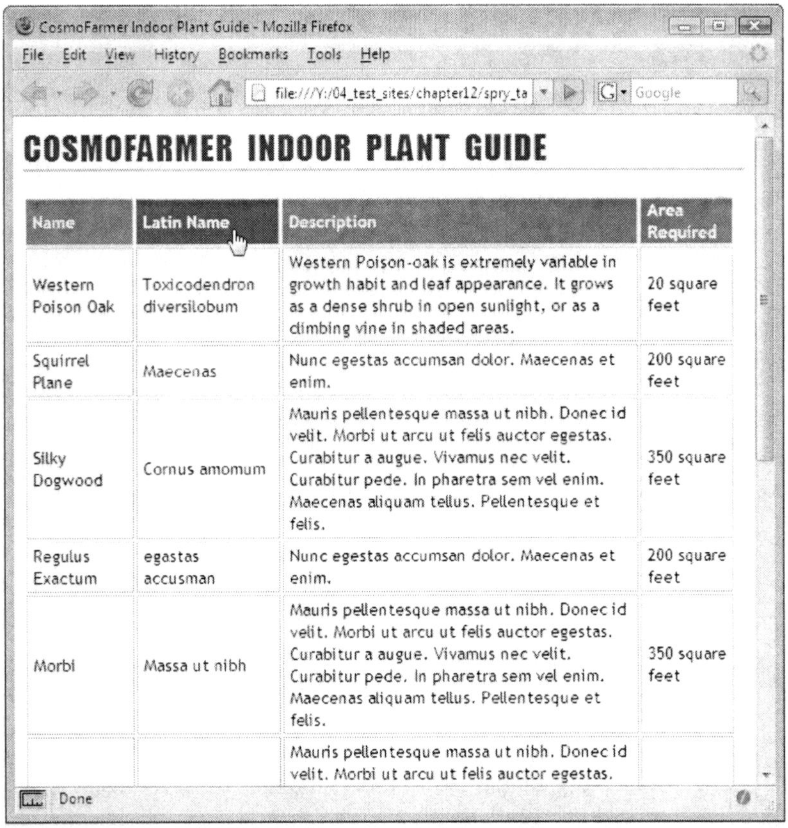

Figure 12-12: *A Spry data table lets visitors interact with your data. Clicking a column header sorts the column in ascending order; click the column again, and data is sorted in descending order. Here, if you wish to view the plants in alphabetical order by their Latin names, then click the Latin Name column header. The table's data is sorted instantly, without loading a new Web page.*

If you often add data tables to your site, or simply have large amounts of related data that you want to display in an interactive format, then the Spry data set is the perfect tool for you. And Dreamweaver CS4 has made it even easier to add Spry data sets to your Web site. In Dreamweaver CS3 you were limited to working with XML files—the data you wanted to display had to be in the XML format. Now, you can use standard HTML Web pages to store your data, and Spry to turn that data into an interactive presentation. In either case, however, you're always dealing with two files: the Web page where the data appears, and a separate file (an HTML file or XML file) containing the data. When the Web page loads, the JavaScript programming provided by the Spry data set downloads the data file, extracts the required data, and then displays it on the page.

Keep in mind that Spry data sets are primarily intended for when you want to display repeating rows of information. Although an HTML or XML file can really hold any type of information, the kind of file you should use with Spry should contain lists of information, like product catalogs, employee records, and so on.

Storing Data in an HTML File

To get started with Spry data sets, you need a file containing data. This file can be an XML file (described next), or a basic HTML file. The ability to use HTML files with Spry data sets is new in Dreamweaver CS4, and makes using Spry data sets much easier for folks who don't normally deal with geek-friendly formats like XML.

Dreamweaver provides two methods for creating a Spry data set from an HTML table. The first method is to create a separate file that contains a basic HTML table containing all of your data. You can then use Spry to load that file and its data, and then display it on another page of your site. In this way you have one simple and easily updated file with the data, and another, fully designed page to display that data using Dreamweaver's Spry data set tools.

The second method is to add the HTML table to the same page on which you wish to add the Spry data set. In other words, on a complete page in your site, insert a basic HTML table's worth of data, and then use the Spry data set tools to reload that table, and then turn it into an interactive super-table.

This second approach might sound a bit weird. After all, why add a table to a page, and then add some fancy JavaScript just to display data from the same table? If all you want to do is display the table's data, this approach isn't a good one—just add a nice-looking table to your Web page, and you're done. But if you want to tap into the interactive capabilities of a Spry data set—for example, to create a sortable table like the one discussed on page 537, or the interactive master/detail data display discussed on page 540—then this approach has a couple of advantages.

First, Spry uses JavaScript to load data into a data set. If the HTML table is in a separate file, and a visitor has JavaScript turned off, then that separate HTML file never loads, and the visitor never sees the data—just an empty space where the data should go. In addition, search engines don't use JavaScript either, so any data that's loaded via JavaScript is lost to a search engine. By putting the HTML table on the same page, search engines and visitors without JavaScript can still access the data (although they lose all of the fancy interactivity provided by JavaScript).

Which method to use? If you're concerned about search engines indexing the data you're displaying, or you want to make sure the data's visible even for people who have JavaScript turned off, then use the second approach: Add the data table to the same page that displays the data. The first approach is good if your data is coming from another source—for example, exported as a HTML table from another program—or if you want someone who's not Dreamweaver-savvy to have a simple method of updating the data in the table.

In either case, you start by adding a basic HTML table containing all your data. The table doesn't have to be fancy—your site's visitors don't actually see this Web page; they just see the data pulled from the table, and either placed onto *another* Web page or completely reformatted and displayed on the same page that Dreamweaver has enhanced with interactive Spry effects. In fact, the table should be as simple as you can get away with (see Figure 12-13). You don't need to worry, for example, about the table's width, the cell padding and spacing, or any of the other formatting choices you make when designing regular HTML tables. Also, do yourself a favor and avoid merged cells and rowspans (page 280) that produce inconsistent results in your data. Finally, don't apply any styles to the rows, columns, or the table itself. This table, if it hasn't sunk in by now, is just for the data—you format the data's appearance when you add it to a Web page using a Spry data set as described on page 529. (The Spry programming actually hides the original table of data if that table is on the same page as the Spry data set.)

Make sure the top row of the table is a header row (see page 267) that includes cells with the description of each column's data. In the table in Figure 12-13, for example, the top row of cells contains table headers. Column 1 has the header named "thumb", column 2 is "large", and so on. Making sure you have header names makes it easier for you, later on, to identify and select the data you wish to use in a Spry data set.

Tip: You can also put images in table cells; just use the same procedure you would for inserting an image into a Web page (page 213). However, in order for those images to show up correctly on a Web page that uses the Spry data tools, you need to make sure that, if you create a separate file for the HTML table, that file is in the same folder as the Web page using the data. Otherwise, the path to the images is different, and they don't display on the final Web page. Alternatively, you can use site root-relative links for your images (see page 163); you can then keep your HTML data file anywhere in your site, and any page on the site can display those images correctly, using the Spry data tools.

Finally, you need to give the table an ID. For some reason, the Spry programming requires this, and if you don't provide an ID, then you can't extract the data from the table. To add an ID, select the table (click the table border, for example, or use one of the other methods mentioned on page 124), and then, in the Property inspector, in the ID box (circled in Figure 12-13), type a name—a simple ID name, like *data*, works just fine.

Dreamweaver also lets you store data in tags other than HTML tables. For example, you could create a series of <div> tags that store the data you wish to display. If you go this route, you need to have one <div> tag that surrounds all your data—it has to have an ID applied to it. You also need separate divs for each row and for each column within a row, and you must apply a class to each of the row divs and another class to each of the column divs. For example, the basic HTML for a data file using divs might look like this:

```
<div id="data">
  <div class="row">
    <div class="column">Godzilla Chia</div>
    <div class="column">1955</div>
  </div>
<div class="row">
    <div class="column">Bambi Chia</div>
    <div class="column">1960</div>
  </div>
</div>
```

You need the class names—*row* and *column* in this example—to let Dreamweaver know which divs hold one row of information, and how many columns are in each row. Of course, if you go to all this trouble, you might as well create an XML file. Unless you already have data set up in the format described in this paragraph, stick to HTML tables for storing data—they're a lot easier to create and maintain.

Note: Because the Spry programming actually downloads the entire data file (the HTML or XML file) and stores it in a browser's memory, Spry data sets work best with relatively few rows of data. If you build a HTML table with 1,000 rows of information, you're better off using a database instead, otherwise you'll find your Spry-driven data sets running slowly in a Web browser.

Storing Data in an XML File

While the HTML table method of storing data is a simple and straightforward way to pipe data into a Spry data set, an XML file can also serve as your data source. In Dreamweaver CS3, this option was the only one, but you still have some reasons to go the XML route in Dreamweaver CS4.

What is XML?

XML is a common method for storing information, and it's routinely used for exchanging data between computers. You might already have XML files that are generated out of the computer systems at your work: Databases can easily save information as XML files, for example. In addition, one of the most common Web-related uses of XML is for RSS feeds—you find them at every news Web site, and if you run a blog on your site, you probably have an RSS feed as well. If so, you can easily post listing of stories and articles from your site's blog directly onto any page of your Web site, using the Spry data set tools.

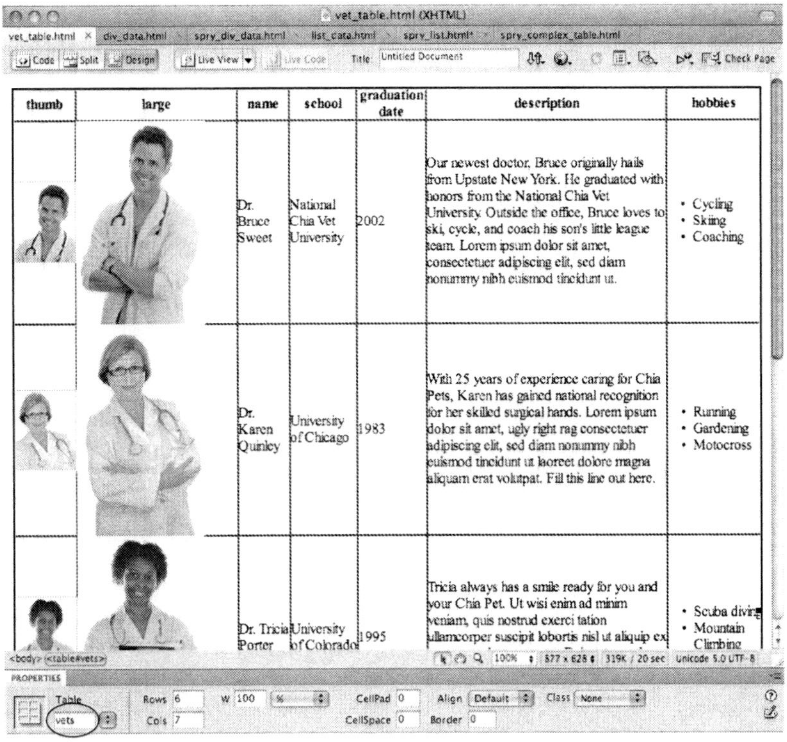

Figure 12-13: *The Spry data set tool lets you extract data from a basic HTML table and manipulate it in fun, interesting, and interactive ways. You can even suck data from an existing table on your site (a nice way to reuse content that's already on your site). The only condition is that any table you want to use for Spry data must have an ID assigned to it. See page 124 for details on how to make that happen.*

Note: Spry lets you access HTML or XML files from the Web for use in Spry data sets. For example, if you want to use your blog's RSS feed to lists your blog postings on other pages of your site, then you can use the RSS feed from your server as the XML source for a Spry data set. Unfortunately, due to security restrictions in Web browsers, you can access HTML and XML files in this way only if both your Web pages (with the Spry data programming on it) and the HTML or XML file are on the same Web server. In other words, you can't use Spry to list the top 10 news stories from CNN.com. (You can, however, use Dreamweaver's server-side programming tools to do that, as described in Chapter 26.)

XML, or Extensible Markup Language, has many similarities to HTML. Like HTML, it's a tag-based language used to identify different pieces of information, and structure data into a meaningful document. For example, HTML has the <h1> tag to identify the most important headline, or the <ul> tag to denote a bulleted list. But HTML has only a handful of tags, and, in many cases, they don't always meaningfully identify the information you're presenting. You can format a news title like "Bigfoot to Wed Super Model" with an <h1> tag, but you could also use the <h1> tag to format the name of a product you're selling, the title of a book, or an event on a calendar. In these cases, you're using the same tag to identify different *types* of information. Technically speaking, there's nothing wrong with using h1 tags in that way. But you can introduce some awfully messy organizational problems into your document, as you'll learn in a moment. Instead, it would be much more informative to use a tag that accurately identifies the type of information, like <product>, <title>, or <event>.

That's where the "X" in XML comes in. XML is not really a markup language like HTML, as much as it is a set of guidelines for creating your own markup languages. The X, or *extensible*, part of XML lets you define your own types of tags—or "extend" the language to fit your needs. In this way, you can create very specific tags to describe different types of information like invoices, books, personnel, and so on.

Note: To learn more about XML, check out *www.w3schools.com/xml*, grab a copy of *Learning XML, Second Edition* (O'Reilly, 2003) by Erik T. Ray, or visit the XMLTopic Center on the Adobe Web site: *www.adobe.com/devnet/topics/xml.html*.

Suppose Chia-Vet.com wants to use XML for storing data about Chia Pets, and so decides to come up with an XML format for storing their list of favorite Chia Pets. That list consists of each Chia Pet's name, when it was issued, how rare it is, a short description of its features, and a path to an image file on the site. In HTML, this information might look like this:

```
<h2>Chia Godzilla <em>1955</em></h2>
<p><img src="images/godzilla.jpg">Chia Godzilla was produced in a limited run
following the release of the classic 1954 movie, Godzilla. <strong>Very rare.
</strong></p>
```

This code is all well and good for display in a Web browser, but it doesn't give any sense of what *kind* of information is being presented. This quality is particularly important when you keep in mind that XML was invented as a way of exchanging data between computers. So if another computer encounters this HTML, it doesn't understand the purpose of the text inside the <h2> tag. In fact, even a human viewing this code might not easily discern what the "1955" means; it's a number, but without some descriptive label, you can't tell that this number refers to the year the product was sold. XML provides a much clearer way of defining the structure and meaning of content.

Chia-Vet.com's IT staff could decide to come up with their own XML format to store this data. In this case, the same information might be written in XML like this:

```
<pets>
<pet>
<name>Chia Godzilla</name>
<issuedate availability="very rare">1955</issuedate>
<description>Chia Godzilla was produced in a limited run following the
release of the classic 1954 movie, Godzilla.</description>
<image>images/godzilla.jpg</image>
</pet>
</pets>
```

Kind of like HTML, right? But with a completely different set of tags. This new markup makes the meaning of each chunk of information clearer. You can easily tell that this data describes a Chia pet (the <pet> tag) with a name, a description, and so on. In a nutshell, that's what XML offers: Tags that meaningfully identify the information inside them.

Rules of the road

Since XML is intended to be an easy way to exchange data between different computers, operating systems, programs, institutions, and people, it has some fairly strict requirements to ensure that everyone's playing by the same rules. If you've done your fair share of writing raw HTML code, much of this will be familiar to you. In fact, if you've written XHTML code (see page 10), then you've already been writing XML. XHTML is an XML version of HTML that just has a few more rules than plain old HTML.

- **Every XML document must have a single "root" element.** A root element is a tag that surrounds all other tags in a document, and appears only once in a document. In an XHTML (and an HTML) document, this tag is the <html> tag. In the example XML format introduced above, this tag is <pets>. If you're creating your own XML-formatted file, then you can make this root element whatever you want: <events>, <employees>, and so on. It makes sense for this tag to describe whatever content you're storing inside the file.
- **All tags must be nested properly, with no overlapping tags.** This rule works just as it does in HTML. You can't have code like this: <b><i>Bold and italics</b> </i>. Since the opening <i> tag appears after the opening <b> tag, its closing tag—</i>—must appear before (or inside of) the closing <b> tag, like this: <b><i>Bold and italics</i></b>.
- **All tags must have both an opening and closing tag, or be self-closing.** In HTML, a paragraph of text is indicated by both an opening <p> and a closing </p>. Some HTML tags, however, don't hold content, like the <img> tag or the line break (<br>) tag. The XML version of these tags include a forward slash at the end of the tag, like this: <br />. This type of tag is called an *empty element*.
- **The property values of all tags must be quoted.** In regular old HTML, you could get away with this line as a way to add a link to a page: <a href=index.html>Home</a>. In XML, this doesn't fly. You need to quote the href property's value like this: <a href="index.html">Home</a>. You're probably used to doing this already, and if you've been using Dreamweaver, the program always does it for you. But when writing your own XML files, make sure to include quotes around a tag's property values.

If your XML file meets these conditions, it's known as (to use the official XML designation) "well-formed." In other words, your XML code is written properly. If you write more complex XML documents, you need to follow additional rules, but these are the basic requirements.

In many cases, you also include what's called a *prolog*—an introduction of sorts that appears at the very top of the document and announces what kind of document it is. In its most basic form, the prolog looks like this:

```
<?xml version="1.0"?>
```

The prolog can also include the type of encoding (useful for indicating different characters for different languages) used in the document.

Here, then, is a basic, complete, and well-formed XML document:

```
<?xml version="1.0" encoding="utf-8"?>
<pets>

<pet>
    <name>Chia Godzilla</name>
    <issuedate availability="very rare">1955</issuedate>
    <description>Chia Godzilla was produced in a limited run following the
release of the classic 1954 movie, Godzilla.</description>
    <image>images/godzilla.jpg</image>
</pet>

<pet>
    <name>Chia Bambi</name>
    <issuedate availability="very rare">1960</issuedate>
    <description>Chia Bambi was produced in a limited run and some units were
packaged as a set with Chia Godzilla.</description>
    <image>images/bambi.jpg</image>
</pet>

</pets>
```

Tip: Dreamweaver can verify whether or not an XML file is well formed. Open the file in Dreamweaver, and then choose File → Validate → As XML. The Results panel opens. If nothing appears inside the Validation panel, the file is OK. If there's an error, then a message explaining the problem appears. Fix the error, and then try to validate the document again. Dreamweaver can even validate XML using a DTD file (see the box below).

If you want to use XML for a data source, then you need to either create an XML file like the one listed above (but hopefully not about Chia Pets or Godzilla), or export data in an XML file format from another program such as a database or Microsoft Excel. Place that XML file (with the file extension of .xml) with the other files in your local site.

Tip: Dreamweaver includes built-in reference material covering XML. See page 422 for more on Dreamweaver's Reference panel.

UP TO SPEED

Taming the Tower of Babel: DTDs and XML Schema

You may be wondering: If anyone can make up her own tags to create her own types of XML files, how can XML help computers, people, and organizations exchange data? After all, if you come up with one way of formatting invoices using XML, and your buddy in accounting uses his own set of tags to create invoices, you'll end up with two different and incompatible types of files for tracking the same information. It's like the Tower of Babel–everyone speaking his own language and unable to talk to each other. Fortunately, XML provides two solutions to this problem: *DTDs* (or Document Type Definitions) and *XML Schemas*. Both solutions are methods of creating a common vocabulary, so everyone can use the same language to talk about the same things.

In fact, you've already been using a DTD when building Web pages in Dreamweaver. When you create a new Web page, Dreamweaver adds a line of code at the beginning of the page, like this:

```
<!DOCTYPE html PUBLIC "-//W3C//DTD XHTML
1.0 Transitional//EN" "http://www.w3.org/
TR/xhtml1/DTD/xhtml1-transitional.dtd">
```

This line varies depending on the type of HTML or XHTML you use. But the concept is the same. The entire line defines the document type for the page–in this example, XHTML 1.0 Transitional–and points to a URL where the DTD can be found–here, it's *http://www.w3.org/TR/xhtml1/DTD/xhtml1-transitional.dtd*.

Essentially, the DTD for each type of HTML or XHTML defines what tags are allowed, and how they should be written. If you don't follow the rules, then the page is considered invalid. In fact, Dreamweaver's validator, discussed on page 651, is doing just that–making sure your code follows the rules of a particular DTD.

XML Schema are just another method of enforcing a language for a particular XML format, with a few bells and whistles that DTDs lack. DTDs have been around a long time and are more common; schemas are a newer concept, but will probably eventually replace DTDs. Both XML Schemas and DTDs are very confusing beasts–difficult to read, and difficult to create. Many DTDs and Schemas are available for describing a wide range of different types of information. A consortium of businesses that agree to a single way of describing information often create these DTDs and Schemas, so that they can easily share data with each other. You probably won't be creating your own anytime soon, but just keep in mind that they exist, and they're a common way to make sure everyone's speaking the same tongue.

Dreamweaver includes a nice feature related to both DTDs and Schemas: If you include a DTD or Schema in an XML file, and then edit that XML file in Code view, then Dreamweaver displays Code Hints for the various XML tags as you type. Code Hints are shortcuts for typing an entire tag or tag property; as you begin to type a tag, Dreamweaver pops up a small window displaying any tags that match what you've typed so far. At that point, you can just select the correct tag, instead of having to type it all out. This feature is also available when working with HTML in Code view, and is described on page 395.

Inserting a Spry Data Set

Dreamweaver CS4 greatly simplifies the process of using Spry data sets. Not only can you now use basic HTML tables to hold your data, but an easy-to-follow wizard lets you create both a complete Spry data set *and* all the HTML needed to display the data using one of four canned layouts. (You can still create your own data set layouts the old fashioned [meaning time-consuming] way as described on page 545.)

To begin using a Spry data set, open a Web page you want to add Spry data to, and then click in the area of the page where you'd like to insert the data. Next, insert the Spry data set object from the Insert panel (Figure 12-14) or by choosing Insert → Spry → Spry Data Set. The new Spry Data Set Wizard opens. The process has three basic steps:

1. **Choose a data source.**

   The data source is the HTML or XML file containing your data (described on pages 520 and 522). You can specify a file on your computer, or even use an absolute URL pointing to a file on your Web server. (Due to security limitations of Web browsers, the data source file and the Web page that displays the Spry data must be located on the same server.) Using an absolute URL is handy when the data isn't in an actual file, but is generated by the server out of a database—for example, an RSS feed's XML data is generated on the fly.

   The exact process of choosing a data source differs depending on whether the data is in an HTML table or an XML file. The specifics for each file type are discussed next.

2. **Set data options.**

   In this step, you can choose various options such as how to sort the data. Again, since the exact options differ between HTML and XML data, you'll learn below about the specifics for each file type.

3. **Choose insert options.**

   This step is the same for both HTML and XML data files. Here's where you choose from four ready-to-use layouts. In other words, the wizard can insert all the necessary HTML and CSS required to display your data. These layout options are discussed on page 536. You can also tell Dreamweaver to just create the data set, leaving you free to manually apply your own design—page 545 has the full scoop.

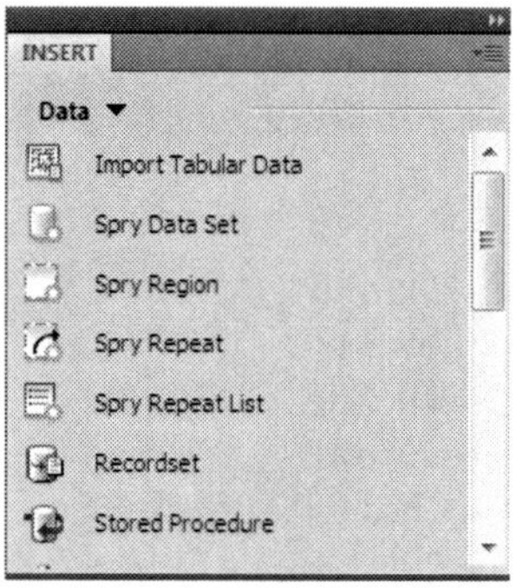

Figure 12-14:
You can find buttons for inserting Spry data set objects under the Insert panel's Data category. (Many of these buttons also hang out in the Spry category.)

Inserting HTML Data

The Spry Data Set window takes you step by step through the process of selecting an HTML data file, and then inserting it into your Web page (see Figure 12-15). This window's many choices can make it a little intimidating, but filling out the options correctly is a pretty simple process:

1. **From the Select Data Type menu, choose HTML.**
2. **In the Data Set Name field, type a name.**

   Dreamweaver supplies a generic name—like *ds1*—but change the name to something more descriptive. If you add multiple data sets to a page, distinguishing among *ds1*, *ds2*, *ds3* isn't as easy as among, say, *dsEvents*, *dsEmployees*, and *dsProducts*.

   However, do leave *ds* as a prefix to the name—*dsEvents*, for example. If you ever go into Code view, then this small step makes it easy for you to identify a reference to a Spry data set.

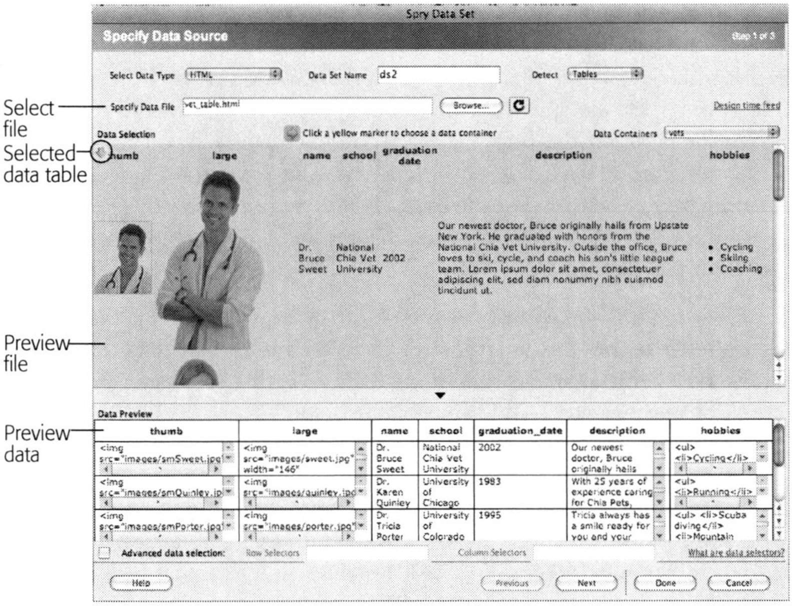

***Figure 12-15:** When you choose an HTML file for a Spry data source, Dreamweaver shows you a preview of the Web page file, and lets you specify which table on the page should be used. While you can specify a complete Web page, including a banner, footer, and logo (as well as the HTML table whose data you want), you're better off creating a plain, simple Web page that contains only the table and the data you want. This way, you let the Spry programming just load the data (and not any other unnecessary HTML) it needs. The result is a faster working Web page.*

3. **From the Detect menu, select Tables.**

   From this menu, you can actually select Divs, List, or Custom. As mentioned on page 522, you can store data inside any nested group of HTML tags, such as a group of <div> tags or even a nested unordered list (the Detect menu lets you specify the HTML tag you used in the data file). However, HTML tables really are the most straightforward method of storing data, so you're better off sticking with the tables option.

4. **Click the Browse button, and then locate and select an HTML file.**

   This file can be a separate file with a table, or even the same file you're working on if it has the data table you want to "Spry-ify." You can also type an absolute URL that points to an HTML file—like *http://www.chia-vet.com/vets/*. This method is handy if you're not pulling data from an actual HTML file, but instead a program on the Web server generates the HTML (for example, out of a database). In that case, you can't point to any real file on your computer; just use the URL of the server-side program that generates the data.

Note: If you specify a URL for the data file, then you can choose a temporary local file while you construct the data set. Click the "Design time feed" link (see Figure 12-15), and then, from your hard drive, select an HTML file. You might choose this option if you're not connected to the Internet and Dreamweaver can't communicate with your Web server, or if the programming that generates the data isn't ready. You need a file that duplicates exactly the HTML produced by the server for this method to work. You can also use the Design Time feed for XML files.

   Keep in mind a couple of caveats for working with absolute URLs, however. First, in order for the Spry data set to work, the Web site the file is located on must be the same site the Web page is on. In other words, if you add a Spry data set that specifies an XML file on *http://www.chiat-vet.com*, to a Web page that will ultimately reside on *http://www.cosmofarmer.com*, then the Spry data set doesn't work. In fact, a browser trying to view that Spry-enabled page displays a nasty error message.

   That error is part of a Web browser's built-in security system. When a Web page on one site tries to use JavaScript to access and display data from another site, the Web browser smells something fishy—"Is this Web page trying to pretend it's on another site?"—and spits out an error.

5. **Identify the data container.**

   The Spry data set tools let you specify any HTML page, including the page to which you're adding the Spry data (as long as it has a data table); you can also specify another fully-designed HTML page on your site that just happens to have a table on it. The page might even have a couple of different tables on it, so you need to tell Dreamweaver which table to use. As mentioned on page 521, when you build an HTML data table for use with Spry, you must apply an ID to the table. If you don't, then Dreamweaver tells you that the file has no valid data containers, and you can't pick a data table.

   You have two ways to identify a data container: The middle part of the Spry Data Set wizard window shows a preview of the HTML file containing the table (see Figure 12-15). A yellow arrow indicates a valid table (that is, any HTML table with an ID). Click the yellow arrow, and it turns green indicating that Dreamweaver will use the information from that table for the Spry data set. If you know the name of the ID you applied to the HTML table, then, in the top right of the window, from the Data Containers menu, you can also select it.

After selecting a table, in the bottom portion of the window, Dreamweaver shows a preview of the table's data (see Figure 12-15). If the table you select has a row of table headers at the top, then the text in that row's cells appears as the name at the top of each column of data. For example, in Figure 12-15 the text "thumb" appears in the Data Preview pane at the top of the first column, because the same text is inside a table header cell in the actual HTML file. (See the HTML preview in the middle of Figure 12-15.)

6. **Optionally specify any advanced data selection rules.**

   If you use HTML tables for data, then, at the bottom of the Specify Data Source window, you probably never need to turn on the "Advanced data selection" checkbox (see Figure 12-15). However, if you're using nested <div> or <ul> tags to store data, then you *have to* choose this option, and then specify which tags are rows and which are columns. For instance, in the nested div example on page 522, each <div> tag that acts as a single row has the class name *row* applied to it; likewise, divs which act as single "cells" of information have the class *column*. So, to use the nested div example, you would need to turn on the "Advanced data selection" box, and in the Row Selectors box, type *.row*, and in the Column Selectors box, type *.column*. (Dreamweaver uses the same syntax as CSS for specifying a class selector.)

   Or, even better, just use HTML tables and skip this entire step!

7. **Click the Next button.**

   The Set Data Options window appears (see Figure 12-16), showing a preview of the data, and providing tools for setting various options for how the data is displayed.

8. **Set column data types.**

   Click each column, and then, from the Type menu, choose an option. This step is necessary only if you want to sort the table before the data is displayed (see the next step) or if you want to give your visitors the ability to sort the table by column. You can choose one of four types of data:

   - **String.** Choose *string* for text. For example, if the column contains people's names, choose this option.
   - **Number.** Choose *number* if a column contains, uh, numbers, of course. For example, if the column displays how many units of a particular product you have in stock, then, from the Type menu, choose *number*. For a sortable table (like the kind described on page 537), a visitor can then click the units column, and view product listings in the order of how many units are in stock.

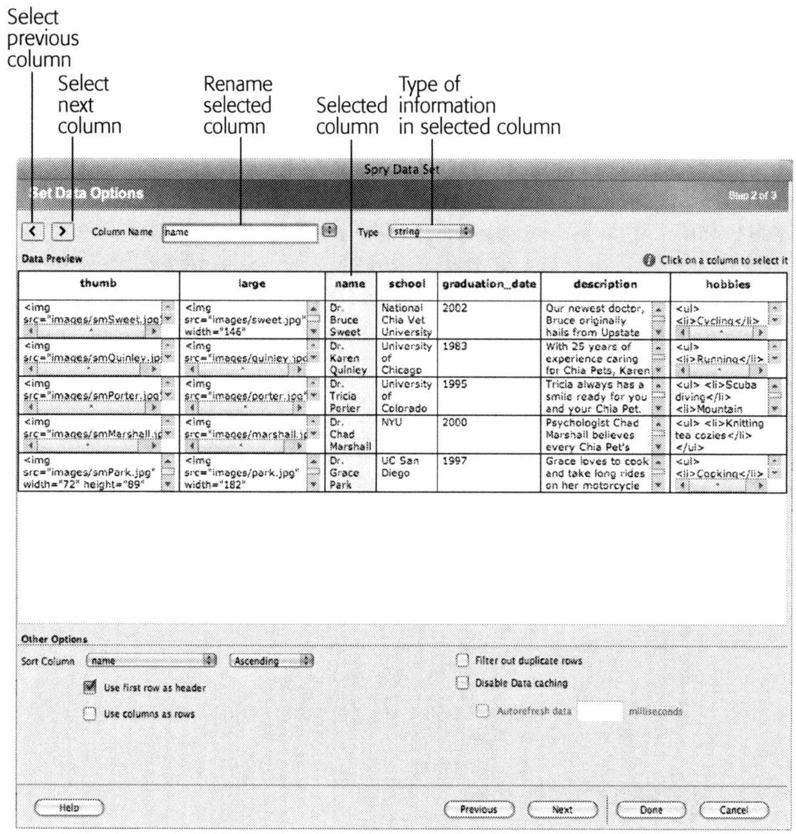

***Figure 12-16:** Use the Set Data Options window to assign data types to each column. You need to do this, however, only if you plan on either making your table sortable (page 537), or if you use the Sort Column option at the bottom of the window; in addition, you need to assign a type only to the columns that you want to sort, and the ones you want your visitors to be able to sort. (As you'll see on page 538, you don't have to make every column sortable for your visitors.)*

- **Date.** Use this option if the column holds dates in the form of 3/29/2009—in other words, the month, followed by a forward slash, the day, another forward slash, and the year. The month and day can be either one or two digits—03 and 3 both work—and the year can be either four or two digits—1999 and 99 both work. However, if the column just has years (such as 1977), then use the *number* option.

- **HTML.** Finally, if the column contains HTML markup (such as <img src="photo.jp">), then you can choose this option. You don't actually have to, though, because Dreamweaver strips out the HTML anyway if you choose the *string* option.

9. **Set additional options.**

   The Set Data Options window's bottom portion has several options that control how the data from the HTML file is displayed:

   - **Sort column.** If you want to sort the data before it's displayed on the page, then choose a column from this menu. For example, if you have an HTML file that includes a table listing employee names and information, you could choose the employee name column to make sure the employees are listed in alphabetical order. From the menu to the right, choose Ascending if you want the data to be sorted A–Z or 1–100; choose Descending to put the data in the opposite order: Z–A or 100–1

- **Use first row as header.** This box is automatically checked if the first row of the table contains table header (<th> tags). Make sure this box is not checked if the first row of table cells contains real data that needs to be displayed.
- **Use columns as rows.** If you've organized your table so each column contains a data on a single record, then turn on this checkbox. This type of configuration is common on pages that compare products. To get an easy-to-read, side-by-side comparison, each table row holds data for *different* records (for example, a row might display the prices of four different cellphones). If your table is set up like this, then turn on this checkbox to make sure the data for each record remains grouped together.
- **Filter out duplicate rows.** Put a check in this box only if the table has the same record with the identical data listed twice.
- **Disable Data caching.** Sometimes data needs to be as fresh as bread from the bakery. Stock prices, sports scores, and other time-sensitive data needs to be as recent as possible. Since Web browsers tend to download and store files in the browser cache (see page 666), when you load a Spry data set page, you may be looking at data that was downloaded a week earlier. Turn on this checkbox to force the Spry programming to download the HTML data file every time the Web page is downloaded. This is especially true if the data is actually coming from a frequently updated database.

  However, if you modify the HTML data table only every now and again, then keep this box unchecked. The Web page performs more quickly if the browser doesn't have to constantly download the HTML data file.
- **Autorefresh data.** This option is available only if you selected the "Disable Data caching" box. Put a check in this box if your data changes *really* frequently—as in every few seconds or so. With this option set, the Web browser re-downloads the data file after the amount of time specified in the milliseconds box. For example, if you type 1000 in the milliseconds box (see Figure 12-16), then the browser downloads the HTML data file every second. Normally, you use this option only when the HTML data is coming from a server program that's receiving constantly updated information.

10. **Click Next, and then select a method for inserting the Spry data.**

The Choose Insert Options screen gives you the same option for HTML and XML data files. Details on how to use it, start on page 536.

Inserting XML Data

The process for using an XML file with a Spry Data Set is similar to the HTML file method just described: Open the Web page to which you want to add Spry data, click in the region on the page where the data should go, and then choose Insert → Spry → Spry Data Set or use the Insert Panel to open the Spry Data Set wizard (Figure 12-17). Then follow these steps:

1. **From the Select Data Type menu, choose XML.**

2. **In the Data Set Name field, type a name.**

   As with HTML data sets (page 529), change the generic name Dreamweaver supplies—ds1, for example—to something that's more descriptive—like *dsEvents*.

3. **Click the Browse button, and then locate and select an XML file.**

   You can also type an absolute URL that points to an XML file—like *http://www.chia-vet.com/rss/*. This way is handy for dynamically generated XML files, such as an RSS feed on a blog. In that case, you don't have a real file you can point to on your computer; just use the URL of the server-side program that generates the data.

Note: If you specify a URL for the data file, the same security restrictions that apply to HTML data (described on page 530) apply to XML data: The URL to the XML file must come from the same domain as the final Web page on which you put the XML data. In addition, see the Note on page 530.

   Dreamweaver loads the XML schema—the structure of the XML file. This structure is pictured in the large "Row element" box. In Figure 12-17, a nested list of names indicates the different tags in the XML file. Each tag is represented by the < > icon. The topmost item (rss) is the root element (see page 525). Inside the root element, you find other nested tags.

   The XML file usually has at least one repeated element, which has a + symbol to the right of its < > icon. In Figure 12-17, the repeated element is named "item". (This XML file contains a list of items from an RSS feed.) Within a repeated element, you can have other elements as well, such as the *title, link, comments*, and *pubDate* tags pictured in this example. The @ symbol indicates an attribute of an element (like a tag's property). In this example, *isPermalink* is an attribute of the <guid> tag. (One example of this tag in the XML file might look like this: <guid isPermalink="false">http://www.sawmac.com/etc/2009/07/25/dreamweaverCS4.</guid>.)

4. **From the list of XML tags, select a Row element.**

   The Spry data set tools are intended to display multiple instances of similar data, such as a list of employee phone numbers, or a list of events. So your job is to tell Dreamweaver which XML tag indicates a repeating item. Basically, you just select an element that has a + symbol. In Figure 12-17, that's the *item* element.

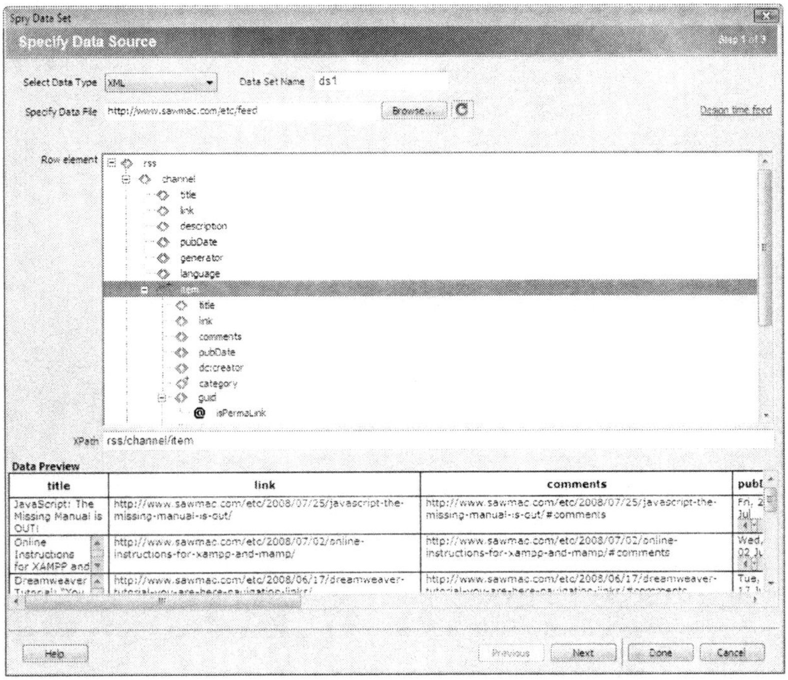

Figure 12-17: *Unless you're an XML pro, don't fill out the XPath field. Dreamweaver does that for you automatically when you identify a repeating row. XPath is a language used to identify particular elements or tags in an XML file. You use XPath to create what's called an "XPath expression," which is kind of like a trail of cookie crumbs that leads from one part of the document (frequently the beginning tag, or "root element") to the particular "node"–tag or tag property–you wish to select. In its most basic form, XPath works very much like the document window's Tag selector: It pinpoints a tag nested in any number of other tags. For instance, in this example, the XPath expression "rss/channel/item" means: Start at the rss element (that's the root element of this particular XML file), move to the channel element, and then find a nested tag named "item". Chapter 26 has more about XPaths.*

After you select a row element, Dreamweaver fills out the Spry Data Set window's XPath field (see Figure 12-17). A preview of the data appears in the lower portion of the window. Each tag that's nested inside the row element tag is treated like a column in a table. In Figure 12-17, the "item" element is like a table row; the "title", "link", "comment", and "pubDate" elements are each like the data you'd find in that row's columns.

5. **Click the Next button to move to the Set Data options screen** (see **Figure 12-18**).

   The options listed here are similar to those for when your data source is an HTML table: Assign data types to the columns of data, choose a sorting option, and then assign caching options for the XML file as described in steps 8 and 9 on page 531.

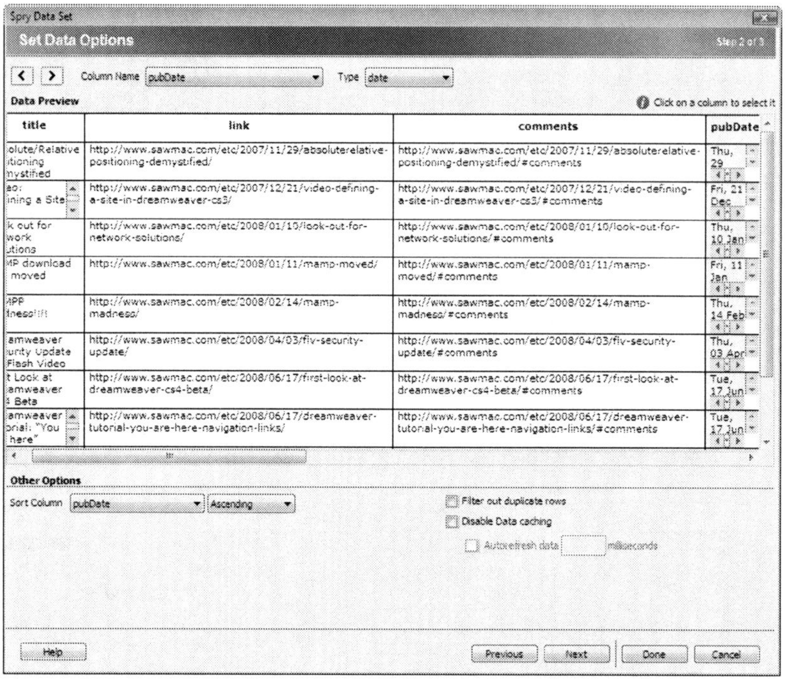

***Figure 12-18:** The options for XML data are simpler than those for HTML data files, but you can still choose whether to sort the data before displaying it and instruct the page to re-download the XML data at set intervals—perfect for up-to-the-minute sports scores.*

6. **Click Next, and then select a method for inserting the Spry data.**

   The Choose Insert Options screen provides the same option for HTML and XML data files, and is discussed next.

Choosing a Data Layout

The last step for the Spry Data Set wizard is selecting how you wish to insert the data into your Web page (see Figure 12-19). To make the process easier, Dreamweaver CS4 now includes four ready-to-use layouts which insert the necessary HTML tags, add the data, attach an external CSS file with some basic formatting, and essentially perform all the heavy lifting so that you just need to massage the CSS to match the look of your site. Each of these four options are covered in the following sections.

Alternatively, you can just add the data set programming as described in the previous sections, and then add the data to your page by hand, using a panel just for this purpose: the Bindings panel (you'll learn this method on page 548). That way was how you had to do things in Dreamweaver CS3; it provides the greatest amount of layout flexibility at the cost of more time, effort, and brain cells.

Note that once you've gone through the Spry Data Set wizard and selected one of the four layouts, you can't return to the wizard and change the layout, or alter any of the layout options you selected when you first inserted the layout onto the page.

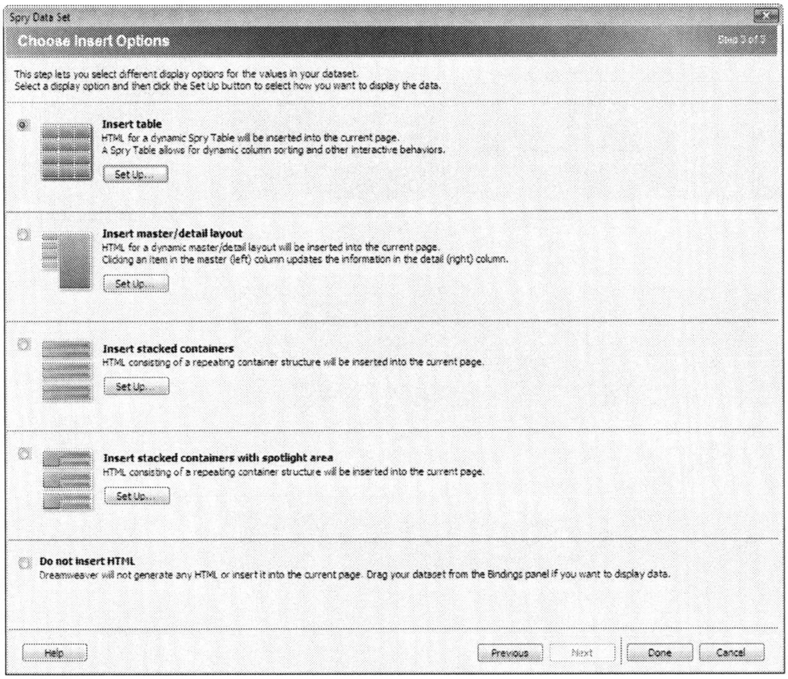

***Figure 12-19:** Dreamweaver CS4's new Spry Data Set wizard makes it easy to insert all the code necessary to create one of four different canned layouts for your data. If you don't like the four that come with Dreamweaver, choose the "Do not insert HTML" button, and then insert the data the way you'd like it.*

You can, however, delete any of the Spry layouts on the page (for example, the Spry table inserted by the wizard). You can then reinsert a different layout (or choose different layout options) by editing the Spry data set as described in the section "The Bindings Panel" on page 548.

Spry Table

The first choice in the Choose Insert Options window (see Figure 12-19) replaces the old Spry Table object from Dreamweaver CS3, and is the easiest way to present rows of information from an XML file in a quick and orderly fashion (see Figure 12-20). While the information might look like a regular HTML table, it's actually interactive, letting visitors click column headers to sort the data and mouse over rows to highlight them.

To add this kind of Spry table, click the "Insert table" button in the Choose Insert Options window (Figure 12-19) and then:

1. **Click the Set Up button.**

   The Insert Table window opens (see Figure 12-21).

2. **Remove and rearrange your table's columns.**

   Dreamweaver lists all the columns from the data set. Each column appears inside a single table cell. If you don't want one of the elements to appear in the

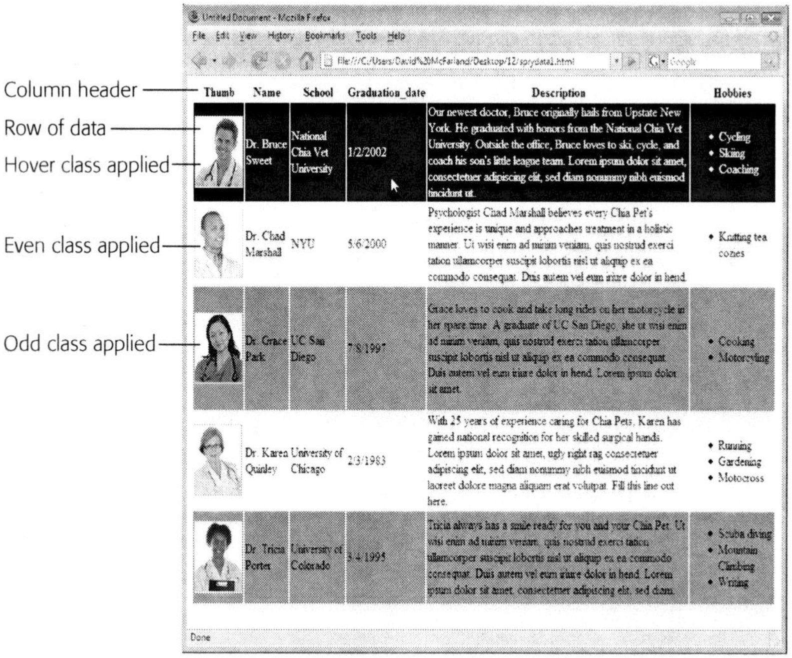

***Figure 12-20:** This is the basic, out-of-the-box look of a Spry Data Table. Dreamweaver adds a style sheet with a couple of CSS styles to identify every other row and highlight a row the visitor mouses over.*

table, in the Columns list, click its name, and then press the minus (–) button to remove it. (If you want to bring back a column you've deleted, press the + button, and then, in the window that appears, select a column name.)

Removing an element from the column list means only that Dreamweaver won't add a column to the table it's about to create. You're free to use the Bindings panel (discussed on page 548) after the table is inserted, to drag missing elements into the table.

You can also rearrange the columns so that they appear in a different order in the table. The name at the top of the list is the table's left-most column; the name at the bottom is the table column on the far right. To rearrange a column, click its name, and then press the up arrow button (to move its column of data to the left in the final table) or the down arrow button (to move the column to the right).

3. **Assign sortable columns.**

   One of a Spry table's coolest features is its ability to instantly re-sort table data simply by clicking a column's header. If someone visiting your Web page wishes to sort the information in a Spry table differently from the way you presented it, he just needs to click a different header to change the data's order.

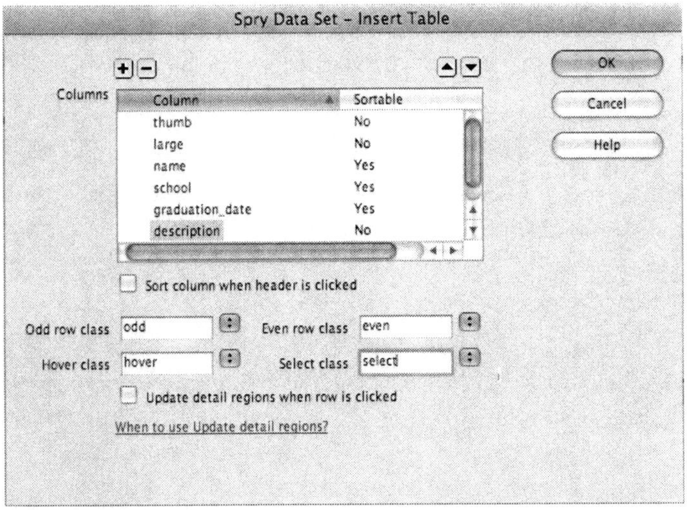

Figure 12-21: *It doesn't always make sense to make a column sortable. For example, it's not useful to sort a column full of descriptive paragraphs (who wants to see a list of items based on whether their description begins with "A", "The", or "This"?), nor would you want to sort a column based on the name of thumbnail images.*

Columns aren't normally sortable—the Insert Spry Table window defaults to listing all columns as non-sortable. To make a column sortable, in the Column list, select its name, and then turn on the "Sort column when header is clicked" checkbox (see Figure 12-21).

4. **Assign CSS classes to table rows.**

   A Spry table provides helpful visual feedback that makes it easier for you to read and interact with a table of data. You can more easily scan all the columns in a single, wide row of data if every other row has a distinct background color (see the Spry table in Figure 12-20). Dreamweaver lets you assign a class style to a table's odd rows and another class style to even rows. For a simple approach, create two classes, *.odd* and *.even*, each with different background colors. Then, in the Insert Spry Table window, select the appropriate class from the "Odd row class" menu and the "Even row class" menu.

   Similarly, you can assign classes to rows based on how someone interacts with a row. For example, you can make a row change color when someone mouses over any column in the row. Or you can change a row's color when it's clicked (a kind of "this row is now selected" indicator). The *hover* class controls the look of a row when the mouse passes over it, while the *select* class is applied by the Spry programming when a row is clicked. Both are useful for master/detail layouts, but since Dreamweaver has a simple tool for creating those types of layouts, you'll probably skip these options for a Spry table (unless you like the eye candy).

   If you haven't yet created any class styles for these rows, then just type in a class name (without the period). Even if you're not sure you want to change the look of the table's rows, assign classes to all four (odd, even, hover, and select) anyway.

Dreamweaver provides no way to return to the Insert Spry Table window, so if you later decide to add styles to the rows, then you have to go into Code view, and add them by hand using specific Spry syntax (see page 508). Save yourself this hardship by assigning the classes while you've got an easy-to-use dialog box.

5. **If you plan on including a detail region (discussed next), then turn on the "Update detail regions when row is clicked" checkbox.**

   This option makes sure that the Spry programming changes a detail region when a visitor clicks a row in the Spry table.

6. **Click OK, and then, in the Spry Data Set window, click the Done button.**

   Dreamweaver inserts a table onto the page. It's just an HTML table with a little extra Spry code. You can resize the table, and then adjust it just as you would a regular HTML table (see Chapter 7). The top row of the table contains a series of table headers (<th> tags) containing each column's name. The names are regular text, and you can change them to a more understandable label if you like.

   The second row of cells represents the data. Just one row is represented in Dreamweaver, but when you preview the page in a Web browser, a table row appears for each row of data in the HTML or XML file. Even better, the new Live View feature (page 553) lets you quickly preview a Spry table without leaving Dreamweaver. In Design view, each cell in this row has a Spry data placeholder (the element's name on a blue background) just as if you had dragged the element from the Bindings panel (page 548) into the table cell. You can select a format for the Spry data placeholder as if it were regular HTML (for example, apply a CSS style to it or make it bold).

Master/Detail Layout

One of the most exciting uses for Spry data is the so-called master/detail layout. From the Choose Insert Options window, when you select this option (Figure 12-19), you can create a page that provides a list of all rows in a data set (the *master* list) accompanied by a region of the page that displays more details from a single, selected row (detailed information for the selected item). For example, in Figure 12-22, clicking Dr. Chad Marshall's box on the left, fills the area on the right with detailed information about the good doctor.

To create a master/detail layout, in the Choose Insert Options screen, select the "Insert master/detail layout" button (Figure 12-19), and then:

1. **Click the Set Up button.**

   The Insert Master/Detail Layout window opens (see Figure 12-23).

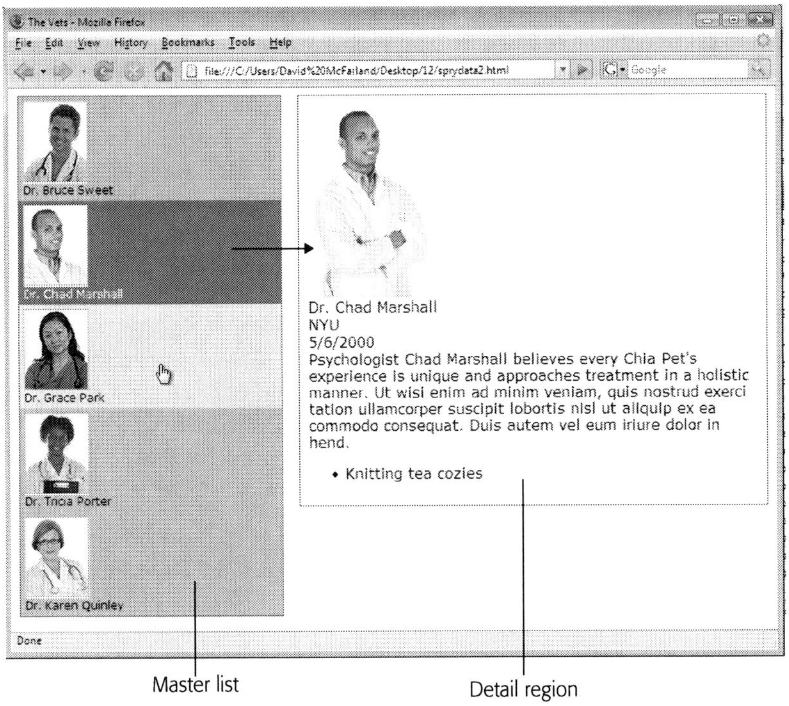

Figure 12-22: *The plain, out-of-the-box design Dreamweaver supplies for a Spry master/detail layout. You can edit the supplied CSS (thankfully) to match the look of your site.*

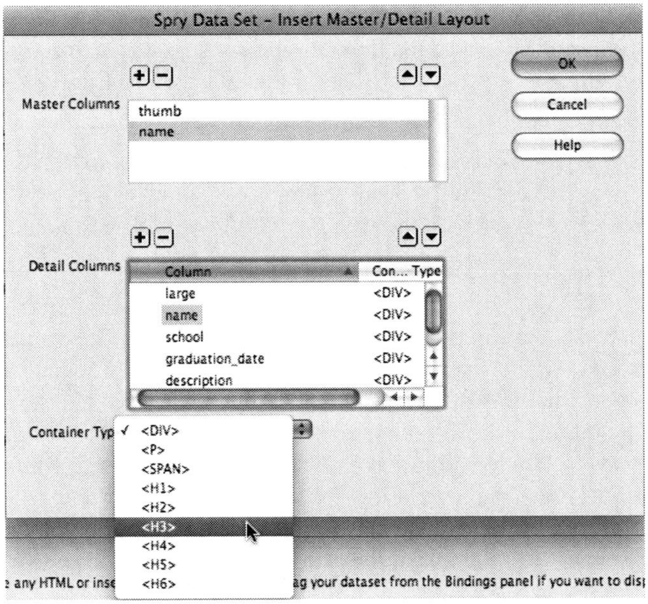

Figure 12-23: *When adding column data to the detail region, you can specify what type of HTML tag the data should be placed in. The normal setting is a <div> tag, which means that each data item appears in its own div. However, once you insert the master/detail layout you can move the Spry data elements around, change the tags they're in and formatting them with additional CSS styles.*

2. **Remove and rearrange the "master" columns.**

   The top portion of the window lets you specify which columns of data appear in the master list. For example, in Figure 12-22, the master columns are the ones containing the thumbnail image and the name of each doctor in the list on the left side of the page. To add a column of data, click the + button, and then, in the window that appears, select a column name. If you don't want one of the elements to appear in the table, in the Columns list, click its name, and then press the minus (–) button to remove it. You can also rearrange the columns by using the up and down arrows, so that they appear in a different order in the list.

3. **Remove and rearrange detail columns.**

   The procedure you use for adding, removing, and rearranging master columns works for detail columns as well. However, in addition to choosing which columns should appear in the detail region, you can also specify which HTML tag you want the data to be placed in. For example, you might want to use a heading (a <h2> tag, for example) to list the title of an article, or a <p> tag for a long description.

4. **Click OK, and then, in the Spry Data Set window, click the Done button.**

   Dreamweaver inserts all the HTML and Spry programming necessary to create the master/detail layout. In addition, Dreamweaver attaches an external style sheet—SpryMasterDetail.css—that provides basic formatting for the different elements on the page.

   Basically, the master list is created with a series of <div> tags stacked one on top of the other. Each item in the master list is in a div with the class *MasterColumn* applied to it. If you want to change the look of each of those boxes (for example, add a top borderline to separate each item in the list), then edit the descendent selector style *.MasterDetail .MasterColumn*.

   Likewise, the detail region is created by a single div with the class *DetailContainer*, while each piece of data in the detail region is contained within a different HTML tag (see step 3), each with the class *DetailColumn* applied to them.

Stacked Containers

The third option in the Choose Insert Options window (Figure 12-19) lets you create a series of stacked <div> tags with information from a Spry data set; Figure 12-24 shows you what this rather pedestrian layout looks like. This layout option really isn't that useful. It doesn't offer any of the interactivity of a Spry table or the master/detail layout. You could just as easily build the same design yourself without imposing all the download overhead—in the form of the data source and Spry files—on your visitors. However, you may want to use this layout if you can't get the data any other way—for example, if the data is spit out of a database from a Web server, and gets updated frequently.

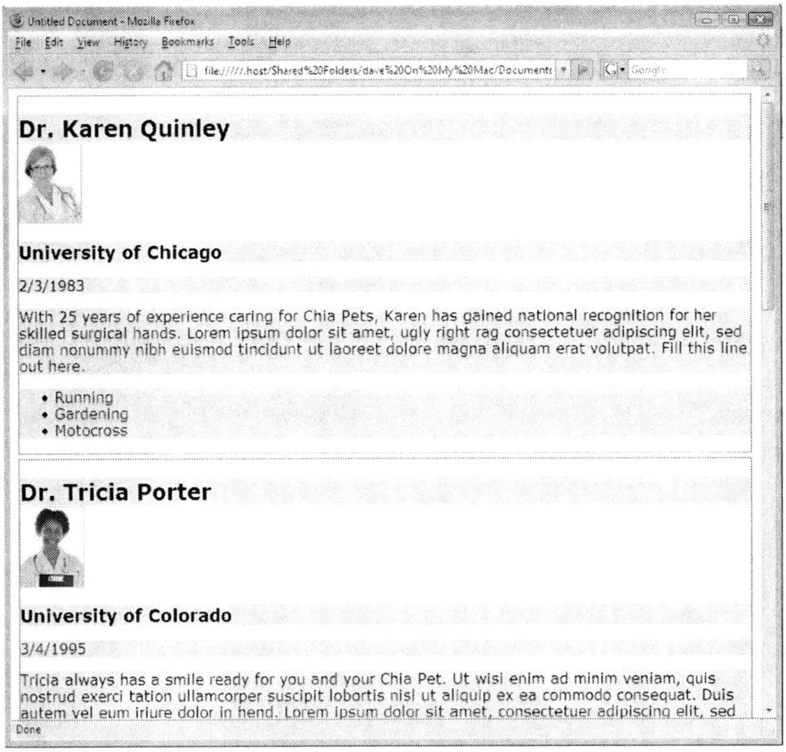

Figure 12-24: *The stacked container layout for Spry data doesn't look like much. Here's an example right out of the box with Dreamweaver's stock CSS applied to it. On top of these design shortcomings, the data isn't interactive as it is with a Spry table or master/detail layout. So if you're going for a design like this, you might want to think about just using plain old HTML and a little elbow grease.*

To create a stacked container layout, in the Choose Insert Options screen, select the "Insert stacked containers" button (Figure 12-19), and then:

1. **Click the Set Up button.**

   The Insert Stacked Containers window opens.

2. **Remove and rearrange columns.**

   As with the Spry table and master/detail layouts, you specify which columns you want to appear on the page. Also, as with step 3 (opoosite page) in the master/detail layouts, you can specify which HTML tag the data should be placed in. For example, you might want to use a heading (a <h2> tag, for example) to list the title of an article, or a <p> tag for a long description.

3. **Click OK, and then, in the Spry Data Set window, click the Done button.**

   Dreamweaver inserts all the HTML and Spry programming necessary to create the layout. In addition, Dreamweaver attaches an external style sheet—SpryStackedContainers.css—that provides basic formatting for the different elements on the page. The style sheet comes with just three styles, and they control the formatting for the overall div container (a class style named *.StackedContainers*), the div containing one row's worth of data (a descendent selector style named

.StackedContainers .RowContainer) and a class style applied to the tag wrapped around each column of information (a descendent selector style named *.Stacked-Containers .RowColumn*).

Stacked Containers with Spotlight Area

Since variety is the spice of life, Dreamweaver includes yet a fourth way to lay out your Spry data. The lovingly-named "stacked container with spotlight area" layout works much like the stacked container layout just discussed, with the addition of one area that floats to the left of the main data. As you can see in Figure 12-25, this particular design is best suited for when your data includes paths to image files, so that you can display a large image on the left (like an employee photograph or a product image), and detailed information on the right.

As with the stacked container option, you could just as easily build this layout without Spry, but, since you asked, you can create one of these babies: First select, in the Choose Insert Options screen, the "Insert stacked containers with spotlight area" button (Figure 12-19), and then:

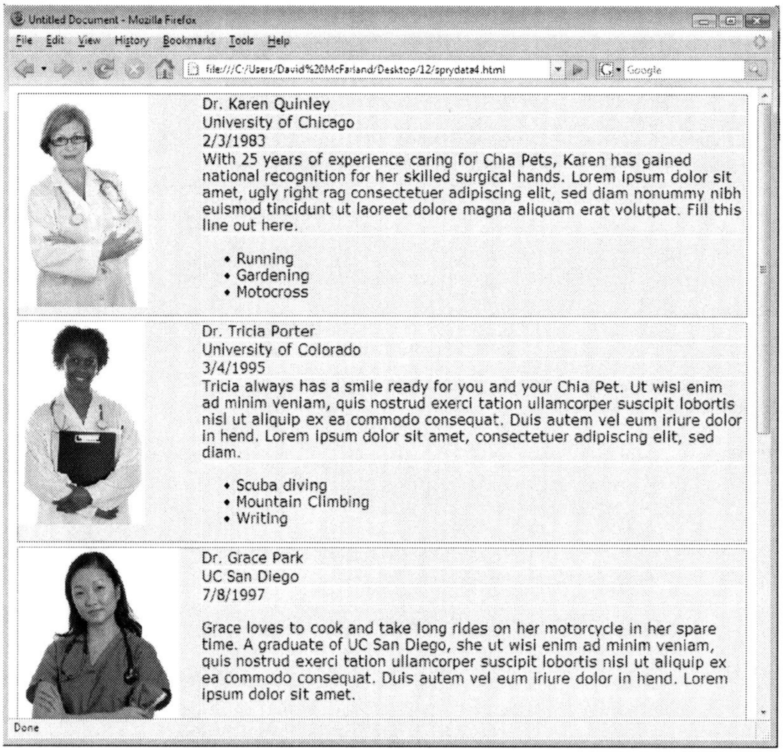

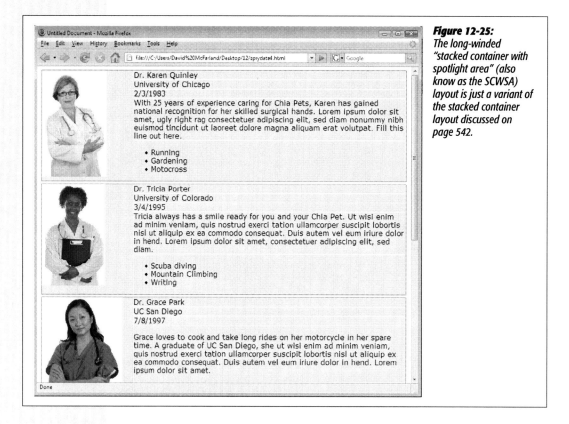

Figure 12-25: *The long-winded "stacked container with spotlight area" (also know as the SCWSA) layout is just a variant of the stacked container layout discussed on page 542.*

1. **Click the Set Up button.**

   The Insert Spotlight Area window opens. This window has two sections, one that lets you specify which columns should appear in the spotlight (left) side of the design and which should appear in the stacked column (right) side of the design.

2. **Remove, rearrange, and assign HTML tags to columns.**

   As with the Spry table and master/detail layouts, you specify which columns you want to appear on the page. Since the left hand area (the spotlight) is small and tall, a path to an image file is a good bet here, and you want only one or two columns of data to display here. The right-hand area, the stacked column region, should display the longer, more detailed data. Also, as with step 3 (page 542) in the master/detail layouts you can specify which HTML tag the data should be placed in. For example, you might want to use a heading (a <h2> tag, for example) to list the title of an article, or a <p> tag for a long description.

3. **Click OK, and then, in the Spry Data Set window, click the Done button.**

   Dreamweaver inserts all the HTML and Spry programming necessary to create the layout. In addition, Dreamweaver attaches an external style sheet—SprySpotlightColumn.css—that provides basic formatting for the different elements on the page.

Creating a Spry Region

If you're not a fan of the four prepackaged layouts offered by the Spry Data Set wizard, then you can manually create a layout using a combination of Spry data (the information drawn from the HTML table cells or an XML file) and HTML. Even if you do use one of the stock layouts, you can continue to refine the design, layout, and data using the do-it-yourself Spry tools offered from Insert panel's Data or Spry category. But first, you need to get the data loaded onto your Web page from the data file. To do that, just follow the steps presented for HTML files (page 529) or XML files (page 534); when you get to the last step (Figure 12-19), select the "Do not insert HTML" option, and then click the Done button. Dreamweaver adds all the necessary programming to access the data in the data file, but none of the HTML. You'll do that yourself in the following pages.

At this point you've told Dreamweaver which HTML or XML file to use to provide the data, and how to process it; none of the information from the file actually appears on the Web page until you add it. You can display multiple items from a data file using one of the Spry tools dedicated to this task: a Spry Repeat List, or a Spry Repeat Region. Each of these tools provides a different way to display multiple records from an HTML table or an XML file. If you want to display a list of employee names, for instance, you can present them in a simple bulleted list, or in a bunch of repeating <div> tags.

Note: The Spry Table object was removed in Dreamweaver CS4. The easiest way to create a sortable table now is to use the Spry Data wizard's Spry Table Layout option (page 537).

But before you use one of these tools, you first need to insert a Spry Region. A Spry Region is simply a tag that marks the beginning and end of a portion of a Web page dedicated to displaying Spry data. You then add the data from your data source—the HTML table or the XML data—inside the region you're about to create.

To insert a Spry Region:

1. **Click the Web page where you wish to insert the Spry Region.**

   This area might be inside a div used for laying out the Web page, such as inside a sidebar or on the main content region of a page. In addition, you can select any HTML that's already on the page, and either replace it with a Spry Region, or wrap the Spry Region around it as described in step 6.

2. **On the Insert panel's Data or Spry category, click the Spry Region button.**

   You can also choose Insert → Spry → Spry Region. Either way, the Insert Spry Region window opens (Figure 12-26).

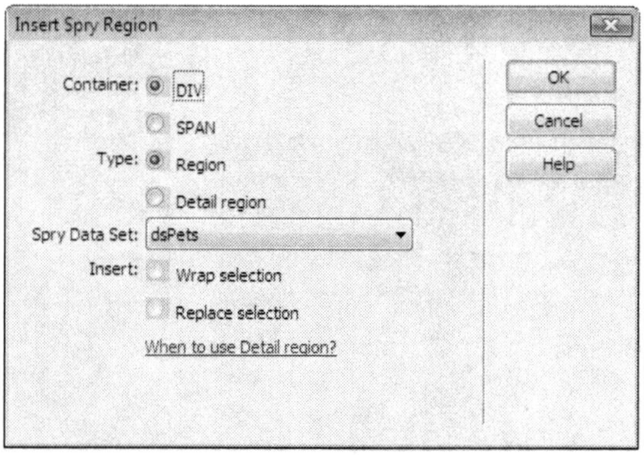

Figure 12-26: *A detail region lets you display more detailed information about individual records from the XML file. It works in conjunction with a Spry table as described on page 540.*

3. **Choose a type of container—div or span.**

   A Spry Region uses either a <div> tag or a <span> tag to hold Spry data content. Div is the most common selection, since a <div> tag can hold block level elements like tables, bulleted lists, and other divs. In other words, a <div> tag provides plenty of room to insert content.

4. **Choose the type of region.**

   To display multiple records from a data file (like a list of employee names, or a catalog of all of your company's products), choose the Region option.

The "Detail region" button is useful when you want to display extra information about one particular record in the data file (like a photo and extra statistics about a particular plant), just as in the master/detail layout provided by the Spry Data wizard. This detail information appears when the person viewing the Web page clicks a row in a Spry table or a row in a Spry repeating region; the detail region is then updated with whatever extra data you want to grab from the data file.

5. **From the Spry Data Set menu, choose a data set.**

   If you've added multiple data sets to a page, use this menu to specify the data set whose data you wish to insert into the region. Dreamweaver lets you insert data from more than one data set into the same Spry Region: from the Bindings panel (page 548), simply drag an element from the different data sets into the Spry Region.

6. **If you selected content on the page before inserting the Spry Region, then choose either "Wrap selection" or "Replace selection."**

   Choose "Wrap selection" if you want to include elements that are already on the page within a Spry Region. Say you want to add a bunch of information from a data file to various locations in the main content area of a page (like inside a div), but you already had some content in that div. Just click the div, click Ctrl+A (⌘-A) to select everything inside the div, insert a Spry Region, and then choose the "Wrap selection" button. Dreamweaver then "spry-ifies" that div.

   Be careful of the "Replace selection" option: It deletes anything that you've selected, and replaces it with an empty Spry Region.

7. **Click OK to insert the Spry Region.**

   Dreamweaver inserts the <div> (or <span> depending upon your choice in step 2) tag in the page, and then adds the proper code to mark it as a Spry Region. You can insert anything inside this region, even non-Spry stuff such as tables, other divs, images, and so on. In addition, you've now enabled that area so that it's ready to accept Spry data using the Bindings panel—or one of the Spry data tools discussed in the following pages.

Warning: Spry data sets add invalid HTML to a Web page. To make all the Spry data magic happen, Dreamweaver inserts invalid HTML attributes like *spry:repeat* and *spry:region* to <div> and <span> tags. The Web page no longer passes muster as proper HTML. The page still works in Web browsers, but it's harder for you to locate any invalid HTML that might actually affect how your page displays in a Web browser (see page 651 for more on validation). Note that the other Spry widgets discussed in this chapter, as well as Spry Effects, Spry Menu Bars, and Spry Validation widgets, do not insert invalid HTML. The Spry data set is the only culprit.

The Bindings Panel

The bindings panel lists the Spry data sets attached to the current Web page (see Figure 12-27). All the elements for a particular data set are also listed there. You can drag an element from the Bindings panel into any Spry Region on a page. In Design view, the element is just a placeholder for either a table cell (for an HTML data file) or XML element (for an XML data file)—its name surrounded by braces like this: {employee} (see Figure 12-28). Dreamweaver adds a blue background to the placeholder so you can easily identify it as a special Spry element. When the page is viewed in a Web browser, that placeholder is replaced with actual data from the HTML or XML file—like Frank Jones.

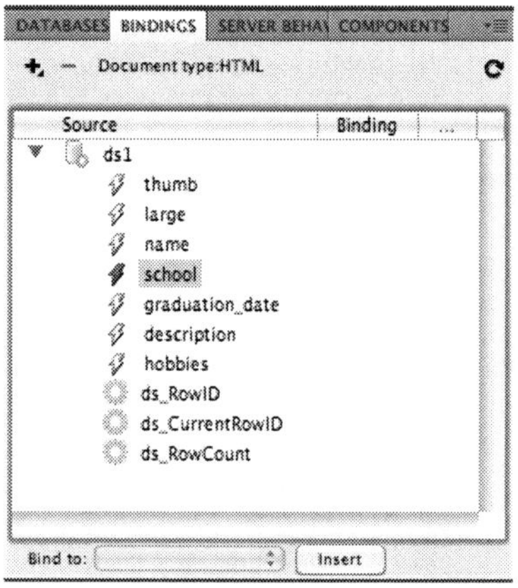

Figure 12-27:
The Bindings panel adds three elements to the bottom of each data set: ds_RowID, ds_CurrentRowID, *and* ds_RowCount. ds_RowCount *is the number of items in the data set. Each item in the data set has its own* ds_RowID *number, and the* fs *indicates the currently active row, which comes into play when using the Master/Detail layout described on page 540.*

You can select a data set element on a Web page, style it with CSS, include it inside other HTML (such as a paragraph or heading 1), and even move it around the page (as long as it remains inside a Spry Region). To delete the element, just select it, and then press Delete.

However, if you insert a Spry Region, and then immediately drag an element from the Bindings panel, you see only the first item from the data set—for example, the first employee listed, not a list of all employees. To see all the records in a data set, you must use one of Spry's repeating region tools, discussed next.

You also use the Bindings panel to edit a Spry data set. Just double-click the data set's name in the Bindings panel to return to the Spry Data Set window you encountered when you first added the data set (Figure 12-15 and Figure 12-17). You can rename the data set, and even choose a different file for the data source—however, don't do either of these things if you already added Spry data from this data set to your Web page; you'll end up with an ugly error message when the page is viewed. However, you can safely change the initial sort order of data and any of the other options mentioned in step 9 on page 532.

Figure 12-28: In Dreamweaver's Design view, a Spry Data Set page isn't much to look at. The data elements appear with a blue background, and their names are surrounded by braces. In this case, {name}, {thumb}, {large}, {school}, {graduation_date}, {hobbies}, and {description} represent data that will be replaced from the data file. This page shows a master/detail layout (see page 540). The left-hand block (the one with {name} and {thumb}) is actually a repeating region (see below) that will list a name and display a small picture for every record in the data file. The right-hand area is a detail region which will display detailed information about a single record.

Spry Repeating Region

Dreamweaver provides several methods for inserting multiple rows of information from a data set. The simplest, though least flexible, are the four stock layouts available from the Spry Data Set wizard. However, there are two do-it-yourself tools as well. The most flexible is the Spry Repeating Region. A Spry Repeating Region is a <div> or <span> tag in which you insert any combination of HTML and Spry Data (using the Bindings panel as described above). The tag and its contents are repeated once per row in the HTML table or the XML file (see Figure 12-29).

To create a repeating region:

1. **Click anywhere inside a Spry Region.**

   Anything related to Spry data sets must be inserted inside of a Spry Region. You can click inside an empty area, or even select HTML inside the Spry Region that you want to be included as part of the repeated region.

2. **On the Insert panel's Data or Spry category, click the Spry Repeat button (Figure 12-14).**

   Alternatively, choose Insert → Spry → Spry Repeat. The Insert Spry Repeat window opens (see Figure 12-30).

Figure 12-29:
A Spry Repeating Region provides a flexible method for displaying data from a data file. This particular page includes four records from an XML file. The repeating region is a <div> tag (outlined), containing three pieces of information from one XML record. However, this same design could just as easily be created using an HTML file with a table as the data source. In that case, each record would actually be a single table row, and each data element would be one cell in that row. For example, this design might be based on a table containing three columns: one for the plant name, one for a photo of the plant, and one for a description of the plant. The flexibility of the Spry Repeating Region means you can lay out this data any way you'd like.

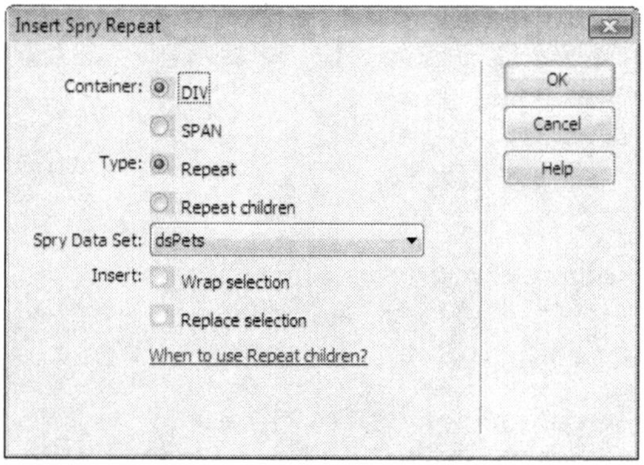

Figure 12-30:
A Spry Repeat region is the most flexible method of inserting multiple records from a data file. However, unlike the layouts available from the Spry Data Set wizard or a Spry Repeat List (discussed next), this tool doesn't insert data automatically; you need to decide which data elements to include, and drag them from the Bindings panel into the Repeat Region.

3. **Choose the type of container for the Repeating Region.**

   In most cases, select DIV, since this inserts a <div> tag in which you can put lots of other HTML elements, such as paragraphs and other divs. The SPAN option can come in handy when you wish to display a single row of data elements side by side.

4. **Select the "Repeat children" button.**

   In practice, you'll find no difference between the Repeat and "Repeat children" options. However, the "Repeat children" option is very useful for adding more complex logic to Spry data. (You may not be ready to jump into Code view and start hand-coding Spry data just yet, but this will at least leave you prepared for the day you do [see the box on page 508 for more on enhancing Dreamweaver's Spry offerings].)

5. **From the Spry Data Set menu, choose a data set.**

   If you're inserting data from multiple data files, then your page has several data sets. Choose the data set whose data you wish to display. Remember, this is a Repeating Region, so each record in the data file appears in its own div as part of the Repeating Region.

6. **If you selected content on the page before inserting the Spry Region, then choose either "Wrap selection" or "Replace selection".**

   Choose "Wrap selection" if you want to include elements that are already on the page within a Spry Region. Be careful of the "Replace selection" option: It deletes anything that you've selected, and replaces it with an empty Spry Region.

7. **Click OK to insert the Spry Region.**

   Dreamweaver inserts the <div> (or <span>, depending upon your choice in step 3) in the page, and then adds the proper code to mark it as a Spry Repeat Region.

At this point, you can add any HTML to the Repeat Region. In addition, to include data (which is, after all, the whole point), drag elements from the Bindings panel (page 548) from the data set into this region. Everything inside the region is repeated once for each row in the data file.

Spry Repeat Lists

If you simply want to list a bunch of repeating elements from an XML file, the Spry Repeat list gives you the simplest method. It inserts either a bulleted list, a numbered list, a form menu, or a definition list full of data (see Figure 12-32). Here's how:

1. **Click inside a Spry Region where you wish to insert a list of repeating elements.**

2. **On the Insert panel's Data category, click the Spry Repeat List button.**

   Alternatively, choose Insert → Spry → Spry Repeat List. The Insert Spry Repeat List window opens (see Figure 12-31).

3. **From the "Container tag" menu, choose the type of container you want for the Repeating Region.**

   Pick from any of the four list types: bulleted lists, numbered lists, form menus, or definition lists.

4. **Choose the data set whose data you wish to repeat.**

   Make your choice from the Spry Data Set menu.

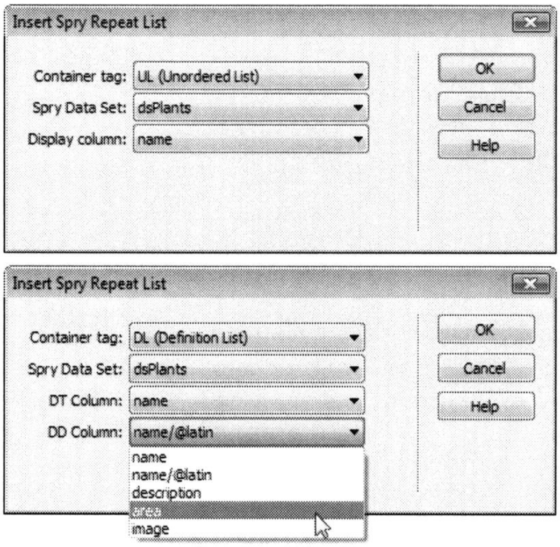

Figure 12-31:
A Spry Repeat List provides four ways of displaying repeating data from an HTML table or XML file.

5. **Choose the column or columns to display.**

   If you're going with a bulleted or numbered list, then you get to pick only one column (Figure 12-31, top). If you're using a form menu or a definition list, then you can pick two data elements (Figure 12-31, bottom). For a menu, you can select one element for the label (what the visitor sees when she views the menu) and another for the value (the information submitted to the Web server when the form is processed). Definition lists include one term (like a word in a glossary) represented by the DT tag, and one definition represented by the DD tag.

6. **Click OK to insert the list.**

   Dreamweaver inserts the list onto the page. In Design view, you don't actually see an entire list of items. You see only one bulleted or numbered item. You have to preview the page, or click the Live View button (see Figure 12-33) to see the final effect with all the items listed.

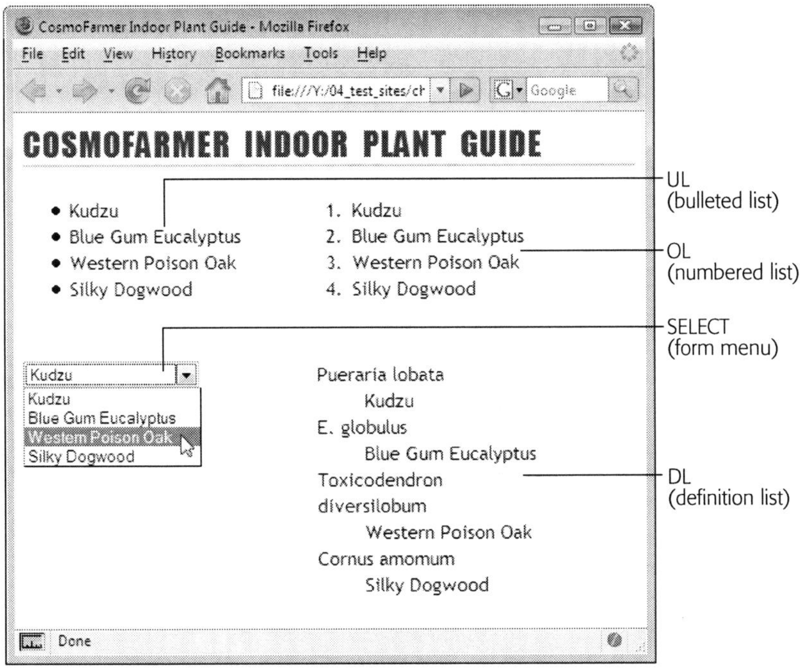

***Figure 12-32:** Dreamweaver provides different options for a Spry Repeat List, depending on the type of list you insert. For a numbered or bulleted list, you choose just one data element to display from the "Display column" menu (top); form menus and definition lists require two data elements (bottom). Once the list is inserted, you can use the Bindings panel to add more data elements to the list. If you want a bulleted list of employee names, but also want to include the employee's phone extension as part of the list item—"Bob Jones (x456)"—insert the Spry list using the employee name, and then, from the Bindings panel, drag the phone extension number.*

You can select and style a Spry Repeat List just like a regular chunk of HTML, and you can even move it (as long as it remains inside the Spry Region).

Live View

Dreamweaver CS4 now includes a built-in Web browser-like view of your Web pages. Called Live View, this new feature lets you view a Web page just as you would in a Web browser; you can interact with the page, view the effect of JavaScript and CSS, and basically preview your designs without leaving Dreamweaver. It's not perfect, however. Since the display is based on Apple's Web Kit (the engine behind the Safari Web browser), you don't really see how the page will look in the most common Web browsers: Internet Explorer 6 and 7. So it's not the best tool for previewing and troubleshooting CSS designs—you still need to test using real browsers for that.

However, Live View is perfect for working with Dreamweaver's Spry widgets, and in particular, seeing how Spry Data pages look and work. To activate Live View, in the document toolbar, click the Live View button (circled in Figure 12-33). Once activated, the page functions like a real Web page—you can interact with JavaScript objects like Spry widgets, see how CSS-based rollover effects (page 248) look, and so on.

You can't, however, continue to work on the Web page in Design view—you can't, for example, select or move HTML around the page. But if you're comfortable with hand coding, then you can choose Split view (see page 395) and get a side-by-side view of the raw HTML and the design's Live View. You can also edit HTML in Code view, click back to the live Design view, and immediately see how the changes you've made affect the final design.

In addition, you can edit CSS while in Live View. In fact, one of Live View's best uses is that you can tweak the CSS styles that control the formatting of dynamic elements like Spry navigation menus, Spry tabbed panels, and Spry data sets. You can use the CSS Styles panel (page 126) to open and edit styles, and immediately see how those changes will look in a Web browser. In fact, you can use the Current View of the CSS Styles panel (see page 315) to identify the styles that affect dynamically generated HTML (like Spry navigation menus, Spry Repeat Regions, and so on). Just turn on Live View, click inside an element on the page, and then see which CSS styles control it's formatting by using the CSS Styles panel. (See page 315 for complete directions on how to use the CSS styles panel's Current view for troubleshooting and editing styles.)

When you're done previewing a page in Live View, make sure you click the Live View button again to return to Dreamweaver's regular Design view.

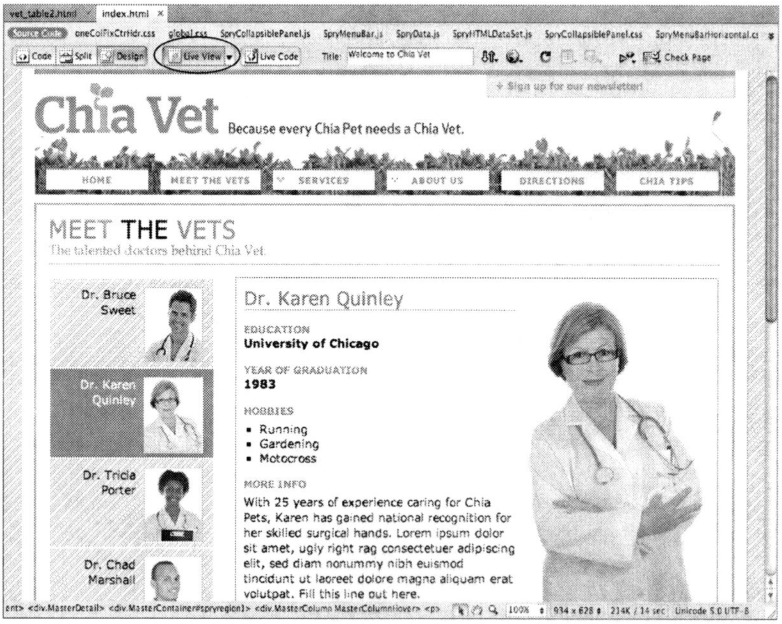

Figure 12-33: *Here's the Live View of a Spry master/detail layout. In fact, this is how the page pictured in Figure 12-28 appears in a Web browser, complete with all of the JavaScript magic that lets you see a complete design. You can even interact with the page within Dreamweaver's Live View–mouse over rows of data, click a record, and see the updated detail information for the selected row.*

CHAPTER

13

Dreamweaver Behaviors

Chapter 6 makes clear how easy it is to add mouse rollover effects using Dreamweaver's Rollover Image object. That and other interactive features rely on *scripts* (small programs) written in the JavaScript programming language. You've already seen some of the JavaScript-powered tools like the Spry menu, Spry form validation, and all of the cool Spry tricks discussed in the previous chapter.

You *could* create the same effects without Dreamweaver, but you'd need to take a few extra steps: buy a book on JavaScript; read it from cover to cover; learn about concepts like arrays, functions, and the Document Object Model; and spend weeks discovering the eccentric rules governing how different browsers interpret JavaScript code differently.

Like the new Spry tools, Dreamweaver's Behaviors let you add dynamic JavaScript programs to your Web pages without doing a lick of programming. Most Dreamweaver Behaviors have been around for a long while, but Dreamweaver CS3 added a new set of behaviors called Spry Effects that let you add dazzling visual touches like fading a photo in or out, highlighting a portion of a page with a flash of color, and shaking a <div> tag to catch a visitor's attention.

Note: What's that you say? You would like to read a book on JavaScript? Happy to oblige: *JavaScript: The Missing Manual*, written by yours truly.

Understanding Behaviors

Dreamweaver behaviors are prepackaged JavaScript programs that let you add interactivity to your Web pages with ease, even if you don't know the first thing about JavaScript. By adding behaviors, you can make your Web pages do things like:

- Make portions of a page appear and disappear.
- Open a new browser window to a specified size, with or without scroll bars, status bar, location bar, and other Web browser "chrome."
- Change the background color of any element on a page.
- Pop open an alert box with an important message for your site's visitors.

Behavior Elements

To use a behavior, you bring together three elements: an action, an event, and an HTML tag:

- The **action** is whatever the behavior is supposed to *do*—such as open a new browser window or hide an absolutely positioned div.
- The **event** is the *trigger* that causes the action to happen. It's usually something your visitor does, like clicking a Submit button on a form, moving the mouse over a link, or even simply loading a Web page into the browser.
- Finally, you apply the event and the action to an **HTML tag** to bring interactivity to your Web page.

An example helps. Let's say that, when a visitor clicks a link, instead of just sending them to another page, you want a new browser window to pop-up with that linked page inside it. In this case, the HTML tag is the link itself—an <a> tag; the *action* is opening another browser window and loading a Web page in it; and the *event* brings the two together so that, when your visitor clicks the link, his browser opens a new window and loads the new page. Voilà—interactivity!

More about Events

When people visit a Web page, they do more than just read it—they interact with it, in all sorts of different ways. You already know that when someone clicks a link, the browser reacts by loading a new Web page or jumping to a named anchor.

But visitors can also interact with a Web page in a variety of other ways. They may resize the browser window, move the mouse around the screen, make a selection from a pop-up menu, click an image, type inside a form field, or click a form's Reset button. Web browsers "listen to" and react to these triggering events with actions.

In JavaScript and Dreamweaver, the names of events always begin with the word "on," which essentially means "when." For example, the onLoad event refers to the moment when an object fully loads into the browser—like when a Web page, its images, and other linked files have downloaded. Events also include the various ways someone can interact with a particular HTML tag (element). For instance, when someone moves the mouse over a link or clicks a link, the corresponding events are called *onMouseOver* and *onClick*.

FREQUENTLY ASKED QUESTION

Behaviors and Added Code

I hear the JavaScript that Dreamweaver produces adds excessive lines of code, unnecessarily adding to a page's file size. Is this a reason not to use behaviors?

It's true that a seasoned JavaScript programmer could write a program that does what a Dreamweaver behavior does using less code.

However, Dreamweaver behaviors were created to work in as many browsers as possible without producing errors in older browsers. The hitch is that JavaScript doesn't work the same in all browsers or even in all versions of browsers.

Indeed, many browsers understand JavaScript so differently that programmers have resorted to elaborate workarounds, requiring a lot of experience, practice, and patience.

Accordingly, the engineers at Adobe used their vast understanding of JavaScript, HTML, and Web browsers to ensure that Dreamweaver behaviors work in as many browsers as possible. At times, this compatibility may lead to larger files with more lines of code, but it also assures that your Web pages will work for the broadest possible audience.

In addition, while the programming code for most behaviors is stored directly within the Web page itself, in the case of Spry Effects and the other Spry tools in Dreamweaver, the majority of the programming magic is stored in an external JavaScript file—that's a good thing too, because the file for Spry Effects alone is a whopping 67k in size. Fortunately, visitors to your site need only download the file once, thanks to their browsers' caches.

Note: Traditionally, JavaScript programmers have capitalized the second word in a JavaScript event—*onMouseOver*, for instance. Trouble is, XHTML doesn't allow uppercase letters for tags or their properties. So if you're creating XHTML pages, events should always be lowercased, like this: *onmouseover*. (Dreamweaver converts such terms to lowercase automatically as you create XHTML pages.)

Applying Behaviors

Dreamweaver makes adding behaviors as easy as selecting a tag and choosing an action from a drop-down menu in the Behaviors panel.

The Behaviors Panel

The Behaviors panel is your control center for Dreamweaver's behaviors (Figure 13-1). On it, you can see any behaviors that are applied to a tag, add more behaviors, and edit behaviors that you've already applied.

You can open the Behaviors panel in any of three ways:

- Choose Window → Behaviors.
- Press Shift+F4.
- If the Tag inspector is open, click the Behaviors tab.

Figure 13-1:
The Behaviors panel lists all of the behaviors applied to the currently selected HTML tag. Because the same event can trigger multiple actions, the actions are grouped by event. In this example, three actions are triggered by the onClick *event for an* <a> *tag (a hyperlink). When a visitor clicks this link, a page element will appear or fade (the Appear/Fade effect), a new browser window will open, and something on the page will either be hidden or shown (the Show-Hide Elements action). The order in which the behaviors occur is determined by their order in this panel. For example, when the link selected in this case is clicked, first, the Appear/Fade effect will happen, followed by the open browser window action, followed by the Show-Hide Elements action. To change the order use the up- and down-pointing arrows.*

To change the type of event, click the event name and then select another event from the pull-down menu. If all of the actions have different events, the order they appear in this panel is irrelevant, since the event determines when the action takes place, not their order in this panel.

Note: Dreamweaver includes two different types of behaviors, and it's important not to get them confused. This chapter describes JavaScript programs (that is, behaviors) that run in your audience's Web browsers–these are called "client-side" programs. The *server behaviors* listed in the Application panel group, on the other hand, run on the Web *server* to let you access information from a database. These are described in Part 6.

The currently selected tag is indicated at the top of the Behaviors panel; a list of all of the behaviors applied to that tag, if any, appears below. Each behavior is listed in two parts: Events and Actions, as described earlier.

The Behaviors panel offers two different views. Switch between them using the buttons at the upper left of the panel:

- **Show set events** (pictured in Figure 13-1) gets down to the specifics: which behaviors you've applied to the tag and which events trigger them. When you're working on a Web page, this view moves extraneous information out of your way.

GEM IN THE ROUGH

Link Events Without Loading a New Web Page

As you start to use behaviors, you'll quickly notice that there are an awful lot of useful events associated with links. Links can respond to interactions of all sorts, like moving the mouse over the link, moving it away from the link, or clicking the link.

Clicking a link, as you know, usually opens a different Web page. But there are times when you may want to use the *onClick* event to trigger an action without leaving the current Web page.

For instance, you may have a Web page with lots of unusual or technical words. It would be great to program the page so that when someone clicks an unfamiliar word, a dialog box displaying its definition pops up on the screen (using the Popup Message action, described on page 586). Unfortunately, a Web browser doesn't know when you click a word, since there's no event associated with regular text. However, browsers do know when you click a link and can respond to this action accordingly.

But in this case, you don't want to use a real link; that would force a new page to load. You just want to use a link's *onClick* event.

The secret is, instead of using a real URL or path for the link, you use a "dummy" link—a link that goes nowhere. This way, you can still take advantage of all of the great events links have to offer without adding links that take you away from the page.

There are two types of dummy (also called *null*) links. The first uses the pound symbol (#). Select the text or graphic you want to add the behavior to, and then, in the Property inspector, instead of adding a URL in the Link field, type in #. You can also create a dummy link by typing *javascript;* into the Link field. Be sure to include both the colon and semicolon. This dummy link doesn't load a new Web page, but provides a link to which you can apply behaviors.

Some browsers (including Internet Explorer for Windows) scroll to the top of the page when a visitor clicks a link that uses the # symbol, which could be disconcerting if you attached a behavior that appears far down a page. Because of this, the second method—typing *javascript;* in the Link field—is better.

- **Show all events** lists all of the events *available* to a particular tag. Someday, should you decide to *memorize* which events apply to which tags, you may no longer need this view.

Applying Behaviors, Step by Step

Open the Behaviors panel, and then proceed as follows:

1. **Select the object or tag you want to apply a behavior *to*.**

   You have to attach a behavior to an HTML tag, such as a link (indicated by the <a> tag) or the page's body (<body> tag). Take care, however: It's easy to accidentally apply a behavior to the wrong tag. Form elements, like checkboxes and text fields, are easy—just click one to select it. For other kinds of tags, consider using the Tag selector, as described on page 24, for more precision.

Tip: You can be sure which tag the behavior is applied to by looking at the Tag inspector's header (above the Behaviors tab). For example in Figure 13-1, "Tag <a>" indicates that the behaviors listed are applied to an <a>, or link, tag.

2. **In the Behaviors panel, add an action.**

   Click the + button in the Behaviors panel and, from the Add Action menu, select the action you wish to add (see Figure 13-2). You'll find a list of these behaviors and what they do beginning on page 567.

   Some actions are dimmed in the menu because your Web page doesn't have elements necessary for the behavior to work. For instance, if you haven't included a form in your Web page, then the Validate Form behavior is grayed out. Others are dimmed because they have to be applied to a particular page element. For example, Jump Menu is off limits until you've added a list/menu field to the page and selected it.

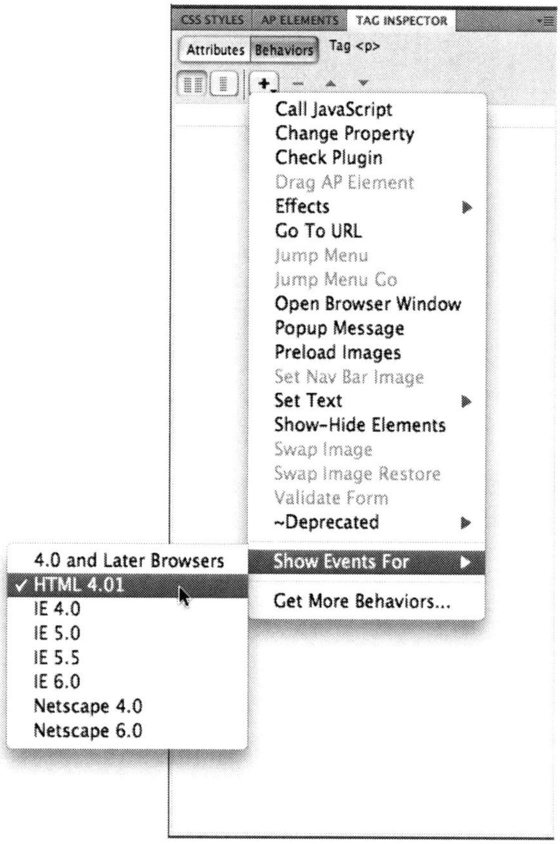

Figure 13-2:
Behaviors you can't currently apply are grayed out. Dreamweaver is trying to tell you that either a necessary object is missing from your page, or you've selected an object that can't have that behavior applied to it. For example, you can't apply the Show-Hide Elements behavior if the page doesn't have at least one tag with an ID applied to it.

3. **In the dialog box that opens, set options for the action.**

   Each action has properties that pertain specifically to it, and you set them to your liking in the dialog box that now appears. For instance, when you choose the Go To URL action, Dreamweaver asks what Web page you want to load. (Once again, the following pages describe each of these actions.)

4. **Click OK to apply the action.**

   At this point, Dreamweaver adds, to the underlying code of your page, the HTML and JavaScript required to make the behavior work. The behavior's action appears in the Behaviors panel.

   Unlike HTML objects, behaviors usually add code to two different places in a document. For behaviors, Dreamweaver usually adds JavaScript code to the head of the document *and* to the body of the page.

5. **Change the event, if desired.**

   When your newly created action shows up in the Behaviors panel, Dreamweaver displays—in the Events column of the panel—a default event (trigger) for the selected tag and action. For example, if you add an Open Browser Window behavior to a link, then Dreamweaver suggests the *onClick* event.

   However, this default event may not be the only event available. Links, for instance, can handle many different events. An action could begin when your visitor's cursor moves *over* the link (the *onMouseOver* event), *clicks* the link (the *onClick* event), and so on.

   To change the event for a particular behavior, click the event's name, and the Events pop-up menu appears (see Figure 13-1). Select the event you want from the list of available events for that particular tag. (See page 563 for a list of all available events in current versions of the most popular browsers.)

When you're done, you can leave the Behaviors panel open to add more behaviors to the tag, or to other tags. Select another tag, using the document window or Tag selector, and repeat steps 2 through 5.

Adding Multiple Behaviors

You're not limited to a single behavior per HTML tag. You can, and often will, apply several behaviors to the same tag. For instance, when a page loads—the onLoad event of the <body> tag—it can preload images to be used in rollover effects, open a small browser window displaying a (shudder) pop-up advertisement, *and* highlight a message on a page with a flash of color.

Nor are you limited to a single *event* per tag—you can add to a link any number of actions that are triggered by different events, such as *onMouseOver*, *onMouseOut*, and *onClick*. For example, if you set things up for a link as shown in Figure 13-1, when you click the selected link in the browser window, some element on the page fades into view, and then a new browser window opens, and finally a custom JavaScript program runs. The link also responds to other events, like moving the mouse over it—in this example, making an invisible element appear on the page.

Editing Behaviors

Once you've applied a behavior, you can edit it anytime. Double-click the behavior in the Behaviors panel to reopen the Settings dialog box, as described in step 3 of the previous instructions. Make any changes you like, and then click OK.

To remove a behavior from your Web page, select it in the Behaviors panel and click the minus sign (–) button or press Delete. (If you *accidentally* delete a behavior, just choose Edit → Undo Remove Behavior.)

A Quick Example

This brief example is designed to give you a clear overview of the behavior-creation process. In it, you'll use a behavior that makes an important message appear automatically when the Web page opens.

1. **Choose File → New to create a new untitled document.**

   You'll start with a new page.

2. **Choose File → Save and save the file to your computer.**

   It doesn't matter where you save the page, since you won't be including any graphics or linking to any pages.

   You start the process of adding a behavior by selecting a specific tag—in this case, the page's <body> tag.

3. **In the Tag selector in the lower-left corner of the document window, click <body>.**

   Once the tag is selected, you can apply one or more behaviors to it. But first, make sure the Behaviors panel is open. If you don't see it, choose Window → Behaviors or press Shift+F4.

4. **Click the + button on the Behaviors panel. From the Add Action menu, choose Popup Message (see Figure 13-2).**

   The Popup Message dialog box appears.

5. **In the message box, type *Visit our store for great gifts!* Then click OK.**

   Dreamweaver adds the required JavaScript code to the page. Notice that the Behaviors panel lists the *action* called Popup Message next to the *event* called *onLoad*. The *onLoad* event triggers an action *after* a page and everything on it—graphics and so on—have loaded.

   To see the page in action, just preview it in a Web browser by pressing the F12 (Option-F12) key. (You can also use the new Live View feature, described on page 553, to see this behavior in action without leaving Dreamweaver.)

Note: Dreamweaver behaviors rely on little JavaScript programs running inside the Web browser. If you've got Windows XP and have Service Pack 2 or later installed, or if you're running Windows Vista, whenever you preview a behavior-using page in Internet Explorer, you'll run into the same problems you encountered with rollover images in Chapter 6. For a solution, turn to the Tip on page 250.

Events

Events are at the heart of interactive Web pages. They trigger behaviors based on how site visitors interact with a Web page: clicking a link, mousing over an image, or simply loading a Web page. But not all events work with all tags. For example, the *onLoad* event only works with Web pages and images, not paragraphs, divs, or any other page element. The Event menu in the Behaviors panel can help: It only lists events available for the tag you're applying the behavior to.

Current browsers—Firefox, Safari, and Internet Explorer 6 and 7—support a wide range of events for many HTML tags. In most cases, you'll find that many of the events listed in the following pages work with all of the tags pictured in Figure 13-3. Many events work with other tags as well, such as headline, paragraph, or div tags. However, don't go crazy. Making an alert message appear when someone double-clicks a paragraph is more likely to win your site the Hard-to-use Web Site of the Month award than a loyal group of visitors.

To help you select a good combination of event and HTML tags, the following pages list and explain the most common and useful HTML tags and events.

Each entry shows you the name of the event as you'll see it listed in the Behaviors panel; a plain-English description of what that event really means; and the list of tags to which this event is most commonly applied. See Figure 13-3 for the visual representations of those HTML tags. For example, you'll find out that the <select> tag represents a pull-down menu.

Mouse Events

Web designers most often use mouse *movement* events to trigger actions (like the familiar rollover image). But mouse *clicks*—on checkboxes, radio buttons, and other clickable form elements—also qualify as mouse events. All current Web browsers can respond to many of these events when applied to most tags—for example, you can trigger a behavior when a visitor moves her mouse over a paragraph of text. Of course, just because you can doesn't mean you should. Most Web surfers aren't accustomed to having things happen when they click on a paragraph or mouse over a headline.

Note: In the following list, the many different types of *input* form elements are listed like this: <input type="button | checkbox | radio | reset | submit">. This notation simply means that *any* of these form elements–buttons, checkboxes, radio buttons, reset buttons, or submit buttons–react to the listed event. Also, when you see an <area> tag, it refers to the hotspots on an image map (see page 245).

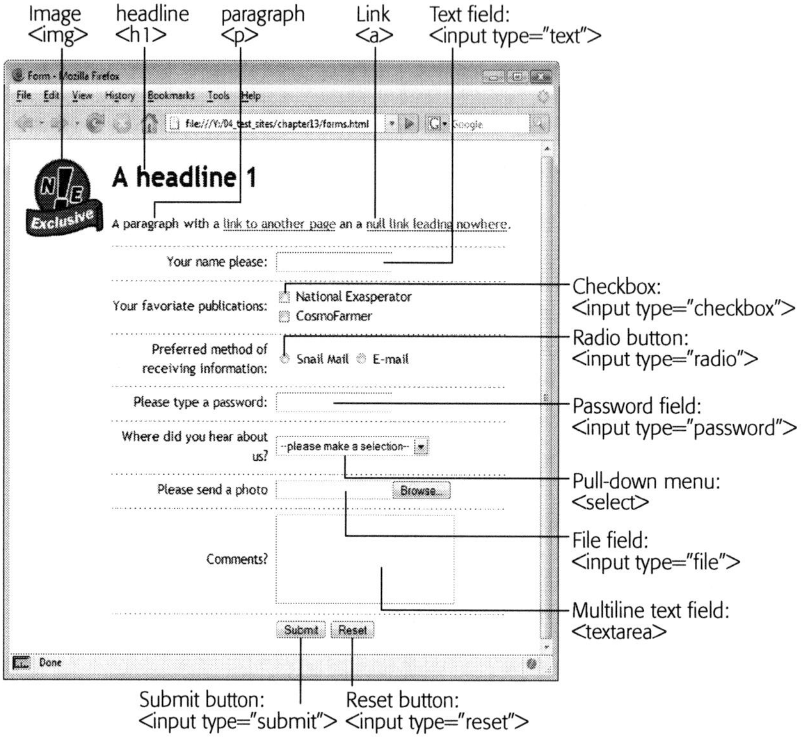

Figure 13-3: *This sample Web page illustrates HTML tags to which you can attach events. Not shown is the body of the Web page (the whole thing, in other words), whose tag is <body>, and the form portion of this page (see Chapter 11), whose tag is <form>. Whenever you set up a behavior, you should attach it to one of the tags shown here. Today's browsers add events to every tag, so you could add a behavior to a level 1 heading or a paragraph of text, but since those tags usually aren't associated with user interactions (like clicking or mousing over), visitors to your site probably won't interact with them.*

onMouseOver

Gets triggered: When the cursor moves over the tag.

Commonly used with these tags: <a>, <area>, <img>

onMouseout

Gets triggered: When the cursor moves off of the tag.

Commonly used with these tags: <a>, <area>, <img>

onMouseMove

Gets triggered: When the cursor moves anywhere inside the tag. Works similarly to *onMouseOver*, but *onMouseOver* is triggered only once—when the mouse first moves over the tag. *onMouseMove* is triggered continually, whenever the mouse moves over the tag. The possibilities for an annoying Web page are endless.

Commonly used with this tag: <body>

onClick

Gets triggered: When a visitor clicks the tag and releases the mouse button.

Commonly used with these tags: <a>, <area>, <input type="button | checkbox | radio | reset | submit">

FREQUENTLY ASKED QUESTION

The Vanishing Events List

I applied a behavior to a link, but the only event available is onMouseOver. *What happened to all the other events?*

To make sure your behavior works in as many browsers as possible, check out the Show Events For submenu (also shown in Figure 13-2). The earlier the browser version you choose here, the fewer events you'll see listed. On the other hand, choosing an earlier browser version ensures that your behavior will work for more of your visitors. If you're developing your site with modern, standards-compliant browsers in mind, you can safely pick the HTML 4.01 specification listed on the Show Events For submenu. Your site will then work with the vast majority of Web browsers in use today.

onDblClick

Gets triggered: When a visitor double-clicks the tag.

Commonly used with these tags: <a>, <area>, <input type="button | checkbox | radio | reset | submit">

onMouseDown

Gets triggered: When a visitor clicks the tag. The mouse button doesn't need to be released for this event to occur (note the contrast with *onClick*).

Commonly used with these tags: <a>, <img>, <input type="button | checkbox | radio | reset | submit">

onMouseUp

Gets triggered: When a visitor releases the mouse button while the cursor is over the tag. The effect is the same as the *onClick* event.

Commonly used with these tags: <a>, <img>, <input type="button | checkbox | radio | reset | submit">

Keyboard Events

Keyboard events respond to key presses and releases. Most Web designers use them in association with form elements that accept text, such as password or text fields. (See Chapter 11 for more on forms.)

onKeyPress

Gets triggered: When a visitor presses and releases a key while the tag is highlighted.

Commonly used with these tags: <textarea>, <input type="file | password | text">, <a>

onKeyDown

Gets triggered: When a visitor presses a key while the tag is highlighted. The key doesn't need to be released for this event to occur.

Commonly used with these tags: <textarea>, <input type="file | password | text">, <a>

onKeyUp

Gets triggered: When a visitor releases a key while the tag is highlighted.

Commonly used with these tags: <textarea>, <input type="file | password | text">, <a>

Body and Frameset Events

Several events relate to actions involving an entire Web page or frameset.

onLoad

Gets triggered: When a Web page *and* any embedded elements—like images and Flash and QuickTime movies—load. Frequently used for triggering actions when a visitor first loads the Web page; can also be used with an image tag to signal when that particular image has finished loading.

Commonly used with these tags:<body>, <frameset>, <image>

onUnload

Gets triggered: When the Web page is about to be replaced by a new Web page—for instance, just before the Web browser loads a new Web page after a visitor clicks a link.

Commonly used with these tags: <body>, <frameset>

onResize

Gets triggered: When a visitor resizes the Web browser window.

Commonly used with these tags: <body>, <frameset>

onError

Gets triggered: When an error occurs while a Web page or an image is loading.

Commonly used with these tags: <body>, <img>

Note: The *onFocus* and *onBlur* events described in the following section also apply to the <body> and <frameset> tags.

Selection and Highlighting Events

Some events occur when the visitor focuses on different parts of a Web page, selects text, or chooses from a menu.

onSelect

Gets triggered: When a visitor selects text in a form field.

Commonly used with these tags: <textarea>, <input type="text">

onChange

Gets triggered: When a visitor changes the text in a form field.

Commonly used with these tags: <textarea>, <input type="file | password | text">, <select>

onFocus

Gets triggered: When an element becomes the focus of the visitor's attention. For instance, clicking in a form text field or tabbing to it gives the text field focus. Also applies to a link when a visitor presses the tab key to reach the link (see the Note on page 183).

Commonly used with these tags: <a>, <body>, <frameset>, <textarea>, <input type="button | checkbox | file | password | radio | reset | submit | text">, <select>

onBlur

Gets triggered: When an element loses the focus. For instance, if the visitor is typing into a form text field and then clicks outside of that field, the onBlur event occurs. The Spry Validation tools (see page 454) can use this event to validate text fields. The onBlur event is also triggered when the visitor sends a window to the background. Suppose your visitor is reading your Web site in one window and has another open in the background. If he clicks the background window, the current page loses focus and an onBlur event occurs.

Commonly used with these tags: <body>, <frameset>, <textarea>, <input type="button | checkbox | file | password | radio | reset | submit | text">, <select>

Form Events

While each element of a form (radio button, text field, checkbox) can respond to a variety of events, the whole form—the entire collection of elements—can respond to only two events:

onSubmit

Gets triggered: When a visitor clicks the Submit button on a form.

Commonly used with this tag: <form>

onReset

Gets triggered: When a visitor clicks the Reset button on a form.

Commonly used with this tag: <form>

The Actions, One by One

While events get the ball rolling, actions are, yes, where the action is. Whether it's opening a 200 × 200 pixel browser window or slowly fading in a photograph, you'll find an action for almost every interactivity need.

In some cases, alas, the actions aren't very good. Dreamweaver CS4 is still saddled with behaviors that were created for (and haven't been updated since) Dreamweaver 4. Although Spry Effects—part of the much newer Spry Framework discussed in the last chapter—offer a fresh set of behaviors to play with, Adobe has only weeded out a few behaviors that aren't very useful or that don't work well. This book makes clear which are the rotten eggs to steer clear of.

Note: You'll find a menu named "~Deprecated" in the behaviors list on the Behaviors panel (see Figure 13-2). This menu includes eight behaviors that have been "deprecated"–meaning AVOID AT ALL COSTS. Those behaviors don't work well (or at all, in some cases). They still appear in the menu to help out the poor Web designers who added these behaviors to their sites using a previous version of Dreamweaver.

After you complete the steps required to set up an action as described on page 559, the new action appears in the Behaviors panel, and your Web page is ready to test. At that point, you can click the behavior's name in the Behaviors panel, where—by clicking the Events pop-up menu, as shown in Figure 13-1—you can change the event that triggers it.

Spry Effects

Spry Effects are a relatively new addition to Dreamweaver's arsenal of behaviors. They first appeared in Dreamweaver CS3 and are sophisticated visual effects that can do things like highlight elements on a page, make a photo fade in, or shake an entire sidebar of information like an earthquake. They're mostly eye candy and work well when you want to draw attention to an element on the page, or create a dramatic introduction. It's easy to abuse these fun effects, however: If every part of your page blinks, shrinks, shakes, and flashes, then most visitors will quickly grow tired of your page's nonstop action.

Spry Effects are part of Adobe's Spry Framework, which you read about in-depth in the previous chapter and have encountered when learning about the Spry menu bar and Spry validation widgets. To use a Spry Effect, you first have to apply an ID to the "target" element—the part of the page you wish to affect. Every effect, except Slide, can target any element (an <img> tag, for instance, for an image). (The Slide effect can target only a <div> tag.)

You're probably thinking of IDs as something you'd use when creating the kinds of CSS layouts discussed in Chapter 9. True, IDs are often associated with Cascading Style Sheets as a way of formatting a unique element on a page. However, IDs are also handy when you want to use JavaScript to add interactivity to a page. In fact, you can add IDs to HTML without ever creating any associated ID styles using CSS.

Recall that the HTML ID attribute marks a tag with a unique name. You can apply CSS to that tag using an ID style, but you can also control that tag using JavaScript. How you apply an ID to a tag differs depending on the tag, but here are the most common techniques:

- **Div tags.** Assign an ID to a div using the Property inspector. Just select the div tag, and then use the ID field in the Property inspector to give it a unique name. In addition, you can wrap any collection of HTML tags (or even a single element like an image) inside a <div> tag and apply an ID at the same time using the Insert Div Tag tool (see page 335).
- **Images.** When you select an image in the document window, you can type an ID for that image in the Property inspector's ID box (see Figure 6-7).
- **Forms.** Select the form and type an ID in the ID field on the left edge of the Property inspector (see Figure 11-3).
- **Form fields.** When you insert a form field, you can set the field's ID in the Input Tag Accessibility Options window (see Figure 11-5). You can later set or change a field's ID by selecting it and then using the ID field on the left edge of the Property inspector.
- **Other elements.** It's not as straightforward to add an ID to paragraphs, headlines, bulleted lists, and other tags. However, it's not that difficult if you use the Tag selector's contextual menu, as described in Figure 4-6.

After you've applied an ID to the target, you then add a Spry Effect behavior to a tag (usually some tag other than the target) which then triggers the effect. For example, you might want the site's banner image to emerge on the page after the Web page loads. The target is the banner image, but you apply the Spry Effect behavior to the <body> tag using the onLoad event (page 566). Any of the tag/event combinations discussed on page 563 will work.

Appear/Fade

To make an element fade in or out, use the Appear/Fade effect. To add a dramatic introduction to your site, you can fade in a large photograph on your site's home page after the page loads. Or you can have an "Important Announcement" box disappear when it's clicked.

To use this effect:

1. **Select the tag that you want to trigger the fade in or out.**

   For example, you could pick a link that triggers the effect, or you could use the <body> tag coupled with the onLoad event (page 566).

2. **From the Actions list on the Behavior panel, choose Effects → Appear/Fade.**

   The Appear/Fade window appears (see Figure 13-4).

3. **Select a target element from the first menu.**

   Here's where you specify which element on the page should appear or fade away. This menu lists every tag on the page that has an ID applied to it. In addition, you may see <current selection> listed, which refers to the tag you selected in step 1. You would choose this option if you wanted to apply the behavior to an absolutely positioned <div> tag that contains some kind of message—like "We'll be closed February 2nd to celebrate Ground Hog's Day!" When a site visitor clicks this <div>, it fades away.

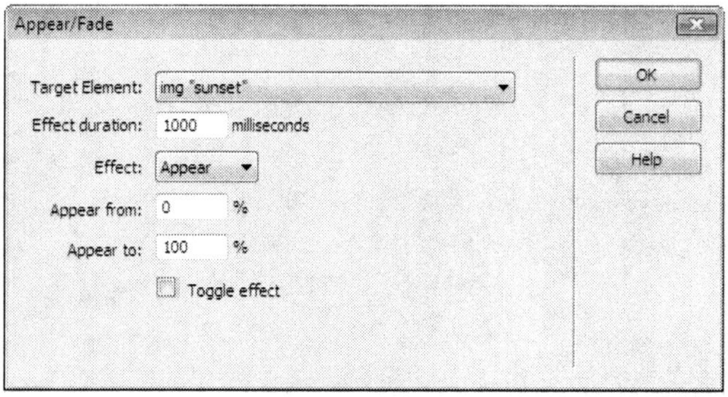

Figure 13-4:
Use the Appear/Fade effect to make an element fade from the page, or have a photograph fade into view on your site's home page.

4. **Type an amount in the "Effect duration" field.**

   This setting controls how long the fade in or out lasts. The duration is measured in milliseconds, so entering *1000* gets you 1 second. If you want the target element to appear or disappear immediately, enter *0*.

5. **Choose the type of effect—Fade or Appear—from the Effect menu.**

   If you want the target element to fade into view, it must be hidden to begin with. Otherwise the fade in effect looks really weird: first you see the photo, then you don't, and *then* it fades in. To make the element invisible, add (or edit) a style for the target element, and then use the CSS *visibility* property (page 362). Set the visibility property to *hidden*. Alternatively, you can use the CSS *display* property and set its value to *none*.

6. **Type a percentage amount in the "from" and "to" fields.**

   Depending on which type of effect you selected, you'll see either "Appear from" or "Fade from" and "Appear to" or "Fade to" in the Appear/Fade window. These two fields let you define the opacity of the target element. You'll commonly type *100* in the "Fade from" field and *0* in the "Fade to" field. Doing so causes an image to fade completely out of view. However, if you like ghostly apparitions, you can fade from 100% to 25%—this makes a solid element become transparent.

7. **Optionally, turn on the "Toggle effect" checkbox.**

   This option turns the trigger tag into a kind of light switch that lets you fade the element in and out. Say you added an absolutely positioned div to a page that contained helpful hints on getting the most out of your Web site. You could then add a link that said "Show/hide hints." Add the Appear/Fade effect, target the AP div, and turn on the Toggle effect checkbox. Now, when that link is clicked, the div would fade into view (if it were hidden) or fade out of view (if it were visible).

8. **Click OK to apply the behavior.**

   Once you've added the effect to a tag, you can edit or delete it just like any other behavior; see page 562 for details.

Blind

Don't worry: The Blind effect won't hurt your eyes. It's actually just a way of simulating a window blind—either being drawn over an element to hide it or opened to reveal an element. The basic concept and functionality is the same as the Appear/Fade effect: It lets you hide or reveal an element on a page. Follow the same basic steps as described in the previous section for Appear/Fade.

Note: Unlike the Appear/Fade effect, which can apply to *any* HTML tag with an ID, you can use the blind effect only to show or hide a <div> tag with an ID. So whatever content you wish to show or hide using this effect must be wrapped in a div. The Insert Div Tag tool described on page 335 makes this step easy.

Once you select Blind from the Effects menu in the Behaviors panel, you can control all of the basic elements of this effect from the Blind dialog box (Figure 13-5).

Use the Effect pull-down menu to choose which direction the blind moves. If you want to display a hidden element on the page, choose "Blind down". To make an element disappear, choose "Blind up." This behavior is totally counter-intuitive—you'd think raising a blind upward would actually reveal something. Fortunately, you can choose either direction for both revealing or hiding an element; the key is entering the correct percentage values in the "from" and "to" fields (Figure 13-5). If you wish to hide an already visible element, then type *100* in the "from" field and *0* in the "to" field.

To make an element appear, first you need to set its *visibility* property (page 362) to *hidden* (or its display property to *none* [page 146]) by creating a CSS style for the target element. Next, apply the Blind effect to a tag (for example, a link or the body tag), and then select the direction you wish the blind to move (up or down) from the Effect menu. Finally, type *0* in the "from" field and *100* in the "to" field. The "Toggle effect" checkbox reverses the effect when the event is triggered again. For example, a link clicked for the first time might reveal a photo on the page; when clicked again, the photo disappears.

Grow/Shrink

The Grow/Shrink effect is another "now you see it, now you don't" type of effect. With it, you can make a photo, a paragraph, or a div full of content grow from a tiny speck on the screen to its full size, or you can make an element disappear by

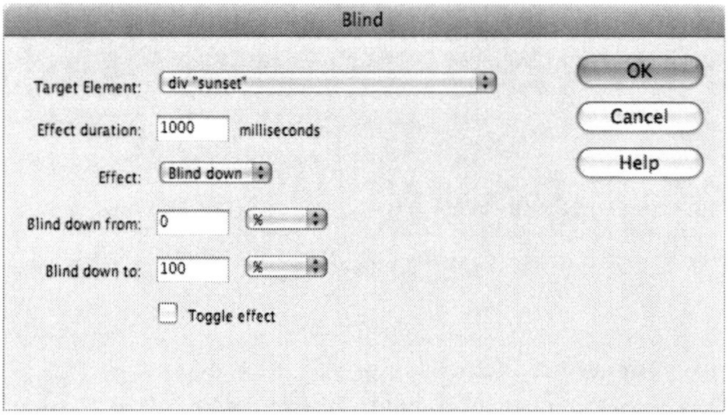

Figure 13-5: *The "from" and "to" fields can also hide or reveal just a portion of a div. If you set "Blind down from" to 0% and "Blind down to" to 50%, the effect will begin to reveal the contents of the div starting at the top and then stop at the halfway mark–in other words, the bottom half of the div will still be invisible.*

shrinking into nothingness. The basic setup is the same as with the Appear/Fade effect described on page 569. The Grow/Shrink window (Figure 13-6) lets you target any element with an ID; set a duration for the effect; and then select whether to make the element appear (grow) or disappear (shrink). You can also have an element grow or shrink to a percentage of its full size. However, unless you're targeting an image, displaying an element at less than its full size is usually unattractive and unreadable.

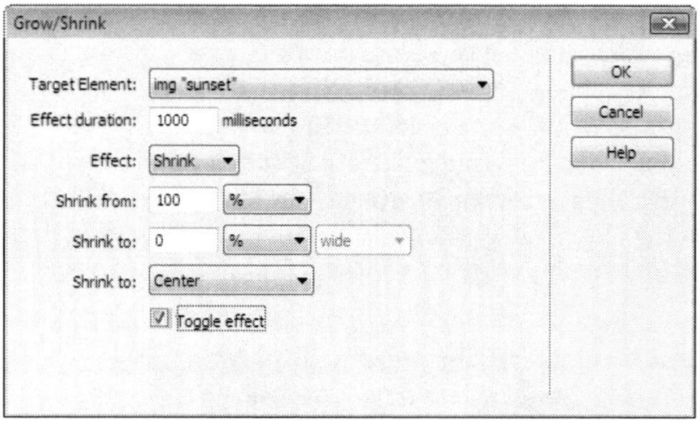

Figure 13-6: *The "Grow from" menu ("Shrink from" if the Shrink effect is selected) determines the point on the page from which the element begins its growth on its way to achieving its full size. You can either make the element grow from its center or from its top-left corner. The "center" option makes the element appear to come straight at you (or recede straight from you when Shrink is selected).*

Tip: You can combine multiple types of effects for a single target element. For example, you could make a photo fade into view when the page loads, shake when the mouse is moved over it, and even slide out of view when a link is clicked. However, be careful assigning multiple effects to the same event on the same element. If you add a Grow/Shrink effect and a Shake effect, both targeting the same element and using the same event, you won't see the element grow and *then* shake–you'll see it shake *as it grows*. In other words, the effects happen simultaneously (and usually bizarrely) instead of one after the other.

Highlight

Adding a background color to a paragraph, headline, or div is one way to create visual contrast and make an important piece of information stand out. A red box with white type will draw the eye quicker than a sea of black type on a white page. But if you really want to draw someone's attention, use the Highlight effect. Highlightling an element lets you add a flash of bright background color to it. For instance, on a form, you may have an important instruction for a particular form field ("Your password must be 10 characters long and not have !, # , or $ in it"). You could add the Highlight effect to the form field so that when a visitor clicks in the field, the instruction's background color quickly flashes, ensuring that the visitor sees the important information.

As with other Spry Effects, you use the Behaviors panel to apply the Highlight effect to some triggering element (like a form field you click in, or a link you mouse over). Then you set options in the Highlight window (see Figure 13-7): a target element (any tag with an ID), the duration of the effect, and background colors.

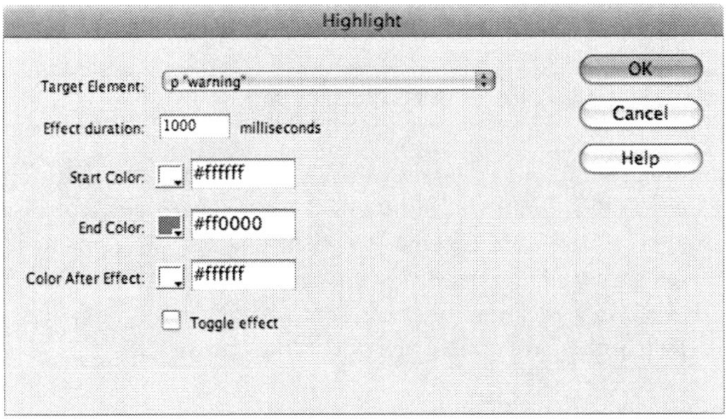

Figure 13-7: *The "Toggle effect" checkbox lets you fade in a background color with one action (for example, a click of a link) and then fade the background color out when the same event occurs again (the same link is clicked a second time, for instance). But in order for it to look good, make sure the Color After Effect is the same as the End Color. Otherwise, the second time the highlight is triggered (in other words, when the effect is toggled) the background won't fade smoothly back to the start color.*

Colors work like this: The Start Color is the background color of the target element when the effect begins. The background subsequently fades from the Start Color to the End Color (the duration of the fade is determined by the Effect duration setting). Finally, the End Color abruptly disappears and is replaced by the Color After Effect. The general settings suggested by Dreamweaver when you apply the effect aren't so good: white, red, white. Assuming the background color of your page is white, you don't get so much of a flash effect as a "fade-to-a-color-that-immediately-disappears" effect. The effect looks a lot better if the Start Color is set to some bright, attention grabbing, highlight color, and the End Color is set to match the current background color of the target element. Then the effect looks like a bright flash that gradually fades away.

However, instead of a flash, you may want an element's background to slowly fade to a different color and stay that color. In that case, set the Start Color to match the target element's current background color, and use the same color for both End Color and Color After Effect.

Shake

The Shake effect is like adding an earthquake to a Web page. The target element shakes violently left to right on the page for a second or so. And that's all there is to it. When you apply this behavior, you have just one option: which element on the page to shake. You can shake any element with an ID—a div or even just a paragraph. It's kind of a fun effect…once…and maybe just for kids.

Slide

The Slide effect is just like the Blind effect. But instead of a "blind" moving over an element to hide it, or moving off an element to reveal it, the element itself moves. Say you have a <div> tag that contains a gallery of photos. If you target that div with a "slide up" effect, then the images will all move upwards and disappear at the top edge of that div. Think of the <div> as a kind of window looking out onto the photos. When the photos move up past the window, you can't see them any longer.

Note: As with the Blind effect (page 571), you can slide only div tags that have IDs.

You can make an element slide up or slide down using the Effect menu in the Slide window (Figure 13-8). And, as with the Blind effect, to make an element disappear, type *100* in the "from" field and *0* in the "to" field. To make an element slide either up or down and *appear* on the page, first create a style for the element's ID; then apply the Slide behavior to some other element (a link or the body tag, for instance). Finally, type *0* in the "from" field and *100* in the "to" field.

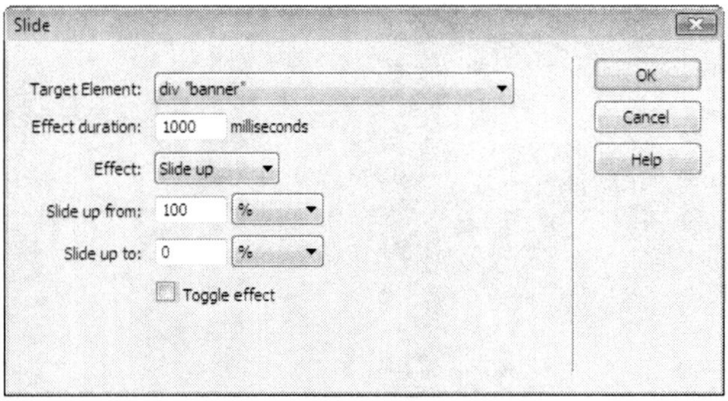

Figure 13-8: *The Slide effect works just like the Blind effect described on page 571. The one difference is that the element itself moves and disappears (as opposed to a blind being drawn over the element).*

Squish

The Squish effect offers no options other than selecting a target element. The effect only works to first hide an element (by shrinking it down until it disappears) and then revealing it by making it grow. It's exactly like the Grow/Shrink effect (page 571) with the "Toggle effect" box turned on and the Shrink effect selected (see Figure 13-6). Since it doesn't provide any controls for timing the effect, you're better off just sticking with the Grow/Shrink effect.

Navigation Actions

Many of Dreamweaver's actions are useful for adding creative navigational choices to your Web sites, giving you the opportunity to go beyond the simple click-and-load approach of a basic Web page.

Open Browser Window

No matter how carefully you design your Web page, chances are it won't look good in every size window. Depending on the resolution of your visitor's monitor and the dimensions of his browser window, your Web page may be forced to squeeze into a window that's 400 pixels wide, or it could be dwarfed by one that's 1200 pixels wide. Designing your Web pages so they look good at a variety of different window sizes is challenging.

Enter the Open Browser Window action (Figure 13-9). Using this behavior, you can instruct your visitor's browser to open a new window to whatever height and width *you* desire. In fact, you can even dictate what elements the browser window includes. Don't want the toolbar, location bar, or status bar visible? No problem; this action lets you include or exclude any such window chrome.

To open a new browser window, you start, as always, by selecting the tag to which you wish to attach the behavior. You can attach it to any of the tags discussed on page 563, but you'll usually want to add this action to a link with an *onClick* event, or to the <body> tag with the *onLoad* event.

Tip: Most browsers have pop-up blockers. This nifty feature prevents the browser from opening a new browser window unless the visitor initiates the request. In other words, you probably won't be able to open a new browser window when a page loads in the current window, but you can open a new browser window based on a visitor's action—like clicking a link.

Once you've selected this action's name from the + menu in the Behaviors panel, you'll see the dialog box shown in Figure 13-10. You have the following choices to make:

- **URL to display.** In this box, type the URL or path of the Web page, or click Browse and find the Web page on your computer (the latter option is a more foolproof method of ensuring functional links). If you're loading a Web page on somebody else's site, don't forget to type an *absolute* URL, beginning with *http://* (see page 162).

Figure 13-9: *You, too, can annoy your friends, neighbors, and Web site customers with these unruly pop-up windows. Just add the Open Browser Window action to the <body> tag of your document. Now, when that page loads, a new browser window opens with the ad, announcement, or picture you specify. To be even more annoying, use the onUnload event of the <body> tag to open a new browser window—with the same Web page—when your visitors try to exit the page. They won't be able to get to a different page, and may even encounter system crashes. Now that's annoying! Most current Web browsers, however, prevent these kinds of automatic window-opening tricks.*

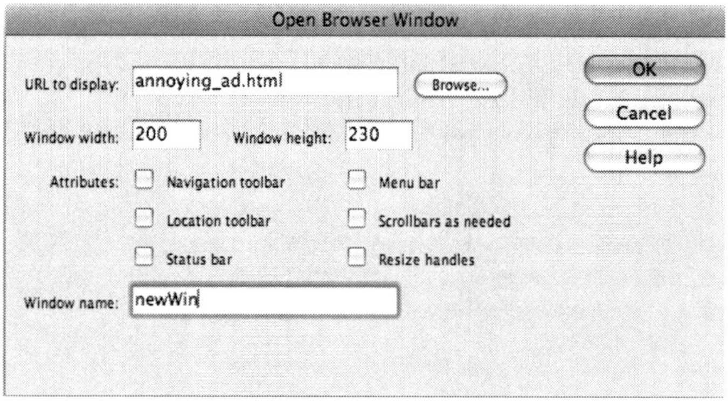

Figure 13-10: *Here, you can define the properties of the new window, including what Web page loads into it, its dimensions, and so on. If you leave the "Window width" and "Window height" properties blank, the new window is the same size as the window it opens from.*

- **Window width, Window height.** Next, type in the width and height of the new window. These values are measured in pixels; in most browsers, 100 × 100 pixels is the minimum size. Also, strange visual anomalies may result on your visitors' screens if the width and height you specify here are larger than the available space on their monitors.

- **Attributes.** Turn on the checkboxes for the window elements you want to include in the new window. Figure 13-11 shows the different pieces of a standard browser window.

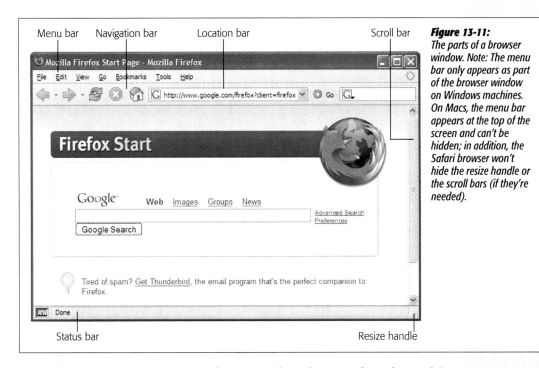

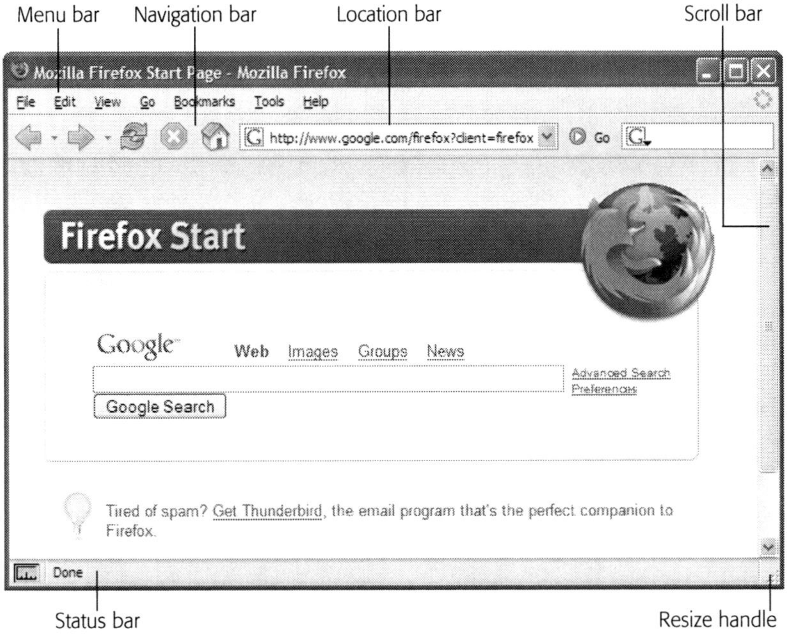

***Figure 13-11:** The parts of a browser window. Note: The menu bar only appears as part of the browser window on Windows machines. On Macs, the menu bar appears at the top of the screen and can't be hidden; in addition, the Safari browser won't hide the resize handle or the scroll bars (if they're needed).*

- **Window name.** Give the new window a name here (letters and numbers only). If you include spaces or other symbols, Dreamweaver displays an error message and lets you correct the mistake. This name won't actually appear on your Web page, but it's useful for targeting links or actions from the original window.

Once a new window is open, you can load other Web pages into it from the original page that opened the window; simply use the name of the new window as the link's target. For example, you could add this behavior to an "Open photo gallery" link that, when clicked, opens a small new window showcasing a photo. You could add links to the main page that then load additional photos into the small window.

If you use more than one Open Browser Window behavior on a single page, make sure to give each new window a unique name. If you don't, you may not get a new window for each Open Browser Window action.

When you click OK, your newly created behavior appears in the Actions list in the Behaviors panel.

Go to URL

The "Go to URL" action works just like a link, in that it loads a new Web page. However, while links work only when you click them, this action can load a page based on an event *other than* clicking. For instance, you may want to load a Web page when your visitor's cursor merely moves over an image, or when she turns on a particular radio button.

Once you've selected a tag and chosen this action's name from the + menu in the Behaviors panel, you can make these settings in the resulting dialog box:

- **Open in.** If you aren't using frames, only Main Window is listed here. But if you're working in a *frameset* file and have named each of your frames, they're listed in the "Open in" list box. Click the name of the frame where you want the new page to appear.
- **URL.** Fill in the URL of the page you wish to load. You can use any of the link-specifying tricks described on "Adding a Link: type in a path or an absolute URL starting with *http://*, or click the Browse button and then select a page from your site.

Jump Menu and Jump Menu Go

Conserving precious visual space on a Web page is a constant challenge for Web designers. Putting too many buttons, icons, and navigation controls on a page can clutter your presentation and muddle a page's meaning. As sites get larger, so do navigation bars, which can engulf a page in a long column of buttons.

The Spry menu bar is one solution to this problem, but you may not want to go through the lengthy process of creating and styling a Spry menu as described on page 184. A simpler way to add detailed navigation to a site without wasting pixels is to use Dreamweaver's Jump Menu behavior. A *jump menu* is a form pop-up menu that lets visitors navigate by choosing from a list of links.

The Jump Menu behavior is listed in the Behaviors panel, but for a simpler, happier life, don't insert it onto your page that way. Instead, use the Insert panel or Insert menu, like this:

1. **Click where you want the jump menu to appear on your Web page.**

   It could be in a table cell at the top of the page, or along the left edge, for example.

2. **Under the Forms category on the Insert panel, click the Jump Menu icon** (see **Figure 11-2). Or choose Insert → Form → Jump Menu.**

   If you use the Behaviors panel instead, you first have to add a form and insert a menu into it. The Insert Jump Menu object saves you those steps.

Note: Even though the jump menu uses a pop-up menu, which is a component of a *form*, you don't have to create a form first, as described in Chapter 11. Dreamweaver creates one automatically when you insert a jump menu.

The Insert Jump Menu dialog box opens, as shown in Figure 13-12.

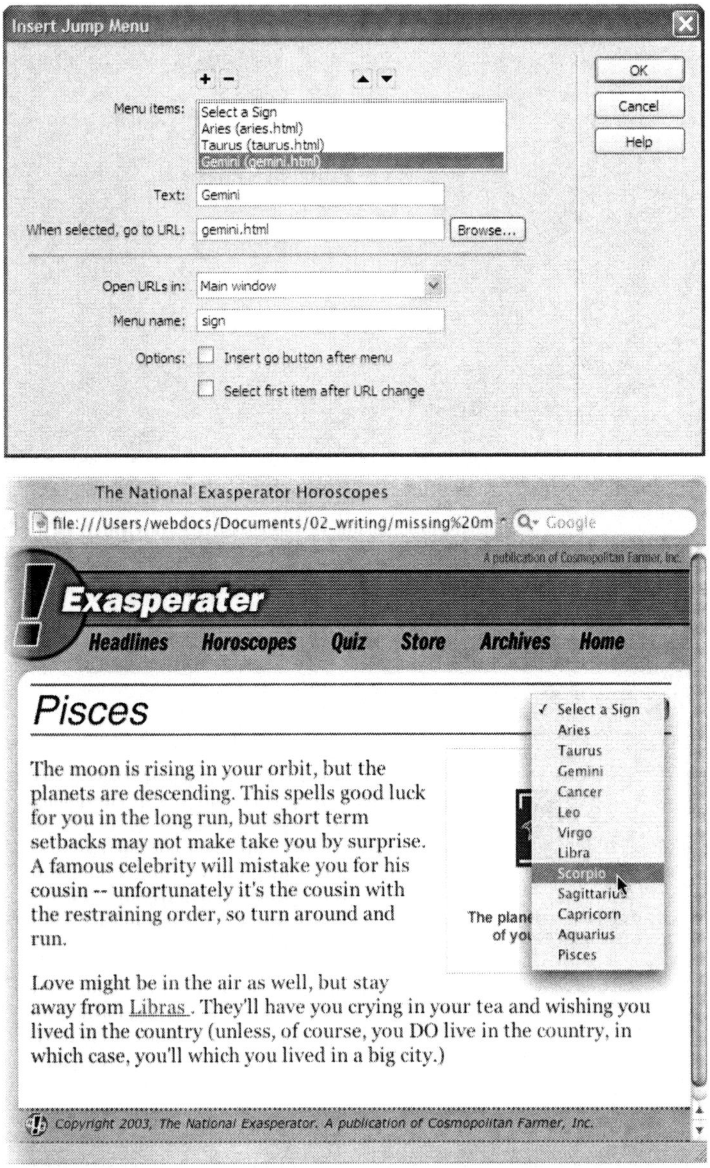

Figure 13-12:
Top: The Insert Jump Menu dialog box is set up so that the onChange *event of the* <select> *tag triggers the Jump Menu action. That is, the Jump Menu behavior works when your visitor selects an item other than the one currently listed.*

Bottom: Unless you turn on the "Insert go button after menu" checkbox, the first item of a jump menu should never be used as a link. Instead, use some descriptive text–such as "Select a Sign"–to let visitors know what the menu does. Then leave the URL blank in the Insert Jump Menu dialog box. When placed on a page, the resulting menu is very compact, but it can offer a long list of pages.

3. **Type an instructive label, like *Select a Destination*, in the Text box.**

   What you enter in the Text box sets the menu's default choice—the first item listed in the menu when the page loads. Dreamweaver provides two methods for triggering the jump-menu behavior: when the visitor makes a selection from the list—which is an *onChange* event, since the visitor changes the menu by selecting a new option—or when the visitor clicks an added Go menu button after making his selection. The second method requires extra effort from the visitor—making a selection *and* clicking a button. The first method, therefore, offers a better visitor experience. But it means that you can't include an actual link in the first item in the menu; after all, the behavior is triggered only when a visitor selects an item other than the one currently listed.

   If you intend to add a Go button, you can skip this step and jump down to step 6.

4. **Leave the "When selected, go to URL" box empty.**

   Since the first item in the list is just an instruction, you don't link it to any page.

5. **To add a link, click the + button.**

   This adds another item to the menu.

6. **Type the name of the link in the text field.**

   You're specifying the first link in your pop-up menu. The name doesn't have to match the page's title or anchor's name; it's whatever you want your menu to say to represent it. For instance, you can call a menu choice *Home* even if the title of your home page is "Welcome to XYZ Corp."

7. **Enter a URL for this link in the "When selected, go to URL" field.**

   Use any of the usual methods for specifying a link (see page 167).

8. **To add the next link in your pop-up menu, click the + button and repeat steps 6 and 7. Continue until you've added all of the links for this menu.**

   If you want to remove one of the links, select it from the "Menu items" list and then click the minus sign (–) button. You can also reorder the list by clicking one of the link names and then clicking the up and down arrow buttons.

9. **If you're using frames, use the "Open URLs in" pop-up menu to specify a frame in which the indicated Web page should appear.**

   Otherwise, the "Main window" option loads links into the entire browser window.

10. **In the "Menu name" box, give the menu a name.**

    This step is optional; you can also just accept the name Dreamweaver proposes. Since Dreamweaver uses this name only for the internal purposes of the JavaScript that drives this behavior, it doesn't appear anywhere on the page.

11. **If you want a Go button to appear beside your jump menu, turn on the "Insert go button after menu" checkbox.**

    You need to use this option only when the jump menu is in one frame and is loading pages into another, or when you want to make the first item in your jump menu a link instead of an instruction.

    When you include a Go button, Dreamweaver adds a small form button next to the menu, which your visitor can click to jump to whatever link is listed in the menu. But most of the time, your visitors won't get a chance to use this Go button. Whenever they make a selection from the menu, their browsers automatically jump to the new page without waiting for a click on the Go button.

    The Go button's handy, however, when there's no selection to make. For example, if the first item in the menu is a link, your visitors won't be able to select it; it's *already* selected when the page with the menu loads. In this case, a Go button is the only way to trigger the "jump."

12. **If you want to reset the menu after each jump (so that it once again shows the first menu command), turn on "Select first item after URL change."**

    Here's another option that's useful only when the jump menu is in one frame, loading pages into another frame. Resetting the menu so that it shows its default command makes it easy for your visitors to make another selection when ready.

13. **Click OK to apply the action and close the Jump Menu dialog box.**

    Your new pop-up menu appears on your Web page, and the new behavior appears in the Actions list in the Behaviors panel.

Note: To edit a jump menu, click the menu in your document and then, in the Behaviors panel, double-click the Jump Menu action in the Actions list. The settings dialog box reappears. At this point, you can change any of the options described in the previous steps, except you can't add a Go button to a jump menu that didn't have one to begin with. Click OK when you're finished.

The Jump Menu Go action (available on the Behaviors panel) is useful only if you didn't add a Go button in step 11. In this case, if there's a jump menu on the page and you wish to add a Go button to it, click next to the menu, add a form button, and then attach this behavior to it. (For more on working with forms, see Chapter 11.)

Check Plugin

The Check Plugin behavior isn't a navigation tool per se, but it helps you guide visitors to the right page if their Web browser is missing software it needs to view your latest Flash animation, QuickTime movie, or Shockwave game. All these multimedia goodies can add a lot of excitement to any Web site. Unfortunately, they don't work unless your visitors have downloaded and installed the corresponding browser plug-ins. In reality, this action doesn't work with Internet Explorer—the most popular Web browser—except in the case of Flash and Shockwave. That's because Internet Explorer doesn't have an easy way to determine which plug-ins are installed. With Flash and Shockwave, however, Dreamweaver adds some additional code in VBScript, a language understood by Internet Explorer.

However, Dreamweaver CS4 has added a very useful tool for checking whether a visitor has the Flash plugin installed...best of all, you don't need to do anything to automatically add this useful feature. As described on page 603, when you insert a Flash movie, Dreamweaver CS4 adds code that not only checks whether the visitor has the Flash plugin, but can even verify that he has the correct *version* of the plug-in. If the visitor is missing the appropriate Flash plug-in, the page will display a message letting him know and provide a quick and easy way to download and install the plug-in.

Image Actions

Images make Web pages stand out. But adding Dreamweaver behaviors can make those same images come to life.

Preload Images

It takes time for images to load over the Internet. A 64 KB image, for instance, takes about 1 second to download over a DSL modem. Add 10 images this size to a page, and it can take a while to actually see the darn Web page. However, once a Web browser loads an image, it stores the image in its *cache*, as described on page 666, so that it loads extremely quickly if a page requires the same graphic again. The Preload Images action takes advantage of this fact by downloading images and storing them in the browser's cache, *even before* they're actually needed.

Preloading is especially important when using mouse rollover effects on a Web page. When a visitor moves the mouse over a particular button, it may, for example, appear to light up. If you couldn't preload the image, then the light-up graphic wouldn't even begin to download until the cursor rolled over the button. The resulting delay would make your button feel less like a rollover than a layover.

If you use the Insert Rollover Image command (see page 248), you won't need to apply this action by hand, since Dreamweaver adds it automatically. But there are exceptions, such as when you use the CSS *background* property (page 231) to add an image to the hover state of a link (see page 181). In this case, a new background image appears when the link is moused over; however, a Web browser only loads that image when the hover state is triggered, not before.

To add the Preload Images action, select the tag you want to attach the behavior to. You'll usually use the <body> tag with an *onLoad* event.

If you've added rollover images to your page, this behavior may already be in the <body> of the page. In this case, just select the body tag (click <body> in the Tag selector, for example) and then double-click the Preload Images action that's already listed in the Behaviors panel. If not, just choose this action's name from the + menu in the Behaviors panel. Either way, you're now offered the Preload Images dialog box.

Click the Browse button and navigate to the graphics file that you wish to preload, or type in the path or (if the graphic is on the Web already) the absolute URL of the graphic. Dreamweaver adds the image to the Preload Images list. If you want to preload another image, click the + button and repeat the previous step. Continue until you've added all the images you want to preload.

You can remove an image from the list by selecting it and then clicking the minus sign (–) button. (Be careful not to delete any of the images that are required for a rollover effect you've already created—the Undo command doesn't work here.)

When you click OK, you return to your document and your new action appears in the Behaviors panel. Here you can edit it, if you like, by changing the event that triggers it. But unless you're trying to achieve some special effect, you'll usually use the *onLoad* event of the <body> tag.

That's all there is to it. When your page loads in somebody's browser, the browser continues to load and store those graphics quietly in the background. They'll appear almost instantly when they're required by a rollover or even a shift to another Web page on your site that incorporates the graphics you specified.

Swap Image

The Swap Image action exchanges one image on your page for another. (See the end of this section for detail on Swap Image's sibling behavior, Swap Image Restore.)

Simple as that process may sound, swapping images is one of the most visually exciting things you can do on a Web page. Swapping images works something like rollover images, except that a mouse click or mouse pass isn't required to trigger them. In fact, you can use *any* tag and event combination to trigger the Swap Image action. For instance, you can create a mini slideshow by listing the names of pictures down the left side of a Web page and inserting an image in the middle of the page. Add a Swap Image action to each slide name, so that the appropriate picture swaps in when your visitor clicks any one of the names.

To make this behavior work, your Web page must already contain a starter image, and the images you want swapped in must be the same width and height as the original graphic. If they aren't, the browser resizes and distorts the subsequent pictures to fit the "frame" dictated by the original.

To add the Swap Image behavior, start by choosing the *starter image* file that you want to include on the page. (Choose Insert → Image, or use any of the other techniques described in Chapter 6.) Give your image an ID in the Property inspector, so that JavaScript knows which image to swap out. (JavaScript doesn't really care about the original graphic image itself, but rather about the space that it occupies on the page.)

Tip: You can swap more than one image using a single Swap Image behavior (Figure 13-13). Using this trick, not only can a button change to another graphic when you mouse over it, but any number of other graphics on the page can also change at the same time. An asterisk (*) next to the name of an image in the Swap Image dialog box (see Figure 13-14) indicates that the behavior will swap in a new image for that particular graphic. In the example in Figure 13-14, you can see that two images–*horoscope* and *ad*, both marked by asterisks–swap with a single action.

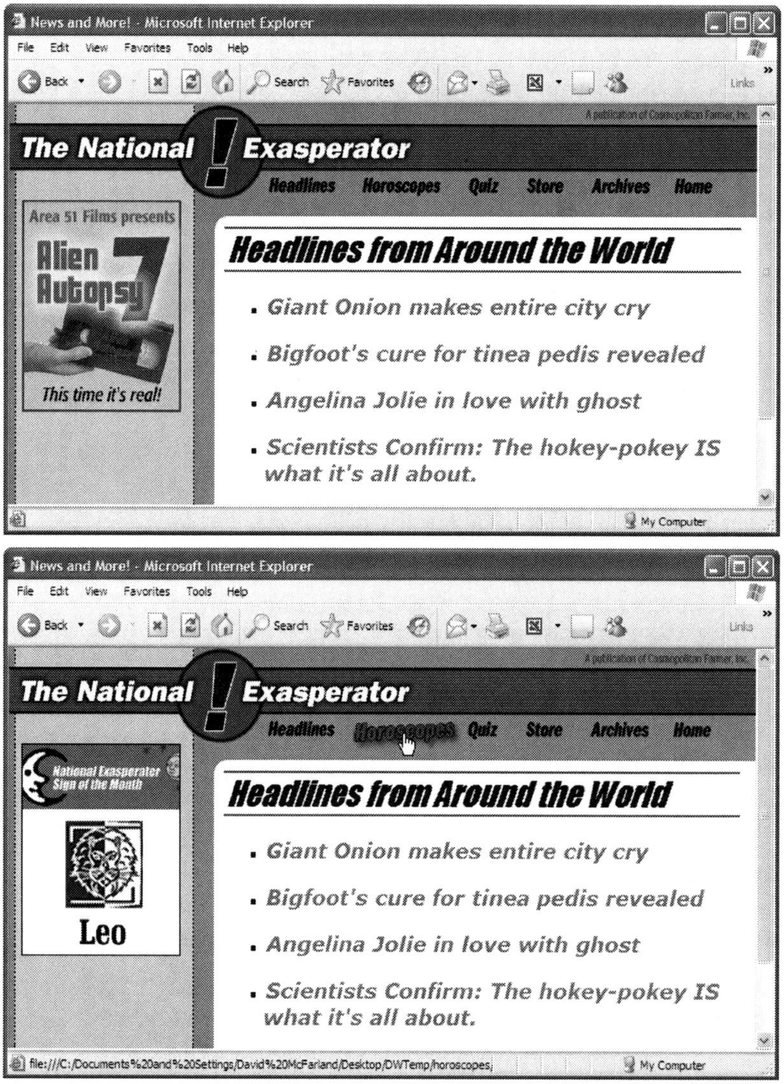

Figure 13-13: *You can use the Swap Image behavior to make multiple graphics change with a single mouseover. A humble Web page (top) comes to life when the mouse is moved over the Horoscopes button (bottom). Not only does the graphic for the Horoscopes button change, but the ad on the left sidebar is also replaced with a tantalizing look at the "Sign of the Month." This type of effect, sometimes called a disjoint rollover, is easy with the Swap Image action.*

Now select the tag you want to attach the Swap Image behavior to. When you choose this action's name from the Behaviors panel, the Swap Image dialog box appears, as shown in Figure 13-14.

- **Images.** From the list, click the name of the starter image.
- **Set source to.** Here's where you specify the *image* file that you want to swap in. If it's a graphics file in your site folder, click Browse to find and open it. You can also specify a path or an absolute URL to another Web site, as described on page 162.
- **Preload images.** Preloading ensures that the swap action isn't slowed down while the graphic downloads from the Internet.
- **Restore images onMouseOut.** You get this option only when you've applied this behavior to a link. When you turn this checkbox on, moving the mouse *off* the link makes the previous image reappear.

Swap Image Restore

The Swap Image Restore action returns the last set of swapped images to its original state. Most designers use it in conjunction with a rollover button so that the button returns to its original appearance when the visitor rolls the cursor off the button.

You'll probably never find a need to add this behavior yourself. Dreamweaver automatically adds it when you insert a rollover image and when you choose the "Restore images onMouseOut" option when setting up a regular Swap Image behavior (see Figure 13-14). But, if you prefer, you can add the Swap Restore Image behavior to other tag and event combinations, using the general routine described on page 559. (The Swap Image Restore dialog box offers no options to set.)

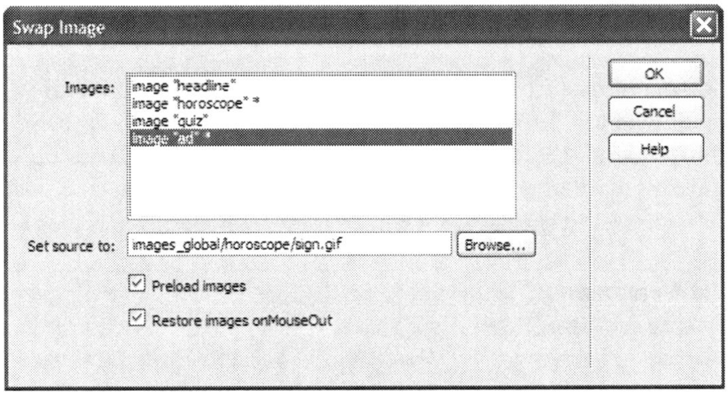

Figure 13-14: *Some actions, like the Swap Image action, can automatically add behaviors to a Web page. In this case, the "Preload images" and "Restore images onMouseOut" options actually add a Swap Image Restore action to the* onMouseOut *event of the currently selected tag, and a Preload Images action to the* onLoad *event of the <body> tag.*

Set Navigation Bar Image

The Navigation Bar object's enticing name tricks many people into thinking that they can quickly and easily build a useful navigation bar for their sites. They can, sort of, but the object adds lots of additional JavaScript code that's easily avoided by simply using Dreamweaver's "Rollover image" feature. The Navigation Bar is really a tool for those outdated dinosaurs—frames-based Web sites (see the box on page 173).

You're better off skipping the Navigation Bar object and using the Spry Menu Bar discussed on page 184 instead.

Message Actions

Communication is why we build Web sites: to tell a story, sell a product, or provide useful information that can entertain and inform our visitors. Dreamweaver can enhance this communication process with actions that provide dynamic feedback. From subtle messages in a browser's status bar to dialog boxes that command a visitor's attention, Dreamweaver offers numerous ways to respond, in words, to the things your visitors are doing on your Web pages.

Popup Message

Use the Popup Message behavior to send important messages to your visitors, as shown in Figure 13-15. Your visitor must click OK to close the dialog box. Because a pop-up message demands immediate attention, reserve this behavior for important announcements.

To create a pop-up message, select the tag to which you want the behavior attached. For example, adding this action to the <body> tag with an *onLoad* event causes a message to appear when a visitor first loads the page; adding the same behavior to a link with an *onClick* event makes the message appear when the visitor clicks the link.

From the Add Action menu (+ button) in the Behaviors panel, choose Popup Message. In the Popup Message dialog box, type the message that you want to appear in the dialog box. (Check the spelling and punctuation carefully; nothing says "amateur" like poorly written error messages, and Dreamweaver's spell-checking feature isn't smart enough to check the spelling of these messages.) Then click OK.

Note to JavaScript Programmers: Your message can also include any valid JavaScript expression. To embed JavaScript code in a message, place it inside braces ({ }). If you want to include the current time and date in a message, for example, add this: {*new Date()*}. If you just want to display a brace in the message, add a backslash, like this: \{. The backslash lets Dreamweaver know that you *really* do want a { character–and not just a bunch of JavaScript–to appear in the dialog box.

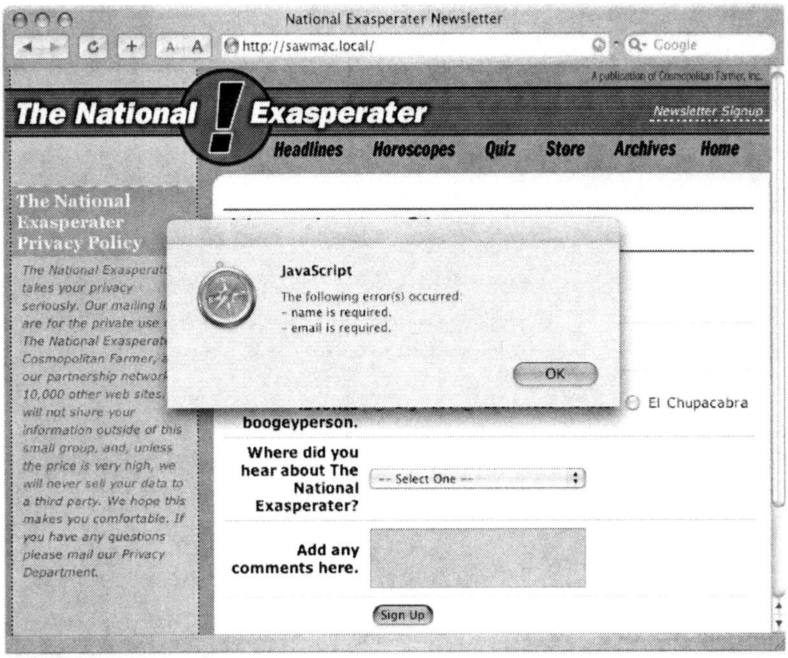

Figure 13-15: *Here, a pop-up message indicates that a Web form wasn't correctly filled out.*

Set Text of Status Bar

Pop-up messages, like those described above, require your visitors to drop everything and read them. For less urgent messages, consider the "Set Text of Status Bar" behavior. It displays a message in the status bar of a browser window—the strip at the bottom of the window. You can add a message to a link, for example, that lets visitors know where the link takes them. Or you could set things up so that when a visitor moves the cursor over a photograph, copyright information appears in the window's status bar.

You should skip this action, however. Many browsers, including Opera, Safari, and Firefox won't let you change the text in the status bar. In addition, many people hide their status bar, and the fact that it's way at the bottom of the browser window means that many visitors wouldn't ever notice the status bar message anyway.

Set Text of Text Field

Normally, a text field in a form (see page 439) is blank. It sits on the page and waits for someone to type in it. The "Set Text of Text Field" behavior, by contrast, can save your visitors time by filling in form fields automatically with obvious answers.

For instance, imagine you've created a Web survey that has a series of questions. The first question might require a yes or no answer, along the lines of "Do you own a computer?" And you've provided radio buttons for Yes or No. The second question might be "What brand is it?" followed by a text field where your visitors can type in the brand.

But if someone answers "No" to question 1, there's no point in her typing a response to the second question. To help keep things moving along, you can set the second question's text field so that it says, "Please skip to Question 3." To do so, simply add the "Set Text of Text Field" action to the *onClick* event of the No radio button of Question 1.

To apply the "Set Text of Text Field" action, make sure your page includes a form and at least one text field. Because this behavior changes the text in a form text field, you won't get very far without the proper HTML on the page.

Select the tag to which you want the behavior attached. In the example above, you'd attach the behavior to the form's No radio button with an *onClick* event. However, you aren't limited to form elements. Any of the tags discussed on pages 563–567 work.

When you choose "Set Text of Text Field" from the + menu in the Behaviors panel, the "Set Text of Text Field" dialog box opens. Make the following changes:

- **Text field.** The menu lists the names of every text field in the form; choose the name of the text field whose default text you want to change. (See Chapter 11 for the full story on building online forms in Dreamweaver.)
- **New text.** Type the text you want that field to display. Make sure you don't make the message longer than the space available in the field. If you leave the New Text field blank, the contents of the field will be erased. Once again, your message can include a JavaScript expression, as described in the Note on page 586.

Set Text of Container

Another way to get your message across is to change the text that appears inside any element with an ID applied. For example, this might be a <div> tag, an absolutely positioned element (see page 358), or just a paragraph with its ID property set. This action also lets you use HTML code to *format* the message that appears in the layer. (Actually, the "Set Text" part of this action's name is a bit misleading, since this action also lets you include HTML code, images, forms, and other objects in the layer—not just text.)

As always, you start by selecting a tag. In this case, you could select a link, for example, so that moving the mouse over the link changes the text inside a <div> to read, "Click here to see our exclusive photos of collectable Chia Pets."

When you choose this action's name from the + menu in the Behaviors panel, you get these controls in a dialog box:

- **Container.** The menu lists the names of every element on the Web page with an assigned ID (see page 114 for more on IDs); choose the name of the container whose text you want to set.

- **New HTML.** In this field, type the text you wish to add to the layer. You can type in a plain-text message or use HTML source code to control the content's formatting.

  For instance, if you want a word to appear bold in the layer, place the word inside a pair of strong tags like this: <strong>important</strong>. Or if you'd rather not mess around with HTML code, you can design the content using Dreamweaver's Design view—that is, right out there in your document window. Copy the HTML source from the Code view (Chapter 10), and then paste it into this action's New HTML field.

Text of Frame

Like the "Set Text of Layer" action, the "Set Text of Frame" action replaces the content of a specified frame with HTML you specify. It's like loading a new Web page into a frame, only faster. Since the HTML is already part of the page that contains this action, your visitors don't have to wait for the code to arrive from the Internet. While frames were once popular, they're best avoided these days. However, if you're really interested here's how to use this action.

To apply the "Set Text of Frame" action, create frameset and frame pages. (For more about frames, see the online chapter about frames, which you can find at *www.sawmac.com/missing/dw8/chapters.php*.) When you select a tag in any of the frames—even the one whose content you intend to replace—and then choose this action from the + menu in the Behaviors panel, the "Set Text of Frame" dialog box opens:

- **Frame.** The menu lists the names of every available frame. Choose the frame where you want the text to appear.
- **New HTML.** Type the text you want the frame to display. You can type in a plain-text message, or use HTML source code to control the content's formatting: <strong> like this </strong> for bold, for example.

  You can also copy the HTML currently in the frame by clicking the Get Current HTML button, which copies the HTML source into the New HTML Field. Once it's there, you can modify it as you see fit. Use this technique if, for example, you want to keep much of the formatting and HTML of the original page. Be careful, however: This action can only update the *body* of the frame; any code in the <head> of the frame is lost. You can't add behaviors, meta tags, or other <head> content to the frame.
- **Preserve Background Color.** This option ensures that the background color of the frame won't change when the new text appears.

Element Actions

Dreamweaver includes several tools that let you manipulate the appearance and placement of any element on a page.

Show-Hide Elements

Do you ever stare in awe when a magician makes a handkerchief disappear into thin air? Now you, too, can perform sleight of hand on your own Web pages, making HTML disappear and reappear with ease. Dreamweaver's Show-Hide Elements behavior is a piece of JavaScript programming that lets you make your own magic.

Show-Hide Elements takes advantage of the Visibility property. You can use it for things like adding pop-up tooltips to your Web page, so that when a visitor's mouse moves over a link, a paragraph appears offering a detailed explanation of where the link goes (see Figure 13-16).

The following steps show how to create this effect:

1. **Add absolutely positioned divs to your Web page using the techniques described on page 358. Use the Visibility setting (page 362) to specify how you want each div to look when the page loads.**

   If you want a layer to be visible at first and then disappear when your visitor performs a specific action, set the layer to Visible. If you want it to appear only *after* some specific event, set it to Hidden.

Note: You don't have to use an absolutely positioned div to take advantage of this behavior; any element with an ID applied to it can be hidden or shown. (See page 114 for more on IDs and page 358 for more on absolute positioning.)

2. **In the Tag selector, click the tag to which you want the behavior attached.**

   Web designers often attach behaviors to link (<a>) tags. But you can also attach them to images or, as in Figure 13-16, to an image map, which defines hotspots on a single graphic.

   To create this effect, attach two behaviors to each hotspot in the document window (that is, to each <area> tag in HTML): one to show the div, using the *onMouseOver* event, and one to hide the div, using the *onMouseOut* event.

Note: If this is all Greek to you, see page 245 for more on image maps and hotspots.

3. **If it isn't already open, choose Window → Behaviors to open the Behaviors panel.**

   The Behaviors panel (as pictured in Figure 13-1) appears. It lets you add, remove, and modify behaviors.

4. **Click the + button on the panel. Select Show-Hide Elements from the menu.**

   The Show-Hide Elements window appears (see Figure 13-17). You'll use this window to tell Dreamweaver what div you intend to work with first.

Figure 13-16: *Using Dreamweaver's Show-Hide Elements behavior, you can make elements appear and disappear. In this example, several elements lay hidden on the page. When a visitor moves the mouse over different parts of the tree cross-section, informative graphics (each placed in a hidden element) suddenly appear. Moving the mouse away returns the element to its hidden state. Notice how the information bubble overlaps the tree image and the text above it—a dead giveaway that this page uses absolutely positioned divs.*

5. **Click an element in the list of named elements.**

   It's useful to give your elements descriptive ID names so you can easily distinguish which is which in a list like this one.

6. **Choose a Visibility setting for the elements by clicking one of the three buttons: Show, Hide, or Default.**

   You're determining what happens to the element when someone interacts with the tag you selected in step 2. Show makes the element visible, Hide hides the element, and Default sets the element's Visibility property to the browser's default value (usually the same as the Inherit value described on page 362).

   The choice you selected appears in parentheses next to the layer's name, as shown in Figure 13-17.

7. **If you like, select another element and then apply another visibility option.**

   A single Show-Hide Elements action can affect several elements at once. A single action can even make some visible and others invisible. (If you apply an action to an element by mistake, select the same option again to remove it from that element.)

8. **Click OK to apply the behavior.**

   The Show-Hide Elements action is now listed in the Behaviors panel, as is the event that triggers it.

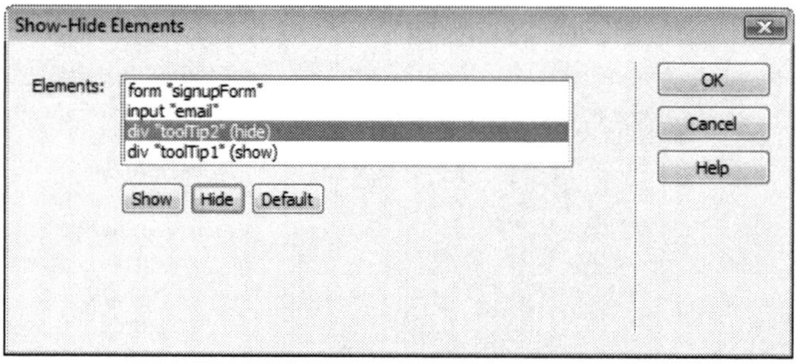

Figure 13-17: *This box lets you hide or show any element on the page. In fact, you can control multiple elements at once. Here, the "toolTip1" div appears, while the div "toolTip2" disappears, when the behavior is triggered. Other elements–like an HTML form and a form field (both have IDs so they appear here)–are unaffected by this particular action.*

Once you've added Show-Hide Elements, you can preview the behavior in a Web browser (Dreamweaver can't display behaviors by itself). Like other Dreamweaver behaviors, you can edit or delete this action; see page 562.

Draggable and Animated Divs

Dreamweaver includes a few other behaviors for working with absolutely positioned divs. The Drag AP Div behavior lets you create pages with AP divs that you can freely position anywhere on the Web page (think interactive jigsaw puzzle). The Timeline behavior lets you create animations, allowing your divs to travel freely around a page. Both of these were cool behaviors in their day, but they haven't been updated for years. Not only do they add lots and lots of JavaScript code that really weighs down your Web page, but they're also based on really old code that isn't guaranteed to work in any new browser. In fact, Adobe recognizes that the code is so old, that they've moved the animation features to the "deprecated bin" (see the Note on page 568) in the list of actions.

At any rate, the tools still sort of work. If you're interested in them, you'll find instructions on how to use them online at *www.sawmac.com/missing/dw8/chapters.php.*

Advanced Behaviors

Dreamweaver has two advanced behaviors that let you call (invoke) custom JavaScript functions and change the properties of various HTML elements. Both of these actions require familiarity with JavaScript and HTML (Chapter 10). Unlike the other Dreamweaver behaviors, these two can easily generate browser errors if used incorrectly.

Call JavaScript

You can use the Call JavaScript behavior to execute a single line of JavaScript code or to call a JavaScript function that you've added to the <head> section of your Web page.

When you select a tag and choose this behavior's name from the Behaviors panel, the Call JavaScript dialog box opens. If you want to execute a single line of JavaScript code, simply type it in. For instance, if you want to make the browser window close, type *window.close( )*. If you want to call a JavaScript function, type the function name, like this: *myFunction( )*.

POWER USERS' CLINIC

Closing Browser Windows with the Call JavaScript Behavior

Suppose you've added an Open Browser Window behavior to your home page, so that when visitors come to your site, a small window opens, displaying a Web page that advertises some new feature of your site.

After they've read the ad, your visitors will want to close the window and continue visiting your site. Why not make it easy for them by adding a "Close this Window" button?

To do so, simply add a graphic button—text works fine, too—and then add a dummy (null) link to it (that is, in the Property inspector, type *javascript:;* in the Link field). Next, add the Call JavaScript behavior; in the Call JavaScript window that appears, type the following line of JavaScript code: *window.close( )*.

Finally, after you click OK, make sure that the event is set to onClick in the Behaviors panel.

That's all there is to it. The link you've added to the pop-up window offers a working close button.

Change Property

The Change Property behavior can dynamically alter the value of a property or change the style of any of the following HTML tags: <div>, <span>, <img>, <form>, <textarea>, or <select>. It can also change properties for radio buttons, checkboxes, text fields, and password fields on forms (see Chapter 11). As with the previous behavior, this one requires a working knowledge of HTML, CSS, and JavaScript. Dreamweaver's built-in HTML, CSS, and JavaScript references (see page 422) can help you get up to speed.

Select a tag, choose this behavior's name from the + menu in the Behaviors panel, and then fill in the following parts of the Change Property dialog box (see Figure 13-18):

- **Type of element**. This pop-up menu lists the 13 HTML tags that this behavior can control. Choose the type of element whose property you wish to change.
- **Element ID**. From this pop-up menu, choose the ID of the object you want to modify. You'll only see elements of the type you selected from the first menu (for example, <div> or <p> tags). Any tag of the selected type that doesn't have an ID applied to it will be listed, but will have the label "unidentified" next to it. Dreamweaver will only let you choose an element with an ID.
- **Property**. Choose the property you want to change (or, if you know enough about JavaScript and CSS, just type the property's name in the Enter field). All of the options in the menu refer to various CSS properties. For example, "colors" refers to the *color* property, which sets the color of text as discussed on page 140.

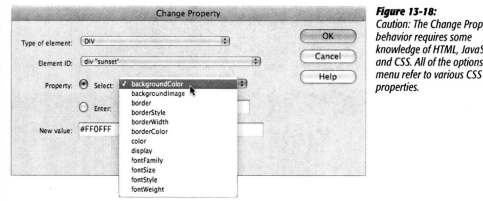

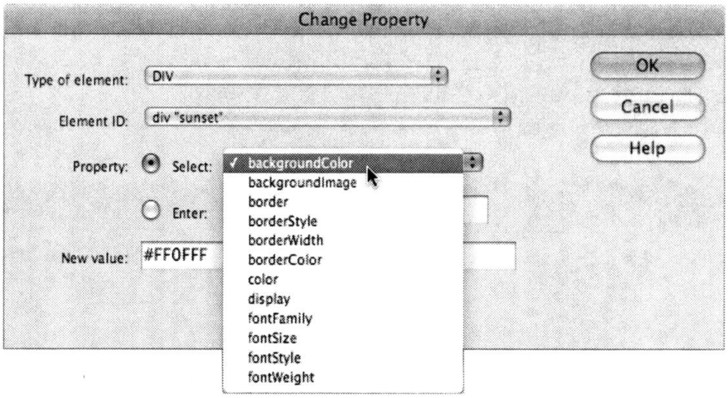

Figure 13-18:
Caution: The Change Property behavior requires some knowledge of HTML, JavaScript, and CSS. All of the options in the menu refer to various CSS properties.

- **New value.** Type the new value you wish to set for this property. This value should be appropriate to the type of property you'll be changing. For example, if you're changing a background color, the value should be a color, like #FF0066. The options in the Property menu refer to CSS properties, so you'll find that the different possible values listed for the different CSS properties in Chapter 4, Chapter 5, and Chapter 6 should work. For example, the *fontWeight* property is the CSS Font Weight property (page 141), so you could enter a value of *bold* to change text in an object (inside a <div> tag, for instance) to bold.

Adding More Behaviors

Dreamweaver's behaviors can open a new world of interactivity. Even if you don't understand the complexities of JavaScript and cross-browser programming, you can easily add powerful and interesting effects that add spice to your Web visitors' experience.

Dreamweaver comes with the preprogrammed behaviors described in this chapter, but you can download many additional behaviors from Adobe's Exchange Web site (*www.adobe.com/exchange*) or any of the Web sites mentioned on page 808. Once you've downloaded them, you can easily add them to Dreameaver, as described in Chapter 21.

CHAPTER

14

Flash and Other Multimedia

With Cascading Style Sheets (Chapter 4), Spry widgets (Chapter 12), Dreamweaver Effects and Behaviors (Chapter 13), and images (Chapter 6), you can bring your Web pages to life with interactivity and animation. But as you probably have noticed, more and more Web pages these days blink, sing, and dance with sound, video, and advanced animation.

You can create these effects too, but you'll need outside help from programs like Flash (see Figure 14-1), Director, or the Java programming language, all of which are designed to create complex multimedia presentations. Dreamweaver provides powerful tools for adding these external media files and embedding them into your Web pages.

Four warnings, however. First, while all the technologies discussed in this chapter let you expand your Web pages into new and exciting territory, they also require that your site visitors have external applications (not just a Web browser). These programs, usually called *plug-ins*, are a bit controversial in the Web development community, mainly because they can limit your audience. Not all Web site visitors have the necessary plug-ins installed on their computers. Those guests must choose from three equally unpalatable options: go to a different Web site to download the plug-in, skip the multimedia show (if you've built a second, plug-in–free version of your site), or skip your Web site entirely. All media types in this chapter require a plug-in of some kind; see each section for more detail.

Second, it's worth noting that these effects can bulk up your Web site considerably, making it slower to load and making it still more likely that some of your visitors (especially those using dial-up modems) won't bother sticking around.

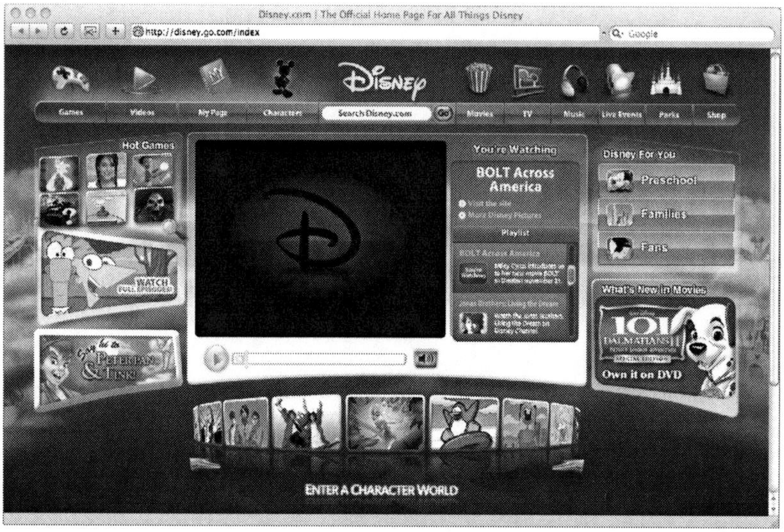

***Figure 14-1:** Some Web pages, like the Disney.com home page, are created almost entirely with Flash. The interactivity, animation, and video playback abilities of Flash make it a great technology for entertainment Web sites. Ultimately, however, you still need an HTML file to display the Flash movie.*

Third, these flashy multimedia effects are easy to overuse. Blink and flash too much, and you'll find your audience beating a hasty retreat for the cyber-exits.

Finally, creating external movies, animations, or applications is an art (and a book or two) unto itself. This chapter is a guide to *inserting* such add-on goodies into your Web page and assumes that a cheerful programmer near you has already *created* them.

Note: For the full scoop on Flash, pick up a copy of *Flash CS4: The Missing Manual.*

Flash: An Introduction

Flash is the standard for Web animation, complex visual interaction, and what has become known as "Rich Internet Applications" (which is just a fancy way of saying you can make a Web page work a lot like a desktop program). Adobe's Flash technology produces high-quality animated images—known as Flash movies—at a relatively small file size. Its drawings and animations are *vector graphics*, which means that they use mathematical formulas to describe objects on the screen. By contrast, *bitmap* technology like GIF and JPEG include data for every pixel of an image, gobbling up precious bytes and adding download time. Flash's vector graphics, on the other hand, save file size with their compact mathematical expressions.

Note: Flash can also use bitmap images, so a Flash movie may not necessarily be populated exclusively with lean vector graphics. In other words, it's possible to create a Flash movie that's full of bitmap imagery, downloads at a glacial pace, and plays back like molasses.

Flash can also handle MP3 audio, video playback, and advanced programming features, providing an added dimension of sound, video, and interactivity that can make a plain HTML page look dull by comparison. For example, sophisticated Flash gurus can build automatic score tracking into an online game or add a cannon-firing animation each time the player clicks the mouse. While Dynamic HTML (see Chapter 13) can do some of these things, Flash movies have a wider range of effects and much better animation control. Another advantage of Flash movies: They look and work exactly the same in every browser, whether on Windows, Mac, or even Linux.

Of course, all this power comes at a price. You need another program, such as Adobe Flash or Swish (*www.swishzone.com*) to produce full-fledged movies for your Web site. These programs aren't necessarily difficult to get started with, but they're more programs to buy and more technologies to get under your belt.

Furthermore, your visitors can't play Flash movies without the Flash Player plug-in. If they don't have it, they'll need to download and install it. Fortunately, Dreamweaver CS4 provides a new method of inserting a Flash movie into a Web page which includes an "express install" feature. That means if your visitor doesn't have Flash (or the correct version of Flash for your movie) installed, then he'll be told this when the page loads. At that point, it's just a simple click of a link on the page to download and install the Flash plugin in, well, a flash!

Inserting a Flash Movie

To insert a Flash movie into a Web page, click where you want to insert the movie, and then choose Insert → Media → SWF (or, on the Common category of the Insert panel, choose SWF from the Media menu [circled in Figure 14-2])—SWF is the file extension used for Flash movies. Either way, a Select File dialog box appears. Navigate to the Flash movie file (look for a .swf extension) and double-click it. Dreamweaver automatically determines the width and height of the movie and generates the appropriate HTML to embed it into the page.

The movie appears as a gray rectangle with the Flash logo in the center; you can adjust its settings as described in the next section.

Tip: You can also drag a Flash movie file from the Files panel into the document window. Dreamweaver automatically adds the correct code.

To preview Flash files directly in Dreamweaver, just select the movie and then click the Play button on the Property inspector (see Figure 14-3). To stop the movie, click the same button, which has now become a Stop button.

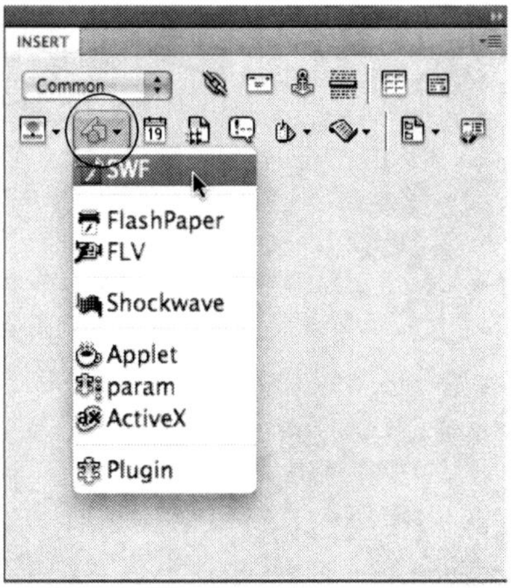

Figure 14-2:
The Media menu on the Insert panel's Common category is where old Web technologies go to die. Only Flash and Flash video are commonly used on Web sites these days.

POWER USERS' CLINIC

The Two Lives of the <object> Tag

If you choose View → Code after inserting a Flash movie, you may be surprised by the amount of HTML Dreamweaver deposits in your page. You may also encounter some HTML tags you've never heard of, including <object>, and <param>. These tags provide browsers with the information they need to launch the Flash Player and play a Flash movie.

Due to differences between Internet Explorer and all the other browsers, Dreamweaver has to insert the <object> tag two times: once for IE (with all the proper settings for that browser) and once for the other browsers. To do this, Dreamweaver uses IE conditional statements like those discussed on page 353.

Using the <object> tag like this is new to Dreamweaver CS4 and replaces the old method which used two tags: the <object> and the <embed> tags. This new method is completely standards compliant, which means that any page you add a Flash movie to with Dreamweaver CS4 will pass W3C validation (see page 651). This wasn't true in earlier versions of Dreamweaver which produced invalid HTML that failed the W3C validator.

Note: When inserting a Flash movie, an Object Tag Accessibility Options window appears. This window lets you set options that are intended to make accessing the Flash content easier, but they don't really work in most browsers. If you don't want to set these options, just click Cancel, and Dreamweaver still inserts the Flash movie. To permanently turn off this window, open the Preferences window–Edit → Preferences (Dreamweaver → Preferences on a Mac)–click the Accessibility category, and then turn off the Media checkbox.

If your page has lots of Flash movies—numerous animated buttons, say—you can play all of them at once by pressing Ctrl+Shift+Alt+P (⌘-Shift-Option-P). Then sit back and watch the show. To stop all running movies, press Ctrl+Shift+Alt+X (⌘-Shift-Option-X). You can also preview Shockwave movies in Dreamweaver. (And no wonder: Adobe makes Shockwave, too.)

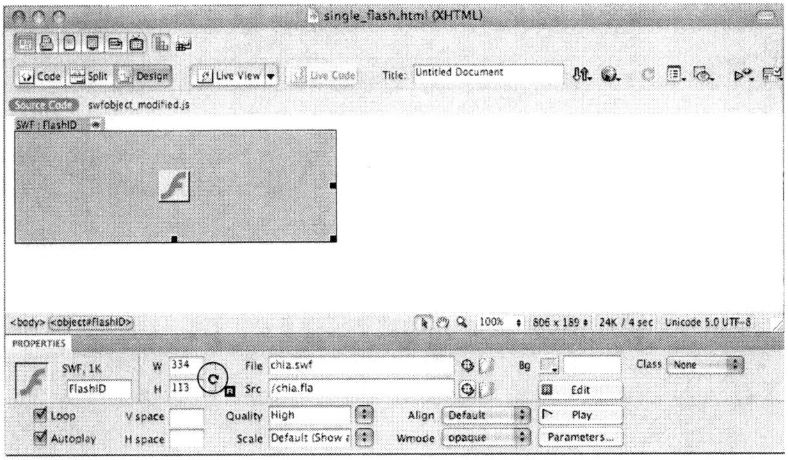

Figure 14-3: *Use the Property inspector to set the controls for the display and playback of a Flash movie. Avoid the V space, H space, and align settings. Those same formatting options are better handled with CSS.*

Flash Movie Properties

You'll rarely have to change the default properties Dreamweaver assigns to Flash movies. But if you ever want to change the movie back to its original size after resizing it, or swap in a different movie, the Property inspector is the place to do it.

Naming a Flash movie

As with images and navigation buttons, you can use JavaScript to control Flash movies. Dreamweaver supplies a generic name—*FlashID*, or *FlashID2*, *FlashID3*, and so on if you have more than one movie on a page. Supplying a name is important—it works with the auto install option discussed on page 603—but the exact name isn't. If you want, you can change the name that appears in the Name field (the box directly below SWF at the top left of the Property inspector; see Figure 14-3). However, there's no real need to change this name since it won't appear to anyone visiting the page.

The movie file

The File field specifies the path to the Flash movie file on your hard drive. To select a different file, type a new path into the File field, or click the folder icon to access your site folder's contents.

Src property

Dreamweaver can keep track of the original Flash file you used when creating a Flash movie. That's fortunate because, once again, Flash movies start off in the program's native format (as .fla files) and then must be exported as .swf (Flash movie) files, which are viewable on the Web.

The Src property field indicates where the original Flash file is stored. This field is blank when you first insert a Flash movie, but when you click the Edit button on the Property inspector, Dreamweaver asks you to locate the original Flash movie file on your computer: you're looking for a file that ends with the .fla extension. Dreamweaver then launches Flash and opens the original Flash file for editing. You can then make any changes you wish to the movie and, in Flash, click Done. Flash exports the updated .swf file into your site, replacing the previous version of the file. In addition, the Src property now points to the original .fla file on your computer. Next time you press the Edit button, Flash launches and your original Flash movie file opens ready for editing.

Movie size

Although dragging to enlarge a GIF or JPEG image can turn it into a pixelated mess, you can usually resize Flash movies without problems, since their vector-based images are based on mathematical formulas that scale nicely. (The exception is when you've included bitmap images—such as GIFs, PNGs, or JPEGs—in your Flash movie. Then, as when resizing an image in a Web page, you'll see distortion and pixelation in the movie.)

To resize a movie, do one of the following:

- Select the movie in the document window; drag one of the three resizing handles that appear at the edges of the movie. To avoid changing the movie's proportions in the process, press Shift as you drag the lower-right corner handle.
- Select the movie in the document window; type new width and height values into the W and H boxes in the Property inspector. You can also use percentage values, in which case Web browsers scale your movie to fit the window.

If you make a complete mess of your page by resizing the movie beyond recognition, just click Reset Size button in the Property inspector (circled in Figure 14-3).

Tip: If you want to insert a Flash movie that fills 100% of the browser window you first need to set the movie's height and width to 100%. Then you need to create a few CSS styles. First, create a tag style for the <body> tag with *padding* (page 343) and *margin* (page 343) set to 0, and *height* (page 341) and *width* (page 341) set to 100%. Next, create a tag style for the <html> tag with the same settings as the <body> tag (a group selector–discussed on page 304–can make the process of creating the styles more efficient). If the Flash movie is contained within other tags, like a <div> or a <p> tag, then you need to remove padding and margin for those tags and set their heights and widths to 100% as well. Finally, choose an appropriate Scaling setting for the movie, as discussed on the opposite page.

Play options

The Loop and Autoplay checkboxes control how the Flash movie plays back. When you turn on Loop, the Flash movie plays over and over again in an endless loop, an approach advertisers often use in animated banner ads.

The Autoplay checkbox instructs the Flash movie to start playing when the page loads.

Note that neither of these options overrides specific programming instructions in the Flash movie. For instance, if you've added a Stop action to the final frame of a movie—an action that stops the movie at that frame—then the Loop option has no effect.

Margins

Skip the V space and H space settings in the Property inspector. They're intended to add space to the top, bottom, left, and right of the Flash movie, but they produce invalid HTML code for strict document types (see page 46 for more on doctypes). In addition, you can't control each of the four margins, individually.

Instead, use Cascading Style Sheets and the CSS *margin* property discussed on page 343. You can create an ID style (page 114) using the name listed in the Property inspector. For example, create an ID style named *#FlashID*.

Quality settings

If your Flash movie's heavy data requirements overwhelm a visitor's computer, it may run slowly and appear choppy, especially if the animation is action-packed and complex. Not every computer on earth has at least a three-gigahertz processor and two gigabytes of RAM. Until then, you may need to adjust the quality settings of your Flash movies to help them look better on all computers, from the sluggish to the speedy.

By default, Dreamweaver sets the quality to High, but you can choose any of the following four settings from the Quality menu in the Property inspector:

- **High** provides the best quality, but the movie may run slower on older computers.
- **Low** looks terrible. This setting sacrifices quality by eliminating all *antialiasing* (edge smoothing) in the movie, leaving harsh, jaggy lines on the edges of every image. Movies set to Low quality look bad on *all* computers; to accommodate both the fast and the slow, use Auto High or Auto Low.
- **Auto Low** forces the movie to start in Low quality mode, but to switch automatically to High if the visitor's computer is fast enough.
- **Auto High** makes the movie switch to Low quality mode only if the visitor's computer requires it. In this way, you can deliver a high-quality image to most visitors, while still letting those with slow computers view the movie. This mode is the best choice if you want to provide a high-quality image but still make your movie accessible to those with older computers.

Scaling

When you resize a Flash movie (see opposite page), changing its original proportions, your visitors' Web browsers scale or distort the movie to fit the newly specified dimensions. Scaling becomes an issue particularly when, for example, you give a Flash movie *relative* dimensions (setting it to, say, 90% of the browser window's width), so that it grows or shrinks as your visitor's browser window grows or shrinks.

The Scale property lets you determine *how* the Flash Player plug-in scales your movie. For example, in Figure 14-4, the top movie's original size is 334 × 113 pixels. But if you resize the movie so that it's *350* × 113 pixels, one of three things may happen, depending on your choice of Scale setting:

- **Show All**. This setting, the default, maintains the original aspect ratio (proportions) of the movie (second from top in Figure 14-4). In other words, although the overall size of the movie may change, the movie's width-to-height proportion remains the same. This setting keeps the movie from distorting, but it may also cause white borders to appear on the top, bottom, or either side of the movie. (To hide the borders, match the movie's background color to the color on the page.)
- **No Border**. This setting resizes the movie according to your specifications *and* maintains its aspect ratio, but may also crop the sides of the movie. Notice how the top and bottom of the Chia Vet logo are chopped off (third from top in Figure 14-4).
- **Exact Fit**. This option may stretch your movie's picture either horizontally or vertically. In Figure 14-4 (bottom), "Chia Vet" is stretched wider. Rookie move.

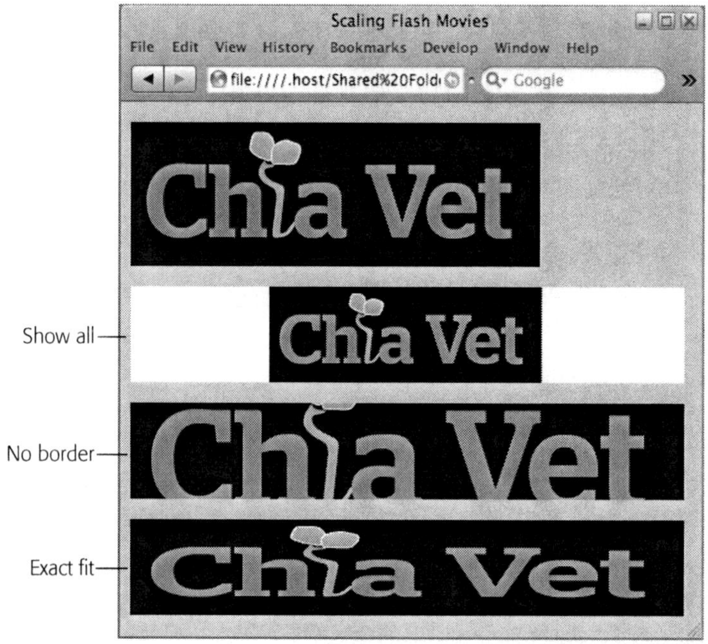

Figure 14-4: *This browser window shows the results of your different choices in the Scale menu on the Property inspector. A Flash movie's Scale property specifies how a movie should be scaled when its width and height properties are set differently than the original movie. If you've resized a movie, press F12 (option-F12) to see how it looks in a Web browser, and then, if necessary, choose a different setting from the Scale pop-up menu in the Property inspector.*

Alignment

You can align Flash movies relative to the paragraphs around them, just as you do with images. In fact, the alignment options in the Property inspector work exactly the same as the text alignment properties. For example, choosing Right from the Align menu positions the movie at the right of the screen and wraps text around its left side. (If the movie is inside a cell, Align Right moves it all the way to the right of the cell.) However, for strict document types (page 46) this property is invalid. As with margins discussed above, you're better off using CSS properties (such as the *float* property [page 229] to align an image to the left or right).

Background color

To set a background color for a Flash movie, use the Bg Color box in the Property inspector. This color overrides any background color set in the movie itself; it fills the space where the movie appears when the page first loads (and the movie hasn't).

Wmode

Wmode stands for "Window mode" and controls how the Flash movie interacts with other HTML on the page. The regular setting, *opaque*, is useful when you include HTML that needs to appear on top of the movie—the classic example is a drop-down menu like the Spry Navigation Bar you learned about on page 184. The opaque setting ensures that the drop-down menu appears on top of the Flash movie. The *transparent* option also lets HTML appear above the movie. But it also lets any HTML underneath the movie—like a page's background color—show through areas of the Flash movie that have a transparent background.

Finally, the *window* option is the exact opposite of the opaque option: It makes sure the Flash movie always appears above any HTML on the page—even above a pop-up navigation menu that should display over the movie.

Making It Easier to Download the Flash Plug-in

When you add a Flash movie to a Web page you can't always be sure that the person visiting your page actually has the Flash plug-in installed in his Web browser. What's worse, you may have created a Flash movie using the latest features of Flash CS4...which only run in the latest versions of the Flash plug-in. In other words, a visitor might have the Flash plug-in, but not the correct *version*. The result? A movie that either doesn't play at all or doesn't function as it should.

Fortunately, Dreamweaver CS4 provides a built-in solution for both these scenarios. When you insert a Flash movie into a page, Dreamweaver adds some additional code. If the visitor either doesn't have the Flash plug-in installed, or doesn't have a version that can play the Flash movie, the code displays a message alerting the person of the problem (see Figure 14-5). The visitor can then click the Get Adobe Flash Player button to download and install the plug-in, or, if the visitor has at least version 6 of the plug-in, they'll be able to use the plug-in's "express install" feature which lets the visitor quickly and painlessly upgrade to the latest version.

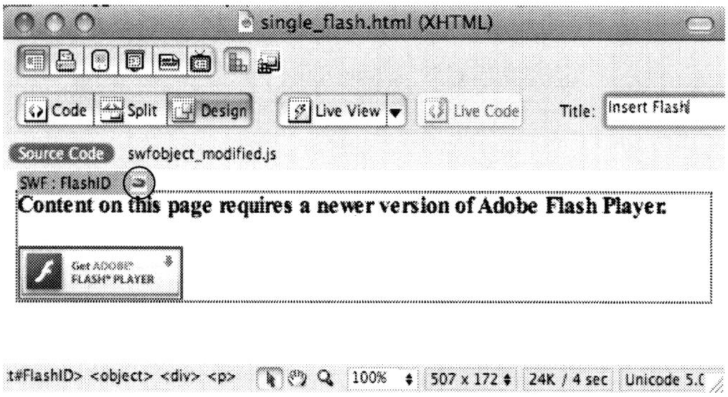

Figure 14-5: *Here's the normal message that a Web browser will display if a visitor to the page doesn't have the Flash player installed, or has an old version of the player installed. You can customize this message by changing the text. However, it's a good idea to leave the Flash Player icon in place–it includes a link to a page on Adobe.com where the visitor can download the player.*

The message only appears if the visitor doesn't have the correct plug-in installed; the majority of people will probably never see it. Even in Design view the message is hidden. However, by clicking the eye icon (circled in Figure 14-5), you can see and edit this message.

To make this all happen, Dreamweaver adds two files to your Web site inside a folder named Scripts: *expressInstall.swf* and *swfobject_modified.js*. When you move your finished Web page and Flash movie to your Web server, be sure to move the Scripts folder with these two files as well. (Chapter 17 covers how to move files to a Web server.)

Note to Dreamweaver CS3 Users: Dreamweaver CS3 used to add a JavaScript file to your site when you added a Flash movie to a page. This file, named *AC_RunActiveContent.js*, was necessary to overcome some relationship problems between Internet Explorer and Flash movies. Microsoft has since worked out those problems in IE 6 and IE 7 (browser therapy?), so that file is no longer needed.

Adding Flash Videos

In addition to animations and games, the Flash player can also project videos. In fact, *Flash video*, as this feature is called, is now one of the most common methods for putting video up on the Web. If you've visited a little Web site named YouTube, you've seen Flash video. High among this format's advantages—compared to competing standards like QuickTime or Windows Media Video—is that you can reasonably count on the fact that visitors won't have to download additional software to view the videos.

Dreamweaver makes it a snap to add these videos to a Web page. Unfortunately, you can't use Dreamweaver to transform existing videos into the appropriate format (called Flash Video; format extension: *.flv*). Nor can you use just any old video format, like MPEG or AVI. Instead, you need to create the Flash Video file using one of several Adobe products. If you bought the Creative Suite, you're in business; it includes the Flash Video Encoder for creating these types of files. Otherwise, you need Flash CS4 Pro or Flash CS3 Pro.

Tip: For a quick intro to creating Flash videos, visit *www.adobe.com/designcenter/dialogbox/encode_video.html*. Adobe also dedicates an entire section of their site to Flash video: *www.adobe.com/devnet/flash/video*.

Fortunately, creating the .flv file is the hardest part. In just a few simple steps, Dreamweaver can insert Flash video directly into a Web page, complete with VCR-like controls (or maybe that's now *DVD*-like controls) for start, stop, pause, and volume control.

1. **Click the page where you'd like to insert the Flash video.**

   Like other Flash movies, you'll want an open area of your page to place the video.

2. **Choose Insert → Media → FLV.**

   Or, from the Common category of the Insert panel, select FLV from the Media menu (see Figure 14-2). The Insert FLV window appears (see Figure 14-6). (You can also just drag the FLV file from the Files panel and drop it onto the document window.)

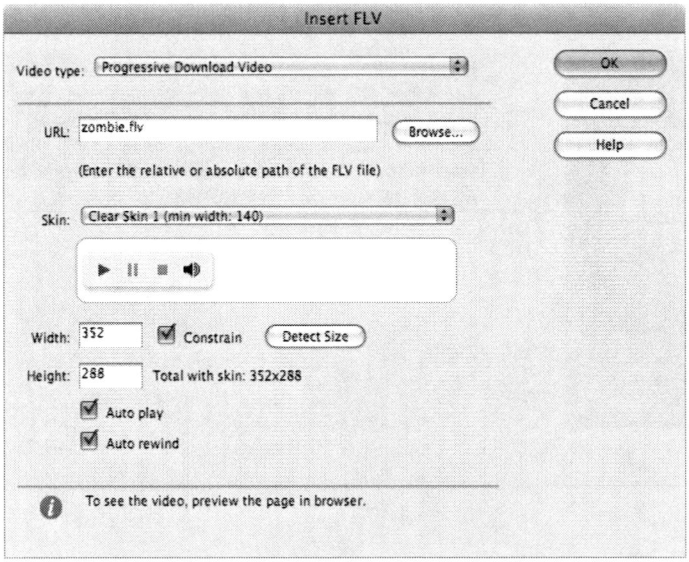

***Figure 14-6:** The Insert Flash Video command is probably the easiest way to add video to your Web site. All your visitors need is the Flash Player, which in many cases comes preinstalled in their browser.*

3. **Select Progressive Download Video from the "Video type" menu.**

   Dreamweaver provides two options, but the second one—Streaming Video—requires some expensive software (the Flash Server) or a Flash video streaming service which can run you anywhere from $10 a month to a couple hundred dollars a month. Streaming Video is best used for live events or to handle very large numbers of viewers. That's why Web sites for TV networks like ABC.com use streaming servers—it's a more efficient method when thousands of people are watching the same video at the same time.

   Choosing Progressive Download means that the video doesn't have to download completely before it begins playing. That way viewers don't have to wait, say, 30 minutes while your 40 MB movie downloads. Instead, the video starts as soon as the first section of the file arrives on their machine; playback proceeds while the rest of the movie downloads.

4. **Click the Browse button and select the Flash Video (.flv) file you wish to add to the page.**

   Due to some differences in how operating systems work, you're better off putting your Flash Video file in the same folder as the Web page you're adding it to. If you want to put your Flash video files elsewhere (for instance in one dedicated Flash Video folder, or even on a different Web server) use absolute links (see page 162) to make sure your video appears.

5. **Select a skin.**

   The *skin* is the visible set of controls that you add to your video: buttons for starting, pausing, and stopping the video; a progress bar; and various volume-adjustment controls (see Figure 14-7).

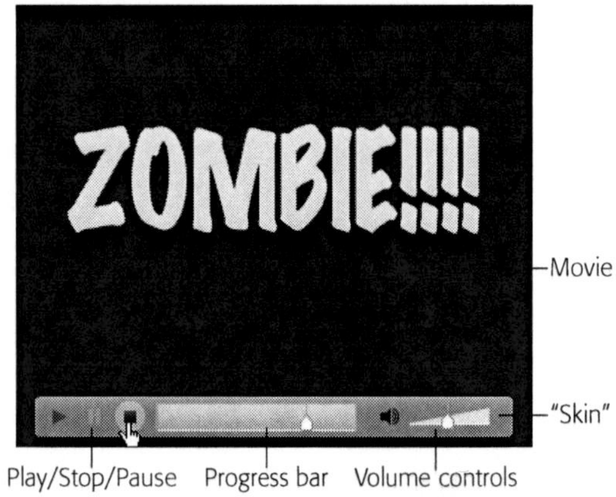

Figure 14-7:
The "Clear" skin controls lie directly over the movie ("Clear Skin 3" is shown here). They disappear if the mouse isn't anywhere inside the movie, but they reappear the moment you mouse back over the video. Try each skin to see which fits your taste.

Dreamweaver adds these controls to your video, and they're offered in nine different styles—actually, three different types of controllers, each with three different graphical styles. Each skin includes controls for starting the video and controlling the sounds. You also get some additional buttons for stopping and pausing the video, and a progress bar that lets you see how far the video has progressed.

6. **Click the Detect Size button.**

   Flash Videos contain *meta-data*—additional information embedded inside the video file that describes features like dimensions, size, and so on. The Flash video encoder adds this meta-data when you create a Flash video file. Clicking the Detect Size button extracts the movie's width and height; adds the width and height of the various elements of the selected skin; and then automatically fills in the width and height boxes in the Insert Flash Video window (see Figure 14-6).

   If for any reason your file doesn't include meta-data, you'll have to enter the width and height values yourself—these settings specify how much space the Flash video occupies on the page. Note that entering these dimensions won't actually distort your video—making it really, really thin, or really, really wide, for example. No matter what size you enter, the original aspect ratio (proportions) of the movie is preserved, and extra, empty space is added to fill any area not filled by the movie. For example, say your movie is 352 pixels wide and 288 pixels tall. If you entered width and height dimensions of 100×288, respectively, the movie won't stretch like you're watching it in fun-house mirror. Instead, the movie appears 100 pixels wide and 82 pixels tall, with 53 pixels of blank space above and below it.

7. **If you want, turn on the "Auto play" checkbox.**

   Doing so makes the movie play as soon as enough video data has downloaded from the Web. Otherwise, your site's visitors need to press the play button to begin the video.

8. **If you want, turn on the "Auto rewind" checkbox.**

   If you want the movie to automatically "rewind" to the beginning after it's done playing, turn on this checkbox. Your movie will then return to the first frame of the video after it's played through. But you may not always want to abide by the video-store credo "Be Kind, Rewind." If your movie ends with a dramatic message—"Stay tuned for the next exciting installment of Blind Mole Rats from Mars!"—you might prefer to leave the movie on its last frame when it's complete.

9. **Click OK to add the Flash Video to your page.**

   This step installs the necessary code not only for the video, but also the same code installed with any Flash movie (see page 603). You can check out the newly inserted video by pressing F12 (Option-F12) to preview the page in a Web browser.

Note: When you upload your Web page and Flash Video to your site (see Chapter 17), you also need to upload four additional files that Dreamweaver secretly added to your site: the two files (and the *Scripts* folder) discussed on page 604, the FLVPlayer_progressive.swf file, and the .swf (Flash movie) file for the skin you selected. That last file is named after the skin you chose–for example, Clear_Skin_1.swf. Save yourself some work: When uploading your Flash-filled Web page (uploading details are on page 678) choose to include "dependent files"; that way Dreamweaver grabs these three files for you.

The Land of Obsolete Web Technology

Dreamweaver CS4 includes many other options on the Media menu of the Insert panel (see Figure 14-2). Some of these options have been around since Dreamweaver was in training pants. Most of them don't see much use on today's Web; they either don't work for many users, or creating the content to work with these technologies is so hard that few Web designers bother. In addition, some of these technologies look like they're being phased out by their creators.

- **FlashPaper**. This simple and useful technology, introduced back in the days when Flash was owned by Macromedia, provides a simple way to export any document (like a Word file or an Excel spreadsheet) into a Web-ready format. Visitors can zoom in on a FlashPaper document, scroll through it, and print it out. It's kind of like a "light" version of a PDF file; in fact, since FlashPaper competes with one of Adobe's premier products—Adobe Acrobat—it may not be around for much longer. The program that creates FlashPaper documents used to be included in the Studio suite of programs along with Dreamweaver and Flash, but now it's only available as a stand-alone product.

  If you happen to have the FlashPaper program, you can still use Dreamweaver to insert a FlashPaper document (which are really just Flash movies, after all): choose Insert → Media → FlashPaper, or choose FlashPaper from the Media menu on the Common tab of the Insert bar. When the Insert FlashPaper window opens, click the browse button and select the FlashPaper document (an .swf file), type a height and width, and then click OK. The height and width you specify determine the size of the "window" that contains the FlashPaper document. Viewers of your page can use the FlashPaper controls to zoom, scroll, and print the document.

  After inserting the FlashPaper document into the page, it acts like a regular Flash movie.

- **Shockwave** is another Web technology that's been around a long time. It's the Internet-ready form for movies created with Macromedia Director. Director has a longer history as a program for creating CD-ROMs. But when the Web exploded onto the scene, Director quickly morphed into a Web authoring tool. As a result of its CD background, Shockwave offers complex programming possibilities, which makes it ideal for detailed, interactive presentations.

However, most people won't find a use for it. Flash provides much of the functionality of Director (at least for Web sites) and is, consequently, the much more common choice for Web designers. In addition, the Shockwave plug-in isn't installed with Web browsers, so visitors have to download the hefty plug-in which weighs in at a hefty 4.5 MB for Windows and 3.5 MB for Mac. One final strike against it: The plug-in hasn't been updated to run natively on Intel Macs. (You might not care about this if you're a Windows user, but it does seem to signal that Adobe isn't too interested in this technology.)

But if you just can't do without Shockwave, you can insert a Shockwave movie into a Web page just as you would any multimedia format. Click where you want to insert the movie, and then choose Insert → Media → Shockwave (or choose Shockwave from the Media menu on the Common category of the Insert panel). Either way, a Select File dialog box appears. Find and double-click the Shockwave movie file (look for the .dcr extension).

- **Other Multimedia Controls.** Dreamweaver also includes tools for inserting other multimedia and plug-in files. In fact, these tools have been around since much earlier incarnations of Dreamweaver, when there really *were* other media types like Java applets, ActiveX controls, and other plug-in technology. However, Java applets never really took off (their performance never quite lived up to the hype), and ActiveX controls are limited to Internet Explorer for Windows.

FREQUENTLY ASKED QUESTION

Adding Sound to Web Pages

Hey man, I'm a rock-star in training, and I want to surprise the world with my cool tunes. How do I put my music on my Web site?

There are lots of different technologies that let you add music and sound to your Web site. Most require plug-ins that severely limit your audience (few people are going to rush off to another Web site and download and install more software just to enjoy your site—unless you're U2 or Miley Cyrus).

Flash provides the best and fastest way to add sound to a site. Flash can import different audio formats such as MP3, WAV (Windows), AIFF (Mac), and if you have QuickTime installed, even more formats. You'll have to dip into the Flash Help files to learn how to import audio, but it's not too hard. If you just want ambient background music on a page, you can even create a very small (like 1 pixel × 1 pixel) Flash movie that simply plays back music. Follow the steps on page 597 for inserting the Flash movie into a Web page.

There are also a few Dreamweaver extensions that let you add sound and music to your site: Speaker from Hot-Dreamweaver (*www.hotdreamweaver.com/speaker*) is a $19.99 extension that lets you insert an MP3 file onto your page that's played back by clicking a small icon. Trio Solutions (*http://components.developers4web.com/*) sells over a dozen different MP3 player extensions; each lets you insert CD-player-like controls (play, pause, stop, fast-forward) to control playback of audio and some let you create a playlist of multiple songs.

4

Part Four: Building a Web Site

CHAPTER

15

Introducing Site Management

As the dull-sounding name *site management* implies, organizing and tracking your Web site's files is one of the least glamorous, most time-consuming, and error-prone aspects of being a Web designer. On the Web, your site may look beautiful, run smoothly, and appear to be a gloriously unified whole, but behind the scenes, it's nothing more than a collection of varied files—HTML, images, Cascading Style Sheets, JavaScript, Flash movies, and so on—that must all work together. The more files you have to keep track of, the more apt you are to misplace one. A single broken link or missing graphic can interfere with the operation of your entire site, causing personal—even professional—embarrassment.

Fortunately, computers excel at tedious organizational tasks. Dreamweaver's site management features take care of the complexities of dealing with a Web site's many files, freeing you to concentrate on the creative aspects of design. In fact, even if you're a hand-coding HTML junkie and you turn your nose up at all visual Web page editors, you may find Dreamweaver worth its weight in gold just for the features described in this chapter and the next two.

Where the first three parts of this book describe how to create, lay out, and embellish a Web site, this part offers a bird's-eye view of the Web production process as you see your site through to completion and, ultimately, upload it to the Internet.

To get the most out of Dreamweaver's site management features, you need to be familiar with some basic principles for organizing Web files, as discussed in the next section.

Structuring a Web Site

When you build a Web site, you probably spend hours providing visitors with carefully planned links, helpful labels, and clear, informative navigation tools. You want your *site architecture*—the organizational structure of your site's various sections—to make it easy for visitors to understand where they are, where they can go, and how to return to where they came from (see Figure 15-1). Behind the scenes, it's equally important to organize your site's files with just as much clarity and care, so that you can find *your* way around when updating or modifying the site later. And, as on your own computer, a Web site's main organizational tool is the humble *folder*.

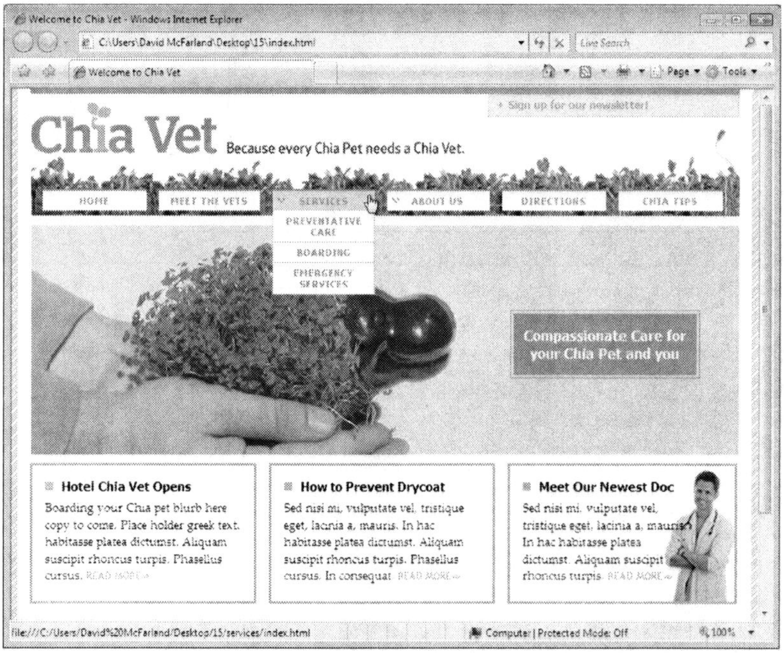

Figure 15-1: *A good site has an easy-to-understand structure. Content is divided into logical sections, and a prominent navigation bar–the row of buttons below the Chia Vet logo in this image–gives visitors quick access to the site's information. When building a site, this "site architecture" provides a useful model for naming and creating the behind-the-scenes folders that hold the site's files.*

You probably organize files on your computer every day, creating, say, a folder called Personal, within which are folders called Financial Planning and Vacation Pictures. Inside the Vacation Pictures folder, you might have separate folders for memories of Maui, Yosemite, and the Mall of America.

The same principle applies to the folders that make up a Web site: All Web sites have one primary folder—the *root folder*—that holds all of the site's Web pages, graphics, and other files used in the site. The root folder usually contains additional folders for further subdividing and organizing the site's files.

A good structure (see Figure 15-2) speeds up the production and maintenance of your site by providing quick access to whatever graphic, style sheet, or Flash movie you're looking for. But don't fall into the trap of becoming so obsessed that you put every graphic or Web page you create in its own separate folder; creating a structure for the files in a site should make your job easier, not harder.

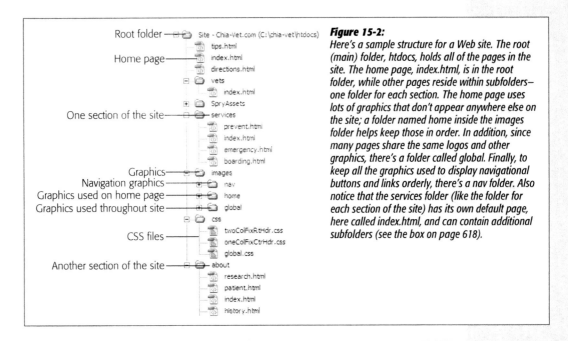

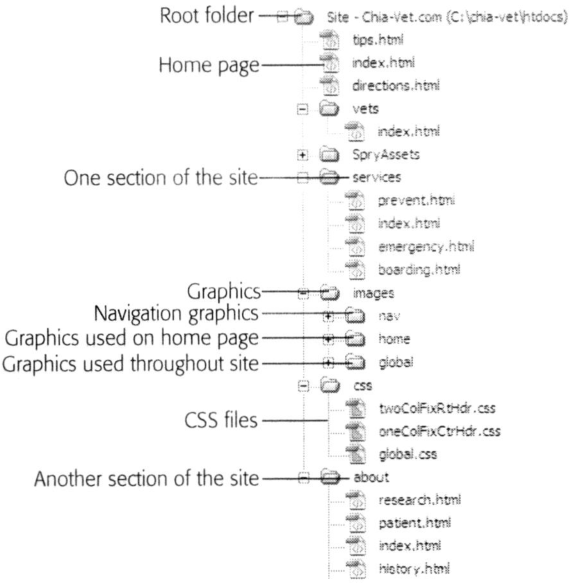

Figure 15-2:
Here's a sample structure for a Web site. The root (main) folder, htdocs, holds all of the pages in the site. The home page, index.html, is in the root folder, while other pages reside within subfolders–one folder for each section. The home page uses lots of graphics that don't appear anywhere else on the site; a folder named home inside the images folder helps keep those in order. In addition, since many pages share the same logos and other graphics, there's a folder called global. Finally, to keep all the graphics used to display navigational buttons and links orderly, there's a nav folder. Also notice that the services folder (like the folder for each section of the site) has its own default page, here called index.html, and can contain additional subfolders (see the box on page 618).

Tip: If you already have a Web site that suffers from lack of organization, it's not too late. Dreamweaver can help you reorganize your files quickly and accurately. Take the following rules to heart and then turn to "Organizing Site Files" on page 625 to learn how Dreamweaver can whip your current site into shape.

Here, then, are some guidelines for effective site organization:

- **Plan for future growth.** Like ever-spreading grapevines, Web sites grow. Today you may have only enough words and pictures for 10 Web pages, but tomorrow you'll put the finishing touches on your new 1,000-page online catalog. It may seem like overkill to create a lot of folders for a small site, but better to start with a solid structure today than find yourself knee-deep in files tomorrow.

  For instance, it's useful to create additional folders for graphics files that appear within each section of the site. If a section of your site is dedicated to promoting your company's products, create a folder called *products* for storing product Web pages. Create an additional folder called *images* to store the pictures of those products. Then, when you add more products or images, you know right where to put them.

Note: While you can start with no organization plan and later use Dreamweaver to bring it all into shape (see page 625), you may run into unforeseen problems if your site is already on the Internet. If your site's been up and running for a while, search engines may have indexed your site, and other Web sites may have linked to your pages. If you suddenly rearrange the pages of your site, those cherished links from the outside world may no longer work, and people who try to access your site from a search engine may be foiled.

- **Follow the site's architecture.** Take advantage of the work you've already done in organizing the content on your site. For instance, the *Chia Vet* site content is divided into five main sections: Meet the Vets, Services, About Us, Directions, and Chia Tips, as shown in Figure 15-1. Following this structure, it makes sense to create folders—*vets, services, about*, and so on—in the site's root folder for each section's respective Web pages. If one section is particularly large, add subfolders.

- **Organize files by type.** After you create folders for each section of your site, you'll probably need to add folders for storing other types of files like graphics, Cascading Style Sheets, external JavaScript files, and PDF files. Most sites, for instance, make extensive use of graphics, with several graphics on each page. If that's the case for you, then you need to file those images neatly and efficiently.

  One way to organize your graphics is to create a folder for images that appear on your home page and another for images that appear elsewhere in the site. Often, the home page is visually distinct from other pages on the site and contains graphics that are not only unique to it, but which might change frequently. You can create a folder—such as *images_home*—in the root folder for images that appear only on the home page. Create another folder—*images_global*, for example—to store graphics that all or most of the pages use, such as the company logo, navigation buttons, and other frequently used icons. When you add these images to other pages of your site, you'll know to look for them in this folder. Alternatively, you could create an *images* folder in the root of your site and add subfolders such as *home, global*, and *nav* (see Figure 15-2). The choice of an organizational system is yours; just make sure you have one.

- **Use understandable names.** While file names like *1a.gif, zDS.html*, and *f.css* are compact, they aren't very explanatory. Make sure file names mean something. Clear, descriptive names like *site_logo.gif* or *directions.html* make it a lot easier for you to locate files and update pages.

  This principle is especially important if you work as part of a team. If you're constantly explaining to your coworkers that *345g.gif* is the banner for the home page, changing the file name to *home_banner.gif* could save you some aggravation. There's a tradeoff here, however, as long file names can waste precious bytes. For instance, a name like *this_is_the_image_that_goes_in_the_upper_right_corner_of_the_home_page.gif* is probably not a good idea.

Note: Dreamweaver employs the industry-standard .html extension for Web pages—as in *index.html*. Another common extension is .htm (a holdover from the days when Windows could only use three-letter extensions). It doesn't really matter which you use, and if you're used to .htm, you can easily change the extension Dreamweaver uses. Just choose Edit → Preferences (Dreamweaver → Preferences on a Mac) to open the Preferences window, select the New Document category, and then type *.htm* in the default extension box.

It's also helpful to add a prefix to related files. For example, use *nav_* at the beginning of a graphic name to indicate that it's a navigation button. In this way, you can quickly identify *nav_projects.png*, *nav_quiz.png*, and *nav_horoscopes. png* as graphics used in a page's navigation bar, or *bg_body.png* and *bg_column.png* for graphics used as backgrounds. As a bonus, when you view the files on your computer or in Dreamweaver's Files panel (see Figure 15-6), they'll appear neatly sorted by name; in other words, all the *nav_* files cluster together in the file list. Likewise, if you have rollover versions of your navigation graphics (see page 248), give them names like *nav_projects_over.gif* or *nav_horoscopes_high.gif* to indicate that they're the highlighted (or over) state of the navigation button. (If you use Fireworks, its button-creation tools automatically use names like *nav_projects_f1.gif* and *nav_projects_f2.gif* to indicate two different versions of the same button.)

- **Be consistent.** Once you've come up with a system that works for you, follow it. Always. If you name one folder *images*, for instance, don't name another *graphics* and a third *pretty_pictures*. And certainly don't put Web pages in a folder named *images* or Flash movies in a folder named *style_sheets*.

  In fact, if you work on more than one Web site, you may want to use a single naming convention and folder structure for all of your sites, so that switching among them goes more smoothly. If you name all your graphics folders *images*, then no matter what site you're working on, you already know where to look for GIFs and JPEGs.

UP TO SPEED

Naming Your Files and Folders

The rules for naming files and folders in Windows and Macintosh are fairly flexible. You can use letters, numbers, spaces, and even symbols like $, #, and ! when naming folders and files on these operating systems.

Web servers, on the other hand, are far less accommodating. Because many symbols—such as &, @, and ?—have special significance on the Web, using them in file names can confuse Web servers and cause errors.

The precise list of no-no's varies from Web server to Web server, but you'll be safe if you stick to letters, numbers, the hyphen (-), and the underscore (_) character when naming files and folders. Stay away from spaces. File names like *company logo.gif* or *This company's president.html* may or may not work on a Web server. Replace spaces with underscores or inner caps—*company_logo.gif* or *companyLogo.gif*—and remove all punctuation marks.

Sure, some operating systems and Web servers permit strange naming conventions, but why take the chance? Someday you may need to move your site to another, less forgiving Web server. Play it safe: keep your file names simple.

Note: It's usually best to put only files that go on your Web site in the root folder and its subfolders. Keep your source files–the original Photoshop, Fireworks, Flash, or Word documents where you created your content–stored elsewhere on your computer. This way, you're much less likely to accidentally transfer a 14.5 MB Photoshop file to your Web server (a move that would *not* gain you friends in the IT department). That said, if you do like keeping all your files files together, check out Dreamweaver's *cloaking* feature (described on page 684). Using it, you can prevent certain file types from being transferred to your Web server when using Dreamweaver's FTP feature.

FREQUENTLY ASKED QUESTION

All Those Index Pages

Why are so many Web pages named index.html *(or* index.htm)?

If you type a URL like *http://www.missingmanuals.com* into a Web browser, the Missing Manuals home page opens on your screen. But how did the Web server know which page from the site to send to your browser? After all, you didn't ask for a particular Web page, like *http://www.missingmanuals.com/index.html.*

When a Web server gets a request that doesn't specify a particular Web page, it looks for a default Web page–often named *index.html* or *index.htm*. It does the same thing even when the URL you've typed specifies (with a slash) a folder inside the site root, like this: *http://www.missingmanuals.com/cds/*. In this case, the Web server looks for a file called *index.html* inside the cds folder and–if it finds the file–sends it to your Web browser.

If the Web server doesn't find an *index.html* file, two things can happen, both undesirable: the Web browser may display either an ugly error message or a listing of all the files inside the folder. Neither result is helpful to your visitors.

While your site still functions without this step, it's good form to give the main Web page inside each folder in your site the proper default page name. Web servers use different names for these default pages–*index.html* or *default.html*, for example–so check with your Web server's administrator or help desk. In fact, you can name any page as a default page, as long as you set up your Web server to look for the correct default name. So if you're creating a dynamic site like those discussed in Part 6, you can set up a server to look for a dynamic page like *index.asp* or *index.php* as the default page. On many Web servers, multiple default page names are specified, so if it doesn't find a file named *index.html*, it may then look for a file called *index.php*.

Defining a Site

Organizing and maintaining a Web site—creating new folders and Web pages; moving, renaming, and deleting files and folders; and transferring pages to a Web server—can require going back and forth between a couple of different programs. With Dreamweaver's site management features, however, you can do it all from within one program. But to take advantage of these features, you must first *define* the site; in other words, give Dreamweaver some basic information about it.

Defining the site involves showing Dreamweaver which folder contains your Web site files (the *root folder*) and setting up a few other options. You've already learned how to do this site-building using Dreamweaver's Site Definition Wizard (see page 38) and you got a quick introduction to the advanced Site Definition window on page 42. Here, you'll get a more detailed explanation of the options available in the advanced Site Definition window.

Start by choosing Site → New Site. This opens the Site Definition window (see Figure 15-3). Click the Advanced tab to access Dreamweaver's advanced settings. There are ten categories of information for your site, but to get up and running, you need to provide information only for the first category: Local Info. (The remaining categories are discussed in Chapter 16 and Chapter 17.)

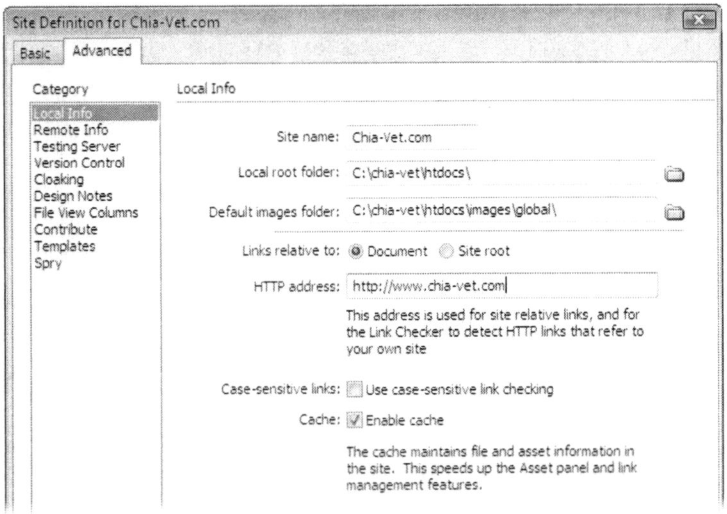

Figure 15-3: *The Basic tab of the Site Definition window provides a simple method for new users to set up a Web site. But Dreamweaver pros can take advantage of the greater options available under the Advanced tab shown here. The ten categories listed on the left side of the window are discussed in this and the next two chapters.*

Here are the options on the Local Info tab:

Site name

Into the "Site name" field, type a name that briefly identifies the site for you—and Dreamweaver. This is the name that appears, among other places, on the Site pop-up menu on the Files panel (skip ahead to Figure 15-6 for a glimpse of that), so that you can tell what site you're working on. It's just for identifying your site while working in Dreamweaver and doesn't have any effect on the actual pages of your site.

Local root folder

Identify your site's local root folder—the folder that contains all files belonging to your site—by clicking the folder icon to the right of the "Local root folder" box. The procedure is described on page 40. (Also see the box on page 623 for more information on local root folders.)

Tip: If you're confused about which folder should be the local root folder, just ask yourself this question: "Which folder on my computer contains (or will contain) my site's home page?" That's the local root folder.

All of Dreamweaver's tools for managing your sites' files rely on the local root folder. Once you've defined a site, you see all of its files listed in the Files panel.

Default images folder

For a graphic image to work properly on the Web, you can't just add it to a Web page (Chapter 6); you also have to store a copy of the graphics file in the local root folder or one of its subfolders. In other words, if you link to a graphic that's sitting on your computer's hard drive *outside* of the root folder, the Web browser will never find it.

Dreamweaver offers a feature that puts images in the right place even if you forget. When you add a stray graphics file to a page in your site, the program automatically copies the file into your default images folder. In fact, even if you drag a graphic from your desktop onto a Web page in progress, Dreamweaver copies the file to the default images folder without missing a beat.

The process of choosing the default images folder is the same as selecting a local root folder. Click the folder icon and select the proper folder, which can be an existing folder in your local root or a new one you create on the spot. (For example, this could be a folder named *images* or *images_global* in your local root folder.)

Links relative to

As discussed on page 161, there are a variety of ways to link to a Web page. When linking to another page in your site, Dreamweaver lets you create document-relative or root-relative links. As explained on page 162, Document-relative is often the easiest way to go, but Dreamweaver offers you the flexibility to choose. Click either the Document or "Site root" radio button. Dreamweaver then uses that method when adding links between pages of your site.

Note: You can override this setting and use whichever type of link you wish–site root-relative or document-relative–when actually creating the link, as described in step 4 on page 169.

FREQUENTLY ASKED QUESTION

Bringing Your Own Web Site

I already have a Web site. Will Dreamweaver work with it?

Yes. In fact, Dreamweaver's site management features are an invaluable aid in organizing the files of an existing site. As you can read in "Organizing Site Files" on page 625, you can use Dreamweaver to rearrange, rename, and reorganize files–tasks that are extremely difficult and time-consuming to do by hand.

Furthermore, Dreamweaver lets you clean up and reorganize a site without breaking links. So Dreamweaver is just as useful for working with a completed site as it is for creating one from scratch.

To work on an existing site, first save a copy of all site files on your computer, all in one folder. When defining the site (see page 37), choose this folder for the local root folder.

HTTP address

This option serves two functions: first, if you use absolute URLs to link to pages within your site (see page 162), you must fill out the "HTTP address" field for Dreamweaver's link-management features to work properly. Type your site's full URL beginning with *http://*. Dreamweaver uses this address to check for broken links within your site and to correctly rewrite links if you move pages around. For example, maybe your Webmaster has told you to link a form to *http://www.yourdomain.com/cgi/formscript.php* instead of using a document-relative link. In this case, you'd type *http://www.yourdomain.com* in the "HTTP address" box. Now, if you move or rename the *formscript.php* page from within Dreamweaver, the program is smart enough to update the link on the page with the form.

This setting is also incredibly valuable for one particular situation: if you're using site root–relative links, but the site you're working on isn't actually located in the site root on the Web server. For example, maybe you're running the marketing department at International ToolCo. You manage just the Web pages for the marketing department, and they're located in a folder called *marketing* on the Web server. In essence you manage a sub-site, which acts as an independent site within the larger International ToolCo site. Maybe your Webmaster demands that you use site root–relative links—man is that guy bossy.

This is potentially a tricky situation. Here's why: site root–relative links always begin with a /, indicating the root folder on the Web server (for a refresher on this concept, see page 163). Normally, if you add a root-relative link, say, to the main page in a folder named *personnel* located inside the local root folder, Dreamweaver would write the link like this: */personnel/index.html*. But in this case, that wouldn't work. The *personnel* folder is actually located (on the Web server) inside the *marketing* folder. So the link should be */marketing/personnel/index.html*. In other words, Dreamweaver normally thinks that the local root folder maps exactly to the Web server's root folder.

You can solve this dilemma by adding a URL that points to the "sub-site" in the Site Definition window's "HTTP address" box. In this example, you'd type *http://www.intltoolco.com/marketing/* in the box. Then, whenever you add a site root–relative link, Dreamweaver begins with */marketing/* and then adds the rest of the path to the URL. In summary, *if* you use site root–relative links *and* you're working solely on pages located inside a subdirectory on the actual Web server, *then* fill out the absolute URL to that subdirectory. Finally, add this whole rigmarole to the list of reasons why document-relative links are easier to manage in Dreamweaver.

Note: Strangely, the first use of the HTTP address box mentioned above–that is, managing absolute URLs pointing to files in your site–doesn't work with the second option–sub-sites. For example, if you specify a sub directory like *http://www.intltoolco.com/marketing/* in the HTTP address box, Dreamweaver isn't able to keep track of absolute links within this site. So if you had to use the URL *http://www.intltoolco.com/marketing/cgi/form.php* to point to a form page within your site, and then move that form page, Dreamweaver will not update the page using that absolute link.

Case-sensitive links

Some Web servers (namely, those of the Unix and Linux variety) are sensitive to the case used in a file name. For example, *INDEX.html* is a different file than *index.html.* In this case, you can turn on the "Use case-sensitive link checking" box to make sure Dreamweaver doesn't mistake one file for another when checking links. Say you link to a file named *INDEX.html*, but change the name of another file named *index.html* to *contact.html.* Without this option turned on, Dreamweaver may mistakenly update any links to *INDEX.html.*

In real-world use, you probably won't need this option. First, it's not possible to have two files with the same name but using different combinations of upper- and lowercase letters in the same folder on a Mac or Windows machine. So if your local root folder is located on your Mac or Windows computer, you'll never be able to get into this situation. In addition, it's confusing (and just plain weird) to use the same name but different cases to name your files. Revisit the rules of file naming (see page 617) if you find yourself tempted to do this.

Cache

The cache is a small database of information about the files in your site. It helps Dreamweaver's site management features work more efficiently; leave this checkbox turned on.

Once you've provided the local information for your site, click OK to close the Site Definition window and begin working. In almost all cases, you'll want to keep this box checked. However, if you have a really large site, composed of tens of thousands of Web pages, Dreamweaver might act pretty sluggishly when you perform basic tasks like moving files around within the site, or checking for broken links.

Editing or Removing Defined Sites

Sometimes you need to edit the information associated with a site. Perhaps you want to rename the site, or you've reorganized your hard drive and moved the local root folder to a different location, and you need to let Dreamweaver know what you've done.

To edit a site, open the Manage Sites dialog box (choose Site → Manage Sites or, in the Files panel, choose Manage Sites from the bottom of the Site pop-up menu) and double-click the name of the site you want to edit. The Site Definition window opens (Figure 15-3). Now you can type a new name in the Site Name box, choose a new local root folder, or make any other changes. Click OK to close the dialog box when you're done.

Tip: If you want to edit the current site's information, there's a shortcut. In the Files panel (Figure 15-6), just double-click the name of the site in the Sites menu. (Mac owners need to click once to select the name in the menu, and then click again to open the Site Definition window.)

UP TO SPEED

Local vs. Remote Root Folders

A root folder is the main, hold-everything folder for your site. It contains every piece of the site: all Web page documents, graphic images, CSS style sheets, flash movies, and so on.

The word "root" implies that this is the master, outer, main folder, in which there may be plenty of subfolders. Remember that, in most cases, your Web site exists in two locations: on your computer as you work on it, and on the Internet where people can enjoy the fruits of your labor. In fact, most Web sites in the universe live in two places at once—one copy on the Internet and the original copy on some Web designer's hard drive.

The copy on your own computer is called the *local site* or the *development site*. Think of the local site as a sort of staging ground, where you build your site, test it, and modify it.

Because the local site isn't on a Web server, and the public can't see it, you can freely edit and add to a local site without affecting the pages your visitors are viewing, meanwhile, on the remote site. The root folder for the version of the site on your computer, therefore, is called the *local root folder*.

When you've added or updated a file, you move it from the local site to the *remote site*. The remote, or live, site mirrors the local site. Because you create it by uploading your local site, it has the same organizational folder structure as the local site and contains the same polished, fully functional Web pages. However, you leave the half-finished, typo-ridden drafts on your local site until you've perfected them. Chapter 17 explains how to use Dreamweaver's FTP features to define and work with a remote site.

Once you've finished a site and are no longer working on it, you may wish to remove it from Dreamweaver's list of sites. To delete a site from the list, open the Manage Sites dialog box as described above, click to select the site you wish to delete, and then click Remove.

A warning appears telling you that this action can't be undone. Don't worry; deleting the site here doesn't actually *delete* the site's images, Web pages, and other files from your computer. It merely removes the site from Dreamweaver's list of defined sites. (You can always go back and define the site again, if you need to, by following the steps on page 37.) Click Done to close the Manage Sites window.

Note: If you do, in fact, want to delete the actual Web pages, graphics, and other site components, you can either switch to the desktop (Windows Explorer or the Finder, for example) and delete them manually, or delete them from within Dreamweaver's Files panel, described on page 633.

Exporting and Importing Sites

When you define a site, Dreamweaver stores that site's information in its own private files. If you want to work on your site using a different computer, therefore, you must define the site again for *that* copy of Dreamweaver. In a design firm where several people are working together on many different sites, that's a lot of extra setup. In fact, even if there's just one of you working on two computers, duplicating your efforts is a pain.

So that you can put your time to better use, Dreamweaver lets you import and export site definitions. For example, you can back up your *site definition* files—in case you have to reinstall Dreamweaver—or export a site definition for others to use.

To export a site definition:

1. **Choose Site → Manage Sites.**

   The Manage Sites window appears, listing all the sites you've defined (Figure 15-4).

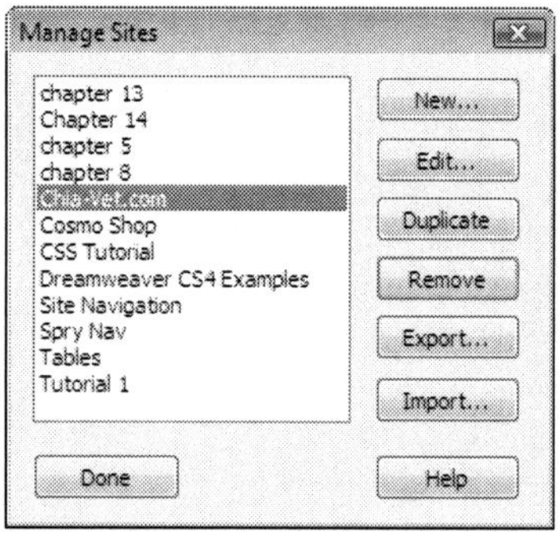

Figure 15-4: *The Manage Sites window is the control center for managing your sites. Add new sites, edit old sites, duplicate a site definition, and even export site definitions for use on another computer, or as a precautionary backup.*

2. **Select a site from the list, and then click Export.**

   If the site definition includes remote site information (see page 668), you'll see a dialog box called "Exporting site" (Figure 15-5). If you're simply making a backup of your site definition because you need to reinstall Dreamweaver, select the "Back up my settings" radio button. (The other option, "Share settings," is useful when, for example, your local root folder is on the C: drive, but the root folder is on the E: drive on someone else's computer, so your setup information doesn't apply to them. It's also handy when you don't want to give someone else your user name and password to the Web server.)

Figure 15-5: *This dialog box lets you back up your settings or share them (minus your login information) with other people.*

3. **Click OK.**

   The Export Site panel appears.

Tip: You can export multiple sites in one step. Just select all of the sites you wish to export (Ctrl-click [⌘-click] the names of the sites you wish to export), and then click the Export button.

4. **In the Export Site panel, specify where you want to save the file and give it a name.**

   If you're making a backup, save the file outside the local root folder (for example, with the Photoshop, Fireworks, and Word source files for the site). Because the export file can potentially contain the username and password you use to move files to your site, you don't want to keep the file anywhere in your local root folder—it might mistakenly be uploaded to the Web server where someone might find the file and discover your username and password.

   Dreamweaver ends site definition files with the file extension *.ste*.

Once you have a *site definition* file, you can import it into Dreamweaver as follows:

1. **Choose Site → Manage Sites.**

   The Manage Sites panel appears.

2. **Click Import.**

   The Import Site panel appears. Navigate to a site *definition* file—look for a file ending in .ste. Select it, and then click OK.

If you're importing the site definition to a computer other than the one you used to export the site, you may need to perform a few more steps. If Dreamweaver can't locate the local root folder in the *site definition* file, it asks you to select a local root folder on the new computer, as well as a new default images folder.

Organizing Site Files

Once you've defined your local site, Dreamweaver helps you organize your files, create folders, and add new Web pages to your site, using the Files panel as your command center. To open the Files panel, choose Window → Files, or just press F8 (Shift-⌘-F).

In its most basic incarnation, the Files panel displays the files in the current site's local root folder (see Figure 15-6). This list looks and acts just like Windows Explorer or the Macintosh Finder; you see names, file sizes, and folders. You can view the files inside a folder by clicking the + (triangle on Mac) symbol next to the folder (or simply by double-clicking the folder). Double-click a Web page to open it in Dreamweaver. You can also see the size of a file, the type of file, and the last time the file was modified. (That's a lot of information to fit in that space, so if you find this new view a little too crammed with information, you can hide any columns you don't like—see page 627.)

Note: You can open certain types of files in an outside program of your choice by defining an external editor for that file type. For example, you can tell Dreamweaver to open GIF files in Fireworks, Photoshop, or another image editor. (See page 239 for more on this feature.)

You can view your site's files in four different ways using the View pop-up menu (shown in Figure 15-6):

Note: Dreamweaver CS4 eliminated the so-very-not-useful "Site Map" view from the Files panel.

- **Local view** shows the files in your local root folder. Folders in this view are green.
- **Remote view** shows files on the Web server in the remote root folder (see page 623). Of course, before you've posted your site on the Web, this list is empty. Information appears here only after you've set up a connection to a remote root folder (see page 668) and connected to a Web server. Folders in this view are yellow on Windows and blue on Macs.
- **Testing Server** view is useful when you're creating the dynamic, database-driven sites discussed in Part 6 of this book. No files appear in this view until you've set up a testing server (see page 811) and connected to it. Folders in this view are red.
- **Repository view** is used for a file versioning system called Subversion. This advanced file management tool is discussed on page 689.

Note: If you've got a small monitor, the Files panel (and other panel groups) might take up too much space to comfortably work on a Web page. You can hide (and show) all panels, including the Property inspector and the Insert bar, by pressing F4.

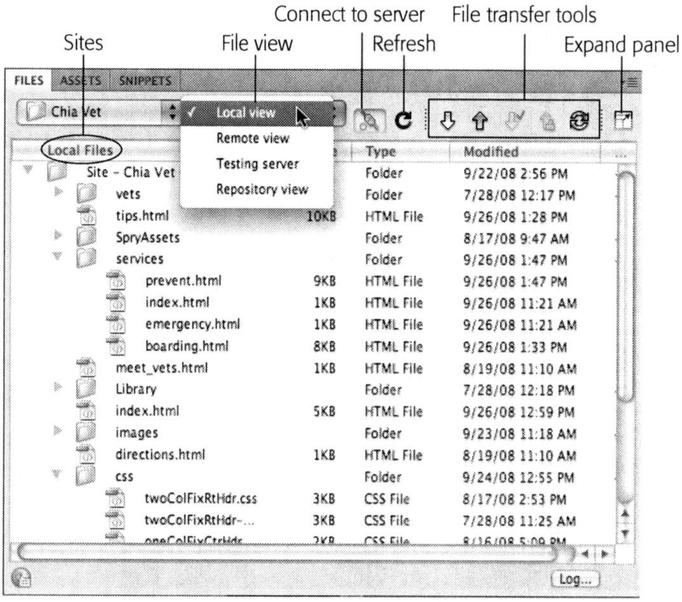

***Figure 15-6:** The Files panel, logically enough, lists files in the currently active Web site. A list of all the Web sites you've defined in Dreamweaver appears in the Sites pop-up menu; to work on a different site, select its name (but be aware you can also select files on your local file system, potentially tripping up Dreamweaver's Site Management tools–see the box on page 634). You can use the Files panel to connect to a Web server and transfer files back and forth between your local and remote sites, as described on page 678. You can tell whether you're looking at the files on your computer, the Web server, the testing server, or a Subversion repository by looking at the name that appears at the top of the file column. For example, in this figure, you're looking at the files on the computer since "Local Files" (circled) is listed.*

Modifying the Files Panel View

Dreamweaver stocks the Files panel with loads of new information: you'll see the file name, the size of the file, the type of file (Web page, graphic, and so on), and the date the file was last modified. This is all useful to know, but if you have a relatively small monitor, you may not be able display everything without having to scroll left and right. What's worse, the filenames themselves can get clipped off as Dreamweaver tries to display the other columns of information.

There are a couple of things you can do to fix this situation. First, you can resize the width of each column by dragging one of the dividers that separates each column name (see Figure 15-6). Using this technique you can at least make the file name column wide enough to display the complete name of each file.

If you don't like the number of columns Dreamweaver displays, you can hide any or all of the columns. After all, how useful is listing the type of each file? The folder icon clearly indicates when you're looking at a folder; a file name ending in .html is a Web page; and a JPEG file's extension, .jpg, is clearly visible as part of the file's name. For most folks, that's enough.

Unfortunately, there's no program-wide setting to control which columns appear. You have to define the visible columns on a site-by-site basis. Start by editing the Site definition, following the instructions on page 622. Next, click the File View Columns category (under the Advanced tab of the Site Definition window; see Figure 15-7). Select a column you wish to hide and turn off the Show checkbox. The column's status under the Show column changes from Show to Hide as shown in Figure 15-7.

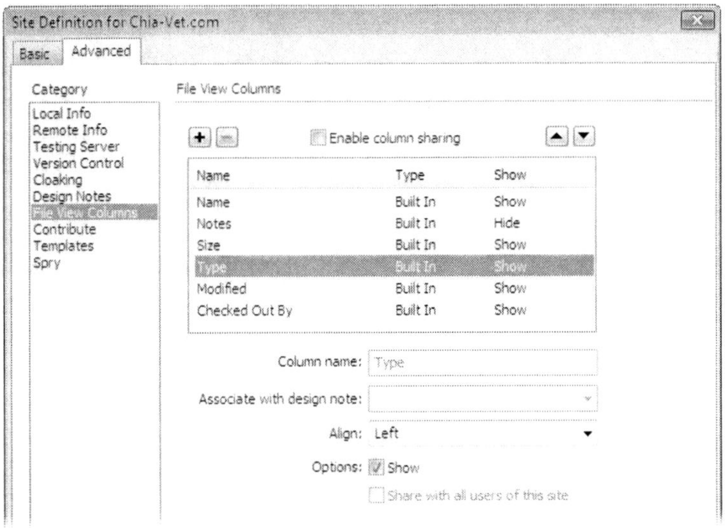

Figure 15-7: *Use the File View Columns category to show or hide columns of information in the Files panel. It's also useful for working with Dreamweaver's collaborative note sharing feature called Design Notes. More on Design Notes and instructions for how to use them start on page 696.*

You can also change the order of the columns—perhaps the Modified date information is more important than the file size to you. Select a column and click the up or down arrow. The up arrow moves the column to the left in the Files Panel, while the down arrow scoots a column over to the right in the Files panel.

FOR WINDOWS PCS

The Windows Files Panel

If you'd like to expand the Files panel, so you can see a side-by-side view of both the *remote site* files and *local site* files, click the Expand/Collapse button (labeled in Figure 15-6). The Files panel fills the screen as shown in Figure 15-8. The obvious drawback is that you can't work on a Web page while the Site window is maximized, because you can't even see it. Click the Expand/Collapse button again to minimize the Files panel and gain access to your document window.

To get around this limitation, you can undock the Files panel before clicking the Expand button: Grab the Files panel group by its grip–the tiny column of dots to the left of the *word* Files–and drag it toward the middle of the screen. (Stay away from the edges of the screen when performing this maneuver; touching there may simply redock the panel group.) The panel group then becomes a floating panel. Now press the Expand button to get the side-by-side files view. You're now free to resize the Files panel even after expanding it.

Adding New Folders and Files

The Files panel provides a fast way of adding blank Web pages to your site. With one click, you can create a new page in any folder you like, saving several steps you'd otherwise have to perform using the File menu.

Adding files

To create a new, blank Web page, open the Files panel using one of the methods described on page 625, and then right-click (Control-click) a file or folder in the Files panel.

In the shortcut menu that appears, choose New File. Dreamweaver creates a new, empty Web page. (Actually, the page doesn't have to be empty; you can edit the file Dreamweaver uses as its default new page, as described in the box below.)

Note: The type of file Dreamweaver creates depends on the type of site you're creating. For a plain HTML site, Dreamweaver creates a blank HTML page. However, if you're building a dynamic, database-driven site like those described in Part 6, Dreamweaver creates a blank page based on the type of server model you've selected. For example, if you're building a site using PHP and MySQL, the page is a blank PHP page (named *untitled.php*).

The new file appears in the Files panel with a highlighted naming rectangle next to it; type a name for the page here. Don't forget to add the appropriate extension (.htm or .html) to the end of its name—if you don't add any extension, Dreamweaver creates a completely empty file (and changing the name again by adding the .html extension won't fix this problem). If this happens, delete the file and create a new one.

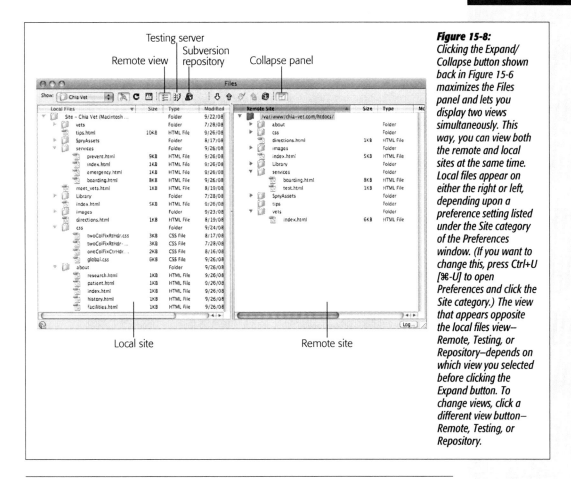

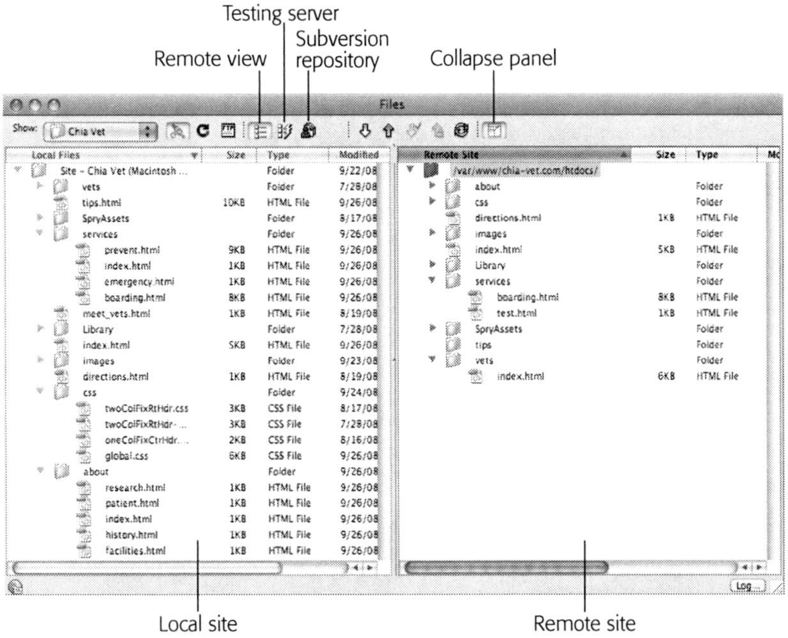

Figure 15-8: *Clicking the Expand/Collapse button shown back in Figure 15-6 maximizes the Files panel and lets you display two views simultaneously. This way, you can view both the remote and local sites at the same time. Local files appear on either the right or left, depending upon a preference setting listed under the Site category of the Preferences window. (If you want to change this, press Ctrl+U [⌘-U] to open Preferences and click the Site category.) The view that appears opposite the local files view–Remote, Testing, or Repository–depends on which view you selected before clicking the Expand button. To change views, click a different view button–Remote, Testing, or Repository.*

Tip: If, immediately after creating a new file in the Files panel, you rename that file and add a new extension, the contents of the file update to reflect the new file type. For example, changing *untitled.html* to *global.css* erases all of the HTML code in the file and turns it into an empty CSS file.

Adding folders

You can add folders to your site directly in Dreamweaver using the Files panel. Just right-click (Control-click) a file or folder in the local files list. From the shortcut menu, choose New Folder. If you clicked a file, Dreamweaver creates the new folder in the same folder as that file; if you clicked a folder, you get a new folder inside it.

If you crave variety, you can add a folder another way. Select a file or folder in the Files panel and then click the contextual menu button (located at the top right of the Files panel) and select File → New Folder. Finally, in the naming rectangle that appears in the Files panel, type a name for the new folder.

POWER USERS' CLINIC

Changing the Default New Page

Whenever you create a new Web page—for example, by choosing File → New or by right-clicking (Control-clicking) an existing file in the Files panel—Dreamweaver gives you a blank, white document window. But what if you always want your pages to have gray backgrounds, or you always want to include a link to the same external style sheet?

Every new Web page you create is actually an untitled copy of a default template document called Default.html. You can find this file in the Dreamweaver configuration folder. On Windows it's in *C:\Program Files\Adobe\Adobe Dreamweaver CS4\configuration\DocumentTypes\NewDocuments*. On a Mac, you can find it in *Applications → Adobe Dreamweaver CS4 → configuration → DocumentTypes → New-Documents* folder.

So that you don't ruin the original, save a copy of this folder to your user folder. In Windows XP: *C:\Documents and Settings\[your user name]\Application Data\Adobe\Dreamweaver CS4\en_US\Configuration*. In Windows Vista: *C:\Users\[your user name]\AppData\Roaming\Adobe\Dreamweaver CS4\en_US\Configuration*. On a Mac: *Volume Name → Users → [your user name] → Library → Application Support → Adobe → Dreamweaver CS4 → en_US → Configuration*.

You can then open a file from the New-Document folders in your personal configuration folder within Dreamweaver and edit it however you like: change its background color, margins, text color, or whatever, so that all subsequent new pages you create inherit its settings. Consider making a backup of this file before editing it, however, so that you can return to the factory settings if you accidentally make a mess of it. (Also, make sure you don't touch an HTML fragment that probably appears to you to be incorrect: namely, the *charset=*" snippet, which appears at the end of the <meta> tag. This fragment of HTML is indeed incomplete, but when you create a new page, Dreamweaver correctly completes this code according to the alphabet—Chinese, Korean, or Western European, for example—that your page uses.)

You'll also notice lots of other files in this folder. Since Dreamweaver can create lots of different file types—Cascading Style Sheets, Active Server Pages, and so on—you'll find a default blank file for each. You can edit any of these—but don't, unless you're sure of what you're doing. You can easily damage some of the more complex file types, especially those that involve dynamic Web sites.

Moving files and folders

Because the Dreamweaver Files panel looks and acts so much like the Windows Explorer and the Macintosh Finder, you may think it does nothing more than let you move and rename files and folders on your computer. You may even be tempted to work with your site files directly on the Mac or Windows desktop, thinking that you're saving time. Think again. When it comes to moving the files and folders in your site, Dreamweaver does more than your computer's desktop ever could.

In your Web travels, you've probably encountered the dreaded "404: File Not Found" error. This "broken link" message doesn't necessarily mean that the page doesn't exist, just that your Web browser didn't find the page at the location (URL) specified by the link you just clicked. In short, someone working on that Web site probably moved or renamed a file without updating the link. Because Web site files are interrelated in such complex ways—pages link to other pages, which include paths to graphics, which in turn appear on other pages—an action as simple as moving one file can wreak havoc on an entire Web site. That's why you shouldn't drag Web site files around on your desktop or rename them in Windows Explorer or the Macintosh Finder.

In fact, moving and reorganizing Web site files is so headache-ridden and error-prone that some Web designers avoid it altogether, leaving their sites straining under the weight of thousands of poorly organized files. But you don't have to be one of them: Dreamweaver makes reorganizing a site easy and error-free. When you use the Files panel to move files, Dreamweaver looks for actions that could break your site's links and automatically rewrites paths of links, images, and other media (see the cautionary box on page 634).

Note to JavaScript Programmers: If your custom JavaScript programs include paths to images, Web pages, or other files in your site, Dreamweaver can't help you. When you reorganize your site with the Files panel, the program updates *links* it created, but not *paths* you've included in your JavaScript programs.

Just be sure to do your moving from within Dreamweaver, like this: In the Files panel, drag the folder or file into its new folder (see Figure 15-9). To move multiple files, Ctrl-click (⌘-click) each of the ones you want to move, and then drag them as a group; to deselect a selected file, Ctrl-click or ⌘-click it again. You can also select one folder or file and Shift-click another to select all files and folders in the list between the two.

Note: Close *all* of your Web documents *before* reorganizing your files in this way. Dreamweaver has been known to not always correctly update links in open files. But if you do end up with malfunctioning links, you can always use Dreamweaver's Find Broken Links tool (see page 643) to ferret out and fix any broken links.

When you release the mouse button, the Update Files dialog box appears (Figure 15-9); just click Update. Dreamweaver updates all the links for you.

Tip: If you accidentally dragged the file or folder to the wrong location, click Don't Update. Then drag the file back to its original location and, if Dreamweaver asks, click Don't Update once again.

Renaming files and folders

Renaming files and folders poses the same problems as moving them. Because links include file and folder names, altering a file or folder name can break a link just as easily as moving or deleting the file or folder.

For example, say you've created a new site with a home page named *home.html*. You cheerfully continued building the other pages of your site, linking them to *home.html* as you went along. But after reading this chapter and checking to find out what default file name your Web server requires (see page 618), you found that

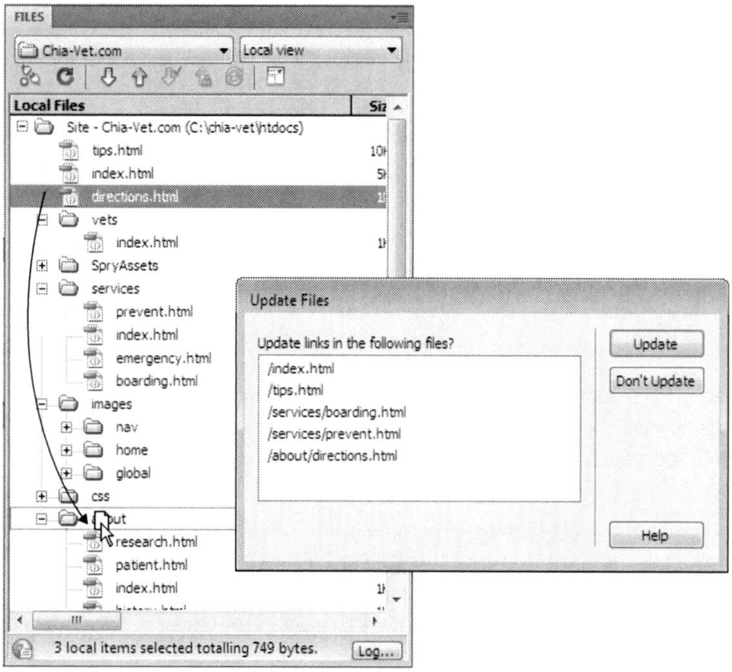

Figure 15-9:
You can move files and folders within the Files panel just as you would in Windows Explorer or the Macintosh Finder. Simply drag the file into (or out of) a folder. But unlike your computer's file system, Dreamweaver constantly monitors the links between Web pages, graphics, and other files. If you move a file using Windows Explorer or the Finder, you'll most likely end up breaking links to that file or, if it's a Web page, links in that file. By contrast, Dreamweaver is smart enough to know when moving files will cause problems. The Update Files dialog box lets you update links to and from the file you're moving, so that your site keeps working.

you need to rename your home page file *index.html*. If you were to rename the file *index.html* using Windows Explorer or the Macintosh Finder, every link to *home.html* would result in a "File not found" error.

Dreamweaver, on the other hand, handles this potential disaster effortlessly, as long as you rename the file in the Files panel instead. To do so, just click the file or folder in the Files panel. Pause a moment, and click the *name* of the file or folder. (The pause ensures that Dreamweaver won't think you just double-clicked the file for editing.)

A renaming rectangle appears; type the new name. Be sure to include the proper extension for the type of file you're renaming. For example, GIFs end with .gif and Cascading Style Sheets end with .css. Although Dreamweaver lets you name files without using an extension, the extensionless files won't work when you move them to a Web server.

Finally, in the Update Files dialog box (Figure 15-9), click Update. Dreamweaver updates all the links to this file or folder to reflect the new name.

Warning: It bears repeating: never rename or move files and folders *outside* of Dreamweaver. If you use Windows Explorer or the Macintosh Finder to reorganize the files in your site, links will break, images will disappear from your pages, and the earth will open underneath your feet. (Well, actually, that last thing won't happen, but it can *feel* that way when your boss comes in and says, "What's happened to our Web site? Nothing works!")

If you've edited files outside of Dreamweaver by accident, see page 643 to learn how to find and fix broken links.

Deleting files and folders

It's a good idea to clean up your site from time to time by deleting old and unused files. Just as with moving and renaming files, you delete files from the Files panel.

To delete a file or folder, just click to select it in the Files panel and press Backspace or Delete. (To select multiple files or folders, Ctrl-click [⌘-click] them as described on page 646.) If the doomed file or folder isn't referenced by any other page on the site, a simple "Are you sure you want to delete this file?" warning appears; click Yes.

However, if other files link to the file—or to files within the folder—that you're deleting, then a warning dialog box (Figure 15-10) appears informing you that you're about to break links on one or more pages in your site.

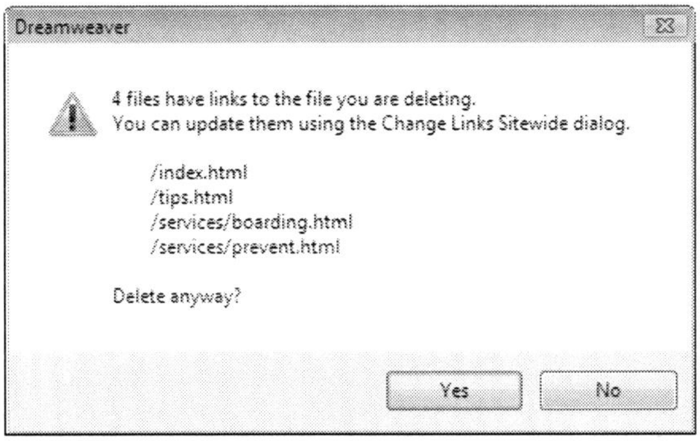

Figure 15-10:
When you delete files in the Files panel, Dreamweaver warns you if other pages reference (link to) the file. If you click Yes, you'll need to go back and repair the links. Dreamweaver gives you a convenient way to do so–the Change Links Sitewide command (see page 650)–and reminds you of it in this dialog box.

The message even lists the first few pages that use the file. If you've made a mistake, click No to leave your site untouched.

If you're sure you wish to delete the file, click Yes. And yes, this move does *break links* in all the pages listed. Repairing those links, which usually means linking them to a new page, requires a separate step: using the Site → Change Links Sitewide command, as described on page 650.

Site Assets

Web pages integrate lots of different elements: PNGs, GIFs, JPEGs, links, colors, JavaScript files and Flash movies, to name just a few. In a large site with lots of files, it's a challenge to locate a particular image or remember an exact color.

To simplify the process, Dreamweaver provides the Assets panel. For want of a better generic term, Dreamweaver defines the term *asset* to mean any element you use on a Web page, such as a GIF file, a link, or even an individual color.

FREQUENTLY ASKED QUESTION

Beware "Site-less" Web Design

Why doesn't Dreamweaver warn me when I delete or move a file?

Dreamweaver's site management tools are always watching your back–unless you're not working in a site. Dreamweaver tries to be a flexible tool for use in all situations. Some developers don't like the whole notion of sites and prefer to just work on their pages in the old (unmonitored) way of most programs. And in cases where you just want to edit a single page, but don't want to go through the whole business of defining a site, Dreamweaver's Files panel lets you browse your files, just like the regular Windows Explorer or Mac Finder. If you click the Sites menu (where you'd normally switch between defined sites) and scroll to the top of the menu, you'll see a list of hard drives and other networked storage devices. For example, you could select your main drive (C: or Macintosh HD, for example). The Files panel then displays all of the files on that drive. Unfortunately, this flexibility can also cause a lot of trouble.

Sometimes people accidentally select their hard drive instead of their site in the Sites menu, and *then* navigate to the folder holding their site's files. They then begin working, blissfully unaware that they're working without Dreamweaver's safety net. When looking at your files in this way, changes you make to your existing site files–like moving, deleting, or renaming–aren't monitored by Dreamweaver (it figures you know better). Similarly, all of Dreamweaver's other site management features like Libraries (Chapter 18), templates (Chapter 19), and file transfers (Chapter 17) don't work when you're off in un-site-managed-land. In other words, it's best to always define a site, and always make sure you've selected the site's name in the Files panel, as you work on your Web site.

Viewing the Assets Panel

Dreamweaver lists your site's assets on the nine category "pages" of the Assets panel (Figure 15-11). To open the panel, choose Window → Assets, or press F11.

You select an asset in the list by clicking its name; a miniature preview appears above the Assets list. To preview a movie, click the green arrow that appears in the preview window.

The Assets panel highlights nine different categories of site elements. To view the assets in a particular category, click its icon at the left of the Assets panel:

- The **Images** category lists all of the GIF, JPEG, and PNG files in your site. Dreamweaver lists the dimensions of each image next to its name, so you can quickly identify whether *logo1.gif*, or *logo2.gif* is your 728 × 90 pixel banner logo. You can also see the images' sizes, types, and where they're located in the site (you may need to scroll to the right to see all of this information).
- The **Colors** category shows all of the colors specified in the Web pages and style sheets of your site. These include link colors, background colors, and text colors.
- The **Links** category lists all *external* links—not just standard *http://* links, but also email links, FTP addresses, and JavaScript links.

- The **multimedia** categories—SWF (meaning Flash movies), Shockwave, and Movies (meaning Flash video or QuickTime)—are roughly equivalent. They each display *movie* files with their corresponding extensions: .swf (Flash), .dcr (Shockwave), .flv (Flash video), and .mov or .mpg (QuickTime and MPEG).
- The **Scripts** category lists JavaScript files. This category only includes external *script* files that Web pages link to; for example, the JavaScript files that are part of the Spry Framework and which are attached to a Web page whenever you use a Spry widget or effect. Scripts that are embedded *into* a Web page—like those created using Dreamweaver behaviors—aren't listed.
- The last two categories—**Templates** and **Library**—are advanced assets that streamline Web site production. They're discussed in Chapter 18 and Chapter 19.

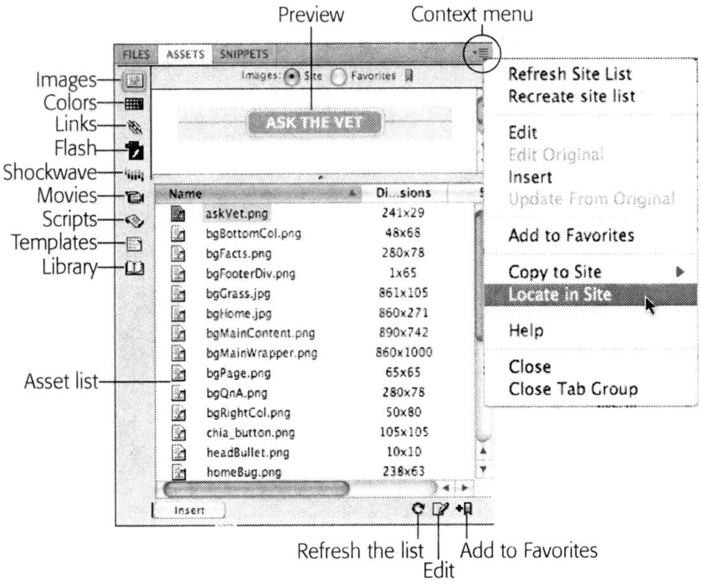

Figure 15-11: *Most of the commands in the contextual menu shown here are duplicated in the panel itself, but three options appear only on this menu. Recreate Site List comes in handy if you've added or deleted files outside Dreamweaver. It rebuilds the site cache and updates the list of assets. "Copy to Site" copies the selected asset to another site. "Locate in Site" opens the Files panel and highlights the file of the asset you selected in the Assets panel. You can also open a contextual menu by right-clicking (Control-clicking) any asset in the list.*

You can switch between two different views for each asset category—Site and Favorites—by clicking the radio buttons near the top of the Assets panel. The Site option lists all the assets that appear in the Site for the chosen category. Favorites lets you create a select list of your most important and frequently used assets (see page 637).

Note: Dreamweaver's cloaking feature lets you hide files from many sitewide tasks, including the Assets panel. So, if you have a folder with thousands of *image* files that you'd rather not display on the Assets panel, you can hide that folder and its files. See page 684 for more on this feature.

If, as you're working on a site, you add additional assets—for example, you create a new GIF image in Fireworks and import it to the site—you'll need to update the Assets panel. Click the Refresh Site List button (see Figure 15-11) to update the list of assets.

Inserting Assets

The Assets panel's prime mission is to make using assets easier. From the Assets list, you can add graphics, colors, and links to your pages with a click of the mouse. Most of the categories on the panel refer to external files that you can include on a Web page: images, Flash, Shockwave, movies, and scripts.

The easiest way to insert an asset file is to drag it from the Assets panel into the document window. You can drag the asset anywhere on the page you'd normally insert an object—in a table cell, a <div> tag, at the beginning or end of a page, or within a paragraph. Script assets can go in the head of a Web page (see Figure 15-12).

(If you're billing by the hour, you may prefer the long way: click in the document window to plant the insertion point, click the asset's name, and then click Insert at the bottom of the Assets panel.)

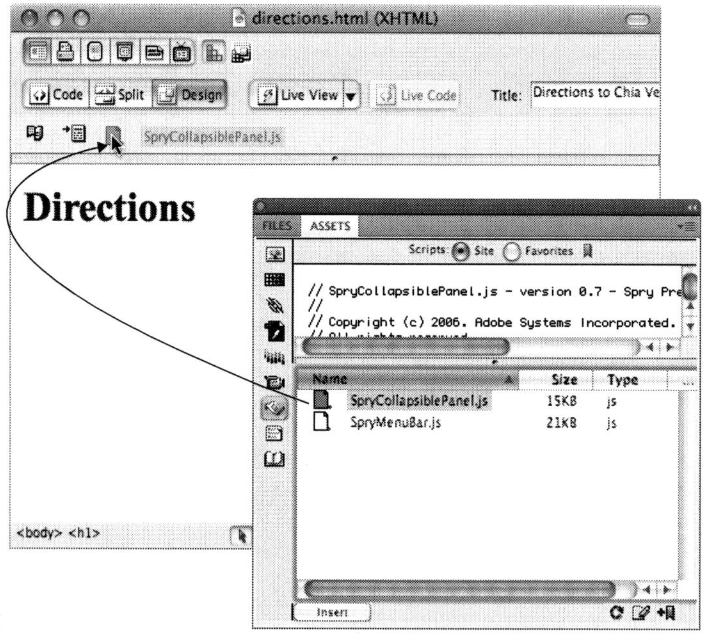

Figure 15-12: *While you'll insert most assets into the body of a Web page, you can (and usually should) place script files in the head of the page. To do this, first choose View → Show Head Content. Then drag the script from the Assets panel into the head pane, as shown here. (Adding a script asset doesn't copy the JavaScript code into the Web page. Instead, just as with external style sheets, Dreamweaver links to the script file so that when a Web browser loads the page, it looks for and then loads the file from the Web site.)*

POWER USERS' CLINIC

The Return of Root-Relative Paths

Chapter 5 explains the different types of link paths—absolute, document-relative, and root-relative—that Dreamweaver understands (see page 161). While, in many cases, it's best to use document-relative paths for linking to pages within your own site, or for adding images and other media to a page, you may notice that Dreamweaver frequently displays root-relative paths in its site management tools.

For instance, the list in the Assets panel includes the full root-relative path of each asset—*/images_home/banner.png*, for example. The initial "/" indicates the root folder of the site, and the information that follows indicates the rest of the path to that asset. In this example, the graphic asset *banner.png* is in a folder called *images_home*, which is itself in the site's root folder. Dreamweaver needs to look no further than the root folder to find the asset in question.

Root-relative paths indicate a precise location within a site and let Dreamweaver know where to find a file. This doesn't mean, however, that when you use the Assets panel to insert an image or other file, that Dreamweaver uses site root-relative links. Dreamweaver uses the type of link you specified for the site as described on page 620.

Adding color and link assets

Color and link assets work a bit differently than other asset files. Instead of standing on their own, they *add* color or a link to images or text you've selected in the document window. (You can add colors to any text selection, or add links to images and text.) In this way, you can quickly add a frequently used link—the URL to download the Flash player or Adobe Reader, for example.

To do so, start by highlighting the text (to change its color or turn it into a link) or image (to turn it into a link). In the Assets panel, click the appropriate category button—Colors or Links. Click the color or link you want, and then click Apply. Alternatively, you can drag the color or link asset from the panel to the selection.

In the case of a link, Dreamweaver simply adds an <a> tag to the selection, with the proper external link. For color, Dreamweaver pops-up the New CSS Rule window (Figure 4-2) and asks you to create a new CSS style—you then need to go through the whole rigmarole described on page 115 to create the style. Unfortunately, Dreamweaver's not smart enough to update the text color of any style that's currently applied to the selected text. In other words, applying colors with the Assets panel is more trouble than it's worth.

Favorite Assets

On a large site, you may have thousands of image files, movie files, colors, and external links. Because scrolling through long lists of assets is a chore, Dreamweaver lets you create a compact list of your favorite, frequently used assets.

For example, you might come up with five main colors that define your site's color scheme, which you'll use much more often than the other miscellaneous colors on the Assets list. Add them to your list of favorite colors. Likewise, adding graphics files you use over and over—logos, for example—to a list of favorites makes it easy to locate and insert those files into your pages. (Don't forget that you can also use Dreamweaver's Library and template features for this function. They're similar, but more powerful tools for keeping frequently used items at the ready. Turn to Chapter 18 for the details.)

Identifying your Favorites

If the color, graphic, or other element to be added to your Favorites list already appears on your Assets panel, highlight it in the list and then click the "Add to Favorites" button (see Figure 15-11).

Even quicker, you can add Favorites as you go, snagging them right from your Web page in progress. If you're working on your site's home page and you insert a company logo, for example, that's a perfect time to make the logo a favorite asset.

Simply right-click (Control-click) the image. From the shortcut menu, choose "Add Image to Favorites;" Dreamweaver instantly adds the graphic to your list of favorites. You can do the same with Flash, Shockwave, and QuickTime files, as well as with links. (Unfortunately, this shortcut doesn't work for colors and script files.)

When it comes to colors and links, there's another way to turn them into Favorites. In the Assets panel, select the Color or URLs category, click the Favorites radio button, and then click the New Asset button (see Figure 15-13). Then:

- If you're adding a favorite color, the Dreamweaver color box appears. Select a color using the eyedropper (see page 59).
- If you're adding a favorite link, the Add URL window opens. Type an absolute URL in the first field, either a Web address starting with *http://* or an email link (for instance, *mailto:subscriptions@nationalexasperator.com*). Next, type a name for the link—such as *Acrobat Download* or *Subscription Email*—in the Nickname field and then click OK.

Your new color or link appears in the Favorites list.

Using your Favorites

You insert assets from the Favorites list into your Web pages just as you would any other assets; see page 636.

Removing Favorites

Removing assets from the Favorites list is just as straightforward as adding them: just select one in the Favorites list of your Assets panel and then press Delete. The "Remove from Favorites" button (see Figure 15-13) on the Assets panel does the same thing. Yet another approach is to use the contextual menu (Figure 15-11).

Don't worry; removing an asset from the Favorites list *doesn't* delete that asset from the Assets panel (or your site)—only from the Favorites list. You can still find it listed if you click the Site radio button.

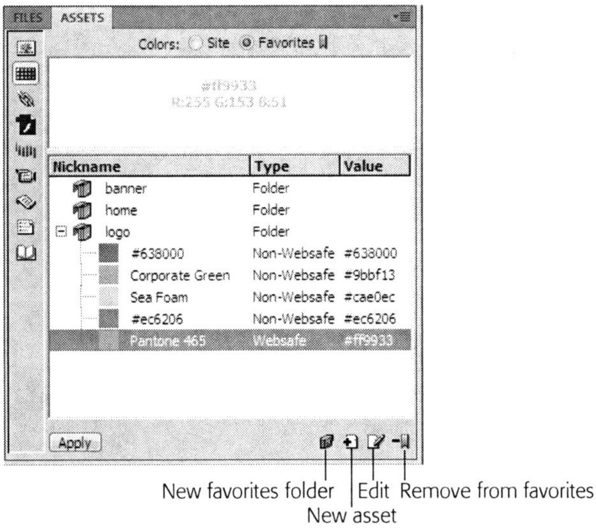

Figure 15-13:
In addition to using folders to organize your favorites, you can give a Favorite asset an easily identifiable nickname. Instead of listing a favorite image using its file name–148593.gif, for instance–use an easily understood name like New Product. Naming favorite colors is particularly helpful; a nickname like Page Background is more descriptive than #FF6633. To name a Favorite asset, click to select it; pause a moment, and then click again to edit its name. (These nicknames apply only in the Assets panel; they don't rename or retitle your files.)

Organizing Favorite assets

On a large site with lots of important assets, even a Favorites list can get unwieldy. That's why you can set up folders within the Assets panel to organize your assets. For example, if you use lots of ads on a site, create a folder in the Image assets Favorites called Ads or, for even greater precision, create multiple folders for different types of ads: Banner Ads, Half Banner Ads, and so on.

You can then drag assets into the appropriate folders, and you can expand or contract the folder to show or hide the assets inside (see Figure 15-13). These folders simply help you organize your Assets panel; they don't actually appear anywhere within the structure of your site. Moving a Favorite asset into a folder in the Assets panel doesn't change the location of files within your site.

To create a Favorites folder, click the appropriate category button at the left edge of the Assets panel (any except the bottom two, since, alas, you can't create folders for templates and Library items). Click Favorites at the top of the Assets panel (you can't create folders in Site view). Finally, click the New Favorites Folder button (see Figure 15-13) at the bottom of the Assets panel. When the new folder appears with its naming rectangle highlighted, type a new name for the folder and then press Enter. (Don't use the same name for more than one folder.)

To put an asset into a folder, just drag it there from the list. And if you're really obsessive, you can even create subfolders by dragging one folder onto another.

EXTENSION ALERT

Nothing Could Be Kuler

Adobe's Kuler Web tool (*http://kuler.adobe.com/*) is an online gallery of color palettes. It lets you build your own favorite sets of colors and offers tools based on the science of color theory to create harmonious color combinations. Even better, you can see thousands of palettes created by *other* Web designers, showcasing everything from cool and subtle schemes, to loud and vibrant color mixes. It's a great site if you're eager for a little color inspiration.

To make it even easier for you to use this Web site, the extension developer WebAssist has a free Dreamweaver extension named PalettePicker. This simple extension is essentially a floating palette within Dreamweaver that lets you browse or search Kuler's large collection of color palettes. When you find colors that you like, you'll be able to use Dreamweaver's color box and eye-drop tool to sample a color from the PalletePicker palette—just as you would sample a color from a picture on a Web page. You can find the extension at *www.webassist.com/professional/products/productdetails.asp?PID=147*. To learn how to use and install extensions, turn to page 804.

CHAPTER

16

Testing Your Site

As you've no doubt realized by now, building a Web site involves quite a few steps. At any point in the process, you can easily introduce errors that affect the performance of your pages. Both small mistakes, like typos, and site-shattering errors, like broken links, occur frequently in the Web development cycle.

Unfortunately, Web designers often don't develop a good procedure for testing their sites. This chapter offers some helpful techniques for testing your site, including using Dreamweaver's wide array of site-testing tools.

Site Launch Checklist

Don't wait until you've finished your site before embarking on a thorough strategy of testing. By that time, serious design errors may have so completely infested your site's pages that you may have to start over, or at least spend many hours fixing problems that you could have prevented early on.

- **Preview early and often.** The single best way to make sure a page looks and functions the way you want is to preview it in as many Web browsers as possible. For a quick test, in the Document toolbar, click the Live View button (page 553) to see how a page looks and works. This way is great for quickly checking JavaScript and viewing complex CSS. However, since the built-in browser for this is WebKit (aka Apple's Safari browser), Live View doesn't necessarily show how your page will look in another Web browser such as Internet Explorer.

To see how your layouts, CSS, and JavaScript hold up in other browsers, use Dreamweaver's Preview command (see page 65) to test your pages in every browser you can get your hands on. Make sure the graphics look right, your layout remains intact, and Cascading Style Sheets and Dreamweaver behaviors work as you intended.

For a thorough evaluation, however, you should preview your pages using every combination of browser *and* operating system you think your site's visitors may use. Enroll coworkers, family members, and household pets, if necessary, in this effort. At the very least, test your pages using Internet Explorer 6 and 7 on Windows, Firefox on Windows or Mac, and Safari on the Mac. According to several sources, including TheCounter.com (*www.thecounter.com/stats/*) and BrowserNews (*www.upsdell.com/BrowserNews/stat.htm*), Internet Explorer 7 for Windows is the most popular Web browser, followed by IE 6, Firefox, Safari, and others.

Tip: If you already have a site up and running, you can find useful browser information in your site's *log files*. These files track information about visits to your site, including which browsers and platforms your visitors are using. Most Web hosting companies provide access to these files, as well as software to analyze the confusing code inside them. You can use this information, for example, to see whether *anyone* who visits your site still uses Internet Explorer 5. If no one does, that's one less browser you have to design for.

Unfortunately, you'll discover that what works on one browser/operating system combination may not work on another. That's why you should preview your designs *early* in the process of constructing your site. If you design a page that doesn't work well in Internet Explorer 6 on Windows, for example, it's better to catch and fix that problem immediately than to discover it after you've built 100 pages based on that design. In other words, once you've created a design you like, don't plow ahead immediately and start building your Web site! Check that page in multiple browsers, fix any problems, and, then, grasshopper, begin to build.

Note: Internet Explorer 6 is usually where most Web pages fall apart. This old and crotchety browser is full of bugs that often cause hair-pulling bouts of hysteria among Web designers. Most of these problems are related to using CSS for layout (see Chapter 9). One approach recommended by professional Web designers is to preview your page in Firefox, Safari, or Internet Explorer 7 first. Get the page working in those browsers, and then preview the page in IE 6 to fix the bugs. If you design just with IE 6 in mind, then you'll find that the site doesn't work in Firefox, Safari, and, in many cases, the ever growing population of IE 7 browsers. Dreamweaver's new Check Browser Compatibility tool gives you one way to track down nasty CSS bugs (see page 130), and if you use Dreamweaver's CSS layouts (Chapter 9), many cross-browser problems have been solved.

- **Validate your pages.** Dreamweaver includes a tool that lets you compare your Web pages against agreed-upon standards for HTML and other Web languages. It checks to make sure your pages are *valid* (that they conform to these standards).

Valid pages are more likely to work in a predictable way on all Web browsers. And if you envision your site on mobile devices such as iPhones, cellphones, and palmtops, valid pages are again a better bet. In addition, one possible cause of page layout problems is invalid HTML, so the validator can help spot otherwise hard to spot errors.

- **Check for accessibility.** Not everyone experiences the Web in the same way. People with poor vision, for example, will miss out on the beautiful, full-color banner and navigation buttons you've created. To help you build Web sites that don't shut out people with disabilities, Dreamweaver can check your Web site to make sure it conforms to Section 508 (a Federal regulation mandating that Web sites built by or for the Federal Government are accessible to those with disabilities).

Some troubleshooting steps should come at the end of the process, when a page (or entire site) is ready to be moved to a Web server:

- **Check spelling on your pages.** Amazingly, people often overlook this simple step. As a result, you can easily find otherwise professional-looking Web pages on the Internet that are undermined by sloppy spelling. To learn how to use Dreamweaver's built-in spell checker, see page 87.
- **Check your links.** A Web site can be a complex and twisted collection of interconnected files. Web pages, graphics, Flash movies, and other types of files all work together. Unfortunately, if one file is moved or deleted, problems can ripple through the entire site. Use Dreamweaver's Check Links command to identify and fix broken links (see below).
- **Run site reports.** It's always the little things. When building a Web site, small errors inevitably creep into your pages. While not necessarily life-threatening, forgetting to title a Web page or to add an Alt property to an image does diminish the quality and professionalism of a site. Use Dreamweaver's site-reporting feature to quickly identify these problems (see page 657).

Find and Fix Broken Links

Broken links are inevitable. If you delete a file from your site, move a page or graphic outside Dreamweaver, or simply type an incorrect path to a file, broken links and missing graphics may result. In the B.D. era (Before Dreamweaver), you could fix such problems only by methodically examining every link on every page in your site. Fortunately, Dreamweaver's link-checking features can automate the process of tracking down broken-link problems.

Note: In this context, a link doesn't mean only a hyperlink connecting one page to another. Dreamweaver also uses the term to include the paths that identify external files incorporated in your Web page, such as PNGs, GIFs, JPEGs, external CSS style sheets, and Flash movies. For example, if a graphic is missing or isn't in the place specified by the Web page, then Dreamweaver reports a broken link.

FREQUENTLY ASKED QUESTION

Testing Your Sites in Multiple Browsers

How can I test my Web site if I have only a couple of the most common browsers on my computer?

If you don't have every browser ever created installed on your Mac, Windows, and Linux machines (you *do* have all three, don't you?), consider the commercial Web site *www.browsercam.com*. This service lets you view screenshots of your site using a wide variety of browsers and operating systems to make sure your site is working. The downside: $40 a month (ouch).

Free alternatives include iCapture (*www.danvine.com/icapture*) for getting screen captures of your Web pages using Apple's Safari browser, and Browsershots (*www.browsershots.org*), which provides a wide-range of Linux screenshots plus Internet Explorer (up to version 8), Safari 3.1 on Windows, and Safari (versions 2–3) on the Mac.

Alternatively, you can download and install the real thing from *http://browsers.evolt.org/*. This site has archived versions of nearly every Web browser created.

Windows XP users can run both IE 6 and IE 7 together (a normally impossible task) with the help of TredoSoft's MultipleIE installer (*http://tredosoft.com/Multiple_IE*). Vista users can't use the TredoSoft solution, but a program named IETester (*www.my-debugbar.com/wiki/IETester/HomePage*) lets you see how your Web pages look in multiple versions of IE including 6, 7, and 8.

If you're a Mac person with an Intel Mac, then you can install Windows on your machine using Apple's Boot-camp technology (*www.apple.com/bootcamp*) or third-party "virtualization" software which lets you run Mac and Windows simultaneously on the same computer (and believe it or not, the universe does *not* implode). VMWare Fusion for Mac (*www.vmware.com/products/fusion/*), for example, lets you run multiple versions of Windows (XP and Vista) as well as Mac OS X.

Finding Broken Links

The Check Links Sitewide command scans an entire site's worth of files, and reports all links and paths that don't lead to a file. (It's one of Dreamweaver's site management features, meaning that you have to define a local site before using this command; see page 37 for instructions on defining a site.) Note that Dreamweaver checks only links and paths *within* the local site folder; it doesn't check links that lead to other people's Web sites (see the Note on the opposite page for a tool that can help with *that* annoying chore).

Note: If your local site contains a lot of pages, you may not want to check links in one or more folders whose pages *you know* have no broken links. You can exclude files from the Check Links Sitewide operation using the Cloaking feature described on page 684. Doing so also makes the link-checking operation go faster.

Checking just one page

To check links on an open page, save it in your local site folder. Then choose File → Check Page → Links (or press Ctrl+F8 [⌘-F8]). Dreamweaver scans the page and opens the Link Checker window, which lists files containing broken links (see Figure 16-1). If Dreamweaver doesn't find any broken links—you HTML god, you—the window comes up empty.

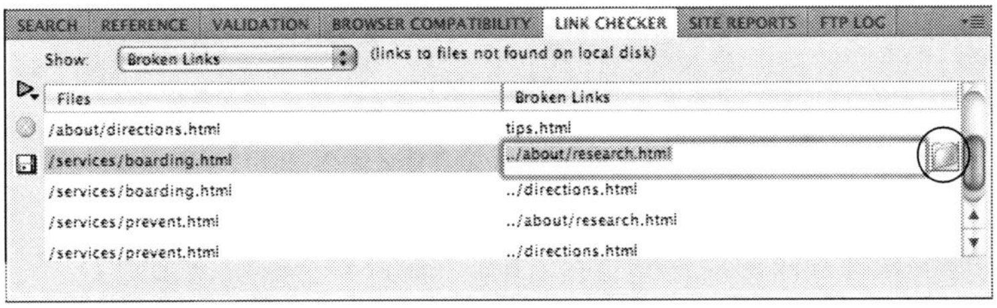

Figure 16-1: *The Check Links Sitewide command generates a list of all external links and orphaned files (files with no links to them). If you wish, click the Save (floppy disk) button to save all this information into a tab-delimited text file. You can also fix a broken link directly inside this panel using the "Browse for File" button (circled) as described on page 167.*

Note: Although Dreamweaver can't check links to the outside world, a free tool from the W3C can. You can find its link checker at *http://validator.w3.org/checklink*. This tool checks both internal links (between pages on the same site) and external links (to other sites). The only possible downside: The pages you wish to check must already be up on the Web. Windows users find that Xenu's Link Sleuth, a free, automated link checker, can help speed up the process of checking external links (*http://home.snafu.de/tilman/xenulink.html*). In addition, Firefox users can download the LinkChecker extension at *www.kevinfreitas.net/extensions/linkchecker/* for quick checking of broken links on a page.

Checking specific pages

You can also check links just on specific pages of your site from the Link Checker panel:

1. **Choose Window → Results to open the Results panel, and then click the Link Checker tab.**

   The Link Checker panel opens.

2. **Use the Files panel to select the site you wish to check (see Figure 15-6).**

   If you're already working on the site you want to check, you can skip this step.

3. **In the Files panel, select the files you'd like to check.**

   For techniques on selecting files and folders in the Files panel, see the box on page 646.

Tip: Selecting a folder makes Dreamweaver scan all files in that folder.

---

4. **In the Link Checker panel, click the green-arrow icon. From the menu that appears, choose "Check Links for Selected Files/Folders in Site".**

   Alternatively, you can right-click (Control-click) the selected files, and then, from the shortcut menu, choose Check Links → Selected Files.

   Either way, Dreamweaver scans the pages, and displays any broken links in the Link Checker panel (Figure 16-1).

Checking the entire Web site

You can check all the links on all pages of your Web site in any of three ways:

- Open the Web site you want to check (press F8 [Shift-⌘-F8] to open the Files panel, and then use the panel's menu to select the site), and then choose Site → Check Links Sitewide. Or use the keyboard shortcut, Ctrl+F8 (⌘-F8).
- Open the Files panel, and then right-click (Control-click) any file. From the shortcut menu, choose Check Links → Entire Local Site.
- Open the Link Checker panel (Window → Results to open the Results panel, and then click the Link Checker tab), click the green-arrow icon, and then, from its menu, choose "Check Links for Entire Current Local Site".

Once again, Dreamweaver scans your site and opens the Link Checker panel, which lists files containing broken links (Figure 16-1).

UP TO SPEED

Selection Shortcuts for the Files Panel

You'll often want to use the tools in the Results panel on more than one page in your Web site. Fortunately, most of these tools can work on multiple pages in the Files panel.

You can probably figure out that you should click a file to select it. But you can also select several files that are listed consecutively: Click the first one, scroll if necessary, and then Shift-click the last one. Dreamweaver highlights all the files between your first and final clicks.

If you want to select several files that aren't consecutive in the list, the trick is to click each one while pressing the Ctrl (⌘) key.

Once you've selected one or more files, you can deselect one by Ctrl-clicking (⌘-clicking) it once again.

Dreamweaver also includes a snazzy command for selecting recently modified files in the Files panel. Suppose you want to select all the files you created or changed today (to see if the links work or to upload them to your Web server). To use this command, in the upper-right corner of the Files panel, you need to click the panel's contextual-menu button. From the menu that appears, select Edit → Select Recently Modified.

The Select Recently Modified window appears. You can either specify a range of dates (for example, files you created or changed between February 1, 2009, and February 7, 2009) or a number of days (to specify all modified files in, say, the last 30 days). (The last option–Modified By–works only with Adobe's Contribute program.) Set the options, click OK, and Dreamweaver selects the appropriate files in the Files panel.

Fixing Broken Links

Of course, simply finding broken links is only half the battle. You also need to *fix* them. The Link Checker panel provides a quick and easy way to do this:

1. **In the Link Checker panel, click a path in the Broken Links column.**

   The path is highlighted, and a tiny folder icon appears to the right (circled in Figure 16-1).

Note: The Link Checker panel shows you which pages *contain* broken links, but doesn't show you the text or images of the broken links themselves, which can make it difficult to figure out how you're supposed to fix them ("Was that a button that links to the home page?"). In such a case, in the Link Checker panel's left column, *double-click* the file name. Dreamweaver opens the Web page and, even better, highlights the link on the page.

Once you've determined where the link should lead ("Oh yeah. That's the button to the haggis buffet menu."), you can fix the link on the page (see page 180) or go back to the Link Checker panel and make the change as described in the next step.

2. **Click the tiny folder icon.**

   The Select File dialog box opens. From here, you can navigate to and (in the next step) select the correct page—the one that *should* have been opened by that link.

   If you prefer, you can type a path directly in the Link Checker panel. Doing so usually isn't a good idea, however, since it's difficult to understand the path from one page to another by just looking at the Link Checker panel. Searching for the proper page using the Select File dialog box is a much more accurate and trouble-free method.

3. **In the Select File dialog box, double-click a Web page.**

   The dialog box disappears, and Dreamweaver fixes the link.

   If your Web site contains other links pointing to the same missing file, Dreamweaver asks if you'd like to fix the same broken link on those pages, too—an amazing timesaver that can quickly repair broken links on dozens of pages.

Note: Dreamweaver's behavior is a bit odd when it comes to fixing the same broken link, however. Once you fix one link, it remains selected in the Link Checker panel. You must click another broken link, or one of the buttons in the window, before Dreamweaver asks if you'd like to fix that same broken link on other pages.

4. **Continue to fix broken links, following steps 1–3.**

   When you've repaired all the broken links, you can close the Results panel by double-clicking anywhere along the top row of tabs (for example, double-click the Link Checker tab). Double-clicking any tab reopens the Results panel.

Listing External Links

Although Dreamweaver doesn't verify links to other Web sites on your pages, it does show you a list of such external links when you run the link checker. To see this list, choose External Links from the Link Checker panel's Show menu (see Figure 16-2). The list includes absolute URLs leading to other sites (like *http://www.yahoo.com*) as well as email links (like *mailto:appointments@chia-vet.com*).

This window is especially useful if you've created a link to a certain external Web site several times throughout your Web site, and you've decided to change the link. For example, if you discovered through testing (or through the W3C Link Checker mentioned in the Note on page 645) that an external link that you've peppered throughout your site no longer works, then:

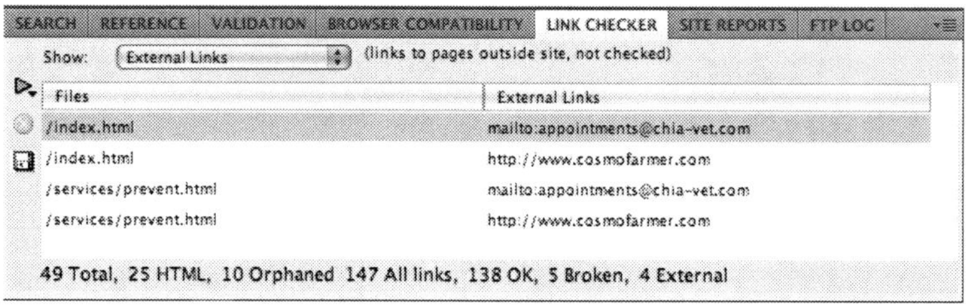

Figure 16-2: *Although Dreamweaver can't check external links, you can use this window to change the URL of an external link.*

1. **Choose Site → Check Links Sitewide (or press Ctrl+F8 [⌘-F8]).**

   Dreamweaver scans your site, and then opens the Link Checker panel.

2. **From the Show pop-up menu, choose External Links.**

   The window lists links you've created to sites outside your own.

3. **Click the external link you want to change.**

   Dreamweaver highlights the link, indicating that you can now edit it.

4. **Type the new URL, and then press Enter (Return).**

   If other pages contain the old URL, Dreamweaver asks if you would like to fix them as well. If so, click Yes; the deed is done.

Orphaned Files

The Link Checker panel also provides a list of files that aren't used by any Web page in the site—*orphaned files*, as they're called. You wind up with an orphaned graphic file when, for example, you save a GIF into your site folder but then never use it on a Web page. Or suppose you eliminate the only link to an old page that you don't need anymore, making it an orphaned file. Unless you think you may link to it in the future, you can delete it to clean up unnecessary clutter in your site.

In fact, that's the primary purpose of this feature: to locate old and unused files, and delete them. Here's how it works:

1. **Choose Site → Check Links Sitewide, or press Ctrl+F8 (⌘-F8).**

   Dreamweaver opens the Link Checker panel.

2. **From the Show menu, choose Orphaned Files.**

   The list of orphaned files appears (see Figure 16-3).

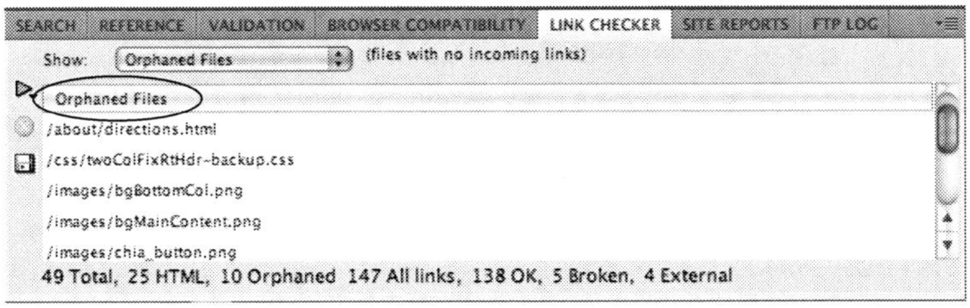

***Figure 16-3:** Identify (and delete) unused files with Dreamweaver's Link Checker panel. This panel lists external links and orphaned files as well as broken links; use the Show menu (circled) to isolate the different types of link.*

3. **Select the files you want to delete.**

   For example, by Ctrl-clicking (⌘-clicking) the files.

4. **Press Delete.**

   Dreamweaver asks if you really want to delete the files. Click OK if you do or Cancel if you suddenly get cold feet.

   Before you get spring-cleaning fever and delete all *orphaned* files in your site, however, keep a few pointers in mind:

   - Just because a file isn't *currently* in use doesn't mean you won't need it again later. For example, say you have an employee-of-the-month page. In March, you included a photo of Robin Albert, your best salesperson. In April, someone else got the award, so you removed Robin's photo from the page. The actual graphic file of the photos is still on your computer; it's just that no Web page is currently using it—that makes it an orphaned file—but next month you may need the photo again, when Robin develops a spurt of motivation. Make sure a file is really useless before deleting it.

   - More important, Dreamweaver may flag files your site actually needs as *orphaned*. For example, some sites include what's called a *splash page*: an introductory page that first appears when someone comes to the site. It can be a page with a bold graphic and the text "Click here to enter the site". Or it may be a fancy Flash movie intended to make a big impact on your visitors. Usually, this page is nothing more than a welcome mat that leads to the *real* home page. Since it's simply an introductory page, no other page in the site links to it. Unfortunately, that's precisely what Dreamweaver considers an *orphaned* file.

   - If you write your own JavaScript code, you may reference graphic files and Web pages. Dreamweaver doesn't keep track of these references, and identifies those files as orphans (unless they're inserted or linked to elsewhere in the page or site).

     On the other hand, Dreamweaver is somewhat smarter when it comes to Spry widgets and Dreamweaver Behaviors. It can track files referenced as part of its own JavaScript programs—for example, graphic files you use in a rollover effect—and doesn't list them as orphaned files.

The bottom line is that while this report can be useful, use it cautiously when deleting files.

Changing a Link Throughout a Site

Suppose you've created a page on your site to teach your visitors about the basics of the HTML language. You think this page would be really, really helpful to your visitors, so you create links to it from every page on your site. After a while, you realize you just don't have the time to keep this page up to date, but you still want to help your visitors get this information. Why not change the link so it points to a more current and informative source? Using Dreamweaver's Change Link Sitewide command, you can do just that:

1. **Choose Site → Change Link Sitewide.**

   The Change Link Sitewide dialog box opens (see Figure 16-4).

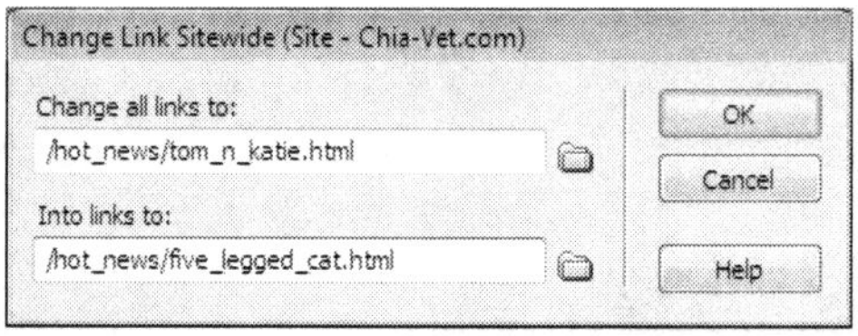

Figure 16-4: *Dreamweaver uses a root-relative link to specify the page whose URL you want to change, as indicated by the slash (/). Don't worry: This doesn't mean Dreamweaver makes the link root-relative. It's just how Dreamweaver identifies the location of the page in the site. See page 163 for more on root-relative links.*

   This dialog box offers two different fields: "Change all links to" and "Into links to". Understanding what you're supposed to do at this point is easier if you imagine that the first label is actually Change All Links That *Currently* Point To. In other words, first you'll indicate where those links point now; then you'll indicate where you'd like them to go instead.

   At this point, you can type the old Web address into the "Change all links to" field. For example, if your aim is to round up every link that now points to Yahoo and redirect it to Google, you could start by typing *http://www.yahoo.com* here.

   If the links you're trying to change refer to a page in your own site, however, proceed to step 2.

2. **To the right of the Change All Links To field, click the folder icon.**

   The "Select Link to Change" dialog box opens. You're about to specify the file that the links point to *now*.

3. **Select a file in the local site folder; click OK (Windows) or Choose (Mac).**

   In the following steps, Dreamweaver will change every link that leads to *this file*, whether it's a graphic, Cascading Style Sheet file, or any other external file that can be part of a Web page.

Note: As a shortcut to following steps 1, 2, and 3, in the Files panel, you can select a file, and *then* choose Site → Change Link Sitewide. Dreamweaver automatically adds the selected file's path to the "Change all links to" field.

Now it's time to substitute the new URL or file—the one to which all those links will be redirected. If you're reassigning them to a different Web site, you can type its URL directly into the "Change all links to" field. For example, in the previous example, you can type *http://www.google.com.*

Note: For another way to change one external link into another, see Figure 16-2.

If you'd like the changed links to point to a file on your own Web site instead, then proceed to step 4.

4. **To the right of the "Into links to" field, click the folder icon.**

   The "Select Link to Change" dialog box opens.

5. **Select a file in the local site, and then click OK (Windows) or Choose (Mac).**

   You've just selected the new file to which you wish to link. In other words, every link that once led to the file you selected in step 3 now links to this file. You can select graphics, Cascading Style Sheet files, and any other external files you can include in a Web page.

   You'll get unpredictable results, however, if you change a link that points to a graphic file into, say, a link that points to a Web page, or vice versa. Make sure the "before" and "after" links share the same file type: Web page, style sheet, or graphic.

6. **Click OK to make the change.**

   The same Update Files dialog box you encountered in the last chapter appears, listing every page that will be affected.

7. **Click Update to update the pages.**

   Dreamweaver scans your site, and updates the pages.

Validating Web Pages

The Web is a far-flung collection of technologies, scripting and programming languages, and people all working together. When you think about it, it's pretty amazing that an 11-year-old in Fargo, North Dakota, can create a Web site viewable by millions of people around the world, or even that hundreds of different browsers, from Internet Explorer to cellphones, can browse the same Web site. This kind of global communication owes its success in large part to the World Wide Web Consortium (the W3C), an organization composed of representatives from universities, research institutions, corporations, and government agencies, dedicated to creating standards for different Internet-related technologies.

The W3C developed standards for HTML, XHTML, CSS, XML, and other Web languages, and continues to create new standards as technologies evolve. Thanks to these standards, companies have a guide to follow when creating new Web browsers and new Web sites.

It sure would be great if all companies followed the standards when building Web browsers, and all Web designers followed the standards when building Web pages. Then anyone with any Web browser could view any Web page. What a wonderful world *that* would be—you'd never have to test your Web pages in different browsers.

Of course, this kind of utopian thinking hasn't always been applied by the major browser makers. As a result, Web developers have been forced to come up with techniques to deal with the way different browsers display HTML. (The Check Browser Compatibility command, covered on page 130, is great for helping you figure out where browsers fail when applying Cascading Style Sheets.)

Fortunately, the situation is improving; browser makers are making more of an effort these days to stick to the W3C's recommended standards. And you can, too: Dreamweaver includes a tool for making sure your pages meet the standards set by the W3C.

Steps for Validating Web Pages

In the Files panel, you can check either an open and saved page or any selected pages by following these steps:

1. **Choose Window → Results → Validation.**

   You can also open the Results panel with the keyboard shortcut F7, and then click the Validation tab. Either way, the Results panel opens, showing the Validation tab (Figure 16-5).

Tip: If you want to validate just the page you're working on, choose File → Validate → Markup.

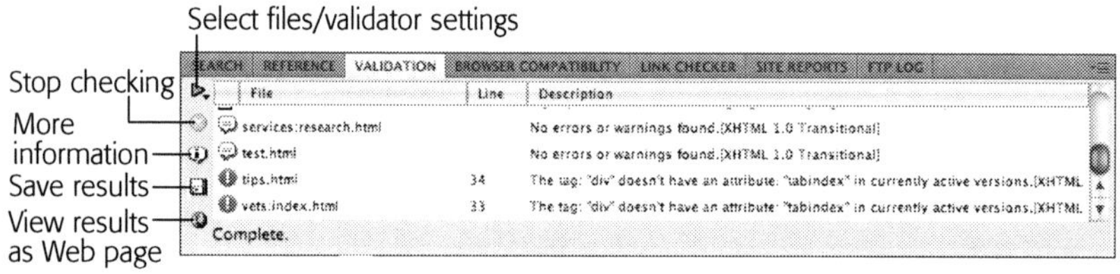

Figure 16-5: *The Validation panel lets you check your Web pages against various W3C standards.*

2. **In the Validation panel, click the green arrow, and then select which files to inspect.**

   The green arrow reveals a menu with four options. The first checks the page you're currently working on. The second option checks all pages in your site, and the third option checks just those files selected in the Files panel.

   The fourth option—Settings—opens the Validator Preferences window, which lets you select which type of standard to validate against if no *doctype* is specified. A doctype (see page 46) is just a line of code that goes in the head of a document and tells a Web browser which standard the particular page is attempting to adhere to. Because Dreamweaver automatically inserts a doctype (as specified by you either in the Site Definition window or when you create the page), you don't need to change any of these settings.

Note: You can also validate the file as an XML file by choosing File → As XML. (To the technically inclined: This command not only checks whether your XML is "well-formed," but can also check the document against the Document Type Definition [DTD] specified in your document.)

3. **Review the results.**

   Dreamweaver displays the results in the Validation panel (Figure 16-5). Each validation message is divided into four columns: The first includes an icon that indicates the severity of the error, the second lists the file, the thirds lists which line in the code the message applies to, and the fourth describes the validation error or message.

   The icon at the beginning of the message helps you determine which errors are important. A red stop sign identifies a violation of the standards for the particular doctype (HTML 4.01 Transitional, XTHML 1.0 Transitional, and so on) the page is attempting to follow. In some cases, this warning can indicate that a mandatory tag (like the <body> tag) is missing—a serious problem.

   Other stop-sign errors aren't necessarily fatal. For example, when inserting a Spry Collapsible Panel (page 508), Dreamweaver adds a *tabindex* property to a <div> tag that represents the panel's tab. Dreamweaver's JavaScript programming relies on this property to control how the panel works when a user tabs through the links on a page, and even though this won't cause a problem for your site's visitors, it's still invalid code since <div> tags have no such property.

   Less serious problems are flagged with little message balloons. These balloons may inform you that the page has *no* problems, or point out optional fixes. (See the following section for a list of common errors and messages.)

   You may also encounter an icon that looks like two pieces of paper placed one on top of the other (who comes up with these things?). These usually occur when you validate against any of the HTML standards and have incorrectly written code—an unclosed <p> tag, for example.

4. **Fix the errors.**

   Alas, Dreamweaver can't fix all these validation errors. For errors related to improperly written code, you can let Dreamweaver automatically fix them as described on page 392.

   For the other errors, it's up to you and your knowledge of HTML to go into the code and fix any problems. For assistance, check out the online HTML reference (see page 422).

To get started, double-click an error in the Validation results panel. The Web page opens in Split view, with the invalid HTML code selected. You can then delete or modify the offending code. Keep in mind, though, that the code Dreamweaver produces is the result of many thousands of hours of engineering and testing. Unless you're sure you know how to fix a problem, you may just want to trust the code Dreamweaver produces.

GEM IN THE ROUGH

Is the Validator Valid?

Dreamweaver's validation feature is a big help in seeing where your code fails to match the standards set by the W3C, but it's an imperfect tool. For example, it doesn't provide very good explanations for errors, it doesn't always catch invalid code, and it can't validate CSS.

For the best source of validation information and tools, turn to the W3C's free validation services and information resources. You can find the HTML (or XHTML) validator at *http://validator.w3.org/*. For CSS validation, visit *http://jigsaw.w3.org/css-validator/*.

With these tools, you can validate files already online or upload a Web page or CSS file for analysis. It's free, and it provides detailed information about the meaning of any errors.

Since Dreamweaver's validator is faster (you don't need to upload files to the Internet or wait for the W3C validator to download files over the Web), start with it. Find and fix errors Dreamweaver identifies, and then try out the W3C validator for the finishing touches.

Cleaning Up HTML (and XHTML)

You've been reading about what great HTML code Dreamweaver writes, and how all you hand coders need to get on the WYSIWYG bandwagon. But there are exceptions to every rule. In the process of formatting text, deleting elements, and—in general—building a Web page, it's quite possible to end up with less-than-optimal HTML coding. While Dreamweaver usually catches potentially sloppy HTML, you may nonetheless run across instances of empty tags, redundant tags, and nested tags in your Dreamweaver pages.

For example, in the normal course of adding, editing, and deleting content on a page (either by hand or even in Dreamweaver's Design view), you can occasionally end up with code like this:

```
<div align="center"> </div>
```

This empty tag doesn't serve any purpose, and only adds unnecessary HTML to your page. Remember, the less code your page uses, the faster it loads. Eliminating redundant tags can improve your site's download speed.

Another possible source of errors is you. When you type HTML in Code view or open pages created by another program, you may introduce errors that you'll need to clean up later.

Note: The Clean Up HTML command doesn't fix really bad errors like missing closing tags, or improperly nested tags. You can have Dreamweaver automatically fix these types of problems when opening a file (see page 392).

Aware of its own limitations (and yours), Dreamweaver provides a command that's designed to streamline the code in your pages: Clean Up HTML (if you're using Dreamweaver's XHTML mode, the command is called Clean Up XHTML). This command not only improves the HTML in your page, it can also strip out other nonessential code such as comments and special Dreamweaver markup code, and it can eliminate a specific tag or tags.

Note: The Clean Up HTML command is extremely useful. Once you've tried it a few times, you'll probably want to use it on all your pages. Unfortunately, it doesn't come with a keyboard shortcut. This case is a classic one when Dreamweaver's *keyboard-shortcut editor* is just the white knight you need; using it, you can add a key combination to trigger this command from the keyboard. See page 799 for details.

To use this command:

1. **Open a Web page to clean up.**

   Unfortunately, this great feature works only on one page at a time. No cleaning up a site's worth of pages in one fell swoop! Accordingly, it's best to first use the Site Reports feature (see page 657) to identify problem pages. *Then* open them in Dreamweaver, and run this command.

2. **Choose Commands → Clean Up HTML (or Clean Up XHTML).**

   The Clean Up HTML/XHTML window appears (see Figure 16-6).

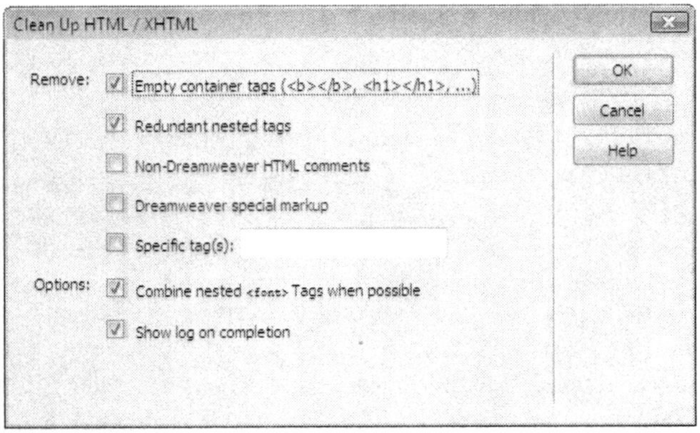

Figure 16-6: *The Clean Up HTML/XHTML command lets you improve the quality and speed of a Web page by stripping out redundant and useless code. You can even use it to strip out unnecessary tags by specifying a tag in the "Specific tag(s)" field (although the "Find and Replace" command provides a much more powerful method of identifying and removing HTML tags; see page 782).*

3. **Turn on the checkboxes for the options you want.**

   Here's a rundown:

   - **Empty Container Tags** deletes any tags that don't actually contain anything. For example, you may delete some text that had been set in boldface, leaving behind opening and closing bold tags without any text in between: <b></b>. Or you may delete an image within a link, leaving behind a useless pair of <a> tags. It's always a good idea to turn on this option.

   - **Redundant Nested Tags** deletes tags that appear within other tags of the same type, like this: <b>You can't get any <b>bolder</b> than bold</b>. The inner set of bold tags does no good, so choosing this option would produce this: <b> You can't get any bolder than bold</b>. This option is extremely useful.

   - **Non-Dreamweaver HTML Comments** deletes any comments *not* inserted by Dreamweaver as part of its site management tools. For example, the Dreamweaver Template tool (Chapter 19) inserts HTML comments to help identify different parts of the template. However, Web designers also place notes within code to give directions or explain parts of the code. (These comments are invisible in a Web browser. They appear only in the Code view, or in Dreamweaver's document window as a gold comment icon.) In addition, Dreamweaver's CSS Layout files (page 345) also add HTML comments to help you learn how those pages work. Since comments are often added as an aid for maintaining a Web page, you may not want to choose this option.

     However, if the page is finished, and you doubt you'll need the information the comments contain, you can decrease the file size of a page by using this option.

Note: Dreamweaver's Clean Up HTML command doesn't strip out CSS comments. If you use Dreamweaver's CSS Layouts, you'll find the style sheets loaded with CSS comments. If you want a quick way to remove those types of comments, visit *www.foundationphp.com/tools/css_comments.php*. On this Web page, you can download a "stored query" (a reusable search) to use with Dreamweaver's "Find and Replace" tool (page 799).

   - **Dreamweaver Special Markup** deletes any special code Dreamweaver inserts. Dreamweaver relies on certain code in some of its features, including tracing images, templates (Chapter 19), and Libraries (Chapter 18). Choosing this option also eliminates the special code that makes those features work, so use this option with care. (Since the template feature can add a fair amount of this specialized code, Dreamweaver includes a Template Export command that lets you export an entire site with all template code removed. See page 764.)

   - **Specific Tag(s)** deletes HTML tags you specify. Type the name of the tag (without brackets) in the field like this: *font*. To remove multiple tags at once, separate each tag name by a comma like this: *font, blink*.

Be careful with this option. Since it lets you remove *any* tag from a page, you could easily delete an important and necessary tag (like the <body> tag) from your page by accident. Furthermore, Dreamweaver's "Find and Replace" command provides much more powerful tools for performing this kind of surgery (see page 799).

- **Combine Nested <font> Tags when Possible** combines multiple *font* properties into a single tag. Hopefully, you've moved to CSS for all of your text formatting needs, so you don't use the <font> tag and don't need this option.
- If you want to see a report of all the changes Dreamweaver makes to a page, turn on **Show Log on Completion.**

4. **Click OK to clean up the page.**

   If you selected "Show Log on Completion", a dialog box appears, listing the types and number of changes that Dreamweaver made to the page.

Note: When running this command on an XHTML page, Dreamweaver also checks to make sure the syntax of the page matches the requirements of an XHTML document. Among other concerns, in XHTML, all tags must be lowercase, and any empty tags must be terminated correctly—
 for the line break tag, for example. Dreamweaver fixes such problems.

As long as you keep the page open, you can undo changes Dreamweaver made. Suppose you asked Dreamweaver to remove any comments, and suddenly realized you really did need them. Ctrl+Z (⌘-Z) does the trick.

Site Reporting

The Clean Up HTML command is a great way to make sure your code is well written. But what if you forget about it until after you've built all 500 pages of your site? Do you have to open each page and run the command—whether there's a problem or not?

Fortunately, no. Dreamweaver's Site Reports feature makes identifying problems throughout a site a snap. As well as locating the problems fixed by the Clean Up HTML command, it makes Dreamweaver check your pages for other problems, such as missing titles, empty Alt properties for images, and other problems that can make your Web site less accessible to disabled Web surfers.

Tip: To save time when running a report, you can exclude select folders from a Site Report operation using the cloaking feature described on page 684.

After running a report, Dreamweaver displays a list of pages with problems. Unfortunately, the Site Reports feature only *finds* problems; it doesn't fix them.

(To see the full life cycle of an HTML error, jump ahead to Figure 16-9.) You have to open and fix each page individually.

To run a report on one or more Web pages, proceed like this:

1. **Choose Site → Reports.**

   The Reports window opens (see Figure 16-7).

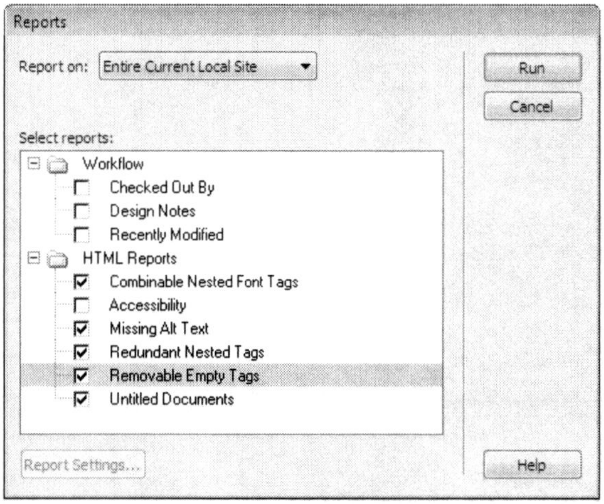

Figure 16-7: *Dreamweaver's Site Reports feature makes quick work of finding common page errors. You won't use all these options, but at the very least make sure you check for missing Alt text (page 225) and any untitled documents before you put a new Web site up on the Internet.*

2. **From the "Report on" menu, select the files to analyze.**

   Dreamweaver can report on a single Web page, multiple pages, or even an entire site. Choose *Current Document* to check the Web page that's open at the moment. *Entire Current Local Site* checks every Web page in the local site folder, including folders inside it. This option is great when you want to check your entire site prior to uploading it to a Web server and making it "live" (more on that in Chapter 17).

   Selected Files in Site checks only the files you choose in the Files panel. You need to open the Files panel, and then select files in the local file list for this option to work. See the box on page 646 for methods on selecting files in the Files panel. Choose this option when you've modified or added pages to a site, and you're ready to move them to the Web server.

   Folder checks all Web pages in a selected folder. After you choose this option, an empty field and a folder icon appear. Click the folder icon; a dialog box gives you the opportunity to locate and select the folder you wish to check, including any folders inside it. You can also use this option when you wish to check pages that aren't actually part of the current site.

3. **Select the types of reports you want Dreamweaver to generate.**

   The Reports window is divided into two types of reports. The first set, Workflow reports, mostly deals with features that facilitate working with others as part of a production team (see the following chapter). The last option in this group—Recently Modified—generates a list of files that have either been created or modified within a certain number of days or within a range of dates (February 1 of last year to the present, say). When you run this type of report, Dreamweaver lists the files in the Site Reports panel *and* opens a Web page listing the files in your browser.

Note: The Recently Modified site report looks for files created or changed in the last seven days, but you can adjust that time frame. In the Reports window, select Recently Modified, and click the Report Settings button (Figure 16-7). A window appears where you can change the range of dates to check.

In fact, you'll find the technique described on page 646 more useful. It not only identifies recently modified files, but also selects them in the Files panel, giving you many more options for acting on this information. For example, with those files selected, you can upload them to your Web server, run find-and-replace operations on just those files, or access many other tools.

   The second type, HTML Reports, is useful for locating common errors, such as forgetting to title a Web page or forgetting to add an Alt property to an image.

   Three of the HTML Report options—*Combinable Nested Font Tags, Redundant Nested Tags*, and *Removable Empty Tags*—search for pages with common code mistakes. These problems are the same ones fixed by the Clean Up HTML command (see page 654).

   The *Accessibility* report lets you see how well people with disabilities can use your site. This command checks to see how well your pages conform to Web accessibility guidelines mandated by the U.S. Government and recommended by the W3C (see page 660). This option produces detailed reports, so it's usually best to run it separately.

   Turn on *Missing Alt Text* to search for pages with images that are missing an alternate text description (see page 225). If you turn on the Accessibility option, then you can leave this option turned off; the Accessibility analyzer already includes missing Alt text.

   Finally, turn on *Untitled Documents* to identify pages that are either missing a title or still have Dreamweaver's default title.

Note: The Site Report command doesn't identify XHTML syntax errors like those fixed by the Clean Up XHTML command (see page 654).

4. **Click Run.**

   Dreamweaver analyzes the pages you specified. Then it produces a report that lists pages that match your report settings (see Figure 16-8). Each line in the Results window displays the name of the file, the line number where the error occurs, and a description of the error.

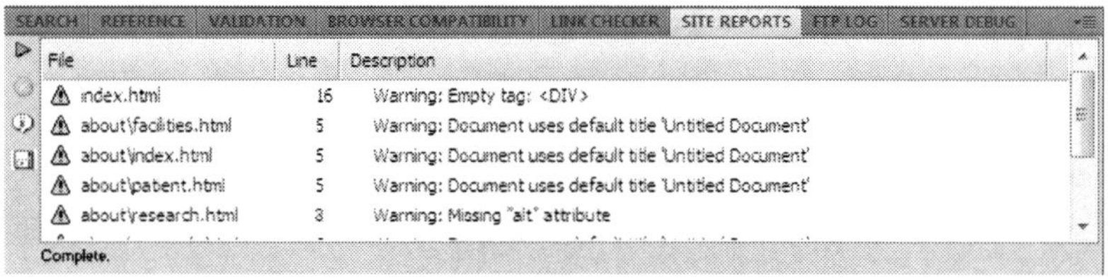

***Figure 16-8:** If you decide that the report is taking too long, you can always stop it. In the Results panel's left-hand toolbar, click the icon that looks like a red stop sign with an X through it.*

5. **In the Results panel, double-click the file to open it.**

   Dreamweaver opens the file, and automatically highlights the offending code.

6. **Fix the problem according to its type.**

   For a page containing Combinable Nested Font Tags, Redundant Nested Tags, or Removable Empty Tags errors, use the Clean Up HTML command as described on page 654.

   For pages missing a title, add one using the technique described on page 47.

   For Accessibility problems, read the detailed discussion starting next.

   You can add missing Alt properties using the Property inspector, as described on page 225, but you may find it faster to use Dreamweaver's powerful "Find and Replace" command (see page 799).

7. **Continue opening files from the Results window and fixing them until you've corrected each mistake.**

   Unfortunately, Dreamweaver doesn't provide a quick, one-step method to fix any of these problems. Except when using the "Find and Replace" tip for adding missing Alt text, you must open and fix each page individually.

If you want to save the results of your report, click the Save Report button. Dreamweaver opens a Save As dialog box, and lets you save the report as an XML file (so you can file it in the "Files I don't really need" folder on your desktop).

Accessibility

Even the clearest, most well-planned Web sites can pose a real challenge to people with vision problems. Likewise, people with motor skill difficulties may be unable to use a mouse, and have to rely on keyboard shortcuts to navigate a Web page.

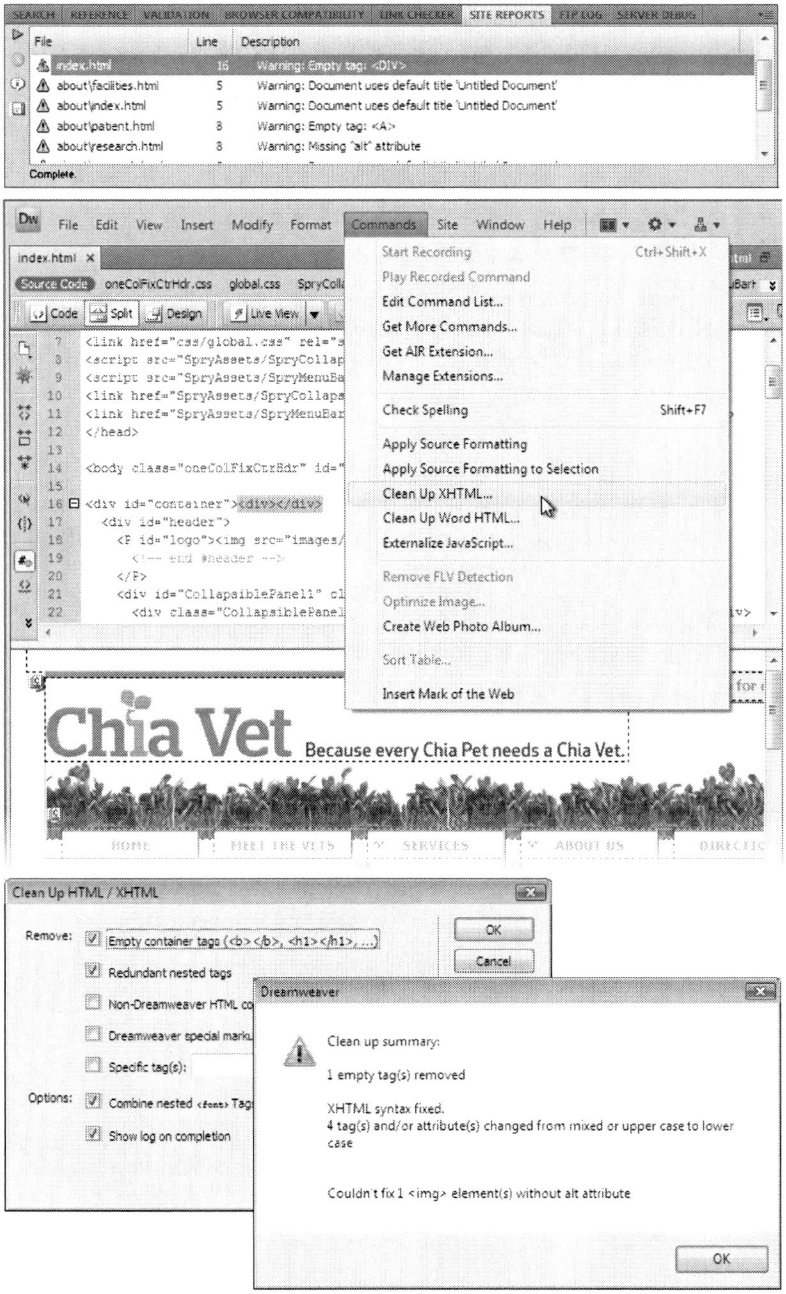

Figure 16-9:
The life cycle of a typical HTML error.

Top: After running a report, you may find a common HTML error, like an empty <div> tag. In the Results window, double-click the page to open it.

Second from top: The page opens with the offending code selected in Split Code view. (Dreamweaver often highlights the problem HTML code so that you can identify the problem.) Since you can fix this particular error—and more—with the Clean Up HTML/XHTML command, choose Commands → Clean Up HTML/XHTML.

Third: The Clean Up HTML/XHTML window opens. Even though you can just clean up the error you identified earlier, it doesn't hurt to clean up other problems that may appear in your code (and somewhere else in the Site Report Results window). Click OK to clean up the HTML.

Bottom: Dreamweaver reports back to you. In this case, Dreamweaver fixed a few other XHTML problems that the Site Report didn't catch, and reported what it couldn't automatically fix: the type attribute for a script tag and the Alt property for an image, both of which require human intervention to fix.

To make Web sites more accessible to those with a variety of disabilities, the Web Accessibility Initiative (WAI)—a part of the World Wide Web Consortium—has proposed guidelines for the design of Web sites. In fact, the U.S. government has mandated its own set of guidelines (Section 508 of the U.S. Rehabilitation Act) for all Web sites built by and for the government (*www.section508.gov*). Some states have even more stringent guidelines, and countries throughout the world are either in the process of developing accessibility standards or already have such standards in place. Following the WAI guidelines improves your site by making it accessible to a larger audience.

Dreamweaver provides several tools for meeting these guidelines and helping Web designers build more accessible sites (see page 228). But for comprehensive analysis of your site, use the Accessibility site report. With it, you can evaluate your Web pages to make sure they comply with W3C guidelines and the requirements of Section 508.

Checking your site against accessibility standards is similar to running any other report. Follow steps 1–4 on page 658, taking care to turn on the Accessibility checkbox. (You can also check accessibility for just the page you're working on: Choose File → Check Page → Accessibility.)

Once the report is complete—which may take awhile for an entire site—the process of identifying and fixing the errors is a little different than with other reports:

1. **In the Results panel's Site Reports tab, select an error (see Figure 16-10).**

   Accessibility errors come with one of two designations: *Failed* and *Manual*. A failure (marked in the Results panel by a red X) indicates that some item on the page fails to meet one of the prescribed guidelines. The most common failure is missing Alt text for graphics.

   "Manual" errors are those about which Dreamweaver isn't sure. Check them manually, and then make corrections, if you deem them necessary.

   In both cases, fixing the problems is up to you; Dreamweaver doesn't do any auto-fixing here.

Tip: The Insert Image command should be set to remind you to add alt text; if you're not prompted to supply alt text when inserting an image, turn to page 228 to learn how to turn on this feature.

---

2. **In the Results panel, click the More Information (i) button (circled in Figure 16-10).**

   The Reference panel shows a description of the problem and techniques for fixing it (see bottom image in Figure 16-10). In addition, you'll find some guidance in the accessibility guide built into the Reference panel (see page 422).

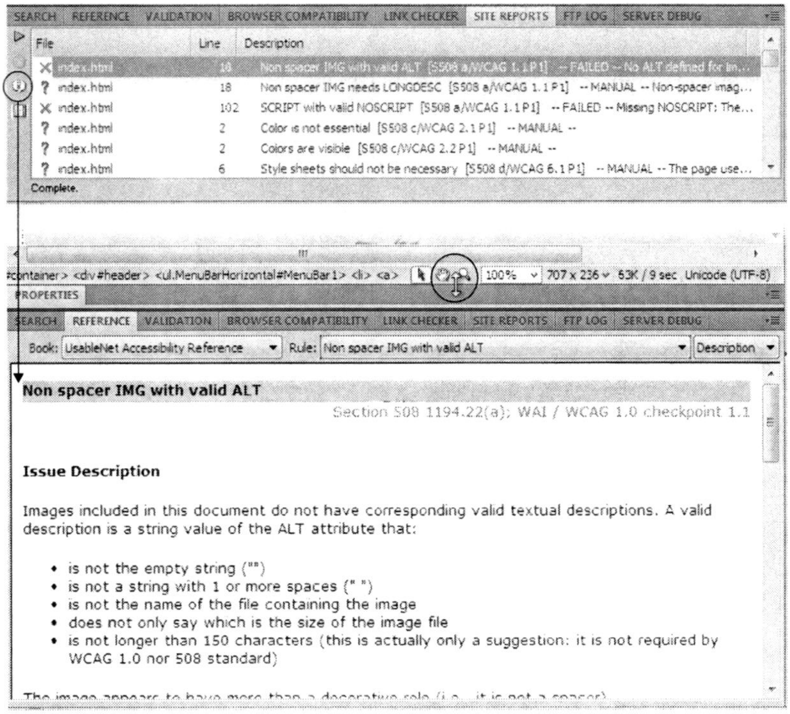

***Figure 16-10:** The UsableNet Accessibility Reference provides diagnosis and recommendations for all accessibility problems encountered by Dreamweaver's Accessibility reporting command. You probably have to stretch the panel to a taller height to read this information: Just drag the dark bar (circled in the middle of the figure) upward to make the Reference panel taller.*

3. **In the Results panel, double-click the name of the file.**

   As with other reports, Dreamweaver opens the file, and automatically highlights the offending code. You can then make the recommended changes and save the page.

Accessibility Priorities

As you'll quickly learn, a *lot* of different guidelines for creating accessible sites are out there. The whole issue can be confusing (some helpful resources are listed in the box on page 664).

To get you started, here are a few of the priority items the WAI recommends:

- **Images, animations.** Use the Alt property to describe the function of each visual element on a page (see page 225).
- **Image maps.** Provide Alt descriptions for each link in an image map (see page 245).
- **Hypertext links.** Use understandable text for all links. Try reading it aloud to make sure the text clearly indicates where the link goes. Avoid "click here" links.
- **Organizing page content.** Use headings, lists, and consistent structure. Avoid the <font> tag and the <table> tag for organizing page content; instead, use Cascading Style Sheets for text styling and page layout.

- **Graphs, charts.** Summarize information contained in informational graphics. You can use the *longdesc* property (see page 228) to help with this goal.
- **Scripts, applets, plug-ins.** Provide alternative content, in case active features are inaccessible or unsupported.
- **Frames.** Use the *noframes* element and title each frame page (though you're better off skipping this quickly dying Web design technique).

POWER USERS' CLINIC

Making Accessible Web Sites

Building Web sites that meet everyone's requirements is a daunting task. Unless you have screen-reader software to simulate the experience of a visually impaired visitor, or a crew of people with a variety of impairments (from colorblindness to repetitive stress injury) to test your site, how do you know what it takes to build a fully accessible Web site?

Fortunately, you can find plenty of resources to get you started. The best place to start is at the Web Accessibility Initiative's Web site, especially their accessibility resources page: *www.w3.org/WAI/Resources*. Here you'll find lots of information, including examples of different disabilities some Web surfers face, plus tips, checklists, and techniques for making sites accessible. You should also check out Dive Into Accessibility (*http://diveintoaccessibility.org*), a Web site dedicated to teaching Web designers the whys and hows of accessibility. For a short checklist that provides information for a basic accessibility evaluation, check out *www.tomjewett.com/accessibility/basiceval.html*.

And if you do want to see how screen readers work with your site, you can download a demo of JAWS, one of the most popular screen readers, at *www.freedomscientific.com/fs_downloads/jaws.asp*. A free alternative is a Firefox extension named Fangs, which displays (in text) what a screen reader like JAWS reads aloud. You can download it from *www.standards-schmandards.com/projects/fangs*.

Finally, Adobe dedicates an entire section of its site to accessibility issues: *www.adobe.com/accessibility/*. Here, you'll find explanations of the issues, tips for using Adobe products, and a showcase of model accessible Web sites.

Accessibility Options

Dreamweaver's accessibility report covers the Section 508 requirements as well as version 1 of the WAI's "Web Content Accessibility Guidelines" (more commonly referred to as WCAG 1.0). This thoroughness is commendable, but it may be more than you need. By all means, pare down the report to include just the guidelines that apply to your site. To do so, choose Site → Reports, and then turn on the Accessibility box. Click the Report Options button to open the window shown in Figure 16-11.

You can disable any rules Dreamweaver uses to evaluate your pages. To turn off an entire category—forms, frames, or tables, for example—click the name, and then click Disable. If you'd like to get more specific, click the + button next to a category name to expand a list of individual rules for that category. You can select and disable one or more rules. For example, if your site doesn't use frames, then you save time and Dreamweaver's energy by turning off the frames category.

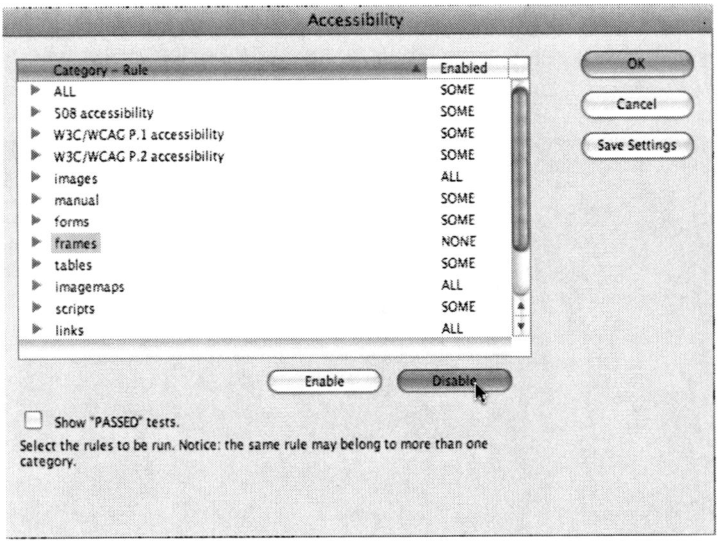

Figure 16-11: *The Accessibility options window lets you control which rules Dreamweaver uses to evaluate a Web site's accessibility. You may want to fine-tune this list based on recommendations in this book or from the online sources mentioned in the box on the opposite page.*

Download Statistics

Remember the old joke that WWW really stands for "World Wide Wait"? Even as more and more people upgrade to speedy DSL and cable modems, file size is the Web designer's constant foe. What takes only a moment to load from your computer's hard drive could take minutes to travel across the Internet. The more information you put into a Web page, the more time it takes to load.

You can judge how big your page is, and therefore how long it'll take to download, by looking at the bottom of the document window, in the status bar, and reading the download stats. You'll see something like this: *9k/2 sec*. This term indicates the file size of the Web page (9k, for instance) and how long it'll take a visitor to download the page (2 seconds) using a 56 Kbps modem.

Note: Because most people now have cable modems or DSL, to get a more realistic view of a visitor's download time you might want to change this 56 Kbps default setting. To do so, choose Edit → Preferences (Dreamweaver → Preferences), click the Status Bar category, and then, from the Connection Speed menu at the bottom of the window, choose a higher setting–a setting of 128 Kbps is a faster, but still conservative setting. You can also manually type in a connection speed (256 Kbps, for instance) to get a setting that Dreamweaver's menu doesn't list.

The file size and download time takes into account linked files like images, external CSS style sheets, and Flash movies. This information provides a realistic picture of download speed, since not only does a page have to download these files, but any files that a page uses (like a photo) also need to travel across the Internet to a visitor's browser. The file size and download time can be misleading, however.

If you use the same external files on *other* pages in the site (for example, a common external style sheet or a logo graphic that appears on each page), then your site's visitors may have already "cached" those files and don't need to spend the time downloading them again (see the box below).

GEM IN THE ROUGH

Caching In

Behind the scenes, Web browsers store the graphics they download onto the computer's hard drive. This is a speed trick. If you click your Back button to return to a Web page whose graphics files the browser has already downloaded, the browser simply pulls them out of the cache—off the hard drive, in other words—instead of re-downloading them. This system makes the page load more quickly, since the hard drive is generally much faster than the modem.

As a Web designer, you can capitalize on this standard Web browser feature by reusing the same graphics files on more than one page of your site. For instance, you can create a navigation bar composed of small graphic buttons (Home, Contact Us, Products, and so on). If you reuse those buttons on other pages of the site, those pages appear to download more quickly.

This same trick works for external CSS style sheets. A browser needs to download a complete style sheet with hundreds of formatting commands only once for any page on a site to reuse it. By putting all your formatting into one or more external files, you can keep your Web pages tidy and lean.

Note: People hate to wait. You may think that the graphic design of your Web site is so compelling that even if it takes a full minute to download that zippy new Flash home page, people will stick around.

Think again. Research shows that 10 seconds is the maximum amount of time that someone stays focused on a task while waiting. That means if you're designing a Web site for people with 128 Kbps modem, you should keep your pages below about 140 KB.

A Firefox plug-in called YSlow is a great tool for testing your download times. It can analyze bottlenecks, and help you determine why a Web page downloads slowly. You can get the plug-in at *http://developer.yahoo.com/yslow/*.

CHAPTER

17

Moving Your Site to the Internet

Building Web pages on your computer is a big accomplishment, but it's not the whole job. Your beautifully designed and informative Web site will simply languish in obscurity on your hard drive unless you move it to a Web server.

Fortunately, once your Web site is ready for prime time, you can put it on a server without ever leaving the comfort of Dreamweaver. The program includes simple commands for transferring files back and forth between the Web server and your desktop.

Depending on how you operate, choose one of these two methods for transferring your files:

- If you're the sole Web developer for a site, Dreamweaver's Get and Put commands are the easiest way to go.
- If, on the other hand, there's a group of people working on your site, Dreamweaver's Check Out and Check In tools let you move files at will without wiping out others' hard work. In addition, this group feature integrates seamlessly with two other industrial-strength Web collaboration tools: Microsoft's Visual SourceSafe, and WebDAV, an open-source file management tool.

Either way, you begin by defining a remote site.

Note: Dreamweaver CS4 has added support for Subversion, a powerful (and complex) file version control system. See the box on page 689 for details.

Defining a Remote Site

As you create your Web site on your computer, you keep it in a *local root folder* (see page 623), often called a *local site* for short. You can think of a local site as a work-in-progress. As your site is under construction—whether you're building it from scratch or adding and modifying pages—you'll routinely have partially finished documents sitting on your computer.

Then, when you've perfected and tested your pages using the techniques described in Chapter 16, you're ready to transfer them to a Web server that's connected to the Internet. Dreamweaver calls the Web server copy of your files the *remote site*, and the program provides five methods for transferring files between it and your local site:

- **FTP.** By far, the most common method is *FTP*, or File Transfer Protocol. Just as HTTP is the process by which Web pages are transferred from servers to Web browsers, FTP is the traditional method of transferring files over the Internet, and it's the one to use if a Web hosting company or Internet Service Provider (ISP) provides the home for your Web pages.
- **Over the local area network.** If you're working on an intranet, or if your company's Web server is connected to the company network, you may also be able to transfer files just as you would any files on your office network (using the Network Neighborhood, My Network Places, or "Connect to Server" command, depending on your operating system).
- The last three options—**RDS, SourceSafe, and WebDAV**—are advanced file management systems used for collaborative Web development. They're discussed on page 674.

FREQUENTLY ASKED QUESTION

Beyond Dreamweaver

Do I have to use Dreamweaver to move my files to the Web server?

No. If you'd like to use another program for this purpose, such as CuteFTP (Windows) or RBrowser (Mac), you can continue to use it and ignore Dreamweaver's Remote Site feature.

However, if you've never before used Dreamweaver to move files to a server, you may want to at least try it; you'll find that Dreamweaver simplifies much of the process. For example, when you want to move a file from your computer to the Web server using a regular FTP program, you must first locate the file on your local machine and then navigate to the proper folder on the Web server. Dreamweaver saves you both steps; when you select the file in the Files panel and click the Put button, Dreamweaver automatically locates the file on your computer and transfers it to the correct folder on the Web server.

Note: Dreamweaver lets you edit *directly* on pages located on a Web server, using an FTP connection (or if you're working with ColdFusion files, an RDS connection). This feature isn't a good way to go: It's slow, leaves your works-in-progress open for the world to see on the Internet, and makes it very easy to save files in the wrong place on your Web server.

Setting Up a Remote Site with FTP

You can set up a remote site only if you've first set up a *local* site on your computer. Even if you're just putting up a temporary site while working on your *real* Web site, you must at least have the temporary site constructed and defined in Dreamweaver (see page 37). Once that's done, here's how you go about creating an Internet-based mirror of your local site folder:

1. **Choose Site → Manage Sites.**

   The Manage Sites dialog box opens, listing all sites that you've defined so far. You're about to create a living, Internet-based *copy* of one of these hard drive–based local sites.

2. **Click the name of the site you want to post on the Internet, and then click Edit.**

   Alternatively, just double-click the site name in the list. The Site Definition window appears for the selected site, as shown in Figure 17-1.

Note: You can also define the remote site and the local site simultaneously, when you first begin creating a Web site (as described on page 42). Even then, however, Dreamweaver requires that you first give the site a name and choose a local root folder. At that point, you rejoin the steps described here.

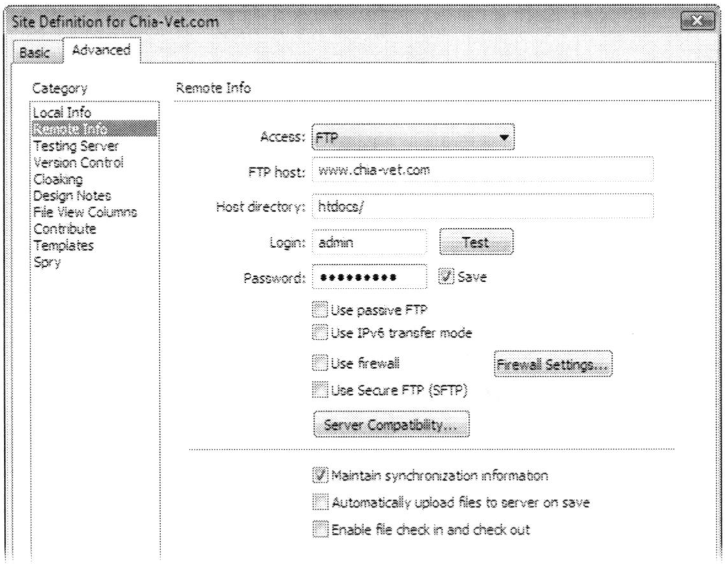

Figure 17-1: *If a Web hosting company or ISP hosts your Web site, you'll most likely use FTP to put your site on the Web. To make sure you have all the information you need to connect to the Web server, ask your ISP for these four pieces of information: (1) the FTP host name of the server, (2) the path to the root directory for your site, (3) your login name, and (4) your password. (If the Web server comes with your email account, your login and password may be the same for both.)*

3. **Click the Advanced tab.**

   You can also use the Site Definition Wizard (Basic tab) to set up a remote site. However, since the wizard requires you to step through screen after screen of setup information—even after you've already supplied most of it—the Advanced tab is faster.

4. **In the Category panel, click Remote Info. From the Access pop-up menu, choose FTP.**

   The Site Definition window now shows menus and fields for collecting your connection information (see Figure 17-1).

5. **Fill in the "FTP host" field.**

   This is the address of the Web server computer. It's usually something like *www.cosmofarmer.com*. It never includes directories, folders, or slashes (like *www.cosmofarmer.com/home*); never includes codes for the FTP protocol (*ftp://ftp.cosmofarmer.com*); and is usually not just a domain name, such as (*cosmofarmer.com*). It can also be an IP address, like *64.226.43.116*. In most cases, it's the address you would enter into a Web browser (minus the *http://*) to get to your site's home page.

   If you don't know the host name, there's only one way to find out: call or email your Web hosting company or ISP, or check its Web site.

6. **In the "Host directory" field, type the path to the root directory.**

   Here you're specifying which *folder* within your Web hosting account will contain your Web page files and serve as the root folder for your site.

   Just as on your own hard drive, all your Web site's files on the Web server are completely contained inside a master folder known as the *root folder*. But when you connect to your Web server using FTP, you're rarely connected to the root folder itself. Instead, you usually connect to a folder that isn't accessible over the Web—some administrative folder for your Web account, often filled with folders for log reports of your site's Web traffic, and other files not visible over the Web.

   You need to make sure Dreamweaver places your site's files in the root folder; that's why you're typing its name here. Common names for the root folder at ISPs or Web hosting companies are *docs, www, htdocs, public_html, or virtual_html.* (Call or email your Web hosting company or ISP to find out.)

   The information you give Dreamweaver here represents the path from the FTP folder to the root folder. It may look like this: *www/htdocs/* (if you leave the trailing forward slash off, Dreameaver adds it when you close the Site Definition window). In effect, you're telling Dreamweaver: "After connecting to the Web server, you'll find a folder named *www*. Inside *this* folder is another folder, *htdocs*. Put my site files in there." In other words, *htdocs* is the Web site's root folder on this particular remote hosting account.

7. **In the Login field, type your user name, and then type your password in the Password field.**

   Dreamweaver uses bullets (•••) to display your password so that passing evildoers in your office can't see what you're typing. If you want Dreamweaver to remember your password each time you use the program, turn on the Save checkbox. This way, you won't have to type your password each time you connect to the Web server.

Warning: For security reasons, don't turn on the Save box if you access the Web using computers at, say, your local library, or anywhere else where people you don't trust may use the machine. Otherwise, you might just awaken one morning to find the following splattered across your home page: "Hi there! Welcome to Jack's house of illegally acquired and unlawfully distributed music, featuring Metallica's greatest hits."

8. **Turn on the "Use passive FTP" or "Use firewall" boxes, if necessary.**

   If you're building sites from your home, home office, or small company, you may never need to use these options.

   Many corporations, however, use *firewalls*: hardware- or software-based gateways that control incoming and outgoing traffic through a network. Firewalls protect the company network from outside hackers; unfortunately, they also limit how computers inside the network—behind the firewall—can connect to the outside world.

Tip: When Dreamweaver can't connect to a Web server, one of the first things you should try is turning on the "Use passive FTP" checkbox. Your first chance to see whether this maneuver is necessary comes below, in step 13.

   If your company's system administrator confirms that you have a firewall, turn on the "Use firewall" checkbox. To overcome any problems caused by the firewall, click the Firewall Settings button, which opens the Site Preferences dialog box; you'll then need to enter the name of the firewall host computer and its port number. Your firewall configuration may also require *passive FTP*—a method of connecting using your local software, rather than the firewall server. Check with your administrator to see if this is the case, and, if so, turn on the "Use passive FTP" checkbox.

Note: You probably won't need to turn on the "Use IPv6 transfer mode" checkbox for several years to come. It's intended for the day when we run out of IP addresses, and Web servers switch from IP addresses that look like *192.168.1.1* to ones that look like this: *1A23:120B:0000:0000:0000:7634:AD01:004D*. Egads.

9. **If your Web server uses SFTP (a secure, encrypted form of FTP), turn on the Use Secure FTP (SFTP) box.**

   Secure FTP encrypts *all* of your data, not just your user name and password, so information transferred in this way is unintelligible to Internet snoops. It's the ideal method of connecting to a Web server, since normal FTP connections send your username and password unencrypted, susceptible to Internet creeps; in many cases, Secure FTP is also faster. Unfortunately, not all Web hosting companies offer this advanced option.

By the way, leave "Automatically upload files to server on save" turned off. Because it makes Dreamweaver upload the file each time you save, it slows you down and runs the risk of putting half-finished Web pages on your server for all the world to see. It's better to just upload the page after you're completely finished with it.

10. **Leave the Server Compatibility options alone.**

    That big Server Compatibility button is useful when you're having trouble connecting to the server or moving files on the server. Dreamweaver, out of the box, is tuned to make FTP run as fast as possible, so leave these options alone, unless you're having trouble. If you are having trouble connecting to your server, start with the Tip on page 671. If that doesn't work, click the Server Compatibility button and turn off the "Use FTP performance optimization" box.

    If everything's okay when you're connecting to your server, but you're getting errors when moving files on the server, you should turn on the "Use alternative FTP move method" box. This method is slower but more reliable. It's also handy if you use Adobe's Contribute program and are taking advantage of the "rollback" feature (to learn more about Contribute, visit *www.adobe.com/contribute/*).

Note: The Server Compatibility button is disabled if you've chose an SFTP connection since the options set with that button don't apply to SFTP.

11. **If you don't want to synchronize files, turn off the "Maintain synchronization information" box.**

    Dreamweaver's synchronization feature is a useful tool for keeping a site up to date. It helps you maintain the most recent versions of a file on the remote server, by keeping track of when you've changed a file on your computer. When you synchronize a site, Dreamweaver can move the more recent files onto the Web server. This feature is described in detail on page 693. If you don't use synchronization, definitely turn off this checkbox. When this feature is on, Dreamweaver inserts little files named *dwsync.xml* throughout your site in folders named *_notes*. These items keep track of synchronization information about each file in your site, but there's no need to clutter things up with these files if you don't use synchronization.

12. **Turn on "Enable file check in and check out," if you like.**

    Turn it on if, for example, you and your team of Web developers all use Dreamweaver. Then fill in the corresponding options as explained in Figure 17-2.

If you do wind up using the "check out" feature (see page 686), you can save yourself some clicks by turning on "Check out files when opening." (Fill in your name and email address, too, as shown in Figure 17-2.) Now you can "check out" a file from the remote server just by double-clicking its name in the Site Files list. If you're not working with other developers on the site, *do not* turn on this setting, since it will slow down the process of moving files back and forth from the server and add unnecessary files (used to determine who has what file checked out) to both your server and your own computer.

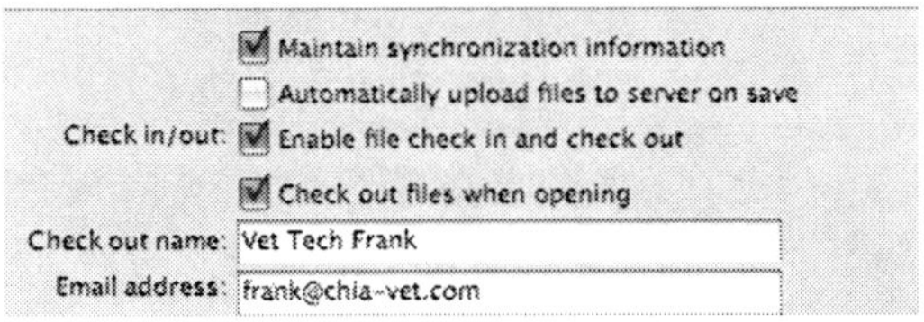

Figure 17-2:
If you're using Dreamweaver's Check In/Check Out feature and you work on your site in several different locations (for example, from home and your office), use a different name for each location (BobAtHome and BobAtWork, for example). In this way, you can identify which files you've checked out to your home computer and which to your computer at work.

13. **Click the Test button to see if Dreamweaver can connect to the Web server.**

    If everything goes according to plan, you'll see a "Dreamweaver connected to your Web server successfully" message. If not, you'll get an "FTP error" message with some additional information that can help you determine the problem (see the box below).

14. **Click OK to return to the Manage Sites dialog box, and then click Done.**

    The Manage Sites dialog box closes, and the Files panel opens.

At this point, you're ready to connect to the Web server and transfer files. If you're the only person working on the site, Dreamweaver's Get and Put commands will do the trick (page 678). If, however, you're part of a development team, use Dreamweaver's Check In and Check Out feature, described on page 686.

Setting Up a Remote Site over a Local Network

If you're working on an intranet, or if your company's Web server is connected to the company network, you may also be able to transfer your Web files just as you'd move any files from machine to machine. Dreamweaver provides the same file-transfer functions as with FTP, but setup is simpler.

Follow steps 1 and 2 of the previous instructions, but in step 4, click the Remote Info category and then choose Local/Network from the Access pop-up menu. Menus and fields for collecting your connection information appear in the Site Definition box (see Figure 17-3).

Now click the folder icon next to the "Remote folder" field. In the resulting dialog box, navigate to and select your site's remote root folder. On a local network, this folder functions as the root folder on your company's Web server, even though it's actually still within the walls of your building.

FREQUENTLY ASKED QUESTION

When Your Remote Site Is Too Remote

Help! I can't connect to my Web server. What should I do?

Things don't always go smoothly. That's doubly true when trying to connect to a Web server, since you depend on a variety of things—your Internet connection, the networks connecting you to your Web server, the Web server itself, and the FTP software—working together in harmony. Dreamweaver presents an error message if you can't successfully establish an FTP connection with your Web server. The error box frequently contains useful information that can help you determine the problem. Here are some of the most common:

- **Remote host cannot be found** usually means you typed an incorrect FTP Host address (step 5 on page 670).
- **Your login or password is incorrect** means just that—you've typed the wrong user name or password (step 7 on page 671).
- **Cannot open remote folder** usually means you mistyped or input the wrong Host directory (step 6 on page 670).

Unfortunately, there are lots of reasons Dreamweaver may not be able to connect, so sometimes the error message isn't particularly helpful. Here are a few other suggestions for troubleshooting: make sure you're connected to the Internet (open a Web browser and see if you can visit a site on the Web); return to the Remote Info category of the Site Definition window, and turn on the "Use passive FTP" option (sometimes this just makes things work); click the Server Compatibility button, and then turn off the "Use FTP performance optimization" box; and if you have another FTP program like CuteFTP or RBrowser, see if you can connect to your Web server using the same settings you gave Dreamweaver. If all these steps fail, you can visit this page on the Adobe Web site for additional troubleshooting tips: *www.adobe.com/cfusion/knowledgebase/index.cfm?id=tn_14834.*

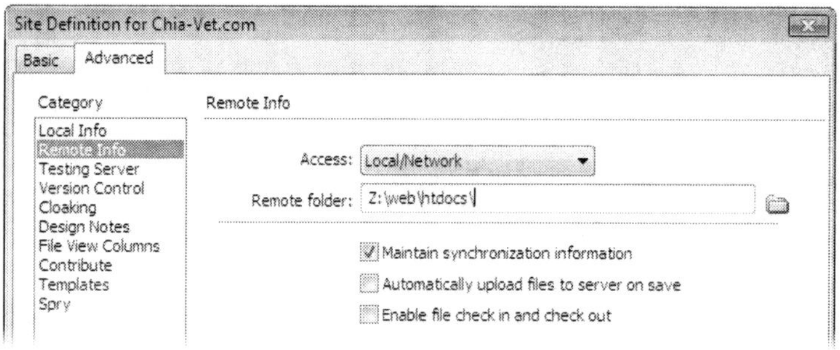

Figure 17-3: *If your company's Web server is hosted in your office, the "remote site" might not be that remote: In this case, choose a folder on your local network as the remote site.*

Wrap up with steps 11, 12, and 14 of the previous instructions. At this point, you're ready to connect to the Web server and transfer files.

Setting Up a Remote Site with RDS

RDS (Remote Development Services) is a feature of Adobe's ColdFusion Server. It lets designers work on Web files and databases in conjunction with a ColdFusion application server. If you aren't using ColdFusion, then this option isn't for you.

To create a remote site in Dreamweaver that works with RDS, follow steps 1 through 3 on page 669. In step 4, click the Remote Info category, and then choose RDS from the Access pop-up menu.

The Site Definition window displays a version number, a short description, and a Settings button. Click Settings to open the Configure RDS Server window, shown in Figure 17-4. Fill in the dialog box as directed by your server administrator or help desk.

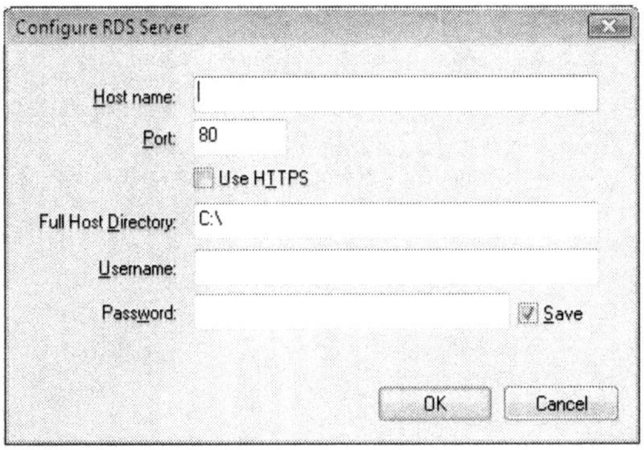

Figure 17-4:
Remote Development Services is a feature of the ColdFusion application server. However, even if you use ColdFusion, you may not be able to use RDS, since many Web hosting companies that offer ColdFusion servers turn off RDS due to potential security problems.

Setting Up a Remote Site with WebDAV

Dreamweaver also allows access to a remote site using *WebDAV*, short for Web-based Distributed Authoring and Versioning. Like FTP, it's a method, or protocol, for transferring files. Like SFTP, it lets you use a secure connection (SSL or Secure Socket Layer) so that all of your data is encrypted as it passes back and forth between your computer and the Web server. But unlike both of those technologies, WebDAV also addresses the kinds of problems you encounter when collaborating on a Web site with other people.

For instance, all kinds of havoc can result if two people edit a page simultaneously; whoever uploads the page to the Web server *second* winds up wiping out the changes made by the first person. WebDAV supports a check-in and check-out system that works similarly to Dreamweaver's Check In/Check Out tool (see page 686) to make sure only one person works on a file at a time and no one tramples on anyone else's files. In fact, Dreamweaver's Check In and Check Out tools work seamlessly with WebDAV.

Both Microsoft Internet Information Server (IIS) and Apache Web Server can work with WebDAV. WebDAV is commonly found at colleges and universities, but it's less common at traditional Web hosting companies. To find out if your Web server can handle WebDAV (and to find out the necessary connection information), consult your Web server's administrator (for example, call or email your Web hosting company).

Setting up WebDAV access to a remote site is very similar to setting up FTP access. Follow steps 1 through 3 on page 669, and then:

1. **Click the Remote Info category, and then choose WebDAV from the Access pop-up menu.**

   The Site Definition window displays the WebDAV settings (Figure 17-5).

2. **In the URL box, type in the URL of the WebDAV server.**

   In most cases, this is the URL of the Web site, so it begins with either *http://* or *https://*. The "s" in *https* means you'll connect securely to the Web server using SSL. The normal *http://* method doesn't use any encryption, which means that, just like with regular FTP, your user name, password, and all data are sent "in the open" as they travel across the Internet. Note that just adding an "s" won't suddenly make your file transfers secure; the Web server needs to be set up to accept https connections (a technically challenging task).

Figure 17-5: *WebDAV, short for Web-based Distributed Authoring and Versioning, is a powerful tool for working on a site with other people. It's built into several Web server packages but, unfortunately, isn't a very common option at most Web hosting companies.*

3. **In the Login field, type your user name, and then type your password in the Password field.**

   Turn on the Save checkbox if you want to save yourself the hassle of having to type in your password each time you move files to your Web server (but heed the Warning on page 671).

4. **Click the Test button to see if your connection works.**

   If Dreamweaver succeeds, it proudly tells you. Unfortunately, if it fails, you'll get an error message that isn't exactly helpful. WebDAV isn't nearly as finicky as FTP, so if there's an error, you most likely just typed the URL, password, or login incorrectly, or WebDAV just isn't available for the server.

Note: However, due to the different possible server configurations for WebDAV, Dreamweaver may not be able to connect at all. If this is the case, you'll need to use FTP or another method to connect to your server.

5. **Leave the "Automatically upload files to server on save" box turned off.**

   This option makes Dreamweaver upload the file each time you save; it slows you down and runs the risk of putting half-finished Web pages on your server for all the world to see. It's better to just upload the page after you're completely finished with it.

The rest of the process is identical to the FTP setup process, so follow steps 11, 12, and 14, starting on page 672. At that point, you're ready to connect to the Web server and transfer files, as described on page 678.

Setting Up a Remote Site with SourceSafe

Microsoft originally created Visual SourceSafe for managing team software development. Like WebDAV, SourceSafe makes sure you don't accidentally stomp on someone else's hard work by overwriting a Web page they just modified. In addition, this sophisticated program tracks different versions of files and lets an administrator "roll back" to previous versions of a Web page, or even an entire site; it's the granddaddy of Undos.

To take advantage of this power, however, you need a Visual SourceSafe (VSS) server and VSS database already setup. In addition, Windows people need to install Microsoft Visual SourceSafe Client version 6 on their PCs.

Note: The Visual SourceSafe option isn't available in the Mac version of Dreamweaver.

Once you've installed the VSS Client software, and you've created and defined a local site, you're ready to configure Dreamweaver for SourceSafe using the Site Definition window. Basically, you tell Dreamweaver where to find the SourceSafe database and how to sign on to the server.

Once again, follow steps 1 though 3 on page 669. But in step 4, click the Remote Info category, and then choose Microsoft® Visual SourceSafe® from the Access pop-up menu. In the resulting dialog box, click Settings to reveal the Open Microsoft® Visual SourceSafe® Database dialog box (Figure 17-6).

Figure 17-6: *This window, sometimes called the "Microsoft's® Lawyers Are Everywhere®" dialog box, lets you set up Dreamweaver for use with the Visual SourceSafe system. Many corporations use this powerful file-control system to control access to files in large projects involving many people.*

Click Browse to select the Visual SourceSafe (VSS) database file on your computer (or type in the file path, if you know it, into the Database Path field)—the *srcsafe.ini* file that Dreamweaver uses to initialize SourceSafe.

Then, in the Project field, fill in the name of the *project* within the VSS database that you wish to use as the remote root folder. (A VSS database can have many projects and Web sites listed in it. Make sure you enter the correct project name for this site. If in doubt, contact the administrator of the Visual SourceSafe database.) Type your user name and password into the appropriate fields; again, ask the administrator for guidance.

Click OK. But before dismissing the Site Definition dialog box, turn on "Check Out Files when Opening," so that Dreamweaver's Check In and Check Out features (see page 686) work with the VSS system. Click OK, and then click Done.

Transferring Files

Once you've told Dreamweaver *how* you plan to ship off your Web page files to the Net, you can now set about actually *doing* it. Thanks to Dreamweaver's Files panel, the whole process takes only a few steps.

Moving Files to the Web Server

To transfer files to your Web server:

1. **Open the Files panel (Figure 17-7).**

   Choose Window → Files (keyboard shortcut: F8 [Shift-⌘-F]).

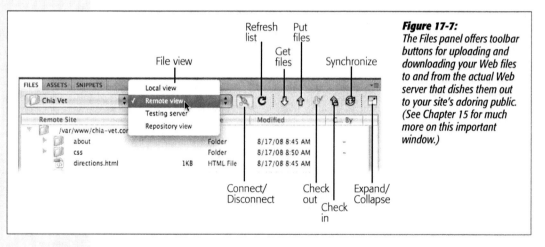

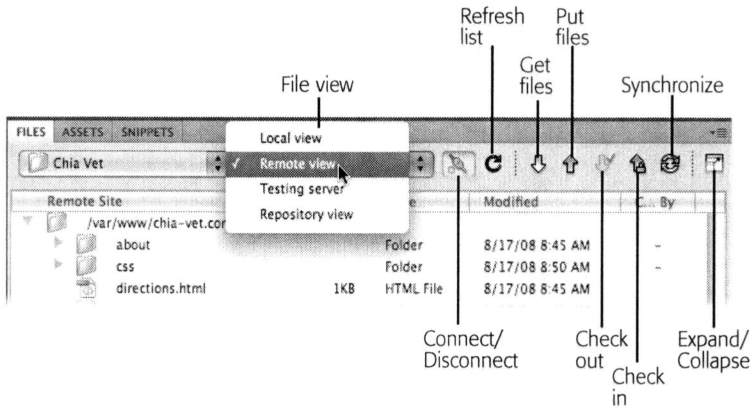

***Figure 17-7:** The Files panel offers toolbar buttons for uploading and downloading your Web files to and from the actual Web server that dishes them out to your site's adoring public. (See Chapter 15 for much more on this important window.)*

2. **From the Site menu, choose the name of the site whose files you wish to move (if it isn't already selected).**

   The Files panel displays files for the selected site. You can use the File View pop-up menu to access either a list of the local files or the remote files on the Web server (see Figure 17-7). You can also see both local and remote files side by side if you first choose "Remote view" from the File View pop-up menu and then click the Expand button on the Files panel, as described on page 629.

Note: The color of the folders in the Site panel lets you know which view you're currently in: green folders mean Local view (your computer), beige (blue on the Mac) folders mean Remote view, and red folders indicate the Testing view for a testing server as described on page 811.

3. **From the file list in the Files panel, select the files you wish to upload to the Web server.**

   To move a folder and every file inside it, just select the folder. (In other words, you can transfer your *entire* Web site to the server by simply selecting the local root folder—the folder listed at the very top of the local file list.) When only a few files have changed, you can also select only certain files or folders for uploading, using any of the techniques described on page 646.

Note: If you don't see the files you wish to upload in the Site Files list, you may have Remote view selected. Select Local view to see only those site files on your computer and click the Refresh button on the Files panel (Figure 17-7).

   When you use do-it-yourself FTP programs like WS_FTP or Fetch, you have to specify a folder location for every file you transfer to the Web server. But here's one of the great advantages of letting Dreamweaver do your file shuffling; it already knows where the files should go on the remote site. The local and remote sites are, after all, mirror images, so Dreamweaver simply puts files in the corresponding folders on the remote site.

   For example, suppose you select the file *mayo.html*, which is in a folder called Condiments, which is itself stored in the local root folder. When you transfer the file, Dreamweaver knows to put this file in the Condiments folder in the root folder on the remote site. In fact, if the folder Condiments doesn't exist on the remote site, Dreamweaver creates it and *then* puts the file into it. Now that's service.

   You're now ready to go live with your Web page.

4. **Click the "Put files" button—the up-arrow icon identified in Figure 17-7—on the Files panel.**

   Alternatively, you can use the keyboard shortcut Ctrl+Shift+U (⌘-Shift-U).

   Several things happen when you do this: First, if you're using an FTP connection, Dreamweaver attempts to connect to your Web server, dialing your modem if necessary. As you can see in the status window that opens, it may take a moment or so to establish a connection; the Connect button (see Figure 17-7) displays a bright green light when Dreamweaver is connected.

   Next, if any of the files you're transferring are currently open and have unsaved changes, Dreamweaver asks if you want to save the files before transferring them to the server. Click Yes to save the file, or, if there are multiple unsaved files, click the Yes To All button to save all of them before posting them online.

In addition, Dreamweaver asks if you wish to transfer any *dependent files* (see Figure 17-8). Dependent files are graphics, external CSS files, or Flash movies that you've placed onto a page and are needed for the page to display properly.

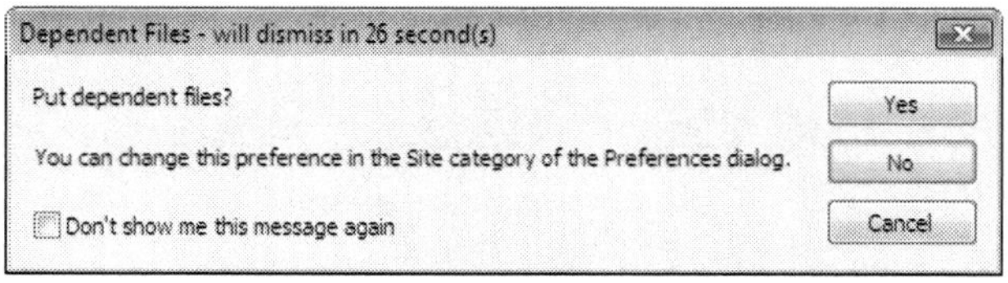

Figure 17-8:
The Dependent Files feature of Dreamweaver's File Transfer command makes sure that all files that are needed for a Web page to display correctly–graphics, Flash movies, external style sheets, and so on–are copied to the Web server along with your Web pages. There's also a countdown–a "will dismiss in xx seconds" message. If you don't click a button within 30 seconds, Dreamweaver assumes you mean "No" and just uploads the selected files.

This feature can save you considerable time and hassle; no need to hunt for and upload each graphic file or external style sheet yourself. On the other hand, if all the dependent files are *already* on the server, having Dreamweaver transfer the same files again is a waste of time. Fortunately, Dreamweaver helps stop this wasted effort as described in the next step.

Note: If you turn on the "Don't show me this message again" box (see Figure 17-8) and then click Yes, from that moment forward, Dreamweaver copies dependent files without asking. On the other hand, if you turn on the "Don't show me this message again" box and click No, Dreamweaver *never* copies dependent files.

If you want the Dependent Files dialog box to appear again after you've turned it off, hold down the Alt (Option) key when you transfer a file (using any method except a keyboard shortcut). Or choose Edit → Preferences → Site Category (Dreamweaver → Preferences → Site Category) to turn this feature on or off.

5. **Click Yes to transfer dependent files, or No to transfer only the files you selected.**

   Dreamweaver copies the files to the Web server. If you're copying a file that's inside a folder that isn't already on the remote site, Dreamweaver creates the folder as well. In fact, Dreamweaver creates as many subfolders as necessary to make sure every file is transferred to the same folder location on the remote site as it is in the local site. (Try doing *that* with a regular FTP program.)

   If you've chosen to transfer dependent files as well, Dreamweaver may or may not put the dependent file on the Web server. If you've turned on the "Maintain Synchronization Information" checkbox when defining your remote site (see step 11 on page 672), Dreamweaver determines if the dependent file is already on the Web server and, if it is, whether your local copy of the file is a newer version. If the dependent file doesn't exist on the server or your local copy is newer (meaning you've made some changes to it locally but haven't yet moved it onto the Web), Dreamweaver puts it on the remote site when you tell it to transfer dependent files.

However, if Dreamweaver thinks that it's the same file, or that the copy of the file on the Web server is newer, it won't transfer the dependent file. This behavior is a huge time-saver, since you won't have to repeatedly upload the same 50 navigation buttons each time you say "Yes" to transferring dependent files; but, best of all, Dreamweaver still transfers those dependent files that really *are* new.

Note: Dreamweaver's ability to correctly determine whether a dependent file on your computer is the same as the file on the remote site depends on its Site Synchronization feature, described on page 693. While Dreamweaver's accuracy with this tool is good, Dreamweaver has been known to get it wrong. If Dreamweaver isn't moving a dependent file that you want moved to the remote server, you can just select that file and upload it manually (for example, select it in the Files panel and click the Put button). Dreamweaver always obeys a direct order to move a selected file to the remote site.

6. **Continue using the Put button to transfer all files in your Web site to the remote site.**

   Depending on the number of files transferred, this operation can take some time. Transferring files over the Internet using FTP isn't nearly as fast as copying files from one hard drive to another (see the box below).

POWER USERS' CLINIC

A Little More Background on File Transfers

Dreamweaver lets you keep working as it dutifully moves files in the background. You can edit a Web page, create a new style sheet, and so on, while the program busily transfers files over the Internet. However, there are some things you *can't* do while Dreamweaver is transferring files. These are mostly logical restrictions: you can't edit the site definition (since this could affect how you connect to the remote server); you can't put or get other files (since Dreamweaver's already busy doing that); you can't delete a file on the local or remote server (since you may be transferring that file). Dreamweaver lets you know if you try to do one of these forbidden actions while it's working with the server.

If you find the background activity window a nuisance, click the Hide button and it temporarily disappears. In addition, if you accidentally start uploading a 10,000 page Web site, you probably won't want to wait until Dreamweaver is finished. Click the Cancel button to stop the process.

Once Dreamweaver's finished moving files around, you can see a record of Dreamweaver's actions by clicking the Log button that appears at the bottom-right corner of the Files panel. This log is a different record than the raw FTP log discussed in the box on page 684. This plain-language window lets you know what Dreamweaver did—"Put successful," "Get successful," and so on. If you see a "not transferred" message, this means that you tried to Get or Put a file, but both the local and remote copies were identical, so Dreamweaver didn't do anything. See the Note above for more information.

Other ways to move files to the Web server

You can also copy your current document to the Web server without using the Files panel at all. You can go directly to the Put command when, say, you finish building or modifying a Web page and want to immediately move it to the Web server. Just choose Site → Put or press Ctrl+Shift+U (⌘-Shift-U); Dreamweaver automatically copies the fresh page to the proper folder online.

The toolbar also provides a quick menu shortcut for this operation, as shown in Figure 17-9.

Figure 17-9: *Click the File Status button (circled) and choose Put to quickly move a file to your Web server. You can also use this menu to retrieve a copy of this file from the server (Get), use Check In and Out features (page 686), or review Design Notes (page 696) for the page. To select this file in the Files panel, choose "Locate in Site".*

Getting Files from the Web Server

So far, this chapter has described getting your hard drive–based Web pages to the Internet. Sometimes, however, you'll want to download one or more files *from* the Web server. Perhaps you've made a horrible (and irreversible) mistake on the local copy of a file, and you want to retrieve the last version from the Web server, using the remote site as a last-ditch backup system. Or perhaps someone else uploaded some files to the site, and you want to download a copy to your own computer (although the Synchronize feature described on page 693 would also work).

To get files from the remote site, open the Files panel (press F8 [Shift-⌘-F]) and proceed as follows:

1. **From the Site pop-up menu, choose the site whose files you wish to retrieve.**

   As with all of Dreamweaver's site management features, downloading files from a Web server depends upon first defining a site.

2. **From the Files panel's View menu (see Figure 17-7), choose "Remote view."**

   Dreamweaver tells you that it's attempting to connect to the Web server. Once the connection has been made, a list of files and folders appears in the Remote Site list, and the Connect button displays a bright green dot. (Dreamweaver automatically disconnects you after 30 minutes of inactivity, at which point the green dot turns black.)

Note: If you'd like to change the disconnect-after-30-minutes-of-inactivity setting, press Ctrl+U (⌘-U) to open the Preferences window. Click the Site category and change the number listed in the Minutes Idle box. Be aware, however, that some Web servers have their own settings and may disconnect you sooner than you've specified.

3. **From the Remote Site file list, select the files you wish to download from the Web server.**

   For techniques on selecting files in the Files panel, see page 646. To download a folder and every file inside it, just click the folder. This technique also lets you get your *entire* Web site from the server; just click the remote root folder, which appears at the very top of the Remote Site file list.

TROUBLESHOOTING MOMENT

Don't Replace the Wrong File

One strange feature of the Files panel's Get and Put commands may get you in trouble. Suppose, having just added new information to the home page (*index.html*), you want to transfer it to the Web server. You select it in the Local Folder list—but then you accidentally click Get instead of Put.

Not knowing your true intention, Dreamweaver dutifully retrieves the file from the Web server and prepares to replace (wipe out) the newly updated home page on your computer.

Fortunately, Dreamweaver also opens a warning message asking if you really want to overwrite the local file. Click No or Cancel to save your hard work.

There may be times when you *do* want to wipe out your local copy—for example, if your cat walks across your keyboard, types illegible code, presses Ctrl+S to save the ruined page, and Ctrl+Q to quit Dreamweaver (keeping you from using Undo to fix the mistakes). In this common situation, you'll want to replace your local copy with the remote copy. To do so, press the Yes key to wipe out your cat's errors. Oh yeah, this is also a useful trick if *you* ever make a mistake on a page you can't fix and want to return to the working copy on your Web server.

Dreamweaver also includes a useful Compare button to help you sort out the differences between the local and remote file. Clicking this button lets you compare the local and remote copies of the page, so you can identify which changes you made. In this way, you can salvage changes you made to the local copy and discard errors you (or your cat) may have introduced to the page. This feature is described on page 416.

4. **Click the Get files button—the down arrow.**

   Alternatively, you can use the keyboard shortcut Ctrl+Shift+D (⌘-Shift-D).

   If the *local* version of any file you're getting from the remote site is currently opened and has unsaved changes, Dreamweaver warns you that you'll lose those changes. (No surprise there; copying a file from the remote site automatically replaces the same file in the local site, whether it's open or not.) Dreamweaver also warns you if you're about to replace a local file that's *newer* than the remote one.

In addition, Dreamweaver offers to transfer any dependent files, as described in Figure 17-8.

5. **Click Yes to transfer dependent files, or No to transfer only the files you selected.**

   Dreamweaver copies the files to the local site folder, creating any folders necessary to replicate the structure of the remote site.

POWER USERS' CLINIC

Troubleshoot with the FTP Log

If you're having problems moving files using Dreamweaver's FTP command, you may be able to find some clues in the records Dreamweaver keeps when transferring files. If you've used other FTP programs, you may have seen little messages that are sent back and forth between the Web server and the FTP program like this:

```
200 PORT command successful. LIST 150
Opening ASCII mode data connection for
/bin/ls.
```

Dreamweaver also sends and receives this information, but it keeps it hidden. In order to see the FTP log, choose Window → Results, and then click the FTP Log tab. Any errors appear in this log.

For example, if you encounter a "cannot put file" error, it may mean that you're out of space on your Web server. Contact your ISP or the administrator of your Web server for help. WebDAV connections also produce a log of file-transfer activity, but it's not very easy to decipher.

And Secure FTP (SFTP) produces no log in Dreamweaver—hush, hush, it's a secret.

Cloaking Files

You may not want *all* files transferred to and from the Remote site. For example, as part of its Library and Template tools, Dreamweaver creates folders inside your local root folder. The Library and templates folders don't do you any good on the Web server; their sole purpose is to help you build the site on your computer. Likewise, you may have Photoshop (.psd), Flash (.fla), or Illustrator (.ai) files in your local root folder. They're inaccessible from a Web browser and can take up a lot of disk space, so they shouldn't be transferred to the Web server when you move your site online.

Note: If you work on a Web site with other people, you probably *will* want to have the Library and templates folders on the server. This way, others who work on the site can access them as well.

To meet such challenges, Dreamweaver includes a feature called *cloaking*. It lets you hide folders and specific file types from many file-transfer operations, including Get/Put files, the Check In/Check Out feature (page 686), and site synchronization (page 693). In fact, you can even hide files from many sitewide Dreamweaver actions, including reports (see page 657), search and replace (page 782), check and change links sitewide (page 643), and the Assets panel (page 633). There's one exception: files that are linked to Library items (see Chapter 18) or templates (Chapter 19) can still "see" items in cloaked Library and template folders.

Dreamweaver lets you cloak specific folders in your site or particular file types (those that end with a specific extension such as .fla or .psd). In addition, Dreamweaver CS4 adds the flexibility to cloak even a single file anywhere in your Web site. Each type of cloak requires a different technique.

To hide specific types of files:

1. **Choose Site → Manage Sites.**

   The Manage Sites window opens, listing all sites you've defined in Dreamweaver.

2. **Select the site you wish to use cloaking on and click Edit.**

   That site's Site Definition window opens.

3. **Click the Cloaking category.**

   The cloaking settings appear (see Figure 17-10). The factory setting is On for every site you define. (If you want to turn it off, just turn off the "Enable cloaking" box.)

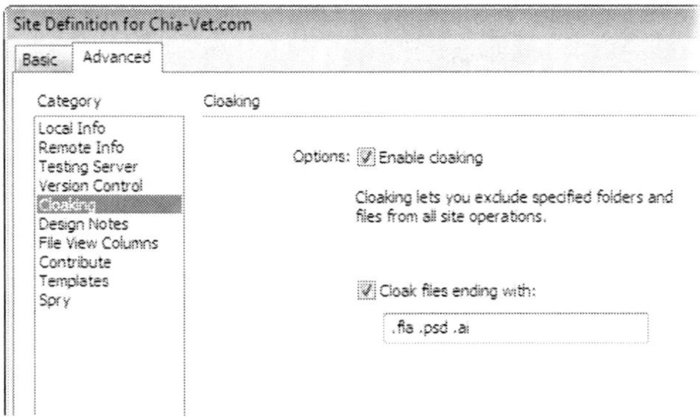

Figure 17-10: *The Cloaking category of the Site Definition window lets you turn cloaking on and off–a feature that lets you hide specific file types, individual files, and folders from sitewide operations like transferring files to a Web server or searching and replacing text. In this window, you can specify which types of files to hide by listing their extensions (.psd for Photoshop files, for example).*

Tip: You can quickly turn cloaking on and off by right-clicking (Control-clicking) any file or folder in the Files panel and selecting Cloaking → Enable Cloaking from the shortcut menu. A checkmark next to Enable Cloaking means cloaking is turned on.

4. **Turn on the "Cloak files ending with" checkbox.**

   Dreamweaver identifies file types by their extensions—.fla for Flash files, for example. If you use Fireworks, don't add the .png extension to this box. Even though you might not want to have your byte-heavy Fireworks files moved to your Web server, cloaking files with the .png extension means you'll also keep graphic files saved in the very common and useful compressed PNG file format (page 218) from being transferred to your server.

Note: Mac programs don't always add these file name suffixes, but without them, Dreamweaver can't cloak, so make sure you add a file extension when saving a file. Some programs have a "Hide File Extension" check box that appears when saving a file—make sure this is *not* checked.

5. **In the text box, type the extensions you wish to cloak.**

   Each extension should start with a period followed by three or four letters. To type multiple extensions in the box, separate them with a space.

6. **Click OK twice to close this window and the Manage Sites window.**

   All cloaked files have a red slash through them in the Files panel.

You can also cloak a single file or folder using the Files panel like this:

1. **Open the Files panel by pressing F8 (Shift-⌘-F).**

   Alternatively, choose Window → Files.

2. **Right-click (Control-click) any file or folder in Local Files view.**

   A shortcut menu appears with many site-related options.

3. **Select Cloaking → Cloak.**

   Dreamweaver adds a red slash through the file or folder's icon in the Files panel. When you cloak a folder, all files and folders inside the cloaked folder are hidden as well, as indicated by the red slashes through their icons.

Once you've cloaked a folder, it and any folders inside it disappear from Dreamweaver's file-transfer functions. Individual files that you've cloaked, as well as files with specific extensions that you specified in the Preferences window, are also hidden.

However, there are exceptions. You can override the cloaking, for example, by selecting a cloaked folder or file and then using the Get or Put file buttons as described on page 678. Dreamweaver assumes that since you specifically selected that file or folder, you intend to override the cloaking feature.

Dreamweaver also ignores cloaking if you answer Yes in the Dependent Files message box (Figure 17-8) when you put or get files. In that case, Dreamweaver transfers all dependent files, even if they're cloaked (this applies to Library and template files as well).

Check In and Check Out

If you're the sole developer for a Web site, the Files panel's Get and Put buttons are fine for transferring your files. But if you're on a team of developers, these simple tools can get you in trouble.

For example, suppose your boss emails you an important announcement that she wants posted on the home page immediately. So you download the home page from the Web server and start to edit it. At the same time, your co-worker Bob notices a typo on the home page. He downloads it, too.

You're a much faster worker than Bob, so you've added the critical news to the home page and moved it back to the Web server. But now Bob transfers his corrected home page to the Web server, *overwriting* your edits and eliminating that urgent notice you just uploaded. (An hour later, your phone rings. It's the boss.)

Without some kind of system to monitor who has what file, and to prevent people from overwriting each other's work, collaborative Web development is a chaotic mess. Fortunately, Dreamweaver's Check In and Check Out system provides a civilized answer to this problem. It works like your local public library: When you check a file out, no one else can have it. When you're finished, you check the file back in, releasing control of it, and allowing someone else on the team to check it out and work on it.

To use the Check In/Check Out feature effectively, it helps to keep a few things in mind:

- When you're developing a Web site solo, your local site usually contains the most recent versions of your files. You make any modifications or additions to the pages on your computer first and *then* transfer them to the Web server.
- But in a collaborative environment where many people are working on the site at once, the files on your hard drive may not be the latest ones. After all, your co-workers, like you, have been updating pages and transferring them to the Web server. The home page file sitting in the local site folder on your computer may be several days older than the file on the remote site, which is why checking out a file from the *remote site*, rather than editing from the copy on your computer, is so important. It guarantees that you have the latest version of the file.
- In a collaborative environment, nobody should post files to the Web server using any method except Dreamweaver's Check In and Check Out system.

  The reason is technical, but worth slogging through: When Dreamweaver checks out a file, it doesn't actually *lock* the file. Instead, it places a small, invisible text file (with the three-letter suffix .lck) on both the remote server and in your local site folder. This text file indicates who has checked out the file. When Dreamweaver connects to a remote site, it uses these files to know which Web files are in use by others.

  But only Dreamweaver understands these .lck files. Other FTP programs, like WSFTP (Windows) or Fetch (Mac), gladly ignore them and can easily overwrite any checked-out files. This risk also applies when you simply copy files back and forth over the office network.

Note: Adobe's word processor–like Web page editing program, Contribute, also takes advantage of this Check In/Check Out feature, so you can use the two programs on the same site.

- All Dreamweaver-using team members must configure their remote site to use Check In and Check Out. If just one person doesn't do it, you risk overwritten files.

Note: Visual SourceSafe and WebDAV people are free of these last two constraints. As long as everyone working on the site uses programs that support the Visual SourceSafe client or the WebDAV protocol, they can work seamlessly with Dreamweaver people, and vice versa.

Checking Out Files

When you want to work on a file in a collaborative site, you check it out from the Web server. Doing so makes sure that *you* have the latest version of the file, and that nobody else can make changes to the file.

Warning: Dreamweaver's Check In/Check Out feature only works if everyone on the team is using it. They must all have Dreamweaver and have turned on this feature as described on page 672. If one person doesn't use this system, you could run into problems.

If you're used to creating sites by yourself, this business may feel a little strange; after all, your local site (the files on your computer) contains the latest versions of all files. When working with a group, however, you should consider the *remote* site—where everyone can access, edit, and add new Web pages—to be the master copy of your site's files.

Note: There's nothing to check out when you're creating a new page for the site. Since the only version of the file in the universe is on your computer, there's no fear that someone else may work on it at the same time as you. In this case, you only need to check the file *into* the site when you're done.

You check out a file using the Files panel; if it's not open, press F8 (Shift-⌘-F) or use choose Window → Files. Then choose the site you wish to work on from the Site pop-up menu (shown at top in Figure 17-11).

Now you're ready to begin. From the Local Folder file list in the Files panel, click to select the files you wish to check out from the Web server—or, to check out an entire folder and every file inside it, just select the folder.

You may in some instances want to select a file from the Remote Site list as well. For example, maybe you need to modify a page that you didn't create, and which you've never before checked out. In this case, the file isn't *in* your local folder, so you must select it from the Remote Site list. Select Remote view from the Files panel (see Figure 17-7); Dreamweaver connects to the server and then displays the remote files in the Files panel. Select the ones you wish to check out.

Tip: If, when you define the remote site (see page 668), you select the "Check Out File when Opening" option, you can also check out (and open) a file by double-clicking it in the Files panel. This is a quick way to open a page for editing while still using Dreamweaver's Check Out feature.

POWER USERS' GEM IN THE ROUGH

Subversion in Dreamweaver

Dreamweaver CS4 adds support for a popular version control system called *Subversion*. Well, at least it's popular among programmers and open-source aficionados. Subversion is a free, open-source program which is usually used to manage files as part of a large programming project. It has powerful features to make sure that multiple users don't overwrite each others' changes and to make it easy to "roll-back" to previous versions of a file if something goes wrong.

To use this new feature, first you need to set up a *Subversion server*—a separate piece of software either running on your own computer, on a server on your network, or even on a server somewhere on the internet. You can download the software at *http://subversion.tigris.org/getting.html*, and there are even companies that offer free or cheap Subversion hosting (in other words, they can take care of the mess of setting up Subversion for you). Next, you need to create what's called a Subversion *repository*—a way of identifying a set of files that belong to a particular project. For example, each Web project would probably be its own repository. You can learn more about how to set up Subversion at *http://svnbook.red-bean.com/*.

For Dreamweaver users, it's important to keep in mind that a Subversion repository is independent of the Web site running on the Web server. In other words, you'll have a Subversion repository, local files on your computer, and another set of files out on the Web (that is, your live Web site).

You can set up Subversion support for a site in Dreamweaver, by choosing Site → Manage Sites, and choosing a site to edit. In the Site Definition window, select the Version Control category and choose Subversion from the Access menu. Then fill out the other settings such as the server address, repository path, your username, and password.

Once this is set up, you'll connect to the repository when you choose Repository View from the File View menu (see Figure 15-6). In addition, when you use the Check Out and Check In buttons on the Files panel, you'll be checking out and checking in files from the Subversion repository. Unfortunately, Dreamweaver doesn't support all of Subversions features and doing basic file management tasks on your local files, such as moving and renaming them, don't have any effect on the files in the repository. Bummer. In addition, if you want to perform site-wide changes like updating Templates, or changing the footer information on all pages of your site, you need to check out the *entire* Web site from the repository.

If you're a lone wolf, developing Web sites on your own, then Subversion is definitely overkill. Even if you work in a small workgroup, unless you have someone with the system administrator know-how to set up a Subversion server and repository, you're probably better off with something simpler like Dreamweaver's Check-in/Check-out system or even WebDav. Probably the most important feature of Subversion is the ability to go back to a previous version of a file that has somehow been wrecked.

If you're not going to use Subversion, it's definitely worth investing in some basic backup software like Retrospect Remote or Apple's Time Machine. Even most simple backup software lets you keep hourly, daily, weekly, or monthly backups of files, and lets you go back in time to retrieve older versions of files. Or, for the low-tech approach, just make a backup of your site every day and store the copied files in a folder named something like *June_10_2009*. That way you'll have a daily backup that you can turn to if you need to recover a lost file.

However, if your company or organization does use Subversion you can get in-depth information on using Dreamweaver with Subversion at *http://help.adobe.com/en_US/Dreamweaver/10.0_Using/WS80FE60AC-15F8-45a2-842E-52D29F540FED.html*.

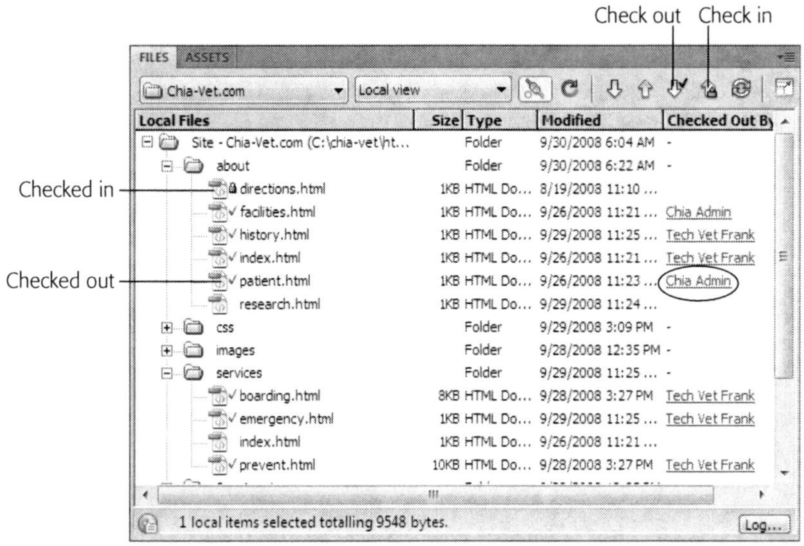

Figure 17-11: *The Check In/Out buttons transfer files between the local site and the Web server. A padlock identifies files that are checked into the remote site. Confusingly, the lock means that the file is open for anyone to check out and edit. If a file is currently checked out, a checkmark appears next to its name. A green checkmark indicates you've checked out the file; a red checkmark means someone else has checked it out.*

In any case, now just click the Check Out files button on the Files panel (see Figure 17-11), or use the keyboard shortcut Ctrl+Alt+Shift+D (⌘-Option-Shift-D). (Not enough fingers? See page 799 to learn how to change Dreamweaver's shortcuts.)

Dreamweaver asks if you wish to also get any dependent files. Click Yes if you think the page you're checking out uses files you haven't yet downloaded. Dreameaver then copies the dependent files to your computer, so the page you've checked out and are working on displays the current images, CSS style sheets, and other linked files correctly. It doesn't *check out* those files, so if you do want to edit a dependent file—for example, you need to also edit styles on a linked external style sheet that's used by the page you checked out—you must also check out that file.

Note: When you edit a Web page that you've checked out, you may run into a weird problem if you edit the CSS for that page. If you're using an external style sheet, and make any changes to it, when you try to save the style sheet, Dreamweaver opens a very confusing "Save As" dialog box. Essentially Dreamweaver is saying, "Hey, you haven't checked that file out, so you can't make changes to it. Please save it as a new file." Of course, it would be a lot better if Dreamweaver just said "You need to check that file out before making changes to it." But alas, Dreamweaver's communication skills aren't always the best. How to avoid this situation? Check out any external style sheets you need to edit in addition to the Web pages you need to work on.

When you check out files, Dreamweaver copies them to your computer and marks them as checked out so others can't change them. As when uploading and downloading files, checking out files can take time, depending upon the speed of your Internet connection.

After you've checked out a file, a green "checked-out" checkmark appears next to its name in the Files panel (see Figure 17-11). You can now open and edit it, and (when you're done) check the file back in.

WORKAROUND WORKSHOP

Manual Checkout Override

Occasionally, you may wish to erase the checked-out status of a file. Suppose, for example, someone who's checked out a lot of files suddenly catches the plague and can't continue working on the site. To free those files so others can work on them, you should undo his checkout (and quarantine his cubicle).

To do this, make sure the Files panel is in Remote view (this trick won't work when looking at the Local Files). Then, right-click (Control-click) the checked-out file in the Files panel and select Undo Checkout from the menu that appears.

Dreamweaver warns you that whoever checked out the file won't be able to check it back in. (This is, in fact, false. That person can still check in the file, overwriting whatever's on the Web server. So you can see why you should override the check-out only when the person who checked it out is very unlikely to check it back in—stranded on a deserted island, perhaps.)

When complete, a padlock icon appears next to the file.

You can also use this technique on a file you've checked out. For example, if, after checking out a file, you've made a horrible mistake on the page and wish to revert to the copy on the Web server.

If you attempt to check out a file someone else has already checked out, Dreamweaver tells you as much. It also gives you the option to override the person's checkout—but unless you're the boss, resist the temptation, for two reasons. First, your colleagues may have made some important changes to the page, which you'll wipe out with your shenanigans. Second, because you so rudely stole the file, they may stop bringing you donuts in the morning.

A better way to work with someone who's checked out a file you need is to use Dreamweaver's email feature. You can see who checked out a file by consulting the Checked Out By column (see the circled entry in Figure 17-11). Even better, if you click the name, Dreamweaver opens your email program and addresses an email to that person, so you can say: "Hey Bob, you've had the home page checked out for two days! I need to work on it, so check it back in!"

The name and email address Dreamweaver uses depends on the information your co-workers provided, just as you did when you configured your computer for remote site use (see step 12 page 672).

Checking In Files

When you're ready to move a page you've edited back onto the server, you check it in. (You also check in *new* files you've created.)

To check in files, open the Files panel (press F8 [Shift-⌘-F]), choose the site you're checking into from the Site pop-up menu, and (using the Local Folder file list in the Files panel) select the files you wish to check in to the Web server. As always, you can click a folder to check it in, along with every file inside it.

FREQUENTLY ASKED QUESTION

Get and Put, In and Out

I'm using Dreamweaver's Check In and Check Out buttons to transfer my files. What do the Get and Put buttons do when the Check In/Out feature is in use?

If you're using Check In and Out, the Get and Put commands function slightly differently than described on page 678. *Get* copies the selected file or files to your local site. However, Dreamweaver draws a small lock icon next to each of these "gotten" files in your Local Folder list. The files are locked, and you shouldn't edit them. Remember, checking out a file is the only way to prevent others from working on it. If you edit a locked file on your computer, nothing is stopping someone else from checking the page out from the Remote site, editing it, and checking it back in.

But using the Get command in such a situation can still be useful. For example, suppose someone just updated the site's external style sheet. Pages you're editing use this style sheet, so you'd like to get the latest version. You don't want to edit the style sheet itself, so you don't need to check it out. If you use Get instead of checking out the pages, you can keep a reference copy on your computer without locking it for anyone else and without having to check it back in later.

Put, on the other hand, simply transfers the file on your local site to the remote site. If you're using the Check In/Check Out feature and you haven't also checked out the file, using Put is a bad idea. The remote site should be your reference copy; several rounds of revisions may have been made to a file since you last checked it out. Your local copy will be hopelessly out of date, and moving it to the server using Put destroys the most recent version of the file.

However, if you do have the file checked out, you can use Put to transfer your local copy to the server so it can be viewed by your site's visitors. For example, say you're updating the home page with 20 new news items. To keep your site "up-to-the-minute" fresh, you can Put the home page after you add each news item. Then the whole world will see each news item as soon as possible. When you're completely finished editing the home page, check it in.

The files you select should be files you've checked out, or brand-new files that have never been on the Web server. If you attempt to check in a file that someone else has checked out, Dreamweaver warns you with a message box. Click Cancel to stop the check-in procedure, so that you won't overwrite the checked-out file on the server. Dreamweaver also warns you if you try to check in a file that's older than the server copy. Again, unless you're sure this is what you want to do, click Cancel.

Tip: If you want to check in the page you're currently working on into the remote site, use the toolbar in the document window (see Figure 17-9).

You can check in the selected files in any of the usual ways:

- Click the Check In files button on the Files panel (see Figure 17-11).
- Use the keyboard shortcut Ctrl+Alt+Shift+U (⌘-Option-Shift-U). (See page 799 to learn how to change the Dreamweaver shortcut to something less cumbersome.)

Note: The Site → Check In menu option checks in only the document you're currently working on, not any files you've selected in the Files panel.

Dreamweaver asks if you wish to also check in any dependent files (see Figure 17-8). You should transfer dependent files only if you first checked them out, or if the dependent files are new and have never been uploaded to the server. If you attempt to check in a dependent file that someone else has checked out, Dreamweaver warns you with a message box—click the No button in this box, so that you don't overwrite someone's checked out file.

After you've clicked through all message boxes, Dreamweaver copies the files to the remote site. Once you've checked in a file, a padlock icon appears next to its name in the Files panel (see Figure 17-11); checking in locks the file so that you don't accidentally change the local copy. If you wish to modify the file in some way, check it out again.

Note: Dreamweaver's Site Report feature (page 657) lets you run a report to see which files are checked out and by whom. Skip it. On a large site, the report can take a long time to run, it isn't always accurate, and the operations you're most likely to perform on checked out files (like checking them back in) can't be accomplished from the Reports panel.

Synchronizing Site Files

As you may suspect, when you keep two sets of files—local folder and remote site—it's easy to lose track of which files are the most recent. For example, say you finish your Web site and move all the files to the Web server. The next day, you notice mistakes on a bunch of Web pages, so you make corrections on the copies in your local site. But in your rush to fix the pages, you didn't keep track of which ones you corrected. So although you're ready to move the corrected pages to the Web server, you're not sure *which* ones you need to transfer.

When you use the Check In/Check Out feature described on page 686, you avoid this problem altogether. Using that system, the version on the Web server is *always* considered the latest and most definitive copy—*unless* you or someone else has checked out that file. In that case, whoever checked out the file has the most recent version.

But if you're operating solo, for example, and don't use the Check In/Check Out feature, you may get good mileage from the Synchronize command, which lets you compare the remote and local sites and transfer only the newer files in either direction. (In fact, since the Synchronize command uses the Get and Put methods of transferring files, you may not get the results you expect if you synchronize your site while also using Check In and Check Out [as described in the box on the opposite page].)

To synchronize your sites:

1. **Make sure the "Maintain synchronization information" checkbox is turned on in the Remote Info category of the Site Definition window (you'll make this choice when you're setting up a new site, as described in step 11 on page 672).**

   This option is turned on automatically when you set up the Remote information for a site (see Figure 17-1).

2. **Choose Site → Synchronize Sitewide.**

   Alternatively, you can right-click anywhere inside the Files panel. From the shortcut menu that appears, select Synchronize. In either case, the Synchronize Files dialog box appears (see Figure 17-12).

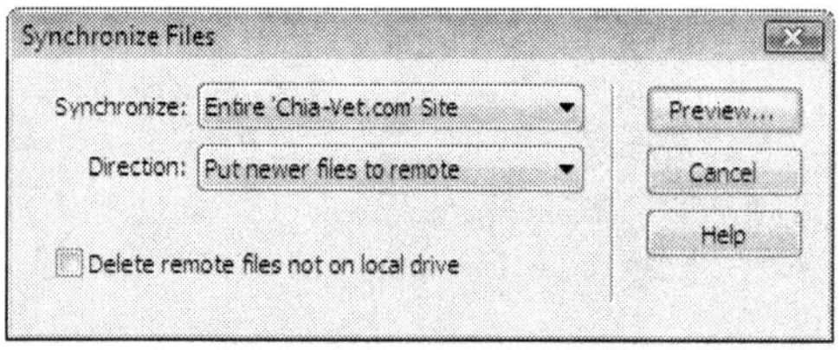

Figure 17-12: *Using the Synchronization command, you can copy newer files from your computer to the Web server, or get newer files from the remote site. (The Synchronization command isn't available if you're using Visual SourceSafe.)*

3. **Using the Synchronize pop-up menu, specify the files to update.**

   You can either synchronize all files in the current Web site, or just files you've selected in the Local Folder list. This last option is good when you have a really big site and want to limit this operation to just a single section of the site—one folder, for example.

4. **Using the Direction pop-up menu, choose where you'd like to copy newer files.**

   You have three choices. *Put newer files to remote* updates the Web server with any newer files from your local site folder. It also copies any *new* files on the local site to the remote site. Use this option when you've done heavy editing to the local site and want to move all new or modified pages to the Web server.

   Get newer files from remote does just the reverse: it updates your local site folder with any newer (or new) files from the remote site. Here's one instance where the synchronize feature comes in handy in team-design situations. If you've been out of the office for a while, click this option to download copies of the latest site files. (Note that this doesn't check any files out; it merely makes sure you have the latest files for your own reference. This is one example where synchronization works well with Check In/Check Out, since it refreshes your local copy of the site with the latest files, including graphics and external CSS style sheets that your checked-out pages may depend on.)

   Get and put newer files is a two-way synchronization. Any new files on the local site are transferred to the remote site and vice versa. For example, if you updated a page on your own computer, that file will move to the Web server; if someone has made changes to a file on the Web server more recently than the copy on your computer, that file will be downloaded to your hard drive. The result is that both "sides" contain the latest files.

5. **Turn on the Delete checkbox, if desired.**

   The wording of this option reflects the option you selected in the previous step. If you're moving newer files to the remote site, it says "Delete remote files not on local drive". It's a useful option when, for example, you've spent the afternoon cleaning up the local copy of your site, deleting old, orphaned graphics files and Web pages, for example, and you want Dreamweaver to update the Web server to match.

If you chose to transfer newer files *from* the remote site, Dreamweaver lets you "Delete local files not on remote server". Use this feature when your local site is hopelessly out of date with the remote site. Perhaps you're working on the site with a team, but you've been on vacation for two months (this is, of course, a hypothetical example). The site may have changed so significantly that you want to get your local copy in line with the Web site.

Warning: Of course, you should proceed with caution when using *any* command that automatically deletes files. There's no Undo for these delete operations, and you don't want to accidentally delete the only copy of a particular page, graphic, or external Cascading Style Sheet.

If you chose the "Get and put newer files" option in step 4, the Delete checkbox is dimmed and unavailable. This option truly synchronizes the two; Dreamweaver copies newer files on the remote site (including files that exist on the Web server but not on your computer) to your local site, and vice versa.

6. **Click Preview to begin the synchronization process.**

   Dreamweaver connects to the remote site and compares the two sets of files—if your site is large, this comparison is a time-consuming process. When it finishes, the Synchronize preview window appears (Figure 17-13), listing which files Dreamweaver will delete and which it will transfer, and providing an additional set of options for working with the listed files.

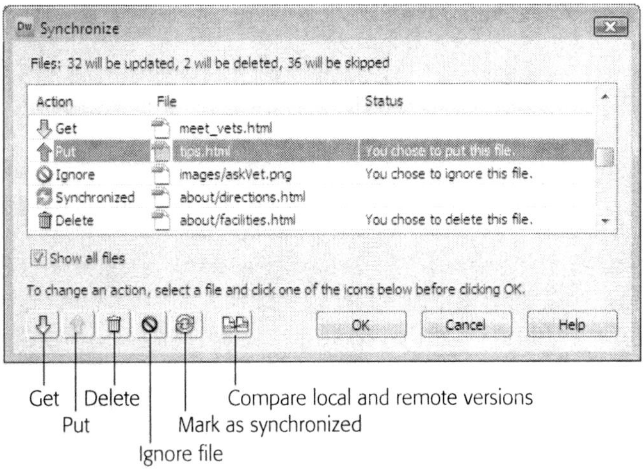

Figure 17-13:
The Synchronize window lets you preview any actions Dreamweaver intends to take to synchronize the files on your local and remote sites. You can change this action on a file-by-file basis. Turning on the "Show all files" checkbox lists all files, including ones Dreamweaver believes are identical on both the remote and local copies of the site: these files are marked Synchronized in the Action column.

7. **Change the action Dreamweaver takes on the listed files.**

   The preview box tells you what Dreamweaver plans to do with a file—get it, put it, or delete it. You can override these actions by selecting a file from the list and clicking one of the action buttons at the bottom of the window. For example, if you realize that Dreamweaver is going to delete a file that you *know* you need, select the file in the list and click the "Ignore file" button (the red circle with a line through it).

Most of these options are useful only if you know Dreamweaver made a mistake: for example, when the program says you should get a file, but you know your local copy is identical to the server's copy. In that case, you could select the file and click the "Mark as synchronized" button, to tell Dreamweaver that they're identical. However, if you knew exactly which files were identical and which ones needed updating, you wouldn't need to use the synchronize feature in the first place, right?

One option can come in quite handy. The "Compare local and remote versions" button lets you compare the code in the local file to the code in the remote file so you can identify exactly what differs between the two. You can use this, for example, to see exactly what changes someone else may have made to the remote copy of the file. This feature is described in detail on page 416.

8. **Click OK to proceed, or Cancel to stop the synchronization.**

   If you click OK, Dreamweaver commences copying and deleting the chosen files. If you want to stop this process after clicking OK, click the Cancel button in the Background File Activity window (see the box on page 681).

9. **Click Close.**

Tip: If you just want to *identify* newer files on the local site without synchronizing them (to run a report on them, for example), click the contextual menu in the top-right corner of the Files panel and choose Edit → Select Newer Local. Dreamweaver connects to the remote site and compares the files, and then, in the Files panel's Local Folder list, highlights files on the Local site that are newer than their remote counterparts.

You can also identify newer files on the remote site: Choose Edit → Select Newer Remote from the Files panel's contextual menu. As with the Synchronization command, these options are unavailable if you're using Visual SourceSafe.

You can also identify files on your computer that you've either created or modified within a given date range, using the new Select Recently Modified command described on page 646.

Communicating with Design Notes

Lots of questions arise when a team works on a Web site: Has this page been proofread? Who is the author of the page? Where did this graphic come from? Usually, you must rely on a flurry of emails to ferret out the answers.

But Dreamweaver's Design Notes dialog box (Figure 17-14) eliminates much of that hassle by letting you attach information, such as a Web page's status or author, to a file.

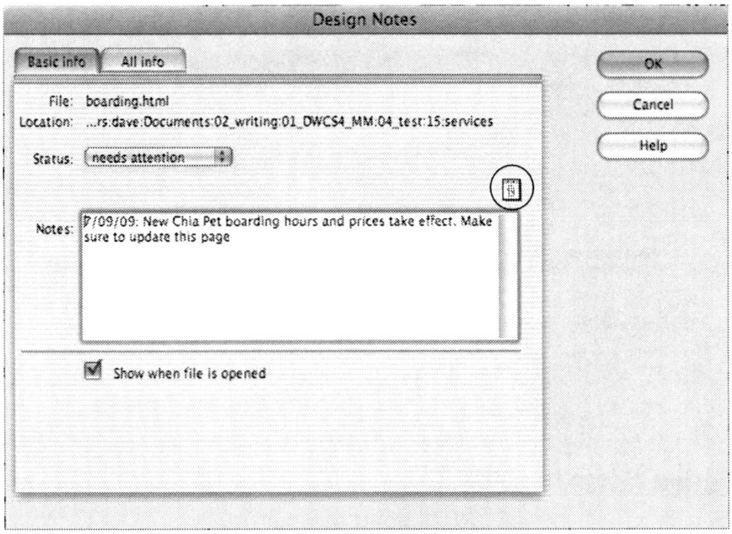

Figure 17-14:
If you want the Design Notes window to open whenever someone opens the page, turn on the "Show when file is opened" checkbox. This option makes sure no one misses an important note attached to a Web page. When the page is opened in Dreamweaver, the Design Notes window appears automatically. (This option has no effect when adding notes to GIFs, JPEGs, Flash movies, or anything other than a file that Dreamweaver can open and edit, such as a Web page or an external CSS style sheet.)

You can open these notes (from the Files panel or from a currently open document), edit them, and even share them with others. In this way, it's easy to leave notes for other people—such as, "Hey Bob, can you make sure that this is the most recent photo of Brad and Angelina?" You can even add notes to files other than Web pages, including folders, images, Flash movies, and external Cascading Style Sheets—anything, in fact, that appears in the Files panel.

Setting Up Design Notes

You can't use Design Notes unless the feature itself is turned on. To find out if it is, open the Site Definition dialog box by double-clicking the site's name in the Manage Sites dialog box (choose Manage Sites from the Site menu or the pop-up menu in the Files panel). In the Category list, click Design Notes; as shown in Figure 17-15, two checkboxes pertain to the notes feature:

- **Maintain Design Notes.** This checkbox lets you create and read notes using Dreamweaver's File → Design Notes command (see page 699).
- **Upload Design Notes for sharing.** If you're using Design Notes as part of a team, turn on this checkbox, which makes Dreamweaver upload design notes to the remote site, so that your fellow team members can read them.

Note: Design Notes are especially useful for keeping track of pages that are built and maintained by a team of developers. But if you're a solo operator and still want to use them—maybe you're the type with a hundred Post-it notes taped to the edges of your monitor—then turn off "Upload Design Notes for sharing." You'll save time and server space by preventing Dreamweaver from transferring note files to the Web server.

Click OK to close the Site Definition dialog box. You can double-click another site in the Manage Sites dialog box to turn on its Design Notes feature, or click Done.

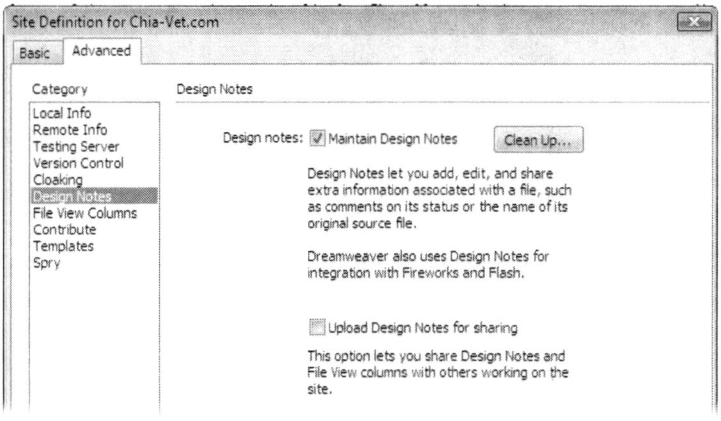

Figure 17-15:
The Clean Up button deletes any notes that were attached to now-deleted files. (To avoid stray notes files in the first place, always delete pages in Dreamweaver's Files panel, as opposed to Windows Explorer or the Mac's Finder.) If you turn off the Maintain Design Notes checkbox, clicking Clean Up removes all Design Notes files for the site.

Adding Design Notes to a File

To add a Design Note to a document you're working on, choose your favorite method:

- Choose File → Design Notes.
- From the File Status menu in the document toolbar, choose Design Notes (see Figure 17-9).
- Right-click (Control-click) a file in the Files panel (or an external object, such as a graphic or Flash movie, in the document window), and choose Design Notes from the shortcut menu.

In any case, the Design Notes window now opens (Figure 17-14). If you like, you can use the Status pop-up menu to let your team members know where the file stands. For example, is it ready to move to the Web server? Is it just a draft version? Or is there something wrong with it that requires specific attention? Dreamweaver provides eight different options: "draft," "revision1," "revision2," "revision3," "alpha," "beta," "final," and "needs attention."

The note itself, which you type into the Note box, could be a simple question you have for the author of the page ("Are you sure 'Coldplay: Defining a New Musical Language for the Modern Age' is an appropriate title for this article?") or more information about the status of the page ("Still need studio shot for Chia Pet bad hair days article").

Tip: Click the calendar icon (circled in Figure 17-14) to pop the date into your note—a great way to keep a running tally of notes and the dates they were made.

When you click OK, Dreamweaver creates a file with all the note information in it. This file ends with the extension .mno and begins with the name of the file; for the file *index.html*, for example, the note would be called *index.html.mno*.

Dreamweaver stores notes in a folder called *_notes* that it keeps in the same folder as the page or file. For example, if you add notes to the home page, Dreamweaver stores the notes file in the *_notes* folder inside the root folder.

Viewing Design Notes

You can view Design Notes in a number of ways. If the note's author turned on "Show when file is opened" (see Figure 17-14), of course, the Design Notes window opens automatically when you open that page (subject to the limitations explained in Figure 17-14).

Otherwise, to look at a note, you have any number of options:

- Choose File → Design Notes.
- Choose Design Notes from the File Status drop-down menu in the document window's toolbar (see Figure 17-9).
- Double-click the small yellow balloon icon in the Notes column of the Files panel (see Figure 17-16). (This column is visible only if you've turned on this option in the Site Definition window, as described below.)
- Right-click (Control-click) an embedded object, like a graphic or Flash movie, right in the document window, and choose Design Notes from the shortcut menu.
- Right-click (Control-click) a file in the Files panel and choose Design Notes from the shortcut menu.

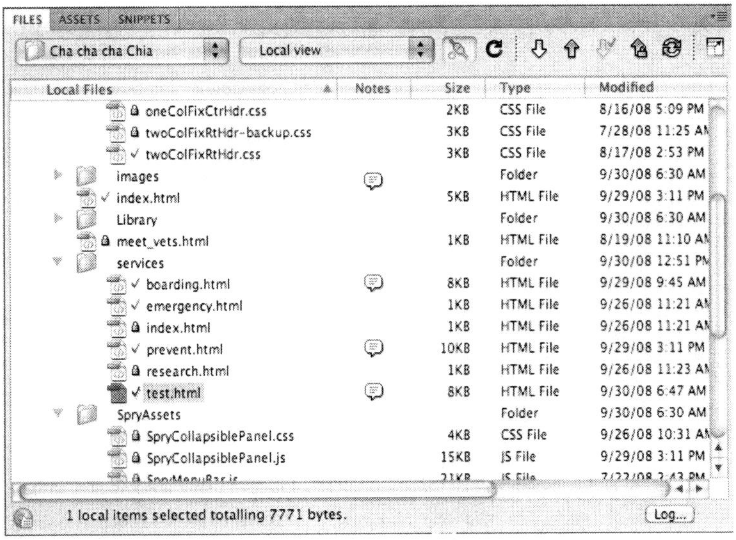

***Figure 17-16:** A yellow speech bubble in the Notes column of the Files panel indicates a Design Notes file. You can even add a note to a folder (in this case, the images folder). The Notes column is normally hidden; you can make it appear by heading to the File View Columns category of the Site Definition window as described below.*

Organizing the Columns in the Files Panel

Columns in the Files panel identify a file's name, file size, modification date, type, and so on.

This may be more information than you're interested in—or it may not be enough. So remember that Dreamweaver lets you show or hide these various columns, change their order, or even create new columns with information retrieved from a file's Design Notes.

Tip: You can adjust the relative widths of these columns by dragging the dividing line between the column names. You can also sort all the pages listed in this window by clicking the relevant column's name. Clicking Modified, for example, sorts the files so that the newest appear first. Click a second time to reverse the sort, placing oldest files first.

When you're setting up a Web site in the Site Definition window, you can view the column setup by clicking the File View Columns category (Figure 17-17).

Once you're looking at the display shown in Figure 17-17, you can perform any of these stunts:

- **Reorder columns.** Click a column name in the Site Definition window to select it. Then click the up and down arrow buttons to move the column one spot to the left or right, respectively, in the Files panel.
- **Hide columns.** You may not care what date a file was last modified or whether it's a folder or Web page. If that's the case, hide the column by clicking its name in the Site Definition window and then turning off the Show checkbox (see Figure 17-17). (You can always return to the Site Definition window and turn the column back on.)

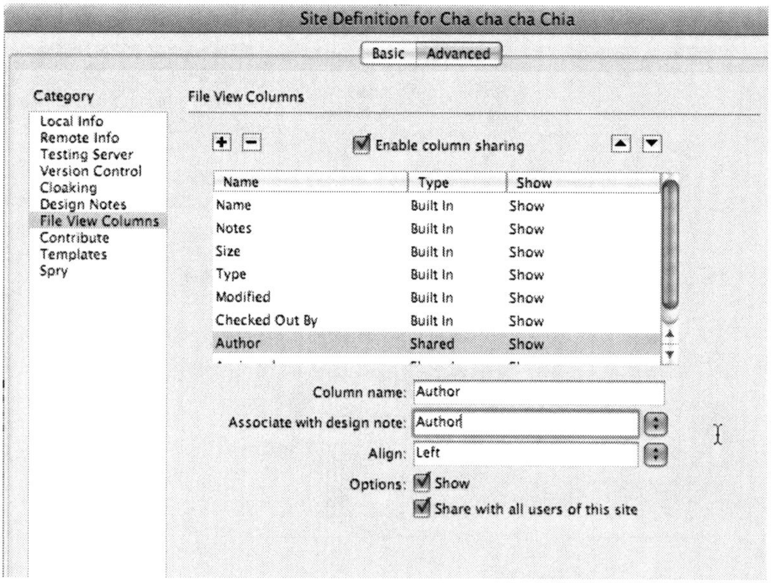

Figure 17-17: *If you're working with others, you might want to share columns you add. Turn on the "Enable column sharing" checkbox; then, you'll be able to see columns that others on your team have added, and they'll be able to see columns you've added (if you've turned on "Share with all users of this site" for each column, of course).*

- **Share a column.** If you work with a team of designers, you may want to make newly added columns visible to them, too. (See Figure 17-17 for details.)
- **Adding Columns.** You can add informational columns of your own, as described next.
- **Deleting columns.** Click the column name, and then click the minus (–) button to delete the column. (Dreamweaver doesn't let you delete the built-in columns: Name, Notes, Type, Modified, and so on.)

"All Info" Design Notes in Column Views

Your Files panel offers columns for all the usual information bits: Name, Checked Out, and so on. But you may someday wish there were a column that showed each page's status, so that your Files panel could show you which files need proofreading, or who wrote each article, or which pages are being held until a certain blackout date.

You can indeed add columns of your own design, although the process isn't streamlined by any means. It involves two broad efforts: First, using an offshoot of the Design Notes feature described earlier, you set up the new columns you want displayed. Then, using the column-manipulation dialog box shown in Figure 17-17, you make the new columns visible in the Files panel.

Phase 1: Defining the new information types

You create new kinds of informational flags—primarily for use as new columns in the Files panel—using the Design Notes dialog box. Here's the rundown:

1. **Choose File → Design Notes.**

   The Design Notes window appears. (You can summon it in various other ways, too, as described on page 699.)

2. **Click the "All info" tab.**

   This peculiar window shows the programmery underbelly of the Dreamweaver Notes feature (see Figure 17-18). It turns out that it stores every kind of note as a name/value pair. If you used the main Notes screen (Figure 17-14) to choose Beta from the Status pop-up menu, for example, you'll see a notation here that says "status=beta". (*Status* is the name of the info nugget; *beta* is the value.) If you turned on the option called "Show when file is opened," you'll see "showOnOpen=true". And if you typed *Badly needs updating* as the note itself, you'll see "notes=Badly needs updating" on this screen.

   But those are just the built-in info types; you're free to create your own.

3. **Click the + button.**

   You may wonder why you'd do this; after all, you can type a lot of information in the Notes box under the Basic Info tab. The primary benefit of creating new types of notes is that you can display that information in the Files panel.

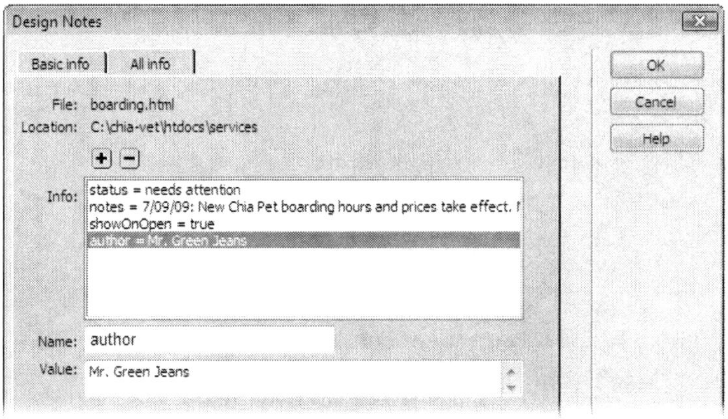

Figure 17-18: *Dreamweaver lets you create your own types of notes in the "All info" tab of the Design Notes window. This lets you add more information to a page, such as its author or designer. If you want to delete a note you've added, it's a simple matter of clicking on the note in the Info box and then clicking the minus (–) button.*

4. **Type the name of the new note in the Name field.**

   It may be *Author*, for example, so that you can note who wrote the text of each page. Or it could be *Artist*, if you wish to add a note to each image specifying who created it. Maybe you need a column called *Hold Until*, which lets you know when certain information is OK to publish online.

5. **Press Tab (to jump to the Value field); type the contents of the note.**

   You can enter the actual name of the author or artist—Jennifer Jones, for example—or the actual "Hold Until" date.

   Repeat steps 3–5 if you want to add more notes to the page or file.

Note: Keep the value short–one or two words. Otherwise, the narrow Files panel column chops off the latter part of it. If you've got enough screen real estate, you can resize the columns by dragging the divider bars between column names.

6. **Click OK.**

   The dialog box closes.

Phase 2: Adding the column

Just creating a new note type gets you only halfway home; now you have to tell Dreamweaver that you want to see that information in the Files panel.

To add a column:

1. **Open the Site Definition window for the particular site and select the File Views category.**

   See page 622 for a reminder of how to edit a site definition. The File Views dialog box appears.

2. **Click the + button (Figure 17-17).**

   A new, untitled column is added to the list, complete with three fields that need filling in (they now say "untitled").

3. **In the Column Name box, type the column-heading name you want to appear in the Files panel.**

   Make it short and descriptive. If possible, it should match the note type (*Author, Artist, Hold Until*, or whatever).

4. **Press Tab. Type the name of the Design Note you wish to use for this column.**

   This is the name part of the name/value pair described in step 4 of the previous instructions. For example, if you added a note named Author to a file, you would type *Author* here. Capitalization matters; so if you named the Design Note *Author*, type it with a capital A.

   There's a pop-up menu here, too, but it always lists the same four options: Status, Assigned, Due, and Priority. If you choose Status, you'll get a column that reflects your choice from the Status pop-up menu. The other three options do nothing *unless* you created a matching note type in step 4 of the previous instructions. (It would be nice if this pop-up menu listed *all* of the note names you've created, so that you didn't have to remember them.)

   Before you wrap up the column-adding procedure, you can, if you wish, choose an alignment option for the text in the column (left, right, or center). Check to make sure that the Show checkbox is turned on (otherwise, your new column won't appear, and you've just defeated the purpose of this whole exercise). Finally, turn on "Share with all users of this site," if you like.

   The Share feature works like this: The next time you connect to the remote site, Dreamweaver uploads a file containing your newly defined column information. The next time another member of the team connects to the remote site, *his* copy of Dreamweaver downloads this file, so that his Files panel shows the same columns yours does.

Note: The column-sharing feature can be very handy; it lets everyone working on a site share the same note information. But it works properly only if everyone on the team has the "Enable column sharing" checkbox turned on (see Figure 17-17).

5. **Click OK.**

   You should now see the new information column in your Files panel. (You may need to widen the panel to see all of the columns. You can also click the Expand Files Panel button [Figure 17-1] to expand the Panel.)

Part Five: Dreamweaver CS4 Power

CHAPTER
18

Snippets and Libraries

You've finished the design for your company's new Web site. It looks great and your boss is ecstatic. But you've really only just begun. You have to build hundreds of pages before you launch. And once the site's online, you'll need to make endless updates to keep it fresh and inviting.

This is where Dreamweaver's Snippets and Library features come in, streamlining the sometimes tedious work of building and updating Web pages.

As you build more and more Web pages (and more and more Web sites), you may find yourself creating the same Web page elements over and over again. Many pages of a site may share certain common elements that always stay the same: a copyright notice, a navigation bar, or a logo, for example. And you may find yourself frequently using more complex items, such as a pull-down menu listing all the countries your company ships products to, or a particular design you use for photos and their captions.

Recreating the same page elements time after time is tiresome and—thanks to Dreamweaver—unnecessary. Dreamweaver provides two subtly different tools for reusing common page elements: *Snippets* and *Library items*.

Snippets Basics

Snippets aren't fancy or complex, but they sure save time. A snippet is simply a chunk of code that you store away, and then plunk into other Web pages. It could be HTML, CSS, JavaScript, or any of the other programming languages you may encounter. Dreamweaver comes with hundreds of snippets organized into different folders, like Footers (canned footer designs), Form Elements (useful form parts like pull-down menus), and JavaScript code (programming code for interesting effects like adding a random image to a page).

For example, say you always use the same table design to list the specifications for a product in your company's catalog. Each time you want to create a similar table, you could go through all the same steps to build it—or you could turn that table into a snippet, and then, with a simple double-click, add it to page after page of your site.

You keep these code chunks in the Files panel's Snippets tab (see Figure 18-1), and you summon them in any of several ways:

- Choose Window → Snippets.
- Windows people can press Shift-F9. (There's no Mac keyboard shortcut for opening the Snippets tab, but you can create your own if you want, as described on page 799.)

Once opened, the Snippets panel appears grouped with the Files and Assets panels. Above and beyond Dreamweaver's preinstalled snippets, you can quickly build a collection of your own.

Using Snippets

Snippets come in two varieties: those that are a simple block of code, and those that wrap around whatever you've currently selected in the document. For example, in the Snippets tab's Text folder, you'll find a snippet called Service Mark. Adding this snippet to a page instantly inserts the code *^{sm}*, creating a superscript service mark (SM) symbol.

But on occasion you may want to wrap code around something you've already typed. You may, for example, want to add an HTML comment to your page (a message that won't appear in a Web browser, but that you can use for helpful notes to yourself or other Web designers). The "Comment, multi-line" snippet (in the Comments folder) can help you quickly add such comments. It wraps whatever you've selected with opening (<!--) and closing HTML comments (-->). Adding an HTML comment is as easy as typing the comment, selecting it, and then inserting this snippet. (This may sound a lot like the Apply Comment button in the Coding toolbar described on page 401. The cool thing about this snippet is that it works in Design view, too, not just Code view.)

Note: Unfortunately, unless the snippet's description (visible in the Snippet Panel's *Description* column) specifies that the snippet wraps, you can't tell whether a snippet is intended to wrap around a selection. You either have to try the snippet or open the snippet in Editing mode to find out. (While you've got the snippet open, you can add a note to its description indicating its ability, or inability, to wrap.)

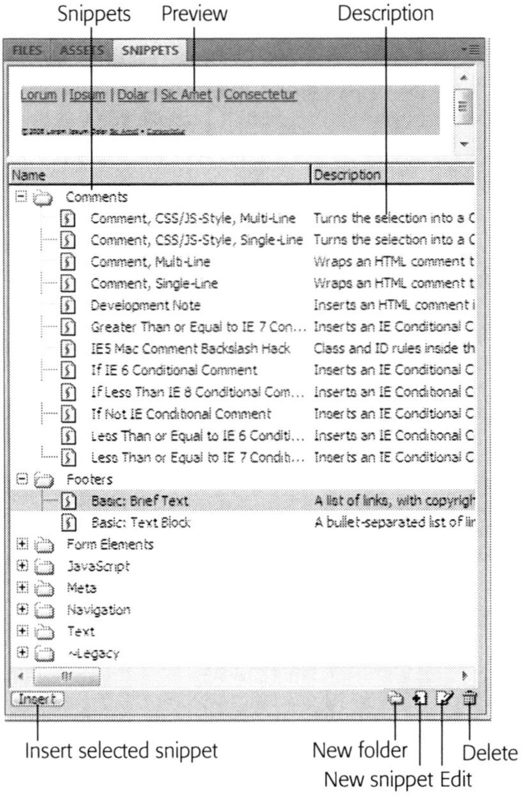

Figure 18-1:
The Files panel's Snippets tab contains reusable chunks of code–snippets–which you can organize into folders. After selecting a snippet from the list, a preview appears in the Preview pane. In this example, you can see a preview of the snippet: a simple footer with a colored background, and dummy text and links. Snippets can have either a graphic preview (as in this example), called Design preview, or a Code preview, which shows the raw code. Code previews are useful for snippets such as JavaScript code that you can't see in Design view. (When you create your own snippets, you specify the preview type.)

To add a snippet to a Web page, click in the document where you want the item to go, or select the object you wish to wrap with a snippet. Then do one of the following:

- On the Files panel's Snippet's tab, double-click the name of the snippet.
- On the Snippets tab, select the snippet, and then click the panel's Insert button.
- Drag the snippet from the panel into the document window. (If the snippet is supposed to wrap a selection, then drag the snippet *onto* the selected object.)

You can use snippets in either Design or Code view, but some snippets make sense only in Code view. For example, the JavaScript snippets that come with Dreamweaver typically have to be inserted in the <head> of a page, inside <script> tags. To use them, you must switch to Code view, insert the script tags, and then put the snippets inside.

Tip: To quickly insert a snippet you've recently used, from the Insert → Recent Snippets menu, select the snippet. Better yet, create a keyboard shortcut for your favorite snippets, and then insert them with a quick keystroke as described on page 799.

Snippets simply dump their contents into a document—essentially copying the snippet code and pasting it into your Web page; Dreamweaver doesn't step in to make sure that you're adding the code correctly. Unless you're careful—and have some knowledge of HTML—you may end up adding snippets that make your Web page impossible to view. (For advice on how to avoid such pitfalls, see the box on page 713.)

Creating Snippets

Dreamweaver comes with a lot of snippets, and you may have no use for many of them. No problem—you can easily create snippets of your own. Here's how:

1. **Create and select the content you wish to turn into a snippet.**

   You could, for instance, select a table in Design view, or select the opening and closing <table> tags (as well as all the code between them) in Code view. Or, if you want to save a pull-down form menu (see page 446) that took you half an hour to build, then, in Design view, just click the form menu.

   If you want to make a snippet out of code that isn't visible in Design view, such as a JavaScript program or content that appears in the <head> of the page, you need to switch into Code view first, and then select the code.

2. **On the Snippets tab, click the New Snippet button (Figure 18-1).**

   The Snippet window appears (Figure 18-2), displaying the code you selected in the Insert field.

Tip: If you skip step 1 and just click the New Snippet button, you can either type the code or, in the Insert box, paste a previously copied selection (see step 6).

3. **Title the snippet.**

   The name you type in the Name field appears in the Snippets tab. Make sure to give it a name that clearly describes its contents.

4. **In the Description field, type identifying details.**

   This step is optional, but useful. Use this field to provide a description of when and how to use the snippet, and whether or not the snippet wraps a selection.

5. **Select a Snippet type.**

   "Wrap selection" makes the code wrap around a selection when you use the snippet in your Web pages. The "Insert block" option is for a snippet that's a single block of code inserted into the document—for example, a simple copyright notice or a form menu.

6. **If necessary, add the code for the snippet.**

   If you initially selected code in the document window, then it already appears in the "Insert before" field for a snippet that wraps around other code. For snippets that are just a single block of code, the code appears in the "Insert code" box.

   If you're creating a wrapping snippet, then some code goes in the "before" field and some in the "after" field. For example, say you want to create a snippet to let you set off a paragraph of text by adding a horizontal rule before the beginning of the paragraph and after the end of the paragraph. In both the "Insert before" and "Insert after" fields, you type *<hr>*—the HTML code for a horizontal rule. (If you're creating XHTML pages as described on page 10, you type *<hr />* in both fields.)

7. **Select a "Preview type".**

   The preview type determines how the snippet appears in the Snippets tab's Preview pane (see Figure 18-1). *Design* means the snippet looks as it would in Design view—a snippet of a table appears as a table, for instance. *Code* means the code itself appears in the Preview pane (in that case, a snippet for a horizontal rule would preview like this: <hr>). Use Code preview for snippets like JavaScript code that aren't visible in Design view.

8. **Click OK.**

   Dreamweaver adds the snippet to the Snippets tab; you can then drop it in your Web pages using any of the techniques described on page 709.

If you need to go back and edit a snippet—change the code, type, description, or name—in the Snippets tab, select the snippet, and then click Edit Snippet (Figure 18-1). You can also right-click (Control-click) the snippet name, and then, from the shortcut menu, select Edit.

Whichever method you chose, the Snippet window (Figure 18-2) appears. Make your changes, and then click OK.

Organizing Snippets

To keep snippets organized, you can create new folders to store them by category. To add a folder to the Snippets tab, click the New Folder button (see Figure 18-1). An untitled folder appears; type a name for it. If you select a folder before clicking New Folder, Dreamweaver creates the new folder *inside* that folder. You can move folders around by dragging them into other folders.

Note: To drag a folder or snippet to the top level of the Snippets list, you have to drag it all the way to the *bottom* of the tab, below any other folders. If you try to drag it to the top, then Dreamweaver puts the folder or snippet inside the list's top folder.

To move a snippet into or out of its folder, simply drag it. If you drag a snippet over a closed folder without releasing the mouse, that folder expands to reveal the folders inside, if any.

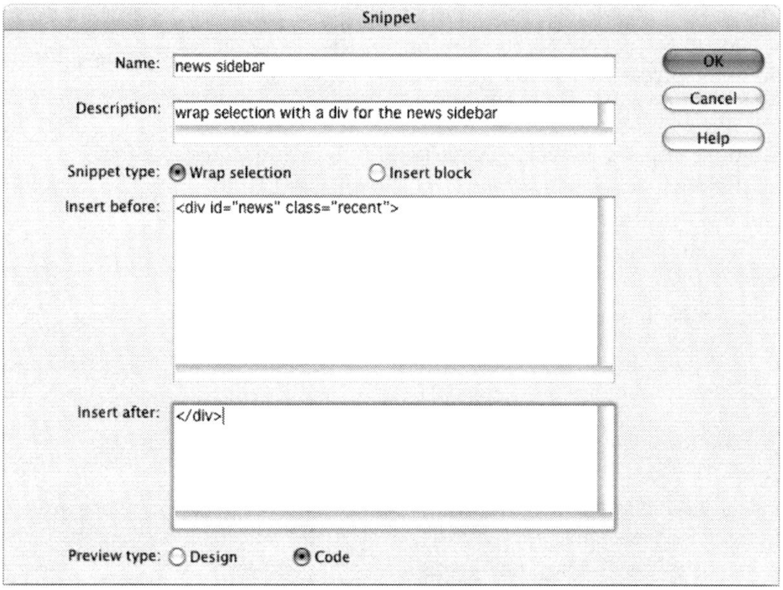

Figure 18-2: *The Snippet window lets you create reusable chunks of HTML called snippets. For snippets that wrap around a currently selected object on the page–for example, a snippet that adds a link to any selected text or graphic–you put code in the two insert boxes. The code that appears before the selected object goes in the top box, and the code that goes after the object appears in the bottom box. In this example, the snippet wraps the current selection in a <div> tag (see page 333) with a predefined ID and class applied to it.*

To delete a snippet, from the Snippets tab, select it, and then click the Delete Snippet (Trash can) button (see Figure 18-1). Quicker yet, press Delete.

Note: Having lots of snippets can slow down the Snippets panel. You'll probably never use many of the snippets that come with the program, so it's best to remove the ones you don't use. If you don't want to permanently delete these snippets, you can move them out of the main Adobe Dreamweaver CS4 → configuration → Snippets folder, and then store them in a separate folder on your hard drive. (For more on the configuration folder and how to find it, see the box on page 811.)

Built-In Snippets

Many of the snippets that come with Dreamweaver offer solutions to specific problems you may never encounter, like a page footer containing two lists of links and a copyright notice. In addition, many use older design techniques (like using tables to lay out content) that are best avoided. However, most Web developers find at least a few snippets worth using. Here are some highlights:

- **Close Window Button.** When you create a pop-up window (page 575), this snippet lets you add a Close button to let people dismiss the window. The "Close Window Button" snippet (in the Form Elements folder) places a form button with the words Close Window on the window page, complete with the JavaScript necessary to close the window when your visitor clicks the button.

- **Drop-down Menus.** If you create a lot of forms for your sites (see Chapter 11), then you'll find some useful snippets in the Form Elements folder, especially in the Dropdown Menus subfolder. For example, the "Numbers 1–12" snippet inserts a menu with the numbers 1–12 already coded into it—great for capturing credit card expiration dates on an e-commerce site. (To create an even more useful drop-down snippet, see the tutorial on page 719.)
- **IE Conditional Comments.** Sometimes Internet Explorer just doesn't get things right. This is frequently the case with CSS. To overcome browser differences, you sometimes need to provide IE with CSS code (or HTML or JavaScript) that differs from the code you send to other browsers. Dreamweaver's CSS layouts use this technique. As described in the box on page 353, you can insert special code (in the form of so-called conditional comments) that only IE understands. Dreamweaver provides a handful of code snippets (the last five snippets listed in the Snippets panel's Comments folder) that create the necessary code for adding IE-oriented conditional comments.

TROUBLESHOOTING MOMENT

A Snippet of Caution

Snippets aren't as smart as other Dreamweaver features. Dreamweaver is usually good about warning you before you make a mistake, but it doesn't make a peep if you're incorrectly adding a snippet.

For instance, when you use one of the program's form snippets to add, say, a text field to a page, Dreamweaver doesn't check to see if you're really putting the snippet into a form. Dreamweaver doesn't let you know if the required <form> tag is missing, and certainly doesn't add it itself. Furthermore, if you're working in Code view, then Dreamweaver lets you add snippets to the <head> (or even outside the <html> tags altogether), which is useful when creating dynamic Web pages that include server-side programming code, but just creates messy and invalid HTML on normal Web pages.

Furthermore, snippets don't take advantage of Dreamweaver's site management features to keep track of links or paths to images. Suppose you create a snippet that includes an image. If you insert that snippet into another page, the image may not show up correctly. If you create a snippet that includes a link from one page to another on your site, that link is also unlikely to work in another page.

So it's best to create snippets without images or links–but there are workarounds. For instance, you can create snippets with fake links–use nothing but the # symbol for the link, for example–and update the link after you insert the snippet into a page. For images, you can use Dreamweaver's Image Placeholder object to simulate a graphic in a snippet (choose Insert → Image Objects → Image Placeholder). After adding the snippet to the page, update the placeholder with your real image file.

If you want to create reusable content that can keep track of links and images, see Dreamweaver's Library feature, described below.

Library Basics

Imagine this situation: You manage a relatively large Web site consisting of thousands of Web pages. At the bottom of each page is a simple copyright notice: "Copyright MyBigCompany. We reserve all rights—national, international, commercial, noncommercial, and mineral—to the content contained on these pages."

Each time you add another page to the site, you *could* retype the copyright message, but this approach invites both typographic errors and carpal tunnel syndrome. And if you must *format* this text too, then you're in for even more work.

Fortunately, Dreamweaver's Library can turn any selection in the document window (a paragraph, an image, a table) into a reusable chunk of HTML that you can easily drop into any Dreamweaver document. The Library, in other words, is a great place to store copyright notices, navigation bars, or any other chunks of HTML you use frequently.

So far, this description sounds pretty much like the snippets described in the previous section. But Library items have added power: When you add HTML to a Web page using a Library item, that code remains linked to the original. Thanks to this link, whenever you update the original Library item, you get a chance to update every page that uses that item.

Suppose your company is bought, for example, and the legal department orders you to change the copyright notice to "Copyright MyBigCompany, a subsidiary of aMuchBiggerCompany" on each of the Web site's *10,000 pages*. If you had cleverly inserted the original copyright notice as a Library item, you could take care of this task in the blink of an eye. Just open the item in the Library, make the required changes, save it, and then let Dreamweaver update all the pages for you (see Figure 18-3).

Compared to Snippets, Library items are much smarter. They possess the unique ability to update the same material on an entire site's worth of files in seconds, and can successfully deal with links and images. Unlike Snippets, however, Dreamweaver's Library feature is site-specific. In other words, each site that you've defined in Dreamweaver has its own Library. You can't use a Library item from one site on a page from a different site.

Creating and Using Library Items

To create a Library item, start by opening the Library window. Click the Assets tab (to the right of the Files panel) or choose Window → Assets, and then click the Library Items button (it looks like an open book, circled in Figure 18-4) to reveal the Library category.

Now select the part of your document that you wish to save as a Library item: a blob of text, a graphic, or whatever.

Note, however, that Library items can contain only page elements that appear in the document window—in other words, only HTML from the <body> of a Web page. You can't include anything that appears in the <head> of a page, like Cascading Style Sheets, Spry widgets (Chapter 12), or meta tags. This means you can't have Dreamweaver behaviors or Spry widgets in your Library items either (but you can in a Dreamweaver Template, discussed in the next chapter). Furthermore,

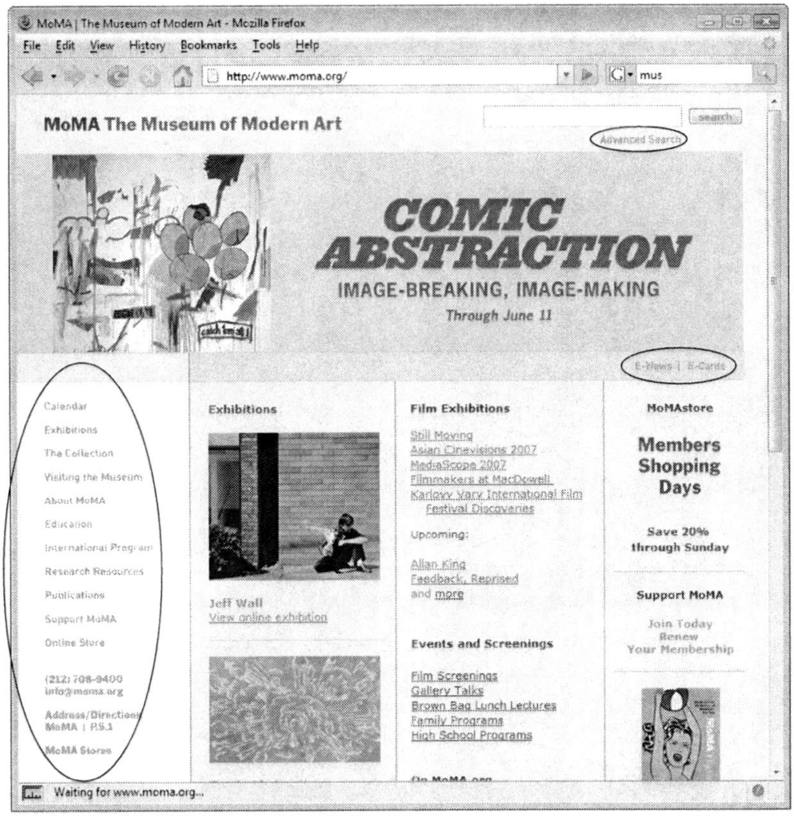

Figure 18-3: *The Museum of Modern Art's home page, which was created with Dreamweaver, takes advantage of Library elements. Many of the navigation options on the page (circled) are Library items. If the Museum decides to add or remove a navigation link, then it can update the Library item to change every page on the site in one simple step. In fact, since a Library item is a chunk of HTML, the Museum could decide to replace the left-hand navigation bar with a Flash movie, plain-text links (instead of graphics), or any other valid HTML code.*

Library items must include a complete set of HTML tags—both an opening and closing tag—as well as all tags necessary to complete the original object. For example, Dreamweaver doesn't let you turn just a single cell, row, or column of a table into a Library item. If you try, then Dreamweaver adds the *entire* table to the Library.

Tip: Use the Tag selector (see page 24) to make sure you select the precise tag information you want. To select *all* the contents of a cell, click at the beginning of the content, and drag until you've selected everything in the cell.

Next, add the selection to the Library. As you may expect, Dreamweaver provides several ways to do this:

- Drag the highlighted selection into the list of Library items.
- Click the New Item button (Figure 18-4).
- Choose Modify → Library → "Add Object to Library".

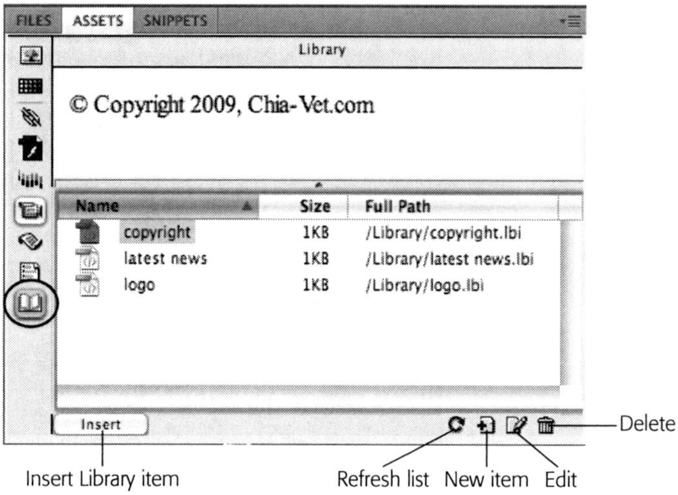

Figure 18-4: *The Assets panel's Library category lists the name, file size, and location of each Library item in the currently opened site. When you select a Library item from the list, you see a small preview. In this example, the Library item "copyright" is, shockingly, a copyright notice.*

The new item appears in the Assets panel, bearing the jaunty name "Untitled". Just type to replace that with a more useful name, such as *Copyright notice* or *Logo*.

(Avoid hyphens in your Library item's name. Hyphens tend to trip up the Firefox Web browser, as described in the box on page 720.) Your new Library element is now ready to use.

Note: Even though you can't turn a CSS style into a Library item, you *can* turn HTML that has been styled with CSS into a Library item. For example, you can add to the Library a paragraph that has a CSS class style applied to it. When you attempt to add this paragraph to the Library, Dreamweaver warns you that the item may not look the same when you place it in other documents—because the style sheet information doesn't come along for the ride. To make sure the Library item appears correctly, make sure that you attach the same style sheet to any page where you use that item. External style sheets (see page 111) make this easy.

Adding Library Items to a Page

To add a Library item to a Web page, drag it directly out of the Assets panel's Library items listing onto your page. (The long way: Click to plant your insertion point in the Web page, click the Library item you want in the Assets panel, and then, on the Assets panel, click the Insert button, shown in Figure 18-4.)

Note: Library items (.lbi files) also appear in the Files panel in a site's Library folder. Dragging a Library item from the Files panel to a page, however, *doesn't* insert it into the page. It adds the name of the library item file (not its contents) with a link to the .lbi file—not something you want to do.

When you insert a Library item into a Web page (or turn a selected item *into* a Library item), it sprouts a light yellow background color. The highlighting indicates that Dreamweaver intends to treat the Library item as a single object, even though it may be made of many different HTML elements. You can select it or drag it around, but you can't change it on the Web page. (Unfortunately, if you turn a nontransparent graphic into a Library item—like a logo, for example—then Dreamweaver doesn't give you this helpful visual cue.)

Remember, too, that the placed Library item is linked to the original copy in the Library. The copy in your document automatically changes to reflect any changes you make to the copy in the Library, using the technique described next.

Tip: Sometimes you may want to sever the connection between the Library and a Library item you've already placed onto a Web page–to modify a copyright notice on a particular page, for example. On the page, select the item, and then, in the Property inspector, click "Detach from original" (Figure 18-5). Dreamweaver removes the comment tags (see the box on page 720), thus breaking the link to the Library.

You can also insert the HTML of a Library item *without* maintaining a link to the Library by pressing the Ctrl (option) key when you add it to your document. Now Dreamweaver doesn't update the HTML on this page when you change the original Library file.

Editing Library Items

You'll appreciate the real power of Library items when it's time to make a change. When you update the file in the Library, all pages that you've graced with that item update themselves, too.

Start by opening the Library, as described on page 714. Then:

1. **Open the Library item that you want to edit.**

   You can do this by double-clicking the Assets panel's Library item, by highlighting it and then clicking the Edit button (Figure 18-4), or by highlighting a Library item on a Web page, and then, on the Property inspector, clicking the Open button (Figure 18-5). (You can also open the Library item file—an .lbi file—in the Library folder of your site's root directly from the Files panel.)

   Dreamweaver opens what looks like a normal Web page document, but it contains only the text, graphics, or other elements of the Library file.

Figure 18-5: *The selected Library item (a .lbi file) is in the site's Library folder. (The path appears after the word "Src.")*

2. **Edit away.**

   A Library item is only a selection of HTML; it's not a complete Web page. That means you shouldn't add *page* properties like the title or background color. (Dreamweaver actually lets you do this, but that adds invalid HTML code to the Library item as well as every page that uses that Library item.) Also, you can insert Library items only in the body of a Web page, so stick with objects that would normally appear in the document window, such as links, images, tables, and text. Don't add any code that appears in the head of a Web page, such as Cascading Style Sheets, meta tags, behaviors, or Spry widgets.

   And since a Library item can't contain a style sheet, if the HTML in your Library item relies on a style, then you'll have trouble previewing it correctly. Dreamweaver's Design Time Style Sheet tool comes in handy here. It lets you temporarily "add" a style sheet while designing a page, without actually adding the CSS code to the page. For more on this cool feature, turn to page 327.

Note: Don't turn any of Dreamweaver's Spry widgets into Library items. For example, if you use the Spry Menu Bar (page 184), then you might be tempted to turn the menu into a Library item that you could reuse on other pages of your site. Problem is, all Spry features combine HTML, JavaScript, and CSS code that are placed in different parts of a page's code. When you select the Spry widget on the page, and then turn it into a Library item, only the HTML comes along for the ride–the CSS which makes the widget look good, and the JavaScript which make the widget work, aren't included. The solution? Use Dreamweaver templates instead (see the next chapter).

3. **Choose File → Save.**

   Dreamweaver checks to see if it can find any pages that use the Library item, and, if it does, then it opens the Update Library Items window. A list of pages in the site that use that Library item appears.

4. **Click Update.**

   Dreamweaver opens the Update Pages window, updates the HTML in all the pages that use the Library item, and then lists all the files that it changed.

   On the other hand, you don't necessarily have to click Update. Perhaps you have a lot of changes to make to the Library item, and you just want to save the work you've done so far. You're not done editing it yet, so you don't want to waste time updating pages you'll just have to update again. You can always update later (see the box on page 763); in that case, click Don't Update. (Once you're finished with the changes and save the file for the final time, *then* update the site.)

5. **Click Done.**

   As you can see, the Library is an incredible timesaver that greatly simplifies the process of changing common page elements.

Renaming Library Elements

To rename something in your Library, on the Assets panel, click its name (Figure 18-4). Pause briefly, click again, and the name highlights, ready to be edited. Type the new name, and then press Enter (Return).

If you've already added the item to your Web pages, then Dreamweaver prompts you to update those pages. Click Update. Otherwise, the link between those pages and the Library breaks.

Tip: If you accidentally click Don't Update, don't panic. Simply change the Library item back to its original name, and then *re*-rename it. Don't forget to click Update this time!

Deleting Library Elements

You can delete unnecessary elements from your Library at any time, but do so with caution. When you delete something from the Library, Dreamweaver leaves behind every copy of it that you've already placed onto your Web pages—complete with links to the now-deleted Library item.

In other words, you can't edit the copies on your Web pages until you break those links. If you do indeed want to edit them, you have to break the links manually on each page where the Library item appears by selecting the item, and then clicking the "Detach from original" button (see Figure 18-5).

Now that you've been warned, here are the instructions. To get rid of a Library item, in the Assets panel, click it, and then do one of the following:

- In the Assets panel, click the Trash can icon.
- Press Delete.
- Right-click (Control-click) the item's name, and then, from the shortcut menu, choose Delete.

Tip: If you ever accidentally delete an item from the Library, you can recreate it, provided you've used it somewhere on one of the Web pages in the site.

Open the page containing the Library item, and then click the Library item to select it. On the Property inspector, click Recreate (Figure 18-5) to make it anew. A new Library item appears in the Library, using the name and HTML from the item you selected.

Snippets and Library Tutorial

In this tutorial, you'll do two things: First, create a useful form pull-down menu snippet, and, second, turn a Chia Vet announcement into a reusable Library item, and then add it to several pages in the site.

TROUBLESHOOTING MOMENT

Under the Hood of Library Items

Behind the scenes, Dreamweaver stores the HTML for Library items in basic text files. Those files' names end with the extension .lbi, and they stay in the Library folder inside your local site folder.

When you insert a Library item into a Web page, Dreamweaver inserts the item's HTML, and adds a set of comment tags. These tags refer to the original Library file, and help Dreamweaver remember where the Library item begins and ends. For instance, if you turn the text "Copyright 2009" into a Library item called *copyright,* and insert it into a Web page, Dreamweaver adds the following HTML to the page:

```
<!-- #BeginLibraryItem "/Library/
copyright.lbi" -->Copyright 2009<!--
#EndLibraryItem-->
```

Avoid the use of hyphens when naming Library items. Why? Since HTML comments use hyphens, <!-- -->, older versions of Firefox, get tripped up by additional hyphens, and respond by hiding the contents of a Library item, or displaying raw HTML code instead.

In addition, although you can't edit a Library item on a page in Design view, you can muck around with the code in Code view. In the example above, you could change 2009 to 2010 in Code view. Don't do it! Dreamweaver obliterates any changes you make the next time you update the original Library item. If you want to make a change to a Library item, then edit the *original* Library item, or detach the item from the Library (as described in the Tip on page 717), and then edit it.

Note: You need to download the tutorial files from *www.sawmac.com/dwcs4/* to complete this tutorial. See the Note on page 48 for more details.

Once you've downloaded the tutorial files and opened Dreamweaver, define a new site as described on page 42: Name the site *Snippets and Library,* and then select the Chapter18 folder (inside the MM_DWCS4 folder). (In a nutshell: choose Site → New Site. In the Site Definition window, click the Advanced tab, type *Snippets and Library* into the Site Name field, click the folder icon next to the Local Root Folder field, navigate to and select the Chapter18 folder, and then click Choose or Select. Finally, click OK.)

Creating a Snippet

1. **With your site freshly defined, make sure the Files panel is open.**

   If the panel isn't open, press the F8 key (Shift-⌘-F) or choose Window → Files.

2. **In the Files panel, double-click the file *snippet.html.***

   A page with several form pull-down menus opens. The page includes menus for the months of the year, names of U.S. states, and the numbers 1–31. These menus are useful for specifying dates when something needs to be done, states for shipping orders to, or simply for selecting a month for one's astrological sign. Dreamweaver's own Snippets don't include these useful menus, but, fortunately, you can add them yourself.

3. **At the top of the page, click the first form menu.**

   This menu appears to the right of the words "Months of the year". You've selected the menu (and its underlying HTML code). To add this as a snippet, you need to open the Snippets panel.

4. **Choose Window → Snippets.**

   The Snippets panel (Figure 18-1) is your control center for adding, editing, and deleting Snippets.

5. **At the bottom of the panel, click the New Snippet button (Figure 18-1).**

   The Snippet window opens. Dreamweaver automatically copies the code for the menu into the window. You just need to name the snippet, and add a few more details.

6. **In the Name box, type *Month Menu*, and in the description box, type *A list of month names, with numeric values* as pictured in Figure 18-6.**

   The name and description appear in the Snippets panel. In this case, the description identifies what appears in the menu on the page (a list of month names) and what value someone submits when selecting a month from the list and submitting the form—in other words, the name/value pair for this form field. (See Chapter 11 for more information on how forms work.)

7. **Select the "Insert block" radio button.**

   This button identifies the snippet as a chunk of HTML that's simply plopped down on a page, as opposed to HTML that wraps around a selected graphic or text like a link or table cell might (if you wanted to do that, then you'd select the "Wrap selection" button).

8. **At the bottom of the window, select the Design button.**

   You've just told Dreamweaver to display the snippet visually when it's selected in the Snippets panel. In other words, when you select this snippet in the panel, you see a preview of the form menu, not a bunch of HTML code.

9. **The window should now look like Figure 18-6. Click the OK button to create your new snippet.**

   The snippet should now appear in the Snippets panel, ready to be inserted into a page.

10. **Select the Files panel by clicking the Files tab or pressing the F8 key (Shift-⌘-F); then double-click the file *preventative.html*.**

    This step opens a page from the Chia Vet Web site. You'll insert the new snippet as part of the "Make an appointment online" form in the right sidebar. Depending on the size of your monitor, you may need to scroll down a little to see the Month area in the form on the right side of the page.

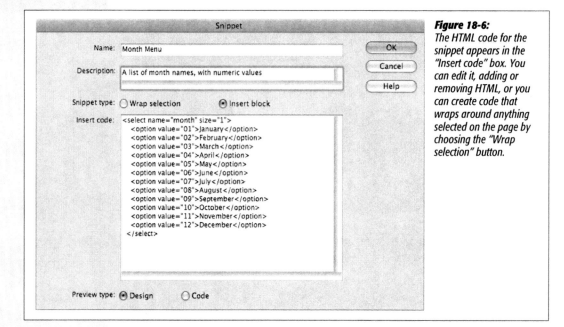

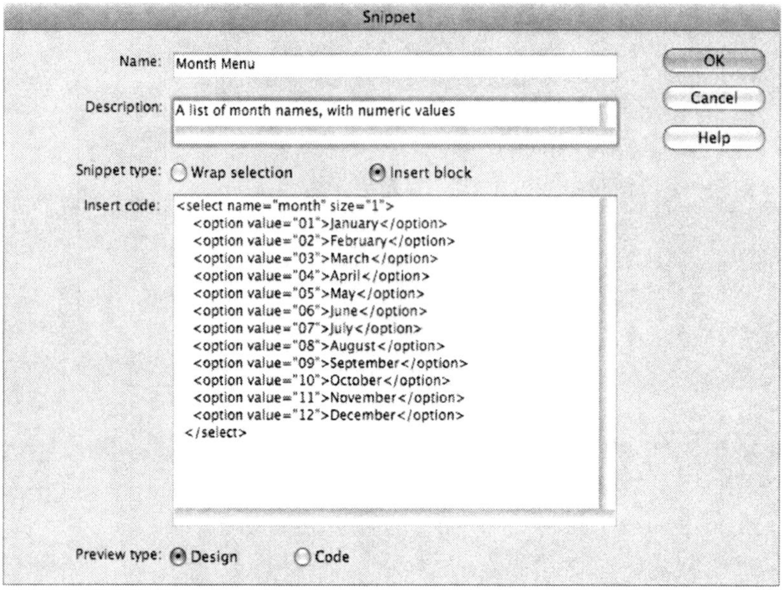

Figure 18-6: *The HTML code for the snippet appears in the "Insert code" box. You can edit it, adding or removing HTML, or you can create code that wraps around anything selected on the page by choosing the "Wrap selection" button.*

11. **Return to the Snippet panel once again by clicking the Snippets tab or choosing Window → Snippets.**

    Now for the moment of truth.

12. **Drag your new snippet—Month Menu—from the Snippets panel to the space just below the bolded word "Month" in the right sidebar.**

    Ta-da, Dreamweaver adds the new menu. Now, whenever you need to add a menu listing the months of the year, don't bother creating it from scratch. Just use the snippet!

Note: If a folder in the Snippets panel was selected when you created the snippet, then Dreamweaver stores the snippet in that folder. To move it out of that folder and up to the top level list of snippets, drag the snippet–Month Menu–to the very bottom of the Snippets panel.

13. **At the top of the document window, click the *snippet.html* tab. Click the third menu (the one with days of the month), and then repeat steps 4-12.**

    Name this new snippet *Days of month* and, as a description for the snippet, type *numerical days of the month.* Insert this new snippet in the empty space directly below the word Day in the form. You can close the file *snippet.html* when you're done.

Creating a Library Item

Now you'll see one way in which Dreamweaver's powerful site management tools can help you create and update your Web sites more effectively:

1. **Make sure the file *preventative.html* is open.**

   This is the same page you added the snippet to in the last section. Here you're going to work on the box with the headline "Meet Our Newest Doc". This box is a simple <div> with a headline, paragraph, and image inside it. It's used for recent Chia Vet announcements, and will appear on various pages of the site. Since these announcements need to be kept up to date, creating an easily updated Library item is an efficient choice.

2. **Click anywhere inside that box (for example in the headline "Meet Our Newest Doc"), and then, in the Tag selector, click <div.announcement> (Figure 18-7).**

   Alternatively, you can click anywhere inside the div, and then choose Edit → Select All *twice* (pressing Ctrl-A or ⌘-A two times also works). You need to use Select All twice because you want to select the actual <div> tag—when the cursor is inside a <div>, the first Select All grabs all the *contents* of the <div>, while the second one actually selects the opening and closing <div> tags.

Figure 18-7: *Click <div.announcement> to select the <div> tag containing the recent Chia Vet announcements.*

3. **Choose Window → Assets, and then click the Library button.**

   The Assets panel opens, and displays the Library category.

4. **On the Assets panel, click the New Library Item button (Figure 18-4).**

   A warning message appears, saying that the Library item may not look the same in other pages. Dreamweaver's trying to tell you that Library items can contain only HTML from the body of a Web page—not Cascading Style Sheets. (You can still include HTML, such as this <div> tag, that's had a style applied to it, as long as you make sure that any *pages* to which you add the Library item have the appropriate style sheets.)

The text in this example *is* formatted using a style sheet, so, sure enough, it won't look the same in pages that don't have the same style sheet. In this exercise, however, this formatting isn't a problem, since all the pages in the site share the same linked external style sheet.

Click OK to dismiss the warning. The copyright notice item appears in the Library list, with an "Untitled" naming rectangle next to it.

5. **Type *news* to name the new item on the Assets panel, and then press Enter.**

   You've just checked this standard blob of text into your Library. It's ready to use anywhere else on your site. Notice that the <div>'s background has changed to yellow in the document window—Dreamweaver's way of letting you know this is a Library item.

6. **In the Files panel, double-click the file called *tips.html*.**

   You'll frequently jump between the Files panel and the Assets panel, so this keyboard shortcut comes in handy: the F8 key (Shift-⌘-F) to open the Files panel. The Assets panel doesn't have a keyboard shortcut, but you can create your own keyboard shortcut to open and close this panel as described on page 799.

   The tips page doesn't have an announcement box, so you'll add one.

7. **Switch back to the Assets panel, and drag the "news" Library item to the left of the letter "L" in the first paragraph of text, as pictured in Figure 18-8.**

   You can recognize the newly inserted Library item by its yellow background. Click the text in the item, and notice that you can't edit it; Dreamweaver treats it like a single object.

8. **Add the "news" Library item to one other page on the site: *boarding.html*.**

   Open the page (by double-clicking its name in the Files window), and then repeat step 7. You can actually insert this Library item anywhere you want on the page.

   (You can close and save the pages as you go, or leave them open. Leave at least one open at the end and go on to step 9.)

9. **This just in!**

   New things are happening at Chia Vet all the time, so it's time to update this announcement. Fortunately, you've used a Library item, so you can easily make the change.

10. **In the Assets panel, double-click the "news" item's icon (not its name).**

    The Library item opens up, ready for editing. Notice that it doesn't have any of the formatting you saw on the Web page—that's because there's no CSS file attached to the library item file, so you see only the plain HTML version of this announcement box.

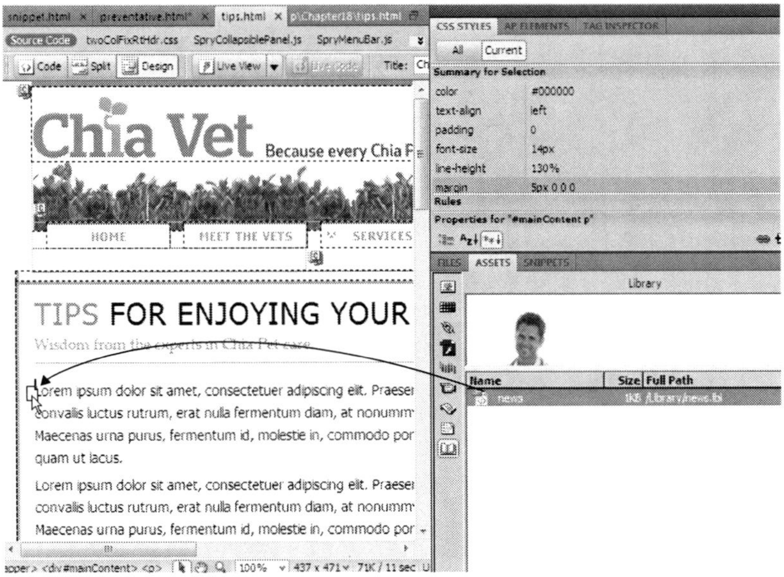

***Figure 18-8:** In addition to dragging a Library item into the document window, you can also insert the item by placing the insertion point in the document window, and then, on the Assets panel, clicking the Insert button.*

11. **Delete the picture of the vet, and change the headline to *Chia Vet nominated for horticulture award of excellence*. Save the file.**

    The Update Library Items dialog box appears, listing the three pages in the site that use this announcement box.

12. **Click Update.**

    Dreamweaver opens the Update Pages dialog box, and then updates all the Web pages that use the "news" item.

13. **Click Close to close the Update Pages dialog box.**

    And *now* if you open *preventative.html*, *tips.html*, and *boarding.html*, you find that the announcement box on all three pages has been updated.

    Now imagine that you just used this auto-update feature on a 10,000-page site. Sit back and smile.

CHAPTER
19

Templates

Some Web designers handcraft sites with loving care, changing layouts, colors, fonts, banners, and navigation from page to page. But that approach isn't always practical—or desirable. Consistency is a good thing. Web pages that look and act similarly reassure visitors; when only important material changes from page to page, readers can concentrate on finding the information they want. Even more importantly, a handcrafted approach is often unrealistic when you're cranking out content on a deadline.

Here's where *templates* come in. Frequently, the underlying design of many pages on a Web site is identical (see Figure 19-1). For instance, a company Web site with an employee directory may dedicate a single Web page to each employee. Each employee page probably has the same navigation bar, banner, footer, and layout. Only a few particulars differ, like the employee name, photo, and contact information. This chapter shows you how templates can make quick work of most, if not all, of these repetitive elements.

Template Basics

Templates let you build pages that share a similar structure and graphic identity, quickly and without having to worry about accidentally deleting or changing elements. Templates come in very handy when you're designing a site for which other, less Dreamweaver-savvy individuals are responsible for adding new pages. If you use a template, these underlings can modify only the areas of a page that you, the godlike Dreamweaver guru, define.

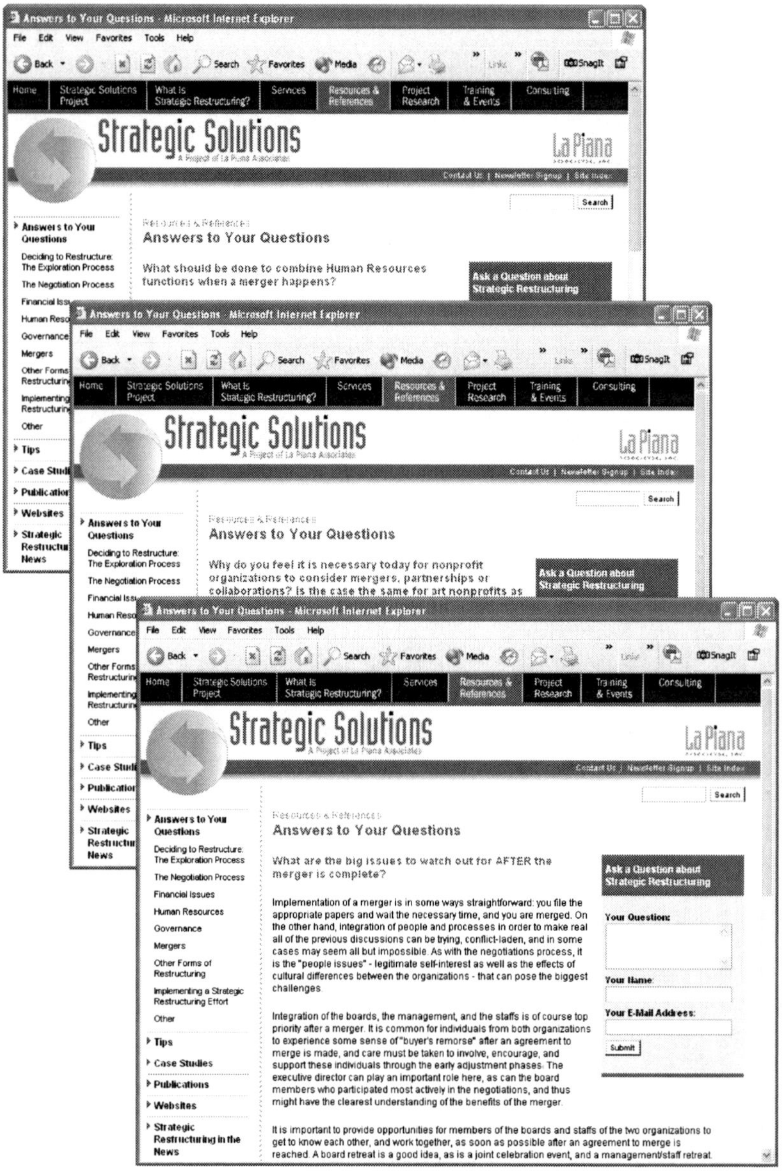

Figure 19-1: *These three Web pages are part of a section of a Web site dedicated to answering frequently asked questions. The pages each provide the answer to a different question, but are otherwise identical, sharing the same banner, navigation buttons, sidebar, and footer. Why rebuild the design for each one? Enter one of Dreamweaver's greatest timesaving features—Templates—which help you quickly build similar looking pages.*

Note: Adobe Contribute, a simple, word processor–like program for updating Web sites, works very well with sites built using Dreamweaver templates. If you build sites that are updated by people who don't know the first thing about Dreamweaver or building Web pages, Contribute can help. The latest version of the program, Contribute CS4, even lets novices use their own Web browser to update pages on their sites. You can find more information about this program at Adobe's Web site: *www.adobe.com/products/contribute*. For another solution, see the box on page 741.

A new page based on a template—also called a template *instance*, or *child page*—looks just like the template, except that you can edit only certain areas of the page, called, logically enough, *editable regions*. In the example shown in Figure 19-1, one editable region includes the question-and-answer text area; the rest of the page remains untouched and is, in fact, locked.

A Dreamweaver template can be very basic: one or more areas of a page (the editable regions) can be changed on pages built from the template, others can't (the *locked regions*). But Dreamweaver also includes many subtle ways for controlling template instances. Here's an overview of the features you'll encounter when creating and using templates:

- **Editable regions.** These are the basic building blocks of a template. An editable region is a part of a page—a paragraph, the contents of a div, or a headline, for example—that people can change on each template instance. A template page can have multiple editable regions—for example, one in a sidebar area and another in the main content section of a page.

- **Editable tag attributes.** There may be times when you want to make a particular *tag* property editable. For instance, you might want to assign an ID to the <body> tag. Then, on each template-based page, you could apply an ID specific to a particular section of the site. For a template-based page that you save as part of an "About Us" section of the site, you could apply an ID with the name *about*. With that in place, you could use a descendent selector (like *#about h1*) to create a custom style for all headlines on that page.

  Or perhaps you've built a template that includes a photo with some complex formatting (left-aligned by a Cascading Style Sheet, perhaps). Turning the entire image into an editable region could pose problems: When someone creates a new page from the template and then inserts a new photo, all of the formatting information can get lost. Instead, you could make just the image's *src* property editable. People would then be able to insert new images for each page without inadvertently ruining the photo's formatting. (You could also make the image's *alt* property editable and, if the *Width* and *Height* properties vary from image to image, you could make those attributes editable as well.)

- **Repeating regions and repeating tables.** Some Web pages include *lists* of items: catalogs of products, lists of news articles, albums of photos, and so on. Dreamweaver lets you define *repeatable* regions for pages like this.

  For example, a page of product listings can include a picture, name, and price for each product in a catalog, organized using a table with multiple rows (Chapter 7).

  As the template builder, you may not know in advance how many products the page will eventually list, so you can't fully design the page. However, you can use Dreamweaver to define a row—or any selection of HTML—as a repeating region, so that page authors can add new rows of product information when needed.

- **Optional regions and editable optional regions.** *Optional regions* make templates even more flexible. They let you show or hide content on a page-by-page basis.

  Suppose you create a template for your company's products. When some products go on sale (but others remain full price), you could add an *optional* region on the template that displays a big "On Sale!" logo. When you create a new product page, you could *show* the optional region for products that are on sale and keep it *hidden* for the others.

  Editable optional regions are similar, but they have the added benefit of being editable. Maybe you're creating a template for an employee directory, giving each employee a separate Web page with contact information. Some employees also want their picture displayed on the page, while others don't (you know the type). Solution: Add an editable optional region that would let you show the space for a photo and add a different photo for each page. For the shyer types, you would simply hide the photo area entirely.

Furthermore, Dreamweaver can create *nested* templates, which inherit design elements from a master template. In this way, you can create a general unified design that's shared by other templates; this feature is described on page 751.

But facilitating page creation is only one of the benefits of templates. You'll also find that templates can greatly simplify the process of updating a Web site's design. Like Library items (page 713), pages based on templates retain a reference to the original template file. Dreamweaver passes any changes you make to the template onto all the pages created from it, which can save you hours of time and trouble when it comes time to update the look or structure of your site. Imagine how much time you'll save when your boss asks you to add "just one more" button to the site's navigation bar. Instead of updating thousands of pages by hand, you need to update only a single template file.

Note: Templates aren't just for building regular, static Web pages. You can also create templates for use with the kinds of dynamic, database-driven Web pages discussed in Part 6 of this book.

Creating a Template

The first step in creating a template requires building a basic Web page and telling Dreamweaver you'd like to use it as a template. You can go about this in two ways: build a Web page and turn it into a template, or create a blank, empty template file and add text, graphics, tables, and other content to it.

Turning a Web Page into a Template

The easiest way to create a template is simply to base it on a Web page in your current site folder. Although you can create templates based on Web pages that *aren't* part of the current local site, you may run into problems with links and paths to images, as described in a moment.

Once you've opened the Web page, just choose File → Save As Template or, on the Common category of the Insert panel (see Figure 19-2), click the Templates button and then select Make Template from the menu. In the Save As Template window (Figure 19-3), the name of the current local site appears in the Site pop-up menu; meanwhile, all templates for that site show up in the Existing Templates field.

Note: At this point, you could theoretically use the Site menu to save a template into any local site folder you've defined (see Chapter 15 for a discussion of local sites), but be careful with this option. If your page contains images and links and you save it as a template for another local site, Dreamweaver doesn't copy the images from the first site folder into the other one. As a result, the paths to the image files and links don't work correctly.

If you must use a page from one site as a template for another, copy the Web page *and graphics* into the new site's root folder, open the page from there, and then create a template as described here.

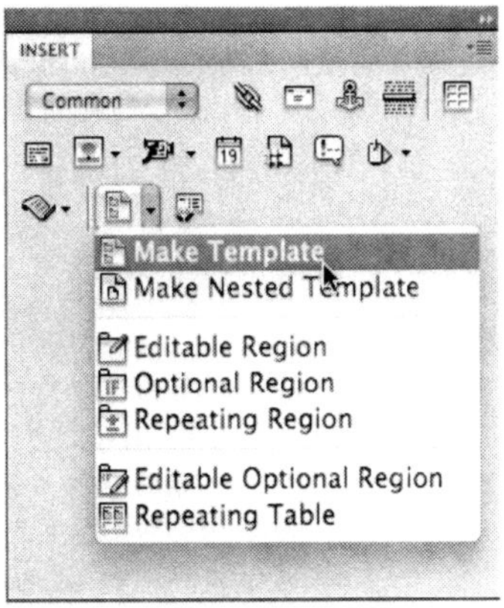

Figure 19-2:
The Templates menu on the Common category of the Insert panel provides access to tools for creating templates and setting up a variety of Dreamweaver template features.

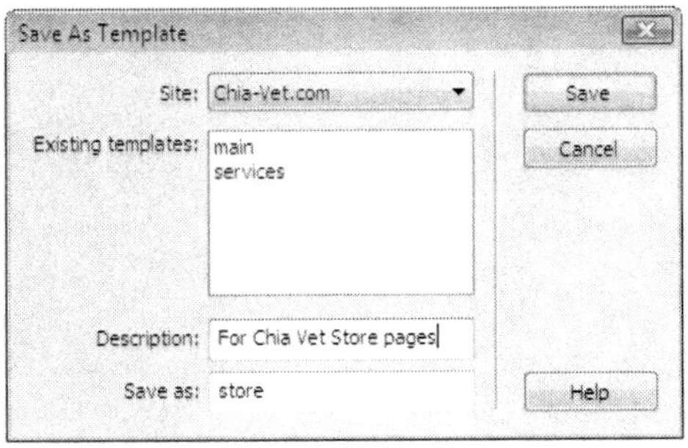

Figure 19-3:
The Save As Template dialog box lets you save your template into any of the local site folders you've defined in Dreamweaver. Stick to your current local site to avoid broken links and similar problems.

Dreamweaver includes a Description field for adding a brief note describing the template. This description appears when you're selecting a template as the basis for a new page you're creating. The description is very useful when *other* people are building a site using your templates and aren't sure whether *templateA1*, *templateA2*, or *templateA3* is the correct choice; a simple "use this template for all FAQ pages" is much clearer.

Finally, in the "Save as" box, type a name for the new template, and then click Save. Choose Yes when Dreamweaver asks if you want to Update Links for the page. If you choose No, all page-relative links break, and all the images on the page appear as broken-image icons.

Dreamweaver saves the page in the Templates folder of your local site root folder. It adds the extension .dwt to the file to indicate that it's a Dreamweaver template. (For dynamic Web pages, Dreamweaver adds the .dwt *before* the file's extension. For example, a PHP template may have a name like *maintemplate.dwt.php*.)

Note: Don't get carried away building too many templates for a site. It doesn't make any sense to create 20 templates for a 20-page Web site. You should only need a handful of templates to cover the different types of pages you have on a site. In fact, you might just need a single template file to dictate the look of all of the pages on your site.

Building a Template from Scratch

It's easiest to create a Web page first and then save it as a template, but you can also build one from scratch. Open the Asset panel's Templates category by choosing Window → Assets and then click the Template assets icon (see Figure 19-4). Then click the New Template button at the bottom of the Assets panel. Once Dreamweaver adds a new, untitled template to the list, type a new name for it. Something descriptive like "press release" or "employee page" helps you keep track of your templates.

After you've created a blank template for the site, you can open it by double-clicking its name in the Assets panel (or selecting its name and then clicking the Edit button at the bottom of the Assets panel). It opens just like any Web page, so that you can get busy designing it.

Defining Editable Regions

Your next task is to specify which parts of your template are locked and which are editable. By default, *everything* on a page is locked. After all, the main reason to use templates is to maintain a consistent, unchanging design and structure among pages. To make a template usable, you must define the area or areas you *can* change.

Figure 19-4:
The Templates category of the Assets panel lists the name, file size, and location of each template in the current local site. The Apply button applies a template to the current open Web page. The Refresh Site List button updates the list of templates: If you've just created a template and don't see it listed, click this button. The New Template button creates a new blank template in the Templates folder. Select a template from the list and click the Edit Template button to open the template for editing.

Adding a Basic Editable Region

To add an editable region to a template, start by selecting the part of the page you want to make changeable. You can designate as editable anything in the document window (that is, any HTML between the <body> tags).

Note: You can always add Cascading Style Sheets, JavaScript code, and meta tag information to the <head> of a template-based page. Any <head> content in the original template files stays put, however. For example, you can't remove an external style sheet applied to the template file from a page based on that template.

Drag across your page to select the elements you wish to make editable, or, for greater precision, use the Tag selector (see page 24) to make sure you select the exact HTML you want.

Now tell Dreamweaver that you want to make the selected elements editable. You can use any of these techniques:

- In the Common category of the Insert panel (Figure 19-2), select Editable Region from the Template menu.
- Choose Insert → Template Objects → Editable Region.
- Press Ctrl+Alt+V (⌘-Option-V).
- Right-click (Control-click) the selection and then choose Templates → New Editable Region from the shortcut menu.

When the New Editable Region dialog box appears, type a name for the region (you can't use the same name twice) and then click OK. You return to your template, where the name you gave the region appears in a small blue tab above the editable region (see Figure 19-5).

FREQUENTLY ASKED QUESTION

The Broken-Link Blues

Why aren't the links in my templates working?

When you created the link in the template file, you probably typed a path into the Property inspector's Link field—a recipe for heartbreak. Instead, always select the target Web page for a link by clicking the folder icon in the Property inspector, or by pressing Ctrl+L (⌘-L). In other words, when adding links to a template, always link to pages within the site by browsing to the desired file.

Dreamweaver saves templates in the Templates folder inside the local root folder; all document-relative links need to be relative to this location. (Absolute links, like those to other Web sites, aren't a problem; neither are root relative links; see page 161 to learn the difference.) The reason you should browse to, rather than type in, your links is so that Dreamweaver can create a proper relative link.

Imagine this situation: You create a template for all the classified ads that appear on your site. You store all the ads for April 2001 inside a series of folders like this: classifieds → 2001 → april, as shown in the site diagram here.

A link from a page in the *april* folder to the home page would follow the path marked 1 here. So when you create a link in your template, you can create a link to the home page by typing the path *../../../index.html*.

That choice is logical if you're thinking about the page (in the *april* folder) you'll create from the template—but it won't work. Dreamweaver stores templates in the Templates folder, so the correct path would be path 2, or *../index.html*. When you create a new page based on the template and save it in the *april* folder, Dreamweaver, in its wisdom, automatically rewrites all paths in the page so that the links function correctly.

The beauty of Dreamweaver is that you don't have to understand how all this works. Just remember to use document-relative links in your templates and create them by clicking the folder icon in the Property inspector.

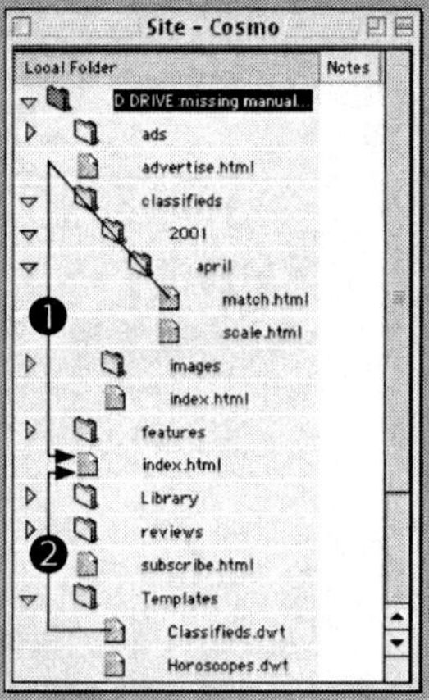

Note: If you use tables to lay out your pages (see Chapter 7), you'll often assign one table cell as the main area to hold the primary content of the page. For example, in the pages shown in Figure 19-1, the Frequently Asked Question and its answer appear in a single cell on the page. This cell makes a perfect editable region for a template. In the Tag selector, just click the <td> tag associated with that cell and use any of the techniques discussed here to convert the contents of that cell into an editable region.

If you use CSS, on the other hand, you can create a separate <div> tag (see page 333) for the main content area. In this case, select just the contents of the <div> tag, not the tag itself. Here's one instance where you want to avoid the Tag selector (page 24), which selects the entire <div>, tags and all. If you turn the <div> tag into an editable region, it's possible for someone modifying the page later to delete the tag entirely, which could wreak untold havoc on your CSS-based layout.

Fortunately, Dreamweaver has a handy shortcut for selecting just the contents of a <div> tag. Click anywhere inside the <div> tag, and then press Ctrl+A (⌘-A) or choose Edit → Select All. Next, turn this selection into an editable region, and the <div> tags will remain *outside* of the editable region, so no one can inadvertently delete a <div> tag that helps define the basic structure of a page.

FREQUENTLY ASKED QUESTION

When Save Won't Behave

I keep getting an error message when I save my template. What's going on?

If you add an editable region *inside* certain block-level elements like a paragraph, or a heading, Dreamweaver pops up a warning message when you save the template, explaining that you can't create additional paragraphs or headings inside this region on any pages you build from this template. This just means that you selected the *contents* of a paragraph or heading (not the actually paragraph or heading tag itself) when you made the region editable. Dreamweaver considers anything outside of the editable region locked, so you can't change those tags. Since it's improper HTML to have a paragraph, heading, or other block-level elements inside *another* paragraph, or heading, Dreamweaver will not let you add a paragraph, a heading, a bulleted list or any other block-level element inside the editable contents of the locked paragraph or heading tag.

This characteristic may not be such a bad thing, however. Imagine you're creating a template that's to be used by other people building a Web site. You have a heading 1 (maybe the title of the page) with a style applied to it, and you want to make sure it looks the same on every page. You wouldn't want anyone changing the heading tag, and possibly erasing the style. In addition, you don't want them to be able to change the heading 1 to a heading 2, or a heading 3; nor do you want them to completely erase the h1 tag and type paragraph after paragraph of their random thoughts. You just want them to type in new text for the page title. Selecting just the text inside the heading (as opposed to the h1 tag *and* the text) and turning it into an editable region does just that. Viva micro-management!

If this is in fact what you want to do, you can save yourself the bother of having to constantly see the "You place an editable region inside a block tag" warning box each time you save the template by simply turning on the "Don't show me this message again" checkbox. However, if you made a mistake and *do* want to allow people to change the heading, or add more headings and paragraphs in this region, you need to do two things: First, unlock the editable region you created (see below); then, select the text *and* tag (the Tag selector [page 24] is the best way to make sure you've selected a tag), and then turn that into an editable region.

You may find that a single editable region is all you need—for example, a single area of the page (a section of a page enclosed by a <div> tag, for example) containing the text for a product review. However, if you need to edit *multiple* areas of a Web page, just add more editable regions to the template. For instance, when you create a template for an employee page, you can create editable regions for the employee's name, telephone number, and photo. If you change your mind and want to lock a region again, select the editable region and then choose Modify → Templates → Remove Template Markup. Dreamweaver removes the code that makes the region editable. You can do the same thing with other types of template regions, like repeating and optional regions.

Warning: You can rename an editable region by clicking the blue tab on the template page and typing a new name into the Property inspector. However, if you've already built pages based on this template, it's not a good idea. Because template-based pages use the name to identify editable regions, Dreamweaver can lose track of where content should go when you rename a region. See Figure 19-18 for a workaround.

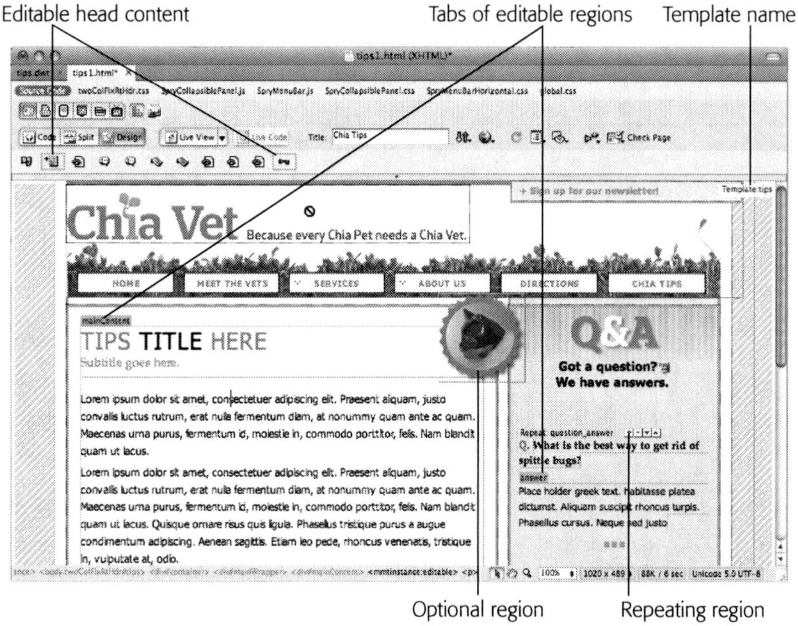

***Figure 19-5:** This page is based on a template called "tips", as you can tell from the little tab in the document window's upper-right corner. You can modify editable regions, which are labeled with small tabs. In this example, one editable region is called "mainContent". An additional editable region (named "answer") appears within a repeating region (labeled "question_answer") that lets you duplicate editable regions to create a list of questions and answers. Optional regions don't have any clear identifier on a template-based page; you can identify them only in the Template properties window, as described on page 744. The title of any page created from a template is also editable. All other parts of the page are locked (circled); you can make changes to these parts only in the original template file.*

Adding a Repeating Region

Some Web pages contain lists of items. A catalog page may display row after row of product information—picture, name, price, and description. An index of Frequently Asked Questions may provide a list of questions and the dates they were posted.

If you were to make a template for either of these pages, you would add an editable region to the area of the page where these lists appear. Just creating an editable region, however, wouldn't give you any ability to enforce (or easily update) the design of these lists, because *everything* within an editable region can be changed.

POWER USERS' CLINIC

Under the Hood of Templates

Dreamweaver saves templates as HTML files in the Templates folder inside your current local site folder (see Chapter 15 for information on local sites). Each template bears the file name extension .dwt to distinguish it from regular Web pages.

The program treats files in the Templates folder differently from normal Web pages, so don't save anything but .dwt files there. In addition, since Dreamweaver expects the Templates folder to be in the local root folder of your site, don't move the Templates folder or change its name in any way (don't even change the capital T in Templates, even if you're a low-key type of person). If you do, your templates won't work.

As with Library items, Dreamweaver uses HTML comment tags to indicate the name of the template. If you inspect the HTML code of a template-based document, you'll see that, immediately following the opening <html> tag, Dreamweaver inserts a comment tag with the text "InstanceBegin" followed by the location and name of the template. Additional comment tags indicate areas of the page that you can modify, plus special template features like template parameters used for optional regions. For instance, the title of a page based on a template is always editable; its comment tag might look like this:

```
<!-- InstanceBeginEditable
name="doctitle" -->
<title>My New Page</title>
<!-- InstanceEndEditable -->
```

The first comment indicates the editable region's beginning and also includes the editable region's name. When editing pages based on the template, you can change only the HTML between these comment tags. Everything else on the page is locked, even when you're working in Code view.

Fortunately, Dreamweaver provides a pair of template tools to overcome this problem: *repeating regions* and *repeating tables*. Both let you create areas of a page that include editable (and uneditable) regions that can be repeated any number of times (see Figure 19-6).

Adding a repeating region is similar to adding an editable region. Select the area of the template page you wish to make repeatable, which usually contains at least one editable region. This could be a single list item (the <li> tag), a table row (<tr> tag), or even an entire <div> tag.

Tip: You can make a repeating region that *doesn't* include an editable region. For example, a template for a movie review Web page could include a repeating region that's simply a graphic of a star. A page author adding a new movie review could repeat the star graphic to match the movie's rating—four stars, for example. (There's just one caveat—see the Tip on page 756.)

Next, tell Dreamweaver that the selected elements are part of a repeating region. You can use any of these techniques:

- On the Common category of the Insert panel (Figure 19-2), select the Repeating Region option from the Templates menu.
- Choose Insert → Template Objects → Repeating Region.
- Right-click (Control-click) the selection and choose Templates → New Repeating Region from the shortcut menu.

FREQUENTLY ASKED QUESTION

Hindered by Highlighting

I'm distracted by the tabs and background colors that Dreamweaver uses to indicate Library items and Templates. How do I get rid of them?

When you use Templates or Library items, you see blue tabs and yellow backgrounds, respectively, to indicate editable regions and Library items. Although these visual cues don't appear in a Web browser, they can still make your page harder to read while you work in Dreamweaver. Fortunately, you can alter the background color of these items and even turn highlighting off altogether.

Choose Edit → Preferences, or press Ctrl+U (⌘-U). In the Preferences Category list, click Highlighting. To change the background color for editable regions, locked regions, and Library items, use the color box (see page 59) or type in a hexadecimal color value. To remove the highlighting, turn off the Show box next to the appropriate item.

Oftentimes, it's useful to keep highlighting on to help you keep track of Library items and editable regions. If you want to turn off highlighting temporarily, simply choose View → Visual Aids → Invisible Elements, or use the keyboard shortcut Ctrl+Shift+I (⌘-Shift-I) to toggle these visual cues off and on. This technique has the added benefit of hiding table borders, layer borders, and image maps, as well as other invisible elements.

When the New Repeating Region dialog box appears, type a name for the region and then click OK. You return to your template, where the name you gave the region appears in a small blue tab above the editable region (see Figure 19-6). (See page 756 for a discussion of using a repeating region when building a new template-based page.)

Warning: Dreamweaver lets you name a repeating region with a name already in use by an editable region. But don't—multiple template areas with the same name make Dreamweaver act unpredictably.

Repeating Tables

The *repeating table* tool is essentially a shortcut to creating a table with one or more repeating rows. If you had time on your hands, you could achieve the same effect by adding a table to a page, selecting one or more rows, and applying a repeating region to the selection. To use the repeating table tool:

1. **Click the template page where you wish to insert the table.**

   You can't insert a repeating table into an already defined editable, repeating, or optional region, as explained in the box on page 742. You must be in an empty, locked area of the template.

2. **On the Common category of the Insert panel (Figure 19-2), select the Repeating Table option from the Templates menu.**

   Alternatively, you can choose Insert → Template Objects → Repeating Table. Either way, the Insert Repeating Table window appears (Figure 19-7).

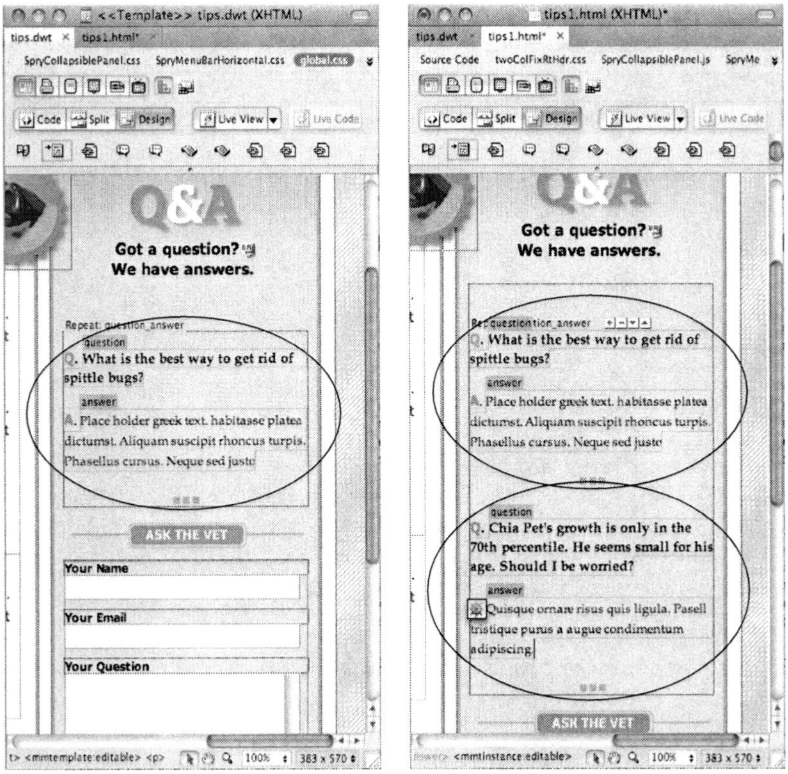

Figure 19-6:
A repeating region lets page authors add multiple selections of repeating information.

Left: In this example, the template has one repeating region, labeled "question_answer" (circled).

Right: A complete page based on this template includes two repeated editable regions (circled). If another page requires more question/answer pairs, you could easily add additional ones to each list by clicking the + button at the top of the repeating region in the template-based page (left). However, the template still controls the basic design. Changing the repeating region's underlying HTML—for example, changing the Q to "Question" at the beginning of the question paragraph, or A to "Answer" in the Answer paragraph in the uneditable part of the template page—automatically changes the same elements in all pages created from the template. From a design perspective, this strategy also means that page authors can't tamper with the design of a repeating region—just the content marked as editable.

3. **Fill out the basic properties of the table.**

   The top part of the window lets you set up the basic structure of the table: rows, columns, cell padding, cell spacing, width, and border. Basically, it's the same information you'd provide when creating any table, as described on page 265. You usually start a repeating table with two rows—one for a heading, and another to contain the information you wish to repeat.

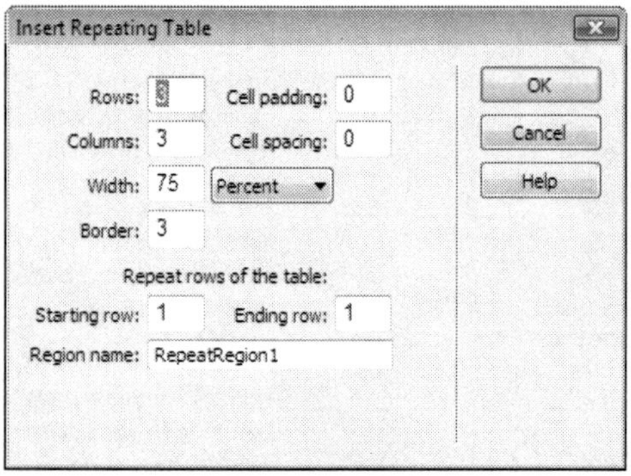

Figure 19-7: *The Insert Repeating Table dialog box lets you kill three birds with one stone: it adds a table to a page, turns one or more rows into a repeating region, and adds editable regions into each table cell inside the repeating region.*

4. **In the "Starting row" box, type the number of the row where the repeating region should begin.**

   Often you'll have just one repeating row: one row of product information, for example. You may want to use the top row for labels indicating the information contained in the rows below. If that's the case, enter *2* at this step, leaving the first row as an uneditable part of the template.

   It's conceivable, however, that you may want each entry to take up *two* rows. The first would list Name and Description; the second would contain a cell for a photo and a cell for the price. You set up this effect in this step and the next.

5. **In the "Ending row" box, type the number of the last repeating row.**

   If you wish to repeat only a single row, enter the same number you provided for step 4. If you're creating a double repeating row, add 1 to the number you provided in step 4. For example, if you need three rows for each repeating entry, add 2 to the number from step 4.

6. **Type a name for this repeating region.**

   Don't use the same name as another template region. You'll run the risk of unpredictable results on template-based pages.

7. **Click OK.**

   Dreamweaver inserts a table into the page. A blue tab with the name of the repeating region appears (see Figure 19-6), as do blue tabs in each cell of each repeated row. These tabs indicate new editable regions—one per cell.

   Since these new editable regions have uninformative names like EditRegion4, you may want to rename them. Click the blue tab and type a new name in the Property inspector. (But do so *before* you create any pages based on the template—see the Warning on page 737.)

To remove a repeating region, select it by clicking the blue Repeat tab, and then choose Modify → Templates → Remove Template Markup. A more accurate way to select a repeating region is to click anywhere inside the region, and then click

GEM IN THE ROUGH

Simple, Web-Based Page Editing

Dreamweaver CS4 includes a few tools to work with a new Adobe service called InContext Editing. This Web-based service lets non-Dreamweaver users edit content on a page using just a Web browser. For example, say your boss (who thinks that CSS is just a Brazilian pop band) wants to update his bio page on the company Web site. Since you don't trust him with Dreamweaver (he might just delete the home page), you can use the new InContext Editing tools in Dreamweaver to create editable regions of a page, which your boss can then edit using just his Web browser.

At this point, InContext Editing is very basic; you can't add new pages to a site or delete a page, for example. However, you can create editable regions and repeating regions just as with Dreamweaver templates. The InContext Editing category of the Insert panel contains the three tools that the InContext Editing service supports.

To use this tool, you need sign to up for an account at Adobe's Web site: *www.adobe.com/products/incontextediting/*. You need to provide basic FTP information about your Web site and create a list of users (people in your organization) who are allowed to edit pages. Even though they'll go to Adobe's site to edit the page, they'll actually be editing pages that exist on your Web server. At the time of this writing, the service is free, but eventually it will be a paid service with a monthly subscription fee (the price has yet to be determined).

Because the InContext Editing service lets you make simple edits to a Web page with nothing more than a Web browser, it may be just the tool if you're overwhelmed with requests for countless, simple page edits. For more complex editing tasks, such as adding new pages to a Web site, Adobe's Contribute program (see the Note on page 728) is a better solution that still lets you pass off some basic Web work to other people while you listen to the soothing sounds of CSS (they really are a Brazilian pop band!).

<mmtemplate: repeat> in the Tag selector (see page 24 for more on the Tag selector). Note that removing a repeating region doesn't remove any editable regions you added inside the repeating region. If you want to rename a repeating region, heed the Warning on page 735.

Making a Tag Attribute Editable

An editable region lets you change areas of HTML—like a paragraph, image, or entire table—on new pages you create from a template. However, when you're creating a template for others to make pages from down the line, you may want to limit these page authors' editing abilities. You may want to allow budding Web designers to change the source of an image used for a banner advertisement without letting them change the width, height, and class applied to the image. Or, you might want to use templates but still let others assign a class or ID to the <body> tag—a move that's normally forbidden on template-based pages. You can use Dreamweaver's Editable Tag Attribute to specify which tag properties your successors can change.

Note: Before making a tag attribute editable, first set that property to a default value in the template. Doing so inserts a default value and makes the attribute appear in the Editable Tag Attribute window (see steps 3 and 7 in the following instructions).

FREQUENTLY ASKED QUESTION

Editable Regions, Repeating Regions, and Errors

When I try to insert an editable region inside a repeating region, I get the following error: "The selection is already in an editable, repeating, or optional region." *What's that about?*

This error message essentially means you're trying to add a template region where it doesn't belong. It appears most often when you attempt to put a repeating or optional region inside an editable region. That kind of nesting is a no-no; anything inside an editable region can be changed on template-based pages, and as such, Dreamweaver can't touch it.

However, you may get this error message seemingly by mistake. For instance, it's perfectly OK to add an editable region inside a repeating region, and it's even OK to add a repeating region inside an optional region, and vice versa.

But say one day you select text inside a repeating region and try to turn it into an editable region, and boom—error message. What probably happened was, when you selected the text, Dreamweaver actually selected part of the hidden code used to define a template region (see the box, "Under the Hood of Templates" on page 737) and thought you were trying to put an editable region inside it. To avoid confusion, use the Tag selector to select the tag you wish to turn into an editable region. In the Tag selector, you can click <p> to select the paragraph inside the repeating region. Alternatively, go into Code view (see page 395), and then select whatever part of the code inside the repeating region you wish to make editable.

To make a tag attribute editable:

1. **Select the tag whose property you wish to make editable.**

   Using the Tag selector (see page 24) is the most accurate way.

2. **Choose Modify → Templates → Make Attribute Editable.**

   The Editable Tag Attributes window opens (Figure 19-8).

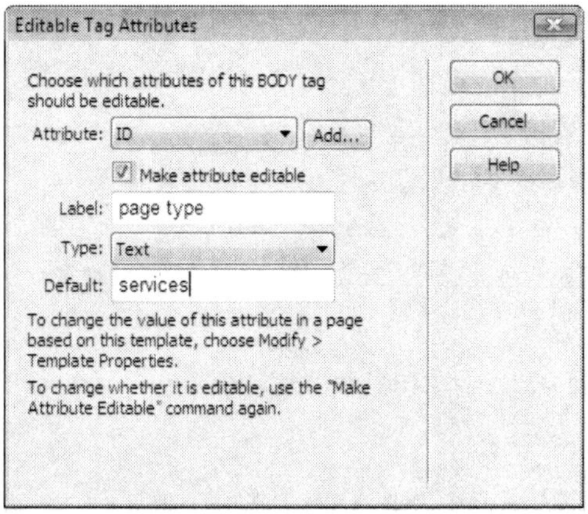

Figure 19-8:
Dreamweaver provides detailed control for template pages. To make just a single property of a single tag editable when pages are later based on your template, turn on the "Make attribute editable" checkbox. In this case, the "id" attribute of the body tag is editable, allowing page designers the freedom to apply different CSS styles to the body of each template-based page.

3. **Select an attribute from the menu or add a new attribute with the Add button.**

   Only properties you've already set for the selected tag appear in the Attribute menu. In other words, if you've selected an image, you probably see the *Src*, *Width*, and *Height* properties listed. But unless you've set the image's alternative text, the *alt* property doesn't appear.

   To add a property, click the Add button. In the window that appears, type the appropriate property name. For example, to make the *alt* (alternate text) attribute of a graphic editable, you'd set the <img> tag's *alt* attribute by typing *alt* here. (If you're not sure of the attribute's name, check out Dreamweaver's built-in HTML reference, described on page 422.)

Note: If you want page editors to be able to change a CSS class or ID applied to the <body> tag on template-based pages–to apply different fonts, background colors, or any of the many CSS formatting options to each template-based page–you *have* to make the Class or ID attribute editable. (See page 114 for more on CSS classes and IDs.)

4. **Make sure the "Make attribute editable" box is turned on.**

   If you decide that you no longer want to allow editing of this property, you can return to this dialog box and turn off editing, as described in a moment.

5. **Type a name in the Label field.**

   What you type here should be a simple description of the editable tag and property, which helps page authors correctly identify editable properties. For example, you could use *Product Image* if you're making a particular image's *source* (Src) property editable.

6. **Choose a value type from the menu.**

   Your choices are:

   - **Text.** Use this option when a property's value is a word. For example, you can change the image tag's *Align* property to *top, middle, baseline*, and so on. Or, when using Cascading Style Sheets, you could make a tag's *Class* property editable to allow page authors to apply a particular custom style to the tag—*content, footer*, and so on.

   - **URL.** Use this option when the editable property is a path to a file, like an image's *Src* property or a link's *Href* property. Using its site management tools, Dreamweaver keeps track of these paths and updates them when you move your pages around your site.

   - **Color.** If the property requires a Web color, like a page's background color, select this option. This option makes Dreamweaver's color box available to people who build pages from the template.

- **True/False.** You shouldn't use this option. It's intended for Dreamweaver's Optional Regions feature (discussed below), and it doesn't apply to *HTML* properties.
- **Number.** Use this choice for properties that require a numeric value, like an image's *Height* and *Width* properties.

7. **Type a default value into the Default field.**

   This step is optional. The default value defines the initial value for this property, when people first create a page based on the template. They can then modify this value for that particular page. If you've already set this property in the template, its value automatically appears in this box.

8. **Click OK to close the window.**

   Dreamweaver adds code to the template page that allows page authors control of the attribute. Setting this attribute on pages created from the template is described on page 757.

If you later decide that you *don't* want a particular tag's property to be editable, Dreamweaver can help. Open the template file, select the tag with the editable attribute, and choose Modify → Templates → Make Attribute Editable. In the window that appears, turn off the "Make attribute editable" checkbox (Figure 19-8). Unfortunately, doing so doesn't remove *all* of the template code Dreamweaver added. Even after you turn off editing for an attribute, Dreamweaver leaves behind the parameter used to control the tag's property. To eliminate *this* extra code, see the box on page 751.

Adding Optional Regions

Templates provide consistent design. While consistency is generally a good thing, it can also get boring. Furthermore, there may be times when you'd like the flexibility to include information on some template-based pages but not on others.

Dreamweaver provides a fairly foolproof way to vary page design: *optional regions.* An optional region is simply part of a template page that you can hide or display on each template-based page (see Figure 19-9.). When creating a new page based on the template, a page author can turn the region on or off.

Creating an optional region is a snap. Just select the HTML code you wish to make optional, and then do one of the following:

- On the Common category of the Insert panel (Figure 19-2), select the Optional Region option from the Templates menu.
- Choose Insert → Template Objects → Optional Region.
- Right-click (Control-click) the selection and choose Templates → New Optional Region from the shortcut menu.

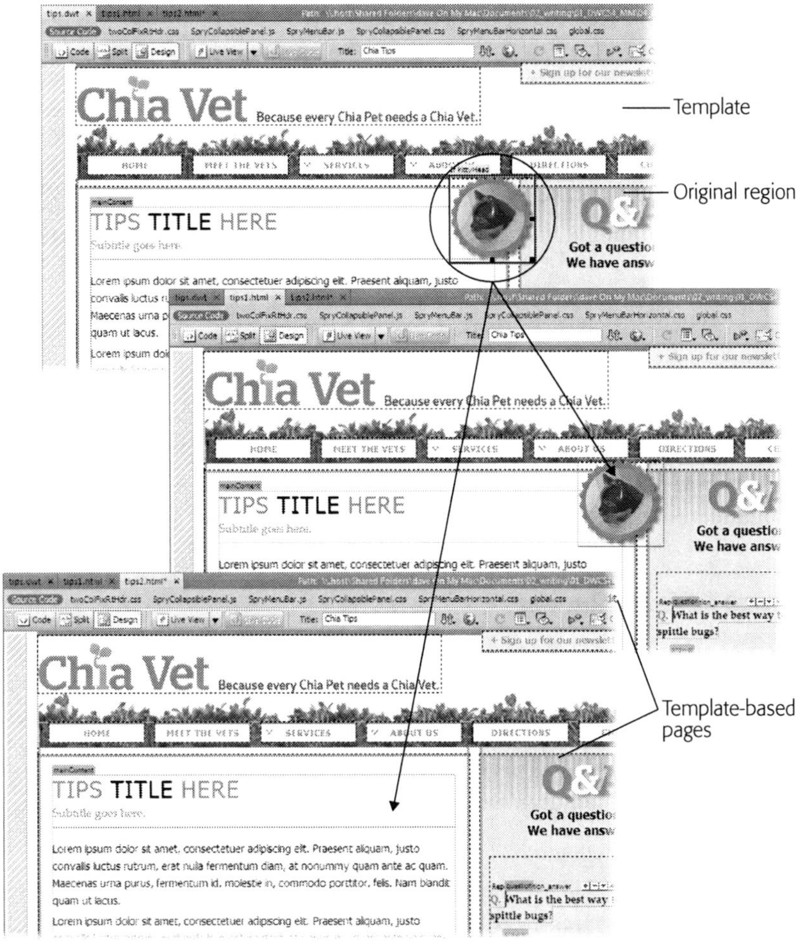

***Figure 19-9:** Now you see it, now you don't. Optional regions let you show or hide content on a page-by-page basis. In these examples, the template page (top) has an optional region containing a "Chia Kitten" icon (circled). When creating a template-based page from this template, you can either display the optional region (middle) or hide it (bottom).*

In the New Optional Region window, type a name (Figure 19-10). Make sure not to use the same name as any other region on the page, and—although Dreamweaver allows it—don't use spaces or other punctuation marks. (Following the rules for naming files as described on page 617 is the best method, and ensures that the optional region works properly.) Click OK to close the window and create the new optional region. Dreamweaver adds a light blue tab with the word "If," followed by the name you gave the region (Figure 19-9).

Locking Optional Regions

An optional region can include editable and repeating regions, *and* locked regions. For example, if you simply want to allow a page editor to turn on or off a graphic ("This item on sale!!!!"), insert the graphic outside an editable region on the page, and then make it an optional region as described above. Since anything not inside an editable region is locked, a page editor can't change the graphic or ruin its formatting—he can only make it visible or hidden.

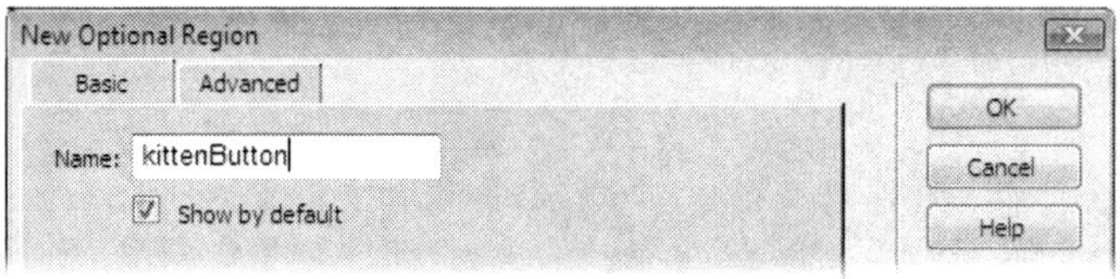

Figure 19-10: *The Optional Regions feature lets you show or hide specific content on template-based pages. Turning on "Show by default" tells Dreamweaver to display the region when a page editor first creates a template-based page. Turn this box on if the optional region needs to show on most pages. You'll save someone the effort of turning the region on each time she creates a new template-based page.*

Repeating Optional Regions

An optional region can also include repeating regions. For example, suppose you create a repeating region (see page 736) that lets a page editor add row after row of links to a list of related articles. You could then turn this repeating region into an optional region, as described above, so that if a particular page had no related articles, the editor could simply hide the entire "related articles" section of the page.

Optional Editable Regions

Dreamweaver's Optional Editable Region command inserts an optional region with an editable region *inside* it. To use it, click in the template at the spot where you'd like to add it, and then choose Insert → Template Objects → Optional Editable Region (alternatively, you can choose this option from the Templates menu on the Common category of the Insert panel). The New Optional Region window appears; give it a name, and then follow the same steps out-lined previously for an optional region.

This technique doesn't offer a lot of control; it's hard to insert HTML *outside* the editable region, for example. So if you want to have an image or table that's optional but *not* editable, it's usually better to just create the editable region as described on page 732 and turn it (and any other HTML you wish to include) into an optional region.

Note: The Optional Editable Region command doesn't let you name the editable region; instead you get a generic name like *EditRegion7*. You can select the editable region and change its name in the Property inspector, but do so *before* you build any pages based on this template (see the Warning on page 735).

Advanced Optional Regions

A basic optional region is a rather simple affair: It either appears or it doesn't. But Dreamweaver offers more complex logic for controlling optional regions. For example, maybe you want several different areas of a page to be either hidden or visible at the same time—perhaps an "On Sale Now!" icon at the top of the page *and* a "Call 1-800-SHIZZLE to order" message at the bottom of the page. When one appears, so does the other.

Because these objects are in different areas of the page, you have to create two separate optional regions. Fortunately, using Dreamweaver's advanced settings for optional regions, you can easily have a single region control the display of one or more additional areas of a page. Here's how to do it:

1. **Create the first optional region using the steps on page 744.**

   Give the region a name using the Basic tab of the New Optional Region window (Figure 19-10).

2. **Select the part of the page—an image, paragraph, or table—that you wish to turn into a second optional region.**

   In this case, you make the display of this region dependent on the optional region added in step 1. If the first region is visible on the page, this second region also shows.

3. **On the Common category of the Insert panel (Figure 19-2), choose the Optional Region item from the Templates menu.**

   The New Optional Region window appears.

4. **Click the Advanced tab.**

   The optional region's advanced options appear (see Figure 19-11). In this case, you want the first optional region you created to control the display of this new region. So instead of giving this region a name, you'll simply select the name of the first optional region in the next step.

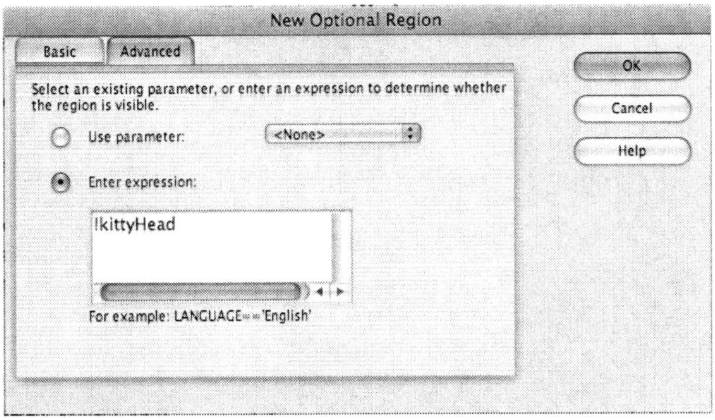

Figure 19-11: *The New Optional Region box lets you more precisely control the display of an optional region. You can make the region appear only when another region is visible, or use Dreamweaver's template expression language to create a more complex behavior. In this case, the selected region appears only when another region—named "kittyHead"—is not visible (the ! is a programming equivalent of "is not").*

5. **Click the "Use parameter" button and select the name of the first optional region from the menu.**

   This step is what makes the first optional region control this region. If a page editor displays the first region, this second region also appears.

6. **Click OK to close the window and create the new optional region.**

   You can continue adding optional regions in this way, using the Advanced tab and selecting the name of the first optional region from the menu. This way, a single region can control the display of many other areas of the page.

Even fancier tricks

You can use these advanced controls for even more elaborate Web page stunts. For example, say your site is composed of several sections. When a visitor is in one section of the site, its navigation button is attractively highlighted and a secondary navigation bar miraculously appears, offering links to other pages in that section.

Using a template, you can add an optional region containing the highlighted section button. When you add the secondary navigation bar to the page, you make *it* an optional region controlled by the highlighted navigation button. Then, when you add a page to that section of the site, you simply show the optional region containing the highlighted button, causing the secondary navigation bar to appear as well (see Figure 19-12 for a look at how this works).

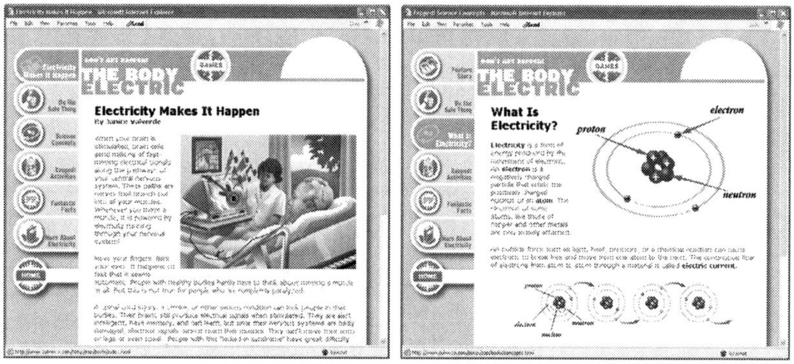

Figure 19-12: *An optional region on the page at left highlights the top navigation button (Electricity Makes It Happen). By turning on a different optional region (right), the navigation system can highlight the site's current section–"What is Electricity?" (the third button from the top).*

Controlling regions with expressions

You can program even more complex behaviors using a basic *expression language*, loosely based on JavaScript, that Dreamweaver understands. For example, instead of having an optional region appear when another optional region is visible (as in the previous example), suppose you want to have a region appear when another region is invisible. This arrangement can come in handy when you're creating a navigation bar. When a page is in a particular section, for instance, the navigation button for that section is highlighted, but the button isn't highlighted if the page is in another section.

In other words, you can build a single template for all the sections of a site, but control the appearance of the navigation bar separately for pages in each individual section (see Figure 19-12).

Here's how you'd control the navigation bar:

1. **Click the page where you wish to insert the navigation buttons.**
2. **Insert the highlighted ("You are in this section") navigation button.**

   This button could be a rollover image (see page 248), or just a single graphic. If you have multiple pages in the section, you probably also want to link this graphic to the main page for that section.
3. **Click next to the highlighted button and insert the plain ("You can go here") navigation button.**

   The button could also be a rollover image with a link to the main page for this section (for example, the main Products page).
4. **In the Property inspector, select the highlighted navigation button and link (if it has one).**

   This button appears on any template-based page for this section.
5. **On the Common category of the Insert panel (Figure 19-2), choose Optional Region from the Template menu.**

   The New Optional Region window appears. Make sure the Basic tab is selected.
6. **Type the name of the section into the Name field. Click OK.**

   For example, if this section of your site advertises your company's products, you can call it *products*. Don't use any spaces or punctuation other than hyphens (–) or underscores (_) for the name. Also make sure the "Show by default" box is *not* turned on. Since you'll be building template-based pages for all the sections of your site, most pages you build will be in other sections of the site. Your work goes faster if this highlighted button starts out hidden. In the next steps, you'll make the plain navigation button appear by default.
7. **Use the Property inspector to select the plain button and link, and then click the Optional Region button on the Insert bar.**

   The New Optional Region window appears again, but this time you'll use the advanced options.
8. **Click the Advanced tab; select "Enter expression" (Figure 19-11).**

   You're going to type an *expression* in the Expression field. An expression is a programming statement that's either true or false. (For an obvious example, 2 is always equal to 2, but it's obviously false to say, "2 is equal to 4." In programming, you express equality using a pair of = signs. So 2==2 is true, but 2==4 is false.) The important thing to remember here is that when an expression is true, the optional region is visible; when it's false, it's hidden.

9. **Type an exclamation point (!) followed by the name you entered in step 6—*!products*, for example.**

   Dreamweaver's template expression language is based on the JavaScript programming language. An exclamation mark means "not," so this code means *not products.* Translation into non-propeller-head language: when the *products* region (remember, that's the highlighted button) is *not* displayed, this region (button) appears on the page.

   The logic gets a little complicated, but have faith. When you add a new page based on this template, the optional region you added in step 6 is *not* visible (because you turned off the "Show by default" box). In other words, because the region—products in this example—is *not* showing, this region, the one with the plain navigation button, by default appears on the page. Turning the *products* region on, *hides* the plain navigation button. In other words, the first optional region works like a light switch, alternately turning on one or the other navigation button.

10. **Click OK to close the window and add the additional optional region.**

    Repeat this process for each button in the navigation bar. Now your template is perfectly suited for displaying customized navigation bars for each section of your site. When you create a new template-based page, simply turn on the region for the particular section in which the page is located. (Hiding and showing optional regions is described on page 758.)

As you can see, optional regions are very powerful—and potentially confusing. But using even basic optional regions, you can exert a great deal of control over your template-based pages. For more information on template expressions and optional regions, take a look in Dreamweaver's Help system. (Choose Help → Dreamweaver Help to open a Web browser and load the online Adobe Help system; then, in the search box, type *template expressions*, and then hit Enter (Return). You'll then get a page that lists several articles related to templates and template expressions [as well as a few articles completely unrelated to the topic!].)

Editing and Removing Optional Regions

After inserting an optional region, you can always return to the New Optional Region dialog box to change the region's name, alter its default settings, or use advanced options. To edit an optional region, first select it using one of these techniques:

- Click the region's blue tab in the document window (Figure 19-9).
- Click anywhere inside the optional region in the document window; click the <mmtemplate:if> tag in the Tag selector (see page 24 for details on the Tag selector).

When you select an optional region, an Edit button appears in the Property inspector. Click it to reopen the New Optional Region window. You can then change the region's properties.

To remove an optional region, select it using one of the techniques listed previously and choose Modify → Templates → Remove Template Markup. Dreamweaver removes most of the code associated with the optional region (but see the box "Understanding Template Parameters" on page 751).

POWER USERS' CLINIC

Understanding Template Parameters

When you insert an optional region, Dreamweaver adds special code to the head of the Web page. Called a *template parameter*, this code is responsible for showing or hiding an optional region.

In fact, Dreamweaver uses parameters when you make a tag attribute editable, too. A typical parameter for an optional region might look like this:

```
<!-- TemplateParam name="SaleBug"
type="boolean" value="true" -->
```

The <!--and --> are HTML comments that hide this code from a Web browser. TemplateParam tells Dreamweaver that the comment is actually part of the program's Template features—specifically, a template parameter.

A parameter is composed of three parts: name, type, and value. The name is the name you gave the editable region. The type—Boolean—indicates that the value of this parameter can be only one of two options: true or false. In this example, the value is "true," which simply means that the optional region called SaleBug is visible. (Don't worry; you don't have to actually edit this code by hand to turn optional regions on and off, as you'll see on page 758.)

In programming jargon, a template parameter is known as a *variable*. In simpler terms, it's just a way to store information that can vary. Dreamweaver reacts differently depending on this value: show the region if the parameter's true, or hide it if the parameter's false.

Editable tag attributes also use parameters to store the values you enter for the tag attribute. For example:

```
<!-- TemplateParam name="PageColor"
type="color" value="#FFFFFF" -->
```

On template-based pages, you can change the value of a parameter used for an editable tag attribute to change that tag's property (see page 757).

Unfortunately, when you delete an optional region from a template, or remove the ability to edit a tag attribute, Dreamweaver always leaves these parameter tags hanging around in the head of the template document. Keeping in mind that Dreamweaver adds these parameter tags directly before the closing </head> tag, you can find and remove unused parameter tags in Code view (see Chapter 10).

Nested Templates

Large sites may have many different sections or types of pages. Each section of the site or type of page may have its own unique look. A Frequently Asked Questions page may have distinct areas for a question, an answer, and links to further resources, while a product page may have a picture, a product description, and ordering information. You could create different templates for each type of page, but even that may be more work than necessary.

Note: Nested templates is a somewhat advanced and potentially confusing topic. Many people happily use Dreamweaver templates without ever using the nested template feature.

While many pages in a site may have subtle differences, they usually share very basic design features. The overall structure of every page, for example, may be the same: same logo, banner, and navigation bar. Even the basic layout may be the same. And there lies the problem with creating individual templates for each section: if you need to make a very basic sitewide change, like adding a new button to the site's overall navigation system or altering the banner, you need to edit *each* template individually, adding extra time, effort, and risk of making a mistake.

Good news—Dreamweaver offers a tool to solve just this problem: nested templates. A *nested template* is a template you make from another template, which then becomes the *master* template (see Figure 19-13).

Imagine a basic software company Web site with three sections: Support, Our Products, and Downloads. Each section has its own kind of information and specific layout needs. However, all three sections share the same banner and navigation.

To create a template system for this site, you must first create a very basic template that includes elements (including editable regions) shared by all pages—the master template. You can then create a nested template based on the master. On the nested templates, you can add further design refinements and additional editable regions for the areas that can be changed on pages created from the nested template.

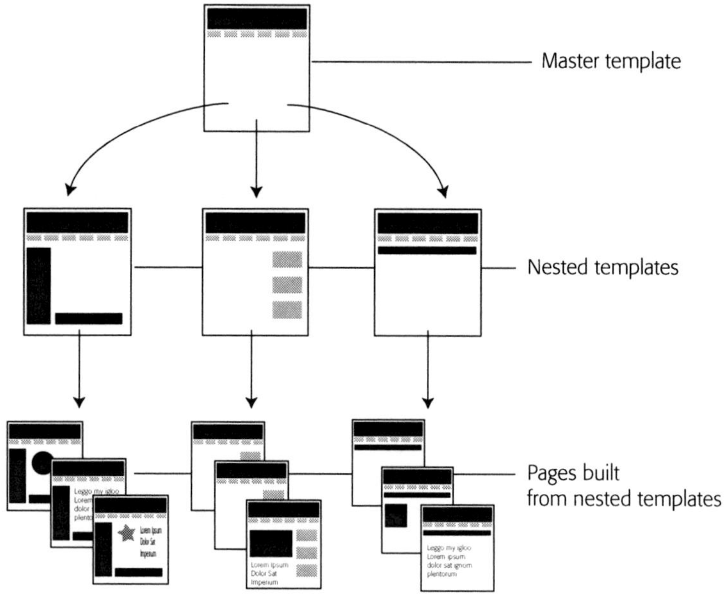

Figure 19-13: *Nested templates (middle row) let you build templates that share common sitewide design elements while providing precise control for particular types of pages or sections of a Web site. A page built from a nested template (bottom row) contains both elements from a master template (top row)–like a banner and a sitewide navigation bar–in addition to elements specific to its nested template–like a section-specific secondary navigation bar. Changes you make to the master template are passed on to all pages of the site, including nested templates. Changes to a nested template, by contrast, pass on only to pages based on the nested template.*

Yes, this process sounds complex—and yes, it is. But when the alternative is hours or days of manual template updating, you can see why serious Web designers are willing to spend the time to master any shortcut they can get.

To create a nested template:

1. **Build a template as described on page 765.**

   This page acts as the master template and controls all nested templates. It should include the basic elements shared by all nested template pages, like your logo and email links. Now is also the time to add editable regions in the areas the nested templates can change, like table cells to hold blocks of text and images.

2. **Name and save this template (File → "Save as Template"), and then close it.**

   Your template is safe on the hard drive.

3. **Choose File → New.**

   The window for creating new documents and template-based pages opens (see Figure 19-14).

4. **On the left side of the New Document window, click the "Page from Template" button. In the Site list, select the Web site on which you're working.**

   You can open templates from any site you've defined in Dreamweaver, but this idea generally isn't a good one, as Figure 19-14 explains.

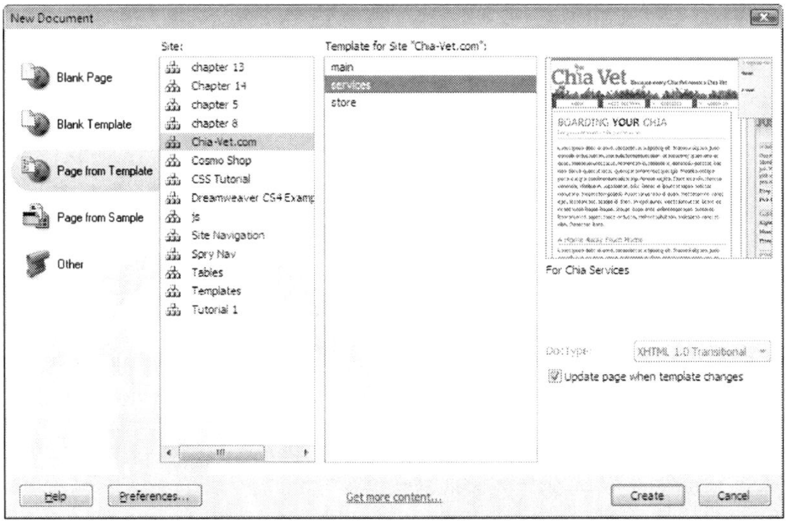

***Figure 19-14:** You can use the "Site" list to choose another site you've defined and reveal the list of templates it uses. However, choosing a template stored in a different site isn't a good idea. Dreamweaver doesn't copy any images on the template to the current site and can't translate relative links correctly. The result is broken links aplenty.*

5. **From the list of templates, select the name of the master template file you created in step 1.**

   Make sure the "Update page when template changes" box is turned on. Otherwise, the nested template doesn't update when you edit the master template.

6. **Click OK.fs**

   Dreamweaver creates a new template-based page. At this point, it's simply a basic Web page based on the original template. Next, you'll turn it into a *nested template*.

7. **Choose File → "Save as Template." Or, on the Common category of the Insert panel (Figure 19-2), select Make Nested Template from the Templates menu.**

   The Save As Template window appears (see Figure 19-3).

8. **Type a name for the template and click the Save button.**

   Voilà! A nested template.

Customizing Nested Templates

When you first create a nested template, there's no difference between it and the master template. They share the same design, content, and template regions.

The next step is adding the design elements that are specific to pages built from that template. For example, you can add a special type of table for displaying a product photo, description, price, and other information. This table appears only in pages built from this nested template, not from the master template or any other nested template.

There are a few things you should keep in mind when planning your template development strategy:

- When creating pages from templates, you can add content only to an editable region. That's true not only for template-based pages, but for nested templates, too. If the master template has *no* editable regions, you won't be able to change anything on the nested template created from it.
- When working on a nested template, you can insert an editable region only into an editable region supplied by the master template. For example, say you've created a master template to provide a consistent banner and navigation bar to the site, all in a locked region of the master template. Then you add a large empty area at the bottom of the page and turn it into an editable region that you can customize to make specific layouts for each nested template. After creating a nested template from the master template, you can then add new editable regions to this open area. In fact, you can add any template region—repeating, optional, or editable—to this area.
- If, when working on a nested template, you insert a template region (editable, optional, or repeating) into an editable region supplied by the master template,

pages based on the nested template can modify *only* those new regions. The rest of the editable region supplied by the master template isn't editable on the pages based on the nested template.

Using the example in the previous paragraph, let's say you next add a repeating table to your nested template (see page 738 for more detail about repeating tables). When you create a page based on this nested template, you can change *only* the editable areas marked out in the repeating table. Of course, the other side of the coin is that if you add an editable region to the master template and then refrain from adding any particular template regions, all the HTML inside that region is editable in the nested template *and* in all pages based on the nested template.

Using Nested Templates

Here's an example of how you can use nested templates. Suppose you want to create a uniform design for your site where every page of the site has a logo as well as a sitewide navigation bar. Each page within one section of the site also has a sidebar containing a *secondary* navigation bar with navigation buttons for just that section. Finally, every page has a large content area to hold the information specific to that page.

Using nested templates, creating a Web site like this couldn't be easier. Create a master template containing the site banner and navigation bar. This template also includes editable regions for the sidebar and main content area.

Next, create a nested template for one *section* of the site, leaving the content area as it is. Since each page has its own content in this area, you don't need to do anything to this region. Then add the secondary navigation bar to the sidebar area. To lock this region so no one can tinker with the sidebar (in pages built from the nested template), add an empty editable region, or see the Tip on the next page. If you want, you can build similar nested templates for the other sections of the site.

Now you're ready to start building the pages of your site. Create a new page based on one of the section templates. Add text or graphics to the editable content area of the page. Should you need to change the site logo or add a button to the sitewide navigation bar, open the master template, make the changes, save the file, and let Dreamweaver update all the pages of your site with the new look. If you simply need to change the secondary navigation for one section of the site, then open the appropriate nested template, change the sidebar, save the template, and let Dreamweaver update all the section pages.

Tip: You can lock an editable region passed from a master template to a nested template, so that pages based on the nested template can't be changed in this region. In the nested template, go into Code view, and then locate the beginning of the editable region, which looks something like, <!--InstanceBeginEditable name="regionName" -->. Then insert the text @@("")@@ directly after the -->.

If you find yourself typing this code often, think about creating a snippet (see page 707) containing the text @@("")@@.

Building Pages Based on a Template

Building a template is only a prelude to the actual work of building your site. Once you finish your template, it's time to produce pages.

To create a new document based on a template, choose File → New to open the New Document window (see Figure 19-14). Click the "Page from Template" button, and then, from the Site list, select the current site you're working on. All templates for the selected site appear in the right column. Select the template you wish to use, and then click Create.

Tip: If you don't want your new Web page linked to the template (so that future changes to the template also affect the Web page), turn off the "Update page when template changes" checkbox. The result is a new page that looks just like the template, but has no locked regions; you can edit the entire page. This method is useful, for example, when you want to start with the general design and structure of a certain template when creating a brand-new design for another template. (Be aware that Dreamweaver remembers this choice the next time you create a new template-based page. In other words, future pages you create from a template will *also* be unlinked–unless you remember to turn the "Update page" box back on.)

A new Web page document opens, based on the template, bearing a tab in the upper-right corner that identifies the underlying template name. Dreamweaver outlines any editable regions in blue; a small blue tab displays each region's name (Figure 19-5).

Dreamweaver makes it obvious which areas you aren't allowed to edit; your cursor changes to a "forbidden" symbol (a circle with a line through it) when it ventures into a locked area.

To add content to an editable region, click anywhere inside the editable region. You can type inside it, add graphics, or add any other objects or HTML you can normally add to a document. You can also change the document's title and add a Spry Menu bar (Chapter 5), Spry widgets (Chapter 12), Behaviors (Chapter 13), Cascading Style Sheets (see Chapter 4), and meta tag information (items that go in the <head> of an HTML document).

Working with Repeating Regions

Repeating regions work a bit differently than editable regions. In most cases, a repeating region includes one or more editable regions (which you can edit using the instructions above). However, Dreamweaver provides special controls to let you add, remove, and rearrange repeating entries (see Figure 19-15).

These regions are intended to let a page editor add repeated page elements—like rows of product information in a list of products. To add a repeating entry, click the + button that appears to the right of the Repeat region's blue tab. You can then edit any editable regions within the entry. Click inside an editable region inside a repeating entry and click + again to add a new entry *after* it.

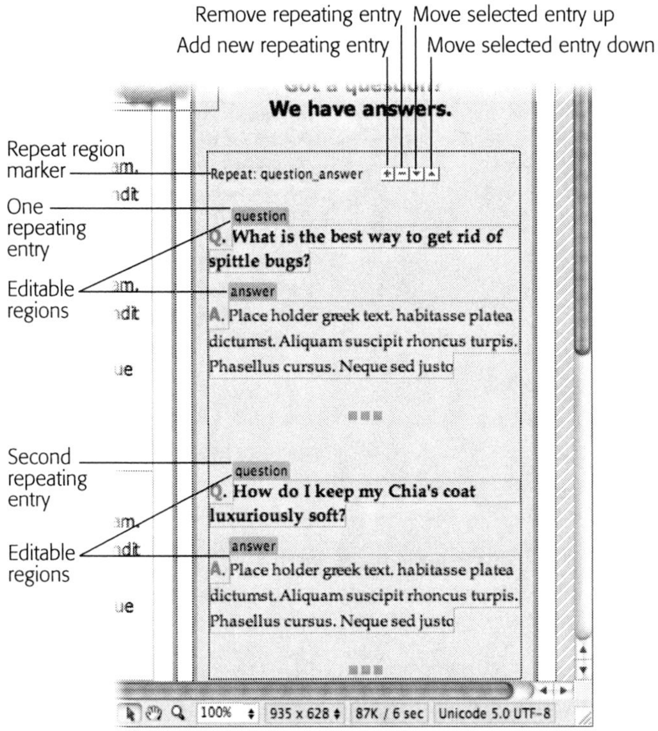

Figure 19-15: *Repeating regions are a great way to quickly add lists to your Web pages. On the page displayed here, repeating regions make it easy to add sets of questions and answers. Each repeating entry has two editable regions–labeled question and answer. Clicking the + button adds an additional question/ answer pair.*

Deleting a repeating entry is just as easy. Click inside an editable region within the entry you wish to delete and click the – sign button.

Tip: You can create repeating regions that don't have any editable regions–for example, repeating a star several times to indicate the rating for a product. Although you can use the + button to repeat such regions, you can't delete those regions with the minus sign (–) button. In other words, you're stuck with any extras you've added. The only workaround is to add an editable region to the repeating region. Then Dreamweaver lets you remove any repeating regions you wish.

To rearrange entries in the list, click inside an entry's editable region. Click the up or down arrows to move the entry up or down in the list (to alphabetize it, for example).

Changing Properties of Editable Tag Attributes

Unlike editable or repeating regions, an editable tag attribute isn't immediately apparent on template-based pages. There's no blue tab to represent it, as there are for editable regions; in fact, nothing appears in Design view to indicate that there are *any* editable *tag* properties on the page. The only way to find out is to choose Modify → Template Properties to open the Template Properties dialog box (see Figure 19-16).

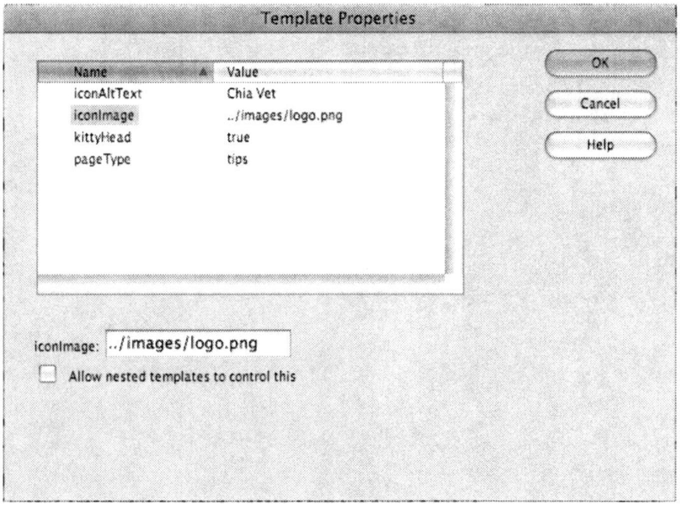

Figure 19-16: *The Template Properties window lets you control editable tag attributes and other parameters for optional regions. Depending on which parameter you select, the options at the bottom of the window change. In this case, the src property of an image tag has been made editable. You can click Dreamweaver's familiar "Browse for File" button to change the image tag's src property by selecting a new graphic file to display on the page.*

All editable tag attributes for this page appear in this window. In addition, all parameters defined for this page, including optional regions, appear here, as discussed in the box on page 751.

To change the value of a template property—in other words, to edit the property of an editable tag—select its name from the list and fill out the option that appears at the bottom of the window. For example, in the case of color properties, use the color box to pick a Web-compatible color. If the property is a path (like a link or an image's *src* property indicating the graphic file's location in the site), click the "select a file" folder icon to browse to select the file.

Once you've finished setting the editable properties for the page, click OK to close the window.

Hiding and Showing Optional Regions

As with Editable Tag Attributes, you use the Template Properties window to control the display of optional regions. On template-based pages, you can show or hide an optional region by choosing Modify → Template Properties to open this dialog box (see Figure 19-17). Next, select the name of the optional region. To make all page elements in the region appear, turn on the "Show" checkbox at the bottom of the window. To hide the optional region, turn off this box.

Applying Templates to Existing Pages

What happens if you create a Web page, and *then* decide you want it to share the look of a template? No problem. Dreamweaver lets you apply a template to any Web page in your site. You can even swap one template for another by applying a template to a page that's already based on a different template

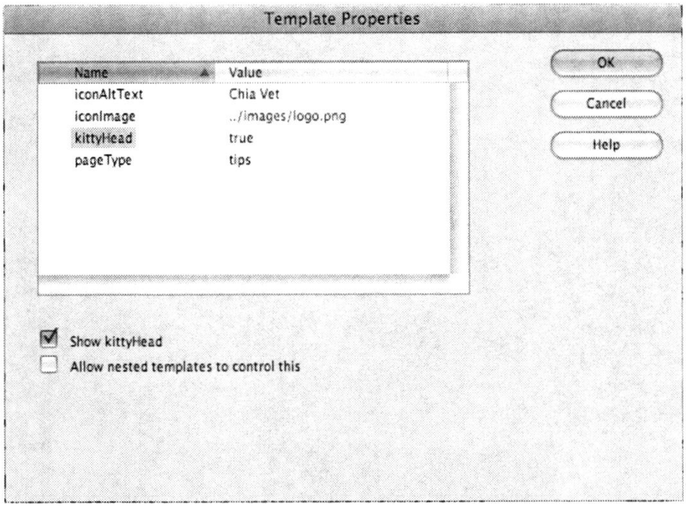

Figure 19-17: *The Template properties window displays optional regions as well as editable tag attributes. A Template property for an optional region–in this example, "kittyHead"–has a value of either true or false. True lets people see the contents of the region on the page, while false hides the region. (The "Allow nested templates to control this" option is described in the box "Controlling the Nest".)*

To apply a template to a page you've already created:

1. **Choose File → Open to open the page you want to alter.**

   The Web page opens.

2. **Choose Window → Assets. Click the Assets panel's Templates button (see Figure 19-4).**

   The Assets panel appears and reveals a list of the site's templates.

Tip: You can also apply a template to a page by choosing Modify → Templates → "Apply Template to Page." Select the name of the template from the window that appears and skip to step 5.

3. **Click a template in the list on the Assets panel, and then click Apply.**

   The Inconsistent Region Names dialog box opens (Figure 19-18).

4. **In the list under "Editable regions," choose "Document body."**

   To the right, in the Resolved column, you see <Not resolved>. This is Dreamweaver's way of saying it doesn't know what to do with the contents of the current page. You need to pick one of the template's editable regions.

5. **From the "Move content to new region" menu, select an editable region.**

   If you want to keep the material, select the name of an editable region in which to place it from the list; otherwise, choose Nowhere, which, in effect, creates a new blank page based on the template.

FREQUENTLY ASKED QUESTION

Controlling the Nest

The Template Properties dialog box includes a checkbox labeled "Allow nested templates to control this." *What does it do?*

Imagine that you create a template and add several optional regions and editable tag attributes to it. You then use this template as a basic design for more refined templates for each section of your site using the nested template feature described on page 751. When you create one of these nested templates based on the master template, it has access to the Template Properties window, where page authors can modify any of the *template* properties created by the original, master template.

For example, to better identify each section of a site, you might assign a different class style to the <body> tag of a section's pages. The class might apply a different background color to each page within a section: blue for the products section, orange for the support section, and so on. In the master template, you make the <body> tag's *class* property editable. Now, when you create a nested template for the products section, you simply open the Template Properties dialog box, and then assign a class style with a blue page background. For the support section's nested template, apply a class that sets the background to orange. Now, when you create a template-based page for the support section, its background is orange, while a page for the products section has a blue background.

However, to let your site's color palette go really wild, you may want every page in the site to have its own unique background color, each defined by a different class style. In this case, you'd want to let every page based on a nested template have an editable *class* property.

To do so, open the nested template, open the Template Properties window, select the property that should be editable in pages built from this template (*color* in this case), and turn on the "Allow nested templates to control this" checkbox. Now this property is uneditable in the nested template, but editable in all pages created from it.

You've probably realized by now that the phrase "Allow nested templates to control this" doesn't make much sense. Turning it on actually *prevents* the nested template from controlling the property. A better way to think of it is "Allow pages created from this nested template to control this property."

The bottom line: Turning on this box makes the attribute uneditable on that page. If it's a nested template, it lets the template property "pass through" to all pages based on this template. In other words, you can't set the background color in the template, but page editors can change it in pages created from the template.

Unfortunately, you can only select a single editable region. If the original has several content regions, then Dreamweaver pushes them all into a single editable region.

6. **If "Document head" also appears in the window, select it and choose "head" from the "Move content to new region" menu.**

   This step preserves any special information you added to the head of your page, like Cascading Style Sheets, meta tags, custom JavaScript programs, and other information that goes in the <head> of the document. Unfortunately, the title of your original page is always replaced with the default title of the template. You have to reenter the title (see page 47) after you apply the template.

7. **Click OK.**

   Your new page appears.

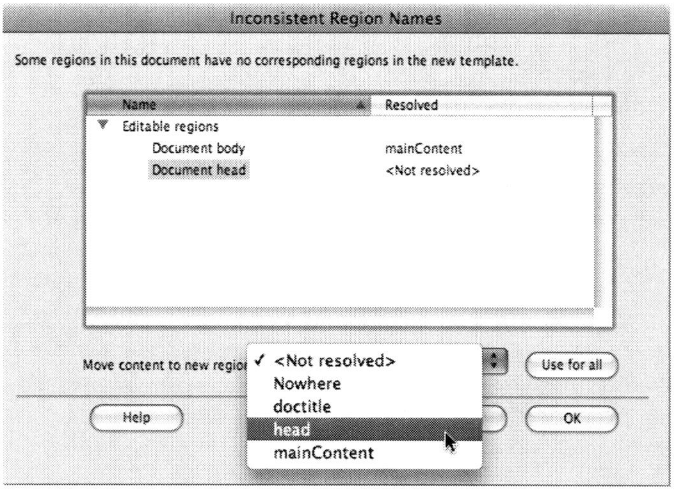

Figure 19-18: *When you apply a template to a page you've already created, you must tell Dreamweaver what to do with the material that's already on the page. Tell it what to do by selecting one of the template's editable regions from a pop-up menu, which takes charge of all editable regions in your page.*

Updating a Template

Templates aren't just useful for building pages rapidly; they also make quick work of site updates. Pages created from templates maintain a link to the original template file; you can automatically pass changes to a template along to every page built from it. If you used templates to build your site, you probably won't cry on your keyboard when the boss asks you to add an additional button and link to the navigation bar. Instead of editing every page, you can simply open the template file, update the navigation bar, and let Dreamweaver apply the update to all the pages.

You update a template (and all the pages based on it) like this:

1. **Choose Window → Assets.**

   The Assets panel appears.

2. **Click the Templates button (see Figure 19-4).**

   A list of the site's templates appears.

3. **Double-click the template's name to open it.**

   Alternatively, you can select the template in the Assets panel, and then click the Edit button to open the original template (.dwt) file (see Figure 19-4). The template opens.

Tip: You can also open a template by double-clicking the appropriate template (.dwt) file located in the Templates folder in the Files panel.

---

4. **Edit the template as you would any Web page.**

   Since this is the original template file, you can edit any of the HTML in the document, including Cascading Style Sheets, meta tags, and layers. You can also add or remove editable regions (see page 735).

   Take care, however, to edit *only* the areas that you did *not* mark as editable regions. The reason: When you update your pages, any region marked as editable in a template file isn't passed on to pages based on that template. After all, the template is supposed to dictate only the design of those pages' *non*-editable regions.

Note: Be careful when you remove editable regions from a template. If you've already built some pages based on the template, Dreamweaver warns you when you save the template. As described below, you can either *delete* the content that was added to that region in each of the pages you created, or move it to another editable region in the page.

5. **Choose File → Save.**

   If you've already created pages based on this template, Dreamweaver opens the Update Template Files dialog box. It lists all the files that use the template.

6. **Click Update to update all files based on the template.**

   Dreamweaver automatically applies the changes you made to the pages based on the template. Then, the Update Pages dialog box opens. If you want to see a list of all files Dreamweaver changed while updating your site, turn on the "Show log" box.

   On a large site, this automatic update feature can be an incredible time-saver, but you may *not* want to click Update, at least not right now. Perhaps you're just saving some of your hard work on the template but aren't quite finished perfecting it—why waste your time updating all those pages more than once? In such a scenario, click the Don't Update button. Remember, you can always update the pages later (see the box "Wait to Update" on page 763).

7. **Click Close.**

   The Update Pages dialog box closes.

Remember that you need to update all your files even if you make a simple change to the template, like changing its name.

Updating Nested Templates

When you build a Web site using nested templates, you have multiple templates affecting your pages. The master template controls design elements of a nested template, which in turn controls pages based on the nested template. (You can even make nested templates *out of* nested templates, but for sanity's sake, you'd better not.) With this level of complexity, updates to nested templates can get confusing fast.

In a nutshell, here's how it works:

- If you edit a locked region in a master template and then update your site, not only does a nested template update, but so do all pages built from it.
- If you edit a locked region in a nested template and then update, those changes pass on only to pages built from that nested template.

However, changes you make to an *editable* region of a master template don't pass on to any page. Neither do changes you make in editable regions of a nested template.

Note: Sometimes after making changes to a master template, Dreamweaver doesn't update pages based on nested templates. To safely verify that all template updates are correct, recreate the Site Cache (Site → Advanced → Recreate Site Cache), choose Modify → Templates → Update Pages, and then select the "Entire Site" option.

POWER USERS' CLINIC

Wait to Update

Whenever you modify and save a Library item or a template, Dreamweaver gives you the option of updating any pages in the site that are descended from it. Very often, you'll say Yes.

But there are times when you want to wait to update the site. If you're making a lot of changes to multiple Library items or templates, you may wish to wait until you've finished all your edits before letting the changes ripple through your pages. After all, it can take some time to update large sites with lots of pages.

Dreamweaver lets you update pages that use Library items and templates at any time. Just choose Modify → Library → Update Pages, or Modify → Templates → Update Pages.

Both menu options open the same window, the Update Pages dialog box.

At this point, you can update pages that use a specific Library item or template by going to the "Look in" menu, choosing "Files that Use," and then selecting the appropriate name from the pop-up menu. If you would like to update all pages in the site, choose Entire Site, and then, from the pop-up menu, select the name of the local site. Turn on both the "Library items" and Templates checkboxes to update all pages.

To see the results of Dreamweaver's work, check the "Show log" box. This box presents a list of all the updated files.

Unlinking a Page from a Template

If you're confident that you won't be making any further changes to a page's template, and you'd like to be able to edit the page's locked regions, you can break the link between a page and its template by choosing Modify → Templates → "Detach from Template".

All the HTML in the page is now editable, just as on a regular Web page—which is what it is now. You've removed all references to the original template, so changes to the template no longer have any effect on this page.

Note: If you unlink a nested template from its master template, Dreamweaver removes only the code provided by the original master template. Any editable regions you added to the nested template remain.

Exporting a Template-Based Site

The good news about Dreamweaver's sophisticated templating features is that they let you build complex Web pages that are easy to create and update. The not so good news is that some behind-the-scenes code is necessary to achieve this ease of use. Dreamweaver's template features rely on HTML comment tags to identify editable, optional, and repeating regions, as well as nested template and editable tag attributes (see the box on page 737).

Although this code is only for Dreamweaver's use and has no effect on how a Web browser displays the page, it does add a small amount to the size of your Web pages. That's probably why Dreamweaver includes a feature that lets you export an entire site into a new folder on your computer *without* any template markup code. The following steps show you how.

Note: While it's certainly possible to perform this file-slimming procedure, truth be told, it's not really necessary—the code Dreamweaver adds is minimal, so it won't have much affect on the download speed of your site.

1. **Choose Modify → Templates → Export Without Markup.**

   Dreamweaver uses the currently active site, so make sure you've got the site you wish to export selected in the Files panel. The Export Site Without Template Markup window appears (see Figure 19-19).

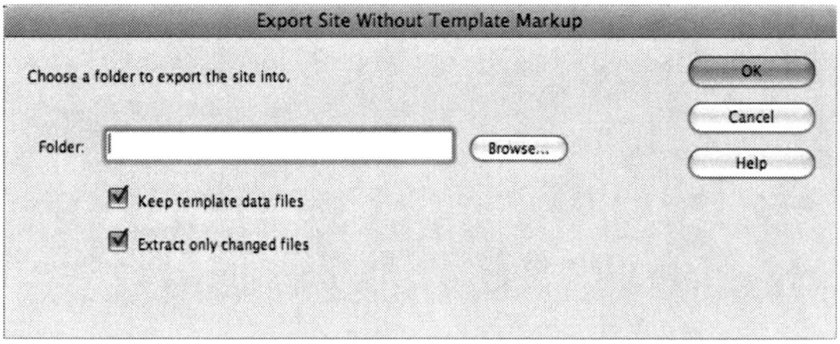

***Figure 19-19:** Dreamweaver lets you strip out template code from template-based pages with the Export Site Without Template Markup command.*

2. **Click the Browse button, and then select a folder for the exported site.**

   Select a folder *other* than the current local site folder. You always want to keep the original files in the local folder, since they're the ones that keep the template markup, making future updates possible.

3. **Turn on the export options you want.**

   The Export window includes two options. The first, "Keep template data files," creates an XML file for each template-based page. In other words, when you export the site, there's one HTML page (without any special template code) and an XML file (which includes all the template code as well as the page content).

Theoretically, you could then go back and choose the File → Import → "XML into Template" to recreate the page, complete with the original template information. However, in practice, you probably won't. For one thing, this process creates lots of additional files that you wouldn't want to move to the Web site. Also, when you want to work on the site to update and edit it, you should use the original files in the site's local folder anyway, since they still have the useful template code in them.

The "Extract only changed files" option speeds up the process of exporting a large template-based site. This option forces Dreamweaver to export only pages that you've changed since the last export. Unfortunately, it doesn't tell you *which* files it exported until after the fact. So, to make sure you get those newly exported files to the Web server, you need to keep track of changes by hand.

4. **Click OK to export the site.**

   Dreamweaver goes through each page of the site, stripping out template code and exporting it to the folder you specified.

You can use Dreamweaver's FTP feature to do the uploading (see page 678), but you need to create a new site and define the folder with the *exported* files as a local root folder. Whenever you need to add or update template-based pages, use the original site files, and then export the changed files. You can then switch to the site containing the exported files and transfer the new or updated files to the Web server.

Template Tutorial

In this tutorial, you'll create a template for the Chia Vet Web site. Then you'll build a page based on that template and enjoy an easy sitewide update courtesy of Dreamweaver's templates feature.

Note: You'll need to download the tutorial files from *http://www.sawmac.com/dwcs4/* to complete this tutorial. See the note on page 48 for more details.

Once you've downloaded the tutorial files and opened Dreamweaver, define a new site as described on page 42: Name the site *Templates*, and then select the Chapter19 folder (inside the MM_DWCS4 folder). (In a nutshell: Choose Site → New Site. In the Site Definition window, click the Advanced tab, type *Templates* into the Site Name field, click the folder icon next to the Local Root Folder field, navigate to and select the Chapter19 folder, and then click Choose or Select. Finally, click OK.)

Creating a Template

1. **Open the Files panel by pressing the F8 key (Shift-⌘-F).**

   Of course, if it was already open, you just closed it. Press F8 (Shift-⌘-F) again.

2. **In the Files panel, find and double-click the page *tips.html*.**

It's usually easier to start with an existing Web page, and then save it as a template. For the purpose of getting to bed before midnight tonight, pretend that you've just designed this beautiful Web page.

3. **Choose File → Save As Template.**

   The Save As Template dialog box opens.

4. **In the description field, type *Use for Chia tips.***

   This description appears in the New Template window when you create a page based on this template.

5. **Name the template *Tips;* click Save. In the Update Links window, click Yes.**

   Behind the scenes, Dreamweaver creates a new folder—Templates—in the site's root folder, and saves the file as Tips.dwt inside it. A new template is born. You can see it in the Templates page of the Assets panel, as well as the new Template folder in the Files panel.

   The template is a model for other pages. But although they'll be *based* on its design, they won't be identical. The next step is to identify those areas of the design that'll change from page to page—the editable regions.

Note: Templates don't always immediately show up in the Templates category of the Assets panel. Sometimes you need to click the Refresh Site List button (the circular arrow in the bottom right of the Assets panel) to see a newly added template.

6. **Drag from the "T" in the heading "Tips Title" down and just to the right of the "e" for "here" in Subtitle.**

   You've just selected the title and subtitle for the page. As people add new tips to the Chia Vet site, you'll certainly want them to add specific titles for each tip, so these two paragraphs should be editable.

7. **Choose Insert → Template Objects → Editable Region.**

   The New Editable Region dialog box appears. Here, as in the following steps, you can also, from the Insert panel's Common category, go to the Templates menu and choose the Editable Region option (Figure 19-2), or just press Ctrl+Alt+V (⌘-Option-V).

8. **Type *Title*; click OK.**

   A small blue tab, labeled *Title*, appears above the headline. You've just added one editable region—the most basic type of template region. You'll make the main text area editable as well.

9. **Drag from the "L" in "Lorem ipsum" in the first paragraph, and drag down until you've selected the two paragraphs of text. Repeat steps 7 and 8; name the region *Text.***

Another small blue tab, labeled *Text*, appears above the paragraphs. You might be wondering why you did this in two chunks? Why not, select the title, subtitle, and paragraphs all in one fell swoop and turn them into a single editable region? Because of the "Related Tips" box. That's a bit of HTML that appears *between* the subtitle and the first paragraph of text. If you'd created just a single editable region, that tips box would also be editable (since its HTML would also have been selected).

However, you've got bigger plans for that box. It's intended to list other Web pages with related information. However, what if there is no related tips for the particular page? In that case, the box shouldn't appear at all—a perfect case for an optional region.

10. **Click anywhere inside the "Related Tips" box (inside the bulleted list for example) and choose Edit → Select All, twice.**

    The first time you choose Edit → Select All (Ctrl-A, or ⌘-A works too), you select the contents of the box; the second time you invoke Select All you grab the <div> tag that creates that box.

    You'll turn this div into an optional region so that it can be hidden on most pages, but displayed when there are related Web pages to link to.

11. **Choose Insert → Template Objects → Optional Region.**

    The New Optional Region window appears. (Again, this same option is available in the Common category of the Insert Panel [Figure 19-2].)

12. **Type *relatedTips* in the name field, turn off the "Show by Default" checkbox, and then click OK.**

    At first, when creating a template-based page, this box won't be visible. When building a page, if there are other related tip pages to link to, you can make the box visible.

    You see a blue tab labeled "If relatedTips" above the "Related Tips" box (see Figure 19-20): this part is the optional region, and represents where the HTML code with the div is located.

    Of course, to let someone add links to related pages, you need to add an editable region as well.

13. **Click anywhere inside the two links—for example in the text "Related Tip 1" or "Related Tip 2". In the Tag selector at the bottom of the document window, click the <ul> tag (circled in Figure 19-20). Choose Insert → Template Objects → Editable Region. Name the new region *relatedLinks*.**

    Now the links listed inside the optional region will be editable.

    Next, you'll add a repeating region to the right sidebar, so that you can add multiple sets of questions and answers. You'll then make the text editable, so that you can add story titles and links.

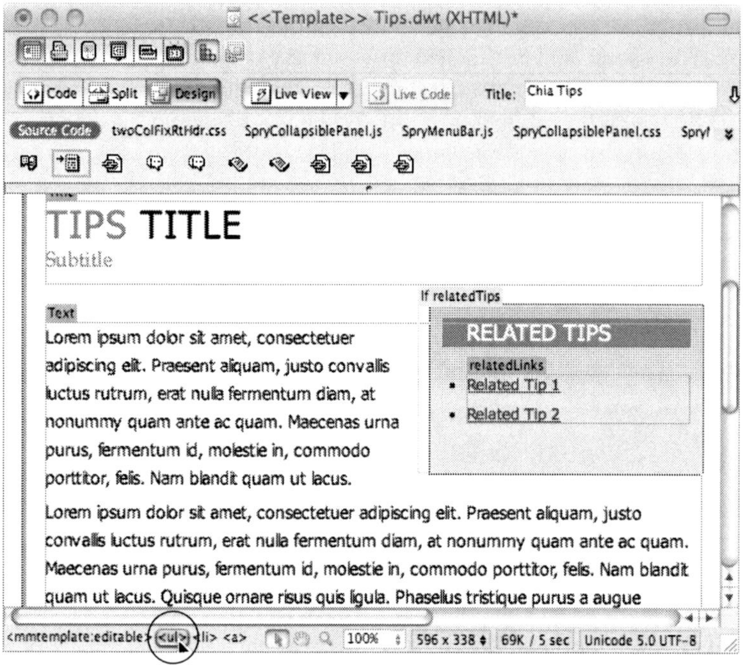

Figure 19-20: *When creating optional, editable, and repeating Template regions, the Tag selector is your best friend. Click a tag (<ul> in this case) to accurately select a tag. You'll also see Dreamweaver-specific tags listed on template files. Here <mmtemplate:editable> indicates the editable region you created in step 13. Because the <ul> tag appears to the right of the <mmtemplate:editable> tag, you know that the <ul> tag and everything inside it can be edited and changed on template-based pages.*

14. **In the right sidebar, click inside the text "Question goes here".**

    Both the question and answer are contained inside a <div> tag. You'll turn that entire <div> tag into a repeating region.

15. **At the bottom of the window, in the Tag selector, click the <div.qa> tag to select that div.**

    (Choosing Edit → Select All twice will also select the div.) The .qa part means that a class named *qa* is applied to that div. You've just selected the <div> tag and the two paragraphs inside it. Because you may want to add any number of question/answer pairs, you'll turn this into a repeating region.

16. **Choose Insert → Template Objects → Repeating Region. In the window that appears, type *repeatQuestions*. Click OK.**

    Dreamweaver inserts a new repeating region with the familiar blue tab. The tab reads "Repeat: repeatQuestions," indicating that it isn't any ordinary template region—it's a repeating region. However, turning a part of the page into a repeating region doesn't automatically make it editable. Since you want to edit the text and add new names to each page, you need to add an editable region *inside* this repeating region.

17. **Select the text "Question goes here". (Don't select the "Q. " at the beginning of the paragraph.) Choose Insert → Template Objects → Editable Region. In the Name field, type *question*, and then click OK.**

Another blue tab, labeled "question," appears inside the repeating region. On template-based pages, you can now change this text. You don't select the "Q. " at the beginning of the paragraph because you don't want that to be editable. That is part of the design, and at some point you might want to change this (for example, spell it out and add a colon: "Question: "). Because it's not part of an editable region, you'll be able to make that change once on the template and have every template-based page display the new "Question: " text.

18. **Choose File → Save.**

    A Dreamweaver dialog box appears, saying that the editable region you just created is inside a block tag and that you won't be able to add new blocks in this region. The reason for this dialog box is discussed on page 735, but in a nutshell it simply means that you won't be able to add additional paragraphs inside this area. Since this editable region is only intended for a single line question, and not multiple paragraphs, this is OK. (If you don't see this warning dialog box then you or someone else using your computer may have already turned off that type of warning, as described in the next step.)

19. **Put a check inside the "Don't show me this message again" box and click OK.**

    You may see another dialog box saying that you've changed a template and asking if you want to update pages on the site. Well, since you haven't yet created any pages from this template, there's nothing to update, so click the No button.

    Dreamweaver saves the file. You'll add another editable region for the answer.

20. **Repeat Step 18 for the text "Answer goes here." Name the editable region, *answer*.**

    The template should now look like Figure 19-21.

21. **Choose File → Save, and close this File.**

    Congratulations! You've created your first template.

Creating a Page Based on a Template

Now it's time to get down to business and build some Web pages. Look at the Files panel and make sure you've selected the site that you defined in step 1 at the beginning of this tutorial. Then proceed as follows:

1. **Choose File → New.**

    The New Document window opens.

2. **On the window's far left side, click the "Page from Template" button.**

    A list of all defined sites appears in the Site list.

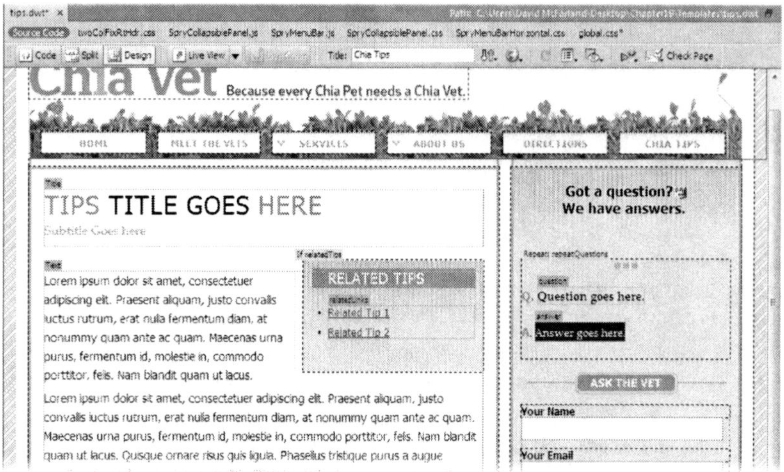

Figure 19-21: *A template file. If you don't see the blue boxes representing editable, optional, and repeatable regions then you may have turned them off. To show these elements choose View → Visual Aids and make sure Invisible Elements is checked.*

3. **Make sure the site you defined for this tutorial is selected is the Site column; also make sure the "Update page when template changes" checkbox (in the bottom right of the window) is turned on.**

   If you don't turn on the "Update page" box, the new page doesn't link to the original template file—and doesn't update when you make changes to the template.

4. **From the templates list, select Tips, and then click Create.**

   And lo, a new, untitled Web page document appears, one that looks (almost) exactly like the template (Figure 19-22).

5. **Choose File → Save. Click the Site Root button and save the file as *tip1.html* in the root folder. In the Document toolbar's Title field (at the top of the document window), type *Repairing Chipped Terra Cotta.***

   To indicate that it's your template's offspring, the document window has a yellow tab in the upper-right corner that reads Template:Tips. You can see your editable and repeating regions indicated by blue tabs. Now it's time to add some content.

6. **Choose File → Open; in the Open file window, click the Site Root button; double-click the file *tip1_text.html.***

   You can also open this file by double-clicking its name in the Files panel. The *tip1_text.html* page contains the content for the new template-based page. It's just a matter of copying and pasting the text from one page to the other.

7. **Select the headline and paragraph immediately following it at the top of the page and choose Edit → Copy. At the top of the document window, click the tip1.html tab to switch to the template-based page.**

Figure 19-22: In template-based pages, blue tabs identify editable areas of the page, and the yellow tab at the top right lists the template's name. In some cases, template tabs may overlap. Here, the tab for the editable region "question" sits on top of the tab for the repeatable region. Notice that the repeating region has small control buttons (+, –, and up and down arrows) and the optional region—the "Related Tips" box—is invisible. (Remember, you deselected the "Show by Default" option for this region.)

Remember that you can add content only to an editable region. If you move your mouse over the banner, navigation, or footer areas of the page, you see a black "forbidden" symbol. You can't insert the cursor anywhere but inside an editable region.

8. **Click the blue tab labeled "Title" (the label is just above the headline "Tips Title Goes Here").**

   This selects everything inside that region. Since it's just placeholder text anyway, you'll replace it with the two paragraphs you just copied.

9. **Choose Edit → Paste.**

   Dreamweaver replaces the dummy content with the title and subtitle for this Chia Tip page. (If the two lines of text look like plain paragraphs, turn the top line into a Heading 1 using the Format menu in the Proptery inspector, and add the class *tagline* to the second paragraph.) Now you'll add the main content of the tip.

10. **Click the *tip1_text.html* tab at the top of the Document window. Repeat steps 7-9, copying the remaining text on the *tip1_text.html* page and pasting it into the Text editable region on the *tip1.html* page.**

    The main tip is in place. This particular page doesn't have any related tips, so you'll leave the hidden optional region hidden (you'll show it on the next page you build).

    Time for some questions and answers.

Note: If, at a later time, Chia-Vet.com does add another page with a tip that's related to this Web page, the Related Tips box can be made visible simply by choosing Modify → Template Properties, and then turning on the "Show relatedTips" checkbox. You'll see this process in action in step 5 on page 761.

11. **In the page's right sidebar, delete the text "Question goes here" and type "Can I dye my Chia Pet?"**

    You've added a question in one editable area, now time for the answer.

12. **Click the "answer" tab and type some suitably silly answer in keeping with the Chia Vet Web site.**

    For example: "You can certainly dye your Chia's body. Since terra cotta is absorbent, any colored liquid will work. However, it's best to use non-toxic dyes like food coloring or beet juice." As it happens, there's another important question for this page. Since you're using a repeating region, it's easy to add another question/answer pair.

13. **Click the + button just to the right of the blue "Repeat: repeatQuestions" tab.**

    You've added another pair of question and answer editable regions to the page, as shown in Figure 19-23.

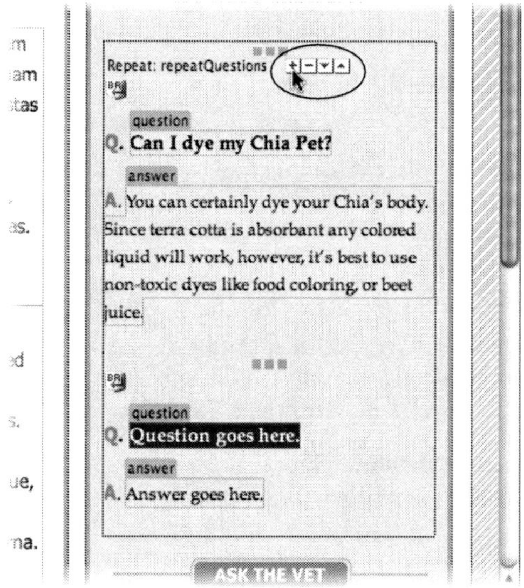

Figure 19-23:
If a page has a lot of elements crowded together–tables, images, text, and so on–Dreamweaver sometimes can't display the small buttons that let you add and remove repeating entries. In this case, you can also use the Modify menu. Click a repeating region, and then choose Modify → Templates → New Entry After Selection to add a new entry after the current one, or New Entry Before Selection to add a new entry before the current one.

14. **Repeat steps 11 and 12, adding an even sillier question and answer.**

    Congratulations, you've just completed a Web page for Chia-Vet.com. Save this page and preview it in a Web browser (press F12 [Option-F12]). Return to Dreamweaver and close this page. Now you'll add another page to the site.

Note: Submit your funniest Chia Vet question and answer to *missing@sawmac.com*. Exceptionally funny submissions will appear on the author's blog. REALLY, REALLY funny submissions will get a free copy of *JavaScript: The Missing Manual*.

Creating Another Template-Based Page

Templates are useful only if you use them to build lots of pages. You'll build one more template-based page for this tutorial, and see how optional template regions let you create very adaptive Web pages.

1. **Choose File → New. In the New Document window, click the "Page from Template" button; from the templates list, select Tips, and then click Create.**

   Another new Web page is born.

2. **Choose File → Save. Save the file as *tip2.html* in the root folder. In the Title field in the Document toolbar (at the top of the document window), type *Trimming Your Chia's Coat.***

   You'll add some already created content to this page.

3. **Repeat steps 6–10 on page 770. Use the file *tip2_text.html* located in the root folder.**

   Because trimming a Chia Pet's mane with sharp scissors is a recipe for chipped terra cotta, you've decided that you should provide a link from this page to the one you created previously. Fortunately, the optional region you created earlier is ready to be used.

4. **Choose Modify → Template Properties.**

   The Template Properties window appears (see Figure 19-24). The optional region you wish to make visible is listed.

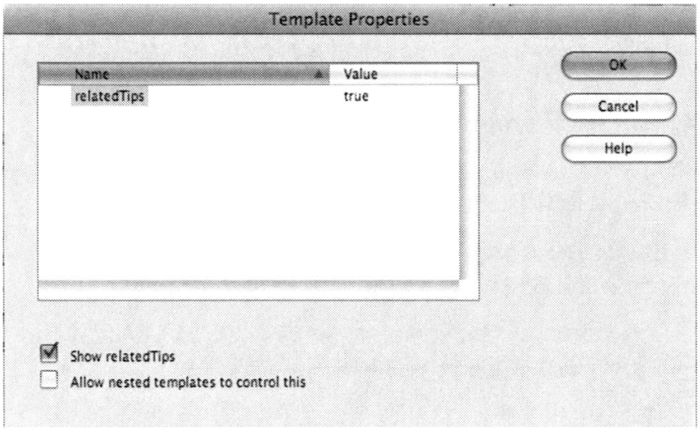

***Figure 19-24:** The Template Properties window does double duty. Not only does it let you hide or show optional regions, it's also the place to set values for editable tag attributes.*

5. **Turn on the "Show relatedTips" checkbox and then click OK to close the window.**

   The Related Tips box suddenly appears. There's only one related page, so you don't need both bulleted items.

6. **Delete the 2nd bullet point ("Related Tip 2") and change the text of the first bullet to "Repairing Chipped Terra Cotta". Link that text to the *tip1.html* page (use any of the link-creation techniques discussed on page 167).**

   This page is nearly complete: just one final item.

7. **Repeat step 14 on page 772 (don't forget the potentially life-changing contest mentioned in the Note on page 773).**

   You're almost done.

8. **Preview the page in a Web browser.**

   While most of the page looks the same as the first template-based page you created, the use of optional regions let you add special content to this page without having to create another template. Next you'll edit the template file and update the Web site.

   Close this page and *tip1.html* when you're ready to move onto the next step.

Updating a Template

Now the fun begins. Remember, this page maintains a reference to the original template. In the final phase, you're going to make a few changes to the template. Choose Window → Assets to open the Assets panel, and then click the Template button to reveal the templates for this site (see Figure 19-4):

1. **Return to Dreamweaver, and in the Assets panel, click the Templates button (see Figure 15-11), and double-click the Tips template to open it.**

   The original template, the Tips.dwt file, opens. You can also open the .dwt file by double-clicking it's name inside the Templates folder in the Files panel.

   There are a couple of things that need changing, first the copyright needs to be updated.

2. **In the footer, locate the *Copyright 2008* and change it to the current year.**

   If it's still 2008 (you early-adopter you), change the year to 2009 or whatever the current year happens to be. You'll also add a link here.

3. **On the same line in the footer, select the text "Cosmofarmer.com". In the Property inspector's link field type *http://www.cosmofarmer.com/*.**

   You've also decided that you don't like the look of the "Q." and "A." in the right sidebar, so you'll change that as well.

4. **In the right sidebar, delete the period at the end of "Q."; select the letter Q, and from the Class menu in the Property inspector select the class style *q*.**

   The Q changes appearance—the letter gets smaller, turns white, and an orange box surrounds it.

Note: If you don't see a Class menu in the Property inspector, you're in CSS view. Click the HTML button on the left side of the Property inspector to reveal the Class menu.

---

5. **Repeat step 4, replacing the "A." with just "A" and applying the class *a* to it.**

   The A changes appearance—the letter gets smaller, turns white, and a green box surrounds it. Because both the Q and A are outside of the editable regions (that is, "question" and "answer"), the changes you just made will pass on to template-based pages.

6. **Choose File → Save.**

   The Update Template Files window appears. This is the moment of truth.

7. **Click Update.**

   Dreamweaver opens the Update Pages dialog box and updates the appropriate Web pages, adding the copyright year, the link, and new Q and A icons to each one. In this case, you based only two pages on the template, so Dreamweaver updates only two pages—as indicated by the list of changes Dreamweaver shows when it's finished.

Note: If, after you update pages based on a template, you don't see the number of updated pages listed in the Update Pages window, turn on the Show Log checkbox.

---

8. **Click Close to close the Update Pages dialog box. Finally, open the files *tip1.html* and *tip2.html*.**

   Notice that the copyright and question/answer sections are updated in both (see Figure 19-25). This series of events happened because you changed the template to which the page was genetically linked. Ah, the power!

Figure 19-25:
The finished tutorial page, complete with a useful Chia tip, a box with a link to a related Web page, and a helpful question and answer.

CHAPTER

20

Automating Dreamweaver

One of Dreamweaver's greatest selling points is that it makes you more productive. You've experienced this firsthand if you've ever labored over tables in an HTML text editor. What once took many keystrokes now takes one click of the Insert panel's Table object.

If you're looking for even more ways to cut time off your work day, Dreamweaver doesn't disappoint. In addition to its Snippets, Library, and Template features (see Chapter 18 and Chapter 19), the program offers two tools that let you automate common and time-consuming tasks: the History panel and the "Find and Replace" command.

The History Panel Revisited

As you work on a Web page, Dreamweaver keeps track of everything you do. You can see a list of your actions—your *history*—in the History panel. Each document has a separate history, which Dreamweaver discards when you close the document or quit the program.

As you read in Chapter 2, You can use the History panel to quickly undo or redo multiple actions (see page 90), but that's only the tip of the iceberg. You can also use it to replay and record a series of actions you wish to repeat. If you've ever used macros in Microsoft Word or actions in Adobe Photoshop, you'll probably get the hang of this feature quickly.

To open the History panel (Figure 20-1), choose Window → History (or, in Windows only, press Shift+F10).

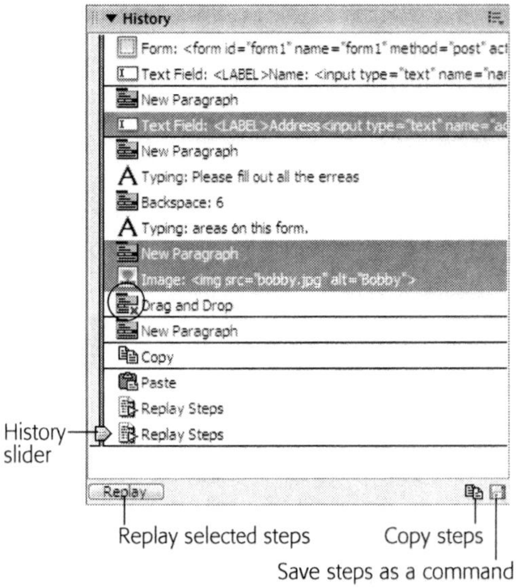

Figure 20-1: *The History panel lists every little step you've taken while working on the current document—even typos. You can replay one or more actions on the list, copy them for use in another document, or save them as a command in the Commands menu. If Dreamweaver can't replay an action, such as a mouse click, it appears with a red X next to it (circled). Furthermore, you can't replay two consecutive steps if you clicked or dragged in the document in between them (you'll see a solid line in the History list separating such steps). Dreamweaver merely replays the first selected step. The History slider indicates where you are in the document's history.*

Replay Your Steps

To replay a step in the History panel, click the step's name to highlight it. You can also select multiple steps by using one of these methods:

- To select a group of consecutive steps, drag over them. You can drag your cursor across either the labels or icons. Take special care not to move your cursor onto the History slider on the left edge of the window, as clicking there undoes or redoes steps.
- You can also select consecutive steps by holding down the Shift key as you click down the list.
- To select steps that aren't consecutive, Ctrl-click (⌘-click) only the ones you want. For example, say you hit Return, typed *hello*, and then inserted a horizontal rule. If you wanted to omit the step where you typed *hello*, you could Ctrl-click (⌘-click) the other two. Dreamweaver ignores unselected steps.

Now, when you click Replay (see Figure 20-1), Dreamweaver replays the selected steps in an encore performance. For example, if you insert an image using the Common category of the Insert panel, that's recorded as one step. You could then add that image to your page again, later, simply by clicking where you want the image to appear and then replaying the "insert image" step. Unfortunately, you can't reorder the steps; they always play from the top of the list of selected steps to the bottom.

Once you've created a series of steps, you can reuse it. For example, say you format a paragraph as a bulleted list and apply a custom style to it. Once Dreamweaver records these steps in the History panel, you can select more text and replay those steps to format it the same way. Now imagine that, instead of a two-step process, you have a 10-step chore that involves not only keystrokes, but multiple visits to the Insert panel and the Property inspector—you can begin to see the power of this feature.

Tip: You probably know that you can repeat your last action by pressing Ctrl+Y (⌘-Y) or choosing Edit → Repeat. For example, if you type the word *hello* in the document window, pressing Ctrl+Y (⌘-Y) will type the word *hello* again. Unless you're Jack Nicholson's character in *The Shining*, this feature may sound less than useful, but used in combination with the History panel's Replay feature, it can be a real time-saver. When you use the History panel to replay several steps, you'll notice the last item in the History list becomes Replay Steps. Dreamweaver treats the replaying of all these steps as a *single action*. Now if you press Ctrl+Y (⌘-Y), you replay all of the steps again.

Exceptions and Errors

Unfortunately, Dreamweaver can't record and play back everything. The exceptions generally involve making changes in certain dialog boxes or moving objects with the mouse. For example, you can't record tasks you perform in the Modify Page Properties dialog box. And you're left to your own devices when you want to click, drag, or drop a graphic in the document window. In addition, only HTML files (or files that contain HTML like Templates or the server-side pages discussed in the next Part of this book) generate a History, and only when you're working in Design view. Dreamweaver doesn't add entries in the History (though you can still undo actions) when working in Code view.

On the other hand, not everything you do with the mouse is off-limits to the History panel. It can track most common tasks, like clicking the Insert panel, choosing a menu item, or clicking in the Property inspector to set a property. Also, you can avoid using many mouse movements by using the equivalent keystrokes, which Dreamweaver *can* record. (See the box below.)

If you take a step, such as a mouse drag, that Dreamweaver *can't* replay, a red X appears next to it in the History panel. A line between two actions also indicates a step that can't be repeated. This problem usually arises when you've clicked in the document window (to deselect an image, for example). One way you can avoid these non-recordable actions is to get into the habit of deselecting an object in the document window by pressing the keyboard's arrow keys instead.

Copying and Pasting Actions

Each document has its own history. So if you work on one page and then switch to another, the History panel changes to reflect only the actions you performed on the new document. The biggest drawback of this behavior is that you can't immediately replicate a series of steps you've made in one document by replaying them in another document.

FREQUENTLY ASKED QUESTION

Keyboard to the Rescue

If Dreamweaver can't track mouse movements, how can I replay an action that involves selecting something?

It's easy to use the mouse to make selections and move items around the screen, but you can do much of the same with the humble keyboard. That's a good thing, because if you can type it, Dreamweaver can record it.

To move up one line, for instance, press the up arrow key; to move down a line, press the down arrow. You can move to the top or bottom of the document window with the Page Up and Page Down keys, or move to the beginning or end of a line by pressing Home or End. Press Shift while pressing the right or left arrow key to select the object or letter to the right or left of the insertion point. Add the Ctrl (⌘) key to that combination to select one word at a time.

Unfortunately, Dreamweaver doesn't record the keystrokes you use for moving between table cells (Tab and Shift-Tab). However, there's a workaround: to move from one cell to the cell on its right, press End, followed by the right arrow key. To move to the cell to the left, press Home, followed by the left arrow key. Arrow keys not only move the cursor but are also a helpful way to deselect an object that's currently highlighted on the page. Best of all, the History panel can track all of these keystrokes.

(You don't have to memorize all of this. You can print out a complete list of keyboard shortcuts, as described in the next chapter on page 804.)

For example, while working on your home page, you might click the Date object in the Insert panel to insert the current date (see page 78), and then choose a format for the date in the dialog box. Then, say you want to place the date on another page using the same format. But when you switch to that page and click Replay on the History panel, your steps aren't there!

Fortunately, there's a workaround: ye olde copy/paste routine. Select the steps you want to copy (see page 778 for selection techniques), and then click the "Copy selected steps" button (see Figure 20-1) on the History panel. (The regular copy shortcut, Ctrl+C or ⌘-C, *doesn't* work in this situation.) Now switch to the new document, select an object (or click to place the insertion point), and then choose Edit → Paste or press Ctrl+V (⌘-V).

Dreamweaver responds by playing the copied steps.

Save Steps as Commands

It's quick and easy to replay and copy steps to automate repetitive tasks, but if you close the document or quit Dreamweaver, your recorded actions disappear—and with them, any chance you had of replaying them in the future. What if you come up with a great sequence of steps that you'd like to use over and over again?

The solution: Before it disappears forever, turn it into a *custom command*. That way, Dreamweaver adds your command to the bottom of the Commands menu, and you can choose it from there whenever you want.

POWER USERS' CLINIC

Copy (and Study) Actions

Dreamweaver is relatively easy to customize, because objects that appear in the Insert panel, behaviors available from the Behaviors panel, and even the Property inspector are all—behind the scenes—combinations of HTML pages and JavaScript programs. If you understand JavaScript, you can add your own commands, behaviors, and objects.

When learning JavaScript, however, you may need all the help you can get. The History panel's Copy Steps feature is a good place to start. To study how Dreamweaver's built-in commands, behaviors, and objects have been programmed, copy one or more actions using the method that's described above.

Switch to a text editor like Notepad or TextEdit (Word will work, too), and then choose Edit → Paste.

What you see is the JavaScript code that Dreamweaver uses to carry out those actions. You'll find out, for example, that while *you* perceive adding a new paragraph to your Web page as a matter of hitting Enter, to Dreamweaver it looks like this: *dw.getDocumentDOM().newBlock()*.

The History panel also has a secret shortcut that lets you view the JavaScript code for each step, right inside the panel: Ctrl+Shift+click (⌘-Shift-click) anywhere inside the History panel and then (Ctrl+Shift+click [⌘-Shift-click] a second time to return to the normal, human-readable description for each step).

To save steps as a command, select the steps you want to copy (see page 778 for selection techniques), and then click the Save Steps button (its icon looks like a little floppy disk) on the History panel. The "Save as Command" dialog box pops open. (If you've selected steps that Dreamweaver can't replay, such as mouse movements, a warning appears. Click Yes to continue without those steps; the valid steps work just fine.) Type a short, descriptive name, and then click OK. Now take a look at the Commands menu—sure enough, your command now appears at the bottom.

To use your custom command, simply select its name from the Commands menu.

Tip: If you decide you want to delete your command or change its name, choose Commands → Edit Command List. In the dialog box that appears, click the command's name to select it. Type a new name or click Delete.

Recording Commands

You can also create a command by telling Dreamweaver to watch and record your actions. This time, Dreamweaver doesn't *let* you perform mouse movements while you're recording, so you can be sure recorded commands will play back properly.

To record a command, make sure the relevant Web page document is front most, and then choose Commands → Start Recording, or press Ctrl+Shift+X (⌘-Shift-X). The cursor turns into a cassette-tape icon (memo to Adobe: we're in the 21st century) to indicate the command is recording. Now's your chance to do whatever you want Dreamweaver to memorize. (If you try to use the mouse to move or select anything in the document window, Dreamweaver complains with a dialog box.)

When you're finished, choose Commands → Stop Recording, or press Ctrl+Shift+X (⌘-Shift-X). Your cursor returns to normal, and Dreamweaver saves the sequence as a command, which you can replay by choosing Commands → Play Recorded Command.

Note, however, that this command disappears when you quit Dreamweaver or record another command. (Dreamweaver can only save one recorded command at a time.) If you want to preserve it for posterity, you have to save it to the Commands menu, like this:

1. **Choose Commands → Play Recorded Command.**

   The History panel lists this action as Run Command.

2. **Click the Run Command step in the History panel.**

   The step is highlighted to indicate you've selected it.

3. **Click the Save Steps button (its icon looks like a little floppy disk).**

   The "Save as Command" dialog box appears.

4. **Type a name for the command, and then click OK.**

   Dreamweaver adds your new command to the Commands menu, where it's ready for action in this or any future Dreamweaver session.

Find and Replace

You've probably encountered find-and-replace tools in word processing programs and even some graphics programs. As the name implies, the command finds a piece of text (*Webmaster*, for example) and then *replaces* it with something else (*Webmistress*). Like Microsoft Word, Dreamweaver can search and replace text in the body of your Web pages. But it also offers variations on this feature that enhance your ability to work within the tag-based world of HTML.

What's more, Dreamweaver lets you find and replace text on *every* page of your Web site, not just the current, open document. In addition, you can *remove* every appearance of a particular HTML tag, or search and replace text that matches very specific criteria. For example, you can find every instance of the word "Aardvark" that appears within a paragraph styled with the class named *animal*. These advanced find-and-replace maneuvers are some of the most powerful—and under appreciated—tools in Dreamweaver. If you learn how to use them, you can make changes to your pages in a fraction of the time it would take using other methods.

Tip: You can use "Find and Replace" to search an entire site's worth of files. This is powerful, but can also be slow, especially if some folders hold files you don't want to search–old archives, for example. You can use Dreamweaver's cloaking feature to hide files from find-and-replace operations. See page 684 for more details.

Find and Replace Basics

To start a search, press Ctrl+F (⌘-F), or choose Edit → "Find and Replace". The "Find and Replace" window opens (see Figure 20-2). Now all you have to do is fill in the blanks and set up the search.

Whether you perform a simple text search or a complex, tag-based search and replace, the procedure for using the "Find and Replace" command is basically the same. First, you need to tell Dreamweaver *where* to search (within text you've selected on the page, in a file, a folder, or an entire Web site). Next, tell it *what* to search for (text, HTML, or a particular tag with a specific attribute). Finally, you can decide what to replace the item with. This last step is optional; you can use the "Find and Replace" window as a way to locate an item on the page, or in your site, without actually changing it to anything.

Tip: After you've entered the "Find and Replace" criteria, click the Save Query button (see Figure 20-2). A Save dialog box appears; you can type in a name for your query, which Dreamweaver saves as a .dwr (Dreamweaver replace query) file. You can save this file anywhere on your computer. If it's a query you'll use for a particular site, you might want to save it with those files. To reuse a query, click the Load Query button and locate the .dwr file. After the search-and-replace criteria load, you can click any of the four action buttons–Find Next, Find All, Replace, or Replace All.

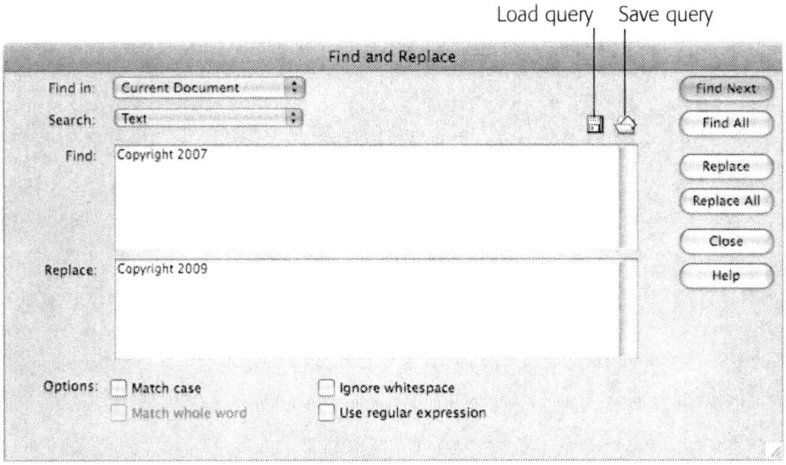

Figure 20-2: *Dreamweaver's "Find and Replace" feature lets you replace text and HTML quickly and accurately. By using the Load Query and Save Query buttons, you can even save complex searches to use in the future.*

Basic Text and HTML Searches

Dreamweaver can either search all of the source code in a page or simply focus on text that appears in the document window.

- **Source code searches** let you find and replace any character in the code of a page, including words, letters, and symbols. This means *anything* you see in Code view, such as HTML, CSS, or server-side programming code used to create the dynamic database-driven sites described in Part 6 of this book.

- **Text** searches are more refined. They look only for text that appears within the body of a page. That is, Dreamweaver ignores HTML tags, properties, and comments when searching—in short, it ignores anything that doesn't appear as actual words in the document window. By using a text search when you want to change the word "table" to "elegant wood table," for example, you won't accidentally change the very useful HTML <table> tag into the browser-will-choke-on <elegant wood table> tag.

If you've used "Find and Replace" in other programs, the following routine will be familiar.

Phase 1: Determine the scope of your search

Using the "Find in" menu (see Figure 20-3), choose any of these options:

- **Selected Text.** Searches only the current selection of the Web page you're working on. This can be useful if you're working in Code view and you want to search the code in just a certain section of the page, such as the head of the document. It's also great when you're writing your own server-side programs (like those described in Part 6 of this book) and you want to search only one part of the code.
- **Current Document.** Searches the Web page you're working on.
- **Open Documents.** Searches all currently open Dreamweaver documents. This option is handy if you're working on a bunch of pages at the same time and realize you've made the same typo on each page.
- **Folder.** Search all Web pages in a particular folder. Dreamweaver also searches Web pages in all folders *within* the selected folder. You can use this option to search pages that aren't part of the current site.
- **Selected Files in Site.** To use this option, open the Files panel and select files that you want to search in the local file list. (See page 646 for details.)
- **Entire Current Local Site.** Searches every Web page in the current site folder, including pages in folders *inside* the site folder. This option is invaluable when some basic piece of information changes throughout your site. For instance, use this when your boss's sex-change operation requires you to replace every instance of "Mark Jones" with "Mary Jones" throughout your company's site.

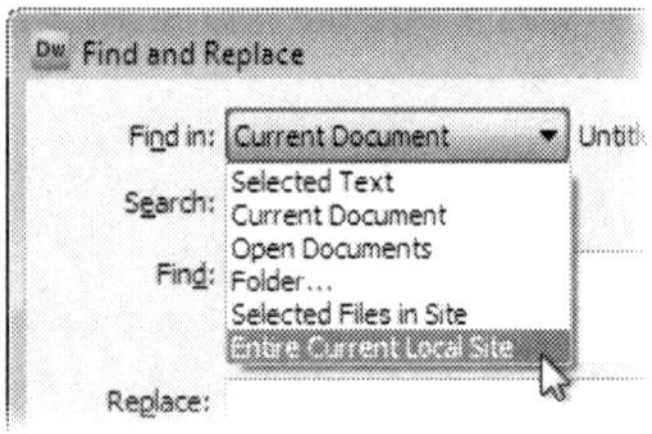

Figure 20-3:
The "Find and Replace" command is not limited to the current document. You can also search multiple Web pages, or even an entire site.

Warning: Using the "Find and Replace" command is one of the best ways to quickly make changes to an entire site, but it's also one of the easiest ways to wreck a site's worth of Web pages. Dreamweaver *can't* undo changes made by the "Find and Replace command to files that aren't open in Dreamweaver. So be careful. If you plan on making extensive changes, make a backup copy of your files first!

Phase 2: Specify what to search for

For your next trick, you'll tell Dreamweaver what you want to search for. Use the Search pop-up menu to choose one of these two options:

- **Text.** This makes Dreamweaver search for a certain word or phrase of text that appears in the *body* of the documents you've specified. Type the text you want to find into the Search field. If you're searching for a pattern in your text, enter a *regular expression* here and turn on the "Use regular expression" checkbox. (See the box on page 792 for more on regular expressions.)

- **Source Code.** Basic text searches are very useful, but they're limited to text that appears in the body of the page (what you see in the document window). If you want to search and replace code, you need the Source Code option.

  Source-code searches work identically to text searches, except that Dreamweaver searches *everything* within the file—text, HTML, JavaScript, CSS, and so on—and replaces any part of the file. Using this option, you could search for any instance of the tag <img src="mark_jones_photo.jpg">, for example, and then replace it with <img src="mary_jones_photo.jpg">.

  (If you're in Code view, Dreamweaver automatically selects the Source Code option.)

  As you fill in the Search field, be aware that some plain English words are also special words in HTML, JavaScript, or CSS. If you try to replace *table* with *desk* using a source-code find and replace, you'll completely destroy any <table> tags on the page.

  You can also enter a regular expression to search for patterns in your HTML source code (see the box on page 792).

Phase 3: Provide the replacement text

If you want to change the text that Dreamweaver finds, type the replacement text into the Replace box. It may be the word or words you'd like to swap in (for a Text search), or actual HTML code if you're performing a source-code search.

Tip: Dreamweaver won't let you create a new line in the search or replace boxes–for example, if you want to replace some source code with two lines of HTML. At least it won't let you do it the normal way. If you hit the Enter key, Dreamweaver begins the search rather than inserting a new line. If you want to add another line use Shift-Enter (Shift-Return).

If you just want to find the text without replacing it, then skip this step.

Tip: If you want to find the specified text and replace it with *nothing* (that is, deleting every occurrence of the text), leave the Replace field blank and perform a replace operation, described in Phase 5.

Phase 4: Choose the search settings

Dreamweaver gives you three options that govern its search and replace; some of them are quite complex:

- The **Match Case** option limits the Find command to text that exactly matches the capitalization you use in the Search field. If you search for the text *The End* with the Match Case box turned on, Dreamweaver finds a match in "The End is near," but not in "You're almost at the end." Use this trick to find every instance of *web* and replace it with *Web*.

- **Match Whole Word** searches for an entire word—not a portion of a larger word. For example, if you turn this option on, a search for *Rob* matches only "Rob," and not any parts of "Robert," "robbery," or "problem." If you don't select this option, Dreamweaver stops on "rob" in all four instances, and could cause serious problems if you also *replace* "rob" with something like "bob". (Note that if you selected the Match Case option, Dreamweaver would match *Rob* in "Rob" and "Robert," but *not* in "robbery" and "problem," since they don't include a capital R.)

- The **Ignore Whitespace** option treats multiple spaces, tabs, non-breaking spaces, and carriage returns as single spaces when searching. For instance, if you search for *the dog* and turn on this option, Dreamweaver matches "the dog" as well as "the dog"—even if the multiple spaces are actually the HTML non-breaking space character * * (see page 77).

Note to Mac Users: Unfortunately, in the Mac version of Dreamweaver, the "Find and Replace" function does not treat non-breaking space characters as spaces, so if you have *the dog* in your HTML and search for *the dog*, even with the Ignore Whitespace box checked, the search will find nothing.

Unless you have a good reason, always leave this option turned on. The HTML of a page can contain lots of extra spaces, line breaks, and tabs that don't appear in a Web browser or in Dreamweaver's document window. For example, in the HTML of a document, it's possible to have two lines of code that look like this:

```
<p>This sentence will appear on one
line in a Web browser</p>
```

Even though this text would appear on a single line in the document window, a search for "one line" *without* the Ignore Whitespace box turned on would find no match. The carriage return after "one" is not an exact match for the space character in "one line."

Note: The Ignore Whitespace option can't be selected when the Use Regular Expression checkbox is turned on.

- The **Use Regular Expression** option is used for matching patterns in text. For a discussion of this advanced technique, see the box on page 792.

Phase 5: Take action

Finally, you're ready to set the search in motion by clicking one of the four action buttons in the "Find and Replace" window (see Figure 20-2):

- **Find Next** locates the next instance of the search term. If you're searching the current document, Dreamweaver highlights the matching text. If you're searching an entire Web site or a folder of pages, Dreamweaver opens the file *and* highlights the match. You can cycle through each instance of the search term by clicking this button repeatedly.

Tip: As in other programs (notably Microsoft Word), you can press Enter to repeat the Find Next function (Windows only). If you've clicked into the document window–or even closed the Find window–you can press F3 (⌘-G) to repeat the Find Next function.

- **Find All** locates every instance of the search terms, all at once, and shows them to you in a list in the Search tab of the Results panel (Figure 20-4). The name and location of each file (if multiple files are searched) appear to the left, and the matched text appears to the right. Dreamweaver displays part of the sentence in which the matched word or words appear. The exact match is underlined with a squiggly red line, so you can see the search in context and identify text you may *not* want to replace.

  Unlike the Find Next action, Find All doesn't automatically open any of the Web pages containing matches. Instead, to open a matched page, double-click its name in the results list. Only then does Dreamweaver open the Web page and highlight the match.

- **Replace** locates the next instance of the search term *and* replaces it with the text in the Replace field, leaving the replaced text highlighted for your inspection.

  You can use this button in combination with Find Next to selectively replace text. First, click Find Next. Dreamweaver locates and highlights the next match. If you want to replace the text, click Replace. If not, click Find Next to search for the next match, and repeat the cycle. This cautious approach lets you supervise the replacement process and avoid making changes you didn't intend.

- **Replace All** is the ultimate power tool. It finds every instance of the search term and replaces it with the text entered in the Replace field. Coupled with the "Find in Entire Local Site" option, you can quickly make sitewide changes (and mistakes—so back up all your files before you Replace All!).

  When you click this button, Dreamweaver warns that you can't undo this operation on any closed files. You can erase mistakes you make with the "Find and Replace" in *open* documents, by choosing Edit → Undo in each document, but

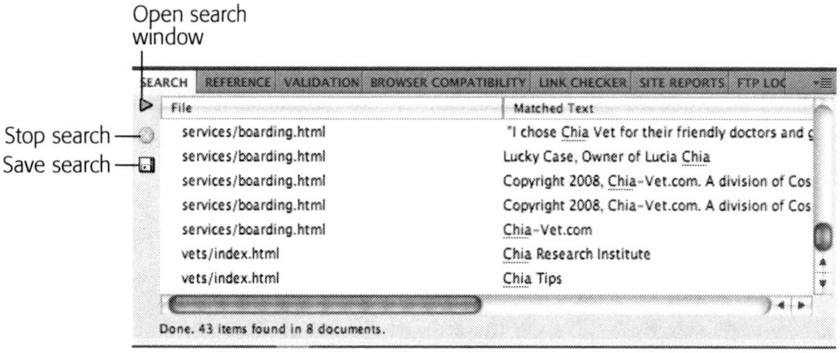

Figure 20-4: *The green-arrow button reopens the "Find and Replace" window. Click the red Stop button to abort the current search (for example, when you inadvertently begin a search for "the" in a 10,000-page Web site). You can also save a rather useless XML file that provides a report of the results of the find-and-replace command (remember the old adage: Just because you can doesn't mean you should).*

Dreamweaver *permanently* alters closed files that you search and replace. So be careful! (On the other hand, changes to open documents aren't permanent until you save those files.)

Tip: Before you take the plunge and click the Replace All button, it's a good precautionary step to click Find All first and then preview the results in the Results panel (Figure 20-4). This way you can be sure that you're going to change exactly what you *want* to change.

If you use the Find All or Replace All commands, the "Find and Replace" window closes, and the results of the search appear in the Search tab (see Figure 20-4). You can reopen the "Find and Replace" window (with all of your previous search criteria still in place) by clicking the green arrow on the Search tab (called the "Find and Replace" button), but only if you haven't selected anything else—like text on a page—first.

Advanced Text Searches

If you want greater control over a text search, you can use the "Find and Replace" command's *advanced* text search option, which lets you confine a search to text either inside or outside a specific tag.

For example, when Dreamweaver creates a new blank document, it sets the page's *Title* property to *Untitled Document*. Unfortunately, if you forget to change it, a site can quickly fill up with untitled Web pages. A basic text search doesn't identify this problem, because it searches only the body of a page; titles appear in the head. And a source-code search for *Untitled Document* would turn up the words "untitled document" *wherever* they appeared in the page, not just inside the <title> tag.

In cases like this, an advanced text search is your best choice. Simply set the "Find and Replace" command to search for *Untitled Document* whenever it appears within the <title> tag. To use the advanced text search, you follow the same general routine as described on the previous pages. But before using one of the action buttons, you make a few additional setup changes to the dialog box.

Limiting the search by tag

Choose Text (Advanced) from the Search pop-up menu to make the expanded controls appear (see Figure 20-5). Now, from the menu next to the + and – buttons, choose either Inside Tag or Not Inside Tag. For example, consider this line of code: "Stupid is as <strong>stupid</strong> does." The first instance of "stupid" isn't inside the <strong> tag, but the second one is.

Note: A more descriptive name for the first option would be "*Enclosed* By Tag"; Dreamweaver actually searches for text that's between *opening and closing* tags. In fact, an advanced text search using this option doesn't identify text that's literally inside a tag. For example, it won't find "Aliens" in this line of code: <img src="ufo.jpg" alt="Aliens live among us.">, but it would find "Aliens" in this one: <strong> Aliens live among us.</strong>. In the first example, *Aliens* appears as part of the <img> tag, while in the second, *Aliens* is enclosed by the opening and closing <strong> tags.

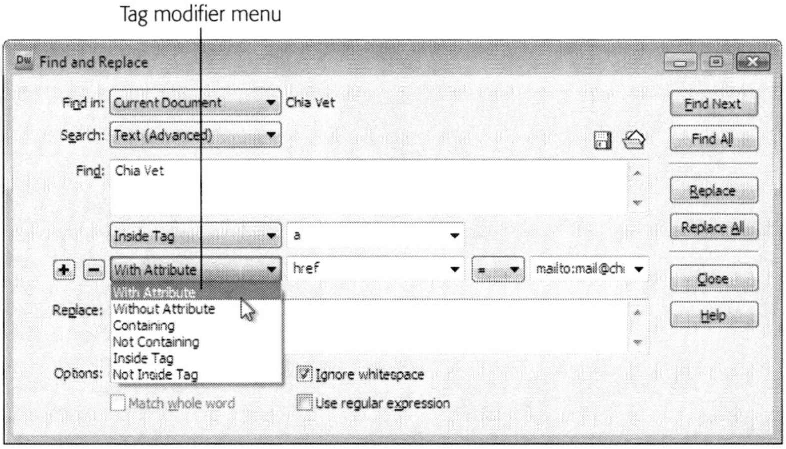

Figure 20-5: *Use an advanced text search to limit your search to text that appears within a particular HTML tag. Or, conversely, use it to search for text that doesn't appear within a tag.*

Once you've specified whether you're looking for text inside or outside tags, you can choose a specific HTML tag from the Tag menu identified in Figure 20-5. The menu lists all HTML tags—not just those with both an opening and closing tag. So the image tag (<img>) still appears, even though Dreamweaver doesn't identify text inside it.

Tip: A great way to search for text in both the title and body of a Web page is to choose the Inside Tag option and then select *html* from the Tag menu. That way, you can search for any text that appears within the opening <html> and closing </html> of the page–which, since those tags start and end any Web document, is *all* text on a page. This trick is handy when you want to change text that might appear in the body *and* the title of a page (for example, a company name).

Limiting the search by attribute

To limit the search further, click the + button (see Figure 20-6); yet another set of fields appears. Using the Tag Modifier menu—next to the + and – buttons (Figure 20-6)—you can choose from any of six options that break down into three groups:

- **With Attribute/Without Attribute.** To limit the search, you can specify that a tag must either have (With Attribute) or not have (Without Attribute) a specific property.

  For example, say the following lines of code appear throughout a Web site:

  ```
  <p>For assistance, please email
  <a href="mailto:mail@chia-vet.com">
  Chia Vet.</a></p>
  ```

  Now, for the sake of argument, say you need to change it to read "For assistance, please email Customer Service." A basic text find-and-replace would incorrectly change the words "Chia Vet" to "Customer Service" *everywhere* on the site.

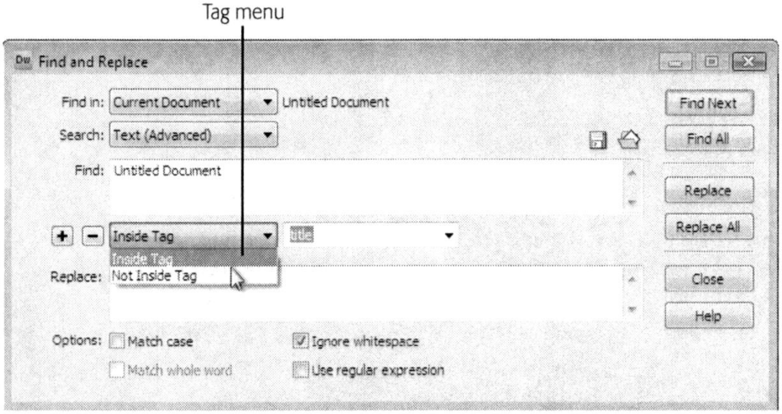

***Figure 20-6:** When you click the + button in the "Find and Replace" window, a new set of fields appears. Use these options to carefully hone your "Find and Replace" commands, and zero in on text that matches precise criteria.*

  However, an advanced text search using the With Attribute option would let you specifically target the text "Chia Vet" wherever it appears inside an <a> tag whose *href* attribute is set to *mailto:mail@chia-vet.com*. You could then just change that text to "Customer Service" while leaving all other instances of "Chia Vet" alone. (To learn about the different HTML tags and attributes, use Dreamweaver's built-in code reference; see page 422.)

After you choose With Attribute, use the menu on the right to select *which* of the tag's properties you want to find. (Dreamweaver automatically lists properties that are appropriate for the tag you've specified.) For example, if you search inside a <table> tag, the menu lists such properties as *align, background, bgcolor*, and so on.

Advance to the next pop-up menu to choose a type of comparison: = (equal to), != (not equal to), > (greater than), or < (less than). These options are useful only when the property's value is a numeric amount, such as the *width* property of a table cell. In this way, you could locate all table cells that are wider than 100 pixels (width > 100). (This setting has no effect on values that are words, such as *center* in this example: <td align="center">.)

Finally, type the value of the property in the last field. If you were searching for a black-colored background, the value would be *#000000* (the hex value for black).

You can also click the menu and choose "[any value]"—a useful option when you want to find tags that have a certain property, but you're not interested in the property's value. For example, if you want to find all <table> tags with a background color (no matter whether the color's #336699, #000000, or #FFFFFF), choose the *bgcolor* attribute and "[any value]".

- **Containing/Not Containing.** These options let you specify whether the tag contains (or does not contain) specific text or a particular tag.

  When you choose this option, a different set of fields appears. Choose either Text or Specific Tag from the menu to the right, and then either enter some text or select a tag in the last field in the row. For example, another solution to the problem above would be to search for the text "Chia Vet" wherever it appears inside a <p> (paragraph) tag that *also contains* the text "please email."

- **Inside Tag/Not Inside Tag.** These last two choices are identical to those described on page 789. They let you specify whether the tag is inside—or not inside—a specific tag. Use these to limit a search, for example, to text that appears only within a <span> tag that's *inside* an <h1> tag.

If you like, you can add even more restrictions to your search, adding new rules by clicking the + button and repeating the setup just described. When you're really on a roll, it's even possible to add so many modifiers that the "Find and Replace" window actually grows past the bottom of your monitor. To remove a modifier, click the minus sign (–) button.

POWER USERS' CLINIC

Turbocharge Your Searches

If you want to find the phone number 555-123-5473, no problem; just type *555-123-5473* into the search field. But what if you wanted to find any and every phone number—555-987-0938, 555-102-8870, and so on—on a Web page or in a site?

In such a case, you need to use *regular expressions*, the geeky name for a delightfully flexible searching language, carried over from early UNIX days, which consists of wildcard characters that let you search for patterns of text instead of actual letters or numbers. Each phone number above follows a simple pattern: three numbers, a dash, three more numbers, another dash, and four more numbers.

To search for a pattern, you use a variety of symbols combined with regular text characters to tell Dreamweaver what to find. For example, in the world of regular expressions, "\d" stands for "any number." To find three numbers in a row, you could search for \d\d\d, which would find 555, 747, 007, and so on. There's even shorthand for this: \d{3}. The number between the braces ({}) indicates how many times in a row the preceding character must appear to match. To finish up the example of the phone numbers, you could use a regular expression like this: \d{3}-\d{3}-\d{4}. The \d{3} finds three numbers, while the hyphen (-) following it is just the hyphen in the phone number, and \d{4} finds four numbers.

Here are some of the other symbols you'll encounter when using regular expressions:

- . (period) stands for any character, letter, number, space, and so on.
- \w stands for any letter or number.
- * (asterisk) represents the preceding character, zero or more times (and is always used after another character). This is best explained with an example: The regular expression colou*r, for instance, matches both colour and color—the * following the u indicates that the u is optional (it can appear zero times). This would also match colouuuuur (handy for those times when you've fallen asleep on the keyboard).

To see a complete list of the regular-expression characters Dreamweaver understands, type "Regular Expressions" in Dreamweaver CS4's new Community Help search box at the top of the Application Bar (see page 31), or choose Help → Dreamweaver Help. A full-length discussion of regular expressions could—and does—fill a book of its own; check out *Mastering Regular Expressions, Third Edition* (O'Reilly, 2006) by Jeffrey E. F. Friedl or, for made-to-order regular expressions, visit the Regular Expression Library at *http://regexlib.com/*.

For an example of using regular expressions in Dreamweaver, see page 794.

Advanced Tag Searches

If you find the number of options an advanced text search offers overwhelming, you haven't seen anything yet. Dreamweaver's tag search adds more choices to help you quickly search for, and modify, HTML tags. You can use a tag search to strip out unwanted HTML tags (for example, if you're migrating an old site to CSS, you could remove the <font> tag), transform one tag into another (you could turn old-style *bold* [<b>] into the more widely accepted *strong* [<strong>] tag), and perform a host of other powerful actions.

In its basic outline, a tag search is much like the regular text search described on page 783. But this time, from the Search menu, you should choose Specific Tag. Now a Tag menu appears next to the Search menu, and the dialog box expands to display a new set of fields (see Figure 20-7). Some of them are the same as the controls you see when performing an advanced text search (page 788), such as the Tag Modifier menu and the + button that lets you add additional restrictions to the search.

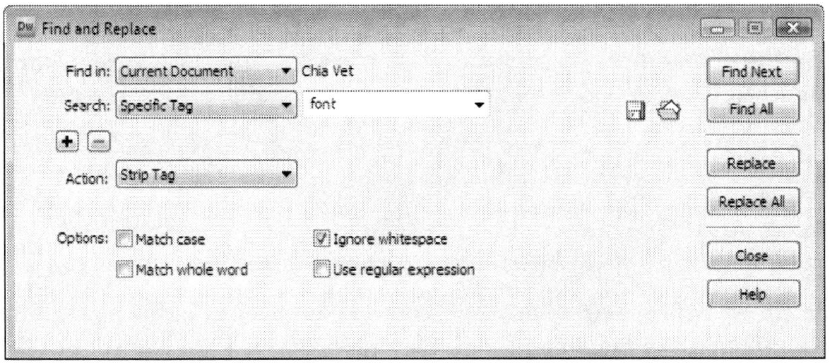

***Figure 20-7:** It's a snap to remove tags when you use the Specific Tag option in Dreamweaver's "Find and Replace" command—just select the Strip Tag action. This option is handy if you're replacing old-style text formatting with Cascading Style Sheets. Use it to strip out unwanted <font> tags from old sites, for example.*

But a key difference here is the Action menu (Figure 20-8), which lets you specify the action Dreamweaver will perform on tags that match the search criteria when you click Replace or Replace All (if you intend to search, but not replace, then these options don't apply):

- **Replace Tag & Contents** replaces the tag, and anything enclosed by the tag (including other tags), with whatever you put into the With box to the right of this menu. You can either type or paste text or HTML here.
- **Replace Contents Only** replaces everything enclosed by the tag with text or HTML that you specify. The tag itself remains untouched.

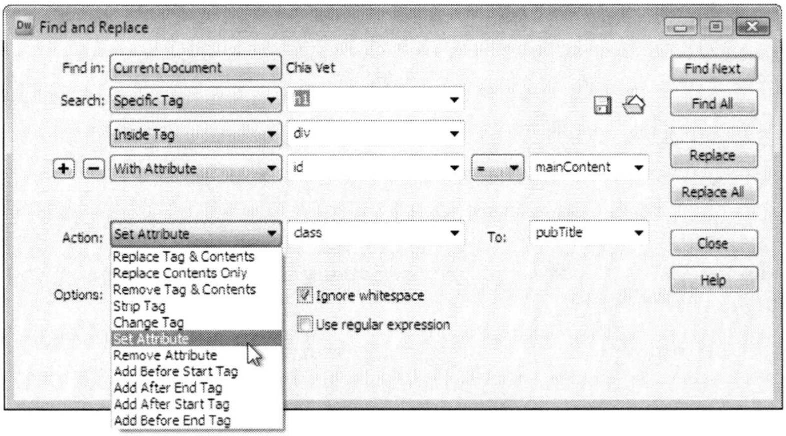

***Figure 20-8:** Once Dreamweaver finds a specific tag, it can perform any of 11 different actions on the tag or its contents.*

Note: Depending on which tag you're searching for, you might not see all the actions listed here. For example, the <img> tag doesn't have both an opening and closing tag like the <p> tag, which surrounds text inside a paragraph, so you won't see any of the options such as "Replace Contents Only" that affect the content between an opening and closing tag.

- **Remove Tag and Contents** deletes the tag and *everything* inside.
- **Strip Tag** deletes the tag from the page, but leaves anything enclosed by the tag untouched. The outmoded <font> tag is a perfect candidate for this action.
- **Set Attribute** adds an attribute to the tag. For example, you could set the *alt* property of an image this way (see the example in the next section).
- **Remove Attribute** removes an attribute from a tag. For example, you could remove the not-so-useful *lowsrc* attribute from all image tags on your pages.
- **Add Before (After) Start (End) Tag.** The last four actions in the menu simply offer variations on the same theme. They each let you place content in a Web page just before or after the tag for which you're searching.

  To understand how these actions work, remember that most HTML tags come in pairs. The paragraph tag, for example, has an opening tag (<p>) and a closing tag (</p>). Say you searched for a paragraph tag; you could add text or HTML *before* or *after* the start tag (<p>), or *before* or *after* the end tag (</p>). (For an example of when you might use this feature, see the box on page 797.)

A Powerful Example: Adding Alt Text Fast

You've just put the finishing touches on the last page of your brand-new, 1,000-page site. You sit back and smile—and then snap bolt upright when you notice you forgot to add an Alt description for the site's banner graphic (see page 225). This graphic, called *site_banner.gif*, appears on every single one of the 1,000 pages. With rising dread, you realize that you'll have to open each page, select the graphic, and add the *alt* property by hand.

And then you remember Dreamweaver's advanced tag-based find-and-replace feature.

Here's what you do. Press Ctrl+F (⌘-F) to open the "Find and Replace window. Set up the dialog box like this:

1. **From the "Find in" menu, choose Entire Current Local Site.**

   You want to fix *every* page on your site.

2. **From the Search pop-up menu, choose Specific Tag; from the pop-up menu to its right, choose "img."**

   You'll start by identifying every image (the <img> tag).

3. **On the next row, use the three pop-up menus to choose With Attribute, "src", and the equals sign (=).**

   This tells Dreamweaver to look for specific images—in this case, images with a src attribute (the path that tells a Web browser where to find the image file on the Web server) with a specific value.

4. **Type *.*site_banner\.gif* in the box next to the = sign.**

   For this exercise, assume the graphic file is stored in a folder called *images* located in the root folder of the site. The name *site_banner.gif* is the name of the image file. The .* is the magic, and you'll learn its purpose in a moment (ditto the backslash hanging out before the second period).

5. **Click the + button.**

   Another row of Tag Modifier menus appears.

6. **From the new row of menus, choose Without Attribute and "alt".**

   You've further limited Dreamweaver's search to only those images that don't already have the *alt* attribute. (After all, why bother setting the *alt* property on an image that already has it?)

7. **From the Action menu, choose Set Attribute; from the Tag menu, choose "alt".**

   You've just told Dreamweaver what to do when you click the Replace or Replace All button. When Dreamweaver finds an <img> tag that matches the search criteria, it will then *add* an *alt* property to that tag.

   In this example, you might type *Chia Vet* in the To field; you've just specified the Alt text for Dreamweaver to add to the image.

8. **Turn on "Use regular expressions".**

   Regular expressions, described on page 792, let you search for specific patterns of characters and, in this case, help you accurately identify the banner graphic file everywhere it appears.

   You know you're looking for the file *site_banner.gif* wherever it appears in the site. Unfortunately, if you just type *site_banner.gif* as the value of the *src* property of step 3, Dreamweaver can't succeed in its task. That's because the src attribute—the part of the <img> tag that includes the name of the file—varies from page to page. Depending on where a page is relative to the graphic, the src might be *site_banner.gif*, *images/site_banner.gif*, or even *../../../images/site_banner.gif*. What you need is a way to match every *src* attribute that ends in *site_banner.gif*.

   A simple regular expression, *.*site_banner\.gif*, does the trick. The period stands for *any* character (6, g, or even %, for example), while the * (asterisk) means "zero or more times." When you add these codes to the graphic name, *site_banner.gif*, you instruct Dreamweaver to find every *src* value that ends in *site_banner.gif*.

In other words .* will match *../../images/*, *images/*, and so on. It will even match nothing at all in the case where the Web page is actually inside the *images* folder and the *src* property is then just *site_banner.gif*.

Note the backslash before the last period: *\.gif*. Since in the world of regular expressions, a period means "any character," simply using *site_banner.gif* would not only match *site_banner.gif*, but also *site_banner1gif*, *site_bannerZgif*, and so on—in other words, any character between *site_banner* and *gif*. The backslash means treat the next character literally; it's just a period with no special regular-expression power.

The dialog box should look like the one in Figure 20-9.

9. **Click the Replace All button and sit back.**

   In a matter of moments, Dreamweaver updates all 1,000 pages.

   To test this out first, you might try a more cautious approach: Click the Find Next button to locate the first instance of the missing *alt* property; verify that it's correct by looking in the Search box (see Figure 20-4); and then click the Replace button to add the proper *alt* value. Double-check the newly updated page to make sure everything worked as planned. You can continue updating pages one at a time this way, or, once you're sure it works correctly, press Replace All.

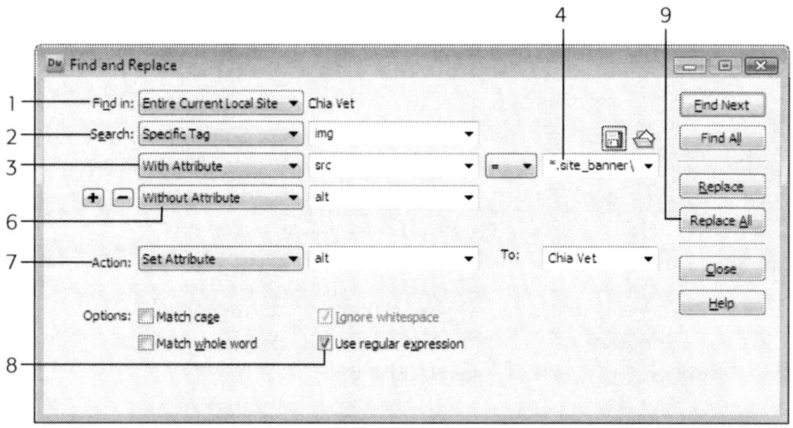

Figure 20-9: *The numbers shown here correspond to the steps in this fictional example, in which you want to add an <alt> tag—for the benefit of people who can't, or don't want to, see graphics in their browsers—to every occurrence of the banner logo.*

FREQUENTLY ASKED QUESTION

Convenient Copyright Notices

I want to add a copyright notice to the bottom of each page in my Web site. Is there a way to automate this process so I don't have to edit every page in my site by hand?

You bet. Use Dreamweaver's "Find and Replace" command to add text or HTML to the bottom of any Web page. The trick is knowing how to use the command's Specific Tag option.

First, choose Edit → "Find and Replace" to open the "Find and Replace" window. Next, choose Entire Current Local Site from the "Find in" menu, and choose Specific Tag from the Search menu. Choose "body" from the Tag menu. Remember, the <body> tag in HTML encloses everything that appears inside a browser window; it's equivalent to what you see in the document window.

From the Action menu, choose Add Before End Tag. The end tag in this case is </body>. Since </body> marks the end of any content in a Web page, whatever appears directly before this closing tag will appear at the bottom of the Web page (you can probably see where this is going).

Now, in the text field next to the Action menu, type (or paste) the copyright notice you'd like to use on each page. You may want to first design the copyright message using Dreamweaver, and then copy and paste the HTML into this field.

Click Replace All. Dreamweaver handles the rest.

You may not want to put the Copyright notice at the *very end* of the page's HTML, as in this example. You might want it to go inside a particular <div> tag that's already on the page. Let's say that that div has an ID of *footer*. In that case, you would search for a <div> tag from the Tag menu and then select "With attribute" ID equal to "footer." Then you could use either the "Add Before End Tag" or "Add After Start Tag" options to place the copyright notice either at the end or beginning of that div.

CHAPTER

21

Customizing Dreamweaver

Whether you're a hard-core HTML jockey who prefers to be knee-deep in Code view, or a visually oriented, drag-and-drop type who never strays from Design view, Dreamweaver lets you work whichever way you want.

By now, you're probably already using the Favorites tab on the Insert panel to store your most frequently used objects in one place, as discussed on page 29. But don't stop there. Dreamweaver also gives you the power to add, change, and share keyboard shortcuts—a simple way to tailor the program to your needs. If that's not enough of an efficiency boost, you can add features that even Adobe's engineers never imagined, from simple productivity add-ons like Quick-Link (see page 175) to advanced Server Behaviors to help power a complete e-commerce Web site. Dreamweaver's design allows amateur and professional programmers alike to write new features and functions using HTML, JavaScript, and XML (Extensible Markup Language). There are hundreds of these extras, called *extensions*, for you to explore. Best of all, you can try many of them for free.

Keyboard Shortcuts

As you use Dreamweaver, you'll hit the same keyboard shortcuts and travel to the same palettes and menus time and again. Perhaps your site uses a lot of graphics and Flash movies, and you're constantly using the keyboard shortcuts to insert them. But you may find that, after the thousandth time, Ctrl+Alt+F (⌘-Option-F) hurts your pinkie and uses too many keys to be efficient. On the other hand, the things you do all the time—like inserting text fields into forms or adding rollover images, for instance—may not have shortcuts at all, so you're forced to go to a menu.

To speed up your work and save your tendons, Dreamweaver comes with a keyboard-shortcut editor that lets you define or redefine shortcuts for most of the program's commands. Dreamweaver stores keyboard shortcuts in sets. It's easy to switch between them— a useful feature when you share your computer with someone who likes different keystrokes.

Four sets come with the program:

- **Dreamweaver Standard.** When you first fire up Dreamweaver, this is the set that's turned on. It's the same set of keyboard shortcuts available since Dreamweaver 8 and it matches the keyboard shortcuts found in Fireworks.
- **Dreamweaver MX 2004.** Some keyboard shortcuts have changed since Dreamweaver MX 2004—for example, Shift-F5 instead of Ctrl-F5 now opens the Tag Editor window. But the changes are so minor, it's not really necessary to use this set.
- **BBEdit.** If you're a Mac user with a code-editing past, you may have spent a lot of time learning shortcuts for Bare Bones Software's popular BBEdit. If so, you can choose this set.
- **HomeSite.** Likewise, if you're adept at the Windows HTML text editor HomeSite, you may want to use its keyboard shortcuts. Don't remember HomeSite? That's because it hasn't been available for years, so you probably won't ever see a need for this.

You can access the shortcut sets from the Keyboard Shortcuts window. Choose Edit → Keyboard Shortcuts. Be patient—the sets can take some time to load. Once the dialog box appears, you can switch sets by choosing a new one from the Current Set menu (see Figure 21-1).

Make Your Own Shortcut Set

What if you want a set that *combines* BBEdit shortcuts with your most-used Dreamweaver ones? Or, you're a radical individualist who wants to remap *every* command to the keys of your liking? You can easily create keyboard shortcut sets that fit the way you work. Dreamweaver doesn't let you alter any of the four standard sets, so if you want to create your own, the first step is to make a copy of an existing one.

To do so, choose Edit → Keyboard Shortcuts (on the Mac, it's Dreamweaver → Keyboard Shortcuts). In the Keyboard Shortcuts window, use the Current Set pop-up menu to choose the set you wish to copy, and then click the Duplicate Set button (see Figure 21-1). Dreamweaver asks you to name the new set; do so, and then click OK.

You can delete or rename any set you create—once you figure out that the button in the Shortcuts window with the cryptic icon is the Rename Set button (see Figure 21-1). The Trash Can button, of course, lets you delete a set.

Tip: Dreamweaver lets you delete the four main keyboard shortcut sets. If you want one of them back, don't worry. The actual file isn't gone. You just need to edit a file called *mm_deleted_files.xml* in your Dreamweaver configuration folder. Remove the line that lists the keyboard shortcut set you want to get back and save the file. Then quit and restart Dreamweaver. (Note that each account holder on Windows and Mac OS X maintains a separate Configuration folder. See the box on page 803 for more details.)

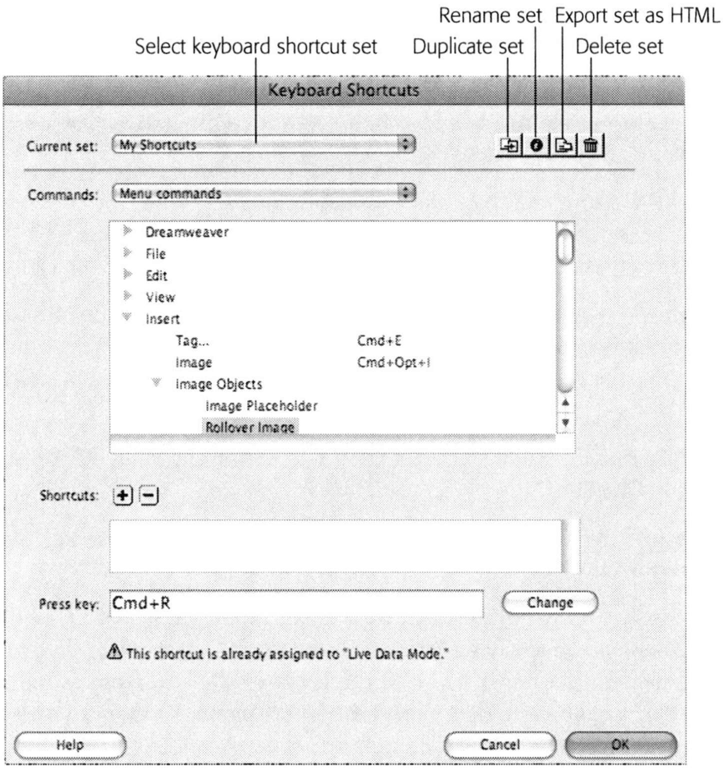

Figure 21-1: *The Keyboard Shortcuts window lets you select or duplicate a shortcut set, as well as add and remove keyboard shortcuts for every menu item in Dreamweaver. You can also create keyboard shortcuts for Snippets (see page 710). When you attempt to create a shortcut that another command's already using, Dreamweaver warns you. If you wish, you can ignore the warning and reassign the keys to the new command.*

Changing Keyboard Shortcuts

Once you've created a new set, you can select any command and alter its shortcut. Start by choosing Edit → Keyboard Shortcuts (Dreamweaver → Keyboard Shortcuts) to open the Shortcuts window, if it's not already open. Then:

1. **From the Commands pop-up menu, choose the command type.**

   Dreamweaver organizes shortcuts into four (Macintosh) or seven (Windows) primary categories. These categories don't always make sense: For example, Copy and Paste appear under the Code Editing category, even though you use them at least as frequently while editing a document in the visual Design view. In addition, you'll find quite a few commands listed under multiple categories (you only need to change a keyboard shortcut once for these redundant listings).

Browse to see which commands have (or could have) keyboard shortcuts associated with them:

- **Menu commands** are the commands in Dreamweaver's menus, such as Insert → Image.
- You might use the **Code editing** commands when editing HTML code. However, you could just as easily use them in Design view. They include Cut, Paste, and "Move to Top of Page," to name a few.
- **Document editing** commands are for selecting text and objects on a page, as well as previewing a page in a Web browser.
- **Files panel options menu** (Windows only) are the commands available when you right-click on a file in the Files panel.
- **Site panel** (Windows only) are the commands available from the contextual menu at the top right of the Files panel, such as Site → New Site. (On the Mac, many of these commands are listed in the Menu Commands category.)
- **Site window** (Windows only) are an odd assortment of commands that apply to situations like closing a window, quitting the application, or canceling FTP. (On the Mac, these commands are listed in the Document Editing group.)
- **Snippets** are reusable code pieces that you select from the Snippets panel, as discussed in Chapter 18.

2. **In the list below the Commands menu, click the command whose keyboard shortcut you want to change.**

   You'll find menu commands grouped by menu name: commands in the File menu, like Open and Save, fall under File. Click the + (Windows) or flippy triangle (Mac) next to the menu name to display the list of commands hidden underneath. For example, in Figure 21-1, the Insert menu is expanded as is its submenu, Image Objects.

   If the command already has a keyboard shortcut, it appears in the right-hand column. If it doesn't have a shortcut, you see an empty space.

3. **Click inside the "Press key" field, and then press the new keystroke.**

   Unless you're assigning the shortcut to an F-key or the Esc key, you must begin your shortcut with the Ctrl key (⌘-key). For example, the F8 key is a valid shortcut, but the letter R isn't; press Ctrl+R (⌘-R) instead.

Note: Some keyboard shortcuts may already be in use by your operating system, so assigning them in Dreamweaver may have no effect. For example, in Windows, Ctrl+Esc opens the Start Menu, while in Mac OS 10.4 and above, Dashboard uses the F12 key.

Of course, many commands already have shortcuts. If you choose a key combination that's in use, Dreamweaver tells you which command has dibs. You can pick a different key combination, or simply click the Change button to reassign the shortcut to your command.

4. **Click the Change button.**

   Dreamweaver saves the new shortcut in your custom set.

   Repeat from step 1 if you want to make other keystroke reassignments. When you're finished, click OK to close the dialog box.

FREQUENTLY ASKED QUESTION

Sharing Shortcuts

How do I share my keyboard set with other people?.

Dreamweaver stores your keyboard shortcuts as XML files—but in Dreamweaver finding them can be tricky. These files are in different locations depending on your operating system. Each keyboard set lives in an XML file; the file's name ends with the extension *.xml*. For example, if you created a new set of keyboard shortcuts name My Shortcuts, the XML file would be named *My Shortcuts.xml*.

In Windows XP, you'll find the custom keyboard set on your main hard drive in *Documents and Settings → [Your Name] → Application Data → Adobe → Dreamweaver CS4 → en_US → Configuration → Menus → Custom Sets*. In Windows Vista, they're in *C:\Users\[your user name]\AppData\Roaming\Adobe\Dreamweaver CS4\en_US\Configuration\Menus\Custom Sets*.

In Mac OS X, these files are squirreled away in your *Home folder → Library → Application Support → Adobe → Dreamweaver CS4 → en_US → Configuration → Menus → Custom Sets*.

Depending upon the language you're using, you might see something other than "en_US" (which stands for English), such as "de_DE" for German, or "ja_JP" for Japanese.

You can copy these files and place them in the Custom Sets folder on other computers. Once you've done so, Dreamweaver users on those machines can use the Keyboard Shortcuts window (Edit → Keyboard Shortcuts or, on the Mac, Dreamweaver → Keyboard Shortcuts) to select the new set, just as though it had been created in that copy of Dreamweaver.

What if a command you use often doesn't have a shortcut at all? It's no problem to create one. As a matter of fact, Dreamweaver lets you assign *two* keyboard shortcuts to every command—one for you, and one for your left-handed spouse, for example.

To give a command an additional shortcut (or its first):

1. **Choose the command.**

   Follow the first two steps of the preceding instructions.

2. **Click the + button next to the word "Shortcuts".**

   The cursor automatically pops into the "Press key" field.

3. **Press the keys of your additional shortcut, and then click the Change button again.**

   Repeat from step 1 if you want to make other keystroke reassignments; when you're finished, click OK.

Deleting shortcuts is just as easy. Simply click the command in the list, and then click the minus sign (–) button next to the word "Shortcuts".

Create a Shortcut Cheat Sheet

Unless your brain is equipped with a 400-gig hard drive, you'll probably find it hard to remember all of Dreamweaver's keyboard shortcuts.

Fortunately, Dreamweaver offers a printable cheat sheet for your reference. At the top of the Shortcuts window, there's a handy "Export Set as HTML" button. (It's labeled with a cryptic icon; see Figure 21-1.) Click this button to name and save a simple HTML page that lists all of the commands and keyboard shortcuts for the currently selected set. Once you've saved the file, print it out or use it as an online reference—a great way to keep a record of your shortcuts for yourself or a team of Web page designers.

Dreamweaver Extensions

While keyboard shortcuts give you an easy way to access frequently used commands, they're not much help if the command you want doesn't exist. Suppose, for example, that you use Dreamweaver's Open Browser Window behavior (page 575) to load a new Web page into a window that's exactly 200 × 300 pixels. But what if you wanted the window to be centered in the middle of the visitor's monitor? Dreamweaver's behavior doesn't do that. What's a Web designer to do? You could go to the Adobe site and request the new feature (*www.adobe.com/cfusion/mmform/index.cfm?name=wishform&product=12*) in hopes that the bustling team of programmers will add the command to the next version. But you'd have to wait—and there's no guarantee that Adobe would add it.

The legions of hard-core Dreamweaver fans have taken this feature wish-list issue into their own hands. As it turns out, amateur (and pro) programmers can enhance Dreamweaver relatively easily by writing new feature modules using the basic languages of the Web: HTML, JavaScript, and XML. (In fact, HTML forms, JavaScript programs, and XML documents constitute much of the program. The objects in the Insert panel, for example, are actually HTML pages stored within Dreamweaver's Configuration folder, and all of Dreamweaver's menus have actually been written as an XML file.)

Because of this "open architecture," you can add new functions and commands—called *extensions*—to Dreamweaver by downloading the work of one of those programmers and installing it in your own copy of Dreamweaver. A Dreamweaver extension can take many forms and work in a variety of ways to change how the program works. It can be an icon on the Insert panel, a behavior listed on the Behaviors panel, or a command in the Commands menu. It might even be an entirely new floating window, like the Property inspector, that you use to alter some aspect of your page.

Best of all, whereas programming ability may be required to *create* extensions, none at all is necessary to use them. You can download hundreds of extensions from the Web and install them on your computer for free. In addition, many sophisticated extensions, like those for creating e-commerce sites, are commercially available.

Note: Extensions have been around for many versions of Dreamweaver. Unfortunately, each version of Dreamweaver added a few kinks for extension developers, so not all extensions out there work with Dreamweaver CS4. (Many extensions that were compatible with Dreamweaver *CS3 do* work with Dreamweaver CS4.) Most extension developers list which versions of Dreamweaver their extensions work with, and you can also check for version compatibility on the Dreamweaver Exchange (see Figure 21-2).

Browse the Exchange

The largest collection of extensions awaits you at the Adobe Exchange Web site, where you'll find hundreds of free and commercial extensions. Although some come from Adobe itself, the vast majority are written by an army of talented Dreamweaver users.

Using the Exchange is a straightforward process:

1. **In your Web browser, go to *www.adobe.com/exchange* and then click the Dreamweaver link under the list of "Exchanges by Product".**

   You can also get there from within Dreamweaver by choosing Commands → Get More Commands.

2. **Sign in (see Figure 21-2).**

   You can *browse* the site without signing in, but to *download* any of the extensions, you need to get a free Adobe ID and sign in, using the Exchange Sign In form—click the *Your account* link in the top-left corner of the Web page (see Figure 21-2).

3. **Browse the extensions.**

   Once you've logged into the site, the home page highlights new and popular extensions. A list of extension categories—Accessibility, DHTML/Layers, Navigation, and so on—appears on the right side of the page. Clicking any of those categories brings you to a list of extensions in that category. Click one of the sorting buttons (circled in Figure 21-2) to view the newest, most popular, or highest rated extensions.

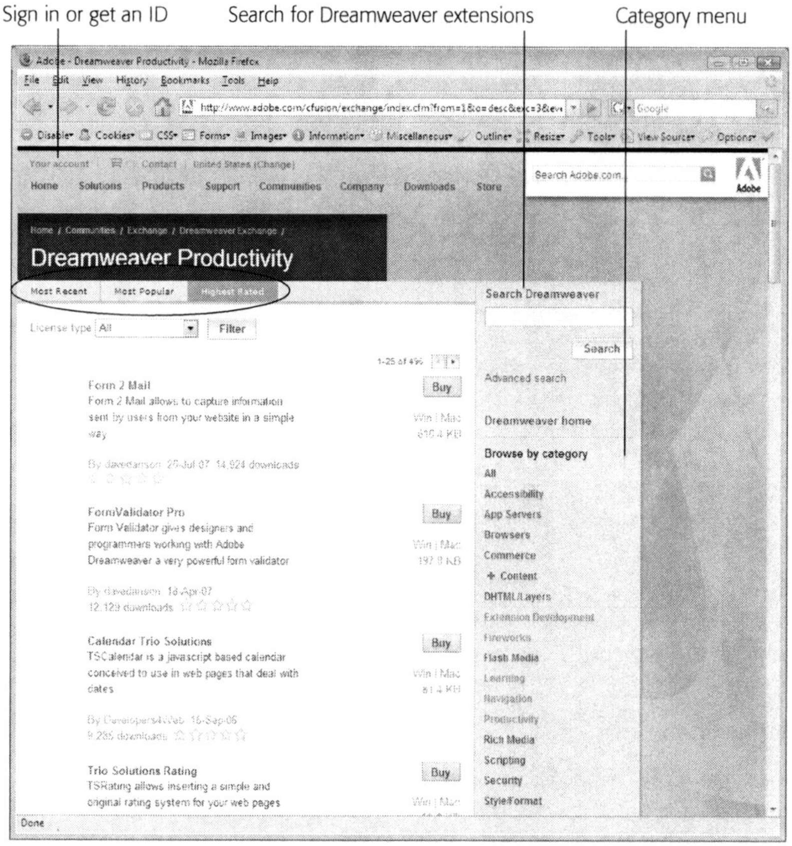

Figure 21-2: *You can peruse the Dreamweaver Exchange freely, check out the offerings, and even buy commercial third-party extensions. However, if you want to download one of the free extensions, you must get an Adobe ID and log into the site. Unfortunately, the marketing machine must be appeased, so you'll need to provide personal information and face a (fortunately optional) survey of your Web development habits.*

Use the menu to the right of "License type" to view extensions that match a particular license—for example, if you're looking for free stuff select Open Source or Freeware and then click the Filter button.

If you're looking for a *particular* extension, the Search command is your best bet (see Figure 21-2). Type the extension's name or a few descriptive words into the Search Dreamweaver field, and then click Search.

4. **Click an extension's name to go to its Web page.**

   On an extension's page, you'll find lots of information about the extension, such as a description of how it works, a button to either purchase or download the extension, information about which version of Dreamweaver and which operating system (Windows or Mac) it's compatible with, and buttons to add the extension to Favorites and Alerts lists. The Favorites option lets you create a personal list of the extensions you like best; the Alerts list feature means you'll receive an email whenever the extension is updated (see Figure 21-3).

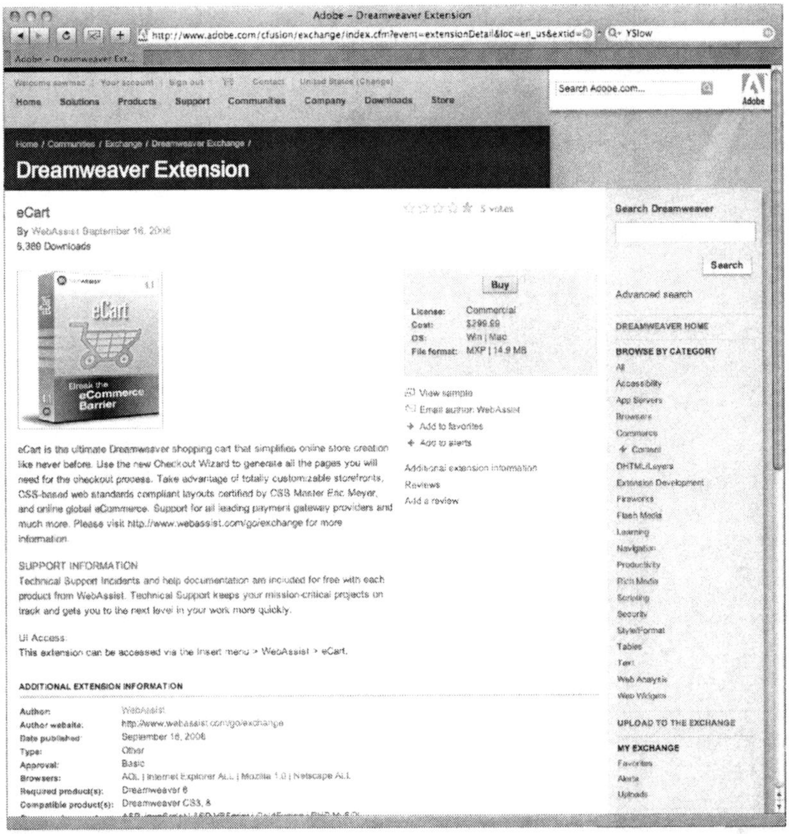

***Figure 21-3:** Each extension has its own page in Adobe Exchange that provides information about the extension and its developer. A helpful voting mechanism (1–5 stars) lets you know what other people think of the extension.*

When you click the Download button for an extension, your Web browser will either start downloading the extension file, or shuttle you off to the Web site of the person or company that created the extension. A Buy button, on the other hand, will always send you off to another Web site where you can then buy the extension directly from its creator.

Find a Good Extension

How do you figure out which extensions are worth checking out? First, you can find some recommendations of the best ones scattered through this book in special boxes labeled Extension Alert (see page 175 and page 451, for instance).

The Exchange also provides information to help you separate the wheat from the chaff. Adobe tests each new extension before posting it. Extensions that pass a basic set of tests—it installs OK, it works, it doesn't blow up your computer—get a Basic approval rating. Some extensions also pass a more rigorous test that determines if the extension works in a way that's "Dreamweaver-like." In other words, these extensions are designed to look, feel, and act like the program, so that you won't need to learn a new interface. These extensions get an Adobe Approved rating, indicated by the word "Adobe" in the approval section of an extension's details page.

Of course, these approval ratings only let you know if an extension works; they don't tell you whether it's *useful.* As an extra aid, Dreamweaver aficionados (including you) can rate each extension on a scale of 1 (worst) to 5 (best) (see Figure 21-3). An extension's average rating gives you a good indication of how handy it is. When you're browsing the Exchange, look for the star rating at the bottom of each extension listing (see Figure 21-2). You can also click the Highest Rated link (circled in Figure 21-2) to sort the list of extensions from most to least number of stars.

Other Extension Sources

Unfortunately, the glory days of totally free extensions are over. You can still find plenty of extensions offered free of charge, but many developers have realized they can't survive by giving away their work. The upside is that there are more excellent, polished, well-documented commercial extensions than ever—many even with customer support. Here are a few highlights:

- **WebAssist** (*www.webassist.com*) is one of the largest and most professional extension development companies. A former Dreamweaver product manager is at the helm, and they offer a wide variety of high quality extensions. (There are even a few free extensions to choose from.)
- If PHP or ASP is your bag, then you'll find an impressive collection of extensions at **Felix One** (*www.felixone.it/extensions/dwextensionsen.asp*).
- **Project Seven** (*www.projectseven.com*) offers free extensions and several excellent commercial extensions for creating animated Dynamic HTML and CSS menus, scrolling text areas, CSS-based page layouts, photo galleries, and more.
- **Trent Pastrana** (*www.fourlevel.com*) sells extensions for building photo galleries, whiz-bang DHTML effects (like menus that slide onto the page), or scrollers that move text up and down (or left and right) across a Web page.
- **Trio Solutions** (*http://components.developers4web.com/*) sells lots of inexpensive Dreamweaver extensions that let you use Dreamweaver to add CSS-style calendars, insert Flash music players into a page, and much more.

Download and Install Extensions

Once you've found a great extension, download it to your computer. You can save the downloaded file anywhere on your computer, but you might want to create a special folder. That way, if you ever need to reinstall Dreamweaver, you can quickly find and add your collection of extensions.

A downloaded extension file's name ends with *.mxp*, which stands for Macromedia Exchange Package (from the days before Adobe bought Macromedia). That's a special file format that works with the Extension Manager—the program, described next, that actually installs the extension into Dreamweaver.

Extension Manager

To add or remove a Dreamweaver extension, use the Extension Manager, a standalone program that's integrated with Dreamweaver. It's designed to manage extensions for many Adobe programs (not just Dreamweaver): you can install extensions, turn them on and off, and remove them. This feature can be quite handy if you also use Adobe's Flash or Fireworks programs—you have a single access point for managing all your extensions.

You can launch the Extension Manager from within Dreamweaver by choosing Help → Manage Extensions, or Commands → Manage Extensions (see Figure 21-4).

To add an extension:

1. **Download an extension package (*.mxp* file) from the Exchange or another Web site.**

   See instructions on page 805.

2. **From Dreamweaver, choose Help → Manage Extensions (or Commands → Manage Extensions).**

   You can also select Extension Manager from the Extension menu in the Application Bar (see Figure 1-31). Either way, the Extension Manager launches. It lists all currently installed extensions (see Figure 21-4).

3. **Choose Dreamweaver CS4 from the left-hand list of Adobe Products.**

   Since the Extension Manager handles extensions for several different programs, you need to specify which program you're using. If you don't have any other Adobe products installed on your machine, Dreamweaver CS4 and Bridge CS4 (which is installed alongside Dreamweaver) are the only options.

4. **Choose File → Install Extension.**

   You can also click the Install Extension button. The Select Extension window appears, listing the folders on your hard drive.

5. **Navigate to and select the extension package (.mxp file) you wish to add.**

   A disclaimer appears with a lot of legal text. In brief, it frees Adobe from liability if your computer melts down as a result of installing the extension.

6. **Click Accept in the Disclaimer window.**

   A message may appear that asks you to quit and restart Dreamweaver. If so, follow the directions.

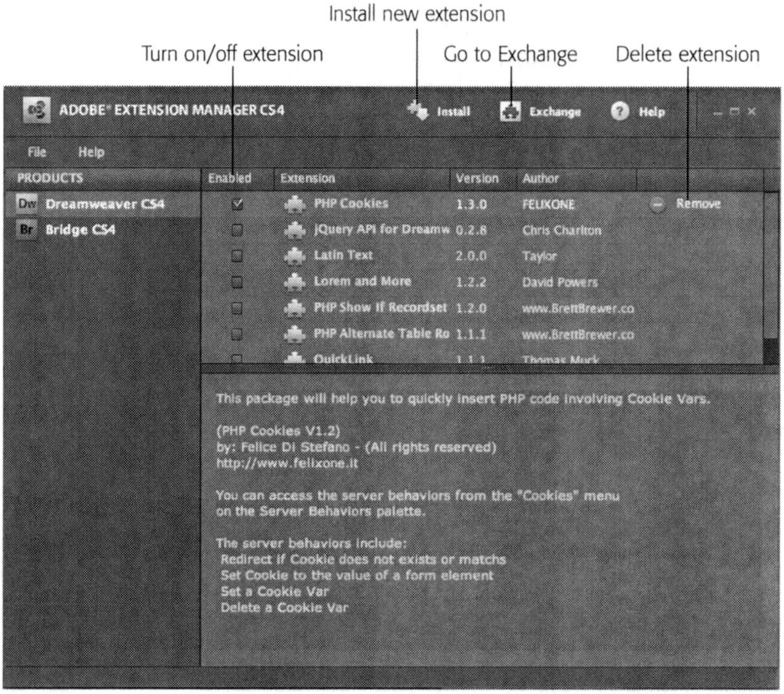

Figure 21-4: *The Extension Manager window lists each extension you've installed, along with its version number, type, and author. If you select an extension from the list, a description appears in the bottom half of the window. Adobe Bridge (listed here on the left) is a program for managing visual "assets" among the various programs that make up the Creative Suite, like Photoshop and Illustrator. Since Bridge's emphasis is on visual media—not Web pages—it's not as useful for Web developers as it is for graphic designers. If you want to learn more about Bridge visit* www.adobe.com/products/creativesuite/bridge/bridgehome/.

Tip: A faster way to install an extension is to simply double-click the .mxp file after you download it. This launchs the Extension Manager and installs the extension.

To remove an extension, select it from the list and choose File → Remove Extension, or click the Remove button (see Figure 21-4).

Note: If you install a lot of extensions, Dreamweaver may take longer than usual to load; it needs to process every extension file as it opens. If you want to temporarily turn off an extension (as opposed to deleting it), open the Extension Manager and turn off the Enable box next to the extension's name. To turn it back on, simply turn on the checkbox again. You may need to restart Dreamweaver to make the extension available again.

Make Your Own Extensions

The Exchange is a great resource for finding useful extensions. But what if you can't find the extension you need? Create your own.

Writing extensions requires in-depth knowledge of JavaScript and HTML. But when you create a command that lets you complete a weekly task in a fraction of the time it previously took, the effort may just be worth it. For more information, visit the the Dreamweaver support center: *www.adobe.com/support/dreamweaver/extend.html.*

POWER USERS' CLINIC

The Secret Life of Extensions

Where do extensions go? The basic answer is: inside the Dreamweaver Configuration folder. But Dreamweaver actually supplies you with multiple configuration folders: the main folder located with the program itself, and account-specific folders for each user account on a computer. Windows and Macs let multiple users have an account on a single computer—one for you, your spouse, and your pet ferret, say. Of course, you may be the only one using your computer, so in that case there'd be just one configuration folder.

On a Windows machine, the main configuration folder is located in *C:\Program Files\Adobe\Adobe Dreamweaver CS4\en_US\configuration* (assuming the C:\ drive is your main drive). On a Mac, you can find it here: *Applications → Adobe Dreamweaver CS4 → en_US → Configuration*. The individual account configuration folders are located in folders dedicated to each user. In Windows XP: *C:\Documents and Settings\[your user name]\Application Data\Adobe\Dreamweaver CS4\en_US\Configuration*. In Windows Vista: *C:\Users\[your user name]\AppData\Roaming\Adobe\Dreamweaver CS4\en_US\Configuration*. On a Mac: *Volume Name → Users → [your user name] → Library → Application Support → Adobe → Dreamweaver CS4 → en_US → Configuration*. (As mentioned in the box on page 803, "en_US" means English. If you installed Dreamweaver using a different language this folder will be named something else, such as "de_DE" for German.)

Some changes you make to Dreamweaver are recorded in your personal configuration folder, such as when you add an extension, delete a keyboard shortcut set (see page 800), or save a workspace layout (see page 34).

The main Configuration folder holds many of the files that control the look and operation of the program. For instance, the entire menu structure, including menu items and submenus, is described in a file called *menus.xml*. When Dreamweaver starts, it reads this file and uses the information inside it to draw the menus on the screen.

The Configuration folder holds many subfolders, each with a special purpose. For example, the Objects folder contains files that tell Dreamweaver which icon buttons appear on the Insert bar and how each one works.

Depending on the type of extension you've downloaded—command, object, behavior, or whatever—the Extension Manager stores the file (or files) required by the extension in one or more folders inside the Configuration folder. Because all of the files inside the Configuration folder are crucial to the way Dreamweaver works, don't delete the folder or any of the files inside it. In fact, because the Extension Manager automatically makes any required changes to the Configuration folder, there's no reason for you to even look inside it.

(The only exception is when you want to copy your keyboard shortcut set to another computer [see page 803] or delete your personal dictionary [see page 91].)

6

Part Six: Dynamic Dreamweaver

CHAPTER
22

Getting Started with Dynamic Web Sites

So far in this book, you've learned to build and maintain Web sites using Dreamweaver's powerful design, coding, and site management tools. The pages you've created are straightforward HTML, which you can immediately preview in a Web browser to see a finished design. These kinds of pages are often called *static*, since they don't change once you've finished creating them (unless you edit them later, of course). For many Web sites, especially ones where you carefully handcraft the design and content on a page-by-page basis, static Web pages are the way to go.

But imagine landing a contract to build an online catalog of 10,000 products. After the initial excitement disappears (along with your plans for that trip to Hawaii), you realize that even using Dreamweaver's Template tool (Chapter 19), building 10,000 pages is a lot of work!

Fortunately, Dreamweaver offers a better and faster way to deal with this problem. Its dynamic Web site creation tools let you take advantage of a variety of powerful techniques that would be difficult or impossible with plain HTML pages. With Dreamweaver, you can build pages that:

- Display listings of products or other items like your record collection, your company's staff directory, or your mother's library of prized recipes.
- Search through a database of information and display the results.
- Require login so you can hide particular areas from prying eyes.
- Collect and store information from visitors to your site.
- Personalize your visitors' experience: "Hello Dave, it's been a while since you've visited. Did you miss us?—Hal."

Visit *Amazon.com*, for example, and you'll find more books than you could read in a lifetime. In fact, you'll find more products—DVDs, CDs, and even outdoor lawn furniture—than could fit inside a Wal-Mart. In just an hour, you could browse through hundreds of products, each with its own Web page. Do you really think Amazon hired an army of Web developers to create each Web page for every product they sell? Not a chance.

Note: Luckily you aren't limited to *either* "static" *or* "dynamic" Web pages. Web sites frequently contain both–static pages for custom designs and handcrafted content, and dynamic pages for mass production of a thousand catalog pages.

Instead, when you search for a book on *Amazon.com*, your search triggers a computer program, running on what's called an *application server*, which searches a large database of products. When the program finds products that match what you're searching for, it merges that information with the HTML elements that make up the page (banner, navigation buttons, copyright notice, and so on). You see a new Web page that's been created on the spot—perhaps for the first time ever (Figure 22-1).

Figure 22-1: *An infinite number of monkeys couldn't create all the Web pages for all the products Amazon sells. The solution? A dynamic Web site, which takes your programmed instructions, and automatically creates pages made up of content chunks pulled from a database. That's the way to go if you've got a site with loads of pages that all present similar information.*

Dynamic Web sites are usually the realm of professional programmers, but Dreamweaver can simplify routine tasks like viewing information from a database and adding, updating, and deleting data. Even if you don't have a programmer's bone in your body, this chapter and the next few give you the basics.

Pieces of the Puzzle

You may be thinking, "Yeah, that sounds fantastic, but so did that time-share in the Bahamas. What's the catch?"

The catch is that dynamic Web sites are more complex and require more technologies to get off the ground. Simple static Web sites require only the computer you use to build them, and a Web server to dish them out. In fact, as you can see by previewing your site from your own computer with a Web browser, you don't even need a Web server to effectively view a static Web site.

Dynamic Web pages, by contrast, require more (see Figure 22-2). Not only is there a Web server that handles requests for Web pages, two other types of servers enter the equation: an *application server* and a *database server*.

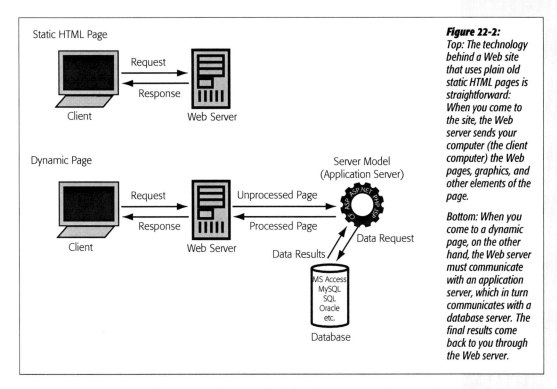

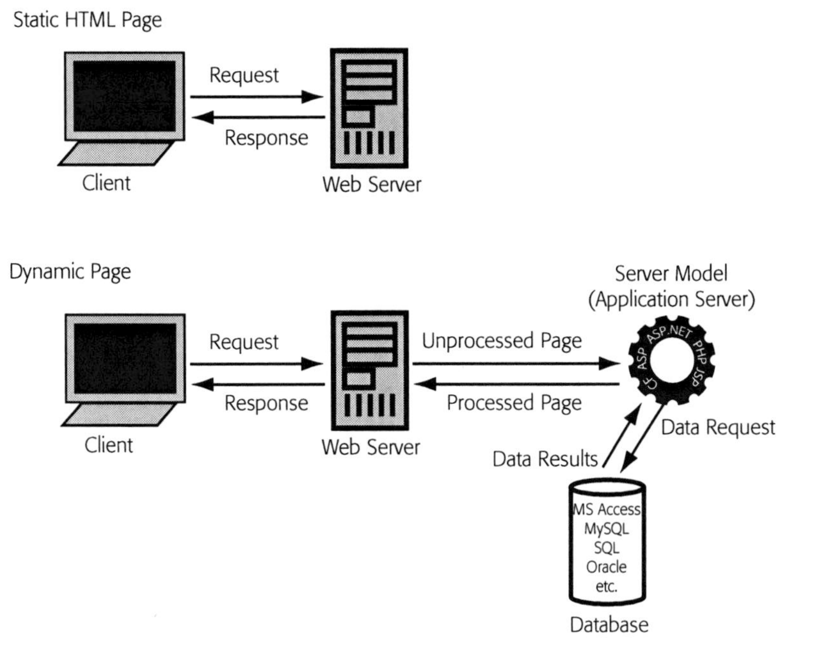

***Figure 22-2:** Top: The technology behind a Web site that uses plain old static HTML pages is straightforward: When you come to the site, the Web server sends your computer (the client computer) the Web pages, graphics, and other elements of the page.*

Bottom: When you come to a dynamic page, on the other hand, the Web server must communicate with an application server, which in turn communicates with a database server. The final results come back to you through the Web server.

You'll still be using a lot of HTML (and CSS) to build a dynamic site—for example, to provide the layout, add banner graphics, and navigation bars. But you'll augment this mix with some form of programming code. The application server processes this code and sends a complete HTML page to the Web server, which, in turn, sends that onto the visitor. In many cases, the programming code requires the application server to retrieve information from a database, and then merge it with the HTML of a page.

Note: In this context, a *server* refers to software that dishes out particular types of information–Web pages, database queries, or a program's output. It doesn't necessarily mean a separate computer; Web hosting firms can (and frequently do) have Web, database, and application servers all running happily together on a single machine.

Because dynamic Web sites require more technology, as you're building these sites you can't just open a dynamic page in your Web browser as you can a regular Web page. You must view a dynamic page through a Web server that has an appropriate application server running.

You also have to set up a database, and connect that database to your application server. Although this can be quite complex, it's not difficult to set up a basic Web server, application server, and database on your own computer, so that you can build and test database-driven Web pages. It's also easy to connect to other computers that are already configured to serve up dynamic, database-driven Web pages.

And once you or your company's system administrator have set up the Web server and other assorted components, Dreamweaver can easily create complex Web pages that access databases, and let you build powerful Web applications, all without ever learning any programming.

Even so, there are literally hundreds of combinations of Web, application, and database servers, and Dreamweaver doesn't work with all of them. However, it's capable of working with three of the most popular and powerful combinations, using four different programming languages!

Note: The term *Web application* refers to Web pages that work together to complete a task. All the various pages that come together to form an online shopping site–which lets visitors do things like search a database of products, view individual product pages, and add products to a shopping cart–would be considered a Web application.

Understanding Server Models

In Dreamweaver lingo, the different application servers combine with a programming language to create a *server model.* Dreamweaver recognizes several server models, including ASP, ColdFusion, and PHP. Each server model has its own set of unique requirements, and its own methods of performing identical tasks.

Each server model also works with one or more programming languages. For example, you can create an ASP page using either VBScript or JScript. PHP can refer both to a programming language named PHP *and* to the application server. Likewise, CFML, or ColdFusion Markup Language, is a programming language, and ColdFusion server is an application server. If your head is hurting trying to make sense of all this, just keep this in mind: An application server processes programming code and carries out various actions, like talking to a database or spitting out a Web page.

FREQUENTLY ASKED QUESTION

The Dynamic Duo

How does a dynamic Web site differ from dynamic HTML?

Dynamic is a word that's thrown around a lot in Web circles, and it has a variety of uses.

For starters, *dynamic* sometimes refers to the power of JavaScript. For example, Dreamweaver CS4's Spry Framework uses JavaScript to create interactive page elements such as the Spry menu bar discussed on page 184, or the animated effects described on page 568. The result is sometimes called "Dynamic HTML," because the elements on the page *change*.

However, in this section of the book, *dynamic* refers to any Web page that's processed by an application server–pages that undergo some form of transformation on the Web server's side of the Internet, like connecting to a database, or collecting information from a form.

What's important to remember is that JavaScript, used for Dynamic HTML, Spry, and Dreamweaver Behaviors (Chapter 13), is a *client-side* programming language. It runs in someone's Web browser, and is limited to changing the way a Web page looks and behaves *after* it's been downloaded over the Internet.

Dynamic Web sites, on the other hand, use *server-side* programs–those that run on an application server, out there on the Web somewhere. The dynamic part (responding to a form or accessing a database, for example) happens *on the Web server*. The visitors to your site never see any programming code, and their computers never have to run the program. They merely enjoy the results of the application server's hard work: a finished HTML page.

Note: Dreamweaver CS4 no longer provides built-in tools for creating database-driven pages for ASP.NET or JSP (Java Server Pages). You can still use Dreamweaver CS4 to work on Web pages using either of those technologies–for example, by writing the programming code yourself–but, you won't have access to the easy-to-use server side programming tools described in this section of the book.

Which server model you use depends on which resources you have available: which type of Web server hosts your site, the operating system it uses, and which application server is available. If you're hosting your site on Linux or Unix, you'll most likely end up using PHP; if you're hosting on Windows, meanwhile, you probably have access to ASP. It all comes down to what you have on your computer, what your company uses, or (if you're using a Web hosting service) what the host computer understands. Here's a brief description of each server model.

PHP

PHP (PHP Hypertext Preprocessor) is a programming language that was created specifically for building dynamic Web pages. It's the most popular and widely available option at Web hosting companies—in other words, when it comes time to place your finished Web site on the Internet, you're most likely to find a Web hosting company that supports PHP. (PHP is also quite often the least expensive hosting option.) The PHP *interpreter*—that's the application server—works in conjunction with a variety of Web servers, including Microsoft's Internet Information Server (IIS), but was initially created for the Apache Web server. PHP can also work with a variety of different database servers, but Dreamweaver understands only the MySQL database server (which is also available at nearly every Web hosting company).

Note: Because Apache, PHP, and MySQL are so commonly used together, you may encounter an acronym frequently used to describe them: AMP.

Apache, PHP, and MySQL are free (one of the reasons they're so popular), and you can find simple installation programs—see page 822 for suggestions—that let you install all three programs on your own desktop computer. The tutorials for this section of the book use the PHP server model.

ASP

ASP (Active Server Pages) used to be one of the most common ways to start building database-driven Web sites. It's a bit long in the tooth now, and is probably not the best choice if you're just starting with database-driven sites. ASP understands two different programming languages: VBScript and server-side JavaScript, both of which Dreamweaver speaks fluently. ASP also works with Microsoft's Web server—IIS.

ASP can work with a variety of databases. For small projects, you can use Microsoft Access (the database program that comes with some versions of Microsoft Office), since it's fairly easy to use. For more demanding projects, where you need to store lots of data, and many people will access your site, Microsoft's SQL Server is a better choice.

ColdFusion

ColdFusion is an application server from Adobe (the maker of Dreamweaver) that's programmed using CFML (ColdFusion Markup Language). ColdFusion works in conjunction with several different Web servers, including IIS and Apache, and uses its own programming language, which resembles HTML. For this reason, some Web designers find it easier to learn than other programming languages.

The downside is that this application isn't free. You *can* download a developer's edition—a free version that runs on your computer—so you can build and test ColdFusion Web pages. But if you want to host the Web site on the Internet, you have to either buy the ColdFusion Server package (which isn't cheap) or find a Web hosting company that offers ColdFusion hosting. Fortunately, in recent years, more and more Web hosting companies have started offering ColdFusion as an option, at rates that are close to or match regular hosting plans.

The Developer Edition of ColdFusion is available for download at *www.adobe.com/go/devcenter_cf_try*.

Like ASP, ColdFusion works with many different databases.

Picking a Server Model

With so many choices, you're probably wondering which server model to choose. If you've never built a dynamic Web site before, your best bet is PHP. You can easily set up a fully operational Web server (Apache), application server (PHP), and database server (MySQL) on your desktop computer, and quickly begin building dynamic pages with Dreamweaver.

In fact, since this is the easiest method, this book's tutorials concentrate on building PHP pages. Once you get the hang of Dreamweaver's dynamic Web-building tools, you can always try any of the other server models to build your sites. (However, switching a single site from one server model to another is difficult and not recommended.)

However, when you're building a real-world Web site, the final decision on which server model to use may be out of your hands. You may be working for a company that's already using ColdFusion for its Web site. Or, if you've already got a Web site up and running, but want to add some database-driven content, you have to use what's installed on that server. If your site is currently hosted at a Web hosting company, you should contact the company to find out which operating system, Web server, and databases it uses. If they're Windows-based, odds are that they use IIS, meaning that you can use ASP, and either Access or SQL Server databases (though PHP and MySQL are also available for Windows). On the other hand, if they're a Unix operation, you'll most likely find the Apache Web server, PHP, and MySQL database.

Fortunately, the tools Dreamweaver provides for the different server models are largely the same. Essentially, you start to build dynamic Web pages using the same techniques you've learned in the earlier sections of this book. For the heavy lifting (like retrieving data from a database or password protecting a Web page), you'll turn to Dreamweaver's menu-driven database tools. They'll help you add the programming code necessary to make an application server do all the server-side magic you need to work with databases and generate dynamic Web pages. Once you learn Dreamweaver, you can build pages for any of the server models with which it works.

Dynamic Web Sites: The Setup

Now that your head is spinning, and you're considering some noble career alternative like farmer, firefighter, or carpenter, it's time to set up Dreamweaver to work with an application server and database.

You can perform this configuration in several different ways. One involves using what Dreamweaver calls a *testing server*. Remember how you can create a Web site on your own computer (the *local site*) before posting it online for all to see (the *remote site*)? Here, the concept is similar. When building Web applications, it's again a good idea to keep all the "work in progress" pages on your own computer. After all, you don't want to fill up an active online database with test data, or put half-finished product pages on the Internet. But because dynamic Web sites require an application server and database, it's a good idea to create a *testing server* for storing and previewing dynamic pages in progress: a real Web server, application server, and database—all running on your own computer.

Then, when you've finished the site, you transfer the pages to the remote site using Dreamweaver's built-in FTP feature (see page 669). If you're working in a group setting with other Web developers, you can set up the testing server on a machine that's part of your group's local network. Each developer can then connect to the testing server and retrieve files to work on. (Using Dreamweaver's Check In/Check Out feature is a good idea when you're working with a group of people on the same site.)

Note: You can always use your remote site as a testing server, as long as it has one of the application servers and databases that Dreamweaver works with. While this method is an easy way to get started, you must contact your Web host to see what application server it uses, and whether it can handle databases. In addition, you should have a fast Internet connection to the server. Otherwise, testing your dynamic pages may just test your patience.

Finally, whenever you work on dynamic files directly on a live Web server, be aware that mistakes you make along the way may affect a database that *other* dynamic pages use. If, while hurriedly trying to complete your Web site, you accidentally create a page that deletes records from your database, important information may no longer be available on your Web site. So whenever possible, the testing server should be separate from the server where the finished and perfected site resides.

In the next four chapters, you'll be building a dynamic Web site using PHP and a MySQL database. The concepts you learn work for all of the other server models as well, though some of the details may be different. Significant differences among various server models are mentioned where applicable.

Setting Up a Testing Server

To get started with the tutorials in this section of the book, you need to install Apache, PHP, MySQL, and a database-administration tool called phpMyAdmin. Don't worry, it's a lot easier than it may sound. There are several simple installers available for both Windows and Macs that make this step a snap.

Windows

For Windows, XAMPP is a good choice. XAMPP is a simple installer for putting Apache, PHP, and MySQL on your computer. It's free and works on both Windows XP and Windows Vista. You can find the software at *www.apachefriends.org/en/xampp-windows.html#641*. Because the software changes somewhat frequently, we've put instructions online at *www.sawmac.com/xampp* that we'll keep up-to-date to match changes to the XAMPP installer.

Mac

For the Mac, MAMP provides a very simple way to get Apache, PHP, and MySQL up and running. MAMP is free and available from *www.mamp.info*. The MAMP software changes (as does the Web site) frequently, so to make sure you've got the most up-to-date directions we've put detailed installation instructions online at *www.sawmac.com/mamp*.

If you plan on following along with the tutorials in this section of the book, it's a good idea to download and install XAMPP or MAMP now.

Localhost and the htdocs Folder

If you followed the previous instructions and installed a testing server on your computer, you've already visited a Web page at either *http://localhost/xampp* or *http://localhost/MAMP* (the home pages for XAMPP or MAMP). You may be wondering, what's this *localhost* thing? For a computer, "localhost" is just another way of saying "me." When you instruct a browser to go to *http://localhost*, you're merely telling it to look for a Web server running on the same computer as the Web browser. Normally, when you visit a Web site, you type a Web address like *http://www.google.com/*. That sends your Web browser out over the Internet looking for a Web page located on some computer identified as *www.google.com*. When you've set up a Web server on your own computer, and you wish to view the Web pages you've placed there, the Web browser need look no further than your own computer.

But once the browser asks the local Web server to give it a Web page, where does the Web server find that page on your computer? When working with static Web pages (like the ones you built earlier in this book), you can keep your Web site files pretty much anywhere you want: on your desktop, in your Documents folder, on an external hard drive, and so on. Dynamic pages, on the other hand, work only with a Web server, and must reside in a particular location on your computer in order for the Web server to find them.

That folder is called the *site root* folder (you may also hear it referred to as the *document root*). The exact name and location of the site root folder varies from system to system. For example, different Web hosting companies have different setups, and might name the folder *htdocs*, *webdocs*, or *public_html*. XAMPP and MAMP both use a folder named *htdocs* as the site root folder. For XAMPP users, that folder is located in the *htdocs* folder in your XAMPP installation (*C:\xampp\htdocs*, for example); for MAMP folks, head over to Applications → MAMP → htdocs.

In the case of XAMPP, if you type *http://localhost/my_page.html* into your browser, the browser requests a file named *my_page.html* from the Web server running on your computer. The Web server then looks inside *C:\Program Files\xampp\htdocs* for a file named *my_page.html;* if it finds it, the server sends the file back to the browser. On a Mac running MAMP, the Web server would look in Applications → MAMP → htdocs for the file *my_page.html*.

Note: If you don't specify a particular file–for example, you just surf to *http://localhost/*–the Web server looks for a "default file" (usually named *index.html* or *index.php*) as described on page 618.

Remember, when you're working on a dynamic, database driven site, you need to keep your Web site files inside the site root folder for your testing server. If you don't, Dreamweaver doesn't let you start building database-driven pages.

Note: You can also put your site files in a folder *inside* the site root folder. If you placed a folder named *store* in the *htdocs* folder, you could visit a Web page named *products.php* inside that folder by browsing to *http://localhost/store/products.php*.

In addition, as you start to build more dynamic sites, you might want to have separate names for each site. For example, you could put the site files for clientX in a folder named *clientX* inside the *htdocs* folder. Then you could test that client's Web pages by typing *http://localhost/clientX/* in a Web browser. However, it's more elegant to have separate local sites for each client; this way you could type something like *http://clientX/* into a Web browser and your local Web server would find the files just for that one client. To do this you create what are called *localhosts* for each sites. You can learn how to do this by following the instructions at *www.sawmac.com/xampp/localhosts* or *www.sawmac.com/mamp/localhosts*.

Setting Up Dreamweaver

To learn how to use Dreamweaver's dynamic features, you'll be building a small Web application for the fictitious Web site *CosmoFarmer.com* (see Figure 22-3). In fact, you'll turn the site's online store into a group of dynamic Web pages that retrieve information from a database, and merge it with existing HTML code.

Before you begin building the page, download the tutorial files. As always, you can find them at *www.sawmac.com/dwcs4/*; click the Tutorials link to go to the tutorials page and download the files. If you've done any of the previous tutorials, you've already downloaded the necessary files. The files for this section of the book are inside the *php_dynamic* folder, which is located inside the MM_DWCS4 folder. Inside the *php_dynamic* folder you'll find another folder named *cosmo_shop*, and a file named *cosmofarmer.sql*.

To begin, move the *cosmo_shop* folder into the newly installed Web server's root folder. If you followed the previous directions, the root folder on Windows should be in *C: \xampp\htdocs*, while the root folder for Macs is in Applications → MAMP → htdocs. Place *cosmo_shop* inside the *htdocs* folder. To make sure you've set this up right, open a Web browser, and then, in the Address bar, type *http://localhost/cosmo_shop/*. If a Web page appears, your Web server is set up correctly.

The first step in working on this dynamic Web application is defining a new site. The process of defining a dynamic site, as outlined in the following steps, is slightly different than for static sites, but no harder:

1. **Start Dreamweaver, and then choose Site → New Site.**

   The Site Definition window opens. Because there are more things to keep track of when setting up a dynamic site, it's easiest to use Dreamweaver's Site Wizard.

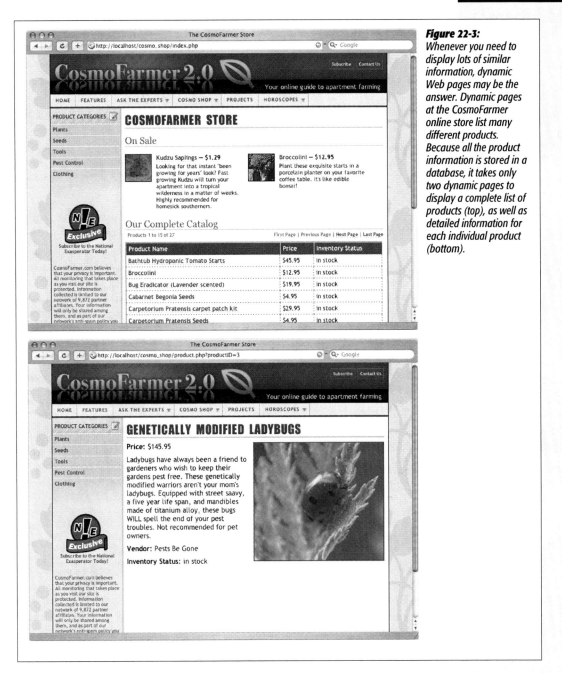

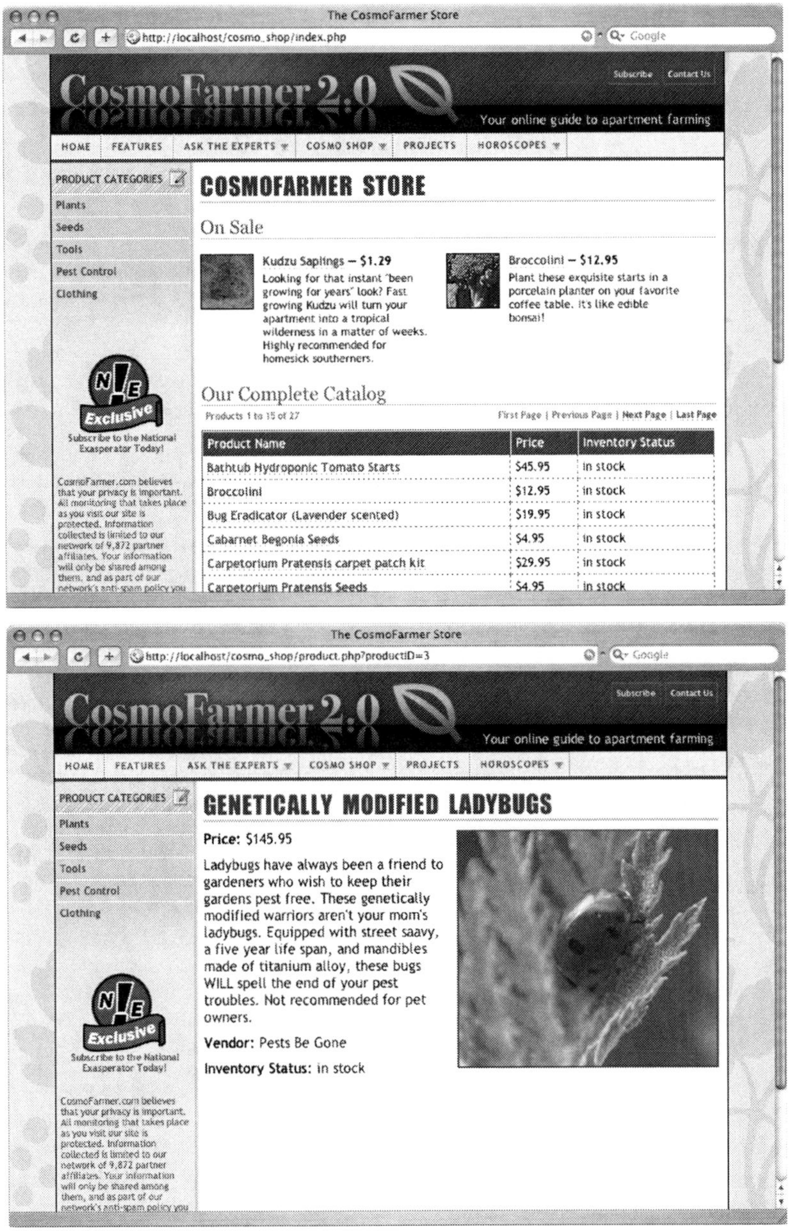

Figure 22-3: *Whenever you need to display lots of similar information, dynamic Web pages may be the answer. Dynamic pages at the CosmoFarmer online store list many different products. Because all the product information is stored in a database, it takes only two dynamic pages to display a complete list of products (top), as well as detailed information for each individual product (bottom).*

2. **If it isn't already selected, click the Basic tab at the top of the window.**

   First, you need to give this new site a name.

3. **Type *Cosmo Shop* in the first box, and *http://www.cosmofarmer.com/cosmo_shop* in the second box.**

   You've just told Dreamweaver the name you want to use while working on this site, and the URL of the Web site. In this case, you're actually just working on one part of the CosmoFarmer site, the store, which is located in a folder (*cosmo_shop*) within the main site. In a real-world scenario, you'd type the address of your Web site.

4. **Click Next.**

   The next screen lets you choose whether you're building a static or dynamic Web site.

5. **Select "Yes, I want to use a server technology," and then, from the pop-up menu, choose PHP MySQL (see Figure 22-4). Click Next to proceed.**

   In the next step, you'll tell Dreamweaver where your local files are, and where you intend to put the files for the testing server.

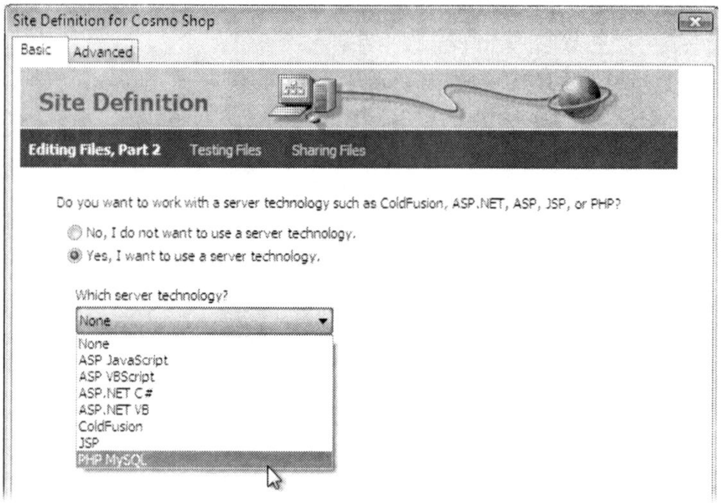

Figure 22-4: *Even though JSP and two versions of .NET are listed in the server technology menu, Dreamweaver CS4 no longer provides "server behaviors" (pre-written programs that make working with dynamic pages and databases very easy) for those server models. In other words, choosing one of those options means you have to do all of the programming yourself, with no help from Dreamweaver.*

6. **Select "Edit and test locally" (see Figure 22-5).**

   Dreamweaver provides three ways to work with dynamic Web page files and a testing server.

   "Edit and test locally" is a good choice when you've set up a Web and application server on your computer (as you've done in this tutorial). Essentially, you're working on Web pages located on a functioning Web server. In this way, you preview the pages running on a real Web server, so you can immediately test out all the nifty dynamic stuff.

Use the other two options when the testing server is located on another computer. This computer may be one on your local network or a full-fledged Web server running on the Internet that you connect to using FTP (see page 669 for more on FTP).

"Edit locally, then upload to remote testing server" is a good option if you already set up a Web site with a Web hosting company, and you can't run a testing server on your computer—for example, if you're building ASP pages but you're on a Mac.

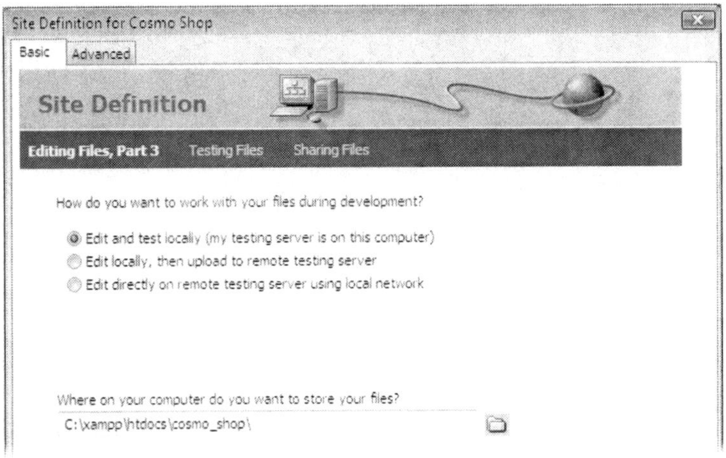

Figure 22-5: *Dreamweaver provides different ways to work with dynamic Web page files on a testing server. If you don't have a working Web server on your computer, but do have an account with a Web hosting company that recognizes one of Dreamweaver's server models, you can use that server to test your files. Choose the second option: "Edit locally, then upload to remote testing server." This method is a bit laborious–you edit the pages on your computer; then, when you test them (a simple F12 [control-F12] to see if they'll work), Dreamweaver connects to your Web server, uploads the file, launches your Web browser, and loads the page from your Web site. But it's one way to get started building dynamic Web sites.*

People don't use the last option often, but if your company happens to have its own in-house Web server, to which you can connect over a local network, then you can use this option. But, in general, it's best not to work on a live Web server—your works-in-progress might be viewable by anyone with a Web browser. In addition, if more than one person is working on the Web site at the same time, you should use some kind of version control system to make sure no two people are working on the same file at the same time (Dreamweaver's Check In/Check Out system is one method—see page 686).

The next step involves telling Dreamweaver where to find the files for the Web site.

7. **Click the folder at the right side of the middle of the window; navigate to and select the *cosmo_shop* folder on the Web server. Click Next.**

   If you're following along using XAMPP, you'll find the *cosmo_shop* folder at *C:\xampp\htdocs\cosmo_shop*; MAMP folks can find it at Applications → MAMP → htdocs → cosmo_shop.

8. **Type *http://localhost/cosmo_shop/* in the box, and then click Test URL.**

   Dreamweaver may have already filled in this box. If the test server is running on your computer, the URL begins with *http://localhost/* and ends with the folder that contains the Web pages. In this case, the URL is *http://localhost/cosmo_shop/*.

Note: If you're running MAMP and can't change the port Apache uses, as described in the MAMP setup instructions at *www.sawmac.com/mamp/*, you need to add the port number 8888 to the URL, like this: *http://localhost:8888/cosmo_shop/*.

   If you get an error message when you click Test URL, you've probably entered the wrong URL. You can make this mistake when the folder following *localhost* in the URL is not actually in the site root folder of the testing server, or the Web server isn't running (to start the XAMPP Web server, see the instructions at *www.sawmac.com/xampp/*; MAMP people visit *www.sawmac.com/mamp/*).

9. **Click Next. Click No, and then click Next one more time.**

   If you were planning to move this site onto a Web server connected to the Internet, you would select Yes at this stage, and provide all the information needed to move your site files to the Internet as described in Chapter 17. But since this tutorial is just an exercise, you won't be putting it up on a live Web server.

Note: If in step 3 you typed *http://www.cosmofarmer.com/cosmo_shop/* (with a forward slash at the end), you may encounter a Dreamweaver error box saying that the URL prefix for the testing server doesn't match the site. You can click the back button until you get to the first screen of the site wizard and remove the forward slash, or just ignore the error message. You haven't really done anything wrong and everything will work just fine even if you ignore this error message.

10. **Click Done.**

   Dreamweaver has successfully set up your site. You're now ready to learn about databases, and set up a new database using the MySQL server.

Creating a Dynamic Page

Once you've set up an application server and a database server, you're ready to connect to a database, retrieve information, and display it on a Web page.

You already know how to handle the first step: Design an HTML page to display the database information. Dynamic pages differ from regular HTML pages in a couple ways. For starters, the name of a dynamic file doesn't end with .html. Depending on which server model you use, dynamic pages end in .php (for PHP pages), .asp (ASP), or .cfm or cfml (Cold Fusion). The file extension you use is important: A Web server uses it to identify the type of page requested. If a Web server gets a request for an .html file, it simply finds it and sends it to the Web browser. But if it gets a request for a page that ends in, say, .php, it will send the page to the application server to sort out all the messy programming.

The good news is that the basic process of creating a new, blank, dynamic page is the same as with a regular HTML page:

- **Choose File → New to open the New Document window. Select the Blank Page category; from the Page Type list, choose a dynamic page type (PHP, ASP VBScript, ASP JavaScript, or ColdFusion). From the Layout list, choose a layout (or none if you wish to start with a fresh, blank page), and then click the Create button.**

  When you save the file, Dreamweaver automatically adds the proper extension: .asp for ASP pages, .cfm for ColdFusion, or .php for PHP pages.

- **Or, more simply, just right-click (Control-click) in the Site panel; choose New File from the shortcut menu.**

  Dreamweaver creates a file in the correct server model format, with the proper extension.

Note: For ASP pages, just renaming a file in the Sites panel (from *about.html* to *about.asp*, for example) does *not* give the file the code necessary to apply the correct server model to the page. However, PHP and ColdFusion pages don't start life within any special code, so you could start with a .html page, change the extension to .php, and then add PHP programming. More importantly, changing the file's extension (from .asp to .php, for example) doesn't change the page to the new server model, either, and usually ends up "breaking" the page.

Once you've created the page, you can then use any of the page-building tools described in this book—Cascading Style Sheets, Spry Widgets, Library items, or whatever—to design the page. Even though the file's officially a PHP page (or ASP or Cold Fusion), it still contains lots of HTML. Unlike a plain-vanilla HTML page, though, this one can also contain the server-side programming code that lets the page communicate with a database.

Finally, you can also edit the newly created page using either Design view or Code view. But before you can add dynamic content to a page, you need to create a connection to a database.

Databases: A Quick Introduction

Simply put, databases store information. You encounter them every day in one way or another, whether charging a dinner on a credit card or calling Moviefone to get local movie listings.

A database is like an electronic filing cabinet that stores related information. At home, you might have a filing cabinet for storing the bits and pieces of your life. You might have a filing folder labeled Insurance, in which you keep information about the various insurance policies you carry. Other folders might contain information on phone bills, car service records, and so on. Databases work more or less the same way, as the following sections explain.

Tables and Records

Databases have an electronic equivalent to filing folders: tables. A *table* is a container that holds information about a set of similar items. In the CosmoFarmer online store database, one table stores information on all the products for sale on the site.

This Products table tracks certain information—the name of the product for sale, its price, a short description, and a few other items. Each piece of information, like price, is stored in a column. All the information for each product (all the columns taken together, in other words) makes up a single *record*, which is stored in a row (see Figure 22-6).

Column

Row

productID	productName	price	description	vendorID	categoryID	image
1	Kudzu Saplings	1.29	Looking for...	1	1	kudzu.jpg
2	CosmoFarmer Tee	20.00	Celebrate...	4	5	cosmo_tee.jpg
3	Indoor Tractor	375.00	The ultimate...	2	3	tractor.jpg
4	Gotcha Cucaracha	2.95	Let this urban...	2	2	cockroach.jpg

Figure 22-6:
This diagram shows part of the Products table's structure, and information for four records. Each row in a table represents a single record, or item, while each piece of information for a record is stored in a single field, or cell.

If you were designing a database, you'd try to model a table on some real-world item you needed to track. If your database was used for generating invoices for your business, you might have a table called Invoices in which you'd store information such as the invoice number, date, and so on. Since your customers are another source of data that needs tracking, you'd also create a table called Customers to store the information about them.

Tip: If you're designing a database to track a business process that you already track on paper, a good place to start is with the paper forms you use. If your company uses a personnel form for collecting information on each employee in the business, you've got a ready-made database table. Each box on the form is the equivalent of a category column in a table.

In addition to the Products table, CosmoFarmer also tracks the vendors who manufactured the products. (After all, after they run out of inventory, the online store staff will need to order more products from their vendors.) Because a product and a vendor are really two different things, the database has a *second* table, called Vendors, that lists all the companies that make the products for sale on the Web site.

Note: Some databases are extremely picky about the names you give your tables and database columns (also called fields). For example, you can't have a database column named Date in an Access database.

You might think, "Hey, let's just put all that information into a single table." After all, you could consider the vendor's information part of the information for each product. While it seems like this method might simplify things (because you'd have one table instead of two), it can actually create a lot of problems.

Imagine a scenario where CosmoFarmer stores both product and vendor information in a single table: CosmoFarmer begins selling a hot new item, *Kudzu seeds*, from Seeds R' Us. All the product information, including the name and price of the plant, as well as the phone number and mailing address for Seeds R' Us, are stored in a single table row. Next month, Seeds R' Us offers another new product, Eucalyptus Saplings, as part of its "invasive plant of the month club." But, in the meantime, Seeds R' Us has moved locations and changed its phone number. So when someone at CosmoFarmer adds the new plant to the Products database, she adds the new phone number and address as part of the new plant's record.

Now the database contains *two* sets of contact information for Seeds R' Us—one for each plant. Not only does this redundant data take up extra space, but the contact information in one record is now wrong.

You could run into an even worse problem when deleting a record. Suppose that the online store decides to discontinue the two plants from Seeds R' Us. If a CosmoFarmer staffer removes those two records from the database, she also deletes any contact information for Seeds R' Us. If the *CosmoFarmer* staff ever decide to stock up on kudzu again, they have no way of contacting the vendor.

So you can see why it's prudent to keep separate classes of information in different tables. With two tables, when Seeds R' Us moves, you have to update only the information in the Vendors table, without touching the Products table at all. This way, if the staff deletes a product, they still have a way of contacting the vendor to learn about new products.

You may be wondering, with a setup like this, how to tell which vendor makes which product. All you have are two distinct tables—one with just product information and one with just vendor information. How do you make the connection?

Note: For a great book on database design, check out *Database Design for Mere Mortals* (Addison-Wesley Professional) by Michael J. Hernandez. For concise, online introductions to database design, visit *www.geekgirls.com/databases_from_scratch_1.htm* and *www.campus.ncl.ac.uk/databases/design/design.html*.

Relational Databases

To connect information between tables, you create a *relationship* between them. In fact, databases that use multiple related tables are called *relational databases*.

The most common way to connect tables is by using what's called a *primary key*—a serial number or some other unique identifying flag for each record in the table. In the case of the *CosmoFarmer* database, the Products table includes a field named *productID*, the product's identification number (see Figure 22-7). Whenever a product is added to the database, it's assigned a new number (usually by the database server itself). If you're building a database that contains a table about employees, you might use an employee's Social Security number as a primary key, or an internal employee ID number based on your company's own cryptic method of identifying employees.

Products table

Primary key — Foreign key

productID	productName	price	description	vendorID	categoryID	image
1	Kudzu Saplings	1.29	Looking for...	1	1	kudzu.jpg
2	CosmoFarmer Tee	20.00	Celebrate...	4	5	cosmo_tee.jpg
3	Indoor Tractor	375.00	The ultimate...	2	3	tractor.jpg
4	Gotcha Cucaracha	2.95	Let this urban...	2	2	cockroach.jpg

Vendors table

Primary key

vendorID	vendorName	vendorStreet	vendorCity	vendorState	vendorZip	vendorPhone
1	Seeds 'R Us	8538 5th Ave.	New York	NV	89173	702-555-1212
2	Gap Plants	237 5th St	New York	NY	21222	212-555-1232
3	Burpee	4578 A St	Portland	OR	97213	503-555-2983
4	John Dear	9988 C Ave	Wilmington	OH	88437	706-555-9348

Figure 22-7:
Each table in your database should have a primary key–a column that contains a unique identifier for each record in a table. To relate information from one table to another, people often add an additional column with information pertaining to another table. In this case, a column called vendorID *in the Products table contains a primary key from the Vendors table. To determine which vendor distributes, say, the Gotcha Cucarache, look at the fifth column in the Products table, which identifies the vendor's ID number as 2. When you check the Vendors table, you see that vendor 2 is Gap Plants. A column that contains the primary key of another table is called a foreign key.*

The Vendors table has a primary key named, not so creatively, *vendorID*. A vendor's primary key is generated automatically whenever a new vendor is added to the database.

To join these two tables, you'd add another column called vendorID to the Products table (see Figure 22-7). Instead of storing *all* the contact information for a vendor within the Products table, you simply store the vendor's ID number. To find out which vendor makes which product, you can look up the product in the Products table, find the vendor's ID number in the vendorID column, and use *that* information to look up the vendor in the Vendors table.

While this hopscotch approach of accessing database tables is a bit confusing at first, it has many benefits. Not only does it prevent the kinds of errors mentioned earlier, it also simplifies the process of adding a new product from a vendor. When Seeds R' Us adds a third plant to their collection, a store staff person determines whether any of Seeds R' Us' info has changed (by checking it against the Vendors table). If not, she simply adds the information for the new product, and leaves the vendor's contact info untouched. Thus, relational databases not only prevent errors, they also make data entry faster.

Databases, of course, can be much more complicated than this simple example. It can take many tables to accurately hold the data needed to run a complex e-commerce site such as *Amazon.com*. In some cases, you may already be working with a previously created database, so you won't have to worry about creating one or even learning more than what's described above. For the tutorials in this section of the book, you'll use the already created CosmoFarmer database.

Loading a Database

You need to install the data for the CosmoFarmer store in your new MySQL server. That process requires a few steps. First you'll create a new database; next, you'll load the data into this new database; finally, you'll create a new *user* for the database (a special account that you'll use for accessing and updating the database). The following steps lead you through everything.

1. **In any Web browser, type *http://localhost/xampp* (*http://localhost/MAMP* if you're on a Mac).**

   This action takes you to the main XAMPP (or MAMP) page on the new testing server. You'll use a program called phpMyAdmin to administer the MySQL server.

2. **Click the "phpMyAdmin" link.**

   In XAMPP, this link is located in the left-hand list of links under the Tools category. The MAMP homepage lists phpMyAdmin in the top navigation bar.

Tip: Since you'll frequently use phpMyAdmin to work with the MySQL database, it's a good idea to bookmark this page, so you can quickly return to it whenever you need.

3. **In the "Create new database" box, type *cosmofarmer* and then press the Create button (see Figure 22-8).**

   This step actually creates a new database on the MySQL server. In addition, it takes you to a new page that includes a row of buttons for working with the new database.

   Next you'll load an SQL file that creates the required tables, and adds the actual data to the database. SQL stands for Structured Query Language, and it's the language you use to communicate with databases: to read, edit, update and generally manipulate the structure and information in a database. You'll learn more about how to use SQL on page 855.

4. **In phpMyAdmin's top navigation bar, click the Import button.**

   Doing so takes you to a page that lets you type in an SQL query (see page 855) or load a text file that has SQL commands in it. You'll do the latter—load a text file that contains all the SQL necessary to create the tables and data for the database.

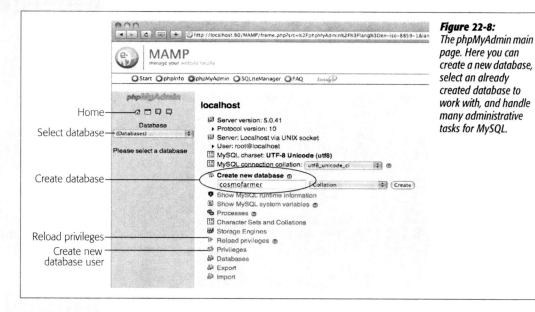

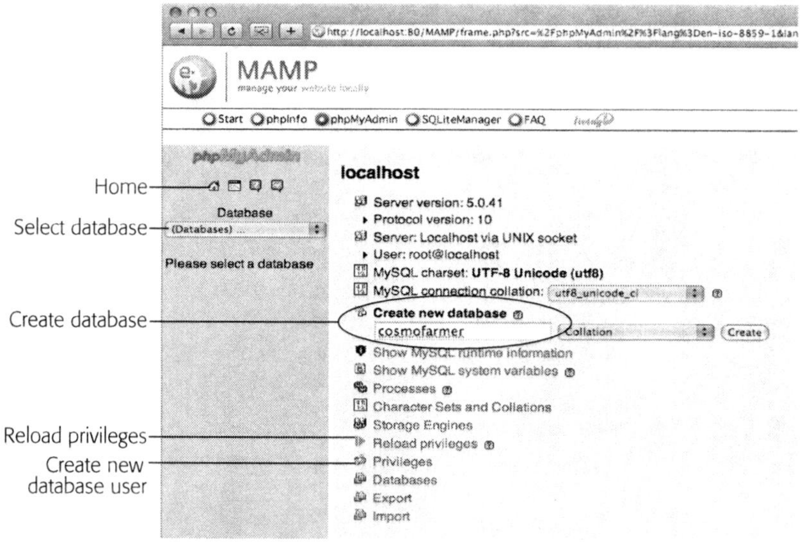

Figure 22-8: *The phpMyAdmin main page. Here you can create a new database, select an already created database to work with, and handle many administrative tasks for MySQL.*

5. **Click the Browse button in XAMPP or the Choose File button in MAMP (circled in Figure 22-9). In the File Upload window that appears, navigate to and select the file *cosmofarmer.sql* in the *php_dynamic* folder you downloaded with the tutorial files.**

   As explained in the previous step, this file contains all the goodies that will appear in your database.

6. **Click the Go button (Figure 22-9, lower-right corner).**

   The MySQL server slurps down the SQL file, and executes the instructions found within it. The result? Four new tables are created (see the list of tables that just appeared on the left side of the phpMyAdmin window), and a bunch of data is added to them. Your last step in prepping the database: Create a new MySQL user that has permission to add to and update the CosmoFarmer database.

7. **Click the link at the top of the page labeled *Server: Localhost* (just *localhost* for MAMP).**

   Alternatively, you can click the small house icon in the left sidebar (see Figure 22-8). In either case, you return to the main phpMyAdmin page.

8. **In the middle column of links, click the Privileges link (see Figure 22-8).**

   This step opens the User page. From here, you can edit current users (for example, change a user password), and add new users.

9. **Click the "Add a new user" link.**

   The link appears under the list of current users. Clicking it opens the "Add a new User" page (see Figure 22-10).

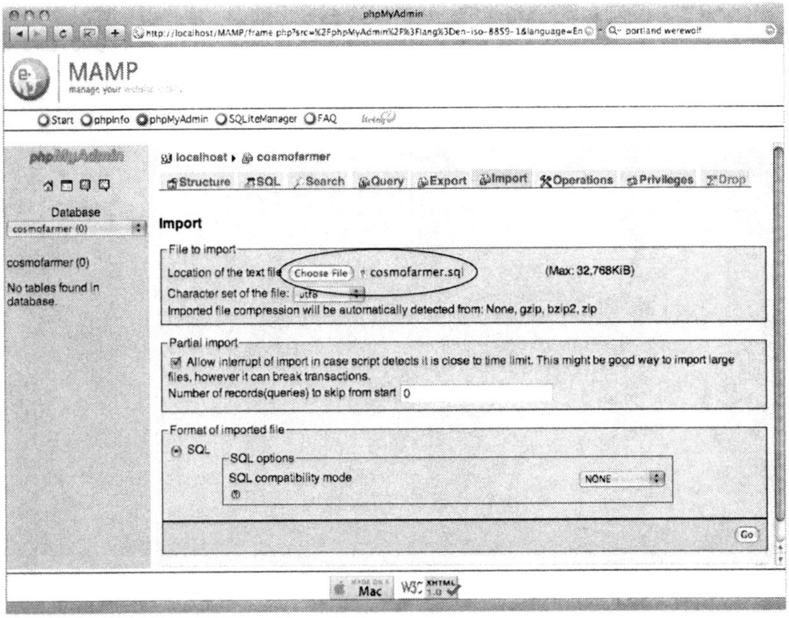

Figure 22-9: *phpMyAdmin lets you load an SQL file, and execute the SQL code inside the file. Translation: Talk to the database server and tell it to create tables and fields, and add data to them. This way is great for replicating data from another database. In addition, you can get data out of your database by exporting all the tables and data from any database to which phpMyAdmin has access.*

10. **Type *cosmo* for the user name and choose *local* from the Host menu. In the password field, type *cosmo*, and in the re-type box, type *cosmo* again. The screen should look like Figure 22-10).**

    This step creates a user whose name is *cosmo*, whose password is *cosmo*, and who can access the database only locally from the server. This means someone out on the Internet can't try to log in to the MySQL server using the cosmo account; only local access—for example, PHP pages being run on the same computer—is allowed.

    In general, it's a very bad idea to make a password the same as a user name (as in this example), or to use any word that could be found in a dictionary, since it doesn't take much imagination for a hacker to figure this out and suddenly gain control of your database. But for this example application, it's best to keep things as simple as possible, so you can quickly get to the more interesting stuff (actually using Dreamweaver, for instance!).

11. **Scroll to the bottom of the page, and then, in the lower-right corner, click the Go button.**

    You've created the new user, cosmo, and now phpMyAdmin has taken you to another Web page so that you can tweak that user's privileges. In MySQL, you can limit which users have access to which databases, and how much power they have to work with the databases they do have access to. You could give a user the ability to read, update, and add data to a database, but prevent him from changing the structure of the database by adding or deleting tables. At this

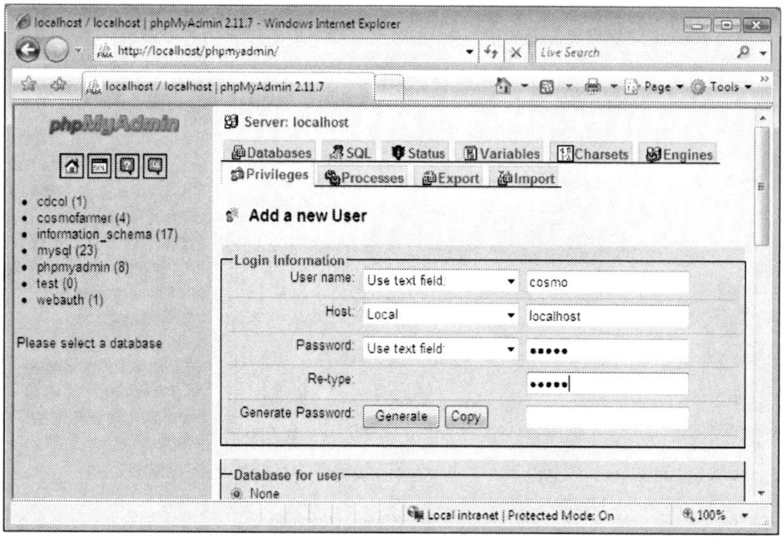

***Figure 22-10:** To create a new database user, just supply a name, choose where the user can access the database from (usually localhost), and then type a password.*

point, the cosmo user doesn't have any privileges, so you need to make sure cosmo can access the CosmoFarmer database.

12. **Scroll down the page to the "Database-specific privileges" section; select "cosmofarmer" from the database menu (circled in Figure 22-11).**

    This step takes you to yet another page, where you can specify what the user can and cannot do to the CosmoFarmer database.

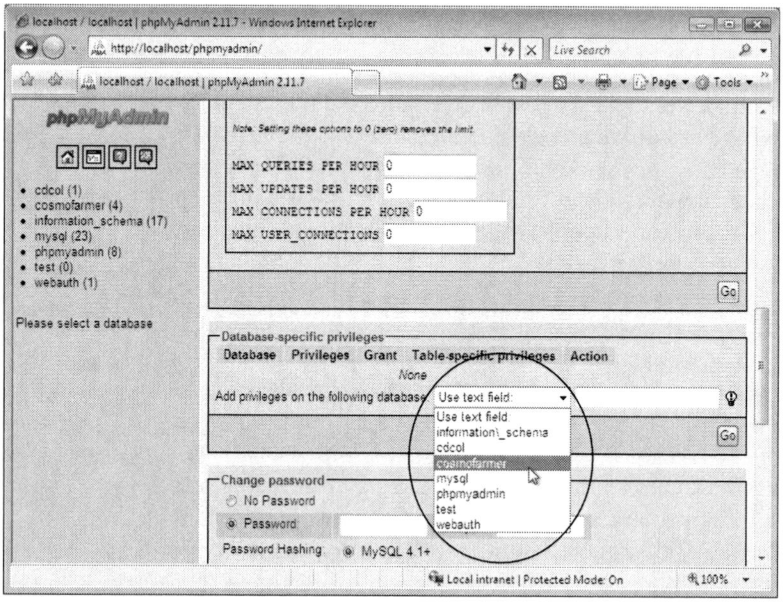

***Figure 22-11:** The MySQL database server can have dozens, even hundreds, of databases running on it at the same time. Usually, only the main MySQL administrator account, called the root user, can access all the databases. Individual users, like the cosmo user you just created, are frequently allowed to access only a single database.*

13. **In the Data column, turn on all the checkboxes circled in Figure 22-12: Select, Insert, Update, and Delete. In the lower-right corner, click the Go button.**

You can give a user many different ways of interacting with a database, including some complex administrative functions that have the potential of wreaking havoc on the database. It's best to limit these "access privileges" to the minimum number each user needs. In this case, all the cosmo user needs to do is select (meaning retrieve data from the database), insert (put data into the database), update (edit data in the database), and delete (remove data from the database).

There's just one final step in setting up this new user: You must "flush" the database's privileges. Although it sounds like a high school prank, flushing privileges just means telling MySQL to activate the new user and its privileges.

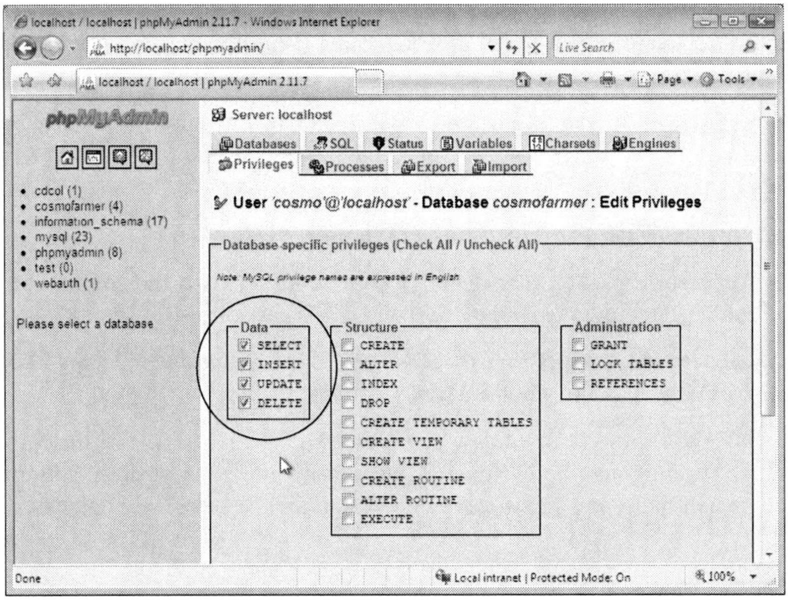

***Figure 22-12:** This page lets you limit user access to just those functions the user needs for the task at hand. In this case, you use the cosmo user account in your PHP pages to access the database for routine database tasks such as adding, editing, deleting, and retrieving information from the database.*

14. **On the left sidebar, click the Home icon to return to the main phpMyAdmin page; once there, click the "Reload privileges" link in the middle list of options (see Figure 22-8).**

Alright, let's take stock of what you've done: set up the database, added the data, and created a new user. Wow. That was a lot of work, and you've barely touched Dreamweaver in this tutorial. Don't worry, all the hard work is behind you. Now it's time to use Dreamweaver to build the site.

Note: In many cases, when you set up an account with a Web hosting company, they supply you with an already created database and a user account for that database. Frequently, the database is named after your domain name or your account name with the Web host. When setting up MySQL on your machine as part of your testing environment, you should use the same user name and database name supplied by your Web hosting company. That way, when you've perfected your site on the testing server, you can simply transfer it to your Web host's server and the database connections should work perfectly.

Connecting to a Database

You've already defined a new site (back on page 824), so Dreamweaver knows that you'll be working on PHP pages, and knows the location the Web server's root folder. Now, you need to tell Dreamweaver how to connect to your newly created database. Fortunately, Dreamweaver makes this a snap.

1. **Return to Dreamweaver. From the Files Panel (Window → Files), double-click the file *index.php*.**

   The main page for the online store opens. This is a dynamic PHP page; you must have a PHP page (or ASP or Cold Fusion depending on your server model) open in order to connect Dreamweaver to a database.

2. **Open the Databases panel by choosing Window → Databases.**

   The Application panel group opens (Figure 22-13). This is the control center for building dynamic Web pages.

3. **At the top left of the panel, click the plus sign (+) button (circled in Figure 22-13). From the pop-up menu, choose MySQL connection.**

   The MySQL Connection window opens (see Figure 22-14). In this dialog box you let Dreamweaver know which database to connect to, where it's located, and the user name and password of the account that can access the database.

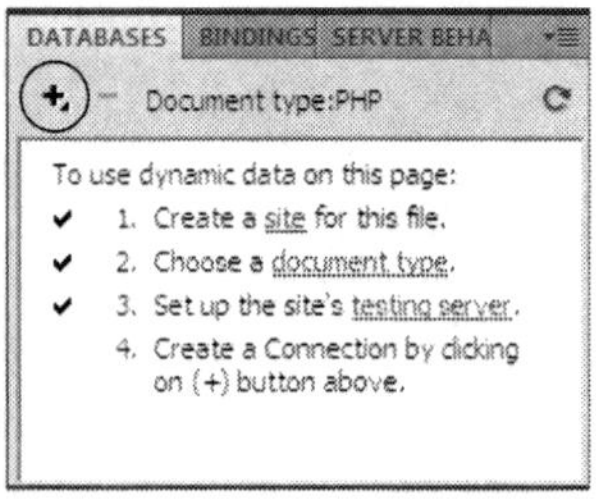

Figure 22-13: *The databases panel lets you connect to databases, and will display the tables and field names of any databases you've already connected to.*

4. **In the "Connection name" box, type *connCosmo*.**

   You can use any name you want as long as it doesn't start with a number and doesn't contain any characters other than letters, numbers, and the underscore character. In this case, *conn* is a helpful indicator that this is a database connection, and makes identifying it easier if you ever need to look into the underlying code of the page.

Next, you'll tell Dreamweaver where the database is located.

5. **In the MySQL server box, type *localhost*.**

   In this case, both the Web server and MySQL are set up on the same computer (namely, yours). So when a dynamic page running on the testing server tries to connect to the MySQL database, the application server needs to look only on the same computer—"localhost"—to find the database.

   In many cases, the MySQL server provided by your Web hosting company is also located on the same server, so when you start building "real" PHP pages to put up on your own site, you can use *localhost* when creating the connection locally. This attribute is helpful, because it means you can develop your sites locally on your computer, move them onto the Internet, and they should be able to connect to the database without a problem.

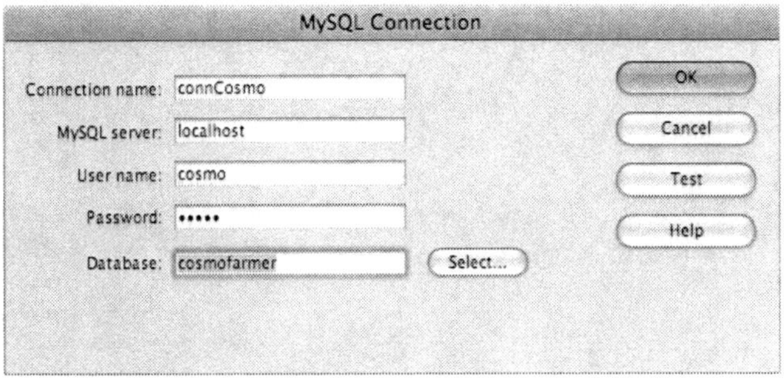

Figure 22-14: *Setting up a Dreamweaver-to-MySQL-database connection requires just a few easy steps.*

However, some Web hosts put their databases on separate machines dedicated to just the task of managing databases. In this case, the database connection on your local computer differs from the one you must put up on the Web server. You would need to edit the database connection, and replace *localhost*, which works for development and testing on your own computer, with the address of the MySQL server—this might be something like *mysql.webhost.com* or it might even be a basic IP address like *192.168.1.2* (don't use http://, or anything besides the server's address).

Your Web hosting company can supply this information. Unfortunately this means that you need to change the connection file Dreamweaver creates to include the new address. Here's how: Before uploading your site, open the connection file. Do this either from the Databases panel (double-click the connection name to open it) or by looking in a folder name *Connections*, located in the local root folder of your site. In that folder you'll find a file named after the connection name you supplied when you created the connection—in this tutorial, that's step 4 above. So in this case the name of the connection file is *connCosmo.php*. Double-click this file, and then change *localhost* to the address of your Web host's MySQL database server. Then upload this file to your site (see page 678 for information on uploading Web files).

You can then open the connection file again, and then change the database address back to *localhost*. This lets you continue to work and test on your local computer—just make sure you don't upload this file to the Web server, or you'll wipe out the connection file that you customized for your Web server, and your dynamic pages won't be able to connect to the database.

This all assumes, of course, that the database and user name you set up on your testing server is the same as the one you use at your Web hosting company (see the Note on page 838). If not, you need to change the user name and password in the connection file before you transfer it to your Web server.

Okay, with all *that* out of the way, back to our regularly scheduled programming: the MySQL Connection dialog box.

6. **Type *cosmo* in the user name box, and *cosmo* in the password box.**

   This is the MySQL user name and password you created earlier when you set up the database.

7. **Click the Select button.**

   The Select Database window appears. This lets you pick which database you wish to connect to. In this case it's the CosmoFarmer online store database.

   If you get an error instead, check that you spelled *localhost* correctly, and that you supplied the right user name and password.

8. **Select *cosmofarmer*, and then click OK.**

   The dialog box closes, and *cosmofarmer* appears in the Database box at the bottom of the window. Click the Test button.

   A window saying "Connection was made successfully" should appear.

9. **Click OK to close the window that appeared when you tested the connection; click OK once more to close the MySQL Connection box.**

   Behind the scenes, Dreamweaver creates a small PHP file and stores it in a folder called Connections in your site's root folder. Whenever you create a dynamic page that communicates with the database, Dreamweaver adds a line of code pointing to this connection file. (The file's name reflects the connection name you typed in step 4—here it's *connCosmo.php*.)

Warning: Don't delete the Connections folder. This folder holds a script that lets your pages connect to your database. If, while cleaning your site, you throw this folder away, you'll break the database connection for all your site's dynamic pages. If this happens, recreate the connection by following steps 3–9.

Exploring the Databases Panel

The Databases panel (Figure 22-15) lets you do more than just connect databases to your site. It also lets you explore a database's structure and data. By clicking the + sign buttons (flippy triangles on Macs), you can view any of three lists:

- **Tables** lists all the tables in the database (see page 830). Expanding a table displays all the columns for that table. You'll use this option most often.
- **Views** lists all *views* stored in the database. A view is a selection of data in the database—a slice of its data. Think of a view as a saved search. Unless you've created views using the database systems tools, this list is empty. Only version 5 and later of MySQL support this feature.
- **Stored Procedures** lists programs that access and manipulate information in the database. Stored procedures are kept right in the database, so they run faster than similar code in a Web page. (Some database systems—like Access and most versions of MySQL—don't recognize this feature.)

Tip: To get a quick peek at the data in a database table, in the Databases panel, right-click (Control-click) the table's name. From the shortcut menu, choose View Data. A window appears, displaying a table of data extracted directly from the database!

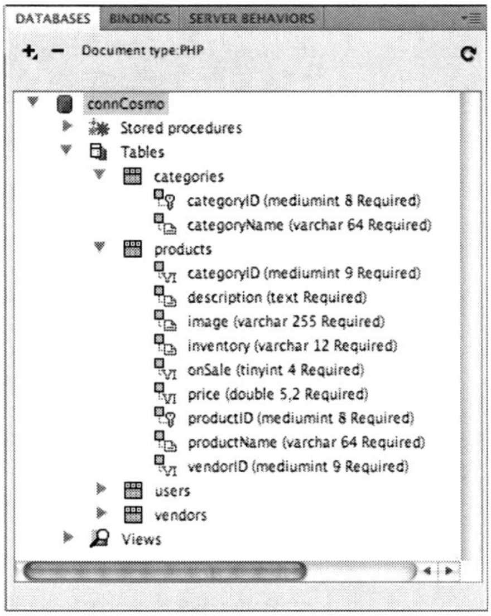

Figure 22-15:
Along with the Databases panel, both the Bindings and the Server Behavior panels provide a quick way for working with dynamic database-driven Web sites. (Another panel that you might see listed under the Window menu is Components. It contains advanced features for use with ColdFusion Web sites.)

In this chapter, you've laid the foundation for a dynamic Web site. In the next chapter, you'll start adding data from a database to the page you created in the preceding tutorial—and building a real, dynamic Web application.

FREQUENTLY ASKED QUESTION

Parenthetical Puzzler

In the Databases panel, I see some weird information in parentheses next to the column names—mediumint 8 Required, *for example. What's that about?*

You're right—there's a notation next to each column name. For example, Figure 22-15 shows a column called *categoryID*, which is followed by (*mediumint 8 Required*).

The information in parentheses denotes the *type* of data in that column. In this instance, it's an *integer* (a whole number like 1, 3, or 5), it's *8* bytes of data long (meaning it can be a very, very large number), and it's *required* (meaning that every new record *must* have a value stored in this field). Within each of these categories, there can be subtypes like timestamp, decimal number, and so on. Different databases recognize different data types, so there's quite a long list of possible data types for all the server models Dreamweaver supports.

These notations may appear cryptic, but they can come in handy. For example, if you're creating a form for updating or inserting a record in a database (as described in Chapter 24), the data type and length can help you figure out what kind of information you're looking for and how long it could be, and help you when you're adding Spry Validation to your form (as described on page 455).

The categoryName column pictured in Figure 22-15 contains text (that's what "varchar" stands for) and is 64 characters long. It's also "required," meaning you can't add a record to the categories table and leave the categoryName field empty. So if you're creating a form to add records to this table, you want to create a required text field that accepts at most 64 characters (you learned how to do this back on page 440).

CHAPTER

23

Adding Dynamic Data to Your Pages

A database is different from a mere pile of facts because it can selectively retrieve information. After all, when you visit Amazon.com, you don't want to see every single book and product they sell. You probably just want to see a list of books on a certain subject or by a particular author, and then view more detail about the books that pique your interest.

This chapter shows you how to use Dreamweaver to display database information on your Web pages. Because these concepts can be tricky, you may prefer to get some hands-on experience by completing the tutorial on page 884 before reading the rest of the chapter.

Retrieving Information

Since databases can contain lots of information, you need a way to find just the data you want to display on a particular Web page. Even though your company keeps information about its products, customers, suppliers, and so on in one database, you may be interested only in, say, an alphabetical list of all your customers. After grabbing that list, you might want to display a particular customer's contact information, or perhaps the list of products that person bought.

Understanding Recordsets

To retrieve specific information from a database, you start by creating what's called a *recordset*. A recordset—also called a *database query*—is a command issued to a database asking for particular information: "Hey Database, show me all the customers listed in the Customers table." It's the heart of many database operations that you'll perform in Dreamweaver (and a piece of jargon you can't escape in the dynamic Web page business).

Recordsets let you retrieve specified columns in a database. Recordsets can also sort records alphabetically or in numerical order, as when viewing a list of products from least to most expensive. In addition, a recordset can zero in on a specific record based on information submitted by a visitor to the site or on information provided in a URL. In essence, recordsets let you winnow down massive amounts of database information in a fraction of a second—a powerful benefit, indeed.

Creating Recordsets

Querying a database can be quite simple or extremely complex. Dreamweaver provides tools to get the novice database developer up and running quickly, while also supplying what's necessary to create more advanced recordsets. Whatever your level of expertise, you start by opening (or creating) a Web page on which to display database information; then you open the Recordset dialog box using one of the following methods (each of which assumes you've set up a server model, as described in Chapter 22):

- On the Data category of the Insert panel, click the Recordset button (see Figure 23-1).
- Choose Insert → Data Objects → Recordset.

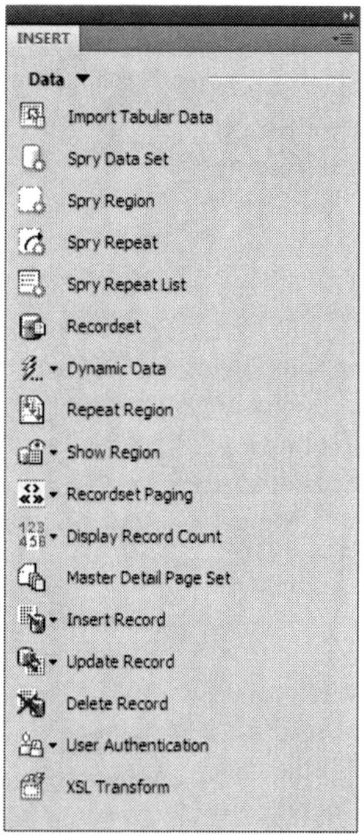

Figure 23-1:
The Insert panel's Data category gives you one-click access to many powerful "application objects," which automate common dynamic Web page-building tasks. Actually, the first five buttons don't require dynamic Web pages: The first is for inserting data from a text file (described on page 282), while the next four are Spry Data objects (see page 518). (The Insert, Update, and Delete records buttons are discussed in the next chapter; the User Authentication features are discussed in Chapter 25; and the last option, XSL Transformation, is presented in Chapter 26.)

- On either the Bindings or Server Behaviors panels, click the + sign button (see Figure 23-9), and then, from the menu that appears, select Recordset.

Whichever technique you choose, the Recordset dialog box opens (Figure 23-2). This box lets you create a database query or recordset, and gives you both simple and advanced modes of operation.

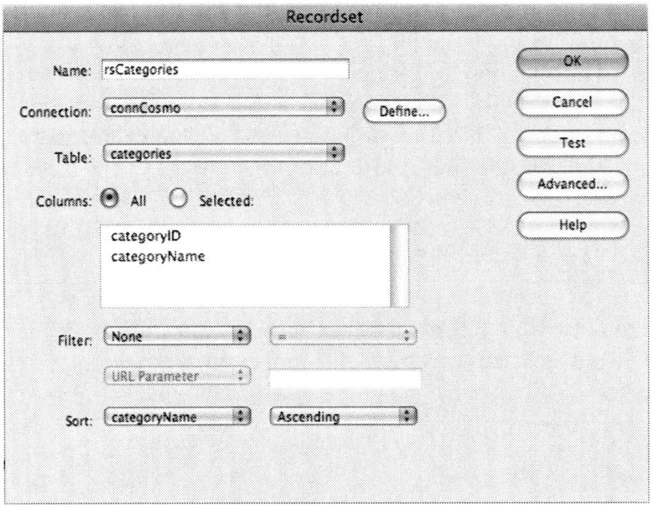

Figure 23-2: *The Recordset window lets you retrieve data from a database. The main window (pictured here) lets beginners search and sort databases for specific information. Advanced options let seasoned database programmers create more complex database queries as described on page 855.*

To create a simple query, make sure you're in the *Simple* mode. (If a button labeled Simple appears at the right edge of the dialog box, click it to make it say Advanced. Now you're in Simple mode.)

1. **In the Name field, type a name for the recordset.**

   You can use any name you want, as long as it doesn't start with a number, and doesn't contain any characters other than letters, numbers, and underscores (_).

Tip: People often begin the name with *rs* (*rsProducts*, for example). The *rs* helps you identify the recordset when you're working in Code view.

2. **From the Connection menu, select a database connection.**

   The menu lists all the database connections you've defined for the site. If you haven't yet created a connection, you can do so now by clicking Define, and then following the instructions on page 838 for creating database connections.

3. **From the Table menu, select the table that'll supply the data.**

   Information in a relational database is usually distributed among different tables, each of which holds information about a particular type of item, such as customer data or product data. For example, to get a list of customers from a database, you'd select the Customers table (or whatever its name happens to be).

Note: To retrieve data from more than one table at a time, you need to create an *advanced* recordset (see page 855).

4. **To select columns from which you want to extract data, click the All or Selected button. If you choose Selected, then click the columns you wish to select.**

   By default, Dreamweaver highlights the All button, but you may not want to get data from *all* the columns in your table. For example, suppose your table contains lots of detailed information for each product your company sells. You may want to create a basic listing of all your products that simply displays names, prices, and descriptions. For this list, you don't need all the details like SKU number, sizes, inventory status, and so on. Therefore, just select the three columns you're interested in.

   To select multiple columns, in the Recordset dialog box's list, Ctrl-click (⌘-click) their names.

   It's always best to limit your recordset to just those columns whose information you need. The more data you retrieve, the more you make the application and database servers work, and the more you slow down your site, especially when the database is large.

5. **Choose a Filter option, if you like.**

   In many cases, you don't want to retrieve *every* record in a table. For example, if you're looking a particular customer's phone number in your database, you don't want the details on every one of your customers. *Filters* let you limit the records retrieved by a recordset. (Details on how to set up filters in a moment.)

6. **Choose a Sort option, if desired.**

   Data from a database may not appear in any particular order. Dreamweaver's sort options let you sort information based on a particular column. For example, maybe you're creating a recordset that gathers the title and release date for every CD you own. You might want to sort the results in alphabetical order by the title of the album, or chronologically by the date they were released.

   To sort database records, from the first Sort menu, choose a column to sort by (Figure 23-2). Then select the sort order: either Ascending (A–Z, 0–10, earliest to latest) or Descending (Z–A, 10–0, latest to earliest).

   The Simple recordset mode lets you sort by only one column. That means, to continue with the previous example, if you want to sort records by date (so the most recent CDs appear first), and then by name (so CDs with the same date are *then* listed in alphabetical order), then you have to use the Advanced mode (see page 855).

To view the results of the recordset, click Test to open the Test SQL Statement window, which contains all records that match that query. If more than 25 matches exist, you can see the next group of results by clicking Next 25 at the bottom of the window. When you're done looking at the test results, click OK to return to the Recordset window.

If the test results look right, click OK to close the Recordset window, and then add the code into the currently opened page.

Note: Unlike a database connection, which is listed in the Databases panel and available to every page on the site, a recordset is specific to a particular page. (See page 861 to learn how to reuse recordsets on other pages.)

Filtering Information

Although you may have selected a limited number of columns when creating a basic recordset, the final results of the recordset still include *all* the records within the table. That's fine when you want a list of all items in a database, like when you're creating a list of all your company's products. But it's not so useful when you want a particular subset of those records, like a list of just the red toupees your company sells, or when you want details on a *single* record—the "Flaming Inferno 78B toupee," for example.

To have Dreamweaver cull specific records from a table, in the Recordset window, use the Filter option (see Figure 23-3). A *filter* lets you compare the information in one database column with a particular value, and then select records that match—in other words, whenever you apply a filter to a recordset you're simply searching through the database for particular records. Suppose, for example, that your products database table contains a column named *price* that contains a product's price. To find all products that cost less than $35, you create a filter that looks for all records where the price column holds a value of less than 35.

Using the Recordset dialog box's Filter feature takes only a few steps:

1. **Create a recordset as described on page 844.**

   To create a filter, you must fill out the Recordset window's Filter options' four form fields—three menus and one text field.

2. **From the first Filter menu, select a column name.**

   This column is the column from the database that Dreamweaver compares to a particular value. In the previous example, you'd select "price" from the menu to indicate the table's price column (see Figure 23-3).

3. **From the next menu, choose a comparison operator (< or >, for example).**

   To find products whose prices are less than $35, for example, you'd use the < (less than) operator. To find an exact value (all products that are exactly $35), use the = sign. Comparison operators are described below.

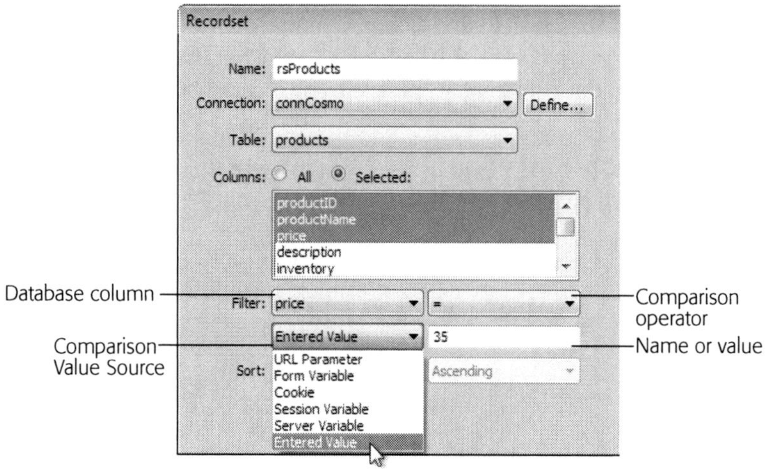

Figure 23-3:
Using a filter, a recordset can identify and retrieve data for a single record in the database, or a collection of records. Dreamweaver gives you several ways to apply filters to your records. The three most common are: information supplied in a URL; via a form submitted by a visitor to your site; or simply based on what you type into the recordset. Three other, more advanced filter options–cookies, session variables, and server variables–are discussed on page 967.

4. **Using the third Filter pop-up menu, select a source for the comparison value.**

   A filter compares the information in a table column against some other value. You find many different sources for such a comparison value. For example, on a Search page, you could create a form that lets visitors type in a search term, and then click a Search button. In this case, the comparison value would come from a form. To set up this arrangement, you, the designer, would select Form Variable from this menu.

   For complete information on selecting a source for a comparison value, see the section "Getting Comparison Values" on the next page.

5. **Into the lower-right Filter box, type a name or value.**

   The value for this field depends on the source you selected in the last step; type in the name of the form variable, cookie, session variable, or whatever. The one exception: If you selected Entered Value in the previous step, then type a specific value in this field. For instance, to compare the "price" column to a specific value, select Entered Value, and then, in the text field, type a number. The Recordset window then looks like Figure 23-3.

6. **Complete the Recordset window by choosing a sort option (if desired), and then clicking OK.**

   You can test the recordset and filter by clicking Test. If you selected anything other than Entered Value from the source menu, then a message prompts you to type in a test value for the source—URL parameter, form variable, and so on.

Comparison Operators for Filters

Dreamweaver provides many different ways to compare information from a database column with information from another source, such as a form, cookie, or simply a value you type into the Recordset window. The type of comparison you choose also depends on the type of data you're comparing: text or numbers.

Comparing text values

You'll often want to create recordsets that find database matches to particular words. For example, a recordset could filter a list of products to find only those records whose descriptions contain the word "green," or you could filter a database of clients to search for a record for "Craig McCord."

Dreamweaver provides the following types of text comparisons:

- **Equality**. To check whether the information in a column is *exactly* the same as another value, from the comparison menu, select the = sign.
- **Inequality**. To find records that don't match a particular piece of text, from the menu, select the <> (doesn't match) operator. You use this, say, if you want to search a database of clothing for items that do *not* match a particular phrase (like "winter" in the Season column).
- **Begins With, Ends With, and Contains.** The last three comparison operators are ideal for locating one or more words within text. For example, a database of movies might have a column containing a short review of each movie. To locate reviews that included the words "horrible acting," you could choose the Contains option, which finds any movie that includes the phrase "horrible acting" anywhere in its review.

  The Begins With and Ends With options are more selective. The former finds records only when the text at the very beginning of a particular record matches; the latter works only when the text appears at the end. You probably won't use these options very often, but they come in handy if you want to search a database for people whose names are Bob or Bobby, but not Joe-Bob. In this example, you use the "Begins With" option, and use Bob as the comparison value.

The other comparison operators (<, >, <=, >=) aren't very useful for searching text in a database. They're intended for comparing numbers, as described next.

Comparing numbers

Filters are particularly useful for numbers: finding products that cost less than $35, albums that were released in 1967, products with more than 3,000 items in stock, and so on. If you've taken basic algebra, these options for comparing numbers should be familiar: = (equal to), <> (not equal to), < (less than), > (greater than), <= (less than or equal to), or >= (greater than or equal to).

Getting Comparison Values

By now it should be clear that the Recordset window's Filter option lets you compare data from one column with some other value. But you're probably wondering where this "some other value" comes from. It depends on which option you selected from the third drop-down menu—the Comparison Value Source menu (see Figure 23-3).

The most straightforward option is the last item in the menu: Entered Value. After selecting it, to the right of the menu, you simply type the value into the field. This value could be a number, a letter, or one or more words. So, to create a recordset that finds a product whose price is more than $50, you select the price column, the > (greater than) comparison symbol, and the Entered Value source option, and then, into the value field, type *50*.

Unfortunately, this kind of recordset is rather limited. The comparison value you specify (50) is hardwired into the recordset, making it very inflexible. What if a visitor wants to see products that cost more than $15, $30, or $100? No joy. This recordset is limited to what you, the designer, entered as a value.

You're better off creating the filter on the fly from information you get when the visitor's Web browser requests the recordset. In this way, you can create very flexible recordsets that are capable of searching databases for a variety of different pieces of information, not just the *one* value selected by a programmer. (After all, how good a search engine would Google be if the *programmers* determined the search criteria? No matter what you searched for—*Web design, Used cars*—it would always find Web sites about Java, Burning Man, and Google's stock valuation.)

Dreamweaver can also draw a filter value from a form, cookie, or even a link's URL. The process is always the same: From the filter's Comparison Value Source menu (Figure 23-3), select the source you want, and then type the name of the appropriate source item. For example, from the source menu, if you select Form Variable, then, in the box to the right, type the name of the form field.

In most cases, you must depend on an additional Web page to provide the source of these values. For example, a search function on a Web site usually requires more than a single page: one (or more) pages containing a Search field and a Submit button to send the information, and another that displays the results of the search. In this example, the form on one page sends information (the search terms) to another page (the results page), which uses the form information to search the database. In essence, Dreamweaver uses the words typed into the search form on one page to create the recordset on another page.

The two commonest ways to pass information from one page to another are forms and URLs. (Three advanced sources—cookies, session variables, and application variables—are discussed on page 967.)

Form variables

A *form variable* is simply the information that a visitor types into a form field (or the value of a selected radio button, menu item, or checkbox). Forms are discussed in depth in Chapter 11, but their use in recordset filters is straightforward:

1. **Create a form page.**

   It can include a text field, pop-up menu, or some other form element. Make sure you *name* the form element. For use in a *simple* recordset filter, you're limited to a single form variable. Using an *advanced* recordset (see page 855), you can use information from more than one form field to filter the data in a recordset.

   If you want to give your site's visitors a chance to look at differently priced products, for example, you can create a menu that includes the values 10, 50, 100, 500, and so on. People can then choose one of those options to look at products below the selected price. (Also be sure to give the menu a name, such as "price," as described on page 446.)

Tip: Name the form field the same as the database column you're filtering. For example, if you're searching a table's *productName* column, name the form field *productName*. If you do, Dreamweaver automatically fills out the correct form field name in step 6 below.

---

2. **Set the Action property of the form (see page 433).**

   You'll want it to point to the results page.

Note: For these steps to work, in the Property inspector, the form's method has to be set to *Post* (see page 434). If *Get* is selected, then the form information appears in the URL when the form is submitted, and that information isn't available as a form variable. (You can, however, use the Get method in conjunction with the URL parameters option discussed next.)

---

3. **Open (or create) the results page.**

   This page displays the results of the recordset that's created using information from the form. This page needs to be a dynamic page using the server model you've chosen—ASP, PHP, and so on. (See page 828 for information on how to create a new dynamic page.)

4. **Add a recordset to the page, using the directions on page 844.**

   You'll also create a filter using a form variable.

5. **From the Filter menu, select a database column. Then choose a type of comparison, as described on page 847.**

   All this is the standard filter-creation routine.

6. **From the source pop-up menu, select Form Variable. In the box to the right of the source menu, type the name of the form field that contains the value for comparison.**

   In keeping with the previous example, type *price* into the box, since that's the name of the menu on the form page.

7. **Add a sort option, if you like, and then click OK to create the recordset.**

   Remember that this kind of recordset's results depend upon information sent from a form. If a visitor just stumbles across the results page without using a form, the recordset most likely produces no results (for a workaround to this problem, see the box on page 854). That's why you should link to this kind of page only by using a form's *Action* property (see page 433).

URL parameters

In your Web travels, you've probably encountered URLs that look kind of strange, along the lines of *http://www.cosmofarmer.com/cart.php?productID=34&quantity=4.* Everything up to the ? probably looks familiar, but you might be wondering what the *?productID=34&quantity=4* means.

Forms aren't the only way to pass information to a dynamic Web page; URLs can do it, too, thanks to information tidbits called *parameters.* Dynamic Web sites can read parameters and use them to create a recordset, among other things. (In fact, using the Get method for a form puts the form's information into the URL.)

You yourself can manually add a URL parameter to a link, but it's even more common to dynamically create a URL parameter from another recordset. This technique is common when you want to link from a long list of items (such as a store's catalog of products) to a single, dynamic page that displays information about a single item (such as the name, description, price, and photograph of a single product).

When a URL parameter is sent along with a link to a dynamic page, that page can use the URL parameter as a filter to search a database. To identify a single record in a database, for instance, the URL could contain a number identifying the record's *primary key* (see page 831 for a definition). You'll find an example of this trick in the tutorial on page 882.

The steps for using URL parameters to filter recordsets are similar to those for form variables. You need two pages, one with a link containing the URL parameter, and another containing the recordset.

Tip: It's possible to add a link with a URL parameter on the *same* page as the recordset. For example, you could have several text links like "Products under $10" and "Products under $100" that link to the same page but have different URL parameters.

Creating a link with a URL parameter

Dreamweaver gives you several ways to create a link that contains a URL parameter. The simplest way is to first highlight the item you wish to turn into a link—usually text or a graphic. Then, in the Property inspector's link box, type the link followed by a ?, a parameter name, an =, and the value (for example: *products.php?category=7*).

However, you'll probably find it easier to browse for the file, and let Dreamweaver write all the complex stuff. To do so, just follow these steps:

1. **Highlight the item you wish to turn into a link.**

   In other words, select a graphic or text on the page.

2. **On the Property inspector, click the folder icon (browse button).**

   The Select File window appears. (For more on creating links, see Chapter 5.)

3. **Browse to and select the page containing the recordset.**

   This page displays the results of the database search.

4. **In the Select File window's lower-right corner, click the Parameters box.**

   The Parameters window appears (see Figure 23-4).

5. **Click in the space below the Name column, and then type the name of the URL parameter.**

   Here you're creating a name of your choosing that describes the data you're searching for. Avoid spaces and any punctuation characters for the name, since you're likely to run into trouble when you try to use such a name in the recordset filter. You could use the name of the table column that you'll be filtering on when you create a recordset. For example, say you create a link to lead to a page listing all the products in a certain category (for instance, plants). Each product might have a column named *categoryID* which identifies the category to which the product belongs. In this case, name the parameter *categoryID*.

6. **Click the space below the Value column, and then type the value for the URL parameter.**

   This value is the value that the filter in the recordset uses to match records in the database.

   Usually this value is a simple one like *17*, *blue*, or *yes*. But you can also use spaces and punctuation marks in the value—for example, *Bob Jones*, in order to search for "Bob Jones" in the database. However, you need to make sure Dreamweaver's Preferences are set accordingly: Choose Edit → Preferences (Dreamweaver → Preferences); click the Code Rewriting category, and then make sure the "Encode using &#" option is selected (the "Encode using %" option also works, but it can have trouble with some characters from some languages). Either of these options rewrites invalid characters in a form that works in a URL. For example, a space is converted to *%20*.

TROUBLESHOOTING MOMENT

The Default Value for a Filter Source

Using a variable source of information for a filter presents a problem. If the filter requires information from a form or URL parameter, what happens if someone comes to the page without first filling out the form or clicking a link with a URL parameter? In most cases, the recordset is empty, and the page displays no records. You can, however, set a *default* value for the form variable or URL parameter, so that at least some records always appear.

Using the steps outlined on page 844, create a basic recordset; include a filter using a form variable or URL parameter. Then, in the Recordset window, click the Advanced button.

Now you get a more complex view of the recordset. The Variables list has a single entry: *colname*. Select *colname*, and then click the Edit button to open the Edit Variable window. The "Default value" box indicates the value used for filtering the recordset if none is supplied (in other words, when the Web browser doesn't give any form or URL variable). The value Dreamweaver supplies is *–1*, which probably doesn't match anything in your database.

Change this value to something that will. For example, if you're filtering on a primary key (to identify one record in the database), then just type a value that you KNOW exists in the primary key field for one particular record. For example, *1*.

You could type a value that matches *all* the records in the database. For example, if the recordset is used to find products under a certain price, then type a value (price) that's larger than the most expensive product in the database. This way, the recordset retrieves all items under that price—in other words, all the products. (This trick also works for the other sources discussed on page 963: cookies, application variables, and session variables.)

One last word of warning. If you switch back to the basic recordset view by clicking the Simple button, then Dreamweaver resets the recordset variable to the default value of *–1*. In other words, if you change the default value in the advanced view, then *don't* switch back to the basic recordset view.

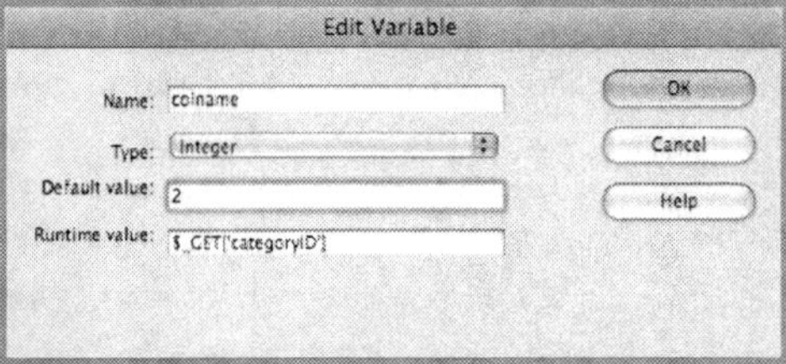

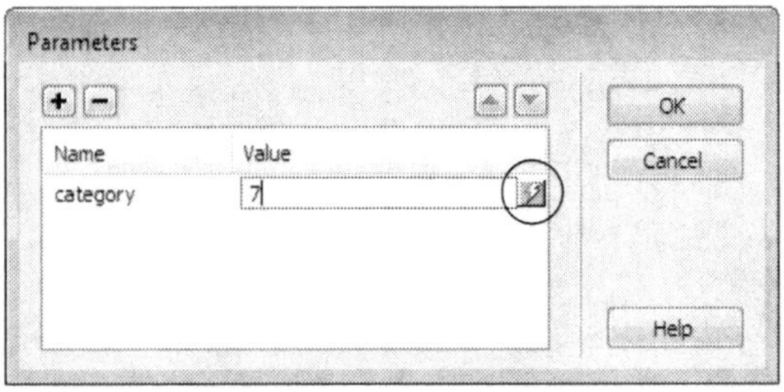

Figure 23-4:
The Parameters window lets you add URL parameters to a link. Recordsets can then use these pieces of information to filter a database query, as discussed on page 847. The lightning bolt button (circled) is used to retrieve dynamic data such as information from a recordset, a cookie, or a server variable, and is especially useful for passing a primary key value to a page that provides detailed information on a single database record.

Note: Forms using the Post method don't suffer from any of these problems, and they can accept all types of punctuation and space characters.

7. **Click OK to close the Parameters window. Click OK to close the Select File window and apply the link.**

Creating the recordset for the results page

Once you've created the link, you need to create an appropriate recordset for the results page. Here's how:

1. **Open (or create) the results page.**

   This page displays the results of the recordset created using information from the URL parameter.

2. **Add a recordset to the page, using the directions on page 844.**

   You'll also create a filter using a URL parameter.

3. **From the Filter menu, select a database column. Choose a type of comparison, as described on page 849. From the source menu, select URL Parameter. In the box to the right of the source menu, type the name of the URL parameter.**

   This name is the name supplied in step 5 of the previous instructions.

4. **Add a sort option, if you like; click OK to create the recordset.**

Like form variables, this recordset depends on information included in the URL of a link. If a visitor just stumbles across the results page without using a link with a URL parameter, then the recordset most probably produces no results. So make sure you link to this kind of page only via a link with a parameter. Otherwise, in the recordset, modify the default value for the URL parameter, as described in the box on page 854.

Tip: Using URL parameters (as opposed to form variables) for retrieving records has an added benefit: since the parameter is embedded in the URL–*http://www.cosmofarmer.com/products.php?productID=20*, for example–you can bookmark or email a link that matches a particular results page. In this way, you could bookmark, say, a page displaying all the products under $50. Then when you want to see if any new products (under $50) have been added to a site, you don't have to search the site again; merely revisit the bookmarked page.

Advanced Recordsets and SQL

Sometimes you need more power than Dreamweaver's simple recordset tool gives you. For example, say you're building an online classified ads system. On one page, you want to present various pieces of information: the name of the sale item, its price, who's selling it, and how to contact the seller, for example. In order to store this kind of information, your database has two tables—one containing the ads themselves, and one containing information about the sellers.

To present all this information, you need to simultaneously access both tables. In addition, you need to connect the records of those two tables so that each item for sale is associated with the correct seller—John Smith is selling the Whirligig 2007, for example. You have only one way to create this kind of complex query: using the advanced options of the Recordset window.

To display these options, insert a recordset using the steps described on page 844. Then, in the Recordset window, click the Advanced button. The Advanced Recordset window should appear (see Figure 23-5). (If you see a Simple button, then you're looking at the advanced options.)

Unfortunately, putting together advanced database queries is not as easy as most other operations in Dreamweaver. The Advanced Recordset window is basically just a way of typing in commands, using a database programming language called *SQL* (Structured Query Language, pronounced "ess-cue-ell"). SQL is a standard language that most database servers use to access, update, delete, and add information to a database.

To create an advanced recordset, in the window's SQL box, type an SQL statement.

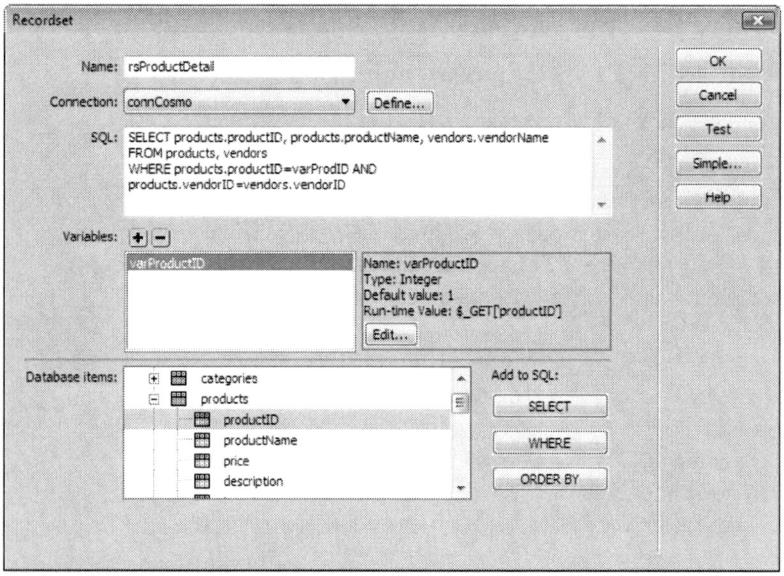

Figure 23-5: *The Recordset window's advanced options aren't for the uninitiated. You need to have a good grasp of SQL– the standard database programming language– to make complex recordsets.*

SQL: the very basics

SQL lets you communicate with a database in order to find, add, update, and delete records. SQL even lets you do more advanced database work, such as adding new tables to a database, and even deleting tables and databases. In the context of the Advanced Recordset window, you need to understand only how SQL *retrieves* information. After all, a recordset is just a selection of data pulled from the database.

To make an SQL query (called an SQL statement), you must first specify:

- **Which columns of data you want to retrieve.** For example, item price, item name, seller name, and seller contact information.
- **Which tables will supply this data.** In the earlier example, the information is stored in two tables: Ads and Sellers.
- **How the search should be limited.** You might just want products that are less than $10 or whose seller is Zachariah Smith. Or you might want to let visitors to your site make these choices themselves, via a form.
- **The sort order.** You could sort items using the Price column to view a list of items from least to most expensive, for example.

Only the first two pieces of information are absolutely necessary. A very basic SQL statement looks like this:

```
SELECT itemPrice, itemName
FROM ads
```

SELECT is an SQL keyword that specifies columns of data for retrieval; FROM indicates which database table contains them. This statement instructs the database server to look inside the Ads table, and retrieve information from two columns: itemPrice and itemName. The result is a list of the price and the name of each item in the database's Ads table.

UP TO SPEED

Getting Your Feet Wet in SQL

SQL isn't difficult to pick up. While you can create very complex SQL queries, a basic SQL statement is straightforward. Once you've reached the limits of Dreamweaver's basic recordset, you may want to expand your skills beyond this simple tool.

Dreamweaver itself is a great place to start learning how to write SQL statements. After you create a simple recordset (see page 844), click the Advanced button. In the SQL box, the SQL statement for the simple query appears.

This chapter introduces the very basics of SQL. For a more complete introduction, check out SQLCourse.com (*www.sqlcourse.com*). Or pick up a book like *SQL Queries for Mere Mortals* (Addison-Wesley Professional) by Michael Hernandez, *SQL in a Nutshell, Second Edition* (O'Reilly) by Kevin Kline, or *Sams Teach Yourself SQL in 10 Minutes* (Sams) by Ben Forta.

Note: SQL keywords are usually written in all caps—SELECT, for example. This is just a convention, not a hard and fast rule; "select" also works. But since you can more easily identify the keywords if they're capitalized, it's best to stick with this practice.

Of course, you may not always want *every* record in a table. You may want to limit the search to a select number of items, such as products under $10. The WHERE keyword lets you do just that:

```
SELECT itemPrice, itemName
FROM ads
WHERE itemPrice < 10
```

Now the SQL statement retrieves only the price and the name of products that cost less than $10. Finally, SQL can sort records into order. In this example, you could also sort all the results from least to most expensive, like this:

```
SELECT itemPrice, itemName
FROM ads
WHERE itemPrice < 10
ORDER BY itemPrice ASC
```

The ORDER BY keywords indicate which column Dreamweaver should use to sort the records. Specifying the prodPrice column sorts the items by price. ASC is short for *ascending*, meaning that the records appear in low-to-high price order. (DESC sorts records into *descending* order, Z–A, or high-to-low.) You can even sort by multiple columns. If, for example, you want a list of all products sorted by price, and *then* alphabetically by product name, you simply change the above ORDER BY keyword to read like this:

```
ORDER BY prodPrice ASC, prodName ASC
```

In this way, all the products with the same price (for example, $10) are presented in alphabetical order (A–Z).

Using the Data Tree view

Although you need to know SQL to use the Recordset window's advanced options, you can get a little help from the data tree in the "Database items" list at the bottom of the window (see Figure 23-5). This area of the window functions just like the Databases panel, and lets you view the tables, columns, views, and stored procedures in the database (see page 841).

Next to the word Tables, click the + (arrow) button to see a list of all tables in the database. Click the + (arrow) next to a table name to see all the columns within that table. This technique is very helpful when you're building an SQL statement, because you may not remember the exact names of every table and column in your database.

To build an SQL statement, you can select a column name, and then click one of the three buttons—SELECT, WHERE, or ORDER BY. The SQL command and column name then appear in the SQL box.

Suppose, for example, you want to create the following SQL statement:

```
SELECT productID, productName
FROM products
```

To build this statement using the data tree, click the + button next to the table named Products, which expands to show a list of all columns. Then click the column named productID, and then click SELECT. Next, click the productName column, and then click SELECT again.

Actually, when you use the Data Tree to insert SQL, Dreamweaver doesn't exactly write it the same as listed above. What you would get after following the previous instructions is:

```
SELECT products.productID, products.productName
FROM products
```

Dreamweaver inserts what are called "qualified" column names. For example, *products.productID* indicates the products table's productID column. When you build a SQL query that involves more than one table, fully qualifying the column name by tacking on the table name as well is a good practice. If the same column name appears in both tables, then your SQL doesn't work—for example, say the Products and the Vendors table both have columns called *name*. Each column refers to different types of data—the item for sale, and the name of the vendor. Without differentiating the two columns (by "pointing to" them, for example as *products.name* and *vendors.name*), the database doesn't know which column you mean, and you end up with a SQL error when you try to test the recordset.

Although these buttons can save you time, they don't check whether the SQL statement is valid. Unless you've got a decent grasp of SQL, you can easily create a statement that generates errors when the test server runs it.

Creating variables for filtering data

Variables let you filter data using information from sources such as forms, URLs, cookies, session variables, and application variables. If you use the basic Recordset window's filtering option, then Dreamweaver creates a variable for you—but in the advanced Recordset window, you must create them yourself.

To add a variable for use in an SQL query, follow these steps:

1. **In the Recordset window, next to Variables, click the + button (see Figure 23-5).**

   The Add Variable window opens (see Figure 23-6).

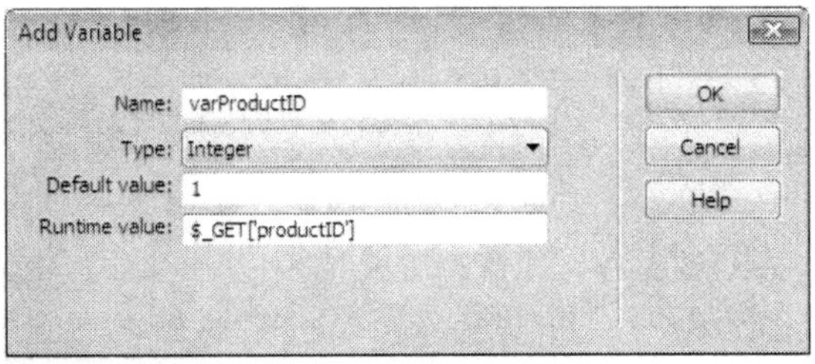

Figure 23-6: *This dialog box lets you create variables to customize how an SQL statement works. You're not limited to just using variables in the filter part of an SQL statement (the WHERE clause) either. You can include a variable as any part of the statement. For example, one variable might determine the order of a sort operation: ASC or DESC.*

2. **In the Name box, type a name for the variable.**

   The name shouldn't include spaces or other punctuation marks.

Tip: As with database connections and recordsets, it's a good idea to add a prefix to the variable's name so you can more easily identify it in Code view. For example, you could begin the variable name with *var*–*varPrice*, for instance–just as you'd begin a recordset name with *rs* (*rsProducts*, for example).

---

3. **From the Type menu, choose a data type.**

   Your options are Integer, Text, Date, and Floating point number. If the variable is going to be used as part of a filtering operation, then the type you choose depends on the type of data stored in the column you're filtering on. For example, if the variable is used as part of a search on the name of a product, choose Text.

   The integer and text options are, of course, for numbers and text. Use Date when the variable contains a date type. This date isn't just any old date, however—it's the type of date defined by your database system. Each database has a different approach to this setting (to find out how MySQL handles date types, visit *http://dev.mysql.com/doc/refman/5.0/en/date-and-time-types.html*). Finally, the Floating point number option is reserved for numbers stored with decimal places—for example, a monetary value like 10.25 or 9.99.

Tip: You can easily determine the type of data stored in a column using the Databases panel, as described in the box on page 842.

---

4. **In the "Default value" box, type a value.**

   A default value comes in handy when the form, URL, cookie, session variable, or application variable is empty. The recordset uses the default value to filter the database records. See page 854 for more on when and why this might happen.

5. **Press Tab to jump to the "Runtime value" box; type the appropriate code.**

   The exact code depends on the server model you selected. For example, to retrieve the value of a form field named *price,* type *$_POST['price']* for PHP or *Request.Form("price"*) for ASP. You can best learn how to create variables when you use the Recordset window's Dreamweaver's filter tool (see instructions on page 847), and then switch to the advanced Recordset window, select the variable, and click the Edit button. The proper code for collecting information from forms, URLs, cookies, and so on appears in the variables' "Runtime value" field.

Note: Keep in mind that if you add more than one SQL variable in the advanced Recordset window, you can't switch back to the simple view.

Once you create a variable, you can include it in your SQL statement. Since variables help filter information, you'll often add them to the SQL *WHERE* keyword.

For example, if you create a variable named *varPrice* that retrieves information from a form, then you can add it to the SQL statement like this:

```
SELECT ads.itemPrice, ads.itemName
FROM ads
WHERE ads.itemPrice < varPrice
```

In this example, whatever information is passed from the form is stored in the *varPrice* variable, and compared to the price stored in the *itemPrice* column in the database's *ads* table.

If you ever need to edit a variable, just select its name from advanced Recordset window's Variables list, and then click the Edit button. That action reopens the Edit Variable window (Figure 23-6).

Reusing Recordsets

You create recordsets on a page-by-page basis. In other words, when you create a recordset, it's added to only the current document. If you create another Web page that requires the same recordset, then you must add the proper code to the new page. You can do this either by recreating the recordset—a potentially laborious process—or by simply copying the recordset from one page and pasting it into another.

Here's how:

1. **Open the Bindings panel by choosing Window → Bindings.**

   Ctrl+F10 (⌘-F10) also works. You can also copy and paste from the Server Behaviors panel.

2. **Right-click (Control-click) the name of the recordset you wish to copy; from the shortcut menu that appears, choose Copy.**

   In the Server Behaviors panel, recordsets appear like this: *Recordset (rsName)*, with the name of the recordset inside the parentheses.

Now switch to the document that'll receive the pasted recordset. Right-click (Control-click) in the Bindings (or Server Behaviors) panel, and then, from the shortcut menu, choose Paste.

Tip: If you need a recordset that's similar to a recordset you've already created–but not identical–you can copy the original recordset, paste it into a new document, and then edit it, following the instructions in the next section.

Editing Recordsets

What if you have to edit a recordset? Maybe you forgot an important column of information when you originally created the recordset, or perhaps you want to modify a recordset you copied from another page. The process is easy: Simply open either the Bindings panel (Ctrl+F10 [⌘-F10]) or Server Behaviors panel (Ctrl+F9 [⌘-F9]), and then double-click the name of the recordset you wish to edit.

The Recordset window appears, looking just as it did when you first created the recordset (see Figure 23-2). Make any changes to the recordset, and then click OK.

Note: If you change the name of a recordset while editing it, then Dreamweaver displays a message indicating that you need to use Find and Replace (see page 782) to locate and update every instance of the recordset's name. Dreamweaver opens the "Find and Replace" window for you when you click OK, but it's up to you to make sure the changes are correct.

This reason is another reason why beginning a recordset with "rs" (*rsProducts*, for example) is a good idea. If you've named a recordset simply "products", you could end up finding and replacing not only the name of the recordset, but also any other cases where the word "products" appears in the page.

The safest (although slowest) way to change a recordset's name is to recreate it. Of course, that's extra effort–a good argument for making sure you're satisfied with a recordset's name when you *first* create it.

Deleting Recordsets

If you add a recordset to a page and later realize that the page isn't using any of the information retrieved by the recordset, you should delete it. Each recordset forces the database server to do some work. Unnecessary recordsets only make your Web pages work harder and more slowly.

You can delete a recordset using either the Bindings or Server Behaviors panel. Just select the name of the recordset in either panel, and then, at the top of the panel, click the minus sign (–) button (pressing Delete on your keyboard has the same effect). However, if you've added dynamic data from that recordset to the page (described next), and then you delete the recordset, Dreamweaver doesn't remove references to the deleted recordset. In most cases, this action breaks the functionality of the page, and it doesn't work when viewed in a browser. You need to make sure you delete that dynamic information (as described on page 866) and remove any server behaviors from the Server Behavior panel that rely on that recordset.

Adding Dynamic Information

Once you've created a recordset, it's a snap to add information retrieved from the recordset to a Web page. In fact, Dreamweaver gives you several ways to add dynamic information. Start in the document window by clicking the spot where you wish to add information from the recordset. Then do one of the following:

- Choose Insert → Data Objects → Dynamic Data → Dynamic Text.
- In the Insert panel's Data category, click the Dynamic Data button, and then, from the menu, select Dynamic Text (see Figure 23-7).

Either way, the Dynamic Text window appears (see Figure 23-8), listing the recordsets on the current page. Click the + sign button next to the recordset from which you wish to get information. This recordset expands to show all columns

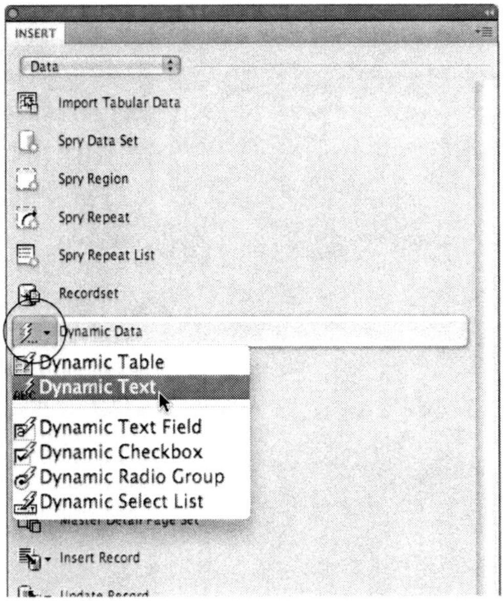

Figure 23-7:
On the Insert panel's Data category, the Dynamic Data button (circled) lets you add a variety of dynamic data to your Web page—from form fields filled in with information retrieved from a database to a complete table based on a recordset. (As discussed on page 26, you have many ways to control the placement and appearance of the Insert Panel, so your setup might not exactly match this figure.)

retrieved in it. Pick the database column (also called Field) containing the information you wish to add to the page. You can pick only one column at a time, but you can repeat this process to add multiple columns to the page.

Note: *Dynamic Text* is a bit of a misnomer. This tool can also insert dates, numbers, and dollar values—not just text.

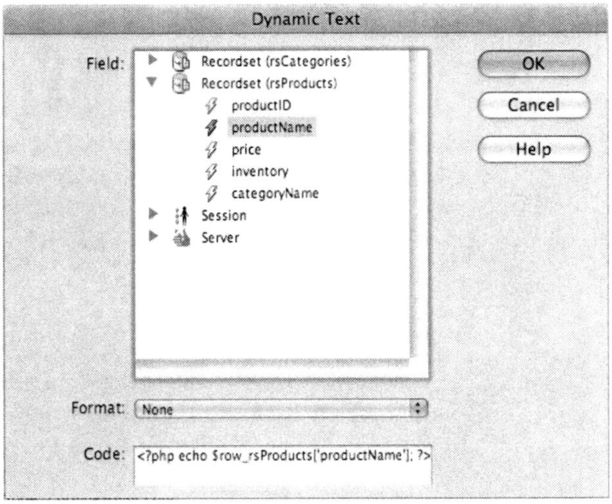

Figure 23-8:
After you select a database field to add to a page, in the Code box, Dreamweaver displays the necessary code. This code is the programming code that makes the data appear on your page. Dreamweaver writes this code using whichever programming language is compatible with the server model you've chosen.

The format menu lets you format the data, like making a date appear as *January 17, 2009*. Formatting is discussed in depth in the section below.

The Bindings Panel

The Bindings panel (Figure 23-9) gives you two other ways to put data from a recordset onto a page. (It's called Bindings because the panel provides a mechanism to "bind" or attach data from a database to a particular spot on a Web page.) Recordsets appear in the Bindings panel. To open this panel, choose Window → Bindings or press Ctrl+F10 (⌘-F10).

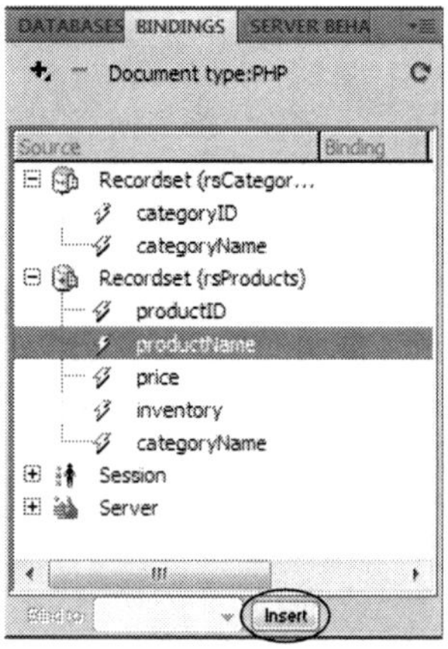

Figure 23-9:
The Bindings panel lists all the different types of dynamic data you can add to your page. Recordsets (and the columns of data they've retrieved) appear here, but so do URL, Form, Cookie, and Session variables, as described on page 963.

To add data from the Bindings panel to a page, click in the document window where you wish to insert the dynamic data. Then, in the Bindings panel, select the column you wish to add, and click Insert (circled in Figure 23-9). But the best and fastest method is to just drag a column's name from the Bindings panel directly into the document window—into a paragraph or table cell, for example. You'll probably use this method most of the time.

After adding dynamic information to a page, it looks something like this: *{rsProducts.productName}*. The information in braces indicates the name of the recordset (rsProducts), and the name of the data column (productName). (You can make "real" data appear—instead of this code—when you use Dreamweaver's Live View, as described on page 875.)

Formatting Dynamic Information

Suppose a database includes a column for a product price, and the raw information is listed in a pretty clunky format—something like *8* or *10.9*. But on your Web page, you want prices properly formatted with a dollar sign and two decimal places, like *$8.00* or *$10.90.*

Dreamweaver includes many different formatting options for numbers, dates, and text. You can choose a formatting option when using the Insert Dynamic Text window (Figure 23-8). You can also apply, remove, or change a formatting option using the Bindings panel.

To set a format using the Bindings panel (Ctrl+F10 [⌘-F10]), proceed as follows:

1. **In the document window, click the dynamic item you wish to format.**

   A down-pointing arrow appears in the Bindings panel, under the Format column.

2. **In the Bindings panel, under the Format column, click the down-pointing arrow, and then, from the menu, select a formatting option** (Figure 23-10).

   Pick an option that's appropriate to the selected piece of data: currency formatting for the price of a product, for example. If you try to apply a formatting option that isn't appropriate for the selected item (Currency to a text description, say), then the page may produce an error when previewed on the testing server.

Tip for PHP Users: Dreamweaver doesn't include date, currency, or number formatting options for the PHP/MySQL server model. Help is available in the form of a free extension called PHP Server Formats. Run, don't walk, to *www.tecnorama.org/document.php?id_doc=51*, and download this extension now! For more information on extensions and how they work, see page 804.

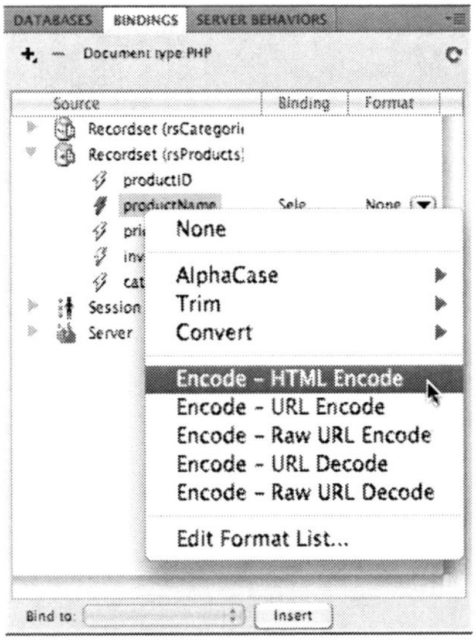

Figure 23-10: *The PHP server model doesn't have too many useful formatting options; however, one of them, "Encode - HTML Encode", may come in handy if your database stores HTML code (this option is called "Encode – Server. HTML Encode" in the ASP server model). For example, maybe you've created a bulletin board whose messages are stored in a database. When you're adding one of those messages to a page, applying the "Encode - HTML Encode" format ensures that Web browsers don't render any code in a message as part of your page. Instead, any HTML in that dynamic text appears to visitors as code. Similarly, if there's any chance a data field might store a bracket like this <, then the Encode formatting option prevents a Web browser from thinking that the opening bracket is the start of an HTML tag–a situation that could make your page not appear at all!*

You can also format selected dynamic data just as you would other text on a page by applying CSS styles, headings, bulleted lists, and so on.

Deleting Dynamic Information

Dynamic information added to a page behaves like a single object. Just click to select it. You can also drag it to another location on the page, copy and paste it, remove it from a page by selecting it and pressing Delete, and so on.

If you remove all the dynamic information from a page, and don't plan on using any information from the recordset, make sure you delete the recordset, too, as described on page 862. Even though you may not display any dynamic information on the page, if a page contains a recordset, it must still communicate with the database server, slowing down your pages.

Dynamic data is also listed in the Server Behaviors panel—you can remove it just like you would any other server behavior, by selecting it from the Server Behaviors panel, and then clicking the minus (–) button (see Figure 23-14).

Displaying Multiple Records

Often, you'll want to create a Web page that displays multiple records, such as a page that lists all the products in your company's catalog.

So far, the techniques you've learned for inserting dynamic data insert information only from a single record. Even if you've created a recordset that retrieves a thousand records, you still just see information from the very first record in the recordset when you simply drag data from the Bindings panel onto a dynamic Web page. You need a bit of extra programming if you want to see information from more than one record (like a long list of all company employees) on a single page. Fortunately, Dreamweaver gives you two tools for displaying multiple records: the Dynamic Table and Repeat Region objects.

Creating a Repeating Table

HTML tables (see Chapter 7) are meant to display data. The columns and rows of tables provide tidy compartments for individual pieces of information. It's not surprising, then, that in database terminology, *row* often refers to a single record in a database, and column indicates a single type of information in a record. Where a row and *column* meet, they form a "cell" that holds one piece of data from a single record.

Dreamweaver's Dynamic Table tool lets you display the results of a recordset in an HTML table. The top row of the table includes the name of each database column to identify the data in the rows below. The bottom row includes the actual dynamic data—one database column per table column (Figure 23-11).

The magic of this tool is that it can duplicate a row for each record in the recordset. In other words, the table displays multiple records, one per table row. Here's how to use it:

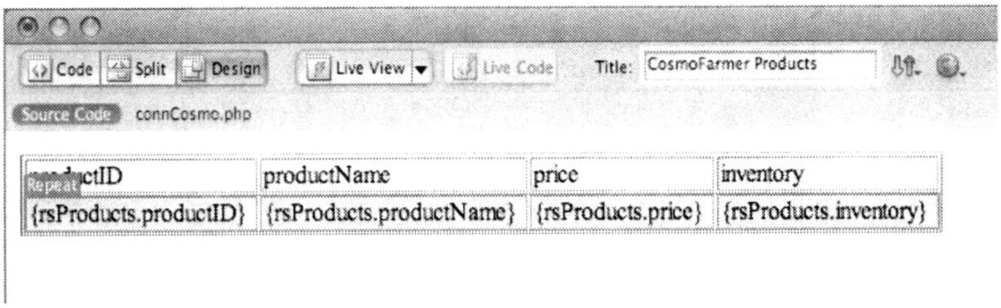

Figure 23-11: *Although the Dynamic Table tool creates a table that displays multiple records, you see only one table row's worth of dynamic data. The Repeat tab that appears above the row indicates that this row will repeat, once for each record in the recordset. To see the effect, use Live View as described on page 875.*

1. **Create a recordset (see page 844). In the Insert panel's Data category, from the Dynamic Data button menu, select Dynamic Table (see Figure 23-7).**

   You can also choose Insert → Data Objects → Dynamic Data → Dynamic Table. Either way, the Dynamic Table window opens (see Figure 23-12).

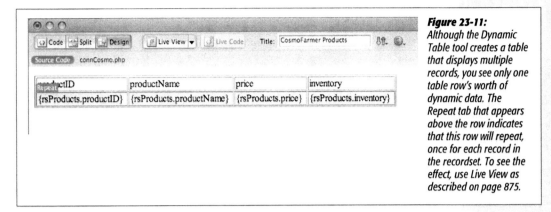

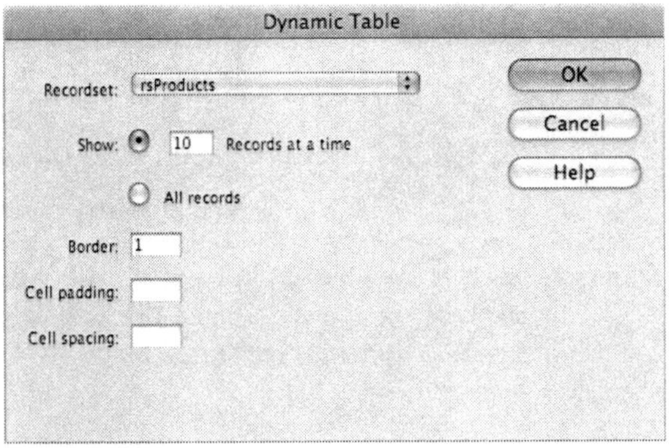

Figure 23-12: *The Dynamic Table tool lets you quickly create a table to display all or some of the records in a recordset.*

2. **From the Recordset menu, choose the recordset you'd like to use.**

   Since a page can contain more than one recordset, you have to indicate which records you want to display.

3. **Using the Show radio buttons, specify the number of records you wish to display.**

   You can show all the records on a single page by clicking the "All records" button. However, if your recordset is huge—if you're creating a Web page to display company employees, and your company has 10,000 employees, say—a single page with all that information could be ridiculously long. In cases like these, you should display only a handful of items at a time.

If you type *10* in this box, you see at most 10 records when previewing the page. (If you choose this method, make sure to add a Recordset Navigation bar, as described on page 871, to give visitors a way to page through the list of results.)

4. **Set the Border, Cell Padding, and Cell Spacing values for the table.**

   These HTML table properties are described on page 264. All you're creating here is a plain old HTML table. You can dress it up later in Design view by changing the border, cell padding, cell spacing, background cell color, and other table properties.

Note: If you insert a Dynamic table, and then later alter the recordset used in this table–for example, by adding a column of information to your query–Dreamweaver doesn't update the repeating table as a result of this change. In fact, if you remove a column of information from a query, you get an error when you try to preview the repeating table. If you edit the recordset, and change the number of columns it retrieves (see page 861), it's usually easiest to delete the current repeating table, and then replace it with a new repeating table.

5. **Click OK.**

   Dreamweaver inserts a table into the page. The top row contains the names of each column from the recordset—one name per table cell. You can, and probably should, edit these names to make them more understandable. After all, *productID* probably doesn't mean anything to your visitors.

   The bottom row of the table contains the dynamic data from the recordset and represents one record. Each table cell in that row simply holds dynamic text for each field in the recordset. You can select each of these placeholders and style them as you would any dynamic text—for example, using the Property inspector's style menu to apply a CSS style. The table row has a Repeat Region object applied to it, which you can edit or delete as described in the next section.

Creating a Repeat Region

While the Repeating Table is easy to use, it doesn't give you the flexibility you might require. For example, what if your dynamic information needs to be presented in a bulleted list (one record per bulleted item) or in individual paragraphs (one paragraph per record)? In these cases, you need to create a *repeating region*—a chunk of HTML that repeats once for each record in a recordset.

Here's an example that can help you understand how to use the Repeat Region object. Imagine you're creating a directory to list your company's staff. This page would include the name, telephone number, email address, and department of each employee. Of course, all this information is stored in a table in a database—one column for each piece of information, and one record for each employee.

In Dreamweaver, you create the basic design of the page, and then add a recordset that retrieves the required information about each employee in the company. The page layout presents each employee's information in a single paragraph, so the finalized page has many paragraphs—one for each employee.

Since this is a dynamic page, you can't predict how many paragraphs you'll need. After all, your company may hire many new employees, which would add records to the database. To allow for this uncertainty, create a single paragraph by adding the dynamic information you want in it, following the steps on page 862. Then tell Dreamweaver to *repeat* that paragraph using information from each record the recordset retrieves.

Just follow these steps:

1. **Using the Bindings panel or one of the techniques described on page 862, insert dynamic text onto the page.**

   You should put these items together on the page, maybe in a single paragraph, in a bulleted or numbered list, or in a <div> tag (see page 333).

2. **Select the dynamic text and any HTML code you wish to repeat.**

   For example, select the paragraph (in the document window's Tag selector, click the <p>) containing the dynamic data. If you're using a bulleted list to present this information, select the list item (<li> tag) containing the dynamic data. For data in a table row, select the table row (<tr> tag).

Note: You need to be very precise when selecting the HTML used in a Repeating Region. If you aren't, the page may not look or work as you expect. For example, if you select the dynamic data in a bulleted list, but don't actually select the <li> tag representing the list item, then when you insert a repeating region, the records repeat within a single bulleted list. In other words, you end up with a bunch of words (data from multiple records) as part of a single bullet. Use the Tag selector (see page 24) to accurately select an HTML tag.

---

3. **In the Insert panel's Data category, click the Repeat Region button (see Figure 23-1).**

   You can also choose Insert → Data Objects → Repeated Region. Either way, the Repeat Region window appears (Figure 23-13).

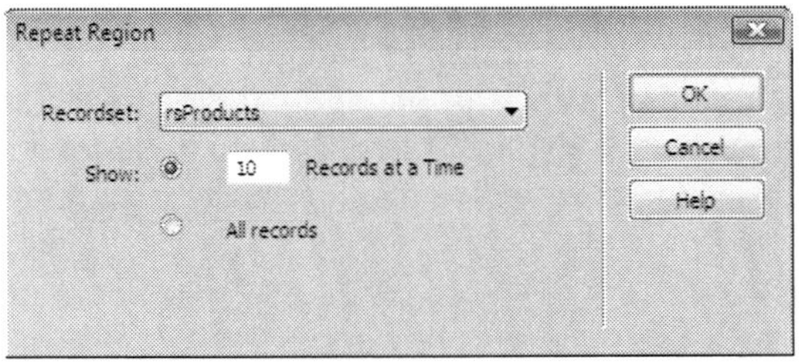

Figure 23-13:
In a Repeat Region that reveals only a limited number of records at a time (in this case, 10), add a Recordset Navigation bar (see the next page). Otherwise, visitors to the page see the first 10 records of a recordset, but don't have any way to view additional records!

4. **From the Recordset menu, choose the recordset you want the page to work with.**

   Since it's possible to have more than one recordset per page, be sure to select the recordset whose data is included in the area you're going to repeat.

5. **Choose the number of records you wish to display.**

   If you decide not to use the "All records" option, make sure that you add a Recordset Navigation bar, as described below, to let visitors page through the list of results.

6. **Click OK.**

   Dreamweaver adds the proper programming code to the Web page.

Editing and Removing a Repeat Region

If you selected the wrong recordset, or want to increase the number of records displayed at a time, you can easily change a Repeating Region. Simply open the Server Behaviors panel (Ctrl+F9 [⌘-F9] or Window → Server Behaviors), and then double-click Repeat Region from the list. In the Repeat Region window (Figure 23-13), make any changes, and then click OK.

To remove a Repeat Region, open the Server Behaviors panel (see Figure 23-14). From the list, select Repeat Region, and then click the minus sign (–) button (or press the Delete key).

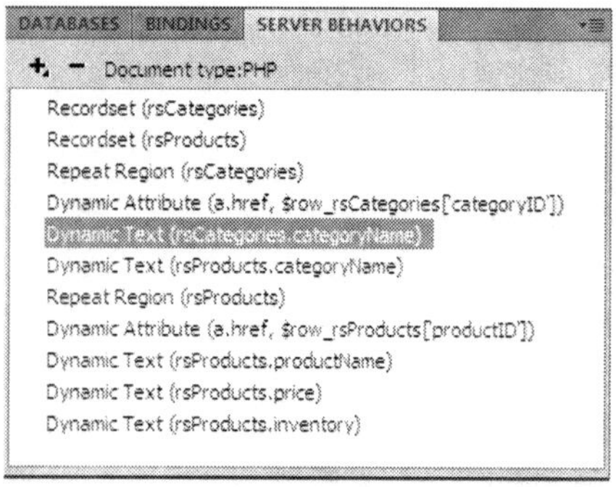

Figure 23-14:
*The Server Behaviors panel lists every dynamic element you add to a page, from recordsets to Repeat Regions. Even when you drag a column from the Bindings panel to add dynamic data to a page, you create a server behavior. In this example, the highlighted element Dynamic Text (*rsCategories .categoryName*) represents data from a recordset that'll appear somewhere on the Web page. You can delete any server behavior by selecting it from the list, and then clicking the minus (–) button.*

Recordset Navigation

Dreamweaver's Repeating Region tool lets you display multiple database records on a single Web page. But a recordset with large amounts of data—like 1,000 employee records—can quickly choke a Web page. A large amount of information takes a long time to download, and forces visitors to scroll for many screens to see it all.

Fortunately, the tool also lets you limit the number of records displayed at once. Of course, this limit presents its own set of problems: How do visitors see additional records, and how do you let them know where they are among all the records in the recordset?

To solve this dilemma, Dreamweaver comes with two handy commands for adding navigation to a recordset—and providing useful feedback about the recordset.

FREQUENTLY ASKED QUESTION

A Little Less Repetition

I applied the Repeat Region object, and when I preview the page, the same record is repeated over and over. That's not what I wanted to do! What's going on?

This scenario can happen when you apply a Repeat Region object, and, from the Repeat Region window, inadvertently select the wrong recordset (see Figure 23-13)—a mistake you can easily make if you've included more than one recordset on a page.

The Repeat Region object adds programming code that steps through each record of a recordset. So, in practice, the Repeat Region object should get the information from the first record in a recordset and write it to the Web page, and then go to the second record and add its info to the page. This process should continue until it's either gone through all the records in the recordset or reached the limit specified in the "Records at a Time" box.

However, if the information you want repeated is retrieved by a different recordset from the one selected in the Repeat Region window, then this system breaks down. Instead, the code continues to cycle through each record from the selected recordset, but doesn't cycle through each record from the recordset containing the dynamic information you want repeated. The result: You get the same information over and over again. The first record of the recordset (the one you want repeated) is repeated for each record in the *other* recordset (the one you don't want repeated).

In other words, to ensure that Repeat Region works, select the recordset whose data is contained in the area you want *repeated*.

Recordset Navigation Bar

Suppose a page contains a recordset that retrieves 100 records from a database, but the Repeating Region on the page limits the display to 10 records at a time. In this case, you should insert a Recordset Navigation Bar to add either text links or graphic buttons to a page. These navigation bars let your audience view the next 10 records in the recordset, jump to the last records in the recordset (see Figure 23-15), jump back to the first record, or move to previous records in the recordset.

To add a Recordset Navigation Bar, follow these steps:

1. **Click in the document window at the location where you want to insert the navigation bar. In the Insert panel's Data category, click the Recordset Paging button, and then, from the menu, select Recordset Navigation Bar (see Figure 23-16).**

   You can also choose Insert → Data Objects → Recordset Paging → Recordset Navigation Bar. In either case, the Recordset Navigation Bar window appears.

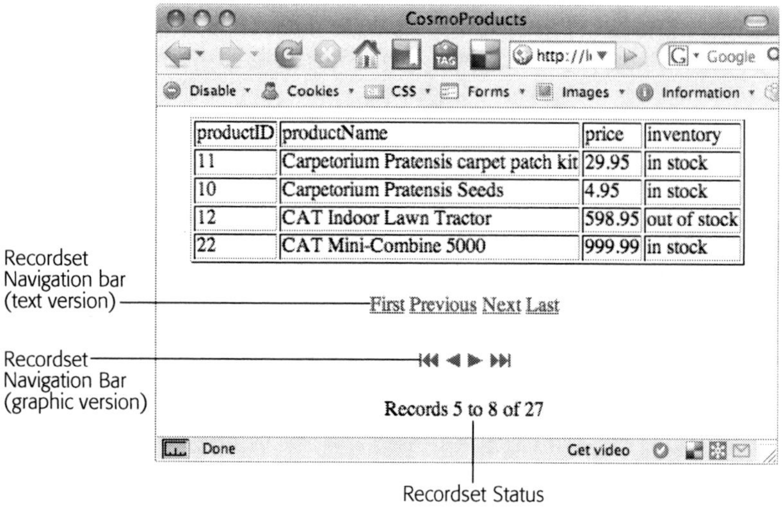

***Figure 23-15:** Dreamweaver's Recordset Navigation Bar object prevents information overload by letting Web page visitors step through smaller chunks of database info. The Recordset Status message also keeps visitors informed about how many records are available.*

***Figure 23-16:** The Recordset Paging button lets you insert a navigation bar for navigating the records returned in a recordset. In addition, if you want to build your own recordset navigation system, you can individually apply server behaviors like "Move to First Page" and "Move to Next Page". These server behaviors are discussed on page 972.*

2. **From the Recordset menu, select the recordset to navigate.**

   If the page contains more than one recordset, select the one that you used when you made the dynamic table or added the Repeating Region.

3. **Select whether to use text or graphic buttons for the navigation bar.**

   If you select Text, Dreamweaver proposes the words First, Previous, Next, and Last to indicate the navigation controls. (You can edit them later.) The graphic buttons resemble standard DVD player controls, representing forward and backward. If you select this option, then Dreamweaver copies the four GIF files into the folder with the dynamic Web page. Later, you can replace these graphics with ones you create.

FREQUENTLY ASKED QUESTION

Behaviors That Serve You Well

What's the difference between Dreamweaver Behaviors (Chapter 13) and a server behavior?

Both are prewritten programs created by Dreamweaver's engineers. They differ mainly in where the programs run and what they attempt to accomplish.

A Dreamweaver Behavior is a JavaScript program that runs in a Web browser. It usually affects the interaction between a visitor and a Web page. For instance, the Swap Image behavior makes the Web browser exchange one image for another when a visitor mouses over a link. The behavior itself runs in the visitor's Web browser, and anyone can see the program by looking in the browser, at the page's source code.

A server behavior, on the other hand, always runs on the *application server*—that is, on the Web-server side of the Internet. Instead of JavaScript, server behaviors can be written in a variety of different languages—VBScript, PHP, and so on, depending on the server model (page 818) your site uses. Server behaviors specifically let you create connections to databases and display, edit, and delete information from databases. Furthermore, since these programs run on the application server, your site's visitors never see the actual programming code. All they see if they look at the source of the page is plain old HTML (the results of the server program).

In a nutshell, Dreamweaver Behaviors add interactive elements to a Web page, like rollovers and JavaScript alert boxes. Server behaviors supply the programming code you need to build sophisticated database-driven Web sites.

4. **Click OK to insert the navigation bar.**

   Dreamweaver inserts a table, consisting of one row and four columns, into the document window. Each cell contains one text or graphic navigation button. You can change the alignment and any other property of the table to fit your design (see Chapter 7 for more information on working with HTML tables).

Tip: If you use the Recordset Navigation Bar frequently, you may long to replace the DVD-control graphics that Dreamweaver displays. Just create your own graphics, and then name them FIRST.GIF, Last.gif, PREVIOUS.GIF, and NEXT.GIF (make sure you capitalize them inconsistently just like Adobe has done). Place these graphic files in the *C:\Program Files\Adobe\Adobe Dreamweaver CS4\configuration\Shared\UltraDev\Images* folder (Applications → Adobe Dreamweaver CS4 → Configuration → Shared → UltraDev → Images folder).

Recordset Navigation Status

When you're viewing hundreds of records, it's nice to know where you are and how many records there are in all. The Recordset Navigation Status tool adds just such information to your pages, as shown in Figure 23-15. Dreamweaver presents the status message in the form of "Records 1 to 10 of 18", indicating which records the visitor is currently viewing, and the total number of records.

Here's how to add a Recordset Navigation Status message:

1. **Click in the document window at the location you want to insert the status message. In the Insert panel's Data category, click the Display Record Count button (circled in Figure 23-17).**

   You can also choose Insert → Data Objects → Display Record Count → Recordset Navigation Status. In either case, the Recordset Navigation Status window appears.

2. **From the menu, select a Recordset.**

   If the page contains more than one recordset, select the one that you used when you inserted the Recordset Navigation Bar.

3. **Click OK to close the window and insert the status message.**

   The Recordset Navigation Status message is simply text with the three dynamic text items (see page 862 for more on dynamic text). Change the words "Records", "to", and "of" to anything you like, such as in "Products 1-10. 149 total products retrieved."

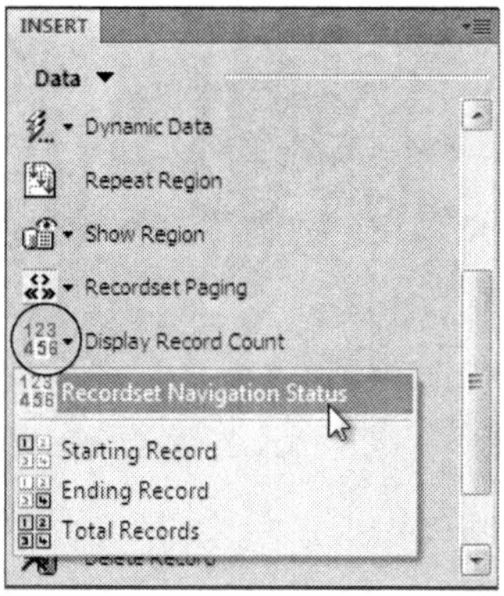

Figure 23-17: *Use the Display Record Count menu to insert status information about a recordset, including the helpful message ("Records 1 to 10 of 18") provided by the Recordset Navigation Status server behavior.*

You can easily build your own recordset navigation status bar using the last three options in the Data tab's Display Record Count menu (see Figure 23-17). Just click in the document window where you'd like to insert the recordset status information, and then, from the menu, select an option.

The Starting Record option displays the number of the first record in a Repeated Region. The exact number depends on where the visitor is within the recordset navigation. For example, say you add a Repeated Region that displays 10 records at a time; you then add a Recordset Navigation Bar (page 871) so visitors can view all the records in the recordset by paging through 10 records at a time. On the first page, the starting record number is 1, but when someone clicks the "next page" button in the Recordset Navigation Bar, the starting record on that page is 11. In other words the starting record number is the "11" in "Showing records 11 to 20 of 100".

The same is true with the Ending Record option. It displays the number of the last record displayed on the page. Again, the exact value depends on the recordset, and which page of records is being viewed. The ending record number is the "20" in "Showing records 11 to 20 of 100".

Finally, the Total Records option is simple: It's just the total number of records retrieved in a recordset. You'll find yourself using this useful option even without a Recordset Navigation Bar. For example, say you want to know how many employees are listed in your database. Create a recordset that retrieves every employee (in other words, don't use a filter [page 847]), and then, from the Record Count menu, use the Total Records option.

Viewing Live Data

After you add dynamic information to a Web page, you see something like this in the document window: *{rsProducts.productID}*. That gives you an idea of what the information is—in this example, the database column productID from a recordset named rsProducts—but it doesn't show any real database information, which can make designing a page more difficult. You're especially far from seeing the actual result when a page contains a Repeating Region: what appears as a single row of dynamic text actually shows up as multiple rows or records when someone views it in a Web browser.

You've already encountered one way to simulate the browser-view of a page: Live View (discussed on page 198). You can use Live View for dynamic pages as well as the JavaScript-enabled pages you learned about in this chapter. Just click the Live View button (see Figure 23-18) to see what the page looks like complete with data directly from your database.

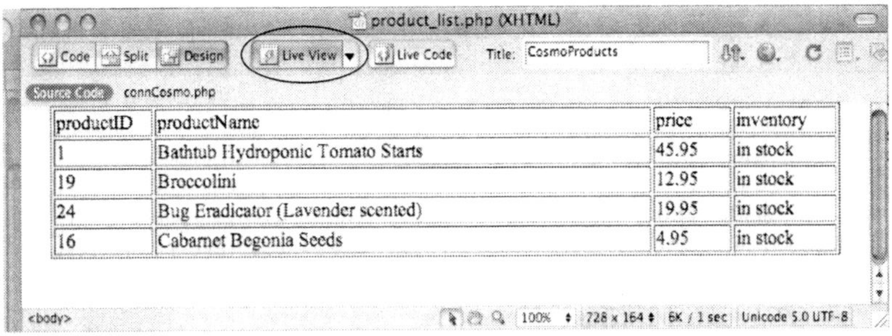

Figure 23-18: *This is the Live View of the dynamic table pictured in Figure 23-11. When the Live View button is highlighted (it looks like it's pressed on Windows, and highlighted in blue on Macs), the page is being displayed in Live View. You can't make any changes to the document until you leave Live View by pressing the Live View button again.*

Note: When using Live View with a local testing server, you may get a message asking if you want to "move" the page to the testing server. This is just a weird behavior of Dreamweaver. This book suggests setting up a testing server on your own computer, and then putting your working files inside the root folder for that server. In other words, both your "local root folder" (the folder which contains the files you're working on) and the root folder on your testing server are one and the same. However, Dreamweaver, for some reason, thinks they're in different locations, and goes through the process of "moving" the files to the testing server. It doesn't actually move anything, but it acts like it does and pops up annoying windows as if it's moving files. Thankfully, you see a "don't ask me again" checkbox on this window, so you can turn it on to avoid being bothered each time you use Live View. This note also applies whenever you preview a Web page using Dreamweaver's "Preview in Browser" feature.

However, you have an even better way to view database-driven pages: Live Data view. Unlike Live View, Live Data view not only lets you preview a page with real database records directly in Dreamweaver, but you can also continue to work on a Web page in this view just as you would in Design view. You can add text and graphics, modify page properties, and even format dynamic data, as described on page 921.

To turn the Live Data view on or off, choose View → Live Data or press Ctrl+Shift+R (⌘-Shift-R). It may take a few seconds for the document window to change, since Dreamweaver must contact the testing server, and retrieve information from the database. After a moment, the page looks just like it will in a Web browser, complete with data pulled straight from the database.

The Live Data toolbar appears (see Figure 23-19), complete with tools for refreshing the displayed data, changing settings for the Live Data view, and adding URL parameters to test recordset filters.

As mentioned earlier, you can continue to work with the Web page while in Live Data view. However, when you're working with a Repeating Region, you can select, delete, or format only the *first set* of dynamic data items. For instance, as you can see in Figure 23-19, a dynamic table displays repeating rows of database records. If you want to apply a CSS style to the name of each product listed, you click the item in the first row of dynamic data—in this example, "Bug Eradicator"—and then apply the style to it. To see the style applied to the other records, in the Live Data view toolbar, click the Refresh button.

Live Data View Settings

Some recordsets depend on information provided by a form or URL. Often when you use the filter option, for instance, a recordset searches a database for records that match information from a form or URL.

This feature can come in handy for pages that provide detailed information about a single record. Frequently, for these types of pages, the URL might appear something like this: *product.php?productID=38*, where the name of the page *(product.php)* is followed by a URL parameter that includes a name *(productID)* and value *(38)*. The recordset then looks for the product whose ID *(productID)* matches 38.

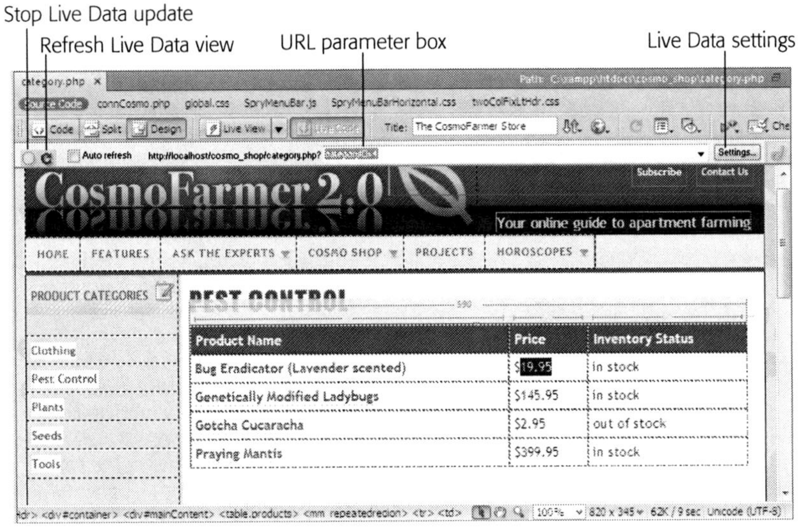

***Figure 23-19:** In Live Data view, you can update the data displayed on the page by clicking the Refresh Live Data view button. Turn on "Auto refresh" if you want Dreamweaver to update the Live Data view automatically whenever you make a change to a dynamic element of the page (but avoid it if your connection to the testing server is slow). Also, if refreshing the data takes too long—or if, when switching into Live Data view, Dreamweaver seems to have stopped working—you can click the Stop Live Data Update button to halt the current update.*

Pages like this can't show up properly without a little outside help, so you need to provide extra information in the Live Data View Setting window, like this:

1. **In the Live Data toolbar, click the Settings button (see Figure 23-19).**

   You can also choose View → Live Data Settings. Either way, the Live Data Settings window appears (Figure 23-20). Click the + button to add a new name and value pair.

   Dreamweaver refers to each name value pair in this window as a "URL request", but essentially it means either a form variable (see page 851) or a URL parameter (see page 852).

2. **Click the Name column, and then type a name for the new "URL request" item.**

   If the "URL request" is being used to filter data in a recordset, you use the name you used when you created the filter in the Recordset window (see step 5 on page 848).

3. **Click the Value column, and then type a value.**

   This value may be a number or text, but the value must retrieve at least one record from the database, according to the filter options you set up in the recordset. For example, if you created a filter to find products under a certain price, then you might type *price* as the name of the URL request, and *10* as its value.

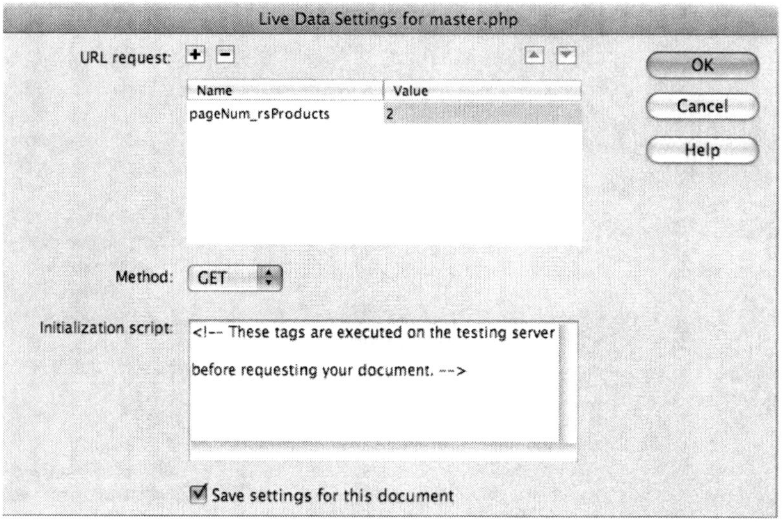

Figure 23-20: *The Live Data Settings window lets you define information that the dynamic page needs to operate correctly. For example, the page may include a recordset that uses information contained in the URL to search records in a database. The "Initialization script" section of the window stores temporary code that the application server executes before viewing the page in Live Data view. Use this advanced option for setting the session and application variables that the application server uses to process the page (see page 963).*

4. **From the Method menu, select either GET or POST.**

   If the filter in your recordset uses a form variable, select POST; if the filter uses a URL parameter, select GET.

5. **Click OK to close the Live Data Settings window.**

   If you haven't turned on the Auto Refresh button, then in the Live Data toolbar, you must click the Refresh button (see Figure 23-19) to see the new results. In addition, if you selected the GET method in step 5, the name and value you supplied in the Live Data Settings window appears in the Live Data toolbar, in the URL Parameter box. You can change the values of the URL parameter directly in this box.

Note: The Recordset Navigation Bar and Status message objects react differently, depending on which records in a recordset are displayed. To see this effect in action, in the Live Data Settings window, add a new URL request item named *pageNum_rsName* (where rsName is the name of the recordset used in the Repeating Region). Set the value to something other than 0. Click OK to return to the Live Data view. You can change this value directly in the Live Data View toolbar, in the URL parameter box (see Figure 23-19), to see how the page reacts with different offset values.

Master Detail Page Set

When you build a database-driven Web site, you often want to give your visitors both an overview and a detailed view of information. Usually, it takes two separate Web pages to do the job: one that lists limited information about all the records in a recordset, and one that links to a second page with detailed information about a single record. Dreamweaver calls these *master* and *detail* pages, and gives you a tool for making quick work of this task. Figure 23-21 shows how these pages work together.

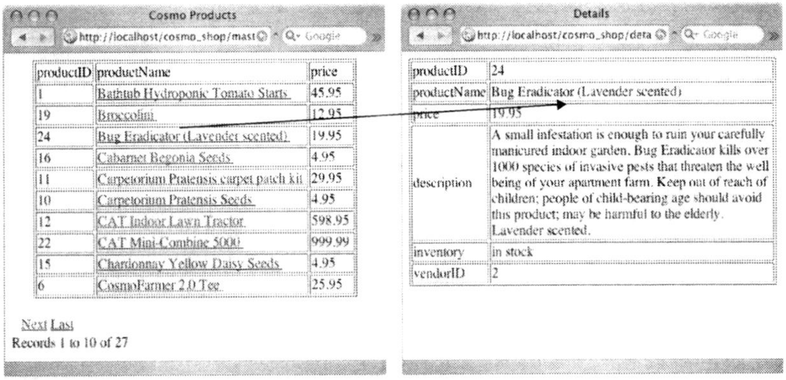

***Figure 23-21:** Here's an example of Dreamweaver's Master Detail Page Set. The screen on the left represents a master page—a list of items retrieved from a recordset. Clicking a link on this page opens a detail page (right), which displays the details of a single record.*

The Master Detail Page Set object automates the process of creating dynamic tables and Recordset Navigation Bars, as well as adding many different server behaviors to your pages. In fact, there's nothing this tool does that you can't do (albeit more slowly) with the other tools you've learned about in this chapter.

To create a Master Detail Page Set, follow these steps:

1. **Create two Web pages—one for the master page and another for the detail page.**

   The pages can be new, blank pages or existing pages that require the dynamic information from the database. It helps to use descriptive names for these pages, such as *productIndex.php* and *productDetails.php.* (Save each page with an extension appropriate for the server model you're using: .asp, .cfm, or .php.)

2. **Open the master page—the one listing all the records—and add a recordset to it.**

   This recordset must include not only all the columns to be displayed on the master page, but also all the columns to appear on the detail page. Both pages use the same recordset, so this one recordset must retrieve *all the* information you want on both pages. Also, make sure you select the primary key for the table (the ID used to identify each record). Even if you won't display this key on the page, you need it to link the master page to a detail page.

3. **In the Data category of the Insert panel, click the Master Detail Page Set button (see Figure 23-1).**

   You can also choose Insert → Data Objects → Master Detail Page Set. Either method opens the Insert Master-Detail Page Set window (see Figure 23-22).

4. **From the Recordset pop-up menu, chose the name of the recordset you created in step 2.**

5. **Select the fields (database columns) you wish to appear on the master page.**

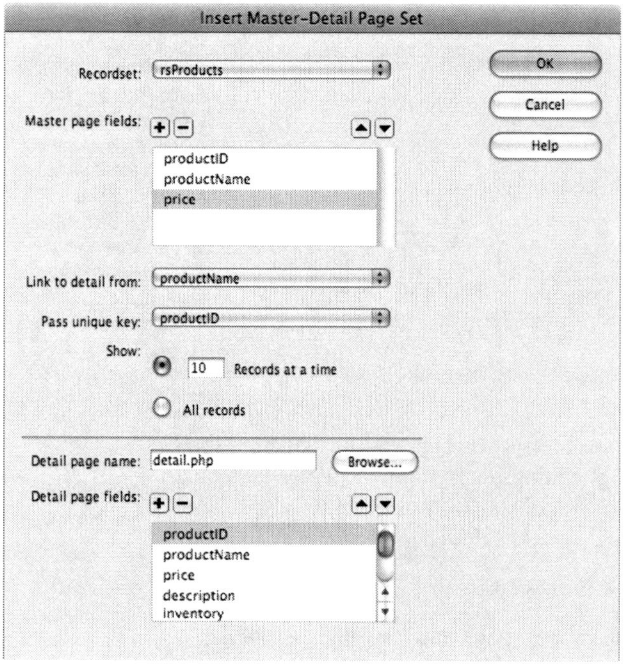

Figure 23-22: *The Insert Master Detail Page Set window lets you quickly create two common types of dynamic pages: one that lists many records in a database, and another that shows detailed information about a single database record.*

   You'll probably remove a bunch of columns from the "Master page fields" box, since most of the information is reserved for the detail page. To remove a column, click its name to select it, and then click the minus (–) button. (If you accidentally delete a column, click the + button to add it back.) You can also change the order of the columns by selecting a column name, and then clicking the up or down arrow buttons. The order the fields are listed in the box dictates the order in which they appear on the master page.

6. **From the "Link to detail from" pop-up menu, choose a column.**

   Here you're determining which item on the master page is linked to the detail page. In Figure 23-21, each product's name has a link to the detail page. If you're creating a staff directory, you might select the column that contains each staff member's name. In this way, visitors can click a name to see a page with that staff person's details.

7. **Using the "Pass unique key" field, select a column.**

   Choose a column that uniquely identifies a single record in the database, such as a product identification number or Social Security number. In most cases, this is the *primary key* in a database table (see page 831 for more on primary keys). You must include the "unique key" column in the recordset you create in step 2 for it to appear in this menu.

8. **Select how many records you wish to show.**

   You can either type a number into the "Records at a time" box or select "All records".

9. **Click Browse. Select the detail page you created in step 1.**

   In this step and the next, you're defining the detail page and what information appears on it.

10. **Select the fields you wish to display on the detail page.**

    The process is the same as step 5, but in this case, you'll probably include most, if not all, of the columns. After all, the detail page is where most of the information for an individual record shows up.

11. **Click OK to close the window and create the pages.**

    It may take a few moments for Dreamweaver to complete this step. It's adding a lot of code to both the master and detail pages.

Once completed, you can (and should) modify the tables, format the dynamic items, and design the page to your liking. Because the Master Detail Page Set tool just automates the process of adding Repeating Regions, Recordset Navigation Bars, and other server behaviors, you must edit those items individually on the page. In other words, you can't return to the Insert Master Detail Page Set window (Figure 23-22) to alter items on either page. For example, if you decide to remove a piece of dynamic information from the detail page, you must make this change on the detail page itself.

While the Master Detail Page Set tool makes building these types of pages a snap, it does have its drawbacks. The primary problem is that Dreamweaver uses the same recordset for both the master and detail pages. This feature can slow down the works, because even though you may want to display only a few columns of data on the master page (the productID, productName, and price fields in Figure 23-21), the recordset added to the page must retrieve *all* the information the detail page needs. The database server is doing a lot of extra work retrieving unused data. However, you have a workaround: After creating the master and details pages, return to the *master page*, edit the recordset, and then select *only* the fields that that page uses. (Editing recordsets is described on page 861.)

Although the Master Detail Page Set makes quick work of creating these types of pages, you can do all the same tasks using the tools you've already learned—Repeating Regions, Recordset Navigation Bars, and so on—with the added benefit of greater design flexibility. For an example of creating a more complex master and detail page set by hand, complete the tutorial at the end of this chapter.

Passing Information Between Pages

Every now and then, you'll want to pass a piece of information from one page to another. The Master Detail Page Set described in the previous section uses this concept: A link on the master page not only points to the detail page, but also passes along a unique ID used to create a filtered recordset on the detail page. In other words, the master page lists a bunch of records from a database. Each record not only links to its own detail page, but also passes along its unique ID. The link might be something like *productDetails.php?productID=7*.

The information after the ? in the URL is a *URL parameter*, which the detail page uses to build a recordset. In this example, the detail page would find only one record—the one whose *productID* is 7—and display its details on the page. The key to the success of the Master Detail Page Set, then, is the ability to pass information to another page, and then use that information to filter a recordset (see page 847 for details on filtering database records).

To retrieve details on only one record, the detail page must include a recordset that filters the records of a database table based on some unique identifier—usually a record's primary key. For example, if every ad in a database of advertisements has its own unique ad ID, then to find info on just a single ad, you simply search for the one record that matches a particular ID number. In other words, you create a recordset that filters the data based on that ID number.

Dreamweaver lets you pass information from a recordset in the URL of a link—for example, *productDetails.php?productID=4*—when creating a link using the "Browse for file" method. Just follow these steps:

1. **Create a page with a recordset and a Repeating Region.**

   This page might be one that lists all the products your company sells, or it might be a list of all company employees.

2. **Select an element on the page to serve as a link to a detailed page.**

   To show the details of a particular product or employee, you'll add a link to each row in a Repeating Region—for example, add a link to the product name's or employee name's detail page. With a Repeating Region, you need to add this link only a single time, since Dreamweaver's programming takes care of the process of actually displaying the multiple rows of repeating information (and therefore the link attached to each row).

3. **In the Property inspector, click the Folder icon.**

   The Select File window appears (Figure 23-23). This method of creating a link is probably very familiar by now.

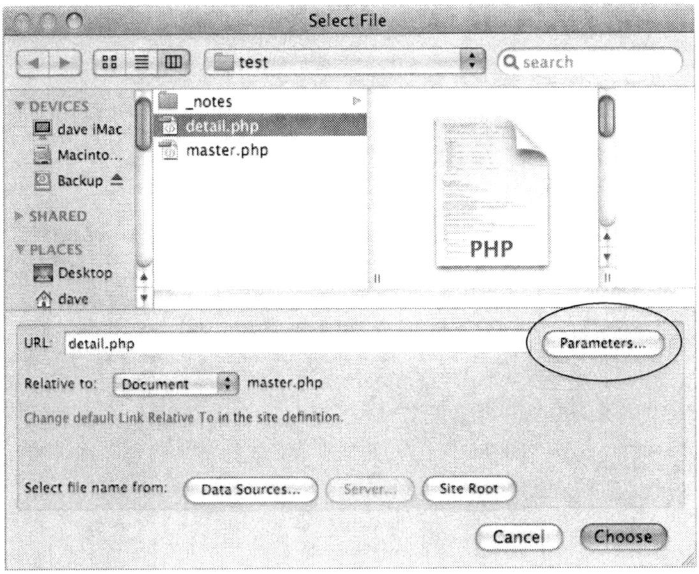

Figure 23-23: *The Select File window provides a quick and error-free way to link to a page. When working with dynamic pages, you can also click the Parameters button (circled) to tack additional information onto the link that can be used by dynamic pages to search a database.*

4. **Select the file you wish to link to, but don't close this window yet.**

   In this step, select the file you wish to pass additional information *to*. Most likely, this file is a detail page that'll use the data in the URL to perform a search of a database, and then return detailed information about a single record from the database.

5. **Click the Parameters button (circled in Figure 23-23).**

   The Parameters window opens (see Figure 23-4). You read about this window on page 852, as a method of adding URL parameters to a link. The basic process described on page 853 applies here, but you'll be using dynamic data from a recordset as the value of the URL parameter.

6. **Click in the space below the Name column, and then type the name of the URL parameter.**

   Since the URL is intended to provide data to another Web page (like a detail page), the name you provide here should match up with the filter name used on the detail page's recordset (see page 847 for more on filtering recordsets). In many cases, the name you provide should match the name of the primary key field used for retrieving a record on the detail page. For example, if you're linking to a page that provides detailed information on an individual product in your catalog, the name might be *productID* to indicate the ID number for the product.

7. **Click the space below the Value column, and then click the lightning bolt button.**

   The Dynamic Data window opens (Figure 23-24). This window lets you select information from a recordset. For example, you can use it to add a record's primary key value to a link. In this way the link can pass the primary key to another page (like a detail page), which then uses that information to retrieve detailed information for that record.

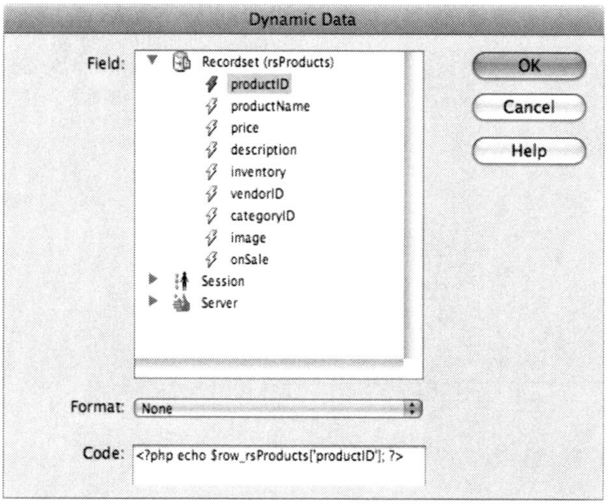

Figure 23-24: *The Dynamic Data window is actually the same as the Dynamic Text window displayed on page 863. It generates the proper programming code to retrieve information from a recordset, or another source of dynamic data, such as cookies or session variables, discussed on page 967.*

8. **From the Dynamic Data window, select an item, and then click OK.**

   Dreamweaver adds the programming code necessary to grab that bit of dynamic data and attach it to the URL.

9. **Click OK to close the Parameters window. Click OK to close the Select File window and apply the link.**

   Now, when you view this page, the link points to the page you specified with the addition of a dynamically generated URL parameter.

Tip: A handy extension simplifies this laborious process of adding a link that includes a URL parameter with dynamic data. The free PHP Missing Tools extension by Felix One (*www.felixone.it/extensions/freeextdetailen.asp?IDProdotto=FX_PHPMissing*) includes a Go To Detail Page server behavior that makes the above nine-step process a matter of a few clicks.

Tutorial: Displaying Database Info

In this tutorial, you'll continue the work you started in the last chapter. Displaying the products available from CosmoFarmer's online store requires two dynamic pages. The first page displays a list of all products available on the site. From that page, visitors can jump to a detailed description of an item for sale by clicking its name. You'll learn how to create both basic and advanced recordsets, and take advantage of some of Dreamweaver's built-in application objects.

This tutorial assumes you've done all of the setup work described in Chapter 22. If you haven't, turn to page 821 and follow the instructions for preparing the application server, database, and Dreamweaver for this project. (Also make sure you have XAMPP or MAMP up and running, as described on pages 882 and 883.)

Creating a Recordset

You'll start by opening an existing page and adding a recordset to it:

1. **In the root folder of the local site you defined in the previous chapter, open *index.php*.**

   Either choose File → Open and navigate to and select *index*, or, in the Files panel, double-click the file name.

   The basic structure of this page is already complete. It was built using CSS layout, the Spry Navigation Bar, a table, Cascading Style Sheets, and the other HTML features you've already learned. Nothing about this page is dynamic yet, so you'll need to create a recordset and insert database information into the page.

2. **Open the Bindings panel (Windows → Bindings or Ctrl+F10 [⌘-F10]).**

   The Bindings panel is your control center for retrieving and using information from a database. It lets you create new recordsets, and add dynamic data to a page.

3. **In the Bindings panel, click the + button, and then choose Recordset.**

   You can also use the Server Behaviors panel (on that panel, click the + button, and then select Recordset); on the Insert panel's Data category, click the Insert Recordset button (see Figure 23-1); or choose Insert → Data Objects → Recordset. Choose whichever method feels easiest for you. In any case, the Recordset box should now be on the screen. (Make sure you're using the *simple* mode—you should see a button labeled Advanced—as shown in Figure 23-25.)

   Next, select the information you want to retrieve.

4. **into the Name box, type *rsProducts*.**

   Since Dreamweaver lets you connect to more than one database, you must now indicate *which* database connection you want it to use.

5. **From the Connections pop-up menu, select "connCosmo".**

   This name is the name of the connection you created in the last chapter. The CosmoFarmer database contains several tables. For this page, you'll create an index of all products for sale. That information is in the Products table.

6. **From the Tables menu, choose "products". Click Selected.**

   You don't need to retrieve *all* the information from the Products table. Since this dynamic page will present a listing of all of the products, you need only basic information, like the name of the product, its price, and its inventory status. More details about each product will appear on a second page, to be created later in this tutorial.

7. **In the Columns list, Ctrl-click (⌘-click) "productName", "price", and "inventory".**

   You want to get these columns of data from the database. You don't have to filter this recordset (meaning you're not trying to search the database for a particular product), so you can ignore these controls in the dialog box—but it would be nice if the product names appeared in alphabetical order.

8. **From the first Sort pop-up menu, choose "productName". From the second menu, choose Ascending.**

   The Ascending option makes certain the records start with products whose names begin with A and end with names that begin with Z. The Recordset window should look like Figure 23-25.

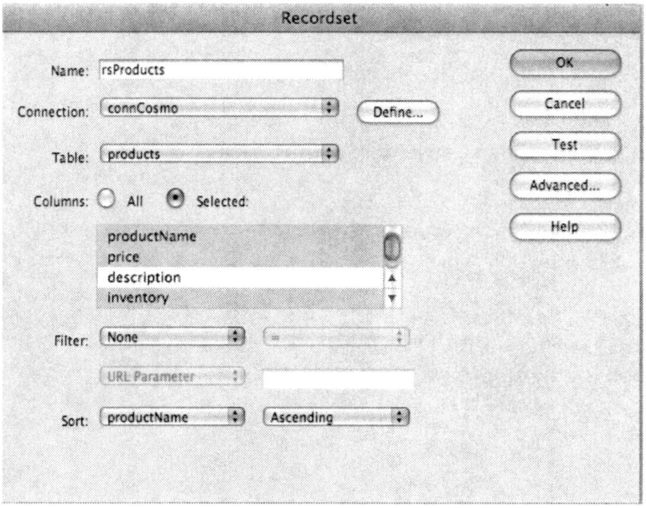

Figure 23-25: *Recordsets let you retrieve information from a database, so that you can display it on a page. This simple recordset retrieves the product name, price, and inventory status of every product in the CosmoFarmer database.*

9. **Click OK to close the Recordset dialog box.**

   The new recordset appears in the Bindings panel. To see the database columns in the recordset, you may need to expand the recordset list.

10. **In the Bindings panel, next to the Recordset icon, click the + icon (flippy triangle on Mac).**

    The Bindings panel should look like Figure 23-26. The page already has an HTML table—below the CosmoFarmer Online Store headline—waiting for the product information.

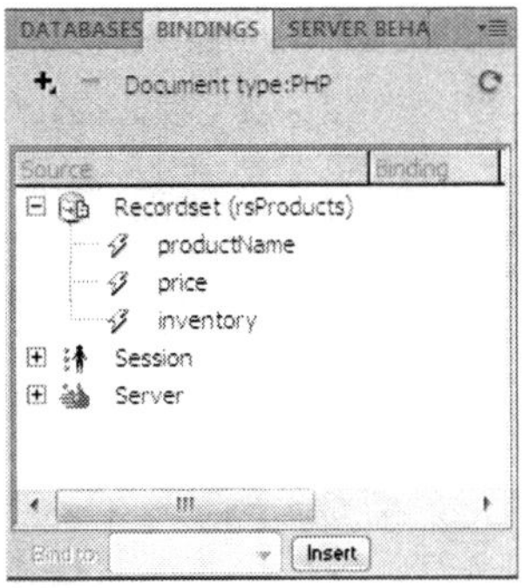

Figure 23-26:
The Bindings panel provides a list of a page's recordsets and data fields. You can use these fields to add dynamic text to a page.

11. **In the document window, click inside the table cell directly below the one labeled Product.**

 In this cell, you'll add the name of the item for sale.

12. **In the Bindings panel, click "productName", and then click Insert.**

 You've just added dynamic data to the page. For the moment, it looks like *{rsProducts.productName}*. You can apply formatting to dynamic data just as you would to regular HTML text—apply a style, change the font, make it bold, and so on.

13. **In the page's table cell, make sure *{rsProducts.productName}* is selected. In the Property inspector, click the HTML button, and then click the B button.**

 Now you'll add both the price and inventory status to the page. Here's an even easier way to insert recordset data.

14. **From the Bindings panel, drag "price" to the empty cell (on the Web page)—below the cell with the label "Price". Repeat this step by dragging "inventory" into the third empty cell ("Inventory Status") on the page.**

 At this point, your page should look like Figure 23-27.

Live Data View and Creating Repeating Regions

When you add dynamic data to a page, it doesn't look like much. All you see is the recordset and column name between braces ({rsProducts.productName}, for example). Not only can this interfere with your design, it certainly doesn't give you a clear picture of what your Web page is actually going to look like.

Thank goodness for Dreamweaver's Live Data view:

1. **Choose View → Live Data.**

 Alternatively you can use the keyboard shortcut: Ctrl-Shift-R (⌘-Shift-R). In either case, Dreamweaver connects to the testing server and database to retrieve the data requested by the recordset (this step may take a few seconds). For the first time, you get to see the page as it'll appear on the Web. But you have a

Figure 23-27: *After you add dynamic information to a page, it appears with a blue background. Here, three pieces of dynamic data appear on the page from the rsProducts recordset: rsProducts.productName, rsProducts.price, and rsProducts.inventory. To change this background color, choose Edit → Preferences (Dreamweaver → Preferences). Click the Highlighting category, and then, at the bottom of the window, change the Live Data colors.*

problem: Only one item is listed. This page is meant to show listings for *all* products. To show more products, you have to add a Repeating Region—a part of the page that repeats for each record in a recordset.

2. **Choose View → Live Data to turn off Live Data view.**

   Dreamweaver runs a little more quickly when Live Data view is off, so it's generally a good idea to turn it on only when you really want to get an accurate view of the page in Design view.

3. **Move your cursor to the left of the table cell with {rsProducts.productName} (you want your cursor to be over the left edge of the table); click when the right-pointing arrow appears.**

   That's how you select the bottom row of the table. (For other methods of selecting a table row, see page 268.) Since this row displays the info for a single product, it's a perfect candidate for a Repeating Region, where an additional row appears in the table for each product.

4. **On the Insert panel's Data category, click the Repeated Region button (see Figure 23-1).**

   The Repeat Region dialog box (Figure 23-13) appears, so that you can select which recordset to use (if the page has more than one) and how many records to display. In this case, since you have only one recordset, you just have to tell Dreamweaver how many records to show.

5. **In the "Records at a Time" box, type *12*. Click OK.**

   You don't know how many products the CosmoFarmer store offers at any time. If it's a lot, you don't want to show them all on a single page—a thousand listings would make a pretty long Web page. In this case, just list 12 records at a time.

If the database has more than 12 products, you need to give people a way to see the other items. You'll do that next.

6. **Click to the right of the table that lists the products. Then, in the Insert panel's Data category, click the Recordset Paging button, and, from the menu, select Recordset Navigation Bar (see Figure 23-16).**

   The Recordset Navigation dialog box appears. You can do only one thing here.

7. **Make sure the Text button is selected; click OK.**

   Dreamweaver plops a table containing four columns onto the page. The columns contain links that let visitors navigate the product listings.

   The table will look better with some CSS style applied to it.

8. **In the document window, select the navigation bar table. In the Property inspector, from the class pop-up menu, choose "paging".**

   For techniques on selecting a table, see page 268.

9. **Click at the end of the headline "CosmoFarmer Online Store", and then press Enter to create a new, empty paragraph; from the Record Count menu, choose Recordset Navigation Status (see Figure 23-17). Click OK when the Recordset Navigation Status window appears.**

   Dreamweaver inserts something that looks like this: *Records {rsProductsFirst Record} to {rsProductLastRecord} of {rsProductsTotalRecords}*. That's placeholder code for this notation: "Records 1 to 10 of 27". In fact, if you choose View → Live Data, that's exactly what you see.

   Now to rework the message a little bit.

10. **Select the word Records, and then change it to Products; select each of the placeholders (*{rsProducts.FirstRecord}*, and so on), and then, in the Property inspector, click the B button to make them bold.**

    You can add or remove any of the non-dynamic text in the navigation status bar. Now to see the results of your hard work.

11. **Press F12 (Option-F12) to preview the page in your Web browser.**

    You may get a warning message titled "Update Copy on Testing Server". Even though when you first defined the site you told Dreamweaver that you're running the testing server on your own computer, it somehow thinks that the testing server is on another computer. Turn on the "Don't show me this message again" checkbox, and then click OK. The page opens in a Web browser, displaying 12 records (see Figure 23-28).

Editing a Recordset and Linking to a Detail Page

Now that the main products listings page is complete, you need to create a link to the name of each product that, when clicked, opens a page with the details for that

***Figure 23-28:** You can easily build dynamic Web pages in Dreamweaver. In just a few short steps–all right, 25 steps– you can create pages for viewing database records. (At the bottom of the page, you can click the Next link to jump to the next set of product listings.)*

item. How does the detail page know which product to display? The link for each product has some additional information—the product's ID number—tacked on to the end. In other words, while all the product links point to the same page, they pass some additional information which helps the detail page know which product to display.

Unfortunately, Dreamweaver doesn't provide a simple, one-click method to add a URL parameter to tell a detail page which recordset's details to display. You'll have to create that yourself, but first you need to add a primary key to the product's recordset.

1. **Open the Server Behaviors panel by pressing Ctrl+F9 (⌘), or, in the Application panel group, clicking the Server Behaviors tab.**

   A list of all the different server behaviors appears; these behaviors were added when you created a recordset, put dynamic text on the page, and used Dreamweaver's other dynamic page creation tools. Instead of adding another server behavior at this point, you can edit one you've already created: the recordset. When you first added this recordset, an important piece of information was missing—the product's ID number. (Actually, it was omitted from the tutorial intentionally, so that you now have this engaging educational opportunity to learn how to edit a recordset.)

   Each product has its own ID number, which you'll use to tell the Details page which item to display.

2. **In the Server Behaviors panel, double-click "Recordset (rsProducts)" to open the Recordset dialog box.**

   You'll just add one additional column to the recordset.

3. **Ctrl-click (⌘-click) "productID" in the columns list, and then click OK.**

   You've just added one additional column (productID) to the recordset. Now the recordset not only retrieves the name, price, and inventory status for each product, but also its unique ID number.

4. **In the document window, select the dynamic data containing the product's name: "{rsProducts.prodName}".**

   A simple link to an already created Web page doesn't work here. Since the page containing a product's details is dynamic—it changes based on which product is being viewed—you need one of Dreamweaver's server behaviors.

5. **In the Property inspector, click the "Browse for file" icon.**

   The Select File window appears. This process is the same as creating a regular link.

6. **Locate and select the file *product.php*, located in the site's root folder.**

   This page will display the detailed records of each product. Next, you'll add a little dynamic information to the link, so that each product's unique ID number can be passed along to the details page.

7. **On the right side of the Select File window, click the Parameters button (it's just to the right of the URL box).**

   The Parameters window opens (see Figure 23-29).

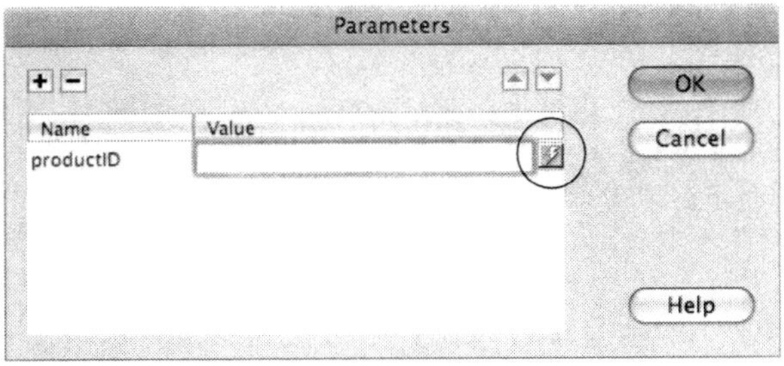

Figure 23-29: *The Parameters window lets you tack on dynamic information to the end of a link. In this way, you can pass information (for example, a product's ID number) off to another dynamic page that uses that information to display dynamic information.*

8. **In the Name column, type *productID*, and then press the Tab key to jump to the Value column. On the right side of the Value column, click the dynamic value button (circled in Figure 23-29).**

   The Dynamic Data window appears (see Figure 23-31). "productID" is the name that'll be added to the link. It will help the details page identify the purpose of the value (which you'll select next).

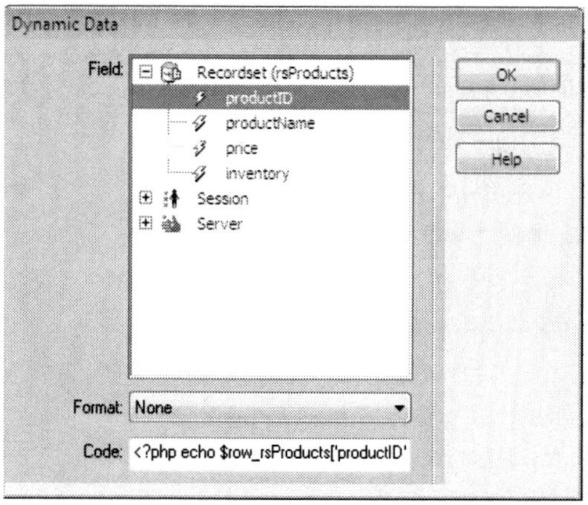

Figure 23-30: *The Dynamic Data window lets you select data from a database recordset to be used as part of the URL of a link.*

9. **Expand the Recordset list (click the + or arrow buttons to the left of the Recordset); select "productID", and then click OK to close the Dynamic Data window.**

   This step selects the "productID" column from the recordset. In other words, this indicates that each link should have the unique ID for a particular product.

10. **Click OK to close the Parameters window, and finally click the OK (Windows) or Choose (Mac) button in the Select File window to finish creating the link.**

    You've just created a dynamic link. Now, preview it.

11. **Press the F12 (Option-F12) key to preview the page in your Web browser. Click the Bathtub Hydroponic Tomato Starts link.**

    The detail page loads...without any details! You'll get to that step in a moment. In the meantime, look at the URL in your Web browser's address bar. It should look something like this: *http://localhost/cosmo_shop/product.php?productID=1*. Notice the *?productID=1* tagged onto the page *product.php*. That's the information the details page needs in order to retrieve the proper product information. The two pieces of information—*productID* and *1*—are what's called a *key/value pair*. The key (*productID*) tells the details page which field to look in, while the value *(1)* identifies a particular product with an ID of 1. Hit your browser's back button, click a different product's link, and you'll see that the ID number is now different.

Note: Sometimes when you preview a Web page from Dreamweaver, the page doesn't display the changes you just made. The browser has cached (see page 666) the old file, and isn't displaying your recent changes. Just press your browser's reload button when this happens. Internet Explorer is particularly prone to this problem.

12. **Save and close this page.**

Building the Detailed Product Page

In this part of the tutorial, you'll build a detail page that displays all the details for a particular product. In addition, you'll create an advanced recordset that combines information from two separate database tables:

1. **Open the file called *product.php* in the site's root folder.**

   Either choose File → Open and navigate to and select *product.php*, or, in the Files panel, double-click the file name.

   Since this page displays the details for a product, it must retrieve data from the database. To set this up, start by creating a recordset.

2. **On the Insert panel's Data category, click the Insert Recordset button** (see Figure 23-1).

   You can also choose Insert → Data Objects → Recordset. Or click the + button on either the Bindings panel or Server Behaviors panel, and then, from the pop-up menu, select *recordset*. In any case, the Recordset dialog box should now be open.

   The CosmoFarmer database contains several database tables—one for product information, one for vendor information, one that lists the different product categories, and one that contains user information (user names and passwords). The details page will list not only information from the Products table (such as the product's name and price) but also the name of the product's vendor. Unfortunately, the Products table contains only the vendor's ID number, not its name, so the recordset must incorporate information from both tables. Since the basic panel of the Recordset dialog box doesn't let you retrieve information from more than a single database table, you have to use the advanced setting.

3. **On the right side of the Recordset window, click the Advanced button.**

   The Advanced Recordset dialog box appears. Unfortunately, Dreamweaver isn't particularly user-friendly in this area. It helps to understand SQL (see page 855)—or you can just take the following steps.

4. **In the Name field, type *rsDetails*. From the Connection menu, choose "connCosmo."**

   In the next few steps, you'll create an SQL query—essentially a line of programming code that asks the database for particular information that matches specific criteria. In this case, it's the information for a particular product.

5. **If there's any text inside the big SQL text box, delete it. Click the + icon (flippy triangle) in the Database Items list, next to the word Tables (at the bottom of the dialog box).**

   It expands to reveal the four tables of the database: Category, Products, Users, and Vendors.

6. **Click the + icon (flippy triangle) to expand the Products table.**

   Your job is to select the information from this table that you want to display on the page.

7. **Select "productID"; click the Select button to the right.**

   Notice that Dreamweaver writes *SELECT products.productID FROM products* in the SQL box. This is SQL code for selecting a particular column of data from a table. You can now choose the other pieces of information.

8. **Repeat step 7 for the following items in the Products table: productName, price, description, inventory, image.**

   These items are all the ones you need to retrieve from the Products table. Now you can choose data from the Vendors table.

Tip: If you understand SQL, then you can bypass this point-and-click approach, and simply write a SQL query directly in the SQL box.

9. **Click the + icon (flippy triangle) to expand the Vendors table. Repeat step 7 for the "vendorName" item in that table.**

   The dialog box should now look like Figure 23-31. Congratulations, you've just created a SQL query.

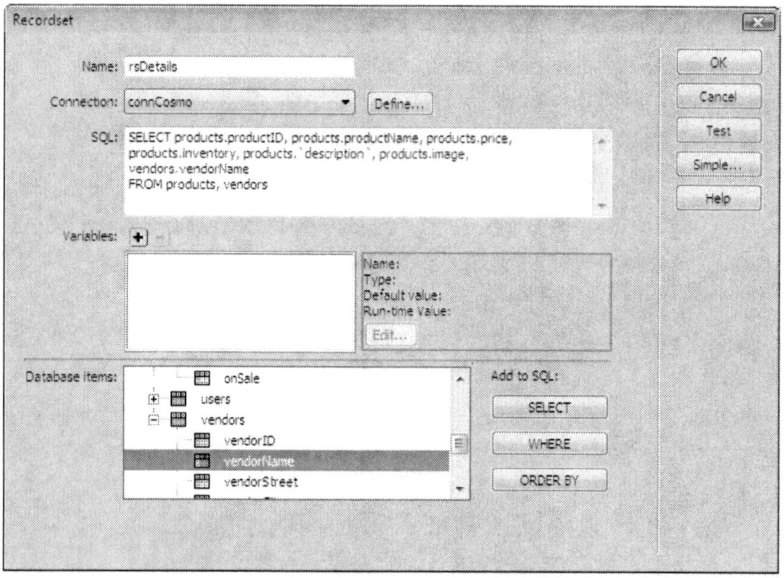

Figure 23-31: *The Recordset window's advanced mode lets you use a data tree (the bottom half of the window) to build an SQL statement. By selecting a column name, and then clicking either the SELECT, WHERE, or ORDER BY buttons, you can get Dreamweaver to do some of the heavy lifting. Unfortunately, you still need to understand a little bit of SQL to create functioning database queries using these advanced options. See page 856 for a brief introduction to SQL.*

But you have a problem here: Because of this query's structure, it retrieves *all* the records for both tables (click the Test button to see for yourself). To remedy the situation, you must do two things: First, combine information from two tables so that you get the vendor information for the corresponding product; and second, retrieve only the information for the particular product specified by the link you created in the last part of this tutorial.

10. **Click inside the SQL box after the word "vendors". Press Enter or Return.**

    Now you have to dive into typing out SQL code.

11. **Type *WHERE products.vendorID = vendors.vendorID*. (Don't include the sentence-ending period.)**

    This little bit of code is called a *WHERE clause*, and it helps filter information in a database. In this instance, you've created what's called a *join*—a statement that joins two or more tables together. When you retrieve product information, you also want to retrieve the name of the vendor who manufactures that product. By matching the vendor ID from the Products table to the identical vendor ID in the Vendors table, the database can produce the proper vendor name.

    If your eyes are glazing over, go get a cup of coffee before plunging ahead.

12. **To the right of the word Variables, click the + button.**

    The Add Variable window appears (see Figure 23-32).

    You're about to expand on the WHERE clause you just wrote. Not only do you need to get the details of a product (plus the vendor's name), you also want to retrieve just a single record—the particular product whose details the visitor wants to review.

13. **Click in the Name box, and then type *varProduct*. Type *1* for "Default value". Type *$_GET['productID']* for the "Runtime value".**

    The Add Variable box should now look like Figure 23-32. Look back to step 8 in "Editing a Recordset and Linking to a Detail Page" (page 889). Remember that the ID number for the product is embedded in the URL that links to this page. In other words, when someone clicks a link on the main product listings page, the ID number for the product is passed along like this: *product.php?productID=12*.

    In this step, you're retrieving that information from the URL—that's the *$_GET ['productID']* part—and storing it in a variable that you'll use in the rest of the SQL query.

14. **Click OK to add the new variable. In the SQL box, click at the end of the WHERE clause (after "vendors.vendorID"), and then type *AND products.productID = varProduct*.**

    The Recordset window should now look like Figure 23-33.

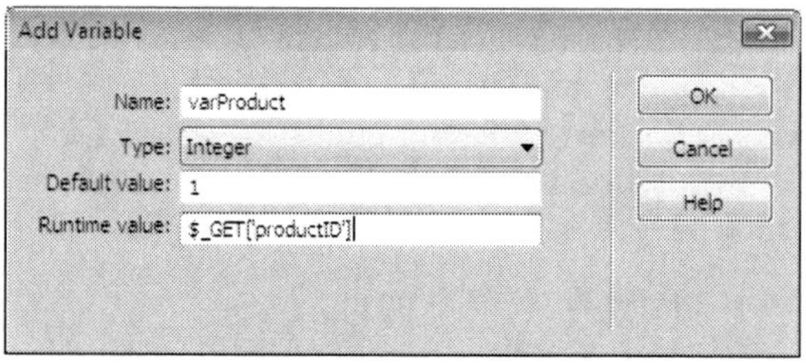

Figure 23-32:
When you add a variable to an SQL query, you're letting that query respond to information from another source. In this example, information that's sent with the URL that's used to link to this page provides the unique ID number for each product. Since that URL will "vary" ("variable," get it?) the recordset produces different results–the specific details for one product.

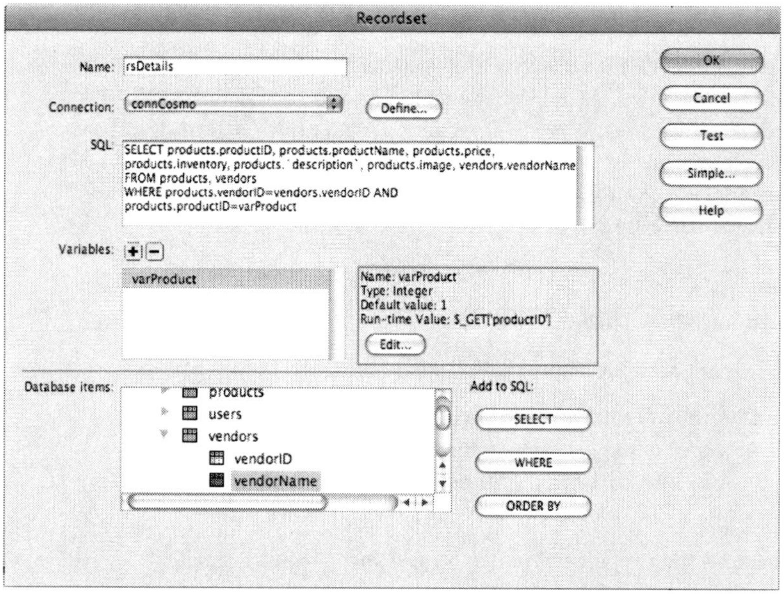

Figure 23-33:
In the Recordset window's advanced mode, you can create highly detailed SQL queries that can retrieve and merge information from multiple database tables.

15. **Click the Test button to see if the SQL query works.**

    A Test SQL Statement window opens, containing a single record. Hallelujah: It includes not only product details but also the vendor's name. (If Dreamweaver spits out an error message instead of a record, there's probably a typo somewhere in the SQL. Either try to identify the problem, or delete the SQL query, and then start again at step 5 above.)

16. **Click OK to close the window. Choose File → Save to save your changes.**

Filling in the Details

Now you just have to add the information retrieved in the recordset to the page:

1. **In the document window, select the words "Product name".**

   You'll add the name of the product here.

2. **Open the Bindings panel.**

   Either press Ctrl+F10 (⌘-F10) or, in the Application panel group, click the Bindings tab.

3. **In the Bindings panel, click the + icon (flippy triangle) next to the recordset to display all the columns retrieved in the recordset. Select "productName", and then click Insert.**

   The placeholder for the dynamic data—*{rsDetails.productName}*—appears in the document window. Next, you'll try the drag-and-drop method of inserting dynamic data.

4. **In the Bindings panel, drag "description" into the empty, blank line just below the product name.**

   Now it's just a matter of adding the additional data to the page.

5. **Continue adding content to this page using these same steps.**

   Add the price, vendor name, and inventory status in the appropriate places in the document window.

   To finish off this page, add a photo to the page.

6. **Click just to the left of the product description (just before {rsDetails.description}). Choose Insert → Image.**

   The Insert Image window appears. You've encountered this dialog box many times before when you inserted a graphic (see Chapter 6). However, in this case, you'll retrieve the image's file name from the database.

7. **Select the Data Sources radio button.**

   In Windows, this button is at the top of the Insert Image window; on a Mac, it's at the bottom. At this point, depending on whether you're using Windows or a Mac, you'll see either the Select Image Source window or the Dynamic Data window (see Figure 23-34).

   A list of all of the different data items from the recordset appears. See the item labeled "image"? The database stores the *name* of the image file for each product in the database. But the image file itself isn't stored there. Although some databases do let you store the actual image data—called binary data—in a database, if you merely want to display an image on a Web page, that's a big waste of database space and processing power. A better method, and the one used here, is to just store the name of an image file that's already in the Web site (for example, in a folder named *images*). In the next two steps, you'll craft a path to an already existing file on the Web server.

8. **Select "image".**

   At the bottom of the window (in the URL box [Windows] and the Code box [Mac]), you see some PHP programming code that looks like this: <?php echo $row_rsDetails['image']; ?>. It looks scary, but it simply prints whatever's stored in the image column for the particular recordset. Since the image column in this table stores the name of a file, this code would print something like *tomatoes.jpg*. This value appears as the *src* property of the image—in other words, specifying where a Web browser should look for the file. (You learned about the src property in Chapter 6.)

Tip: One benefit of this only-store-the-file-name-in-the-database approach is that you can store different size images for the same record in different locations, yet still use the same recordset field for each. For example, say you have a dynamic page that displays thumbnails of all the products in your database. And you also have a page that displays a larger picture of the same product. Use the same file name in each case (*tomato.jpg* for example) but store the thumbnail file in one location (perhaps *images/small/*) and the larger file in another folder (*images/large/*). When you want to insert a thumbnail, you use the database field used to store the image, but add the appropriate path (for example, *images/small/*). When you want to insert the larger image, you use the same database field (*image*, for example), but supply the path that points to the larger file (*images/large/*).

For the CosmoFarmer store, the images are actually stored inside a folder named large, which is inside the images folder. (Thumbnails for each image are stored in the small folder.) So for the image to appear correctly, you need to add a little additional information to this window.

9. **In the URL (Code) box, click before the text "<?php", and then type *images/large/* as pictured in Figure 23-34.**

   Don't omit the forward slash after the word large. You'll then have this code: *images/large/<?php echo $row_rsDetails['image']; ?>*.

10. **Click OK. (If the Image Tag Accessibility Attributes window appears, just click OK to dismiss it.)**

    A little square icon appears in the document window. This icon is an image placeholder icon, and represents the space where an image appears when the page is viewed in a Web browser. Next you'll add a style to this graphic.

11. **Make sure the little square icon is still selected (if not, click it), and then, from the Class menu, choose "productImage".**

    The image placeholder floats to the right side of the page. One last thing to do: Since you're a Web design expert (or at least an aspiring expert), you know that images should always have their *alt* properties (page 60) set. But since the exact image that appears varies based on which product is being viewed—it might be a tomato or a picture of an indoor lawn mower—how can you specify alt text that matches the picture? As with most things in this section of the book, the answer is, "You do it dynamically, of course!"

    To set alt text dynamically you need to use the Tag inspector window.

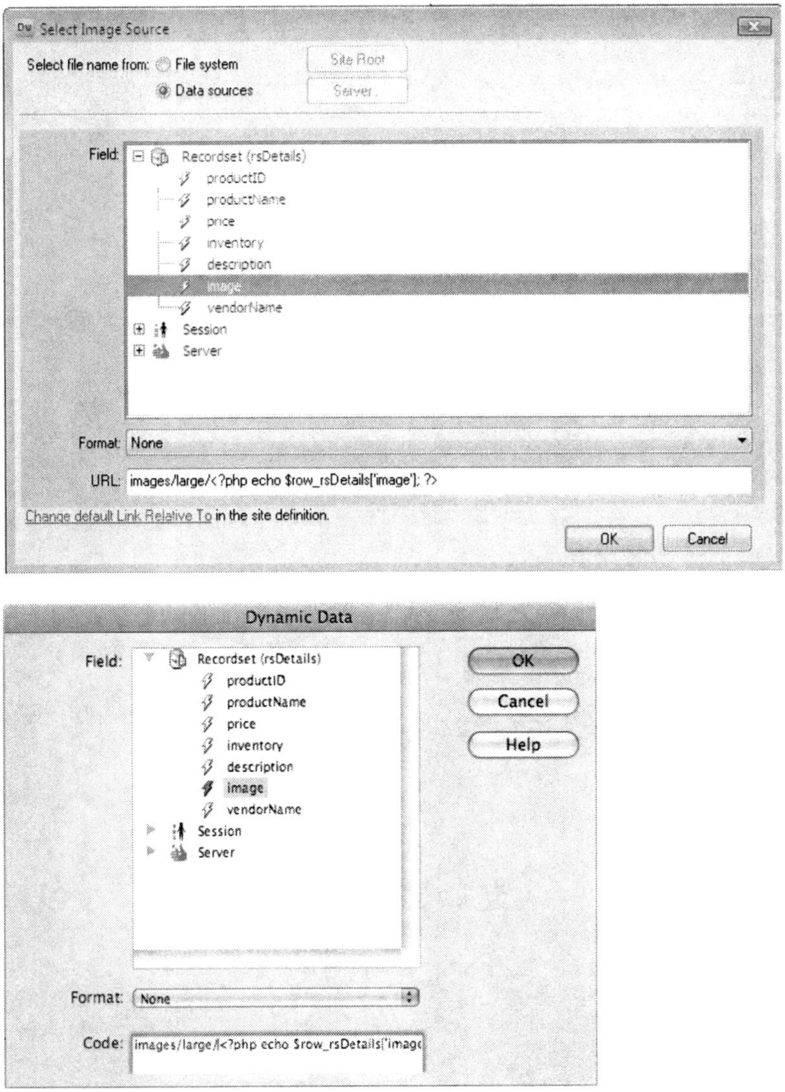

Figure 23-34: *Paths for links and images needn't be hardwired into a Web page. You can craft custom paths and links using information retrieved from a database. A good technique when working with images and a database is to store just the name of the image file in the database. Then, when you insert an image using a data source from a database, you select the field that contains the file name, and then precede the PHP code that appears in the URL (Windows, top) or Code (Mac, bottom) box with the information necessary to create a complete path to the image.*

12. **Make sure the image placeholder is still selected, and then choose Window → Tag Inspector (or press F9).**

    The Tag inspector is a kind of super Property inspector. It lets you set every conceivable HTML property for a particular tag (not just the most common ones listed in the Property inspector).

13. **Click the Show List View button (the icon with A-Z on it), and then, to the right of "alt", click the empty area.**

    You could just type the alt text here, but notice that our friend, the lightning bolt icon, appears. This is your clue that we can access some dynamic data.

14. **Click the lighting bolt icon to open the Dynamic Data window.**

    The Dynamic Data window works just like the Dynamic Text window pictured back in Figure 23-8. It lets you insert information from a field in a recordset. In this case, the appropriate text description for each product's photo is the product's name.

15. **In the Dynamic Data window, click "productName"; click OK.**

    Now whenever the page is viewed, the alt text for the image matches the product's name. Time to see how it looks.

16. **Choose View → Live Data. If everything looks good (Figure 23-35), choose File → Save.**

To see the results of your hard work, open the *index.php* page in Dreamweaver, and then press the F12 key (Option-F12) to preview the page in a browser. Now click a link to see the details for that product.

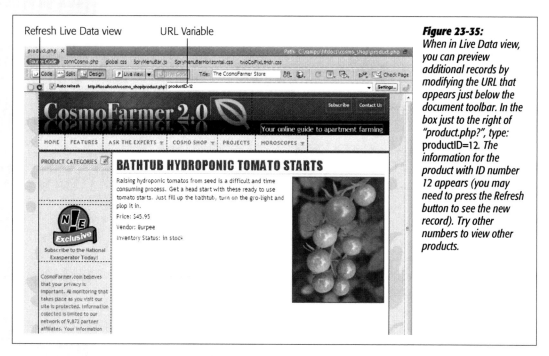

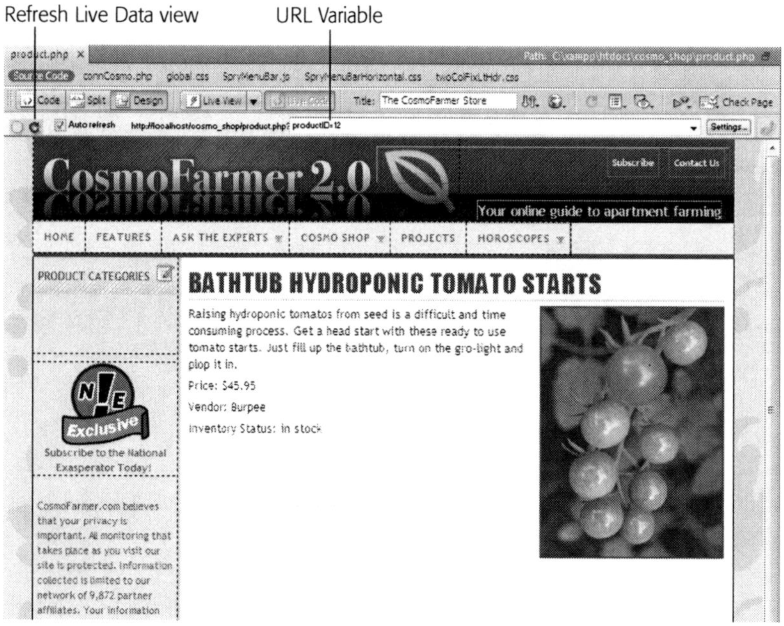

Figure 23-35: *When in Live Data view, you can preview additional records by modifying the URL that appears just below the document toolbar. In the box just to the right of "product.php?", type:* productID=12. *The information for the product with ID number 12 appears (you may need to press the Refresh button to see the new record). Try other numbers to view other products.*

Operators Standing By

One final touch would make the products page perfect. Each product sold at the CosmoFarmer online store belongs to a category—plants, seeds, pest control, and so on. Shoppers might find it useful to view a list of products in a particular category they're interested in—just the plants, for instance.

Since category information is stored in the database, you can use this info to create such a feature. In this final part of the tutorial, you'll add a category navigation bar along the left side of the products page, so that when a visitor clicks a category name, a list of the products within that category appears:

1. **Open the *index.php* page.**

   This is the page to which you add the category links. The first step is to add a new recordset that retrieves all the category names from the database.

2. **If it's not open, open the Bindings panel (press Ctrl+F10 [⌘-F10], click the big + button, and then, from the pop-up menu, select Recordset.**

   You can also, on the Insert panel's Data category (see Figure 23-1), click the Insert Recordset button; choose Insert → Data Objects → Recordset; or, on the Server Behaviors panel, click the + button, and then, from the pop-up menu, select Recordset. In any case, the Recordset dialog box opens. (You may need to click the Simple button to switch the Recordset dialog box out of advanced mode.)

3. **Type *rsCategories* into the Name box.**

   The *CosmoFarmer* database includes a table with the names of each category of products sold. You'll use this table to dynamically generate the list of category names.

4. **From the Connections pop-up menu, select "connCosmo".**

   This is the same connection you've used throughout this tutorial. In this case, you're going to retrieve information from a different table in that database.

5. **From the Table menu, select Categories.**

   The Categories table is very basic: just a name and ID number. The Categories table identifies a category by using a Category ID number—the table's "categoryID" field. You may wonder why a separate table is even necessary. Why not just store the category name with the product information?

   This design has two advantages. First, because the table is just a list of category names, you can easily retrieve an alphabetized list of those names by creating a recordset. That ability is useful, for example, when you want to add a list of categories to a page—as in these tutorial steps. In addition, the separate category table makes changes to categories easier. If you decide you want to change a name—say "Pest Control" to "Pest and Weed Control"—you need to update it only in one record in the Category table. If "Pest Control" were stored in the Products table, you would have to change the name to "Pest and Weed Control" in potentially hundreds of records.

6. **Make sure the All radio button is selected, and then, from the Sort box, choose "categoryName".**

   At this point, the dialog box should look like Figure 23-36.

7. **Click OK to apply the recordset to the page.**

   Now the page has two recordsets—one to retrieve product info, the other to retrieve the list of categories. You'll add the category name to the page next.

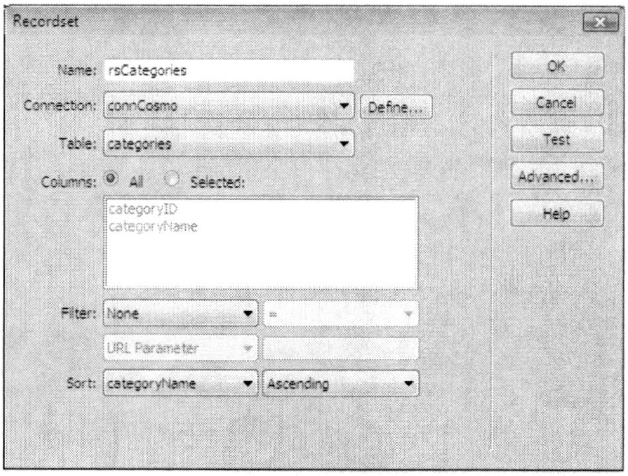

Figure 23-36:
By storing all the product category names in a single table, you can build a dynamic category navigation bar with the help of a simple recordset.

The Bindings panel should look like Figure 23-37. The list of category links will appear in the left-hand sidebar on the page; currently the text "Product Categories" appears in that space. You'll add the links below that. However, to make the job easier, you'll first hide the style sheets that create the design for this page.

8. **Choose View → Style Rendering → Display Styles.**

   Doing so turns off the Display Styles option, and temporarily hides the style sheets applied to this page. Why? Sometimes, the styles you create can make such a drastic change to the look of the page that it's hard to select, edit, and insert text and other HTML in Dreamweaver's Design view. This left-hand sidebar is a good example. The list of category links is a bulleted list of names, but the current styles hide the telltale sign of a list item (the actual bullet) and make it hard for you to see exactly where to place your cursor at the beginning of a list item. (Bulleted lists are discussed on page 100, and you can learn more about Dreamweaver's style rendering options on page 324.)

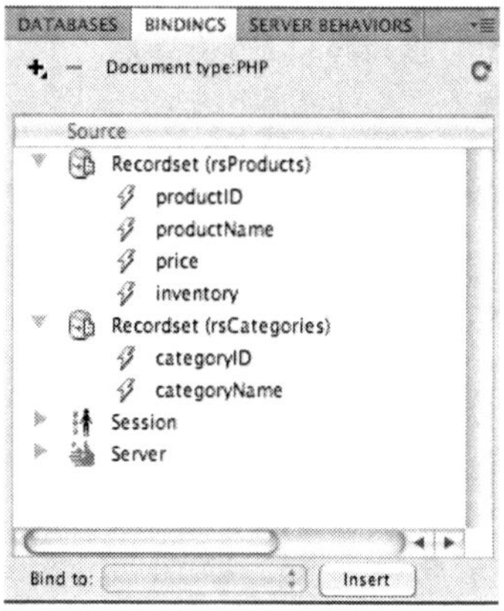

Figure 23-37:
The Bindings panel displays all recordsets currently applied to a page. To hide the recordset's field names, to the left of the recordset icon, click the minus (–) sign (arrow on the Mac).

9. **Scroll down the page a bit, until you spot the empty bullet that appears in the left sidebar below the "Product Categories" headline and directly above the National Exasperator logo (the "N!E" graphic).**

   That's an empty bulleted item—you'll place the category name there.

10. **From the Bindings panel, drag "categoryName" just to the right of the bullet.**

    This step adds the dynamic text for the category name to the page. Next, you'll add a Repeating Region so that *all* the category names appear.

11. **At the bottom of the document window, in the Tag selector, click the <li> tag.**

    The Tag selector (page 24) is the most accurate way to select an HTML tag. When working with Dreamweaver's Repeat Region server behavior, you have to be particularly careful that you've selected exactly what you want to repeat for each record in a recordset. In this case, you want each category name to appear as its own bulleted item in the list—that means the <li> tag (or list item) needs to be selected before applying the Repeat Region server behavior.

12. **On the Insert panel's Data category, click the Repeat Region button (see Figure 23-1).**

    The Repeat Region window appears.

13. **From the menu, select "rsCategories". Click the All records radio button, and then click the OK button to create the Repeating Region.**

    If you preview the page at this point, you see a list of categories along the left side of the page. To make this list a functional navigation bar, you'll add a link to the category name.

14. **In the document window, select the dynamic text {rsCategories.categoryName}. In the Property inspector, click the "Browse for file" icon.**

    The Select File window appears. This is the same process as creating a regular link.

15. **Locate and select the file *category.php*, located in the site's root folder.**

    This page will display the list of products within a particular category. You'll next add a little dynamic information to the link, so that each category's unique ID number can be passed along.

16. **On the right side of the Select File window, click the Parameters button (it's just to the right of the URL box).**

    The Parameters window opens.

17. **In the Name column, type *categoryID*, click the Value column to the right, and then click the Dynamic Value button (the lightning bolt).**

    The Dynamic Data window appears (see Figure 23-30).

    categoryID is the name that'll be added to the link. It helps the details page identify the purpose of the value (which you'll select next).

18. **Expand the "rsCategories" recordset list (click the + or arrow buttons to the left of the Recordset); select "categoryID", and then click OK to close the Dynamic Data window.**

    This step selects the "categoryID" column from the recordset. In other words, this indicates that each link should have the unique ID for a particular category.

19. **Click OK to close the Parameters window and, finally, in the Select File window, click the OK (Windows) or Choose (Mac) button to finish creating the link.**

    You've just created a dynamic link. Since the hard work is now done, you can turn the style sheets back on.

20. **Choose View → Style Rendering → Display Styles.**

    The document window returns to all its green and blue glory. Now, preview the page.

21. **Press F12 (Option-F12). When the page opens, click any of the category names at the left side of the page.**

    A new page should open, listing all the products within a particular category, as shown in Figure 23-38. If you're feeling adventurous, open the *product.php* page and follow steps 2-21 above to add the same category list to that page.

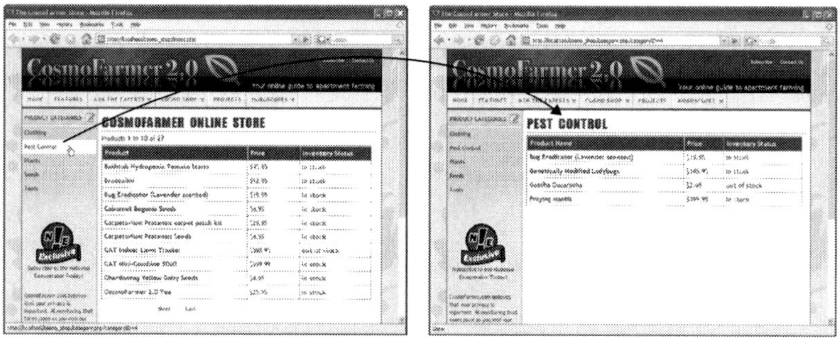

***Figure 23-38:** URL parameters aren't just used to link to a page with the details of a single record. You can use URL parameters to pass any information that can be used to search a database. In this case, the link on the products page (left) provides an ID number to the categories page (right), so that just the products within a particular category appear.*

Congratulations! You've just built two powerful, complex, dynamic Web pages (and probably watched three presidential administrations pass). As you can see, Dreamweaver has an impressive array of tools for building dynamic pages. And even though there were some twists and turns to negotiate, you never once had to resort to the dreaded Code view.

CHAPTER

24

Web Pages that Manipulate Database Records

Just displaying database information on a Web page is useful, but you may be more interested in using the Web to *collect* information from your site's visitors (see Figure 24-1). Maybe something as simple as an online registration form will do the trick. Other times, you may have something more ambitious in mind—like a full-fledged e-commerce system that provides a way to collect product orders and credit card numbers.

Once you've got data in the database, clearly you need a way to update and delete that information. After all, prices change, products are discontinued, and you may suddenly want to remove any record of "Harvey the Wise Guy" from your site's online guestbook. Thankfully, Dreamweaver makes changing information in a database simple and painless.

Note: You may feel more comfortable learning these concepts by *doing* them. If so, turn to the tutorial on page 932 before reading this next section.

Adding Data

As noted in Chapter 11, the primary method of collecting information over the Internet is the *HTML form*. Its basic elements—text boxes, radio buttons, pop-up menus, and so on—can collect a wide assortment of data. But to funnel this information into a database, you need to either write your own program or, more simply, use Dreamweaver's built-in tools. With its Record Insertion Form wizard and Insert Record server behavior, Dreamweaver makes adding data a simple process.

Warning: You might not want just anyone adding, editing, or deleting database information. To control access to these types of pages—or any page, for that matter—use Dreamweaver's User Authentication server behaviors, as discussed on page 953.

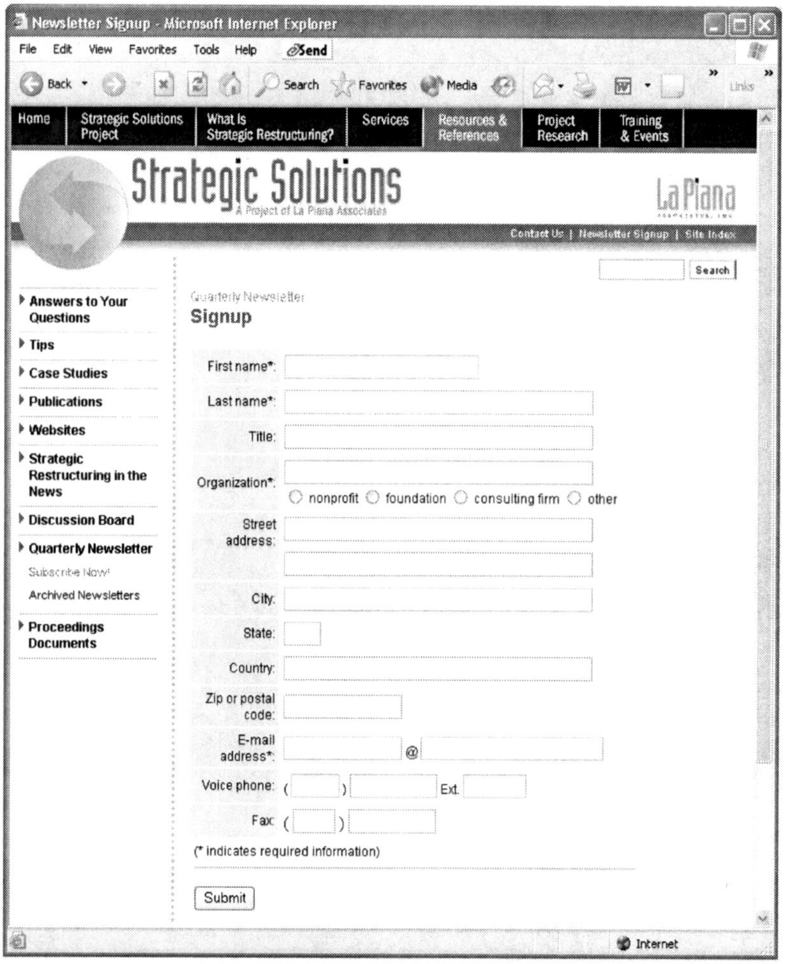

Figure 24-1: Whether you're looking to accept credit cards on an e-commerce site or gather sign-up information for an online newsletter, Dreamweaver simplifies the process of creating forms that funnel info into a database.

Dreamweaver's Record Insertion Form Wizard

Dreamweaver's Record Insertion Form wizard is the quickest way to build a page for adding records to a database. It builds a form, creates a table, and then adds all the necessary programming code in just a couple of steps. To use it:

1. **Create a new Web page, and save it to your site (or open a dynamic Web page that you've already created).**

   Make sure the page uses the extension (.asp, .cfm, .php) that matches the server model (page 818) of your site. (See page 828 for info on creating new dynamic pages.)

2. **In the document window, click where you want the form to appear. Choose Insert → Data Objects → Insert Record → Record Insertion Form Wizard.**

   You can also select Record Insertion Form Wizard from the Insert Record menu on the Insert panel's Data category. Either way, the Record Insertion Form window opens (Figure 24-2).

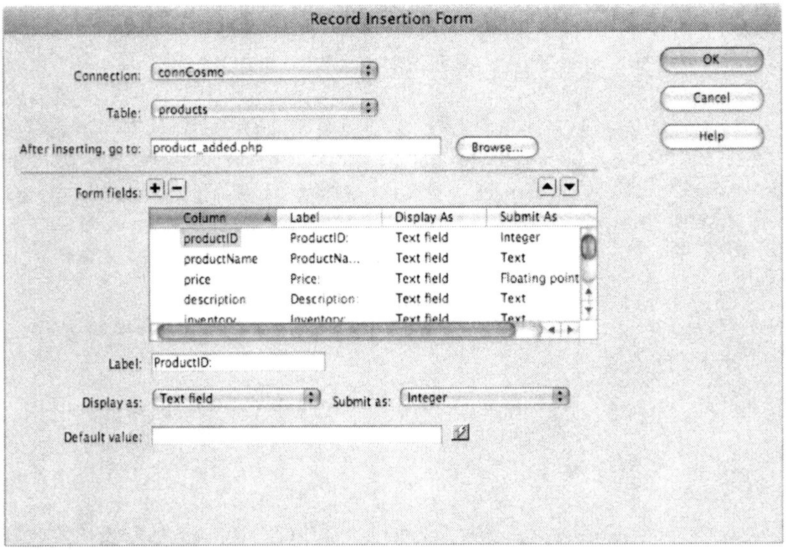

***Figure 24-2:** When creating a form, it's a good idea to remove columns that the database creates for its own use, such as record ID numbers. Here, the column "productID" is a unique ID number created by the database. Whenever someone adds a new record, the database automatically creates a new, unique product ID number. You wouldn't want anyone to tamper with this number, so leave it off the form.*

3. **From the Connection menu, select the database connection.**

   Dreamweaver needs a place to put the data your forms are collecting. If your site works with several databases, select the connection for the database to which this form will add information. (Database connections are described on page 838.)

4. **From the Table menu, choose a table.**

   A list of all tables available in the database appears in this menu. Dreamweaver lets you insert data only into a single table at a time. You can, however, add multiple record insertion forms to a single page. So it's possible to create one "add data" page that contains separate insert record forms for each table in the database. You would still have to input records one at a time for each table, but at least your would have to visit only a single page in order to add a record to any table. (Of course, if your database has 20 tables, it would be a good idea to create several "add record" pages so you don't end up with one gigantic Web page containing 20 different forms.)

Tip: You can use Dreamweaver CS4's Spry Tabs to display multiple insert forms on a single page without wasting a lot of precious screen real estate. The tutorial starting on page 932 shows how.

5. **Click the Browse button and select a file from your site.**

   Choose the page you want your visitors to see after adding a record to the database. It could simply be a page saying, "Thanks for signing up with our Web site." Or, if the insertion form adds a new employee to your company's employee database, you could choose the page that lists all the employees (including the one just added to the database). If you want people to be able to add multiple records, one right after the other, you might also select the record insertion form itself; that way, once visitors add one record, they'll return to the form again, ready to continue the very pleasant work of data entry.

Note: Unfortunately, Dreamweaver doesn't provide a way to, post-form submission, immediately display just the details of the newly added record. For example, you can't create an "insert new record" page that directs visitors to a detail page listing the details of the record they just entered. The best you can do is present a page showing all the records in a particular database table (in other words, a Master page, as described on page 879). The newly added record will then appear on a page listing all records.

   You can also change how the menu item for each database column is formatted on the page, as follows.

6. **In the "Form fields" box, select a database column, and change its settings, if you like.**

   Your options include:

   - **Remove the field.** Click the minus (–) button to remove the field from the form. It doesn't appear on the final form page, and users can't manually submit a value for this field. You should remove any fields that the database automatically fills out, such as a primary key field (see page 831). (If you accidentally delete a field, click the + button to add it back.)

Tip: Use the up and down arrow buttons (see Figure 24-2) to rearrange the order in which the fields appear in the form on the Web page.

   - **Label** is the text Dreamweaver adds next to the form field on the page. It identifies what someone should type in the field, like First Name. Dreamweaver just uses the name of the column in the database—"fName", for instance—so it's usually best to change this text to something more understandable.

   - The **Display as** menu lets you select the *type* of form element you want to use to collect the column's information. If the column is someone's first name, select Text Field. This selection will add a text box, where visitors can type their names, to the form. On the other hand, if people are supposed to choose from a limited number of choices (*U.S. Postal Service, FedEx–2 day,* and *FedEx–next morning,* for example), you might select Radio Group instead.

Radio buttons or pop-up menus can also ensure consistency and rule out typos. On a form that asks visitors to indicate the state they live in, you could offer a pop-up menu that lists the 50 states. If you provided a text box instead, your visitors would be able to type in every conceivable abbreviation and misspelling. (For a description of the different types of form elements, see page 835.)

Note: Dreamweaver can also create *dynamic* menus, which display data taken from a database. See page 925.

- The **Submit as** menu is automatically determined according to how you've set up your database. It tells Dreamweaver what kind of data the field contains: text, number, date, and so on. Dreamweaver figures this information out correctly, so you don't need to change anything.
- The **Default value** text box lets you preload a form field with information. It's actually the same as a text field's *initial value*, as described on page 441. You can also add a dynamic value generated by your server model's programming language. If you had a field called *date*, then you could automatically add today's date to the field by typing *<?php echo date("Y-m-d") ?>* (in the PHP/MySQL server model).

  Depending on what type of field you selected from the "Submit as" menu, the Default value text box might be replaced with one of three different types of controls: For a checkbox, radio buttons provide the simple choice of either checked or not checked; if you selected Menu or Radio Group, a Properties button appears, which lets you set the options that appear in the drop-down menu or radio group on the Insert form—the process is the same as adding a dynamic menu or dynamic radio button group, as described on page 922.

  In most cases, you'll change the label of every column. But for now, leave the other options alone.

7. **Click OK to close the window and create the form.**

   Dreamweaver inserts a table, form, all the form elements you specified and the programming code to add records to the specified database table. At this point, the page is complete and ready to accept information. Unfortunately, Dreamweaver doesn't let you return to this window to make any changes. (If you quickly realize that you made a mistake, you can always use Ctrl+Z [⌘-Z] to undo the operation, and then reapply the Insert Record Form wizard. (Otherwise you need to delete the table and the form and remove the Insert Record server behavior from the Server Behaviors panel. Do that by selecting Insert Record Server behavior in the panel and then press the Delete key. You can then reapply the Insert Record Form wizard.)

To ensure your form works correctly and doesn't produce any errors when it's submitted, add form validation. The powerful Spry validation tools make this easy (see page 455).

Warning: Once you've added the form, don't rename any form fields. You'll break the programming code responsible for inserting the record. If you forget and rename a form field, here's what you need to do: edit the Insert Record sever behavior by double-clicking Insert Record on the Server Behaviors panel. This action re-opens the Insert Record window. You can make changes in this window, like associating a database column to a form field that you renamed.

Using the Insert Record Behavior

Dreamweaver's Record Insertion Form wizard makes quick work of adding the table, form, and programming code required to create a Web page for adding data to a database table. At times, though, you might want a more customized approach. Perhaps you've already designed a form that you'd like to use, or created a beautiful CSS-based design for your form. Rather than relying on Dreamweaver's rather pedestrian table and form design, you can supercharge your own design with the Insert Record server behavior.

To build a page for adding database records, start by creating a Web page for your server model (ASP, PHP, or ColdFusion). Add a form to the page (see Chapter 11). Make sure it has one form field for every column to which you wish to add data. Every time a visitor fills out the form, the database acquires a new record.

In some cases, you don't include certain form fields. For example, a database table's primary key (a unique identifier for each record) is usually generated automatically by the database for each new record. In this case, you wouldn't add a field for this column.

In other cases, you might add *hidden* fields (see page 450) that aren't set by someone filling out the form. Suppose someone signs up for your online newsletter, and you want to store the date of registration. Instead of letting the visitor fill out the date, add a hidden form field with the current date.

Once you've created the form, add the Insert Record server behavior like this:

1. **Choose Window → Server Behaviors to open the Server Behaviors panel.**

   The keyboard shortcut is Ctrl+F9 (⌘-F9). You can also use the Insert Record menu (circled in Figure 24-3).

2. **Click the + button on the panel, and then select Insert Record.**

   The Insert Record window opens (see Figure 24-4). It's very similar to the Insert Record Form window, but one key difference is that you must manually associate a form element with the correct database column. (If you name your form fields the same as the corresponding fields in your database, Dreamweaver will help you out with this.) (Another difference is that you can't define default values for each form element in this window. You can, however, still apply default values to a form field using the Property inspector, as described on page 922.)

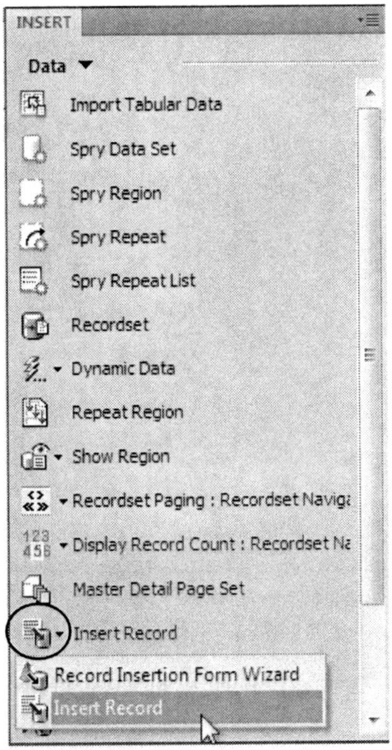

Figure 24-3:
The Insert Record menu (found on the Insert panel's Data category) lets you use either an automated wizard (Record Insertion Form wizard) or a basic server behavior (Insert Record) to add a record to a database.

3. **Choose the name of the form that will collect the information for the new record.**

   If there's only a single form on your Web page, you don't have an option here. However, if you have multiple forms (like a search box at the top of the page, as well as the form used to insert a new record), make sure you select the name of the form used for adding data to the database.

4. **Choose a database connection and table.**

   They're the same options described in steps 3 and 4 for the Record Insertion Form Wizard (see page 906). You're telling Dreamweaver which database to use and which table to add data to.

5. **From the Columns list, select a database column. From the Value menu, choose the name of the form field that collects data for that column.**

   For the form's information to end up in the proper database columns, you must tell Dreamweaver which form field will collect the data for which database column. You can let Dreamweaver choose the proper type from the "Submit as" pop-up menu. As with step 6 on page 908, this choice depends on how your database is set up (which Dreamweaver can figure out).

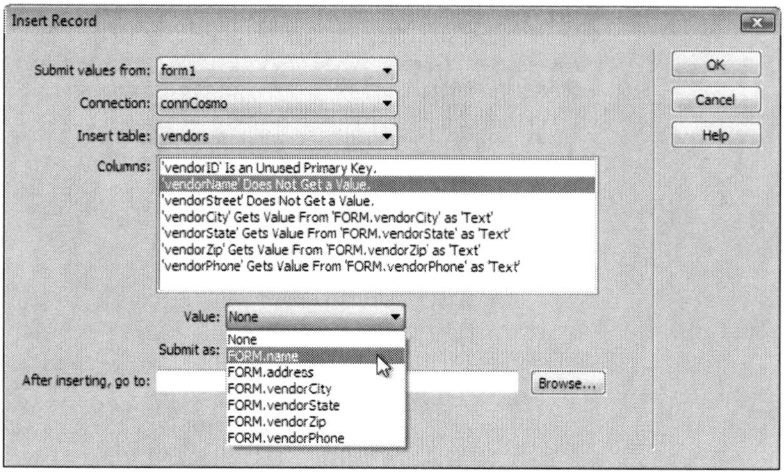

Figure 24-4: *The Vendors database table contains a column named "vendorName". To ensure that the correct data is stored in the database, from the Value menu, choose the corresponding form field–in this example, FORM.name. (The actual name of the form field is "name;" Dreamweaver, for whatever reason, tacks on FORM at the beginning.) (You may not have to worry about selecting anything; see the Tip following step 5.)*

Tip: You need to perform step 5 only if the names of the form fields *differ* from the names of the columns in the database. If you name a form field "productName", and there's also a database column named "productName", Dreamweaver automatically connects the two in the Insert Record window.

6. **Click the Browse button, and then select a Web page.**

   This step is the same as step 5 on page 908, and indicates which page someone sees after adding a new record to the database.

7. **Click OK to close the window and apply the server behavior.**

   The page is now capable of adding information directly to the database.

If you change the name of a form field, add a form field, or wish to change any of the settings for this behavior, you can edit the Insert Record server behavior by double-clicking Insert Record on the Server Behaviors panel. This action opens the Insert Record window once again.

Updating Database Records

Maybe someone made an error while entering info into the database. Maybe the price of your product changes. Or maybe you want to provide a way for your Web visitors to update their email addresses. In any case, the time will come when you have to edit an online database.

Creating Update Record Forms in Dreamweaver is very similar to creating Insert Record Forms. Both require an HTML form that your audience can fill out and submit. The primary difference is that an update form is *already* filled out with information from the database. It's like a combination of an Insert Record Form and a record detail page (such as the one created by the Master Detail Page set described on page 879).

The first step in creating an update form is to add a *recordset* to the update page (page 844). The recordset will retrieve the data that appears in each field of the update form.

The recordset should contain only a single record—the one to be updated. Therefore, you must use a form or URL parameter to filter the recordset (see page 847 for more on filtering). For example, on a page listing company employees, you could add an Edit button that would link to the page containing the update form. Use the technique discussed on page 852 for adding a URL parameter to a link—in this case, you'd pass the primary key from each record in the link to the update page. For example, in a page listing employees, link to the update page and pass the employee record's primary key. In turn, the update page would use that primary key to filter the database for a single record, and display the employee information in the form. (If all of this sounds confusing on paper, try the tutorial starting on page 932, which takes you step by step through the process.) After you add the recordset to the update form page, you have two options for building an update form. You can either let Dreamweaver automate the process with its Insert Update Record Form wizard, or build a form yourself, and then add the Update Record server behavior. The following pages cover both methods.

The Update Record Form Wizard

Dreamweaver can automate most of the steps involved in creating an update form:

1. **Open a dynamic page with a recordset already added.**

   Remember, the recordset should contain only a single record—the one to update. So you must add a filter when you create the recordset (see page 849 for more on filtering recordsets).

2. **In the document window, click where you want the insertion form to appear. Choose Insert → Data Objects → Update Record → Record Update Form Wizard.**

   You can also, from the Update Record menu on the Insert panel's Data category, select Record Update Form Wizard (Figure 24-5). Either way, the Record Update Form window opens (Figure 24-6).

3. **From the Connection menu, select the database connection.**

   If your site works with several databases, select the connection for the database to which this form will add information.

4. **From the "Table to update" menu, choose a table that matches the recordset you created in step 1.**

   A list of all tables available in the database appears in this menu. You can edit data only from a single table at a time, so select the table that matches the filtered recordset.

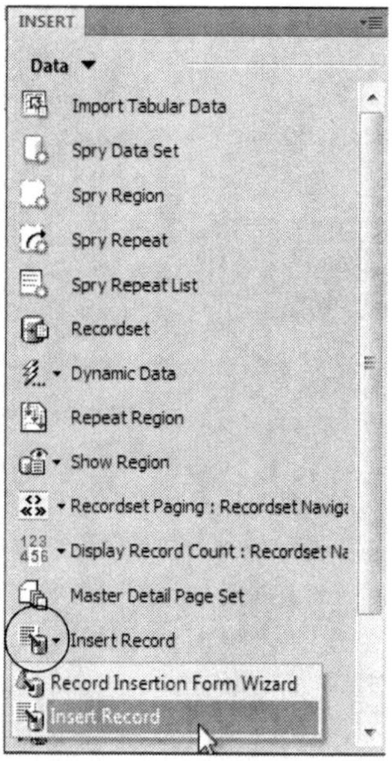

Figure 24-5:
As discussed on page 26, there are many ways to display the Insert Panel. Shown here is the normal, out-of-the-box, way that Dreamweaver displays the Insert Panel icons. To save screen space, click the category menu (for example, Data, in this case) and choose Hide Labels. Only the small icons will appear, freeing up lots of space for other important panels–or that YouTube video you've been meaning to watch.

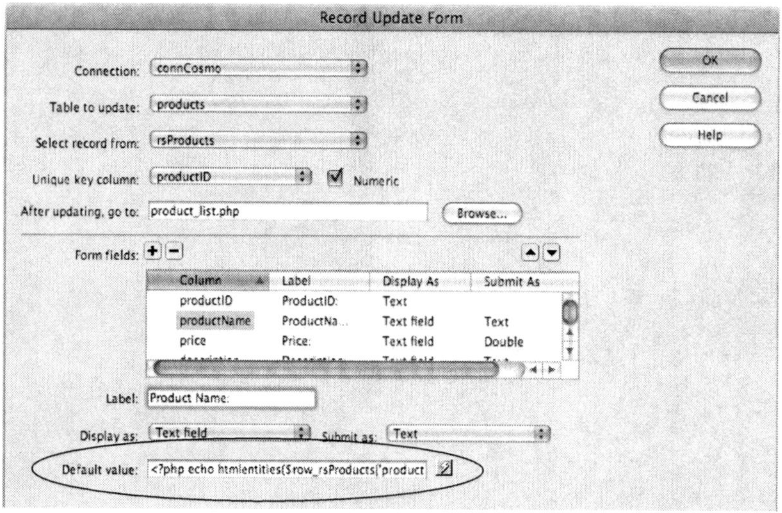

Figure 24-6:
A form field's default value is the information visible when the form first appears on the Web page. In the case of an update form, each form element is already filled out with information from the database. After all, this page is meant for editing data that already exists, not for adding a new record. When using the Update Record Form wizard, Dreamweaver is smart enough to fill out the "Default value" (circled) for each form field using the proper information from the database.

Tip: You can include multiple update forms on a single page, so it's possible to create one page that lets you update all the different tables in a database. You'll need to add filtered recordsets for each table you wish to update, and provide links that identify which table you're updating. In one case a URL may include the primary key for one table (*update.php?productID=2*, for example). Meanwhile, another link passes a different primary key (*update.php?categoryID=1*) to the same page in order to update a record in a different table.

One way to keep a page like this from appearing overly cluttered with forms is to use the "Show if Recordset Not Empty" server behavior (see page 974). Select one update form, apply the server behavior, and in the "Show if Recordset Not Empty" dialog box, select the recordset that matches the update form. In this way, the page only ever displays one form–the one used to update the record from the specified recordset.

5. **In the "Select record from" menu, make sure the recordset you created earlier is selected.**

   The recordset should be selected already. If it's not, you must have created another recordset first.

6. **In the "Unique key column" pop-up menu, make sure the table's primary key column is selected. If the column contains a number—and it usually does—verify that the Numeric checkbox is turned on.**

   The "Unique key column" is used to identify which record to change during the update process. (For a description of primary keys, see page 831.)

7. **Click the Browse button; select a file from your site.**

   This file represents the page that will appear after a record has been updated. A good technique is to select a page that lists the details of the record that's being edited (like the detail page in the master/detail pages discussed on page 879). Then, after updating the page, the visitor immediately sees a page showing the changes.

8. **If you like, change a column's settings.**

   After clicking a row in the "Form fields" list, you can change the Label, Display As, and Submit As properties of the database column, the same as when inserting a record as described on page 909. If the table includes a Description column that might hold a fair amount of text, then select Text Area from the "Display as" menu. This way, the form includes a larger text box that can display all of the description.

   Don't change the "Submit as" pop-up menu option, which determines what kind of data to submit—text, a number, and so on—because Dreamweaver automatically gets this information from the database. In addition, you would rarely change the "Default value" property. Since this represents the data pulled out of the database for a particular record, modifying the default value *always* changes that information in the database.

Note: Sometimes you might want to change the "Default value" for a column. Say a table includes a column to track the date a record was last updated. In this case, you would make the value show the current date (instead of the date already stored in the database). When someone updates a record, the database automatically records the current date in the "last update" field.

To delete a field so it doesn't appear in the form, click the Remove (minus sign [–]) button. For example, you might want to remove the primary key column—the column you selected in step 5. Since the key identifies the record, letting someone edit this could cause problems to your database, such as overwriting data for another record. Fortunately, Dreamweaver is aware of this potential problem; when you use the Update Record Form wizard, Dreamweaver doesn't create an editable form field for the primary key. Instead it simply displays the number on the page for your reference.

9. **Click OK to close the window.**

   Dreamweaver inserts a table, form, and all the form elements you specified.

Note: If you get the following error–"Please choose a unique key from the selected Recordset, or Click Cancel"–then the recordset you added to the page didn't include the table's primary key. You should cancel the Update wizard, edit the recordset, and then click the "All" button next to the word Columns. Then reapply the Record Update Form wizard.

Once you click OK to close the Record Update Form dialog box, you can never again return to it. From now on, you make any changes by editing the Update Record server behavior, as described next. You're also free to use any of Dreamweaver's editing tools to format the table, labels, and form elements any way you wish.

Warning: After using the Update wizard, don't change the name of the form or its fields. Because the program that updates the database relies on these names, changing them stops the update code from working. If for some reason you do change a form or field name, you can edit the Update Record sever behavior by double-clicking Update Record on the Server Behaviors panel. This action opens the Update Record window once again. You can make changes in this window, like associating a database column to a form field that you renamed.

The Update Record Server Behavior

Dreamweaver's Record Update Form wizard makes it delightfully easy to add the table, form, and programming code required to create a Web page for editing database records. But when you need more flexibility—if you've already designed a form that you'd like to use or created a CSS-based design for your form—the Update Record server behavior lets you keep your own beautiful design and give it the power to update a database.

You must start with a page that has a filtered recordset, as described on page 847. Then add a form to the page (see Chapter 11). Make sure the form has one form field for every database column to be edited. Don't include an editable form field for the database table's primary key. (Allowing anyone to change the primary key could have disastrous effects on your database.) You will, however, need to add a hidden field containing the primary key, as described in step 6 below.

Tip: Giving your form fields the same names used for the database table's columns speeds up the process of adding the Update Record server behavior.

At this point, the form is full of empty fields. If you preview the page, none of the data you retrieved from the recordset appears. To fill the form with data, you must *bind* data from the recordset to each form field, as follows:

1. **In the document window, select a form field.**

   Just click the form field to select it.

Note: These instructions apply to text and hidden fields. Information on binding data to radio buttons, checkboxes, and menus appears on page 922.

2. **In the Property inspector, click the dynamic data button (the lightning bolt) to the right of the "Init val" box.**

   The Dynamic Data window appears (Figure 24-7).

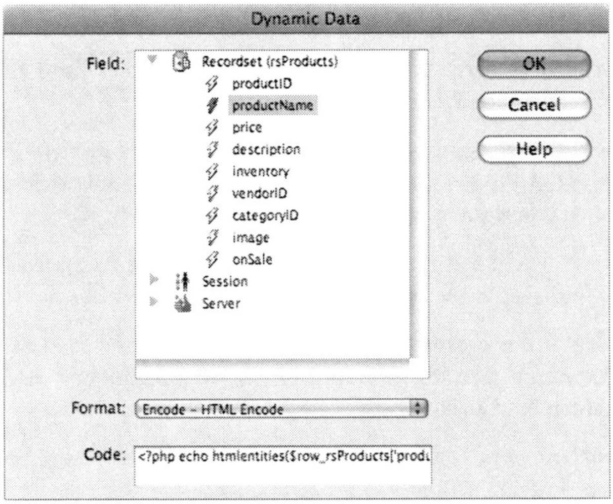

Figure 24-7: *The Dynamic Data window lets you add information from a recordset to form fields, so parts of a form can be pre-filled out. This ability is exactly what you want when updating information already in the database. In fact, the Dynamic Data window displays and lets you use additional data sources (like URL variables) that you've added to the page (see page 963).*

Note: You can also bind data from a recordset to a form field by dragging the database column from the Bindings panel (see page 864), and then dropping it onto the form field. Then use the Bindings Panel's Format menu (page 864) to set the format to "Encode–HTML Encode" (see step 5 below).

3. **Click the + button next to the recordset used for the update page.**

   A list of all columns retrieved by the recordset appears.

4. **Select the name of the table column you wish to bind to the form field.**

   To make sure the page displays correctly, you need to change the format in which the data is displayed.

5. **Select "Encode—HTML Encode" from the Format menu. Click OK.**

   This step is necessary only when inserting database content that includes text that might be misinterpreted as HTML by a Web browser (so skip ahead to step 6 if the database field only holds numbers). For example, if you had the following text inside a database field—"I think 5<3"—a Web browser will think that the less-than sign—<—is actually the beginning of an HTML tag. If that text was output, as is, to the Web page, the browser might completely mess up the display of the page. By choosing the HTML Encode formatting option, you're telling Dreamweaver to change HTML characters like < or > to their safe-to-display equivalents such as *<* or *>*.

   Ignore the Code box (which just shows you the actual PHP code that Dreamweaver will add to the page). The form field is now set to display information from the recordset.

6. **Repeat steps 1–5 for each field in the form.**

   There's one final step—providing the record's primary key. Although you don't want to let anyone edit this number in the form, you still need to include the primary key so that the programming that updates the database knows which record to update.

7. **Click somewhere inside the form (between the dashed red lines) and then choose Insert → Form → Hidden Field.**

   You can also use the Forms category of the Insert Panel to insert a hidden field, as described on page 451. A hidden form field—represented by a gold shield—is added to the form. Now you need to give it a name and a value.

8. **In the Property inspector, change the name of the hidden field to match the name of the primary key field in the appropriate table.**

   For example, if the field in the database table is named "productID", then name the hidden field "productID" (see page 450 for more on naming hidden fields). Next, you give the hidden field a value.

9. **In the Property inspector click the dynamic data button (the lightning bolt) and, from the Dynamic Data window (Figure 24-7) choose the recordset's primary key field.**

   In other words, you're telling Dreamweaver to make the hidden field match the primary key of the record that will be updated.

Once you've created the form and added recordset information to each field, add the Update Record server behavior:

10. **Choose Window → Server Behaviors to open the Server Behaviors panel.**

    The keyboard shortcut is Ctrl+F9 (⌘-F9).

11. **Click the + button on the panel, and then select Update Record.**

    The Update Record window opens (see Figure 24-8).

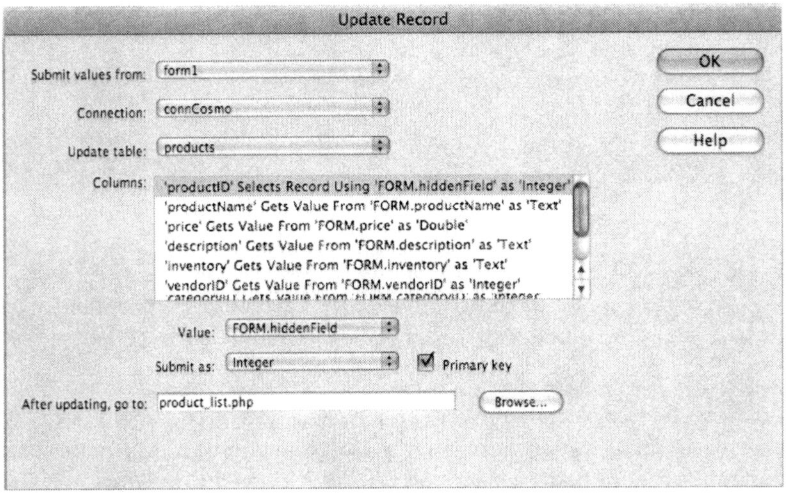

Figure 24-8: *The Update Record window is very similar to the Record Update Form window (Figure 24-6). The main difference is that here you must manually associate a form element with the correct database column.*

12. **From the "Submit values from" menu, select the name of the form.**

    It's possible to have multiple forms on a single page: a form for editing a record and a form for searching the site, for example. Select the name of the form used for editing data.

13. **Select the database connection and the table you want to update.**

    They're the same as described in steps 3 and 4 for the Record Update Form wizard on page 913. They tell Dreamweaver which database to use, and which table to update data to.

14. **Select a form element from the list, and then, from the Columns menu, select the matching database.**

    For the form's information to end up in the proper database columns, you must tell Dreamweaver which database column you want to store the selected form field's information.

Tip: If you use the name of your database columns to name the form fields too, Dreamweaver automatically associates the two, so you can skip this step.

From the "Submit as" menu, let Dreamweaver choose the proper type. As with step 6 on page 908, this choice depends on how your database is set up (which Dreamweaver can figure out).

15. **Click the Browse button; select a file from your site.**

    This file represents the page that appears after a record has been updated. A good technique is to select a page that lists the details of the record that's being edited (like the detail page in the master/detail pages, discussed on page 879).

16. **Click OK to close the window and apply the server behavior.**

    The page is now capable of editing information from the database.

As with any server behavior, double-clicking its name on the Server Behaviors panel—in this case, Update Record—opens the behavior's dialog box so you can make changes to its properties.

Dynamic Form Fields

Form fields don't necessarily have to be empty. For example, the record update forms covered in the previous section are already filled out with data pulled from the database. Likewise, you don't necessarily have to manually create the options in a pull-down menu; they could come from information in a database.

Imagine a scenario where you create an Employee Directory section for your company's Web site. On the Insert New Employee page, you build a pop-up menu that lets the Human Resources department select a department for the new employee.

You, the designer, *could* create a menu like this department list by manually typing the name of each department (as described in the Forms chapter on page 429). But what if the names of the departments change, or new departments are added? You'd have to reopen the page and edit the form field each time. But if you opted for a dynamic menu instead, the page would build the Departments pop-up menu automatically by retrieving the current list of departments from the database. Figure 24-9 shows a similar example of a form pull-down menu that's been dynamically created.

In essence, a dynamic form field is a form element whose value, labels, or other settings come from dynamic data in the Bindings panel. The dynamic data can come from a recordset (as with an update form), a form or URL parameter, or even a cookie or session variable (see page 967).

Whenever you wish to use a dynamic form field, start by creating a form. Add all form fields that might include dynamic content. (Not all the fields have to be dynamic, however. In the employee directory example discussed earlier, only the Department menu on the Insert New Employee form would be dynamic. The other fields for entering an employee's information would be empty.)

Figure 24-9: *Dynamic form fields come in handy with update forms. Form fields are already filled out with database information that's ready to be edited. Menus can also be dynamically generated from records in a recordset. In this case, the Vendor menu (shown open) lists records retrieved directly from a database table containing the names of all vendors who supply the CosmoFarmer online store.*

Next, add a recordset, request variable, session variable, or application variable to the Bindings panel (see page 963 for information on those last three choices). Then, finally, attach the dynamic data to the form field. The process for binding dynamic data depends on the type of form field.

Dynamic Text Form Fields

Any form field that accepts typing—text, text area, and password fields—can be dynamic. For example, if a site requires a user login, you could include a "remember me" feature, so that when a visitor who's previously signed in returns to the site, the user name and password are already filled out.

Tip: If you like the idea of a "remember me" feature for password-protected pages, try the free Save Password Login Form extension, which works with ASP, PHP, and ColdFusion. You can find it on the Adobe Exchange Web site (see page 804).

You can add dynamic data (also called *binding* data) to a text field using any of the methods described below. (Remember, you must first have added the form field to the page and added the dynamic data to the Bindings panel, which means adding a recordset to a page, as described on page 844, or creating additional data sources [like cookies or session variables], as described on page 963.)

- In Design view, drag the dynamic data item from the Bindings panel, and drop it onto the form field.
- In Design view, select the text field. In the Bindings panel, select the dynamic data item, and then click the Bind button.
- Select the text field. In the Property inspector, click the dynamic data button (the lightning bolt). The Dynamic Data window appears (see Figure 24-7); select the dynamic data item from the list, and then click OK.
- In the Server Behaviors panel, click the + button, and then select Dynamic Form Elements → Dynamic Text Field. In the window that appears, you see a text field menu. Select the text field to which you wish to add dynamic data; then click the lightning bolt button to open the dynamic data window. Select the dynamic data item from the list, and then click OK. (Insert → Data Objects → Dynamic Data → Dynamic Text Field works, too.)

Note: You can bind dynamic data to a *hidden* field using the same steps (for an example, see steps 9–12 on page 950).

After binding the data to the field, the name of the data item appears inside the field—{rsDetails.adName}, for example. If you're using Live view (page 875), the actual data from the database appears inside the field.

Note: Dreamweaver lets you format dynamic data in a form field just like dynamic text you add to a page, as described on page 864. As mentioned in step 5 on page 864, if there's a chance that the database field contains any text that has special meaning for a Web browser, like an opening < or closing >, then use the "Encode–HTML Encode" formatting option. This makes sure that those special characters are translated in a way that won't cause the browser to think you're trying to include *real* HTML and ruin the display of the page.

To remove dynamic data from a text field, just select the field, and then, in the Bindings panel, click the Unbind button. (Deleting the contents of the field's "Init val" box in the Property inspector also works.)

Dynamic Checkboxes and Radio Buttons

With a text field, you can dynamically change the *value* of the field. With checkboxes and radio buttons, however, you can control only their status (checked or unchecked) dynamically.

You can use this value to select one radio button in a group based on a value in the database. As part of a product ordering system, shoppers could select a particular shipping option: USPS, FedEx, or UPS. But after reviewing her orders, what if a customer changes her mind and chooses a different shipping option? When she returns to the order page, you'd want the Shipping Option radio button to reflect the choice she had made earlier. In other words, you want the page to read the shipping option for the order from the database, and highlight the radio button that matches. (See an example of this in the "Building a Page for Editing Database Records" section of the tutorial starting on page 940.)

Dynamic radio buttons

You add dynamic radio buttons like this:

1. **Add a group of radio buttons to the page.**

   You should have as many radio buttons as there are possible values stored in the database column. Remember, if you wish to create a group of related radio buttons, you must give every button in the group the same name (see page 445).

   Note, too, that the value of each radio button must also exactly match the values stored in the database. If a Shipping column in the database stores USPS, FedEx, or UPS, then the radio group should have three buttons. Each button would share the same name—*shipping*, for instance—but their checked values would match the different values stored in the database: USPS, FedEx, and UPS. Capitalization counts, so if the value in the database is UPS, the radio button value must be UPS, not Ups, ups, or UpS.

2. **Open the Server Behaviors panel (Window → Server Behaviors). Click the + button, and then select Dynamic Form Elements → Dynamic Radio Group.**

   You can also find this option under Insert → Data Objects → Dynamic Data, or under the Dynamic Data menu in the Data category of the insert bar (Figure 23-1). The Dynamic Radio Group window appears (see Figure 24-10).

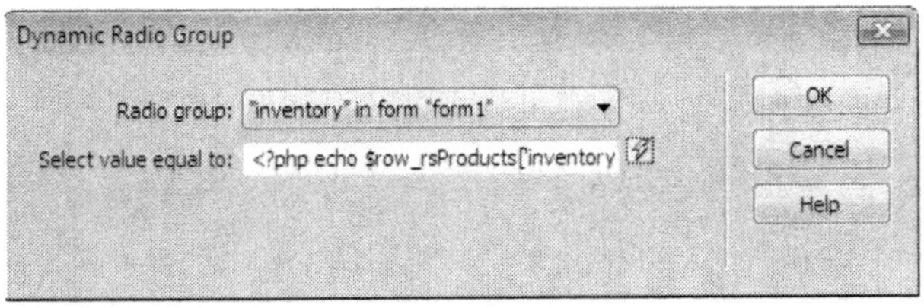

Figure 24-10: *The Dynamic Radio Group window lists the values of each button in the group. By selecting a button from the list, you can change its value in the Value field.*

3. **From the first menu, choose the radio button group.**

   In other words, select the name assigned to every button in the group. If your form has more than one group of radio buttons, select the one you wish to be dynamic.

4. **Click the dynamic data button (the lightning bolt) to the right of the "Select value equal to" field.**

   The Dynamic Data window opens (see Figure 24-7). Select the dynamic data item for this radio group. In a nutshell, the radio button whose value matches the dynamic data is selected. If no radio buttons contain the same value, then no buttons are selected.

Note: You set the "Select value equal to" field only once per radio group (not once per button in the group).

5. **Click OK to close the window.**

   Dreamweaver adds a Dynamic Radio Buttons server behavior to the page. If you change the value of one of the buttons in the radio group, you need to reapply the server behavior like this: Open the Server Behaviors panel and then double click the Dynamic Radio Group item. This opens the Dynamic Radio Group window again (Figure 24-10). Click the OK button and Dreamweaver updates the code to reflect the change you made to the button's value.

Note: If you find that the Dynamic Radio button doesn't highlight correctly when you preview the Web page in a browser, odds are that you didn't type the correct value for one of the buttons. Double-check the radio button values to make sure they match the data in the database (including the case of the letters). You then need to reapply the Dynamic Radio Group server behavior as described in step 5 above.

Dynamic checkboxes

Dynamic checkboxes work almost the same way:

1. **Add a checkbox to the page.**

   This process is described on page 442.

2. **Select the Checkbox, and in the Property inspector, click the Dynamic button.**

   The Dynamic CheckBox window appears (Figure 24-11).

Tip: You can also open the Dynamic CheckBox on the Server Behaviors panel under Dynamic Form Elements → Dynamic CheckBox, or in the Dynamic Data menu in the Data category of the Insert Panel (Figure 23-1). Heck, you can even open the window by choosing Insert → Data Objects → Dynamic Data → Dynamic Checkbox.

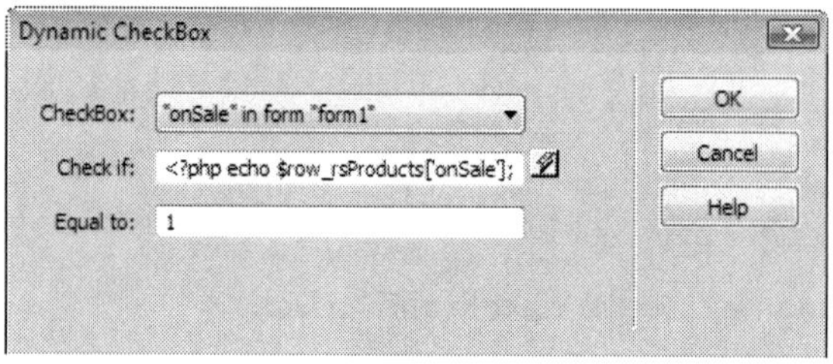

***Figure 24-11:** The Dynamic CheckBox server behavior lets you control whether or not a checkbox is turned on, based on information from a database, cookie, URL parameter, or other piece of dynamic data.*

3. **If the form has more than one checkbox, select a checkbox from the first menu.**

   Select the checkbox you wish to control dynamically.

4. **Click the dynamic data button (the lightning bolt) to the right of the "Check if" field.**

   The Dynamic Data window opens (see Figure 24-7). Select the dynamic data item for this checkbox.

5. **Type a value into the "Equal to" box.**

   If the value from the dynamic data (previous step) matches the value you provide here, the checkbox is turned on. (If the checkbox is part of an update form, this should match the value you gave the checkbox from step 1.)

6. **Click OK to close the window.**

   Dreamweaver adds a Dynamic CheckBox server behavior to the page.

To *remove* the dynamic properties from a group of radio buttons or a checkbox, open the Server Behaviors panel (Window → Server Behaviors). Among the list of server behaviors, you see the dynamic radio button or checkbox behavior. It looks something like "Dynamic Radio Buttons(group_name)" or "Dynamic Check Box(checkbox_name)"—where *group_name* or *checkbox_name* is replaced with whatever name you gave the buttons or checkbox. Select it, and then click the Remove (minus sign [–]) button. (Pressing the Delete key does the same thing.)

Dynamic Menus and Lists

Dynamic menus and lists are among the most common form elements. You can use them for more than just update forms. Even a form used to add information to a database can use a dynamic form to display a list of options stored in the database. They save you the effort of having to rebuild traditional menus or lists every time your company opens a store in a new state, adds a new employee department, or adds a new category to its product line.

To create a dynamic menu or list, proceed as follows:

1. **Create a form, and then add a menu or list to the page.**

   For example, choose Insert → Form → Form, and then Insert → Form → List/Menu. This process is the same as adding a menu or list, as described on page 446. Don't add any items to the list, though. That's the whole point of this exercise: Dreamweaver builds the menu or list automatically.

Tip: If the dynamic menu is part of a form that updates or adds a record to a database, name the menu the same as the corresponding field in the database table. For example, if the database table has a field named "employeeCategoryID", then name the menu in the form "employeeCategoryID". This will make it easier for Dreamweaver to associate this menu with the proper database field to be updated.

---

2. **Add a recordset to the page, which includes the information you wish to appear in the menu or list.**

   Perhaps you want to create a menu listing the different categories of products your company sells—books, DVDs, CDs, lederhosen, clogs, and so on. If the database has a table containing the categories, you could then create a recordset that retrieves the name of each category. (In most cases, you also retrieve a primary key, like the category ID field. The name of the category appears in the menu, while the primary key is the value submitted with the form.)

3. **In the document window, select the menu or list, and then, on the Property inspector, click the Dynamic button.**

   The Dynamic List/Menu window opens (see Figure 24-12). The name of the menu or list you selected appears in the Menu box.

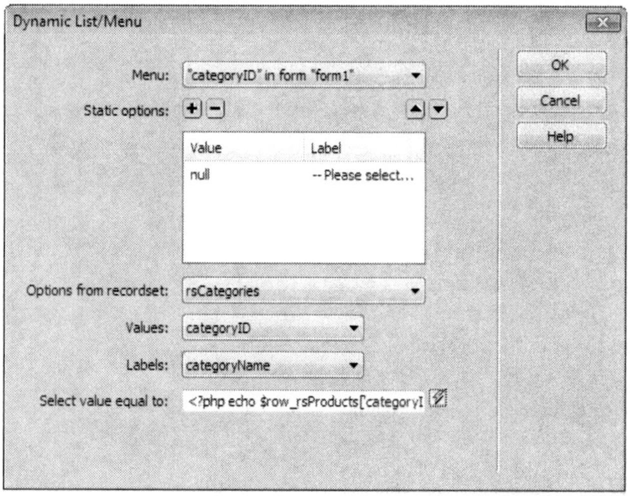

Figure 24-12: *Dreamweaver simplifies the process of creating automatically generated menus like the one pictured in Figure 24-9. Using information pulled from a database, you may never have to create another menu by hand.*

4. **If you like, add some static options to the menu or list.**

   A *static option* is simply a value and a label that you enter by hand—menu or list items, appearing at the top of the list, that don't change. This option doesn't come from the recordset you created.

   You could use this feature for options not likely to change—Amazon.com may begin to sell electronics, hors d'oeuvres, and dermatology services, but chances are good that books will always be among its categories. You can also use it to provide clear instructions about operating this menu: "Pick a state," or "Choose an option from this list," for example. This step is optional—the menu options can come entirely from the database. (Adding static options works just like it does in a regular menu's List Values box, as described on page 446.)

5. **From the Options From Recordset menu, choose the recordset you created in step 2.**

   You've just told Dreamweaver where the items to be listed in the menu are coming from.

6. **From the Values menu, choose a table column; choose another column from the Labels menu.**

   Menu and list items consist of a *label* (what someone actually sees in the menu) and a *value* (the information that's transmitted when the form is submitted). For example, in Figure 24-12, "categoryID" is the recordset's primary key, so that's what's selected from the Values menu. The label that appears on the menu should be the category's name, so "categoryName" is selected from the Labels menu. If the label and value are the same, choose the same table column from both menus.

7. **If you want your menu to have one item preselected, then click the dynamic data button (the lightning bolt). In the Dynamic Data window (Figure 24-7), select a dynamic data item.**

   This step is optional and most frequently used for an update form. Suppose you create a form for updating information on your catalog of products. When the update page loads, all the form fields would already be filled out with information about a particular product. The menu that lets you specify the product's category, therefore, should have the name of the category that matches the database record displayed and preselected.

8. **Click OK.**

   Dreamweaver adds a Dynamic List/Menu server behavior to the page.

You can remove the dynamic menu or list by selecting and deleting it. To leave the menu but remove its dynamic properties, open the Server Behaviors panel (Window → Server Behaviors). Here, you see the dynamic list/menu behavior; it's listed as "Dynamic List/Menu(menu_name)," where "menu_name" is the name you gave the menu or list. Select it, and then click the Remove (minus sign [–]) button or press the Delete key.

To edit the behavior, just select the menu in the document window, and then, once again, in the Property inspector, click the Dynamic button.

Deleting Records

Dreamweaver's Delete Record server behavior lets you build pages that let people remove records from a database. Depending on which server model you use, the method of adding this server behavior varies. There's one server behavior for ASP and another (that offers a bit more flexibility) for PHP and ColdFusion.

Deleting Records for ASP

The setup is similar to using the Update Record server behavior, in that you must create a page with a recordset that retrieves a single record—the item to delete. This page is just like a detail page, as described on page 446. Another page must link to the delete page, and provide the proper key for filtering to a single record on the delete page.

One way you can do this is by adding a link—Delete This Record, perhaps—on a record detail page. The link should pass the primary key for the condemned record to another page (the "Go to Detail Page" server behavior described on page 972 can help with this). This page—the delete page—would include a recordset that retrieves the file to be deleted. To confirm the deletion, the page might say something like, "Are you sure you wish to delete this record?" (Adding some dynamic text from the recordset, such as a name column, will help identify the record.)

A delete page differs from a regular detail page because it includes a form with a single Submit button, and a Delete Record server behavior.

To create a delete page, proceed as follows:

1. **Create a dynamic page containing a filtered recordset.**

   As noted above, the recordset should retrieve a single record—the one to be deleted. However, you don't need to retrieve *all* the columns for the record. At a minimum, the recordset must retrieve the record's primary key, since the Delete Record server behavior needs it to know which record to remove. But beyond that, you should probably include some identifying information on the delete page, so that your visitor can make sure she's really deleting the right record. If the page deletes an employee from the database, consider putting the employee's name on the page as one final check.

2. **Add a form to the page with a single Submit button (see page 431).**

   Change the label of the button so that it reflects the action it will perform—Delete This Record, for example.

3. **Open the Server Behaviors panel (Window → Server Behaviors). Click the + button, and then select Delete Record.**

   The Delete Record window appears (see Figure 24-13).

4. **From the Connection menu, select a database. From the "Delete from table" menu, select the table with the record to be deleted.**

   These steps should be familiar by now; the table you select should be the same one you used when creating the detail recordset for this page.

5. **From the "Select record from" menu, select the recordset you added to this page.**

   This step specifies the recordset on the page (if there's more than one) that Dreamweaver should use for specifying the record to be deleted.

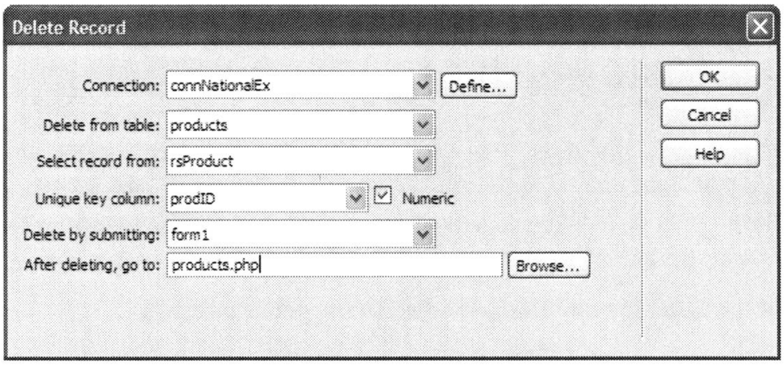

Figure 24-13: *Dreamweaver's Delete Record server behavior simplifies the process of removing information from a database.*

6. **From the "Unique key column" menu, choose the table's primary key. If it's a number, make sure the Numeric checkbox is also turned on.**

   The "Unique key column" identifies which record to delete. (For a description of primary keys, see page 831.) Make sure you retrieved this primary key information when you created the recordset, or the server behavior doesn't work.

7. **Select the name of the form that contains the Delete button.**

   Unless the page has more than one form, the name of the form you created in step 2 should automatically appear here.

8. **Click the Browse button; navigate to the Web site, and then select a file.**

   This file represents the page that will appear after a record has been deleted. This could either be a page with a confirmation message ("The Record has been successfully deleted") or a page that lists the remaining records in the database.

9. **Click OK.**

   Dreamweaver inserts the code necessary to delete a record from the database.

Deleting Records for PHP and ColdFusion

The Delete Record server behavior for PHP and ColdFusion offers a lot of flexibility, so you can implement it in a variety of ways. You don't have to add a recordset to a page to delete a record, nor do you have to add a form with a delete button.

The main requirement: The page with the Delete Record server behavior must have some way to retrieve the primary key for the record you wish to delete. This can be a form, a URL, a cookie, a session variable, or any of the other data sources discussed on page 963.

On a page that lists the details of a particular record, for example, you could include a link to a delete page and pass the ID of that record in the URL (see page 882). The delete page could then use the ID number in the URL to delete the record, and then send the visitor off to another page—perhaps a page verifying that the record was successfully deleted.

Note: Because of this flexibility, under the PHP and ColdFusion server models, you could place a Delete Record server behavior on a blank dynamic page. All the page would do is delete the specified record, and then send the visitor off to another page on the site.

There are many ways, therefore, that you could delete a record in this server model. Here's a method that would provide the same experience as the ASP model discussed above—that is, a delete page that lets people confirm the item they wish to delete by clicking a button on a form:

1. **On one of the pages in your site, add a link to the delete page.**

   On a page that provides the details of a single record, you could add a link to the delete page—maybe the word "Delete" or a button with a picture of a trash can. Alternatively, you could add a "delete this record" link as part of a repeating region (see page 736). In this way, you would have multiple records on a single page, each with its own link to the delete page. In both cases, you'd attach the record's primary key to the link, as described on page 882.

Note: Unfortunately, Dreamweaver doesn't provide a tool for deleting more than one record at a time.

2. **Create a dynamic page—the delete page—containing a filtered recordset.**

   This recordset should retrieve a single record—the one to be deleted. As mentioned for the ASP model, you don't need to retrieve *all* the columns for the record. At a minimum, the recordset must retrieve the record's primary key, since the Delete Record server behavior needs it to know which record to remove. You may want to include some identifying information, such as the name of the item to be deleted, so that your visitors can see what they're about to delete.

3. **Add to the page a form consisting of a single Submit button (as described on page 451).**

   When you create the button, change its label to reflect what it does—Delete This Record, for example.

4. **Select the form. Then, in the Property inspector's Action box, type the page's file name.**

   If the page is called *delete.php*, type *delete.php*.

   The *Action* property indicates where the form should be sent (see page 433). In this case, when the visitor clicks the Submit button, the form information goes *back* to the same page.

   This kind of trickery is common in dynamic pages. When your visitor clicks the Delete button, the form is sent to the same page—but this time the form doesn't show up. Instead, the Delete Record server behavior (which you're going to add in step 6) deletes the record, and then sends the visitor off to another page.

5. **Add a hidden field to the form (page 450). Name this field whatever you wish, but bind (attach) to it the primary key from the recordset you created in step 2.**

   This hidden field is what tells the Delete Record server behavior which record to delete. (For instructions on binding dynamic data to a form field, see page 920.)

6. **Open the Server Behaviors panel (Window → Server Behaviors). Click the + button, and then, from the list of server behaviors, select Delete Record.**

   The Delete Record window appears (Figure 24-14). This window differs slightly between PHP and ColdFusion. However, the basic steps described here are the same.

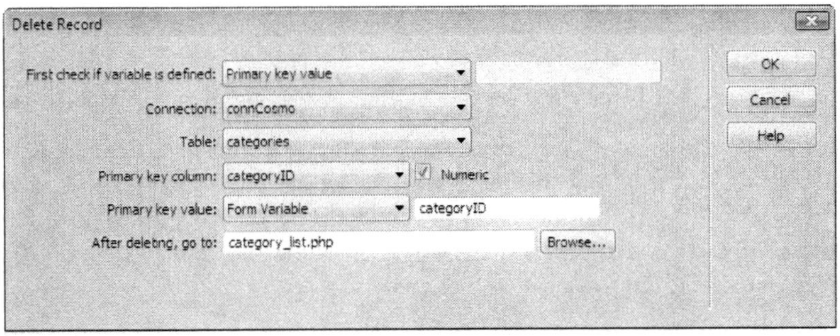

***Figure 24-14:** The Delete Record window for PHP (pictured here) differs slightly from its ColdFusion counterpart. ColdFusion lets you specify a user name and password for the database.*

7. **From the "First check if variable is defined" menu, choose "Primary key value".**

   This step may seem like putting the cart before the horse, because you won't define the primary key value until step 10 below. However, this option lets you control *when* the record is deleted, by making sure the proper variable is defined *before* the server behavior deletes the record. In this case, the record doesn't go away until the visitor clicks the Delete button, causing the server to send a form variable containing the record's primary key.

   This precaution is necessary; without this option, the record would be deleted whenever the page loads. Since the page really serves two functions—letting visitors confirm that they wish to delete the record, and actually deleting the record from the database—you need to make sure the visitor has first visited the page, and *then* clicked the Submit button you added in step 3.

8. **From the Connection menu, select a database. From the Table menu, select the table with the record to be deleted.**

   These steps should be familiar by now. The table you select should be the same one you used when creating the detail recordset for this page.

9. **From the "Primary key column" menu, select the table's primary key.**

   This tells Dreamweaver which database field contains the unique key that identifies which record to zap from the table.

10. **From the "Primary key value" menu, select Form Variable. In the box just to the right of that menu, type the name of the hidden field you added in step 5.**

    This step is the final piece of the puzzle. It tells the server behavior where to find the ID number for the doomed record. In this case, the form with its hidden field supplies the ID number.

11. **Click the Browse button; navigate to the Web site, and then select your confirmation page.**

    The confirmation page appears after a record has been deleted. It's a page you've created in advance—either a page with a confirmation message ("The Record has been successfully deleted"), or a page that lists the records of the database—a *master* page.

12. **Click OK.**

    Dreamweaver inserts the code necessary to remove a record from the database.

As with any of the other server behaviors that change content in a database, you should carefully control who has access to the delete page. Going to work one morning and finding that someone has deleted all the products from your company's e-commerce site is enough to ruin your whole day. Dreamweaver's User Authentication behaviors, discussed in the next chapter, can help.

If you ever need to change any of the properties of the Record Delete action, such as picking a different page to go to after a record is deleted, you can go to the Server Behaviors panel, and then double-click Delete Record. The Delete Record window opens; make any changes, and then click OK.

Tutorial: Inserting and Updating Data

In this tutorial, you'll continue working on CosmoFarmer's online store. You'll work on two administrative pages that allow employees of CosmoFarmer to add new products to the database, and to edit products already in the database.

This tutorial assumes you've already completed the tutorials for Chapter 22 and Chapter 23. If not, turn to page 821, follow the instructions for preparing the application server, database, and Dreamweaver for this project. Then turn to page 821 and build the product catalog pages.

Adding an Insert Product Page

Start by opening a page that's already been created:

1. **Open the file named *add.php* in the admin folder of the local site you defined in Chapter 22.**

   This page contains three Spry tabbed panels like the ones you learned about on page 494. Instead of having several Web pages, each dedicated to inserting one record into one database table, you can collect all the insert forms on a single page. Clicking a tab opens the tabbed panel with the appropriate insert form.

You'll also notice that this page is stored inside a folder named *admin*. Pages for adding and editing the online store's products shouldn't be accessible to the public; you wouldn't want just anyone adding products—"The Electric Whoopee Cushion, by Mr. Hacker," for example—to the store. Accordingly, these pages are kept in a folder reserved for administrators of the Web site. (In the next chapter, you'll learn how to password-protect these pages.)

Each new product requires an ID number for the vendor who manufactures the product. The database for these products actually contains several tables: Products, Vendors, and Category. Information about each vendor (name and contact info) is in the Vendors table, while information on each product (price, description, and so on) is in the Products table. A third table contains a list of product categories, which you used in the last tutorial to create the category navigation bar.

To keep the Vendors and Products tables connected, so that you know which vendor manufactures which product, the Products table includes a field containing the vendor's ID number. Whenever you add an item to the Products table, then, you also need to insert the vendor's ID number. One way would be to have a CosmoFarmer employee type the vendor *number* each time a product is added to the page. But that approach is prone to error, since the employee needs to remember which number belongs to which vendor: "Is Gap Plants vendor 2 or 3?" A better method is to provide a pull-down menu that lists the name of each vendor, but which submits the vendor's number when the product is added to the database. To make this kind of dynamic menu, start by creating a recordset.

2. **Make sure the Bindings Panel is open (Window → Bindings). In the Bindings Panel, click the + button, and then select Recordset.**

   Or use any of the methods described on page 844 to add a new recordset; for example, choosing Insert → Data Objects → Recordsets; clicking the + button in the Server Behaviors panel, and then choosing Recordset (Query); or using the Recordset button on the Insert panel's Data category. Either way, the Recordset window opens. Make sure that the simple recordset options show up (see Figure 24-15). Next, you'll define this recordset's properties.

3. **In the Name box, type *rsVendors*. From the Connection menu, select "connCosmo". From the Table menu, select "vendors."**

   These three steps set up the name, database, and table required for the recordset. For a recap of creating recordsets, turn to page 844.

4. **Click the Selected radio button; from the Columns list, select "vendorID" and "vendorName".**

   You can do this step by holding down the Ctrl (⌘) key while clicking the name of each column. Finally, pick an order for sorting the list of vendors.

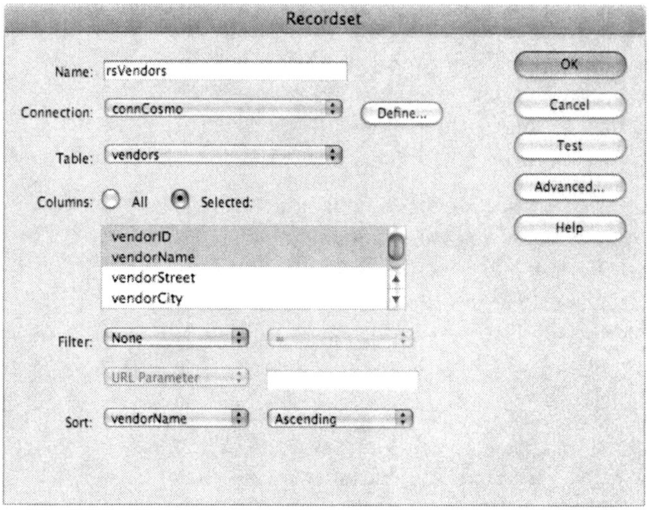

Figure 24-15: *When creating this recordset, make sure you're using the window's Simple options. If you see a button labeled Advanced, you're in the right place. (If that button's missing, click the Simple button to access the basic recordset options.)*

5. **From the Sort menu, choose vendorName. Make sure that in the Order menu, Ascending is selected.**

   The Recordset window should now look like Figure 24-15.

6. **Click OK to close the window and insert the recordset in the page.**

   You've just created a recordset that retrieves a complete list of vendor names and ID numbers in alphabetical order.

   Each product also belongs to a particular category. In the Products table in the database, the category is represented by a number, but the category names are stored in the Categories table. This situation is the same as vendors, so you'll create a dynamic menu for inserting the proper category name.

7. **Add another recordset to the page by following steps 2–6: Name the recordset *rsCategories*, select the "category" table, choose the All columns radio button, and then sort by CategoryName.**

   You've just added a second recordset to this page. Now you're ready to add a form for inserting a new record. The page contains three Spry tabbed panels. You'll add a form for inserting new products into the database via the tab that's visible when you open the page—the Add Product tab.

8. **Click the empty area of the gray box directly below the Add Product tab. Choose Insert → Data Objects → Insert Record → Record Insertion Form Wizard.**

   The Record Insertion Form Wizard is also available from the Data category of the Insert panel (see Figure 24-3). The Record Insertion Form window opens (Figure 24-16). Next, you'll tell Dreamweaver which database to connect to, and which table will receive data from the form.

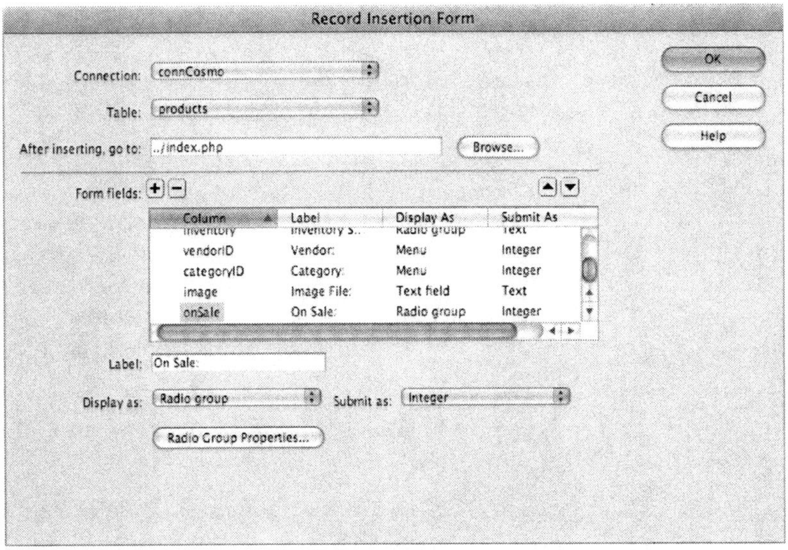

Figure 24-16: *While you can manually create a form and program it to insert a new record in a database, Dreamweaver's Record Insertion Form wizard makes the task a whole lot easier.*

9. **From the Connection menu, choose "connCosmo." From the Table menu, choose Products.**

   You can insert data into only one table at a time. In this case, you've selected the Products table because it holds all the information for each item at the store. After information is added to the database, Dreamweaver redirects the visitor to another page. You'll set this up next.

10. **Click the Browse button. In the site's root folder, select the file *index.php*.**

    After adding a new product to the database, your staff is taken to the Products page (the one you created in the previous chapter). Since the newly added product is part of the database, browsing the products catalog reveals the newly added item.

Note: You could also choose *add.php* for Step 10 if you wanted to quickly add multiple product records. Then, after one product was inserted into the database, the administrator would return to the product insertion form again, ready to input the next product.

11. **In the "Form fields" list, select "productID." Click the Remove (minus sign [–]) button to remove this field.**

    In some cases, the database itself fills in certain fields. For instance, every product in the database has its own unique ID—the table's primary key, which is generated by the database. When a new record is added, the database creates a new, unique number and stores it in the productID column. Since you don't want anyone entering the wrong information here, you should remove it from the form Dreamweaver is about to create.

12. **Select the "productName" column. In the Label field, change the label to *Product Name:*.**

The label you type here doesn't affect your database in any way. It's just the text that visitors see next to the form field. (You'll do the same thing with each field, to make the labels reader-friendly.)

You don't need to change any of the other "Form fields" options such as Display As or Submit As. You'll often change the "Display as" pop-up menu, which changes what type of form element—like a checkbox or menu—Dreamweaver displays (you'll see this in the next step). However, you'll probably never change the "Submit as" pop-up menu, which determines how Dreamweaver submits the data to the database. Dreamweaver figures this out correctly based on the design of your database.

13. **Select the "description" column. From the "Display as" menu, choose "Text area".**

The label for this column is fine, but since a description may be anywhere from several sentences to several paragraphs, it's a good idea to provide a large text box for collecting the product description. A regular text box is just one line, so changing the "Display as" option to a "Text area" (a multiline text box) provides plenty of space to accept visitor input (see page 439 for more information on multi-line text boxes).

14. **Select the inventory column, and then, in the Label field, change the label to *Inventory Status:*.**

The database tracks a product's inventory status: whether the product is in the warehouse or on back order with the manufacturer. You could let a store administrator type in the correct status, but that would take time, and, besides, he might make a mistake. (It wouldn't do for shoppers to see that the "Kudzu seeds" are on "Gack Order.") So you'll simplify the process by adding radio buttons.

15. **From the "Display as" menu, choose Radio Group, and then click the Radio Group Properties button.**

The Radio Group Properties window appears (Figure 24-17). Here you're going to add the radio buttons you want to appear on the form. Remember, the value of each button must match the data stored in the database (see page 923).

16. **In the Label field, replace *button1* with *in stock*. Type *in stock* in the Value field as well.**

Make sure you enter the value in all lower case (that's how it appears in the database's inventory field). The label is what appears on the page, while the value is the information that gets stored in the database. You need to add one more button.

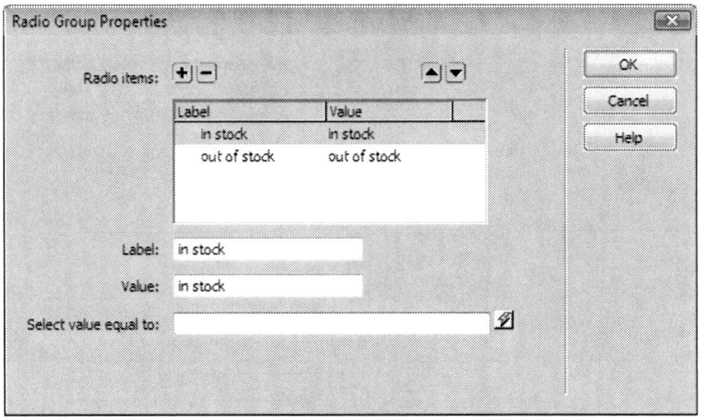

Figure 24-17: *Use the Radio Group Properties window to add radio buttons to a form. Radio buttons make data entry faster and less error-prone.*

17. **Click the + button to add another radio button; repeat step 15, but type *out of stock* for the label and value of the second button.**

    The window should look like Figure 24-17.

18. **Click OK to close the Radio Group Properties window.**

    Again, in an effort to speed up data entry and make sure the form is filled out correctly, the next two fields will be pull-down menus. First, you'll create a dynamic menu to display the list of vendors, as follows.

19. **Select the "vendorID" column, and then change its label to *Vendor:*.**

    This column only stores a number; the vendor's name and contact information are stored in a different table. To make entering this information easier, you'll make a dynamic menu that lists all of the vendors' names. When somebody chooses a name from the menu, the appropriate *vendorID* number is submitted to the database.

20. **From the "Display as" menu, choose Menu. Then click the Menu Properties button.**

    The Menu Properties window opens (see Figure 24-18). Use this window to build the menu.

21. **Click the "From database" radio button. Make sure that in the Recordset menu, "rsVendors" is selected.**

    You're telling Dreamweaver that the items to be listed in the menu are actually coming from a database query. In fact, they come from the recordset you created at the beginning of this tutorial—"rsVendors".

22. **From the "Get labels from" menu, choose "vendorName". Then, from the "Get values from" menu, choose "vendorID".**

    The labels—the text that appears in the menu—are the names of each vendor. The value that's submitted with the form, meanwhile, is the vendor's ID number.

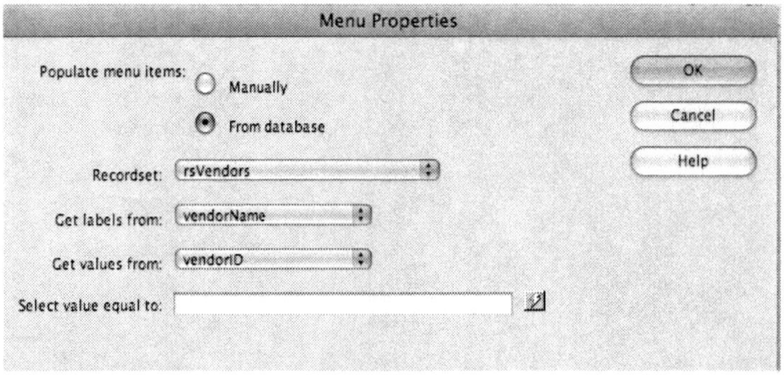

Figure 24-18: *Dreamweaver can create dynamic pull-down menus (also known as pop-up menus) that get their labels and values from a database.*

You can skip the "Select value equal to" field. It's useful if you want a particular value to be preselected when the form loads, which is usually the case when you're *updating* a record in the database, since you need to display the current database information in order to update it.

23. **Click OK to close the window.**

    The product category is another instance where a pull-down menu makes sense. You'll follow the same procedure to add a pop-up menu listing the names of all the categories available at the store.

24. **Select the categoryID column, and then change its label to *Category:*.**

    The next few steps should feel familiar.

25. **Repeat steps 20–23; use the "rsCategories" recordset, retrieve the label from the "categoryName" field, and set the value to "categoryID".**

    For the final field, you'll change the label and manually enter a default value.

26. **Select the "image" column, and then change its label to *Image File:*.**

    Because not every product has an image, you'll change the default value to point to a graphic that's already been created—one used to indicate that no graphic is available.

27. **In the "Default value" box, type *none.gif*.**

    Finally, each product can be marked as "On Sale" or not.

28. **Select the "onSale" category, and then change the label to *On Sale:*.**

    Either the product is on sale or it isn't. This kind of yes or no option is best represented by radio buttons.

29. **From the "Display as" menu, choose Radio Group, and then click the Radio Group Properties button.**

    Numbers in the database represent a product's sale status: If the onSale field has a value of 1, the product is on sale; if the value is 0, the product isn't on sale.

Because 1 and 0 might not make sense to anyone using this Web page to add a product to the database, you'll use plain language words as labels.

30. **In the Label field, replace *button1* with *Yes*. Type *1* in the Value field as well.**

    Just one more button to add.

31. **Click the + button to add another radio button; repeat step 30, but type *No* for the label and *0* for the value of the second button. Click OK to close the radio button window.**

    At this point, the Record Insertion Form window should resemble Figure 24-16.

Note: Dreamweaver doesn't provide any way to return to the Insert Record Form wizard. If you accidentally close the window and insert the form before completing each of the steps in this section of the tutorial, you have to finish the form manually. Unless you're really sure how to do that, your best bet is to delete the form from the page, remove all server behaviors except for "rsVendors" and "rsCategories", and then start at step 8 on page 934. Practice makes perfect, right?

---

32. **Click OK again to insert the form.**

    Dreamweaver adds a table, a form, and all the programming code necessary to add a new product to the database. The form has a blue background—one of Dreamweaver's signals that this form is special—and indicates that this form uses one of Dreamweaver's server behaviors (see Figure 24-22 on page 947 for information on how to hide or change this color).

33. **Choose File → Save.**

    You're nearly finished. You just have to finish up the design and take it for a test drive.

Finishing the Insert Form

To make your form ready for prime time, you'll spruce up its appearance and test it:

1. **Select the table containing the form fields.**

   The fastest method is to click anywhere inside the table and then, in the Tag selector, click the <table> tag (the one farthest to the right in the Tag selector). For other table selection techniques, see page 268.

2. **In the Property inspector, from the Align pop-up menu, choose Default.**

   The Default option aligns the table to the left without adding bandwidth-hogging HTML code. In addition, a little extra space is added around and inside each cell in a table. You'll remove that next.

3. **With the table still selected, in the Property inspector's CellPad, CellSpace, and Border boxes, type *0*.**

   You could repeat this step with the tables used for the two sets of radio buttons. In addition, if you don't like the way the buttons appear one on top of the other, you can move them. At this point, the labels, form fields, and tables in the form are fully editable. You could, for example, remove the labels and radio buttons from the table, place them side by side, and delete the small table.

   Now you'll apply a style to the table to improve its appearance.

4. **In the Property inspector, from the Class menu, choose "insertForm".**

   The text inside the table should now be formatted to better match the site's style.

5. **Select each of the table cells in the left-hand column, and then, in the Property inspector, click the Header box.**

   You can select the cells by clicking the top cell, and then dragging down until all the cells in the left column are selected; Ctrl-clicking (⌘-clicking) each cell works as well. For other methods for selecting table cells, see page 269.

   The finished page should resemble Figure 24-19. Now you're ready to take the page for a spin.

6. **Press F12 (Ctrl-F12) to preview the page in a Web browser. Type information into each of the fields, and then click the "Insert record" button.**

   If you filled out all the fields correctly, you should see the product page you built in the last chapter. Click the category name of the new product you just added, or navigate through the product pages until you find the newly added item.

Note: If, when you submit the form, you get a page full of errors, you may be attempting to preview the page using a temporary file. See the Note on page 159 for an explanation.

You can enhance this page in many ways. For example, you can make sure that no one at CosmoFarmer accidentally inserts a new product without a price, a description, or any of the other required pieces of information; just add Dreamweaver CS4's Spry Validation tools discussed on page 454. In addition, you could use the Insert Record Form wizard to add insert forms in the Add Category and Add Vendors tabbed panels. (See page 494 for information on how to work with Spry tabbed Panels.)

Building a Page for Editing Database Records

If employees at CosmoFarmer type the wrong information for a particular product and have no way to correct it, they could be in a lot of trouble. After all, they'd be losing money hand over fist if the site were selling those $598 CAT Indoor Lawn Tractors for only $5.98. That said, here's how to add an update-record page to the site.

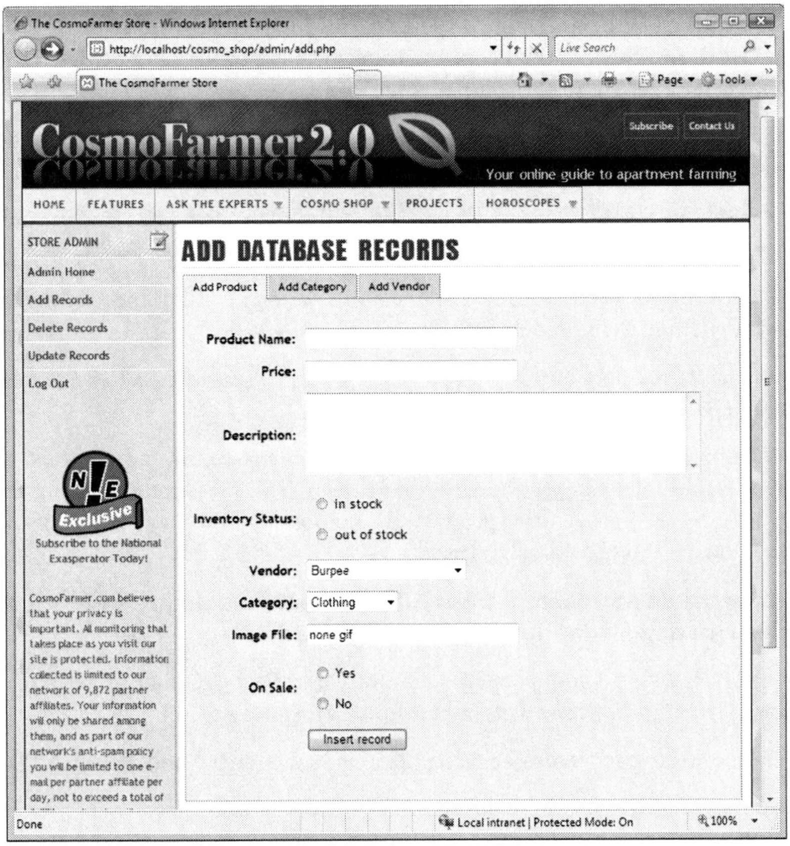

Figure 24-19: *No database-driven site would be complete without a way to add new records to the database. Use forms like this one to collect newsletter sign-up information, collect order and payment details, or just create an online guest book.*

Linking to the update page

An update page is very much like an insert-record page; the only difference is that the form is already filled out with information about a particular record. First, you have to tell the update page which product it's supposed to update. To do so, you must add a link to the product-details page you built in the last chapter.

1. **In the local site's root folder, open the file named *product.php*.**

   This page lists details for a particular product. As you may recall from last chapter, this page is itself accessed from the *index.php* page, which displays a listing of all products in the database. By clicking the name of a product on that page, the *product.php* page retrieves and displays information on just that product.

   Now you need to create a link on this page that, when clicked, takes a visitor to an update page for the particular product.

2. **Click to the right of the Inventory Status line, and then hit Enter (Return) to create a new, blank paragraph. Type *Edit This Information.* Select the text you just typed, and then, in the Property inspector, next to the Link field, click the "Browse for File" button (the little folder icon).**

   The standard Open File dialog box appears. (If you installed the extension described on page 882, you could also use the Go To Detail Page server behavior.)

3. **In the admin folder, navigate to and select the file called *edit.php*, but don't close the window yet.**

   You need to add some additional information, which identifies the product that needs updating, to the end of the URL.

4. **Click the Parameters button to open the Parameters window. Click the name column, and then type *productID.***

   The Parameters button lets you add a URL parameter to the end of a link, letting you pass information on to another page. In this case, you're passing on a dynamic piece of data—the product ID number for the item currently displayed on the Product Details page.

5. **Click in the Value column. Click the dynamic data button that appears to the right of the column (the lightning bolt).**

   The Dynamic Data window opens. Here you can select data that you've already added to the Bindings panel, such as columns from a recordset.

6. **From the "rsDetails" recordset, select the item "productID," and then click OK.**

   (You may need to click the + button to the left of the word Recordset to see this option.) The link is nearly complete.

7. **Click OK to close the Parameters window. Click OK (or Choose on a Mac) once again to close the Select File window and apply the link.**

   When you're all done, the Property inspector's link box should look like this:

   ```
   admin/edit.php?productID=<?php echo $row_rsDetails['productID']; ?>
   ```

8. **Choose File → Save.**

Note: You probably wouldn't want a link like this to appear for the average visitor to your site. After all, customers shouldn't be changing information on the products you sell. In the next chapter on page 984, you'll learn how to hide this link from unauthorized eyes.

Creating the update page

Now that the initial legwork is out of the way, you're ready to build the actual Record Update Form. To start, you'll add a filtered recordset to retrieve information for the product to be updated:

1. **In the admin folder, open the file *edit.php*.**

2. **Add a recordset, using any of the methods described on page 844. For example, choose Insert → Data Objects → Recordset.**

   The Recordset window opens. Make sure the Simple (as opposed to Advanced) options are displayed, as shown in Figure 24-20.

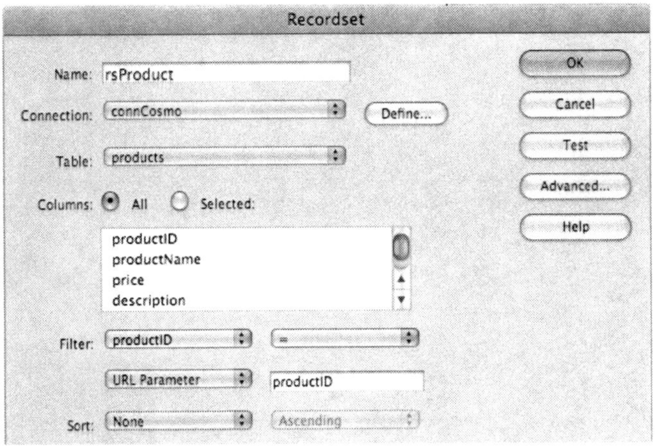

Figure 24-20: *When you filter on a table's primary key ("productID", in this case) using the = operator, the recordset never retrieves more than one record.*

3. **In the Name field, type *rsProduct*; from the Connection menu, choose "connCosmo", and from the Tables menu, select Products. Leave the All button selected.**

   Next, add a filter to the recordset. This filter ensures that the recordset retrieves only a single record—the product you wish to update.

4. **From the Filter menu, select "productID". From the Comparison menu, select "=". From the Source menu, choose URL Parameter. Finally, make sure the last field in the Filter area of the window says "productID".**

   After you selected "productID", Dreamweaver most likely filled in the other three options for you. When creating a filtered recordset, Dreamweaver assumes you'll use a URL parameter with the same name as the selected field. The Recordset window should now look like Figure 24-20. In essence, it instructs the recordset to retrieve only the record whose productID matches the number passed in the URL parameter named "productID" (that's the name you supplied as part of the link in step 4 on page 942).

5. **Click OK to close the window and add the recordset to the page.**

   Next, you'll create two more recordsets—a listing of all vendors and a listing of product categories. You'll use them to create dynamic menus, just as you did on the insert form.

6. **Follow steps 2–7 from the "Adding an Insert Product Page" part of this tutorial (see page 933) to create new "rsVendors" and "rsCategories" recordsets.**

   (You can also copy those recordsets from the insert product page as described on page 861.) The hard part's behind you. You can now use Dreamweaver's Update Record Form tool to finish the page.

7. **Click directly underneath the green line of the Edit Record headline. Choose Insert → Data Objects → Update Record → Record Update Form Wizard.**

   The Record Update Form window opens (see Figure 24-21). Next, you'll specify the recordset and fields the form should update.

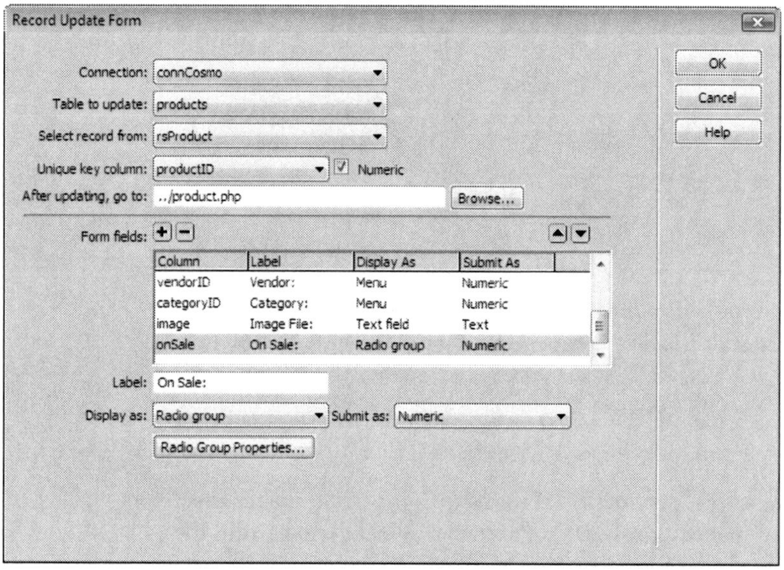

***Figure 24-21:** Dreamweaver's Record Update Form wizard makes very quick work of creating pages to update records in a database.*

8. **From the Connection menu, select "connCosmo". Make these selections for the next three menus: "products" in the "Table to update" menu, "rsProduct" in the "Select record from" menu, and "productID" in the "Unique key column."**

   Next, you need to specify which page appears after someone updates the record. Since the update page lets you edit a single product, it makes sense that after submitting any changes, you should see the newly updated information on that product's detail page.

Note: As with the Insert Record Form wizard, once you close the Update Record Form wizard window, there's no way to return to it (see the Note on page 939).

9. **Click the Browse button. In the Select File window, navigate to and select the file *product.php*. Click OK to choose the file.**

   Now you must specify which fields appear in the form. You also need to change which type of form element they should use, and edit their labels. This process is very similar to the Insert Record form; it's summarized in the following steps.

10. **In the "Form field" list, select "productID"; click the Remove (minus sign [–]) button to remove this field from the list.**

    Since "productID" is a primary key generated by the database, no one should be allowed to change it. Next, you'll change the text label that appears next to a couple of the fields.

11. **Select the "productName" form field, and then change its label to *Product Name*.**

    Next, you'll provide some more room for lengthy descriptions of each product.

12. **Select the "description" column. From the "Display as" menu, choose Text Area.**

    As with the insert product page, inventory status information is better displayed with a simple pair of radio buttons. You'll add those now.

13. **Select the "inventory" column. Change the label to *Inventory Status:*, from the "Display as" menu, choose Radio Group.**

    You now need to give Dreamweaver a bit of information about the radio buttons you wish to add to the page.

14. **Click the Radio Group Properties button.**

    The Radio Group Properties window appears (Figure 24-17). You need to add the radio buttons you want to appear on the form. The value of each button must match the data stored in the database.

15. **In the Label field, replace *button1* with *in stock*. Type *in stock* into the Value field, too.**

    The label appears on the page, while the value is stored in the database. You need to add one more button.

16. **Click the + button to add another radio button; repeat step 15, but type *out of stock* for the label and value of the second button.**

    The window should look like Figure 24-17, except that the "Select value equal to" box is filled with the programming code necessary to select the correct button. Since this is an update form, one of the buttons should *already* be selected when the page loads—information stored in the recordset determines which button is selected.

17. **Click OK to close the Radio Group Properties window.**

    Again, in an effort to speed up data entry and make sure the form is filled out correctly, the next two fields will be pull-down menus. First, you'll create a dynamic menu to display the list of vendors.

18. **Select the "vendorID" column, and then change the label to *Vendor:*. From the "Display as" menu, choose Menu; click the Menu Properties button.**

    The Menu Properties window opens (see Figure 24-18).

19. **Click the "From database" radio button, make sure "rsVendors" is selected in the Recordset menu, and then, from the "Get labels from" menu, choose "vendorName". Now, from the "Get values from" menu, choose "vendorID".**

    Leave the "Select value equal to" field as is. Dreamweaver automatically selects the appropriate choice, based on which vendor manufactures the product.

20. **Click OK to close the Menu Properties window.**

    You need to repeat the process for the product categories menu.

21. **Select the "categoryID" column, and then change the label to *Category:*. From the Display As menu, choose Menu; click the Menu Properties button.**

    The Menu Properties window opens.

22. **Click the "From database" radio button, make sure "rsCategories" is selected in the Recordset menu, and then choose "categoryName" from the "Get labels from" menu. Now, from the "Get values from" menu, choose "categoryID". Click OK to close the Menu Properties window.**

    As with the previous menu, Dreamweaver automatically adds the correct code to make sure the category for the product being edited is correctly selected when this update page loads.

23. **Select the "image" form field, and then change its label to *Image File:*.**

    Finally, you'll provide a way to indicate whether a product is on sale.

24. **Select the "onSale" category, and then change the label to *On Sale:*.**

    Either the product is on sale or it isn't. You can best represent this kind of yes or no option by radio buttons.

25. **From the "Display as" menu, choose Radio Group, and click the Radio Group Properties button.**

    Numbers in the database represent the sale status of a product: if the "onSale" field has a value of 1, the product is on sale; if the value is 0, the product isn't on sale. Because 1 and 0 might not make sense to anyone using this Web page to add a product to the database, you'll use plain language words as labels.

26. **In the Label field, replace *button1* with *Yes*. Type *1* in the Value field as well.**

    Just one more button to add.

27. **Click the + button to add another radio button; repeat step 30, but type *No* for the label and *0* for the value of the second button. Click OK to close the radio button window.**

    At this point, the Record Update Form window should resemble Figure 24-21.

28. **Click OK to close the Record Update Form window.**

    Dreamweaver inserts a table, form, form fields, and programming code to the update page. All that's left are some final cosmetic touches.

29. **Repeat steps 1–5 from the "Finishing the Insert Form" part of this tutorial (page 939).**

    Doing so properly formats the form. Your finished page should resemble Figure 24-22.

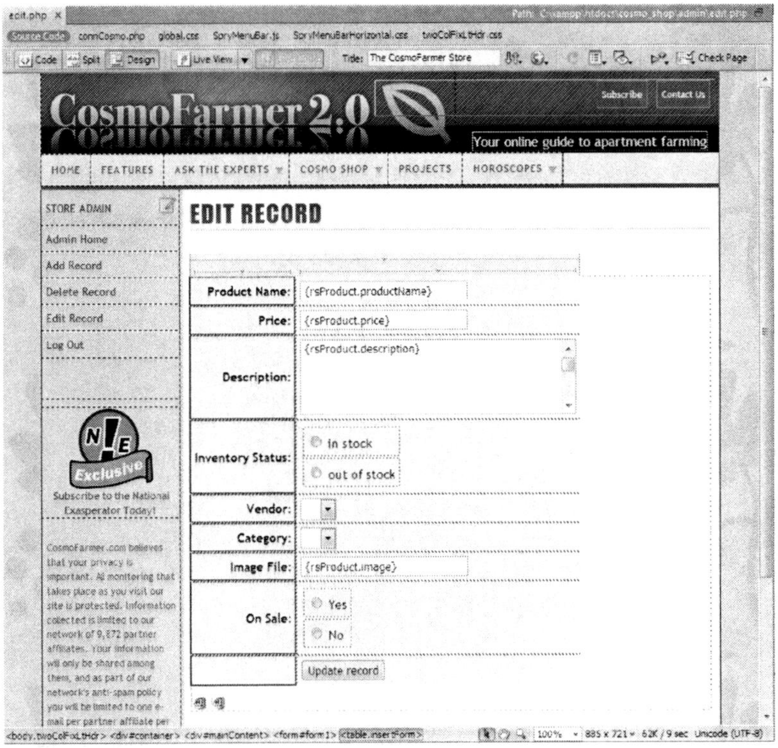

***Figure 24-22:** When you're working in Design view, Dreamweaver highlights dynamic areas of the page—like this update form—in light blue. In Live Data view (see page 875), the same areas change to yellow. If you'd like to hide this coloring, open the Preferences window (Edit → Preferences [Dreamweaver → Preferences]), select the Highlighting category, and then turn off the two Live Data checkboxes.*

30. **Save this page and close it.**

    To get a feel for what you've done, it's time to test your application.

31. **In the local root folder (the *cosmo_shop* folder), open the *index.php* page. Press F12 (Option-F12) to preview it in a browser.**

    The page lists the products in the database. Take a close look at one product in particular.

32. **Click the name of any product in the list.**

    A details page for that product appears.

33. **Click the Edit This Information link near the bottom.**

    The Update Product page appears, with the form already completed.

34. **Change some of the information on the form, and then click the "Update record" button.**

    Voilà! You're taken back to the details page for this product listing, which proudly displays the freshly edited content.

Creating and Linking to the Delete Page

Obviously, if a vendor stops manufacturing a product, or the staff at CosmoFarmer decides to discontinue an item, you need a way to remove a product listing from the database.

Adding a link on the details page

To begin, you must provide a link to delete the product. A good place for this would be on the details page of each product. Since you've already added an Edit This Information link to this page, you must now add a Delete This Product link:

1. **Open the file *product.php*.**

   Add a link that leads to a delete page.

2. **Near the bottom of the page, click to the right of the text you added earlier: Edit This Information. Press the Space bar, followed by the | character and another space; type *Delete This Product*.**

   Now you'll link this phrase to the delete page.

Note: It's easy to accidentally click into the "Edit This Information" link. Doing so will make any text you type a part of that link. If you're in this situation, just delete the new text you typed, click the <a> in the Tag selector at the bottom of the document window, and then press the right arrow key. This moves the insertion point to the right of the link.

3. **Select the text "Delete This Product", and then, in the Property inspector, click the "Browse for File" button (the little folder icon). In the *admin* folder, navigate to and select the file *delete.php*, but don't close the window yet.**

   You need to add the information that lets the delete page form know which product it should delete.

4. **Follow steps 4–7 in the "Linking to the update page" part of this tutorial (page 942).**

   Doing so creates a link that not only goes to the delete page, but also passes along the ID number of the product to be deleted.

5. **Save and close this page.**

   You'll probably find yourself needing to use the same recordset on several pages on a site. For example, on the product detail page you created in the last tutorial, you created a filtered recordset which retrieved information on a single product (based on an ID number passed in the URL). You recreated that same recordset on the update record page you created on page 942. You'll also need it for the delete page (in order to select a single product to delete). Instead of recreating that recordset yet again, you'll just copy it from another page.

6. **Open the file *edit.php*.**

   You'll copy the recordset from the Bindings panel, so make sure it's open (Window → Bindings).

7. **Right-click (Ctrl-click) on the "rsProduct" recordset, and then, from the pop-up menu, choose Copy.**

   You can also select the recordset in the Bindings panel, click the shortcut menu that appears in the panel's top-right corner, and then select Copy. Either way, you've copied the programming code necessary for the delete page.

Creating the delete page

You've just created a link to the delete page; now you need to make the delete page do its stuff:

1. **Open the file *delete.php*.**

   This is where you'll paste the recordset that you copied a moment ago.

2. **Make sure the Bindings panel is open. Right-click (Control-click) in the empty area of the panel; from the shortcut menu, choose Paste.**

   Dreamweaver pastes all the programming code to create a recordset. This method is a fast way to reuse a recordset.

3. **In the Bindings panel, expand the recordset listing by clicking the small + button (arrow on Macs) to the left of the recordset.**

   Don't click the *large* + button, which lets you add additional recordsets. You just want to see an expanded listing of recordset columns so you can add some dynamic data to the page.

4. **Drag the "productName" column from the Bindings panel and drop it onto the document window, just to the right of the text "Product to delete".**

   This action inserts dynamic data into the page. When this page appears in a Web browser, the name of a product appears in bold type.

5. **Click the empty space just below the name of the product. Choose Insert → Form → Form.**

   A red, dotted line—the boundaries of the form—appears on the page. You need to set the form's *action* property (a URL to the page that collects the form information).

6. **In the Property inspector, click the action box, and then type *delete.php*.**

   Now when this form is submitted, its contents will be sent...to itself! This is a common maneuver with dynamic pages, which often do double duty depending on how you access them. In this case, when the form is submitted, the programming code (which you'll add in a minute) receives the request to delete a particular product. Instead of displaying the page and form again, it merely deletes the record from the database, and then redirects the browser to a different page (see page 929 for more detail on how this works).

7. **Click in the empty space between the form's red dotted boundaries. Choose Insert → Form → Button. (If the "Input Tag Accessibility Attributes" window appears, click Cancel to close it.)**

   Currently the button's label says Submit, but a more descriptive term like Delete would be better.

8. **In the Property inspector, change the Value box to read Delete.**

   This button, when clicked, will remove one product from the database. However, you need to identify the product as well. A hidden form field containing the product's ID number will do the trick.

9. **In the document window, click to the right of the button you just added, and then choose Insert → Form → Hidden Field.**

   When you view the Web page, you don't see a hidden field, but it provides useful information when the form is submitted. In this case, it needs to supply the product ID.

10. **With the hidden field selected, change its name in the Property inspector from *hiddenField* to *productID*.**

    This step and the next are similar to adding a parameter to the end of a URL (for example, to link from a list of records to a detail page for a single record). The only difference is that instead of placing the product's ID number in a URL, it's now embedded within a form. Now you need to add the product ID that's retrieved from the database.

11. **In the Property inspector, click the lightning bolt to the right of the value box.**

    The Dynamic Data window opens, displaying the rsProduct recordset.

12. **From the list of fields, select "productID", and then click OK to close the Dynamic Data window.**

    Now when someone views this page, the doomed product's ID number is stored in this hidden field.

13. **Open the Server Behaviors panel (Window → Server Behaviors). Click the + button, and then select Delete Record.**

    The Delete Record window appears (see Figure 24-23).

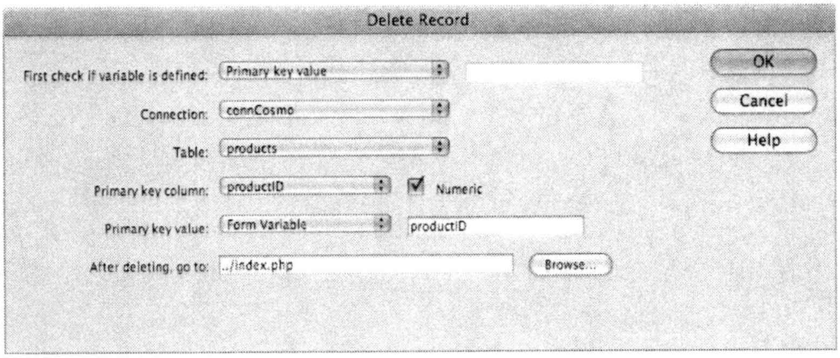

Figure 24-23: *The Delete Record behavior adds all the necessary programming code to remove a record from the database. All you need to make it work is a recordset that retrieves a single record—and a form with a Delete button and a hidden field containing the record's primary key value.*

14. **From the first menu, select Primary Key Value.**

    This step tells the server behavior that it shouldn't delete the record until it's given a primary key value (you define when this happens in steps 17 and 18 below).

15. **From the Connection pop-up menu, choose "connCosmo".**

    Now tell Dreamweaver which table the record belongs to.

16. **From the Table menu, choose "products".**

    This menu indicates the table containing the record that is to be deleted. You next have to specify the primary key (see page 831) of the record to delete.

17. **From the "Primary Key Column" menu, select "productID," and make sure the Numeric box is checked.**

    Now you need to let the server behavior know where the primary key value will be coming from. In this case, the ID number for the product to be deleted is embedded in a hidden form field named "productID".

18. **From the Primary Key Value field, choose Form Variable, and make sure "productID" appears in the box to the right.**

    To finish filling out this window, you'll just tell Dreamweaver which page should appear after someone deletes the record.

Note: It's important to choose Form Variable in step 18. Dreamweaver starts with the option "URL variable" selected. If you don't change this option, as soon as this page encounters a URL variable with the product ID number, it will delete that record. In other words, as soon as you get to this page (with the productID passed in the URL [see step 4 on page 949]) the product will be deleted and the innocent CosmoFarmer administrator will never have a chance to confirm the deletion.

19. **In the Property inspector, click the "Browse for File" button. In the root folder (cosmo_store), navigate to and select the file *index.php*.**

    The Delete Record window should now look like Figure 24-23.

20. **Click OK.**

    Dreamweaver adds the Delete Record server behavior to the page. You've done it! Now you need to test it out.

21. **Save and close this page. Open the *index.php* page. Press the F12 key (Option-F12) to preview it in a browser.**

    The page lists the products in the database. Take a closer look now at a specific item.

22. **Click the name of any product in the list.**

    A details page for that product appears.

23. **Click the Delete This Product link near the bottom.**

    The Delete Product page appears (see Figure 24-24). Notice that both the product name and a Delete button appear.

Figure 24-24: *When you first access the page (from a link on a product details page), it displays the confirmation shown here. But when the Delete button is clicked, the page is reloaded, and a Delete command is sent to the database.*

24. **Click the Delete button to remove the item.**

    Don't worry, you can always insert more products later! In any case, you'll note that that the product is no longer listed in the Product listings.

Of course, in the real world, you wouldn't want just anybody deleting, adding, or editing products on an e-commerce Web site. So in the next chapter, you'll learn how to keep prying eyes and mischievous fingers away from your coveted insert, update, and delete pages.

CHAPTER

25

Advanced Dynamic Site Features

Dreamweaver's basic database capabilities are impressive. But there may come a time when you need to dig deeper into the program to build successful Web applications. Dreamweaver's advanced features let you, the mere mortal, do things that the pros do every day, like password-protect pages; display (or hide) content based on database results; and access information from forms, cookies, and URLs.

Password-Protecting Web Pages

Although Dreamweaver lets you create Web pages that let others add, edit, and delete records from a database, your e-business wouldn't last very long if just *anyone* could remove orders from your online ordering system or view credit card information stored in your customers' records. And certainly your company's executives wouldn't be happy if someone accessed the staff directory database, and changed the boss's title to Chief Bozo. For these and other reasons, Dreamweaver provides a simple set of tools for locking your pages away from prying eyes.

The User Authentication server behaviors can password-protect any page on your site. With this feature, you can limit areas of your site to registered users only, let customers access and update their contact information, create maintenance pages accessible only to administrators, or personalize Web pages with customized messages ("Welcome back, Dave").

To password-protect pages on your site, you need to get several elements in order:

- A database table containing visitors' login information.

- A registration form for adding new visitors. (This is an optional step, but it's frequently useful when you want to automate the process of adding user login information to the database.)
- A login form.
- One or more pages that need to be password-protected.

The Users Table

To password protect your Web pages, your database must hold several pieces of information about the people who can access those secret pages. For example, each visitor must have a user name and password to type in when he attempts to log into your site. If the name and password match a record in the database, then Open Sesame: He's logged into the site and can access password-protected pages.

You might also need to include a field in the record for assigning an *access level* to each person. This way, your site can have multiple sections, accessible by different groups of people. Dreamweaver provides tools not only to require a proper name and password, but also to allow access to only those with the proper clearance level.

For example, if your site has a members-only section that publishes special content to registered visitors, you could assign the level of "member" to people who register, and give them access to these pages. However, you want only your site's administrators and staff to be able to update a product database or retrieve sales records, so you would give these users a level of "administrator" for access to these areas.

At a minimum, then, your database needs a users table with three fields (user name, password, and access level). You can either use a standalone table or incorporate this information into another table. For example, if you require people to provide their names, addresses, email addresses, and so on when registering, you could include the three login fields in this table. For an e-commerce system, login information could be stored in the table holding customer information.

Tip: Most database systems let you assign a default value to a column. That way, when someone creates a new record and supplies no information for the column, the application enters the default value instead.

For starters, it's a good idea to assign a default value for the access-level field. You can set your database to assign the lowest access level—"guest," say—whenever someone creates a new user record. In this way, if you use a Web form for collecting and creating a new member, you can omit a form field for assigning an access level. This method is a good security precaution, as adept (and malicious) Web surfers could submit a fake form with a higher access level, potentially granting them access to sensitive areas of your site.

Creating a Registration Form

Once you've added a users table to your database, you'll need a way to add new members. If you plan to use password protection for sensitive pages that only your site's staff should access, you probably *shouldn't* create a Web form for adding new administrative members. You'd run the risk of someone finding the form and adding herself to the list of administrators. In such cases, you're better off adding the proper login records in the database system itself—using phpMyAdmin, Microsoft Access, SQL Server, or MySQL Monitor, for example.

Note: If you do create a Web form for adding new members with a high access level, password-protect this form! Otherwise, anyone stumbling upon it could add new administrative members–and from there, Pandora's box would be open.

On the other hand, if you want to let *lots* of people sign up as members of your site, you might want to add a registration form that *automatically* adds them to the list of the site's members. This setup would free you from the headache of manually assigning user names and passwords for everyone who wants to become a member.

If the site already includes a form for collecting visitor information, then you can simply add the proper user fields to this form. Say your site includes a "Sign up for our email newsletter" page that collects a visitor's name, email address, and other contact information. You could add a field called *user name* and another called *password.*

Tip: Organizations often use an email address as a person's user name for password-protected pages. If you're already collecting an email address, then exclude the user name field from the form.

When the visitor submits the form, the Web application adds all these fields to the database. (To add records to a database using a Web form, see page 905.) While the process of creating a new member for password-protected pages is basically the same as adding a new record to a database, you do need to make sure that every visitor has a unique user name. That's because if more than one person has the same name, then you can't distinguish them from each other.

Fortunately, Dreamweaver's Check New User Name server behavior ensures that each user name submitted in the form is unique. If the name already exists, then the server doesn't add the new record to the database, and it redirects the visitor to another page. To apply this server behavior, follow these steps:

1. **Add an insert-record form to a dynamic page.**

   The form should include fields for a user name and password. You might also add a field for an access level, if that's how you've structured your site. However, for a form that's accessible to the public, it's best to use the database to set a default value for this; see the Tip on page 954. (You'll need to use Dreamweaver's Insert Record server behavior. Creating insert-record forms is described on page 906.)

2. **Make sure the Server Behaviors panel is open (Window → Server Behaviors). Click the Add (+) button and, from the pop-up menu, choose User Authentication → Check New Username.**

   In the Insert panel's Data category, you can also use the User Authentication menu (see Figure 25-1). Either way, the Check New Username window appears (see Figure 25-2).

Figure 25-1:
Dreamweaver provides access to all user-authentication server behaviors from the Insert panel's Data category. (Here, the Insert panel appears in one of its many guises: Classic view, as described on page 35.)

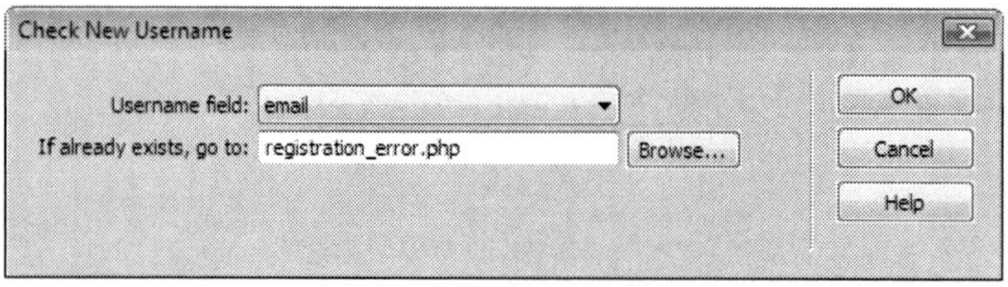

Figure 25-2:
When adding a new person to your database, the Check New Username server behavior lets you verify that the user name isn't already in use by another person.

3. **Select the name of the form field that captures the user name.**

   Note that this is the name of the form field *on the Web page*—not the name of the column in the *database*. Dreamweaver already knows which form field applies to which database column—the Insert Record server behavior takes care of that.

4. **Click Browse, and then select a Web page.**

   Here, choose the page that opens if the user name is already assigned to someone else. This page (which you should create before applying this behavior) should include a note to your visitor, clearly spelling out the problem (the user name just supplied is already in use and therefore unavailable). To make re-entering information easier for your guest, you should include the insert form on this page as well, or provide a link back to the registration form page.

5. **Click OK to close the window and add the server behavior to the page.**

   Now when someone fills out the registration form, this behavior kicks in and makes sure that no one else has the same user name.

Note: Registering a new member doesn't automatically log him into the site. He still needs to go to a login page (described next).

After inserting the server behavior, Dreamweaver lists it in the Server Behaviors panel. If you wish to change any of its properties, then in the panel, double-click Check New Username to reopen the Check New Username window (Figure 25-2). To delete the behavior, in the Server Behaviors panel, select it, and then click the Remove (minus sign [–]) button.

Creating the Login Page

To access a password-protected page, your visitor must first log into the site using a Web form. This simple Web form should contain just two fields—a user name field and a password field—and a Submit button.

When someone attempts to log in, the values she types into the form are compared with the user name and password columns in the database. If there's a match, then she's transported to another page—often the main page of a password-protected area of the site. If there's no matching record, then the visitor is carted away to a page of your creation—an "Access Denied!" page or maybe just the original login page.

To create a login page:

1. **Add a Web form to a dynamic Web page.**

   If your site includes password-protected pages aimed at a general audience of Web visitors, you could place this form on your home page. Or you could create a dedicated login page (remembering to provide links to this page throughout your site). However, if you're creating a login for administrators, you might want to put the login form out of the way, so that the average visitor doesn't notice it.

   Either way, the form should contain only a user name field, a password field, and a single Submit button. Naming the fields "username" and "password" (rather than keeping Dreamweaver's factory-set field names) helps with step 3.

2. **Open the Server Behaviors panel (Window → Server Behaviors). Click the + button, and then choose User Authentication → Log In User.**

   You can also use the Insert panel's Data category (see Figure 25-1) or choose Insert → Data Objects → User Authentication → Log In User to open the Log In User window (see Figure 25-3).

3. **From the first three menus, select the names of the login form, the form field for collecting the user name, and the password field, respectively.**

   You're telling Dreamweaver which form (if the page has more than one) and which fields to use for comparison to the users table in the database.

Tip: Dreamweaver automatically makes these first three menu selections for you if the following things are in place: You've got just one form on the page; the first field on that form is the user name field; and the second field is the password field.

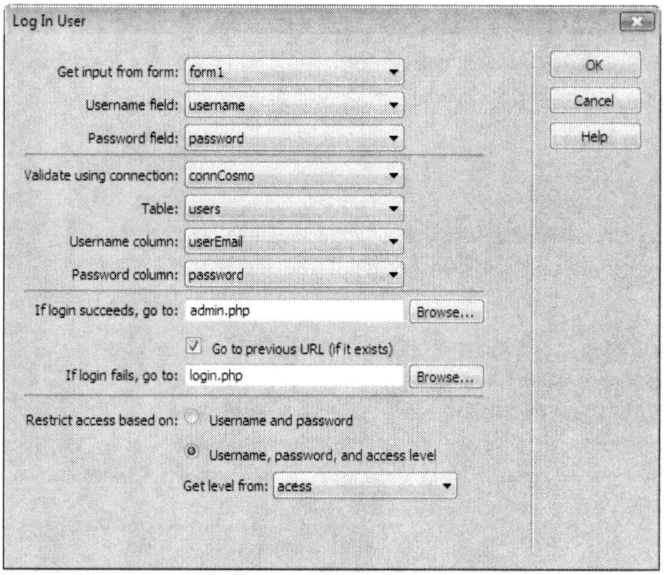

Figure 25-3: *Dreamweaver's Log In User server behavior gives visitors a way to log into your Web site, so they can visit password-protected pages. You have quite a few items to fill out here, but they're all straightforward. The last option lets you use access levels to limit pages of the site to particular groups of visitors–administrators, for example.*

4. **From the "Validate using connection" menu, choose the name of the database connection.**

   This name should be the database that contains the table with user login information.

5. **From the Table menu, choose the name of the users table.**

   This is the table described on page 954, which includes the username, password, and access level for anyone attempting to log in.

6. **From the "Username column" menu, select the database column that stores names. From the "Password column" menu, choose the database column for passwords.**

   The User Authentication server behavior searches these two database columns for a record that matches the values your visitor types into the form.

7. **To the right of the "If login succeeds" field, click the Browse button; navigate to and select a page from your site.**

   Most of the time, this is the main page for a password-protected area of the site. If the site contains a members-only section, then, after logging in, the visitor arrives at the Members page. If you're adding features for administering the site—adding, deleting, and editing database info, for example—then create a main Administrators page with links to all of the database administration pages.

8. **Turn on the "Go to previous URL" checkbox.**

   This option is a little confusing, but very convenient. Imagine a visitor stumbling across a password-protected page (you'll learn how to protect pages in the next section). He simply comes across a link to a password-protected page, and clicks it. Of course, since he hasn't logged in, he's denied access to the page and sent to another page. At this point, you're probably redirecting him to the login page, so he can log in and continue clicking his way through your site.

   That's where this feature comes in handy. By turning on this box, you permit the login form to take the visitor *back* to the page he couldn't get past at the outset. In other words, the visitor tries to access a password-protected page (*any* password-protected page in the site); he's not logged in, so he's sent to the login page. After successfully logging in, he's taken directly to the page he first tried to access (*not* the page you specified in step 7). This is very convenient for visitors who bookmark password-protected pages in your site, since it saves them the hassle of having to log in and then navigate to the page they wanted in the first place!

Note for PHP Users: While the "Go to Previous URL" option is convenient, it doesn't remember URL parameters from the previous page (this limitation is an issue in the PHP/MySQL server model only). For example, say you try to visit a page used for updating a record in a database: *update_record.php?recordID=2*. If the page is password-protected and you're not logged in, then you're sent to a login page. After successfully logging back in, you're returned to *update_record.php*, but the URL parameter *recordID=2* isn't available. In other words, returning to the previous URL doesn't end up giving you the page you wanted—for example, an edit form for record number 2.

---

9. **To the right of the "If login fails" field, click Browse; navigate to and select a page from your site.**

   This page, which you need to create in advance, should explain that the user name and password were not correct. Since the visitor may have just made a typo, it's polite to either include another login form on this page or a link back to the login page.

10. **If the database includes a column for storing an access level, then select the "Username, password, and access level" radio button.**

    This option not only lets folks log into the site, but also tracks their access levels. In this way, you can limit areas of your site to people with the proper access level—administrators, for example.

11. **From the "Get level from" pop-up menu, select the name of the database column that contains visitors' access levels.**

    Dreamweaver lists all the columns in the table you selected in step 5. If the table doesn't have a column for this information, then go to your database application and add it, or deselect the Access Level radio button. (Even if you don't currently have plans for offering different levels of access, it's a good idea to keep this option in mind. In the future, you may very well want to add special pages for administrators or Super Premium Members. Without an access level, anyone who has a user name and password can visit those pages.)

12. **Click OK to close the window and apply the behavior to the page.**

You can edit or delete this behavior by double-clicking its name in the Server Behaviors panel.

POWER USERS' CLINIC

Logging In: Behind the Scenes

The Log In User server behavior checks to see if the user name and password submitted by a form matches a user name and password in the database. If it does, the behavior generates two session variables (see page 968): MM_Username and MM_UserGroup for the PHP/MySQL server model, and MM_Username and MM_UserAuthorization for the other server models. The first one (MM_Username) stores the user name of the logged-in visitor; the second (MM_UserGroup or MM_UserAuthorization) stores the visitor's access level. (The MM stands for Macromedia, for the company that owned Dreamweaver before Adobe.) The variables follow visitors from page to page of the site, until they log out, close the browser, or don't do anything on the Web site for at least 20 minutes.

The password-protection scripts use these session variables to allow or deny access to a page. But you can take advantage of these variables in other ways. You can add MM_Username to the Bindings panel (see page 963), for example. You can then add it to your pages, like other dynamic data, for customized pages: "Welcome back *Kotter176@aol.com.*"

Furthermore, since each user name is unique—just like a primary key—you can use the session variable to filter records in a recordset (see page 847). You could use this technique, for instance, when a logged-in visitor wishes to see all his contact information. Create a recordset that filters the user table by the session variable.

You can also use the MM_UserGroup (PHP) or MM_UserAuthorization variable to control the display of certain areas of a page. For example, while regular members of your Web site might see a simple listing of products on a dynamic catalog page, administrators might see additional items like "Edit this product" and "Delete this product" buttons. The tutorial at the end of this chapter has an example of this scheme in action (see page 984).

The Log Out User Behavior

Dreamweaver's Log Out User server behavior lets someone log out by clicking a link. Thereafter, her Web browser can't load any password-protected pages in the site until she logs back in.

This setup is useful when a visitor shares her computer with others, maybe at the library or at school, because it provides a sense of security that she can log out. (It's not absolutely necessary, though; her computer destroys the cookie used to identify the session variable used to keep track of her login status, anyway, as soon as she quits her browser. Furthermore, if a certain amount of time passes without any activity—usually 20 minutes—the Web server automatically destroys the session variable, effectively logging out the visitor. Again, though, a logout link can be reassuring to your audience.)

To add a Log Out server behavior:

1. **Open a dynamic page.**

   Note that since this adds programming code to the page, it works only on dynamic pages. You can't add a logout link to a static HTML page. So if you want to provide this option on all pages of your site, then you have to save each page in your site as a PHP, ASP, or Cold Fusion page.

2. **Click the page where you'd like to add a logout link.**

   The logout link is just a regular link, so you can place this anywhere that makes sense, such as an option in the navigation bar, or a link in the page's footer. In addition, you can select text or an image that's already on the page to turn it into a logout link.

3. **Open the Server Behaviors panel (Window → Server Behaviors). Click the + button and, from the pop-up menu, choose User Authentication → Log Out User.**

   Alternatively you can use the Insert panel's Data category (see Figure 25-1) or choose Insert → Data Objects → User Authentication → Log Out User. In any case, the Log Out User window appears (see Figure 25-4).

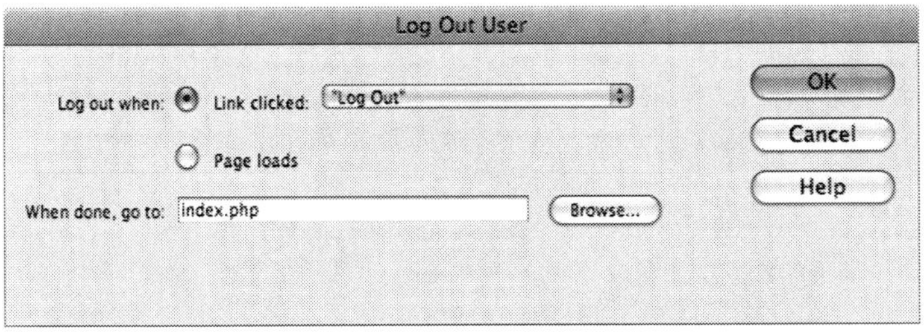

Figure 25-4: *To add a logout function to text or an image that's already on a page, simply select it, and then apply the Log Out User server behavior.*

4. **Select one of the two radio buttons.**

   A visitor can be logged out in two ways. You can log him out when a page loads or when he clicks a link. Use the first method when you want to automatically log someone out when he reaches a specific page. For example, say you create an online testing application, where students sit at a computer and answer page after page of questions. When students reach the last page of the quiz—maybe a page summarizing their results—you could automatically log them out. The next student sitting down at the same computer would have to log in, preventing the testing application from thinking the new test taker is the same person as the previous student.

   The second method lets visitors log themselves out by clicking a link, so the menu starts out reading, "Create new link: 'Log out'", which adds a new link with the words "Log out" to the page. After adding the behavior, you can then edit the page and change *Log out* to any text you like, or even add a graphic button to the link.

Tip: You can also first add some text like "Quit system", select it, and then apply the Log Out User server behavior. Dreamweaver automatically uses that text instead of its standard "Log Out" text when creating the link.

5. **Click Browse; navigate to and select a page from your site.**

   Good choices for this page are the login page—so the next visitor can log in—or the home page.

6. **Click OK.**

   You've just applied the link and server behavior.

Protecting Individual Pages

To password-protect a Web page, apply the "Restrict Access to Page" server behavior. You have to do this for each page you wish to protect, and you can apply it only to dynamic Web pages. In other words, you can't password-protect regular HTML files, text files, graphics, or any other file that isn't first processed by the application server.

Note: Although some Web servers let you password-protect an entire folder's worth of files, Dreamweaver doesn't give you any tools to do so. (If your site runs on an Apache Web server, however, you can use *.htaccess* files to password-protect an entire folder. You'll find a quick tutorial at *www.sitedeveloper.ws/tutorials/htaccess.htm*, and a free online tool for creating these files at *www.webmaster-toolkit.com/htaccess-generator.shtml*. Visit *http://apache.org/docs/howto/htaccess.html* for more information.)

The "Restrict Access to Page" behavior works like this: When someone attempts to load a password-protected page, programming code in the page determines whether she's already logged in. If the page also requires a particular access level—administrators only, for instance—it checks to see whether the visitor has the proper clearance as well; if so, the browser displays the page. If the visitor isn't logged in, however, or doesn't have the proper access level, then she's redirected to another page—like an "Access Denied" page or back to the login page.

To apply this server behavior, follow these steps:

1. **Open the dynamic page you wish to protect.**

   It must be a dynamic page that uses the site's server model (see page 818).

2. **Open the Server Behaviors panel (Window → Server Behaviors). Click the + button, and then choose User Authentication → "Restrict Access to Page".**

   The "Restrict Access to Page" window appears (see Figure 25-5).

3. **Turn on one of the two radio buttons.**

   If you want to allow access to anyone in the users table, then select the Username and Password buttons. However, if you want to limit the page to visitors with a particular access level, then turn on the second button.

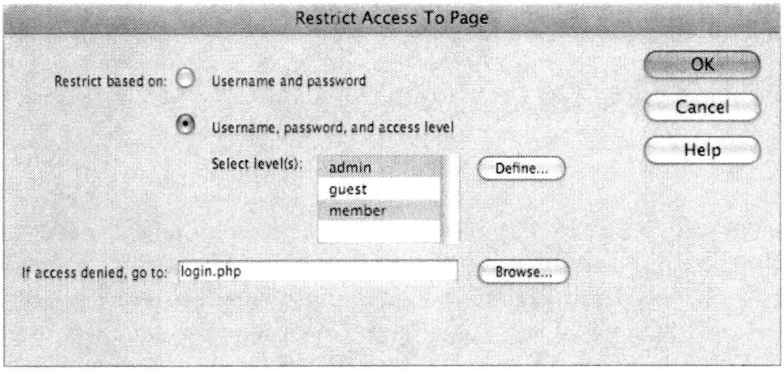

Figure 25-5:
If you want to give access to more than one group, you can Ctrl-click (⌘-click) more than one level in the Select Levels list to highlight them simultaneously.

The first time you use this behavior, you have to define the different access levels, so click Define. You must type in each access level exactly as it appears in the database—*admin, member*, and *guest*, for example. Capitalization counts.

You need to define these access levels only once. Dreamweaver remembers these settings for other dynamic pages in the same site.

4. **Click Browse; navigate to and select the page people see if they aren't logged in.**

   It's often a good idea to simply dump unregistered visitors onto the login page. That way, if they're legitimate customers, they can simply log in and return to the page. (Dreamweaver can help with this. See step 8 on page 958.)

5. **Click OK to apply the link and server behavior.**

Like the other server behaviors, Dreamweaver lists the "Restrict Access to Page" behavior in the Server Behaviors panel after it's applied. If you wish to change any of its properties, in the panel, double-click its name. To delete the behavior, in the Server Behaviors panel, select it, and then click the minus (–) button.

Additional Data Sources

So far, you've been using Dreamweaver's dynamic page-building features to retrieve information from databases to build catalog pages, product detail pages, and other pages that require database-generated content. But occasionally you want to collect data from other sources and add them to your page. For example, when someone logs into a site (see the Log In User server behavior on page 957), her user name travels along with her from page to page in what's called a *session variable*. Using the Bindings panel, you can capture this session name, and then use it on a Web page.

Similarly, you can create *cookies* to store small pieces of information on a person's computer—such as a counter tracking how many times he's been to your site—and use Dreamweaver's Bindings panel to add that information to a Web page.

The Bindings panel lets you access these sources of data, as well as information submitted from form fields and embedded in URLs. You can add any number of other data sources to the Bindings panel (see Figure 25-6), and then add those data sources to your Web page. Adding one of these sources to a page automatically inserts the programming code needed to retrieve the information stored in the data source. It's important to make clear that Dreamweaver isn't *creating* these various data sources—such as cookies, URL variables, or session variables—when you add them to the Bindings panel. Dreamweaver is just providing an easy way to add the programming necessary to access the value of already created variables. For example, adding a cookie variable to the Bindings panel doesn't actually create a cookie on a visitor's system; it just lets you add the programming necessary to read a cookie and use the cookie's contents on a page. (For information on creating cookies, see page 967.)

Regardless of the type of dynamic data you wish to add, the process of accessing these data sources is essentially the same. It differs only among server models; details in the sections that follow.

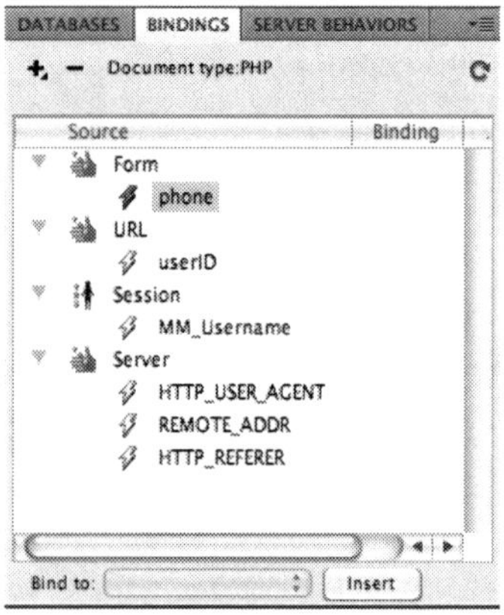

Figure 25-6:
Once you add a data source to the Bindings panel, you can add that data source to your page, just as you would dynamic data from a recordset (see page 921). For example, you can drag the source from the Bindings panel and drop it onto a page, or click somewhere on a page, select the item in the Bindings panel, and then click the panel's Insert button. The result? Dreamweaver adds the proper programming code required to access the value stored in that data source.

For PHP and ColdFusion

1. **In the Bindings panel, click the + button, and then select the proper variable type: URL, Form, Cookie, or whatever (see Figure 25-7).**

   A window appears for the particular type of data source.

2. **In the Name field, type the name of the variable.**

   Capitalization matters; *username, UserName*, and *USERNAME* are all different variables. Find a system you're comfortable with (all lowercase, all uppercase, or mixed case) and stick with it.

3. **Click OK.**

   Dreamweaver adds the variable to the Bindings panel.

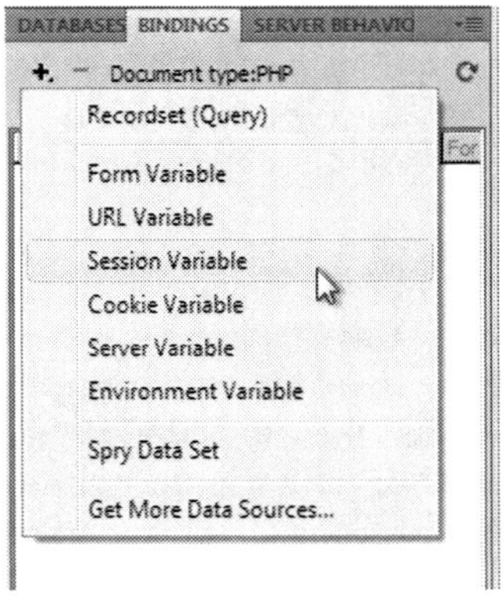

Figure 25-7:
Recordsets aren't the only type of data you can add to the Bindings panel. You can add the names of cookies, session variables, form fields, and other data sources to the Bindings panel, and then drag them onto the page. The XML Dataset option is new in Dreamweaver CS4, and it's part of the Spry data tools discussed on page 518.

For ASP

1. **In the Bindings panel, click the + button. Depending on the type of dynamic data you're interested in, select either Request Variable, Session Variable, or Application Variable.**

   In ASP, Request Variable covers a wide range of data sources, including form variables, URL variables, cookies, and server variables, so there's an extra step you must perform. After selecting Request Variable to open the Request Variable window (see Figure 25-8), from the Type menu, choose a type of variable.

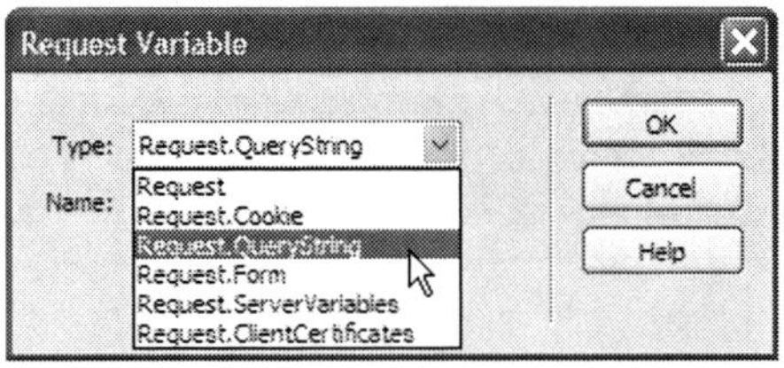

Figure 25-8:
The Request Variable window (for the ASP server model only) lets you add a wide variety of variable types for use in an ASP page. "Request.QueryString" is ASP's way of referring to a URL variable.

2. **Into the Name field, type the name of the variable.**

   Capitalization doesn't matter. To ASP, *username, UserName*, and *USERNAME* are all the same.

3. **Click OK.**

   Dreamweaver adds the variable to the Bindings panel.

Tip: You can drag data sources listed in the Bindings panel into Code view, as well. Once you've got your programming chops sharpened, this trick is helpful for quickly adding data to your own server-side programs.

URL Variables

Some URLs include information tagged onto the end of the name of a Web page, like this: *www.cosmofarmer.com/product.php?productID=10&action=delete.* The information following the ? is known as a *query string*, and it provides additional information to a dynamic page.

In most cases, this information comes in the form of one or more name/value pairs, which Dreamweaver refers to as *URL variables*. This example has two URL variables: The first is named *productID*, and its value is *10*; the second is named *action*, and its value is *delete*. URL variables are often used to transfer specific information for use in a recordset. You saw an example of this in the tutorial in Chapter 23: The number of a particular product was passed in a URL to the product details page, which used this number to retrieve details on a particular item.

You can also add a URL variable to the Bindings panel, and then include it in a Web page or use it anywhere you'd use a dynamic data source. For example, you can use it as a parameter added onto the end of a link to hand off the information to another page.

Keep in mind that a page that links *to* the page using the URL variable must include the proper query string in the link. For example, say you add a URL variable named "username" to the page *crop_circles.html*; the page uses the query string to personalize the page: "Welcome, [username]". For this to work, you then need to link to the *crop_circles.html* page with the query string attached to the URL, like this: *crop_circles.html?username=bob*. You can add a URL variable to a link using the methods described on page 853.

Tip: Don't use this method for accessing private or sensitive data. For example, suppose you use a URL variable as a method for accessing the personal data of one of your customers, like this: *customer_data.asp?customerID=78*. A nefarious visitor could just change the number in the URL to, say, 79 to view all the personal data for customer number 79.

Form Variables

You can also add information from *forms* to the Bindings panel, and use them on your page. If you add a form on one page, you can then collect that information on the page the form submits to (the same page specified in the form's *Action* property, as described on page 433). In other words, the page receiving the form data can display that information on the page *or* use it in some other fashion—such as inserting the information into the database, or creating a cookie or session variable.

If you're mainly using forms in conjunction with Dreamweaver's Insert Record and Update Record server behaviors, you won't generally take advantage of form variables. Those two behaviors work by collecting data from a form, adding or updating a database record, and then redirecting the Web browser to another page. The page the visitor finally sees never has access to the form information, so you can't add any form variables to that page.

However, adding a form variable to the Bindings panel can come in handy when you create a search page. For example, suppose you've created a page for searching a database. The search form lets the visitor type in a name—of an author or musician, for instance. You could then create a search *results* page that looks in the database for any records that match the search term. On that page, along with the database results, you could add text like "Search Results for: [search_term]", where *search_term* would be the word the visitor typed into the form. Just add the form variable to the Bindings panel, and then drag it to the spot in the search page where you wish it to appear.

Note: If you use the GET method for submitting a form, the names and values of each form field are included in the URL. In this case, they're considered URL variables, so if you wish to add any of these fields to the Bindings panel, use the URL variable method instead. (For the difference between GET and POST, see page 434.)

Cookies

One problem with Web servers is that they have no memory.

Suppose, for example, that a site has a particularly long and annoying Flash movie that welcomes visitors with an ear-pounding, eye-throbbing multimedia display. Even if the designer was kind enough to include a "Skip this nauseating display" button, the Web server doesn't remember that you clicked it the *last* time you were there.

To overcome this limitation, most Web browsers can store *cookies*—small text files containing specific information—that Web servers create and read. In the example above, the Web server could drop a cookie onto your computer when you click the "Skip intro" button. The next time you visit the site, the Web server reads the cookie and kindly ushers you past the Flash movie and directly to the home page.

You can use cookies to store information on visitors' computers, too. They're a great way to store customer ID numbers, the number of visits to a particular page, and other bits of identifying information.

Cookies play by a few rules:

- **A single cookie is stored on just one browser and one computer at a time.** If you log onto a site that adds a cookie to your computer, and then log on again later from the public library, that computer doesn't have access to the cookie. In fact, if you use a different Web browser on the *same computer*, the Web server can't read the original cookie from the other browser. (A variation: In some corporations, a Web browser stores cookies on a network server. This kind of cookie *can* be accessed by a particular browser—Internet Explorer, for example—on different computers on the network.)
- **Only the domain that created the cookie can read it.** *You* can't create dynamic pages that read a cookie set by Amazon.com, for example. Fortunately, that means other Web sites can't read the cookies you set on your visitors' computers, either.

- **Web browsers limit the size of a cookie to 4 KB**, and allow only a limited number of total cookies (usually 300) per computer so that hard drives don't crumble under their weight.

You can add a cookie to the Bindings panel using the method described on page 963. Unfortunately, Dreamweaver doesn't give you any tools for creating cookies (you can submit feature requests for the next version of Dreamweaver on the Adobe Web site at *www.adobe.com/cfusion/mmform/index.cfm?name=wishform*). Several third-party developers have risen to the occasion, however:

- **PHP developers.** Dreamweaver Extension developer Felice Di Stefano has developed a free cookie extension for the PHP server model. It includes server behaviors for adding and deleting cookies from a PHP page. In addition, it can set a cookie to the value of a form field, or redirect a visitor to another page if a specific cookie doesn't exist, or if it matches a particular value. You can find it at the Adobe Exchange (page 814) or at *www.felixone.it*.
- **JavaScript cookies.** You can also use JavaScript to set cookies. This technique works with any type of page—even non-dynamic pages. The only catch is that the visitor's browser must both understand JavaScript and have JavaScript enabled (most do). Dreamweaver comes with two Snippets for setting and reading cookies using JavaScript. They're in the Snippets panel's JavaScript folder, in the cookies folder. See Chapter 18 to learn about Snippets. For the king of JavaScript cookie creators, check out WebAssist's Cookies Toolkit at *www.webassist.com/professional/products/productdetails.asp?PID=109* (this is a commercial product that runs around $50 and also includes tools for adding cookies using server-side tools for PHP).

Session Variables

Web servers don't know or care whether the person requesting your company's home page just placed a $10 million order or is a first-time visitor. Of course, *you* probably care, and so do most Web applications, which need to follow visitors as they travel through a site. For example, in a typical e-commerce site, people use a "shopping cart" to store items they're interested in purchasing. For this to work, however, you need to track each shopper's movement from page to page.

To make this possible, most Web servers recognize what are called *session variables*. A session variable is created by the Web developer (or, more accurately, by a dynamic Web page that creates the variable) and follows the visitor from page to page. This type of variable lasts, logically enough, for a single *session*: If the visitor closes the browser, then the session ends and the variable disappears. Most Web servers also add a limited time that the variable sticks around—usually 20 minutes. In other words, if the visitor doesn't hit any page in the site for 20 minutes, the Web server assumes that he's no longer around, and destroys the session variable.

Note: Session variables take up resources from the Web server. That's why a Web server gets rid of them as soon as it can. Creating lots of session variables for a busy Web site can slow down the server.

POWER USERS' CLINIC

Adding and Deleting Cookies Using PHP Pages

While Dreamweaver doesn't provide a tool for adding the scripts necessary to create and delete cookies with PHP pages, it isn't difficult to add the code yourself. (Dreamweaver can easily retrieve cookie information, as described on page 967.)

First, decide which page should add the cookie. The script runs when a visitor's browser *requests* the page, sending the cookie to the browser before the page content. Thus, you could add a script like this at the beginning of a page that receives and processes form information. For example, if someone registers at your site, then your script can store the name he enters in the registration form as a cookie on his computer. When he returns to the site, the home page can then read the cookie and display a message like "Welcome back, Bob."

To add a cookie, switch into Code view (page 395), and then put the following code (all on one line) above the <!DOC-TYPE> declaration in the HTML code of the page.

```
<?php setcookie("name_of_cookie", "value_
of_cookie", time()+2419200); ?>
```

Remember to include the opening "<?php" and closing "?>", which tell the application server that everything in between is programming code and not HTML. Replace *name_of_cookie* with whatever name you wish to give the cookie: *username*, for example. Also replace *value_of_cookie* with whatever you want to store in the cookie. In many cases, this is a dynamic value—information from a recordset, a URL variable, or a form variable, for example. Using the steps described on page 963, add the appropriate dynamic data to the Bindings panel, and then drag it into the code, replacing the text (including the quote marks) "value of cookie".

Finally, you can set the amount of time the cookie stays on the visitor's computer. That's the *time()+2419200* in the code above. Essentially you're saying that the cookie should stick around for a certain number of seconds (2419200) after the current moment (time()). In this case, 2419200 is 30 days or about 1 month. If you want the cookie to stick around for an hour, use 3600; for 1 day, use 86400.

PHP is a little persnickety about where you place this code: It has to come before all the code in the page, with the exception of other PHP code. If there's even just a single blank line (not within the <?php ?> tags), you end up with the much-dreaded "Headers already sent" error.

You can, however, place the code *after* other PHP code at the beginning of the file. For example, if you want to set the value of a cookie using information retrieved from a recordset, then you need to place the cookie code *after* the recordset code.

You may also want to delete a cookie at some point. For example, on an e-commerce site, you can use a cookie to store items a visitor adds to her shopping cart. When she wants to empty her cart—after she purchases everything in it, for example—you could simply delete the cookie. Just assign no value and a time in the past (no kidding) to the cookie you wish to delete, like this:

```
<?php setcookie('name_of_cookie', '',
time()-3600); ?>
```

Again, make sure you type the above code on a single line in the Code view of your page.

When it creates a session variable, the Web server sends a cookie to the visitor's machine. The cookie contains a unique number (not the actual data contained in the variable), which the server uses to keep track of each visitor. When that person requests a page, the Web server reads the cookie with the unique ID. It can then retrieve session variables for that individual. For this reason, session variables don't work if the visitor's Web browser doesn't accept cookies. (PHP, however, has a built-in method for maintaining session information even when cookies aren't turned on.)

Note: Dreamweaver itself creates session variables when you use the User Authentication server behaviors. See the box on page 960 for a discussion of these session variables, and how you can use them.

You may be wondering how cookies and session variables differ, and when you'd want to use one over the other. The difference is that cookies can last between visits. If you want access to a piece of information when a visitor comes back tomorrow, or next week, or next month, use a cookie. For example, you'd use a cookie to remember a selection someone made from a previous visit, such as "Skip this crazy Flash Intro."

Session variables, on the other hand, provide better security. The actual information stored in the session variable stays on the Web server, while cookies exist as text files on a visitor's computer and can be opened and read by anyone with access to the computer. Accordingly, if you need to keep track of a confidential piece of information (someone's bank account password, for example), use a session variable.

You can add a session variable to the Bindings panel using the method described on page 963.

Unfortunately, as with cookies, Dreamweaver doesn't provide any tools for creating or destroying session variables. To find third-party extensions that work with session variables, try the Adobe Exchange (*www.adobe.com/exchange*). Click the Dreamweaver link, and search using the term *session*.

Note for PHP Users: Felice Di Stefano has developed a free session extension for the PHP server model. It includes server behaviors for adding and deleting session variables from a PHP page. You can find it at the Adobe Exchange or at *www.felixone.it*.

Server Variables

Web servers collect and produce lots of information, much of which is hidden from the everyday Web surfer (and even the everyday Webmaster). Some of that information is obscure, but some can come in handy. For example, you can find out which Web browser the visitor is using, or which language the browser uses. While the exact list of server variables differs by Web server, here are some useful variables that work on many Web servers:

- HTTP_USER_AGENT. Information about the browser visiting the page. Unfortunately, you don't get a neat little summary like *Firefox 2 for Windows*. Instead, browser info is usually rather long-winded, like: *Mozilla/5.0 (Windows; U; Windows NT 6.0; en-US; rv:1.8.1.2) Gecko/20070219 Firefox/2.0.0.2*. To decipher this confusing jumble of information, visit *www.user-agents.org*.
- REMOTE_ADDR. The IP address of the computer requesting the Web page. It'll look something like 65.57.83.12. Depending on the visitor's setup, this could be the exact address of the computer. (Big Brother, where art thou?)

POWER USERS' CLINIC

Adding and Deleting Session Variables Using PHP Pages

While Dreamweaver doesn't provide a simple wizard for adding the code necessary to create and delete session variables with PHP pages, it isn't difficult to add it yourself. (Dreamweaver does, however, make quick work of *retrieving* session variables; see page 968.)

The procedure is much like the one for adding cookies (see the box on page 969)—for example, here again, the script runs when a visitor requests the page. When people register at your site, therefore, the email addresses they enter in the registration form could be stored as a session variable.

To add a session variable, you must do two things. First, in Code view (page 395), add this code (on a single line) near the top of the file:

```
<?php if (!isset($_SESSION)) session_
start(); ?>
```

This code simply alerts PHP that you wish to use session variables on this page (if you omit this line, you can't set or read session variables). As when setting a cookie, you can't have any HTML or even empty space before this line or you get a "Headers already sent" error. Next, you set the session variable.

```
<?php $_SESSION['name_of_variable']
='value_of_variable'; ?>
```

Replace *name of variable* with whatever name you wish to give the session variable: *email*, for example. Also replace *value of variable* with whatever you want to store in the session variable. In many cases, this value will be a dynamic value, like information from a recordset, a URL variable, or a form variable. Using the steps described on page 962, add the appropriate dynamic data to the Bindings panel, and then drag it into the spot in the code in the previous column just after the = sign (in this case, omit the set of quote marks: ''). As with cookies, *where* you place the session-creating code determines *when* it kicks in. So if you want to set a session with a value from a recordset, then place the session code after the code that creates the recordset.

You may also want to delete a session variable to conserve server resources. (Dreamweaver's Log Out User server behavior uses this method to log a visitor out of a site.) To delete a server variable, add this code to the beginning of a page:

```
<?php unset($_SESSION['name_of_
variable']); ?>
```

To delete all session variables for a particular individual in one fell swoop, use this code:

```
<?php
if (isset($_SESSION)) {
  session_destroy();
}
?>
```

Knowing this address has its uses. If someone frequently causes problems on your site—posts phony information to registration forms, say, or submits offensive messages to a message board—one potential solution is to prevent submissions to your database from that particular IP address. (However, since many users' IP addresses frequently change, this solution isn't foolproof.)

- **HTTP_REFERER**. This is the URL of the page that *leads* to the current page. For example, say you click a link on page A to get to page B. Page B's HTTP_REFERER server variable would be A.

You can use this knowledge to create the ultimate Back button. Simply add the HTTP_REFERER server variable to the Bindings panel. Then add a link to whatever you wish to be the Back button—graphic or text—and use the server variable as the link. When visitors click this link, it takes them back to whichever page brought them there in the first place.

For a list of server variables for use with the Apache Web server (the server most commonly used with PHP), visit *www.php.net/reserved.variables*. For a list of server variables supported by Microsoft's IIS Web server, visit the Microsoft Developer's Network site at *http://msdn2.microsoft.com/en-us/library/ms524602*.

Advanced Server Behaviors

In addition to the server behaviors described already, two other sets of behaviors come in handy on dynamic Web pages.

Tip: You can download many more third-party server behaviors from the Adobe Exchange. In the Server Behaviors panel, click the + button, and then choose Get More Server Behaviors. Dreamweaver launches your Web browser and connects to the Dreamweaver Exchange site.

Not all extensions listed here work with Dreamweaver CS4. On the other hand, many of the server behaviors for Dreamweaver 8 also work with Dreamweaver CS4.

Recordset Paging

This set of four different behaviors lets you add links for jumping to different records in a recordset (straight to the last record, for example). In fact, Dreamweaver makes use of these same behaviors as part of its Recordset Navigation Bar object (page 870). You use these for moving through a long list of records, like a complete listing of products in a database.

To begin, add a recordset to a page. It should contain multiple records, since jumping to the *next* record when there's only one doesn't make much sense. The page could also contain a repeating region, so that several records appear.

You can add the recordset-paging server behaviors from the Server Behaviors panel, or on the Insert bar's Data category, from the recordset-paging menu (circled in Figure 25-9):

- **Move to First Page** adds a link that jumps to the first record in the recordset.

Note: In ASP, you see the word "Record" instead of "Page" in this example and the following ones. For instance, you see "Move to First Record" instead of "Move to First Page".

- **Move to Previous Page** adds a link that jumps to the record before the current record. If you use a Repeating Region, then it jumps to the previous *set* of records. For example, say you create a Repeating Region that displays five records at a time. If the page currently displays records 6–10, clicking a link with this server behavior applied to it causes records 1–5 to appear.
- **Move to Next Page** adds a link that jumps to the next set of records in the recordset.
- **Move to Last Page** adds a link that goes to the last set of records in the recordset.

Figure 25-9:
You can create your own recordset navigation controls using the recordset-paging server behaviors.

Using any of the four behaviors involves the same steps:

1. **Create a recordset, and then add dynamic content to the page.**

   For example, you could create a list of all the products your company sells. The recordset should contain at least enough records to span several pages. (You wouldn't use any of these behaviors if you displayed *all* the records on a single page.)

2. **Click the page where you wish to insert the link.**

   You can also select an item on the page—text or a graphic—that you'd like to turn into a link.

3. **From the Server Behaviors panel, click the + button. Select Recordset Paging, and then choose a behavior from the submenu.**

   The window for the particular server behavior appears (see Figure 25-10).

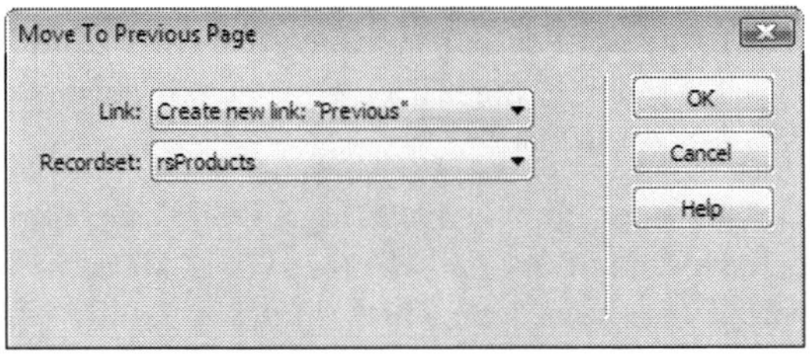

Figure 25-10:
The recordset-paging behaviors–like the "Move to Previous Page" behavior–can add a new link with preset text (for example, "Previous"), or add a link to text or an image you've selected on the page. You can also use the menu to select any link already on the page. That's usually not a good idea, however, since Dreamweaver erases whatever link was previously applied.

4. **From the Recordset menu, choose a recordset.**

   This is the recordset the behavior will move through.

5. **Click OK.**

   Dreamweaver adds the server behavior to the page, and adds its name to the Server Behaviors panel.

Show Region Server Behaviors

At times, you'll want to display different information on a page based on the results of a recordset. For example, if a visitor searches your site's database of products for a product you don't sell, then the search results page should say something like, "Sorry, we don't carry alligator skin bicycle seats." But if someone searches for a product you *do* sell, then the page should present the relevant details for that product. The Web page displays different text depending upon whether the search item was in the recordset.

Dreamweaver provides three sets of server behaviors that let you display any selection of HTML based on the results of a recordset (Figure 25-11):

- **Show If Recordset Empty.** If the recordset retrieves no records, then this behavior makes the selected HTML appear in the browser window.

  This behavior comes in handy for a search page. On the search results page, apply it to some text like "We're sorry, your search retrieved no results", and you've got yourself a friendly solution for searches that turn up empty. This sever behavior is also handy for any page that displays detailed information about a single record, such as a detail page (page 879) or an update record page (page 912). Both those pages depend on retrieving data from the database, and are most often accessed using a URL variable like *product_details.php?productID=14*. If someone visits a page like that without the URL variable (for example, *product_details.php*), then she'll end up with a blank page. Use the Show If Recordset Empty behavior to list a message like "No product specified. Click here for a list of products."

- **Show If Recordset Not Empty.** If the recordset retrieves *any* records, then this behavior causes the selected HTML to appear in the browser window: a list of search results or details on a specific database record, for example. You'll often use this server behavior along with the Show If Recordset Empty server behavior. In this case, select the stuff you want to appear when a record is found: From the previous examples, you'd select all the HTML and code displaying the details of the record, or the record update form.

- **Show If First Page.** This server behavior, like the next three, works in conjunction with recordset-paging behaviors. It makes the selected HTML appear when the page displays the *first* record of a recordset, which comes in handy when you want to let people step through several pages of records.

- **Show If Not First Page** is the opposite of the previous one. If the page *does not* contain the first record in a recordset, then the selected HTML appears.

Dreamweaver makes use of this behavior in its Recordset Navigation Bar (see page 870). In that case, if the page displays anything *except* the first set of records in a recordset, then the First Item and Previous Page links appear. If the page *does* display the first item in a recordset, those links are hidden. (After all, you can't very well view the Previous Page if you're on page 1.)

- **Show If Last Page** functions just like the Show If First Page behavior, but for the last record in a recordset.
- **Show If Not Last Page** functions just like the Show If Not First Page behavior, but for the last record in a recordset. Dreamweaver uses this behavior to hide or show the Next Page and Last Item links in the Recordset Navigation Bar on the last page of records (page 870).

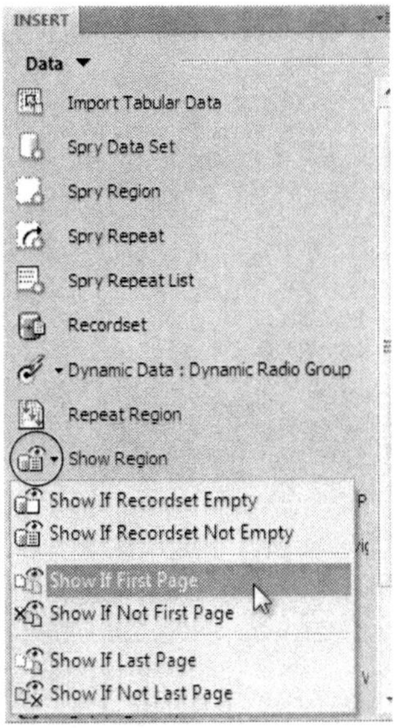

Figure 25-11:
The Show Region server behaviors are available on the Insert panel's Data category (shown here), the Insert → Data Objects → Show Region menu, and the Server Behaviors panel.

You can use these behaviors to show any selected object on the page—a paragraph of text, an image, a table, and so on. Your page can contain any combinations of these behaviors, and you can use any behavior two or more times to display multiple areas of a page. For example, maybe you'd like two things to appear when the recordset successfully retrieves a record: a graphic in the page's sidebar, and a message in the main area of the page. You'd apply the Show If Recordset Not Empty server behavior twice; once for each selection of HTML (the graphic and the message).

You'll often use these behaviors in pairs. For example, a search results page should include both the Show If Recordset Empty behavior to display a "no results" message, and a Show If Recordset Not Empty behavior to display the search results.

To apply any of these behaviors:

1. **Create a dynamic page containing a recordset.**

   This page could be a search results page or a master page that lists many records from the database.

2. **Select the HTML you wish to show based on a recordset outcome.**

   For example, when applying a Show If Recordset Is Empty server behavior to a search result page, select the message that should appear if the search returns no results.

3. **Open the Server Behaviors panel (Window → Server Behaviors). Click the + button, select Show Region, and, from the submenu, choose one of the six behaviors.**

   A window looking like Figure 25-12 appears. While the title of the window varies depending on which behavior you selected, each of the six behaviors has just this one option.

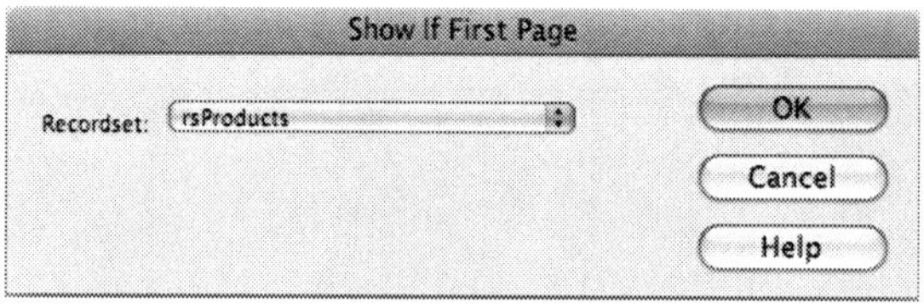

Figure 25-12: *Regardless of which of the Show Region server behaviors you apply, you can choose only one option: the recordset whose results control the display of the region.*

Note: The last four behaviors–Show If First Page, Show If Not First Page, Show If Last Page, and Show If Not Last Page–work only on pages that also have one of the recordset-paging server behaviors (discussed on page 972) applied.

4. **Select the name of the recordset from the menu, and then click OK.**

   The recordset you select should be the one whose results you're interested in. For example, on a search results page, you'd select the recordset you created to perform the search.

After applying one of these behaviors to a selection of HTML, a gray line appears around the selection, and a gray tab appears bearing the words "Show If". That area appears if the given recordset condition is met (for example, if the page is displaying the last record of the recordset).

To remove a Show Region server behavior, in the Server Behaviors panel, select its name, and click the minus (–) button (or press the Delete key). Doing so removes the gray tab and outline. Now the affected HTML appears regardless of the recordset results.

Note for PHP Users: An extension called PHP Show If Recordset Field Condition Is True (available for free on the Adobe Exchange site) lets you display part of a page when a field from a recordset matches a certain condition. Suppose, for example, that you have a products database with a field that records whether a particular item is for sale. If the item is indeed for sale, then you can use this behavior to display a large "For Sale" graphic on the product's detail page.

Tutorial: Authentication

In the tutorial at the end of Chapter 24, you created Web pages that could add, delete, and update records in the *CosmoFarmer* database. But you don't want to allow just anyone who visits the Web site to access these pages, let alone delete products from the site. So in this tutorial, you're going to learn how to password-protect these sensitive, mission-critical Web pages.

The following steps assume that you've worked through the tutorial in Chapter 24, and you have all the completed files ready to go. You'll build on them in the following steps.

Building a Login Page

The first step is to create a login page—a simple form with fields for a user name and password. After a successful login from this page, an administrator can access the administration pages:

1. **In the site's admin folder, open the file *login.php*.**

   This page contains the form for typing in an administrator's user name and password. You'll add the form next.

2. **Click in the empty space directly below the headline "Administrator Login". Choose Insert → Form → Form.**

   Dreamweaver adds a red dashed line to the page, indicating the beginning and ending <form> tags.

3. **In the Property inspector, type *login* as the name of the form.**

   While this step isn't required, it's good to get into the habit of assigning your forms descriptive names. Next, you'll add a box for entering a user name.

Note: The next steps assume you have the Form Accessibility feature turned on (see page 435). To make sure this is in fact the case, open the Preferences window by choosing Edit → Preferences (Dreamweaver → Preferences), select the Accessibility category, and make sure the Form Objects checkbox is turned on.

4. **Choose Insert → Form → Text Field.**

   The Input Tag Accessibility Attributes window appears (Figure 25-13). You'll add a label that'll appear next to the form field on the page.

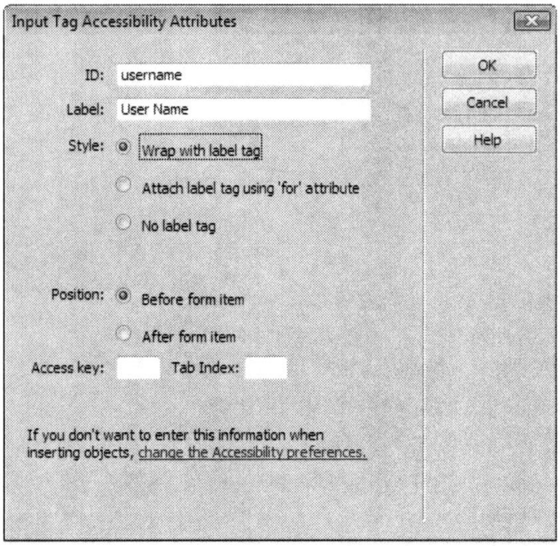

Figure 25-13:
Dreamweaver's Accessibility features let you add helpful controls–including a descriptive label–to form elements. Setting the ID adds an ID property to the field (see step 3 on page 436), which is useful for adding CSS or using JavaScript to control the field. In addition, Dreamweaver uses the ID you supply for the field's name.

Note: You can also use the Insert panel's Forms category to add forms and form objects to your page, as described on page 431.

5. **In the ID box, type *username*; in the Label box, type *User Name:*; select the "Wrap with label tag" and "Before form item" buttons, and then click OK.**

   Dreamweaver inserts a text field with a descriptive label.

6. **In the Property inspector, from the Formatting menu, choose Paragraph.**

   This step wraps a paragraph tag around the label and form field. You now need to add a password field.

7. **Click to the right of the form field you just inserted, and then press the Enter (Return) key to add a new paragraph.**

   The routine for adding the next form field is the same.

8. **Choose Insert → Form → Text Field. In the window that appears, in the ID box, type *password*; in the label box, type *Password:;* and then click OK.**

   This step inserts another form field and label.

9. **Select the new form field and, in the Property inspector, turn on the Password radio button.**

   By turning this form element into a password field, anything your visitors type in the field is displayed like this **** or this ••••, hiding the secret password from nosy passersby watching over their shoulders.

   To complete the form, you'll add a Submit button.

10. **In the document window, click to the right of the password field, and then press the Enter (Return) key. Choose Insert → Form → Button.**

    The Accessibility window appears yet again. In this case, however, you don't need to add a label, since text appears directly on the button.

11. **Click Cancel to close the Accessibility window and insert a Submit button. Select the new button and, in the Property inspector, change its value to Login.**

    The form is complete. Now it's time to let Dreamweaver do its magic.

12. **Choose Window → Server Behaviors to open the Server Behaviors window.**

    Alternatively, you can use the keyboard shortcut Ctrl+F9 (⌘-F9).

13. **Click the + button, and then choose User Authentication → Log In User.**

    The Log In User window appears (see Figure 25-14). The first three items should already be filled out: the name of the form, the name of the user name field, and the name of the password field. If you had more than one form on the page, or additional fields inside the one form, you'd have to tell Dreamweaver which form and which fields to use for collecting the login information.

14. **From the "Validate using connection" pop-up menu, select "connCosmo".**

    This step indicates which database contains the login information. You also need to specify which table and columns contain the user name and password.

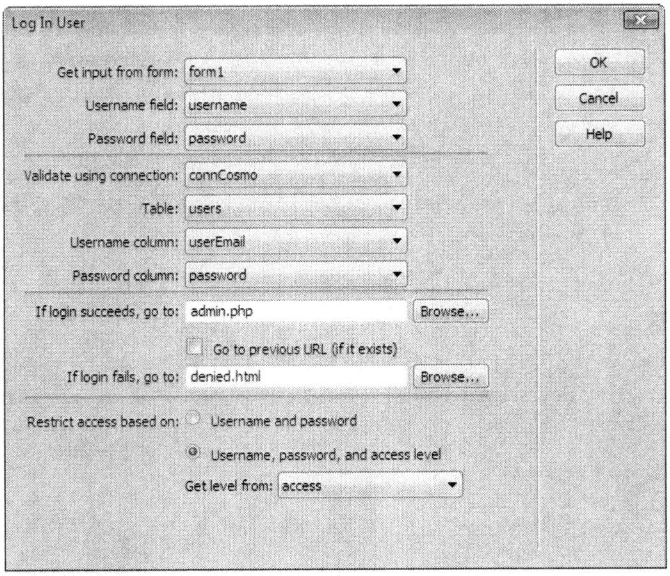

Figure 25-14:
Before visitors can access password-protected pages, they first need to log into the site. Dreamweaver's Log In User server behavior makes adding this feature a snap.

15. **From the Table menu, select "users". From the "Username column" pop-up menu, choose "userEmail". From the "Password column" pop-up menu, choose "password".**

 You've just established the basic logic of the login behavior: Whatever a visitor types into the two form fields is compared with data stored in the *CosmoFarmer* database, inside the Users table.

 Next, you need to specify what happens when there's a match—when your visitor types a valid user name and password into the form—and what happens when the visitor types in an invalid user name or password.

16. **To the right of the "If login succeeds, go to" field, click the Browse button. In the Select File window, navigate to and select the file *admin.php* inside the admin folder. Click OK.**

 You've just chosen the page that appears if the login is successful; your visitor's browser displays an administration page. (For the purposes of this tutorial, it doesn't matter if the "Go to previous URL" checkbox [see step 8 on page 958] is turned on.)

17. **To the right of the "If login fails, go to" field, click the Browse button. In the Select File window, navigate to and select the file *denied.html* inside the admin folder. Click OK.**

 This, of course, is the "access denied" page that appears when somebody types in an invalid user name or password.

 Because this section of the site is for administrators only, you'll add an additional layer of security by restricting administrative pages using an access level as well as a password and user name. In this way, you can also have other password-protected pages—such as a special "paid subscribers" section—for registered visitors, without letting them access administrative areas of the site.

18. **Select the "Username, password, and access level" button. From the "Get level from" pop-up menu, choose "access".**

 The database table includes a special field for defining the access privileges of each registered member. For example, in the *users* table, each administrator record, in the Access field, also includes the value *admin*.

19. **Click OK. Save this file. Press F12 (Option-F12) to preview it in your Web browser.**

 You'll now try out your newly created login page.

20. **In your Web browser, type anything you want in the two fields; click Submit.**

 Unless you've just made an incredible guess, you just typed in a user name and password that doesn't exist in the database. If the technology gods are smiling, an "Access Denied" page appears.

 Now try it again.

21. **Click the "Try logging in again" link to return to the login page. In the Username field, type *dibble@cosmofarmer.com*; in the Password field, type *sesame*; then submit the form.**

    This time, you're in; the browser takes you to the main administration page. Here, you can jump to the pages you created earlier for adding, updating, and deleting products.

Tip (Important!): *sesame* is simply an awful password. Don't ever use it, or any word you can find in a dictionary, as a password. The reason? Web vandals often launch so-called "Dictionary attacks," in which they run through different terms pulled from a dictionary until they find a match.

The login script works just fine—you end up at the right page when you type in a valid user name and password. However, none of those pages are protected yet. You can go to any of them, even if you haven't logged in. In the next part of this tutorial, you'll lock down each admin page, so only logged-in administrators can access them.

Password-Protecting the Administration Pages

The password-protection features offered by Dreamweaver require you to add a server behavior to each page you wish to protect:

1. **In the admin folder, open the file *admin.php*.**

   This page is the main jumping-off point for adding, deleting, and updating products. Only administrators should be able to access it, so you'll add password protection to it.

2. **Make sure the Server Behaviors window is open (Window → Server Behaviors). Click the + button, and then choose User Authentication → Restrict Access To Page.**

   (Alternatively, in the Insert panel, you can use the User Authentication menu, as pictured in Figure 25-1.)

   The Restrict Access To Page window appears (see Figure 25-15). Since you want to limit access to administrators only, make sure the page is restricted to those with the proper access level.

3. **Select the "Username, password, and access level" radio button.**

   You want to specify which type of user has access to this page, but first you must tell Dreamweaver what the different levels *are*.

4. **Click Define to open the Define Access Levels window. In the Name field, type *admin*. Next, click OK to close the window.**

   In the "Select level(s)" box, the word *admin* appears. If you had other areas of the site with different access privileges, such as a subscriber area of the site only paying subscribers could access, you could continue to add levels by repeating this step.

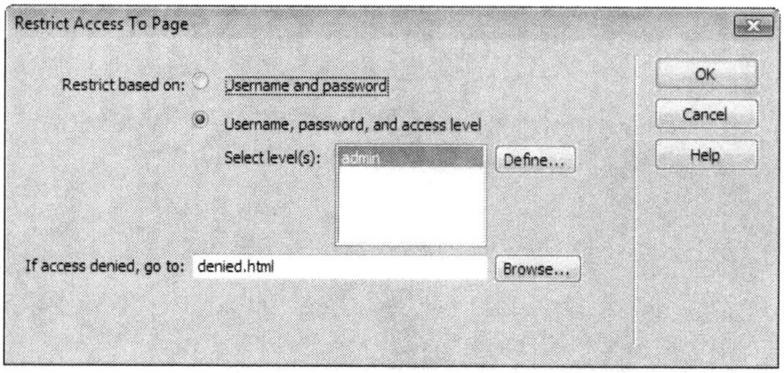

Figure 25-15: *Administrative pages can be reserved for those with the access level "admin," while regular subscribers to CosmoFarmer have access to pages intended for subscribers.*

5. **Click Browse; in the admin folder, select the *denied.html* file, and then click OK. Click OK again to close the Restrict Access To Page window.**

   To finish this page, you'll add a "Log out" link.

6. **Select Log Out (in the page's left navigation bar, the last link).**

   You'll turn this text into a "Log out" link.

7. **On the Server Behaviors panel, click the + button, and then select User Authentication → Log Out User.**

   Again, this option is also available from the Insert bar, as pictured in Figure 25-1. In any case, the Log Out User window appears (see Figure 25-16). The first radio button should already be selected. The text "Log Out" appears in the menu.

   These are the proper settings; you're simply adding the logout script to the words you selected on the page.

   Next, you'll tell Dreamweaver which page to go to after the visitor logs out.

8. **Click the Browse button; in the root folder of the site, navigate to and select the file *index.php,* and then click OK.**

   When people log out, they simply end up at the main products page. Since they're no longer logged in as administrators, they can't access any of the administrative pages without logging back in. The Log Out User window should now look like Figure 25-16.

9. **Click OK to close the Log Out User window.**

   Now it's time to test the result.

10. **Choose File → Save; press F12 (Option-F12) to preview the page in your browser.**

    One of two things happens: either you end up on the Access Denied page, or you see the CosmoFarmer administration page.

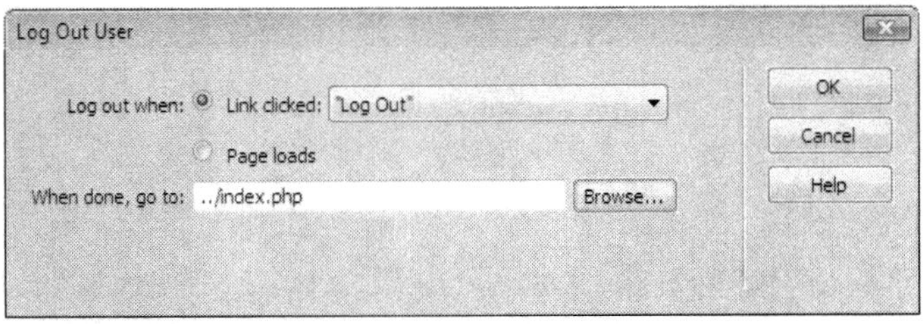

Figure 25-16: *This server behavior lets you offer visitors the polite option of logging out from your site. It destroys the session variables that track a visitor's login status.*

If you quit your Web browser after the previous section of this tutorial, or never logged in to begin with, then the Restrict Access To Page server behavior is working: It doesn't recognize you as a registered administrator, and denies you access to this page. Click the "Try logging in again" link to go to the login page. In the Username field, type *dibble@cosmofarmer.com*; in the Password field, type *sesame;* and then submit the form. You're now logged in, and taken to the admin page.

However, if you logged in following the instructions from the previous section in this tutorial, and you haven't quit your Web browser in the meantime, you're still logged in. In this case, the Restrict Access To Page server behavior is again doing its job. You're allowed onto this admin page, because you *are* a registered administrator.

11. **In the left navigation bar, click the Log Out link.**

    The site logs you out, and takes you to the main products page. To make sure you really are logged out, you'll open the administration page again.

12. **Return to Dreamweaver and the *admin.php* page. Press F12 (Option-F12) to preview the page again.**

    You're immediately redirected to the Access Denied page. You're not logged in, so you can't see the administration page. Hooray! The page is successfully protected from snoops.

Note: Some browsers "cache," or store, the previously viewed administration page, so you might not actually see the Access Denied page. In this case, reload the page by clicking your browser's refresh button.

Of course, the most vulnerable pages (the update-, delete-, and add-product pages) are still accessible to everyone. You need to lock down those pages as well.

13. **Open the *add.php* page, and then repeat steps 2–5 on page 981.**

    Repeat this step for all other dynamic pages (*delete.php* and *edit.php*) in the *admin* folder, with the exception of *login.php*. (After all, *that page* should be visible to those who haven't yet logged in.)

    If you want, you can also add a Log Out link to each of these pages by repeating steps 6–9 on page 982.

Now all of the administrative pages in the site are password-protected. Only authorized administrators who log into the site can add, edit, or delete records from the database.

Displaying a Portion of a Page to Logged-In Users

Even though unauthorized users can't access any of the pages that can change the database, they can still see the links you added to the Product Details page in the last chapter—"Edit this Information" and "Delete this Product". Nothing particularly earth-shattering happens if they click these links—unauthorized users just end up at the Access Denied page—but even that's not very elegant. Wouldn't it be tidier if those links didn't even *show up* except to people logged in as administrators?

You'll set that up next:

1. **Open the *product.php* page.**

   You'll be doing a little painless programming in Code view at this point.

2. **In the document window, click inside the text "Edit this Information"; in the Tag selector, click the <p>.**

   You've just selected the paragraph containing the two links. This paragraph should appear only to administrators.

3. **Choose View → Code.**

   You can also click the Code button in the document window's top left. Either way, the document window switches into Code view (see Figure 25-17). If your monitor's big enough, you can use Split view instead (View → Split Code) so you can see Code and Design view side by side (see page 395 for more on Split view).

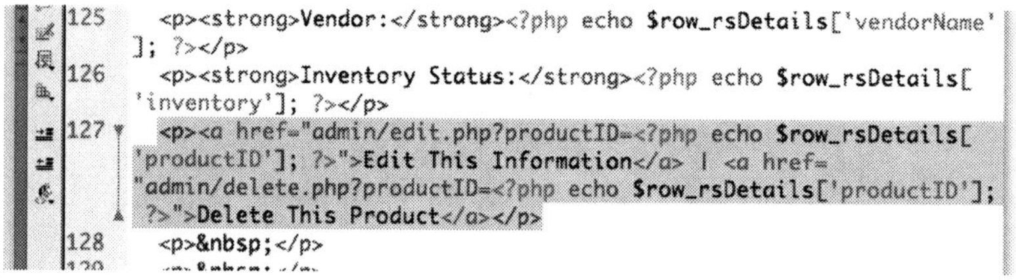

Figure 25-17: *When you enter Code view, whatever you had selected in the document window is highlighted in the code. The HTML code outlined here includes the Edit and Delete product links you wish to hide from unregistered visitors.*

4. **Click at the beginning of the selection, just before the opening <p>.**

   The insertion point is now at the start of the paragraph. You'll add some programming code here.

5. **On a single line, type *<?php if (isset($_SESSION['MM_UserGroup']) && $_SESSION['MM_UserGroup']=='admin') { ?>*.**

   The opening *<?php* tells the application server that some PHP code is coming. In other words, this code isn't HTML—it's a program that the application server must process. The IF part of this code indicates what's called a *conditional statement*. In this case, it means, "*If* this person is logged in with an access level of 'admin', *then* the paragraph will appear on the page."

   To determine if the visitor is logged in with the proper access level, the code sneaks a peak at a session variable called MM_UserGroup. As mentioned on page 968, when someone logs into the site, the server behavior creates a session variable called MM_UserGroup. This variable follows the visitor around the site, and contains a word that indicates what level of access he has. The programming you just added first checks to see if the session variable exists (that's the *isset* weirdness), and then verifies that the session variable is "admin", which indicates that the visitor is logged in as an administrator. If all of that is true, then the paragraph letting the visitor access the edit and delete links appears.

6. **Click to the right of the closing </p> tag (just after "Delete this product"), and then type *<?php } ?>*.**

   This code concludes the conditional statement. In other words, all the HTML between the first line of code you added in the previous step and this final *<?php } ?>* appears *only* if the user is logged in as an administrator.

   The code should now look like Figure 25-18. You need to do one last thing on this page.

***Figure 25-18:** Here's the finished code that hides the "Delete this Product" paragraph from unregistered users.*

7. **Stay in Code view, and scroll to the top of the page. Place your cursor after the very beginning of the file, before the very first line, which begins with "<?php".**

   Next, you'll add a little code that lets the page access the session variables.

8. **Type** ***<?php session_start( ); ?>*****, and then press Return to move the existing code after this onto the next line. The first two lines in Code view should now look like this:**

```
<?php session_start( ); ?>
<?php require_once('Connections/connCosmo.php'); ?>
```

The code you just added makes PHP turn on its magical session-handling powers. Now this page can "see" any session variables set for the current visitor—such as whether the visitor is logged in, and if she is an "admin" user.

9. **Choose File → Save; press F12 (Option-F12) to preview the page.**

Since you logged out earlier, the links should now be invisible. To see them, you must log in, and then return to the product details page.

10. **Go back to Dreamweaver, and then open the** ***login.php*** **page. Press F12 (Option-F12) to preview the page. In the Username field, type** ***dibble@cosmofarmer.com.*** **In the Password field, type** ***sesame.*** **Click Submit.**

You're now logged in, and taken to the main administration page. If you return to a product details page, then the links miraculously return.

11. **In the top navigation bar on the page, click the Cosmo Shop button to go to the product listings page. Click the name of any product to see its details.**

Voilà! The links are back. You can freely edit or delete any product in the database. If you return to the administration page, and click the Log Out button, then you don't see these links until you log back in.

You could also use this trick to add "Log out" links to every page on the site, but make them visible only if the visitor is logged in. With no programming experience, you can use Dreamweaver's server behaviors together (and perhaps bring in server behaviors from extension developers) to build sophisticated database-driven Web sites.

Now go forth and electrify your sites!

CHAPTER

26

Server-Side XML and XSLT

XML is everywhere. You'll find it used in countless files on your computer; for everything from tracking information in your iTunes music library to providing the structure and options in Dreamweaver's menus. On the Web, XML is used to broadcast newsfeeds, and provide product, pricing, and availability information from Amazon.com and eBay using a technology known as *Web services*. In fact, probably the best use of Dreamweaver's server-side XML tool is for adding news, blog posts, or other information broadcast from *other* Web sites to your own.

So what exactly is XML? XML, or Extensible Markup Language, is a tag-based language, somewhat like HTML, used to organize data in a clear, easy to understand way so that different computers, operating systems, and programs can quickly and easily exchange data.

Dreamweaver's Spry XML Data Set tools (covered in Chapter 12) let you work with XML on the "client-side." Translation: someone visiting your site downloads a Web page, some Spry JavaScript programming, and an XML file; then, thanks to some fancy JavaScript magic, the Web page can display and interact with the XML data in a variety of ways. For example, you can publish a table of data that the visitor can sort dynamically, simply by clicking a particular column's header (see page 518 for more about this trick).

Note: For a detailed introduction to XML, flip back to page 522.

The tradeoff with the client-side approach is that it forces a visitor's Web browser to download the entire XML file. If the file is large, that can take a fair amount of time, since the browser downloads the whole enchilada (even the stuff you never intend to display). In addition, a Spry Data Set can only use an XML file that's stored on the same Web server as your Web page. In other words, you can't access the RSS feed (an XML format for broadcasting news, blog posts, and other information) of CNN.com or your favorite blogger.

Fortunately, you can use Dreamweaver's server-side XML and XSLT tools to overcome these limitations. The program's XSLT server behavior produces regular HTML out of XML and XSLT style sheets. (Hang in there: more in a moment on what XSLT is all about.) And, fortunately, since Dreamweaver handles all the complex programming required to make this happen, it's no more difficult for you than building a dynamic Web page.

Understanding the Technologies

Although XML is very much like HTML in many ways, it doesn't have any inherent formatting capabilities. Unlike with HTML, where an <h1> tag is at least displayed differently—bolder and bigger—than text inside a paragraph, a Web browser doesn't know how to display an XML tag. XSLT and XPath are two complementary (and very complex) languages that let you define how XML tags should look. Fortunately, even though these languages are hard to master, Dreamweaver takes care of the entire process. All you need to know is how to use Dreamweaver's Design view to create cool-looking Web pages.

XPath provides the means to identify particular elements or tags in an XML file (see Figure 12-17 on page 535). In other words, it's like a set of directions for specifying a particular piece of information in an XML file.

XSLT is the magic dust that transforms an XML document into an HTML document. In fact, it's used to create any number of different types of documents for Web browsers, smart phones, printers, and so on, out of a single XML file. XSLT stands for Extensible Style Language Transformations, which is just a really geeky name for a programming language that converts XML tags—<event>Halloween Social</event>, for example—into something else, like the code a Web browser understands—<h1>Halloween Social</h1>. In a nutshell, that's what Dreamweaver's XML tools do: They use XSLT to transform XML into HTML.

Note: Because XSLT adds formatting to XML, much like Cascading Style Sheets add formatting to HTML, you'll often see an XSLT file referred to as an *XSLT style sheet*.

Think of it this way: XPath is used to identify the XML tags that XSLT transforms into HTML. XSLT does the actual conversion to HTML, but XPath tells XSLT which tags to convert. They work hand in hand to get the job done. And, fortunately, that's all you need to know. In fact, it's more than you need to know to use Dreamweaver to turn XML into great-looking Web pages.

Tip: Dreamweaver includes built-in reference material covering XML and XSLT. See page 422 for more on Dreamweaver's Reference panel.

Creating Dynamic Pages with XSLT and XML

Dreamweaver's XSLT server behavior processes all of those "X" files and produces nothing but clean HTML for your visitors. To take advantage of this feature, you'll need to set up an application server, as described in Chapter 22, so that you can run ASP, PHP, or ColdFusion pages with the necessary programming code.

Next, you need to either have an XML file in your site, or know the URL of an XML file out on the Web that you'd like to use—for example, *www.amazon.com/gp/blog/A31FYGCJNYUWYQ/rss.xml*. One option is to create an entire page that's an XSLT file—it will contain all the HTML for the general look of the page, and the XML information you wish to display. But this is generally an inefficient technique, since the server has to process the entire file (plain HTML and all) and you can't take advantage of Dreamweaver templates to enforce the look of your site.

Note for PHP Users: For server-side XSLT to work, the version of PHP you're using must have XSLT support. PHP 5 has this capability built in, but PHP 4 requires extra work to get this going. Unfortunately, some Web hosting companies still use PHP 4, and many of those don't offer XSLT support. So before moving ahead with your XML-fueled dynamic-page-creation efforts, call or email your Web hosting company to see if their PHP installation supports XSLT.

A better method is to create what's called an *XSLT fragment*, which lets you add a "chunk" of formatted XML to just one part of a dynamic page. For example, say you want to list the top 10 headlines from CNN.com's RSS feed on your home page. Using Dreamweaver, you can transform the newsfeed from XML into HTML code. Of course, that won't be the only thing you want on your home page. Most of the page will consist of information related to your site. In this case, you only need to dedicate a fragment of the page—like a sidebar on the right edge of the page—to these headlines.

Note: RSS and Atom (a competing standard) are simply two different XML-based formats used to identify document information–like an author's name, a title, or a brief article description–and provide a link to a complete article on a Web site. These formats are commonly used on news sites and blogs to provide readers with a syndicated news feed. RSS stands for "Rich Site Summary" or "Really Simple Syndication" (depending on whom you ask). Atom is another, more complex standard that competes with RSS but pretty much does the same thing. For more information on RSS, see *www.w3schools.com/rss/*, and for Atom, see *www.atomenabled.org/developers/syndication/*.

The process for creating and inserting an XSLT fragment is simple: create the fragment, add and format the XML information, open a dynamic page, and then insert the XSLT fragment into it. When your visitors view the dynamic page, the application server will process the XSLT fragment and add its contents to the rest of the page.

Here's how to create and use an XSLT fragment:

1. **Choose File → New.**

   The New Document window appears.

2. **Click the Blank Page button on the left side of the window. From the Blank Page list, select XSLT (Fragment), and then click the Create button.**

   The Locate XML Source window appears (Figure 26-1). Because XSLT is meant to make an XML file look great, you need to tell Dreamweaver which XML file to use. You have two choices when working with server-side XSLT: select a local file or type the URL of an XML file out on the Web.

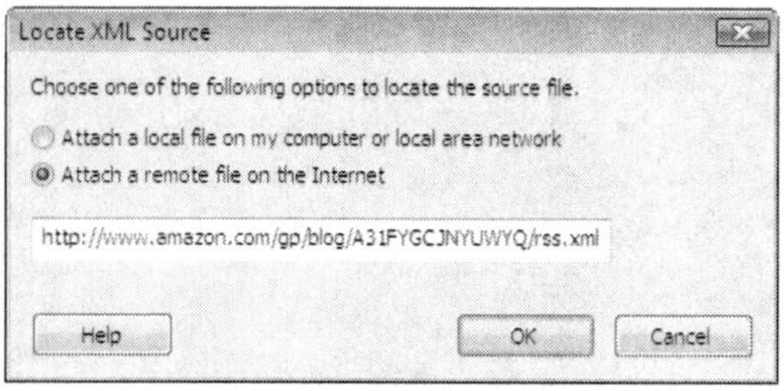

Figure 26-1:
You can use either an XML file stored locally on your own site, or type the absolute URL of an XML file on the Web, such as the location of an RSS feed from a blog or news Web site.

3. **Select either "Attach a local file..." or "Attach a remote file on the Internet".**

   If the XML file is on your site, choose the first option. Select the second option if the XML file is on another Web site.

4. **If you're using an XML file on your site, click the Browse button to locate the file. Otherwise, type an absolute URL—*http://www.the_site.com/xml_file.xml*, for example—in the box. Click OK.**

   If you're pointing to a file out on the Internet, you *must* use a full, absolute URL including the *http://* part (Dreamweaver helps you out by adding *http://* to the box when you select the "Attach a remote file" button). Dreamweaver finds the file in your local site (or looks for the file out on the Internet), reads its contents, and displays the file's tags and properties in the Bindings panel. At this point, jump to page 534 to learn how to add XML data to the page.

   Although Dreamweaver claims that it's "attaching" the XML file to the XSLT document, it's really just adding a comment tag to the XSLT file, like this: <!--DWXML-Source="news.xml" -->. This comment helps Dreamweaver know which XML file to use with the XSLT document—so don't delete it. Technically, you actually attach an XSL file to an XML file to make this whole process work (as described below).

Note: If you want to try this out for fun, you can load an XML file from the author's Amazon.com blog: *http://www.amazon.com/gp/blog/A31FYGCJNYUWYQ/rss.xml*.

5. **Save the new XSLT style sheet fragment.**

   Make sure the file ends in the extension .xsl. In addition, make sure you save it in the same folder as the dynamic page you wish to attach the XSLT style sheet fragment to. Otherwise, if the style sheet contains links, graphics, and other linked elements, they may not show up when the XML file is viewed.

Note: One way to get around this limitation of needing to store everything in the same folder is to use root-relative or absolute URLs (see page 161) for links, and to add graphics and external CSS files to your XSLT style sheet. Of course, taking these steps is probably more work than simply saving the XSL file in the same folder as your dynamic Web page.

6. **Add XML elements to the XSLT style sheet as described on page 992.**

   You can also add regular Web page content—like images, tables, CSS styles, and so on—to the page, and format the XML just as you would text on any other dynamically generated page. Once you've finished the design of your XSLT fragment, you then add it to your dynamic Web page.

Note: Because the XSLT fragment will be part of a larger Web page, you won't be able to see the effects of that page's CSS styles as you format your XML data. Fortunately, if you're using external CSS style sheets, you can use Dreamweaver's Design Time Stylesheets feature to temporarily attach, preview, and use the same CSS styles you're using on your final Web page. See page 327 for instructions.

7. **Open the dynamic page that you wish to add the XSLT fragment to.**

   This must be a dynamic page using the same server model as your site—for example PHP, ASP, or ColdFusion. Because the XML transformation magic occurs via programming that Dreamweaver inserts in the page, you can't add an XSLT fragment to a regular Web page (an .html file).

8. **Click where you wish to insert the XSLT fragment.**

   The spot you pick could be inside a table cell or within another layout region—such as a sidebar—on your page. The XSLT fragment will be added to this spot, just like a Dreamweaver Library item (see page 713)—that is, it will just be a chunk of HTML inside your page.

9. **Make sure the Server Behaviors panel is open (Window → Server Behaviors), click the + button, and then select XSL Transformation.**

   The XSL Transformation window appears (see Figure 26-2). Next, you select the XSL file you created earlier.

10. **Click the top Browse button to open the Select XSLT File window. Navigate to and select the XSL file you created; click OK (Choose on the Mac) to choose the file, and then close the Select XSLT File window.**

    This tells Dreamweaver which fragment to use. In addition, Dreamweaver should automatically fill out the path to the XML file (it reads the comment inserted in the XSLT file identifying which XML file to use—see the Note below). If the XML file path doesn't appear, you can click the Browse button

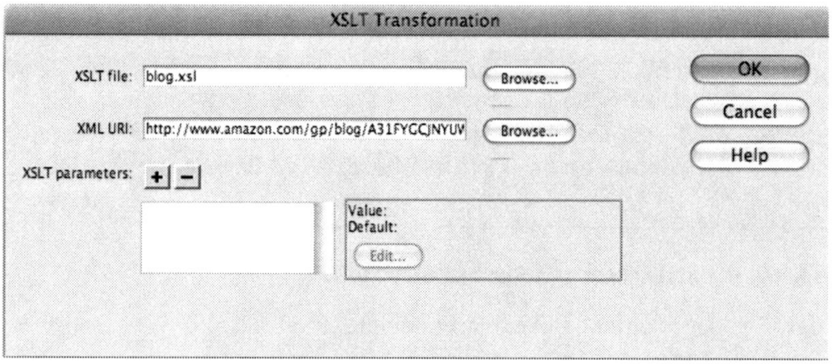

Figure 26-2: *The XSL Transformation window lets you attach an XSLT style sheet to a dynamic page. You can also send special information–XSLT parameters–to the style sheet that affects the display of the page (this process is described on page 1006).*

next to the XML file box and select the proper XML file yourself. In addition, if you're using XML from another Web site, you'll see the URL of that file, and the Browse button will disappear.

The "XSLT parameters" option lets you pass information to the XSL file that can be used to alter how the XML file is displayed. This advanced feature is discussed on page 1006.

11. **Click the OK button to close the window and insert the fragment.**

 Dreamweaver displays the XSLT fragment in your Web page. If you've set up a testing server (see page 821), you can preview the effect by pressing F12 (Option-F12).

You can't directly edit the fragment inside the dynamic Web page. Dreamweaver treats it like a single element on the page. To make changes to the fragment—to add graphics, change links, or reformat the XML—you must open the XSL file and make changes directly to it.

Note: Dreamweaver adds additional folders and files to your site when you use the XSLT server behavior. These additions contain the necessary programming code to successfully embed XML data into a Web page. That means when you're moving everything to your Web server–the dynamic page, the XSLT fragment file, and the XML file–you also need to upload these files, which you'll find stored in a folder named *includes* in your site's local root folder. Upload this folder to your Web server. (See Chapter 17 for instructions on using Dreamweaver's FTP tool.)

Inserting and Formatting XML

Now you know the basics of creating and using XSLT style sheets. But how do you actually add and format XML data? Dreamweaver makes this process easy, and if you've used the program's database tools, you already know how to do it: just use the Bindings panel. Once you create an XSL file and attach the XML file to it, Dreamweaver reads all of the tags in the XML file and adds them to the Bindings panel (see Figure 26-3).

You can drag any element in the Bindings panel into your XSLT style sheet page, just as you'd drag information from a database recordset. That means you can place XML information in a table cell, a footer, or a banner—anywhere you can place regular HTML elements on a page.

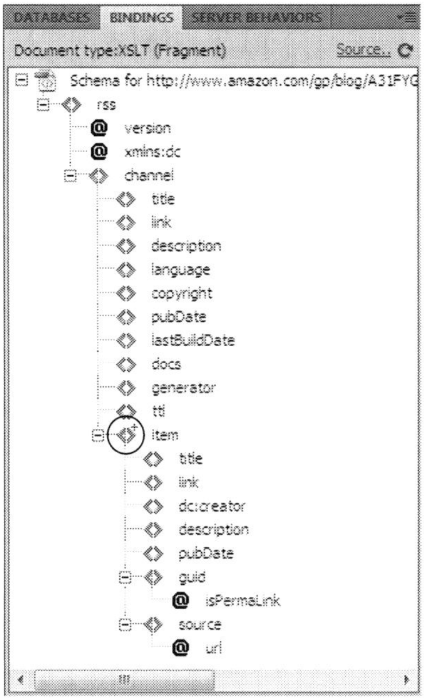

Figure 26-3:
When using Dreamweaver's XSLT tools, the Bindings panel lists all the tags and properties in the XML file you're formatting. Dreamweaver includes a few visual clues about the XML file: < > represents an XML tag and is the most common icon you'll encounter; the @ sign represents a tag property (also called an attribute; for example, in the tag <rss version="2.0">, "version" is an attribute); and next to some tags, you'll see a small + sign (circled in this image) or a ?. The + indicates that the tag is repeated multiple times; for example, an RSS feed usually has multiple news items, so in the feed's XML file each news item will have its own tag. The ? (not shown here) means the tag is optional, and it appears next to tags inside of other repeated tags (the ones with the +).

You should keep a couple things in mind when inserting XML using this dragging method:

- Only the contents of the XML tags and properties are inserted, not the tags or property names themselves. For example, in Figure 26-3, dragging the <title> tag that appears inside the <channel> tag onto a document just prints the text inside this tag, not the tag itself. This is a good thing: You don't usually want to include the tags: <title>An Important Story</title>. Instead, you just want the text: *An Important Story.*

- Dragging a tag that includes *other* tags often results in a hard-to-read mess. That's because Dreamweaver includes text from each of the nested tags, as well. For example, dragging the root element—"rss"—from the Bindings panel pictured in Figure 26-3 adds the simple label {rss} to the page in Dreamweaver's Design view. But when the page is actually viewed in a Web browser, you'll end up with one long paragraph composed of the text from all of the tags—the channel, the title, the description, and so on, as well as each of the repeated "item" tags as pictured in Figure 26-4. Dreamweaver treats this as a single big blob. To get around this, drag tags that don't include other nested tags. (Nested tags are called *child* tags.) For example, in Figure 26-3, the "title" tag that appears directly inside the "channel" tag doesn't have any tags inside it. Likewise, a repeating tag—item, for example—includes tags that don't have any children: "title," "link," "description," and "pubDate." These are all good candidates for adding to a document.

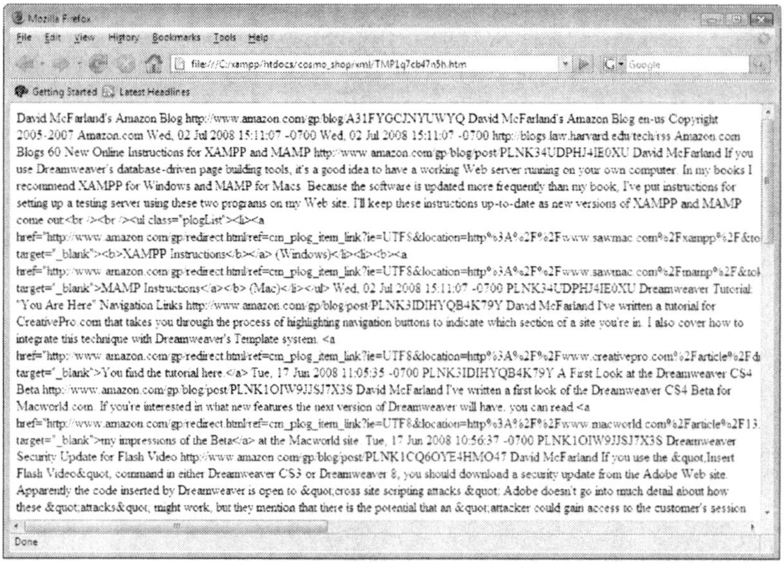

***Figure 26-4:** If you use an XML tag that's too high up on the food chain—that is, one that has other tags nested inside of it—you can end up with a large chunk of hard-to-read text.*

You can also insert XML into a Web page by choosing Insert → XSLT Objects → Dynamic Text or by clicking the Dynamic Text button on the Insert panel's XSLT category (see Figure 26-5). Either method opens the XPath Expression Builder window (Figure 26-6). An XPath Expression is just a way of identifying a particular element—called a *node*—inside an XML file (see Figure 12-17 on page 535).

To add the dynamic text, select the XML tag or property you wish to insert. In the Expression box in the bottom half of the window, you'll see the XPath code required to locate your selection. For example, in Figure 26-6, the expression is *rss/channel/item/title/*. This is shorthand for "Find the title tag, which is inside the item tag, which is inside the channel tag, which is located inside the rss tag." In other words, this expression lists the order in which the tags are nested (in this sense, it's very much like the document window's Tag selector [see page 24]).

Dreamweaver also lets you apply some formatting options to the selected text using the Format menu. Almost all the options have to do with formatting numbers, so if you're inserting content from a tag that's actually a numeric value, these formatting controls can come in handy. For example, say you add a tag that's used to indicate a price: <price>3.25</price>. Selecting any of the currency options will

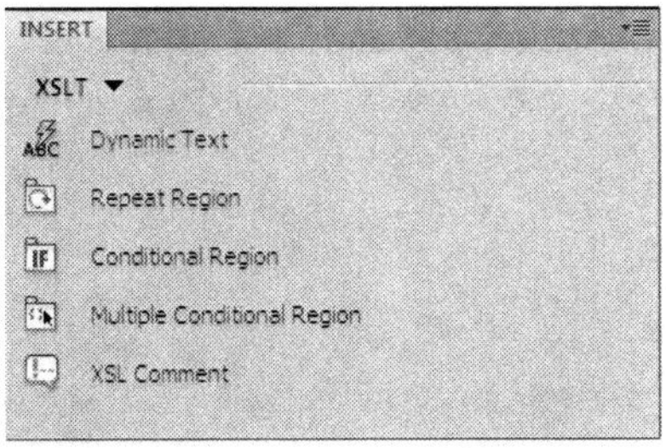

Figure 26-5:
The Insert panel's XSLT category includes five buttons for adding XSLT objects. The XSL Comment object just inserts an XSL comment–like an HTML comment (see page 401)–so you probably won't use it much, if ever.

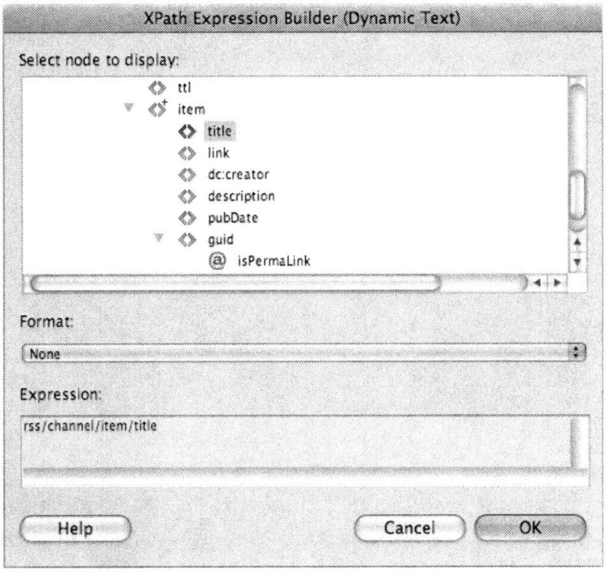

Figure 26-6:
Use the Format drop-down menu to apply a format to the XML data. Unfortunately, the formats are aimed almost entirely at formatting numbers–adding a $ sign to currency data, for example–so they won't do anything for text-only XML data.

add a $ sign in front of the number when it's displayed on the page. If you're dealing with big sums of money—<price id="Federal Bailout">84317589585</price> —then the "Currency group to 3 digits, 2 decimal places" is a good option. Then, the output would be something like this: $84,317,589,585.00. Again, all but two of the options are for formatting numbers, and the two that help format text aren't very useful.

After selecting a tag and setting a formatting option (if desired), click OK to insert the dynamic text. Dreamweaver adds a placeholder to the page; it has a blue background and displays the XPath expression inside of curly brackets, like this: {rss/channel/item/title}.

Tip: You can summon the XPath Expression Builder window again by double-clicking any dynamic XML text placeholder on the page.

Click an XML text placeholder to select it. You can then apply a CSS style to it, format it as a header or paragraph, or drag it to another spot on the page, just as you would any other HTML element.

Inserting a Repeat Region

XML files frequently contain the same tag repeated multiple times. For example, an XML file that's a list of employees might use the tag <employee> to begin each employee listing. For every employee in the company, the <employee> tag will appear once. The XML might look something like this:

```
<companyInfo>
<company>
<name>Big Co.</name>
<phone>555-3333</phone>
</company>
<employeeList>
<employee id="485734">
<name>Mark</name>
<phone>555-3333 x405</phone>
</employee>
<employee id="38753">
<name>Jane</name>
<phone>555-3333 x406</phone>
</employee>
</employeeList>
</companyInfo>
```

If you added the <name> tag inside the first <employee> tag to an XSLT style sheet, attached that XSL file to a dynamic page, and then previewed it in a Web browser, you would see just a single name: the first employee name in the XML file. But just as with recordsets, you usually want to display multiple XML records. The answer is Dreamweaver's XSLT Repeat Region object. To use it:

1. **Insert elements that appear within a tag that is repeated multiple times.** (Use **any of the methods described on page 992.**)

   The Bindings panel lets you know if an XML tag is repeated multiple times: check for a tiny + symbol floating just above the right side of the <> icon in the panel (see Figure 26-3).

   So, in the above employee list example, you wouldn't insert the <name> tag that appears inside the <company> tag, since <company> appears only once in the file. You would, however, insert the <name> tag and perhaps the <phone> tag inside the <employee> tag, since these are both "children" of a tag that's repeated twice in the document.

Note: This example points out a sometimes confusing aspect of XML: Tags with the same name may appear as children within different kinds of tags. The <name> tag in the above example, for instance, appears both within the <company> and <employee> tags, but obviously refers to two different things–the name of a business and the name of a person.

Articles in a Web feed are another case. For example, the RSS standard (see page 989) requires that each news item delivered in an RSS XML document be surrounded by an <item> tag with the following children: <title>, <link>, and <description>. Therefore, for an RSS feed, the elements you'd want to add to the page (and repeat once for each news item) would be <title>, <link>, and <description>.

2. **Select (by dragging, for example) the XML placeholders and any other content that you want to be repeated once for each instance in the XML file.**

   At the very least, this includes the XML placeholders you inserted in step 1, but may also include other HTML elements, such as a graphic that's repeated once for each item or a <div> tag that contains the XML data you're repeating. You can select only elements that are together: You can't, for instance, select an XML element at the top of the page and another at the bottom of the page, and use the same Repeat Region object.

Note: You can, however, include multiple repeat regions on a page, so you could repeat the same XML data in several locations on a page by adding multiple Repeat Region objects.

3. **Choose Insert → XSLT Objects → Repeat Region, or click the Repeat Region button on the XSLT category of the Insert Panel (see Figure 26-5).**

   The XPath Expression Builder window appears (see Figure 26-7). This is a similar window to the one that appears when you insert dynamic text (Figure 26-6). However, instead of a format menu, the window includes a "Build Filter" option.

4. **Select the repeating tag.**

   This tag will always have a + to the right of its <> icon, and is usually the parent tag of the tags you inserted in step 1. So, in the employee list example above, you would select the <employee> tag; in the case of an RSS feed, it would be the <item> tag.

5. **Build a filter to limit the information retrieved from the XML file.**

   An XSLT filter works similarly to filters on recordsets (see page 845). It's a way to select only certain information from the XML file. For example, you might want to select only employees whose last name is Smith, or product tags that have only an <instock> XML tag containing the word "true." Filters are discussed on page 998.

6. **Click OK to insert the repeat region.**

   Dreamweaver adds a gray border around the repeating elements and adds a gray tab labeled "xsl: for-each". (If you don't see these, make sure invisible elements are turned on: View → Visual Aids → Invisible Elements.)

You can see the effect by pressing F12 (Option-F12): Dreamweaver translates all of that XSLT gobbledygook into a temporary HTML file. But to see the final presentation, you need to attach the XSLT style sheet to a dynamic page (steps 8–11 on page 991) and preview it in a browser.

If you want to edit the repeat region, click the gray tab to select it and, in the Property inspector, click the lightning-bolt icon to open the Repeat Region window again (Figure 26-7).

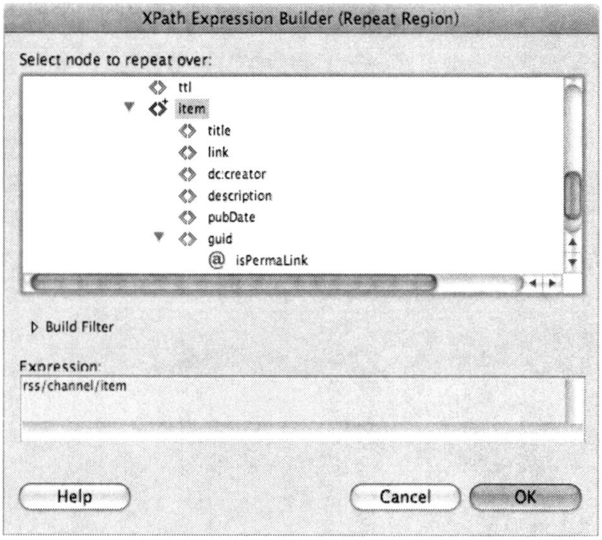

Figure 26-7: *Display repeating XML data using the XPath Expression Builder for repeat regions.*

To remove a repeat region, right-click (Control-click) on the gray "xsl: for-each" tab and select "Remove Tag: <xsl:for-each>". You can also click anywhere inside the repeat region, right-click (Control-click) on "xsl: foreach" in the Tag selector (see page 24), and then choose Remove Tag. Don't try to remove the tag by hand in Code view: The code used to specify the tags inside the region also must be changed; Dreamweaver does this automatically and accurately.

Building a repeat-region filter

If the XML file you're using has lots and lots of repeating items, or you just want to hone in on a single item, you can build an XSLT filter that lets you search and select XML elements that match certain criteria. Say you want to display only employee tags with a "department" property whose value is "marketing." Fortunately, Dreamweaver lets you create very complex filters. In a nutshell, to filter a repeat region:

1. **Follow steps 1–4 on page 996–997 to insert a repeat region.**
2. **In the "XPath Expression Builder (Repeat Region)" window, click Build Filter to display the filter tools (see Figure 26-8), and then click the + button to add a filter.**

   You build a filter by first selecting a tag that contains the information you wish to compare to a certain value.
3. **Click in the Filter By column and, from the pop-up menu, select a tag.**

   This menu lists the repeating tag, its parent tag, its parent's parent tag, and so on, up the food chain, until it reaches the top (root) element. You'll just leave it as the repeating tag you selected in step 4 on page 997 (finish reading these steps and then read the following note to understand why this is the case).

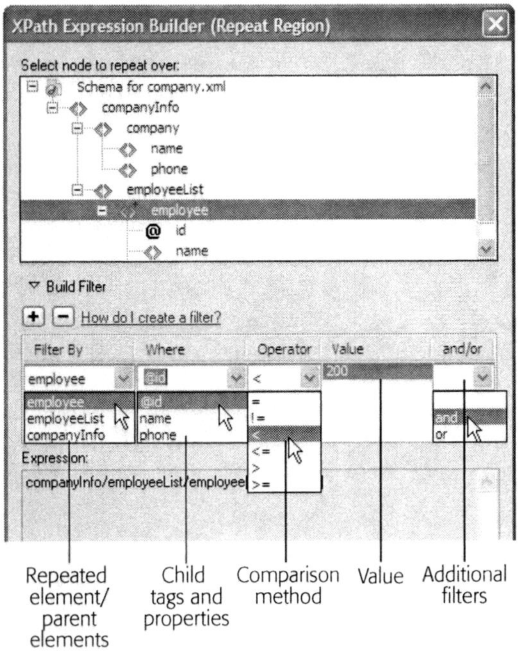

Figure 26-8:
Limit the XML data displayed by creating a filter that includes only XML tags that match certain criteria. Here's an example using the employee list XML code on page 996.

Note (hold onto your thinking caps): A filter lets you select criteria that each repeated region is tested against. If it passes the test, then the XML data is displayed. For example, the "id" property of the <employee> tag will vary with each employee listing. In a repeated region, the only elements that change are either a property of the tag that's repeated or the contents of other tags inside the repeated tag. That's why you should always select the repeated tag from the Filter By menu; the parent (and grandparent, and so on) of the repeated tag doesn't change with each region that repeats. If the parent has a property named "version," that property value will be the same whenever the filter is applied to a repeat region. In other words, the filter will either always be true or never be true, and you'll either get all of the XML data or none of the XML data from the repeated tags. Dreamweaver includes a more flexible tool for displaying or hiding information based on some "test" or condition: conditional regions (see page 1001).

4. **Click in the Where column, and select an option from the pop-up menu.**

   This menu lists any properties of the repeated tag, and all the repeated tag's child tags. In the employee list code (page 996), for example, each <employee> tag has a property named "id" and child tags called <name> and <phone>. So in this case, those options are listed in the "Where" menu. Tag properties begin with an @ symbol, so in this example, the "id" property is listed as "@id" in the menu (see Figure 26-8).

   To continue with the employee list example, if you want to display only employees whose employee IDs are below a certain number (perhaps to list the company's first 200 employees), then choose "@id" from the menu.

Note to Power Users: If you're up on your XPath expressions (and who isn't?), you can actually click in the Where column and type your own path to identify tags and properties located deeper in the tag structure.

5. **Select a comparison method from the Operator menu.**

   Your options are = (equal to), != (not equal to), < (less than), <= (less than or equal to), > (greater than), and >= (greater than or equal to). If the property or tag you selected in step 4 contains a number, you can use any of these *comparison operators*. So if you want to find employees whose IDs are below 200, then select <.

   For properties and tags that contain text (<department>marketing</department>, for example) stick to either the = or != options. That way, a repeat region shows only employees who are either in the "marketing" department (use the = sign) or not in it (use the != operator).

6. **Type a comparison value in the Value box.**

   The value is what you're testing against. If you're looking for employee IDs that are below 200, type *200*; for <department> tags that contain the word "marketing" type *marketing*.

7. **If you want to add more filters, select either "and" or "or" from the "and/or" menu, click the + button to add another filter, and then repeat steps 4–7.**

   This lets you add additional conditions that must be met in order to select XML data to include in the repeat region. Say you want to display employees who are both in the marketing department *and* are one of the first 200 employees. In that case, select the "and" option and add another filter. Or suppose you want to display a list of employees who are *either* in the marketing department *or* the finance department: Select "or" and add a filter where the <department> tag is equal to "finance".

   The ability to add multiple filters lets you build up complex filters that either let you narrow the number of regions that are repeated (by adding more and more *and* options) or that include more and more data from the XML file (by using additional *or* filters).

8. **After adding one or more filters, click the Close button to create a filtered repeat region.**

   Dreamweaver inserts the repeat region into the XSLT style sheet. You can edit or remove this region as described on page 998.

Inserting a Conditional Region

At times, you may want to display a part of a page only if certain conditions are met. The "Filter" feature of the Repeat Region tool (see page 998) offers some help, since it can display select XML data when a tag's property or contents pass a particular test: an *id* property that's less than 200, for example. But there are other occasions when the filter doesn't help. Say you want to display only the last item in a repeat region; there's no tag or property containing this information, so a filter won't work.

Note to Power Users: If you use Dreamweaver templates, this problem may sound familiar. It's the same concept as a template optional region (see page 744).

Or maybe you want to display a graphic or another part of a page only when a certain XML property appears. Suppose an XML document listing products has a tag like this: <product stock="in">. The product tag's "stock" property serves to indicate whether a product is available (in which case, it's value is "in") or when it's not ("out"). In such cases, you can use a conditional region to display an "out of stock" button next to each product that's not available.

To use a conditional region:

1. **Select the part of the page—the XSLT fragment—you want to display if a condition is true.**

   A simple example is an "out of stock" or "on sale" graphic. But you could also select XML data placeholders: Maybe you want to display just the first five items inside a repeat region. In this case, select all the XML placeholders inside the repeat region (you need to add the repeat region first).

Note: Many Web designers find it useful to place conditional regions inside of repeat regions, since this lets them fine-tune the display of information on a per-item basis. For example, in a repeating list of products, showing an "on sale" graphic only for those products that are actually on sale.

2. **Choose Insert → XSLT Objects → Conditional Region or click the Conditional Region button in the XSLT category of the Insert panel (see Figure 26-5).**

   The Conditional Region window opens (see Figure 26-9).

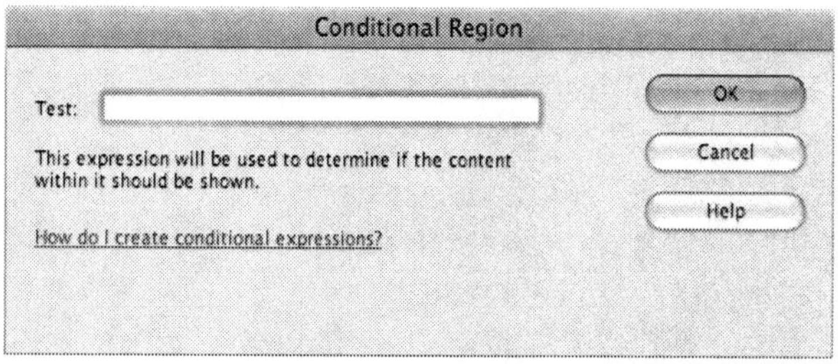

Figure 26-9:
The Conditional Region window lets you show or hide content on your page based upon certain conditions in the XML or XSL files.

3. **Type a test condition in the Test box.**

   "But what am I supposed to type?" you're asking. This is the tricky part, since Dreamweaver doesn't really give you much help. Your test condition can actually be a number of different things, many of which can be quite complex. Here are a few examples:

   - **An XPath expression followed by some kind of comparison.** For example, say you're working with the XML document on page 998. You've created a repeat region listing all of your company's employees, and you want an "employee of the month" graphic to appear in the listing, but only next to the employee whose ID is, say, 38753. To make that happen, the condition you'd type would be *@id=38753*. *@id* refers to the "id" property (@ is used before a property name) of the repeated tag (<employee>, in this example.) Likewise, if you wanted to highlight all employees named Jane (that is, the text inside the <name> tag is *Jane*), the condition would be *name='Jane'*. (Note that whenever you're testing whether a tag has text inside it—as opposed to just numbers—you must place quotes around the word, like this: *'Jane'*.)

   - **The position of an item in a repeated region.** When applying conditions to content that comes from a repeat region, you can access an item's position using *position( )*. So if you wanted to have the selected page elements inside a repeat region appear only when the first item is displayed, you could type *position( )=first( )*; for the last item, the condition would be *position( )=last( )*. And if you wanted to limit the repeat region to just 5 items (if you want to show only the first 5 headlines from a newsfeed, say), you could use this expression: *position( )<=5*.

- **An XPath expression to determine if a tag or property exists.** You can also just enter an XPath expression for a particular *node* (page 994) in the document. If the node exists, then the selected element is displayed; otherwise, it's hidden. For example, say you have a repeat region that contains some optional tags. Again, using the employee list example, imagine that some employees have their own offices. For those employees, you might add an XML tag called <office> that includes the office number, like so: <office> Room 222</office>. You'd like to include the text "Office:" followed by the actual office number in your final Web page. However, if someone doesn't have an office (meaning that her entry in the XML file has no <office> tag), you don't want the word "Office:" to appear. To make that happen with a conditional region, type *Office*: somewhere inside the repeat region (perhaps on a line below the employee phone number); next, drag the <office> tag from the Bindings panel to the page, and then select both the text and the XML placeholder. Finally, add a conditional region as described on page 1001 and simply type *office* as the condition. Now "Office:" and the office number will appear only for <employee> tags that have an <office> tag inside them.

- **Tag or property values that begin with one or more particular characters.** Say you want to display only those employees whose names begin with 'M'. You can do this easily with the *starts-with( )* function. In the Conditional Region box, you'd type *starts-with(name, 'M')*. Translated from XSLT-speak, this means any <name> tag whose contents start with the letter M will appear on the final Web page; so <name>Mark</name> and <name> Mary</name> would match, but <name>Andrea</name> wouldn't.

4. **Click OK to insert the conditional region.**

   Dreamweaver adds a gray border around the page elements you selected in step 1 and adds a gray tab labeled "xsl:if" to indicate the conditional region. (If you don't see these, make sure invisible elements are turned on by choosing View → Visual Aids → Invisible Elements.)

You can still edit the page elements inside the conditional region's gray border: You can edit, add, or remove text, images, and XML placeholders. If you want to edit the conditional test, click the gray "xsl:if" tab to select the conditional region, and then change the test listed in the Property inspector.

To remove a conditional region, right-click (Control-click) the gray "xsl:if" tab, and then select "Remove Tag <xsl:if>". You can also click anywhere inside the conditional region, right-click "xsl:if" in the Tag selector (see page 24), and then choose "Remove Tag".

Using Multiple Conditional Regions

A conditional region is pretty straightforward: It either shows or hides part of the page based on the results of a simple test. But what if you want to display one thing if the condition is true, but show different stuff if the condition is false? Say you have two graphics called "In Stock" and "Out of Stock" that need to appear next to each product name in a repeat region. You can use two conditional regions: the first to display the "In Stock" image if the product tag's stock property is set to "in" (<product stock="in">) and another for out-of-stock products (<product stock="out").

Note: If you've ever done any computer programming, you'll recognize the upcoming maneuver as a variation on the venerable "if-then-else" statement.

But using conditional regions in that way requires far too much work on your part. Fortunately, Dreamweaver's Multiple Conditional Region tool makes it easy to deal with these "either/or" situations. Here's how to use it:

1. **Select the part of the page you want to display if a condition is true.**

   This could be a graphical button with the text "In Stock" printed across it. This step is the same as a conditional region described on page 1001. In fact, most of the steps are the same.

2. **Choose Insert → XSLT Objects → Multiple Conditional Region or click the Multiple Conditional Region button in the XSLT category of the Insert panel (see Figure 26-5).**

   The Multiple Conditional Region window opens. Except for its title, this window is identical to the Conditional Region window (see Figure 26-9).

3. **Type a test condition in the Test box.**

   For instance, *@stock="in"* would cause the region to display if the value of the repeating tag's *stock* property was "in." For more examples, see page 1002.

4. **Click OK.**

   Dreamweaver inserts three different sections of XSL code, each marked with their own gray tab: "XSL:choose", "XSL:when", and "XSL:otherwise". The "XSL:when" section contains the actual condition or test you set in step 3 and the content you selected in step 1.

   The "XSL:otherwise" section is the part of the page that will display if the test *isn't* true. Dreamweaver adds "Contents goes here" to that area.

5. **Select and delete "Content goes here" and then add the page elements you wish to display if the test from step 3 isn't true.**

   This is the alternative to the content selected in step 1—for example, an "Out of Stock" icon.

You can edit the contents of either the "XSL:when" or "XSL:otherwise" sections. To edit the test, either click the gray "XSL:when" tab or click anywhere inside the "XSL:when" section and use the Tag selector (see page 24) to select the <xsl:when> tag. The Property inspector displays the test condition; edit it, and then press Enter or Return.

Removing a multiple conditional region is a bit trickier. You can't just right-click (Control-click) the gray "XSL:choose" tab and then select "Remove Tag <xsl: choose>" to remove all of the multiple conditional region code. You must remove each of the three sections separately. To do so, follow the same process as required when removing a conditional tag, as described on page 1004.

Advanced XSLT Tricks

XSLT is a complex language with lots of bells and whistles—and just as many pitfalls. It's all too easy to head ambitiously into Code view and, with just a few keystrokes, completely break your XSLT style sheet. But since Dreamweaver's XSLT tools take you only so far, you'll undoubtedly find yourself wanting to dip into the code. Here are a couple of examples to help your explorations go a little more smoothly.

Sorting Data in a Repeat Region

The Repeat Region feature normally works by spitting out data that it retrieves from an XML document in the order it appears in the XML file. In the case of an RSS feed, that's usually OK, since items in an RSS feed are sorted in chronological order with most recent first. But what if you want information sorted in another way, or you have an XML file with other kinds of data like the employee listing on page 996? In that example, you might want employees listed in alphabetical order. Dreamweaver doesn't have a visual tool to let you accomplish this common goal. Fortunately, adding the code yourself is pretty easy:

1. **Click inside a repeat region and then click the "Code" or "Split" buttons in the document window's toolbar.**

   Alternatively, you can choose View → Code or View → "Code and Design". Doing so drops you into the scary world of XSLT code.

2. **Locate the beginning of the repeat region.**

   What you're looking for is something like this: <xsl:for-each select="company-Info/employeeList/employee">, where the stuff in quotes after "select" is the XPath expression pointing to the repeating tag. You need to add your new code directly after this tag.

3. **Click immediately after the closing bracket (>), hit Enter, and then type *<xsl: sort select="xml_tag_to_sort_on" data-type="text" order="ascending" />*.**

   Replace *xml_tag_to_sort_on* with the XML tag inside the repeat region that you wish to use as the basis for sorting. For example, pick a tag used for a name or a price.

Note: Don't forget the forward slash at the end of the sort tag: />. The tag you're adding is an *empty tag* (meaning there's no accompanying closing tag). In XML, these types of tags must be "self closed" using the forward slash (see page 525 for details).

The value for *data-type* can be either "text" or "number." Pick the one that matches the type of data contained in the XML tag you're using as a sorting key—use "text" if you're sorting names and "number" if you're sorting prices.

Depending on how you want to sort the data—smallest number to largest, or largest number to smallest—type either *ascending* or *descending*, respectively, for the *order* property. "Ascending" gets you smallest number to largest, or A–Z; "descending" results in largest number to smallest, or Z–A.

Using XSLT Parameters

The Repeat Region's filter feature is very useful. With it, you can winnow down a mass of XML data to a smaller collection of useful facts. But what if you wanted the data retrieved from the XML file to *change* based on information from a database or information submitted by a visitor? Say you've already created an employee list page, and now you want to create separate pages for each employee (kind of like the master-detail pages described on page 879). You could create an XSLT style sheet for each employee, thereby filtering the XML file based on the employee's ID number. But creating one page for each employee is a lot of work. A better approach is to use an *XSLT parameter*.

XSLT parameters provide a way of passing information from an outside source to the XSLT style sheet; the parameters can affect how the XSLT style sheet processes and displays the XML file. You've already encountered one way to pass a parameter to an XSLT style sheet—the XSL Transformation server behavior (see Figure 26-2). You can use the server behavior to pass either a value you manually enter, a dynamic value pulled from a database, or any of the other sources of data accessible in dynamic Web pages (see page 963). In this way, you could present a separate page for each employee simply by passing the employee's ID number to the XSLT style sheet (instead of manually creating separate XSLT files for each employee).

For this maneuver to work, you need to string together several different concepts involving both dynamic pages and XSLT files that you've already learned in this book. Here's an example of how to use XSLT parameters to dynamically filter XML data:

1. **Create an XSLT fragment as described on page 989.**

   You'll eventually include this fragment on a dynamic page (PHP, ASP, or ColdFusion) to display the final, filtered data.

2. **Follow steps 1–5 on page 996 to insert a repeat region and create a filter.**

   With this technique, all the steps in creating a filter are the same as those on page 998, except for entering the value in the Value box, as explained in the next step.

3. **In the filter's Value box type *$your_param* (see Figure 26-10).**

   Change *your_param* to a name you'd like to use for the parameter. For example, if you want to filter for an ID that matches a particular value, then you'd type *$id*. You must include the $ sign, but you can come up with whatever name you like. It helps if it's descriptive, like *$id*, *$name*, or *$price*. It also has to follow a few rules: use only numbers and letters, always start the name with a letter (not a number), don't use spaces, and stay away from punctuation marks, except for hyphens and underscores.

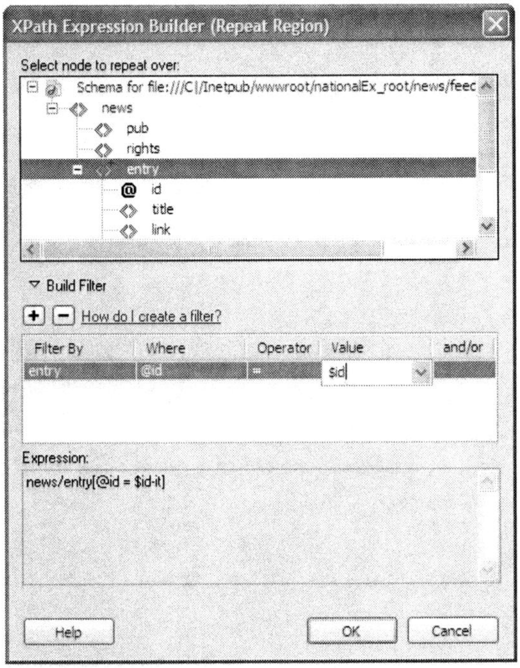

Figure 26-10:
You can use an XSLT parameter as a filter value. The parameter always begins with the $ sign and lets you dynamically filter the contents of an XML file.

Unlike a static value that you type into the Value box, like *38*, *Dave*, or *marketing*, a parameter can be different each time the XSLT style sheet does its magic. But to get it to work, you need to dip (just a bit) into Code view.

4. **Click the Code or Split button to view the XSLT code. Locate the line <xsl: template match="/">, and then click just before the opening bracket (<).**

   In XSLT, you first need to tell the style sheet that you'll be using a parameter.

5. **Type *<xsl:param name="your_param"/>*.**

   Replace "*your_param*" with the text you typed in step 3. Note that you leave off the $ sign. Also, make sure you include the forward slash before the final bracket, like this: />.

You're done with the XSLT style sheet. It's all primed to have dynamic data sent to it. The next steps involve adding the XSLT fragment to a dynamic page.

6. **Repeat steps 8–10 on page 991.**

   This step is the same process as adding any XSLT fragment to a dynamic page—that is, using the XSL Transformation server behavior.

   In the next step, you add the XSLT parameter.

7. **In the XSL Transformation window, click the + button next to the label XSLT Parameters (see Figure 26-2).**

   The Add Parameter window opens (Figure 26-11).

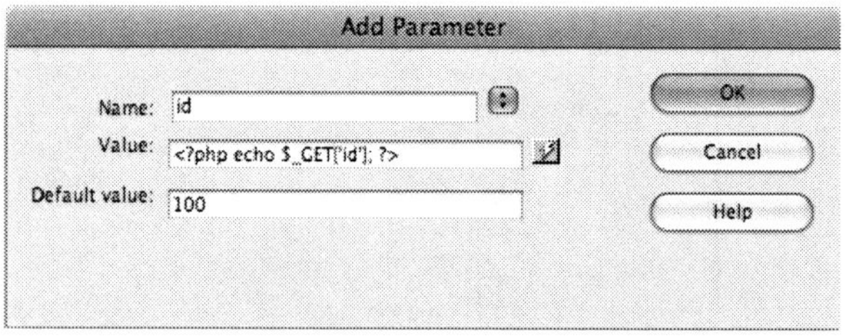

Figure 26-11: *While inserting the XSLT server behavior, you can add one or more parameters that let you pass information to the XSLT fragment. That way, you can control which data from the XML file is displayed on the Web page.*

8. **In the Name box, type the name you used in steps 3 and 5 above (don't include the $ sign).**

   The value you enter here defines the name of the parameter that the dynamic page will pass off to the XSLT style sheet. Next (and this is the magic part), you'll add the value.

9. **Click the lightning-bolt icon to the right of the Value box to open the Dynamic Data window.**

   This is the same Dynamic Data window you've encountered with dynamic pages (see Figure 24-7). Don't get it confused with the XSLT Dynamic Text box (Figure 26-6). Here, "dynamic" refers to any of the many sources of dynamic information you've used when creating database-driven pages—recordsets, URL variables, form variables, cookies, session variables, and so on. (For a recap on creating recordsets, see page 884; the other types of dynamic data can be added to the Dynamic Data window as described on page 953.)

10. **Select a source from the Field list and then click OK.**

    What you select here is the crucial part of the puzzle. You're telling the dynamic page where to get the information that will be passed off to the XSLT style sheet. To use the employee list example again, you would need to identify where the ID number used to select just a single employee comes from. Here are a few examples:

- **Recordsets.** You could use the value from a field in a recordset. For this to work, you'll need to add a recordset (pgae 884) to the dynamic page first.
- **Form fields.** One way to pass a value to a page is via a form. For example, you could add a form to a separate Web page. The form submits to this dynamic page (the one with the XSL Transformation) and includes a form menu that lists every employee's name (and includes the employee ID in the menu's value column—see page 446 for more on form menus). When a visitor selects a name from the menu, the employee ID is submitted to the dynamic page, which turns it into an XLST parameter and hands it off to the XSLT style sheet for use in the repeat region filter. (Turn to page 953 to see how to add a form field name to the dynamic data window.)
- **URL variables.** You can apply the same idea to URL variables, but instead of getting the employee ID from a menu, you'd attach it to a link to the dynamic page. For example, you might use a URL variable that looks something like this: *employee.php?id=15*. (Turn to page 953 to see how to add a URL variable to the Dynamic Data window.)

These are just a few examples. You can use dynamic data from any dynamic source: cookies, session variables, and so on.

11. **Type a value in the "Default value" box.**

    This is the value the dynamic page will use if the source you picked in step 10 doesn't come through—for example, if the dynamic page is accessed without adding a URL variable (in which case you'd be passing just *employee.php*, instead of *employee.php?id=15*). Entering a default value will ensure that the XSLT style sheet has some value to work with. If, as in this example, you're using this technique to dynamically control XML filtering, the default value should match at least one record in the XML file.

12. **Click OK to close the Add Parameter box, and then click OK once again to close the XSL Transformation window.**

    Dreamweaver adds the new server behavior and the new parameter to your page.

Note: If you want to remove or change the XSLT parameter, just re-open the XSL Transformation window by double-clicking its name in the Server Behaviors panel.

13. **Provide a way to pass the dynamic data to the page.**

    For example, if you selected a URL variable as the data source for step 10, you would add links to other pages on your site that would point to the page with the XSL Transformation—*products.php?sku=10294* or *employee.asp?id=15*, for example.

Hopefully, by this point, your brain hasn't completely melted. As you can see, XML, XSLT, and all of the other X's can be pretty X-hausting.

Part Seven: Appendixes

7

APPENDIX

A

Getting Help

Hard as it may be to believe, even a book as voluminous and detailed as this one may not answer all your questions about Dreamweaver. Fortunately, a wide range of other resources awaits when a particular feature doesn't work for you.

Getting Help from Dreamweaver

There's plenty of assistance built right into the program, from beginner tutorials to a complete browser-based help system. You can also access Dreamweaver's electronic help system and online support center from the Help menu.

Detailed Assistance

In Dreamweaver CS4, Adobe has moved all of its help documents online. There's no longer a built-in help system. Instead, when you choose Help → Dreamweaver Help (or press the F1 key), your favorite Web browser launches and takes you to a Web-based help system—it's actually structured just like the old electronic help system and is even searchable. There's a list of categories such as "Creating Pages with CSS" and "Previewing pages" that you can access to get more detailed information on various aspects of the program.

Tip: If you prefer your documentation printed, you can download a PDF of the entire Dreamweaver documentation. Just choose Help → Dreamweaver Help (or press the F1 key) to access the online help documents. In the upper right corner of the page that loads is a PDF icon–click it to download 20 megabytes worth of documentation.

Adobe also has a more interactive version of their oline help system called Community Help (the old LiveDocs system is gone). Community help is kind of like a Google for Dreamweave (in fact, Google provides the underlying technology for it.) When you search for a Dreamweaver-related topic in the Community Help system—templates, for example—you'll receive a list of pages that have something to do with Dreamweaver templates. However, rather than searching the entire Web, including Joe's "I just learned Dreamweaver two seconds ago and now I'm an expert" blog in the search, only selected Web sites are searched. Adobe has determined which Web sites actually have good and accurate information on Dreamweaver—this includes not only Adobe's Web site, but also other useful sites such as CreativePro.com and CommunityMX (*www.communitymx.com*).

You can even search the Community Help offerings from directly within Dreamweaver. The new Application toolbar includes a simple search box (see Figure A-1.) Type a term in the box and click the magnifying glass icon to launch a Web browser and retrieve a list of results that match your search term. Of course, as with all things available for free on the Internet, you may or may not find an exact answer to your question.

Figure A-1: *The Application toolbar, new in Dreamweaver CS4, provides a quick method for searching the Web for Dreamweaver tips, tricks, and information.*

The Help menu provides other useful jumping off points for exploring specific topics such as the Spry Framework, InContext Editing, and Cold Fusion. If you're interested in writing your own Web code, Dreamweaver's Reference window (select Help → Reference or Window → Reference, or press Shift-F1) provides in-depth information on HTML, CSS, JavaScript, ASP, JSP, ColdFusion, and Web accessibility.

Getting Help from Adobe

You can also get more up-to-date and personalized support from Adobe, ranging from technical notes on the Adobe Web site to pay-as-you-ask support plans.

Adobe Web Site

www.adobe.com/support/dreamweaver/

The Dreamweaver support page (also available from Help → Dreameaver Support Center) is your command center for finding help from Adobe. You can click the Contact Customer Service or Contact Technical Support links to enter the "Customer Support Portal" and create an ominous sounding "Customer Service Web Case" to request support and track your support requests. In addition, the

Support Center page lists the top support issues and recent Dreamweaver-related documents that have been added by the support team. You can also search the vast database of technical notes (short articles on specific, tweaky problems) that just may hold the answer you're seeking.

For tutorials and in-depth articles on using Dreamweaver, turn to either Adobe's Dreamweaver Design Center (*www.adobe.com/cfusion/designcenter/search.cfm?product=Dreamweaver&go=Go*) or the Dreamweaver Developer Center (*www.adobe.com/devnet/dreamweaver/*). The Developer Center includes sample database applications, video tutorials, and in-depth articles. It's worth checking out frequently.

Paid Support

www.adobe.com/support/programs/dreamweaver/

If you have deep pockets, then you can also turn to three levels of personalized, fee-based support, ranging from $39 for a single incident to the whole-hog luxury of the Gold Support program (for pricing on this option you are instructed to "contact your Adobe reseller"—watch out!). For more information on these programs, go to the Web page whose address appears above. Each program has its own phone number, so read the Web site to determine the type of support (Bronze to Gold) that you need. If you have just a single nagging question, the single-incident help program gets you an Adobe technician who will work with you to resolve the issue. But at $39, make sure you've tried to answer the question yourself first using one of the free resources listed in this appendix. Customers in the U.S. and Canada should call 1-866-MYADOBE to order this service.

The Forums

Adobe provides both online forums that you get to with a browser and newsgroups that require newsgroup-reading software like the software built into Outlook Express. To get to either of these, choose Help → Adobe Online Forums. The forums are a terrific source of information, offering almost real-time answers on Dreamweaver and related Web design techniques. Adobe sponsors several forums and news-groups. Of most interest to average Dreamweaver users are the General Discussion forum—for answers to basic questions—and the Application Development forum, where people discuss Dreamweaver's dynamic Web page features. If you're struggling with Dreamweaver's Spry tools, the Dynamic HTML General Discussion forum is a good place to seek help. Odds are one of the many knowledgeable experts who always seem to be hanging around will come back with an answer, sometimes within minutes. (If you're new to forums, *www.adobe.com/support/forums/using.html* explains how to use them.)

You can access the Web forums for Dreamweaver directly on this page: *www.adobe.com/cfusion/webforums/forum/index.cfm?forumid=12.*

Help from the Real World

If Adobe doesn't have the answer, there's probably a Web site somewhere that does. In fact, you're likely to find more honest critiques of the program on some of these sites. Here are two of the best non-Adobe sites for answers.

DMX Zone

www.dmxzone.com

The DMX Zone includes tutorials, extensions, and Adobe-related news. It also offers "Premium Content," a subscription-based service that provides more in-depth information on Dreamweaver.

Community MX

www.communitymx.com

Another subscription service (it's so hard to find free help these days). This site has lots of material for all things MX (Dreamweaver once had "MX" in its name), including Flash and other Adobe programs. It does have some free content as well, and it's updated regularly.

APPENDIX

B

Dreamweaver CS4, Menu by Menu

Dreamweaver CS4: The Missing Manual is quite complete; in its pages, you'll find descriptions of every major Dreamweaver function (and most minor ones). In the interests of completeness, however, here's a quick reference to every command in every menu—and the answer to the occasional "What does that mean?" mystery.

File Menu

The commands in the File menu control the open Dreamweaver document as a whole. They also include basic file functions like saving and quitting:

- **New.** Opens the New Document window, which lets you select a new, blank document among many different types, from basic HTML pages to dynamic pages like ASP or PHP. This window also lets you access templates you've created for your site.
- **Open.** Opens the standard Open File dialog box so you can choose an existing Dreamweaver document to open. You can set the Show pop-up menu to show only specific types of documents—only HTML or style sheets, for example. The Preview button displays a thumbnail image of the document, if one's available.
- **Browse in Bridge.** Bridge is Adobe's file manager program. It's like the Windows Explorer or Mac Finder. Bridge is a way to browse, find and open documents. It's part of Adobe's graphic heritage and works best with image files—in other words, Photoshop and Illustrator files, *not* Dreamweaver documents.

- **Open Recent.** Displays a submenu that lists the 10 most recently opened documents. Selecting a document from the list opens it. The last option in this menu, "Reopen Documents on Startup," is kind of cool. If you quit Dreamweaver when any documents are still open (and this option is checked), those documents automatically reopen the next time you start up Dreamweaver.
- **Open in Frame.** Opens an existing HTML page within one frame of a frameset. To make this command available, you must first have a frameset open and click inside a frame to select it—not just in the Frameset document. The Select HTML file dialog box opens and lets you navigate to the file you wish to insert into the frame. You can also choose to make the file's URL relative to the document or the root folder, as described in Chapter 5. (See note about frames in the box on page 171.)
- **Close.** Closes the open Dreamweaver document. If you have unsaved changes, Dreamweaver gives you the opportunity to save them.
- **Close All.** Closes *all* currently open documents. If you have unsaved changes, Dreamweaver gives you the opportunity to save them.
- **Share My Screen.** This option is new in Dreamweaver CS4 and works with Adobe's ConnectNow Web conferencing service. You can share your Dreamweaver screen with students, colleagues, or your Aunt who's learning how to create Web sites. The service lets you provide real-time demonstrations of Dreamweaver in action. It's free for up to three people viewing the demonstration. Learn more about ConnectNow at *www.adobe.com/acom/connectnow/*.
- **Save (Save Frameset/Save Frame).** Saves any changes you've made to your document. The Save command is dimmed if you haven't made any changes to the document since the last time you saved it.

Note: If you're working on a frames-based document, this command may say Save Frameset or Save Frame, depending on what's selected.

- **Save As (Save Frameset As/Save Frame As).** Saves a copy of the current document under a new name. The behavior of this command has changed in Dreamweaver CS4—the original document you're saving a copy of reverts to its *last* saved state. In other words, only the Save As copy has the most recent changes you made to the original…weird. Here again, if you're working on a frames-based document, this command says either Save Frameset As or Save Frame As, depending on what's selected.
- **Save All.** Saves changes to all the open documents, including files like external CSS and JavaScript files listed in the Related Files bar (page 410). This is a great command to make sure you save all changes to a Web page and any linked style sheets.

- **Save to Remote Server.** Lets you save the current file to *any* site for which you've defined a remote site. In other words, if you use Dreamweaver's FTP feature to move your files to a Web server (see Chapter 17), this option lets you directly access that Web server. In fact, it lets you access any Web server for any Web site you've defined in Dreamweaver. Because of this behavior, this option can be risky. You can accidentally save a file into the wrong Web site, or in the wrong folder of the right Web site. Therefore, it's generally better to use the Files panel and its Put Files button—see page 678.
- **Save as Template.** Saves the current document as a template file with the suffix .dwt. The "Save as Template" dialog box appears, so you can specify the template's file name, and indicate which site it belongs to. Dreamweaver automatically saves all template documents in a Templates folder in the selected site's folder. Templates are discussed in Chapter 19.
- **Revert.** Undoes any changes you've made to the document since the last time you saved it. Edit → Undo is often a better choice; it might take a few more steps to undo all the changes you've made, but it can actually undo changes *past* your last save. So if you're one of those gotta-save-it-every-5-seconds types, the Undo command is for you.
- **Page Setup.** Lets you set up printer settings (like what size paper you wish to print on) for the Print Code command listed next.
- **Print Code.** Prints the code (that is, what you see in Code view) of the current document.
- **Import.** Lets you import data from other sources into your Dreamweaver document, such as XML data into a Template document or tabular data from a CSV (comma separated value) file. Windows users can also choose to import text from a Microsoft Word document or tabular data from an Excel Spreadsheet.
- **Export.** Extracts tabular data or template data as XML from your Dreamweaver document, for use in other applications.
- **Convert.** Converts older HTML pages into a variety of more modern formats like HTML 4.01 Strict and two forms of XHTML. Unfortunately, it's kind of hit-or-miss: this feature can't always update older files to more modern standards.
- **Preview in Browser.** Opens the current document in your Web browser. By selecting Edit Browser List, you can add new browsers to, or delete browsers from, your browser list, or specify a preferred browser. This command also includes an option to preview your page in a program called Device Central—this Adobe program is meant to let a Web designer preview a Web page in mobile devices. It works well if you're working on a Flash movie, but it's not so good for regular Web pages.

- **Check Page.** Checks the current page for a variety of problems, such as broken links, code that's incompatible with various browsers, and accessibility limitations. These same tools are available from the Results panel for checking an entire site's worth of files—choose Window → Results, and then click an appropriate tab—like the Link Checker to check links.
- **Validate.** Lets you check an HTML or XML file to make sure it conforms to the proper Web standards and document type definition (see page 46). In other words, it checks to make sure your HTML or XML is correct.
- **Compare with Remote/Compare with Testing.** Lets you use a third-party code-comparison tool to see how a local copy of a page differs from either the remote copy (on the Web server) or a copy on your testing server. This lets you see exactly what code differs between two copies of the same page. This feature is discussed on page 416.
- **Design Notes.** Opens the Design Notes window (Chapter 17), where you can add additional information about the document, set the status, and choose to have the Design Note appear whenever the document is opened.

Note: To use Design Notes on your site, you must make sure that in the Site Definition window's "Design notes" section, the Maintain Design Notes option is selected.

- **Exit/Quit.** Exits Dreamweaver. If any of your open Dreamweaver documents have unsaved changes, the program prompts you to save them before quitting. (Mac users will find this option under the Dreamweaver menu.)

Edit Menu

The Edit menu applies common document changes like copying and pasting:

- **Undo.** Undoes the most recent change made to your document. You can choose this command repeatedly to move progressively backwards through your changes, even *after* you've saved the document.
- **Redo (Repeat).** Restores whatever changes you just made by using the Undo command. Selecting Redo multiple times moves you progressively forward through changes you've undone. If you've just performed an operation other than Undo, Repeat appears instead of Redo. This property lets you repeat the last action. For example, if you just pressed Delete, the Repeat command presses it again.
- **Cut.** Deletes the selected text or objects from the document, and copies them to the invisible Macintosh or Windows Clipboard so they can be pasted elsewhere. (The Clipboard holds only one selection at a time.)
- **Copy.** Copies the selected text or object to the Clipboard so it can be pasted elsewhere—without disturbing the original.

- **Paste.** Places the most recent selection from the Clipboard into your document at the insertion point.
- **Paste Special.** Opens the Paste Special window, which lets you choose how you wish to paste the Clipboard into your document. Options range from Text Only for just plain text to increasingly more elaborate options, which force Dreamweaver to attempt to preserve various levels of formatting, such as styles, bold, italics, bulleted lists, and so on.
- **Clear.** Deletes the selected text or objects from the document without placing it on the Clipboard.
- **Select All.** Selects everything in the document so you can make document-wide changes in one fell swoop.
- **Select Parent Tag.** Increases the current selection to include everything within the *parent tag*, including its content. If you had a table cell selected, this command would increase the selection to the entire table *row*. Choosing the command a second time would increase the selection to include the entire table. In short, this command ensures that any changes you make apply to the entire tag.
- **Select Child.** Decreases the current selection to include everything within the child tag, including its contents. If you selected a table row, choosing this command would decrease that selection to include only the first table *cell* and its contents.
- **Find and Replace.** Opens the "Find and Replace" window, which you can use to search the document—or entire site—for a specific word, tag, or source code, and replace it with something different (see page 782). This command lets you make such changes either en masse or one instance at a time.
- **Find Selection.** This command lets you find another instance of the current selection. Say you've selected the word "Mothball" on the page. With this command, you search the page for another example of "Mothball."
- **Find Next.** Uses the most recent search settings from the "Find and Replace" window to search the current document, highlighting the next instance of the requested search item.
- **Go to Line.** Opens the Go To Line dialog box. Type a number, and Dreamweaver positions the cursor at the beginning of the specified line of code. (Available only in Code view.)
- **Show Code Hints.** Immediately displays any code hints (overriding the delay set in the Preferences window) available for the current tag. Code Hints, described in Chapter 10, provide a pop-up menu of tag properties appropriate for the current tag (available only in Code view, and when using the Insert Tag command [Ctrl-T]).
- **Refresh Code Hints.** Doesn't seem to do much of anything.

- **Code Hint Tools.** When working in Code view, lets you access Dreamweaver's color picker, "Browse for File" button, and list of fonts so you don't have to type things like *#FF6633, ../../images/dog.gif*, or *Arial, Helvetica, sans-serif*, every time you use a color, link to a file, or want to use a font.
- **Indent Code.** Adds one indent before the selected line of code. (Available only in Code view.)
- **Outdent Code.** Removes one indent from the selected line of code. (Available only in Code view.)
- **Balance Braces.** When you're editing a script in Code view, this command helps you check for unbalanced braces (that is, an introductory "{" without a closing "}") by highlighting the matching tags enclosing the selected code. It doesn't do anything for plain HTML, but if you're writing a JavaScript program or using a dynamic programming language like PHP or ASP, it can help identify missing braces—a common source of programming errors. Works with ( ) as well.
- **Repeating Entries.** Lets you cut, copy, paste, and delete repeating regions in templates. Repeating regions are described in Chapter 19.
- **Code collapse.** Hides a selection of code in Code view, so you need to see only the code you're interested in working on. This feature is discussed on page 404, and since the same options are available more directly from the coding toolbar, you can skip these menu options.
- **Edit with External Editor.** If you haven't already specified an external HTML code editor, such as BBEdit or Notepad, to use when editing large amounts of source code, this command opens the Preferences window so that you can find and select one on your hard drive. Once you've specified an editor, this command opens the current document in that editor.
- **Tag Libraries.** Lets you modify the way Dreamweaver writes code for various types of tags: HTML, ColdFusion, ASP, and so on. You can create new tag libraries for working with other types of tag-based languages, or modify the ones that ship with Dreamweaver.
- **Keyboard Shortcuts.** Opens the Keyboard Shortcuts window, and shows you all Dreamweaver's current keyboard shortcuts. You can create a new set of shortcuts for specific sites or programs, or export the settings to HTML to share with others. (You must duplicate the factory settings before you can add or delete your own shortcuts.) Details are in Chapter 21. (On the Mac, this option appears under the Dreamweaver menu.)
- **Preferences.** Opens the Preference window, which is full of options that customize the way Dreamweaver works. There are 20 categories of preferences, including the color and format of different HTML tags, shorthand for CSS styles, and the order in which panels appear on the screen. (On the Mac, this option appears under the Dreamweaver menu.)

View Menu

The View menu controls the document window's appearance. A checkmark in the menu lets you know which view you're in:

- **Zoom In.** Zooms in on the document in 50% increments. If you're looking at a document at normal size (100%), selecting this option zooms in to 150%; selecting it again zooms in to 200%.
- **Zoom Out.** Zooms out from the document in 50% increments.
- **Magnification.** Lets you choose from a list of magnification levels from the absurdly small and illegible 6% all the way to a ridiculously large, land-of-the-giant-pixels 6,400%.
- **Fit Selection, Fit All, Fit Width.** Additional magnification options that zoom in or out, depending on the size of the document or selected element.
- **Code.** Displays the file's source code.
- **Design.** Displays the file's visual design.
- **Code and Design.** Splits the document window into two panes: source code on the left (or top), visual design at the right (or bottom). You can adjust where the split panes appear (see page 396), and can adjust how much of each pane is visible by dragging the center divider up or down.
- **Switch Views.** Switches between the Code and Design views.
- **Refresh Design View.** Updates the Design view to reflect changes you've made directly to the source code in either Code view or split ("Code and Design") view.
- **Live View.** Displays the Web page as it would appear in a Web browser (actually as it would appear in Apple's Safari browser). You can preview JavaScript, Flash movies, and other interactive page features.
- **Live View Options.** Lets you control the display of Live View. You can pause JavaScript—a useful way to see the HTML that JavaScript creates on the fly—disable JavaScript, turn off plug-ins, and control settings that affect how the page is displayed while in Live View.
- **Head Content.** Opens a new menu bar in the main document window that contains shortcuts to accessing the file's Head contents. You can use these menu items to highlight your document's Title tags, meta tags, and scripts, and then, in the Property inspector, edit their content.
- **Noscript Content.** When inserting JavaScript code into the document window, you can also include what's called "Noscript" tags—information that appears in browsers that don't understand JavaScript (of which there are very few), or which have their JavaScript turned off. After selecting this option, all information inside noscript tags appears in the document window. To hide this information, select this menu option again.

- **Table Mode.** Lets you switch between the standard Table view, Expanded Tables view, and something called Layout Table view. Layout Table view is a holdover from earlier versions of Dreamweaver. This view is intended to make creating table-based layouts easier, but more often creates hard-to-edit HTML. Layout Table View used to appear front and center in the program, but the Adobe engineers have hidden it away in this menu, so that those who used the tool in the past can continue to use it. But don't you be tempted to use it! CSS is a far superior way of laying out Web pages (see Chapter 9 for the details).
- **Visual Aids.** Lets you summon onscreen symbols that represent typically invisible page elements like image maps, anchors, and borders.
- **Style Rendering.** Lets you hide or show the effect of all style sheets on a page, or selectively display the formatting changes caused by a style sheet that's applied for a particular media—for example, screen only or printer only.
- **Code View Options.** Lets you adjust the appearance of your HTML code in Code view. You can turn on (or off) options that wrap lines of text to fit in the document window, add line numbers, highlight invalid HTML, turn on syntax coloring, or indent lines of code.
- **Rulers.** When you choose Show, Dreamweaver displays rulers along the top and left sides of the document window. Using the options you find here, you can choose your ruler units: pixels, inches, or centimeters. You can also reset the orientation of the two rulers so that both start from zero in the screen's upper-left corner.
- **Grid.** Places a grid of vertical and horizontal lines over the document window to use as a guide when building your layouts. Selecting Edit Grid opens the Grid Setting dialog box, where you can adjust your grid's colors, spacing, behaviors, and line appearance.
- **Guides.** Shows, hides, locks, and erases user-added guidelines that have been dragged from a ruler onto the page. Also controls options for guides, and displays guidelines that mark the visible area of a Web browser window on monitors of different resolutions.
- **Tracing Image.** Adjusts the document's background tracing image. You can load a new tracing image, make a current one visible, or adjust its position.
- **Plugins.** Lets you "play" browser plug-ins within the document window to test embedded media. You can choose to play a document's plug-ins one at a time, or all at once, to simulate how the page will look to your viewers.
- **Display External Files.** You can insert images and other files from your own or other Web sites on the Internet. When you insert an image, for example, instead of selecting a file from your site, you can type or paste an absolute URL (page 162) to a graphic located on the Internet. Dreamweaver even displays the image in Design view, but only if this option is checked. Because it depends on an

Internet connection to display the image, pages with links to external files may take longer to display in Dreamweaver (since it has to get the images and files over the Web). If you have lots of external images and files, and your pages open sluggishly in Dreamweaver, uncheck this option.

- **Color Icons.** Dreamweaver's interface underwent an overhaul in CS4—the once bright icons are now hip, dull, and gray. If you miss the colorful icons from Dreamweaver CS3 turn this option on.
- **Hide Panels (Show Panels).** Hides all open panels. If panels are already hidden, the command says Show Panels instead, and restores the panels to their original positions.
- **Toolbars.** Displays toolbars for use with Dreamweaver. Select Document from the submenu to display the Toolbar menu at the top of the document window. This menu offers common commands like the document's View settings, page title, file management options, code navigation options, and browser preview. The Standard toolbar option displays a toolbar with common buttons for common commands, such as opening files; closing files; and cutting, copying, and pasting content. The Style Rendering toolbar lets you toggle style sheets off and on like the Style Rendering menu described earlier in this section.
- **Related Files.** Lists all external CSS, JavaScript, and server-side programming files used by the current Web page. Select one and you'll see the code for that file. Better yet, just use the Related Files toolbar that appears in the document window—it's much faster than using this hidden away menu.
- **Code Navigator.** Pops open the Code Navigator window so you can scan all CSS rules that apply to the current HTML element (see page 320).
- **Show Spry Tooltips.** Shows or hides Spry tooltips on a Web page in Design view (see page 513 for more on Spry Tooltips).

Insert Menu

The Insert menu adds selected page elements to the document at the insertion point's position. The commands listed here correspond to the buttons on the Objects panel:

- **Tag.** Opens the Tag Chooser window, which provides access to all the tags—not only HTML, but any tag Dreamweaver has stored in its Tag Library (see entry under the Edit menu on page 1020). You can insert any tag and set any of its properties from this window. However, Dreamweaver doesn't make sure you're inserting the tag correctly, so you should understand HTML (or the tag language you're using) before trying this option.
- **Image.** Inserts an image file, such as a JPEG, PNG or GIF, into the document. The Select Image Source window appears, and lets you navigate to the file you want on your hard drive. You can choose to make the URL for the file relative to either the document or the Site Root.

- **Image Objects**. Lets you insert placeholder graphics, rollover images, or HTML from Fireworks. These options are discussed in Chapter 6. Avoid the Navigation Bar listed here—it's left over from earlier versions of Dreamweaver and it's just plain bad. You're much better off using the new Spry Navigation Bar discussed in Chapter 5.
- **Media**. Inserts other types of media files, including Flash, Shockwave, Generator Applets, Plug-ins, and Active X. In most cases, the standard Select File window appears, which you can use to navigate to the desired file. This menu also lets you insert Flash text, Flash buttons, and the Image Viewer Flash element (an old and clunky Flash-based slideshow tool).
- **Table**. Inserts a new table into the document. The Insert Table dialog box appears, and lets you format the table by specifying the number of rows and columns; the table width; measurements for cell padding, cell spacing, and the table border; and whether or not and where to include table headers.
- **Table Objects**. Provides methods to insert tabular data (see the Import entry under the File menu on page 1017) and add other table-related tags such as the <th>—table header—tag into the page. The tag options listed under this menu item assume you understand HTML and let you just insert the tags, without making sure you're doing it correctly.
- **Layout Objects**. Lets you insert absolutely positioned divs, regular divs, table lay-out cells, and table layout tables. This menu also includes the new Spry Widgets like the Spry Navigation bar discussed in Chapter 5, and the Spry panel widgets discussed in Chapter 12.
- **Form**. Inserts Form Objects—the <form> tag, text fields, buttons, checkboxes, or lists—into the document. (If you haven't already inserted the <form> tag, Dreamweaver prompts you to do so.)
- **Hyperlink**. Inserts a link. The Insert Hyperlink dialog box lets you specify the text that should appear inside the link, the file to link to, as well as many other link options such as target and tab index.
- **Email Link**. Creates a new email link at the insertion point. The Insert Email Link dialog box appears; specify both the email address and the link's text (such as "Click to email me").
- **Named Anchor**. Inserts a named anchor for adding links *within* a page. See page 176.
- **Date**. Inserts the current date into the document. The Insert Date dialog box lets you format the appearance of the day of the week, the date, and the time. You can also elect to have the date automatically updated each time the document is saved.
- **Server-Side Include**. Opens a Find File window, from which you select a file that's dynamically added to the content of your page. Works only with special server setup, such as the dynamic server-driven pages discussed in Part 6 of this book.

- **Comment.** Inserts an HTML comment into your page. This comment isn't viewable in Web browsers, but in Dreamweaver's Design view, it appears as a little gold shield. Use these to leave notes for yourself and others about specific information about a page. For example, a comment indicating where an ad should be placed can help someone updating the page.

- **HTML.** Menu including lots of specific HTML tags, such as a horizontal rule, frames, text objects (many of which are also available under the Text menu), script objects for JavaScript, and head tags that go in the *head* portion of a Web page—including meta tags such as keywords and descriptions used by some search engines.

- **Template Objects.** When working on a template file, this menu option lets you insert many of Dreamweaver's template features, such as Optional, Editable, and Repeating Regions.

- **Recent Snippets.** Lists the most recently inserted snippets. Selecting a snippet from the list inserts it into the document. Snippets are discussed in Chapter 18.

- **Spry.** Inserts any of Dreamweaver's Spry objects, including the Spry Navigation bar (Chapter 5), Spry Form Validation widgets (Chapter 11), and Spry Data and Layout widgets (Chapter 12).

- **InContext Editing.** Lets you insert tags related to Adobe's InContext Editing service. This online, commercial (as in you gotta pay) service lets non-Web saavy individuals update specially created Web pages. In other words, you can create Web sites and have your clients do all the boring updates themselves. You can learn more about this service at *www.adobe.com/products/incontextediting/.*

- **Data Objects.** Used for inserting server behaviors associated with Dreamweaver's dynamic database-driven Web site tools—discussed in Part 6 of this book.

- **XSLT Objects** (visible only when working on an XSL file). Inserts various objects for converting XML data into a Web browser–readable format. This feature is discussed in Chapter 26.

- **Customize Favorites.** Lets you add your favorite objects from the Insert panel into a special "favorites" tag, so your most common objects, images, divs, roll-overs, tables, and so on can be just one click away. See page 28 for more information.

- **Get More Objects.** Opens the Adobe Exchange for Dreamweaver Web site in your browser. There you can search for and download new extensions and objects to add new features to your copy of Dreamweaver. Use the Commands → Manage Extensions command to add downloaded extensions to Dreamweaver.

Modify Menu

You can use the commands in the Modify menu to adjust the properties of common document objects like links, tables, and layers:

- **Page Properties.** Opens the Page Properties window, where you can specify document-wide attributes—such as the page title, background and link colors, page margins, and background image—or select a *tracing image* to use as a reference for designing the page.

- **Template Properties.** Opens the Template Properties window, where you can modify settings for various template features, such as controlling the visibility of optional regions, the properties of editable attributes, and the values of any template expressions you've created. Available only when you're working on a template-based page, as described in Chapter 19.

- **Selection Properties.** When this item is selected (as indicated by a checkmark in the menu), the Properties inspector palette is on the screen; you use it to edit the current settings for selected page elements. This command is the same as choosing Window → Properties.

- **CSS Styles.** Controls the display of the CSS Styles Panel. A checkmark tells you that the panel is open. This item has the same effect as choosing CSS Styles from the Window menu.

- **Edit Tag.** Opens a dialog box with detailed options for the HTML tag that's active in the current document. This advanced feature is for the true HTML geek—it gives access to *all* the properties for a specific tag (not just the ones Dreamweaver displays in the Property inspector). But skip this option: The Tag inspector, which provides a less intrusive panel with all the same options, is better. Choose Window → Tag Inspector to open it.

- **Quick Tag Editor.** Lets you edit an HTML tag without leaving Design view. If nothing on the page is selected, the Quick Tag editor prompts you to enter a new HTML tag at the insertion point (by choosing from the alphabetical menu). But if text or an object is already selected when the Quick Tag Editor is opened, the window displays the selection's HTML tags for editing.

- **Make Link.** Turns a highlighted page element (graphic or text) into a link. The standard Select File dialog box appears; choose the document you want to open when someone clicks the link.

- **Remove Link.** This command is available only when a link is selected or the insertion point is inside a link. Remove Link deletes hyperlinks by removing the <a href> tag from the selected text or image.

- **Open Linked Page.** Opens the linked page in a new document window. This command is available only when a link is selected or the insertion point is inside a link. (You can, however, hold down the Ctrl key [⌘] and double-click a link to open the page to which it's linked.)

- **Link Target.** Sets a link's target and defines whether the linked page appears in the same browser window or a new one. You can choose from blank, parent, self, or top targets, or manually define the target in the Set Target dialog box. This command is available only when a link is selected or the insertion point is inside a link. (See Chapter 5 for details on links.)

- **Table.** Opens a list of options for modifying a selected table. You can adjust the number of rows and columns, add row or column spans, or completely clear cells' defined heights and widths (see Chapter 7).
- **Image.** Opens a list of options for modifying a selected image, including optimizing it in Fireworks, or using one of the new built-in image-editing tools, such as the crop, resample, and sharpen tools. See page 236.
- **Frameset.** Offers options for splitting the current page into *frames*. Or choose the Edit No Frames Content command to create alternative Web-page material that can be read by older browsers that don't support frames. Frames aren't used much any more, and they're best avoided by the professional Web designer.
- **Arrange.** Lets you change the Z-index (the front-to-back order) of overlapping absolutely positioned elements. You can choose to send one element in front of another absolutely positioned element, send it to the back, and so on. You can also tell Dreamweaver to prevent overlapping elements altogether. If two or more layers are selected, you can also choose from one of this menu's alignment options to align things like the tops of two elements. See Chapter 9 for more on absolutely positioned elements.
- **Convert.** Don't use this menu! It's meant to take a table-based layout and turn it into a layout using CSS absolute positioning. It doesn't work well at all. Better to recreate your design using the CSS layout techniques described in Chapter 9. The other option—converting absolutely positioned elements to table layout—produces awful HTML and no benefit (unless you're building a "Retro Web Design Circa 1998" Web site).
- **Navigation Bar.** Skip this option. It's meant to help edit the navigation bar available from the Insert → Image Objects (see "Image Objects" on page 1025). The Spry Navigation bar discussed in Chapter 5 is far superior.
- **Library.** Lets you add selected document objects to the site's Library file (Chapter 18). You can also update the current document, or multiple documents, to reflect any changes you've made to a Library object.
- **Templates.** These commands affect *template* documents (Chapter 19). Using these commands, you can apply a pre-existing template to the current page, separate the page from its template, or update the page to reflect changes made to its template. If the open document is a template file, you can use this menu to create or delete editable regions (remove template markup), and update all site files based on that template. You can also use this menu to add repeating template regions and editable tag attributes.

Format Menu

The commands in this menu let you format and modify the document's text:

- **Indent.** Adds one level of indentation to everything within the current block-level element (paragraph, headline, bulleted list).

- **Outdent.** Removes one level of indentation from everything within the current block-level element.
- **Paragraph Format.** Applies a paragraph format, such as Heading 1, Heading 2, or preformatted text, to all the text in the current block-level element. You can also go to the submenu, and choose None to remove the paragraph formatting.
- **Align.** Aligns text in the selected paragraph to the left margin, center, or right margin of the document. If the paragraph is inside a table cell or layer, Dreamweaver aligns it with the left, center, or right of that cell or layer.
- **List.** Turns the selected paragraph into an ordered, unordered, or definition *list*. You can edit the list's format by selecting the submenu's Properties option.
- **Font.** Lets you choose from a list of common font combinations for application to the selected text. When displaying text, your visitor's browser moves down the list of assigned paragraph fonts until it finds one installed on its system (Chapter 3). You can create your own combination of paragraph fonts by going to the submenu, and choosing Edit Font List.
- **Style.** Applies predefined text styles—such as Bold, Italic, or Strikethrough—to the selected text.
- **CSS Styles.** Lets you create new CSS styles, and then apply them to selected text (Chapter 4). You can also choose to attach an existing style sheet to the current document, or export the document's own style sheet for use in other sites.
- **Color.** Opens the standard Mac or Windows color picker dialog box, so that you can choose a color to apply to the selected text. *Macintosh*: You can choose from a variety of color palettes, including CMYK, RGB, HTML (Web safe), HSV, and HLS. *Windows*: In general, the Property inspector's color box is a better way to assign Web colors to text.

Commands Menu

You can use the Commands menu to apply advanced features to your Dreamweaver document. Some menu items, such as the Record commands, eliminate repetitive tasks; others, such as the Clean Up HTML command, fix common problems in a single sweep:

- **Start/Stop Recording.** Records a series of actions that can then be reapplied to other parts of the document (Chapter 20). When you select the Start Recording command, Dreamweaver records each of your actions until you choose Stop Recording. Note that Dreamweaver retains only one recorded command at a time.
- **Play Recorded Command.** Reapplies the most recently recorded command.
- **Edit Command List.** Opens a list of all saved commands. You can rename the commands, or delete them permanently.

- **Get More Commands.** Opens the Adobe Exchange for Dreamweaver Web site in a new browser window so that you can search for and download new extensions or commands. Extensions are downloaded to your Extension Manager (see Chapter 21).
- **Get AIR Extension.** Takes you to Adobe's Web site where you can download a Dreamweaver extension that lets you use Dreamweaver to create Adobe AIR applications—desktop-based programs that work (without a Web browser) using common Web technologies like HTML, JavaScript, and Flash.
- **Manage Extensions.** Opens the Extension Manager, a program that lets you manage extensions you download from the Adobe Exchange Web site (Chapter 21). The Extension Manager helps you install, delete, and selectively disable extensions.
- **Check Spelling.** Checks the current document for possible spelling errors (see page 87).
- **Apply Source Formatting.** Changes you make to Dreamweaver's HTML source formatting (which is defined in the Preferences window and the SourceFormat.txt file) apply only to newly created documents. This command, on the other hand, offers a way to apply these formatting preferences to existing HTML documents.
- **Apply Source Formatting to Selection.** Same as the previous command, "Apply Source Formatting", but applies only to whatever you've selected. In this way, you can make sure the HTML for, say, a <table> is nicely formatted (by selecting it and applying this command), while the rest of your finely crafted HTML is left alone.
- **Clean Up HTML/XHTML.** Opens a list of options for correcting common HTML problems, such as empty tags or redundant nested tags. Once you've selected what you'd like to fix, Dreamweaver applies those changes to the current document, and, if requested, provides a log of the number and type of changes made (see Chapter 16).
- **Clean Up Word HTML.** If you import HTML that was generated by Microsoft Word, you often end up with unnecessary or cluttered HTML tags that can affect your site's performance. This command opens a list of options that can correct common formatting problems in Microsoft Word's HTML. Dreamweaver applies your selected changes to the document and, if requested, displays a log of the number and type of changes it made.
- **Externalize JavaScript.** Let's you take all the JavaScript code that's written in a Web page and dump it into an external JavaScript file. This can make Web pages download more quickly and lets you reuse common JavaScript programs throughout the site. Page 426 discusses this new Dreamweaver CS4 tool.
- **Remove FLV Detection.** If you've added Flash Video to your page as described on page 604, Dreamweaver inserts some JavaScript code to help make sure your site's visitors can view the video. Unfortunately, if you just delete the movie from your page, the JavaScript code is left in the page. This command removes it.

- **Optimize Image.** Opens the selected image in the Image Preview window, where you can experiment with different compression settings to find the best balance between file size and image quality. See page 217.
- **Create Web Photo Album.** Lets you turn a folder of images into a Web-based photo album. The Create Web Photo Album window appears; specify a title for your album, the source folder, and so on.

Note: This command requires Adobe's Fireworks image-editing program, which creates thumbnail and full-size versions of each image. Dreamweaver then creates a Web site with one page displaying all the thumbnail images. The thumbnails are linked to individual HTML pages containing the full-size images.

- **Sort Table.** Sorts the information in a selected table. You can choose to sort alphabetically or numerically, in ascending or descending order. You can't apply this command to tables that include *rowspans* or *colspans*.
- **Insert Mark of the Web.** This slightly Satanic-sounding menu option is applicable only to Windows XP with Service Pack 2 and Vista. The Service Pack 2 update for XP inserted code into Internet Explorer to "protect" it from malicious Web page code. Unfortunately, this also has the effect of preventing you from previewing JavaScript effects—like the image rollovers discussed in Chapter 6—or Flash movies. Strangely, this happens only when you preview a local page (on your own computer), not when you view a page on the Internet. This menu option lets you overcome that peculiar problem.
- **Attach an XSLT Stylesheet.** This menu option, available only when working on a XML file, lets you attach an XSL file, which miraculously transforms cryptic XML into a beautiful, browser-viewable page. This feature is discussed in Chapter 26.

Site Menu

As its name suggests, the commands in this menu apply to your entire Web site, rather than one document at a time. These commands can help keep your Web site organized, and promote collaboration between large workgroups:

- **New Site.** Opens the New Site window, where you can set up a site for working in Dreamweaver.
- **Manage Sites.** Opens the Manage Sites Panel where you can create, delete, or edit site definitions. See Chapter 15.

Note: The next five menu commands let you transfer files between your computer (the *local* site) and a Web server (the *remote* site). These commands, in other words, don't work unless you've first defined a remote site in the Site Definition window. In addition, these operations work only on files that you've *selected* in the Site window.

- **Get.** Copies files (those you've selected in the Site window) from the remote server to the local site folder for editing. Note that if the File Check In and Check Out feature is active, the downloaded files aren't editable.

- **Check Out.** Copies files (those you've selected in the Site window) from the remote server to your local site, and marks them on the remote server as *checked out*. No one else can make changes to the document until you upload it back onto the remote server.

- **Put.** Uploads files (those you've selected in the Site window) from the local site to the remote site. The uploaded file replaces the previous version of the document.

- **Check In.** Uploads checked-out files from the local site to the remote site, and makes them available for others to edit. Once a file is checked in, the version on your local site becomes read-only (you can open it, but you can't edit it).

- **Undo Check Out.** Removes the checked-out status of selected files. The file isn't uploaded back to the remote server, so any changes you made to the file aren't transmitted to the Web server. Your local copy of the file becomes read-only.

- **Show Checked Out By.** Lets you see who's checked out a particular file.

- **Locate in Site.** When working on a document, selecting this option opens the Site window and highlights that document's file in the site's local folder.

Note: See Chapter 17 for the full scoop on remote sites, local sites, and checking files in and out.

- **Reports.** Opens the Reports window, and lists options for generating new reports (Chapter 16). Reports can monitor workflow (such as design notes and checkout status) and common HTML problems (such as missing Alt text, empty tags, untitled documents, and redundant nested tags). You can generate a report on just the open document, multiple documents, or the entire site.

- **Synchronize Sitewide.** Opens the Synchronization window, which lets you compare all your local files with all the files on your Web server. Use this to make sure all the most recent files you've updated locally are transferred to the Web server, or vice versa.

- **Check Links Sitewide.** Analyzes the current site for broken links, external links, and orphaned pages. Dreamweaver then generates a report listing all the found problems. You can fix problematic links directly in the Report window—or click the file name to open the errant file in a new document window, with the link highlighted and ready to repair.

- **Change Link Sitewide.** In one step, replaces a broken link that appears multiple times throughout your site. In the Change Link dialog box, you first specify the incorrect link; below it, enter the link with which you'd like to replace it. Dreamweaver searches your site, replacing every instance of the old link.

- **Advanced.** Provides access to advanced site options, such as the FTP Log—a record of all FTP file transfer activity; "Recreate Site Cache", which forces Dreamweaver to rescan the site's files and update its cache file to reflect any changes to the files or links in the site; "Remove Connection Scripts" for removing the script files Dreamweaver creates to work with dynamic, database-driven Web sites; and "Deploy Supporting Files" to move necessary programming files to the Web server when using Dreamweaver's ASP.NET server model to build dynamic pages. (Since Dreamweaver CS4 no longer provides the tools to easily build .NET web pages, this last menu option is, uh, useless.)

Window Menu

This menu controls which panels and windows are visible or hidden at the moment. (A checkmark in the menu denotes open panels.)

- **Insert.** Opens the Insert panel, from which you can insert various types of objects (such as images, layers, or forms) into your document. The Insert panel also contains options for switching between Layout and Standard table views, and accessing options for dynamic Web pages.
- **Properties.** Opens the Property inspector, where you can edit the relevant properties for a selected object. The options in the Property inspector depend on which page element's selected.
- **CSS Styles.** Opens the CSS (Cascading Style Sheet) Styles panel, from which you can define and edit CSS styles, or apply existing ones to selected text.
- **AP Elements.** Opens the AP Elements panel, which lists all elements that have been positioned on the page using CSS positioning. See Chapter 9 for more details.
- **Databases.** Opens the Databases panel for working with dynamic Web sites. This panel lets you connect your site to a database, view the structure of a database, and even preview data currently stored in the database.
- **Bindings.** Opens the Bindings panel, which lets you create database queries for working with dynamic sites. In addition, the panel displays and lets you add dynamic data to a Web page.
- **Server Behaviors.** Opens the Server Behaviors panel, the control panel for viewing, editing, and adding advanced functionality to dynamic Web pages.
- **Components.** Opens the Components panel, for use with ColdFusion sites. This advanced feature lets ColdFusion developers take advantage of prewritten, self-contained programs, which makes building complex dynamic sites easier.
- **Files.** Opens the Files panel. From this window, you can open any file, and transfer files between your computer and the remote server.
- **Assets.** Opens the Assets panel, which conveniently groups and lists all the assets (such as colors, links, scripts, graphics, library items, and templates) you've used in your site.

- **Snippets.** Opens the Snippets panel, which contains snippets of HTML, JavaScript, and other types of programming code. You can create your own snippets to save your fingers from having to retype frequently repeated code.
- **Tag Inspector.** Opens the Tag inspector panel, which provides a listing of *all* properties available for the currently selected HTML tag. This uber-geek option is like the Property inspector on steroids.
- **Behaviors.** Opens the Behaviors panel, which lets you associate *behaviors* (such as swapping images in a rollover, or checking for necessary plug-ins) to selected page elements (see Chapter 13).
- **History.** Displays the History panel for viewing a record of actions performed in the current document.
- **Frames.** Displays the Frames panel for selecting frames and framesets for editing.
- **Code Inspector.** A window displaying the HTML code for the current document. You can edit the code directly in the window, while still looking at the Design view. It's often easier to just use Dreamweaver's "Code and Design" view (View → "Code and Design").
- **Results.** Lets you open Dreamweaver's many site-wide tools, such as the "Find and Replace" command, Link Checker, and Reports command. Pick the type of action you'd like to perform using the submenu.
- **Extensions.** This mysterious menu item (new in Dreamweaver CS4) houses add-ons to Dreamweaver. Currently there's only one item listed, Connections; when selected, it opens a small window asking you to connect with the Adobe mothership and enter your Adobe ID and password. Supposedly this just lets you check for updates to Dreamweaver (though the Updates option on the Help menu is easier). All in all, it sounds kind of fishy.
- **Workspace Layout.** Lets you save the position and size of Dreamweaver's panels and windows in any arrangement you like.
- **Hide Panels.** Closes all currently open panels. Choosing Show Panels reopens only those panels that were displayed before you selected Hide Panels.
- **Application Bar (Mac only).** Opens and closes the Application bar at the top of the screen just below Dreamweaver's menu items.
- **Cascade.** By default, when there are multiple documents open, you switch from page to page by clicking on tabs that appear at the top of the document area. If you prefer to have all open documents floating and resizable within this space, this and the next two options let you "undock" the current documents. The cascade option resizes each open document and places them one on top of the other. Windows folks can redock pages by clicking the Maximize button on any currently opened document. Mac people can select the Combine As Tabs option.

- **Tile Horizontally (Windows Only).** Places all open documents one on top of the other. The documents don't float on top of each other; rather, they fill the available document area as row upon row of thin, horizontal windows. With more than a few documents open, this option displays so little of each page that it's difficult to work on any one page.
- **Tile Vertically (Windows Only).** Just like the previous command, except that documents are placed vertically like stripes going across the screen.
- **Tile (Mac Only).** This has the same effect as Tile Vertically above.
- **Combine As Tabs (Mac Only).** Returns documents that either tile or cascade (see those options above) on the screen into the single, unified tab interface.
- **Next document, Previous document (Mac Only).** This pair of commands let you step through all your open documents, bringing each document in turn to the front of the screen for editing.
- **List of Currently Open Documents.** All the documents that are currently open are listed at the bottom of this menu. Selecting a document brings it to the front for editing. But with the easy document tabs, why bother?

Help Menu

The Help menu offers useful links and references for more information about using, troubleshooting, and extending Dreamweaver:

- **Dreamweaver Help.** Launches a Web browser and loads Dreamweaver's online help system. You can search for help in this online documentation repository or within a handful of other useful Dreamweaver-related Web sites. In addition, you can download a 20 MB PDF file containing the program's documentation.
- **Spry Framework Help.** An online reference to working with and programming Spry widgets like those discussed in Chapter 12. It doesn't have any information on how to use the Spry tools built into Dreamweaver. Instead, it provides more in-depth information for programming-oriented Web designers who wish to jump into Code view, and expand on Dreamweaver's Spry features.
- **Get started with InContext Editing.** Takes you to the home page for the InContext Editing service, a new program from Adobe that provides a Web interface for editing Web pages. This service is useful for those Web designers who want to offload the tedious task of updating Web pages to their clients, co-workers, underlings, and pet hamsters.
- **ColdFusion Help.** Takes you to an online reference to Adobe's server-side programming language, ColdFusion, on Adobe.com.
- **Reference.** Opens the Reference panel, a searchable guide to HTML tags, Cascading Style Sheets, and JavaScript commands. The guides are culled from the popular O'Reilly reference books and include an explanation of what specific

tags do, when you can use them, and what additional components are required, as well as tips for getting the most out of them.

- **Dreamweaver Exchange.** Launches a Web browser and loads the home page for the Dreamweaver Exchange at Adobe.com. Here you can download extensions for adding new features to Dreamweaver (see Chapter 21 for details).
- **Manage Extensions.** Same as the Manage Extensions menu option listed under the Commands menu (see page 1030).
- **Dreamweaver Support Center.** Opens Adobe's online Dreamweaver Support Center Web page in your browser. This Web site offers technical support for known bugs or common questions, downloadable updates to the program, and a link to online forums.
- **CSS Advisor.** Takes you to Adobe's online CSS advisor. This Web site provides information about common (and not so common) CSS bugs. The site works in conjunction with Dreamweaver's check browser compatibility tool discussed on page 130.
- **Adobe Online Forums.** Opens an index of available online forums from Adobe's Web site (in your Web browser). You can use the forums to interact with other Adobe customers, post questions, share techniques, or answer questions posted by others. Requires Internet access and a newsgroup reader.
- **Adobe Training.** Opens Adobe's Training Web page, where you can spend even more money learning how to use the program. Cool! Advertising, built right into Dreamweaver.
- **Registration.** Opens a registration form window, so you can register your copy of the program with Adobe. Adobe provides a few free gifts if you register.
- **Activate.** As part of Adobe's attempt to stop piracy of their software, Software Activation contacts Adobe and makes sure that the copy you're using isn't activated on any other computers. You're limited to installing the software on one desktop and one laptop of the same operating system. If you don't activate your software, it won't run on your computer after 30 days.
- **Deactivate.** If you're moving a new computer, *do not forget* to deactivate the software on your old computer. Use this menu option to do it. Deactivating the software lets you install it on another computer.
- **Updates.** Launches the oh-so-slow-and-annoying Adobe updater. It will eventually find any updates for Dreamweaver (and every other Adobe product installed on your computer), and then ask you to close Internet Explorer, Firefox, Safari, Microsoft Word, and just about every other program on your computer before updating Dreamweaver.
- **About Dreamweaver (Windows Only).** Opens an About Dreamweaver window, showing your software's version number. (On the Macintosh, this command is in the Dreamweaver menu.)

Index

D

G

I

J

M

N

O

P

Q

R

T

U

V

W

X

Y

Z

Colophon

Adam Witwer provided quality control for *Dreamweaver CS4: The Missing Manual.* Production assistance provided by Leah Hatten and Caitlin Metzger .

The cover of this book is based on a series design originally created by David Freedman and modified by Mike Kohnke, Karen Montgomery, and Fitch (*www.fitch.com*). Back cover design, dog illustration, and color selection by Fitch.

David Futato designed the interior layout, based on a series design by Phil Simpson. This book was converted by Abby Fox to FrameMaker 5.5.6. The text font is Adobe Minion; the heading font is Adobe Formata Condensed; and the code font is LucasFont's TheSansMonoCondensed. The illustrations that appear in the book were produced by Robert Romano and Jessamyn Read using Macromedia FreeHand MX and Adobe Photoshop CS.

Dreamweaver CS4

THE MISSING CD
There's no
CD with this book;
you just saved $5.00.
Instead, every single Web address, practice file, and
piece of downloadable software mentioned in this
book is available at *www.missingmanuals.com*
(click the Missing CD icon).
There you'll find a tidy list of links,
organized by chapter.

Don't miss a thing!
Sign up for the free Missing Manual email announcement list at www.missingmanuals.com. We'll let you know when we release new titles, make free sample chapters available, and update the features and articles on the Missing Manual Web site.

CPSIA information can be obtained at www.ICGtesting.com
Printed in the USA
BVOW081640181011

273915BV00012B/4/P

9 780596 522926